AILA's Asylum Primer, Fifth Edition

AILA Titles of Interest

AILA's Occupational Guidebooks

Immigration Options for Artists and Entertainers

Immigration Options for Physicians

Immigration Options for Nurses & Allied Health Care Professionals

Immigration Options for Religious Workers

Immigration Options for Academics and Researchers

Immigration Options for Investors and Entrepreneurs

Statutes, Regulations, Agency Materials & Case Law

Immigration & Nationality Act (INA)

Immigration Regulations (CFR)

Agency Interpretations of Immigration Policy (Cables, Memos, and Liaison Minutes)

AILA's Immigration Case Summaries

Core Curriculum

Navigating the Fundamentals of Immigration Law

Immigration Law for Paralegals*

AILA's Guide to Technology and Legal Research for the Immigration Lawyer

CD Products & Toolbox Series

AILA's Immigration Practice Toolbox

AILA's Litigation Toolbox

For Your Clients

Client Brochures (10 Titles)

U.S. Tax Guides for Foreign Persons and Those Who Pay Them, 4 volumes— (H-1Bs, L-1s, J-1s, B-1s)*

Online Research Tools

AILALink Online

AILA's Focus Series

EB-2 & EB-3 Degree Equivalency
by Ronald Wada

Waivers Under the INA
by Julie Ferguson

Private Bills & Pardons in Immigration
by Anna Gallagher

Treatises & Primers

Kurzban's Immigration Law Sourcebook
by Ira J. Kurzban

Professionals: A Matter of Degree
by Martin J. Lawler

AILA's Asylum Primer
by Regina Germain

Immigration Consequences of Criminal Activity
by Mary E. Kramer

Essentials of Removal and Relief
by Joseph A. Vail

Essentials of Immigration Law
by Richard A. Boswell

Litigating Immigration Cases in Federal Court
by Robert Pauw

Other Titles

David Stanton Manual on Labor Certification

AILA's Global Immigration Guide: A Country-by-Country Survey

Immigration & Nationality Law Handbook

The Visa Processing Guide

Ethics in a Brave New World

Immigration Practice Under NAFTA and Other Free Trade Agreements

Government Reprints

BIA Practice Manual

Immigration Judge Benchbook

Citizenship Laws of the World

ICE Inspector's Field Manual

Adjudicator's Field Manual

Tables of Contents and other information about these publications can be found at *www.ailapubs.org*. Orders may be placed at that site or by calling 1-800-982-2839.

*An AILA-distributed title

AILA's Asylum Primer
Fifth Edition

A Practical Guide to U.S. Asylum Law and Procedure

Regina Germain

AMERICAN IMMIGRATION LAWYERS ASSOCIATION

1.800.982.2839
www.ailapubs.org

> **Website for Corrections and Updates**
>
> Corrections and other updates to AILA publications
> can be found online at: *www.aila.org/BookUpdates.*
>
> If you have any corrections or updates to the information in this book,
> please let us know by sending a note to the address below, or e-mail us at
> *books@aila.org*.

This publication is designed to provide accurate and authoritative information in regard to the subject matter covered. It is distributed with the understanding that the publisher is not engaged in rendering legal, accounting, or other professional service. If legal advice or other expert assistance is required, the services of a competent professional should be sought.

—from a Declaration of Principles jointly adopted by a Committee of the American Bar Association and a Committee of Publishers

Copyright © 2007 by the American Immigration Lawyers Association

All rights reserved. No part of this publication may be reproduced or transmitted in any form or by any means, electronic or mechanical, including photocopy, recording, or any information storage retrieval system, without written permission from the publisher. No copyright claimed on U.S. government material.

Requests for permission to make electronic or print copies of any part of this work should be mailed to Director of Publications, American Immigration Lawyers Association, 918 F Street NW, Washington, DC 20004, or e-mailed to *books@aila.org*.

Printed in the United States of America

ISBN 978-1-57370-219-5
Stock No. 52-19

In Memory of Aunt Rose (Witko) Gerko
(1927–2007)

PREFACE

What a difference two and one-half years make in the field of asylum law. The years 2005, 2006, and 2007 have brought a number of positive changes along with new obstacles for asylum-seekers in the United States. At the time the last edition went to press, the REAL ID Act had just gone into effect, increasing the already heavy burden of proof shouldered by asylum-seekers. At the same time, the REAL ID Act removed the asylee adjustment cap and the long waiting periods asylees endured before they could obtain their permanent residency. It's a mixed and ever-changing bag we thrust upon refugees arriving on our shores.

Recent changes at the time of this edition show us that modest gains for asylum-seekers can be erased with the stroke of a pen by the Board of Immigration Appeals. The lesson boils down to this: there are sweet victories from time to time, but also much work that still needs to be done.

Whether you are tackling your very first asylum claim, or your 100th, I hope you will keep in mind:

- You are the voice for the voiceless. Your representation ensures that refugees are afforded due process. You are a Godsend to your client and the asylum system.

- DHS attorneys have a duty to uphold international refugee law and ensure that justice is done. Sometimes they forget this, and when they do, a gentle reminder never hurts.

- The law is a mighty weapon and a shield. Use it fully and wisely. Re-read the statute, re-read the regulations, negotiate, object, make arguments no one has ever made before, find the perfect country expert, give openings and closings, file motions, and appeal when you have to.

- Take good care of yourself. Representing asylum-seekers is hard work. Harder than you may have ever dreamed. Exercise, meditate, and commiserate with others. Enjoy your life. You will be a better advocate.

Regina Germain
December 2007

Summary Table of Contents

AILA's Asylum Primer
Fifth Edition

Preface vii
Table of Federal Court Decisions, State Court Decisions, and
Decisions of Foreign Tribunals 583
Table of Administrative Decisions 601
Table of Court and Administrative Decisions Sorted by Country 607
Subject-Matter Index 623

Chapter One

1.1. International Law 1
1.2. U.S. Statutes 10
1.3. Regulations 14
1.4. Operations Instructions and Field Manuals 15
1.5. BIA Decisions 16
1.6. Office of Legal Counsel Decisions 17
1.7. Federal Court Decisions 17
1.8. Legacy INS, DHS, and EOIR Policy Directives, Memoranda, and Statements 18
1.9. Legacy INS's *Basic Law Manual* and Asylum Officer Basic Training Course 20
1.10. Laws of Other Countries 20

Chapter Two

2.1. History 23
2.2. Asylum Standard—Relief Available 25
2.3. Withholding Standard—Relief Available 26
2.4. Definitions 27
2.5. Current Issues in U.S. Asylum Cases 59
2.6. Burden of Proof 79
2.7. Ineligibility for Asylum and Withholding of Removal 102
2.8. Standard of Review 130

CHAPTER THREE

3.1. Who Is Eligible to Apply 140
3.2. Affirmative Procedures 145
3.3. Immigration Court (Defensive) Procedures 155
3.4. Asylum Procedures for Stowaways 188
3.5. Asylum Procedures for Children 189
3.6. Reinstatement of Removal 195
3.7. Expedited Removal for Aggravated Felons 203
3.8. Release from Detention 211
3.9. Employment Authorization 219
3.10. Appeals to BIA 225
3.11. Motions to Reopen and Reconsider 231
3.12. Judicial Review 239
3.13. Adjustment of Status for Asylees and Refugees 246
3.14. Refugee Travel Document 248
3.15. Refugee/Asylee Relative Petition (I-730) 250
3.16. Termination of Asylum and Withholding 252
3.17. Termination of Refugee Status 254

CHAPTER FOUR

4.1. The Implementing Legislation 260
4.2. Convention Against Torture—Key Provisions, U.S. Understandings, and Regulations 263
4.3. Procedures for Applying for Relief Under the Convention Against Torture 279

CHAPTER FIVE

5.1. Statutory Provisions—INA §235(b) 295
5.2. How Expedited Removal Works in Practice 304
5.3. Oversight of the Expedited Removal Process 318

CHAPTER SIX

6.1. "T" and "U" Visas for Victims of Trafficking in Persons 328
6.2. INA §209(c) Waiver for Refugees and Asylees 332
6.3. Temporary Protected Status 333

6.4. Humanitarian Parole 334
6.5. *ABC* Settlement.. 337
6.6. Nicaraguan Adjustment and Central American Relief Act.................... 339
6.7. Haitian Refugee Immigration Fairness Act 341
6.8. Cuban Adjustment Act.. 343
6.9. Cancellation of Removal... 344
6.10. Voluntary Departure 348
6.11. Registry.. 351
6.12. Waiver of Inadmissibility Under INA §212(h)..................................... 352
6.13. Family-Sponsored, Employment-Based, and Other Means
       of Regularizing Immigration Status in the United States..................... 353
6.14. Citizenship 355
6.15. Private Bills... 357

APPENDICES

Appendix 1—Interviewing and Intake... 361
Appendix 2—The Asylum Application 371
Appendix 3—Applying Affirmatively... 391
Appendix 4—Supporting Documentation 401
Appendix 5—Preparing for the Hearing.. 423
Appendix 6—Contacts 473
Appendix 7—Charts 509
Appendix 8—Resources 523
Appendix 9—Forms 527

Acknowledgments

No one can write or update a book like this alone. So many wonderful and knowledgeable people contributed to the final product, I am almost sure I will miss someone.

Let me start with the many hours of research, writing, and cite checking provided by Latham & Watkins LLP. Simply put, this book could not have been produced without this firm. In particular, I thank from the bottom of my heart Angela M. Olsen, a dedicated and accomplished associate at the Washington, D.C. office of Latham & Watkins, who specializes in environmental matters. She also has handled numerous pro bono asylum cases at the firm and was able to convince partner Claudia M. O'Brien to take on this project. I can attest to the weekends and late nights that Angela worked on this to meet our summer production deadlines. For all of Angela's and her team's hard work, I am eternally grateful.

Next, I must thank Richard Link, Legal Editor at AILA Publications, for his crisp editing, for cracking the whip and moving this along in the nicest way possible, and for making great suggestions for improving the content of the *Primer*. The fifth edition of the *Primer* is better than ever and Richard is to thank for that. I also wish to thank Tatia L. Gordon-Troy, Director of AILA Publications, and Mary Johnson, Marketing Associate at AILA, for all their help and support on this edition. Additionally, I thank AILA's Liaison and Information department, particularly Robin Williamson Thiel and Dominique Kaschak, who collected and verified much of the information in the appendices.

As I do in every edition, I thank Nadine Wettstein, who first suggested to AILA and to me that I write this book. That was 10 years ago, and my life has been forever changed. I view every change in the law, every newly issued policy, and every announcement by U.S. Citizenship and Immigration Services (USCIS), with a little more attention. I believe I am a better lawyer because of it. So, thank you again, Nadine.

I also wish to thank the following people who have contributed in some way to the publication of this book: Liz Barna, David Cleveland, Elizabeth Dallam, Ernie Duff, Paige Gardner, Mark Hetfield, Anwen Hughes, Kate Jastram, Larry Katzman, Stephen Knight, Jane Kochman, Karen Musalo, Christopher Nugent, Andrew Painter, Gail Pendleton, Sarnata Reynolds, Joe Vail, and Beth Werlin. They were all helpful in answering questions, forwarding an interesting case, reading over sections of the book, and/or answering my questions. A special thanks also goes to the following individuals at USCIS Asylum Headquarters who were helpful in answering my questions regarding forms, Asylum Officer Basic Training Course materials, and Quality Assurance: Deputy Director Joanna Ruppel, Jedidah Hussey, and Lisa Flanagan.

Last, but not least, I thank my daughter, Isadora, for her patience in this process. We did not have a summer vacation this year because I used that time to work on the book. She never complained once throughout the long, hot Denver summer. We stayed in town and cheered on the Colorado Rockies baseball team and learned that miracles do happen when you least expect it.

Regina Germain
December 2007

DETAILED TABLE OF CONTENTS

AILA's ASYLUM PRIMER
FIFTH EDITION

Preface vii
Table of Federal Court Decisions 583
Table of Administrative Decisions 601
Table of Court and Administrative Decisions Sorted by Country 607
Subject-Matter Index 623

Chapter 1: Sources of Asylum Law 1
   1.1. International Law 1
      1.1.1. The 1951 Convention/1967 Protocol Relating to the Status of
Refugees 1
         The Definition of Refugee 4
         The Principle of Nonrefoulement 4
         UNHCR's Handbook on Procedures and Criteria for Determining
Refugee Status 5
            UNHCR Executive Committee Conclusions 6
            Other UNHCR Publications 6
      1.1.2. Customary International Law 7
      1.1.3. Convention Against Torture and Other Cruel, Inhuman or
Degrading Treatment or Punishment 8
      1.1.4. Other Treaties 9
   1.2. U.S. Statutes 10
      1.2.1. Refugee Act of 1980 10
         Definition of Refugee 11
         Asylum 11
         The Principle of Nonrefoulement 11
      1.2.2. Illegal Immigration Reform and Immigrant Responsibility Act 12
         Revised Definition of Refugee 12
         Revised Nonrefoulement Provision 12

Additional Statutory Bars to Asylum 13
Expedited Removal Proceedings 13
1.2.3. USA PATRIOT Act 13
1.2.4. The REAL ID Act 14
1.3. Regulations 14
1.4. Operations Instructions and Field Manuals 15
1.5. BIA Decisions 16
1.6. Office of Legal Counsel Decisions 17
1.7. Federal Court Decisions 17
1.8. Legacy INS, DHS, and EOIR Policy Directives, Memoranda, and Statements 18
1.9. Legacy INS's *Basic Law Manual* and Asylum Officer Basic Training Course 20
1.10. Laws of Other Countries 20

Chapter 2: U.S. Asylum Law 23
2.1. History 23
2.2. Asylum Standard—Relief Available 25
2.3. Withholding Standard—Relief Available 26
2.4. Definitions 27
2.4.1. Refugee 27
2.4.2. Country of Nationality and Statelessness 28
2.4.3. Unable or Unwilling to Return 30
2.4.4. Well-Founded Fear 30
2.4.5. Persecution 32
Definition of Persecution 32
Examples of Persecution 34
Past Persecution as a Basis for Asylum 38
2.4.6. "On Account of"; Mixed Motives 39
"On Account of" 39
Mixed Motives 41
Imputed Protected Grounds 42
2.4.7. Race 42
2.4.8. Religion 43
2.4.9. Nationality 46

2.4.10. Membership in a Particular Social Group 47
2.4.11. Political Opinion 52
Actual: Acts, Words, and Beliefs 52
Unexpressed 53
Imputed 53
Neutrality 54
Coercive Population Control 55
2.5. Current Issues in U.S. Asylum Cases 59
2.5.1. Gender-Based Claims 59
2.5.2. Children 63
2.5.3. Sexual Orientation 66
2.5.4. HIV-Positive/AIDS Status 67
2.5.5. Disabilities—Physical and Mental 68
2.5.6. Gang-Related Claims 69
2.5.7. Conscription; Refusal to Serve 70
2.5.8. Nongovernmental Actors 72
2.5.9. Countrywide Persecution 73
2.5.10. Prosecution vs. Persecution 75
Punishment for Criminal Conduct 75
Punishment for Illegal Departure; Unauthorized Stays 77
2.5.11. Refugee Sur Place 77
2.5.12. Remaining in Home Country for an Extended Period of Time 78
2.6. Burden of Proof 79
2.6.1. On Applicant 79
2.6.2. Testimony and Credibility 80
2.6.3. Corroboration: Evidence and Country Conditions Documentation 84
2.6.4. Benefit of the Doubt 88
2.6.5. Specific Threat of Harm 89
2.6.6. Persecution of Family and Friends 91
2.6.7. "Similarly Situated" Standard 92
2.6.8. Possession of a Valid Passport 94
2.6.9. Changed Country Conditions; Administrative Notice 94
2.6.10. Past Persecution; Presumption of Future Persecution 96
Fundamental Change in Circumstances 97

Reasonableness of Internal Relocation Alternative 98
Humanitarian Asylum 100
2.6.11. Foreign Law 101
2.7. Ineligibility for Asylum and Withholding of Removal 102
2.7.1. Asylum—Discretionary Denials 102
2.7.2. Mandatory Bars to Both Asylum and Withholding of Removal 104
Particularly Serious Crimes 105
Aggravated Felonies 105
Nonaggravated Felonies 108
Serious Nonpolitical Crimes 109
Participation in Persecution of Others 110
Danger to Security of the United States 112
Terrorism 113
    Engaging in Terrorist Activity 113
    Representative of a Foreign Terrorist Organization 115
    Representatives of Political or Social Groups That Endorse Terrorist Activity 116
    Individuals in Positions of Prominence Who Endorse Terrorist Activity 116
    Members of Terrorist Organizations 116
    Waiver of Certain Grounds of Inadmissibility 117
    Alien Terrorist Removal Courts 118
    Mandatory Detention of "Suspected Terrorists" 119
2.7.3. Bars to Asylum Only 119
Prior Asylum Denial 119
One-Year Filing Deadline 120
    Extraordinary Circumstances 122
    Changed Circumstances 124
Firm Resettlement 126
Safe Third Country 129
2.7.4. Bars to Withholding Only 130
Participation in Nazi Persecution 130
Participation in Genocide 130
2.8. Standard of Review 130
2.8.1. Before the BIA 130

2.8.2. Before the Attorney General 132
2.8.3. Before the Federal Courts 132
    Limited Review of Certain Asylum Bars... 133
    No Review for Persons Convicted of Crimes 134
    Revised Statutory Standards of Review.. 135
    De Novo Standard of Review 136
    Abuse of Discretion 136
    Statutory Construction 136
    Deference in Credibility Determinations 137
    Review of Factual Findings 138
    Review of "Changed Circumstances" Determinations 138

Chapter 3: Asylum and Withholding of Removal Procedures 139
3.1. Who Is Eligible to Apply 140
    3.1.1. In General.. 140
        Asylum... 140
        Withholding of Removal.. 140
        Overseas Processing and Refugee Admissions....................................... 141
    3.1.2. Ineligibility for Asylum and Withholding of Removal...................... 142
        Bars to Asylum Only.. 142
        Bars to Asylum and Withholding.. 142
        Bars to Withholding Only 142
    3.1.3. Required Notices.. 142
        Notice of Right to Be Represented 142
        Notice of Consequences of Filing a Frivolous Application 143
        Notice That Information May Be Used to Initiate Removal
        Proceedings and Satisfy the Government's Burden of Proof 144
        Notice of Confidentiality 144
3.2. Affirmative Procedures 145
    3.2.1. Who Is Eligible 145
    3.2.2. Where to File.. 146
    3.2.3. No Filing Fee 147
    3.2.4. Incomplete Applications 147
    3.2.5. Interview 147
        Time Period.. 147

Nonadversarial	147
Biometrics	148
Interpreter	148
Role of Attorney or Representative	149
Department of State Comments	150
Failure to Appear	150
Identity Check	151
Decision—Grant, Denial, or Referral	151
Grant	152
Denial	152
Referral	153
No Appeal/Motions to Reopen or Reconsider/Quality Assurance	153
3.2.6. Affirmative Procedures for Children	155
3.3. Immigration Court (Defensive) Procedures	155
3.3.1. Who Is Eligible	156
3.3.2. Where to File	157
3.3.3. No Filing Fee	157
3.3.4. Biometrics	157
3.3.5. Hearing	158
Time Period	158
Master Calendar Hearings	158
Entry of Appearance	158
Continuances	159
Advisals	159
Ascertain Desire for Representation	160
Pleadings	160
Designation of a Country of Removal	160
Motions	161
Removability	162
Deportability	162
Inadmissibility	162
Mandatory Denials	162
Department of State Comments	162
Merits Hearing	163

        Closed Hearings 163
        Videoconferenced Hearings 163
        Headquarters Immigration Court 164
        Location of Hearings 164
     Rights 165
        Fourth Amendment Rights 165
        Right to Due Process 166
        Right Not to Incriminate Oneself 168
        Right to Representation 169
        Right to Competent Interpreter 171
        Right to Present, Examine, and Object to Evidence 171
        Right to Cross-Examine Witnesses 172
        Right to Appeal 173
        "Right" to Confidentiality 173
     Incompetents 176
     Unaccompanied Minors 177
     Consequences of Failure to Appear 178
        Within 180 Days of the Date of the In Absentia Order 179
        Any Time After the Date of the In Absentia Order 180
     Evidence 181
        Experts and Witnesses 182
        Hearsay 184
        Discovery 184
        Classified Evidence 184
        Authentication of Documents 185
        Affidavits vs. Declarations 186
        Foreign Language Documents 187
        Foreign Law 187
     IJ Decision and Order 187
  3.4. Asylum Procedures for Stowaways 188
     3.4.1. Credible Fear 188
     3.4.2. No Credible Fear 188
     3.4.3. IJ Review of Negative Credible Fear Determination 189
  3.5. Asylum Procedures for Children 189

- 3.5.1. Exception to One-Year Filing Deadline 192
- 3.5.2. Exception to Expedited Removal 192
- 3.5.3. Aged-Out Children 193
  - Children Who Age Out Before the Asylum Interview 193
  - Children Who Age Out Before Adjustment of Status 193
  - Children Who Age Out Before I-730 Is Filed 194
- 3.5.4. Detention of Children 194
- 3.6. Reinstatement of Removal 195
  - 3.6.1. Preliminary Procedures 196
  - 3.6.2. Definition of Reasonable Fear 197
  - 3.6.3. No Bars Considered 197
  - 3.6.4. Interview 197
    - Orientation 198
    - Scheduling of Interview 198
    - Representation 198
    - Evidence 199
    - Interpretation 199
    - Record 200
  - 3.6.5. Decision 200
    - Reasonable Fear—Withholding-Only Proceeding Before an IJ 200
    - No Reasonable Fear—Removal or IJ Review 201
    - Withdrawals 201
  - 3.6.6. Review of Negative Reasonable Fear Determination by IJ 201
    - Reasonable Fear 202
    - No Reasonable Fear 202
- 3.7. Expedited Removal for Aggravated Felons 203
  - 3.7.1. Administrative Removal Proceedings 203
    - Initiation 203
    - Response to Notice of Intent (I-851) 204
    - Initiation of §240 Removal Proceedings 204
    - Termination of §240 Removal Proceedings 204
    - Judicial Review 204
  - 3.7.2. Reasonable Fear Determination by an Asylum Officer 205
    - Preliminary Procedures 205

Definition of Reasonable Fear 205
No Bars Considered 205
Interview 206
Orientation 206
Scheduling of Interview 206
Representation 207
Evidence 207
Interpretation 207
Record 208
Decision 208
    Reasonable Fear—Withholding-Only Proceeding Before an IJ 208
    No Reasonable Fear—Removal or IJ Review 209
Withdrawals 209
3.7.3. Review of Negative Reasonable Fear Determination by IJ 209
    Reasonable Fear 210
    No Reasonable Fear 211
3.8. Release from Detention 211
  3.8.1. Who Is Eligible for Release 212
    Individuals Found to Have a Credible Fear 212
    Noncriminals Who Have Made a Lawful or Illegal Entry or Who Fall Within the Definition of "Arriving Alien" 212
    Individuals Who Completed Their Criminal Sentences Prior to October 9, 1998, or with Final Orders of Removal Who Cannot Be Returned to Their Home Countries 212
    Children 213
  3.8.2. Who Is *Not* Eligible for Release 213
    Individuals in Expedited Removal 214
    Individuals Subject to Criminal Grounds of Deportation or Inadmissibility 214
    Terrorists 214
    Individuals with Final Orders of Removal 215
  3.8.3. Bond Hearings vs. Parole Requests 215
  3.8.4. Bond Hearings 215
    Procedure 216
        Application for an Initial Bond Redetermination 216

Venue 216
Separate Proceeding..216
Basis for Decision 216
Decision 216
Appeal..216
Request for a Subsequent Bond Redetermination...............................217
Burden of Proof..217
3.8.5. Requests for Release (or Parole) to ICE District Directors 218
Eligibility and Burden of Proof..218
Expedited Removal..218
Credible Fear Finding 218
Others Arriving at a Port of Entry...219
Arriving Individuals Subject to Criminal Grounds for Detention 219
Procedure 219
3.9. Employment Authorization..219
3.9.1. Eligibility 220
3.9.2. Time for Filing..220
3.9.3. What to File..221
3.9.4. Where to File..221
3.9.5. Fee..221
3.9.6. Adjudication Period 221
3.9.7. Renewals..221
3.9.8. Asylees and Withholding Grantees..222
3.9.9. Social Security Cards...223
Asylum Applicants..223
Asylees..223
3.9.10. Federal Individual Tax ID Numbers 224
Asylum Applicants and Asylees 224
3.9.11. Termination..225
Asylum Officer Denial..225
IJ, BIA, or Federal Court Denial...225
3.10. Appeals to BIA 225
3.10.1. Notice of Right to File an Appeal 226
3.10.2. When to File..226

3.10.3. Where to File	227
3.10.4. What to File	227
3.10.5. Fee	227
3.10.6. Streamlined Process	228
3.10.7. Service on DHS	229
3.10.8. Automatic Stay of Removal	229
3.10.9. Briefs	230
3.10.10. Oral Argument	230
3.10.11. Ineligibility/Waived Appeal	230
3.10.12. Departure from United States	231
3.10.13. Interlocutory Appeal	231
3.11. Motions to Reopen and Reconsider	231
3.11.1. Who May Make a Motion	232
3.11.2. Where to File	232
3.11.3. Jurisdiction	232
3.11.4. Standard of Review; Burden of Proof	232
3.11.5. Limit on Number	233
3.11.6. Time Limit for Filing	234
Motion to Reconsider—30 Days	234
Motion to Reopen—90 Days	234
3.11.7. Exceptions to the Numerical and Time Limitations	234
Motion to Reopen an Order Entered In Absentia	234
Changed Circumstances	234
Consent by All Parties	235
DHS Motions Regarding Fraud or Crimes	236
Equitable Tolling	236
3.11.8. Contents of Motions	236
Contents of Motion to Reconsider	237
Contents of Motion to Reopen	238
3.11.9. Stay of Removal	238
3.11.10. Reply to Motion	238
3.11.11. Rulings on Motion	239
3.11.12. Departure from the United States	239
3.12. Judicial Review	239

- 3.12.1. *Chevron* Deference 240
- 3.12.2. No Review 241
  - Negative Credible Fear Determination 241
  - Noncitizens Convicted of Certain Crimes 241
  - Reinstatement 241
- 3.12.3. Restrictions on Judicial Review 241
  - Safe Third Country 241
  - One-Year Deadline 241
  - Previous Denial 242
  - Terrorist Bar 242
  - Expedited Removal 242
  - Discretionary Determinations by the IJ and BIA 242
- 3.12.4. Procedures 243
  - Time Limit 243
  - Venue 243
  - What to File 243
  - Briefing Schedule 244
  - Scope of Review 244
  - Stay of Removal 245
  - Motions to Reopen or Reconsider 246
- 3.13. Adjustment of Status for Asylees and Refugees 246
  - 3.13.1. Asylees 246
  - 3.13.2. Refugees 247
- 3.14. Refugee Travel Document 248
  - 3.14.1. Who May File 249
  - 3.14.2. Where to File 249
  - 3.14.3. Fee 249
  - 3.14.4. What to File 249
- 3.15. Refugee/Asylee Relative Petition (I-730) 250
  - 3.15.1. Relationship 250
  - 3.15.2. Who May File 251
  - 3.15.3. Where to File 251
  - 3.15.4. When to File 251
  - 3.15.5. Fee 251

 3.15.6. What to File 251
 3.15.7. Burden of Proof 252
 3.15.8. No Appeal 252
3.16. Termination of Asylum and Withholding 252
 3.16.1. Grounds for Terminating Asylum 252
 3.16.2. Grounds for Terminating Withholding 253
 3.16.3. Procedures 253
  Asylum Office 253
  BIA or IJ 254
 3.16.4. Termination of Derivative Status 254
3.17. Termination of Refugee Status 254
 3.17.1. Procedure 254
 3.17.2. No Appeal 255

Chapter 4: Convention Against Torture 259
4.1. The Implementing Legislation 260
 4.1.1. Regulations 261
 4.1.2. Possible Bars to Relief 261
 4.1.3. Judicial Review 262
 4.1.4. Detention 262
 4.1.5. Definitions 262
 4.1.6. Number of Cases Granted 262
 4.1.7. Prior Procedures for Relief Under the Convention 262
4.2. Convention Against Torture—Key Provisions, U.S. Understandings, and Regulations 263
 4.2.1. The Definition of Torture 264
  Intentional Act 264
  Infliction of Severe Pain or Suffering 266
   Physical Torture 266
   Mental Torture 267
  Under the Custody or Control of the Offender 267
  For a Broad Array of Wrongful Purposes 267
  By or Sanctioned by a Public Official 268
   Public Official or Person Acting in Official Capacity 268
   Acquiescence 269

Not Arising Out of Lawful Sanctions 271
4.2.2. *Nonrefoulement* (Nonreturn) Provision 272
"More Likely Than Not" Standard 273
Prospective Only 273
No Internal Relocation Option 274
Evidence to Support Claim 274
Credibility 274
All Evidence Relevant to the Possibility of Torture 275
Torture Only 278
No Bars to Protection 278
4.3. Procedures for Applying for Relief Under the Convention
Against Torture 279
4.3.1. Who Is Eligible to Apply 279
Individuals Physically Present 279
Individuals Not Physically Present 279
Diplomatic Assurances 280
4.3.2. Types of Relief Available 281
Withholding Under the Convention Against Torture 281
Deferral Under the Convention Against Torture 282
4.3.3. Applying for Convention Against Torture Relief 280
Where to File 283
No Filing Fee 283
4.3.4. The Immigration Court Hearing 283
Time Period 283
Steps in the Decision-Making Process 283
Right to Appeal 284
Administrative Review 284
Judicial Review 284
Continued Detention After Grant of Deferral of Removal 285
4.3.5. Termination of Convention Against Torture Protection 285
Withholding of Removal Under the Convention Against Torture 286
Deferral of Removal Under the Convention Against Torture 286
Motion for Hearing on Termination 286
Notice of Hearing 287
Submission of Supplemental Information 287

      Scheduling of Hearing 287
      Department of State Comments 287
      De Novo Hearing 287
      Burden of Proof 288
      Decision 288
      Appeal 288
      Termination at the Request of the Individual 288
      Diplomatic Assurances 288
  4.3.6. Motions to Reopen 289
      Individuals with Final Orders of Deportation, Exclusion, or
      Removal Before March 22, 1999 289
      Individuals with Final Orders of Deportation, Exclusion, or
      Removal After March 22, 1999 289
      Individuals with Requests for Convention Against Torture Relief
      Pending with Legacy INS on or Before March 22, 1999 290
          No Final Decision 290
          Denial by Legacy INS 290
          Grant by Legacy INS 290
  4.3.7. Expedited Administrative Procedures 290
      Special Procedures for Stowaways Under INA §235(a) 291
      Expedited Removal Under INA §235(b) 291
      Reinstatement of Removal Under INA §241(b) 291
      Expedited Removal for Persons Convicted of an Aggravated Felony
      Under INA §238(b) 292
      Alien Terrorist Administrative Removal Procedures Under
      INA §235(c) 293
      Terrorist Removal Proceedings Under INA §501 *et seq.* 293
  4.3.8. Employment Authorization 293
      Employment Authorization When Removal Withheld Under the
      Convention Against Torture 293
      Employment Authorization When Removal Deferred Under the
      Convention Against Torture 293

Chapter 5: Expedited Removal 295
  5.1. Statutory Provisions—INA §235(b) 295
    5.1.1. What Is Expedited Removal 295

- 5.1.2. Who Is Subject to Expedited Removal 296
  - Noncitizens Arriving at a Port of Entry with False or No Documents 296
  - Noncitizens Interdicted in International or U.S. Waters and Brought to the United States 296
  - Noncitizens Who Have Not Been "Admitted" or "Paroled" into the United States and Who Have Not Resided in the United States for Two Years or More 296
    - Individuals Paroled into the United States After April 1, 1997 298
- 5.1.3. Who Is *Not* Subject to Expedited Removal 298
  - Cuban Citizens or Nationals Arriving at a Port of Entry or Apprehended Within 100 Miles of the Border 298
    - Pre–April 1, 1997, Parolees 298
    - Unaccompanied Minors 298
    - Stowaways 299
    - Crewmembers 299
    - Individuals Seeking Entry under VWPP 299
    - Noncitizens Paroled into the United States with Advance Parole 299
    - Individuals with Additional Charges of Inadmissibility 299
    - LPRs, Asylees, Refugees, and Others with Additional Protections 300
- 5.1.4. Credible Fear Standard 300
- 5.1.5. Withdrawal of Application for Admission 301
- 5.1.6. Judicial Review 301
  - Habeas Corpus Proceedings 301
  - Limitations on Declaratory, Injunctive, and Equitable Relief 302
  - Prohibition on Certification of a Class Under Rule 23 302
  - Challenges to Validity of the System 302
  - Relief 302
- 5.1.7. Consequences of Removal 302
- 5.1.8. Expedited Removal and Credible Fear Statistics 303
- 5.2. How Expedited Removal Works in Practice 304
  - 5.2.1. Primary Inspection 304
  - 5.2.2. Secondary Inspection 304
    - Background 304
    - No Right to Representation 304
    - Record of Sworn Statement—Form I-867AB 305

  Final Order 307
 5.2.3. Expression of Fear and Form M-444 308
 5.2.4. Exceptions to Expedited Removal 308
  Applicants Permitted to Withdraw Their Applications for Admission 308
   Factors 309
   Unaccompanied Minors 309
  LPRs, Refugees, Asylees, and U.S. Citizens 309
  Unaccompanied Minors 310
  Pre–April 1, 1997, Parolees 311
  Stowaways 311
  Crewmembers 311
  Individuals Seeking Entry under VWPP 311
 5.2.5. Detention 311
 5.2.6. Credible Fear Interviews 312
  Rest Period 312
  Location 312
  Interviewers 312
  Interview Procedures 313
  Role of Attorney, Representative, or Consultant 314
  Interpretation 315
  Dependents 315
  Confidentiality 315
 5.2.7. Asylum Officer's Credible Fear Decision 316
 5.2.8. Review by an IJ 316
  Standard of Review 316
  Procedures 317
  Role of Attorney, Representative, or Consultant 317
  Interpreters 318
  Decision 318
  No Appeal 318
 5.2.9. Credible Fear Reinterviews Prior to Departure 318
5.3. Oversight of the Expedited Removal Process 318
 5.3.1. Quality Assurance 319
 5.3.2. Government Accountability Office Reports 320

5.3.3. U.S. Commission on International Religious Freedom Report 321
5.3.4. Nongovernmental Organizations 323
5.3.5. United Nations High Commissioner for Refugees 324

Chapter 6: Other Forms of Relief 327
6.1. "T" and "U" Visas for Victims of Trafficking in Persons 328
    6.1.1. T Visas 328
    6.1.2. U Visas 330
6.2. INA §209(c) Waiver for Refugees and Asylees 332
6.3. Temporary Protected Status 333
6.4. Humanitarian Parole 334
    6.4.1. Who May File 335
    6.4.2. What to File 335
    6.4.3. Fee 336
    6.4.4. Where to File 336
    6.4.5. When to File 336
    6.4.6. No Appeal 336
6.5. *ABC* Settlement 337
    6.5.1. Eligibility for *ABC* Class Member Benefits 337
        Salvadoran Nationals Who: 337
        Guatemalan Nationals Who: 338
    6.5.2. Exclusions from Class Member Benefits 338
    6.5.3. Detention 338
6.6. Nicaraguan Adjustment and Central American Relief Act 339
    6.6.1. Cuba 340
    6.6.2. Nicaragua 340
    6.6.3. El Salvador 340
    6.6.4. Guatemala 341
    6.6.5. Former Soviet Union and Warsaw Pact Countries 341
6.7. Haitian Refugee Immigration Fairness Act 341
6.8. Cuban Adjustment Act 343
6.9. Cancellation of Removal 344
    6.9.1. Relief for Permanent Residents 344
        Former §212(c) 344
        New INA §240A(a) 345

6.9.2. Relief for Nonpermanent Residents 346
    Old §244 346
    New §240A(b) 346
6.10. Voluntary Departure 348
    6.10.1. Before the Conclusion of Removal Proceedings 349
    6.10.2. At the Conclusion of Removal Proceedings 350
    6.10.3. Consequences for Failure to Depart 351
    6.10.4. Revocation 351
6.11. Registry 351
6.12. Waiver of Inadmissibility Under INA §212(h) 352
6.13. Family-Sponsored, Employment-Based, and Other Means of Regularizing Immigration Status in the United States 353
    6.13.1. Family-Sponsored Immigration 354
    6.13.2. Employment-Based Immigration 354
    6.13.3. Diversity Visas 355
    6.13.4. Nonimmigrant Visas 355
    6.13.5. Special Immigrant Juvenile Visas 355
6.14. Citizenship 355
    6.14.1. Derivative Citizenship 356
    6.14.2. Naturalization 356
6.15. Private Bills 357

APPENDICES

Appendix 1—Interviewing and Intake
1A	Interviewing Techniques	361
1B	Sample Intake Form	365
1C	Checklist for Bars to Asylum and Withholding of Deportation	369

Appendix 2—The Asylum Application
2A	Checklist for Asylum Application (Form I-589)	371
2B	Practice Pointers for Completing the Asylum Application	375
2C	Sample Declaration	385

Appendix 3—Applying Affirmatively
3A	Sample Letter to USCIS Service Center	391
3B	Checklist for Preparing for the Asylum Interview	393
3C	Sample Closing Statement	395

Appendix 4—Supporting Documentation

4A	Checklist for Supporting Documentation	401
4B	Sample Index of Supporting Documentation for Asylum Applicant from Iran	403
4C	Sample Expert Affidavits (Country Conditions; Medical)	405
4D	UNHCR Advisory Opinion on Cessation and Cancellation of Refugee Status	415

Appendix 5—Preparing for the Hearing

5A	Practice Pointers on Direct and Cross-Examination of the Asylum Applicant	423
5B	Sample Motion, Sample Petition for Review, and Sample Brief	429

Appendix 6—Contacts

6A	Asylum Offices	473
6B	Executive Office for Immigration Review	475
6C	Address for Service of a Petition for Review	483
6D	ICE Offices of Chief Counsel	487
6E	Detention Facilities	495
6F	Selected Resources for Country Condition Information	497
6G	Useful Websites	499
6H	Torture Treatment Programs	503

Appendix 7—Charts

7A	Affirmative and Defensive Asylum Process Chart	509
7B	Flowchart of Expedited Removal/Credible Fear Process	513
7C	A Comparison of the Forms of Protection Available Under U.S. Law	515
7D	Temporary Protected Status	517
7E	Benefits or Assistance Available to Asylees	519

Appendix 8—Resources

8A	Recommended Texts and Tools	523
8B	Resource Availability	525

Appendix 9—Forms

9A	Form I-589 and Instructions	527
9B	Form I-730 and Instructions	551
9C	Form I-765 and Instructions	557
9D	Form I-131 and Instructions	571

GLOSSARY OF ACRONYMS

ABC	*American Baptist Churches* Settlement
AEDPA	Antiterrorism and Effective Death Penalty Act
AG	Attorney General
AO	Asylum Officer
APSO	Asylum Prescreening Officer
BIA	Board of Immigration Appeals
CAT	Convention Against Torture
CFR	Code of Federal Regulations
DD	District Director
DED	Deferred Enforced Departure
DHS	Department of Homeland Security
DOS	Department of State
EOIR	Executive Office for Immigration Review
FARRA	Foreign Affairs Reform and Restructuring Act
HRIFA	Haitian Refugee Immigrant Fairness Act
ICE	Immigration and Customs Enforcement
IFM	Inspector's Field Manual
IIRAIRA	Illegal Immigration Reform and Immigrant Responsibility Act
IJ	Immigration Judge
INA	Immigration and Nationality Act
INS	Immigration and Naturalization Service (dismantled by DHS)
IRFA	International Religious Freedom Act
LPR	Lawful Permanent Resident; Legal Permanent Resident
NACARA	Nicaraguan Adjustment and Central American Relief Act
NGO	Nongovernmental Organization
NOID	Notice of Intent to Deny
NTA	Notice to Appear
OSC	Order to Show Cause

SAO	Supervisory Asylum Officer
TPCR	Transitional Period Custody Rules
TPS	Temporary Protected Status
UNHCR	United Nations High Commissioner for Refugees
USA PATRIOT	Uniting and Strengthening America by Providing Appropriate Tools Required to Intercept and Obstruct Terrorism Act
USC	United States Code
USCIRF	United States Commission on International Religious Freedom
USCIS	United States Citizenship and Immigration Service
VAWA	Violence Against Women Act
VTVPA	Victims of Trafficking and Violence Protection Act
VWPP	Visa Waiver Pilot Program
VWP	Visa Waiver Program

ABOUT AILA

The American Immigration Lawyers Association (AILA) is a national bar association of more than 11,000 attorneys who practice immigration law and/or work as teaching professionals. AILA member attorneys represent tens of thousands of U.S. families who have applied for permanent residence for their spouses, children, and other close relatives for lawful entry and residence in the United States. AILA members also represent thousands of U.S. businesses and industries who sponsor highly skilled foreign workers seeking to enter the United States on a temporary or permanent basis. In addition, AILA members represent foreign students, entertainers, athletes, and asylum-seekers, often on a pro bono basis. Founded in 1946, AILA is a nonpartisan, not-for-profit organization that provides its members with continuing legal education, publications, information, professional services, and expertise through its 36 chapters and over 50 national committees. AILA is an affiliated organization of the American Bar Association and is represented in the ABA House of Delegates.

American Immigration Lawyers Association
918 F Street, NW
Washington, DC 20004
Tel: (202) 216-2400
Fax: (202) 783-7853
www.aila.org

CHAPTER 1
SOURCES OF ASYLUM LAW

The law is a weapon.*

1.1. International Law 1
1.2. U.S. Statutes 10
1.3. Regulations 14
1.4. Operations Instructions and Field Manuals 15
1.5. BIA Decisions 16
1.6. Office of Legal Counsel Decisions 17
1.7. Federal Court Decisions 17
1.8. Legacy INS, DHS, and EOIR Policy Directives,
     Memoranda, and Statements 18
1.9. Legacy INS's Basic Law Manual and Asylum Officer
     Basic Training Course 20
1.10. Laws of Other Countries 20

This chapter provides an overview of the sources of law that may be useful in preparing asylum, withholding of removal, and Convention Against Torture claims. They are sources that should be consulted on a continuing basis—after your initial client interview and throughout the development of your case. These sources should be cited in your briefs and motions and raised in your oral arguments and closing statements. Use them creatively. Asylum law is in a state of flux, constantly evolving to conform to changes in international, as well as national, law. These sources of law are more than just tools for constructing your case; they can also be your ammunition in court.

1.1. INTERNATIONAL LAW

1.1.1. The 1951 Convention/1967 Protocol Relating to the Status of Refugees

U.S. asylum law is unique because it is derived directly from international law. The principal international instruments that provide protection to persons fleeing persecution are the 1951 United Nations Convention relating to the Status of Refugees (Refugee Convention)[1]

---

* Sam Williamson, the legendary Houston immigration attorney, known for his sharp wit, deep compassion, and fighting spirit.

[1] Convention Relating to the Status of Refugees, July 28, 1951, 189 U.N.T.S. 150 (entered into force Apr. 22, 1954).

and the 1967 United Nations Protocol relating to the Status of Refugees (Protocol).[2] The Protocol, to which the United States acceded in 1968, incorporates by reference Articles 2 through 34 of the Refugee Convention, including the refugee definition (Article 1) and the *nonrefoulement* provision (Article 33). A provision often invoked by refugee advocates is Article 31, which prohibits countries from imposing penalties on refugees for their illegal entry or presence. Also included in the Refugee Convention and Protocol are various rights that countries should accord to refugees, such as education (Article 22), travel (Article 28), employment (Articles 17 and 18), housing (Article 21), and social security rights (Article 24). To date, more than 146 countries are parties to the Refugee Convention, the Protocol, or both.

If you are pursuing a novel claim or one that may have been rejected by one or more courts or administrative tribunals, it may be helpful to look to the Refugee Convention and Protocol, as well as other sources of international human rights law, for guidance. Under U.S. law, courts are required, whenever possible, to construe domestic legislation in a way that is consistent with international obligations.[3] Moreover, international human rights are so important to asylum adjudications that asylum officers (AOs) are required to receive specialized training in international human rights law.[4]

---

[2] Protocol Relating to the Status of Refugees, 606 U.N.T.S. 267 (entered into force Oct. 4, 1967).

[3] *Weinberger v. Rossi*, 456 U.S. 25, 32 (1982); *Murray v. The Charming Betsy*, 6 U.S. (2 Cranch) 64, 118 (1804); *Ali v. Ashcroft*, 346 F.3d 873, 885 (9th Cir. 2003).

[4] 8 CFR §§208.1(b), 1208.1(b).

CHAPTER 1 • SOURCES OF ASYLUM LAW

Sources of Asylum Law: An Overview

International Instruments

- 1951 UN Convention Relating to the Status of Refugees
- 1967 UN Protocol Relating to the Status of Refugees
- UN Convention Against Torture and Other Cruel, Inhuman or Degrading Treatment or Punishment
- International Covenant on Civil and Political Rights
- Convention on the Rights of the Child
- Universal Declaration of Human Rights

Other International Sources

- Customary international law
- Office of the United Nations High Commissioner for Refugees (UNHCR), *Handbook on Procedures and Criteria for Determining Refugee Status* (Geneva, 1992)
- UNHCR Executive Committee conclusions
- UNHCR guidelines, training modules, reports, and comments
- Interpretations of the Refugee Convention and Protocol by other countries
- Decisions from the UN Committee Against Torture

U.S. Statutes

- Section 101(a)(42) of the Immigration and Nationality Act (INA), 8 USC §1101(a)(42)—definition of refugee
- INA §208, 8 USC §1158—asylum procedures and eligibility
- INA §235(a)(2), 8 USC §1225(a)(2)—asylum for stowaways
- INA §235(b), 8 USC §1225(b)—expedited removal procedures
- INA §241(b)(3), 8 USC §1231(b)—withholding of removal
- Section 2242(b) of the Foreign Affairs Reform and Restructuring Act of 1998, Pub. L. No. 105-277, div. G—requiring the implementation of article 3 of the Convention Against Torture
- Homeland Security Act of 2002, Pub. L. No. 107-296—created DHS and split legacy INS functions among USCIS, ICE, and CBP; provides statutory authority for EOIR within DOJ.

Code of Federal Regulations

- 8 CFR §§208, 1208 *et seq.*—asylum and withholding of removal procedures and eligibility (includes procedures for stowaways)
- 8 CFR §§235, 1235 *et seq.*—expedited removal procedures (includes procedures for stowaways)
- 8 CFR §§238.1, 1238.1—expedited removal for aggravated felons
- 8 CFR §§241.8, 1241.8—reinstatement of removal procedures (withholding of removal)
- 8 CFR §§208.16, 208.17, 208.18, 1208.16, 1208.17, and 1208.18—Convention Against Torture relief

Administrative and Federal Court Decisions

- IJ and BIA unpublished decisions
- BIA precedent decisions
- U.S. District Court decisions
- U.S. Circuit Courts of Appeals decisions
- U.S. Supreme Court decisions

Other Sources

- DHS field manuals and operations instructions
- USCIS, ICE, CBP, and EOIR policy directives and memoranda
- Asylum Officer Basic Training Course
- Legacy INS's *Basic Law Manual—U.S. Law and INS Refugee/Asylum Adjudications*
- Citizenship, immigration, and asylum laws of other countries

The Definition of Refugee

Under the Protocol, a "refugee" is a person who:

> owing to a well-founded fear of being persecuted for reasons of race, religion, nationality, membership of a particular social group or political opinion, is outside the country of his [or her] nationality and is unable or, owing to such fear, is unwilling to avail himself [or herself] of the protection of that country; or who not having a nationality and being outside the country of his [or her] former habitual residence . . . , is unable or, owing to such fear, is unwilling to return to it.[5]

A person is a refugee as soon as he or she fulfills the criteria contained in the definition and not when he or she is declared or determined to be a refugee by a particular country. In other words, a person does not become a refugee when he or she is recognized, but is recognized because he or she is a refugee.[6] This distinction is important when utilizing provisions of the Convention or Protocol that use the term "refugee," but not "asylum seeker" or "asylum applicant."

The Protocol definition is virtually identical to the definition of refugee found at §101(a)(42) of the Immigration and Nationality Act (INA),[7] 8 USC §1101(a)(42), *added by* the Refugee Act of 1980, Pub. L. No. 96-212. Congress was keenly aware of the United States' international treaty obligations when it drafted the Refugee Act of 1980. As the U.S. Supreme Court noted:

> If one thing is clear from the legislative history of the new definition of "refugee," and indeed the entire 1980 Act, it is that one of Congress' primary purposes was to bring United States refugee law into conformance with the [Protocol], to which the U.S. acceded in 1968.[8]

The Principle of Nonrefoulement

The fundamental protection provided by the Refugee Convention and Protocol is the prohibition on returning refugees to countries where they would face persecution. Article 33 of the Refugee Convention sets forth this principle of *nonrefoulement*, or nonreturn, as follows:

> No Contracting State shall expel or return (refouler) a refugee in any manner whatsoever to the frontiers of territories where his [or her] life or freedom would be threatened on account of his [or her] race, religion, nationality, membership of a particular social group or political opinion.[9]

---

[5] Protocol, *supra* note 2, art. I(2), incorporating by reference article 1(A)(2) of the Refugee Convention.

[6] *See* United Nations High Commissioner for Refugees, *Handbook on Procedures and Criteria for Determining Refugee Status* (1992) at ¶28.

[7] Immigration and Nationality Act of 1952 (INA), Pub. L. No. 82-414, 66 Stat. 163 (codified as amended at 8 USC §1101 *et seq.*).

[8] *INS v. Cardoza-Fonseca*, 480 U.S. 421, 436–37 (1987) (citations omitted).

[9] Refugee Convention, *supra* note 1, art. 33, incorporated by reference in article I(1) of the Protocol.

Similarly, this principle also has a counterpart in U.S. law, embodied in the withholding of removal (deportation) provision.[10]

UNHCR's Handbook on Procedures and Criteria for Determining Refugee Status

The Office of United Nations High Commissioner for Refugees (UNHCR) was established by the United Nations General Assembly in 1951 to provide international protection to refugees and to seek permanent solutions to their problems. UNHCR currently has offices in more than 120 countries, including the United States. UNHCR's *Handbook on Procedures and Criteria for Determining Refugee Status* (*Handbook*) was first published in 1979 as a resource for governments and has become an important source of interpretation and authority in U.S. refugee and asylum law. Although the *Handbook* lacks the "force of law," the Supreme Court has held that it provides "significant guidance" in construing U.S. obligations under the Protocol.[11] The *Handbook* is frequently cited by immigration judges (IJs), the Board of Immigration Appeals (BIA), and federal courts in decisions interpreting the refugee definition and construing U.S. obligations under international law. Although it is a small, pocket-sized book composed of just 223 paragraphs, the *Handbook* provides invaluable insight on topics ranging from the meaning of persecution and "serious" crime to the standard for assessing the availability of an internal flight alternative and procedures for adjudicating claims of unaccompanied minors. It also contains the Refugee Convention and Protocol. The *Handbook* is a "must" for every asylum practitioner's law library.[12]

As a complement to the *Handbook*, UNHCR has provided additional guidance on a number of topics relevant to asylum determinations. UNHCR issued the following six publications as part of this process:

- *Operational Protections in Camps and Settlements: A Reference Guide to Good Practices in the Protection of Refugees and Other Persons of Concern* (UNHCR, Geneva, June 2006);
- *Guidelines on International Protection: Victims of Trafficking and Persons at Risk of Being Trafficked* (UNHCR, Geneva, Apr. 2006);
- *Procedural Standards for Refugee Status Determination under UNHCR's Mandate* (UNHCR, Geneva, September 2005);
- *Guidelines on International Protection: Religion-Based Refugee Claims* (UNHCR, Geneva, April 2004);
- *Guidelines on International Protection: Membership of a Particular Social Group* (UNHCR, Geneva, May 2002);
- *Guidelines on International Protection: Gender-Related Persecution* (UNHCR, Geneva, May 2002).[13]

---

[10] INA §241(b)(3); 8 USC §1231(b)(3).

[11] *INS v. Cardoza-Fonseca*, 480 U.S. at 439 n.22; *INS v. Aguirre-Aguirre*, 526 U.S. 415, 427 (1999) (finding that the *Handbook* provides "some guidance" in construing the refugee provisions of the INA).

[12] The *Handbook* is available free of charge from UNHCR's Washington office: UNHCR, 1775 K Street, N.W., Suite 300, Washington, DC 20006, Fax: (202) 296-5660; e-mail: *usawa@unhcr.org*. The *Handbook* is also available on UNHCR's website at *www.unhcr.org/publ/PUBL/3d58e13b4.pdf*.

[13] All these publications are available on UNHCR's website, *www.unhcr.org*.

UNHCR Executive Committee Conclusions

Another source for interpreting the Refugee Convention and Protocol is UNHCR's Executive Committee Conclusions. The Executive Committee consists of more than 60 member states—including the United States—that meet on an annual basis and reach conclusions by consensus on a variety of refugee issues. Although these conclusions are not formally binding, they represent the views of the international community. Past Executive Committee Conclusions have addressed the protection of stateless persons,[14] women and girls at risk,[15] local integration,[16] protection measures for intercepted asylum-seekers,[17] the principle of *nonrefoulement*,[18] procedures for determining refugee status,[19] protection of asylum-seekers at sea,[20] the problem of manifestly unfounded or abusive claims,[21] and the detention of refugees and asylum-seekers.[22] These Conclusions often set forth minimum procedural standards that member states are expected to meet and are often cited by UNHCR and others when commenting on U.S. legislation and regulations.

Other UNHCR Publications

UNHCR periodically issues reports, guidelines, training modules, and comments on refugee issues. In addition to those listed on the previous page, publications from UNHCR that may be useful in preparing or presenting your asylum claim include:

- *Guidelines on Detention of Asylum Seekers* (UNHCR, Geneva, Feb. 1999);
- *Guidelines on Policies and Procedures in Dealing with Unaccompanied Minors Seeking Asylum* (UNHCR, Geneva, Feb. 1997); and
- *Guidelines on the Protection of Refugee Women* (UNHCR, Geneva, July 1991).

UNHCR's Executive Committee Conclusions and UNHCR publications may be obtained from:

- UNHCR's website: *www.unhcr.org*.
- UNHCR's RefWorld website: *www.unhcr.org/cgi-bin/texis/vtx/refworld/rwmain*.
- asylumlaw.org website: *www.asylumlaw.org*.
- Law libraries with an international law collection.

---

[14] Executive Committee Conclusion No. 106 (2006).
[15] Executive Committee Conclusion No. 105 (2006).
[16] Executive Committee Conclusion No. 104 (2005).
[17] Executive Committee Conclusion No. 97 (2003).
[18] Executive Committee Conclusion No. 6 (1977).
[19] Executive Committee Conclusion No. 8 (1977).
[20] Executive Committee Conclusion No. 20 (1980).
[21] Executive Committee Conclusion No. 30 (1983).
[22] Executive Committee Conclusion No. 44 (1986).

1.1.2. Customary International Law

Customary international law encompasses basic norms of international law that are followed by countries from a sense of legal obligation, regardless of whether they are obligated to do so by treaty or domestic law.[23] Customary international law, in the absence of conflicting domestic law, is binding on the United States.[24]

Courts have sometimes looked to customary international law when adjudicating claims of individuals fleeing persecution.[25] The Supreme Court has long recognized that:

> International law is part of our law, and must be ascertained and administered by the courts of justice of appropriate jurisdiction, as often as questions of right depending upon it are duly presented for their determination. For this purpose, where there is no treaty and no controlling executive or legislative act or judicial decision, resort must be had to the customs and usages of civilized nations; and, as evidence of these, to the works of jurists and commentators who by years of labor, research and experience have made themselves peculiarly well acquainted with the subjects of which they treat.[26]

Courts have held, however, that customary international law is not controlling where Congress has specifically enacted a law on the issue.[27]

The BIA has held that customary international law does not create a remedy from deportation or an independent basis for granting protection to persons who are not refugees.[28]

The principles of customary international law may be ascertained from the following sources:[29]

---

[23] *See generally* T. Buergenthal, *International Human Rights* (2002).

[24] *The Paquete Habana*, 175 U.S. 677, 700 (1900).

[25] *See, e.g., Matter of Abu*, A29 499 143 (IJ Feb. 19, 1997) (Phoenix, AZ) (Richardson, IJ) (holding that return to torture violates customary international law); *Matter of Santos*, A29 564 781 (IJ Aug. 24, 1990) (Arlington, VA) (Nejelski, IJ) (recognizing right of safe haven under customary international law), *reported in* 67 *Interpreter Releases* 982 (Aug. 31, 1990)); *Beharry v. Reno*, 183 F. Supp. 2d 584 (E.D.N.Y 2002), *reversed on other grounds*, 329 F.3d 51 (2d Cir. 2003) (ordering a hearing incorporating the customary international law principle of "best interests of the child" in determining whether the father of a U.S. citizen child should be deported). For an in-depth discussion of the customary international law principle prohibiting the removal of a person to a country where he or she faces torture, see K. Rosati, "The United Nations Convention Against Torture: A Detailed Examination of the Convention as an Alternative for Asylum seekers," 97-12 *Immigration Briefings* 1 (Dec. 1997).

[26] *See The Paquete Habana*, supra note 24, at 700; *Filartiga v. Pena-Irala*, 630 F.2d 876, 884 (2d Cir. 1980) (finding that official torture violates customary international law based on the court's examination of "the usage of nations, judicial opinions and the works of jurists").

[27] *See, e.g., Echeverria-Hernandez v. INS*, 923 F.2d 688, 694 (9th Cir. 1991), *vacated on other grounds*, 946 F.2d 1481 (1991) (holding that the customary norm of safe haven in times of civil war and conflict was preempted by the enactment of the Refugee Act of 1980 and the executive act of extended voluntary departure).

[28] *Matter of A–E–M–*, 21 I&N Dec. 1157, 1162 (BIA 1998); *Matter of Medina*, 19 I&N Dec. 734, 746 (BIA 1988). *Medina* was distinguished in *Matter of Abu*, A29 499 143 (IJ Feb. 19, 1996) (Phoenix, AZ) (Richardson, IJ), in which the immigration judge noted that he was not "granting relief" under customary international law, but that he was prohibited from entering an order of deportation against a person who would face torture upon return to his country of nationality. *Id.* at 15.

- the customs and practices that nations actually observe, to the extent that these practices flow from a sense of international legal obligation;
- general principles widely recognized as law by civilized nations, even if these principles are not always observed in practice;
- decisions of national and international courts in cases involving international legal issues; and
- the writings of scholars and other most highly qualified publicists.

1.1.3. Convention Against Torture and Other Cruel, Inhuman or Degrading Treatment or Punishment

The United States is also a signatory to the Convention against Torture and Other Cruel, Inhuman and Degrading Treatment or Punishment (Convention against Torture). Although the Senate adopted its resolution of advice and consent on October 27, 1990, the Convention against Torture did not become effective in the United States until November 20, 1994.[30] Article 3 of the Convention against Torture, the *nonrefoulement* (or nonreturn) provision, is unqualified in providing:

> No State Party shall expel, return (refouler) or extradite a person to another State where there are substantial grounds for believing that he [or she] would be in danger of being subjected to torture.
>
> For the purpose of determining whether there are such grounds, the competent authorities shall take into account all relevant considerations including, where applicable, the existence in the State concerned of a consistent pattern of gross, flagrant or mass violations of human rights.[31]

Unlike the Refugee Convention and Protocol, the Convention against Torture does not exclude certain classes of individuals deemed to be undeserving of protection, such as individuals convicted of serious crimes. Nor does it require a showing that the torture feared be for particular reasons, such as race, religion, nationality, membership in a particular social groups, or political opinion.

On October 21, 1998, President Bill Clinton signed legislation requiring the legacy Immigration and Naturalization Service (INS) and other government agencies to issue regulations implementing Article 3 of the Convention against Torture.[32] Legacy INS and the Executive Office for Immigration Review (EOIR) issued an interim rule on February 19, 1999, which became effective March 22, 1999, setting forth procedures for applying for

---

[29] *See The Paquete Habana, supra* note 24, at 700; *Matter of Medina*, supra note 28, at 744; United States Citizenship and Immigration Services, Asylum Officer Basic Training Course Lesson Plan on International Human Rights Law (Dec. 4, 2002) at 5–6; Immigration and Naturalization Service (INS), *Basic Law Manual, U.S. Law and INS Refugee/Asylum Adjudications* (1994) at 11–12. For more details about the Asylum Officer Basic Training Course and legacy INS's *Basic Law Manual*, see *infra* this chapter.

[30] *See* U.N. Doc. No. 571 Leg/SER. E/13, IV.9 (1995).

[31] Convention Against Torture and Other Cruel, Inhuman or Degrading Treatment or Punishment, Dec. 10, 1984, art. 3, 1465 U.N.T.S. 85 (entered into force June 26, 1987).

[32] *See* Foreign Affairs Reform and Restructuring Act of 1998, Pub. L. No. 105-277, div. G, §2242(b), 112 Stat. 2681, 2681-822, *reprinted infra* ch. 4.

relief under the Convention against Torture. Additional changes were made in final regulations issued on December 6, 2000.[33]

1.1.4. Other Treaties

Treaties *ratified* by the United States are the "supreme law" of the United States under Art. IV, Section 2 of the Constitution. Courts must distinguish, however, between treaties that are self-executing and those that are not.[34] A determination that a treaty is not self-executing means only that, absent implementing legislation, the treaty does not provide a rule that courts must enforce.[35] The BIA, in *Matter of H–M–V–*, 22 I&N Dec. 256 (BIA 1998), held that it lacked jurisdiction to adjudicate Convention against Torture claims because as of the date of the decision there had been no legislation to implement Article 3, no regulations had been promulgated with respect to Article 3, and the U.S. Senate had declared that Article 3 was not self-executing.

Although legacy INS declared that the Convention against Torture was not self-executing, it took the position that the executive branch, as one of the political branches, may "act to protect rights a person may have under a treaty that is not self-executing."[36] As a result, prior to the passage of implementing legislation, legacy INS had established informal procedures for presenting a claim under the Convention against Torture. With regard to treaties that have been signed by the United States, but not ratified—such as the Convention on the Rights of the Child—legacy INS/USCIS has taken the position that the United States must refrain from acts that would defeat the object and purpose of the treaty.[37]

Other human rights treaties signed *or* ratified by the United States include:

- International Covenant on Civil and Political Rights;
- International Covenant on Economic, Social and Cultural Rights;
- Convention on the Prevention and Punishment of the Crime of Genocide;
- Convention on the Elimination of All Forms of Racial Discrimination;
- Convention on the Rights of the Child;
- Convention on the Elimination of All Forms of Discrimination Against Women; and
- Convention on the Political Rights of Women.

While courts, EOIR, and the Department of Homeland Security (DHS) may not be able to enforce these treaties without implementing legislation, they are useful for other purposes. For example, they are useful in determining if an act amounts to persecution,

---

[33] For information on the legislation, case law, regulations, and policy memoranda for seeking protection under the Convention Against Torture, see ch. 4.

[34] *See, e.g., Foster v. Neilson*, 27 U.S. (2 Pet.) 253, 314 (1829), *overruled on other grounds, U.S. v. Percheman*, 32 U.S. 51 (1833).

[35] *Id.*

[36] *Basic Law Manual, supra* note 29, at 11.

[37] INS Memorandum, "Guidelines for Children's Asylum Claims" (Dec. 10, 1998), *published on* AILA InfoNet (*posted* Jan. 25, 1999), *reproduced in* 76 *Interpreter Releases* 5, 6 n. 2 (Jan. 4, 1999), and available at *www.asylumlaw.org/docs/united_states/guidelines/children.pdf.*

what procedures should be used when adjudicating women's or children's asylum claims, or even whether the provisions of the treaty have become customary international law.[38]

It may also be useful in asylum cases to consult sources of international humanitarian law. If the asylum applicant is from a country engaged in a civil war or conflict, the treatment of noncombatants, the conduct of combatants, and whether the harm experienced or inflicted amounts to persecution may be issues that arise in such claims.

The most important conventions governing wartime conduct are:

- Geneva Convention for the Amelioration of the Condition of the Wounded and Sick in Armed Forces in the Field;
- Geneva Convention for the Amelioration of the Condition of the Wounded, Sick, and Shipwrecked Members of the Armed Forces at Sea;
- Geneva Convention Relative to the Treatment of Prisoners of War;
- Geneva Convention Relative to the Protection of Civilian Persons in Time of War;
- Protocol Additional to the Geneva Conventions of 2 August 1949, and relating to the Protection of Victims of International Armed Conflict (Protocol I); and
- Protocol Additional to the Geneva Conventions of 2 August 1949, and relating to the Protection of Victims of Non-International Armed Conflict (Protocol II).

An excellent source for information about these and other human rights treaties is the Office of United Nations High Commissioner for Human Rights website—*www.ohchr.org/english*.

1.2. U.S. STATUTES

1.2.1. Refugee Act of 1980

The Refugee Act of 1980 is contained within the INA.[39] The Refugee Act significantly revised U.S. law in an effort to bring the United States into compliance with its obligations under the 1967 United Nations Protocol relating to the Status of Refugees, to which the United States had acceded in 1968.[40] Prior to the passage of the Refugee Act, U.S. law provided protection to individuals fleeing persecution from Communist countries and the Middle East.[41] The principal provisions of the Refugee Act that concern asylum applicants in the United States are found in INA §101(a)(42), the definition of refugee; §208, asylum; and former §243(h), the *nonrefoulement* provision.[42] These provisions of the Refugee Act have been modified and in some cases moved to new sections of the INA by the Illegal

---

[38] *See, e.g.*, International Covenant on Civil and Political Rights, Dec. 16, 1966, 999 U.N.T.S. 171, 1057 U.N.T.S. 407 (entered into force Mar. 23, 1976), art. 6 (the right not to be arbitrarily deprived of life), art. 18 (the right to freedom of thought and conscience), art. 14 (the right to a fair trial), art. 22 (freedom of association).

[39] Refugee Act of 1980, Pub. L. No. 96-212, 94 Stat. 102.

[40] *See, e.g.*, *INS v. Cardoza-Fonseca*, 480 U.S. 421, 436–37 (1987).

[41] *See* former INA §203(a)(7); 8 USC §1153(a)(7) (repealed 1980).

[42] 8 USC §§1101(a)(42), 1158, and former §1253(h).

CHAPTER 1 • SOURCES OF ASYLUM LAW

Immigration Reform and Immigrant Responsibility Act of 1996 (IIRAIRA).[43] More recently, under the REAL ID Act of 2005, provisions were added to §208 of the INA regarding credibility determinations, corroboration, the burden of proof, and judicial review.[44]

Definition of Refugee

Under the Refugee Act, a "refugee" is defined as:

any person who is outside any country of such person's nationality or, in the case of a person having no nationality, is outside any country in which such person last habitually resided, and who is unable or unwilling to return to, and is unable or unwilling to avail himself or herself of the protection of, that country because of persecution or a well-founded fear of persecution on account of race, religion, nationality, membership in a particular social group, or political opinion.[45]

IIRAIRA amended this definition by adding a sentence regarding persons fleeing coercive population control measures.[46] The definition also explicitly excludes:

any person who ordered, incited, assisted, or otherwise participated in the persecution of any person on account of race, religion, nationality, membership in a particular social group, or political opinion.[47]

Asylum

Section 208 of the INA authorizes the granting of asylum to individuals who are physically present or arriving in the United States, regardless of their status, and who meet the definition of refugee.[48] This section was substantially revised by IIRAIRA[49] and the REAL ID Act.[50]

The Principle of Nonrefoulement

The *nonrefoulement* provision of the Refugee Act, previously known as withholding of deportation, provides protection to individuals whose lives or freedom "would be threatened" on account of race, religion, nationality, membership in a particular social group, or political opinion if returned to their home countries. This provision, previously INA §243(h), 8 USC §1253(h), was revised by IIRAIRA and is now found at INA §241(b)(3), 8 USC §1231(b)(3)(B). The provision is now referred to as withholding of removal or restriction on removal.[51]

---

[43] Illegal Immigration Reform and Immigrant Responsibility Act of 1996 (IIRAIRA), Pub. L. No. 104-208, div. C, 110 Stat. 3009, 3009-546 to 3009-724, discussed *infra* this chapter.

[44] REAL ID Act of 2005, Pub. L. No. 109-13, div. B, 119 Stat. 231, 302–23, discussed *infra* this chapter.

[45] INA §101(a)(42); 8 USC §1101(a)(42).

[46] *See* this chapter, at 1.2.2.

[47] INA §101(a)(42); 8 USC §1101(a)(42).

[48] 8 USC §1158.

[49] *See* this chapter, at 1.2.2.

[50] *See* ch. 2.6.

[51] *See* this chapter, at 1.2.2.

1.2.2. Illegal Immigration Reform and Immigrant Responsibility Act

The asylum amendments to IIRAIRA have been described as the most significant revision to U.S. asylum law since the adoption of the Refugee Act.[52] The new provisions include a revised definition of refugee, a revised *nonrefoulement* provision, new bars to asylum eligibility, and a new expedited removal process. Listed below are highlights of the most significant changes under IIRAIRA.

Revised Definition of Refugee

Under IIRAIRA, the term "refugee" was amended to include that:

> a person who has been forced to abort a pregnancy or to undergo involuntary sterilization, or who has been persecuted for failure or refusal to undergo such a procedure or for other resistance to a coercive population control program, shall be deemed to have been persecuted on account of political opinion, and a person who has a well founded fear that he or she will be forced to undergo such a procedure or subject to persecution for such failure, refusal, or resistance shall be deemed to have a well founded fear of persecution on account of political opinion.[53]

The number of individuals who may be admitted to the United States as refugees or granted asylum under this new provision was limited to 1,000 per year.[54] This numerical limitation was removed by the REAL ID Act.[55]

Revised Nonrefoulement Provision

The withholding of removal or *nonrefoulement* section of IIRAIRA was amended to preclude from protection any individual who "has been convicted of an aggravated felony (or felonies) for which [he or she] has been sentenced to an aggregate term of imprisonment of at least 5 years." Such individuals are deemed to have committed a "particularly serious crime" and are ineligible for withholding of removal.[56] Individuals barred from such relief may wish to pursue a claim for relief under the Convention against Torture.[57]

For a few months prior to the enactment of IIRAIRA, the Antiterrorism and Effective Death Penalty Act (AEDPA)[58] permitted the U.S. Attorney General (AG) to grant withholding of removal "to ensure compliance" with the 1967 Protocol, "notwithstanding any other provision of law." Nevertheless, in *Matter of Q–T–M–T–*, 21 I&N Dec. 639, 655 (BIA 1996), the BIA construed the aggravated felony bar to be in compliance with the Protocol, thereby barring individuals from *nonrefoulement* protection even though the crime would not be particularly serious under international law standards.[59]

---

[52] *See* D. Horne and L. Weitzhandler, "Asylum Law after the Illegal Immigration Reform and Immigrant Responsibility Act," 97-4 *Immigration Briefings* (Apr. 1997).

[53] INA §101(a)(42)(B); 8 USC §1101(a)(42)(B).

[54] INA §207(a)(5); 8 USC §1157(a)(5).

[55] For additional information, see ch. 2.4.11.

[56] INA §241(b)(3)(B); 8 USC §1231(b)(3)(B).

[57] *See* ch. 4.

[58] Antiterrorism and Effective Death Penalty Act of 1996, Pub. L. No. 104-132, 110 Stat. 1214.

[59] For additional information on the aggravated felony bar, see ch. 2.7.2.

Additional Statutory Bars to Asylum

Under INA §208(a), an individual is ineligible to apply for asylum in the United States if the asylum-seeker: (1) may be removed to a safe third country; (2) did not file within one year after his or her arrival in the United States; or (3) was previously denied asylum.[60]

Under §208(b), asylum may not be granted if the applicant has committed a particularly serious crime or a serious nonpolitical crime, is found to be a danger to the security of the United States, has engaged in terrorist activities, is affiliated with a terrorist organization, or is found to be firmly resettled in a third country. After the September 11, 2001, attacks, Congress added additional bars to asylum for individuals associated with terrorist activities.[61]

Expedited Removal Proceedings

One of the most controversial provisions in IIRAIRA is the section on expedited removal. Under this process, sometimes referred to as summary exclusion, a noncitizen who arrives at a port of entry with purportedly false documents or no documents will be removed from the United States without further hearing or review, unless the individual indicates a fear of persecution or a desire to apply for asylum, or alleges that he or she was previously granted permanent residency or refugee/asylee status.[62] These provisions have been expanded in recent years to include individuals apprehended in the interior of the United States.[63]

1.2.3. USA PATRIOT Act

Just six weeks after the September 11 terrorist attacks, Congress enacted sweeping changes to the INA with the passage of the Uniting and Strengthening America by Providing Appropriate Tools Required to Intercept and Obstruct Terrorism Act (USA PATRIOT Act).[64] The act added to the already extensive list of bars to asylum and withholding of removal.[65] Now, any individual who "used [his or her] position of prominence within any country to endorse or espouse terrorist activity, or to persuade others to support terrorist activity" is barred if the Secretary of State determines that such actions undermine U.S. efforts to reduce or eliminate terrorist activities.[66]

The USA PATRIOT Act also expands the definition of terrorist activity to include the use of "any weapon or dangerous device," in addition to those previously listed, which included chemical, biological, and nuclear weapons, as well as explosives and firearms.[67]

---

[60] For several exceptions to these provisions, see ch. 2.7.2.

[61] For more detail on all of these bars, see ch. 2.7.2., and this chapter, at 1.2.4.

[62] For a more detailed discussion, see ch. 5.

[63] For more information on the expansion of expedited removal, see ch. 5.

[64] Pub. L. No. 107-56, 115 Stat. 272.

[65] For a more in-depth look at the potential consequences of the USA PATRIOT Act for refugees and asylum seekers, see ch. 3. *See also* R. Germain, "Rushing to Judgment: The Unintended Consequences of the USA PATRIOT Act for Bona Fide Refugees," 16 *Geo. Immigr. L.J.* 505 (Winter 2002).

[66] INA §212(a)(3)(B)(i)(VI); 8 USC §1182(a)(3)(B)(i)(VI).

[67] INA §212(a)(3)(B)(iii)(V); 8 USC §1182(a)(3)(B)(iii)(V).

This bar only applies if the weapon is used "other than for mere personal monetary gain" and "with the intent to endanger, directly or indirectly, the safety of one or more individuals or to cause substantial damage to property."[68]

Perhaps the most controversial provision of the act is the mandatory detention section that allows the AG to certify and detain, perhaps indefinitely, noncitizens deemed to be a threat to national security.[69] Those who could be certified include individuals granted asylum or individuals who merely have a familial relationship with someone deemed to be a threat to national security.[70]

1.2.4. The REAL ID Act

On May 11, 2005, more changes were made to asylum law under the REAL ID Act, a law that also has sweeping repercussions in other areas of immigration and national security law. The new provisions that impact asylum-seekers include a statutory description of the burden of proof for asylum,[71] the elimination of the cap on the number of coercive population control asylum cases that could be granted each year (previously 1,000),[72] changes to the definition of "terrorist activity,"[73] changes to the definition of "engage in terrorist activity,"[74] a waiver for the material support bar,[75] and a broadening of judicial review.[76] Some provisions were effective immediately; others apply only to asylum applications filed on or after May 11, 2005.[77] The impact of these provisions is discussed in chapters 2 and 3, *infra*.

1.3. REGULATIONS

Since 2000, final regulations regarding procedures, definitions, and the burden of proof in asylum, withholding of removal, and Convention against Torture claims have been issued.[78] In preparing your case, it is important to review carefully the applicable regulations. The regulations often set forth definitions and additional procedural requirements that will assist you in preparing your claim. Beware! Immigration regulations change frequently. You should never rely on outdated sources.

---

[68] *Id.*

[69] INA §236A, 8 USC §1226a.

[70] *See generally* INA §§236A(a)(2), (3); 8 USC §§1226a(a)(2), (3).

[71] REAL ID Act §101(a)(3)(B), codified at INA §208(b)(1)(B).

[72] *Id.* at §101(g)(2), codified by removing INA §207(a)(5).

[73] *Id.* at §103(a)(i), codified at INA §212(a)(3)(B)(i).

[74] *Id.* at §103(b), codified at INA §212(a)(3)(B)(iv).

[75] *Id.* at §103(b)(iv)(VI), codified at INA §212(a)(3)(B)(iv)(VI).

[76] *Id.* at §101(f), codified at INA §242(a)(2)(D).

[77] *See, e.g., Matter of S–B–*, 24 I&N Dec. 42 (BIA 2006) (holding that the provisions regarding credibility determinations only apply to asylum applications filed on or after May 11, 2005).

[78] *See, e.g.,* 65 Fed. Reg. 76121–38 (Dec. 6, 2000).

Note that regulations that do not fall within the scope of a statutory delegation of authority are *ultra vires* and may be challenged in court. Even a long-standing agency regulation is not entitled to deference if it conflicts with the plain language of the statute.[79]

Additionally, if DHS violates a regulatory requirement, IJs and the BIA are permitted to exclude evidence or invalidate the proceedings if the purpose of the regulation is to benefit the individual and the violation prejudiced his or her interests.[80]

1.4. OPERATIONS INSTRUCTIONS AND FIELD MANUALS

Legacy INS had its own internal guidelines, called Operations Instructions (OIs). The sections relevant to asylum procedures included §§209 (adjustment) and 223a (travel documents). OI §208, which was somewhat out of date, was removed from the OIs in 1997. DHS is now in the process of issuing a series of field manuals to replace the OIs.[81]

The first such manual to be issued is the *Inspector's Field Manual* (*IFM*) (first published Mar. 13, 1998), which deals with issues arising at ports of entry. Some of the sections relevant to asylum claims are §16.3 (asylees and asylum applicants), §17.11 (asylum claims), and §23.18 (asylum claims by stowaways). Other recently issued manuals are the *Adjudicator's Field Manual* (Feb. 2001) and the *Detention and Deportation Officer's Field Manual* (May 19, 1999) (which contains §17.2 on asylum). There is also a *Detention Operations Manual* (Sept. 20, 2000) that includes information on grievance procedures, group rights presentations, and access to legal materials. U.S. Citizenship and Immigration Services (USCIS) has also published an *Affirmative Asylum Procedures Manual*,[82] a comprehensive manual with information ranging from scheduling interviews to motions to reopen.

OIs did not have the force of law, but provided general guidance for legacy INS employees. While federal courts have jurisdiction to review the validity of agency practices and internal procedures,[83] they did not appear to have the authority to enforce OIs.[84] Similarly, the new manuals will probably not have the force of law. To emphasize this point, the first page of the *IFM* specifically states: "Nothing in this manual shall be con-

---

[79] *See Brown v. Gardner*, 513 U.S. 115, 120–21 (1994) ("legislative silence as to [an agency's] practice over the last 60 years" is trumped by the plain language of the statute); *Demarest v. Manspeaker*, 498 U.S. 184, 190 (1991) (a long-standing agency interpretation of a statute is not entitled to deference, and even subsequent reenactment of the statute does not constitute an adoption of a previous administrative construction where the law is plain).

[80] *Matter of Garcia-Flores*, 17 I&N Dec. 325 (BIA 1980).

[81] *See* INS Memorandum, C. Sale, IIRAIRA Wire #25 (Mar. 31, 1997), *published on* AILA InfoNet at Doc. No. 97033192 (*posted* Mar. 31, 1997).

[82] The *Affirmative Asylum Procedures Manual* (Feb. 2003) is available online at www.uscis.gov/files/nativedocuments/AffrmAsyManFNL.pdf, and in hardcopy from AILA Publications, www.ailapubs.org. As of Fall 2007, USCIS is preparing an updated version of the *Manual* for imminent publication.

[83] *McNary v. Haitian Refugee Center, Inc.*, 498 U.S. 479, 491–94 (1991).

[84] *Fano v. O'Neill*, 806 F.2d 1262, 1263–64 (5th Cir. 1987) (holding that OIs are only internal guidelines that do not confer substantive rights nor establish procedures on which a petitioner for immigration benefits may rely); *Pasquini v. Morris*, 700 F.2d 658, 661–62 (11th Cir. 1983) (holding that OIs are for the administrative convenience of the INS and do not confer substantive rights).

strued to create any substantive or procedural right or benefit that is legally enforceable by any party against the United States or its agencies or officers or any other person."

1.5. BIA DECISIONS

In preparing your asylum claim, it is essential to review decisions issued by the BIA. The BIA is the administrative appellate body charged with reviewing decisions by IJs and interpreting immigration statutes and regulations. The BIA does not, however, have authority to review credible-fear determinations made by AOs and IJs in the expedited removal process under INA §235(b)(1)(C), 8 USC §1225(b)(1)(C).

Decisions of the BIA are binding on all officers and employees of DHS and IJs.[85] The AG, however, has the authority to review decisions made by the BIA.[86] For example, the AG exercised this authority in his decision to vacate the BIA's bond determination in *Matter of D–J–*.[87]

Select decisions are designated by the BIA as precedents.[88] These precedent decisions are first designated as interim decisions and later published in *Administrative Decisions Under Immigration & Nationality Laws of the United States* (abbreviated as I&N Dec.). Sometimes BIA precedent decisions are cited by their interim decision number.[89] Although unpublished BIA decisions are not binding on the BIA, IJs, or AOs, at least one court has recognized the BIA's nonprecedent decisions as an expression of the BIA's position on a particular issue.[90] Courts also have held that the BIA abuses its discretion if it inexplicably departs from prior precedent.[91]

Although the BIA lacks jurisdiction to rule on the constitutionality of the INA and the regulations,[92] where possible, it must construe statutes to achieve results that are consistent—rather than in conflict—with constitutional protections. The BIA also lacks the authority to ignore or disregard regulations promulgated by the AG.[93]

---

[85] 8 CFR §1003.1(g).

[86] 8 CFR §1003.1(h); *Matter of Leon-Orosco and Rodriguez-Colas*, 19 I&N Dec. 136 (A.G. 1984), *reversed on other grounds, Fernandez-Roque v. Smith,* 599 F. Supp. 1103 (N.D.Ga. 1984).

[87] *Matter of D–J–*, 23 I&N Dec. 572 (AG 2003) (holding that a Haitian asylum seeker's release on bond was unwarranted due to national security concerns).

[88] 8 CFR §1003.1(g).

[89] *See, e.g., Matter of Acosta*, 19 I&N Dec. 211 (BIA 1985), *overruled in part on other grounds, Matter of Mogharrabi,* 19 I&N Dec. 439 (BIA 1987).

[90] *Davila-Bardales v. INS*, 27 F.3d 1, 5–6 (1st Cir. 1994) ("[W]e see no earthly reason why the mere fact of nonpublication should permit an agency to take a view of law that is flatly contrary to the view it set out in earlier cases . . . without explaining why it is doing so.").

[91] *See, e.g., Margalli-Olvera v. INS*, 43 F.3d 345, 357 (8th Cir. 1994); *Yepes-Prado v. INS*, 10 F.3d 1363, 1372 (9th Cir. 1993).

[92] *See, e.g., Matter of L–S–J–*, 21 I&N Dec. 973 (BIA 1997).

[93] *Matter of Anselmo*, 20 I&N Dec. 25, 30 (BIA 1989).

1.6. OFFICE OF LEGAL COUNSEL DECISIONS

On occasion, the AG has directed the Office of Legal Counsel at the Department of Justice to prepare formal opinions for issuance to federal agencies, including DHS and legacy INS.[94]

1.7. FEDERAL COURT DECISIONS

Federal courts often are the final arbiters in asylum cases. Decisions by U.S. district courts, U.S. circuit courts of appeals, and the U.S. Supreme Court have interpreted key provisions in the Refugee Act and asylum regulations, and have ruled on constitutional issues raised by asylum-seekers. DHS and the BIA lack the authority to make decisions on constitutional issues and claims that question the validity of their own regulations or statutes. Such claims may only be brought in the federal courts. While decisions of the Supreme Court are binding throughout the United States, decisions of U.S. circuit courts of appeals are binding only in their own circuits.

The BIA has historically followed a circuit court's precedent in cases arising within the jurisdiction of that circuit.[95] When the BIA disagrees with a court's position on a given issue, it has declined to follow it outside the court's jurisdiction. The BIA has held, however, that it is not bound to follow the published decision of a U.S. district court in cases arising within the same district.[96]

Changes under IIRAIRA and the USA PATRIOT Act have limited federal court review for asylum applicants in several areas. For example, amendments to INA §208 (statutory bars to asylum) bar judicial review of the AG's determinations regarding the availability of a safe third country, the applicability of exceptions to the filing deadline, and the bar for previously denied claims. Section 208 also bars judicial review of the AG's determination that an individual is ineligible for asylum based on terrorist-related grounds. Section 242(b)(4)(D) of the INA, added by IIRAIRA, provides that the AG's discretionary judgment whether to grant asylum under §208(a) is conclusive unless "manifestly contrary to the law and an abuse of discretion." The REAL ID Act gave back some limited jurisdiction to the federal courts, allowing the courts to review constitutional claims and questions of law on issues previously barred from judicial review, such as the one year filing deadline.[97] Under the USA PATRIOT Act, the AG's determination that an individual is subject to detention as a suspected terrorist is reviewable only in habeas corpus proceedings and appeals may only be to the U.S. Court of Appeals for the D.C. Circuit or the U.S. Supreme Court.[98]

---

[94] *See, e.g.*, Legal Obligations of the United States under Article 33 of the Refugee Convention, 15 Op. O.L.C. 86 (1991); *Deportation Proceedings of Joseph Patrick Thomas Doherty*, 12 Op. O.L.C. 1 (1988). These opinions are available on Lexis and Westlaw.

[95] *Matter of Anselmo*, *supra* note 93, at 31–32.

[96] *Matter of K–S–*, 20 I&N Dec. 715, 718–20 (BIA 1993).

[97] INA §242(a)(2)(D); 8 USC §1252(a)(2)(D), as modified by the REAL ID Act.

[98] INA §236A(b); 8 USC §1226a(b).

Judicial review of the expedited removal process is even more limited.[99] In most cases, federal courts are barred by statute from reviewing the individual credible-fear determinations of AOs or IJs. Section 242(e) of the INA provides for very limited judicial review of final removal orders entered under the new "expedited" removal process. Judicial review of an individual expedited removal order is only available through habeas corpus and is limited to whether the petitioner is an alien, whether the petitioner was ordered removed under the expedited removal process, and whether the petitioner can prove by a preponderance of the evidence that he or she is a lawful permanent resident, or has been admitted as a refugee or granted asylum.[100] Judicial review of the implementation of the expedited removal process is only available in the U.S. District Court for the District of Columbia and must be filed within 60 days after the date that a challenged section, regulation, directive, guideline, or procedure is first implemented.[101]

Despite limits on judicial review under IIRAIRA and the USA PATRIOT Act, the role of the federal courts should not be underestimated. Federal courts have, in the past, played an important role in defining the rights of noncitizens subject to deportation even before Congress created a statutory right to judicial review. The right to judicial review, as noted by one commentator, is grounded in the long-standing recognition that a noncitizen facing deportation is threatened with loss of a fundamental liberty interest protected by the U.S. Constitution.[102]

1.8. LEGACY INS, DHS, AND EOIR POLICY DIRECTIVES, MEMORANDA, AND STATEMENTS

From time to time, DHS and EOIR (composed of the BIA and the immigration courts) issue policy directives in the form of memoranda or guidelines to their employees. These directives have addressed both procedural and substantive topics. While not legally binding on DHS or EOIR, they do provide insight into the views of these agencies on particular topics that may be at issue in your case.

In May 1995, for example, legacy INS issued guidelines to all AOs for adjudicating women's asylum claims.[103] These guidelines state:

> [R]ape . . . , sexual abuse and domestic violence, infanticide and genital mutilation are forms of mistreatment primarily directed at girls and women and they may serve as evidence of past persecution on account of one or more of the five grounds.

Another example is the former INS general counsel's memorandum concerning HIV infection and relief from deportation issued in February 1996. In that memorandum, the then-

---

[99] INA §242(a)(2); 8 USC §1252(a)(2).

[100] INA §242(e)(2); 8 USC §1252(e)(2).

[101] INA §§242(e)(3)(A), (B); 8 USC §§1252(e)(3)(A), (B).

[102] *See* L. Guttentag, "The 1996 Immigration Act: Federal Court Jurisdiction—Statutory Restrictions and Constitutional Rights," 74 *Interpreter Releases* 245 (Feb. 10, 1997).

[103] *See* INS Memorandum, P. Coven, "Considerations for Asylum Officers Adjudicating Claims from Women" (May 25, 1995), *published on* AILA InfoNet (*posted* May 31, 1995), and *reproduced in* 72 *Interpreter Releases* 771 (June 5, 1995).

INS general counsel adopted recommendations made by the Presidential Advisory Council on acquired immune deficiency syndrome (AIDS) in 1995. The Presidential Advisory Council suggested that INS's efforts against AIDS-related discrimination should include the granting of asylum based on the social group category of HIV-positive individuals.[104]

In response to asylum reform measures implemented in 1995, the Chief Immigration Judge issued Operating Policies and Procedures Memorandum No. 96-1, Asylum Request Processing (Mar. 15, 1996), which set forth procedures for various stages of an asylum claim, including filing applications, scheduling hearings, filing change of venue motions, and obtaining comments from the Department of State.[105]

After the passage of IIRAIRA, legacy INS issued a detailed memorandum on the implementation of the expedited removal process and how officers should handle persons asserting a fear of persecution or intent to apply for asylum.[106]

With regard to the Convention against Torture,[107] both legacy INS and EOIR issued memoranda regarding the implementation of Article 3 relief under the Convention.[108]

Other topics of memoranda include:

- USCIS Fact Sheet, "Traveling Outside the United States as an Asylum Applicant, Asylee, or a Lawful Permanent Resident Who Obtained Such Status Based on Asylum Status" (Jan. 4, 2007 (revised)), available at *www.uscis.gov/files/pressrelease/Asylum Travel122706FS.pdf*;

- EOIR Memorandum, M. Creppy, "Operating Policies and Procedures Memorandum (OPPM) 05-07: Definitions and Use of Adjournment, Call-up and Case Identification Codes" (June 16, 2005), *published on* AILA InfoNet at Doc. No. 05070660 (*posted* July 6, 2005);

- ICE Memorandum, M. Garcia, "Detention Policy Where an Immigration Judge Has Granted Asylum and ICE Has Appealed" (Feb. 9, 2004), *published on* AILA InfoNet at Doc. No. 04022462 (*posted* Feb. 24, 2004);

- EOIR Memorandum, M. Creppy, "Cases Requiring Special Procedures" (Sept. 21, 2001) (requiring closed hearing in some post-September 11 cases); and

- INS Office of International Affairs Memorandum, "Persecution of Family Members" (June 30, 1997).

---

[104] *See* INS General Counsel Memorandum, D. Martin, "Seropositivity for HIV and Relief From Deportation" (Feb. 16, 1996), *reproduced in* 73 *Interpreter Releases* 901, 909 (July 8, 1996).

[105] This memorandum is reproduced in 73 *Interpreter Releases* 479 (Apr. 12, 1996).

[106] INS Memorandum, *supra* note 81, at 646.

[107] See ch. 4 for further discussion of relief under the Convention Against Torture.

[108] INS Memorandum, J. Langlois, "Implementation of Amendments to Asylum and Withholding of Removal Regulations, effective March 22, 1999" (Mar. 18, 1999); EOIR Memorandum, M. Creppy, "Operating Policies and Procedures Memorandum No. 99-5: Implementation of Article 3 of the UN Convention Against Torture" (May 14, 1999), *published on* AILA InfoNet (*posted* June 4, 1999), and available at *www.usdoj.gov/eoir/efoia/ocij/oppm99/99_5.pdf*.

Other sources of useful information are public statements and press releases issued by USCIS, ICE, U.S. Customs and Border Protection (CBP), and EOIR public affairs offices, often in question-and-answer format.[109]

1.9. Legacy INS's *Basic Law Manual* and Asylum Officer Basic Training Course

In the past, a useful tool in preparing asylum claims was the *Basic Law Manual: U.S. Law and INS Refugee/Asylum Adjudications* (1994) (*Basic Law Manual*), which was prepared by the Asylum Division and Office of the General Counsel of legacy INS as a training manual for its AOs. USCIS has expanded on the *Basic Law Manual* in its Asylum Office Basic Training Course (AOBTC), the lesson plans for which are available on the Rocky Mountain Survivors Center website.[110] Although neither the *Basic Law Manual* nor the AOBTC have the force and effect of law, they set forth, in detail, the position of USCIS on a wide range of legal issues.

Previously, the *Basic Law Manual* had been cited with approval by the BIA for recognizing the need for an asylum adjudicator to acquire general country condition information.[111] Similarly, in *Matter of H–*,[112] the BIA noted that the *Basic Law Manual* acknowledges that a Somali clan may constitute a "particular social group," and that clan membership is a highly recognizable, immutable characteristic that is acquired at birth and is inextricably linked to family ties. Therefore, not only AOs, but IJs and the BIA as well, are likely to look to the AOBTC for guidance, as they did with the *Basic Law Manual*.

1.10. Laws of Other Countries

If your claim involves a novel or evolving issue or a firm resettlement question, it may be advantageous or even essential for you to consult the case law and statutes of other countries.

It is not uncommon for courts to look to the law of other countries when interpreting a treaty. The Supreme Court has held that in construing a treaty, it is necessary to "look beyond the written words to . . . the practical construction adopted by the parties."[113] As one commentator has suggested, "[t]he examination of foreign jurisprudence by courts interpreting common terms under the 1951 Refugee Convention and 1967 Protocol should be a standard exercise, and not an occasional occurrence."[114]

---

[109] *See, e.g.*, INS Public Statement, *The 208 Final Rule: Questions and Answers* (Dec. 6, 2000).

[110] *www.rmscdenver.org*.

[111] *Matter of S–M–J–*, 21 I&N Dec. 722 (BIA 1997) (quoting from the *Basic Law Manual* that "[t]he asylum officer should be fully familiar with the reports and country profiles developed by the INS Resource Information Center, with the Department of State's Country Reports of Human Rights Practices for the country being considered, and with reports from Amnesty International and other reputable organizations, including academic institutions.").

[112] 21 I&N Dec. 337 (BIA 1996).

[113] *Air France v. Saks*, 470 U.S. 392, 396 (1985).

[114] A. Helton, "The Use of Comparative Law and Practice under the International Refugee Treaties," *Asylum Law and Practice in Europe and North America: A Comparative Analysis* (G. Koll & J. Bhabha eds., 1992).

In cases regarding the issue of "firm resettlement," *i.e.*, whether the asylum-seeker is barred from asylum because he or she was offered or obtained residency or citizenship in a third country prior to arrival in the United States, the asylum, residency, and citizenship laws of other countries are often in question. If your case involves an asylum-seeker who has resided in another country before coming to the United States or who has documents that appear to confer refugee or other status, the laws of that country should be carefully reviewed.

Chapter 2
U.S. Asylum Law

Every spot of the world is overrun with oppression. Freedom hath been hunted round the globe. Asia, and Africa have long expelled her. —Europe regards her like a stranger, and England hath given her a warning to depart. O! receive the fugitive, and prepare in time an asylum for mankind.*

2.1. History	23
2.2. Asylum Standard—Relief Available	25
2.3. Withholding Standard—Relief Available	26
2.4. Definitions	27
2.5. Current Issues in U.S. Asylum Cases	59
2.6. Burden of Proof	79
2.7. Ineligibility for Asylum and Withholding of Removal	102
2.8. Standard of Review	130

2.1. History

Americans often take for granted that we are a nation that offers refuge to the persecuted. Our national symbol, the Statue of Liberty, may have beckoned our great grandparents or even parents from oppressive conditions in their home countries. Indeed, our nation, even before it was a nation, offered sanctuary to individuals persecuted for religious and other reasons.

Throughout our first 100 years, the United States had a generous, open-door immigration policy. One interesting, but little known, community in the early years of our nation that exemplifies this generous policy was a French refugee settlement called Asylum (or Azilum), settled in 1793 in northeastern Pennsylvania by refugees from the French Revolution.[1] As one commentator has noted, this tradition of welcoming the persecuted was easier to honor when global population was low, travel was expensive and hazardous, and there were no immigration quotas.[2] Yet even the earliest federal controls on U.S. immi-

---

* Thomas Paine, *Common Sense* (1776).

[1] *See* E. Murray, *Azilum: French Refugee Colony* (1940).

[2] *See* D. Martin, *Asylum Case Law Sourcebook* (1998), at xvii.

gration, in the 19th century, provided protection for individuals fleeing persecution for political reasons.[3]

The Immigration and Nationality Act of 1952 (INA),[4] which is the foundation of our immigration law today, likewise allowed the admission of persecution-fleeing individuals who came to the United States outside of the formal refugee resettlement program. The 1952 Act also included a seventh preference category, §203(a)(7), which allowed refugees who were fleeing persecution from communist or communist-dominated countries or from the Middle East to be admitted to the United States.[5] This law may be attributed in part to international efforts, in the aftermath of World War II, to alleviate the plight of refugees and find lasting solutions to their uncertain legal and physical situation. Such efforts culminated in the adoption of the 1951 United Nations Convention Relating to the Status of Refugees (Convention), an instrument that limited protection to refugees fearing persecution as a result of events occurring in Europe before January 1, 1951.[6]

The 1967 United Nations Protocol Relating to the Status of Refugees (Protocol) incorporated Articles 2 through 34 of the Convention and removed its temporal and geographic limitations.[7] In 1968, the United States acceded to the Protocol and became obliged to abide by its provisions, including the broadened definition of "refugee" and the principle of *nonrefoulement*.[8] It was not until 1980, however, that Congress passed the Refugee Act[9] in an effort to bring U.S. law into conformity with international obligations under the Protocol. The act created a legal framework for refugees to apply from abroad and for asylum-seekers to apply from within the United States. The definition of "refugee" in the Refugee Act is virtually identical to the Protocol definition. In addition, revisions were made to the INA's withholding of removal section—the *nonrefoulement* provision—to make it mandatory and to include exceptions or exclusion clauses found in the Convention and Protocol.

In 1996, Congress amended the INA explicitly to provide protection to individuals fleeing coercive population control methods and to permit the expedited removal of asylum-seekers who fail to establish a "credible fear" of persecution shortly after their arrival in the United States. This law, the Illegal Immigration Reform and Immigrant Responsibility Act (IIRAIRA),[10] also expanded the number of offenses deemed to be particularly serious crimes, thereby barring otherwise eligible individuals from asylum and withholding of removal. Moreover, for the first time, U.S. law imposed a deadline for filing an asylum application. Applicants must file within one year after their arrival in the

---

[3] *Id.*

[4] Immigration and Nationality Act of 1952 (INA), Pub. L. No. 82-414, 66 Stat. 163 (codified as amended at 8 USC §1101 *et seq.*).

[5] 8 USC §1153(a)(7) (repealed 1980).

[6] *See* Convention Relating to the Status of Refugees, July 28, 1951, 189 U.N.T.S. 150 (entered into force Apr. 22, 1954), art. 1A.

[7] Protocol Relating to the Status of Refugees, 606 U.N.T.S. 267 (entered into force Oct. 4, 1967).

[8] *See* ch. 1.1.1.

[9] Refugee Act of 1980, Pub. L. No. 96-212, 94 Stat. 102.

[10] Illegal Immigration Reform and Immigrant Responsibility Act of 1996 (IIRAIRA), Pub. L. No. 104-208, div. C, 110 Stat. 3009, 3009-546 to 3009-724.

CHAPTER 2 • U.S. ASYLUM LAW

United States, unless they are able to establish extraordinary circumstances for the delay or the existence of changed circumstances that materially affect their eligibility for asylum. In 1998, Congress passed the Foreign Affairs Reform and Restructuring Act,[11] which contains a provision prohibiting the United States from returning an individual to a country where he or she would be subjected to torture.[12] In 2001, Congress passed the USA PATRIOT Act,[13] which again expanded the bars to asylum and allowed for the detention of "suspected terrorists" even if they have been granted asylum. More recently, the REAL ID Act of 2005 made additional changes regarding credibility determinations and corroboration in asylum claims.[14]

Asylum law in the United States continues to evolve. Congress is considering several changes to the INA that would provide greater protection to children in removal proceedings, as well as changes that would allow for exceptions to the material support bar for asylum. The Department of Homeland Security (DHS) is also expected to issue regulations regarding gender-based asylum claims. Asylum applicants and their representatives also play an important role in the evolution of asylum law as they strive for fairer and more generous applications of the law in their individual cases.

2.2. ASYLUM STANDARD—RELIEF AVAILABLE

Under §208(b) of the INA, the attorney general (AG) may, in his or her discretion, grant asylum to an individual who qualifies as a "refugee" within the meaning of INA §101(a)(42). Under the Homeland Security Act of 2002, this discretion to grant asylum extends to the DHS secretary and other DHS officials.[15] The definition includes the requirement that the asylum applicant demonstrate that he or she is unwilling or unable to return to his or her home country because of past persecution or a "well-founded fear" of persecution on account of race, religion, nationality, membership in a particular social group, or political opinion.[16]

The asylum applicant's burden of proof is to demonstrate that there is a "reasonable possibility" that he or she will be persecuted.[17] An applicant for asylum may establish a well-founded fear by showing that a reasonable person in his or her circumstances would fear persecution.[18] A fear may be well-founded "even if there is only a slight, though dis-

---

[11] Foreign Affairs Reform and Restructuring Act of 1998, Pub. L. No. 105-277, div. G, §2242(b), 112 Stat. 2681, 2681-822.

[12] *See* ch. 4.

[13] Uniting and Strengthening America by Providing Appropriate Tools Required to Intercept and Obstruct Terrorism (USA PATRIOT ACT) Act of 2001, Pub. L. No. 107-56, 115 Stat. 272.

[14] REAL ID Act of 2005, Pub. L. No. 109-13, div. B, 119 Stat. 231, 302–23.

[15] *See* Homeland Security Act of 2002, Pub. L. No. 107-296, §§456, 1512, 1517, 116 Stat. 2135, 2200, 2310, 2311.

[16] The definition of "refugee" is set forth and explained in more detail in this chapter, at 2.4.

[17] *INS v. Cardoza-Fonseca*, 480 U.S. 421, 438–39 (1987) (rejecting argument by INS that the standard should be a "clear probability" of persecution).

[18] *See Matter of Mogharrabi*, 19 I&N Dec. 439, 445 (BIA 1987); *see also Guevara-Flores v. INS*, 786 F.2d 1242, 1249 (5th Cir. 1986); *Matter of D–V–*, 21 I&N Dec. 77, 78 (BIA 1993).

cernible, chance of persecution."[19] An applicant must also establish that race, religion, nationality, membership in a particular social group or political opinion "was or will be one central reason for persecuting the applicant."[20] Asylum, unlike withholding of removal, may be denied in the exercise of discretion to a person who establishes eligibility for relief.[21] "The danger of persecution," however, "should generally outweigh all but the most egregious of adverse factors."[22]

Asylum also provides more permanent protection than withholding of removal. A person granted asylum, known as an "asylee," may apply for permanent residency after one year under INA §209 and may eventually become a U.S. citizen. An asylee may also bring his or her spouse and children to the United States under 8 CFR §1208.21.[23]

> *Tip*—Every application for asylum is also considered to be an application for withholding of removal.[24] In most affirmative cases, however, the asylum office does not have authority to grant withholding of removal.[25]

2.3. WITHHOLDING STANDARD—RELIEF AVAILABLE

Under INA §241(b)(3)(A), the AG may not remove a person to a country where his or her life or freedom would be threatened because of the person's race, religion, nationality, membership in a particular social group, or political opinion. Under the Homeland Security Act of 2002, this prohibition on removal extends to the DHS secretary and other DHS officials.[26] The applicant for withholding of removal must show a clear probability of persecution or that it is more likely than not that he or she would be persecuted if removed to his or her home country.[27] This standard is more difficult to satisfy than the well-founded-fear standard for asylum.[28] While the granting of asylum is discretionary,

---

[19] *Diallo v. INS*, 232 F.3d 279, 284 (2d Cir. 2000).

[20] INA §208(b)(1)(B)(i); 8 USC §1158(b)(1)(B)(i).

[21] *See Cardoza-Fonseca, supra* note 17, at 441; *Mogharrabi, supra* note 18, at 449; *see also* this chapter, at 2.7.1.

[22] *Matter of Pula*, 19 I&N Dec. 467, 474 (BIA 1987).

[23] *See* ch. 3.15.

[24] 8 CFR §1208.3(b).

[25] *See* ch. 3.2.

[26] *See* Homeland Security Act of 2002, Pub. L. No. 107-296, §§456, 1512, 1517, 116 Stat. 2135, 2200, 2310, 2311.

[27] *See Cardoza-Fonseca, supra* note 17, at 423; *INS v. Stevic*, 467 U.S. 407, 429–30 (1984).

[28] *Cardoza-Fonseca, supra* note 17, at 431; *see Niang v. Gonzales*, 492 F.3d 505 (4th Cir. 2007) (observing that a petition for withholding of removal "cannot be based on a fear of psychological harm alone"); *Capric v. Ashcroft*, 355 F.3d 1075, 1095 (7th Cir. 2004) (noting that the "clear probability" standard is "a much more demanding burden"); *Lim v. INS*, 224 F.3d 929, 938 (9th Cir. 2000) (finding that although the applicant was eligible for asylum, because his risk of persecution was less than 50 percent, he did not qualify for withholding). *But see Wang v. Ashcroft*, 341 F. 3d 1015, 1022–23 (9th Cir. 2003) (an applicant who was subjected to two forced abortions, who had taken steps to have more children, and who would be subject to forced sterilization upon return to China qualified for withholding of removal).

withholding of removal to a particular country is mandatory if the AG determines that the applicant's life or freedom would be threatened in that country.[29]

The grant of withholding of removal, unlike asylum, does not give an individual an automatic right to remain in the United States, nor may he or she apply for permanent residency, obtain many federally funded benefits and assistance, or bring his or her spouse or children to the United States.[30] An individual granted withholding may be removed to a third country in which he or she would not face persecution if the United States is able to find such a country willing to accept the individual.[31]

2.4. DEFINITIONS

This section focuses on the definition of "refugee," the terms that are included in that definition, and their interpretation by legacy INS, DHS, the Board of Immigration Appeals (BIA), the federal courts, and the Office of United Nations High Commissioner for Refugees (UNHCR). The refugee definition has evolved over time to conform to changes in law, as well as changes in the causes of and responses to refugee crises throughout the world.

2.4.1. Refugee

A "refugee," as defined by the INA, is:

any person who is outside any country of such person's nationality or, in the case of a person having no nationality, is outside any country in which such person last habitually resided, and who is unable or unwilling to return to, and is unable or unwilling to avail himself or herself of the protection of, that country because of persecution or a well-founded fear of persecution on account of race, religion, nationality, membership in a particular social group, or political opinion.[32]

The definition of refugee was amended in 1996 to ensure protection for individuals fleeing coercive population control methods. The revised definition includes the following provision:

For purposes of determinations under this Act, a person who has been forced to abort a pregnancy or to undergo involuntary sterilization, or who has been persecuted for failure or refusal to undergo such a procedure or for other resistance to a coercive population control program, shall be deemed to have been persecuted on account of political opinion, and a person who has a well-founded fear that he or she will be forced to undergo such a procedure or subject to persecution for such

---

[29] *Cardoza-Fonseca, supra* note 17, at 429; *Gonzales-Neyra v. INS*, 122 F.3d 1293, 1297 (9th Cir. 1997), *amended by* 133 F.3d 726 (9th Cir. 1998). *But see Salazar v. Ashcroft*, 359 F.3d 45, 52 (1st Cir. 2004) (denying withholding of removal claim based on finding that Peruvian asylum applicant "may" be able to voluntarily depart to Venezuela).

[30] *But see* 8 CFR §§208.16(e), 1208.16(e) (requiring asylum officers and immigration judges to reconsider their discretionary denial of asylum in cases in which withholding of removal is granted, if such a decision effectively precludes the admission of the applicant's spouse or minor children).

[31] 8 CFR §§208.16(f), 1208.16(f); *see also Cardoza-Fonseca, supra* note 17, at 428, n.6; *Choeum v. INS*, 129 F.3d 29, 40 n.9 (1st Cir. 1997).

[32] INA §101(a)(42)(A); 8 USC §1101(a)(42)(A).

failure, refusal, or resistance shall be deemed to have a well-founded fear of persecution on account of political opinion.[33]

The refugee definition specifically excludes any individual "who ordered, incited, assisted, or otherwise participated in the persecution of any person on account of race, religion, nationality, membership in a particular social group or political opinion."[34]

2.4.2. Country of Nationality and Statelessness

There are two references to the term "nationality" in the refugee definition. The first refers to a status akin to, but not exactly, citizenship. In interpreting what it means for an applicant to be outside his or her country of nationality, the BIA has looked to the definition of "national" found within the INA. Section 101(a)(21) defines "national" as a person owing permanent allegiance to a state. In *Matter of Fatoumata Toure*, the BIA concluded that an applicant who was a citizen of Guinea and feared persecution there was eligible for asylum despite the fact that she possessed a passport from the Ivory Coast.[35] The BIA looked to the INA definition of "national," UNHCR's *Handbook*,[36] and the refugee definition and found that a contrary result would require the deportation of the asylum applicant to a country where she has little or no connection.[37] An applicant's nationality, or lack of nationality, is a threshold question in determining eligibility for asylum.[38] One recent change to the law, however, allows North Korean citizens to apply for asylum, even if they have a right to legal citizenship in South Korea.[39] The failure of the immigration judge (IJ) or the BIA to address nationality may be grounds for remand.[40] In contrast, when interpreting nationality for purposes of determining the motivation of the persecution, *i.e.*, persecution on account of "nationality," courts have defined the term more broadly to include ethnicity and race.[41]

---

[33] INA §101(a)(42); 8 USC §1101(a)(42). This amendment is addressed further in this chapter, at 2.4.11.

[34] INA §101(a)(42)(B); 8 USC §1101(a)(42)(B). For a further discussion of this bar to asylum and withholding of removal, see this chapter, at 2.7.2.

[35] *Matter of Fatoumata Toure*, A24 876 244 (BIA 1990), *reprinted in* 8 *Bender's Immigr. Case Rep.* B1-105.

[36] United Nations High Commissioner for Refugees (UNHCR), *Handbook on Procedures and Criteria for Determining Refugee Status* (1992), available at *www.unhcr.org/publ/PUBL/3d58e13b4.pdf*.

[37] *Matter of Fatoumata Toure, supra* note 35.

[38] *Wangchuck v. DHS*, 448 F.3d 524, 528 (2d Cir. 2006) (applicant was born in India to Tibetan refugee parents); *Dhoumo v. BIA*, 416 F.3d 172, 173 (2d Cir. 2005) (applicant was born in India of Tibetan parents in Tibetan refugee camp).

[39] North Korean Human Rights Act of 2004, Pub. L. No. 108-333, 118 Stat. 1287 (2004). Section 302(a) provides: "North Koreans are not barred from eligibility from refugee status or asylum in the United States on account of any legal right to citizenship they may enjoy under the Constitution of [South Korea]." *But see Matter of K–R–Y– and K–C–S–*, 24 I&N Dec. 133 (BIA 2007) (finding natives of North Korea who became citizens of South Korea were precluded from establishing eligibility for asylum based on their firm resettlement in South Korea).

[40] *Matter of K–R–Y– and K–C–S–, supra* note 39.

[41] *See* this chapter, at 2.4.9.

CHAPTER 2 • U.S. ASYLUM LAW

The refugee definition also specifically allows for protection of individuals who have no nationality and who are outside of their country of last habitual residence.[42] The United Nations defines "stateless person" as "a person who is not considered a national by any State under the operation of its law."[43] The mere fact that a stateless applicant's country of last habitual residence refuses to allow the applicant to return does not negate an asylum claim from that country.[44]

The BIA has adopted the definition of "last habitual residence" as "a place of general abode" or the applicant's "principal, actual dwelling place in fact, without regard to intent" based on the INA definition of residence.[45] This definition was accorded *Chevron* deference by the Third Circuit in *Paripovic v. Gonzales*, which held that a stateless Croatian last habitually resided in Serbia, where he had lived for two years.[46]

The Asylum Officer Basic Training Course (AOBTC) notes that even though an applicant may have resided in more than one country and may fear persecution in more than one country, his or her claim "should be analyzed based on the country of *last* habitual residence only."[47] The AOBTC also cautions that "last habitual residence" is distinct from and should not be confused with firm resettlement.[48] The AOBTC states that an applicant may have last habitually resided in a country, even if he or she has not been firmly resettled there.[49] Nevertheless, at least two courts have held that the BIA's determination that a person was firmly resettled in a country is an implicit finding that the person last habitually resided there.[50]

The break-up of the Soviet Union and unresolved land and nationality issues in the Middle East have contributed to a rising number of stateless persons. Such persons are afforded protection under U.S. asylum law if they are able to establish a well-founded fear of persecution in their country of last habitual residence. For example, Palestinians who resided in Saudi Arabia, Qatar, and the United Arab Emirates—and who, following the Persian Gulf War, were expelled, denied re-entry, and/or had their property confiscated—are eligible for asylum in the United States.[51]

---

[42] *See* INA §101(a)(42); 8 USC §1101(a)(42); *see also* UNHCR *Handbook*, *supra* note 36, at ¶¶101–05.

[43] *See* Convention Relating to the Status of Stateless Persons, 360 U.N.T.S. 117 (1954), art. I(1).

[44] *Ouda v. INS*, 324 F.3d 445, 452–53 (6th Cir. 2003) (noting that refusal to accept the applicant could be further evidence of persecution).

[45] INA §101(a)(33); 8 USC §1101(a)(33).

[46] *Paripovic v. Gonzales*, 418 F.3d 240, 244 (3d Cir. 2005).

[47] Asylum Officer Basic Training Course (AOBTC), Lesson: Asylum Eligibility Part I, at 11 (Dec. 5, 2002) (emphasis in original), available at www.rmscdenver.org/aobtc/Elig1persecution6de02lp links.pdf.

[48] *Id.* at 10.

[49] *Id.* For a further discussion of firm resettlement, see this chapter, at 2.7.3.

[50] *Tesfamichael v. Gonzales*, 469 F.3d 109, 115 (5th Cir. 2006); *Al Najjar v. Ashcroft*, 257 F.3d 1262, 1294 (11th Cir. 2001).

[51] *See* Immigration and Naturalization Service (INS) Office of General Counsel, Legal Opinion: Palestinian Asylum Applicants (Oct. 27, 1995), *reprinted in* 72 Interpreter Releases 1553 (Nov. 13, 1995); *see also Ouda v. INS*, 324 F.3d 445 (6th Cir. 2003) (granting asylum to a Palestinian forced to leave Kuwait).

2.4.3. Unable or Unwilling to Return

The definition of refugee includes the requirement that the asylum applicant demonstrate that he or she is unwilling or unable to return to, or avail him- or herself of the protection of, his or her country because of persecution or a well-founded fear of persecution.[52] Being "unwilling" to return relates to an asylum applicant's fear of return. As UNHCR's *Handbook* provides:

> [A]n applicant's well-founded fear of persecution must be in relation to the country of his nationality. As long as he has no fear in relation to the country of his nationality, he can be expected to avail himself of that country's protection. He is not in need of international protection and is therefore not a refugee.[53]

Being "unable" to avail oneself of such protection implies circumstances that are beyond the will of the person concerned. The *Handbook* recognizes that when a country is in a state of war, including civil war, or other grave disturbance, it may be prevented from extending protection or such protection may be ineffective.[54] Moreover, in cases in which protection by the country of nationality may be purposely denied to the applicant, such denial of protection may confirm the applicant's fear of persecution, and may even be an element of persecution.[55] Therefore, a denial of services, such as a refusal of a national passport or extension of its validity, or denial of admittance to the home territory may constitute a refusal of protection within the refugee definition.[56] In contrast, the term "unwilling" refers to individuals who refuse to accept the protection of their home countries.[57]

2.4.4. Well-Founded Fear

To establish a "well-founded fear of persecution," an asylum applicant must show that a reasonable person in the same circumstances would fear persecution if removed to his or her home country.[58] The U.S. Supreme Court noted that "[o]ne can certainly have a well-founded fear of an event happening when there is less than a 50% chance of the occurrence taking place."[59] The Court suggested that even a 1-in-10 chance of suffering persecution would make an applicant's fear well-founded.[60] The Court, however, did not hold that a well-founded fear requires *at least* a 1-in-10 chance of persecution, but only that the persecution feared must be a reasonable possibility.[61] It could, therefore, be argued that even a less than 1-in-10 chance is sufficient to meet the well-founded-fear stan-

---

[52] INA §101(a)(42); 8 USC §1101(a)(42); *see also Matter of D–V–*, 21 I&N Dec. 77, 78 (BIA 1993).

[53] UNHCR *Handbook*, *supra* note 36, at ¶90.

[54] *Id.* at ¶98.

[55] *Id.*

[56] *Id.* at ¶99.

[57] *Id.* at ¶100.

[58] *See Matter of Mogharrabi*, 19 I&N Dec. 439, 445 (BIA 1987); *see also Ahmed v. Gonzales*, 467 F.3d 669, 674 (7th Cir. 2006); *Tesfamichael v. Gonzales*, 469 F.3d 109, 113 (5th Cir. 2006); *Gao v. Ashcroft*, 299 F.3d 266, 272 (3d Cir. 2002); *Korablina v. INS*, 158 F.3d 1038, 1044 (9th Cir. 1998); *M.A. v. INS*, 899 F.2d 304, 311 (4th Cir. 1990).

[59] *INS v. Cardoza-Fonseca*, 480 U.S. 421, 431 (1987).

[60] *Id.* at 440.

[61] *Id.*

dard. A fear may be well-founded "even if there is only a slight, though discernible, chance of persecution."[62]

A well-founded fear of persecution has both a subjective and an objective component. An asylum applicant's subjective fear of persecution must be objectively reasonable.[63] The subjective component requires a showing that the applicant's fear is genuine.[64] The objective component requires a showing that the fear is reasonable.[65] Mere irrational apprehension is insufficient.[66]

An asylum applicant may establish the objective basis of his or her fear by submitting evidence regarding conditions in his or her home country.[67] A number of BIA decisions have highlighted the increasing importance of such evidence.[68] A recent change to the INA by the REAL ID Act of 2005 provides that "[w]here a trier of fact determines that the applicant should provide evidence that corroborates otherwise credible testimony, such evidence *must* be provided unless the applicant does not have the evidence and cannot reasonably obtain the evidence."[69]

The BIA in *Matter of Mogharrabi* set forth the following four elements that an applicant for asylum must show in order to establish a well-founded fear of persecution: (1) the applicant possesses a belief or characteristic a persecutor seeks to overcome in others by means of punishment of some sort; (2) the persecutor is already aware, or could become aware, that the applicant possesses this belief or characteristic; (3) the persecutor has the capability of punishing the applicant; and (4) the persecutor has the inclination to punish the applicant.[70]

Asylum regulations further define "well-founded fear." The regulations provide that an applicant has a well-founded fear of persecution if:

---

[62] *Diallo v. INS*, 232 F.3d 279, 284 (2d Cir. 2000).

[63] *Kratchmarov v. Heston*, 172 F.3d 551, 553 (8th Cir. 1999); *Bhatt v. Reno*, 172 F.3d 978, 981 (7th Cir. 1999); *Mikhael v. INS*, 115 F.3d 299, 304 (5th Cir. 1997).

[64] *Samedov v. Gonzales*, 422 F.3d 704, 708 (8th Cir. 2005) (upholding IJ's finding that the applicant lacked a subjective fear because he entered and exited the United States several times before applying for asylum); *Knezevic v. Ashcroft*, 367 F.3d 1206, 1213 (9th Cir. 2004); *Bhatt, supra* note 63, at 981.

[65] *Samedov, supra* note 64; *see also Francois v. INS*, 283 F.3d 926, 930 (8th Cir. 2002) ("The objective element requires a showing of credible, direct, specific evidence that a reasonable person would fear persecution . . . .").

[66] *Gonahasa v. INS*, 181 F.3d 538, 541 (4th Cir. 1999).

[67] *See* this chapter, at 2.6.3.

[68] *See, e.g., Matter of S–M–J–*, 21 I&N Dec. 722, 724 (BIA 1997) (observing that the burden is on asylum applicants to provide evidence to buttress their claims); *Matter of Dass*, 20 I&N Dec. 120, 124–25 (BIA 1989) (highlighting the importance of background information in evaluating the applicant's testimony); *see also Banks v. Gonzales*, 453 F.3d 449, 453 (7th Cir. 2006) (stressing the need for "concrete, case-specific evidence" to demonstrate the risk faced by the applicant in the country from which he or she is seeking asylum); *Matter of Y–B–*, 21 I&N Dec. 1136, 1139 (BIA 1998) (the weaker an applicant's testimony, the greater the need for corroborative evidence).

[69] INA §208(b)(1)(B)(ii); 8 USC §1158(b)(1)(B)(ii) (emphasis added).

[70] *Matter of Mogharrabi*, 19 I&N Dec. 439, 446 (BIA 1987).

- The applicant has a fear of persecution in his or her country of nationality or, if stateless, in his or her country of last habitual residence, on account of race, religion, nationality, membership in a particular social group, or political opinion;
- There is a reasonable possibility of suffering such persecution if he or she were to return to that country; and
- He or she is unable or unwilling to return to, or avail him- or herself of the protection of, that country.[71]

An applicant does *not* have a well-founded fear if the applicant could avoid persecution by relocating to another part of the country, "if under *all* circumstances it would be reasonable to expect the applicant to do so."[72] In determining the "reasonableness" of an internal relocation option, adjudicators should consider, among other things, the possibility of other serious harm, ongoing civil strife, the country's infrastructure, geographic limitations, and social and cultural constraints.[73] The same factors are considered in determining whether a person's life or freedom would be threatened in a withholding of removal claim.[74] The regulations also note that these factors "may, or may not, be relevant, depending on all the circumstances of the case, and are not necessarily determinative" of whether relocation is reasonable.[75]

2.4.5. Persecution

Definition of Persecution

In order to qualify for asylum, an applicant must demonstrate past persecution or a well-founded fear of future persecution. "Persecution" is a broad term that is not defined in the INA, nor has it been defined by the BIA.[76] As UNHCR acknowledges in its *Handbook*, "persecution" is difficult to define:

> There is no universally accepted definition of "persecution," and various attempts to formulate such a definition have met with little success. . . . [I]t may be inferred that a threat to life or freedom on account of race, religion, nationality, political opinion or membership of a particular social group is always persecution. Other serious violations of human rights—for the same reasons—would also constitute persecution.[77]

In addition, the *Handbook* states that "various measures not in themselves amounting to persecution (*e.g.*, discrimination in different forms), in some cases combined with

---

[71] 8 CFR §§208.13(b)(2)(i), 1208.13(b)(2)(i).

[72] 8 CFR §§208.13(b)(2)(ii), 1208.13(b)(2)(ii) (emphasis added).

[73] 8 CFR §§208.13(b)(3), 1208.13(b)(3).

[74] 8 CFR §§208.16(b)(3), 1208.16(b)(3).

[75] 8 CFR §§208.13(b)(3), 208.16(b)(3), 1208.13(b)(3), and 1208.16(b)(3). For further discussion and prior case law regarding internal relocation alternatives, see this chapter, at 2.6.10.

[76] *Sahi v. Gonzales*, 416 F.3d 587, 588–89 (7th Cir. 2005) (criticizing the BIA for failing to discharge its duty as an agency to define "persecution" and adding, "[W]e haven't a clue as to what it thinks religious persecution is.").

[77] UNHCR *Handbook*, *supra* note 36, at ¶51; *see also Chen v. INS*, 359 F.3d 121, 128 (2d Cir. 2004) (non–life threatening violence and physical abuse also constitute torture).

other adverse factors, such as a general atmosphere of insecurity in the country of origin, may amount to persecution on 'cumulative grounds.'"[78]

The BIA has held that persecution is the infliction of harm or suffering by a government, or by persons a government is unwilling or unable to control, to overcome a characteristic of the victim.[79] It also has held that incidents of "harassment" do not amount to persecution, but has not explained the distinction between mere harassment and persecution.[80] The Seventh Circuit's definition of persecution is "punishment or the infliction of harm for political, religious or other reasons that this country does not recognize as legitimate."[81] The Eighth Circuit's definition is "the infliction or threat of death, torture, or injury to one's person or freedom. . . ."[82] Persecution does not require bodily harm.[83] Nor does it require a threat to life or freedom.[84] The term "persecution," however, does not encompass all treatment that our society regards as unfair, unjust, or even unlawful or unconstitutional.[85] Nor does the term embrace harm solely arising out of civil strife or anarchy.[86] Persecution, however, does include violent conduct that generally goes beyond the mere annoyance and distress that characterize harassment.[87]

---

[78] UNHCR *Handbook*, *supra* note 36, at ¶53; *see also Krotova v. Gonzales*, 416 F.3d 1080, 1084 (9th Cir. 2005) (the combination of sustained economic pressure, physical violence and threats against the applicant and her close associates, and the restrictions on her ability to practice her religion cumulatively amount to persecution); *Chand v. INS*, 222 F.3d 1066, 1074 n.15 (9th Cir. 2000) (finding BIA erred by considering each incident of harm "in isolation, without analyzing the cumulative harm Chand suffered"); *Korablina v. INS*, 158 F.3d 1038, 1045 (9th Cir. 1998) (finding that, cumulatively, the experiences suffered by the petitioner compel the conclusion that she suffered persecution where, in conjunction with the political and social turmoil in her country, she received many threats against her life); *Matter of [name not provided]*, (IJ Dec. 20, 2000) (Baltimore, MD) (Gossart, IJ), *reported in* 78 *Interpreter Releases* 233 (Jan. 15, 2001) (finding that refusal to render medical aid, firing or refusing to hire a person, and forcing someone to leave their community or state, due to their HIV status, when viewed cumulatively, amounts to persecution).

[79] *See Matter of Kasinga*, 21 I&N Dec. 357, 365 (BIA 1996) (finding that female genital mutilation is a form of persecution).

[80] *Matter of A–E–M–*, 21 I&N Dec. 1157, 1159 (BIA 1998), *cited in Sahi v. Gonzales*, 416 F.3d 587, 589 (7th Cir. 2005) (criticizing the BIA for its failure to define persecution).

[81] *Bace v. Ashcroft*, 352 F.3d 1133, 1137 (7th Cir. 2003) (noting that the actions must rise above the level of mere harassment).

[82] *Ngure v. Ashcroft*, 367 F.3d 975, 989–90 (8th Cir. 2004).

[83] *Singh v. INS*, 134 F.3d 962, 967 (9th Cir. 1998).

[84] *Bhatt v. Reno*, 172 F.3d 978, 981 (7th Cir. 1999); *Singh*, *supra* note 83, at 967.

[85] *See, e.g., Ahmed v. Gonzales*, 467 F.3d 669, 673 (7th Cir. 2006) (finding that general conditions of hardship that affect entire populations are not persecution); *Fatin v. INS*, 12 F.3d 1233, 1240 (3d Cir. 1993) (finding that the applicant failed to establish that the treatment she would face upon return to Iran amounts to persecution); *Matter of V–T–S–*, 21 I&N Dec. 792, 798 (BIA 1997) (holding that kidnapping was not persecution where the sole motivation was to make money).

[86] *See Matter of Acosta*, 19 I&N Dec. 211, 222 (BIA 1985), *modified on other grounds by Matter of Mogharrabi*, 19 I&N Dec. 439 (BIA 1987).

[87] *Ivanishvili v. Gonzales*, 433 F.3d 332, 340 (2d Cir. 2006) (finding that the IJ failed to distinguish between harassment and persecution in the case of a Jehovah's Witness who was subjected to threats and attacks).

The lack of a precise definition or enumeration of acts that constitute persecution enables adjudicators to examine the circumstances in each case. As a result, in recent years a number of cases have expanded asylum protection to previously unprotected groups, such as children, homosexuals, and women. As one commentator has observed:

> There being no limits to the perverse side of human imagination, little purpose is served by attempting to list all known measures of persecution. Assessments must be made from case to case by taking account, on the one hand, of the notions of individual integrity and human dignity and, on the other hand, of the manner and degree to which they stand to be injured.[88]

> ➢ *Note*—On December 7, 2000, legacy INS published proposed regulations that define persecution as: "the infliction of objectively serious harm or suffering that is subjectively experienced as serious harm or suffering by the applicant . . . ."[89] The proposed regulations did not contain an effective date and it is not known when, or if, final regulations will be issued.

Examples of Persecution

Customary international law is generally considered to forbid the following conduct, even in the absence of a treaty: genocide; slavery; torture and other cruel, inhuman, or degrading treatment; and prolonged detention without notice of and an opportunity to contest the grounds for the detention.[90] Asylum applicants who can show that they have reasonable grounds to fear that they will be subjected to any of these practices because of race, religion, nationality, membership in a particular social group, or political opinion could establish eligibility for asylum.[91]

Persecution comes in many forms. It may be:

- Threats to life, confinement, and torture;[92]
- Rape or sexual assault;[93]
- Forced abortion, which is per se persecution;[94]
- Female genital mutilation;[95]
- Threats and attacks even if the applicant has not been beaten or physically harmed;[96]
- Ethnic cleansing;[97]

---

[88] G. Goodwin-Gill, *The Refugee in International Law* 69 (2d Ed. 1996).

[89] 65 Fed. Reg. 76588–98 (Dec. 7, 2000).

[90] AOBTC Lesson: Asylum Eligibility Part I, *supra* note 47, at 20–21.

[91] *Id.*

[92] *Chang v. INS*, 119 F.3d 1055, 1066 (3d Cir. 1997).

[93] *Shoafera v. INS*, 228 F.3d 1070, 1074 (9th Cir. 2000).

[94] *Wang v. Ashcroft*, 341 F.3d 1015, 1020 (9th Cir. 2003).

[95] *Barry v. Gonzales*, 445 F.3d 741, 745 (4th Cir. 2006); *Mohammed v. Gonzales*, 400 F.3d 785, 796 (9th Cir. 2005); *Abay v. Ashcroft*, 368 F.3d 634, 638 (6th Cir. 2004); *Abankwah v. INS*, 185 F.3d 18, 23 (2d Cir. 1999); *Matter of Kasinga*, 21 I&N Dec. 357, 365 (BIA 1996).

[96] *Baballah v. Ashcroft*, 367 F.3d 1067, 1074 (9th Cir. 2004).

- Detention in a concentration camp that includes detention in an underground cell, forced labor, and lack of access to family and friends for a period of several years;[98]
- Inability to earn a livelihood, travel safely within a country, and forced expulsion from the country;[99]
- A country's program of denaturalization and deportation;[100]
- Forbidding one from practicing his or her religion;[101]
- Kidnapping, coupled with beatings and threatening phone calls, cumulatively.[102]

Persecution may also include non–life threatening violence and physical abuse.[103] While threats alone may amount to persecution, in order to do so they must be "highly imminent and menacing in nature."[104] Severe economic deprivation may also constitute persecution.[105] In making a claim that economic deprivation rises to the level of persecution, the applicant must offer some proof he or she suffered a "deliberate imposition of substantial economic

---

[97] *Knezevic v. Ashcroft*, 367 F.3d 1206, 1212 (9th Cir. 2004) (ethnic Serb applicants suffered past persecution by Croats engaged in a campaign of ethnic cleansing).

[98] *Phommasoukha v. Gonzales*, 408 F.3d 1011, 1015 (8th Cir. 2005) (finding that the IJ's determination that imprisonment in a concentration camp does not constitute past persecution was not supported by substantial evidence).

[99] *Un v. Gonzales*, 415 F.3d 205, 210 (1st Cir. 2005) (finding that verbal death threats may amount to persecution); *Ouda v. INS*, 324 F.3d 445, 454 (6th Cir. 2003).

[100] *Giday v. Gonzales*, 434 F.3d 543, 553–56 (7th Cir. 2006).

[101] *See, e.g., Bucur v. INS*, 109 F.3d 399, 405 (7th Cir. 1997).

[102] *Martinez-Ruiz v. Gonzales*, 479 F.3d 762, 766 n.2 (11th Cir. 2007).

[103] *See Vladimirova v. Ashcroft*, 377 F.3d 690, 696 (7th Cir. 2004) (finding that the IJ's statement that the conduct must involve a "threat to the life or freedom of the victim" is "simply wrong;" and that the beating that the applicant suffered, which resulted in a miscarriage, amounted to persecution); *Chen v. INS*, 359 F.3d 121, 128 (2d Cir. 2004).

[104] *Chavarria v. Gonzales*, 446 F.3d 508, 518 (3d Cir. 2006) (finding the second threat the applicant received because of his imputed political opinion was highly imminent, concrete, and menacing).

[105] *See Matter of T–Z–*, 24 I&N Dec. 163 (BIA 2007) (finding that the deliberate imposition of severe economic disadvantage or the deprivation of liberty, food, housing, employment, or other essentials of life may amount to persecution); *Li v. Gonzales*, 405 F.3d 171, 177 (4th Cir. 2005) (finding that deliberate imposition of severe economic disadvantage may rise to the level of persecution); *Baballah v. Ashcroft*, 367 F.3d 1067, 1075 (9th Cir. 2004) (noting that the IJ erred as a matter of law by requiring the applicant to show an absolute inability to support his family); *Berdo v. INS*, 432 F.2d 824, 847 (6th Cir. 1970); *Kovac v. INS*, 407 F.2d 102, 107 (9th Cir. 1969); *Dunat v. Henry*, 297 F.2d 744, 746 (3d Cir. 1961); *Matter of Salama*, 11 I&N Dec. 536 (BIA 1966); AOBTC Lesson: Asylum Eligibility Part I, *supra* note 47, at 24. *But see Damko v. INS*, 430 F.3d 626, 628 (2d Cir. 2005) (finding that economic restrictions must be so severe that they constitute a threat to life or freedom in order to amount to economic persecution); *Sharif v. INS*, 87 F.3d 932, 934–35 (7th Cir. 1996) (finding that inability to attend college and losing job but finding another does not amount to economic persecution); *see also Mirzoyan v. Gonzales*, 457 F.3d 217, 221–22 (2d Cir. 2006) (criticizing the BIA for not applying a consistent standard for economic persecution claims).

disadvantage."[106] In addition, harm to an asylum applicant's family member may constitute persecution of the applicant.[107]

In the Asylum Officer Basic Training Course, U.S. Immigration and Citizenship Services (USCIS) also notes that the following types of harm may be significant in determining if human rights have been violated or discrimination has become overwhelming:

> Serious restrictions on the right to earn a livelihood; arbitrary interference with a person's privacy; relegation to substandard dwellings; serious restrictions on access to normally available educational facilities; enforced social or civil inactivity; passport denial; constant surveillance; pressure to become an informer; or confiscation of property.[108]

Cases finding that the harm suffered by the applicant amounted to persecution include:[109] *Voci v. Gonzales*,[110] *Abay v. Ashcroft*,[111] *Bellido v. Ashcroft*,[112] *Jahed v. INS*,[113] *Rios v. Ascroft*,[114] *Begzatowski v. INS*,[115] *Tarubac v. INS*,[116] *Duarte de Guinac v. INS*,[117] *Kojevnikova v. Reno*,[118] *Borja v. INS*,[119] *Garrovillas v. INS*,[120] *Pitcherskaia v. INS*,[121] *Mat-*

---

[106] *Shan Liao v. U.S. Dept. of Justice*, 293 F.3d 61, 70 (2d Cir. 2002) (finding applicant should have submitted proof of income in China, net worth, and other personal financial information).

[107] *See Navas v. INS*, 217 F.3d 646, 658 (9th Cir. 2000) (persecution of applicant included murder of two family members and beating of mother); INS Memorandum, "Persecution of Family Members" (June 30, 1997).

[108] AOBTC Lesson: Asylum Eligibility Part I, *supra* note 47, at 22–23.

[109] *See also* INS Office of General Counsel, Legal Opinion: Palestinian Asylum Applicants (Oct. 27, 1995), *reprinted in* 72 Interpreter Releases 1553 (Nov. 13, 1995) (noting that expulsion from a country, denial of re-entry, and the uncompensated confiscation of property may be violations of basic human rights amounting to persecution).

[110] *Voci v. Gonzales*, 409 F.3d 607, 609 (3d Cir. 2005) (finding multiple beating by the Albanian police, including one in which the applicant suffered a broken knee, amounted to persecution).

[111] *Abay v. Ashcroft*, 368 F.3d 634, 642 (6th Cir. 2004) (threat of female genital mutilation to daughter amounts to a well-founded fear for daughter *and* mother).

[112] *Bellido v. Ashcroft*, 367 F.3d 840, 845 (8th Cir. 2004) (an illegal arrest, a death threat from the military, and the government's search for the applicant amount to persecution).

[113] *Jahed v. INS*, 356 F.3d 991, 999 (9th Cir. 2004) (threats of exposing the applicant's past participation in the Mojahedin and extortion amount to persecution).

[114] *Rios v. Ascroft*, 287 F.3d 895, 900 (9th Cir. 2002) (death threats by anonymous callers is sufficient basis to find persecution).

[115] *Begzatowski v. INS*, 278 F.3d 665, 669–70 (7th Cir. 2002) (finding that ethnic Albanian who was physically abused, deprived of bathing facilities, forced into battle without ammunition, and deprived of basic survival tools suffered persecution by the Yugoslavian army).

[116] *Tarubac v. INS*, 182 F.3d 1114, 1118 (9th Cir. 1999) (finding applicant who was kidnapped, beaten, held without food, and repeatedly threatened was subjected to persecution).

[117] *Duarte de Guinac v. INS*, 179 F.3d 1156, 1162 (9th Cir. 1999) (repeated beatings coupled with explicit expressions of ethnic hatred and death threats amounts to persecution).

[118] *Kojevnikova v. Reno*, No. 97-4214, 1999 U.S. App. LEXIS 6368, at *4–*5 (2d Cir. Apr. 6, 1999) (detention for some months at a "psychiatric" institution amounts to past persecution).

[119] *Borja v. INS*, 175 F.3d 732, 738 (9th Cir. 1999) (finding that beatings and assaults for the purpose of financial extortion constitute persecution).

ter of S–A–,[122] *Matter of V–T–S–*,[123] *Matter of Kasinga*,[124] *Matter of D–V–*,[125] and *Matter of Toboso-Alfonso*.[126]

Mere harassment or discrimination, however, does not rise to the level of persecution.[127] Nor do generalized conditions of hardship that affect entire populations constitute persecution.[128] Short periods of detention also do not amount to persecution.[129] Persecution does not encompass all treatment that society regards as unfair, unjust, or even

---

[120] *Garrovillas v. INS*, 156 F.3d 1010, 1016 (9th Cir. 1998) (finding that recruitment attempts and death threats are sufficient to show persecution).

[121] *Pitcherskaia v. INS*, 118 F.3d 641, 647–48 (9th Cir 1997) (finding that forced institutionalization, electroshock treatments, and drug injections to "treat" the applicant's homosexuality constitute persecution, thereby rejecting the BIA's requirement that the applicant demonstrate that her persecutors intended to harm her).

[122] *Matter of S–A–*, 22 I&N Dec. 1328, 1335 (BIA 2000) (finding that repeated physical assaults, imposed isolation, and deprivation of an education amounted to persecution).

[123] *Matter of V–T–S–*, 21 I&N Dec. 792, 798-99 (BIA 1997) (finding that kidnapping is a serious offense that may constitute persecution, but it must be on account of one of the five enumerated grounds).

[124] *Matter of Kasinga*, 21 I&N Dec. 357, 365 (BIA 1996) (finding that female genital mutilation is a form of persecution).

[125] *Matter of D–V–*, 21 I&N Dec. 77, 79–80 (BIA 1993) (finding pro-Aristide activist who was gang-raped and beaten because of her political views and religion suffered grievous harm and had a well-founded fear of persecution).

[126] *Matter of Toboso-Alfonso,* 20 I&N Dec. 819 (BIA 1990) (detention and threat of imprisonment is persecution).

[127] *See Ciorba v. Ashcroft*, 323 F.3d 539, 545 (7th Cir. 2003) (questioning by police and searches of house amounted to harassment, not persecution); *Nelson v. INS*, 232 F.3d 258, 264 (1st Cir. 2000) (three episodes of solitary confinement of less than 72 hours [each accompanied by physical abuse], periodic surveillance, threatening phone calls, occasional stops and searches, and visits to applicant's place of work do not amount to past persecution); *Tamas-Mercea v. Reno*, 222 F.3d 417, 424 (7th Cir. 2000) (tapping phone lines, opening mail, questioning of wife does not rise to level of persecution); *Singh v. INS*, 134 F.3d 962, 968–69 (9th Cir. 1998) (rock throwing; damage to property; burglary of home; and stolen laundry, coconuts, and other items did not amount to persecution); *Bradvica v. INS*, 128 F.3d 1009, 1012 (7th Cir. 1997) (arrest and detention following a pro-democracy rally is harassment, not persecution); *Matter of A–E–M–*, 21 I&N Dec. 1157, 1159 (BIA 1998) (finding that a painted threat on the door of an applicant's house, while regrettable, was not persecution).

[128] *Capric v. Ashcroft*, 355 F.3d 1075, 1084 (7th Cir. 2004). *But see Popova v. INS*, 273 F.3d 1251 (9th Cir. 2001) (repeated harassment by the police and hospital co-workers, arrests, detentions, and disconnection of telephone amount to persecution); *Matter of O–Z– & I–Z–*, 22 I&N Dec. 23, 25–27 (BIA 1998).

[129] *See, e.g., Kibinda v. Att'y. Gen. of U.S.*, 477 F.3d 113, 119 (3d Cir. 2007) (finding that five days of detention, which did not result in serious injury, is not persecution); *Zheng v. U.S. Att'y. Gen.*, 451 F.3d 1287, 1290 (11th Cir. 2006) (finding that five days of detention of a Falun Gong activist who was not physically harmed did not amount to persecution); *Diallo v. Ashcroft*, 381 F.3d 687, 698 (7th Cir. 2004) (short detentions or detentions without physical abuse seem less apt to reach the "persecution" threshold); *Fesseha v. Ashcroft*, 333 F.3d 13, 19 (1st Cir. 2003) (occasional 24-hour detentions did not amount to persecution). *But see Beskovic v. Gonzales*, 467 F.3d 223, 226 (2d Cir. 2006) (noting that any physical degradation designed to cause pain, humiliation, or other suffering, may rise to the level of persecution if it occurred in the context of an arrest or detention).

unlawful or unconstitutional.[130] Nevertheless, lack of past persecution does not foreclose a finding that the applicant has a well-founded fear.[131]

Past Persecution as a Basis for Asylum

An applicant for asylum may establish eligibility by presenting evidence of past persecution alone.[132] To establish eligibility for asylum based on past persecution, an applicant must prove an incident that: (1) rises to the level of persecution; (2) is on account of one of the five protected grounds; and (3) is committed by the government or by private actors the government is unable or unwilling to control.[133] While proof of particularized persecution, *i.e.*, evidence that the applicants were singled out, may sometimes be needed to show a well-founded fear of future persecution, it is not required to establish past persecution.[134] Moreover, if the IJ or BIA fails to provide a reasoned discussion of whether an individual was subjected to past persecution, the reviewing court is unable to provide a meaningful review of the decision.[135]

If the applicant establishes that he or she has suffered past persecution, the applicant is presumed to have a well-founded fear of future persecution unless a preponderance of the evidence establishes there has been a fundamental change in circumstances or the applicant could reasonably be expected to relocate to another part of the country.[136] In cases involving past persecution, it is the government's burden to rebut the presumption, unless the future harm feared is unrelated to the past persecution claim.[137] A similar presumption and allocation of the burden of proof applies in withholding of removal claims.[138]

---

[130] *See Fatin v. INS*, 12 F.3d 1233, 1240 (3d Cir. 1993).

[131] *See Abdel-Masieh v. INS*, 73 F.3d 579, 584 (5th Cir. 1996) (in reversing the denial of asylum based on the BIA's finding that an individual's fear was not well-founded where the individual was detained twice but not mistreated to the degree that would constitute persecution, the court found that these past actions do not create an "outer limit" on the government's future actions against the individual).

[132] 8 CFR §1208.13(b)(1); *see also Matter of H–*, 21 I&N Dec. 337, 345–46 (BIA 1996) (a Somali national whose father and brother were murdered and who was detained and tortured because of his clan membership suffered past persecution); *Matter of D–V–*, 21 I&N Dec. 77, 79–80 (BIA 1995) (a Haitian woman gang-raped and beaten in her home suffered past persecution); *Matter of Chen*, 20 I&N Dec. 16, 18–19 (BIA 1989) (finding that the son of a Christian minister in China suffered severe past persecution that included denial of education, deprivation of food, denial of medical care, mistreatment of his father, ransacking of his home, and confiscation of papers and personal effects).

[133] *Knezevic v. Ashcroft*, 367 F.3d 1206, 1211 (9th Cir. 2004).

[134] *Id.* at 1211–12 (noting that the applicants' town was specifically targeted for bombing, invasion, occupation, and ethnic cleansing of Serbs by Croats).

[135] *See, e.g.*, *Phommasoukha v. Gonzales*, 408 F.3d 1011, 1015 (8th Cir. 2005); *Hernandez-Barrera v. Ashcroft*, 373 F.3d 9, 13 (1st Cir. 2004).

[136] 8 CFR §§208.13(b)(1)(i), 1208.13(b)(1)(i); *see, e.g.*, *Balliu v. Gonzales*, 467 F.3d 609, 612 (7th Cir. 2006); *Un v. Gonzales*, 415 F.3d 205, 209 (1st Cir. 2005) (finding that the agency's failure to address past persecution precluded meaningful review of the applicant's entitlement to a presumption of fear of future persecution and was reversible error).

[137] 8 CFR §§208.13(b)(1), (b)(1)(ii), 1208.13(b)(1), (b)(1)(ii); *see, e.g.*, *Bace v. Ashcroft*, 352 F.3d 1133, 1137 (7th Cir. 2003).

[138] 8 CFR §§208.16(b)(1)(i), (ii), 1208.16(b)(1)(i), (ii). For a more detailed discussion, see this chapter, at 2.6.10.

CHAPTER 2 • U.S. ASYLUM LAW

If the past persecution causes a harm that is "permanent and continuing," such as with forced sterilization[139] or female genital mutilation (FGM),[140] courts have held that the presumption of well-founded fear cannot be rebutted.

Even if a preponderance of the evidence demonstrates a fundamental change in circumstances or an internal relocation alternative, an applicant may still be granted asylum in the discretion of the adjudicator, if:

- The applicant has demonstrated *compelling reasons* for being unwilling or unable to return to the country, arising out of the severity of the past persecution; or

- The applicant has established that there is a reasonable possibility that he or she may face *other serious harm* upon removal to that country.[141]

According to legacy INS, "other serious harm" means "harm that is not inflicted on account of race, religion, nationality, membership in a particular social group, or political opinion, but is so serious that it equals the severity of persecution."[142] The BIA has held that a favorable exercise of discretion in an asylum application may be warranted for humanitarian reasons, notwithstanding the fact that there is little likelihood of future persecution.[143]

2.4.6. "On Account of"; Mixed Motives

"On Account of"

An asylum applicant must demonstrate that the persecution he or she suffered or fears is "on account of" his or her race, religion, nationality, membership in a particular social group, or political opinion. The "on account of "requirement was addressed by the Supreme Court in *INS v. Elias-Zacarias*.[144] The Court in *Elias-Zacarias* held that the persecution must be "on account of" the victim's political opinion or other enumerated ground, *i.e.*, the persecutor must be motivated by the race, religion, nationality, social group, or political opinion of the victim.[145] While an asylum applicant is not re-

---

[139] *Matter of Y–T–L–*, 23 I&N Dec. 601 (BIA 2003).

[140] *Mohammed v. Gonzales*, 400 F.3d 785, 799–800 (9th Cir. 2005). *But see Matter of A–T–*, 24 I&N Dec. 296, 299–301 (BIA 2007) (finding that FGM does not qualify as "continuing persecution").

[141] 8 CFR §§208.13(b)(1)(iii), 1208.13(b)(1)(iii).

[142] *See* 65 Fed. Reg. 76121, 76127 (Dec. 6, 2000) ("Supplementary Information"). For more detailed discussion about this form of relief, sometimes called humanitarian asylum, see this chapter, at 2.6.10.

[143] *Matter of Chen*, 20 I&N Dec. 16, 19 (BIA 1989); *see also Lal v. INS*, 255 F.3d 998, 1003, *amended on reh'g*, 268 F.3d 1148 (9th Cir. 2001) (finding applicants were eligible for asylum based on the severity of their past persecution, which included repeated arbitrary detentions, painful and humiliating torture, sexual assault, threats, and severe intimidation); *Vongsakdy v. INS*, 171 F.3d 1203 (9th Cir. 1999) (finding that a Laotian national suffered egregious past persecution, including imprisonment in a labor camp, beatings, torture, inadequate food and water, denial of medical treatment, and a severed thumb); *Matter of H–*, 21 I&N Dec. 337, 347–48 (BIA 1996) (finding that humanitarian reasons may include the applicant's age, health, or family ties in the United States). *But see Francois v. INS*, 283 F.3d 926, 932 (8th Cir. 2002) (finding that applicant who was interrogated, threatened that her father would be killed, and denied an exit visa failed to demonstrate severe or long lasting harm sufficient to warrant humanitarian asylum).

[144] *INS v. Elias-Zacarias*, 502 U.S. 478 (1992).

[145] *Id.* at 482.

quired to prove the exact motivation of his or her persecutor, he or she must "provide *some* evidence of it, direct or circumstantial."[146]

The BIA has held that an asylum applicant must establish facts upon which a reasonable person would fear that the danger arises on account of one of the five grounds.[147] Federal courts have recognized, however, the difficulty in proving motivation.[148] At least one circuit has held that if persecution is by the government and there is no legitimate prosecutorial purpose for the harm inflicted, there is a presumption that the government's motive is political.[149] Adjudicators may not base their "on account of" determinations on a "'non-evidence-based assumption[]' regarding conduct in another culture."[150] Use of ethnic slurs by interrogators does not necessarily prove a nexus to a protected ground.[151] If an asylum applicant is unable to provide sufficient proof that the motivation of his or her persecutor is one of the five enumerated grounds, the claim will be denied.[152]

---

[146] *Id.* at 483 (emphasis in original). *But see* G. Goodwin-Gill, *The Refugee in International Law* 50 (2d Ed. 1996) ("Nowhere in the drafting history of the 1951 Convention is it suggested that the motive or intent of the persecutor was ever to be considered as a controlling factor in either the definition or the determination of refugee status."); *see also* "The Michigan Guidelines on Nexus to a Convention Ground," 23 *Mich. J. Int'l L.* 210 (2002), available at *www.refugeecaselaw.org/nexus.asp*.

[147] *Matter of Fuentes*, 19 I&N Dec. 658, 662 (BIA 1988).

[148] *See Guo v. Ashcroft*, 361 F.3d 1194, 1203 (9th Cir. 2004) (holding that resistance to discriminatory government action that results in persecution is persecution on account of a protected ground); *Baballah v. Ashcroft*, 367 F.3d 1067, 1077 (9th Cir. 2004) (noting that the use of the derogatory term "goy" by the Israeli marines demonstrated they were motivated by the applicant's ethnicity); *Bace v. Ashcroft*, 352 F.3d 1133, 1138 (7th Cir. 2003) (statements made by assailants suggesting that attacks were politically motivated were sufficient to meet "on account of" requirement); *Gailius v. INS*, 147 F.3d 34, 45 (1st Cir. 1998) ("Persecutors have not been given adequate notice that our government expects them to sign their names and reveal their identities when they deliver threatening messages."); *Gonzales-Neyra v. INS*, 122 F.3d 1293, 1296 (9th Cir. 1997), *amended at* 133 F.3d 726 (9th Cir. 1998) (threats to an applicant's life and business made after applicant expressed his political opinion were on account of this opinion and were not motivated solely by economic reasons); *Bolanos-Hernandez v. INS*, 767 F.2d 1277, 1285 (9th Cir. 1984) (finding that because authentic refugees are rarely able to offer direct corroboration of specific threats, the applicant's own credible testimony is sufficient).

[149] *Navas v. INS*, 217 F.3d 646, 658 (9th Cir. 2000).

[150] *Popova v. INS*, 273 F.3d 1251, 1258 (9th Cir. 2001) (rejecting the BIA's reliance on facts that applicant was able to pursue her medical education, travel outside of Bulgaria, and work in government-run medical facilities in finding that she was not persecuted "on account of" a protected ground).

[151] *Mitreva v. Gonzales*, 417 F.3d 761, 764 (7th Cir. 2005). *But see Azhgirevich v. Gonzales*, 185 Fed. Appx. 72, 74–75 (2d Cir. 2006) (finding sufficient nexus between an assault of a Russian woman and a protected ground of persecution where the attacker allegedly called the victim a "Russian whore" and said, "You should satisfy not only . . . one Muslim . . . [but] all the Muslims") (alteration in original).

[152] *See, e.g., Tamara-Gomez v. Gonzales*, 447 F.3d 343, 349–350 (5th Cir. 2006) (finding that the applicant failed to establish a nexus between the persecution and one of the five grounds and that claims based on dangers by policemen are not on account of a protected ground); *Oliva-Muralles v. Ashcroft*, 328 F.3d 25, 27 (1st Cir. 2003) (Guatemalan applicant could not tie the crimes that were committed against her or her neighbors to one of the five protected grounds); *Ontunez-Tursios v. Ashcroft*, 303 F.3d 341, 350–53 (5th Cir. 2002) (upholding BIA's determination that feared persecution over a land dispute was not on account of political opinion or membership in a particular social group); *Debab v. INS*, 163 F.3d 21, 27 (1st Cir. 1998) (holding that the applicant failed to establish a nexus between the threats he received and clandestine antigovernment organizations); *Matter of C–A–L–*, 21 I&N Dec.

continued

Mixed Motives

The persecutor may also be motivated by several reasons, one or more of which may be a ground enumerated in the refugee definition. As UNHCR's *Handbook* notes:

> It is evident that the reasons for persecution under these various headings will frequently overlap. Usually there will be more than one element combined in one person, *e.g.*, a political opponent who belongs to a religious or national group, or both, and the combination of such reasons in his person may be relevant in evaluating his well-founded fear.[153]

The persecutor may have several motives for engaging in acts of persecution—some tied to reasons protected under the INA and others not.[154] An asylum applicant does not bear the unreasonable burden of establishing the exact motivation of a persecutor where different grounds for the persecutor's actions are possible.[155] Prior to the passage of the REAL ID Act, the applicant had to produce evidence from which it was reasonable to believe that the harm was motivated, at least in part, by an actual or imputed protected ground.[156] Language added by the REAL ID Act requires an applicant to "establish that

---

754, 756–57 (BIA 1997) (finding that a former Guatemalan soldier was not targeted on account of one of the five grounds where guerrillas sought to obtain information from him and attempted to recruit him due to his expertise as an artillery specialist); *Matter of R–*, 20 I&N Dec. 621, 624 (BIA 1992) (finding that the purpose of the mistreatment by police was to extract information regarding Sikh militants and not because of the applicant's political opinion or because the applicant was a Sikh); *Matter of T–*, 20 I&N Dec. 571, 575 (BIA 1992) (finding that an ethnic Tamil was not persecuted on account of his ethnicity or political views).

[153] UNHCR *Handbook*, *supra* note 36, at ¶67; *see, e.g.*, *Matter of D–V–*, 21 I&N Dec. 77, 79–80 (BIA 1993) (finding that the applicant, an activist in a pro-Aristide church group, had a well-founded fear of persecution based on her political opinion and religion); *see also Osorio v. INS*, 18 F.3d 1017, 1028 (2d Cir. 1994) (finding that "persecution on account of the victim's political opinion" does not mean persecution solely on account of the victim's political opinion).

[154] *See Matter of S–P–*, 21 I&N Dec. 486, 489 (BIA 1996).

[155] *Matter of Fuentes*, 19 I&N Dec. 658, 662 (BIA 1988).

[156] *Id.*; *see also Uwais v. Gonzales*, 478 F.3d 513, 517–18 (2d Cir. 2007) (finding BIA erred in finding that officer's motives were not motivated, even in part, by a protected ground); *Mohideen v. Gonzales*, 416 F.3d 567, 570 (7th Cir. 2005) (persecution on account of a protected ground does not mean persecution "solely" on account of one of those grounds); *Jahed v. INS*, 356 F.3d 991, 998 (9th Cir. 2004) (extortion coupled with the threat of political exposure satisfies the "on account of" requirement); *Girma v. INS*, 283 F.3d 664, 668 (5th Cir. 2002) (finding that despite being questioned by armed abductors about her political activities, substantial evidence supported BIA's finding that the applicant had not established that persecution was "on account of" a protected ground where motivation could have been economic); *Bandari v. INS*, 227 F.3d 1160, 1168–69 (9th Cir. 2000) (finding that accusations made by Iranian police demonstrate their beatings were based on applicant's religion, not enforcement of a neutral law); *Agbuya v. INS*, 219 F.3d 962, 965–66 (9th Cir. 2000), *amended at* 241 F.3d 1224 (9th Cir. 2001) (holding that "persecutory conduct may have more than one motive, and so long as one motive is one of the statutory grounds, the requirements have been met") (citations omitted); *Briones v. INS*, 175 F.3d 727, 729 (9th Cir. 1999) (en banc) (finding that the asylum applicant's "activity as a confidential informer who sided with the Philippine military in a conflict that was political at its core certainly would be perceived as a political act by the group informed upon"); *Tarubac v. INS*, 182 F.3d 1114, 1119 (9th Cir. 1999) (finding that the applicant's expression of opposition to communism led to the most extreme persecution that she suffered and that the persecution was, therefore, not solely for economic or recruitment reasons).

race, religion, nationality, membership in a particular social group, or political opinion was or will be *at least one central reason* for persecuting the applicant."[157] A 2007 BIA decision further clarified what was meant by "one central reason" for persecution. The BIA held that Congress "purposely did not require that the protected ground be *the* central reason for the actions of the persecutors" but that aliens who were persecuted by someone motivated by more than one reason may be protected under INA §208 if they can show a nexus to a protected ground.[158] The BIA stated that the REAL ID Act did not radically alter the standard in mixed motive cases, because the protected ground must still be a central reason for persecution, and that the burden of proof may be met by testimonial evidence.[159]

Imputed Protected Grounds

USCIS takes the position that *any* of the five protected grounds may be imputed to an asylum applicant, not just political opinion. When the persecution inflicted on the asylum applicant is because of an imputed characteristic related to any one of the five protected grounds, the persecution is "on account of" that characteristic, regardless of whether the applicant possesses it.[160]

2.4.7. Race

The term "race" in the refugee definition should be interpreted in its widest sense to include "all kinds of ethnic groups that are referred to as 'races' in common usage."[161] UNHCR has noted that "[d]iscrimination for reasons of race has found world-wide condemnation as one of the most striking violations of human rights" and "will frequently amount to persecution."[162] Legacy INS in its *Basic Law Manual* cites apartheid in South Africa, the Holocaust, and slavery as examples of persecution on the basis of race.[163]

In finding that a Guatemalan member of the indigenous Quiche ethnic group suffered past persecution on account of race, the Ninth Circuit noted that the applicant was persecuted because of his "'ethnicity,' a category which falls somewhere between . . . 'race' and 'nationality.'"[164]

---

[157] INA §208(b)(1)(B)(i); 8 USC §1158(b)(1)(B)(i) (emphasis added).

[158] *Matter of J–B–N– & S–M–*, 24 I&N Dec. 208, 212–13 (BIA 2007).

[159] *Id.* at 214.

[160] AOBTC, Lesson: Asylum Eligibility Part III: Nexus and the Five Protected Characteristics, at 14 (Jan. 23, 2007).

[161] UNHCR *Handbook*, *supra* note 36, at ¶68, cited with approval in AOBTC Lesson: Asylum Eligibility Part III, *supra* note 160, at 15.

[162] UNHCR *Handbook*, *supra* note 36, at ¶¶68 and 69.

[163] INS, *Basic Law Manual, U.S. Law and INS Refugee/Asylum Adjudications* (1994) at 37.

[164] *Duarte de Guinac v. INS*, 179 F.3d 1156, 1159 n.5 (9th Cir. 1999); *see also Knezevic v. Ashcroft*, 367 F.3d 1206, 1210 (9th Cir. 2004) (persecution was based on applicants' Serbian ethnicity); *Baballah v. Ashcroft*, 367 F.3d 1067, 1075 n.10 (9th Cir. 2004) (in case of an Israeli applicant who was the child of a Muslim father and Jewish mother, the court noted that "ethnicity" falls between race and nationality); *Gafoor v. INS*, 231 F.3d 645, 653–54 (9th Cir. 2000) (granting asylum to Fijian of Indian descent); *Shoafera v. INS*, 228 F.3d 1070, 1074 n.2 (9th Cir. 2000) (persecution based on Amhara ethnicity); *Andriasian v. INS*, 180 F.3d

continued

> *Tip*—**Imputed Race**—USCIS takes the position that race, as one of the five protected grounds, may be imputed to an asylum applicant.[165]

2.4.8. Religion

Asylum law is also evolving with regard to claims based on religious persecution, especially in light of the passage of the International Religious Freedom Act (IRFA) in 1998.[166] IRFA created within the State Department the Office of International Religious Freedom, which is responsible for assisting the secretary of state in preparing an annual report for Congress on international religious freedom on September 1 of each year. The report describes the nature and extent of violations of religious freedom committed or tolerated by foreign governments.[167] The IRFA also called for the creation of the United States Commission on International Religious Freedom (USCIRF), an independent federal government agency, for the purpose of ensuring that the president and Congress receive independent recommendations and, where necessary, criticism of American policy that does not promote international religious freedom. The USCIRF is independent of the executive branch and is not part of the State Department. It compiles an annual report of its policy recommendations, including critiques on religious freedom abuses committed in numerous countries.[168]

Persecution on account of religion may assume various forms, including the prohibition of membership in a religious community, of worship in private or in public, of religious instruction, or serious discriminatory measures imposed on persons because they practice their religion or belong to a particular religious community.[169] Some courts have held that forbidding one from practicing his or her religion amounts to persecution.[170] As noted in UNHCR's *Handbook*, the Universal Declaration of Human Rights and the International Covenant on Civil and Political Rights proclaim the right to freedom of thought, conscience, and religion—including the freedom of a person to change his or her religion and his or her freedom to manifest it in public or private, in teaching, practice, worship, and observance.[171] More recently, in 2004 UNHCR issued *Guidelines on International Protection: Religion-Based Refugee Claims Under Article 1A(2) of the 1951 Convention and/or 1967 Protocol Relating to the Status of Refugees*[172] to complement the

---

1033, 1042 n.15 (9th Cir. 1999) (persecution based on Armenian ethnic origin treated as on account of race); *Singh v. INS*, 94 F.3d 1353 (9th Cir. 1996) (claim of Indo-Fijian analyzed as on account of race).

[165] *See supra* note 160 and accompanying text.

[166] International Religious Freedom Act of 1998, Pub. L. No. 105-292, 112 Stat. 2787.

[167] Annual reports are available at *www.state.gov/g/drl/rls/irf*. Paper copies are available from the Superintendent of Documents, U.S. Government Printing Office, Washington, DC 20402, Tel: (202) 512-1800; Fax: (202) 512-2250.

[168] USCIRF annual reports are available at *www.uscirf.gov/countries/publications/currentreport/index.html*. Countries of particular concern listed in the 2007 report include Burma, China, Eritrea, Iran, North Korea, Pakistan, Saudi Arabia, Sudan, Turkmenistan, Uzbekistan, and Vietnam.

[169] UNHCR *Handbook*, *supra* note 36, at ¶72.

[170] *See, e.g.*, *Bucur v. INS*, 109 F.3d 399, 405 (7th Cir. 1997).

[171] UNHCR *Handbook*, *supra* note 36, at ¶71.

[172] Available at *www.unhcr.org/publ/PUBL/40d8427a4.pdf*.

Handbook. These *Guidelines* offer guidance on defining "religion," defining religion-based "persecution," and assessing credibility based on knowledge of the religion.[173]

Conscientious objectors who refuse to perform military service for religious reasons and who are punished for their refusal must show that the motivation of their persecutor is to harm them because of their religious beliefs.[174]

Federal court cases in which applicants have been found to be at risk of persecution or torture because of their religion include: *Lhanzom v. Gonzales*,[175] *Ivanishvili v. Gonzales*,[176] *Guo v. Ashcroft*,[177] *Baballah v. Ashcroft*,[178] *Popova v. INS*,[179] *Bandari v. INS*,[180] *Maini v. INS*,[181] *Kojevnikova v. Reno*,[182] *Korablina v. INS*,[183] *Abdel-Masieh v. INS*,[184] *Cordero-Trejo v. INS*,[185] and *Bastanipour v. INS*.[186] See also *Chen v. INS*[187] and *Kanivets v. Riley*.[188]

---

[173] *See also* T.J. Gunn, "The Complexity of Religion and the Definition of 'Religion' in International Law," 16 *Harv. Hum. Rts. J.* 189 (2003).

[174] *Canas-Segovia v. INS*, 970 F.2d 599, 601 (9th Cir. 1992). For a more detailed discussion, see this chapter, at 2.5.7.

[175] *Lhanzom v. Gonzales*, 430 F.3d 847–48 (7th Cir. 2005) (overturning negative credibility determination in which government conceded that there was "no question" that the Chinese government continues to persecute Tibetan Buddhists).

[176] *Ivanishvili v. Gonzales*, 433 F.3d 332, 340 (2d Cir. 2006) (finding that IJ failed to distinguish between harassment and persecution in case of Jehovah's Witness who was subjected to threats and attacks).

[177] *Guo v. Ashcroft*, 361 F.3d 1194, 1197–99 (9th Cir. 2004) (Chinese applicant persecuted because of his Christian faith).

[178] *Baballah v. Ashcroft*, 367 F.3d 1067, 1077–78 (9th Cir. 2004) (Israeli Muslim faced persecution in part because of his parents' mixed marriage).

[179] *Popova v. INS*, 273 F.3d 1251, 1254–56 (9th Cir. 2001) (Bulgarian applicant suffered persecution, in part, because of her religion and religious connotations of her name).

[180] *Bandari v. INS*, 227 F.3d 1160, 1168–69 (9th Cir. 2000) (finding Iranian Christian tortured for interfaith dating was persecuted on account of religion).

[181] *Maini v. INS*, 212 F.3d 1167, 1175 (9th Cir. 2000) (finding punishment for interfaith marriage is without question persecution on account of religion).

[182] *Kojevnikova v. Reno*, No. 97-4214, 1999 U.S. App. LEXIS 6368, at *4–*5 (2d Cir. Apr. 6, 1999) (not selected for publication in the Federal Reporter) (finding that an applicant who was detained for some months at a "psychiatric" institution because of her Jewish ethnicity and her involvement with a Jewish dissident group suffered past persecution).

[183] *Korablina v. INS*, 158 F.3d 1038, 1045 (9th Cir. 1998) (finding that Jewish applicant who suffered various forms of discrimination and threats suffered past persecution).

[184] *Abdel-Masieh v. INS*, 73 F.3d 579, 586 (5th Cir. 1996) (holding that a Sudanese Christian who demonstrated that his government persecutes Christians was not required to demonstrate countrywide persecution).

[185] *Cordero-Trejo v. INS*, 40 F.3d 482, 492 (1st Cir. 1994) (remanding to the BIA for further consideration the case of a Guatemalan religious worker who was placed under surveillance, accused of inciting rebellion, and whose family members were attacked).

[186] *Bastanipour v. INS*, 980 F.2d 1129, 1133–34 (7th Cir. 1992) (recognizing that persecution feared by an Iranian national for abandoning Islam and converting to Christianity is a basis for asylum).

BIA cases finding persecution on account of religion include: *Matter of G–A–*,[189] *Matter of S–A–*,[190] and *Matter of D–V–*.[191] In a case that received national media attention, an IJ granted asylum to a German woman based on her membership in the Church of Scientology.[192]

Cases based on claims of religious persecution that have been rejected include: *Quomsieh v. Gonzales*,[193] *Chakir v. Gonzales*,[194] *Gu v. Gonzales*,[195] *Gomes v. Gonzales*,[196] *Ngure v. Ashcroft*,[197] *Pop v. INS*,[198] *Ahmad v. INS*,[199] *Saleh v. INS*,[200] *Elnager v. INS*,[201] *Khalaf v. INS*,[202] and *Gumbol v. INS*.[203] Mere membership in a particular religious community will not normally be enough to establish an asylum claim.[204]

---

[187] *Chen v. INS*, 359 F.3d 121, 128 (2d Cir. 2004) (remanding claim of Chinese Roman Catholic to BIA where BIA had failed to consider beatings suffered by applicant and relied on State Department reports that were contrary to the evidence presented by the applicant).

[188] *Kanivets v. Riley*, 320 F. Supp. 2d 297, 300 (E.D. Pa. 2004) (remanding to IJ who erred by requiring applicant to present objective evidence that there was a "clear-cut tradition" of anti-Semitism in Kyrgyzstan where the applicant experienced past persecution and presented testimony by an expert witness).

[189] *Matter of G–A–*, 23 I&N Dec. 366 (BIA 2002) (in granting Convention Against Torture relief, the BIA relied on State Department reports indicating that the persecution of Armenian Christians was on the rise in Iran).

[190] *Matter of S–A–*, 22 I&N Dec. 1328, 1335 (BIA 2000) (granting asylum to a Moroccan woman with liberal Muslim beliefs who was persecuted by her father who held more orthodox Muslim views).

[191] *Matter of D–V–*, 21 I&N Dec. 77, 79–80 (BIA 1993) (finding that the applicant, an activist in a pro-Aristide church group, had a well-founded fear of persecution based, in part, on her religion).

[192] *See* D. Frantz, "U.S. Immigration Court Grants Asylum to German Scientologist," *N.Y. Times,* Nov. 8, 1997, at front page (noting that the German authorities consider Scientology an extremist organization and bar Scientologists from membership in major political parties).

[193] *Quomsieh v. Gonzales*, 479 F.3d 602, 606 (8th Cir. 2007) (rejecting claim of Palestinian Christians for failure to show past persecution or a well-founded fear).

[194] *Chakir v. Gonzales*, 466 F.3d 563, 569-70 (7th Cir. 2006) (denying asylum claim of Moroccan Christian convert who failed to show a well-founded fear of persecution).

[195] *Gu v. Gonzales*, 454 F.3d 1014, 1021 (9th Cir. 2005) (finding Chinese Christian who was subjected to interrogation and who was struck on the back ten times with a rod had not suffered past persecution and did not have a well-founded fear).

[196] *Gomes v. Gonzales*, 429 F.3d 1264, 1267 (9th Cir. 2005) (finding Catholic from Bangladesh had not established a pattern or practice of persecution or that relocation within Bangladesh was unreasonable).

[197] *Ngure v. Ashcroft*, 367 F.3d 975, 990 (8th Cir. 2004) (finding claim based on Kenyan applicant's Christian Science beliefs without merit).

[198] *Pop v. INS*, 270 F.3d 527, 530–32 (7th Cir. 2001) (finding claim of Jehovah's Witness from Romania not credible).

[199] *Ahmad v. INS*, 163 F.3d 457, 463 (7th Cir. 1999) (rejecting applicant's claim of per se persecution of Ahmadis in Pakistan).

[200] *Saleh v. INS*, 962 F.2d 234, 239 (2d Cir. 1992) (rejecting Yemeni Moslem's claim of religious persecution arising out of death sentence for murder imposed by a religious court).

[201] *Elnager v. INS*, 930 F.2d 784, 788 (9th Cir. 1991) (finding that an Egyptian Muslim who converted to Christianity failed to establish a well-founded fear of persecution).

[202] *Khalaf v. INS*, 909 F.2d 589, 592 (1st Cir. 1990) (holding that a Jordanian Moslem whose American wife was of Jewish and Christian ancestry failed to establish a well-founded fear of persecution).

In assessing credibility of religious-based claims, asylum adjudicators at times rely on tests or quizzes regarding the religion in question. Adjudicators often believe there is only one correct answer to a question and that an adherent of the religion would know the answer. This practice has been criticized by the advocacy community[205] and the federal courts.[206] At least one court has vacated a negative outcome in a religious persecution case based on clear bias on the part of the IJ, who referred to the applicants as "religious zealots."[207] The court found that the IJ departed from his judicial rule and his conduct amounted to a denial of due process.[208]

> *Tip*—**Imputed Religion**—USCIS takes the position that religion, as one of the five protected grounds, may be imputed to an asylum applicant.[209]

2.4.9. Nationality

According to UNHCR's *Handbook*, the term "nationality" includes citizenship, as well as membership in an ethnic or linguistic group, and may occasionally overlap with the term "race."[210] The *Handbook* provides that persecution for reasons of nationality may consist of adverse attitudes and measures directed against a national (ethnic, linguistic) minority.[211] Conflict due to the presence of two or more ethnic or linguistic groups within the same country has resulted in persecution of groups such as ethnic Albanians in former Yugoslavia, Kurds in Iraq, indigenous populations in Central America, and ethnic groups in the former Soviet Union.[212]

---

[203] *Gumbol v. INS*, 815 F.2d 406, 412–13 (6th Cir. 1987) (finding that an Iraqi Christian failed to establish a well-founded fear of persecution).

[204] *Ahmad*, *supra* note 199, at 463; *Refahiyat v. INS*, 29 F.3d 553, 557 (10th Cir. 1994) (holding that the mere assertion that one is aligned with a minority religion is not sufficient to establish a prima facie case of religious persecution); *see also* UNHCR *Handbook*, *supra* note 36, at ¶73.

[205] *See, e.g.*, Lawyers Committee for Human Rights, *Testing the Faithful: Religion and Asylum* (Nov. 2002), available at *www.humanrightsfirst.org/refugees/reports/religion_surv_1102.pdf*.

[206] *See Yan v. Gonzales*, 438 F.3d 1249, 1256 (10th Cir. 2006) (finding that "notwithstanding his stumbling over a few points of Christian doctrine, [the applicant] presented a coherent, personal testimony of his conversion to faith in Jesus Christ"); *Mezvrishvili v. U.S. Att'y. Gen.*, 467 F.3d 1292, 1296–97 (11th Cir. 2006) (finding that the IJ assumed facts not in the record when he held the applicant to a level of religious devotion that the applicant did not assert); *Rizal v. Gonzales*, 442 F.3d 84, 90 (2d Cir. 2006) (rejecting the approach that a certain degree of doctrinal knowledge is necessary to establish eligibility for asylum on grounds of religious persecution); *Ahmadshah v. Ashcroft*, 396 F.3d 917, 920 n.2 (8th Cir. 2005) ("[W]e are not convinced that a detailed knowledge of Christian doctrine is relevant to the sincerity of an applicant's belief; a recent convert may well lack detailed knowledge of religious custom.").

[207] *Floroiu v. Gonzales*, 481 F.3d 970, 976 (7th Cir. 2007) (court vacated and remanded claim of Seventh Day Adventists from Romania, encouraged the BIA to send the case to a different IJ, and instructed the court clerk to send a copy of the decision to the attorney general).

[208] *Id.*

[209] *See supra* note 160 and accompanying text.

[210] UNHCR *Handbook*, *supra* note 36, ¶74.

[211] *Id.*

[212] *See, e.g.*, *Knezevic v. Ashcroft*, 367 F.3d 1206, 1210 (9th Cir. 2004) (finding that persecution was based on applicant's Serbian ethnicity); *Baballah v. Ashcroft*, 367 F.3d 1067, 1077 n.10 (9th Cir. 2004) (persecu-
continued

The *Handbook* cautions:

It may not always be easy to distinguish between persecution for reasons of nationality and persecution for reasons of political opinion when a conflict between national groups is combined with political movements, particularly where a political movement is identified with a specific "nationality."[213]

Moreover, the *Handbook* notes that while in most cases persecution for reasons of nationality is feared by persons belonging to a national minority, there have been many cases where a person belonging to a majority group may fear persecution by a dominant minority.[214]

> *Tip*—**Imputed Nationality**—USCIS takes the position that nationality, as one of the five protected grounds, may be imputed to an asylum applicant.[215]

2.4.10. Membership in a Particular Social Group

According to UNHCR's *Handbook*, a particular social group consists of "persons of similar background, habits or social status."[216] The *Handbook* notes that membership in a particular social group "may be at the root of persecution because there is no confidence in the group's loyalty to the Government or because the political outlook, antecedents or economic activity of its members, or the very existence of the social group as such, is held to be an obstacle to the Government's policies."[217] In addition, claims based on an applicant's social group "may frequently overlap with a claim to fear of persecution on other grounds, *i.e.*, race, religion or nationality."[218]

In recently issued guidelines that complement its *Handbook*, UNHCR has expounded further on this ground. Notably, these guidelines define "particular social group" as:

a group of persons who share a common characteristic other than their risk of being persecuted, or who are perceived as a group by society. The characteristic will often be one which is innate, unchangeable, or which is otherwise fundamental to identity, conscience or the exercise of human rights.[219]

---

tion based on being child of mixed marriage between a Muslim and a Jew); *Shoafera v. INS*, 228 F.3d 1070, 1074 n.2 (9th Cir. 2000) (persecution based on Amhara ethnicity); *Perkovic v. INS*, 33 F.3d 615, 622–23 (6th Cir. 1994) (granting asylum to an ethnic Albanian from Yugoslavia); *Matter of O–Z– & I–Z–*, 22 I&N Dec. 23, 26 (BIA 1998) (finding anti-Semitic threats and beatings rise to level of persecution on account of Jewish "nationality").

[213] UNHCR *Handbook*, *supra* note 36, ¶75.

[214] *Id.* at ¶76.

[215] *See supra* note 160 and accompanying text.

[216] UNHCR *Handbook*, *supra* note 36, ¶77.

[217] *Id.* at ¶78.

[218] *Id.* at ¶77.

[219] UNHCR, *Guidelines on International Protection: "Membership of a Particular Social Group" Within the Context of Article 1A(2) of the 1951 Convention and/or its 1967 Protocol Relating to the Status of Refugees* (2002) at ¶11, available at *www.unhcr.org/publ/PUBL/3d58de2da.pdf*.

In addition, UNHCR highlights that the size of the particular social group is not relevant in determining whether a group exists, noting that a majority of the population could, under certain circumstances, constitute a particular social group.[220]

The BIA, in *Matter of Acosta*,[221] interpreted the phrase "persecution on account of membership in a particular social group" to mean:

> persecution that is directed toward an individual who is a member of a group of persons all of whom share a common, immutable characteristic. The shared characteristic might be an innate one such as sex, color, or kinship ties, or in some circumstances it might be a shared past experience such as former military leadership or land ownership. The particular kind of group characteristic that will qualify under this construction remains to be determined on a case-by-case basis. However, whatever the common characteristic that defines the group, it must be one that the members of the group either cannot change, or should not be required to change because it is fundamental to their individual identities or consciences.

The BIA has recently found that an important consideration is the "social visibility" of the members of claimed particular social group.[222] Moreover, it is not enough simply to identify the common characteristic of a group found to be at risk. The applicant also must show that the claimed persecution is "on account of" the group's identifying characteristics.[223]

> ➢ *Tip*—**Imputed Membership in Social Group**—USCIS takes the position that membership in a particular social group, as one of the five protected grounds, may be imputed to an asylum applicant.[224]

The Ninth Circuit has set forth a four-part test for determining a particular social group claim. Under this test the applicant must: (1) identify a cognizable social group; (2) prove that the applicant is a group member; (3) prove that the persecution is aimed at one of the group's unifying characteristics; and (4) show "special circumstances" that merit the recognition of a group-based claim.[225] In the case in which it established this test, the Ninth Circuit found that

---

[220] *Id.* at ¶18.

[221] *Matter of Acosta*, 19 I&N Dec. 211, 233 (BIA 1985), *modified on other grounds by Matter of Mogharrabi*, 19 I&N 439 (BIA 1987).

[222] *Matter of C–A–*, 23 I&N Dec. 951, 959–61 (BIA 2006) (noting that UNHCR's *Guidelines* confirm that "visibility" is an important element), *aff'd Castillo-Arias v. U.S. Att'y. Gen.*, 446 F.3d 1190 (11th Cir. 2006), *cert. denied*, 127 S. Ct. 977 (Jan. 8, 2007).

[223] *Matter of Sanchez and Escobar*, 19 I&N Dec. 276, 285–86 (BIA 1985), *aff'd, Sanchez-Trujillo v. INS*, 801 F.2d 1571 (9th Cir. 1986); *see also Lukwago v. Ashcroft*, 329 F.3d 157, 170 (3d Cir. 2003).

[224] *See supra* note 160 and accompanying text.

[225] *Sanchez-Trujillo v. INS*, 801 F.2d 1571, 1574–75 (9th Cir. 1986); *see also Rivera-Castaneda v. INS*, 6 Fed. Appx. 604, 605 (9th Cir. 2001) (not selected for publication in the Federal Reporter); *Olarte v. INS*, 1995 U.S. App. LEXIS 7796, at *5–*6 (9th Cir. 1995) (not selected for publication in the Federal Reporter). The Seventh Circuit has articulated a three-part test for proving persecution based on membership in a social group. *See Lwin v. INS*, 144 F.3d 505, 510 (7th Cir. 1998) ("An alien must: (1) identify a particular social group; (2) establish that [he or she] is a member of that group; and (3) establish that [his or her] well-founded fear of persecution is based on membership in that group.") (internal quotation marks and citations omitted) (alteration in original).

the class of young, urban, working class males in El Salvador did not constitute a particular social group.[226] It further held that a social group "implies a collection of people closely affiliated with each other, who are actuated by some common impulse or interest."[227]

However, many circuits—including the Ninth Circuit itself—have shifted their focus in defining social groups from the "voluntary associational relationship" to whether the members of the purported social group share an essential or immutable characteristic. These circuits embrace the test articulated by the BIA in *Matter of Acosta*,[228] which requires that the common characteristic be one that the members of the group cannot change or should not be required to change. The *Acosta* approach has been endorsed by the First,[229] Second,[230] Third,[231] Sixth,[232] Seventh,[233] Eighth,[234] Ninth,[235] Tenth,[236] and Eleventh[237] Circuits—and the Fourth and Fifth Circuits have cited its language approvingly without explicitly endorsing the approach.[238]

Particular social groups may include: Somalian females,[239] the educated, landowning class of Colombian cattle farmers,[240] former U.S. Embassy employees,[241] former child soldiers,[242] families,[243] persons with disabilities,[244] gay men with female sexual identities,[245] a

---

[226] *Sanchez-Trujillo*, *supra* note 225, at 1577.

[227] *Id.* at 1576.

[228] *Matter of Acosta*, 19 I&N Dec. 211 (BIA 1985), *modified on other grounds by Matter of Mogharrabi*, 19 I&N Dec. 439 (BIA 1987). The BIA continues to use this definition of "social group" today. *See, e.g., Matter of A–M–E– & J–G–U–*, 24 I&N Dec. 69, 73 (BIA 2007).

[229] *Elien v. Ashcroft*, 364 F.3d 392, 396–97 (1st Cir. 2004).

[230] *Koudriachova v. Gonzales*, 490 F.3d 255, 2007 U.S. App. LEXIS 15177, at *13–*15 (2d Cir. 2007).

[231] *Fatin v. INS*, 12 F.3d 1233, 1239–40 (3d Cir. 1993).

[232] *Castellano-Chacon v. INS*, 341 F.3d 533, 546-48 (6th Cir. 2003), *superseded by statute on other grounds as stated in Chen v. United States*, 434 F.3d 144, 151 (2d Cir. 2006).

[233] *See, e.g., Lwin v. INS*, 144 F.3d 505, 512 (7th Cir. 1998).

[234] *Safaie v. INS*, 25 F.3d 636, 640 (8th Cir. 1994). Note: The Eighth Circuit's definition of a social group centers on *both* a "voluntary associational relationship" *and* a "common characteristic" that is "essentially beyond the petitioner's power to change or is so fundamental to the individual's identity or conscience that he or she ought not to be required to change."

[235] *Thomas v. Gonzales*, 409 F.3d 1177, 1184–87 (9th Cir. 2005) (en banc), *vacated on other grounds*, 547 U.S. 183 (2006).

[236] *Niang v. Gonzales*, 422 F.3d 1187, 1199 (10th Cir. 2005).

[237] *Castillo-Arias v. U.S. Att'y Gen.*, 446 F.3d 1190, 1196–97 (11th Cir. 2006), *cert. denied*, 127 S. Ct. 977 (Jan. 8, 2007).

[238] *See Lopez-Soto v. Ashcroft*, 383 F.3d 228, 235 (4th Cir. 2004); *Ontunez-Tursios v. Ashcroft*, 303 F.3d 341, 352–53 (5th Cir. 2002).

[239] *Mohammed v. Gonzales*, 400 F.3d 785, 798 (9th Cir. 2005).

[240] *Tapiero de Orjuela v. Gonzales*, 423 F.3d 666, 672 (7th Cir. 2005).

[241] *Ang v. Gonzales*, 430 F.3d 50, 56 (1st Cir. 2005) (agreeing that applicant's work at the Embassy and support for Americans could serve as basis for particular social group claim, but rejecting claim because no past persecution or well-founded fear).

[242] *Lukwago v. Ashcroft*, 329 F.3d 157, 178–79 (3d Cir. 2003).

[243] *See Vumi v. Gonzales*, 502 F.3d 150 (2d Cir. 2007).

family that plays a prominent role in a minority group that is the object of widespread hostile treatment,[246] parents of Burmese student dissidents,[247] Filipinos of Chinese ancestry,[248] young women who are members of the Tchamba-Kunsuntu tribe who have not been subjected to female genital mutilation and who oppose the practice,[249] female members of a tribe,[250] members of a Somali clan,[251] homosexuals,[252] Guatemalan street children,[253] Honduran street children,[254] married women in India who have contracted HIV, who fear their families will disown them or force them to get a divorce, and who wish to or need to be employed,[255] social outcasts in Colombia,[256] unmarried Chinese women who have been subjected to arranged marriages according to feudal practices and who oppose such practices,[257] women who have been subjected to or face being subjected to the practice of Trokosi, a system of indentured sexual servitude to fetish shrines,[258] young, Westernized, educated, Muslim women who voice their political opinion,[259] persons who are HIV positive,[260] students,[261] members of a royal tribal family,[262] members of a tribe, professionals,

---

[244] *Tchoukhrova v. Gonzales*, 404 F.3d 1181, 1189–90 (9th Cir. 2005) (finding "persons with disabilities are precisely the kind of individuals that our asylum law contemplates by the words 'particular social group'"), *rehearing en banc denied*, 430 F.3d 1222 (9th Cir. 2005) (dissent criticized court for creating a reverse derivative asylum claim by imputing harm suffered disabled child to parents). Although the Supreme Court vacated the Ninth Circuit's opinion in *Tchoukhrova* because the Ninth Circuit erred by reaching issues that the BIA had not ruled on in the first instance, *Gonzales v. Tchoukhrova*, 127 S. Ct. 57 (2006), the Ninth Circuit's opinion suggests that courts may be willing to view persons with disabilities as a particular social group.

[245] *Hernandez-Montiel v. INS*, 225 F.3d 1084 (9th Cir. 2000), *overruled on other grounds by Thomas v. Gonzales*, 409 F.3d 1177, 1187 (9th Cir. 2005) (en banc).

[246] *Mgoian v. INS*, 184 F.3d 1029, 1036 (9th Cir. 1999).

[247] *Lwin v. INS*, 144 F.3d 505, 512 (7th Cir. 1998).

[248] *Matter of V–T–S–*, 21 I&N Dec. 792, 798 (BIA 1997).

[249] *Matter of Kasinga*, 21 I&N Dec. 357, 365–66 (BIA 1996).

[250] *Niang v. Gonzales*, 422 F.3d 1187, 1199 (10th Cir. 2005).

[251] *Matter of H–*, 21 I&N Dec. 337, 342–43 (BIA 1996).

[252] *Matter of Toboso-Alfonso*, 20 I&N Dec. 819 (BIA 1990).

[253] *Matter of A–M–L–, [number not provided]* (IJ Nov. 21, 2001) (Phoenix, AZ) (Richardson, IJ), *reported in* 79 *Interpreter Releases* 440 (Mar. 25, 2002).

[254] *Matter of Reyes-Diaz, [number not provided]* (IJ Aug. 2, 2001) (Los Angeles, CA) (Munoz, IJ).

[255] *Matter of [name not provided]*, (IJ Dec. 20, 2000) (Baltimore, MD) (Gossart, IJ), *reported in* 78 *Interpreter Releases* 233 (Jan. 15, 2001).

[256] *Matter of Faronda-Blandon*, A74 979 517 (IJ June 15, 2001) (York County Prison, PA) (Van Wyke, IJ), *reported in* 78 *Interpreter Releases* 1173 (July 16, 2001).

[257] *Matter of [name not provided]*, A76 512 001 (IJ Oct. 18, 2000) (Chicago, IL) (Zerbe, IJ), *reported in* 77 *Interpreter Releases* 1634 (Nov. 20, 2000); *see also Gao v. Gonzales*, 440 F.3d 62, 70–71 (2d Cir. 2006) (finding women who have been sold into marriage and who live in a part of China where forced marriages are considered valid and enforceable constitute a particular social group).

[258] *See* "IJ Grants Asylum to Former 'Trokosi' Slave," 75 *Interpreter Releases* 165 (Feb. 2, 1998).

[259] *Matter of Sharmin*, A73 556 833 (IJ Sept. 27, 1996) (New York, NY) (IJ Bukszpan), *reported in* 74 *Interpreter Releases* 174 (Jan. 27, 1997).

[260] *Matter of [name not provided]*, A71 498 940 (IJ Oct. 31, 1995) (New York, NY), *reported in* 73 *Interpreter Releases* 901 (July 8, 1996).

business people, and highly educated individuals,[263] former members of the national police,[264] government employees,[265] and union members.[266] UNHCR also takes the position that victims of trafficking and persons at risk of being trafficked might also qualify for refugee status under certain circumstances.[267]

Groups found not to be particular social groups, under the facts presented, include: criminal deportees,[268] Honduran street children,[269] noncriminal drug informants working against the Cali drug cartel,[270] young, attractive Albanian women forced into prostitution,[271] indigenous people comprising a large percentage of the population of a disputed area,[272] mentally ill Jamaicans or mentally ill female Jamaicans,[273] former members of the military,[274] cooperative taxi drivers,[275] Tamil males between the ages of 15 and 45,[276] Salvadoran women previously raped and beaten by guerrillas,[277] Iranian women whose claims were based solely on gender and the harsh restrictions placed upon them as women,[278] Chinese citizens of low economic status,[279] members of the criminal class,[280] cheese makers who supplied guerrillas with food,[281] and family members of military deserters.[282]

---

[261] *Matter of Villalta*, 20 I&N Dec. 142 (BIA 1990).

[262] *Adebisi v. INS*, 952 F.2d 910, 913 (5th Cir. 1992).

[263] *Ananeh-Firempong v. INS*, 766 F.2d 621, 623 (1st Cir. 1985).

[264] *Matter of Fuentes*, 19 I&N Dec. 658 (BIA 1988).

[265] *Aguilera-Cota v. INS*, 914 F.2d 1375, 1380 n.3 (9th Cir. 1990).

[266] *Bernal-Garcia v. INS*, 852 F.2d 144 (5th Cir. 1988).

[267] See UNHCR, *Guidelines on International Protection: The Application of Article 1A(2) of the 1951 Convention and 1967 Protocol Relating to the Status of Refugees to Victims of Trafficking and Persons at Risk of Being Trafficked* (2006), available at *www.unhcr.org/publ/PUBL/443b626b2.pdf*.

[268] *Toussaint v. Gonzales*, 455 F.3d 409, 417–18 (3d Cir. 2006); *Elien v. Ashcroft*, 364 F.3d 392, 397 (1st Cir. 2004).

[269] *Escobar v. Gonzales*, 417 F.3d 363, 367–68 (3d Cir. 2005).

[270] *Matter of C–A–*, 23 I&N Dec. 951 (BIA 2006), *aff'd Castillo-Arias v. U.S. Att'y. Gen.*, 446 F.3d 1190 (11th Cir. 2006), *cert. denied*, 127 S. Ct. 977 (Jan. 8, 2007).

[271] *Rreshpja v. Gonzales*, 420 F.3d 551, 555–56 (6th Cir. 2005).

[272] *Pedro-Mateo v. INS*, 224 F.3d 1147, 1151 (9th Cir. 2000).

[273] *Raffington v. INS*, 340 F.3d 720,723 (8th Cir. 2003).

[274] *Arriaga-Barrientos v. INS*, 937 F.2d 411, 414 (9th Cir. 1991).

[275] *Matter of Acosta*, 19 I&N Dec. 211, 234 (BIA 1985), *modified on other grounds by Matter of Mogharrabi*, 19 I&N Dec. 439 (BIA 1987).

[276] *Ravindran v. INS*, 976 F.2d 754, 761 n.5 (1st Cir. 1992).

[277] *Gomez v. INS*, 947 F.2d 660, 664 (2d Cir. 1991).

[278] *Safaie v. INS*, 25 F.3d 636, 640 (8th Cir. 1994).

[279] *Li v. INS*, 92 F.3d 985, 987 (9th Cir. 1996).

[280] *Bastanipour v. INS*, 980 F.2d 1129, 1132 (7th Cir. 1992).

[281] *Alvarez-Flores v. INS*, 909 F.2d 1, 7 (1st Cir 1990).

[282] *DeValle v. INS*, 901 F.2d 787, 792 (9th Cir. 1990).

2.4.11. Political Opinion

Asylum is often referred to as "political asylum." Political opinion, of course, is just one of the five grounds enumerated in the refugee definition. While a substantial number of asylum cases are political opinion claims, the four other grounds noted above should not be overlooked. Indeed, it is quite common for asylum applicants to base their claims on two or more of the enumerated grounds.

Actual: Acts, Words, and Beliefs

Political opinion, in many cases, has been interpreted to encompass a wide spectrum of views. It would include, of course, any opinion regarding the government, its laws, or its policies. One commentator has further noted that it should also include "any opinion on any matter in which the machinery of State, government, and policy may be engaged."[283] UNHCR's *Handbook* provides that political opinions are "opinions not tolerated by the authorities, which are critical of their policies or methods."[284]

A person may express his or her political opinion through actions as well as words. In *Chang v. INS*,[285] the Third Circuit held that the asylum applicant had "manifested" his political opinion through his actions in defying the orders of the Chinese government. The court reasoned that "[s]imply because he did not call himself a dissident or couch his resistance in terms of a particular ideology renders his opposition no less political."[286] Political opinion may also be expressed through the act of whistleblowing against corrupt government officials.[287]

Persecution on account of political opinion means "persecution on account of the *victim's* political opinion, not the persecutor's."[288] To meet this burden, an asylum-seeker must show, through direct or circumstantial evidence, that there is a causal connection between the persecution suffered or feared and his or her political opinion or imputed

---

[283] G. Goodwin-Gill, *The Refugee in International Law* 49 (2d Ed. 1996).

[284] UNHCR *Handbook*, *supra* note 36, at ¶80.

[285] *Chang v. INS*, 119 F.3d 1055, 1063 (3d Cir. 1997).

[286] *Id.*; *see also Grava v. INS*, 205 F.3d 1177 (9th Cir. 2000) (whistleblowing found to be an expression of political opinion); *Tarubac v. INS*, 182 F.3d 1114, 1119 (9th Cir.1999) (finding that the applicant's expression of opposition to communism led to the most extreme persecution that she suffered); *Osorio v. INS*, 18 F.3d 1017, 1029 (2d Cir. 1994) (holding that resistance is no less political simply because the asylum applicant did not state he belonged to a political party or which political philosophy he supported); *Montecino v. INS*, 915 F.2d 518, 520 (9th Cir. 1990) (holding that an ex-soldier's fear of reprisals by guerrillas was political persecution).

[287] *Fedunyak v. Gonzales*, 477 F.3d 1126, 1129 (9th Cir. 2007) (noting that to qualify as a whistleblower, the applicant need not expose government corruption to the public at large). *But see Pavlyk v. Gonzales*, 469 F.3d 1082, 1089 (7th Cir. 2006) (rejecting applicant claim based on whistleblowing because he did not take his evidence of corruption "to the public in quest of a political decision" and because as a public employee he would have limited First Amendment rights even within the United States).

[288] *INS v. Elias-Zacarias*, 502 U.S. 478, 482 (1992) (emphasis in original).

political opinion. In other words, it is not sufficient to demonstrate merely that the persecutor is motivated by political reasons.[289]

Unexpressed

An asylum applicant's beliefs may also constitute a political opinion even though they are not expressed. UNHCR's *Handbook* provides:

> There may, however, also be situations in which the applicant has not given any expression to his opinions. Due to the strength of his convictions, however, it may be reasonable to assume that his opinions will sooner or later find expression and that the applicant will, as a result, come into conflict with the authorities. Where this can reasonably be assumed, the applicant can be considered to have fear of persecution for reasons of political opinion.[290]

Similarly, the BIA has noted that an applicant's fear may be well-founded if the persecutor "could" become aware of the applicant's belief.[291]

Imputed

Individuals may also be persecuted for political opinions that they are erroneously believed to hold. Courts have recognized that persecution based on an "imputed" political opinion can satisfy the refugee definition.[292] Such claims are also recognized by UNHCR's *Handbook*, which states that persecution based on political opinions may include situations in which "such opinions have come to the notice of the authorities or are *attributed* by them *to the applicant*."[293]

USCIS also takes the position that *any* of the five protected grounds may be imputed to an asylum applicant, not just political opinion. According to USCIS, when the persecution inflicted on the asylum applicant is because of an imputed characteristic related to any one of the five protected grounds, the persecution is "on account of" that characteristic, regardless of whether the applicant possesses it.[294]

Claims based on imputed political opinion have been accepted in cases in which the applicant was erroneously believed to support Falun Gong,[295] to be a member of a subversive

---

[289] *See, e.g.*, *Leva-Montalvo v. INS*, 173 F.3d 749 (9th Cir. 1999) (finding that where all of the applicant's discussions with the "Recontras" centered on politics and ideology, there was no evidence indicating that their motives were purely criminal); *see also Vera-Valera v. INS*, 147 F.3d 1036 (9th Cir. 1998) (in establishing an imputed political opinion, court considers the political views the persecutor rightly or wrongly attributes to his or her victims).

[290] UNHCR *Handbook*, *supra* note 36, at ¶82.

[291] *Matter of Mogharrabi*, 19 I&N Dec. 439, 446 (BIA 1987). *But see Sharif v. INS*, 87 F.3d 932, 935 (7th Cir. 1996) (denying claim of a Westernized woman from Iran because "there [is no] evidence to suggest that she will voice her opposition to Iranian law when she returns to Iran").

[292] *Uwais v. U.S. Att'y Gen.*, 478 F.3d 513, 517 (2d Cir. 2007); *Mulanga v. Ashcroft*, 349 F.3d 123, 133 n.7 (3d Cir. 2003); *Sangha v. INS*, 103 F.3d 1482, 1489 (9th Cir. 1997); *Singh v. Ilchert*, 69 F.3d 375, 379 (9th Cir. 1995); *Canas-Segovia v. INS*, 970 F.2d 599, 601–02 (9th Cir. 1992); *Matter of S–P–*, 21 I&N Dec. 486, 497 (BIA 1996).

[293] UNHCR *Handbook*, *supra* note 36, at ¶80 (emphasis added).

[294] *See supra* note 160 and accompanying text.

[295] *Lu v. Ashcroft*, 2004 U.S. App. LEXIS 3003 (9th Cir. 2004) (unpublished).

group,[296] to be involved with the military,[297] to hold antiguerrilla beliefs,[298] to be an opponent of communism,[299] to be a government supporter,[300] to be a dissident because he benefited from a U.S.-led airlift out of Iraq,[301] and to have transported weapons for a rebel group.[302]

Claims that have been rejected include cases in which the applicant has failed to demonstrate that the persecutor had attributed a political opinion to him or her[303] or that the persecution feared was not a "reasonable possibility."[304]

Neutrality

Several federal courts have recognized that neutrality that is a conscious choice is a political opinion.[305] In *Rivera-Moreno*, the Ninth Circuit noted that it follows the doctrine of "hazardous neutrality," which recognizes that neutrality may constitute a political opinion in an environment fraught with hazard from government or antigovernment forces.[306] Similarly, in *Umanzor-Alvarado*, the First Circuit held that neutrality may be considered a political opinion upon a showing that the applicant affirmatively chose to remain neutral, articulated this opinion, and had been or could reasonably be singled out for persecution on this basis.[307] An asylum applicant, however, must establish that the persecution he or she fears or suffered was because of his or her neutrality.[308]

---

[296] *Maldonado-Cruz v. INS*, 883 F.2d 788 (9th Cir. 1990); *Matter of S–P–*, 21 I&N Dec. 486, 497 (BIA 1996).

[297] *Molina v. INS*, 170 F.3d 1247, 1249 (9th Cir. 1999).

[298] *Ventura v. INS*, 264 F.3d 1150, 1156 (9th Cir. 2001), *rev'd on other grounds*, 537 U.S. 12 (2002).

[299] *Agbuya v. INS*, 219 F.3d 962, 967 (9th Cir. 2000), *amended by* 241 F.3d 1224 (9th Cir. 2001).

[300] *Aguilera-Cota v. INS*, 914 F.2d 1375 (9th Cir. 1990).

[301] *Al-Harbi v. INS*, 242 F.3d 882 (9th Cir. 2001).

[302] *Blanco-Lopez v. INS*, 858 F.2d 531 (9th Cir. 1988); *see also Briones v. INS*, 175 F.3d 727, 729 (9th Cir. 1999) (en banc) (finding that the asylum applicant's "activity as a confidential informer who sided with the Philippine military in a conflict that was political at its core certainly would be perceived as a political act by the group informed upon").

[303] *Estrada-Escobar v. Ashcroft*, 376 F.3d 1042, 1047 (10th Cir. 2004); *Huaman Cornelio v. BIA*, 979 F.2d 995, 1000 (4th Cir. 1992); *Estrada-Posadas v. INS*, 924 F.2d 916, 919 (9th Cir. 1991), *overruled on other grounds by Thomas v. Gonzales*, 409 F.3d 1177, 1180 (9th Cir. 2005); *Arriaga-Barrientos v. INS*, 937 F.2d 411, 414 (9th Cir. 1991); *Matter of R–*, 20 I&N Dec. 621 (BIA 1992).

[304] *Aruta v. INS*, 80 F.3d 1389, 1395 (9th Cir. 1996).

[305] *See, e.g., Rivera-Moreno v. INS*, 213 F.3d 481, 483–84 (9th Cir. 2000); *Umanzor-Alvarado v INS*, 896 F.2d 14, 15–16 (1st Cir. 1990); *Arteaga v. INS*, 836 F.2d 1227, 1231–32 (9th Cir. 1988).

[306] *Rivera-Moreno*, *supra* note 305, at 483 (finding, however, that the applicant had not established that the guerrillas sought to persecute her because of her neutrality).

[307] *Umanzor-Alvarado v INS*, *supra* note 305, at 15.

[308] *See Sagarminaga v. INS*, 113 F.3d 1247 (10th Cir. 1997) (holding that the applicant failed to establish that the guerrillas would persecute her because of her decision to remain neutral); *Lopez-Zeron v. U.S. Department of Justice*, 8 F.3d 636 (8th Cir. 1993) (holding that Honduran asylum applicants failed to demonstrate they were targeted by the government because of their political neutrality); *Matter of Vigil*, 19 I&N Dec. 572, 576–77 (BIA 1988) (holding that applicant failed to show that he had articulated his neutrality previously and that he received some threat or could be "singled out" for persecution because of his neutrality).

Coercive Population Control

In 1996, the definition of refugee was amended to provide protection to people who have suffered or who fear persecution for resistance to coercive population control measures in their home countries. Under the amended definition, these individuals are deemed to have been persecuted or to have a well-founded fear of persecution on account of their political opinion.

IIRAIRA amended the term "refugee" to provide that:

[A] person who has been forced to abort a pregnancy or to undergo involuntary sterilization, or who has been persecuted for failure or refusal to undergo such a procedure or for other resistance to a coercive population control program, shall be deemed to have been persecuted on account of political opinion, and a person who has a well-founded fear that he or she will be forced to undergo such a procedure or subject to persecution for such failure, refusal, or resistance shall be deemed to have a well-founded fear of persecution on account of political opinion.[309]

The provision applies retroactively.[310] The BIA announced in *G–C–L–*, however, that it would no longer grant untimely motions to reopen for asylum claims based on coercive population control policies because, at the time of the BIA's decision, more than five years had passed since the law changed under IIRAIRA.[311]

The BIA has decided several cases interpreting this provision. In *Matter of X–P–T–*, the BIA found that the applicant, who had violated China's one-child policy by having three children and who, as a result, was forcibly sterilized, was statutorily eligible for asylum.[312] The BIA also found that the applicant was eligible for withholding of deportation.[313] In *Matter of C–Y–Z–*,[314] the BIA held that an asylum applicant whose spouse was forced to undergo sterilization was able to establish past persecution on account of political opinion and qualified as a refugee within the definition of INA §101(a)(42). Similarly, in *Matter of G–C–L–*, an applicant who violated the one-child policy by having two children and whose spouse was forced to undergo an abortion, as well as forced sterilization, was eligible for asylum.[315] The Asylum Division similarly takes the position that forced abortion or forced sterilization of an asylum applicant's spouse could be considered persecution of the applicant.[316]

---

[309] INA §101(a)(42)(B); 8 USC §1101(a)(42)(B).

[310] *Zhang v. Reno*, 27 F. Supp. 2d 476, 477 (S.D.N.Y. 1998).

[311] *Matter of G–C–L–*, 23 I&N Dec. 359, 361–62 (BIA 2002).

[312] *Matter of X–P–T–*, 21 I&N Dec. 634, 638 (BIA 1996).

[313] *Id.*

[314] *Matter of C–Y–Z–*, 21 I&N Dec. 915, 919–20 (BIA 1997); *but see Lin v. U.S. DOJ*, 494 F.3d 296 (2d Cir. 2007) (holding that spouses of those subjected to or threatened with coercive birth control procedures are not *automatically* eligible for asylum, as suggested by *Matter of C–Y–Z–*).

[315] *Matter of G–C–L–*, *supra* note 311; *see also Ge v. Ashcroft*, 367 F.3d 1121, 1127 (9th Cir. 2004); *Matter of Y–T–L–*, 23 I&N Dec. 601 (BIA 2003) (forced sterilization of spouse is grounds for asylum despite the fact that applicant faces no future threat).

[316] *See* AOBTC Lesson: Asylum Eligibility Part I, *supra* note 47, at 26; *see also Ma v. Ashcroft*, 361 F.3d 553, 559 (9th Cir. 2004) (overturning a BIA decision that a husband whose marriage was not *legally* registered with the Chinese government was ineligible for asylum based on his wife's forced abortion and finding that the government's refusal to allow the marriage was part of China's coercive population control program).

The BIA has also taken the position that forcible insertion of an intrauterine device (IUD) is a "cognizable claim" of persecution under the amended definition of refugee.[317] But at least one court has found that one routine medical insertion of an IUD, absent allegations of force or physical abuse, does not constitute persecution.[318]

The BIA and the federal courts have recognized asylum claims by the spouses of individuals forced to undergo population control procedures,[319] but at least one circuit court has ruled that spouses should not *automatically* receive asylum based on these grounds.[320] In those circuits that do automatically extend asylum to spouses of those forced to undergo sterilization or an abortion, it is not clear whether boyfriends, fiancés, and nonspouses may also claim such protection.[321] The BIA has rejected claims by unmarried partners,[322] and the circuits are divided on this issue.[323] The Second Circuit has held that parents and in-laws of persons persecuted under coercive family planning policies are not per se eligible for asylum.[324] That same court has found that the forced sterilization of the applicant's mother is not per se persecution of that

---

[317] *Zheng v. Gonzales*, 409 F.3d 804, 810 (7th Cir. 2005) (in overturning an adverse credibility determination, the court noted that the BIA took the position that the involuntary insertions of IUDs constituted a "cognizable claim" of persecution on account of political opinion under the amended refugee definition).

[318] *Li v. Gonzales*, 405 F.3d 171, 179 (4th Cir. 2005). *But see Li v. Ashcroft*, 356 F.3d 1153, 1158 (9th Cir. 2004) (a forced gynecological exam that the victim resisted by kicking and screaming constituted persecution).

[319] *See Matter of C–Y–Z–*, 21 I&N Dec. 915 (BIA 1997); *see also, e.g., Qu v. Gonzales*, 399 F.3d 1195, 1203 (9th Cir. 2005); *Qui v. Ashcroft*, 329 F.3d 140, 144–45 (2d Cir. 2003).

[320] *Lin v. U.S. DOJ*, supra note 314 (holding that spouses of those subjected to or threatened with coercive birth control procedures are not *automatically* eligible for asylum, as suggested by Matter of C–Y–Z–; rather, applicants must demonstrate "other resistance to a coercive population control program" or "a well founded fear that he or she will be . . . subject to persecution for such . . . resistance . . . .").

[321] *See, e.g., Pan v. Gonzales*, 449 F.3d 408, 415 (2d Cir. 2006) (noting the inadequacy of the reasoning by the BIA in *Matter of C–Y–Z–* and a circuit court split on the issue).

[322] *Matter of S–L–L–*, 24 I&N Dec. 1 (BIA 2006) (requiring that a spouse must have been opposed to the abortion or sterilization and legally married; but noting that unmarried applicants may qualify for asylum based on "other resistance" to coercive population control measures), *overruled in part by Lin v. U.S. DOJ*, 2007 WL 2032066 (2d Cir. 2007) (agreeing that unmarried partners do not automatically qualify for asylum but going further to state that *no relatives* of the individual who underwent the coercive population control procedure should automatically qualify for asylum).

[323] *See, e.g., Zhang v. Gonzales*, 434 F.3d 993, 1001–02 (7th Cir. 2006) (granting asylum to husband of woman who was forced to have an abortion, even though the couple had divorced and the wife had subsequently remarried); *Ma v. Ashcroft*, 361 F.3d 553, 559 (9th Cir. 2004) (extending asylum to applicants whose common-law spouses suffered persecution). *But see Chen v. Gonzales*, 457 F.3d 670, 674 (7th Cir. 2006) (finding that refugee status does not extend to boyfriends of women forced to have abortions); *Wang v. Gonzales*, 152 Fed. Appx. 761, 769 (11th Cir. 2005) (finding that marriage to spouse must have existed at the time of the spouse's forcible abortion to qualify for per se eligibility for asylum); *Chen v. Ashcroft*, 381 F.3d 221, 235 (3d Cir. 2004) (refusing to grant asylum to unmarried applicant whose fiancée was forced by Chinese officials to have an abortion, even though the applicant and his fiancée were unable to marry due to China's inflated age requirements for marriage).

[324] *Ai Feng Yuan v. U.S. Dept. of Justice*, 416 F.3d 192, 197 (2d Cir. 2005).

child.³²⁵ In contrast, the Eighth Circuit has granted asylum to individuals whose siblings and siblings' spouses suffered forced sterilizations.³²⁶

A person who engages in "other resistance to a coercive population control program" is also eligible for asylum.³²⁷ There are few precedential decisions defining what "other resistance" is. One court has found that writing an article critical of population control practices and exposing the practice of infanticide constitutes such "other resistance."³²⁸ Another court has held that a woman's vocal resistance to a marriage-age restriction, which resulted in forced gynecological examination that she physically resisted, constitutes "other resistance."³²⁹ In addition, a forced injection and forced IUD procedures have also been considered to be "other resistance."³³⁰ A claim based on "other resistance" does not require proof that the resistance was motivated by opposition to coercive population control policies.³³¹

Additional federal court cases regarding coercive population control include: *Wang v. Gonzales*,³³² *Yang v. Gonzales*,³³³ *Qui v. Ashcroft, Li v. Ashcroft*,³³⁴ *Lin v. Ashcroft*,³³⁵ *Wang v. Ashcroft*,³³⁶ *Shan Liao v. U.S. Dept. of Justice*,³³⁷ *Chen v. INS* (9th Circuit),³³⁸ *Zhao v. U.S. Dept. of Justice*,³³⁹ and *Chen v. INS* (4th Circuit).³⁴⁰

---

³²⁵ *Chen v. Gonzalez*, 417 F.3d 303, 305 (2d Cir. 2005).

³²⁶ *Yang v. Gonzales*, 427 F.3d 1117, 1118 (8th Cir. 2005).

³²⁷ INA §101(a)(42); 8 USC §1101(a)(42).

³²⁸ *Cao v. U.S. Att'y. Gen.*, 407 F.3d 146, 153 (3d Cir. 2005).

³²⁹ *Li v. Ashcroft*, 356 F.3d 1153, 1160 (9th Cir. 2004) (en banc).

³³⁰ *Yang v. U.S. Att'y. Gen.*, 418 F.3d 1198, 1205 (11th Cir. 2005).

³³¹ *Lin v. Gonzales*, 472 F.3d 1131, 1134 (9th Cir. 2007) (an applicant must show: (1) the government was enforcing a coercive population program at the time of the events, and (2) the applicant resisted the program).

³³² *Wang v. Gonzales*, 152 Fed. Appx. 761, 769 (11th Cir. 2006) (finding that marriage to spouse must have existed at the time of the spouse's forcible abortion to qualify for per se eligibility for asylum.)

³³³ *Yang v. Gonzales*, 427 F.3d 1117, 1118 (8th Cir. 2005) (finding Chinese couple with two U.S. citizen children, who wished to have two more children, had a well-founded fear of persecution if they returned to China).

³³⁴ *Li v. Ashcroft*, 356 F.3d 1153 (9th Cir. 2004) (finding that a woman who opposes the Chinese government's population control policies and was subjected to a forced gynecological exam and threatened with future abortions and sterilization of her boyfriend is eligible for asylum).

³³⁵ *Lin v. Ashcroft*, 377 F.3d 1014, 1031 (9th Cir. 2004) (finding that the "discrimination or abusive treatment of children in families with more than one child may qualify them for refugee status" based on language in the INA that defines a refugee as someone who is persecuted for "other resistance" to a coercive population control program).

³³⁶ *Wang v. Ashcroft*, 341 F.3d 1015, 1020 (9th Cir. 2003) (finding that forced abortions are per se persecution and trigger asylum eligibility).

³³⁷ *Shan Liao v. U.S. Dept. of Justice*, 293 F.3d 61 (2d Cir. 2002) (denying asylum to an applicant who failed to prove he would face economic persecution, that his 51-year-old wife was in danger of sterilization, or that he would be subjected to detention upon return).

³³⁸ *Chen v. INS*, 266 F.3d 1094 (9th Cir. 2001) (granting withholding to an applicant who married and had a child without the permission of the Chinese government).

³³⁹ *Zhao v. U.S. Dept. of Justice*, 265 F.3d 83 (2d Cir. 2001).

A hotly contested issue in coercive population control cases is whether having more than one child, one or more of whom are born in the U.S. or elsewhere outside of China, establishes a claim for asylum.[341] Documents presented in *Shou Yung Guo v. Gonzales* suggested that there may be an official policy of forced sterilization in the Fujian Province and that the documents may undermine the court's reliance on State Department reports.[342] The BIA, however, has rejected such a claim in *Matter of J–W–S–*.[343] In addition, courts have grappled with whether having two children alone, both of whom were born in China, is sufficient grounds for a well-founded fear of persecution.[344] The BIA, however, has also rejected this argument.[345]

In September 2001, the Resource Information Center, now part of USCIS, published a comprehensive report entitled *Chinese State Birth Planning in the 1990s and Beyond*, by Susan Greenhalgh, Ph.D. and Edwin Winckler, Ph.D., as part of its Perspective Series, designed to provide country condition information to asylum and immigration officers.[346] For UNHCR's views on coercive population control as a basis for asylum, see *UNHCR Note on Refugee Claims Based on Coercive Family Planning Laws and Policies* (Aug. 2005).[347]

Finally, for applicants seeking to reopen asylum proceedings based on "changed circumstances arising in the country of nationality," evidence of coercive population control policies may not be sufficient to meet the applicant's burden of proof if such evidence does not specifically show any likelihood that the applicant or similarly situated nationals will be persecuted.[348]

---

[340] *Chen v. INS*, 195 F.3d 198 (4th Cir. 1999) (rejecting claim of applicant with three children where record showed forced sterilizations were on decline in China, were limited to rural areas, and couples returning from abroad may be "excused" from paying penalties), *vacated on other grounds*, 537 U.S. 1016 (2002).

[341] *See, e.g., Matter of C–C–*, 23 I&N Dec. 899 (BIA 2006) (finding evidence submitted with motion to reopen did not indicate that Chinese national returning to that country with foreign born children have been subjected to forced sterilization); *Huang v. INS*, 421 F.3d 125, 129 (2d Cir. 2005) (rejecting claim of Chinese applicant with two U.S.-born children for failure to meet his burden of proof).

[342] *Shou Yung Guo v. Gonzales*, 463 F.3d 109 (2d Cir. 2006); *see also Tian Ming Lin v. Gonzales*, 473 F.3d 48, 51 (2d Cir. 2007).

[343] *Matter of J–W–S–*, 24 I&N Dec. 185 (BIA 2007) (finding that the evidence of record did not demonstrate that the Chinese government had a national policy of requiring forced sterilization of a parent who returns with a second child born outside of China).

[344] *See, e.g., Jian Hui Shao v. BIA*, 465 F.3d 497, 503 (2d Cir. 2006).

[345] *Matter of J–H–S–*, 24 I&N Dec. 196 (BIA 2007).

[346] The 258-page report can be found at *www.uscis.gov/graphics/services/asylum/ric/documentation/pschn01001.pdf*.

[347] This note is available on UNHCR's website at *www.unhcr.org/cgi-bin/texis/vtx/refworld/rwmain/opendocpdf.pdf?docid=4301a9184*.

[348] *See, e.g., Matter of S–Y–G–*, 24 I&N Dec. 247 (BIA 2007) (rejecting applicant's motion to reopen asylum proceedings where applicant claimed that the birth of her second child in the United States would lead to persecution in her home province in China, which enforces general population control policies).

2.5. CURRENT ISSUES IN U.S. ASYLUM CASES

2.5.1. Gender-Based Claims

For more than a decade, gender-related asylum claims have received increasing attention by advocates, the U.S. immigration authorities, and the federal courts.[349] The tide began turning in May 1995, when legacy INS issued a memorandum to all asylum officers setting forth guidelines for adjudicating women's asylum claims.[350] In this memorandum, legacy INS acknowledges that women often experience gender-specific types of persecution. The memorandum reviews the human rights context in which guidance on gender-related adjudications has evolved internationally, emphasizes the importance of gender-sensitive interviewing techniques, and outlines how gender-related claims should be analyzed under U.S. law.

Courts, however, have admonished government attorneys for failing to adhere to the principles set forth in the 1995 legacy INS memorandum.[351] More recently, DOJ has been criticized for perpetuating the myth that "rape is just forceful sex by men who cannot control themselves."[352]

Legacy INS, in drafting its memorandum, relied in part on UNHCR's *Guidelines on the Protection of Refugee Women*,[353] in which UNHCR recommends gender-sensitive interviewing techniques and advises asylum adjudicators, in evaluating a gender-based claim, to be aware of the following factors in an applicant's country of origin: the position of women before the law, the political rights of women, the social and economic rights of women, the incidence of reported violence against women, and the consequences that may befall a woman on her return in light of the circumstances described in her claim.[354] In 2002, UNHCR issued *Guidelines on International Protection: Gender-Related Persecution Within the Context of Article 1A(2) of the 1951 Convention and/or its 1967 Protocol Relating to the Status of Refugees*.[355] These *Guidelines* complement UNHCR's *Handbook* and give further guidance how gender-based claims should be analyzed. The *Guidelines* note, for example, that trafficking women or minors for the pur-

---

[349] For a concise overview of recent developments, see S. Knight, "Seeking Asylum from Gender Persecution: Progress Amid Uncertainty," 79 *Interpreter Releases* 689 (May 13, 2002).

[350] *See* INS Memorandum, P. Coven, "Considerations For Asylum Officers Adjudicating Claims From Women" (May 25, 1995), *published on* AILA InfoNet (*posted* May 31, 1995), and *reproduced in* 72 *Interpreter Releases* 771 (June 5, 1995).

[351] *See, e.g., Angoucheva v. INS*, 106 F.3d 781, 793 n.2 (7th Cir. 1997) (Rovner, J., concurring) ("I was taken aback by the argument that a sexual assault like this one could be attributed to sexual attraction alone."); *Matter of Sharmin*, A73 556 833 at 20 (IJ Sept. 27, 1996) (New York, NY) (IJ Bukszpan) (noting that legacy INS's closing argument, which referred to the domestic violence suffered by the applicant as a mere "family matter," is a position in direct contravention of its own gender guidelines).

[352] *Garcia-Martinez v. Ashcroft*, 371 F.3d 1066, 1076 (9th Cir. 2004) (citations omitted).

[353] UNHCR, *Guidelines on the Protection of Refugee Women* (1991), available at *www.unhcr.org/publ/PUBL/3d4f915e4.pdf*.

[354] *Id.* at ¶¶72–73.

[355] UNHCR, *Guidelines on International Protection: Gender-Related Persecution Within the Context of Article 1A(2) of the 1951 Convention and/or its 1967 Protocol Relating to the Status of Refugees* (2002), available at *www.unhcr.org/publ/PUBL/3d58ddef4.pdf*.

poses of forced prostitution or sexual exploitation is a form of persecution.[356] They also offer guidance on procedural issues such as interviewing techniques and evidentiary matters.[357]

> *Tip*—**Need Help with a Gender-Based Asylum Claim?**—The Center for Gender and Refugee Studies at the University of California, Hastings College of the Law provides legal expertise and resources to attorneys representing women asylum-seekers fleeing gender-related harm, and tracks decisions in these cases. Attorneys representing women fleeing persecution linked to their gender—such as honor killing, rape, gang violence, domestic violence, sexual trafficking, female genital cutting—should fill out the "Assistance" form on the Center's website at *www.uchastings.edu/cgrs* or contact the Center at (415) 565-4877. The Refugee Law Center, in coordination with the Harvard Immigration and Refugee Clinic Program, maintains a database of gender-based asylum claims and provides documentation support, advice, and referrals to attorneys representing women applying for asylum for gender-related reasons. Anyone seeking advice or information about their cases may contact them at (617) 983-2700 or via their website, *www.refugeelawcenter.org*.

Over the past several years, as more gender-related asylum cases have been raised, immigration judges, the BIA, and federal courts have grappled with a variety of gender-related issues. The BIA, for example, found that female genital mutilation (FGM), also known as female genital cutting (FGC), is a form of persecution, relying in part on legacy INS's 1995 memorandum on considerations for adjudicating claims from women,[358] which acknowledges that FGM is a form of persecution.[359] Several federal courts have held that FGM performed on a daughter could amount to persecution of the parent.[360] In *Abay v. Ashcroft*, the Sixth Circuit held that "where a parent and protector is faced with exposing her child to [FGM]" she could establish eligibility for asylum.[361] But at least one federal

---

[356] *Id.* at ¶18.

[357] *Id.* at ¶¶35–37.

[358] *Supra* note 350.

[359] *Matter of Kasinga*, 21 I&N Dec. 357, 365 (BIA 1996).

[360] *Abay v. Ashcroft*, 368 F.3d 634, 641–42 (6th Cir. 2004) (threat of FGM to daughter amounts to a well-founded fear for daughter *and* mother); *see also Abebe v. Gonzales*, 432 F.3d 1037, 1043 (9th Cir. 2005) (finding evidence indicated U.S. citizen daughter was at risk of FGM if she returned to Ethiopia with her parents); *Kebede v. Ashcroft*, 366 F.3d 808, 811 (9th Cir. 2004) (acknowledging that a victim of sexual assault does not irredeemably compromise his or her credibility by failing to report the assault at the first opportunity); *Abankwah v. INS*, 185 F.3d 18, 23–24 (2d Cir. 1999) (finding that Ghanaian woman of the Nkumssa tribe had a well-founded fear of FGM for engaging in premarital sex); *Matter of Quist*, A79 468 512 (BIA July 9, 2004), available at *www.lexisnexis.com/practiceareas/immigration/ pdfs/web581%20Quist.pdf* (Gambian women married to Mandinka men who have not been subjected to FGM and who oppose the practice are a particular social group). *But see Matter of A–K–*, 24 I&N Dec. 275 (BIA 2007) (finding that an applicant may not establish eligibility for asylum based solely on the fear that his or her daughter will be subject to FGM upon return).

[361] *Abay v. Ashcroft*, *supra* note 360, at 641–42.

court has refused to extend that protection to female children who remain in the home country and are at risk of FGM.[362] More recently, courts have found that past FGM is persecution and a continuing form of harm that allows for a finding of a well-founded fear.[363] The BIA, however, has disagreed with such findings.[364]

The BIA also granted asylum to a Haitian woman who had been gang-raped, holding that she was not merely a victim of general conditions of violence, as the IJ had found.[365] In addition, an IJ has granted asylum to a 16-year-old girl who feared being subjected to a forced marriage in China.[366] Similarly, a woman who suffered repeated rapes after being sold as a slave to a fetish shrine was granted asylum by an IJ, based on her membership in a particular social group.[367] The Chicago Asylum Office granted asylum to a Jordanian man who feared he would be subjected to an "honor killing" for his intimate, nonmarital relationship with a Bedouin woman.[368]

> **FGM Notice**—It is against the law in the United States to perform FGM on a person under 18 years of age. A parent who knowingly allows FGM to be performed on his or her child may also be subject to criminal penalties.[369] The Department of State has identified the following 30 countries where FGM is prevalent: Benin, Burkina Faso, Cameroon, Central African Republic, Chad, Cote d'Ivoire, Democratic Republic of Congo, Djibouti, Egypt, Ethiopia, Eritrea, Gambia, Ghana, Guinea, Guinea-Bissau, Indonesia, Kenya, Liberia, Mali, Mauritania, Niger, Nigeria, Senegal, Sierra Leone, Somalia, Sudan, Tanzania, Togo, Uganda, and Yemen.[370]

---

[362] *Bah v. Gonzales*, 462 F.3d 637, 643 (6th Cir. 2006).

[363] *Mohammed v. Gonzales*, 400 F.3d 785, 795–96 (9th Cir. 2005); *Niang v. Gonzales*, 422 F.3d 1187, 1189 (10th Cir. 2005) (finding that opposition to FGM need not be proved to establish nexus and adopting the rationale in *Mohammed v. Gonzales*, 400 F.3d at 796 n. 16).

[364] *Matter of A–T–*, 24 I&N Dec. 296, 299–301 (BIA 2007) (finding that FGM does not qualify as "continuing persecution").

[365] *Matter of D–V–*, 21 I&N Dec. 77, 78–79 (BIA 1993). *But see Nelson v. INS*, 232 F.3d 258, 264 (1st Cir. 2000) (finding that a political activist and supporter of women's rights who suffered three episodes of solitary confinement of less than 72 hours (each accompanied by physical abuse), periodic surveillance, threatening phone calls, occasional stops and searches, and visits to her place of work was not subject to past persecution).

[366] *See Matter of [name not provided]*, A76 512 001 (IJ Oct. 18, 2000) (Chicago, IL) (Zerbe, IJ), *reported in* 77 *Interpreter Releases* 1634 (Nov. 20, 2000).

[367] *See* "IJ Grants Asylum to Former 'Trokosi' Slave," 75 *Interpreter Releases* 165 (Feb. 2, 1998).

[368] Letter Opinion by Robert Esbrook, A77 827 289 (Chicago Asylum Office, Feb. 25, 2002) *cited in* 79 *Interpreter Releases* 594 (April 22, 2002).

[369] 18 USC §116.

[370] 63 Fed. Reg. 13433 (Mar. 19, 1998); *see also* State Department Report, "Prevalence of the Practice of Female Genital Mutilation (FGM), Laws Prohibiting FGM and Their Enforcement, Recommendations on How to Best Work to Eliminate FGM" (2001) at 8–10, available at www.state.gov/documents/organization/9424.pdf (adding Indonesia and Yemen as countries where FGM is prevalent).

In 2001, Attorney General Janet Reno vacated the BIA's controversial decision in *Matter of R–A–*, in which the BIA had denied asylum to a Guatemalan woman who had fled after 10 years of brutal beatings by her husband. The AG's reason for vacating the decision was to allow for the claim to be considered after final regulations regarding gender-based claims are issued.[371] Although proposed regulations were issued in December 2000 for public comment,[372] it is not known when (or if) interim or final regulations will be issued. In February 2004, former Attorney General John Ashcroft accepted new briefs by the parties. Astonishingly, DHS took the position in its brief that the applicant should be granted asylum. A copy of the DHS brief is available online[373] and should be read and used by all advocates making similar claims. After accepting briefs, Attorney General Ashcroft remanded the case to the BIA "for reconsideration following final publication of the proposed rule" on gender-based claims.[374] To date, *Matter of R–A–* remains in limbo.

Since the AG vacated *Matter of R–A–* in 2001, there have been a number of BIA and immigration judge decisions granting asylum to applicants fleeing domestic violence. In *Matter of S–A–*, the BIA granted asylum to a Muslim woman from Morocco who suffered domestic abuse at the hands of her father on account of her religious beliefs, which differed from her father's orthodox beliefs.[375]

Immigration judges also have granted asylum to women who have been subjected to domestic violence in countries in which their governments were unable or unwilling to protect them.[376] For additional unpublished BIA and IJ decisions, contact the Center for Gender and Refugee Studies (see *Tip* above).

Federal courts have found that women who refuse to conform to their government's gender-specific laws may satisfy the definition of particular social group.[377] However, in *Fisher v. INS*,[378] the Ninth Circuit, sitting en banc, reversed its previous decision and found that the applicant, an Iranian woman, had failed to establish a well-founded fear of

---

[371] *Matter of R–A–*, 22 I&N Dec. 906 (AG 2001).

[372] *See* 65 Fed. Reg. 76588–98 (Dec. 7, 2000).

[373] http://cgrs.uchastings.edu//documents/legal/dhs_brief_ra.pdf.

[374] *Matter of R–A–*, 23 I&N Dec. 694 (AG 2005).

[375] *Matter of S–A–*, 22 I&N Dec. 1328, 1335 (BIA 2000); *see also* UNHCR, *Guidelines on International Protection: "Membership of a Particular Social Group," supra* note 219, at ¶22 (noting that in situations of domestic abuse, an applicant who cannot show that her persecutor is abusing her on a protected ground, may still qualify for refugee status upon a showing that her government is unwilling to extend protection based on one of the five grounds).

[376] *See, e.g., Matter of A–N–*, A73 603 840 (IJ Dec. 22, 2000) (IJ Grussendorf), *reported in* 78 *Interpreter Releases* 409 (Feb 26, 2001) (granting asylum to a Jordanian woman); *Matter of Sharmin*, A73 556 833 (IJ Sept. 27, 1996) (New York, NY) (IJ Bukszpan), *reported in* 74 *Interpreter Releases* 174 (Jan. 27, 1997) (granting asylum to a Bangladeshi woman); *Matter of A– and Z–*, A72 190 893, A72 793 219 (IJ Dec. 20, 1994) (Arlington, VA) (IJ Nejelski), *reported in* 72 *Interpreter Releases* 521 (Apr. 17, 1995) (granting asylum to a Jordanian woman).

[377] *See, e.g., Fatin v. INS*, 12 F.3d 1233, 1241 (3d Cir. 1993) (holding that an Iranian woman who finds gender-specific laws and repressive social norms objectionable or offensive may belong to a "particular social group" if her opposition is so profound that she would choose to suffer the severe consequences for noncompliance).

[378] *Fisher v. INS*, 79 F.3d 955 (9th Cir. 1996).

persecution on account of religion, political opinion, or membership in a particular social group. The harm suffered by the applicant did not amount to persecution, according to the Ninth Circuit, because the applicant failed to establish that she would receive disproportionately severe punishment or that the laws were especially unconscionable.[379]

Often in gender-based claims the persecution is alleged to be on account of the individual's membership in a particular social group, though claims may be brought on any of the five enumerated grounds. A particular social group may comprise: women subjected to FGM;[380] young women who are members of the Tchamba-Kunsuntu tribe who have not been subjected to FGM and who oppose the practice;[381] women who have been sold into marriage;[382] women who have been subjected to or face being subjected to the practice of Trokosi, a system of indentured sexual servitude to fetish shrines;[383] or young, Westernized, educated, Muslim women who voice their political opinion.[384]

Persons found not to be members of a particular social group, under the facts presented, include: Salvadoran women previously raped and beaten by guerrillas,[385] and Iranian women whose claims were based solely on gender and the harsh restrictions placed upon them as women.[386]

2.5.2. Children

Minors often gain asylum derivatively from a successful asylum application filed by a parent or legal guardian.[387] Unaccompanied children often base applications for refugee status on one of the following enumerated grounds for asylum: nationality, race, religion,

---

[379] *Id.* at 961–62; *see also Yadegar-Sargis v. INS*, 297 F.3d 596 (7th Cir. 2002) (holding that an Iranian Christian woman who opposed wearing Islamic garb did not have a well-founded fear of persecution); *Sharif v. INS*, 87 F.3d 932 (7th Cir. 1996) (holding that an Iranian woman failed to establish past persecution or a well-founded fear of future persecution based on her status as a "Westernized woman").

[380] *Mohammed v. Gonzales*, 400 F.3d 785, 795–96 (9th Cir. 2005); *Niang v. Gonzales*, 422 F.3d 1187, 1189 (10th Cir. 2005).

[381] *Matter of Kasinga*, 21 I&N Dec. 357, 365 (BIA 1996).

[382] *Gao v. Gonzales*, 440 F.3d 62, 70–71 (2d Cir. 2006) (finding women who have been sold into marriage and who live in a part of China where forced marriages are considered valid and enforceable constitute a particular social group).

[383] *See* "IJ Grants Asylum to Former 'Trokosi' Slave," 75 *Interpreter Releases* 165 (Feb. 2, 1998).

[384] *Matter of Sharmin*, A73 556 833 (IJ Sept. 30, 1996) (New York, NY) (IJ Bukszpan), *reported in* 74 *Interpreter Releases* 174 (Jan. 27, 1997).

[385] *Gomez v. INS*, 947 F.2d 660, 664 (2d Cir. 1991) (finding that they did not compose a particular social group because they lacked a "recognizable and discrete" attribute to enable their persecutors to distinguish them from other women).

[386] *Safaie v. INS*, 25 F.3d 636, 640 (8th Cir. 1994); *see also* Anker, Kelly, and Willshire-Carrera, "Defining 'Particular Social Group' in Terms of Gender: The *Shah* Decision and U.S. Law," 76 *Interpreter Releases* 1005 (July 2, 1999). For a recent overview of how U.S. immigration laws have a negative impact on women asylum-seekers, see Lawyers Committee for Human Rights, *Refugee Women at Risk: Unfair U.S. Laws Hurt Asylum Seekers* (2002), available at www.humanrightsfirst.org/refugees/reports/refugee_women.pdf.

[387] J.K. Dalrymple, "Seeking Asylum Alone: Using the Best Interests of the Child Principle to Protect Unaccompanied Minors," 26 *B.C. Third World L.J.*, 131, 133–35 (2006).

political opinion, and sometimes, social group.[388] UNHCR has noted that applications filed by minors seeking refugee status should be granted more liberal review than those submitted by adults.[389] Legacy INS and a growing number of courts have recognized that harm suffered or feared by a child may be less than that experienced or feared by an adult but still qualify as persecution.[390] Minors, similarly, are entitled to a liberal application of the benefit of the doubt.[391]

There is also a growing body of case law recognizing that children are eligible for asylum based on membership in a "particular social group." In an opinion vacated by the Supreme Court because the Ninth Circuit erred by reaching issues that the BIA had not ruled on in the first instance,[392] the Ninth Circuit held that Russian disabled children, and parents who provide care for their disabled children, both constitute "a particular social group" due to their well-documented mistreatment by the state and society in general.[393] Similarly, in *Lukwago v. Ashcroft*, the Third Circuit held that membership in a group of former child soldiers who have escaped captivity by rebels in Northern Uganda "fits precisely within the BIA's recognition that a shared past experience may be enough to link

---

[388] *See e.g., Lusingo v. Gonzalez*, 420 F.3d 193, 200 (3d Cir. 2005) (explaining that applicant's argument of well-founded fear of persecution was not based on the Tanzanian government's persecution of children, but instead on an imputed political opinion and fear of retaliation against him for causing embarrassment to the Tanzanian government); *Baballah v. Ashcroft*, 335 F.3d 981, 990–91 (9th Cir. 2003) (persecution of Israeli-Arab child of an intermarriage due to his mixed parentage is on account of either ethnicity or religion as a protected ground).

[389] UNHCR *Handbook, supra* note 36, at ¶¶214–17 (observing that a minor's refugee status must be determined in the context of the minor's degree of mental development and maturity); *see also Matter of Devison*, 22 I&N Dec. 1362 (BIA 2000) (asserting that, in considering mandatory bars to asylum, courts do not treat a child's adjudication of delinquency as a conviction for immigration purposes). *But see Cruz-Diaz v. INS*, 86 F.3d 330, 331 (4th Cir. 1996) (stating that a 15-year-old asylum-seeker must show "a reasonable possibility of persecution or that a reasonable person in similar circumstances would fear persecution on account of his political beliefs or one of the other enumerated provisions of the statute" and finding no error in applying the same standard of proof to juveniles as is applied to adults because the standard necessarily includes consideration of age).

[390] *See* INS Memorandum, J. Weiss, "Guidelines for Children's Asylum Claims" (Dec. 10, 1998), *published on* AILA InfoNet *(posted* Jan. 25, 1999), *reproduced in* 76 Interpreter Releases 1, appx. I (Jan. 4, 1999), and available at *www.abanet.org/publicserv/immigration/ins_guidelines_for_children.pdf*; *Hernandez-Ortiz v. Gonzales*, 496 F.3d 1042 (9th Cir. 2007) (finding that IJ should have considered applicant's case from perspective of a small child); *Jorge-Tzoc v. Gonzales*, 435 F.3d 146, 147–48 (2d Cir. 2006) (considering the harm suffered by the applicant from the perspective of a small child); *Liu v. Ashcroft*, 380 F.3d 307, 314 (7th Cir. 2004) (finding that age can be a critical factor in the adjudication of asylum claims and may bear heavily on whether the applicant was persecuted or has a well-founded fear); *Abay v. Ashcroft*, 368 F.3d 634, 640 (6th Cir. 2004) (overturning, on the basis of age, the IJ's finding that nine-year-old had not adequately expressed a fear of persecution).

[391] UNHCR *Handbook, supra* note 36, at ¶219, *cited with approval by Abay v. Ashcroft*, 368 F.3d 634, 640 (6th Cir. 2004).

[392] *Gonzales v. Tchoukhrova*, 127 S. Ct. 57 (2006).

[393] *Tchoukhrova v. Gonzales*, 404 F.3d 1181, 1189–90 (9th Cir. 2005) ("[J]ust as their children's disabilities are 'immutable,' so is a parent's relationship to a disabled child. Because the parents and their disabled child incur harm as a unit, it is appropriate to combine family members into a single social group for purposes of asylum and withholding.").

members of a 'particular social group.'"³⁹⁴ Notably, the court specifically stated that this group is "*not* dependent on a member's current age, but rather the shared experience of abduction, persecution and escape at a time when he was a child."³⁹⁵ In the same case, the court upheld the BIA's determination that the applicant was abducted by the rebels due to their need for labor, and that the applicant failed to demonstrate that he was targeted by the rebels because he was a child.³⁹⁶ In a subsequent Third Circuit case, a juvenile applicant relied on *Lukwago* to argue that juvenile informants against international alien smuggling rings are similarly members of a "particular social group" based on a shared past experience.³⁹⁷ Finding that the BIA had failed to provide a principled reason for denying the applicant's claim, the court of appeals remanded the case, noting that "once 'shared personal experience' is recognized as a legitimate immutable characteristic for defining 'a particular social group,' [that principle] is not easy to limit."³⁹⁸

Other courts have held that children are not considered to be a "particular social group" for purposes of establishing eligibility for asylum.³⁹⁹ One court explained that children do not qualify as a "particular social group" because "unlike innate characteristics, such as sex or color, age changes over time, possibly lessening its role in personal identity."⁴⁰⁰ For example, many jurisdictions have held that groups of young urban males do not constitute a "particular social group" within the meaning of the INA.⁴⁰¹ Youth asylum-seekers have been similarly unsuccessful in arguing membership in a social group of street children and fear of persecution based on pervasive violence against the group by government officials and street gangs.⁴⁰² Children of those directly victimized by coercive family planning policies are not per se eligible for immigration relief in their own right on the basis of their parent's persecution.⁴⁰³

---

³⁹⁴ *Lukwago v. Ashcroft*, 329 F.3d 157, 179 (3d Cir. 2003).

³⁹⁵ *Id.* (emphasis added).

³⁹⁶ *Id.* at 173.

³⁹⁷ *Hong v. Attorney General*, 165 Fed. Appx. 995 (3d Cir. 2006).

³⁹⁸ *Id.* at 1002.

³⁹⁹ *Gomez v. INS*, 947 F.2d 660, 664 (2d Cir. 1991) ("Possession of broadly-based characteristics such as youth and gender will not by itself endow individuals with membership in a particular group.").

⁴⁰⁰ *Lukwago, supra* note 394, at 179.

⁴⁰¹ *See, e.g.*, *Matter of Vigil*, 19 I&N Dec. 572, 575 (1988) (finding that a group of young, male, urban, unenlisted Salvadorans does not constitute a particular social group because "the factors that identify the respondent's group in the instant case (age, living environment, military status) are not factors that are 'fundamental to individual identity or conscience.'"); *Sanchez-Trujillo v. INS*, 801 F.2d 1571, 1576–77 (9th Cir. 1986) ("The class of young, working class, urban males of military age does not exemplify the type of 'social group' for which the immigration laws provide protection from persecution. Individuals falling within the parameters of this sweeping demographic division naturally manifest a plethora of different lifestyles, varying interests, diverse cultures, and contrary political leanings.").

⁴⁰² *See e.g.*, *Escobar v. Gonzales*, 417 F.3d 363 (3d Cir. 2005) ("Poverty, homelessness, and youth are far too vague and all encompassing to be characteristics that set the perimeters for a protected group within the scope of the INA."); *Flores-Portillo v. Ashcroft*, 103 Fed. Appx. 852, 853 (5th Cir. 2004) (finding that Honduran street children was "so broad that it was questionable whether it was a cognizable social group with a characteristic innate or fundamental to the group's identity.").

⁴⁰³ *See, e.g., Chen v. Gonzalez*, 417 F.3d 303, 305 (2d Cir. 2005) (holding that the applicant, a native and citizen of the People's Republic of China, could not establish eligibility for refugee status on the

continued

2.5.3. Sexual Orientation

Asylum officers, immigration judges, the BIA, and federal courts all recognize that individuals may qualify for asylum based on their sexual orientation. In June 1994, Attorney General Janet Reno designated as precedent *Matter of Toboso-Alfonso*,[404] a decision in which the BIA found that a gay man from Cuba who had been detained and threatened with imprisonment because of his sexual orientation was eligible for withholding of deportation based on his membership in a particular social group. In 2000, the Ninth Circuit granted asylum to a gay man with a female sexual identity.[405] More recently, courts have recognized the viability of sexual orientation asylum claims from Albania,[406] Argentina,[407] Lebanon,[408] and Uganda.[409] Courts, however, have denied petitions for review of applicants from Peru[410] and Zimbabwe.[411]

In March 1996, legacy INS granted asylum to a gay man from Jordan on the grounds that he would suffer persecution because of his sexual orientation. The applicant had demonstrated that neither his native country nor Saudi Arabia, where he had acquired permanent residency, was able or willing to protect him because both governments have strict laws that criminalize homosexual activity.[412] Legacy INS granted asylum to an HIV-positive gay man from Brazil in August 1996.[413]

In a decision interpreting the term "persecution," the Ninth Circuit found that a Russian lesbian is not required to show that her persecutors intended to punish her in order

---

basis of his mother's alleged forced sterilization); *Wang v. Gonzalez*, 405 F.3d 134, 144 (3d Cir. 2005) (stating that in a case where the applicant's parents were subject to government persecution after violating China's one-child-per-family policy, the child-applicant could not obtain relief because he did not show that the persecution threatened his own "life or freedom").

[404] *Matter of Toboso-Alfonso*, 20 I&N Dec. 819 (BIA 1990).

[405] *Hernandez-Montiel v. INS*, 225 F.3d 1084 (9th Cir. 2000) (finding the applicant was a member of a particular social group in Mexico), *overruled on other grounds by Thomas v. Gonzales*, 409 F.3d 1177, 1180 (9th Cir. 2005).

[406] *Shahinaj v. Gonzales*, 481 F.3d 1027 (8th Cir. 2007) (remanding claim and requesting assignment to a different immigration judge because of bias).

[407] *Maldonado v. Attorney Gen. of the United States*, 188 Fed. Appx. 101 (3d Cir. 2006).

[408] *Karouni v. Gonzales*, 399 F.3d 1163 (9th Cir. 2005) (finding that the persecution the applicant fears is on account of his membership in a particular social group regardless of whether it is characterized as being a homosexual or engaging in homosexual acts).

[409] *Nabulwala v. Gonzales*, 479 F.3d 972 (8th Cir. 2007).

[410] *Salkeld v. Gonzales*, 420 F.3d 804, 809 (8th Cir. 2005) (upholding IJ's finding that applicant failed to demonstrate past persecution or a clear probability of future persecution for withholding of removal).

[411] *Kimumwe v. Gonzales*, 431 F.3d 319 (8th Cir. 2005) (finding applicant failed to satisfy his burden of proof; one judge dissent).

[412] *See* "INS Grants Asylum to Gay Jordanian," 73 *Interpreter Releases* 365 (Mar. 25, 1996); *see also Matter of A–G–F–F–, [number not provided]* (IJ July 9, 2004) (New York, NY) (McManus, IJ) (granting asylum to a gay, HIV-positive man from Indonesia; for more information contact the Asian American Legal Defense and Education Fund, www.aaldef.org); "INS Grants Asylum to Iranian Lesbian Feminist," 72 *Interpreter Releases* 1483 (Oct. 30, 1995).

[413] *See* "INS Grants Asylum to Gay Brazilian with HIV," 73 *Interpreter Releases* 1140 (Aug. 26, 1996).

to qualify for asylum.[414] The BIA, in denying her claim, had held that although she had been subjected to involuntary psychiatric treatments, the militia and psychiatric institutions intended to "cure" her and, thus, their actions did not constitute persecution within the meaning of the INA. In its decision, the Ninth Circuit held that the definition of persecution is objective and that a subjective "punitive" or "malignant" intent is not required for harm to constitute persecution.[415]

> *Tip*—An invaluable resource for sexual orientation claims is the LGBT/HIV Asylum Manual, *Winning Asylum, Withholding and CAT Cases Based on Sexual Orientation, Transgender Identity and/or HIV Positive Status* (3d Ed. 2006), published by Immigration Equality and the Midwest Immigrant and Human Rights Center. It is available free at *www.immigrationequality.org/manual_template.php*.

2.5.4. HIV-Positive/AIDS Status

In February 1996, the former INS General Counsel issued a memorandum concerning HIV infection and relief from deportation. In that memorandum, the INS General Counsel adopted recommendations made by the Presidential Advisory Council on acquired immune deficiency syndrome (AIDS) in 1995. The Presidential Advisory Council suggested that the legacy INS's efforts against AIDS-related discrimination should include the granting of asylum based on the social group category of HIV-positive individuals.[416]

In one of few published decisions, the Ninth Circuit found that a gay may with AIDS was eligible for asylum based on the persecution he suffered in Mexico and his inability to relocate within Mexico for health reasons.[417] In an unpublished decision, an IJ granted asylum to an HIV-positive woman from India, finding that she would face ostracism and lack of appropriate medical care if she returned to her home country.[418] The IJ found that the applicant was a member of a particular social group comprised of married women in India who have contracted HIV, who fear their families will disown them or force them to get a divorce, and who wish to or need to be employed.[419] In a case involving a gay man with AIDS from Lebanon, the Ninth Circuit cited with approval the INS General

---

[414] *Pitcherskaia v. INS*, 118 F.3d 641, 647 (9th Cir. 1997).

[415] *Id.* at 646.

[416] *See* INS Memorandum, D. Martin, "Seropositivity for HIV and Relief from Deportation" (Feb. 16, 1996), *reprinted in* 73 Interpreter Releases 901, 909 (July 8, 1996).

[417] *Boer-Sedano v. Gonzales*, 418 F.3d 1082, 1091 (9th Cir. 2005); *see also Karouni v. Gonzales*, 399 F.3d 1163, 1178 (9th Cir. 2005).

[418] *Matter of [name not provided]*, (IJ Dec. 20, 2000) (Baltimore, MD) (Gossart, IJ), *reported in* 78 Interpreter Releases 233 (Jan. 15, 2001); *see also Matter of [name not provided]*, (IJ Nov. 3, 2005) (Cordova, IJ) (granting asylum to an HIV positive man from Republic of Congo).

[419] *See also Matter of A–G–F–F–*, *supra* note 412; *Matter of [name not provided]*, A71 498 940 (IJ Oct. 31, 1995) (New York, NY), *reported in* 73 Interpreter Releases 901 (July 8, 1996) (granting asylum to an HIV-positive man from Togo, finding that he would suffer persecution upon return to either Togo or the Ivory Coast).

Counsel memorandum, which noted persons with AIDS may constitute a particular social group under refugee law.[420]

Legacy INS also had a policy to ease the standards for admission of HIV-positive refugees who seek resettlement in the United States through the overseas refugee processing program.[421] Asylum applicants applying within the United States, however, are not required to file for such a waiver. A waiver, however, may be required at the time of adjustment of status for individuals granted asylee status.[422]

> *Tip*—An invaluable resource for HIV-positive claims is the LGBT/HIV Asylum Manual, noted *supra* in the *Tip* for sexual orientation claims.

2.5.5. Disabilities—Physical and Mental

A disability or mental health problem may also be a consideration in asylum claims. The BIA recently affirmed a case granting asylum to a Peruvian man, finding that he had at least a 10 percent likelihood that his bipolar disorder would cause him to be persecuted in a state psychiatric hospital, where he would be forced to undergo electric shock therapy without anesthesia.[423] Asylum-seekers have also claimed that they would be tortured, within the meaning of the Convention Against Torture, due to inadequate access to necessary mental health care. While several of these claims have been denied, courts appear to implicitly recognize that such a claim, if supported by adequate evidence, would be viable.[424]

---

[420] *Karouni v. Gonzales*, 399 F.3d 1163, 1178 (9th Cir. 2005) (holding that the IJ's finding that the applicant did not have a well-founded fear of persecution was not supported by substantial evidence).

[421] *See* "INS Eases Waiver Standards for HIV Positive Refugees," 76 *Interpreter Releases* 1551 (Oct. 25, 1999).

[422] *See* ch. 3.13.

[423] *Matter of J–M–*, [number not provided] (BIA May 31, 2007), available at http://bibdaily.com/pdfs/BIAu%205-31-07%20Jobe%20J-M-.pdf. The panel also held that "Peruvian psychiatric patients with serious and chronic mental illness" constituted a social group, which may be entitled to protection. *Id.* But see *Baptiste v. Attorney General of the U.S.*, 229 Fed.Appx. 66, 2007 U.S. App. LEXIS 9400, at *3–*4 (3rd Cir. Apr. 25, 2007) (holding that petitioner, a Haitian citizen, failed both to show that disabled Haitians constituted a particular social group and that he was a member of such a group, given that his conditions, a limp and depression, were exceedingly minor); *Akhtar v. Attorney General of the United States*, 138 Fed. Appx. 481, 483 (3rd Cir. 2005) (finding that an alien pointed to no evidence showing that the treatment of disabled individuals in Pakistan rose to the level of persecution).

[424] *See, e.g., Lin v. Gonzales*, 2007 U.S. App. LEXIS 3041, at *4–*5 (2d Cir. 2007) (affirming BIA's decision to deny petitioner's motion to reopen, and finding that the evidence in the record did not support petitioner's contention that mental health patients in China were subject to abuse); *Raffington v. Cangemi*, 399 F.3d 900, 904 (8th Cir. 2005) (holding that while petitioner may not have access to the same level of public and private mental health care in Jamaica as in the United States, that does not constitute torture within the meaning of the Convention Against Torture); *Matter of J–F–F–*, 23 I&N Dec. 912, 918 (BIA 2006) (holding that respondent's uninformed guess that he could not procure his medication in the Dominican Republic and a single sentence about the general shortage of mental health resources is not sufficient to demonstrate that he would be tortured if returned to the Dominican Republic under the Convention Against Torture). But see *Lavira v. U.S. Att'y Gen.*, 478 F.3d 158, 166–72 (3d Cir. 2007) (finding Haitian government's placement of an HIV-positive, above-the-knee amputee in a prison with "wholly inadequate" medical care constituted persecution because the government

continued

The psychological harm or physical harm resulting from lack of medical care may also be a factor to support a claim for humanitarian asylum due to a "reasonable possibility" that an applicant will suffer "other serious harm" if removed to his or her home country.[425] In addition, humanitarian asylum may be granted to an applicant who has been disabled by torture and the denial of medical care.[426] Finally, emotional and physical disabilities may be evidence of "extraordinary circumstances" to justify untimely filing of asylum applications.[427]

2.5.6. Gang-Related Claims

One controversial area in recent years has been the emergence of asylum claims on the basis of persecution tied to a person's current or former membership in a gang. The cases so far have involved asylum-seekers from Central American countries, where notorious criminal gangs such as MS-13 and the 18th Street Gang (*Mara* 18) have gained a foothold.[428] While courts have long dealt with persecution of asylees by gangs that the government is unable or unwilling to police, it is a more recent phenomenon for claimants to seek asylum on account of their current or former membership in a gang. One reason for this is that former gang members and unaffiliated youths increasingly face detention and harassment at the hands of police in their home countries due to the *Mano Duro* ("Iron Fist") laws that have been enacted throughout Central America to counter the pervasiveness of criminal gangs.[429]

In addition to the presumptions and other legal obstacles that all other asylum-seekers face, current and former gang members are faced with the added difficulty of proving that they were not involved in any way in the persecution of others on account of grounds pro-

---

was "placing an individual in such conditions with the intent to inflict severe pain and suffering on that individual") (internal quotation marks and citation omitted); *Gomez-De Leon v. INS*, 2002 U.S. Dist. LEXIS 13606, at *14–*15 (D. Conn. 2002) (holding that under the Convention Against Torture, a person claiming that he or she would be tortured because of inadequate mental health care would have to show that the alleged torture would be inflicted by public officials or that it would be for the purpose of obtaining information, punishing or intimidating the person, or for a discriminatory reason); *Matter of Andy Taylor*, 24 *Immigr. Rptr.* B1-184 (BIA 2002) (holding that under the Convention Against Torture, the torture must be inflicted by public officials and there was no evidence that the Nicaraguan government either inflicts or acquiesces in torturous acts against persons who are vulnerable because of emotional problems).

[425] *See* 8 CFR §§208.13(b)(1)(iii)(B), 1208.13(b)(1)(iii)(B).

[426] *See Matter of Chen*, 20 I&N Dec. 16 (BIA 1989).

[427] *See, e.g., Mukamusoni v. Ashcroft*, 390 F.3d 110, 117 (1st Cir. 2004) (holding that a woman from Rwanda with post-traumatic stress disorder met the extraordinary circumstances exception to excuse failure of timely filing).

[428] *See* the Capital Area Immigration Rights (CAIR) Coalition, *Seeking Asylum from Gang-Based Violence in Central America: A Resource Manual* (2007), available at *www.refugees.org/uploadedFiles/Participate/National_Center/Resource_Library/Revised_Gang%20_Resource_Manual_Aug07.pdf*; *see also* M. James, "Fleeing the Maras: Child Gang Members Seeking Refugee Status in the United States," 25 *Child. Legal Rts. J.* 1 (2005).

[429] *See* M. *James, supra note* 428.

tected under the INA.⁴³⁰ If an asylum-seeker cannot make such a showing, the law bars the courts both from granting asylum and withholding removal for such a person.

In one of the earliest published decisions, the BIA found that a member of a child gang established membership in a protected social group, as all of the members of such a gang "share a common, immutable characteristic."⁴³¹ On the other hand, the Sixth Circuit found that a young, tattooed male from Honduras who had belonged to MS-13 was not eligible for withholding of removal because members of the alleged social group did not share any common and immutable characteristics.⁴³² While the court found it possible to conceive of the members of MS 13 as a particular social group under the INA, sharing for example the common immutable characteristic of their past experiences together, their initiation rites, and their status as Spanish-speaking immigrants in the United States, it viewed the evidence presented as establishing, at best, that "tattooed youth" are targeted and prosecuted. The court declined to hold that "tattooed youth" constitute a particular social group.⁴³³

Where asylum-seekers have shown extenuating circumstances to explain their membership in a gang or explain the persecution that former members face, they have had a better chance, at least before an immigration judge. For example, in one case, a young Guatemalan woman successfully argued that she had been forced to join a gang merely to survive, after being abandoned on the streets at age 10, and facing daily and increasingly more violent persecution at the hands of both street gangs and the police.⁴³⁴ In another case, a Honduran male who had escaped from his gang, was eligible for withholding of removal based on the fact that he had been forcibly tattooed and inducted into a gang, had not been involved in violence against others, and had a well-founded fear of persecution by his former gang members as well as the police in his country.⁴³⁵ In this case, the court found that the social group of former gang members constituted a protected social group.

> *Tip*—An invaluable resource for gang-related claims is *Seeking Asylum from Gang-Based Violence in Central America: A Resource Manual*, published by the Capital Area Immigration Rights (CAIR) Coalition, which is available online.⁴³⁶

2.5.7. Conscription; Refusal to Serve

Many asylum claims are based on an individual's refusal to perform compulsory military service, desertion from government or rebel forces, or his or her desire to avoid

---

⁴³⁰ *See* INA §§208(b)(2), 241(b)(3).

⁴³¹ *Matter of Acosta*, 19 I&N Dec. 211, 233 (BIA 1985), *modified on other grounds by Matter of Mogharrabi*, 19 I&N Dec. 439 (BIA 1987).

⁴³² *See Castellano-Chacon v. INS*, 341 F.3d 533, 546 (6th Cir. 2003), *overruled in part on other grounds by Almuhtaseb v. Gonzales*, 453 F.3d 743 (5th Cir. 2006).

⁴³³ *See id.*

⁴³⁴ *See Matter of E–S– and A–M–* [file no. redacted] (IJ Mar. 20, 2003) (Phoenix, AZ) (Richardson, IJ), available at *www.refugees.org/uploadedFiles/Participate/National_Center/Resource_Library/G.005.pdf*.

⁴³⁵ *See Matter of Enamorado*, A77 530 541 (IJ Nov. 22, 1999) (Harlingen, TX) (Burkhart, IJ), available at *www.refugees.org/uploadedFiles/Participate/National_Center/Resource_Library/H.008.pdf*.

⁴³⁶ *See supra* note 428.

forced recruitment into a rebel army. Punishment for failure to perform compulsory military service is generally not considered to be a basis for asylum in the United States.[437]

Courts have recognized exceptions to this general rule where conscription places an individual in a position in which he might be forced to commit acts that the international community condemns, or where refusal to serve could lead to disproportionate punishment because of an actual or imputed political opinion.[438] A person also qualifies if, when performing military service, he or she is singled out for harsh treatment because of one of the protected grounds.[439]

Similarly, UNHCR's *Handbook* provides that:

Fear of prosecution and punishment for desertion or draft-evasion does not in itself constitute well-founded fear of persecution under the definition. Desertion or draft-evasion does not, on the other hand, exclude a person from being a refugee, and a person may be a refugee in addition to being a deserter or draft-evader.[440]

In contrast to government conscription, forced recruitment by a revolutionary army has been found to be "tantamount to kidnapping, and is therefore persecution."[441] An applicant must still show, however, that the persecution is "on account of" one of the five

---

[437] *See, e.g., Djedovic v. Gonzales,* 441 F.3d 547, 549 (7th Cir. 2006); *Foroglou v. INS,* 170 F.3d 68, 71 (1st Cir. 1999); *Castillo v. INS,* 951 F.2d 1117, 1122 (9th Cir. 1991); *M.A. v. INS,* 899 F.2d 304, 312 (4th Cir. 1990); *Matter of R–R–,* 20 I&N Dec. 547, 551 (BIA 1992); *Matter of Vigil,* 19 I&N Dec. 572, 578 (BIA 1988).

[438] *See, e.g., Zehatye v. Gonzales,* 453 F.3d 1182, 1187 (9th Cir. 2006) (finding that the applicant, an Eritrean Jehovah's Witness, failed to demonstrate that she would be singled out for disproportionately severe treatment when serving in the military); *Islami v. Gonzales,* 412 F.3d 391, 397 (2d Cir. 2005) (finding that fear of retribution for refusing to participate in a military known to perpetrate crimes against humanity clearly rose to the level of persecution); *Matter of A–G–,* 19 I&N Dec. 502, 506 (BIA 1987), *aff'd sub nom. M.A. v. INS,* 899 F.2d 304 (4th Cir. 1990).

[439] *Giday v. Gonzales,* 434 F.3d 543, 555–56 (7th Cir. 2006) (finding that the applicant raised the issue of whether Eritrean national service was particularly dangerous or deadly for those of Ethiopian descent, which was erroneously ignored by IJ); *Begzatowski v. INS,* 278 F.3d 665 (7th Cir. 2002) (finding that an ethnic Albanian who deserted from the Yugoslavian army suffered past persecution during his military service); *Vujisic v. INS,* 224 F.3d 578 (7th Cir. 2000) (finding that a deserter from the Yugoslavian army established a well-founded fear of persecution on account of his political beliefs in opposition to the war against Slovenia); *Duarte de Guinac v. INS,* 179 F.3d 1156, 1162 (9th Cir. 1999) (finding that an indigenous Guatemalan suffered persecution while performing military service on account of race); *see also Matter of Salim,* 18 I&N Dec. 311, 313 (BIA 1982) (finding that the applicant sufficiently established that he might have be singled out for persecution in his native Afghanistan for opposing the ongoing Russian invasion and refusing to join the Soviet-controlled Afghan army in its war against the Afghan rebels opposing the invasion).

[440] UNHCR *Handbook, supra* note 36, at ¶167.

[441] *Cifuentes-Villatoro v. Ashcroft,* 71 Fed. Appx. 750, 752 (9th Cir. 2003) (citing *Arteaga v. INS,* 836 F.2d 1227 (9th Cir. 1988)) ("petitioner must prove something more than violence plus disparity of views" to show guerrilla persecution "on account of political opinion"); *see also Lukwago v. Ashcroft,* 329 F.3d 157, 168–69 (3d Cir. 2003) (noting that the applicant did not violate a legitimate conscription requirement established under Ugandan law, but was forcibly abducted by the guerrillas and subjected to physical and psychological abuse).

enumerated grounds.[442] In *INS v. Elias-Zacarias*, the Supreme Court rejected the lower court's finding that a guerrilla organization's attempt to conscript a person into its military forces necessarily constitutes persecution on account of political opinion.[443]

An individual may also qualify for asylum if his or her refusal to serve in the military is based on a sincerely held religious belief. UNHCR's *Handbook* provides:

> Refusal to perform military service may also be based on religious convictions. If an applicant is able to show that his religious convictions are genuine, and that such convictions are not taken into account by the authorities of his country in requiring him to perform military service, he may be able to establish a claim to refugee status. Such a claim would, of course, be supported by any additional indications that the applicant or his family may have encountered difficulties due to their religious convictions.[444]

2.5.8. Nongovernmental Actors

Asylum claims are, in many cases, based on persecution by the government or authorities in the applicant's home country. Claims may also be based, however, on persecution by nongovernmental actors if the government is unable or unwilling to provide protection to the asylum applicant.[445]

---

[442] *See Pedro-Mateo v. INS*, 224 F.3d 1147, 1151 (9th Cir. 2000) (rejecting claim of indigenous Guatemalan who failed to show that forcible recruitment was on account of a protected ground).

[443] *INS v. Elias-Zacarias*, 502 U.S. 478 (1992); *see also Matter of C–A–L–*, 21 I&N Dec. 754 (BIA 1997); *Matter of R–O–*, 20 I&N Dec. 455, 458–59 (BIA 1992); *Matter of Vigil*, 19 I&N Dec. 572, 577 (BIA 1988). *But see Rivas-Martinez v. INS*, 997 F.2d 1143 (5th Cir. 1993) (finding that an applicant—who testified that her refusal to assist guerrillas was based on her political beliefs, which were well known to the guerrillas—had produced "some evidence" that her persecution would be on account of her political opinion).

[444] UNHCR *Handbook*, *supra* note 36, at ¶172; *see also* UNHCR, *Guidelines on International Protection: Religion-Based Refugee Claims Under Article 1A(2) of the 1951 Convention and/or 1967 Protocol Relating to the Status of Refugees* (2004), which addresses the issue of conscientious objection to military service at ¶¶25–26. These *Guidelines* are available at www.unhcr.org/publ/PUBL/40d8427a4.pdf. *But see Foroglou v. INS*, 170 F.3d 68, 71 (1st Cir. 1999) (punishment for refusal to serve is not persecution based on the objector's religious or political beliefs, but instead is because of his or her refusal to fight).

[445] *See, e.g., Menjivar v. Gonzales*, 416 F.3d 918, 922–23 (8th Cir. 2005) (finding that the applicant's claim failed because the record did not compel the conclusion that the Salvadoran government was unable or unwilling to protect her from a gang member); *Castro-Perez v. Gonzales*, 409 F.3d 1069, 1072 (9th Cir. 2005) (finding that the applicant's claim failed because did not show the Honduran government was unable or unwilling to control or prosecute rape in the country); *Avetova-Elisseva v. INS*, 213 F.3d 1192 (9th Cir. 2000) (finding that "it does not matter that financial considerations may account" for Russian government's inability to stop ethnic persecution, but that what matters is that the government "is unwilling or *unable*" to stop it) (emphasis in original); *Sotelo-Aquije v. Slattery*, 17 F.3d 33, 37 (2d Cir. 1994) (denying asylum for a man attacked by criminal thugs); *Matter of S–A–*, 22 I&N Dec. 1328 (BIA 2000) (finding that the applicant suffered persecution at the hands of her father and could not rely on the Moroccan authorities to protect her); *Matter of Villalta*, 20 I&N Dec. 142, 147 (BIA 1990) (finding that the Salvadoran government appeared to be unable to control the paramilitary death squads); *see also* UNHCR *Handbook*, *supra* note 36, at ¶65 ("Where serious discriminatory or other offensive acts are committed by the local populace, they can be considered as persecution if they

continued

The BIA has recognized claims based on persecution by such nongovernmental actors as a rival clan in Somalia[446] and a Togolese tribe that practiced female genital mutilation.[447] Similarly, recent federal decisions have granted petitions for review based on persecution by anti-Semitic gangs or skinheads,[448] Revolutionary Armed Forces of Colombia (FARC),[449] the New People's Army in the Philippines[450] and the Communist Party Marxist (CPM) of India.[451] In addition, despite a group's demographics or diversity, courts have found that a person could suffer persecution "at the hands of his [or her] own people."[452] Generally, in these cases, the asylum applicant must show that it is not reasonable to seek protection elsewhere in his or her country.

2.5.9. Countrywide Persecution

Under regulations that became effective January 5, 2001, an applicant may be denied asylum or withholding of removal if the applicant "could avoid future persecution by relocating to another part" of his or her home country and if "under *all* the circumstances, it would be reasonable to expect the applicant to do so."[453] In determining the "reasonableness" of an internal relocation option, adjudicators should consider, among other things:

- whether the applicant would face other serious harm in the place of suggested relocation;
- any ongoing civil strife within the country;
- administrative, economic, or judicial infrastructure;
- geographical limitations;
- social and cultural constraints, such as age, gender, health, social, and familial ties.[454]

The regulations also note that these factors "may or may not be relevant, depending on all the circumstances of the case, and are not necessarily determinative" of whether relocation is reasonable.[455]

Recent cases interpreting this regulation have found that the FARC operates countrywide in Colombia and that internal relocation is not a reasonable option,[456] relocation

---

are knowingly tolerated by the authorities, or if the authorities refuse, or prove unable, to offer effective protection.").

[446] *Matter of H–*, 21 I&N Dec. 337 (BIA 1996).

[447] *Matter of Kasinga*, 21 I&N Dec. 357, 365 (BIA 1996).

[448] *Krotova v. Gonzales*, 416 F.3d 1080, 1087 (9th Cir. 2005).

[449] *Arboleda v. U.S. Atty. Gen.*, 434 F.3d 1220, 1226 (11th Cir. 2006).

[450] *Agbuya v. INS*, 219 F.3d 962 (9th Cir. 2000), *amended by* 241 F.3d 1224 (9th Cir. 2001).

[451] *Maini v. INS*, 212 F.3d 1167, 1175 (9th Cir. 2000).

[452] *Id.* (punishment for interfaith marriage is without question persecution on account of religion); *see also Matter of S–A–*, 22 I&N Dec. 1328 (BIA 2000) (granting asylum to a Moroccan woman with liberal Muslim beliefs who was persecuted by her father, who held more orthodox Muslim views).

[453] 8 CFR §§208.13(b)(1)(i)(B), (2)(ii), 208.16(b)(1), (2), 1208.13(b)(1)(i)(B), (2)(ii), and 1208.16(b)(1), (2) (emphasis added).

[454] 8 CFR §§208.13(b)(3), 208.16(b)(3), 1208.13(b)(3), and 1208.16(b)(3).

[455] 8 CFR §§208.16(b)(3), 1208.16(b)(3).

within Mexico is unreasonable for a gay man with AIDS,[457] and hiding in the Republic of Congo is not a reasonable option.[458]

In cases in which the persecutor is the government or government-sponsored, or the applicant has suffered persecution in the past, it will be presumed that internal relocation would not be reasonable unless the presumption is rebutted by the asylum officer or U.S. Immigration and Customs Enforcement (ICE) attorney.[459] Courts have found that internal relocation is not an option for applicants who fear the Chinese government,[460] that a native of Afghanistan who repeatedly experienced anti-foreigner threats and violence while living in Germany could not avoid persecution by relocating in Germany,[461] and that a man persecuted in the past by the Shining Path revolutionary group could not safely relocate within Peru.[462]

Prior case law adjudicating claims in which an applicant fears a nongovernmental actor remain relevant. In those cases, courts have considered whether an applicant has the ability to or can reasonably be expected to relocate to another area in his or her home country.[463] If the applicant has demonstrated a well-founded fear of a nongovernmental authority, the BIA has also considered whether the applicant, if ordered removed, would have to pass through any unsafe part of his or her home country before arriving in a safe area.[464]

According to UNHCR's *Handbook*, "a person will not be excluded from refugee status merely because he could have sought refuge in another part of the country, if under all the circumstances it would not have been *reasonable* to expect him to do so."[465] UNHCR has noted that an internal flight alternative must be accessible in safety and durable in character.[466] Moreover, according to UNHCR, the possibility to find safety in other parts of the country must have existed at the time of flight and continue to be avail-

---

[456] *Arboleda v. U.S. Atty. Gen.*, 434 F.3d 1220, 1226 (11th Cir. 2006) (finding the record in this case compelled the conclusion that the FARC operates countrywide in Colombia and that relocation was not a viable option).

[457] *Boer-Sedano v. Gonzales*, 418 F.3d 1082, 1090 (9th Cir. 2005).

[458] *Bockou Essohou v. Gonzales*, 471 F.3d 518, 522 (4th Cir. 2006).

[459] 8 CFR §§208.13(b)(3)(ii), 208.16(b)(3)(ii), 1208.13(b)(3)(ii), and 1208.16(b)(3)(ii).

[460] *Yang v. Gonzales*, 427 F.3d 1117 (8th Cir. 2005) (finding Chinese couple with two U.S. citizen children, who wished to have two more children, had a well-founded fear of persecution if they returned to China and could not reasonably relocate within China).

[461] *Mashiri v. Ashcroft*, 383 F.3d 1112, 1123 (9th Cir. 2004).

[462] *Cardenas v. INS*, 294 F.3d 1062 (9th Cir. 2002).

[463] *See, e.g., Lopez-Gomez v. Ashcroft*, 263 F.3d 442 (5th Cir. 2001) (finding applicant failed to show countrywide threat in Guatemala); *Etugh v. INS*, 921 F.2d 36, 39 (3d Cir. 1991); *Matter of A–E–M–*, 21 I&N 1157, 1177 (BIA 1998); *Matter of H–*, 21 I&N Dec. 337, 349 n.7 (BIA 1996); *Matter of [name not provided]*, A76 512 001 (IJ Oct. 18, 2000) (finding that applicant fleeing forced marriage in China could not be expected to relocate within the country), *reported in* 77 *Interpreter Releases* 1634–36 (Nov. 20, 2000).

[464] *Matter of H–*, 21 I&N Dec. 337, 349 n.7 (BIA 1996).

[465] UNHCR *Handbook, supra* note 36, at ¶91 (emphasis added).

[466] *See* UNHCR, "An Overview of Protection Issues in Western Europe: Legislative Trends and Positions Taken by UNHCR," 1 *European Series* no. 3 (1995) at 32.

able when the refugee status determination is made.[467] In addition to physical safety, the applicant should have access to basic civil, political, and socioeconomic rights in the area of relocation.[468] According to one commentator, determinations of reasonableness should include consideration of the financial and logistical barriers to relocating internally and whether the refugee would be placed in an illusory or unpredictable situation.[469]

Prior to the issuance of the 2001 regulations, in cases in which the applicant was persecuted by or feared harm at the hands of the government of his or her home country, courts held that there was no requirement for the applicant to establish countrywide persecution.[470] In *Singh v. Moschorak*, the Ninth Circuit noted, "It has never been thought that there are safe places within a nation when it is the nation's government that has engaged in the acts of punishing opinion that have driven the victim to leave the country."[471] In *Matter of R–*, however, the BIA denied asylum to a Sikh from the Punjab who had been subjected to brutal physical abuse by Indian police, because he failed to demonstrate he would face countrywide persecution.[472]

2.5.10. Prosecution vs. Persecution

In asylum claims, the issue often arises of whether the harm inflicted or feared is merely prosecution for an unlawful act or persecution for one of the protected grounds. Individuals fleeing prosecution are generally not refugees. However, what may at first glance appear to be prosecution may upon further examination amount to persecution. Careful consideration should be given to the reasons for and type of punishment imposed or feared.

Punishment for Criminal Conduct

In general, fear of prosecution under laws that are "fairly administered" does not qualify an individual as a refugee or make that individual eligible for refugee status.[473] As noted in UNHCR's *Handbook*, persecution is not the same as "punishment for a common law offense."[474] Courts have rejected asylum and withholding claims of individuals who feared prosecution for the following offenses: bribing a passport official,[475] evading con-

---

[467] *Id.*

[468] *Id.*; *see also* G. Goodwin-Gill, *The Refugee in International Law* 74 (2d Ed. 1996) (noting that "for various reasons it may be unreasonable to expect the asylum seeker to move internally").

[469] J. Hathaway, *The Law of Refugee Status* 134 (1991).

[470] *See, e.g., Singh v. Ilchert*, 63 F.3d 1501 (9th Cir. 1995); *Singh v. Moschorak*, 53 F.3d 1031 (9th Cir. 1995); *see also Abdel-Masieh v. INS*, 73 F.3d 579, 587 (5th Cir. 1996) (holding that when a party seeking asylum demonstrates that a government is the "persecutor," the burden falls on the INS to show the government's persecutory actions are "truly limited to a clearly delineated and limited locality and situation").

[471] *Singh v. Moschorak*, *supra* note 470, at 1034.

[472] *Matter of R–*, 20 I&N Dec. 621, 627 (BIA 1992).

[473] *Ngure v. Ashcroft*, 367 F.3d 975, 991 (8th Cir. 2004); *Chang v. INS*, 119 F.3d 1055, 1060 (3d Cir. 1997); *see also Abedini v. INS*, 971 F.2d 188, 191 (9th Cir. 1992); *Behzadpour v. U.S.*, 946 F.2d 1351, 1353 (8th Cir. 1991).

[474] UNHCR *Handbook*, *supra* note 36, at 56.

[475] *Janusiak v. INS*, 947 F.2d 46, 48 (3d Cir. 1991).

scription laws,[476] distributing Western films,[477] murder committed in the United States,[478] and violating currency laws.[479]

In addition, harm inflicted by police to extract information concerning criminal matters is not persecution unless it is on account of one of the five enumerated grounds.[480] A person who has been subjected to or fears such harm, but who is ineligible because the harm is not on account of one of the five enumerated grounds, may be eligible for protection under the Convention Against Torture.[481]

Prosecution under some laws, however, such as those not in conformity with accepted human rights standards or those that are applied in a discriminatory manner, may constitute persecution.[482] Criminal prosecution may amount to persecution where the punishment is arbitrary or excessive, indicating that the motive, in part, may be on account of one of the five enumerated grounds.[483] Criminal prosecution also may be a pretext for persecution if the crime is political.[484]

Lack of a fair trial or punishment imposed without the benefit of a judicial process may also constitute persecution.[485] In addition, if there is no legitimate means for changing a nondemocratic government, violent rebellion in an attempt to overthrow the gov-

---

[476] *M.A. v. INS*, 899 F.2d 304, 312 (4th Cir. 1990).

[477] *Abedini*, *supra* note 473, at 191.

[478] *Saleh v. INS*, 962 F.2d 234 (2d Cir. 1992).

[479] *Matter of H–M–*, 20 I&N Dec. 683 (BIA 1993).

[480] *See, e.g.*, *Prasad v. INS*, 47 F.3d 336, 340 (9th Cir. 1995); *Ozdemir v. INS*, 46 F.3d 6, 8 (5th Cir. 1994); *Matter of T–*, 20 I&N Dec. 571 (BIA 1992).

[481] See ch. 4 for more information regarding relief under the Convention Against Torture.

[482] UNHCR *Handbook*, *supra* note 36, at ¶59.

[483] *See, e.g.*, *Tagaga v. INS*, 228 F.3d 1030, 1034–35 (9th Cir. 2000) (finding that prosecution for treason for refusal to participate in persecution of Indo-Fijians constitutes persecution); *Bandari v. INS*, 227 F.3d 1160, 1168 (9th Cir. 2000) (finding that while the police's initial stop may have been for law enforcement, subsequent beatings were on account of religion); *Zahedi v. INS*, 222 F.3d 1157, 1165 (9th Cir. 2000) (prosecution by Iranian authorities for translating and copying the book *The Satanic Verses* is persecution on account of a political opinion, finding that the IJ failed to properly consider the documentary evidence submitted by the applicant); *Singh v. Ilchert*, 63 F.3d 1501, 1509 (9th Cir. 1995); *Matter of S–P–*, 21 I&N Dec. 486 (BIA 1996); *Matter of Izatula*, 20 I&N Dec. 149, 157 (BIA 1990) (Vacca, concurring) ("Torture" and "conduct such as beating with bats and forcing one to drink one's own urine when thirsty ought not be mistaken for legitimate governmental investigations . . . ."); *Senathirajah v. INS*, 157 F.3d 210, 221 (3d Cir. 1998).

[484] *See Chang v. INS*, 119 F.3d 1055, 1064 (3d Cir. 1997) (finding that the evidence of record suggested that China punished political dissidents under its State Security Law); *Perkovic v. INS*, 33 F.3d 615, 622 (6th Cir. 1994) (holding that punishment under laws against peaceful political expression is "on account of" political opinion); UNHCR *Handbook*, *supra* note 36, at ¶86 (stating that adjudicators should examine, inter alia, the nature of the act committed, the nature of the prosecution, and its motives in determining whether a political offender is a refugee). *But see Ngure v. Ashcroft*, 367 F.3d 975, 990 (8th Cir. 2004) (three prior arrests did not amount to persecution); *Kapcia v. INS*, 944 F.2d 702, 707–08 (10th Cir. 1991) (holding that punishment for the illegal distribution of political pamphlets is a legitimate government act and not persecution).

[485] *Bellido v. Ashcroft*, 367 F.3d 840, 845 (8th Cir. 2004); *Behzadpour v. U.S.*, 946 F.2d 1351, 1353 (8th Cir. 1991).

ernment need not be considered criminal, and any actions taken by the government to punish such acts may amount to persecution.[486]

Punishment for Illegal Departure; Unauthorized Stays

Some countries impose severe penalties on nationals who depart unlawfully from the country or who remain abroad without authorization. An individual may be eligible for asylum or withholding of removal if he or she would be subject to such penalties based on one of the five enumerated grounds.[487] Some courts have held that a country that severely punishes unlawful departure views persons who illegally leave as disloyal and subversive.[488] In determining whether punishment rises to the level of persecution, courts have held that punishment of up to one year imprisonment for violation of state security laws in China constitutes persecution,[489] as does three years' imprisonment for violating the Cuban exit laws.[490]

Previous regulations promulgated by legacy INS and EOIR required that asylum officers and IJs give "due consideration" to evidence that the government of the applicant's country of nationality or last habitual residence persecutes its nationals or residents if they leave the country without authorization or seek asylum in another country. The final regulations implementing IIRAIRA removed these sections, previously found at 8 CFR §§208.13(b)(2)(ii) and 208.16(b)(4). Several commenters to the proposed regulations objected to the elimination of these sections. Legacy INS and EOIR responded that while the United States "continues to deplore and oppose certain countries' practice of severely punishing their citizens for illegal departure or for applying for asylum in another country," the regulations were "ambiguous" and did not clearly implement this policy.[491]

2.5.11. Refugee Sur Place

An asylum applicant may not meet the definition of refugee at the time the applicant leaves his or her home country. As noted in UNHCR's *Handbook*, "[t]he requirement that a

---

[486] *Matter of Izatula*, 20 I&N Dec. 149, 153–54 (BIA 1990) (citing *Dwomoh v. Sava*, 696 F. Supp. 970, 979 (S.D.N.Y. 1988)) (prosecution, beating, or torture of a coup participant may qualify as persecution). Such conduct, however, may result in a denial of asylum and withholding of removal under the new terrorism-related bars. See this chapter, at 2.7.2.

[487] *See, e.g., Chang*, supra note 484, at 1067; *Matter of Exilus*, 18 I&N Dec. 276, 278 (BIA 1982) (applicant failed to demonstrate the harm feared for illegal departure from Haiti would be on account of one of the five enumerated grounds).

[488] *Chang*, supra note 484, at 1064 (citing *Rodriguez-Roman v. INS*, 98 F.3d 416, 430–31 (9th Cir. 1996)) (holding that the BIA erred in concluding that the severe punishment an individual would suffer upon return to Cuba following illegal departure would be merely criminal prosecution, rather than persecution on account of political opinion).

[489] *Id.* at 1067. *But see Chen v. Gonzales*, 434 F.3d 212, 221 (3d Cir. 2005) (finding that Chinese law barring illegal emigration is generally applicable to all illegal emigrants who return to China and nothing in the record supports the conclusion that the applicant would be singled out for persecution or torture).

[490] *Rodriguez-Roman v. INS*, 98 F.3d 416, 431 (9th Cir. 1996). *But see Kozulin v. INS*, 218 F.3d 1112, 1117–18 (9th Cir. 2000) (finding that the applicant failed to demonstrate that he would be subjected to punishment by the Russian authorities for his illegal departure).

[491] *See* 62 Fed. Reg. 10311, 10317 (Mar. 6, 1997) (supplementary information).

person must be outside his country to be a refugee does not mean that he [or she] must necessarily have left that country . . . on account of well-founded fear."[492] An asylum applicant who was not a refugee when leaving his or her home country, but who becomes a refugee at a later date, is called a refugee "*sur place*."[493] An individual becomes a refugee *sur place* because of circumstances arising in the individual's country of origin during his or her absence or as a result of actions taken by the individual while abroad.[494] The *Handbook* notes that "[d]iplomats and other officials serving abroad, prisoners of war, students, migrant workers and others have applied for refugee status during their residence abroad and have been recognized as refugees."[495] In its asylum officer basic training course, USCIS recognizes that "changes occurring in an applicant's country . . . and/or activities by an applicant outside his or her country may make the applicant a refugee *sur place*."[496]

In the United States, there is little case law on the issue of refugee *sur place*. In *Azarshahy v. Ilchert*, the court found that the petitioner could establish his asylum claim as a refugee *sur place*, finding that "refugee status can be established based on facts arising after the applicant has left her country."[497] UNHCR's *Handbook* advises that "[r]egard should be had in particular to whether such actions may have come to the notice of the authorities of the person's country of origin and how they are likely to be viewed by those authorities."

2.5.12. Remaining in Home Country for an Extended Period of Time

In determining whether an applicant has a well-founded fear of persecution, some courts have looked to the length of time an individual remained in his or her home country after suffering persecution or becoming aware that he or she may become a target of persecution. In *Lim v. INS*, the applicant had remained in the Philippines for six years after receiving his first death threat.[498] The court found that his extended stay, although

---

[492] UNHCR *Handbook*, *supra* note 36, at ¶94; *see also Wiransane v. Ashcroft*, 366 F.3d 889, 899 (10th Cir. 2004) ("[A]n applicant need not have fled his home country out of fear of persecution to qualify as a refugee.").

[493] UNHCR *Handbook*, *supra* note 36, at ¶94.

[494] *Id.* at ¶¶95, 96.

[495] *Id.* at ¶95.

[496] AOBTC, Lesson: One-Year Filing Deadline (Sept. 14, 2006) at 10–11, available at *www.rmscdenver.org/documents/Oneyear14Sept06LP.pdf*.

[497] *Azarshahy v. Ilchert*, 1994 WL 446040, at *5 (N.D. Cal., Aug. 10, 1994); *see also Lukwago v. Ashcroft*, 329 F.3d 157, 180 (3d Cir. 2003) (in remanding claim, court instructed BIA to determine what effect the widespread publicity of the applicant's case has on his fear of future persecution); *Matter of G–A–*, 23 I&N Dec. 366 (BIA 2002) (en banc) (finding antiregime activities abroad were relevant in a Convention Against Torture claim by an Iranian national); *Matter of Ngum*, A27 709 543 (BIA Dec. 13, 1999) (finding that adjudicators may consider political activities engaged in after entry into the United States that jeopardize an applicant's life or freedom in the applicant's native country, citing *Makonnen v. INS*, 44 F.3d 1378, 1384 (8th Cir. 1995)), and *reported in* D. Cleveland, "Protesting in the U.S. Can Establish a Well-Founded Fear of Future Persecution," available at *www.ilw.com/articles/2005,0208-cleveland.shtm*; *Matter of Mogharrabi*, 19 I&N Dec. 439 (BIA 1987) (an Iranian student who visited the Iranian interests section of the Algerian embassy in the United States and was threatened by an official there was found to be eligible for asylum).

[498] *Lim v. INS*, 224 F.3d 929, 935 (9th Cir. 2000).

CHAPTER 2 • U.S. ASYLUM LAW

relevant, did not render his fear unreasonable, especially where the evidence suggested the threats he received became more menacing.[499]

2.6. BURDEN OF PROOF

2.6.1. On Applicant

The burden of proof is on the applicant for asylum or withholding of removal to establish that he or she is eligible for relief.[500] The asylum applicant must meet this burden by demonstrating that he or she has suffered past persecution or has a well-founded fear of future persecution.[501] The applicant bears the evidentiary burdens of proof and persuasion.[502] The applicant for asylum must demonstrate that a reasonable person in the applicant's circumstances would fear persecution if returned to his or her home country.[503] The burden of proof required to establish eligibility for asylum is lower than the "clear probability" burden of proof that is required to establish eligibility for withholding of removal.[504]

The applicant must establish that race, religion, nationality, membership in a particular social group or political opinion was or will be "one central reason" for persecuting the applicant.[505] The testimony of the applicant may be sufficient to sustain the applicant's burden without corroboration, but only if the applicant satisfies the trier of fact that the applicant's testimony is credible, persuasive, and refers to specific facts sufficient to demonstrate that the applicant is a refugee.[506] In determining whether the applicant has met his or her burden, the trier of fact may weigh the credible evidence along with other evidence of record.[507] Where the trier of fact determines that the applicant should provide evidence that corroborates otherwise credible testimony, such evidence must be provided unless the applicant does not have the evidence and cannot reasonably obtain the evidence.[508]

---

[499] *Id.*; *see also Reyes-Guerrero v. INS*, 192 F.3d 1241, 1243–44 (9th Cir. 1999) (granting asylum to an applicant who received death threats over seven years before fleeing); *Vongsakdy v. INS*, 171 F.3d 1203, 1207 (9th Cir. 1999) (finding the fact that the applicant's continued stay in Laos for a considerable period of time following his release from the labor camp was "irrelevant" to evaluating the "atrocity" of his past persecution). *But see Daneshvar v. Ashcroft*, 355 F.3d 615, 625 (6th Cir. 2004) (finding that applicant did not have a well-founded fear of future persecution because he "enjoyed as close to a normal life during his eight years in Iran after his release, as can be expected of a person living in a totalitarian Islamic state").

[500] *Matter of C–A–L–*, 21 I&N Dec. 754, 756 (BIA 1997); *see also* 8 CFR §§208.13(a), 1208.13(a).

[501] *Matter of O–D–*, 21 I&N Dec. 1079, 1080 (BIA 1998), *modified on other grounds by Kourski v. Ashcroft*, 355 F.3d 1038 (7th Cir. 2004); *Hanaj v. Gonzales*, 446 F.3d 694 (7th Cir. 2006).

[502] *Matter of S–S–*, 21 I&N Dec. 121, 122 (BIA 1995) (citing *Matter of Acosta*, 19 I&N Dec. 211 (BIA 1985), *modified on other grounds by Matter of Mogharrabi*, 19 I&N Dec. 439 (BIA 1987)).

[503] *Id.* at 122.

[504] *See INS v. Cardoza-Fonseca*, 480 U.S. 421 (1987).

[505] INA §208(b)(1)(B)(i); 8 USC §1158(b)(1)(B)(i).

[506] INA §208(b)(1)(B)(ii); 8 USC §1158(b)(1)(B)(ii).

[507] INA §208(b)(1)(B)(ii); 8 USC §1158(b)(1)(B)(ii).

[508] INA §208(b)(1)(B)(ii); 8 USC §1158(b)(1)(B)(ii).

Despite this burden of proof, an applicant for asylum or withholding of removal should be given the "benefit of the doubt" where the applicant is unable to substantiate his or her statements, but where the testimony is generally credible and does not run counter to generally known facts.[509] Moreover, justice requires that an applicant for asylum or withholding of removal be afforded a meaningful opportunity to establish his or her claim.[510] The procedures for requesting such relief should not be a search for a justification to deport an applicant.[511] There should be no rule that prevents an asylum applicant from elaborating on the circumstances underlying an asylum claim when given the opportunity to take the witness stand.[512]

2.6.2. Testimony and Credibility

An applicant for asylum cannot meet his or her burden of proof unless the applicant testifies under oath regarding the application for asylum.[513] The applicant's right to present testimony cannot be nullified by a preliminary negative credibility determination by the IJ.[514] The testimony of an asylum applicant, "if credible in light of general conditions in the applicant's country of nationality or last habitual residence, *may* be sufficient to sustain the applicant's burden of proof without corroboration."[515]

An applicant, however, cannot meet his or her burden of proof by presenting general and meager testimony.[516] An applicant must show "specific, detailed facts supporting the reasonableness of his or her fear.[517] Moreover, it is error for the BIA to deny a claim based on insufficient testimonial detail if the IJ and trial attorney failed to elicit such tes-

---

[509] *Matter of S–M–J–*, 21 I&N Dec. 722, 725 (BIA 1997). *See* this chapter, at 2.6.4; *see also Matter of Pula*, 19 I&N Dec. 467, 476 (BIA 1987) (Heilman, concurring) (recognizing that asylum provisions are humanitarian in their essence and that the "normal" immigration laws cannot be applied in their usual manner to refugees).

[510] *Senathirajah v. INS*, 157 F.3d 210, 221 (3d Cir. 1998).

[511] *Id.*

[512] *Id.*

[513] *Matter of Fefe*, 20 I&N Dec. 116 (BIA 1989).

[514] *Kerciku v. INS*, 314 F.3d 913, 919 (7th Cir. 2003) (remanding case to BIA where IJ did not allow applicant to present testimony in support of his claim after determining that the applicant's testimony regarding how he obtained documentary evidence was not credible).

[515] 8 CFR §§208.13(a), 1208.13(a) (emphasis added); *see also Mulanga v. Ashcroft*, 349 F.3d 123, 133 (3d Cir. 2003) (holding that "the most natural meaning of the word 'may' . . . is that credible testimony is neither per se sufficient nor per se insufficient"); *Georgis v. Ashcroft*, 328 F.3d 962, 969 (7th Cir. 2003) (noting that it is not necessary for an applicant to submit corroborating evidence to sustain her burden of proof); *Abankwah v. INS,* 185 F.3d 18 (2d Cir. 1999) (finding that the BIA was too exacting in the quantity and quality of evidence that it required); *Sangha v. INS*, 103 F.3d 1482, 1487 (9th Cir. 1997); *Matter of Mogharrabi*, 19 I&N Dec. 439, 445 (BIA 1987) (an applicant's own testimony may be sufficient, without corroborating evidence, to prove a well-founded fear of persecution where that testimony is believable, consistent, and sufficiently detailed to provide a plausible and coherent account of the basis for his or her fear). **Note**: These cases were decided before changes to the INA under the REAL ID Act of 2005. The outcome could have been different if the courts were applying INA §208(b)(1)(B); 8 USC §1158(b)(1)(B).

[516] *Matter of Y–B–*, 21 I&N Dec. 1136 (BIA 1998).

[517] *Bhatt v. Reno*, 172 F.3d 978, 982 (7th Cir. 1999).

timony at the hearing.[518] Nevertheless, a finding that an asylum applicant's testimony is credible is not necessarily dispositive.[519] If an applicant's testimony on an issue is found credible for determining whether he or she is a refugee eligible for asylum, he or she cannot be found incredible on the same issue in determining whether he or she merits asylum as a matter of discretion.[520]

Under recent changes set forth in the REAL ID Act of 2005, a trier of fact may base a credibility determination on (1) demeanor, candor, or responsiveness of the applicant's or witness's account; (2) the consistency between the applicant's or witness's written and oral statements, (3) the internal consistency of each such statement, (4) the consistency of such statements with other record evidence (including Department of State reports); and (5) any inaccuracies or falsehoods in such statements, without regard to whether an inconsistency, inaccuracy or falsehood goes to the heart of the applicant's claim, or (6) any *other relevant* factor.[521] The reference to "any other relevant factor" implies that if the trier of fact wishes to rely on any of the first five factors, they must be relevant to the adjudication of the asylum claim. These provisions apply only to applications filed on or after May 11, 2005.[522] In one recent case, the Eleventh Circuit rejected the applicant's argument that the inconsistencies and discrepancies relied on by the IJ were "trivial" and "irrelevant to the dispositive issues," citing to this new provision added by the REAL ID Act.[523] In another, the Ninth Circuit stated that the result it reached would have been different if the REAL ID provision applied to the case.[524]

An IJ's credibility determination is given significant deference by reviewing courts since an IJ is in the best position to observe the demeanor of the witness.[525] A credibility finding based on the applicant's demeanor will be accorded a high degree of deference by the BIA, especially in cases in which there are legitimate reasons for doubting the veracity of the applicant's testimony.[526] Each case, however, must be evaluated on its own merits.[527] Boilerplate or "cookie cutter" credibility findings are not tolerated.[528]

---

[518] *Qiu v. Ashcroft*, 329 F.3d 140, 152–53 (2d Cir. 2003).

[519] *Matter of E–P–*, 21 I&N Dec. 860, 863 (BIA 1997) (finding that although the applicant's testimony was credible, the content of her testimony and the relevant evidence of record were not sufficient to meet her burden of proof).

[520] *Kalubi v. Ashcroft*, 364 F.3d 1134, 1135 (9th Cir. 2004).

[521] INA §208(b)(1)(B)(iii); 8 USC §1158(b)(1)(B)(iii).

[522] *Matter of S–B–*, 24 I&N Dec. 42 (BIA 2006) (finding that where respondent initially filed with the Asylum Office and renewed his application in removal proceedings subsequent to May 11, 2005, the REAL ID Act provision was not applicable to credibility determinations made in his case).

[523] *Chen v. U.S. Atty. Gen.*, 463 F.3d 1228, 1233 (11th Cir. 2006).

[524] *Jibril v. Gonzales*, 423 F.3d 1129, 1138 n.1 (9th Cir. 2005) (reluctantly remanding case because IJ's adverse credibility determination was based on speculation, but noting that "relief is on its way in the form of the REAL ID Act" and "were it in effect today we would be obliged to deny Jibril's petition").

[525] *Matter of A–S–*, 21 I&N Dec. 1106 (BIA 1998); *Matter of Kulle*, 19 I&N Dec. 318, 331 (BIA 1985); *Matter of Boromand*, 17 I&N Dec. 450, 452 (BIA 1980).

[526] *Matter of A–S–, supra* note 525, at 1131.

[527] *Paramasamy v. Ashcroft*, 295 F.3d 1047, 1050 (9th Cir. 2002).

In finding an applicant not credible, an IJ must offer a specific, cogent reason for his or her disbelief of the applicant's testimony.[529] An IJ's negative credibility determination has been overturned where an asylum-seeker's testimony was plausible, detailed, internally consistent, consistent with the asylum application, and unembellished.[530] A negative credibility determination has also been overturned when an asylum applicant's hearing was found to be fundamentally unfair.[531] An adjudicator, however, is not required to ignore repeated and blatant inconsistencies throughout an applicant's hearing testimony, simply because when viewed individually, each consistency weakened her claim for re-

---

[528] *Id.* (reversing negative credibility determination where IJ had made identical demeanor findings in two other cases).

[529] *Tewabe v. Gonzales*, 446 F.3d 533, 540 (4th Cir. 2006) (noting that the requirement that the IJ provide a specific and cogent reason for an adverse credibility determination "leaves ample room for the IJ to exercise common sense in rejecting [an applicant's] testimony"); *see also Mulanga v. Ashcroft*, 349 F.3d 123, 138 (3d Cir. 2003) (holding that IJ's mere "disbelief" of applicant's testimony regarding how she escaped from detention is unsound in light of testimony and country condition reports); *Secaida-Rosales v. INS*, 331 F.3d 297, 307 (2d Cir. 2003) (overturning IJ's negative credibility determination based on minor inconsistencies and insubstantial omissions); *Paramasamy v. Ashcroft*, supra note 527, at 1054 (finding that use of false documents for travel is not a proper basis for an adverse credibility finding); *Daiga v. INS*, 183 F.3d 797, 798 (8th Cir. 1999) (finding that the IJ articulated valid reasons for discrediting testimony, including that the applicant could not remember dates, her inconsistent testimony, and her submission of questionable documents); *Matter of O–D–*, 21 I&N Dec. 1079, 1082 (BIA 1998) (finding that the applicant's submission of a counterfeit identity document generally discredits his testimony regarding asylum eligibility and specifically discredits his claim of identity), *distinguished by Kourski v. Ashcroft*, 355 F.3d 1038 (7th Cir. 2004) *and Hanaj v. Gonzales*, 446 F.3d 694 (7th Cir. 2006) (holding that if the applicant does not know that the documents are forged, it does not discredit the testimony).

[530] *Matter of B–*, 21 I&N Dec. 66, 70–72 (BIA 1995) (holding that IJ erred in finding that an Afghani asylum applicant was not truthful because he would not look at the IJ when he testified, failed to provide precise dates, and did not corroborate his testimony with the testimony of other witnesses); *see also Uwase v. Ashcroft*, 349 F.3d 1039 (7th Cir. 2003).

[531] *Al Khouri v. Ashcroft*, 362 F.3d 461 (8th Cir. 2004) (finding that IJ prejudiced an unrepresented applicant's claim by not allowing him to testify regarding his whole asylum claim); *see also Kebede v. Ashcroft*, 366 F.3d 808, 811 (9th Cir. 2004) (acknowledging that a victim of sexual assault does not irredeemably compromise his or her credibility by failing to report the assault at the first opportunity); *Mulanga v. Ashcroft*, 349 F.3d 123, 137 (3d Cir. 2003) (holding that the IJ's reliance on airport statement of applicant to impeach her credibility was not supported by the record because the statement was not necessarily inconsistent with her asylum hearing testimony); *Wang v. Ashcroft*, 341 F. 3d 1015, 1021 (9th Cir. 2003) (overturning an adverse credibility determination where the inconsistent statements were not material to whether the applicant was subjected to two forced abortions); *Hartooni v. INS*, 21 F.3d 336, 342 (9th Cir. 1994) (finding no credibility problem when a 14-year-old girl with poor English skills indicated on an application that neither she nor her family had been mistreated in Iran, but the applicant offered testimony regarding mistreatment); *Matter of S–A–*, 22 I&N Dec. 1328 (BIA 2000) (in overturning an IJ's negative credibility determination, the BIA noted that the IJ failed to identify any internal discrepancies in the applicant's testimony or between her testimony and the asylum application); *Matter of Kasinga*, 21 I&N Dec. 357 (BIA 1996) (holding that the IJ erred in finding the applicant not credible where she had adequately and reasonably explained several incidents where the IJ found such explanations to be irrational, unpersuasive, or inconsistent).

lief.⁵³² An adjudicator, however, cannot base an adverse credibility determination on non-record testimony.⁵³³

Prior to the enactment of the REAL ID Act of 2005, minor inconsistencies and minor omissions in an individual's asylum application or in his or her testimony would not support an adverse credibility finding.⁵³⁴ Previous inconsistent statements made by the applicant to immigration officials were also not sufficient to support an adverse credibility finding when the record of the statement might not be reliable, the questions posed were not designed to elicit the "details" of any asylum claim, and the applicant, who was abused by government officials in his or her home country, might be reluctant to speak to U.S. government officials.⁵³⁵ Would the REAL ID Act have changed the outcome in these cases? Maybe.⁵³⁶ Discrepancies involving the heart of the asylum claim, however, have always supported a negative credibility determination.⁵³⁷

An applicant's untrue statements by themselves, however, are not a sufficient reason for refusal of refugee status. According to UNHCR's *Handbook*, "[a] person who, because of his experiences, was in fear of the authorities in his own country may still feel apprehensive vis-à-vis any authority. He may therefore be afraid to speak freely and give a full and accurate account of his case."⁵³⁸ The *Handbook* further provides that "[u]ntrue statements by themselves are not a reason for refusal of refugee status and it is the examiner's responsibility to evaluate such statements in the light of all the circumstances of the

---

⁵³² *Kaur v. Gonzales*, 418 F.3d 1061, 1068 (9th Cir. 2005) (finding that IJ's credibility determination was supported by substantial evidence).

⁵³³ *Gao v. Bd. Of Immigration Appeals*, 482 F.3d 122, 134 (2d Cir. 2007) (finding that the IJ did not tether any of the inferences leading to his adverse credibility determination to anything in the record).

⁵³⁴ *See Bellido v. Ashcroft*, 367 F.3d 840, 843–44 (8th Cir. 2004); *Georgis v. Ashcroft*, 328 F.3d 962, 968 (7th Cir. 2003); *Bandari v. INS*, 227 F.3d 1160, 1165–67 (9th Cir. 2000); *Senathirajah v. INS*, 157 F.3d 210, 221 (3d Cir. 1998); *Osorio v. INS*, 99 F.3d 928, 931 (9th Cir. 1996); *Aguilera-Cota v. INS*, 914 F.2d 1375, 1382 (9th Cir. 1990); *Damaize-Job v. INS*, 787 F.2d 1332, 1337 (9th Cir. 1986); *Zavala-Bonilla v. INS*, 730 F.2d 562, 566 (9th Cir. 1984); *Basic Law Manual*, *supra* note 163, at 104–05.

⁵³⁵ *Balasubramanrim v. INS*, 143 F.3d 157 (3d Cir. 1998) (reversing the BIA's negative credibility determination); *see also Ememe v. Ashcroft*, 358 F.3d 446, 453 (7th Cir. 2004) (testimonial inconsistencies alone do not support IJ's negative credibility determination where applicant was interviewed initially in Italian, and her native language was Amharic); *Singh v. INS*, 292 F.3d 1017, 1021 (9th Cir. 2002) (finding the applicant's airport interview lacked sufficient indicia of reliability and accuracy to support an adverse credibility determination); *Senathirajah*, *supra* note 534, at 218 (finding that reliance on an airport interview for a credibility determination "seriously undermined the reliability of the administrative process").

⁵³⁶ *See supra* note 524 and accompanying text.

⁵³⁷ *Krouchevski v. Ashcroft*, 344 F.3d 670, 673 (7th Cir. 2003) (although the applicant offered explanations for the inconsistencies, the reviewing court refused to overturn the negative credibility determination simply because an alternative finding could be supported by substantial evidence); *Disu v. Ashcroft*, 338 F.3d 13, 17–18 (1st Cir. 2003) (upholding a negative credibility determination where harm alleged was not mentioned in applicant's asylum application or at his initial interview); *De Leon-Barrios v. INS*, 116 F.2d 391, 393 (9th Cir. 1997) (upholding IJ and BIA finding that a Guatemalan asylum applicant was not credible where the applicant failed to present a satisfactory explanation for discrepancies in his two asylum applications); *see also Singh-Kaur v. INS*, 183 F.3d 1147 (9th Cir. 1999); *Hajiani-Niroumand v. INS*, 26 F.3d 832, 838 (8th Cir. 1994); *Khano v. INS*, 999 F.2d 1203, 1208 (7th Cir. 1993); *Ceballos-Castillo v. INS*, 904 F.2d 519, 520 (9th Cir. 1990).

⁵³⁸ UNHCR *Handbook*, *supra* note 36, at ¶198.

case."[539] Similarly, legacy INS's *Basic Law Manual* provides that even where an applicant lies in one part of the claim, the asylum officer may give weight to parts of the testimony found to be credible and approve the claim based on those parts.[540] Moreover, an applicant should be given the opportunity to address any apparent inconsistencies and explain any misrepresentations or concealment of material facts.[541]

If the BIA sua sponte raises concerns about an applicant's credibility, it must give the applicant an opportunity to offer an explanation of any perceived inconsistencies.[542] Failure to do so is a violation of due process.[543]

2.6.3. Corroboration: Evidence and Country Conditions Documentation

Supporting or corroborating evidence regarding an applicant's claim is an essential component in every asylum case. This evidence may be in the form of expert or lay testimony, documentation from the applicant's home country, newspaper articles, or human rights reports from the Department of State, Amnesty International, Human Rights Watch, or other reputable organizations.[544] IJs are not experts on country conditions and are prohibited from relying on their own views on how foreign regimes conduct themselves.[545] The Seventh Circuit has even suggested that the "immigration bureaucracy" needs its own expert, similar to the experts employed by the Social Security Administration.[546]

Recent changes to the INA under the REAL ID Act of 2005 provide that a trier of fact, in determining whether an applicant's or witness's statements are credible, may rely on "the consistency of such statements with other evidence of record (including reports of the Department of State on country conditions)."[547] In addition, "[w]here the trier of fact determines that an applicant should provide evidence that corroborates otherwise credible testimony, such evidence must be provided unless the applicant does not have the evidence and cannot reasonably obtain the evidence."[548] Will this new provision change the way adjudicators handle cases? At least one court thinks not. The Seventh Circuit has stated in dicta that "[i]t is possible that the change is less than meets the eye, since now there is no dispute

---

[539] *Id.* at ¶199.

[540] *Basic Law Manual, supra* note 163, at 106.

[541] UNHCR *Handbook, supra* note 36, at ¶199; *see also Garrovillas v. INS*, 156 F.3d 1010, 1073 (9th Cir. 1998) (untrue statements by themselves are not reason for refusal of refugee status).

[542] *Stoyanov v. INS*, 172 F.3d 731, 735 (9th Cir. 1999).

[543] *Id.*

[544] *See* 8 CFR §§208.12(a), 1208.12(a) (providing that adjudicators may rely on "other credible sources" for information on country conditions, such as international organizations, private voluntary agencies, news organizations, or academic institutions).

[545] *Banks v. Gonzales*, 453 F.3d 449, 453–54 (7th Cir. 2006); *Kllokoqi v. Gonzales*, 439 F.3d 336, 344 (7th Cir. 2005).

[546] *Banks, supra* note 545, at 454.

[547] INA §208(b)(1)(B)(iii); 8 USC §1158(b)(1)(B)(iii). A similar provision exists for withholding of removal claims. *See* INA §208(b)(3)(C); 8 USC §1158(b)(3)(C); *see also* INA §240(c)(4)(c); 8 USC §1229a(c)(4)(c).

[548] INA §208(b)(1)(B)(ii); 8 USC §1158(b)(1)(B)(ii). A similar provision exists for withholding of removal claims. *See* INA §208(b)(3)(C); 8 USC §1158(b)(3)(C).

about the appropriateness of asking for corroboration in the common situation when the IJ has some doubt about an applicant's credibility."[549]

In the past, courts have raised concerns that the State Department "soft-pedals human rights violations by countries the United States wants to have good relations with."[550] One court has advised the BIA to treat State Department reports with "a healthy skepticism" rather than as "Holy Writ."[551] It is unclear how the new provisions added by the REAL ID Act would affect such decisions.

It is well-established that knowledge of conditions in the applicant's country of origin is an important element in assessing the applicant's credibility.[552] Other evidence that may corroborate an asylum claim includes the applicant's identity documents, if available, as well as other official records and letters from the applicant's home country.[553] If the applicant bears physical or emotional scars from his or her mistreatment, testimony or affidavits from a medical or mental health professional should be presented to the asylum officer or immigration judge. Also, the testimony or affidavit of an expert on country conditions who is able to corroborate the applicant's testimony and assess the risk of harm upon return is invaluable.[554] Whenever possible, expert testimony is preferable, in addition to an affidavit. Most courts and asylum officers will allow experts to testify in person or by telephone. Having your expert testify at the hearing or asylum officer interview adds weight to the evidence and avoids objections by opposing counsel.

The BIA, in *Matter of S–M–J–*,[555] examined the role of documentation in asylum adjudications. According to the BIA, although an asylum applicant's own testimony alone may be sufficient to sustain his or her burden of proof, an applicant should provide "supporting evidence, both of general conditions and of the specific facts sought to be relied on by the applicant, where such evidence is available."[556] If such evidence is unavailable,

---

[549] *Dawoud v. Gonzales*, 424 F.3d 608, 613 (7th Cir. 2005).

[550] *Gailius v. INS*, 147 F.3d 34, 46 (1st Cir. 1998) (citation omitted); *see also Shah v. INS*, 220 F.3d 1062, 1069–70 (9th Cir. 2000).

[551] *Galina v. INS*, 213 F.3d 955, 959 (7th Cir. 2000); *see also Chen v. INS*, 359 F.3d 121, 130 (2d Cir. 2004) (noting that observations in State Department reports do not automatically discredit contrary evidence presented by the applicant and are not binding on the immigration court); *Niam v. Ashcroft*, 354 F.3d 652, 659 (7th Cir. 2004) (noting that the authors of the State Department reports are anonymous and cannot be cross-examined). *But see Gonahasa v. INS*, 181 F.3d 538 (4th Cir. 1999) ("If it is reasonable to suspect the State Department has a tendency to soft-pedal human rights violations, it may be just as reasonable to suspect that Amnesty International exaggerates them so they will not go without notice.")

[552] *See, e.g., Cordero-Trejo v. INS*, 40 F.3d 482, 491 (1st Cir. 1994); UNHCR *Handbook, supra* note 36, at ¶42.

[553] *See, e.g., Camara v. Ashcroft*, 378 F.3d 361, 370–71 (4th Cir. 2004) (IJ erred by failing to consider independent evidence of persecution: *inter alia*, a notice of escape, a political party membership card, an arrest warrant, and State Department reports corroborating the applicant's claim).

[554] *See, e.g., Niam v. Ashcroft*, 354 F.3d 652, 658 (7th Cir. 2004) (noting that the scholar proffered by the applicant should have been considered an expert and that it was error for the IJ to refuse to allow her to testify telephonically from overseas).

[555] *Matter of S–M–J–*, 21 I&N Dec. 722 (BIA 1997).

[556] *Id.* at 724; *Matter of M–D–*, 21 I&N Dec. 1180, 1182–83 (BIA 1998), *reversed by Diallo v. INS*, 232 F.3d 279 (2d Cir. 2000) (holding BIA misapplied its corroboration standard by failing to rule on credibility of applicant's testimony); *Matter of S–P–*, 21 I&N Dec. 486 (BIA 1996); *Matter of Dass*, 20 I&N

continued

the applicant is required to provide an explanation of why it is unavailable.[557] The IJ must ensure that the applicant's explanation is included in the record.[558] The BIA has taken the position that these requirements are consistent with UNHCR's *Handbook*, which provides that an "applicant's statements cannot, however, be considered in the abstract, and must be viewed in the context of the relevant background situation."[559]

In cases in which an applicant's claim is based primarily on personal experiences not reasonably subject to verification, corroborating documentary evidence of the applicant's particular experiences is not required.[560] Where, however, it is reasonable to expect corroborating evidence for certain alleged facts, such evidence should be provided.[561] According to the BIA, an applicant should be expected to provide easily obtainable documentary evidence such as evidence of his or her place of birth, media accounts of large demonstrations, evidence of publicly held office, or documentation of medical treatment.[562] Courts have been critical of IJs and the BIA for their unrealistic demands on asylum applicants, finding that in the circumstances of some cases it is unreasonable to expect an applicant to provide corroborating documentation.[563]

Prior to the passage of the REAL ID Act, minor discrepancies or typographical errors in official documents could not serve as a basis for a negative credibility finding.[564] Nor could an applicant be found not credible for submitting a fraudulent document if there was no evidence that the applicant knew or suspected that the document was fraudulent.[565] Similarly, documents could not be rejected on the basis that the applicant's testi-

---

Dec. 120, 124 (BIA 1989). The BIA has held that the weaker an applicant's testimony, the greater the need for corroborative evidence. *Matter of Y–B–*, 21 I&N Dec. 1136, 1139 (BIA 1998).

[557] *Matter of O–D–*, 21 I&N Dec. 1079, 1081 (BIA 1998), *vacated on other grounds by Hanaj v. Gonzales*, 446 F.3d 694, 700 (7th Cir. 2006); *Matter of S–M–J–*, *supra* note 555, at 724; *see also Salaam v. INS*, 229 F.3d 1234, 1239 (9th Cir. 2000) (finding that the applicant provided a reasonable explanation for the absence of documents, including his haste in fleeing the country and the danger in carrying documents critical of the Nigerian government).

[558] *Matter of S–M–J–*, *supra* note 555, at 724.

[559] *Id.* (citing *Handbook* at ¶42); *see also Wiransane v. Ashcroft*, 366 F.3d 889, 898 (10th Cir. 2004) (finding that IJ erred by rejecting claim of Indonesian applicant because he failed to provide documentation that he was ethnically Chinese).

[560] *Matter of S–M–J–*, *supra* note 555, at 725.

[561] *Id.*; *see also Eta-Ndu v. Gonzales*, 411 F.3d 977, 984 (8th Cir. 2005) (finding that "the IJ and BIA may require corroborative evidence 'where it is reasonable to expect corroboration'") (internal quotation omitted).

[562] *Matter of S–M–J–*, *supra* note 555, at 725.

[563] *See, e.g., Hor v. Gonzales*, 421 F.3d 497, 501 (7th Cir. 2005) ("the notion that documentation is as regular, multicopied, and ubiquitous in disordered nations as in the United States . . . is unrealistic"); *Gjerazi v. Gonzales*, 435 F.3d 800, 809 (7th Cir. 2006) (finding that "it seems illogical to require a family fleeing a country to take precious time to search for and collect documents"); *Kabamba v. Gonzales*, 162 Fed. Appx. 337, 341 (5th Cir. 2006) (finding that given the country conditions in the Democratic Republic of Congo, it was unreasonable to require the applicant to provide further corroborating documents of her husband's political party affiliation).

[564] *Shah v. INS*, 220 F.3d 1062, 1068 (9th Cir. 2000).

[565] *Kourski v. Ashcroft*, 355 F.3d 1038, 1039–40 (7th Cir. 2004).

mony was vague or inconsistent.[566] If U.S. authorities wished to dispute the authenticity of documents submitted by the applicant, they had to do so in a manner that did not violate due process. The provisions of the REAL ID Act that relate to corroboration and credibility[567] may change these rulings.

The Third Circuit established the following "three-part inquiry" to determine whether the IJ or BIA properly applied the rule in *S–M–J–*,[568] requiring corroborating evidence in certain circumstances. The Third Circuit asked whether the IJ or BIA made (1) "an identification of facts for which it is reasonable to expect corroboration," (2) an inquiry as to whether the applicant has provided information corroborating those facts; and if not, (3) an analysis of whether an applicant has adequately explained why he or she was unable to do so.[569] The Third Circuit has held that the REAL ID Act has not changed this required test.[570]

In addition to documents related specifically to the asylum claim, an applicant is also expected to provide, if available, general corroborating evidence of persecution of similarly situated individuals.[571] An example provided by the BIA is that of a union vice-president who would be expected to provide documentation regarding the persecution of union members in her home country.[572]

In *Matter of S–M–J–*, the BIA also acknowledged the roles of the IJ and trial attorneys in introducing evidence. The role of the trial attorney, according to the BIA, is to uphold international refugee law and to ensure that justice is done.[573] The BIA further stated that it expects the trial attorney "to introduce into evidence current country reports, advisory opinions, or other information readily available from the Resource Information Center."[574] With regard to IJs, the BIA held that they should state for the record how the testimony comports

---

[566] *Zahedi v. INS*, 222 F.3d 1157, 1165 (9th Cir. 2000) (finding that the IJ failed to properly consider the documentary evidence submitted by the applicant).

[567] INA §§208(b)(1)(B)(ii), (iii); 8 USC §§1158(b)(1)(B)(ii), (iii).

[568] *Matter of S–M–J–*, supra note 555.

[569] *Toure v. Atty. Gen. of U.S.*, 443 F.3d 310, 323 (3d Cir. 2006); *see also Mulanga v. Ashcroft*, 349 F.3d 123, 135–36 (3d Cir. 2003) (reversing the IJ's determination that the applicant failed to adequately corroborate her claim because the IJ failed to explain what corroborating evidence would be reasonably expected and failed to provide the applicant with an opportunity to explain its absence); *Bellido v. Ashcroft*, 367 F.3d 840, 844 (8th Cir. 2004) (noting the difficulty applicants have in obtaining documentation and holding "this should never serve to close the door on a grant of asylum").

[570] *Toure*, supra note 569, at 325 (interpreting INA §242(b)(4); 8 USC §1252(b)(4), as amended by the REAL ID Act).

[571] *Matter of S–M–J–*, supra note 555, at 726.

[572] *Id. But see Abankwah v. INS*, 185 F.3d 18 (2d Cir. 1999) (finding that the BIA was too exacting in the quantity and quality of evidence that it required); *Duarte de Guinac v. INS*, 179 F.3d 1156, 1162 (9th Cir. 1999) (criticizing the BIA for concluding that reports of widespread racial discrimination against Indians in Guatemala did not support the applicant's claim, where country condition reports could not corroborate specific acts of persecution).

[573] *Matter of S–M–J–*, supra note 555, at 727.

[574] *Id.* The Asylum Resource Information Center is a part of USCIS and posts country condition information on its website at *www.uscis.gov* ("Education and Resources" tab; then "Asylum Resources" hyperlink); *see also Matter of Fuentes*, 19 I&N Dec. 658, 662 (BIA 1988).

with background information and, if no such background information is part of the record, they must explain how the testimony was assessed without such information.[575] The BIA concluded that IJs have the authority to introduce evidence regarding country conditions and that both UNHCR's *Handbook* at ¶196 and the *Basic Law Manual* at 100 recommend the introduction of evidence by the adjudicator.[576]

In *Matter of S–M–J–*, the BIA held that a Liberian asylum applicant had failed to meet her burden of proof where she did not provide any background information about country conditions in Liberia and did not explain whether such evidence was unavailable. As a result, there was no evidence of record to establish that the asylum applicant's tribe exists or why anyone associated with an individual known as "Prince Anderson" would be targeted for persecution.[577] The BIA, however, remanded the case to the IJ because the IJ relied on information not included in the record regarding conditions in Liberia and because the Department of State's report submitted as part of the record related to Zaire and not Liberia.[578]

In contrast, the asylum applicant in *Singh v. Ilchert*[579] presented documents regarding widespread and arbitrary arrest, detention, and abuse of persons suspected of affiliation with separatists and, thereby, demonstrated the reasonableness of his assertion that his persecution was on account of a political opinion imputed to him.[580]

2.6.4. Benefit of the Doubt

In recognition of the fact that bona fide refugees often are unable to provide documentation in support of their claims, UNHCR's *Handbook* provides:

> After the applicant has made a genuine effort to substantiate his story there may still be a lack of evidence for some of his statements. . . . [I]t is hardly possible for a refugee to "prove" every part of his case and, indeed, if this were a requirement the majority of refugees would not be recognized. It is therefore frequently necessary to give the applicant the benefit of the doubt.[581]

---

[575] *Matter of S–M–J–*, *supra* note 555, at 729–30.

[576] *Id.* at 729; *see also Secaida-Rosales v. INS*, 331 F.3d 297, 306 (2d Cir. 2003) (the IJ has an affirmative obligation to help establish and develop the record). *But see* INA §240(b); 8 USC §1229a(b), which no longer provides that immigration judges may "present" evidence.

[577] *Matter of S–M–J–*, *supra* note 555, at 730.

[578] *Id.*; *see also Shan Liao v. U.S. Dept. of Justice*, 293 F.3d 61 (2d Cir. 2002) (finding that the general background information in the case did not support the applicant's claim that he would be harmed upon return); *Matter of B–B–*, 22 I&N Dec. 309, 311 (BIA 1998) (in denying the respondent's motion to reopen to apply for asylum, the BIA found that previous counsel's insistence on corroborating evidence did not amount to egregious conduct or ineffective assistance of counsel); *Matter of V–T–S–*, 21 I&N Dec. 792, 797 (BIA 1997) (finding that an asylum applicant's failure to provide corroborating evidence, when such corroboration was available to him, weakened the persuasiveness of his testimony).

[579] *Singh v. Ilchert*, 63 F.3d 1501, 1511–12 (9th Cir. 1995).

[580] *See also Matter of S–P–*, 21 I&N Dec. 486 (BIA 1996) (relying on a Department of State report regarding conditions in Sri Lanka in finding that the applicant was persecuted on account of imputed political opinion).

[581] UNHCR *Handbook*, *supra* note 36, at ¶203.

The benefit of the doubt should only be given, however, after "all available evidence has been obtained and checked and when the examiner is satisfied as to the applicant's general credibility."[582] These paragraphs were cited with approval by the BIA in *Matter of S–M–J–*.[583] In cases in which there is some ambiguity regarding an aspect of the applicant's claim, the BIA may give the applicant the benefit of the doubt.[584] The BIA will not do so in cases in which the applicant has failed to meet his or her burden of proof.[585]

The *Handbook* also addresses the application of this principle in the case of minors as follows:

> If the will of the parents cannot be ascertained or if such will is in doubt or in conflict with the will of the child, then the examiner, in cooperation with the experts assisting him, will have to come to a decision as to the well-foundedness of the minor's fear on the basis of all the known circumstances, which may call for a *liberal application* of the benefit of the doubt.[586]

This paragraphed was relied on by the Sixth Circuit in finding that a minor girl who feared genital mutilation if she returned to Ethiopia was eligible for asylum.[587]

In the case of an unaccompanied minor, particular regard should be given to factors such as "the child's stage of development" and "his/her possibly limited knowledge of conditions in the country of origin."[588]

2.6.5. Specific Threat of Harm

A specific threat of harm to an asylum applicant on account of one of the five enumerated grounds is usually sufficient to demonstrate a well-founded fear of persecution. Courts have asserted various thresholds that applicants must meet to show that threats of harm constitute *past* persecution, but courts will also consider unfulfilled threats of harm as part of a determination of a well-founded fear of *future* persecution. For example, although the Ninth Circuit found that repeated death threats did not amount to *past* persecution where neither the applicant nor his family were ever "touched, robbed, imprisoned, forcibly recruited, detained, interrogated, trespassed upon, or even closely confronted" during a period of six years,[589] the court found that this threat of harm suggests that the applicant had a well-founded fear of *future* persecution.[590]

---

[582] *Id.* at ¶204.

[583] *Matter of S–M–J–*, *supra* note 555, at 725 (BIA 1997); *see also Matter of Pula*, 19 I&N Dec. 467, 476 (BIA 1987) (Heilman, concurring) (recognizing that asylum provisions are humanitarian in their essence and that the "normal" immigration laws cannot be applied in their usual manner to refugees).

[584] *Matter of Y–B–*, 21 I&N Dec. 1136, 1139 (BIA 1998).

[585] *Id.*

[586] UNHCR *Handbook*, *supra* note 36, at ¶219 (emphasis added).

[587] *Abay v. Ashcroft*, 368 F.3d 634, 640 (6th Cir. 2004).

[588] UNHCR, *Guidelines on Policies and Procedures in Dealing with Unaccompanied Children Seeking Asylum* (Feb. 1997), at ¶8.6, available at *www.unhcr.org/publ/PUBL/3d4f91cf4.pdf*.

[589] *Lim v. INS*, 224 F.3d 929, 936 (9th Cir. 2000).

[590] *Id.* at 935.

In evaluating claims of past persecution, the Third Circuit, for example, limits the type of threats sufficient to show past persecution to those "that are so menacing as to cause significant actual 'suffering or harm.'"[591] The court also requires that threats include only those that are "highly imminent and menacing in nature," holding that those that are not imminent or concrete or did not result in physical violence or harm to the applicant do not constitute past persecution.[592] Therefore, the court found that a death threat combined with a robbery at gunpoint that mimicked attacks of other members of the targeted group constituted past persecution because it was highly imminent and concrete and the applicant suffered harm from it.[593] However, the Third Circuit did not characterize threats of sterilization and physical violence as past persecution because they were neither imminent nor concrete and neither the applicant nor his family were imprisoned, sterilized, or physically harmed, but the court did note that unfulfilled threats should be considered by the court in its determination of whether the applicant has a well-founded fear of future persecution.[594] The Seventh Circuit has a similar requirement that threats be of a highly immediate and menacing nature in order to constitute past persecution, but observed that unfulfilled threats are more likely to be viewed as danger of future persecution.[595] The court held that an applicant who criticized the communist government, had a friend disappear and later turn up murdered after a confrontation with government police, and who subsequently was threatened that he would "lose his job and his apartment, 'and something even worse could happen'" did not endure conduct that could be categorized as past persecution.[596] Finally, the Ninth Circuit also held that mere threats only amount to past persecution where they "are so menacing as to cause significant actual 'suffering or harm.'"[597] For example, the Ninth Circuit has held that "repeated and especially menacing death threats can constitute a primary part of a past persecution claim, particularly where those threats are combined with confrontation or other mistreatment."[598] Where the applicant's life and business had been threatened by a rebel group because of the applicant's political opinion, the Ninth Circuit found that the person had suffered past persecution.[599]

---

[591] *Chavarria v. Gonzales*, 446 F.3d 508, 518 (3d Cir. 2006) (quoting *Li v. Atty Gen'l of the U.S.*, 400 F.3d 157, 159 (3d Cir. 2005)).

[592] *Id.*

[593] *Id.* at 520.

[594] *Li v. Atty Gen'l of the U.S.*, 400 F.3d 157, 163–65, 165 n.3 (3d Cir. 2005).

[595] *Boykov v. INS*, 109 F.3d 413, 416–17 (7th Cir. 1997).

[596] *Id.*

[597] *Lim v. INS*, 224 F.3d 929, 936 (9th Cir. 2000).

[598] *Id.*(citing cases finding past persecution with a combination of repeated bribe attempts, personal confrontations and death threats; murder of family members, recruitment attempts, and death threats; attack on family, personal confrontation, and death threats).

[599] *Gonzales-Neyra v. INS*, 122 F.3d 1293, 1296 (9th Cir. 1997), *amended by* 133 F.3d 726 (9th Cir. 1998); *see also Ventura v. INS*, 264 F.3d 1150, 1154 (9th Cir. 2001) (threats spray-painted on walls of applicant's house by guerrillas amount to well-founded fear of persecution); *Garrovillas v. INS*, 156 F.3d 1010, 1016 (9th Cir. 1998) (three death threats in four months sufficient to establish persecution); *Sangha v. INS*, 103 F.3d 1482, 1487 (9th Cir. 1997) (threats of death and violence from a terrorist

continued

2.6.6. Persecution of Family and Friends

Courts have also looked to the treatment of an applicant's family members and friends in assessing whether the applicant has a well-founded fear of persecution. Courts have held that the mistreatment of family members is a basis for a well-founded fear of persecution.[600] UNHCR's *Handbook* similarly provides: "What . . . happened to [the applicant's] friends and relatives and other members of the same racial or social group may well show that his fear that sooner or later he also will become a victim of persecution is well-founded."[601]

Harm to an applicant's family member may also constitute persecution of the applicant. At least one federal court has held that FGM performed on a daughter could amount to persecution of the parent. In *Abay v. Ashcroft*, the Sixth Circuit held that "where a parent and protector is faced with exposing her child to [FGM]" she could establish eligibility for asylum.[602] Similarly, legacy INS has taken the position that if the persecutor's motives in harming the applicant's family member or friend was to punish or harm the applicant, the harm may constitute persecution of the applicant.[603] The Asylum Division also takes the position that forced abortion or forced sterilization of an asylum applicant's *spouse* or severe psychological harm suffered by an applicant from mere knowledge of or actually witnessing harm to another person could be considered persecution of the applicant.[604]

---

group sufficient to establish persecution). *But see Matter of A–E–M–*, 21 I&N Dec. 1159, 1159 (BIA 1998) (painted threat on house does not rise to the level of persecution).

[600] *See, e.g., Ventura v. INS*, 264 F.3d 1150, 1154 (9th Cir. 2001) (past political persecution of family members provides evidence of imputed political opinion of the applicant), *rev'd on other grounds by INS v. Ventura*, 537 U.S. 12, 18 (2002); *Mgoian v. INS*, 184 F.3d 1029, 1036–37 (9th Cir. 1999) (evidence that all of the applicant's principal family members were subjected to forms of violence, persecution, and harassment gives rise to the inference that the family has become a target); *Rodriguez-Matamoros v. INS*, 86 F.3d 158 (9th Cir. 1996) (finding that the applicant had established a well-founded fear due in part to the threats to her family and the torture and killing of her sister); *see also Li v. INS*, 92 F.3d 985, 987 (9th Cir. 1996) (arrest of family member in church may provide basis for claim based on religious persecution); *Gebremichael v. INS*, 10 F.3d 28 (1st Cir. 1993) (finding a link between family membership and persecution); *Arriaga-Barrientos v. INS*, 937 F.2d 411, 414 (9th Cir. 1991) ("Acts of persecution against a petitioner's friends and family may establish a well-founded fear, notwithstanding an utter lack of persecution against the petitioner . . . ."); *Matter of Villalta*, 20 I&N Dec. 142 (BIA 1990) (finding that the threats to the applicant's immediate family members and the murder of applicant's brother establish a well-founded fear of persecution).

[601] UNHCR *Handbook*, *supra* note 36, at ¶43.

[602] *Abay v. Ashcroft*, 368 F.3d 634, 641–42 (6th Cir. 2004) (threat of FGM to daughter amounts to a well-founded fear for daughter *and* mother); *see also Baballah v. Ashcroft*, 367 F.3d 1067, 1074–75 (9th Cir. 2004) ("[V]iolence directed against an applicant's family members provides support for a claim of persecution . . . ."). *But see Matter of A–K–*, 24 I&N Dec. 275 (BIA 2007) (an applicant may not establish eligibility for asylum based solely on the fear that his or her daughter will be subjected to FGM).

[603] *See* INS Memorandum, "Persecution of Family Members" (June 30, 1997); *see also Chouchkov v. INS*, 220 F.3d 1077 (9th Cir. 2000) (harm to father and mother-in-law and threats against wife amount to persecution of the applicant).

[604] *See* AOBTC Lesson: Asylum Eligibility Part I, *supra* note 47, at 26 (emphasis added).

In other cases, where the mistreatment of the applicant's family is not linked to the applicant, courts have found that the applicant does not have a well-founded fear.[605] Similarly, if conditions in the country have changed substantially since the harm to the family members occurred, the applicant cannot rely on the past harm to establish a well-founded fear.[606]

Some courts have relied on the lack of harm or mistreatment of family members in finding that an applicant's claim is not well-founded.[607] In contrast, other courts have held that the lack of harm or mistreatment of other family members is not relevant in cases in which the applicant has been singled out for mistreatment.[608] In *Cordero-Trejo v. INS*, the court found that to infer that an asylum applicant is unlikely to be persecuted because he and his relatives were not killed during attempts to terrorize them leads to the absurd result of denying asylum to those who have actually experienced persecution.[609]

2.6.7. "Similarly Situated" Standard

Asylum applicants may also establish a well-founded fear even if they have not been individually targeted by their persecutors.[610] A well-founded fear can be based on harm that has been suffered by others who are similarly situated to the asylum applicant.[611] Courts have held that where a number of similarly situated individuals face a similar type of harm, this strengthens rather than weakens an applicant's claim.[612] With regard to similarly situated claims, the asylum regulations provide:

---

[605] *See, e.g., Arriaga-Barrientos v. INS*, 937 F.2d 411 (9th Cir. 1991) (holding that the disappearance, for unknown reasons, of the applicant's two brothers who resided 800 kilometers away from the applicant did not demonstrate a well-founded fear); *Matter of E–P–*, 21 I&N Dec. 860, 862 (BIA 1997) (finding that the applicant failed to provide evidence linking the murder of her family members and the harm she fears upon return to her home country).

[606] *Francois v. INS*, 283 F.3d 926, 931–32 (8th Cir. 2002).

[607] *See, e.g., Agada v. Ashcroft*, 368 F.3d 867, 869 (8th Cir. 2004) (relying on evidence that the applicant's wife, sons, and siblings lived in Nigeria without harm); *Bhatt v. Reno*, 172 F.3d 978, 982 (7th Cir. 1999) (finding that the absence of evidence of harm to the applicant's family members undermines claim of well-founded fear); *Abedini v. INS*, 971 F.2d 188, 192 (9th Cir. 1992) (court relied on the applicant's testimony that none of his family members had been subject to persecution in finding that the applicant's fear was not well-founded); *Matter of A–E–M–*, 21 I&N Dec. 1157, 1160 (BIA 1998) (finding that applicant lacked a well-founded fear, in part, because his family members remained unharmed in Peru since his departure).

[608] *See, e.g., Nakibuka v. Gonzales*, 421 F.3d 473, 479 (7th Cir. 2005) (noting that there was no evidence that the applicant's relatives were politically active or closely associated with known opponents of the government); *Bellido v. Ashcroft*, 367 F.3d 840, 844 (8th Cir. 2004) (noting that the applicant should not suffer simply because his government has chosen to focus its efforts on persecuting only him); *Rios v. Ashcroft*, 287 F.3d 895, 902 (9th Cir. 2002).

[609] *Cordero-Trejo v. INS*, 40 F.3d 482, 489 (1st Cir. 1994); *see also Lim v. INS*, 224 F.3d 929, 935 (9th Cir. 2000) (finding that lack of harm to family refutes a well-founded fear only if the family members are similarly situated to the applicant).

[610] *Knezevic v. Ashcroft*, 367 F.3d 1206, 1213 (9th Cir. 2004).

[611] *Matter of Mogharrabi*, 19 I&N Dec. 439, 446 (BIA 1987); *see also Wiransane v. Ashcroft*, 366 F.3d 889, 894–95 (10th Cir. 2004) (an applicant is permitted to show that a person in his position, as opposed to himself specifically, could be subject to persecution).

[612] *See, e.g., Bolanos-Hernandez v. INS*, 767 F.2d 1277, 1285 (9th Cir. 1984).

In evaluating whether the applicant has sustained his or her burden of proving that he or she has a well-founded fear of persecution, the asylum officer or immigration judge shall *not* require the applicant to provide evidence that he or she would be singled out individually for persecution if:

(A) The applicant establishes that there is a pattern or practice in his or her country of nationality or last habitual residence of persecution of groups of persons similarly situated to the applicant on account of race, religion, nationality, membership in a particular social group, or political opinion; and

(B) The applicant establishes his or her own inclusion in and identification with such group of persons such that his or her fear of persecution upon return is reasonable.[613]

In establishing a "pattern or practice," the applicant is *not* required to show that "*every* individual in the vulnerable group must face [] serious persecution."[614] The pattern or practice, however, must be systematic, pervasive, or organized.[615] The applicant must also show that that persecution is perpetrated or tolerated by state actors.[616] The BIA has been reversed where it has failed to consider evidence concerning a pattern or practice of persecution of similarly situated persons.[617]

Even if an applicant is unable to establish a pattern or practice, an applicant may be able to establish membership in a "disfavored" group. Factors that are considered are: (1) the risk level of membership in the group, *i.e.*, the extent and severity of persecution suffered by the group; and (2) the applicant's individual risk level, *i.e.*, whether he or she has a special role in the group or is more likely to come to the attention of the persecutors, making him or her a more likely target for persecution.[618] The more serious and widespread the threat of persecution to the group, the less individualized the threat of persecution needs to be.[619]

---

[613] 8 CFR §§208.13(b)(2), 1208.13(b)(2)(iii) (emphasis added).

[614] *Avetova-Elisseva v. INS*, 213 F.3d 1192, 1201 (9th Cir. 2000) (emphasis in original).

[615] *Mitreva v. Gonzales*, 417 F.3d 761, 765 (7th Cir. 2005); *Ngure v. Ashcroft*, 367 F.3d 975, 991 (8th Cir. 2004).

[616] *Mitreva*, *supra* note 615, at 765.

[617] *See, e.g.*, *Thavendran v. Gonzales*, 211 Fed. Appx. 74, 75 (2d Cir. 2007) (BIA erred in failing to consider whether there was a pattern or practice of persecution in Sri Lanka against individuals of Tamil ethnicity); *Cordero-Trejo v. INS*, 40 F.3d 482, 491–92 (1st Cir. 1994). *But see Gomes v. Gonzales*, 429 F.3d 1264, 1267 (9th Cir. 2005) (finding applicant failed to show that BIA's finding that there was no pattern or practice of persecution of Christians or Catholics was not supported by substantial evidence); *Capric v. Ashcroft*, 355 F.3d 1075, 1094 (7th Cir. 2004) (rejecting claim of applicant who relied on "State Department reports addressing [the former Federal Republic of Yugoslavia] generally and detailed ethnic cleansing campaigns in *other* regions") (emphasis in original).

[618] *See Kotasz v. INS*, 31 F.3d 847, 853 (9th Cir. 1994).

[619] *Id.* at 853–54; *see also Yong Hao Chen v. INS*, 195 F.3d 198, 204 (4th Cir. 1999) (noting the correlation between the seriousness of the threat of persecution to the "disfavored" group and the individualized nature of the threat).

2.6.8. Possession of a Valid Passport

Asylum applicants may have left their home countries by obtaining a passport from their government. Courts have sometimes relied on the applicant's possession of a passport as evidence that the applicant would not be persecuted by his or her government.[620] In other cases, courts have recognized that the applicant's possession of a passport does not necessarily mean that the applicant would not be in danger upon return to his or her home country.[621] With regard to this issue, UNHCR's *Handbook* provides:

> Possession of a passport cannot therefore always be considered as ... an indication of the absence of fear. A passport may even be issued to a person who is undesired in his country of origin, with the sole purpose of securing his departure, and there may also be cases where a passport has been obtained surreptitiously. ... [T]he mere possession of a valid national passport is no bar to refugee status.[622]

In addition, the holder of a valid passport may not necessarily be a citizen of the country that issued the passport. Countries may issue "passports of convenience" to individuals in order to facilitate travel. Jordan, for example, has issued many passports to Palestinians. While passports may be evidence of citizenship, they are not conclusive. "They 'may be overcome by sufficient evidence that the holder of the passport is not a citizen' of the issuing country."[623] In this regard, UNHCR's *Handbook* also provides:

> Possession of a passport creates a *prima facie* presumption that the holder is a national of the country of issue, unless the passport itself states otherwise. A person holding a passport showing him to be a national of the issuing country, but who claims that he does not possess that country's nationality, must substantiate his claim, for example, by showing that the passport is a so-called "passport of convenience" (an apparently regular national passport that is sometimes issued by a national authority to non-nationals).[624]

2.6.9. Changed Country Conditions; Administrative Notice

Many asylum applicants have claims pending when significant events occur, for better or worse, in their home countries. Peace may be declared, civil war may erupt, or new elections may take place. Administrative agencies may take administrative notice of commonly known facts.[625] The BIA, in many cases, has taken administrative notice of changed country conditions. The concept of changed country conditions is also important in determining whether there should be a presumption of future persecution,[626] whether a

---

[620] *See, e.g., Kratchmarov v. Heston*, 172 F.3d 551, 555 (8th Cir. 1999); *Huaman-Cornelio v. BIA*, 979 F.2d 995, 1000 (4th Cir. 1992); *Ravindran v. INS*, 976 F.2d 754, 760 (1st Cir. 1992).

[621] *See, e.g., Damaize-Job v. INS*, 787 F.2d 1332, 1336 (9th Cir. 1986); *Matter of Pula*, 19 I&N Dec. 467, 472 (BIA 1987) (finding the applicant eligible for asylum even though the Yugoslav government issued him a passport).

[622] UNHCR *Handbook*, *supra* note 36, at ¶48.

[623] *Palavra v. INS*, 287 F.3d 690, 692 (8th Cir. 2002) (vacating the BIA's finding that holders of Croatian passports were Croatian citizens, citing *Matter of Maccaud*, 14 I&N Dec. 429, 432 (BIA 1973)).

[624] UNHCR *Handbook*, *supra* note 36, at ¶93.

[625] *Matter of R–R–*, 20 I&N Dec. 547, 551 n.3 (BIA 1992).

[626] *See* this chapter, at 2.6.10.

motion to reopen will be granted,[627] and whether the one-year filing deadline will be waived.[628]

The BIA and courts have addressed the issue of changed conditions with regard to pending claims in a variety of ways. In some cases the BIA has taken administrative notice of changed conditions without introducing any evidence into the record or affording applicants the opportunity to respond to the noticed facts. In *Castillo-Villagra v. INS*,[629] the Ninth Circuit held that the BIA improperly took administrative notice when it failed to afford the asylum applicant the opportunity to rebut the noticed facts.[630] Where, however, the applicant has had an opportunity to introduce evidence that country conditions have changed (or have not changed), the opportunity to rebut the noticed facts is not necessary.[631] In contrast, the Seventh Circuit in *Kaczmarczyk v. INS*[632] held that the BIA's taking of administrative notice was proper, and concluded that the asylum applicant could rebut the noticed facts through a motion to reopen.[633]

Where the BIA has relied on country condition information that is several years old in determining that an applicant does not have a well-founded fear and ignores nonrecord evidence suggesting that conditions have changed, courts have remanded cases to the BIA for further consideration.[634] Other courts have taken judicial notice of the changed conditions.[635] A third approach has been to require the applicant to file a motion to reopen.[636]

The BIA and IJs have also been instructed to avoid reliance on general changes in country conditions and to conduct an individualized analysis of how any changes might affect the specific asylum applicant's situation.[637] In cases involving past persecution, the

---

[627] *See* ch. 3.11.

[628] *See* this chapter, at 2.7.3.

[629] *Castillo-Villagra v. INS*, 972 F.2d 1017, 1029 (9th Cir. 1992).

[630] *See also Francois v. INS*, 283 F.3d 926, 933 (8th Cir. 2002) (approving of the BIA's use of administrative notice if the BIA gives notice and an opportunity to respond); *De La Llana-Castellon v. INS*, 16 F.3d 1093, 1097–98 (10th Cir. 1994) (finding that the BIA erred in taking administrative notice of changed conditions without giving due regard for potential persecution from a group the government cannot control); *Gutierrez-Roque v. INS*, 954 F.2d 769, 773 (D.C. Cir. 1992) (due process guarantees an asylum applicant the right to challenge an officially noticed fact).

[631] *See, e.g., Acewicz v. INS*, 984 F.2d 1056, 1061 (9th Cir. 1993); *Matter of H–M–*, 20 I&N Dec. 683, 689–90 (BIA 1993).

[632] *Kaczmarczyk v. INS*, 933 F.2d 588, 593–97 (7th Cir. 1991).

[633] *But see Vujisic v. INS*, 224 F.3d 578, 582 (7th Cir. 2000) (finding that the BIA erred in taking administrative notice of changed country conditions where it did not engage in an "individualized review" of the applicant's case); *Galina v. INS*, 213 F.3d 955, 958–59 (7th Cir. 2000) (finding that BIA erred in taking administrative notice of items in the State Department report which were not "facts," but merely pronouncements or summaries of laws).

[634] *See, e.g., Yang v. McElroy*, 277 F.3d 158, 161–62 (2d Cir. 2002).

[635] *See Dobrota v. INS*, 195 F.3d 970, 973 (7th Cir. 1999); *Ivezaj v. INS*, 84 F.3d 215, 218–19 (6th Cir. 1996).

[636] *See Sivaainkaran v. INS*, 972 F.2d 161, 165–66 (7th Cir. 1992); *Chavarria v. U.S. Dept. of Justice*, 722 F.2d 666, 669 (11th Cir. 1984).

[637] *See Bace v. Ashcroft*, 352 F.3d 1133, 1141 (7th Cir. 2003); *Rios v. Ashcroft*, 287 F.3d 895, 901–02 (9th Cir. 2002); *Gailius v. INS*, 147 F.3d 34, 36 (1st Cir. 1998).

BIA must not only consider the current situation in the country of origin, but should address the ways in which the situation differs from the one in which the applicant experienced persecution in the past.[638]

2.6.10. Past Persecution; Presumption of Future Persecution

Asylum regulations promulgated in 2001 changed the burden of proof and exceptions for the well-founded fear presumption in past persecution claims. Under the 2001 regulations, if it is determined that the applicant has suffered past persecution, the applicant is presumed to have a well-founded fear of persecution on the basis of the original claim.[639] That presumption may be rebutted if the asylum officer or IJ, in his or her discretion, finds by a preponderance of the evidence that:

> There has been a fundamental change in *circumstances* such that the applicant no longer has a well-founded fear of persecution . . . on account of race, religion, nationality, membership in a particular social group, or political opinion; or

> The applicant could avoid future persecution by relocating to another part of the applicant's country . . . and under all circumstances it would be *reasonable* to expect him to do so.[640]

If the applicant has established past persecution, the trial attorney or asylum officer bears the burden of proving a fundamental change in circumstances or a reasonable internal relocation option.[641] Similarly, for purposes of withholding of removal, if an applicant has suffered past persecution in the proposed country of removal, it is presumed that the applicant's life or freedom would be threatened in the future on the basis of the original claim.[642] This presumption likewise may be rebutted if the trial attorney or asylum officer establishes by a preponderance of the evidence there has been a fundamental change in circumstances or the applicant could avoid future persecution by relocating, if it would be reasonable under all circumstances.[643] If the IJ or BIA fails to provide a reasoned discussion of whether an individual was subjected to past persecution, the reviewing court is unable to provide a meaningful review of the decision and the case must be remanded.[644]

For both asylum and withholding claims, if the applicant's fear of future persecution is "unrelated" to the past persecution, the applicant bears the burden of establishing that the fear is well-founded.[645] This change appears to codify the BIA's decision in *Matter of N–M–A–*, which held that when the record reflects that the applicant no longer has a well-

---

[638] *Margos v. Gonzales*, 443 F.3d 593, 598 (7th Cir. 2006) (upholding the IJ's taking of administrative notice of changed circumstances in Iraq as of April 2003); *Kojevnikova v. Reno*, 173 F.3d 844 (2d Cir. 1999).

[639] 8 CFR §§208.13(b)(1), 1208.13(b)(1).

[640] 8 CFR §§208.13(b)(1)(i), 1208.13(b)(1)(i) (emphasis added).

[641] 8 CFR §§208.13(b)(1)(ii), 1208.13(b)(1)(ii).

[642] 8 CFR §§208.16(b)(1)(i), 1208.16(b)(1)(i).

[643] 8 CFR §§208.16(b)(1)(i), (ii), 1208.16(b)(1)(i), (ii).

[644] *See, e.g.*, *Hernandez-Barrera v. Ashcroft*, 373 F.3d 9, 22 (1st Cir. 2004).

[645] 8 CFR §§208.13(b)(1), 208.16(b)(1)(iii), 1208.13(b)(1), and 1208.16(b)(1)(iii).

founded fear of persecution from his or her original persecutors, the applicant bears the burden of demonstrating a well-founded fear of persecution from a new source.[646]

Fundamental Change in Circumstances

A "fundamental change in circumstances" required to rebut the presumption of a well-founded fear in claims involving past persecution is intended to be broader than the previously required changed country conditions. According to legacy INS, it includes other changes, including changes in "personal" circumstances, if "those changes are fundamental in nature and go to the basis of the fear of persecution."[647] In explaining the reason for the change in the regulation, legacy INS noted that it was designed to comply with the United States' international obligations under the 1967 Protocol Relating to the Status of Refugees.[648] The phrase "fundamental change in circumstances" is found in Article 1C(5) of the 1951 United Nations Convention Relating to the Status of Refugees, incorporated by reference into the 1967 Protocol.[649] In interpreting this particular clause, which outlines when a person may cease to be a refugee, legacy INS looked to UNHCR's *Handbook*.[650]

The *Handbook*, however, seems to undercut legacy INS's assertion that personal circumstances should be considered. Paragraph 135 provides:

> "Circumstances" refer to fundamental changes in the *country*, which can be assumed to remove the basis of the fear of persecution. A mere—possibly transitory—change in the facts surrounding the individual refugee's fear, which does not entail such major changes in circumstances, is not sufficient to make this clause applicable.[651]

It is possible, therefore, to argue that a fundamental change in circumstances refers only to country conditions, since the regulation itself does not include the word "personal."

The BIA has recently interpreted this regulation in the context of coercive population measures.[652] It found that an asylum applicant whose wife was forcibly sterilized and who remained in China for seven years after the sterilization without additional harm occurring was nevertheless eligible for asylum.[653] The BIA reasoned that the IJ had failed to take into account the continuing nature of the persecution inflicted on the applicant and his wife.[654] In addition, the BIA noted that the IJ's rationale could lead to the anomalous result that the

---

[646] *Matter of N–M–A–*, 22 I&N Dec. 312, 318 (BIA 1998). For a comprehensive overview of these changes, see P. Schmidt, "The Presumption of Future Persecution Under the 2001 Asylum Regulations," 21 *Immigration Law Today* 225 (Apr. 2002). The author of this article, Paul Schmidt, is a former member of the BIA.

[647] *See* 65 Fed. Reg. 76121, 76127 (Dec. 6, 2000) (supplementary information).

[648] *Id.*

[649] *Id.*

[650] *Id.*

[651] UNHCR *Handbook*, *supra* note 36, at ¶135 (emphasis added).

[652] *See Matter of Y–T–L–*, 23 I&N Dec. 601 (BIA 2003).

[653] *Id.* at 605.

[654] *Id.*

very act of persecution itself would also constitute the change in circumstances and that it was "highly unlikely" Congress contemplated such an interpretation.[655] In a case involving the fall of the Taliban in Afghanistan, the Eighth Circuit held that it was not enough for the government to show a change in government, but it was required to show that the legal system had changed to such an extent that Christian converts would not be subjected to death for their religious beliefs under Afghanistan's current laws.[656] In the case of an Iraqi Assyrian, however, the court did find it was proper for the IJ to take administrative notice of that Saddam Hussein's regime ceased control of Iraq in April 2003.[657] Similarly, in the case of a Kosovar Muslim, the Fifth Circuit upheld the IJ's finding of a fundamental change in circumstances in Kosovo.[658]

Prior to the change in the regulation, there were a number of cases interpreting changed country conditions that are still relevant. In *Matter of H–*, for example, the BIA held that as a practical matter it is the trial attorney's burden to rebut the presumption based on past persecution, either by submitting additional evidence or by resting on the evidence already in the record.[659]

Reasonableness of Internal Relocation Alternative

Under regulations issued in 2001, an internal relocation alternative sufficient to rebut a presumption of a well-founded fear (or that the applicant's life or freedom would be threatened) must be "reasonable" "under *all* the circumstances."[660] In determining the "reasonableness" of an internal relocation option, adjudicators should consider, among other things:

- whether the applicant would face other serious harm in the place of suggested relocation;
- any ongoing civil strife within the country;
- administrative, economic, or judicial infrastructure;
- geographical limitations;

---

[655] *Id.*; *see also Hernandez-Barrera v. Ashcroft*, 373 F.3d 9, 23 (1st Cir. 2004) (noting the burden is *not* on the applicant to show his fear of persecution is not negated by changed circumstances; the burden is on the government).

[656] *Ahmadshah v. Ashcroft*, 396 F.3d 917, 921 (8th Cir. 2005) (finding that the government's evidence of changed conditions does not address the fear of persecution for apostasy).

[657] *Margos v. Gonzales*, 443 F.3d 593, 598 (7th Cir. 2006).

[658] *Shehu v. Gonzales*, 443 F.3d 435, 439–40 (5th Cir. 2006).

[659] *Matter of H–*, 21 I&N Dec. 337 (BIA 1996); *see also Tarubac v. INS*, 182 F.3d 1114, 1120 (9th Cir. 1999) (Legacy INS failed to demonstrate that, in light of applicant's past persecution, the State Department profile provided sufficient evidence of changed country conditions to rebut the presumption of a well-founded fear); *Korablina v. INS*, 158 F.3d 1038, 1046 (9th Cir. 1998) (finding that the fact that members of the applicant's family were severely beaten soon after she left the Ukraine, with specific threats regarding her absence, indicates that the persecution would continue); *Fergiste v. INS*, 138 F.3d 14 (1st Cir. 1998) (the BIA erred as a matter of law in *not* applying the rebuttable presumption of future persecution to an individual who established that he suffered past persecution in Haiti).

[660] 8 CFR §§208.13(b)(1)(i)(B), 208.16(b)(1)(i)(B), 1208.13(b)(1)(i)(B), and 1208.16(b)(1)(i)(B) (emphasis added).

- social and cultural constraints, such as age, gender, health, and social and familial ties.[661]

The regulations also note that these factors "may, or may not, be relevant, depending on the all the circumstances of the case and are not necessarily determinative" of whether relocation is reasonable.[662]

In *Knezevic v. Ashcroft*, the Ninth Circuit held that the IJ failed to consider all of the factors for determining reasonableness for Serbian applicants to relocate to Serb-held parts of Bosnia-Herzegovina and should have considered their advanced age, lack of a home, destruction of their business, and lack of family members in the area.[663]

Countries in which internal relocation has been found to be reasonable under the specific evidence presented include: Bangladesh,[664] Guatemala,[665] Indonesia,[666] and the Ukraine.[667] Countries in which internal relocation was found *not* to be a reasonable option under the specific evidence presented include: China,[668] Colombia,[669] Republic of the Congo,[670] Mexico,[671] and Pakistan.[672]

---

[661] 8 CFR §§208.13(b)(3), 208.16(b)(3), 1208.13(b)(3), and 1208.16(b)(3).

[662] 8 CFR §§208.13(b)(3), 208.16(b)(3), 1208.13(b)(3), and 1208.16(b)(3).

[663] *Knezevic v. Ashcroft*, 367 F.3d 1206, 1214–15 (9th Cir. 2004); *see also Vladimirova v. Ashcroft*, 377 F.3d 690, 697 (7th Cir. 2004) (noting that the State Department report makes clear that individuals practicing unsanctioned religions face harassment throughout Bulgaria); *Hagi v. Ashcroft*, 359 F.3d 1044 (8th Cir. 2004) (remanding the case to the BIA because the BIA failed to properly consider the factors outlined in this regulation). For further discussion and prior case law regarding internal relocation alternatives, see this chapter, at 2.5.9.

[664] *Gomes v. Gonzales*, 429 F.3d 1264, 1267 (9th Cir. 2005) (finding that applicants, who claimed asylum based on being Catholics and Christians, failed to show by compelling evidence that they could not safely relocate within Bangladesh).

[665] *Lopez-Gomez v. Ashcroft*, 263 F.3d 442, 446 (5th Cir. 2001) (holding that the BIA's determination that the petitioners, who feared persecution based on political affiliation, could have relocated within Guatemala was supported by substantial evidence); *see also Mazariegos v. Office of the United States AG*, 241 F.3d 1320, 1328 (11th Cir. 2001) (finding substantial evidence supporting the BIA's determination that the petitioner, a soldier in the Guatemalan army who feared persecution at the hands of guerrillas, had a reasonable prospect of resettling safely within Guatemala).

[666] *Setiadi v. Gonzales*, 437 F.3d 710, 714 n.3 (8th Cir. 2006) (finding that the record supported the BIA's determination that the applicant, who claimed asylum as a Christian fearing persecution, could relocate within Indonesia).

[667] *Yakovenko v. Gonzales*, 477 F.3d 631, 637 (8th Cir. 2007) (upholding the BIA's determination that the petitioner, who claimed asylum because of past persecution based on her Jewish faith, failed to show that it would be unsafe or unreasonable to relocate in the Ukraine where BIA and the IJ found a lack of evidence to corroborate that anti-semitism was "sanctioned, supported, or tolerated by the Ukrainian government.").

[668] *Gao v. Gonzales*, 440 F.3d 62, 71 (2d Cir. 2006) (vacating and remanding the BIA's determination that a Chinese asylum applicant fleeing domestic violence and human trafficking could reasonably relocate within the country. The court held that the BIA determination was contradicted by the record. The applicant testified that she had attempted unsuccessfully to relocate within China. The court further held that the BIA cannot solely determine whether the applicant could avoid persecution by relocating, but must also determine whether it would be *reasonable* to require relocation). *See also Tu Kai Yang v. Gonzales*, 427 F.3d 1117, 1122 (8th Cir. 2005) ("The IJ's suggestion that petitioners could potentially avoid persecution by relocating within China is incorrect.").

Humanitarian Asylum

Even if a preponderance of the evidence demonstrates a fundamental change in circumstances or an internal relocation alternative, an applicant may still be granted asylum, in the discretion of the adjudicator, if:

(A) The applicant has demonstrated *compelling reasons* for being unwilling or unable to return to the country arising out of the severity of the past persecution; or

(B) The applicant has established that there is a reasonable possibility that he or she may face *other serious harm* upon removal to that country.[673]

According to legacy INS, "other serious harm" means "harm that is not inflicted on account of race, religion, nationality, membership in a particular social group, or political opinion, but is so serious that it equals the severity of persecution."[674] One court has found that this regulation provides "a second avenue of relief" for victims of past persecution whose fear of future persecution has been rebutted by evidence of changed country conditions or of safe harbors within his or her home country.[675] Courts have held, however, that eligibility for asylum on this basis is reserved for "the most atrocious abuse."[676]

Case law interpreting the "compelling reasons" standard under prior regulations remains relevant. It should be noted, however, that the new regulations require a nexus between the "compelling reasons" and the severity of the past persecution. In *Lal v. INS*, the Ninth Circuit found that the applicants were eligible for asylum based on the severity of

---

[669] *Arboleda v. United States AG*, 434 F.3d 1220, 1224 (11th Cir. 2006) (vacating and remanding the BIA's denial of asylum where "the record in [the] case compels the conclusion that the FARC operates country-wide in Colombia, and that relocation was therefore not a viable option for the petitioners to escape persecution").

[670] *Essohou v. Gonzales*, 471 F.3d 518, (4th Cir. 2006) (vacating and remanding the BIA's denial of asylum based on the reasonableness of internal relocation where the court found that the facts on the record suggested that "[a]ny intermittent period in which Bockou Essohou was not specifically troubled by the Cobras was not due to a reasonable, internal relocation; rather, it was due to her efforts to hide in conjunction with the timing of the Cobras' forays").

[671] *Boer-Sedano v. Gonzales*, 418 F.3d 1082, 1091 (9th Cir. 2005) ("We hold, therefore, that after considering the cumulative evidence on the social and cultural constraints Boer-Sedano would face as a homosexual man in Mexico, his current health, and the likelihood that serious harm would come to him if forced to relocate to Mexico where he could not obtain his required medication, no reasonable factfinder could conclude that the INS has carried its burden of showing that such relocation was reasonable.").

[672] *Kaiser v. Ashcroft*, 390 F.3d 653, 660 (9th Cir. 2004) ("Thus, the evidence compels the conclusion that Petitioners could not relocate safely anywhere in Pakistan.").

[673] 8 CFR §§208.13(b)(1)(iii), 1208.13(b)(1)(iii).

[674] *See* 65 Fed. Reg. 76121, 76127 (Dec. 6, 2000) (supplementary information). Note, however, that this supplementary information is not part of the regulations and is not binding on adjudicators. *See also Krastev v. INS*, 292 F.3d 1268, 1271 (10th Cir. 2002); S. Heller, "'Other Serious Harm'—Asylum Protection for Refugees Who No Longer Fear Persecution," 22 *Immigration Law Today* 35 (Jan./Feb. 2003).

[675] *See Liti v. Gonzales*, 411 F.3d 631, 641–42 (6th Cir. 2005); *Belishta v. Ashcroft*, 378 F.3d 1078, 1081 (9th Cir. 2004).

[676] *See, e.g., Naizgi v. Gonzales*, 455 F.3d 484, 488 (4th Cir. 2006).

their past persecution, which included repeated arbitrary detentions, painful and humiliating torture, sexual assault, threats, and severe intimidation.[677] Similarly, in *Vongsakdy v. INS*, the court found that a Laotian national who had been imprisoned in a labor camp and had suffered beatings, torture, inadequate food and water, denial of medical treatment, and a severed thumb had been subjected to egregious past persecution.[678] The court also found the fact that the applicant remained in Laos for a considerable period of time following his release from the labor camp was "irrelevant" to evaluating the "atrocity" of his past persecution.[679]

2.6.11. Foreign Law

Increasingly, foreign law is at issue in an asylum or withholding of removal case. An applicant may have had a legal immigration status in a third country prior to arriving in the United States and may have to prove she was not "firmly resettled." She may be fleeing what at first glance looks like prosecution, but on closer examination of the law rises to the level of persecution. She may be stateless because the country she was born in does not confer citizenship by virtue of being born on its territory. These and other scenarios will require reference to foreign law.

The BIA has held that foreign law is a matter to be proven by the party seeking to rely on it.[680] In *Soleimani*, the BIA found that legacy INS had produced no evidence of record to establish that the applicant had been "offered" permanent resettlement under Israel's Law of Return.[681] Absent any such documentation, the BIA held that it could not find that the applicant had been offered permanent resettlement in Israel within the meaning of the firm resettlement concept. In *Abdille v. Ashcroft*, the Third Circuit held that legacy INS, as the party seeking to rely on foreign law for firm resettlement purposes, carries the initial burden of proof.[682] Once the trial attorney submits evidence of foreign law sufficient to indicate that the firm resettlement bar will apply, the burden shifts to applicant.[683]

---

[677] *Lal v. INS*, 255 F.3d 998, 1003, *amended on reh'g*, 268 F.3d 1148 (9th Cir. 2001).

[678] *Vongsakdy v. INS*, 171 F.3d 1203 (9th Cir. 1999).

[679] *Id.* at 1207; *see also Matter of Chen*, 20 I&N Dec. 16, 18–19 (BIA 1989) (finding that a favorable exercise of discretion may be warranted for humanitarian reasons despite changed country conditions), *codified by* 8 CFR §§208.13(b)(1)(iii), 1208.13(b)(1)(iii); *Matter of H–*, 21 I&N Dec. 337, 347–48 (BIA 1996) (finding that humanitarian reasons may include the applicant's age, health, or family ties in the United States); *Matter of B–F–O–*, A78 677 043 (BIA Nov. 6, 2001) (in this unpublished decision, the BIA found that a Nicaraguan street child suffered atrocious forms of persecution, meriting a grant of asylum without regard to current country conditions), *reported in* 21 Immigration Law Today 135 (Mar. 2002). *But see Francois v. INS*, 283 F.3d 926, 932 (8th Cir. 2002) (finding that applicant, who was interrogated, threatened that her father would be killed, and denied an exit visa, failed to demonstrate severe or long-lasting harm sufficient to warrant humanitarian asylum); *Matter of N–M–A–*, 22 I&N Dec. 312, 326 (BIA 1998) (finding no compelling reasons where the applicant suffered a month-long detention, beatings, and the disappearance and likely death of his father, but where there was no evidence of severe psychological trauma).

[680] *Matter of Soleimani*, 20 I&N Dec. 99, 106 (BIA 1989).

[681] *Id.*

[682] *Abdille v. Ashcroft*, 242 F.3d 477, 490–91 (3d Cir. 2001).

[683] *Id.* (citing 8 CFR §208.13(c)(2)(ii)); *see also Matter of Annang*, 14 I&N Dec. 502 (BIA 1973).

2.7. Ineligibility for Asylum and Withholding of Removal

2.7.1. Asylum—Discretionary Denials

Even if an asylum applicant establishes statutory eligibility for asylum, *i.e.*, that he or she has a well-founded fear of persecution on account of one or more of the five enumerated grounds, the applicant may be denied asylum as a matter of discretion.[684] An applicant for asylum has the burden of establishing that the favorable exercise of discretion is warranted.[685] In determining whether an applicant merits asylum in the exercise of discretion, the danger of persecution will outweigh all but the most egregious adverse factors.[686] The IJ may consider and evaluate both *favorable* and unfavorable factors.[687] In the absence of any adverse factors, asylum should be granted in the exercise of discretion.[688]

The BIA has held in *Matter of Pula* that the totality of the circumstances and the actions of the applicant should be examined in determining whether a favorable exercise of discretion is warranted.[689] There is no definitive list of factors that must be considered.[690] However, all relevant favorable and adverse factors must be considered and weighed.[691] Among the factors that could be considered are whether the applicant passed through any other countries after leaving his or her home country, whether orderly refugee procedures were available to the applicant in any of those countries, and whether the applicant made any attempts to seek asylum before coming to the United States.[692] In addition, the length of time the applicant remained in a third country and the applicant's living conditions, safety, and potential for long-term residency there are also relevant.[693] Another factor mentioned by the BIA is whether the applicant has relatives legally residing in the United States or other personal ties to this country that motivated the applicant to seek asylum here rather than elsewhere.[694] Also considered is whether the applicant engaged in fraud to circumvent orderly refugee procedures and the seriousness of the fraud.[695] The BIA noted that the "use of fraudulent documents to escape the country of persecution itself is not a significant adverse factor."[696] One court

---

[684] *See* INA §208(b)(1); 8 USC §1158(b)(1); 8 CFR §§208.14(a), (b), 1208.14(a), (b).

[685] *Matter of Shirdel*, 19 I&N Dec. 33, 38 (BIA 1984).

[686] *See, e.g., Matter of Kasinga*, 21 I&N Dec. 357 (BIA 1996) (finding that the applicant, who feared female genital mutilation, merited a favorable exercise of discretion despite her use of a false passport and her failure to seek asylum in Germany or Ghana); *Matter of Pula*, 19 I&N Dec. 467, 474 (BIA 1987).

[687] *Kalubi v. Ashcroft*, 364 F.3d 1134, 1138 (9th Cir. 2004) (emphasis added).

[688] *Matter of Pula*, *supra* note 686, at 474.

[689] *Id.* at 473 (finding that the applicant merited a grant of asylum despite his use of a false document to gain entry to the United States); *see also Matter of H–*, 21 I&N Dec. 337, 348 (BIA 1996); *Matter of A– H–*, 23 I&N Dec. 774, 782–83 (AG 2005).

[690] *Kalubi v. Ashcroft*, *supra* note 687, at 1139.

[691] *Id.*

[692] *Matter of Pula*, *supra* note 686, at 473–74.

[693] *Id.* at 474.

[694] *Id.*

[695] *Id.*

[696] *Id.*

found that the following reasons given by the IJ for denying asylum as a matter of discretion were insufficient as a matter of law: (1) that the applicant embellished aspects of his testimony and (2) that he used a professional smuggler to flee his home country.[697]

At least one court held that *Matter of Pula* had been modified by regulations adopted in 1997, which controlled discretionary denials of asylum on the basis of an applicant's stay or opportunity to stay in a third country.[698] The regulation regarding discretionary denials provided:

> An asylum application may be denied in the discretion of the Attorney General if the [individual] can be removed to a third country which has offered resettlement and in which the [individual] would not face harm or persecution.[699]

The Ninth Circuit held that this regulation precluded the discretionary denial of an asylum claim by an ethnic Armenian from Azerbaijan who had resided in Armenia on and off for a total of 22 months. The court found that the applicant was not offered resettlement in Armenia and that the applicant would face harm if returned to Armenia.[700] According to the Ninth Circuit, an asylum applicant may *not* be denied as a matter of discretion on the basis of a stay in a third country *unless* resettlement has been offered and the individual would not face harm or persecution if returned there.[701] Because the regulation has been rescinded as of 2001, it is unlikely that the court's decision would be applied to future cases. But an argument could be made that it still applies. In commenting on the removal of this regulation, the Department of Justice noted that "while the Department finds that the regulatory provision [8 CFR §208.13(d)] would be fully in keeping with the [INA], it has decided to remove it from the regulations to avoid confusion."[702]

Adverse factors that have resulted in a denial of asylum include criminal convictions,[703] criminal convictions for dangerous or violent crimes,[704] and failure to attend an asylum hearing in another country.[705]

Positive factors to consider include general humanitarian considerations, such as the applicant's tender age or poor health, and whether the applicant can meet the higher burden required for withholding of removal.[706] Additional positive factors include the applicant's legal entry in the United States, an application for asylum submitted while in legal

---

[697] *Huang v. INS*, 436 F.3d 89, 97 (2d Cir. 2006).

[698] *Andriasian v. INS*, 180 F.3d 1033, 1043–46 (9th Cir. 1999).

[699] 8 CFR §208.13(d) (rescinded 2001).

[700] *Andriasian, supra* note 698, at 1045.

[701] *Id.* at 1046.

[702] 65 Fed. Reg. 76121, 76126 (Dec. 6, 2000) (supplementary information).

[703] *Dhine v. Slattery*, 3 F.3d 613, 619–20 (2d Cir. 1993).

[704] *Matter of Jean*, 23 I&N Dec. 373 (AG 2002).

[705] *Matter of Gharadaghi*, 19 I&N Dec. 311, 315 (BIA 1985). *But see Kalubi v. Ashcroft*, 364 F.3d 1134, 1138–39 (9th Cir. 2004) (stating that if an applicant's testimony on a particular issue is not found incredible for purposes of determining whether he is eligible for asylum, it cannot be found incredible for determining whether he merits a favorable exercise of discretion).

[706] *Matter of Pula, supra* note 686, at 474.

status, and severe past persecution.[707] Because this is not an exhaustive list, an asylum applicant should present evidence on any relevant factors that support the favorable exercise of discretion. In *Matter of Chen*, the BIA stated that "*all* other factors, both *favorable* and adverse, should [] be considered."[708] Advocates have submitted evidence regarding employment, certificates of achievement, school records, attendance at English classes, community involvement, and letters from the applicant's church, synagogue, or mosque attesting to membership, volunteer work, and attendance at services.[709]

A grant of asylum may be founded solely on the basis of past persecution in select circumstances and as a matter of discretion.[710] To establish eligibility for asylum based on past persecution alone, an applicant must show "compelling reasons for being unwilling or unable to return to the country arising out of the severity of the past persecution" or that he would suffer other serious harm upon return.[711]

If an applicant is denied asylum solely in the exercise of discretion and the applicant is subsequently granted withholding of removal, thereby precluding the applicant's spouse or minor children from following to join him or her, the denial of asylum must be reconsidered.[712] Factors that should be considered include the reasons for the denial and reasonable alternatives available to the applicant, such as reunification with his or her spouse and minor children in a third country.[713] A mere statement that this regulation was considered, without an explanation, is insufficient.[714] The duty is on the BIA, moreover, to reconsider the denial of asylum after a timely appeal by the applicant.[715]

It is therefore very important to accentuate the positive aspects of the applicant throughout the asylum proceedings. The asylum claim should always include information about the applicant's contributions to the community and to his or her workplace, place of worship, and family.

2.7.2. Mandatory Bars to Both Asylum and Withholding of Removal

Persons seeking asylum or withholding of removal may be barred from receiving and, in some cases, from applying for such relief for reasons outlined below. A bar to asylum is not necessarily a bar to withholding of removal, and vice versa, although several of the bars apply to both forms of relief.[716] Individuals who are barred from both asylum and withhold-

---

[707] *Matter of Soleimani*, 20 I&N Dec. 99, 108 (BIA 1989).

[708] *Matter of Chen*, 20 I&N Dec. 16, 19 (BIA 1989).

[709] *See, e.g.*, *Tamara-Gomez v. Gonzales*, 447 F.3d 343, 348 n.4 (5th Cir. 2006) (noting that the applicants submitted letters from teachers, pastors, and friends confirming that the applicants were model members of the community).

[710] *Matter of H–*, 21 I&N Dec. 337, 339 (BIA 1996) (citing *Matter of B–*, 21 I&N Dec. 66 (BIA 1995)); *Matter of Chen*, 20 I&N Dec. 16, 18 (BIA 1989).

[711] 8 CFR §§208.13(b)(1)(iii), 1208.13(b)(1)(iii). For further discussion, see this chapter, at 2.6.10.

[712] 8 CFR §§208.16(e), 1208.16(e); *see also Huang v. INS*, 436 F.3d 89, 92–93 (2d Cir. 2006).

[713] 8 CFR §§208.16(e), 1208.16(e).

[714] *See Kalubi v. Ashcroft*, 364 F.3d 1134, 1141 (9th Cir. 2004).

[715] *Huang*, *supra* note 712, at 93–94.

[716] For asylum-only bars, see this chapter, at 2.7.3. Withholding-only bars are discussed in this chapter, at 2.7.4.

ing of removal and who fear harm if they are returned to their home countries should consider applying for deferral of removal under the Convention Against Torture.[717]

Particularly Serious Crimes

An individual is ineligible for asylum and withholding of removal if he or she "having been convicted by a final judgment of a particularly serious crime, constitutes a danger to the community of the United States."[718]

In applying this bar, courts have focused on whether the crime is a particularly serious crime and not whether the individual is a danger to the community. The BIA and numerous federal courts have rejected the argument that an adjudicator is required to make a separate determination regarding whether an individual is a danger to the community.[719]

> ➤ **Tip**—Has an asylum applicant been "convicted of" or "arrested" for a crime? One way to find out is to submit a request for his or her rap sheet. The request must be sent to: Federal Bureau of Investigation (FBI), CJIS Division—Record Request, 1000 Custer Hollow Road, Clarksburg, WV 26306. The request should include a cover letter, a fingerprint card (Form FD-258, available at *www.fbi.gov/hq/cjisd/pdf/fpcardb.pdf*), and certified check or money order for $18, payable to the "Treasurer of the United States." If the request is for a couple, family, etc., all persons must sign the cover letter. The fingerprint card must include rolled impressions of all 10 of the applicant's fingerprints taken simultaneously. The card should include the applicant's full name, date of birth, and place of birth, and be signed by the applicant.

Aggravated Felonies

Under IIRAIRA, an individual convicted of an aggravated felony, as defined in INA §101(a)(43) (8 USC §1101(a)(43)), is deemed to have been convicted of a particularly serious crime for purposes of asylum.[720] IIRAIRA also expanded the definition of aggravated felony to include many minor, nonviolent offenses. For example, a theft offense for which the term of imprisonment imposed is one year or more, regardless of any suspension of sentence, is an aggravated felony.[721]

For purposes of withholding of removal, an individual who has been convicted of an aggravated felony (or felonies) for which he or she has been sentenced to an aggregate

---

[717] See ch. 4 for additional information on applying for relief under the Convention Against Torture.

[718] INA §§208(b)(2)(A)(ii), 241(b)(3)(B)(ii); 8 USC §§1158(b)(2)(A)(ii), 1231(b)(3)(B)(ii).

[719] *Choeum v. INS*, 129 F.3d 29, 40–43 (1st Cir. 1997); *Hamama v. INS*, 78 F.3d 233, 240 (6th Cir. 1996); *Ahmetovic v. INS*, 62 F.3d 48, 52–53 (2d Cir. 1995); *Kofa v. INS*, 60 F.3d 1084, 1088–91 (4th Cir. 1995); *Feroz v. INS*, 22 F.3d 225, 227 (9th Cir. 1994); *Mosquera-Perez v. INS*, 3 F.3d 553, 558–59 (1st Cir. 1993); *Martins v. INS*, 972 F.2d 657, 660–61 (5th Cir. 1992); *Crespo-Gomez v. Richard*, 780 F.2d 932, 934–35 (11th Cir. 1986); *Matter of C–*, 20 I&N Dec. 529, 533 (BIA 1992); *Matter of K–*, 20 I&N Dec. 418 (BIA 1991). *But see Matter of Q–T–M–T–*, 21 I&N Dec. 639 (BIA 1996) (Rosenberg, concurring and dissenting) (noting that legislative amendments highlighted a focus by Congress on "endangerment").

[720] INA §208(b)(2)(B)(i); 8 USC §1158(b)(2)(B)(i).

[721] *See* INA §101(a)(43)(G); 8 USC §1101(a)(43)(G).

term of imprisonment of at least five years is considered to have committed a particularly serious crime.[722] Even if an individual received less than a five-year sentence, the adjudicator may find, notwithstanding the sentence imposed, that the individual has been convicted of a particularly serious crime.[723]

In 2002, the attorney general ruled that all drug trafficking offenses, regardless of the sentence imposed, are presumptively particularly serious crimes.[724] The presumption may be rebutted upon a demonstration of "extraordinary and compelling circumstances" that would need to include a showing that the crime involved a small amount of drugs and money; the applicant was only peripherally involved; the absence of violence, organized crime involvement, and terrorist organization involvement; and the absence of harm to juveniles.[725] If the IJ fails to consider these factors, the claim must be remanded for additional findings.[726] In determining whether a state drug offense should be considered a drug trafficking crime falling within the definition of "aggravated felony," the BIA has held that adjudicators must look to decisions from the federal circuit courts.[727]

For withholding cases not involving drug trafficking offenses for which the sentence (or aggregate sentences if more than one offense) is less than five years, the adjudicator must consider nature of the conviction, the sentence imposed, and the circumstances and underlying facts of the crime.[728]

In *Matter of Q–T–M–T–*,[729] a decision applying a provision in the Antiterrorism and Effective Death Penalty Act (AEDPA)[730] that was superseded by IIRAIRA, the BIA found that a categorical classification of per se "particularly serious crimes" did not violate Article 33 of the Refugee Convention.[731]

UNHCR has suggested that the following elements be considered in determining the seriousness of an offense:

> minority of the offender; parole; elapse of five years since the conviction or completion of sentence; general good character (for example, one offense only); of-

---

[722] INA §241(b)(3)(B); 8 USC §1231(b)(3)(B).

[723] *Id.*

[724] *Matters of Y–L–, A–G–, R–S–R–*, 23 I&N Dec. 270 (AG 2002).

[725] *Id.* at 276.

[726] *Lavira v. U.S. Atty. Gen.*, 478 F.3d 158, 166 (3d Cir. 2007).

[727] *Matter of Yanez-Garcia*, 23 I&N Dec. 390 (BIA 2002); *see, e.g., Matter of Santos-Lopez*, 23 I&N Dec. 419 (BIA 2002) (finding that two misdemeanor offenses for marijuana possession under Texas law do *not* fall within the definition of "drug trafficking crime" under federal law).

[728] *See Matter of L–S–*, 22 I&N Dec. 645 (BIA 1999) (conviction for bringing a noncitizen into the United States in violation of the law for which the individual received a three-and-a-half-month sentence is not a particularly serious crime).

[729] *Matter of Q–T–M–T–*, 21 I&N Dec. 639 (BIA 1996).

[730] Antiterrorism and Effective Death Penalty Act of 1996 (AEDPA), Pub. L. No. 104-132, 110 Stat. 1214.

[731] *Matter of Q–T–M–T–*, *supra* note 729, at 651.

fender was merely accomplice; other circumstances surrounding the offense (for example, provocation and self-defense).[732]

Although UNHCR provided these suggestions in the context of whether crimes committed outside of the country of refuge constitute serious nonpolitical crimes, they are also useful in assessing whether a crime is a particularly serious crime.[733]

Whenever possible, because of the harsh consequences that result from a finding that an individual has committed an aggravated felony, an asylum applicant should argue that his or her offense does not constitute an aggravated felony. Particular attention should be paid to the effective dates of any amendments to the aggravated felony definition.[734]

An excellent resource for information regarding the immigration consequences of criminal conduct or convictions is the National Immigration Project of the National Lawyers Guild.[735] Another resource for immigration practitioners grappling with a criminal law question is the National Legal Aid & Defender Association's (NLADA) Defending Immi-

---

[732] G. Goodwin-Gill, *The Refugee in International Law* 107 (2d Ed. 1996).

[733] *See, e.g., Matter of Frentescu*, 18 I&N Dec. 244, 245 (BIA 1982) (holding that a particularly serious crime is more serious than a serious nonpolitical crime).

[734] Although ICE or legacy INS alleged that the individual in each of the following cases had been convicted of an aggravated felony, the courts found that the offense committed did not constitute an aggravated felony: *Lopez v. Gonzales*, 127 S.Ct. 625, 633 (2006) (finding that a drug offense that is a felony under state law but only a misdemeanor under federal law is not an aggravated felony); *Leocal v. Ashcroft*, 543 U.S. 1, 125 S.Ct. 377 (2004) (finding that DUIs under statutes requiring a mens rea of negligence or less are not crimes of violence and, therefore, not aggravated felonies); *Smith v. Gonzales*, 468 F.3d 272, 278 (5th Cir. 2006) (two New York misdemeanor marijuana offenses are not aggravated felonies); *Lee v. Ashcroft*, 368 F.3d 218 (3d Cir. 2004) (filing a false tax return is not an aggravated felony); *Nugent v. Ashcroft*, 367 F.3d 162 (3d Cir. 2004) (theft by deception under Pennsylvania law is not a "theft offense" aggravated felony under the INA); *Jobson v. Ashcroft*, 326 F.3d 367 (2d Cir. 2003) (manslaughter in the second degree under New York law is not an aggravated felony); *Valansi v. Ashcroft*, 278 F.3d 203 (3d Cir. 2002) (embezzlement if no intent to defraud); *Dalton v. Ashcroft*, 257 F.3d 200, 208 (2d Cir. 2001) (a felony DUI under New York law is not an aggravated felony); *Xiong v. INS*, 173 F.3d 601 (7th Cir. 1999) (second-degree sexual assault of a child); *Matter of Sanudo*, 23 I&N Dec. 968 (BIA 2006) (domestic battery under the California Penal Code does not qualify as a crime of violence); *Matter of Gutierrez-Martinez*, A17 945 476 (BIA Mar. 9, 2004), available at *www.lexisnexis.com/practiceareas/immigration/pdfs/web487.pdf* (digital penetration is not rape); *Matter of Santos-Lopez*, 23 I&N Dec. 419 (BIA 2002) (two misdemeanor offenses for marijuana possession); *Matter of Ramos*, 23 I&N Dec. 336 (BIA 2002) (DWI under Massachusetts law); *Matter of Sweetser*, 22 I&N Dec. 709 (BIA 1999) (criminally negligent child abuse); *Matter of Alvarado-Alvino*, 22 I&N Dec. 718 (BIA 1999) (alien smuggling under INA §275(a)); *Matter of [name not provided]*, A43 163 062 (IJ Oct. 3, 2000) (Florence, AZ) (Jeffries, IJ) (domestic violence-related misdemeanors not "crimes of violence"), *reported in* 77 Interpreter Releases 1633 (Nov. 20, 2000). *But see St. John v. Ashcroft*, 43 Fed. Appx. 281 (10th Cir. 2002) (use of false Social Security card is aggravated felony when loss to victims exceeds $10,000); *Matter of Small*, 23 I&N Dec. 448 (BIA 2002) (sexual abuse of a minor under New York law is an aggravated felony); *Matter of Martinez-Recinos*, 23 I&N Dec. 175 (BIA 2001) (perjury under California law is an aggravated felony).

[735] National Immigration Project of the National Lawyers Guild, 14 Beacon Street, Suite 506, Boston, MA 02108; (617) 227-9727; *www.nationalimmigrationproject.org*.

grants Partnership. NLADA's website[736] contains state and federal law reference charts, key decisions, model pleadings, and practice tips.

An applicant convicted of an aggravated felony should also consider seeking various forms of postconviction relief available in criminal court.[737] If, however, a court vacates a conviction for reasons solely related to rehabilitation or immigration hardship, rather than for a procedural or substantive defect in the underlying criminal proceeding, the conviction is not eliminated for immigration purposes.[738]

Nonaggravated Felonies

If an asylum applicant has been convicted of a crime that does not constitute an aggravated felony, the adjudicator will make a determination of whether the crime should be considered a "particularly serious crime."[739] The balancing test to apply in such circumstances is found in *Matter of Frentescu*.[740] The adjudicator should consider such factors as the nature of the conviction, the circumstances and underlying facts of the conviction, the type of sentence imposed, and, most importantly, whether the type and circumstances of the crime indicate that the applicant will be a danger to the community.[741] The BIA in *Frentescu* noted that a "particularly serious crime" is more serious than a "serious nonpolitical crime" and that UNHCR's *Handbook* defines a "serious" crime as "a capital crime or a very grave punishable act."[742] It is also important to note that an adjudication of delinquency is not a conviction for immigration purposes.[743]

In *Matter of Jean*, the attorney general determined that asylum applicants who have committed violent or dangerous crimes should not be granted asylum, even if they are technically eligible, except in extraordinary circumstances.[744] The AG found that an asylum applicant convicted of second-degree manslaughter for killing a 19-month old toddler in her care was ineligible for asylum. According to the AG, extraordinary circumstances in the case of violent or dangerous crimes would include those involving

---

[736] www.nlada.org/Defender/Defender_Immigrants.

[737] *See, e.g.*, M. Kenmore, "Getting Comfortable with Post-Conviction Relief," 1 *Immigration & Nationality Law Handbook* 197 (AILA 2004–05 Ed.).

[738] *Pickering v. Gonzales*, 454 F.3d 525, 526 (6th Cir. 2006) (finding that the "BIA correctly interpreted the law by holding that, if a court vacates an alien's conviction for reasons solely related to rehabilitation or to avoid adverse immigration hardships, rather than on the basis of a procedural or substantive defect in the underlying criminal proceedings, the conviction is not eliminated for immigration purposes").

[739] *Matter of C–*, 20 I&N Dec. 529 (BIA 1992). *But see Alaka v. Att'y Gen. of the U.S.*, 456 F.3d 88, 105 (3d Cir. 2006) (finding that for withholding purposes a crime must be an aggravated felony in order to be classified as a particularly serious crime).

[740] *Matter of Frentescu*, 18 I&N Dec. 244 (BIA 1982) (finding that an applicant sentenced to three months imprisonment and one year probation for a burglary offense was not convicted of a "particularly serious crime").

[741] *Id.* at 245.

[742] *Id.*

[743] *Matter of Devison*, 22 I&N Dec. 1362 (BIA 2000).

[744] *See Matter of Jean*, 23 I&N Dec. 373 (AG 2002).

national security or foreign policy considerations, or cases in which the applicant clearly demonstrates exceptional or extremely unusual hardship.[745]

According to the *Handbook*, "[m]inor offenses punishable by moderate sentences are not grounds for exclusion . . . even if technically referred to as 'crimes' in the penal law of the country concerned."[746] The *Handbook* recommends that the adjudicator balance the degree of persecution feared against the nature of the offense committed and take all relevant factors, including mitigating circumstances, into account.[747] The Supreme Court rejected this approach in the context of assessing whether an offense is a serious nonpolitical crime.[748] Mitigating factors, according to the *Handbook*, include the fact that the applicant has already served his or her sentence or has been granted an amnesty or pardon.[749]

Crimes found by courts to be "particularly serious crimes" include armed robbery,[750] kidnapping and burglary,[751] and aggravated battery.[752] Crimes found *not* to be "particularly serious crimes" have included burglary,[753] assault with a deadly weapon,[754] and possession of cocaine.[755] If the conviction occurred in a criminal proceeding that was demonstrably a "travesty of justice," the conviction can be questioned and the offense may not amount to particularly serious crime.[756]

Serious Nonpolitical Crimes

A person is also ineligible for asylum and withholding of removal if he or she committed a serious nonpolitical crime outside of the United States prior to his or her arrival.[757] Congress intended this bar to be consistent with article 1(F)(b) of the 1951 United Nations Convention Relating to the Status of Refugees.[758] According to UNHCR's *Handbook*, the purpose of this bar "is to protect communities . . . from the danger of admitting a refugee who has committed a serious common crime."[759] It also seeks "to render due justice to a refugee who has committed a common crime (or crimes) of a less se-

---

[745] *Id.* at 385.

[746] *Frentescu, supra* note 740, at 245 (citing UNHCR *Handbook, supra* note 36, at ¶155).

[747] UNHCR *Handbook, supra* note 36, at ¶¶156, 157.

[748] *INS v. Aguirre-Aguirre*, 526 U.S. 415 (1999).

[749] UNHCR *Handbook, supra* note 36, at ¶157.

[750] *Matter of Rodriguez-Coto*, 19 I&N Dec. 208, 210 (BIA 1985).

[751] *Choeum v. INS*, 129 F.3d 29 (1st Cir. 1997).

[752] *Matter of B–*, 20 I&N Dec. 427 (BIA 1991).

[753] *Frentescu, supra* note 740, at 244.

[754] *Matter of Juarez*, 19 I&N Dec. 664, 665 (BIA 1988).

[755] *Matter of Toboso-Alfonso*, 20 I&N Dec. 819 (BIA 1990).

[756] *Doe v. Gonzales*, 484 F.3d 445, 451–52 (7th Cir. 2007) (finding that the applicant's murder conviction in El Salvador should not be a bar to asylum).

[757] INA §§208(b)(2)(A)(iii), 241(b)(3)(B)(iii); 8 USC §§1158(b)(2)(A)(iii), 1231(b)(3)(B)(iii).

[758] *McMullen v. INS*, 788 F.2d 591, 595 (9th Cir. 1986), *overruled in part on other grounds by Barapind v. Enomoto*, 400 F.3d 744, 751 (9th Cir. 2005).

[759] UNHCR *Handbook, supra* note 36, at ¶151.

rious nature or has committed a political offense."[760] Nonserious offenses and political offenses are, therefore, exceptions to this bar to asylum and withholding of removal.

In determining whether a crime outside of the United States falls within the political offense exception, courts have looked to whether "the political aspect of the offense outweighs its common-law character."[761] Whether a crime is of a political character is primarily a question of fact.[762] UNHCR also recommends that an adjudicator balance "the nature of the offense . . . committed by the applicant and the degree of persecution feared," noting that "[i]f a person has well-founded fear of very severe persecution, . . . a crime must be very grave in order to exclude him."[763] The Supreme Court, however, has rejected this approach.[764]

Acts that have constituted serious nonpolitical crimes for purposes of this bar include acts of violence against civilians,[765] a theft offense for which the sentence imposed was 15 years,[766] and a robbery for which the sentence imposed was two years.[767] In contrast, acts that have been found *not* to constitute serious nonpolitical crimes include participation in resistance activities and supporting a coup against a military government.[768]

Participation in Persecution of Others

An individual is barred from both asylum and withholding of removal if he or she "ordered, incited, assisted, or otherwise participated in the persecution of any person on account of race, religion, nationality, membership in a particular social group, or political opinion."[769] A growing number of cases have addressed this so-called persecutor exception.

The Ninth Circuit in *Miranda-Alvarado v. Gonzales* held that in determining whether an applicant engaged in the persecution of others an adjudicator must conduct a particularized evaluation of both personal involvement and purposeful assistance in order to assess culpability.[770] The court upheld the denial of asylum and withholding of

---

[760] *Id.*

[761] *Matter of McMullen*, 19 I&N Dec. 90, 97 (BIA 1984), *aff'd McMullen v. INS (II)*, 788 F.2d 591 (9th Cir. 1986) (finding that the applicant's participation in random acts of violence directed against civilians were acts of an atrocious nature out of proportion to the political goal of achieving a unified Ireland and were not within the political offense exception).

[762] *Id.* (citing *Ornelas v. Ruiz*, 161 U.S. 502 (1896)).

[763] *Handbook* at ¶156.

[764] *INS v. Aguirre-Aguirre*, 526 U.S. 415 (1999).

[765] *McMullen*, *supra* note 761.

[766] *Matter of Ballester-Garcia*, 17 I&N Dec. 592 (BIA 1980), *modified in part by Matter of Gonzalez*, 19 I&N Dec. 682, 685 n.3 (BIA 1988) (modifying this precedent to the extent that it supports the practice of pretermitting asylum applications in cases involving applicants convicted of particularly serious crimes because the nature and gravity of the conviction "is not the only evidence that should be received and considered by an immigration judge or this Board in evaluating whether an otherwise eligible applicant warrants a grant of asylum as a matter of discretion").

[767] *Matter of Rodriguez-Palma*, 17 I&N Dec. 465 (BIA 1980) *modified in part by Matter of Gonzalez*, 19 I&N Dec. 682, 685 n.3 (BIA 1988).

[768] *Dwomoh v. Sava*, 696 F. Supp. 970, 979 (S.D.N.Y. 1988).

[769] INA §§208(b)(2)(A)(i), 241(b)(3)(B)(i); 8 USC §§1158(b)(2)(A)(i), 1231(b)(3)(B)(i).

[770] *Miranda-Alvarado v. Gonzales*, 449 F.3d 915, 927 (9th Cir. 2006).

removal for a Peruvian interpreter who provided Quechua interpretation for the Peruvian military while the military engaged in the torture of suspected members of the Shining Path. The court reasoned that the applicant's actions went beyond mere membership because he was a regular part of the interrogation teams and without him the interrogation could not proceed.[771] Similarly, the Second Circuit in *Xie v. INS* found that the applicant, a driver who transported women to forced abortions, assisted in the persecution of others because his actions contributed directly to the persecution.[772]

In contrast, in *Hernandez v. Reno*,[773] the court found that the BIA had not evaluated all pertinent evidence to determine whether the applicant had engaged in the persecution of others when he participated in the killing of suspected government informants. According to the court, the BIA failed to consider the *involuntariness* of the applicant's involvement with the guerrilla group, the death threats he received, that he shared no persecutory motives with the guerrillas, that he expressed his disagreement to his commander, and that he fled at the first available opportunity.[774] Although the case was remanded, the court concluded that based on the record, the applicant "may be seen to have met his burden of proving that he did not assist or participate in the persecution of others.[775] In contrast, if the applicant willingly engages in acts that he knows are likely to result in torture or death over an extended period of time, he will be barred as a persecutor of others.[776]

The Seventh Circuit has recently looked at the issue of whether mere presence at an event may be considered participation in the persecution of others.[777] In *Doe v. Gonzales*, the court noted that the BIA has used "assist" and "participate" as interchangeable when interpreting the persecutor bar.[778] The court reasoned that the applicant who was present at the murder of Jesuit priests and their cook in El Salvador probably did not assist or participate in the persecutions of others, but remanded the case to the BIA to make findings of fact.[779]

In *Matter of Rodriguez-Majano*,[780] the BIA found that if an applicant's action or inaction furthers persecution in some way, he or she is ineligible for relief. However, if the

---

[771] *Id.* at 928.

[772] *Xie v. INS*, 434 F.3d 136, 143 (2d Cir. 2006) (finding that the applicant "played an active and direct, if arguably minor, role").

[773] *Hernandez v. Reno*, 258 F.3d 806, 813–14 (8th Cir. 2001).

[774] *Id.* at 814.

[775] *Id.* at 815.

[776] *See Ofosu v. McElroy*, 933 F. Supp. 237 (S.D.N.Y. 1995).

[777] *Doe v. Gonzales*, 484 F.3d 445, 449 (7th Cir. 2007).

[778] *Id.* at 450 (citing *Matter of Rodriguez-Majano*, 19 I&N Dec. 811, 814 (BIA 1988) and *Matter of A–H–*, 23 I&N Dec. 774, 784–85 (AG 2005)).

[779] *Id.* at 453.

[780] *Matter of Rodriguez-Majano*, 19 I&N Dec. 811 (BIA 1988).

harm or injury inflicted arose as the natural consequence of civil strife, the harm resulting from such generalized civil strife is not persecution.[781]

According to the BIA, "[m]ere membership in an organization, even one which engages in persecution, is not sufficient to bar one from relief."[782] The person is barred only if his or her action or inaction furthers that persecution in some way.[783] The IJ or BIA must engage in a particularized evaluation in order to determine if the individual's behavior was culpable to such a degree that he or she could be deemed to have assisted or participated in the persecution of others.[784] It is the objective effect of the individual's actions that is controlling.[785] Likewise, acts of self-defense do not constitute persecution for purposes of this bar to asylum and withholding of removal.[786]

Danger to Security of the United States

An applicant is barred from receiving asylum and withholding of removal if "there are reasonable grounds for regarding the [applicant] as a danger to the security of the United States."[787] The withholding of removal section further provides that an applicant who has engaged in terrorist activity (as defined in INA §212(a)(3)(B)) is considered to be an individual with respect to whom there are reasonable grounds for regarding as a danger to the security of the United States.[788]

These bars to asylum and withholding of removal mirror the bar found in Article 33(2) of the 1951 United Nations Convention Relating to the Status of Refugees, which provides that the protection of *nonrefoulement* may be denied to "a refugee whom there are reasonable grounds for regarding as a danger to the security of the country."[789]

In a highly publicized case, Sheik Abdel Rahman, whose followers were linked to the 1993 World Trade Center bombing, was found to be a danger to the security of the

---

[781] *Id.* at 815 (finding that the applicant, who was forced to join the guerrillas and covered them with his weapon while they burned cars, was not a persecutor of others).

[782] *Id.* at 814–15.

[783] *Id.*

[784] *Vukmirovic v. Ashcroft*, 362 F.3d 1247, 1252 (9th Cir. 2004); *Hernandez v. Reno*, 258 F.3d 806, 813 (8th Cir. 2001).

[785] *Laipenieks v. INS*, 750 F.2d 1427, 1437 (9th Cir. 1985) (holding that the INS must show by clear and convincing evidence that the individuals harmed were persecuted solely because of their political opinion (or other enumerated ground)); *Matter of Fedorenko*, 19 I&N Dec. 57, 69–70 (BIA 1984).

[786] *Vukmirovic, supra* note 784, at 1253 (finding that the IJ erred as a matter of law in determining categorically that acts of self-defense constitute persecution under the INA); *see also Chen v. Ashcroft*, 94 Fed. Appx. 930, 2004 WL 835786 (3d Cir. 2004) (finding that a physician who administered anesthesia to women undergoing forced late-term abortions did not properly preserve for appeal the issue of whether he engaged or assisted in the persecution of others).

[787] INA §§208(b)(2)(A)(iv), 241(b)(3)(B)(iv); 8 USC §§1158(b)(2)(A)(iv), 1231(b)(3)(B)(iv).

[788] INA §241(b)(3)(B); 8 USC §1231(b)(3)(B). For a further discussion of terrorist activity, see *infra* this section.

[789] Convention Relating to the Status of Refugees, July 28, 1951, 189 U.N.T.S. 150 (entered into force Apr. 22, 1954), art. 33(2).

United States and ineligible for asylum and withholding of deportation.[790] Other cases of individuals considered to be a danger to the security of the United States include a Palestine Liberation Organization (PLO) member[791] and an anti-Communist Cuban who had been convicted of placing explosives on vessels in Miami, firing upon a Polish vessel, and threatening heads of state.[792]

Terrorism

The September 11, 2001, terrorism attacks on the Pentagon and the World Trade Center have made this bar to asylum a priority for ICE and EOIR. Soon after the attacks, Congress passed the USA PATRIOT Act of 2001, which expanded the already broad definition of terrorist activity and allows for the mandatory detention of "suspected terrorists," even if they have been granted asylum or other relief from removal. More recently, the REAL ID Act amended these provisions further.[793] The terrorism-related bars to asylum are outlined below.[794]

Engaging in Terrorist Activity

An applicant is barred from asylum and withholding of removal if he or she is found to have engaged in, is likely to engage in, or incited terrorist activity.[795] The REAL ID Act of 2005 made several changes to terrorism-related bars to asylum. First, it broadened the INA definitions of "terrorist organization" and "engage in terrorist activity." Second, it expanded the bases for inadmissibility based on a person's support of terror-related activity. Finally, it made terror-related grounds for removability the same as those for inadmissibility.[796]

Individuals who engage in terrorist activity are both inadmissible and removable. "Engaging in terrorist activity" is defined under INA §212(a)(3)(B)(iv) and includes committing, inciting, preparing, and planning terrorist activities, as well as soliciting funds, soliciting individuals, and providing material support for a "terrorist organization" or a terrorist activity.[797] The definition has become stricter under the REAL ID Act, which added that an applicant who provided material support or acted as a solicitor for a person engaged in terrorist activity or a nondesignated terrorist organization has engaged in terrorist activity himself. The change by the REAL ID Act requires an applicant to demonstrate

---

[790] *Ali v. Reno*, 829 F. Supp. 1415, 1434 (S.D.N.Y. 1993); *see also* "Sleuthing Shows Significant Slip-ups in Sheik Saga," 70 *Interpreter Releases* 1202 (Sept. 13, 1993).

[791] *Azzouka v. Meese*, 820 F.2d 585 (2d Cir. 1987).

[792] *Avila v. Rivkind*, 724 F. Supp. 945 (S.D. Fla. 1989). *But see Cheema v. Ashcroft*, 383 F.3d 848 (9th Cir. 2004) (finding that the BIA failed to apply both prongs of its own test of who constitutes a danger to the security of the United States).

[793] *See* INA §212(a)(3)(B); 8 USC §1182(a)(3)(B).

[794] For a more in-depth analysis, *see* R. Germain, "Rushing to Judgment: The Unintended Consequences of the USA PATRIOT Act for Bona Fide Refugees," 16 *Geo. Immigr. L.J.* 505 (2002), and N. Chang & A. Kabat, "Summary of Recent Court Rulings on Terrorism-Related Matters Having Civil Liberty Implications" (2004), available at *www.ccr-ny.org/v2/legal/september_11th/docs/summaryofcases2-4-04.pdf.*

[795] INA §§208(b)(2)(A)(v), 241(b)(3)(B); 8 USC §§1158(b)(2)(A)(v), 1231(b)(3)(B).

[796] INA §§212(a)(3)(B)(i)(I), 237(a)(4)(B); 8 USC §§1182(a)(3)(B)(i)(I), 1227(a)(4)(B).

[797] INA §212(a)(3)(B)(iv); 8 USC §1182(a)(3)(B)(iv).

by clear and convincing evidence that he did not and should not have reasonably known that his material support or solicitation would further either a terrorist activity or organization.[798] Another change is that the definition of "engage in terrorist activity" was expanded to include the provision of material support to a member of a designated terrorist organization; before, a person providing material support to the organization directly was more likely to be found to have engaged in terrorist activity himself.[799]

The REAL ID Act also amended the definition of "terrorist organization."[800] Before the REAL ID Act, a "terrorist organization" could be one designated by the secretary of state or could be a group of two or more individuals, whether organized or not, which engages in terrorist activity. Under the REAL ID Act, the secretary of state may consult with both the secretary of homeland security and the attorney general to designate a group as a terrorist organization, after finding that the organization "engages in terrorist activity."[801] It is important to note that the definition of "engages in terrorist activity" was also expanded by the REAL ID Act, and includes either direct participation or support of terrorist activity, or indirect support of terrorist activity or organizations.[802] In addition, a group that solicits funds or membership for a terrorist activity or terrorist organization, or otherwise provides material support for a terrorist activity or organization, may also be considered a terrorist organization, even if not otherwise designated as such.[803] Any officer, official, representative, or spokesman of the Palestine Liberation Organization is deemed "to be engaged in terrorist activity."[804] For purposes of withholding of removal, a person found to have engaged in terrorist activity is deemed to be a threat to the security of the United States and is barred from relief under the withholding of removal section.[805] "Terrorist activity," as defined by the INA and expanded under the USA PATRIOT Act, includes hijacking, sabotage, hostage taking, assassination, use of biological, chemical, or nuclear weapons, and use of explosives, firearms, or other weapons or dangerous devices (other than for mere personal monetary gain), and the threat, attempt, or conspiracy to do any of these activities.[806]

In one of the few reported cases interpreting this provision, the BIA found that there were "reasonable grounds to believe" that an Iranian national who was a supporter and member of the Mujahedin-e Khalq (MEK) was engaged in or was likely to engage in "terrorist activity."[807] More recently, the Third Circuit denied asylum and withholding of

---

[798] INA §§212(a)(3)(B)(iv)(IV)(cc), (V)(cc), (VI)(dd); 8 USC §§1182(a)(3)(B)(iv)(IV)(cc), (V)(cc), (VI)(dd).

[799] INA §212(a)(3)(B)(iv)(VI); 8 USC §1182(a)(3)(B)(iv)(VI).

[800] INA §212(a)(3)(B)(vi); 8 USC §1182(a)(3)(B)(vi).

[801] INA §212(a)(3)(B)(vi)(II); 8 USC §1182(a)(3)(B)(vi)(II).

[802] INA §212(a)(3)(B)(iv); 8 USC §1182(a)(3)(B)(iv).

[803] INA §212(a)(3)(B)(iv)(IV)–(VI); 8 USC §1182(a)(3)(B)(iv)(IV)–(VI).

[804] INA §212(a)(3)(B)(i)(IX); 8 USC §1182(a)(3)(B)(i)(IX).

[805] See INA §240A(c)(4); 8 USC §1229b(c)(4).

[806] INA §212(a)(3)(B)(iii); 8 USC §1182(a)(3)(B)(iii).

[807] *Matter of U–H–*, 23 I&N Dec. 355 (BIA 2002) (holding that the USA PATRIOT Act does not impose a new and higher standard of proof and that "reasonable grounds to believe" is akin to a "probable cause" standard).

removal to a former member of the Irish National Liberation Army who served as an armed lookout while other members shot at a Royal Ulster Constabulary (RUC) officer.[808] In contrast, an IJ granted asylum to a convicted Irish Republican Army (IRA) bomber, finding that he had engaged in a "political offense" and not "terrorist activity."[809] In reaching this conclusion, the IJ noted that no one had been injured in the bombing and that the applicant's acts were in furtherance of an ongoing conflict to rid Northern Ireland of British rule.[810] In addition, the IJ found that because the RUC had engaged in "atrocious acts" against the Catholic population, the RUC was a "legitimate target" conforming to international law precepts of proportionality, necessity, and respect for the combatant/noncombatant distinction.[811] The IJ reasoned that a "political offense" is "legitimate political violence," whereas terrorism that targets unarmed civilians is "illegitimate political violence."[812] This is one of six Irish deportation cases that were terminated by the AG on December 11, 2000, in order to serve the interests of U.S. foreign policy.[813]

In a series of cases for which they came under criticism, asylum officers found that victims of extortion by rebel groups in Colombia were ineligible for asylum because by paying ransom for kidnapped family members they had provided "material support" to a terrorist organization.[814] The U.S. Committee for Refugees, in a letter to former Attorney General John Ashcroft, stated that it was "ludicrous" to label the payment of ransom or other extortion fees "material support." DHS later reversed the decision in these cases. Under the USA PATRIOT Act, the attorney general or secretary of state may choose, in their unreviewable discretion, not to apply the "material support" bar.[815]

Representative of a Foreign Terrorist Organization

An applicant is barred from asylum if he or she is found to be a representative of a foreign terrorist organization.[816] This ground may be waived by the AG as a matter of discretion if the AG determines that the applicant is not a danger to the security of the United States.[817] As of 2007, there were 40 organizations designated as "foreign terrorist organizations" by the secretary of state, including Al-Qaida, which was added in October 1999. Other designated organizations include: Basque Homeland and Freedom (ETA), Harakat al-Muqawama al-Islamiyya (Hamas), the Liberation Tigers of Tamil Eelam

---

[808] *McAllister v. Attorney General*, 444 F.3d 178, 191 (3d Cir. 2006) (finding the applicant removable for having engaged in terrorist activity).

[809] *Matter of Pearson*, A72 472 870 (IJ Mar. 27, 1997) (New York, NY) (IJ, Williams), at 34.

[810] *Id.* at 33.

[811] *Id.* at 34 (citing *In re Doherty*, 599 F. Supp 270 (S.D.N.Y. 1984)).

[812] *Id.* at 36.

[813] *See* 78 Interpreter Releases 16 (Jan. 3, 2001); *see also Cheema v. Ashcroft*, 372 F.3d 1147, 1155 (9th Cir. 2004), *amended by* 383 F.3d 848 (9th Cir. 2004) (finding that wife's actions of sending money to widows and orphans does not constitute terrorist activity); *Humanitarian Law Project v. Gonzales*, 380 F. Supp. 2d 1134, 1138 (C.D. Cal 2005) (holding that the person must know of the organization's terrorist activities or classification).

[814] *See* INS Statement, Colombian Asylum (Apr. 11, 2001) (on file with author).

[815] INA §212(a)(3)(B)(iv); 8 USC §1182(a)(3)(B)(iv).

[816] INA §212(a)(3)(B)(i)(IV)(aa); 8 USC §1182(a)(3)(B)(i)(IV)(aa).

[817] INA §208(b)(2)(A)(v); 8 USC §1158(b)(2)(A)(v).

(LTTE), the Real IRA, Revolutionary Forces of Colombia (FARC), the Shining Path, and the United Self-Defense Forces of Colombia (AUC).[818] The secretary of state designates organizations as "foreign terrorist organizations" pursuant to his authority under INA §219, 8 USC §1189. A designation under §219 is effective for a period of two years and is subject to limited judicial review. Generally, due process rights do not apply to such organizations because they lack sufficient ties to the United States.[819] In refusing to set aside the designations of the People's Mojahedin Organization of Iran and the LTTE, the D.C. Circuit held that such designations were political judgments, "decisions of a kind for which the Judiciary has neither aptitude, facilities nor responsibilities and have been long held to belong in the domain of political power not subject to judicial intrusion or inquiry."[820]

Representatives of Political or Social Groups That Endorse Terrorist Activity

An applicant is also barred if he or she is a representative of a political, social, or other similar group and his or her public endorsement of acts of terrorist activity undermine U.S. efforts to reduce or eliminate terrorism.[821] Under the USA PATRIOT Act, only the secretary of state could make this determination. However, under the REAL ID Act, the determination may be made by a consular officer, the attorney general, or the secretary of homeland security.[822]

Individuals in Positions of Prominence Who Endorse Terrorist Activity

The USA PATRIOT Act also added an additional bar to asylum for individuals for hold positions of prominence and who "endorse or espouse terrorist activity," or who "persuade others to support terrorist activity or a terrorist organization."[823]

Members of Terrorist Organizations

Despite the expansion of bars to asylum on terrorism grounds, being a member of a terrorist organization is not a per se bar to asylum or withholding of removal. Members of such organizations are, however, inadmissible to the United States and could be removed because of their membership.[824] The BIA has held that "mere membership in an organization, even one which engages in persecution, is not sufficient to bar one from asylum, but only if one's action or inaction furthers that persecution in some way. It is the objective effect of the [individual's] actions which is controlling."[825] Even legacy INS conceded that members of terrorist organizations are eligible for asylum. In 1996, legacy INS issued a detailed memorandum on the terrorism provisions of AEDPA that stated that "members" of

---

[818] See U.S. Department of State, *Country Reports on Terrorism and Patterns of Global Terrorism 2006* (Apr. 2007), ch. 6, available at *www.state.gov/s/ct/rls/crt/2006/82738.htm*.

[819] See, e.g., *32 County Sovereignty Committee v. U.S. Dept. of State*, 292 F.3d 797 (D.C. Cir. 2002).

[820] *People's Mojahedin Organization of Iran v. U.S. Dept. of State*, 182 F.3d 17 (DC Cir. 1999) (citation omitted).

[821] INA §212(a)(3)(B)(i)(IV)(bb); 8 USC §1182(a)(3)(B)(i)(IV)(bb).

[822] INA §212(a)(3)(B)(i)(II); 8 USC §1182(a)(3)(B)(i)(II).

[823] INA §212(a)(3)(B)(i)(VII); 8 USC §1182(a)(3)(B)(i)(VII).

[824] INA §212(a)(3)(B)(i)(V); 8 USC §1182(a)(3)(B)(i)(V).

[825] *Matter of Rodriguez-Majano*, 19 I&N Dec. 811, 814–15 (BIA 1988).

terrorist organizations may still be eligible for asylum, as long as they have not engaged in terrorist activities.[826] Such membership, however, could be a factor in determining whether the applicant merits asylum in the exercise of discretion.[827]

The REAL ID Act made some other changes to the bars to asylum. While the mere membership exception to automatic disqualification for asylum is preserved for inadmissible applicants who are members of designated terrorist organizations, it is not available for removable applicants. INA §208(b)(2)(A)(v) makes applicants who are either inadmissible on specified terrorism grounds[828] or are removable for terrorist activities (under INA §237(a)(4)(B)) ineligible for asylum. Inadmissibility on the grounds of membership in a designated terrorist organization[829] is not among the grounds for denying asylum, nor is inadmissibility on the grounds of endorsement or espousal of terrorist activity.[830] Therefore, the REAL ID Act makes some applicants who are inadmissible because of terror-related activities eligible for asylum relief, but applicants who are removable for terror-related activities are categorically ineligible for asylum.

Although members of designated terrorist organizations may be eligible for asylum, under the REAL ID Act, inadmissibility for mere membership in a *nondesignated* terrorist organization[831] will bar an applicant from eligibility for asylum, unless the applicant can demonstrate by clear and convincing evidence that he or she did not know and should not reasonably have known that the organization was a terrorist organization.[832]

Waiver of Certain Grounds of Inadmissibility

The REAL ID Act gives certain designated officials waiver authority over some of the terrorism-related immigration provisions. Either the secretary of state or secretary of homeland security, in consultation with each other and the attorney general, may waive (1) inadmissibility of representatives of political, social, or other groups that endorse or espouse terrorist activity; (2) inadmissibility of those who endorse or espouse terrorist activity, or persuade others to do so; (3) the application of the definition of "terrorist organization" to groups who constitute one solely because a subgroup has engaged in terrorist activity; and (4) the application of the material support bar.[833]

---

[826] *See* "INS Sends Instructions on Terrorist Exclusions, New Law Amends AEDPA," 73 *Interpreter Releases* 1439 (Oct. 11, 1996).

[827] *See Kalubi v. Ashcroft*, 364 F.3d 1134, 1139 (9th Cir. 2004).

[828] INA §208(b)(2)(A)(v); 8 USC §1158(b)(2)(A)(v), providing that an applicant may be denied asylum for terror-related grounds if he or she is inadmissible under INA §§212(a)(3)(B)(i)(I), (II), (III), (IV), or (VI). The asylum bar does not apply to inadmissible representatives of terrorist organizations or political or social groups that endorse terrorist activity (INA §212(a)(3)(B)(i)(IV)) if the attorney general determines, in his or her discretion, that there are not reasonable grounds for regarding the alien as a danger to the security of the United States. INA §208(b)(2)(A)(v); 8 USC §1158(b)(2)(A)(v).

[829] INA §212(a)(3)(B)(i)(V); 8 USC §1182(a)(3)(B)(i)(V).

[830] INA §212(a)(3)(B)(i)(VII); 8 USC §1182(a)(3)(B)(i)(VII).

[831] INA §212(a)(3)(B)(vi)(III); 8 USC §1182(a)(3)(B)(vi)(III).

[832] INA §§208(b)(2)(A)(v), 212(a)(3)(B)(i)(VI), (vi)(III); 8 USC §§1158(b)(2)(A)(v), 1182(a)(3)(B)(i)(VI), (vi)(III).

[833] INA §212(d)(3)(B)(i); 8 USC §1182(d)(3)(B)(i), waiving the applicability of INA §§212(a)(3)(B)(i)(IV)(bb), (VII), (iv)(VI), and (vi)(III) in certain circumstances.

On April 27, 2007, the secretary of the Department of Homeland Security exercised his waiver authority and decided that the material support bar would not apply to certain individuals who provided material support to certain terrorist organizations while under duress, if the waiver of the bar was warranted by the totality of the circumstances.[834] The eight groups that Secretary Chertoff stated the material support bar will not apply to include: Karen National Union/Karen National Liberation Army (KNU/KNLA), Chin National Front/Chin National Army (CNF/CAN), Chin National League for Democracy (CNLD), Kayan New Land Party (KNLP), Arakan Liberation Party (ALP), Tibetan Mustangs, Cuban Alzados, or the Karenni National Progressive Party (KNPP).[835] The Department of Homeland Security will identify the terrorist organizations that may be included, and USCIS will evaluate whether the material support provided to the organization was provided while under duress.[836] When determining if the applicant for asylum provided material support to a terrorist organization under duress, USCIS will consider certain factors, including whether the applicant could reasonably have avoided providing material support; the severity and type of harm inflicted or threatened; to whom the harm was directed; and the perceived imminence of the harm threatened and the perceived likelihood that harm would be inflicted.[837]

USCIS has issued a memo that serves as guidance on obtaining asylum for applicants who are eligible but for the provision of material support to a terrorist organization.[838] When an applicant who has provided material support to any terrorist organization is otherwise eligible for asylum, the adjudicating asylum officer must fill out the Material Support Exemption Worksheet,[839] regardless of whether the terrorist organization is designated by the secretary of homeland security as exempt. The USCIS Headquarters Asylum Division (HQASM) Training, Research, and Quality (TRAQ) Branch will review all cases for possible applications of exemptions to the material support bar.[840]

> ➢ *Tip*—To access the latest information on material support waivers, visit the Human Rights First website at *www.humanrightsfirst.org/asylum/asylum.htm*.

Alien Terrorist Removal Courts

Changes made to the INA in 1996 allow for special removal proceedings for noncitizen "terrorists" in which the U.S. government has the authority to use classified in-

---

[834] USCIS Fact Sheet, "Concerning the Secretary's Exercise of Authority Under Sec. 212(d)(3)(B)(i)" (May 10, 2007), *published on* AILA InfoNet at Doc. No. 07051164 (*posted* May. 11, 2007).

[835] USCIS Interoffice Memorandum, J. Langlois, "Processing of Asylum Division Cases Involving Material Support" (June 1, 2007), *published on* AILA InfoNet at Doc. No. 07070573 (*posted* July 5, 2007).

[836] *Id.*

[837] 72 Fed. Reg. 26138 (May 8, 2007) (effective Apr. 27, 2007).

[838] *See* USCIS Interoffice Memorandum, *supra* note 835.

[839] *Published on* AILA InfoNet at Doc. No. 07070573 (*posted* Jul. 5, 2007), and available at *www.rcusa.org/uploads///pdfs/MS%20Exemption%20Worksheet,%205-11-07.pdf*.

[840] *See* USCIS Interoffice Memorandum, *supra* note 835.

formation.⁸⁴¹ Under these procedures, applications for removal are submitted *ex parte* and *in camera*, and filed under seal with the removal court. Noncitizens have a right to be present at such a hearing and to be represented by counsel. Any noncitizen financially unable to obtain counsel is entitled to appointed counsel. The noncitizens are not permitted to have access to classified information used against them but are permitted to view unclassified summaries of the information. Noncitizens are not entitled to suppress evidence that they allege was unlawfully obtained, and the Federal Rules of Evidence do not apply in such hearings. Moreover, judges in these proceedings may not consider or grant asylum or withholding of removal claims. To date, the U.S. government has not used these special removal proceedings. ICE and legacy INS have, however, resorted to the use of secret, or classified, evidence in asylum proceedings. The use of such evidence has been successfully challenged in a small number of cases.⁸⁴²

Mandatory Detention of "Suspected Terrorists"

Under a controversial section of the USA PATRIOT Act, the attorney general or deputy attorney general may certify a noncitizen as a "suspected terrorist" if he or she has "reasonable grounds to believe" the individual falls within one of seven security-related grounds of inadmissibility or deportability, or engages in any other activity that endangers the national security of the United States.⁸⁴³ This new section would allow for the detention of noncitizens who seek to overthrow the U.S. government by force or violence, and those who have or are likely to engage in terrorist activity. It also permits the detention of noncitizens who are merely the spouse or child of a "suspected terrorist" or who are mere members of foreign terrorist organizations, without any allegations that they actually engaged in culpable conduct.⁸⁴⁴ The person may be detained even if "relief from removal [is] granted."⁸⁴⁵ A person granted asylum or withholding of removal who has been found not to be a threat to national security could, nevertheless, be detained as a "suspected terrorist." To date, no noncitizens have been subject to detention under this new provision.

2.7.3. Bars to Asylum Only

Prior Asylum Denial

An individual is not eligible to apply for asylum if he or she "has previously applied for asylum and had such application denied," unless he or she is able to demonstrate changed circumstances.⁸⁴⁶ For this bar to apply, the application must have been denied by an IJ or the BIA.⁸⁴⁷ An application may be considered, despite a previous denial, if the applicant "demonstrates to the satisfaction of the [AG] . . . the existence of changed cir-

---

[841] *See* INA §501 *et seq.*; 8 USC §1531 *et seq.*

[842] *See, e.g.*, *Kiareldeen v. Reno*, 71 F. Supp. 2d 402 (D.N.J. 1999).

[843] INA §236A(a)(3)(A); 8 USC §1226a(a)(3)(A).

[844] INA §236A(a)(3)(A); 8 USC §1226a(a)(3)(A).

[845] INA §236A(a)(2); 8 USC §1226a(a)(2).

[846] INA §§208(a)(2)(C), (D); 8 USC §1158(a)(2)(C), (D).

[847] 8 CFR §§208.4(a)(3), 1208.4(a)(3).

cumstances which materially affect the applicant's eligibility for asylum."[848] According to the Asylum Officer Basic Training Course, in order to meet the "to the satisfaction of the [AG]" requirement, the applicant is *not* required to establish beyond a reasonable doubt or by clear and convincing evidence that an exception applies.[849] The applicant need only demonstrate that "it is *reasonable* for the asylum officer to conclude that the exception applies under the circumstances."[850] There is no such bar for an individual seeking withholding of removal.

The asylum regulations provide that changed circumstances may include, but are not limited to:

- Changes in conditions in the applicant's country of nationality or, if the applicant is stateless, country of last habitual residence; or
- Changes in the applicant's circumstances that materially affect the applicant's eligibility for asylum, including changes in applicable U.S. law and activities the applicant becomes involved in outside of the country of feared persecution that place the applicant at risk; or
- In the case of an applicant who had previously been included as a dependent in another applicant's pending asylum application, the loss of the spousal or parent-child relationship to the principal applicant through marriage, divorce, death, or attainment of age 21.[851]

The regulations require that the applicant must apply for asylum within a "reasonable period" given those changed circumstances.[852] If the applicant can establish that he or she did not become aware of the changed circumstances until after they occurred, such delayed awareness must be taken into account in determining what constitutes a "reasonable period."[853]

If the applicant is initiating a new claim by filing a motion to reopen beyond the 90-day period for filing such motions, he or she must demonstrate "changed circumstances arising in the country of nationality or in the country to which deportation has been ordered, if such evidence is material and was not available and could not have been discovered or presented at the previous hearing."[854] This provision appears mistakenly to have omitted changes in the applicant's circumstances and changes in U.S. law, specifically referred to in the regulation noted above.

One-Year Filing Deadline

An individual is barred from applying for asylum if he or she fails to demonstrate "by clear and convincing evidence that the application has been filed within one year after the

---

[848] INA §208(a)(2)(D); 8 USC §1158(a)(2)(D).

[849] AOBTC, Lesson: Eligibility Part IV: Burden of Proof, Standards of Proof, and Evidence (Dec. 5, 2002) at 10, available at *www.rmscdenver.org/aobtc/Elig4burden5dec02lplinks.pdf*.

[850] *Id.* (emphasis in original).

[851] 8 CFR §§208.4(a)(4)(i), 1208.4(a)(4)(i).

[852] 8 CFR §§208.4(a)(4)(ii), 1208.4(a)(4)(ii).

[853] 8 CFR §§208.4(a)(4)(ii), 1208.4(a)(4)(ii).

[854] 8 CFR §1003.2(c)(3)(ii); *see also Matter of J–J–*, 21 I&N Dec. 976 (BIA 1997).

date of [his or her] arrival in the U.S."[855] There is no such bar for an individual seeking withholding of removal. The statute imposing the one-year filing requirement took effect on April 1, 1997.[856] Accordingly, all asylum applicants filing on or after April 1, 1998, have had to demonstrate arrival within a year prior.

According to the AOBTC,[857] testimony alone, when credible, is sufficient to meet the clear and convincing standard.[858] "Clear and convincing evidence" has been defined as a degree of proof that will produce a "firm belief or conviction as to allegations sought to be established."[859] It is higher than the preponderance of evidence standard used in civil cases, but lower than the "beyond a reasonable doubt" standard used in criminal cases.[860]

The one-year period is calculated from the date of the applicant's last arrival in the United States, and the application is considered to be filed on the date it is received or, under certain circumstances, the date it is mailed.[861] For purposes of calculating the one-year period, if the applicant arrived on November 5, 2006, he or she must file on or before November 4, 2007.[862] The Fifth Circuit, in addressing the issue of the mailing date as the filing date, found that an IJ had no legal authority to reject an application that was mailed before the one-year filing deadline based on his interpretation that the regulation allowing this applied only to applications that the agency never received.[863]

There are two exceptions for individuals who fail to file within one year of arrival. Specifically, an application may be considered if filed beyond the one-year deadline if the applicant "demonstrates . . . either the existence of changed circumstances which materially affect the applicant's eligibility for asylum or extraordinary circumstances relating to the delay in filing the application within the [one-year] period."[864] Moreover, the applicant must also demonstrate to the "satisfaction of the [AG]" that he or she qualifies for an exception.[865] According to the Asylum Officer Basic Training Course, in order to meet the "to the satisfaction of the [AG]" requirement, the applicant is *not* required to establish beyond a reasonable doubt or by clear and convincing evidence that an exception applies.[866] The applicant need only demonstrate that "it is *reasonable* for the asylum officer to conclude that the exception applies under the circumstances."[867]

---

[855] INA §208(a)(2)(D); 8 USC §1158(a)(2)(D).

[856] IIRAIRA, *supra* note 10, at §604(c), 110 Stat. 3009-694.

[857] AOBTC, Lesson: One-Year Filing Deadline, *supra* note 496, at 4.

[858] *Id.* at 7.

[859] AOBTC, Lesson: Eligibility Part IV, *supra* note 849, at 9 (citing *Black's Law Dictionary* (5th Ed.)).

[860] *Id.*

[861] *See* 8 CFR §§208.4(a)(2)(ii), 1208.4(a)(2)(ii).

[862] *See* AOBTC, Lesson: One-Year Filing Deadline, *supra* note 496, at 5.

[863] *Nakimbugwe v. Gonzales*, 475 F.3d 281, 285 (5th Cir. 2007).

[864] INA §208(a)(2)(D); 8 USC §1158(a)(2)(D).

[865] 8 CFR §§208.4(a), 1208.4(a).

[866] AOBTC, Lesson: Eligibility Part IV, *supra* note 849, at 10.

[867] *Id.* (emphasis in original).

An additional exception may exist for Salvadoran and Guatemalan ABC class members.[868]

Under the REAL ID Act, federal appeals courts have held that they have jurisdiction to review the BIA's denial of asylum based on failure to meet the one-year deadline if the one-year deadline issue constitutes a constitutional claim or a question of law.[869] The REAL ID Act eliminated habeas corpus jurisdiction over all final orders of deportation, exclusion, and removal; instead, it provides that a petition of review filed with an appropriate court of appeals is the sole and exclusive means for judicial review of such orders.[870] Appeals pending before courts of appeal involving habeas corpus petitions are properly converted to petitions for review and retained by the appropriate court.[871]

Extraordinary Circumstances

The asylum regulations define "extraordinary circumstances" as "events or factors directly related to the failure to meet the 1-year deadline."[872] Such circumstances may excuse the failure to file within the one-year period as long as the applicant files the application "within a reasonable period given those circumstances."[873] The burden of proof is on the applicant to establish to the satisfaction of the AO, the IJ, or the BIA that the circumstances were "not intentionally created by the [applicant] through his or her own action or inaction, that those circumstances were directly related to the [applicant's] failure to file the application within the 1-year period, and that the delay was reasonable under the circumstances."[874]

Under the regulations, "extraordinary circumstances" include, but are not limited to:

(i) Serious illness or mental or physical disability, including any effects of persecution or violent harm suffered in the past, during the 1-year period after arrival;

(ii) Legal disability (*e.g.*, the applicant was an unaccompanied minor or suffered from a mental impairment) during the 1-year period after arrival;

(iii) Ineffective assistance of counsel, provided that:

---

[868] *See* "Settlement Provides Potential Relief for *ABC* Registrants Who Missed Asylum Filing Deadline," 79 *Interpreter Releases* 904 (June 10, 2002).

[869] Pursuant to INA §242(a)(2)(D); 8 USC §1252(a)(2)(D), the courts have found jurisdiction despite the bar on judicial review at INA §208(a)(3); 8 USC §1158(a)(3). *See Lin v. Gonzales*, 190 Fed. Appx. 301 (4th Cir. 2006); *Krisman v. Gonzales*, 199 Fed. Appx. 299 (4th Cir. 2006).

[870] *See Spina v. Dep't of Homeland Sec.*, 70 F.3d 116, 123 (2d Cir. 2006); *Iasu v. Chertoff*, 426 F. Supp. 2d 1124 (D. Cal. 2006); *Walters v. Ashcroft*, 198 Fed. Appx. 78 (2d Cir. 2006); *Restrepo v. Winfrey*, 162 Fed. Appx. 311 (5th Cir. 2006); *Tilley v. Chertoff*, 144 Fed. Appx. 536 (6th Cir. 2005); *see also INS v. St. Cyr*, 533 U.S. 289 (2001); *Kanivets v. Riley*, 320 F. Supp. 2d 297, 300 (E.D. Pa. 2004) (holding that the IJ erred in finding that the asylum application was time barred); American Immigration Law Foundation (AILF) Practice Advisory, Judicial Review Provisions of the REAL ID Act (June 7, 2005), available at *www.ailf.org/lac/lac_pa_realid_051205_final.pdf*.

[871] REAL ID Act of 2005, *supra* note 14, at §106(c), 119 Stat. 311.

[872] 8 CFR §§208.4(a)(5), 1208.4(a)(5).

[873] 8 CFR §§208.4(a)(5), 1208.4(a)(5).

[874] 8 CFR §§208.4(a)(5), 1208.4(a)(5).

(A) The alien files an affidavit setting forth in detail the agreement that was entered into with counsel with respect to the actions to be taken and what representations counsel did or did not make to the respondent in this regard;

(B) The counsel whose integrity or competence is being impugned has been informed of the allegations leveled against him or her and given an opportunity to respond; and

(C) The alien indicates whether a complaint has been filed with appropriate disciplinary authorities with respect to any violation of counsel's ethical or legal responsibilities, and if not, why not;

(iv) The applicant maintained Temporary Protected Status, lawful immigrant or non-immigrant status, or was given parole, until a reasonable period before the filing of the asylum application;

(v) The applicant filed an asylum application prior to the expiration of the 1-year deadline, but that application was rejected by the Service as not properly filed, was returned to the applicant for corrections, and was refiled within a reasonable period thereafter;

(vi) The death or serious illness or incapacity of the applicant's legal representative or a member of the applicant's immediate family.[875]

A BIA precedent decision addressing "extraordinary circumstances" is *Matter of Y–C–*.[876] In *Y–C–*, the BIA found that an applicant who entered the United States as an unaccompanied minor and who failed to file his application within one year of his arrival established that such failure was due to "extraordinary circumstances." The BIA set forth the following three-part test: the applicant (1) "must establish the existence or occurrence of the extraordinary circumstance;" (2) "must show that those circumstances directly relate to his failure to file the application within the 1-year period;" and (3) "must demonstrate that the delay in filing was reasonable under the circumstances."[877] In finding that the applicant had met this test, the BIA noted that the applicant was 15 years old when he arrived in the United States as an unaccompanied minor, that he remained in the status of unaccompanied minor throughout the one-year period, that he was in legacy INS custody for one year, that five months after his release an IJ rejected his application for asylum, and that the application that was finally accepted by the IJ was filed within one year of his release from INS custody.[878] In another important case, *Mukamusoni v. Ashcroft*, the First Circuit affirmed the IJ's decision that a woman from Rwanda with post-traumatic stress disorder had an "extraordinary circumstance" for failing to file her asylum application in a timely fashion.[879] Finally, in an unpublished decision, the BIA found that a woman from the Gambia who had been subjected to female genital mutilation at 15 years

---

[875] 8 CFR §§208.4(a)(5), 1208.4(a)(5).

[876] *Matter of Y–C–*, 23 I&N Dec. 286 (BIA 2002).

[877] *Id.* at 288.

[878] *Id.*; *see also El Himri v. Ashcroft*, 378 F.3d 932, 936 (9th Cir. 2004) (noting that the claim of a minor living with his parents was not time-barred).

[879] *Mukamusoni v. Ashcroft*, 390 F.3d 110, 117 (1st Cir. 2004).

of age and who suffered abuse at the hands of her spouse met the extraordinary circumstances exception.[880]

With regard to maintaining lawful immigrant or nonimmigrant status prior to filing the asylum application, legacy INS took the position that an individual should file an asylum application as soon as possible after the expiration of his or her valid status. It further maintained that waiting six months was "clearly" not reasonable and that shorter periods of time should be considered on a case-by-case basis.[881]

Other possible extraordinary circumstances are addressed in the AOBTC's lesson plan on the one-year filing deadline. The lesson plan notes that extraordinary circumstances may include "severe family or spousal opposition, extreme isolation within a refugee community, profound language barriers, or profound difficulties in cultural acclimatization."[882]

Changed Circumstances

According to regulations, "changed circumstances," which will excuse a late filing of an asylum application, may include but are not limited to:

- Changes in conditions in the applicant's country of nationality or, if the applicant is stateless, country of last habitual residence; or
- Changes in the applicant's circumstances that materially affect the applicant's eligibility for asylum, including changes in applicable U.S. law and activities the applicant becomes involved in outside of the country of feared persecution that place the applicant at risk; or
- In the case of an applicant who had previously been included as a dependent in another applicant's pending asylum application, the loss of the spousal or parent-child relationship to the principal applicant through marriage, divorce, death, or attainment of age 21.[883]

Types of changed circumstances also are addressed in the AOBTC.[884] The lesson plan on the one-year filing deadline notes that changed circumstances may include:

- A change of government that is now hostile to the applicant's profession, such as journalism;
- The applicant's involvement in political organizing or other activities in the United States that are critical of the applicant's government;

---

[880] *Matter of [name not provided]*, *[file no. redacted]* (BIA Aug. 8, 2007) (noting that applicant was currently undergoing treatment for depression and post-traumatic stress disorder), available at *http://bibdaily.com/pdfs/Gambia%20FGM%20excep.%20circ.%20BIA%208-8-06.pdf*.

[881] *See* 65 Fed. Reg. 76121, 76123–24 (Dec. 6, 2000) (supplementary information); *see also* AOBTC, Lesson: One-Year Filing Deadline, *supra* note 496, at 18–20 (noting that delayed awareness, illness, and difficulty in obtaining legal assistance are factors in determining reasonableness).

[882] AOBTC, Lesson: One-Year Filing Deadline, *supra* note 496, at 17. For an excellent overview of the one-year deadline provision, see M. Pistone and P. Schrag, "The New Asylum Rule: Improved But Still Unfair," 16 *Geo. Immigr. L.J.* 1 (2001).

[883] 8 CFR §§208.4(a)(4)(i), 1208.4(a)(4)(i).

[884] AOBTC, Lesson: One-Year Filing Deadline, *supra* note 496, at 8–11.

- The applicant's conversion from one religion to another, or abandonment of religion altogether;
- Recent antagonism in the applicant's country toward the applicant's race or nationality; and
- Threats against the applicant's family members living abroad.[885]

The regulations require that the applicant must apply for asylum within a "reasonable period" given those changed circumstances.[886] If the applicant can establish that he or she did not become aware of the changed circumstances until after they occurred, such delayed awareness must be taken into account in determining what constitutes a "reasonable period."[887]

In a 2004 decision by former Attorney General Ashcroft, in which he overturned a BIA summary affirmance of an IJ decision denying asylum to a Lebanese applicant, the attorney general elaborated on the "changed circumstances" exception.[888] The applicant entered the United States on a visitor's visa in 1986, but did not apply for asylum until 13 years later, in 1999. Interestingly, two of the changes relied on by the AG as "changed circumstances" sufficient to merit an exception to the one-year deadline occurred a year or more after the applicant actually applied for asylum.[889] The changed circumstances were (1) withdrawal of the Israeli Defense Forces from Lebanon in 2000; (2) the increased influence and autonomy of Hezbollah, and of the Syrian government and its proxies within Lebanon, and (3) the addition of Hezbollah, on Nov. 21, 2001, to the list of terrorist organizations covered by Executive Order No. 13224, which blocked access to its assets.[890] More recently, the Ninth Circuit found that a female Egyptian asylum applicant failed to establish changed personal circumstances after her arrival in the United States, finding that her past harassment in Egypt was on account of her political views, so that her outspokenness in the United States was not a change in circumstances.[891] Similarly, the Seventh Circuit found that an applicant from Zimbabwe failed to show changed circumstances, since the Mugabe government and oppressive climate in Zimbabwe were the same in 2006 as they were when the applicant arrived in the United States in 1999.[892]

If the applicant is initiating a new claim by filing a motion to reopen beyond the 90-day period for filing such motions, he or she must demonstrate "changed circumstances arising in the country of nationality or in the country to which deportation has been ordered, if such evidence is material and was not available and could not have been discovered or presented

---

[885] *Id.* at 9–10; *see also* this chapter, at 2.5.11.

[886] 8 CFR §§208.4(a)(4)(ii), 1208.4(a)(4)(ii).

[887] 8 CFR §§208.4(a)(4)(ii), 1208.4(a)(4)(ii); *see also Kanivets v. Riley*, 320 F. Supp. 2d 297, 300 (E.D. Pa. 2004) (remanding one-year deadline issue because IJ failed to consider arguments regarding changed circumstances and delayed awareness).

[888] *See Matter of Marshi*, A26 980 386 (AG Feb. 13, 2004), *published on* AILA InfoNet at Doc. No. 04021390 (*posted* Feb. 13, 2004).

[889] *Id.* at 7–8.

[890] *Id.*

[891] *Ramadan v. Gonzales*, 479 F.3d 646, 657 (9th Cir. 2007) (en banc).

[892] *Mabasa v. Gonzales*, 455 F.3d 740 (7th Cir. 2006).

at the previous hearing."[893] This provision appears mistakenly to have omitted changes in the applicant's circumstances and changes in U.S. law, specifically referred to in the regulations noted above.

Firm Resettlement

An individual is barred from receiving asylum if it is determined that the individual was "firmly resettled" in another country prior to arriving in the United States.[894] Firm resettlement, however, is not a bar to withholding of removal.

An applicant is considered to be "firmly resettled" if "prior to arrival in the United States, he [or she] entered into another country with, or while in that country received, an offer of permanent resident status, citizenship, or some other type of permanent resettlement."[895] An applicant is not considered to be firmly resettled if the applicant establishes:

- That his or her entry into that country was a necessary consequence of his or her flight from persecution, that he or she remained in that country only as long as was necessary to arrange onward travel, and that he or she did not establish significant ties in that country; or

- That the conditions of his or her residence in that country were so substantially and consciously restricted by the authority of the country of refuge that he or she was not in fact resettled.[896]

In making this last determination, the adjudicator must consider:

- The conditions under which other residents of the country live;
- The type of housing, whether permanent or temporary, made available to the refugee;
- The types and extent of employment available to the refugee;
- The extent to which the refugee received permission to hold property; and
- The extent to which the refugee enjoyed other rights and privileges, such as travel documentation that includes a right of entry and/or re-entry, education, public relief, or naturalization, ordinarily available to others resident in the country.[897]

According to the Ninth Circuit, DHS must first make a threshold showing that the asylum applicant received an offer of some type of official status permitting the applicant to reside in a third country indefinitely.[898] This showing may be made by direct or circumstantial evidence.[899] Once DHS has produced some evidence, the burden shifts to the applicant to show that he or she falls within one of the regulatory exceptions to firm resettlement. A similar approach also has been used by the First,[900] Third,[901] Eighth,[902] and

---

[893] 8 CFR §1003.2(c)(3)(ii); *see also Matter of J–J–*, 21 I&N Dec. 976 (BIA 1997).

[894] INA §208(b)(2)(A)(vi), 8 USC §1158(b)(2)(A)(vi).

[895] 8 CFR §§208.15, 1208.15.

[896] 8 CFR §§208.15, 1208.15.

[897] 8 CFR §§208.15, 1208.15.

[898] *Maharaj v. Gonzales*, 450 F.3d 961, 964 (9th Cir. 2006) (en banc).

[899] *Id.*

[900] *Salazar v. Ashcroft*, 359 F.3d 45, 50–51 (1st Cir. 2004).

Tenth[903] Circuits. Other courts have adopted a totality of the circumstances approach.[904] Courts, however, have refused to allow applicants who have severed ties with countries that offered permanent status to bootstrap a claim for asylum on the rationale that they can no longer return to the country that offered them status.[905]

An applicant who was accepted as a refugee by Denmark and who resided in the country for six months before coming to the United States was found to be ineligible for asylum.[906] The court relied on the fact that Denmark issued her a passport and that her family was residing in Denmark as refugees.[907] In addition, the court rejected her argument that she met the exception under 8 CFR §1208.15(a), *i.e.*, that she did not establish "significant ties" in Denmark and only remained there "as long as was necessary to arrange onward travel."[908] The court noted that when she was questioned regarding her reasons for leaving Denmark, she stated that she wanted to be with her husband, who was studying in the United States.[909] The court also held that a declaration by the Danish authorities that they were no longer obligated to accept the applicant into their country did not undermine the firm resettlement determination.[910] The court noted that the regulations look only to the applicant's status prior to his or her entry into the United States and thus preclude an applicant from "bootstrapping an asylum claim by unilaterally severing her existing ties with a third country after arriving in the U.S."[911] Other reported cases finding an individual has been firmly resettled include: *Matter of K–R–Y– and K–C–S–*,[912] *Sultani v. Gonzales*,[913] *Nahrvani v. Gonzales*,[914] *Mussie v. INS*,[915] *Vang v. INS*,[916] and *Abdalla v. INS*.[917]

---

[901] *Abdille v. Ashcroft*, 242 F.3d 477 (3d Cir. 2001).

[902] *Rife v. Ashcroft*, 374 F.3d 606, 611 (8th Cir. 2004).

[903] *Elzour v. Ashcroft*, 378 F.3d 1143, 1151 (10th Cir. 2004).

[904] *See, e.g., Sall v. Gonzales*, 437 F.3d 229, 232 (2d Cir. 2006).

[905] *Firmansjah v. Gonzales*, 424 F.3d 598, 604 (7th Cir. 2005); *Abdalla v. INS*, 43 F.3d 1397, 1400 (10th Cir. 1994).

[906] *Ali v. Reno*, 237 F.3d 591 (6th Cir. 2001).

[907] *Id.* at 595.

[908] *Id.*

[909] *Id.*

[910] *Id.* at 596.

[911] *Id.; see also Salazar v. Ashcroft*, 359 F.3d 45, 51 (1st Cir. 2004) (finding that the IJ's determination that the applicant was firmly resettled in Venezuela based on a residency stamp in his passport, residence there for one year, and several recent trips to Venezuela with that passport, as well as his marriage to a Venezuela citizen, was supported by substantial evidence); *Desta v. Ashcroft*, 329 F.3d 1179, 1187 (10th Cir. 2003) (petition for review denied where the asylum applicants lived for 18 months in Canada, received landed immigrant status there, and their son's birth there made him a Canadian citizen); *Abdille v. Ashcroft*, 242 F.3d 477, 480 (3d Cir. 2001) (holding that a prime element in firm resettlement inquiry is existence *vel non* of a government offer of permanent status; court rejected totality of circumstances approach and remanded to BIA for consideration of South African law). *But see Diallo v. Ashcroft*, 381 F.3d 687 (7th Cir. 2004) (holding that the IJ erred in finding Mauritanian applicant had firmly resettled in Senegal because IJ failed to determine whether the applicant received an offer of permanent resettlement there).

[912] *Matter of K–R–Y– and K–C–S–*, 24 I&N Dec. 133 (BIA 2007) (finding applicants who became citizens of South Korea and had significant ties there were firmly resettled in South Korea).

In contrast, the Ninth Circuit has rejected a finding by an IJ that a Somali asylum applicant was firmly resettled in Ethiopia where the evidence credited by the IJ established that although she remained in Ethiopia for five years, she had no right to remain there permanently.[918] The court in that case found that the IJ erred in applying the *Cheo* presumption, which allows an adjudicator to presume that an applicant is firmly resettled if she has resided for a number of years in a third country without being bothered.[919] The court held that because the applicant offered evidence, which the IJ found credible, that she was not firmly resettled, the *Cheo* presumption did not apply.[920]

In cases decided before firm resettlement was a mandatory bar to asylum, courts considered the issue of firm resettlement in determining whether an applicant merited asylum in the exercise of discretion. In *Matter of D–L– & A–M–*,[921] the BIA denied asylum as a matter of discretion to Cuban nationals who had lived and worked in Spain for six years as lawful temporary residents with the option to become permanent residents of that country.[922] In contrast, the BIA found, in *Matter of Soleimani*,[923] that an Iranian Jew who had resided in Israel for 10 months prior to her arrival in the United States was not firmly resettled in Israel. During her stay in Israel, she lived with her grandmother, studied Hebrew, and recuperated from an illness, but did not work or seek any benefits from the government. The BIA noted that the applicant had closer relatives in the United States and that her arrival in the United States was "reasonably proximate to her flight from Iran."[924]

---

[913] *Sultani v. Gonzales*, 455 F.3d 878, 883 (8th Cir. 2006) (finding a family from Afghanistan granted refugee status in Australia was firmly resettled in Australia).

[914] *Nahrvani v. Gonzales*, 399 F.3d 1148, 1150 (9th Cir. 2005) (finding that an Iranian national was firmly resettled in Germany where he was offered permanent residency, married a German citizen, and worked and traveled freely in Germany).

[915] *Mussie v. INS*, 172 F.3d 329 (4th Cir. 1999) (finding firm resettlement despite incidents of racial taunting and threats, because applicant was granted asylum in Germany, resided there for six years, and received language schooling, transportation, rent assistance, travel documentation, and food from the German government).

[916] *Vang v. INS*, 146 F.3d 1114 (9th Cir. 1998) (because applicant lived in France for 12 years with refugee status).

[917] *Abdalla v. INS*, 43 F.3d 1397 (10th Cir. 1994) (because applicant lived in United Arab Emirates for 20 years with residence visa).

[918] *Ali v. Ashcroft*, 394 F.3d 780, 782 (9th Cir. 2005).

[919] *Id.* at 790 (citing *Cheo v. INS*, 162 F.3d 1227, 1229 (9th Cir. 1998)).

[920] *Id.*; *see also Makadji v. Gonzales*, 470 F.3d 450, 452 (2d Cir. 2006) (finding IJ's determination that Mauritanian applicant was firmly resettled in Mali was not supported by substantial evidence and that IJ improperly placed burden of proof on the applicant to show he was not firmly resettled).

[921] *Matter of D–L– & A–M–*, 20 I&N Dec. 409 (BIA 1991).

[922] *See also Farbakhsh v. INS*, 20 F.3d 877 (8th Cir. 1994) (finding that an Iranian's four-year residence in Spain under a pending application for refugee status reasonably constituted firm resettlement even though he had no permission to work or study).

[923] *Matter of Soleimani*, 20 I&N Dec. 99 (BIA 1989).

[924] *Id.* at 107.

Safe Third Country

An applicant is barred from applying for asylum if he or she may be removed to a "safe third country."[925] The removal must be "pursuant to a bilateral or multilateral agreement," and must be to a country other than the individual's home country or, in the case of a stateless person, other than the country of the individual's last habitual residence.[926] The "safe third country" must also be a country where the individual's "life or freedom would not be threatened on account of race, religion, nationality, membership in a particular social group, or political opinion," and where the individual would have "access to a full and fair procedure for determining a claim to asylum or equivalent temporary protection."[927] The attorney general may waive this bar upon finding that it is in the "public interest" for the individual to receive asylum in the United States.[928] Under the Homeland Security Act of 2002, this waiver authority would extend to the DHS secretary and other DHS officials.[929]

The United States signed a safe-country agreement with Canada on December 5, 2002.[930] The agreement allows the United States to return "arriving aliens" to Canada, if that was their country of last presence, to seek protection under Canadian law, rather than under U.S. law. Similarly, the agreement allows Canada to return asylum-seekers to the United States, if the United States was their country of last presence.

Final U.S. regulations implementing this agreement were published on November 29, 2004.[931] The regulations became effective on December 29, 2004.[932] Exceptions to the agreement include: citizens of Canada, asylum-seekers with close relatives in the United States, unaccompanied minors, holders of valid visas or admission documents to the United States, and persons for whom a determination has been made by the USCIS director that it is in the public interest to allow them to seek asylum, withholding, or Convention Against Torture (CAT) relief in the United States.[933] The regulations allow for not only asylum applicants, but also applicants for withholding of removal and CAT relief, to be subject to the safe-third-country bar if none of the exceptions apply.[934] In addition, the regulations also set forth procedures for stowaways and noncitizens subject to expedited removal.[935]

---

[925] INA §208(a)(2)(A); 8 USC §1158(a)(2)(A).

[926] INA §208(a)(2)(A); 8 USC §1158(a)(2)(A).

[927] INA §208(a)(2)(A); 8 USC §1158(a)(2)(A).

[928] INA §208(a)(2)(A); 8 USC §1158(a)(2)(A).

[929] *See* Homeland Security Act of 2002, Pub. L. No. 107-296, §§456, 1512, 1517, 116 Stat. 2135, 2200, 2310, 2311.

[930] Agreement Between the Government of the United States and the Government of Canada For Cooperation in the Examination of Refugee Status Claims from Nationals of Third Countries (Dec. 5, 2002), available at *www.uscis.gov/files/article/appendix-c.pdf*.

[931] 69 Fed. Reg. 69479 (Nov. 29, 2004).

[932] *Id.*

[933] 8 CFR §208.30(e)(6)(iii).

[934] 8 CFR §1240.11(g)(4).

[935] 8 CFR §§208.30, 1208.30.

➢ Canadian regulations implementing the Agreement were published in the Canada Gazette.[936] Some notable exceptions include unaccompanied minors, individuals subject to the death penalty in their home countries, and countries to which Canada has temporarily suspended removals (currently Afghanistan, Burundi, Democratic Republic of Congo, Haiti, Iraq, Liberia, Rwanda, and Zimbabwe).

2.7.4. Bars to Withholding Only

While the following two bars apply only to withholding of removal, it is reasonable to conclude that such individuals would be denied asylum as a matter of discretion or would be subject to other bars such as the serious nonpolitical crime bar.

Participation in Nazi Persecution

An applicant is barred from withholding of removal if, under the direction of or in cooperation with the Nazi government of Germany, he or she ordered, incited, assisted, or otherwise participated in the persecution of any person because of race, religion, national origin, or political opinion, during the period beginning March 23, 1933, and ending on May 8, 1945.[937]

Participation in Genocide

An applicant is barred from withholding if he or she has engaged in conduct that is defined as genocide for purposes of the International Convention on the Prevention and Punishment of Genocide.[938] Genocide is defined in the convention as "any of the following acts committed with intent to destroy, in whole or in part, a national, ethnic, racial or religious group, such as: killing members of the group; causing serious bodily or mental harm to members of the group; deliberately inflicting on the group conditions of life calculated to bring about its physical destruction in whole or in part; imposing measures intending to prevent births within the group; forcibly transferring children from the group to another group."[939]

2.8. STANDARD OF REVIEW

2.8.1. Before the BIA

The Board of Immigration Appeals is the appellate body authorized to review asylum and withholding of removal decisions made by immigration judges.[940] The BIA does not,

---

[936] Regulations Amending the Immigration and Refugee Protection Regulations, SOR/2004-217 (Can.), 138 C. Gaz. no. 22 (Nov. 3, 2004), available at *http://canadagazette.gc.ca/partII/2004/20041103/html/sor217-e.html*. For an overview of the exceptions that apply to asylum-seekers seeking entry into Canada, see the Canadian Council for Refugees website, *www.ccrweb.ca/eng/engfront/frontpage.htm*.

[937] INA §241(b)(3)(B); 8 USC §1231(b)(3)(B) (referencing INA §237(a)(4)(D)).

[938] INA §241(b)(3)(B); 8 USC §1231(b)(3)(B).

[939] International Convention on the Prevention and Punishment of Genocide (Dec. 9, 1948), art. II, 78 U.N.T.S. 277 (entered into force Jan. 12, 1951).

[940] *See* 8 CFR §1003.1.

however, have the authority to review credible-fear determinations made by IJs.[941] Nor does the BIA have authority to review withholding of removal decisions made by asylum officers during the reinstatement-of-removal process.[942]

Under regulations issued in 2002, the BIA applies a "clearly erroneous" standard of review to all factual determinations by IJs, including to determinations on credibility of testimony.[943] This standard applies only to appeals filed on or after the effective date of the new regulations, *i.e.*, September 25, 2002.[944] It should be noted that the BIA still employs the "de novo" standard of review for all questions of law, discretion, and judgment.[945] In addition, all questions arising in appeals from decisions by DHS officers may be reviewed "de novo."[946]

The BIA also, at times, employs an abuse-of-discretion standard.[947] The BIA has noted, however, that it does not employ an abuse-of-discretion standard when reviewing discretionary determinations by an IJ, but rather relies upon its "own independent judgment."[948]

Prior to the issuance of the 2002 regulations, an IJ's findings with respect to the credibility of witnesses was given considerable deference.[949] Although the BIA could defer to the IJ's credibility determination, it was not required to do so and did not have to defer when such deference was not supported by its own independent review of the record.[950] On occasion, the BIA had reversed an IJ's credibility determination.[951] Now the BIA must, by regulation, apply a "clearly erroneous" standard.[952] If the BIA sua sponte raises concerns about an applicant's credibility, it has to give the applicant an opportunity to offer an explanation of any perceived inconsistencies.[953] Failure to do so is a violation of due process.[954]

The BIA lacks jurisdiction to rule upon the constitutionality of the INA and the regulations,[955] but where possible it must construe statutes to achieve results that are consistent, rather than in conflict, with constitutional protections.

---

[941] INA §235(b)(1)(B)(iii); 8 USC §1225(b)(1)(B)(iii). *See* ch. 5.

[942] INA §241(a)(5); 8 USC §1231(a)(5). *See* ch. 3.

[943] *See* 8 CFR §1003.1(d)(3); *Matter of S–H–*, 23 I&N Dec. 462, 464 (BIA 2002).

[944] 8 CFR §1003.3(f).

[945] 8 CFR §1003.1(d)(3)(ii).

[946] 8 CFR §1003.1(d)(3)(iii).

[947] *See Yepes-Prado v. INS*, 10 F.3d 1363, 1367, 1372 n.18 (9th Cir. 1993) (in which the court criticized the BIA for its inconsistent use of de novo and abuse-of-discretion standards).

[948] *Matter of Burbano*, 20 I&N Dec. 872 (BIA 1994).

[949] *See, e.g., Matter of A–S–*, 21 I&N Dec. 1106 (BIA 1998); *Matter of Kulle*, 19 I&N Dec. 318 (BIA 1985); *Matter of Boromand*, 17 I&N Dec. 450, 452 (BIA 1980).

[950] *Senathirajah v. INS*, 157 F.3d 210, 216 (3d Cir. 1998); *Matter of S–A–*, 22 I&N 1328, 1331 (BIA 2000).

[951] *See, e.g., Matter of S–A–*, *supra* note 950, at 1331; *Matter of B–*, 21 I&N Dec. 66, 72 (BIA 1995).

[952] *See* 8 CFR §1003.1(d)(3).

[953] *Stoyanov v. INS*, 172 F.3d 731, 735 (9th Cir. 1999).

[954] *Id.*; *see also Campos-Sanchez v. INS*, 164 F.3d 448, 450 (9th Cir. 1998).

[955] *See, e.g., Matter of L–S–J–*, 21 I&N Dec. 973, 974 (BIA 1997).

2.8.2. Before the Attorney General

The attorney general has the authority to review BIA cases referred to him or her under 8 CFR §1003.1(h)(1). The AG's review of BIA decisions is *de novo* and he or she retains full authority to receive additional evidence.[956]

2.8.3. Before the Federal Courts

Asylum and withholding of removal claims may be reviewed by the federal courts in several ways. Review of removal orders in federal courts of appeal is perhaps the most common avenue of review.[957] When reviewing removal orders, the court of appeals considers only the decision of the BIA, unless the BIA has merely adopted the IJ's decision or reviewed it for abuse of discretion, rather than conducting de novo review.[958] Recently, reviewing courts have harshly criticized the poor quality of decisions from IJs and the BIA and, in several circuits, have resorted to recommending that remanded cases be sent to immigration judges other than the ones who initially heard the claim.[959]

AEDPA and IIRAIRA restricted the availability of judicial review of removal orders. They restricted judicial review of decisions relating to expedited removal of arriving aliens, certain denials of discretionary relief, and removal orders for individuals removable for certain criminal offenses.[960] However, the Supreme Court held that there is a strong presumption in favor of judicial review of administrative actions, and that eliminating any judicial review, without any substitute for review of questions of law, would raise constitutional issues.[961] Therefore, cases decided under AEDPA and IIRAIRA allowed judicial review of removal orders relating to expedited removal, certain denials of discretionary relief, and orders for aliens removable for certain criminal offenses insofar as they raised claims of constitutional or statutory error.[962]

---

[956] *See Matters of Y–L–, A–G–, R–S–R–*, 23 I&N Dec. 270, 270 n.1 (AG 2002); *Deportation Proceedings of Joseph Patrick Thomas Doherty*, 12 Op. O.L.C. 1, 4 (1988).

[957] *See generally* INA §242; 8 USC §1252.

[958] *See, e.g., Girma v. INS*, 283 F.3d 664, 666 (5th Cir. 2002); *Lata v. INS*, 204 F.3d 1241 (9th Cir. 2000) (because the BIA did not review the case de novo, the court reviewed the decision of the IJ); *De Leon-Barrios v. INS*, 116 F.2d 391, 393 (9th Cir. 1997); *Ghaly v. INS*, 58 F.3d 1425, 1430 (9th Cir. 1995) (where BIA conducts de novo review of record, court is limited to BIA's opinion, except to extent BIA adopts IJ's opinion).

[959] *See, e.g., Shahinaj v. Gonzales*, 481 F.3d 1027 (8th Cir. 2007); *Floroiu v. Gonzales*, 481 F.3d 970 (7th Cir. 2007); *Niam v. Ashcroft*, 354 F.3d 652 (7th Cir. 2004); *Kerciku v. INS*, 314 F.3d 913, 919 (7th Cir. 2003).

[960] AEDPA, *supra* note 730, at §440(c), 110 Stat. 1277; IIRAIRA, *supra* note 10, at §306(a)(2), 110 Stat. 3009-607, 3009-608.

[961] *INS v. St. Cyr*, 533 U.S. 289 (2001); *Calcano-Martinez v. INS*, 533 U.S. 348 (2001). *See generally* 28 USC §2241; U.S. Const. art. I, §9, cl. 2. *But see Hose v. INS*, 180 F.3d 992 (9th Cir. 1999) (holding that INA §242(g) does not give the district court jurisdiction to hear a habeas petition where the petitioner could have appealed directly to the circuit court of appeals).

[962] *See, e.g., Gutierrez-Chavez v. INS*, 298 F.3d 824, 827 (9th Cir. 2002); *see also* "Judicial Review Under IIRAIRA and AEDPA: A Litigation Update," 76 *Interpreter Releases* 1450 (Sept. 30, 1999); L. Guttentag, "The 1996 Immigration Act: Federal Court Jurisdiction—Statutory Restrictions and Constitutional Rights," 74 *Interpreter Releases* 245 (Feb. 10, 1997).

After the REAL ID Act was enacted, habeas review and other review of certain removal was further restricted,[963] but it was clarified that these restrictions do not preclude appellate review of constitutional claims and other questions of law raised in accordance with review procedures under the INA.[964] Consequently, the constitutional issues raised by the Supreme Court previously seem to be resolved, inasmuch as the REAL ID Act provides that questions of law still have a forum for review.

Limited Review of Certain Asylum Bars

Changes to the INA under IIRAIRA eliminated judicial review of certain determinations made by legacy INS, DHS, IJs, and the BIA. Federal courts were prohibited by statute from reviewing (1) whether an asylum applicant is ineligible for asylum based on the availability of a safe third country, (2) whether an applicant timely filed an asylum application under the one-year filing deadline, (3) whether an applicant demonstrated extraordinary circumstances for failing to apply within one year after entry, (4) whether an applicant established that changed circumstances materially affected his or her eligibility for asylum to excuse a late filing, or (5) whether the applicant's application was previously denied.[965] In addition, IIRAIRA barred judicial review of determinations that an asylum applicant is ineligible for asylum based on the terrorism bar.[966] Courts, however, have found jurisdiction and remanded cases where the IJ and BIA failed to address the timeliness issue and ignored the applicant's argument that extraordinary circumstances excused her delay.[967]

Under provisions added by the REAL ID Act of 2005, the federal appeals courts regained jurisdiction over constitutional claims and questions of law, despite the restriction on judicial review found elsewhere in the INA.[968] A question of law includes not only statutory interpretation, but also questions involving the application of statutes or regulations to undisputed facts.[969] Based on the REAL ID Act, courts have found jurisdiction to consider one-year deadline claims.[970] Courts have refused to review one-year deadline cases where the issue presented is an issue of fact.[971] Habeas corpus review, however,

---

[963] INA §§242(a)(2)(A)–(C); 8 USC §§1252(a)(2)(A)–(C).

[964] INA §242(a)(2)(D); 8 USC §1252(a)(2)(D).

[965] INA §208(a)(3); 8 USC §1158(a)(3).

[966] INA §208(b)(2)(D); 8 USC §1158(b)(2)(D).

[967] *See, e.g., Sagaydak v. Ashcroft*, 405 F.3d 1035, 1040 (9th Cir. 2005).

[968] INA §242(a)(2)(D); 8 USC §1252(a)(2)(D).

[969] *Ramadan v. Gonzales*, 479 F.3d 646, 648 (9th Cir. 2007). *See, e.g., Brue v. Gonzales*, 464 F.3d 112 (10th Cir. 2006); *Boakai v. Gonzales*, 447 F.3d 1 (1st Cir. 2006); *see also Nakimbugwe v. Gonzales*, 475 F.3d 281, 284 (5th Cir. 2007) (holding that when an IJ's determination is based entirely on construction of a federal regulation, it is a question of law over which the court of appeals has jurisdiction); *Almuhtaseb v. Gonzales*, 453 F.3d 743, 748 (6th Cir. 2006) (holding that a question regarding construction of a statute is a question of law).

[970] *See, e.g., Liu v. INS*, 475 F.3d 135, 138 (2d Cir. 2006); *Nakimbugwe v. Gonzales*, 475 F.3d 281, 284 (5th Cir. 2007); *Almuhtaseb v. Gonzales*, 453 F.3d 743, 748 (6th Cir. 2006); *Mabasa v. Gonzales*, 455 F.3d 740 (7th Cir. 2006); *Diallo v. Gonzales*, 447 F.3d 1247, 1281 (10th Cir. 2006).

[971] *Jarbough v. Atty. Gen. of U.S.*, 483 F.3d 184, 189 (3d Cir. 2007); *Yakovenko v. Gonzales*, 477 F.3d 631, 6350 (8th Cir. 2007); *Hayek v. Gonzales*, 445 F.3d 501, 507 (1st Cir. 2006); *Xiao Ji Chen v. U.S.*
continued

was eliminated as a mechanism for reviewing final orders of removal in federal district courts by the REAL ID Act.[972]

The REAL ID Act also restricts federal court review of corroborating evidence findings. No court may reverse a determination made by a trier of fact with respect to the availability of corroborating evidence, unless the court finds that "a reasonable trier of fact would be compelled to conclude that such corroborating evidence is unavailable."[973] One court interpreting this provision has held that the IJ's determination regarding corroboration is entitled to deference, but only if the IJ explains (unless it is obvious) why he or she thinks corroborating evidence would be available to the applicant.[974]

No Review for Persons Convicted of Crimes

In IIRAIRA, Congress restricted the availability of judicial review of removal orders for aliens removable for certain criminal offenses. Under the INA, federal courts do not have jurisdiction to review any final order of removal against a person who is removable for having committed certain criminal offenses including an aggravated felony; a crime involving moral turpitude (unless such crime falls within a narrow exception); two crimes of moral turpitude; two or more crimes for which the aggregate sentence to confinement is five years or more; controlled-substance offenses; controlled-substance trafficking offenses; prostitution and prostitution-related offenses; commercialized vice offenses; certain firearms offenses; and miscellaneous treason, sedition, and sabotage offenses; or if the individual is a drug abuser or a drug addict.[975] However, federal courts do have jurisdiction to determine questions of law and constitutional claims.[976] This includes determination of whether the crime committed does in fact fall within one of the above-mentioned categories.[977] In addition, courts also have jurisdiction to review the IJ or BIA's denial of asylum and withholding claims, despite the finding of removability for a criminal offense.[978]

DOJ, 434 F.3d 144, 154 (2d Cir. 2006); *Chacon-Botero v. U.S. Atty. Gen.*, 427 F.3d 954, 957 (11th Cir. 2005); *Vasile v. Gonzales*, 417 F.3d 766, 768 (7th Cir. 2005).

[972] *See Spina v. Dep't of Homeland Sec.*, 70 F.3d 116, 123 (2d Cir. 2006); *Iasu v. Chertoff*, 426 F. Supp. 2d 1124 (D. Cal. 2006); *Walters v. Ashcroft*, 198 Fed. Appx. 78 (2d Cir. 2006); *Restrepo v. Winfrey*, 162 Fed. Appx. 311 (5th Cir. 2006); *Tilley v. Chertoff*, 144 Fed. Appx. 536 (6th Cir. 2005); *see also* AILF Practice Advisory, *supra* note 870.

[973] INA §242(b)(4); 8 USC §1252(b)(4).

[974] *Hor v. Gonzales*, 421 F.3d 497, 500–01 (7th Cir. 2005).

[975] INA §242(a)(2)(C); 8 USC §1252(a)(2)(C).

[976] INA §242(a)(2)(D); 8 USC §1252(a)(2)(D).

[977] *See, e.g.*, *Lee v. Ashcroft*, 368 F.3d 218 (3d Cir. 2004) (finding that filing a false tax return is not an aggravated felony); *see also Silva v. Gonzales*, 455 F.3d 26 (1st Cir. 2006) (holding that determining whether a crime is an aggravated felony poses an abstract legal question that is reviewable by the court).

[978] *Morales v. Gonzales*, 472 F.3d 689, 695 (9th Cir. 2007) ("Although we lack jurisdiction to review the IJ's finding that Morales was removable, we have jurisdiction to review the IJ's denial of Morales's applications for asylum and withholding of removal.").

Revised Statutory Standards of Review

Judicial review provisions under IIRAIRA, which became effective on April 1, 1997, provide that administrative findings of fact (made by the IJ or the BIA) are "conclusive unless any reasonable adjudicator would be compelled to conclude to the contrary."[979] This standard has been compared to the standard for review of factual finding set forth in *INS v. Elias-Zacarias*.[980] When the BIA finds a fact without mentioning or analyzing significant evidence, the case will be remanded to the BIA for further consideration.[981] In addition, IIRAIRA provides that discretionary judgment exercised on whether to grant asylum is "conclusive unless manifestly contrary to the law and an abuse of discretion."[982]

The REAL ID Act amended the INA to limit judicial review where an appellant seeks to reverse certain evidentiary determinations of the IJ for asylum, withholding of removal, or other removal relief.[983] The REAL ID Act bars a court from reversing a decision of an IJ regarding the availability of corroborating evidence in those instances, unless it can find that a reasonable IJ was compelled to conclude that the evidence was unavailable.[984]

Federal courts have held, however, that they cannot give meaningful review to a BIA decision reversing the IJ if the BIA does not explain its reasons for the reversal.[985] If the BIA summarily affirms the IJ's decision or offers little analysis, the federal appeals court

---

[979] INA §242(b)(4)(B); 8 USC §1252(b)(4)(B).

[980] *INS v. Elias-Zacarias*, 502 U.S. 478, 481 n.1, 483–84 (1992) (superseded by statute that codifies the substantial evidence standard set forth by the Court); *see also Bace v. Ashcroft*, 352 F.3d 1133, 1137 (7th Cir. 2003); *Lukwago v. Ashcroft*, 329 F.3d 157, 167 (3d Cir. 2003); *Shan Liao v. U.S. Dept. of Justice*, 293 F.3d 61 (2d Cir. 2002); *Girma v. INS*, 283 F.3d 664, 666 (5th Cir. 2002) (although applicant presented "*some* evidence" that her persecutors were motivated by a protected ground, it was not sufficient to warrant a reversal of the BIA's decision); *Chen v. INS*, 195 F.3d 198, 202 (4th Cir. 1999) (holding that it can reverse the BIA "only if the evidence presented was 'so compelling that no reasonable factfinder could fail to find the requisite fear of persecution,'" citing *Elias-Zacarias, supra*, at 483–84); *Gonzales-Neyra v. INS*, 122 F.3d 1293, 1296 (9th Cir. 1997), *amended by* 133 F.3d 726 (9th Cir. 1998); *see also* S. Knight, "Shielded from Review: The Questionable Birth and Development of the Asylum Standard of Review under Elias-Zacarias," 20 *Geo. Immigr. L.J.* 133 (2005).

[981] *Palavra v. INS*, 287 F.3d 690, 693 (8th Cir. 2002).

[982] INA §242(b)(4)(D); 8 USC §1252(b)(4)(D); *see also Kalubi v. Ashcroft*, 364 F.3d 1134, 1137 (9th Cir. 2004). For an excellent overview of judicial review under the previous law, the transition rule, and IIRAIRA, see "Judicial Review Under IIRAIRA and AEDPA: A Litigation Update," 76 *Interpreter Releases* 1450 (Sept. 30, 1999); L. Guttentag, "The 1996 Immigration Act: Federal Court Jurisdiction—Statutory Restrictions and Constitutional Rights," 74 *Interpreter Releases* 245 (Feb. 10, 1997).

[983] INA §242(b)(4)(B); 8 USC §1252(b)(4)(B).

[984] INA §242(b)(4)(B); 8 USC §1252(b)(4)(B). It is unclear whether this provision of the REAL ID Act significantly changed the status of the law, since the previous statutory and case law already stated that administrative findings of fact that include a conclusion about the availability of evidence may not be reversed unless a reasonable adjudicator would be compelled to find otherwise. *See, e.g., Hoxha v. Ashcroft*, 319 F.3d 1179, 1181 n.4 (9th Cir. 2003).

[985] *See, e.g., Awolesi v. Ashcroft*, 341 F.3d 227 (3d Cir. 2003) (vacating the BIA's reversal of the IJ's grant of asylum where the BIA's decision was a terse, four-sentence decision that did not adequately indicate the reasons for the reversal).

will review the IJ's decision directly, and will not search for an independent basis to affirm the BIA.[986]

De Novo Standard of Review

Courts review due process claims de novo.[987] Determinations of purely legal questions regarding the INA are reviewed de novo, as well.[988] Questions of law regarding what evidence will suffice to carry an asylum applicant's burden of proof are also reviewed de novo.[989] In addition, courts will review the administrative record in its entirety, including evidence that contradicts the BIA's findings.[990]

Abuse of Discretion

Prior to the changes to the INA under IIRAIRA, federal courts reviewed discretionary decisions of the BIA under the abuse of discretion standard.[991] The INA now provides that the AG's discretionary judgment on whether to grant asylum is "conclusive unless manifestly contrary to the law and an abuse of discretion."[992] The denial of a motion to reopen is subject to an abuse of discretion standard of review.[993]

Statutory Construction

If Congress's intent is clear and unambiguous, the federal court must give effect to the intent of Congress.[994] Deference to the agency's interpretation of the immigration laws is only appropriate if Congress's intent is unclear.[995] If the statute is silent or ambiguous, the court must defer to the agency's interpretation if it is based on a "permissible construction of the statute."[996] The court must reject any interpretation by the agency that is

---

[986] *Secaida-Rosales v. INS*, 331 F.3d 297, 305 (2d Cir. 2003).

[987] *Velazquez v. Ashcroft*, 103 Fed. Appx. 142 (9th Cir. 2004); *Kerciku v. INS*, 314 F.3d 913, 917 (7th Cir. 2003); *Morales v. INS*, 208 F.3d 323, 327 (1st Cir. 2000).

[988] *Jahed v. INS*, 356 F.3d 991, 997 (9th Cir. 2004) ("[W]e review de novo . . . the BIA's interpretation of the [INA]."); *Shan Liao v. U.S. Dept. of Justice*, 293 F.3d 61 (2d Cir. 2002); *Girma v. INS*, 283 F.3d 664, 666 (5th Cir. 2002); *Bradvica v. INS*, 128 F.3d 1009, 1012 (7th Cir. 1997); *see also Gailius v. INS*, 147 F.3d 34, 43 (1st Cir. 1998); *Ghaly v. INS*, 58 F.3d 1425, 1429 (9th Cir. 1995) (holding that the BIA's purely legal interpretations of the INA are reviewed de novo, but are generally entitled to deference).

[989] *Qiu v. Ashcroft*, 329 F.3d 140, 146 n.2 (2d Cir. 2003).

[990] *See Mgoian v. INS*, 184 F.3d 1029, 1034–35 (9th Cir. 1999); *see also Velarde v. INS*, 140 F.3d 1305 (9th Cir. 1998); *Turcios v. INS*, 821 F.2d 1396, 1398 (9th Cir. 1987).

[991] *See, e.g., Huang v. INS*, 421 F.3d 125, 127 (2d Cir. 2005); *Gilaj v. Gonzales*, 408 F.3d 275, 288 (6th Cir. 2005); *Etchu-Njang v. Gonzales*, 403 F.3d 577, 580 (8th Cir. 2005); *Nasir v. INS*, 122 F.3d 484 (7th Cir. 1997).

[992] INA §242(b)(4)(D); 8 USC §1252(b)(4)(D).

[993] *INS v. Doherty*, 502 U.S. 314, 317 (1992); *Bolshakov v. INS*, 133 F.3d 1279, 1281 (9th Cir. 1998); *Hernandez-Vivas v. INS*, 23 F.3d 1557, 1560 (9th Cir. 1994).

[994] *INS v. Aguirre-Aguirre*, 526 U.S. 415 (1999).

[995] *Jahed v. INS*, 356 F.3d 991, 997 (9th Cir. 2004).

[996] *INS v. Aguirre-Aguirre*, supra note 994, at 422 (citing *Chevron, USA, Inc. v. Natural Resources Defense Council*, 467 U.S. 837, 843 (1984)); *see also Lukwago v. Ashcroft*, 329 F.3d 157, 167 (3d Cir. 2003) ("[I]f the statute is silent or ambiguous . . . the question for the court is whether the agency's answer is based on a permissible construction of the statute.").

"arbitrary, capricious or manifestly contrary to the statute."[997] Now, after the breakup of legacy INS, there are two separate agencies interpreting U.S. immigration law—DHS and DOJ. There is the potential that their views may conflict. Courts may have to decide which agency merits greater deference.

Deference in Credibility Determinations

Federal courts give considerable deference to the BIA's and IJ's credibility determinations. Such determinations are overturned by some reviewing courts only when "extraordinary circumstances so require,"[998] or the determinations are based on "insufficient or incomplete evidence."[999] Generally, courts have treated credibility questions as questions of fact subject to the "substantial evidence" standard.[1000] Credibility findings that rest on an analysis of testimony, rather than demeanor, may deserve less than usual deference.[1001] A demeanor determination will not be upheld if it is compromised by factual error.[1002] The REAL ID Act amended the INA to limit judicial review by barring a court from reversing decisions by adjudicators regarding the availability of corroborating evidence in certain instances, unless the court finds that a reasonable adjudicator would be compelled to decide that such evidence was unavailable.[1003] This amendment seems to establish standards for credibility determinations and the use of corroborating evidence to provide a uniform standard for judicial review.[1004]

Deference is not due where findings and conclusions are based on inferences or presumptions that are not reasonably grounded in the record when viewed as a whole.[1005] Deference is not due when the IJ has not made an express credibility finding, but has only

---

[997] *Chang v. INS*, 119 F.3d 1055, 1060 (3d Cir. 1997) (citing *Chevron*, 467 U.S. at 844).

[998] *Nasir v. INS*, 122 F.3d 484, 486 (7th Cir. 1997).

[999] *Uwase v. Ashcroft*, 349 F.3d 1039, 1041 (7th Cir. 2003); *see also Krouchevski v. Ashcroft*, 344 F.3d 670, 673 (7th Cir. 2003) (although the applicant offered explanations for the inconsistencies, the reviewing court refused to overturn the negative credibility determination simply because an alternative finding could be supported by substantial evidence); *Singh-Kaur v. INS*, 183 F.3d 1147, 1149 (9th Cir. 1999) (holding that review of credibility findings by an IJ or the BIA is "extremely deferential" and that "special deference" is given to credibility determinations based on demeanor); *Hartooni v. INS*, 21 F.3d 336, 340 (9th Cir. 1994) (holding that credibility findings are entitled to "considerable deference").

[1000] *Secaida-Rosales v. INS*, 331 F.3d 297, 307 (2d Cir. 2003).

[1001] *Id.*

[1002] *Guan v. INS*, 453 F.3d 129, 136 (2d Cir. 2006).

[1003] INA §242(b)(4)(B); 8 USC §1252(b)(4)(B).

[1004] *See* Congressional Research Service Report, *Immigration: Analysis of the Major Provisions of the REAL ID Act of 2005*, at 13 (May 25, 2005), available at *www.ilw.com/immigdaily/news/2005,1101-crs.pdf* (observing that preexisting statutory and case law already followed this principle but that the REAL ID Act may have been intended to standardize judicial review of the evidentiary decisions of immigration fact finders).

[1005] *See Guo v. Ashcroft*, 361 F.3d 1194, 1199 (9th Cir. 2004) ("[W]e review adverse credibility findings under a substantial evidence standard."); *Gailius v. INS*, 147 F.3d 34, 44 (1st Cir. 1998) ("Although our review [of credibility determinations] is deferential . . . we have rejected the notion that the INS is 'a unique kind of administrative agency entitled to extreme deference.'").

made implicit credibility observations in passing.[1006] Minor inconsistencies and omissions in an individual's application or in his or her testimony will not support an adverse credibility finding.[1007] It is also error for the BIA to deny asylum based on "insufficient testimonial specificity" where neither the IJ nor the trial attorney questioned the applicant about the details of an act of persecution against a family member.[1008]

In cases in which the IJ has expressly found the testimony of the asylum applicant credible, and the BIA has made no finding to the contrary, courts will accept the testimony given before the IJ as undisputed.[1009] If neither the IJ nor the BIA make an adverse credibility finding, the applicant's testimony is accepted as true by the reviewing court.[1010] At least one court has rejected the government's argument on appeal that when an applicant's testimony is found credible, that finding only means that the applicant "believed his or her testimony to be true."[1011] The Ninth Circuit reasoned that under this theory, the IJ's positive credibility determination would be rendered meaningless.[1012]

Review of Factual Findings

Factual findings in asylum and withholding proceedings are reviewed for substantial evidence.[1013]

Review of "Changed Circumstances" Determinations

Federal courts review the BIA's determination that circumstances have changed in the applicant's country for substantial evidence.[1014] The BIA must provide an "individualized analysis of how changed conditions will affect the [applicant's] situation."[1015]

[1006] *Manimbao v. Ashcroft*, 329 F.3d 655, 660–61 (9th Cir. 2003) (holding that failure to make a sufficient credibility determination violates due process).

[1007] *See, e.g.*, *Osorio v. INS*, 99 F.3d 928, 931 (9th Cir. 1996).

[1008] *Qiu v. Ashcroft*, 329 F.3d 140, 152–53 (2d Cir. 2003); *see also* this chapter, at 2.6.2.

[1009] *See Mgoian v. INS*, 184 F.3d 1029, 1033 (9th Cir. 1999); *Singh v. Ilchert*, 63 F.3d 1501, 1506 (9th Cir. 1995).

[1010] *See Lopez v. Ashcroft*, 366 F.3d 799, 802 (9th Cir. 2004).

[1011] *Garcia-Martinez v. Ashcroft*, 371 F.3d 1066, 1069 n.1 (9th Cir. 2004).

[1012] *Id.*

[1013] *INS v. Elias-Zacarias*, 502 U.S. 478, 481; *Capric v. Ashcroft*, 355 F.3d 1075, 1086 (7th Cir. 2004); *see also Wiransane v. Ashcroft*, 366 F.3d 889, 897 (10th Cir. 2004) ("[W]e review the IJ's resolution of the initial refugee status question under a substantial evidence standard.").

[1014] *Lopez v. Ashcroft*, 366 F.3d 799, 805 (9th Cir. 2004).

[1015] *Id.*

Chapter 3
Asylum and Withholding of Removal Procedures

> *[B]efore the Law stands a doorkeeper. To this doorkeeper comes a man from the country who begs for admittance to the Law. But the doorkeeper says that he cannot admit the man at the moment ... [The doorkeeper says] ... "[N]ote that I am powerful. And I am only the lowest doorkeeper. From hall to hall, keepers stand at every door, one more powerful than the other...." These are difficulties which the man from the country has not expected to meet; the Law, he thinks, should be accessible to every man and at all times.***

3.1. Who Is Eligible to Apply	140
3.2. Affirmative Procedures	145
3.3. Immigration Court (Defensive) Procedures	156
3.4. Asylum Procedures for Stowaways	189
3.5. Asylum Procedures for Children	190
3.6. Reinstatement of Removal	196
3.7. Expedited Removal for Aggravated Felons	204
3.8. Release from Detention	213
3.9. Employment Authorization	221
3.10. Appeals to BIA	227
3.11. Motions to Reopen and Reconsider	234
3.12. Judicial Review	242
3.13. Adjustment of Status for Asylees and Refugees	249
3.14. Refugee Travel Document	251
3.15. Refugee/Asylee Relative Petition (I-730)	253
3.16. Termination of Asylum and Withholding	255
3.17. Termination of Refugee Status	258

This chapter provides an overview of asylum and withholding of removal procedures for applicants applying affirmatively before an asylum officer (AO) and those applying defensively before an immigration judge (IJ) or, in some instances, applying defensively before an AO. The process can be completed within a few months or may last for several years. In some instances, the procedures may seem counterintuitive or cumbersome. It is

---
* Franz Kafka, *The Trial*.

necessary and, indeed, crucial to follow the instructions, rules, and regulations throughout the process. If you are confused or unsure about a particular procedure, it is useful to consult the statutes, regulations, and agency policies outlined below. It may also be helpful to call a colleague, the immigration court, and/or a nonprofit organization specializing in immigration and asylum law for assistance in getting past one or more of the many doorkeepers to asylum.

> ➤ *Tip*—**Expedited Removal**—If an asylum applicant arrived at a port of entry with false or no documents on or after April 1, 1997, the applicant may be subject to expedited removal proceedings.[1]

3.1. Who Is Eligible to Apply

3.1.1. In General

For an overview of the standard of proof required and relief available to individuals applying for asylum and withholding of removal, see chapter 2.2 and 2.3.

Asylum

Any noncitizen who is "physically present" or "arrives" in the United States may apply for asylum.[2] Of course, there are more than a few exceptions to this general rule.[3] A person granted asylum is generally referred to as an asylee. Asylees may confer derivative asylee status on their spouses and children under 21 years of age who are either inside or outside of the United States.[4] A person applying for asylum may have a lawful immigration status, may have fallen out of status, or may have no immigration status. In some cases, a lawful permanent resident (LPR) may benefit from a grant of asylum if the LPR has been found to be removable from or inadmissible to the United States, or if the children or spouse of the LPR are at risk overseas and the grant of asylum would allow for them to enter the United States more quickly. Asylum is available to all, regardless of age, mental capacity, or immigration status.

Withholding of Removal

Unlike for asylum, there is no statutory requirement that a noncitizen seeking withholding of removal be physically present in the United States.[5] Nevertheless, the U.S. Supreme Court has held that the right to apply for withholding does not extend to noncitizens outside of the United States.[6] Persons granted withholding of removal, unlike asylum, cannot confer derivative status on their spouse or unmarried children.[7]

---

[1] See ch. 5 for more information about the expedited removal process.

[2] INA §208(a)(1); 8 USC §1158(a)(1).

[3] *See* ch. 2.7.

[4] INA §208(b)(3); 8 USC §1158(b)(3); 8 CFR §§208.21(a)–(f), 1208.21(a)–(f).

[5] INA §241(b)(3); 8 USC §1231(b)(3).

[6] *See Sale v. Haitian Centers Council, Inc.*, 509 U.S. 155 (1993) (holding that neither domestic nor international law prohibited the United States' repatriation of Haitians interdicted beyond U.S. territorial waters); *see also Cuban-American Bar Assn., Inc. v. Christopher*, 43 F.3d 1412 (11th Cir. 1995) (holding that Cubans

continued

> *Tip*—**Statistics on Interdiction**—The Coast Guard reported that it had interdicted a total of 4,330 migrants in fiscal year (FY) 2007, including the following nationalities: Haitians (1,221); Ecuadorians (50); Cubans (1,580); mainland Chinese (73); and Dominicans (1,261). For the most up-to-date statistics on interdictions, see the U.S. Coast Guard website at *www.uscg.mil*. For the United Nations High Commissioner on Refugees' (UNHCR) position on interception (or interdiction) of refugees, see UNHCR Executive Committee, Report of the 54th Session of the Executive Committee of the High Commissioner's Programme (Geneva, 29 September–3 October 2003), Conclusion on Protection Safeguards in Interception Measures (Oct. 10, 2003), available online at *www.unhcr.org*.

Overseas Processing and Refugee Admissions

When a person is outside the United States, he or she may apply for refugee status under procedures that differ greatly from the asylum and withholding procedures set forth in this chapter. To be granted refugee status, a person must be outside the United States and must meet the definition of refugee under U.S. law.[8] The refugee must also fall within one or more of the "priority" categories established by the U.S. State Department. The first priority allows UNHCR or U.S. embassies to identify urgent individual cases; the second is for groups of special concern; and the third priority enables U.S. citizens or persons lawfully admitted to the United States to petition for family members to enter pursuant to the refugee resettlement program.[9] Under this overseas process, the number of refugee admissions each year is set by the president after consulting with Congress.[10] For FY 2007, the Bush administration proposed that the United States admit up to 70,000 refugees.[11] The United States has been criticized for the low number of Iraqi refugees—just 7,000—that it has agreed to resettle.[12] UNHCR reported in 2007 that for the first time in five years the number of refugees in the world had risen and was estimated to be nearly 10 million. Less than one percent will be resettled by the United States, Canada, and other Western countries in any given year. The chances of any refugee obtaining resettlement to the

---

receiving temporary safe haven at the U.S. naval base in Guantanamo Bay, Cuba, cannot assert rights under the INA, the U.S. Constitution, or international law to be paroled or otherwise admitted to the United States).

[7] *See, e.g., Delgado v. U.S. Att'y Gen.*, 487 F.3d 855, 2007 U.S. App. LEXIS 12210, at *13–14 (11th Cir. 2007).

[8] INA §101(a)(42); 8 USC §1101(a)(42).

[9] *See generally www.uscis.gov* (click on the "Services and Benefits" tab, and then the "Humanitarian Benefits" link, the "Refugees" link, and finally the "Worldwide Priority System" link); *see also* J. Guilfoyle, "The Refugee Resettlement Program: How It Might Help the Relatives of Your Asylee Clients," 23 *Immigration Law Today* 48 (Sept./Oct. 2004).

[10] INA §207(e); 8 USC §1157(e).

[11] *See* Department of State, Oversight of U.S. Refugee Admissions and Policy (Sept. 27, 2006), available at *www.state.gov/g/prm/rls/2006/73264.htm*.

[12] *See, e.g.*, Amnesty International USA Urges United States to Provide More Assistance to Refugees (Feb. 14, 2007), available at *www.amnestyusa.org/document.php?lang=e&id=ENGUSA2007 0214001*.

United States through overseas refugee processing are minute at best. The procedures for applying for refugee status overseas are beyond the scope of this *Primer*.[13]

3.1.2. Ineligibility for Asylum and Withholding of Removal

A noncitizen physically present in the United States may be ineligible to apply or be barred from seeking asylum and/or withholding of removal if he or she falls within one or more of the categories set forth below.[14]

Bars to Asylum Only

- prior asylum denial
- one-year filing deadline
- safe third country
- firm resettlement
- aggravated felony

Bars to Asylum and Withholding

- particularly serious crime
- serious nonpolitical crime
- persecutor of others
- danger to the security of the United States
- terrorism-related grounds

Bars to Withholding Only

- participation in Nazi persecution
- participation in genocide

3.1.3. Required Notices

Notice of Right to Be Represented

At the time the applicant files for asylum and withholding of removal, the U.S. attorney general (AG) is required to notify the applicant of the privilege of being represented by counsel and to provide the applicant with a list of pro bono representatives.[15] Under

---

[13] For additional information on the overseas refugee resettlement process, visit the website for the U.S. Committee for Refugees and Immigrants at *www.refugees.org*, or U.S. Citizenship and Immigration Services at *www.uscis.gov* (click on the "Services and Benefits" tab, and then the "How do I?" link, and finally the "I am a Refugee or Asylee, How Do I . . . ?" link). For a comprehensive overview and critique of the current U.S. resettlement program and recommendations for reform, see D. Martin, The United States Refugee Admissions Program: Reforms for a New Era of Refugee Resettlement, available at *www.state.gov/documents/organization/36495.pdf*.

[14] For additional information regarding these bars, see ch. 2.7.

[15] INA §208(d)(4); 8 USC §1158(d)(4); 8 CFR §1240.11(c)(1)(iii) (regarding IJ's duty to notify); *see also* appx. 9A, I-589 filing instructions, section IV: Right to Counsel (containing this notice and a toll-free number and website address to access for a list of attorneys and accredited representatives).

the Homeland Security Act of 2002, this responsibility to give notice extends to the Department of Homeland Security (DHS) Secretary and other DHS officials.[16] In proceedings before an asylum officer, an immigration judge, or the Board of Immigration Appeals (BIA), asylum and withholding of removal applicants may be represented by attorneys, law school students or graduates, reputable individuals of good moral character, accredited representatives, or accredited officials.[17]

Notice of Consequences of Filing a Frivolous Application

At the time the applicant files for asylum (if on or after April 1, 1997), the AG is also required to notify the applicant of the consequences of knowingly filing a frivolous application.[18] Under the Homeland Security Act of 2002, this responsibility to give notice extends to the DHS secretary and other DHS officials.[19]

If the IJ or BIA determines that the applicant knowingly filed a frivolous application after receiving such notice, the applicant is "permanently ineligible for any benefits" under the Immigration and Nationality Act (INA),[20] effective on the date of the final determination regarding the application.[21] This provision was added to the INA by the Illegal Immigration Reform and Immigrant Responsibility Act of 1996.[22] The regulations provide that an asylum application is "frivolous" if "any of its material elements is deliberately fabricated."[23]

An applicant may be permanently barred only if a final order by an IJ or the BIA specifically finds that the applicant knowingly filed a frivolous application.[24] The IJ or the BIA must be "satisfied" that during the course of the proceedings the applicant "has had sufficient opportunity to account for any discrepancies or implausible aspects of the claim."[25] An IJ may not base a frivolous determination on merely an adverse credibility

---

[16] *See* Homeland Security Act of 2002, Pub. L. No. 107-296, §§456, 1512, 1517, 116 Stat. 2135, 2200, 2310, 2311.

[17] *See generally* 8 CFR §§292.1, 1292.1.

[18] INA §208(d)(4)(A); 8 USC §1158(d)(4)(A); *see also* 8 CFR §§208.3(c)(5), 1208.3(c)(5), 1240.11(c)(1)(iii) (regarding DHS and IJ duty to notify).

[19] *See* Homeland Security Act of 2002, Pub. L. No. 107-296, §§456, 1512, 1517, 116 Stat. 2135, 2200, 2310, 2311; *see also* appx. 9A, I-589 filing instructions (containing the following warning: "Applicants determined to have knowingly made a frivolous application for asylum will be permanently ineligible for any benefits under the [INA].").

[20] Immigration and Nationality Act of 1952, Pub. L. No. 82-414, 66 Stat. 163 (codified as amended at 8 USC §1101 *et seq.*).

[21] INA §208(d)(6); 8 USC §1158(d)(6).

[22] Illegal Immigration Reform and Immigrant Responsibility Act of 1996 (IIRAIRA), Pub. L. No. 104-208, div. C, 110 Stat. 3009, 3009-546 to 3009-724.

[23] 8 CFR §§208.20, 1208.20.

[24] 8 CFR §§208.20, 1208.20.

[25] 8 CFR §§208.20, 1208.20; *see also Matter of Y–L–*, 24 I&N Dec. 151 (BIA 2007) (holding that an IJ must make a separate and specific finding regarding frivolousness and must give the applicant the opportunity to account for discrepancies); *Matter of [name not provided]*, A94 097 292 (BIA June 21, 2000), *reported in* 77 *Interpreter Releases* 1091–92 (July 31, 2000) (in this unpublished decision, the BIA over-

continued

assessment.[26] The IJ must give specific and convincing reasons for determining that a preponderance of the evidence supports a frivolousness finding.[27] Note, however, that a finding that an applicant filed a frivolous application is not a bar to withholding of removal.[28] It is also not a bar to relief under the Convention Against Torture.

> *Tip*—The knowing placement of false information on the application may also subject the applicant (or the person who placed the information on the application) to criminal and civil penalties.[29]

Notice That Information May Be Used to Initiate Removal Proceedings and Satisfy the Government's Burden of Proof

The information provided by an applicant in an asylum application filed on or after January 4, 1995, may be used as a basis for initiating removal proceedings and to satisfy DHS's burden of proof in exclusion, deportation, or removal proceedings.[30]

Notice of Confidentiality

The Application for Asylum and Withholding of Removal (I-589) provides:

---

turned the IJ's "frivolous" finding based on a determination that the claim was "baseless" and exaggerated); *Aziz v. Gonzales*, 478 F.3d 854, 857 (8th Cir. 2007) (upholding IJ's finding that the applicant from Iraq filed a frivolous asylum application); *Sterkaj v. Gonzales*, 439 F.3d 273, 279 (6th Cir. 2006) (upholding frivolous finding where applicant submitted a fraudulent summons and "wanted" document); *Kifleyesus v. Gonzales*, 462 F.3d 937, 945 (8th Cir. 2006) (upholding IJ's frivolousness finding where the applicant filed a false application, failed to modify it, swore to the truth of the application, and was given sufficient opportunity to account for discrepancies); *Meidiansyah v. U.S. Att'y Gen.*, 468 F.3d 763, 770 (11th Cir. 2006) (finding that IJ failed to give the applicants a proper opportunity to explain any discrepancies); *Selami v. Gonzales*, 423 F.3d 621, 622 (6th Cir. 2005) (upholding the IJ's finding that the applicant submitted a frivolous application where the applicant submitted a fraudulent newspaper article and was given an opportunity to explain, but failed to articulate any explanation); *Farah v. Ashcroft*, 348 F.3d 1153 (9th Cir. 2003) (overturning frivolous determination where applicant was not given the opportunity to explain discrepancies); *Efe v. Ashcroft*, 293 F.3d 899 (5th Cir. 2002) (upholding frivolousness determination where applicant was given ample opportunity to clarify his testimony); *Barreto-Claro v. U.S. Attorney Gen.*, 275 F.3d 1334 (11th Cir. 2001) (upholding the finding of frivolousness).

[26] *Alexandrov v. Gonzales*, 442 F.3d 395, 407 (6th Cir. 2006) (finding that the IJ violated the applicant's due process rights by relying on two State Department reports in finding that the applicant's asylum application was frivolous); *Muhanna v. Gonzales*, 399 F.3d 582, 589 (3d Cir. 2005) (the court found that "by imposing a frivolousness finding based not on a thorough examination of the application but instead on her assessment of [the applicant's] credibility, and by consequently refusing to allow further testimony, the IJ . . . deprived [the applicant] of due process.")

[27] *Matter of Y–L–*, 24 I&N Dec. 151 (BIA 2007).

[28] 8 CFR §§208.20, 1208.20.

[29] 8 CFR §§208.3(c)(4), 1208.3(c)(4).

[30] 8 CFR §§208.3(c)(1), 1208.3(c)(1); *see also* appx. 9A, I-589 filing instructions (containing the following warning: "Any information provided in completing this application may be used as a basis for the institution of, or as evidence in, removal proceedings, even if the application is later withdrawn").

[N]o information indicating that you have applied for asylum will be provided to any government or country from which you claim a fear of persecution. Regulations at 8 CFR §208.6 protect the confidentiality of asylum claims.[31]

Under 8 CFR §§208.6, 1208.6, DHS and the Executive Office for Immigration Review (EOIR) are required to keep confidential all records indicating that an applicant has applied for asylum or similar forms of protection. There are exceptions, however, outlined in 8 CFR §§208.6, 1208.6(c). The broadest exception, found at 8 CFR §§208.6(a), 1208.6(a), allows for the disclosure of asylum information and records "*at the discretion of the Attorney General.*"[32] Under the Homeland Security Act of 2002, this duty of confidentiality extends to the DHS secretary and other DHS officials.[33]

3.2. AFFIRMATIVE PROCEDURES

3.2.1. Who Is Eligible

An applicant may file an affirmative application for asylum if he or she is not currently in removal, deportation, or exclusion proceedings and has not been previously issued a removal, deportation, or exclusion order. One exception to this general rule is *American Baptist Churches v. Thornburgh (ABC)* class members[34] who are entitled under the *ABC* Settlement to an affirmative asylum interview.[35] An applicant may file if he or she currently holds a valid immigration status (such as a visitor's visa or temporary protected status), his or her status has lapsed or expired (except for Visa Waiver Program cases), or even if he or she holds no immigration status (*e.g.*, if he or she entered the country without inspection). During the affirmative process, the asylum officer will determine whether the applicant is barred from asylum or withholding of removal based on one or more of the grounds of ineligibility.[36]

> *Note*: Visa Waiver Status—Does the Asylum Division have jurisdiction to adjudicate visa waiver cases? If the applicant is in status and not otherwise removable, the Asylum Division should adjudicate the application. Under 8 CFR §217.4(b)(1), it appears that the district director may only refer cases to the IJ after determining that the asylum applicant is deportable.[37]

---

[31] Appx. 9A, I-589 filing instructions, section III.

[32] 8 CFR §§208.6(a), 1208.6(a) (emphasis added).

[33] *See* Homeland Security Act of 2002, Pub. L. No. 107-296, §§456, 1512, 1517, 116 Stat. 2135, 2200, 2310, 2311. For further discussion of confidentiality, see this chapter, at 3.3.5.

[34] *See* ch. 6.

[35] *See* D. Smith, "The *ABC* Settlement: A Guide for Class Members and Advocates," 72 *Interpreter Releases* 1497 (Nov. 6, 1995); *see also* American Immigration Law Center, The American Baptist Churches v. Thornburgh (ABC) Settlement Agreement, available at www.ailc.com/services/residency/abc-1.htm.

[36] *See* ch. 2.7.

[37] *See* 8 CFR §§208.2(c)(1), 208.4(b)(5), 1208.2(c)(1), and 1208.4(b)(5).

An applicant who has filed affirmatively, but has been issued a Notice To Appear (NTA) or other charging document that has been filed with an immigration court, is ineligible to proceed with the application pending before the Asylum Division.[38] On rare occasions, DHS may file a motion to dismiss on the grounds that, among other reasons, the NTA was improvidently issued or that circumstances have changed to such an extent that the continuation of the case is no longer in the best interest of the government.[39] The motion, however, must be adjudicated on the record like any other motion before the IJ or the BIA.[40] If the immigration court proceedings are dismissed, the applicant might be able to pursue an affirmative claim, if other bars do not apply. Other categories of individuals ineligible for the affirmative asylum process are: (1) certain alien crewmembers; (2) certain stowaways, (3) Visa Waiver Program applicant for admission, (4) Visa Waiver Program overstays and status violators, (5) certain individuals ordered removed under INA §235(c) on security-related grounds, and (6) certain nonimmigrants admitted under INA §101(a)(15)(S) (*e.g.*, witnesses and informants).[41]

If the applicant has received a previous order of removal, the asylum application, in conjunction with a motion to reopen, should be filed with the immigration court or the Board of Immigration Appeals, depending on where jurisdiction has vested.[42] If the applicant has been previously removed, deported, or excluded from the United States and illegally re-entered the United States, upon filing for asylum, he or she may be placed in reinstatement of removal proceedings and may only be eligible for withholding of removal.[43]

> ➤ *Tip*—Asylum officers generally do have authority to grant withholding of removal. The only exception is for *ABC* claims adjudicated under the *American Baptist Churches* settlement.[44]

3.2.2. Where to File

Affirmative asylum applications should be filed with the appropriate U.S. Citizenship and Immigration Services (USCIS) regional service center by mail.[45] A list of the regional service centers and the geographic areas they cover is found in the filing instructions of the I-589, "Where to File."[46] It is strongly recommended that an application be

---

[38] *See, e.g., Matter of P–L–P–*, 21 I&N Dec. 887 (BIA 1997) (finding that an applicant who was issued a charging document on the day he filed his asylum application with the INS could not proceed with his affirmative application).

[39] 8 CFR §§239.2(a)(6), (7), (c), and 1239.2(c); *see also Matter of G–N–C–*, 22 I&N Dec. 281 (BIA 1998), *criticized on other grounds by Castro-Cortez v. INS,* 239 F.3d 1037, 1052 (9th Cir. 2001).

[40] *Matter of G–N–C–*, 22 I&N Dec. 281 (BIA 1998), *criticized on other grounds by Castro-Cortez v. INS,* 239 F.3d 1037, 1052 (9th Cir. 2001).

[41] *See* 8 CFR §§208.2(c)(1), 1208.2(c)(1); *see also* appx. 9A, I-589 filing instructions, p. 9.

[42] *See generally* 8 CFR §§208.4(b)(3)(ii), (4), 1208.4(b)(3)(ii), (4); *see also* this chapter, at 3.11.

[43] *See* this chapter, at 3.6.

[44] For more information on the *ABC* settlement, see ch. 6.5.

[45] 8 CFR §§208.4(b)(1), 1208.4(b)(1).

[46] *See* appx. 9A, I-589 filing instructions.

sent by certified mail, return receipt requested, in order to have proof of where and when the application was filed. The regulations also allow for an application to be filed directly with the Asylum Office having jurisdiction over the matter, but only if express consent is given by the director of asylum.[47]

> ➤ *Tip*—**Asylum Application Form**—The Application for Asylum and Withholding of Removal (Form I-589) is revised about every two years. It is important to check the USCIS website for the most recent version and to determine what previous versions, if any, are acceptable for submission.[48]

3.2.3. No Filing Fee

To date, there is no fee for filing an affirmative application for asylum.[49] Nor is there a fingerprinting fee.[50] The statute, however, permits the AG to impose a fee.[51] Under the Homeland Security Act of 2002, this authority would extend to the DHS Secretary.[52]

3.2.4. Incomplete Applications

An asylum application is incomplete if it does not include a response to each question, is unsigned, or is unaccompanied by the required supporting documents or copies.[53] Incomplete applications will be returned to the applicant within 30 days of receipt.[54] If USCIS does not return the application within 30 days, it will be deemed to be complete.[55] An incomplete application will not commence the 150-day period after which the applicant may file an application for employment authorization.[56]

3.2.5. Interview

For tips on preparing for an asylum interview, see appendix 3B.

Time Period

By statute, the initial interview must commence "not later than 45 days" after the application is filed, unless there are exceptional circumstances.[57]

---

[47] 8 CFR §§208.4(b)(2), 1208.4(b)(2).

[48] *See* appx. 9A, I-589 application.

[49] 8 CFR §1103.7.

[50] *Id.*

[51] INA §208(d)(3); 8 USC §1158(d)(3).

[52] *See* Homeland Security Act of 2002, Pub. L. No. 107-296, §§456, 1512, 1517, 116 Stat. 2135, 2200, 2310, 2311.

[53] 8 CFR §§208.3(c)(3), 1208.3(c)(3).

[54] 8 CFR §§208.3(c)(3), 1208.3(c)(3).

[55] 8 CFR §§208.3(c)(3), 1208.3(c)(3).

[56] 8 CFR §§208.3(c)(3), 1208.3(c)(3); *see also* this chapter, at 3.9.

[57] INA §208(d)(5); 8 USC §1158(d)(5).

Nonadversarial

Affirmative asylum interviews are conducted by asylum officers, and, unlike hearings for defensive claims, are (or should be) conducted in a nonadversarial manner.[58] The purpose of the interview, according to the regulations, is "to elicit all relevant and useful information bearing on the applicant's eligibility for asylum."[59] The applicant may present witnesses and may submit affidavits of witnesses or other evidence.[60] Asylum officers are given special training in nonadversarial interview techniques.[61]

> ➤ *Tip*—**Special Procedures and Interviewing Techniques for Children's Claims**—On December 10, 1998, legacy Immigration and Naturalization Service (INS) issued guidelines for children's asylum claims, which provide additional procedural protections for children in the affirmative asylum process.[62] In addition, on May 22, 2007, the Office of the Chief Immigration Judge issued an operating policies and procedures memorandum (OPPM) on policies and procedures for immigration cases involving children.[63] While the IJs are not bound by legacy INS's guidelines, this OPPM incorporates by reference some of the child-questioning techniques referred to in the guidelines.

Biometrics

After the application is filed and accepted, the applicant will receive an appointment letter to be fingerprinted at a USCIS office. An unexcused failure to appear for an appointment to provide biometrics (such as fingerprints) within the time allowed may result in the asylum officer dismissing the application or referring the case to the immigration court.[64]

Interpreter

If the applicant is unable to proceed with the interview in English, the applicant must provide, at no expense to DHS, a competent interpreter.[65] The interpreter must be fluent in English and the applicant's native language or any other language in which the applicant is

---

[58] 8 CFR §§208.9(b), 1208.9(b).

[59] 8 CFR §§208.9(b), 1208.9(b).

[60] 8 CFR §§208.9(b), 1208.9(b).

[61] 8 CFR §§208.1(b), 1208.1(b); *see also* Asylum Officer Basic Training Course, Lesson: Interviewing Part I: Overview of Nonadversarial Asylum Interview (Sept. 14, 2006).

[62] *See* this chapter, at 3.5.

[63] *See* EOIR Memorandum, D. Neal, "Operating Policies and Procedures Memorandum No. 07-01, Guidelines for Immigration Court Cases Involving Unaccompanied Alien Children" (May 22, 2007), *published on* AILA InfoNet at Doc. No. 07052360 (*posted* May 23, 2007).

[64] Appx. 9A, I-589 filing instructions, p. 7; *see also* USCIS Interoffice Memorandum, J. Langlois, "Securing Compliance with Fingerprinting Requirements Prior to Asylum Interview and Amending Procedures for Issuance of Recommended Approvals" (Sept. 12, 2006), *published on* AILA InfoNet at Doc. No. 06091360 (*posted* Sept. 13, 2006).

[65] 8 CFR §§208.9(g), 1208.9(g).

fluent.[66] The interpreter must be at least 18 years of age and may not be the applicant's attorney or representative, a witness testifying on the applicant's behalf, or a representative or employee of the applicant's country of nationality (or, if the applicant is stateless, the applicant's country of last habitual residence).[67] The applicant's failure to provide an interpreter at the time of the interview, if without "good cause," may be considered by the Asylum Office to be a failure to appear.[68]

> *Tip*—Hearing-impaired applicants will be provided with a sign language interpreter by the asylum office. To obtain this service, the applicant should contact the asylum officer with jurisdiction over his or her case as soon as notice of the interview date is received.[69]

USCIS contemplates issuing regulations to provide government-funded interpreter services for affirmative asylum interviews.[70] In the meantime, USCIS has been conducting a pilot program under which it contracts with providers of interpretation services who monitor affirmative asylum interviews by telephone.[71]

Role of Attorney or Representative

The applicant has the privilege of being represented by counsel during the affirmative asylum process.[72] One study has shown that asylum applicants in removal proceedings who are represented by counsel are four to six times more likely to be granted asylum than applicants who are not represented.[73] Having an attorney may make the difference between an applicant winning or being placed in removal proceedings. For a listing of free or low cost legal counsel, call (800) 870-3676 or visit the EOIR website at *www.usdoj.gov/eoir/probono/states.htm*.

The counsel or representative should file a Notice of Appearance, Form G-28 (traditionally printed on blue paper), at the time the application is filed, or prior to or at the asylum interview.[74] The applicant's counsel or representative may be present during the interview, and upon the completion of the interview may make a statement or comment on the evidence presented.[75] The asylum officer has the discretion to limit the length of

---

[66] 8 CFR §§208.9(g), 1208.9(g).

[67] 8 CFR §§208.9(g), 1208.9(g).

[68] 8 CFR §§208.9(g), 1208.9(g); *see also infra* this section.

[69] Appx. 9A, I-589 filing instructions, p. 10.

[70] *See* 72 Fed. Reg. 22601 (Apr. 30, 2007) (DHS's semiannual regulatory agenda).

[71] Information on the status and particulars of the pilot program, and of the proposed regulations implementing a permanent program, is often available in the minutes of meetings between USCIS Headquarters Asylum Division and nongovernmental agencies, coordinated by Human Rights First.

[72] INA §208(d)(4); 8 USC §1158(d)(4).

[73] *See* A. Schoenholtz and J. Jacobs, "The State of Representation: Ideas for Change," 16 *Geo. Immigr. L.J.* 739 (Summer 2002). U.S. immigration laws have been called "second only to the Internal Revenue Code in complexity." *U.S. v. Ahumada-Aguilar*, 295 F.3d 943, 950 (9th Cir. 2002) (citations omitted).

[74] 8 CFR §§292.4, 1292.4.

[75] 8 CFR §§208.9(b), (d), 1208.9(b), (d).

such a statement or comment and may require the counsel or representative to submit the statement or comment in writing.[76] Although practices vary among and even within asylum offices, some asylum officers also permit the attorney or representative to ask the applicant follow-up questions at the end of the interview. The asylum officer may also grant a brief extension of time following an interview for the applicant or the applicant's counsel to submit additional evidence.[77] For tips on representing an applicant at an asylum interview, see appendix 3B.

Department of State Comments

USCIS must forward to the Department of State (DOS) a copy of each asylum application filed affirmatively. DOS has the option of providing detailed country condition information, an assessment of the accuracy of the applicant's assertions regarding conditions in the applicant's home country, information about whether individuals similarly situated to the applicant are persecuted in his or her home country, and any other information DOS believes to be relevant.[78] All such comments must be made part of the record.[79] The applicant must be given an opportunity to review and respond to the comments, unless they are classified.[80] In addition, an asylum officer may request specific comments regarding individual cases or types of claims, or other information the asylum officer deems appropriate.[81] The advice of DOS, however, is not binding on the Asylum Division or the courts.[82]

Failure to Appear

An applicant's failure to appear for a scheduled interview without prior authorization may result in a dismissal of the asylum application or the waiver of the right to an interview.[83] A dismissal may also result if the applicant fails to comply with fingerprint processing requirements and appointments.[84] If the applicant or the applicant's counsel is unable to attend a scheduled interview or appointment, the Asylum Office should be contacted immediately. A failure to appear will be excused if the notice of the interview or fingerprint appointment was not mailed to the applicant's current address and the address was provided to Office of Refugee, Asylum, and International Operations prior to the date the notice was mailed. However, this failure to appear will not be excused if the ap-

---

[76] 8 CFR §§208.9(d), 1208.9(d); *see also* appx. 3C, Sample Closing Statement.

[77] 8 CFR §§208.9(e), 1208.9(e).

[78] 8 CFR §§208.11(a), (b), 1208.11(a), (b).

[79] 8 CFR §§208.11(d), 1208.11(d).

[80] 8 CFR §§208.11(d), 1208.11(d).

[81] 8 CFR §§208.11(c), 1208.11(c).

[82] *See* ch. 2.6.3. *But see* INA §208(b)(1)(B)(iii); 8 USC §1158(b)(1)(B)(iii), added by the REAL ID Act of 2005, specifically allowing adjudicators to rely on DOS reports when assessing credibility.

[83] 8 CFR §§208.10, 1208.10.

[84] 8 CFR §§208.10, 1208.10.

plicant received "reasonable notice" of the interview or fingerprint appointment.[85] A failure to appear will also be excused if the failure was the result of exceptional circumstances.[86]

Changes of address for applications pending with the Asylum Division must be filed on Form AR-11 and submitted to the Asylum Office with jurisdiction over the applicant's claim within 10 days after the applicant changes his or her address.[87] If an applicant files a nonelectronic Form AR-11, this will legally change the applicant's address but will not automatically update the applicant's address on pending applications and petitions filed with USCIS.[88] Therefore, if an applicant chooses to file a paper copy of Form AR-11, the applicant will also need to call customer service at (800) 375-5283 to update his or her address on pending applications and petitions.[89] An applicant can also change his or her address on the USCIS website at *https://egov.uscis.gov/crisgwi/go?action=coa*.[90] By using the online tool, an applicant is able to change his or her address for both legal purposes and for pending applications and petitions.[91]

Identity Check

At the time of the interview, the applicant must provide complete information regarding his or her identity, including name, date and place of birth, and nationality.[92] Asylum cannot be granted until the identity of the applicant has been checked against all appropriate records or databases maintained by the AG or secretary of state, including the Automated Visa Lookout System.[93] These records and databases are checked to determine if the applicant is inadmissible to or deportable from the United States, or ineligible for asylum.[94]

Decision—Grant, Denial, or Referral

At the end of the interview, the applicant will be informed where and when he or she must appear in person to receive and acknowledge receipt of the asylum officer's deci-

---

[85] 8 CFR §§208.10, 1208.10; *see also* appx. 6A for Office of Refugee, Asylum, and International Operations contact information.

[86] 8 CFR §§208.10, 1208.10.

[87] *See* appx. 9A, I-589 filing instructions, pt. 2, sec. I; *see also* How Do I Report a Change of Address to the USCIS?, at *www.uscis.gov/addresschange* (stating that failure to give written notice to USCIS within 10 days of a change of address is a misdemeanor crime).

[88] Filing a paper copy of the AR-11 form will delay the process of notifying USCIS of the change of address significantly. *See* How Do I Report a Change of Address to the USCIS?, at *www.uscis.gov/addresschange*.

[89] Calling this customer service line by itself does not meet the legal requirement of completing an AR-11. *Id.*

[90] *Id.*; *see also* USCIS Online Change of Address, at *https://egov.uscis.gov/crisgwi/go?action=coa*.

[91] Welcome to Change of Address on the Internet for USCIS, at *https://egov.uscis.gov/crisgwi/go?action=coa.Terms*.

[92] 8 CFR §§208.9(b), 1208.9(b).

[93] INA §208(d)(5)(A)(i); 8 USC §1158(d)(5)(a)(i).

[94] INA §208(d)(5)(A)(i); 8 USC §1158(d)(5)(a)(i).

sion.[95] The asylum officer may grant, deny, or refer an asylum claim. The decision of the asylum officer to grant, deny, or refer an asylum application must be communicated in writing to the applicant.[96] An applicant must appear in person to receive and acknowledge receipt of the decision.[97] In the asylum officer's discretion, the decision may be served by mail if appropriate, but generally decisions will be served on the applicant in person.[98]

In reaching a decision on the asylum application, the asylum officer may rely on material provided by DOS, the Office of Refugee, Asylum, and International Operations, other DHS offices, or other credible sources, such as international organizations, private voluntary agencies, news organizations, or academic institutions.[99]

Grant

The asylum officer has the authority to grant asylum in the exercise of discretion to an applicant who qualifies as a refugee under INA §101(a)(42), unless the applicant is prohibited from receiving asylum under 8 CFR §1208.13(c), *i.e.*, the mandatory bars.[100] The grant of asylum is effective for an indefinite period, subject to termination under certain conditions.[101] An applicant who is granted asylum, *i.e.*, an asylee, is authorized to work and, after one year, is eligible for adjustment of status.[102] The asylee may confer derivative asylee status on his or her spouse and unmarried children under 21 years of age.[103]

Denial

An asylum officer may issue a denial to an applicant who is maintaining valid nonimmigrant status at the time the application is decided.[104] The decision denying an application must state the basis for the denial. The denial must also contain an assessment of the applicant's credibility, unless the denial is due to the applicant's conviction of an aggravated felony. Prior to issuing the denial, the asylum officer will issue a Notice of Intent to Deny (NOID) to allow the applicant an opportunity to rebut the reasons for the denial. A NOID, like a denial, may only be issued to an individual maintaining valid nonimmigrant status. One exception to this general rule is that an *ABC* class member must be issued a NOID before a referral may be made to an immigration judge.[105]

---

[95] 8 CFR §§208.9(d), 1208.9(d).

[96] 8 CFR §§208.19, 1208.19.

[97] 8 CFR §§208.19, 1208.19.

[98] 8 CFR §§208.19, 1208.19.

[99] 8 CFR §§208.12(a), 1208.12(a).

[100] 8 CFR §§208.14(b), 1208.14(b). *See* ch. 2.7.

[101] 8 CFR §§208.14(e), 1208.14(e); *see also* this chapter, at 3.16.

[102] *See infra* 3.9 and 3.13.

[103] INA §208(b)(3); 8 USC §1158(b)(3).

[104] 8 CFR §§208.14(c)(1), 1208.14(c)(1).

[105] See ch. 6.5 for more information on *ABC*; *see also* D. Smith, "The *ABC* Settlement: A Guide for Class Members and Advocates," 72 *Interpreter Releases* 1497 (Nov. 6, 1995); American Immigration
continued

The denial of an application filed by the principal applicant will result in the denial of asylum status to any dependents of the principal applicant who are included in the same application.[106] Such a denial, however, will not preclude a grant of asylum for a dependent who has filed a separate application, nor will such a denial bar the dependent from seeking asylum on the basis of having been previously denied asylum.[107]

Referral

If the case is not granted and the applicant appears to be deportable, excludable, or removable, the asylum officer must refer the application to an IJ for adjudication in deportation, exclusion, or removal proceedings.[108] The referral may be made after an interview has been conducted or if the applicant, by failing to appear or provide an interpreter, is deemed to have waived his or her right to an interview.[109] In referral cases, the asylum officer issues a referral notice, containing a checklist of the reasons for the referral, and a Notice to Appear (NTA) to initiate immigration court proceedings. Numerous DHS officers, including supervisory asylum officers, are authorized to issue an NTA.

No Appeal/Motions to Reopen or Reconsider/Quality Assurance

An applicant may not appeal a decision by an asylum officer. Any problems arising in a case may be raised with the director of the Asylum Office where the case was adjudicated.[110]

An applicant may file a motion to reconsider or reopen a decision with the Asylum Office that denied or referred the application.[111] The motion alternatively may be filed with the Asylum Division headquarters office in Washington, D.C.[112] In some cases, the Asylum Division has requested the local Immigration and Customs Enforcement (ICE) office to terminate removal proceedings so that the claim could be readjudicated by the Asylum Office.

Under the Asylum Division's Quality Assurance Program, the following cases must be referred to Headquarters for review: [113]

- *Gender cases* (grants, referrals, and NOIDs of domestic violence cases where gender forms the basis of a particular social group, the applicant is found credible, and mandatory bars do not apply);

Law Center, *The American Baptist Churches v. Thornburgh (ABC) Settlement Agreement,* at www.ailc.com/services/residency/abc-1.htm.

[106] 8 CFR §§208.14(f), 1208.14(f).

[107] 8 CFR §§208.14(f), 1208.14(f).

[108] 8 CFR §§208.14(c), 1208.14(c).

[109] 8 CFR §§208.14(c), 1208.14(c).

[110] See appx. 6A for a list of Asylum Office directors and their telephone numbers.

[111] Procedures for filing a motion to reopen and reconsider can be found in USCIS's *Affirmative Asylum Procedures Manual* at 118–20 (Feb. 2003), available at *www.uscis.gov/files/nativedocuments/ AffrmAsyManFNL.pdf.*

[112] *See* appx. 6A for address and fax number.

[113] USCIS Asylum Division, Quality Assurance Referral Sheet (revised Feb. 9, 2007).

- *Contiguous territory and visa waiver grants* (grants of Mexican or Canadian asylum-seekers, and grants from countries participating in the Visa Waiver Program);
- *National security-related* (grants of cases in which (1) the applicant claimed to have been involved, or was falsely accused of involvement, in terrorist acts or with a terrorist organization; (2) the applicant claims to be related to an individual who is a possible terrorist/security risk; or (3) other evidence indicated a possible security risk, and the individual meets the burden of proof to demonstrate that he or she should not be barred as a terrorist/security risk);
- *Material support provided to a terrorist organization* (grants, referrals, and NOIDs);
- *Persecutors* (grants of cases where evidence indicates that the applicant may have participated in persecution or human rights violations, and the individual meets the burden of proof to demonstrate that he or she should not be barred as a persecutor; referrals and NOIDS of cases involving an individual where the case may be publicized nationally or who may pose a threat to others);
- *Discretionary denials and referrals* (referrals and NOIDS of an applicant who meets the definition of a refugee and is otherwise eligible for asylum, but is denied or referred because of acts that are not a bar to asylum);
- *Those that have been or are likely to be publicized* (grants, referrals, and NOIDS of cases likely to have national exposure, not just local interest; such as where the applicant has publicized that he or she has filed or intends to file for asylum; cases involving notable applicants; or cases involving areas of law perceived in the media to be novel);
- *Diplomats* (grants, referrals, and NOIDS of cases involving sitting diplomats to the United States or United Nations, or other high-level government or military officials and/or their family members; high-ranking diplomats to other countries);
- *Reasonable fear of persecution or torture* (all reasonable fear of persecution or torture determinations; all withdrawals of requests for protection);
- *Credible fear of persecution or torture cases* (all negative decisions; fear of torture/no fear of persecution found; high-profile cases; all solely domestic violence cases;[114] positive determinations in certain cases[115]);
- *NACARA*[116] (grants of cases where there are strong negative factors present, including where evidence indicates that the applicant may have participated in persecution or human rights violations or there is evidence of significant criminal activity; referrals of cases involving an individual barred as a persecutor where the case may be publicized nationally or who may pose a threat to others; all decisions in which the applicant provided material support to a terrorist organization; discretionary referrals; re-

---

[114] *See* ch. 5.

[115] *See* USCIS Interoffice Memorandum, J. Langlois, "Increase of Quality Assurance Review for Positive Credible Fear Determinations and Release of Updated Asylum Office Basic Training Course Lesson Plan, *Credible Fear of Persecution and Torture Determinations*" (Apr. 14, 2006).

[116] *See* ch. 6.6.

ferrals based on good moral character (unless the negative determination is based on a criminal conviction); referral or approval involving an unusual legal issue);

- *Cases with a prior denial by EOIR* (grants, referrals, and NOIDs);
- *Juvenile cases* (grants, referrals, and NOIDs of all cases in which the principal applicant is less than 18 years old at the time of filing); and
- *Asylum Office requests* (any case that the Asylum Office director decides should be reviewed).

An applicant who is not granted asylum and is referred to an IJ may renew his or her request for asylum before the IJ. An applicant who has been denied and who maintains a valid nonimmigrant status may file a new application with the Asylum Division. A new application may be filed with the Asylum Division, for example, in cases in which the applicant has obtained additional evidence in support of his or her claim.

3.2.6. Affirmative Procedures for Children

Children, as well as adults, suffer persecution and torture throughout the world. In some countries, children are subjected to abusive child labor practices, are recruited by regular or irregular armies, are sold into prostitution or indentured servitude, or are subjected to various other human rights abuses. As a result, a small but increasing number of children are seeking asylum in the United States.[117] According to the Department of Justice, in 2006 approximately 8,000 unaccompanied children came to the United States.[118] To address issues that arise in children's claims, the Office of International Affairs (now Office of Refugee, Asylum, and International Operations) issued guidelines for children's asylum claims on December 10, 1998.[119] In addition, the Office of the Chief Immigration Judge issued a memorandum on policies and procedures for immigration cases involving children on May 22, 2007.[120] This memorandum provides nonbinding procedural guidance on cases involving unaccompanied children, defined as children who have not yet

---

[117] *See, e.g.*, J. Bhabha and W. Young, "Through a Child's Eyes: Protecting the Most Vulnerable Asylum Seekers," 75 *Interpreter Releases* 757 (June 1, 1998); *see also* UNHCR, *2006 Global Trends: Refugees, Asylum-seekers, Returnees, Internally Displaced and Stateless Persons*, (revised July 16, 2007), available at *www.unhcr.org/statistics/STATISTICS/4676a71d4.pdf* (stating that 45 percent of refugees, asylum-seekers, returnees, internally displaced and stateless persons are children under the age of 18; 11 percent being under the age of 5).

[118] EOIR Fact Sheet, "Unaccompanied Alien Children in Immigration Proceedings" (Aug. 8, 2007), *published on* AILA InfoNet at Doc. No. 07081563 (*posted* Aug. 15, 2007).

[119] *See* INS Memorandum, J. Weiss, "Guidelines for Children's Asylum Claims" (Dec. 10, 1998), *published on* AILA InfoNet (*posted* Jan. 25, 1999), *reproduced in* 76 *Interpreter Releases* 1, appx. I (Jan. 4, 1999), and available at *www.abanet.org/publicserv/immigration/ins_guidelines_for_children.pdf*. For more information on the adjudication of children's claims in defensive and affirmative proceedings, see this chapter, at 3.3.4 and 3.5.

[120] EOIR Memorandum, D. Neal, "Operating Policies and Procedures Memorandum No. 07-01, Guidelines for Immigration Court Cases Involving Unaccompanied Alien Children" (May 22, 2007), *published on* AILA InfoNet at Doc. No. 07052360 (*posted* May 23, 2007).

attained 18 years of age and have no parent or legal guardian in the United States available to provide care and physical custody.[121]

3.3. IMMIGRATION COURT (DEFENSIVE) PROCEDURES

An application for asylum and withholding of removal in immigration court proceedings is referred to as defensive because these forms of relief are a defense to DHS's efforts to remove the individual from the United States.[122] The removal proceedings are held in immigration court before an immigration judge.

> ➤ *Tip*—For a complete list of immigration courts and judges, see appendix 6B. For links to local court procedures and other court information, go to *www.usdoj.gov/eoir/sibpages/ICadr.htm*.

3.3.1. Who Is Eligible

An individual served with a Notice to Appear (NTA), Form I-862, or other charging document that has been filed with the immigration court may apply defensively for asylum and withholding of removal before an IJ.[123] Some asylum applicants, such as individuals refused admission at a port of entry under the Visa Waiver Pilot Program (VWPP) or the Visa Waiver Program (VWP), are permitted "asylum only" hearings before an IJ.[124] Even if the applicant filed affirmatively, he or she must proceed before an IJ if the charging document has been filed with the immigration court.[125] By regulation, any application for asylum is deemed to be an application for withholding of removal.[126] Unlike asylum officers, IJs may grant withholding of removal or Convention Against Torture protection to any individual who qualifies for such relief. The IJ will also determine whether an applicant is barred from asylum or withholding of removal based on one or more of the grounds of ineligibility.[127]

---

[121] *Id.*

[122] See ch. 6 for other forms of relief in removal proceedings. For practice pointers on preparing direct and cross-examination for an immigration court hearing, see appx. 5A.

[123] 8 CFR §§208.2(b), 1208.2(b), 1240.1(a).

[124] *See* 8 CFR §§208.2(b), (c)(1)(iii), 1208.2(b), (c)(1)(iii); *see also Matter of Kanagasundram*, 22 I&N Dec. 963 (BIA 1999) (finding that legacy INS had improperly placed an asylum applicant from Sri Lanka in expedited removal proceedings and that applicant was entitled to an immediate referral to an IJ for an asylum hearing, despite the fact that he sought entry on a passport from the Netherlands under the VWPP).

[125] 8 CFR §§208.2(b), 1208.2(b); *see also, e.g., Matter of P–L–P–*, 21 I&N Dec. 887 (BIA 1997) (finding that an applicant who was issued a charging document on the day he filed his asylum application with legacy INS could not proceed with his affirmative application).

[126] 8 CFR §§208.3(b), 1208.3(b).

[127] *See* ch. 2.7.

If the applicant had applied affirmatively, the NTA filed with the immigration court will contain a copy of the asylum application, along with any supporting documentation.[128] Under no circumstances, however, should any document containing references to the asylum officer's credibility findings be filed with the immigration court.[129] The information provided by an applicant in an asylum application filed on or after January 4, 1995, may be used as a basis for initiating removal proceedings and to satisfy ICE's burden of proof in exclusion, deportation, or removal proceedings.[130]

On rare occasions, ICE may file a motion to dismiss on the grounds that, among other reasons, the NTA was improvidently issued or that circumstances have changed to such an extent that the continuation of the case is no longer in the best interest of the government.[131] The motion, however, must be adjudicated on the record like any other motion before the IJ or the BIA.[132] If the immigration court proceedings are dismissed, the applicant may be able pursue an affirmative claim, if other bars do not apply.

3.3.2. Where to File

If the applicant already filed an initial application with an Asylum Office, there is no need to file a new application if the claim is referred to an IJ. As noted above, the Asylum Office will submit the previously filed application to the IJ along with the NTA. If there are errors in the previously filed application, or the applicant would like to provide additional details, the applicant may amend his or her application before the IJ.

If, however, the applicant is applying for the first time in removal proceedings, an application for asylum and withholding of removal should be filed directly with the immigration court that has jurisdiction over the applicant's case.[133] An IJ has exclusive jurisdiction over asylum applications filed by applicants who have been served with an NTA or other charging document, after the charging document has been filed with the immigration court.[134] Generally, an applicant will be given a date for filing the application by the IJ at a master calendar hearing. According to a memorandum by Chief Immigration Judge Creppy, an applicant filing for asylum and withholding of removal on or after January 4, 1995, must file his or her application at a master calendar hearing, not at the immigration court filing window.[135]

---

[128] *See* EOIR Memorandum, M. Creppy, "Revised Operating Policy and Procedures Memorandum No. 00-01, Asylum Request Processing" (Aug. 4, 2000) at 14, available at *www.usdoj.gov/eoir/efoia/ocij/oppm00/OPPM00-01Revised.pdf*.

[129] *Id.*

[130] 8 CFR §§208.3(c)(1), 1208.3(c)(1).

[131] 8 CFR §§239.2(a)(6), (a)(7), (c), and 1239.2(c); *see also Matter of G–N–C–*, 22 I&N Dec. 281 (BIA 1998), *criticized on other grounds by Castro-Cortez v. INS*, 239 F.3d 1037, 1052 (9th Cir. 2001).

[132] *Matter of G–N–C–*, 22 I&N Dec. 281 (BIA 1998), *criticized on other grounds by Castro-Cortez v. INS*, 239 F.3d 1037, 1052 (9th Cir. 2001).

[133] 8 CFR §§208.4(b)(3), 1208.4(b)(3).

[134] 8 CFR §§208.2(b), 1208.2(b).

[135] *See* EOIR Memorandum, *supra* note 128, at 15.

3.3.3. No Filing Fee

To date, there is no fee for filing an application for asylum.[136] Nor is there a fingerprinting fee.[137] The statute, however, permits the AG to impose an asylum application fee.[138] Under the Homeland Security Act of 2002, this authority would extend to the DHS Secretary.[139]

3.3.4. Biometrics

At the time the asylum application is filed with the IJ, the IJ will usually make a determination whether fingerprints are needed to proceed with the claim. If so, DHS will supply the applicant with a form, completion of which will generate a biometrics appointment letter. Failure to comply with processing requirements for biometrics will result in dismissal of the application unless the applicant demonstrates that such failure was the result of good cause.[140] Moreover, the IJ cannot grant asylum unless the applicant is in compliance with biometrics requirements under 8 CFR §1003.47.[141]

3.3.5. Hearing

Time Period

By statute, the initial hearing must commence "not later than 45 days" for applications initially filed with the IJ, unless there are exceptional circumstances.[142] Applications filed on or after January 4, 1995, are placed on an expedited docket and should be completed, in the absence of exceptional circumstances, within 180 days after the application is filed with the court.[143] IJs have been instructed to allow for a minimum of 14 days between the master calendar and the individual calendar hearing, unless a two-week delay would prevent the court from completing the case in 180 days or the applicant requests an earlier date.[144] The 180-day period is tied to the 180-day period during which an asylum applicant is ineligible for employment authorization.[145]

---

[136] *See* 8 CFR §103.7.

[137] *See id.*

[138] INA §208(d)(3); 8 USC §1158(d)(3).

[139] *See* Homeland Security Act of 2002, Pub. L. No. 107-296, §§456, 1512, 1517, 116 Stat. 2135, 2200, 2310, 2311.

[140] 8 CFR §§208.10, 1208.10.

[141] 8 CFR §§208.14, 1208.14. For more information, see DHS Fact Sheet, "USCIS and ICE Procedures Implementing EOIR Regulations on Background and Security Checks on Individuals Seeking Relief or Protection from Removal in Immigration Court or Before the BIA" (Aug. 8, 2006), *published on* AILA InfoNet at Doc. No. 06081767 (*posted* Aug. 17, 2006), and available at *www.uscis.gov/files/ article/JointFactsheet080806.pdf.*

[142] INA §208(d)(5); 8 USC §1158(d)(5).

[143] INA §208(d)(5)(a)(iii); 8 USC §1158(d)(5)(a)(iii); *see also* EOIR Memorandum, *supra* note 128, at 8.

[144] INA §208(d)(5)(a)(iii); 8 USC §1158(d)(5)(a)(iii).

[145] *See* this chapter, at 3.9.

> *Tip*—For information on the status of an asylum case, hearing dates, appeal information, and the 180-day work authorization "clock," call the EOIR toll-free number at (800) 898-7180.

Master Calendar Hearings

An asylum applicant may be scheduled for one or more master calendar hearings. The following are preliminary matters addressed at these hearings.

Entry of Appearance

The applicant's representative, if any, enters an appearance before the IJ on Form EOIR-28, Notice of Appearance (traditionally submitted on green paper).[146] The representative must also serve a copy of the Notice of Appearance on the DHS trial attorney.[147] The representative may also file a G-28, Notice of Appearance with DHS (traditionally submitted on blue paper).[148]

Continuances

If the applicant is unrepresented at the initial master calendar hearing, the IJ may grant a continuance to give the applicant an opportunity to obtain representation.[149] The IJ may also grant a continuance for other good cause.[150] Any delay caused by the applicant will stop the "asylum clock."[151] An applicant is eligible to apply for employment authorization when the "asylum clock" reaches 150 days.[152]

Advisals

The IJ must advise the applicant of his or her right to representation; the availability of free legal services; and his or her rights to examine, object to, and present evidence, as

---

[146] 8 CFR §1003.17.

[147] *Id.*

[148] *See* 8 CFR §§292.4(a), 1292.4(a).

[149] 8 CFR §1240.6.

[150] *Id.*; *see also Gjeci v. Gonzales*, 451 F.3d 416, 424 (7th Cir. 2006) (refusal to continue hearing resulted in a denial of due process). *But see Alsamhouri v. Gonzales*, 484 F.3d 117, 123 (1st Cir. 2007) (finding that the denial of a continuance did not result in a fundamentally unfair hearing where the applicant had 16 months to obtain counsel and file his applications); *Berri v. Gonzales*, 468 F.3d 390, 395 (6th Cir. 2006) (finding applicants failed to show good cause where they had two years to prepare for their merits hearing); *Al Khouri v. Ashcroft*, 362 F.3d 461, 464 (8th Cir. 2004) (noting that IJs have wide discretion in managing their dockets and finding no abuse of discretion where the applicant was given ample opportunity to find another attorney).

[151] *See* EOIR Memorandum, Office of the Chief Immigration Judge, "Operating Policies and Procedures Memorandum (OPPM) 05-07, Definitions and Use of Adjournment, Call-up and Case Identification Codes" (June 16, 2005), *published on* AILA InfoNet at Doc. No. 05070660 (*posted* July 6, 2005), and available at *www.usdoj.gov/eoir/efoia/ocij/oppm05/05-07.pdf* (codes marked with an asterisk will stop the asylum clock until the next hearing).

[152] For a more in-depth look at this issue, *see* American Immigration Law Foundation (AILF) Practice Advisory, Employment Authorization and Asylum: Strategies to Avoid Stopping the Asylum Clock (Feb. 28, 2006), available at *www.ailf.org/lac/lac_pa_022806.pdf*.

well as to cross-examine witnesses.[153] If the applicant has not previously filed an application for asylum or withholding of removal with DHS and expresses a fear of returning to his or her home country, the IJ must also: (1) advise the applicant that he or she may apply for asylum and withholding of removal; (2) make the appropriate forms available; (3) provide the applicant with a list of persons who provide pro bono representation; and (4) advise the applicant of the consequences of knowingly filing a frivolous application for asylum.[154] The following cases have examined whether an applicant has knowingly filed a frivolous application: *Farah v. Ashcroft*,[155] *Efe v. Ashcroft*,[156] *Barreto-Claro v. U.S. Attorney Gen.*,[157] *Yuanliang Liu v. United States DOJ*,[158] *Juiang Hui v. U.S. Attorney Gen.*,[159] and *Chandi v. Gonzales*.[160]

Ascertain Desire for Representation

The IJ is required to ask the applicant whether he or she desires representation.[161] Failure to do so may be grounds for the BIA to remand the claim to the IJ.[162]

Pleadings

The IJ will read the factual allegations and charges in the Notice to Appear (NTA) or other charging document and will ask the applicant or his or her representative to respond to them. The applicant or representative must admit or deny the allegations and the charges.[163] Based on the admissions made by the applicant or the applicant's representative, the IJ may determine that removability has been established by the admissions.[164] If

---

[153] 8 CFR §1240.10(a).

[154] 8 CFR §1240.11(c)(1).

[155] *Farah v. Ashcroft*, 348 F.3d 1153 (9th Cir. 2003) (overturning frivolous determination where applicant was not given the opportunity to explain discrepancies).

[156] *Efe v. Ashcroft*, 293 F.3d 899 (5th Cir. 2002) (upholding frivolousness determination where applicant was given ample opportunity to clarify his testimony).

[157] *Barreto-Claro v. U.S. Attorney Gen.*, 275 F.3d 1334 (11th Cir. 2001) (upholding the finding of frivolousness).

[158] *Yuanliang Liu v. United States DOJ*, 455 F.3d 106, 115-16 (2d Cir. 2006) (remanding the case to the BIA to set down clear standards by which a frivolous determination will be judged).

[159] *Juiang Hui v. U.S. Attorney Gen.*, 174 Fed. Appx. 627, 629 (2d Cir. 2006) (upholding the finding of frivolousness where the applicant was given an opportunity to explain the numerous inconsistencies between his application and his testimony).

[160] *Chandi v. Gonzales*, 227 Fed.Appx. 651, 2007 U.S. App. LEXIS 8593 (9th Cir. 2007) (overturning frivolous determination where the IJ did not identify specific discrepancies on which he based his determination that the application was frivolous and where the IJ did not give the applicant a chance to address any discrepancies).

[161] 8 CFR §1240.10(a)(1).

[162] *See Matter of Michel*, 21 I&N Dec. 1101 (BIA 1998).

[163] 8 CFR §1240.10(c).

[164] *Id.*

removability is not established by the admissions of the applicant, the IJ will conduct a hearing on any unresolved issues.[165]

If the applicant had applied affirmatively, the NTA filed with the immigration court will contain a copy of the asylum application, along with any supporting documentation.[166] Any information provided by an applicant in an asylum application filed on or after January 4, 1995, may be used as a basis for initiating removal proceedings and to satisfy ICE's burden of proof in exclusion, deportation, or removal proceedings.[167]

Designation of a Country of Removal

Most asylum applicants decline to designate a country of removal in the event that removal is ordered. If the applicant declines, the IJ is required to designate a country for the applicant.[168] If the IJ designates a country other than the country of claimed persecution, the IJ must advise the applicant that he or she has the right to seek asylum and introduce evidence to contest removal to the country designated by the IJ.[169] An IJ may designate a country even if the applicant is not a citizen or national of the country[170] and regardless of whether the receiving country has made a commitment to accept the applicant.[171]

> *Note*: IJs must inform asylum applicants and other noncitizens in removal proceedings that they can be removed to another country under INA §241(b) in the discretion of the secretary of the Department of Homeland Security.[172]

Motions

An IJ may entertain one or more motions during the preliminary hearing stage, such as motions to change venue, to terminate proceedings, or to suppress evidence. All motions should be in writing and must state the grounds for the motion, the relief sought, and the jurisdiction of the court.[173] A motion must be deemed unopposed unless a timely response

---

[165] 8 CFR §1240.10(d).

[166] *See* EOIR Memorandum, *supra* note 128, at 13–14.

[167] 8 CFR §§208.3(c)(1), 1208.3(c)(1).

[168] 8 CFR §1240.10(f).

[169] *See, e.g., Gebrekidan v. Clark*, 2006 U.S. Dist. LEXIS 83687, at *4–5 (W.D. Wash. 2006) (granting stay of removal to applicant who sought asylum from Eritrea after ICE attempted to remove him to Ethiopia); *see also Kossov v. INS*, 132 F.3d 405, 408 (7th Cir. 1998) (finding that the lack of such advice was a fundamental failure of due process). *But see Desta v. Ashcroft*, 329 F.3d 1179 (10th Cir. 2003) (finding that the BIA has the authority to designate an alternate country of deportation).

[170] INA §§241(b)(2)(E)(i)–(vii); 8 USC §§1231(b)(2)(E)(i)–(vii); *see also Pavlovich v. Gonzales*, 476 F.3d 613, 616 (8th Cir. 2007) (noting that INA §§241(b)(2)(E)(i)–(vii) allow the AG to remove an applicant to any country that falls within one of seven categories if the applicant cannot be removed to his or her country of citizenship or nationality, citing *Jama v. Imm. & Customs Enforcement*, 543 U.S. 335, 342 (2005)).

[171] 8 CFR §§241.15(d), 1240.10(f); *see also Zahren v. Gonzales*, 487 F.3d 1039, 2007 U.S. App. LEXIS 11542, at *9–10 (7th Cir. 2007).

[172] 8 CFR §1240.10(f).

[173] 8 CFR §1003.23(a).

is filed.[174] The decision of whether to grant a change of venue motion rests solely in the discretion of the IJ.[175] In determining whether good cause exists, an IJ may consider a number of factors, including administrative convenience, location of witnesses, the applicant's place of residence, and DHS's interests.[176] The Office of the Chief Immigration Judge has issued a policy memorandum on motions to change venue that noted that the large number filed has created problems in caseload management. The memorandum urges IJs to "make an effort to ensure good cause has been shown."[177]

> *Note*: For regulations regarding exclusion proceedings initiated before April 1, 1997, see 8 CFR §§1240.30–1240.38. For regulations regarding deportation proceedings initiated before April 1, 1997, see 8 CFR §§1240.40–1240.53.

Removability

Immigration court proceedings are bifurcated proceedings, separated into the removability and relief phases. The proceedings advance to the relief phase only if the IJ determines that the applicant is deportable or inadmissible.

Deportability

DHS must establish that the applicant, if other than an "arriving alien," is deportable by clear and convincing evidence.[178] If the applicant has not been admitted or paroled into the United States, DHS must prove the applicant's alienage.[179] Usually this is done through the applicant's own admission at the hearing, but it may also be done by the submission of prior statements made by the applicant to legacy INS, DHS, or other government agencies.[180] If the applicant was searched, apprehended, or questioned in an unlawful manner prior to the applicant's hearing, it may be possible to have the evidence or prior statements excluded from consideration.[181]

---

[174] *Id.* For a sample motion, see appx. 5B.

[175] *Matter of Rivera*, 19 I&N Dec. 688, 690 (BIA 1988).

[176] *Id.*; *see also Baires v. INS*, 856 F.2d 89 (9th Cir. 1988) (IJ's denial of a change of venue motion may violate an applicant's statutory and regulatory procedural rights to present evidence in support of the asylum claim by, among other things, depriving the applicant of the testimony of an expert and other witnesses); *Garcia-Guzman v. Reno*, 65 F. Supp. 2d 1077 (N.D. Cal. 1999) (finding that allowing counsel to appear telephonically was "woefully inadequate" where counsel notified legacy INS prior to the commencement of proceedings of the special needs of his mute client).

[177] *See* EOIR Memorandum, Office of the Chief Immigration Judge, "Operating Policy and Procedure Memorandum 01-02—Changes of Venue" (Oct. 9, 2001) at 1–2, *reprinted in* 79 *Interpreter Releases* 66, 84–85 (Jan. 14, 2002), and available at *www.usdoj.gov/eoir/efoia/ocij/oppm01/OPPM01-02.pdf*.

[178] INA §240(c)(3)(A); 8 USC §1229a(c)(3)(A); 8 CFR §1240.8. *But see Woodby v. INS*, 385 U.S. 276 (1966) (holding that legacy INS must establish deportability by evidence which is clear, *unequivocal*, and convincing).

[179] 8 CFR §1240.8(c).

[180] *See, e.g.*, 8 CFR §1240.7(a); *see also Matter of Ponce-Hernandez*, 21 I&N Dec. 784 (BIA 1999) (finding that the INS met its burden of proof in establishing a minor's deportability on the basis of a Record of Deportable Alien (Form I-213) that documented his identity and alienage).

[181] *See infra* this section.

Chapter 3 • Asylum and Withholding of Removal Procedures

Inadmissibility

If the applicant is an "arriving alien," the applicant must establish that he or she is clearly and beyond a doubt entitled to be admitted to the United States and is not inadmissible as charged.[182] An "arriving alien" is defined as a noncitizen "who seeks admission to or transit through the [United States] . . . or who is interdicted in international or [U.S.] waters . . . [or who is] paroled [into the United States] pursuant to [INA] §212(d)."[183]

Mandatory Denials

If an applicant is subject to the mandatory bars set forth in 8 CFR §1208.13(c) and §1208.16(d)(2), he or she is not eligible for asylum or withholding of removal, but may be eligible for relief under the Convention Against Torture. Deferral of removal under the Convention Against Torture has no such bars.[184]

Department of State Comments

After the applicant has filed his or her asylum application with the immigration court, the court must forward a copy of the application to the Department of State (DOS) pursuant to 8 CFR §1208.11 and must then calendar the case for a merits hearing.[185] The reply from DOS, if any, must be given to both the applicant and DHS, unless the reply is classified.[186] The advice of DOS, however, is not binding on DHS or the courts.[187]

Merits Hearing

The merits hearing, as well as other evidentiary hearings on applications for asylum, are generally open to the public, unless the applicant expressly requests that the hearing be closed.[188]

Closed Hearings

Despite the rule that requires open hearings, shortly after the September 11, 2001, terrorist attacks, Chief Immigration Judge Creppy issued a memorandum to all IJs requiring closed hearings for cases requiring "additional security," *i.e.*, presumably related to the September 11 investigations.[189] The memorandum instructs: "The courtroom must be closed for these cases—no visitors, no family, no press."[190] According to the Department

---

[182] 8 CFR §1240.8(b).

[183] 8 CFR §§1.1(q), 1001.1(q).

[184] *See* ch. 4. See ch. 2.7 for a list of bars to asylum and withholding of removal.

[185] 8 CFR §1240.11(c)(2).

[186] *Id.*

[187] *Gailius v. INS*, 147 F.3d 34, 46 (1st Cir. 1998) (citations omitted) (noting concern that the DOS softpedals human rights violations by countries with which the United States wants to have good relations).

[188] 8 CFR §1240.11(c)(3)(i).

[189] *See* EOIR Internal Memorandum, M. Creppy, "Cases Requiring Special Procedures" (Sept. 21, 2001), *reproduced in* 78 Interpreter Releases 1816 (Dec. 3, 2001).

[190] *Id.* at 1819.

of Justice, as of July 2002, IJs had conducted over 600 of these closed hearings.[191] Not surprisingly, these closed hearings have generated lawsuits and a split in the circuit courts regarding their constitutionality.[192] IJs also have the authority to issue protective orders or seal records regarding law enforcement or national security information. The interim regulations issued on May 28, 2002, require IJs to close hearings to the public "if information subject to a protective order . . . may be considered."[193]

Videoconferenced Hearings

An applicant need not be physically present before the IJ during his or her hearing. Increasingly, IJs are resorting to the use of video removal hearing, where the detained applicants are often miles away.[194] At least one court has held that although such hearings do not violate due process, they do have "the potential of creating certain problems" and seem to place lawyers in a Catch-22 situation that diminishes their effectiveness.[195] The chief immigration judge has given guidance to IJs on how they should conduct video hearings in a memorandum issued in August 2004.[196]

Headquarters Immigration Court

On July 19, 2004, EOIR established the Headquarters Court (HQIC), based in Falls Church, VA. At present, HQIC has four immigration judges who hear cases via video-teleconferencing. The purpose behind this new immigration court is to address short-time resource needs as they arise in the immigration courts nationwide. The HQIC will hear both master calendar and merits hearings.[197]

---

[191] *See* 79 *Interpreter Releases* 1154 (July 29, 2002); *see also* Illinois Coalition for Immigrant and Refugee Rights, *Losing Ground: The Loss of Freedom, Equality, and Opportunity for America's Immigrants since September 11* (Sept. 2003) at 10, available at *www.icirr.org/publications/losingground03.pdf* (stating that "[a] Justice Department letter to Sen. Carl Levin (D-MI) revealed that 611 detainees had been subjected to at least one closed hearing, with 419 going through multiple closed hearings").

[192] *See, e.g., North Jersey Media Group, Inc. v. Ashcroft*, 308 F.3d 198 (3d Cir. 2002); *see also Detroit Free Press v. Ashcroft*, 303 F.3d 681 (6th Cir. 2002).

[193] 8 CFR §1003.27(d); 67 Fed. Reg. 36802 (May 28, 2002); *see also* 8 CFR §§1003.31, 1003.46 regarding the procedures for sealing records or issuing protective orders.

[194] *See* J.T. Hong, Practice Advisory, "Video Removal Hearings: A Violation of Due Process?" 20 *Immigration Law Today* 545 (Nov. 2001) (providing a helpful list of objections to make on the record to a video hearing).

[195] *See Rusu v. INS*, 296 F.3d 316, 322 (4th Cir. 2002). For more information on video hearings and strategies for objecting to them if they fail to comport with due process principles, see AILF Practice Advisory, Objecting to Video Merits Hearings (Dec. 2003), available at *www.ailf.org/lac/lac_pa_121203.pdf*.

[196] *See* EOIR Memorandum, Office of the Chief Immigration Judge, "Interim Operating Policies and Procedures Memorandum No. 04-06: Hearings Conducted Through Telephone and Video Conference" (Aug. 18, 2004), available at *www.usdoj.gov/eoir/efoia/ocij/oppm04/04-06.pdf*.

[197] For more information, see EOIR Fact Sheet, "EOIR Headquarters Immigration Court" (July 21, 2004), available at *www.usdoj.gov/eoir/press/04/HQICFactSheet.htm*.

Location of Hearings

Jurisdiction vests, and proceedings before an IJ commence, when the charging document is filed with the immigration court by DHS.[198] However, sometimes removal proceedings may take place in a location different from where the charging document is filed.[199] IJs conducting telephonic or videoconference hearings are instructed to make a clear record of where the hearing is taking place. According to the Office of the Chief Immigration Judge, the hearing location is the location where the case is docketed for a hearing.[200] The IJs must also note the locations of the applicant, the applicant's representative, if any, and the DHS trial attorney.[201] The law that is to be applied by the IJs is the law of the hearing location (which may be different from the law where the IJ is sitting).[202]

During the hearing, whether in person or via video, the applicant will be examined under oath on his or her application and may present evidence or witnesses on his or her own behalf.[203] The applicant has the burden of establishing that he or she is a refugee as defined in INA §101(a)(42).[204] The DHS trial attorney may call witnesses and present evidence, including classified information.[205]

The decision to grant or deny asylum or withholding of removal must be communicated to both the applicant and DHS.[206] The decision of the IJ may be rendered orally or in writing.[207] Such decisions are usually given orally, immediately after the hearing. Decisions must include a finding on inadmissibility or deportability, the reasons for granting or denying relief, and an order by the IJ.[208] An IJ may issue a summary decision in lieu of an oral or written decision, but only if the applicant has admitted the charges of removability and is clearly ineligible for relief or chooses not to apply for relief.[209]

---

[198] 8 CFR §1003.14.

[199] 8 CFR §1003.11.

[200] *See* EOIR Memorandum, M. Creppy, "Operating Policies and Procedures Memorandum No. 04-04: Hearings Conducted Through Telephone Conference and Video Conference" (July 22, 2004), available at *www.usdoj.gov/eoir/efoia/ocij/oppm04/04-04.pdf*.

[201] *Id.*

[202] *Id.*; *see also Ramos v. Ashcroft*, 371 F.3d 948 (7th Cir. 2004) (denying DOJ's motion to transfer case to Eighth Circuit, where IJ was sitting in Chicago and conducting hearing via teleconference with respondent in Iowa; holding location of hearing was Chicago).

[203] 8 CFR §1240.11(c)(3)(iii).

[204] *Id.*

[205] 8 CFR §1240.11(c)(3)(iv). Regarding the use of classified evidence, see the discussion of the right to due process in this chapter at 3.3.5.

[206] 8 CFR §1240.11(c)(4).

[207] 8 CFR §1003.37(a).

[208] 8 CFR §1240.12(a).

[209] *See* 8 CFR §1240.12(b); *Matter of A–P–*, 21 I&N Dec. 468 (BIA 1999) (finding the IJ properly issued a summary decision in the case an individual from Laos who was ineligible for asylum and withholding of removal because of a conviction for a particularly serious crime).

Rights

Individuals subject to removal proceedings have certain constitutional and statutory rights. Among these rights are:

Fourth Amendment Rights

Evidence obtained as a result of an egregious Fourth Amendment violation may be excluded in an immigration court proceeding.[210] Similarly, a violation of a regulatory requirement by a DHS officer can result in evidence being excluded or proceedings invalidated where the regulation at issue benefits the noncitizen and the violation prejudiced his or her interests that were protected by the regulation.[211]

Right to Due Process

Due process protections under the Fifth Amendment extend to noncitizens who have entered the United States, whether lawfully or unlawfully.[212] Such protections do not extend to noncitizens seeking entry or admission to the United States.[213] One exception to this general rule is that returning lawful permanent residents are entitled to due process protection.[214]

The Fifth Amendment's due process clause requires that removal hearings be fundamentally fair.[215] Recent cases in which courts have found due process violations in re-

---

[210] *See Orhorhaghe v. INS*, 38 F.3d 488 (9th Cir. 1994); *see also Gonzalez-Rivera v. INS*, 22 F.3d 1441 (9th Cir. 1994); *INS v. Lopez-Mendoza*, 468 U.S. 1032 (1984) (holding that the exclusionary rule does not apply in civil deportation proceedings to nonegregious violations of the Fourth Amendment); *U.S. v. Arvizu*, 122 S. Ct. 744 (2002) (although Fourth Amendment protections extend to brief investigatory stops, there is no violation if law enforcement officers have a "reasonable suspicion" of criminal activity); *Perez-Quiroz v. Gonzales*, 221 Fed.Appx. 676, 2007 U.S. App. LEXIS 4515, at *2–3 (9th Cir. 2007). For more detailed information, see R. Chiao, "Fourth Amendment Limits on Immigration Law Enforcement," 93-2 *Immigration Briefings* (Feb. 1992); *see also* J. Wong, "Egregious Fourth Amendment Violations and the Use of the Exclusionary Rule in Deportation Hearings: The Need for Substantive Equal Protection Rights for Undocumented Immigrants," 28 *Colum. Human Rights L. Rev.* 431, 442 (1997).

[211] *Matter of Garcia-Flores*, 17 I&N Dec. 325 (BIA 1980), *disapproved by Montilla v. INS*, 926 F.2d 162, 169 (2d Cir. 1991) ("[A]n alien claiming the INS has failed to adhere to its own regulations regarding the right to counsel in a deportation hearing is not required to make a showing of prejudice before he is entitled to relief. All that needs to be shown is that the subject of the regulations were for the alien's benefit and that the INS failed to adhere to them.").

[212] *See, e.g., Accardi v. Shaughnessy*, 347 U.S. 260 (1954), *superseded on other grounds by La Guerre v. Reno*, 164 F.3d 1035, 1038 (7th Cir. 1998).

[213] *See Shaughnessy v. Mezei*, 345 U.S. 206 (1953) (holding that "whatever the procedure authorized by Congress is, it is due process as far as an alien denied entry is concerned"); *see also Knauff v. Shaughnessy*, 338 U.S. 537, 543 (1950).

[214] *Landon v. Plasencia*, 459 U.S. 21 (1982).

[215] *See, e.g., Reno v. Flores*, 507 U.S. 292, 306 (1993); *see also Al Khouri v. Ashcroft*, 362 F.3d 461, 464 (8th Cir. 2004).

moval hearings include: *Gjeci v. Gonzales*,[216] *Circu v. Gonzales*,[217] *Subhan v. Ashcroft*,[218] *Lin v. Ashcroft*,[219] *Kerciku v. INS*,[220] *Andriasian v. INS*,[221] *Selgeka v. INS*,[222] and *Stoyanov v. INS*.[223]

A neutral judge is one of the most basic due process protections.[224] The Ninth Circuit has reopened an asylum case where it was apparent from the record that the IJ had pressured the *pro se* applicant, off the record, to withdraw his asylum application before taking any testimony in the case.[225] The court held that the IJ had not behaved as a neutral fact-finder interested in hearing the applicant's evidence because he indicated that he had already judged the asylum claim.[226] Similarly, the Sixth Circuit found that an IJ abandoned her role as an impartial arbiter and became a zealous advocate by uncovering a witness that DHS did not reveal or present.[227] A neutral arbiter is, at a minimum, one who has not predecided the case and is not predisposed to disregard a witness's testimony based on that witness's participation in an advocacy group.[228] Other circuit courts that have been critical of the behavior and/or bias exhibited by IJs include: the Second Cir-

---

[216] *Gjeci v. Gonzales*, 451 F.3d 416, 424 (7th Cir. 2006) (refusal to continue hearing resulted in a denial of due process).

[217] *Circu v. Gonzales*, 450 F.3d 990, 995 (9th Cir. 2006) (finding IJ violated applicant's due process rights by taking administrative notice without giving the applicant the opportunity to rebut)

[218] *Subhan v. Ashcroft*, 383 F.3d 591, 595 (7th Cir. 2004) (denial of request for a continuance was arbitrary and a denial of due process).

[219] *Lin v. Ashcroft*, 377 F.3d 1014, 1034 (9th Cir. 2004), *overruled on other grounds by Thomas v. Gonzales*, 409 F.3d 1177, 1187 (9th Cir. 2005) (finding that the ineffective assistance of counsel in a deportation proceeding was a denial of due process because the proceeding was so fundamentally unfair that the applicant was prevented from reasonably presenting his case).

[220] *Kerciku v. Ashcroft*, 314 F.3d 913, 918 (7th Cir. 2003) (the IJ excluded so much of the asylum applicants' testimony that he violated their right to due process).

[221] *Andriasian v. INS*, 180 F.3d 1033, 1041 (9th Cir. 1999) (holding that the last minute designation of Armenia as a country of deportation deprived applicant of the opportunity to prepare and present relevant arguments and evidence regarding harm he would suffer in Armenia).

[222] *Selgeka v. INS*, 184 F.3d 337 (4th Cir. 1999) (finding that the denial of opportunity for a stowaway from Kosovo to have his asylum claim heard before an impartial immigration judge violated due process).

[223] *Stoyanov v. INS*, 172 F.3d 731, 735 (9th Cir. 1999) (finding that by raising the issue of the applicant's credibility sua sponte without affording the applicant an opportunity to offer an explanation of any supposed inconsistencies, the BIA violated the applicant's right to due process).

[224] *Cano-Merida v. INS*, 311 F.3d 960 (9th Cir. 2002).

[225] *Id.*

[226] *Id.* at 964–65 (citations omitted); *see also U.S. v. Aguirre-Tello*, 353 F.3d 1199 (10th Cir. 2003) (finding that the IJ adequately advised the respondent of his rights and eligibility for relief).

[227] *Vasha v. Gonzales*, 410 F.3d 863, 873-75 (6th Cir. 2005) (finding applicant's due process rights were violated by the IJ's off-the-record discussions with the court clerk and the inclusion of evidence regarding the applicant's relationship with a prominent member of the local Albanian community).

[228] *Tun v. Gonzales*, 485 F.3d 1014, 1017, 1026 (8th Cir. 2007) (finding IJ erred in excluding testimony of witness from Physicians for Human Rights).

cuit,[229] the Third Circuit,[230] the Sixth Circuit,[231] the Seventh,[232] the Eighth Circuit,[233] and Ninth Circuit.[234]

In response to this growing chorus of criticism, the attorney general issued a memorandum to IJs expressing concern about their conduct and the quality of their work.[235] The AG then proposed measures to improve the immigration courts and the Board of Immigration Appeals.[236] One recent change has been the development of a code of conduct for IJs and members of the BIA that, inter alia, requires IJs to be "patient, dignified and courteous."[237]

> *Tip*—**Recusal of an IJ**—When is it appropriate to request that an IJ recuse himself or herself? According to the Office of the Chief Immigration Judge, "a judge should recuse him or herself when it would appear to a reasonable person, knowing all the relevant facts, that a judge's impartiality might reasonably be questioned."[238]

As noted above, the DHS trial attorney is authorized by regulation to call witnesses and present evidence, including classified information.[239] If classified information is received, the IJ must inform the applicant.[240] DHS or the agency providing the classified information may provide an unclassified summary for release to the applicant, but they are not required

---

[229] *Huang v. Gonzales*, 453 F.3d 142, 143 (2d Cir. 2006) (finding IJ Chase appeared biased and hostile to Chinese asylum applicant and requesting a remand to a different immigration judge).

[230] *Cham v. Gonzales*, 445 F.3d 683, 686, 691 (3d Cir. 2006) (finding that the applicant under the bullying nature of the IJ was "ground to bits" and requesting the presence of the deputy attorney general at oral argument to answer what procedures are in place to address the IJ's repeated poor conduct).

[231] *Mapouya v. Gonzales*, 487 F.3d 396 (6th Cir. 2007) (finding IJ failed to properly consider the evidence or the legal standards and requesting that the case be remanded to a different IJ).

[232] *Floroiu v. Gonzales*, 481 F.3d 970, 971-73 (7th Cir. 2006) (criticizing the IJ for departing from his judicial role and manifesting a clear bias that constituted a denial of due process).

[233] *Shahinaj v. Gonzales*, 481 F.3d 1027, 1029 (8th Cir. 2007) (remanding case to BIA, which failed to explain how IJ's findings and credibility determination as a whole were not tainted by the IJ's bias, and recommending that the case be assigned to a different IJ).

[234] *Recinos de Leon v. Gonzales*, 400 F.3d 1185, 1187 (9th Cir. 2005) (criticizing IJ for "incomprehensible" and "incoherent" opinion).

[235] AG Memorandum, A. Gonzales, "Memorandum to Immigration Judges" (Jan. 9, 2006), *published on* AILA InfoNet at Doc. No. 06011064 (*posted* Jan. 10, 2006).

[236] DOJ Announcement, "Measures to Improve the Immigration Courts and the Board of Immigration Appeals" (Aug. 9, 2006), *published on* AILA InfoNet at Doc. No. 06080968 (*posted* Aug. 9, 2006).

[237] 72 Fed. Reg. 35510 (June 20, 2007).

[238] EOIR Memorandum, Office of Chief Immigration Judge, Operating Policies and Procedures Memorandum 05-02: Procedures for Issuing Recusal Orders in Immigration Proceedings (Mar. 21, 2005) at 2, available at *www.usdoj.gov/eoir/efoia/ocij/oppm05/05-02.pdf*.

[239] 8 CFR §1240.11(c)(3)(iv).

[240] *Id.*

to do so.²⁴¹ At least one court has held that the use of classified or secret evidence violates due process.²⁴²

> ➤ *Tip*—**Off-the-Record Remarks**—The chief immigration judge has advised IJs that they must maintain and preserve a thorough and complete record of proceedings. If IJs do go off the record during proceedings, they must summarize what was discussed on the record.²⁴³

Right Not to Incriminate Oneself

An individual in removal proceedings has the right to assert the Fifth Amendment privilege against self-incrimination.²⁴⁴ If the individual is other than an "arriving alien," DHS must establish the individual's alienage. The individual's refusal to testify, in the absence of any other evidence of record, is insufficient to constitute prima facie evidence of the individual's alienage and, therefore, insufficient to establish his or her deportability by clear, unequivocal, and convincing evidence.²⁴⁵ The right not to incriminate oneself also applies during custodial interrogations.²⁴⁶ An individual who, at a port of entry, was taken into an interrogation room, stripped of her passport and visa, and shackled at the ankles was found to be in the custody of legacy INS; her right against self-incrimination was thus violated by legacy INS questioning that was reasonably likely to inculpate her.²⁴⁷

Right to Representation

Noncitizens do not have a Sixth Amendment right to be represented in removal proceedings.²⁴⁸ The right to counsel in removal proceedings is, however, grounded in the

---

²⁴¹ *Id.*

²⁴² *See Kiareldeen v. Reno*, 71 F. Supp. 2d 402 (D.N.J. 1999), *rev'd on other grounds by Kiareldeen v. Ashcroft*, 273 F.3d 542 (3d Cir. 2001) (use of secret evidence to support continued detention violates due process).

²⁴³ *See* EOIR Memorandum, Office of the Chief Immigration Judge, "Revised Operating Policy and Procedures Memorandum No. 03-06: Procedures for Going Off-Record During Proceedings" (Oct. 10, 2003), available at *www.usdoj.gov/eoir/efoia/ocij/oppm03/03-06.pdf*.

²⁴⁴ *Kastigar v. United States*, 406 U.S. 441, 444 (1972) (right against self-incrimination applies in civil and administrative proceedings); *Bilokumsky v. Tod*, 263 U.S. 149, 154–55 (1923), *overruled in part by INS v. Lopez-Mendoza*, 468 U.S. 1032 (1984); *Rios-Berrios v. INS*, 776 F.2d 859 (9th Cir. 1985).

²⁴⁵ *Matter of Guevara*, 20 I&N Dec. 238 (1991).

²⁴⁶ *Miranda v. Arizona*, 384 U.S. 436, 444 (1966).

²⁴⁷ *U.S. v. Gonzalez-DeLeon*, 32 F. Supp. 2d 925 (W.D. Tex. 1998); *see also Hernandez-Montiel v. INS*, 225 F.3d 1084, 1098–99 (9th Cir. 2000), *overruled on other grounds by Thomas v. Gonzales*, 409 F.3d 1177 (9th Cir. 2005) (finding that BIA drew improper negative inference regarding persecution claim from applicant's failure to respond to questions about his arrests in the United States).

²⁴⁸ *See Ponce-Leiva v. Ashcroft*, 331 F.3d 369, 374 (3d Cir. 2003); *see also Castro-O'Ryan v. INS*, 847 F.2d 1307, 1312 (9th Cir. 1988).

Fifth Amendment's guarantee of due process.[249] In certain circumstances, depriving a noncitizen of the right to counsel may rise to the level of a due process violation.[250] The right to counsel is also a statutory right.[251] The INA provides for the right to representation in immigration court proceedings, but at no expense to the government.[252]

The regulations specify who is eligible to provide representation in removal proceedings.[253] The categories of representation include: attorneys, law students and law graduates not yet admitted to the bar (if supervised), organizations recognized by the BIA that charge nominal fees (such as nonprofit, religious, or social service organizations), and accredited representatives who are affiliated with a recognized organization and accredited by the BIA.[254]

In the asylum context, the right to counsel has been characterized as "fundamental."[255] As one court has noted, "With only a small degree of hyperbole, the immigration laws have been termed, 'second only to the Internal Revenue Code in complexity.' A lawyer is often the only person who could thread the labyrinth."[256] The BIA has held that "since the right to counsel is . . . often essential to the fundamental fairness of a hearing, meticulous care must be exercised to ensure that a waiver of this right is competently and understandably made."[257] One study has shown that asylum applicants in removal proceedings who are represented by counsel are four to six times more likely to be granted asylum than applicants who are not represented.[258] Another study found that nonrepresented asy-

---

[249] *Prichard-Ciriza v. INS*, 978 F.2d 219, 222 (5th Cir. 1992).

[250] *Tawadrus v. Ashcroft*, 364 F.3d 1099, 1103 (9th Cir. 2004) (holding there must be a knowing and voluntary waiver of the right to counsel); *Al Khouri v. Ashcroft*, 362 F.3d 461, 464 (8th Cir. 2004) (finding no due process violation where applicant waived his right to counsel).

[251] *Ponce-Leiva, supra* note 248, at 374–75.

[252] INA §§240(b)(4), 292; 8 USC §§1229a(b)(4), 1362; *see also* 8 CFR §§1240.3, 1292.1. *But see Machado v. Ashcroft*, No. Cs-02-0066-FVS, Preliminary Injunction Order (E.D. Wash., Mar. 5, 2002) (legacy INS ordered to hire a lawyer for a child in its custody at government expense or release him from detention). For more information regarding this class action suit seeking appointed counsel for children in immigration detention, see "Advocates File Class Action Suite to Compel INS to Provide Counsel for Detained Minors," 79 *Interpreter Releases* 622 (Apr. 29, 2002).

[253] 8 CFR §§292.1, 1292.1.

[254] For more information on recognized organization and accredited representatives, see 8 CFR §§292.2, 1292.2; EOIR Fact Sheet, "Representation of Aliens in Immigration Proceedings" (revised Mar. 20, 2006), *published on* AILA InfoNet at Doc. No. 05072760 (*first posted* July 27, 2005), and available at *www.usdoj.gov/eoir/press/06/AccreditationFactSheetMarch202006.htm*.

[255] *Orantes-Hernandez v. Thornburgh*, 919 F.2d 549, 554 (9th Cir. 1990).

[256] *U.S. v. Ahumada-Aguilar*, 295 F.3d 943, 950–51 (9th Cir. 2002).

[257] *Matter of Gutierrez*, 16 I&N Dec. 226, 228 (BIA 1977).

[258] *See* A. Schoenholtz and J. Jacobs, "The State of Representation: Ideas for Change," 16 *Geo. Immigr. L.J.* 739 (Summer 2002). For a listing of free or low cost legal counsel, call (800) 870-3676 or visit the EOIR website at *www.usdoj.gov/eoir/probono/states.htm*.

lum-seekers had a much lower chance of being granted asylum (2%) than those with an attorney (25%).[259]

The right to counsel may be infringed by violating other statutory or regulatory provisions, such as by denying a motion for change of venue or denying a continuance necessary to permit representation by counsel of one's choice.[260] In addition, to waive the right to counsel, an IJ must: (1) inquire whether the applicant wishes to proceed without a lawyer and (2) receive a knowing, voluntary, affirmative response from the applicant.[261]

When an applicant is unrepresented, however, IJs have a duty to "fully develop the record."[262] Courts have found that noncitizens appearing *pro se* in removal proceedings often lack the legal knowledge to navigate "the morass of immigration law" and have found it critical for IJs to "scrupulously and conscientiously probe into, inquire of, and explore for all relevant facts.[263] Where the IJ failed to develop the record fully by curtailing the applicant's testimony, failed to instruct the applicant that he or she should provide detailed responses, and failed to give the unrepresented applicant adequate time to review a 200-page court submission, the applicant's hearing was found to be fundamentally unfair.[264]

Right to Competent Interpreter

If an individual in immigration court proceedings cannot speak English fluently, the presence of a competent interpreter is essential for his or her meaningful participation in the hearing and to ensure the fundamental fairness of the proceedings.[265] Even where

---

[259] United States Commission on International Religious Freedom, Asylum Seekers in Expedited Removal: A Study Authorized by Section 605 of the International Religious Freedom Act of 1998 (Feb. 2005), available at *www.uscirf.gov/countries/global/asylum_refugees/2005/february/execsum.pdf*.

[260] *See Garcia-Guzman v. Reno*, 65 F. Supp. 2d 1077 (N.D. Cal. 1999) (finding that requiring counsel to appear telephonically was "woefully inadequate" where counsel notified legacy INS prior to the commencement of proceedings of the special needs of his "mute" client); *see also Ahumada-Aguilar*, 295 F.3d at 950–52 (finding that lack of a knowing and intelligent waiver of the right to counsel is a violation of due process where prejudice is shown). *But see Al Khouri v. Ashcroft*, 362 F.3d 461, 464 (8th Cir. 2004) (finding that the applicant was given ample opportunity to obtain new counsel and the IJ did not abuse his discretion in denying applicant's request for a continuance).

[261] *Hernandez-Gil v. Gonzales*, 476 F.3d 803, 804 (9th Cir. 2007) (finding that the applicant was denied his statutory right to counsel where he told the IJ he was not prepared to go forward, that he did not want to proceed without his lawyer, and that he wanted a continuance so that he could proceed with his attorney present).

[262] *Al Khouri*, *supra* note 260, at 464 (citing *Jacinto v. INS*, 208 F.3d 725, 733–34 (9th Cir. 2000)). *But see Kalaj v. Gonzales*, 201 Fed. Appx. 345, 349 (6th Cir. 2006) ("Even were this court to hold with the Ninth Circuit . . . that an IJ in an adversarial hearing must 'develop the record' according to a rule developed for non-adversarial social security hearings, that rule would not seem to apply here since the applicant did not appear 'without counsel.'").

[263] *Al Khouri*, *supra* note 260, at 464–65 (citing *Key v. Heckler*, 754 F.2d 1545, 1551 (9th Cir. 1985)).

[264] *Id.* at 465.

[265] *See Matter of Tomas*, 19 I&N Dec. 464 (BIA 1987) (asylum claim of a Kanjobal speaker from Guatemala remanded because applicant could not adequately present his claim through the Spanish interpreter provided by the court); *see also Tun v. Gonzales*, 485 F.3d 1014, 1030 (8th Cir. 2007) ("Com-
continued

there is no due process violation, faulty or unreliable translations can undermine the evidence on which an adverse credibility determination is based.[266] In reversing a negative credibility determination, the Ninth Circuit noted that "some portions of the transcript read like, 'Who's on First.'"[267]

The interpreter, however, is not required to translate the entire proceeding for the applicant.[268] Nor is the court required to provide an interpreter to assist the applicant in completing the asylum application.[269] In an unpublished decision, the BIA held that it was improper for the IJ to terminate proceedings in the case of a detained individual who was unable to complete his asylum application in English.[270]

Right to Present, Examine, and Object to Evidence

In removal proceedings, noncitizens are entitled to a reasonable opportunity to present evidence on their own behalf and to examine the evidence against them unless it is classified national security information.[271] Refusal to hear evidence in an asylum claim is a denial of the right to present evidence under the INA and regulations.[272] The regulations further provide that noncitizens are entitled to a reasonable opportunity to object to the evidence presented against them.[273] It is a denial of due process for IJs to interrupt applicants and to refuse to hear testimony regarding particular elements of the claim.[274]

---

mon sense informs us that evidence of improper translation may include direct evidence of mistranslated words, evidence that a witness is unable to understand a translator, or unresponsive answers from a witness."); *Singh v. Ashcroft*, 367 F.3d 1139, 1143–44 (9th Cir. 2004) (noting that standard for remand in an incompetent translation claim is whether a better translation would have made a difference in the outcome); *Augustin v. Sava*, 735 F.2d 32, 37 (2d Cir. 1984) (holding that asylum-seekers have a due process right to a translator in their hearings).

[266] *See He v. Ashcroft*, 328 F.3d 593, 598 (9th Cir. 2003).

[267] *Id.* at 597.

[268] *El Rescate Legal Services, Inc. v. EOIR*, 959 F.2d 742 (9th Cir. 1992) (finding that this policy does not deny applicants a reasonable opportunity to be present, to examine unfavorable evidence, to present favorable evidence, or to cross-examine government witnesses).

[269] *Matter of Singh*, A78 494 845 (BIA Nov. 23, 2001).

[270] *Id. But see Matter of Liao*, A44 197 294 (BIA Oct. 22, 1999) (BIA, in unpublished decision, upheld IJ's decision to terminate proceedings where applicant did not have access to an interpreter).

[271] INA §240(b)(4); 8 USC §1229a(b)(4); 8 CFR §1240.11(c)(3)(iii). *But see Kiareldeen v. Reno*, 71 F. Supp. 2d 402 (D.N.J. 1999), *rev'd on other grounds by Kiareldeen v. Ashcroft*, 273 F.3d 542 (3d Cir. 2001) (use of secret evidence to support continued detention violates due process); "Federal Court Rules against Government in Secret Evidence Case," 76 *Interpreter Releases* 1657 (Nov. 15, 1999).

[272] *Pronsivakulchai v. Gonzales*, 461 F.3d 903, 908 (7th Cir. 2006) (finding that IJ's refusal to hear evidence in asylum case denied the applicant the opportunity to be heard and to present evidence on her behalf in violation of INA §249(b)(4)(B) and 8 CFR §1240.1(c)).

[273] 8 CFR §1240.10(a)(4).

[274] *See Colmenar v. INS*, 210 F.3d 967, 971 (9th Cir. 2000) (finding IJ behaved as a "partisan adjudicator" who sought to intimidate the applicant and his counsel); *see also Podio v. INS*, 153 F.3d 506 (7th Cir. 1999) (finding IJ's frequent interruptions of the applicant's testimony and refusal to permit the testimony of the applicant's witnesses also violate an applicant's right to due process); *Zhu v. Ashcroft*, 382 F.3d 521, 526 n.2 (5th Cir. 2004) (in remanding case, court noted that the commentary on the ap-
continued

> *Tip*—**Are Asylum Officer's Notes and Assessments Admissible?**—One unpublished BIA decision has held that they are not. The BIA in a June 14, 2005, asylum appeal remanded the case for a new hearing because the IJ had admitted into evidence an asylum officer's completed assessment that included numerous credibility findings.[275] The BIA found that this admission was precluded by a revised operating policy and procedures memorandum issued in 2000.[276]

Right to Cross-Examine Witnesses

In removal proceedings, noncitizens also have the right to cross-examine witnesses presented by DHS.[277] An IJ is not required, however, to permit cross-examination regarding documents prepared by immigration agents without evidence that the agent is an unfriendly witness or an inaccurate recorder.[278] IJs will permit cross-examination if there is evidence of coercion or that the information contained in the form is incorrect.[279] DHS must also make a reasonable effort to afford the noncitizen a reasonable opportunity to confront the witnesses against him or her.[280]

Right to Appeal

Noncitizens generally have the right to appeal an IJ decision to the BIA.[281] Two notable exceptions to this rule are: (1) in absentia orders;[282] and (2) IJ reviews of negative credible-fear determinations.[283] If an applicant waives his or her right to appeal, the IJ's order becomes final.[284] However, the waiver of the right to appeal, if not "considered and

---

plicant's case by the IJ was "highly inappropriate" and "facially sexist"). *But see Ciorba v. Ashcroft*, 323 F.3d 539 (7th Cir. 2003) (holding that when IJ cut off pre-1991 testimony, attorney for applicant should have made an offer of proof to court or show any prejudice that resulted); *Morales v. INS*, 208 F.3d 323, 327 (1st Cir. 2000) (finding that although the judge was somewhat impatient, applicant was not denied a full hearing on his asylum application). For additional cases, see the discussion of evidence *infra* this section.

[275] This BIA case is available at *www.lexisnexis.com/practiceareas/immigration/pdfs/web846.pdf*.

[276] EOIR Memorandum, M. Creppy, "Revised Operating Policy and Procedures Memorandum No. 00-01, Asylum Request Processing" (Aug. 4, 2000), available at *www.usdoj.gov/eoir/efoia/ocij/oppm00/OPPM00-01Revised.pdf*.

[277] INA §240(b)(4); 8 USC §1229a(b)(4); *see also* 8 CFR §1240.10(a)(4).

[278] *Cruz-Espinoza v. INS*, 45 F.3d 308, 311 (9th Cir. 1995).

[279] *Id.* at 310.

[280] *Saidane v. INS*, 129 F.3d 1063, 1065–66 (9th Cir. 1997) (legacy INS's reliance on a damaging hearsay affidavit rendered the hearing fundamentally unfair); *see also Kiareldeen v. Reno*, 71 F. Supp. 2d 402 (D.N.J. 1999), *rev'd on other grounds by Kiareldeen v. Ashcroft*, 273 F.3d 542 (3d Cir. 2001) (finding that legacy INS's reliance on secret evidence and the denial of a meaningful opportunity to cross-examine even one witness violated the right to due process).

[281] 8 CFR §1240.15; *see also* this chapter, at 3.10.

[282] *See infra* this section.

[283] *See* ch. 5.

[284] *See Matter of L–V–K–*, 22 I&N Dec. 976 (BIA 1999), *rev'd on other grounds by Konstantinova v. INS*, 195 F.3d 528 (9th Cir. 1999).

intelligent," violates due process.[285] Although the BIA does not ordinarily entertain interlocutory appeals, it will rule on the merits of such appeals where it is necessary to address important jurisdictional questions regarding the administration of the immigration laws or to correct recurring problems in the handling of cases before IJs.[286]

Asylum-seekers in removal proceedings may appeal a negative BIA decision to a federal appeals court, unless they are barred because of a criminal conviction.[287] If, however, the appeal concerns whether a particular offense is a bar to review, federal courts have permitted review.[288]

"Right" to Confidentiality

Is there a right to confidentiality in asylum adjudications? According to the regulation on confidentiality:

> Information contained in or pertaining to any asylum application . . . shall not be disclosed without the written consent of the applicant . . . .[289]

Section III of the Instructions to the Application for Asylum and Withholding of Removal (Form I-589) provides:

> [N]o information indicating that you have applied for asylum will be provided to any government or country from which you claim a fear of persecution. Regulations at 8 CFR sections 208.6 and 1208.6 protect the confidentiality of asylum claims.

Remarkably, no exceptions are listed on the application form. There are exceptions, however, most of which are outlined in 8 CFR §§208.6(c), 1208.6(c). The broadest exception is found at 8 CFR §§208.6(a), 1208.6(a) and allows for the disclosure of asylum information and records "*at the discretion of the Attorney General.*"[290] Under the Homeland Security Act of 2002, this discretion would extend to the DHS secretary.[291] In *Matter of Jean*, the AG invoked the discretion to disclose in publishing the asylum applicant's name in his precedent decision.[292] Normally, BIA and AG precedent decisions list only the asylum applicants' initials.

---

[285] *See U.S. v. Zarate-Martinez*, 133 F.3d 1194, 1097–98 (9th Cir. 1998) *questioned on other grounds by United States v. Balleteros-Ruiz*, 319 F.3d 1101, 1104 (9th Cir. 2003) (holding that an IJ's request that an individual raise his or her hand if he or she wishes to appeal violates due process).

[286] *See, e.g., Matter of Morales*, 21 I&N Dec. 130 (BIA 1995) (finding that the immigration court did not have jurisdiction to proceed with the case of an *ABC* class member).

[287] *See* this chapter, at 3.12.

[288] *See, e.g., Coronado-Durazo v. INS*, 123 F.3d 1323 (9th Cir. 1997).

[289] 8 CFR §§208.6(a), 1208.6(a). In *Lewis v. DOJ*, 34 Fed. Appx. 774 (Fed Cir. 2002) (unpublished), the Merits Systems Protection Board concluded that a breach of the confidentiality provision found at 8 CFR §208.6 was a firing offense, irrespective of whether the breach was harmless.

[290] 8 CFR §§208.6(a), 1208.6(a) (emphasis added).

[291] *See* Homeland Security Act of 2002, Pub. L. No. 107-296, §§456, 1512, 1517, 116 Stat. 2135, 2200, 2310, 2311.

[292] *Matter of Jean*, 23 I&N Dec. 373, 373 n.1 (AG 2002).

Asylum advocates have reported a marked increase in the number of overseas investigations of asylum claims. At the request of DHS and legacy INS, overseas investigators (often nationals of the home country) have been sent out to verify the authenticity of arrest warrants, political party documents, and medical records. The Ninth Circuit has held in an unpublished decision that an applicant for Convention Against Torture (CAT) relief did not have his right to confidentiality violated when an immigration official informed the Salvadoran Interpol office that the applicant was in immigration proceedings, because the information provided revealed nothing about the nature of the application for relief.[293]

When do overseas investigations cross the line and violate confidentiality? The Second Circuit has held in a recent case that the U.S. government breached the confidentiality owed to an asylum applicant when it provided the Chinese government with an unredacted copy of the applicant's prison release certificate.[294] The court found that this breach potentially exposed the applicant and his family to a new risk and ordered the BIA to consider this new risk on remand.[295]

In June 2005, the director of the Asylum Division issued a fact sheet on confidentiality to all Asylum Office directors and deputy directors.[296] The fact sheet notes that if information is disclosed publicly regarding an asylum applicant, it could subject the applicant to retaliatory measures by government authorities or nonstate actors. It further states that confidentiality is breached when "information contained in or pertaining to an asylum application is disclosed to a third party . . . ."[297] The only exceptions are: (1) consent by the applicant, (2) authorization by the Secretary of DHS, or (3) disclosure to U.S. government officials on a need-to-know basis.[298] Similarly, a memorandum from former INS General Counsel Bo Cooper, states that 8 CFR §208.6 "prohibits INS [now DHS] personnel from commenting to any third party on the nature or even the existence of individual applications for asylum."[299] Although there is an exception for disclosures "at the Attorney General's discretion," this does not extend, the memorandum noted, to INS [now DHS] personnel.[300] The memorandum contains nine guidelines for conducting overseas investigations. The following are three of those guidelines:

---

[293] *Velasco v. INS*, 87 Fed. Appx. 35, 2004 WL 78208 (9th Cir. 2004). See ch. 4 for more information on Convention Against Torture relief.

[294] *Zhen Nan Lin v. United States DOJ*, 459 F.3d 255, 262 (2d Cir. 2006) (rejecting the BIA's finding that a breach occurs only when sensitive information is revealed).

[295] *Id.* at 268.

[296] USCIS Asylum Division Fact Sheet, "Federal Regulations Protecting the Confidentiality of Asylum Applicants" (June 3, 2005), *published on* AILA InfoNet at Doc. No. 05062440 (*posted* Jun. 24, 2005), and available at *www.uscis.gov/files/pressrelease/FctSheetConf061505.pdf*.

[297] *Id.* at 2.

[298] *Id.*

[299] *See* INS Memorandum, B. Cooper, "Confidentiality of Asylum Applications and Overseas Verification of Documents and Application Information (Confidentiality Memo)" (June 21, 2001), at 2.

[300] *Id.*

(1) If an investigation cannot be accomplished without compromising the confidentiality of the application, the investigation should be abandoned and the investigator should inform the requestor of the investigation of this fact.

(2) Generally, confidentiality of an asylum application is breached when information contained therein or pertaining thereto is disclosed to a third party, and the disclosure is of a nature that allows the third party to link the identity of the applicant to: (1) the fact the applicant has applied for asylum; (2) specific facts or allegations pertaining to the individual asylum claim contained in the asylum application; or (3) facts or allegations that are sufficient to give rise to a reasonable inference that the applicant has applied for asylum. If one or the other part of this link is missing, then no breach has occurred.

(9) The content of the investigative report . . . must contain at a minimum:

    (i) the name and title of the investigator;

    (ii) a statement that the investigator is fluent in the relevant language(s) . . . ;

    (iii) any other statements of the competency of the investigator . . . ;

    (iv) the specific objective of the investigation;

    (v) the location(s) of any conversation or other searches conducted;

    (vi) the name(s) and title(s) of the people spoken to in the course of the investigation;

    (vii) the method used to verify the information;

    (viii) the circumstances, content and results of each relevant conversation or searches; and

    (ix) a statement that the Service investigator is aware of the confidentiality provisions found in 8 CFR §208.6.[301]

UNHCR, however, imposes a more bright-line rule. In an October 29, 1998, advisory opinion, UNHCR advised that governments "not share any information relating to individual cases with the country of origin."[302] One reason for this is that sharing such information "could increase the likelihood of retaliatory or punitive measures by the national authorities in the event the individuals are repatriated."[303] Another reason is that "sharing information with the countries of origin may endanger the security of any family members who may be residing in those countries."[304] As a general rule, according to UNHCR, dialogue with countries of origin on individual cases is *absolutely excluded*.[305] The only exception to the duty of confidentiality, according to UNHCR, is in the case of voluntary

---

[301] *Id.* at 3–7.

[302] UNHCR Advisory Opinion (Oct. 29, 1998), at 1. For a copy of this advisory opinion, contact UNHCR at: 1775 K Street, NW, Suite 300, Washington, DC 20006; (202) 295-5191; *usawa@unhcr.ch*.

[303] *Id.*

[304] *Id.*

[305] *Id.* (emphasis added).

repatriation, when, with the consent of the individual, UNHCR shares information with the country of origin.[306]

Incompetents

The AG is required to prescribe safeguards for protecting the rights and privileges of mentally incompetent noncitizens in removal proceedings.[307] Under the Homeland Security Act of 2002, this authority would extend to the DHS Secretary and other DHS officials.[308] The IJ may not accept an admission of removability from a person who is incompetent and who is not represented by an attorney or legal representative, a near relative, legal guardian, or friend.[309] In such cases, the IJ is required to hold a hearing on the issue of removability.[310] In an unpublished decision, the BIA has held that in cases in which a mentally incompetent person is not represented by a guardian or other representative, the IJ may be required to appoint one on his or her behalf.[311]

In determining whether an individual is competent for purposes of a removal hearing, an IJ may have to receive evidence regarding the individual's mental competency. The Sixth Circuit has held that the only time a hearing is required is when an *"unrepresented alien shows sufficient evidence of incompetency to require an attorney or guardian to represent the alien's interests . . . ."*[312] The standard of competency in federal *criminal* trials is whether the accused (1) has sufficient present ability to consult with counsel with a reasonable degree of rational understanding, and (2) has a rational as well as a factual understanding of the proceedings.[313] In an unpublished decision, the BIA remanded a case to the IJ to determine whether an individual was "mentally competent to *meaningfully participate* in her own hearing."[314] If the IJ determined that he or she could not so participate, the IJ must appoint a guardian or representative for the individual and hold a new hearing to determine if he or she is eligible for relief from removal.[315] If an individual is unable to participate in his or her own defense, proceeding with a removal hearing

---

[306] *Id.* at 2.

[307] INA §240(b)(3); 8 USC §1229a(b)(3).

[308] *See* Homeland Security Act of 2002, Pub. L. No. 107-296, §§456, 1512, 1517, 116 Stat. 2135, 2200, 2310, 2311.

[309] 8 CFR §1240.10(c).

[310] *Id.*

[311] *See Matter of M–V– [number withheld]* (BIA Feb. 19, 2002), *reported in* 21 Immigration Law Today 229 (Apr. 2002).

[312] *Jadaan v. Gonzales,* 211 Fed. Appx. 422, 431 (6th Cir. 2006) (emphasis in original).

[313] *Dusky v United States,* 362 U.S. 402, 403 (1960).

[314] *See Matter of M–V–, supra* note 311 (emphasis added).

[315] *Id. But see Nelson v. INS,* 232 F.3d 258, 261–62 (1st Cir. 2000) (finding applicant's statements that she has a "bad memory," that she "forget[s] things," and that she "get[s] pain" were "limited" symptoms that would *not* require IJ to request a custodian or other party to appear on her behalf); *Nee Hao Wong v. INS,* 550 F.2d 521, 523 (9th Cir. 1977) (holding due process does not require that proceedings be postponed until an incompetent individual is able to participate intelligently in the proceedings where he was accompanied by a state-appointed conservator who testified fully on his behalf).

may violate an individual's right to due process. Due process requires a meaningful opportunity to be heard,[316] but may not protect an incompetent from deportation.[317]

In cases in which it is impracticable for an individual to be present for his or her removal proceedings because of mental incompetency, the attorney, legal representative, legal guardian, near relative, or friend who was served with a copy of the NTA will be permitted to appear on behalf of the individual.[318] If such a person cannot be found, the custodian of the individual will be requested to appear on his or her behalf.[319] If a person confined to a penal or mental institution is competent to understand the nature of the proceedings initiated against him or her, DHS must personally serve both the individual confined and the person in charge of the institution or hospital.[320] If the person confined is not competent to understand the nature of the proceedings, DHS must serve only the person in charge of the hospital or institution.[321] Whether or not the mentally incompetent person is confined, DHS must also personally serve the person with whom the incompetent individual resides.[322] Whenever possible, DHS should also serve the near relative, guardian, committee, or friend of the incompetent individual.[323]

In certain circumstances, mental issues can constitute grounds for inadmissibility or deportation.[324] The Ninth Circuit has stressed the importance of having an incompetent individual's rights protected through necessary and proper safeguards.[325]

Unaccompanied Minors

An immigration judge may not accept an admission of removability from an individual under 18 years of age who is not accompanied by an attorney or legal representative, a near relative, legal guardian, or friend.[326] This regulation does not preclude the IJ from accepting a minor's admissions to factual allegations, which may properly form the basis

---

[316] *See, e.g., Mathews v. Eldridge*, 424 U.S. 319, 348 (1976); *Kaczmarczyk v. INS*, 933 F.2d 588, 595 (7th Cir. 1991).

[317] *See Nee Hao Wong v. INS*, 232 F.3d 521, 523 (9th Cir. 1977) (stating that deportation is "not a criminal proceeding, and the full trappings of procedural protections that are accorded criminal defendants are not necessarily constitutionally required for deportation proceedings"); *see also United States v. Mandycz*, 199 F. Supp. 2d 671, 675 (D. Mich. 2002) (finding that because due process does not protect incompetent defendants from deportation, a fortiori, it does not protect incompetent defendants from denaturalization).

[318] 8 CFR §1240.4.

[319] *Id.*

[320] 8 CFR §103.5a(c)(2)(i).

[321] *Id.*

[322] 8 CFR §103.5a(c)(2)(ii).

[323] *Id.*

[324] *See* INA §§212(a)(1)(A)(iii), 237(a)(1)(A); 8 USC §1182(a)(1)(A)(iii), 1227(a)(1)(A).

[325] *Nee Hao Wong v. INS*, 550 F.2d 521, 523 (9th Cir. 1977).

[326] 8 CFR §1240.10(c); *see also Flores-Chavez v. Ashcroft*, 262 F.3d 1150, 1156 (9th Cir. 2004) (stating that "juveniles are presumed unable to appear at immigration proceedings without the assistance of an adult").

of a finding that the minor is removable.[327] The BIA has cautioned that an IJ must exercise "particular care" in determining a minor's removability and must take into account the minor's age and unaccompanied status.[328] In the case of a minor under 14 years of age, DHS must personally serve the NTA on the person with whom the minor resides.[329] Whenever possible, DHS should also personally serve the near relative, guardian, committee, or friend.[330]

The parent or guardian of a child must establish his or her own identity, as well as the identity of the child, and must also establish his or her parentage or provide a court order establishing guardianship.[331] At least one court has found that it was not an error for the IJ and BIA to refuse to appoint a guardian ad litem for a minor aged 16 when he was represented by counsel and in the custody of legacy INS.[332]

There are certain methods by which an unaccompanied minor may remain in the United States legally.[333] One of these ways is by applying for special immigrant juvenile status.[334]

Consequences of Failure to Appear

A noncitizen who fails to attend immigration court proceedings after having been properly served with a Notice to Appear or whose counsel has been served pursuant to INA §239(a) will be ordered removed in absentia, *i.e.*, in his or her absence, if DHS establishes by clear, unequivocal, and convincing evidence that written notice was provided and that the noncitizen is removable.[335] Written notice is not required if the noncitizen failed to provide the required address,[336] but only if he or she has received the appropriate warnings about the consequences of not providing the required address.[337]

---

[327] *Matter of Amaya-Castro*, 21 I&N Dec. 583 (BIA 1996).

[328] *Id.* at 6. *But see Matter of Ponce-Hernandez*, 21 I&N Dec. 784 (BIA 1999) (in the case of a 15-year-old minor who failed to appear for his deportation hearing, the BIA found that legacy INS met its burden of proof in establishing deportability on the basis of a Record of Deportable Alien (Form I-213), which documented the minor's identity and alienage).

[329] 8 CFR §103.5a(c)(2)(ii).

[330] *Id.*; *see also Mejia-Andino*, 23 I&N 533 (BIA 2002) (proceedings against a minor were properly terminated because service of the Notice to Appear was made on the minor's uncle, not her parents). *But see Flores-Chavez v. Ashcroft*, 362 F.3d 1150 (9th Cir. 2004) (finding DHS erred in not serving Notice of Hearing and charging document on the adult to whom the child was released from DHS custody).

[331] 8 CFR §103.21(c).

[332] *Chitay-Pirir v. INS*, 169 F.3d 1079, 1081 (7th Cir. 1999); *see also* this chapter, at 3.5.

[333] *See In re Zaim R.*, 13 Misc.3d 180, 822 N.Y.S.2d 368 (N.Y. Fam. Ct. 2006); *see also* ch. 6.13.5.

[334] A minor may apply for this status when he or she entered the country illegally or "without inspection." *Matter of Zaim R.*, 2006 NY Slip Op 26247, 1 (N.Y. Misc. 2006).

[335] INA §240(b)(5)(A); 8 USC §1229a(b)(5)(A).

[336] INA §240(b)(5)(B); 8 USC §1229a(b)(5)(B).

[337] *See Matter of G–Y–R–*, 23 I&N Dec. 181 (BIA 2001) (upholding an IJ's refusal to issue an in absentia order against an individual who was never advised of the consequences of her failure to provide legacy INS with a mailing address and who never received actual service of the NTA). *But see Matter continued*

> *Tip*—**Late Arrival?**—Arriving 15 to 20 minutes late to court has been found to be a "brief and innocent" absence that is not a "failure to appear."[338]

Such failure to appear after receiving the required notice of the consequences of failing to appear will bar an individual from the following forms of relief for a period of 10 years: cancellation of removal, voluntary departure, adjustment of status to lawful permanent residence, change of nonimmigrant status, and registry.[339]

An in absentia order may be rescinded upon the filing of a motion to reopen with the immigration court under the conditions outlined below.[340] The normal numerical and time limitations do not apply, however, when an individual seeks to reopen exclusion proceedings conducted in absentia.[341]

Within 180 Days of the Date of the In Absentia Order

Within this time period, the individual must demonstrate that the failure to appear was because of "exceptional circumstances."[342] Exceptional circumstances are defined as circumstances beyond the individual's control, "such as serious illness of the [individual] or serious illness or death of the spouse, child, or parent of the [individual], but *not* including less compelling circumstances."[343] When determining whether exceptional circumstances caused the applicant's failure to appear, the BIA may not rely on newly created evidentiary standards.[344]

---

of Ponce-Hernandez, 21 I&N Dec. 784 (BIA 1999) (in the case of a minor who failed to appear for his deportation hearing, the BIA found that legacy INS met its burden of proof in establishing deportability on the basis of a Record of Deportable Alien (Form I-213), which documented the minor's identity and alienage); *Matter of Gomez-Gomez*, 23 I&N Dec. 522 (BIA 2002) (service on father by mail was proper service on minor).

[338] *Abu-Hasirah v. Dep't of Homeland Sec.*, 478 F.3d 474, 475 (2d Cir. 2007) (15 minutes late was not a failure to appear); *Cabrera-Perez v. Gonzales*, 456 F.3d 109 (3d Cir. 2006) (15- to 20-minute delay not a failure to appear); *Alarcon-Chavez v. Gonzales*, 403 F.3d 343 (5th Cir. 2005) (20 minute late arrival not a failure to appear).

[339] *See* INA §240(b)(7); 8 USC §1229a(b)(7).

[340] *See* AILF Practice Advisory, Rescinding an In Absentia Order of Removal (Sept. 21, 2004), available at *www.ailf.org/lac/lac_pa_092104.pdf*; *Matter of Guzman-Arguera*, 22 I&N Dec. 722 (BIA 1999).

[341] *See Matter of N–B–*, 22 I&N Dec. 590 (BIA 1999). *But see Matter of M–S–*, 22 I&N Dec. 349 (BIA 1998) (finding that an asylum applicant who did not receive oral notice in a language she understands need not file a motion to rescind the in absentia order, but may file a regular motion to reopen).

[342] INA §240(b)(5)(C)(i); 8 USC §1229a(b)(5)(C)(i).

[343] INA §240(e)(1); 8 USC §1229a(e)(1).

[344] *Singh v. INS*, 213 F.3d 1050, 1053 (9th Cir. 2000), *reversing Matter of B–A–S–*, 22 I&N Dec. 57 (BIA 1998) (denying motion to reopen that was not accompanied by medical evidence or affidavit of employer).

Courts have found exceptional circumstances when failure to appear was due to erroneous advice by an attorney,[345] the applicant waiting for an interpreter to return to his office;[346] ineffective assistance of counsel;[347] and an illness of the applicant's stepson that caused a 15-minute delay in appearing at the hearing.[348]

Exceptional circumstances do not include a car breaking down on the way to a hearing;[349] traffic difficulties;[350] the general assertion that the individual was prevented from reaching the hearing on time because of heavy traffic;[351] a long-standing minor illness;[352] unsuccessful communications with an attorney regarding the next hearing date after a change of venue was granted, where the individual has failed to demonstrate ineffective assistance of counsel;[353] or pursuit of employment.[354]

Any Time After the Date of the In Absentia Order

Applicants must demonstrate that they did not receive notice in accordance with INA §239(a), or that they were in federal or state custody and the failure to appear was through no fault of their own.[355] Courts have recently examined what proof is needed in cases where the applicant alleges he or she did not receive notice of the hearing.[356] The Eighth Circuit has held that where notice is sent by regular mail (*not*, as previously required, by certified mail), it was error for the IJ to require documentary evidence from the U.S. Postal Service or third-party affidavits demonstrating that service was improper.[357] The court reasoned that in cases where notice is sent by regular mail, the only proof of nondelivery is the applicant's statement that he did not receive delivery.[358] Similarly, in *Salta v. INS*,[359] the Ninth Circuit held that regular mail was not entitled to the same presumption of effective delivery. It further held that:

---

[345] *Galvez-Vergara v. Gonzales*, 484 F.3d 798, 801–02 (5th Cir. 2007).

[346] *Nazarova v. INS*, 171 F.3d 478, 484 (7th Cir. 1998).

[347] *Matter of Grijalva*, 21 I&N Dec. 472 (BIA 1996).

[348] *Matter of Singh*, 21 I&N Dec. 998 (BIA 1997).

[349] *De Morales v. INS*, 116 F.3d 145, 149 (5th Cir. 1997).

[350] *Sharma v. INS*, 89 F.3d 545, 547 (9th Cir. 1996).

[351] *Matter of S–A–*, 21 I&N Dec. 1050 (BIA 1997).

[352] *Matter of Ali*, 21 I&N Dec. 1058 (BIA 1997) (interpreting the phrase "exceptional circumstances" as applied to the individual's failure to depart during the period of voluntary departure).

[353] *Matter of Rivera*, 21 I&N Dec. 599 (BIA 1996).

[354] *Matter of W–F–*, 21 I&N Dec. 503 (BIA 1996).

[355] INA §240(b)(5)(C)(ii); 8 USC §1229a(b)(5)(C)(ii).

[356] *See, e.g., Matter of M–D–*, 23 I&N Dec. 540 (BIA 2002) (applicant can be charged with receipt of notice to appear and notice of hearing date where the notice is sent by certified mail to applicant's correct address, but is returned by Postal Service as unclaimed).

[357] *Ghounem v. INS*, 378 F.3d 740, 744–45 (8th Cir. 2004); *see also Nibagwire v. Gonzales*, 450 F.3d 153, 156 (4th Cir. 2006) (finding BIA abused its discretion in requiring applicant to rebut "string presumption" of delivery where NTA was sent by regular mail).

[358] *Ghounem, supra* note 357, at 744.

[359] *Salta v. INS*, 314 F.3d 1076, 1079 (9th Cir. 2002).

Where a petitioner actually initiates a proceeding to obtain a benefit, appears at an earlier hearing, and has no motive to avoid the hearing, a sworn affidavit from [the petitioner] that neither she nor a responsible party residing at her address received the notice should ordinarily be sufficient to rebut the presumption of delivery and entitle [the petitioner] to an evidentiary hearing to consider the veracity of her allegations.[360]

Another issue arising in cases regarding lack of notice is how soon the motion to reopen must be filed after the applicant learns of the in absentia order. By statute, a motion to reopen may be filed "at any time."[361] Courts have interpreted this to mean, literally, "at any time" and have reversed IJs who have denied motions to reopen if there has been a significant delay after the applicant learns of the in absentia order.[362]

A motion to reopen to rescind an in absentia order will automatically stay the removal of an individual.[363] The BIA has no jurisdiction to review directly an in absentia order, except for a review of an IJ's denial of a motion to reopen.[364] Any petition for judicial review in federal court must be confined to the following issues: the validity of the notice, the reasons for failing to appear, and whether the individual is removable.[365] One exception to this rule is for individuals who claim to be nationals of the United States.[366]

Evidence

Asylum applicants have the right to a reasonable opportunity to examine the evidence against them, to present evidence on their own behalf, and to cross-examine witnesses against them.[367] The only exception is that they are not entitled to examine national security information if such information is used to deny them admission to the United States or in determining their eligibility for discretionary relief.[368] By regulation, IJs may receive in evidence any oral or written statement that is material and relevant to any issue in the case that was obtained during an investigation, examination, hearing, or trial.[369] IJs are

---

[360] *Id.* at 1079; *see also Matter of G–Y–R–*, 23 I&N Dec. 181 (BIA 2001) (upholding an IJ's refusal to issue an in absentia order against an individual who was never advised of the consequences of her failure to provide legacy INS with a mailing address and who never received actual service of the NTA); *Flores-Chavez v. Ashcroft*, 362 F.3d 1150 (9th Cir. 2004) (finding error where DHS failed to serve Notice of Hearing on adult to whom child was released).

[361] INA §240(b)(5)(C)(ii); 8 USC §1229a(b)(5)(C)(ii).

[362] *See Andia v. Ashcroft*, 359 F.3d 1181, 1184 (9th Cir. 2004) (finding error where IJ denied motion to reopen as a matter of discretion where the delay in filing was seven months); *see also Matter of A–A–*, 22 I&N Dec. 140, 144 n.4 (BIA 1998) (noting there is no statutory time limit where lack of notice is alleged and motion to reopen was filed 10 years after the in absentia order was issued).

[363] INA §240(b)(5)(C); 8 USC §1229a(b)(5)(C).

[364] *Matter of Gonzalez-Lopez*, 20 I&N Dec. 644 (BIA 1993).

[365] INA §240(b)(5)(D); 8 USC §1229a(b)(5)(D).

[366] INA §242(b)(5); 8 USC §1252(b)(5).

[367] INA §240(b)(4); 8 USC §1229a(b)(4).

[368] *Id.*

[369] 8 CFR §1240.7(a).

instructed that "[t]he general rule with respect to evidence in immigration proceedings favors admissibility as long as the evidence is shown to be probative of relevant matters and its use is fundamentally fair so as not to deprive the alien of due process of law."[370]

The Federal Rules of Evidence are not controlling in immigration court proceedings.[371] However, they should always be kept in mind when preparing and presenting a claim. As noted above, the test for the admissibility of evidence in immigration court proceedings is whether the evidence is probative and whether its use is fundamentally fair.[372] "[F]airness is closely related to the reliability and trustworthiness of the evidence."[373] The Federal Rules of Evidence are pertinent in determining whether the applicant was denied a fundamentally fair hearing as a result of evidence admitted or rejected by the IJ. Hearsay, for example, while generally admissible in immigration court proceedings, may constitute a due process violation under some circumstances.[374] Below are a few of the evidence issues that may arise when presenting an asylum claim. The list is by no means exhaustive.[375]

Experts and Witnesses

As noted above, asylum applicants have the right to a reasonable opportunity to present evidence on their own behalf.[376] Increasingly, asylum applicants are relying on the testimony of expert and other witnesses to establish their eligibility for asylum. The testimony of experts and other witnesses must be under oath or affirmation administered by the IJ.[377] It is error for an IJ to refuse to allow testimony if it would have had a potential effect on the outcome of the hearing.[378] The AG has noted that experts in immigration

---

[370] *Immigration Judge Benchbook* (Oct. 2001), ch.1, at I.A.2., available at *www.usdoj.gov/eoir/statspub/benchbook.pdf;* see also *Doumbia v. Gonzales*, 472 F.3d 957, 962 (7th Cir. 2007); *Espinoza v. INS*, 45 F.3d 308, 310 (9th Cir. 1995).

[371] *Matter of D–*, 20 I&N Dec. 827, 831 (BIA 1994).

[372] *See Ezeagwuna v. Ashcroft*, 301 F.3d 116, 127 (3d Cir. 2002), *rev'd on other grounds by Ezeagwuna v. Ashcroft*, 325 F.3d 396 (3d 2003); *see also Bustos-Torres v. INS*, 898 F.2d 1053, 1055 (5th Cir. 1990); *Matter of Ponce-Hernandez*, 21 I&N Dec. 784 (BIA 1999).

[373] *Felzcerek v. INS*, 75 F.3d 112, 115 (2d Cir. 1996).

[374] *See, e.g., Saidane v. INS*, 129 F.3d 1063, 1065–66 (9th Cir. 1997) (reliance on a damaging hearsay affidavit rendered the hearing fundamentally unfair).

[375] For additional guidance, see D. Smith and B. Hake, "Evidence Issues in Asylum Cases," 90-10 *Immigration Briefings* (Oct. 1990); *see also* T. Elliott, "Strategies and Tactics in Deportation Proceedings," 90-05 *Immigration Briefings* (May 1990); *Immigration Judge Benchbook, supra* note 370, ch.1.

[376] INA §240(b)(4); 8 USC §1229a(b)(4).

[377] 8 CFR §1240.7(b).

[378] *See, e.g., Tun v. Gonzales*, 485 F.3d 1014, 1017, 1026 (8th Cir. 2007) (finding the IJ erred in excluding a medical doctor's testimony because she had not been to Burma, she did not specialize in trauma or psychiatry, and her organization, Physicians for Human Rights, was an "advocacy group"); *Koval v. Gonzales*, 418 F.3d 798, 808 (7th Cir. 2005); *Boyanivskyy v. Gonzales*, 450 F.3d 286, 293 (7th Cir. 2006) (finding the IJ erred by excluding the testimony of corroboration witnesses); *Kerciku v. INS*, 314 F.3d 913, 918 (7th Cir. 2003). *But see Myslymi v. Gonzales*, 216 Fed. Appx. 571, 576 (7th Cir. 2007) (finding IJ properly disregarded expert whose testimony was "speculative and provided no insight into any specific threat [the applicants] might face . . . .").

court proceedings do not need to be formally "qualified" as experts.[379] Nor is there a requirement that an academic, to be qualified as an expert, have published academic books or articles on the precise subject matter of his or her testimony.[380]

But some degree of competency is necessary. Judge Posner in the Seventh Circuit criticized the use of a document expert by DHS who did not speak or read Albanian, but testified as an expert at the hearing that the applicant's Albanian documents were probably fakes.[381] He based this conclusion in part on the lack of accent marks and the type of technology used to make them.[382] Judge Posner noted that the "spirit of *Daubert*"[383] is applicable in proceedings before administrative agencies and "junk science" has no place. The court concluded that the expert, not knowing Albanian, should not have been allowed to testify that Albanian is always written with diacritical marks, nor should he have been allowed to testify about the printing technology when he stated that he did not know what printing resources the Albanian government had.[384] Courts have also held that it is not necessary for an expert have traveled recently to the country in question.[385] Nor is there an absolute requirement that experts be present to be cross-examined in immigration court proceedings.[386]

It is important to provide information to the court on the witness's qualifications and expertise on the matter. And, if at all possible, it is preferable and a best practice to have the expert and witnesses physically or telephonically present for cross-examination purposes. IJs have been criticized by federal courts for disregarding expert testimony and relying instead on nonrecord evidence, in most cases speculation and conjecture, when adjudicating cases.[387] The Seventh Circuit, in response, has called for administrative country experts to be appointed by the immigration courts, similar to vocational experts

---

[379] *See Matter of Marshi*, A26 980 386 (AG Feb. 13, 2004), at 5 (finding IJ erred in disallowing testimony from a U.S. Marine colonel who had extensive and impressive experience and qualifications, where his testimony would have been material and supportive of the applicant's asylum claim), *published on* AILA InfoNet at Doc. No. 04021390 (*posted* Feb. 13, 2004).

[380] *Niam v. Ashcroft*, 354 F.3d 652, 660 (7th Cir. 2004).

[381] *Pasha v. Gonzales*, 433 F.3d 530, 532 (7th Cir. 2005).

[382] *Id.* at 531–32.

[383] *Id.* at 535; *see also Daubert v. Merrell Dow Pharmaceuticals*, 509 U.S. 579 (1993) (allowing for the exclusion of expert testimony of one who lacks expertise or uses questionable methods).

[384] *Pasha, supra* note 381, at 535.

[385] *See, e.g., Tun*, 484 F.3d at 1026 (8th Cir. 2007) (finding the IJ erred in excluding a medical doctor's testimony, in part, because she had not been to Burma); *see also Koval v. Gonzales*, 418 F.3d 798, 803 (7th Cir. 2005) (finding that although the expert had not been to Ukraine in 12 years, the IJ erred in refusing to admit his testimony).

[386] *Tun*, 484 F.3d at 1025-26 (finding that fairness rather than the rules of evidence govern admissibility and that the use of a report from a qualified witness, in the absence of any specific objections, is generally fair); *Yang v. Gonzales*, 427 F.3d 1117, 1121-22 (8th Cir. 2005) (finding error where IJ and BIA failed to accord weight to an affidavit from a nontestifying, facially qualified country condition expert).

[387] *See Banks v. Gonzales*, 453 F.3d 449, 454 (7th Cir. 2006) (finding that the IJ played the role of country specialist, "a role for which an overworked lawyer who spends his life in the Midwest is . . . poorly suited[]").

in Social Security cases.[388] Courts have also criticized the IJs' reliance on Department of State reports because the authors of the reports are anonymous and decision makers do not know the credentials of the individuals who assemble the reports or the trustworthiness of the evidence they have relied on.[389]

Hearsay

As noted above, hearsay evidence is generally admissible, unless its admission would be fundamentally unfair.[390]

Discovery

While the Federal Rules of Civil Procedure do not apply in administrative proceedings, the following are measures that may be taken to obtain documents or testimony from DHS: (1) *always* file a Freedom of Information Act (FOIA) request (Form G-639) with the USCIS National Records Center;[391] (2) ask the trial attorney for a copy of pertinent documents in the applicant's case;[392] (3) ask the IJ to order prehearing statements pursuant to 8 CFR §1003.21, including copies of exhibits; (4) ask the IJ to issue a subpoena for DHS to produce one or more specific documents or witnesses pursuant to 8 CFR §1287.4; and (5) ask the IJ to order the taking of a deposition pursuant to 8 CFR §1240.7(c).

The BIA has held that, notwithstanding allocation of the burden of proof, the party with more ready access to evidence substantiating a party's burden should come forward with it.[393] In addition, the BIA has recently recognized that the trial attorney's role in an asylum hearing is to produce any relevant evidence that would further adjudication of the individual's asylum claim.[394]

---

[388] *Id.* at 453.

[389] *See Koval v. Gonzales*, 418 F.3d 798, 807 (7th Cir. 2005) (noting that the reports are prepared in general terms and offer more of a statement on the relationship of the U.S. government to that country than an account of individual circumstances).

[390] *Matter of Grijalva*, 19 I&N Dec. 713 (BIA 1988); *see also Cunanan v. INS*, 856 F.2d 1373 (9th Cir. 1988) (the test for hearsay is whether it is probative and whether its admission is fundamentally fair); *Saidane v. INS*, 129 F.3d 1063 (9th Cir. 1997) (reliance on a damaging hearsay affidavit rendered the hearing fundamentally unfair); *Kiareldeen v. Reno*, 71 F. Supp. 2d 402 (D.N.J. 1999), *rev'd on other grounds by Kiareldeen v. Ashcroft*, 273 F.3d 542 (3d Cir. 2001) (reliance on five reports by the FBI's Joint Terrorism Task Force in conjunction with the failure to produce any witness in support of the allegations in the reports violated due process).

[391] Individuals in removal proceedings are eligible for expedited processing of their FOIA request under the "Notice to Appear" track, effective March 30, 2007. For complete instructions, see USCIS Form G-639 and USCIS Fact Sheet, "Freedom of Information Act" (Feb. 28, 2007), *published on* AILA InfoNet at Doc. No. 07030165 (*posted* Mar. 1, 2007).

[392] See appx. 6D for a list of district counsel addresses and telephone numbers.

[393] *Matter of Vivas*, 16 I&N Dec. 68 (BIA 1977).

[394] *See Matter of S–M–J–*, 21 I&N Dec. 722 at 7–8 (BIA 1997).

Classified Evidence

The DHS trial attorney may present classified evidence in an asylum hearing to either the IJ or BIA.[395] The IJ or BIA, before admitting the evidence, must determine that the classified evidence is relevant to the hearing.[396] The asylum applicant must be notified that classified evidence has been given to the IJ.[397] The agency that provides the classified evidence to the IJ or BIA may provide an unclassified summary to the applicant.[398] At least one IJ has requested that the agency also provide any exculpatory evidence, and when it failed to do so, found that the classified evidence would be viewed with "respectful skepticism."[399]

Authentication of Documents

8 CFR §287.6 appears to require that official records and public documents from foreign countries be "certified," in the form of an official publication or a copy attested to by an authorized foreign officer, in order to be admissible. Limited case law on this issue suggests that it is *not* an absolute requirement, especially in asylum cases. An asylum applicant may be afraid to ask officials from his or her home country to certify an arrest warrant or conviction. The type of certification that may be required under this section varies depending on whether the country is a signatory to the 1961 Hague Convention Abolishing the Requirement of Legalisation for Foreign Public Documents.[400] Certification may be needed for "official records" from countries that are signatories to the Hague Convention. If the country at issue is not a signatory to the Convention, then certification may be needed for any "public documents" sought to be introduced. In determining whether 8 CFR §287.6 applies in a particular case, the IJ should first determine whether the document at issue is an "official record" or public document.[401] Official records include foreign vital statistics records, military records, census records, and judicial records. Public documents are defined in 8 CFR §287.6(c)(3) and include, inter alia, administrative documents and notarial acts.

Even if a document is found to be an official record or public document, courts have held that 8 CFR §287.6 is not the *sole* means of authentication available to an asylum applicant.[402] In both *Georgis v. Ashcroft*[403] and *Khan v. INS*,[404] the reviewing courts found

---

[395] 8 CFR §1240.33(c)(4).

[396] *Id.*

[397] *Id.*

[398] *Id.*

[399] *Cheema v. Ashcroft*, 383 F.3d 848, 852 (9th Cir. 2004). For more cases regarding the use of classified evidence, see *supra* this section.

[400] For a list of countries that are signatories to this Convention, see *www.hcch.net/index_en.php?act=states.listing*.

[401] *Georgis v. Ashcroft*, 328 F.3d 962, 969 (7th Cir. 2003).

[402] *Id.* at 969; *see also Gui Cun Liu v. Ashcroft*, 372 F.3d 529, 533 (3d Cir. 2004) (finding that 8 CFR §287.6 is not an absolute rule of exclusion and is not the exclusive means of authenticating records before the IJ); *Khan v. INS*, 237 F.3d 1143, 1144 (9th Cir. 2001) ("[D]ocuments may be authenticated in immigration proceedings through any recognized procedure, such as those required by INS regulation or by the Federal Rules of Civil Procedure.").

it was error for the IJs to exclude documents based on lack of authentication when basing the denial of asylum on a lack of corroborating documents.[405] One alternative is to allow the opposing party to inspect the document, as provided under Federal Rule of Evidence 902(3). A similar alternative is found in Federal Rule of Civil Procedure 44. Another recognized exception to authentication is "good cause."[406] It is error for an IJ to reject a document solely because it was not authenticated in strict conformity with the regulation.[407]

At least one IJ has also found the authentication provisions under 8 CFR §287.6 to be permissive rather than mandatory in the asylum context. In *Matter of Long Sheng*,[408] the IJ applied a two-part test in the claim of an asylum applicant from China. The IJ held that "where the applicant's testimony if (1) credible and consistent concerning the circumstances of his or her past persecution and/or well-founded fear of future persecution and (2) the applicant satisfactorily explains the failure to properly certify foreign documents offered to the court as evidence, the foreign documents should be admitted." This approach is a reasonable one and is similar to the approach in *Matter of S–M–J–*[409] that allows for an applicant to provide an explanation of why corroborating evidence is not available.[410]

Affidavits vs. Declarations

Some immigration judges prefer to have personal statements from witnesses in the form of an "affidavit," *i.e.*, a sworn statement signed before a notary. This may be a difficult or even deadly requirement for witnesses in foreign countries. According to 28 USC §1746, the substitute for an affidavit is an unsworn declaration under penalty of perjury. The statute provides:

> Whenever, under any law of the United States or under any rule, regulation, order, or requirement made pursuant to any law, any matter is *required* or permitted to be supported, evidenced, established, or proved by the sworn declaration, verification, certificate, statement, oath or affidavit . . . such matter may with like force and effect, be supported, evidenced, established, or proved by the unsworn declaration, certificate, verification, or statement, in writing of such person, which is subscribed by him, as true under penalty of perjury and dated, in substantially the following form:

---

[403] *Georgis v. Ashcroft*, 328 F.3d 962 (7th Cir. 2003).

[404] *Khan v. INS*, 237 F.3d 1143 (9th Cir. 2001).

[405] For an in-depth discussion of this issue, *see* V. Wiebe and S. Parker, "Asking for a Note from Your Torturer: Corroboration and Authentication Requirements in Asylum, Withholding and Torture Convention Claims," 1 *Immigration & Nationality Law Handbook* 414 (AILA 2001–02 Ed.).

[406] *See* 31 C. Wright & C. Gold, *Federal Practice and Procedure* §7137, as cited in V. Wiebe and S. Parker, *supra* note 405, at 428.

[407] *Jiang v. Gonzales*, 474 F.3d 25, 29 (1st Cir. 2007).

[408] *Matter of Long Sheng*, A71 800 016 (IJ Baltimore, June 23, 1993), as cited in V. Wiebe and S. Parker, *supra* note 405, at 425.

[409] *Matter of S–M–J–*, 21 I&N Dec. 722 (BIA 1997).

[410] V. Wiebe and S. Parker, *supra* note 405, at 425–26.

If executed without the United States: I declare (or certify, verify, or state) under penalty of perjury under the laws of the United States of America that the foregoing is true and correct.

Executed on (date).

(Signature).

Foreign Language Documents

Any foreign language documents offered by a party in a proceeding must be accompanied by English language translation and a certification signed by the translator.[411] The certification must include a statement that the translator is competent to translate the document, and that the translation is true and accurate to the best of the translator's abilities.[412]

Foreign Law

According to the BIA, foreign law is a matter to be proven by the party seeking to rely on it.[413] In *Abdille v. Ashcroft*,[414] the Third Circuit held that legacy INS, as the party seeking to rely on foreign law for firm resettlement purposes, carries the initial burden of proof. Once it submits evidence of foreign law sufficient to indicate that the firm resettlement bar will apply, however, the burden shifts to the applicant.[415]

IJ Decision and Order

The decision of the IJ may be oral or written.[416] It must include a finding as to admissibility or deportability.[417] It must also contain reasons for granting or denying the request.[418] A decision that lacks sufficient factual findings and legal analysis will be remanded by the BIA to the IJ to correct the deficiencies.[419] The decision must conclude with an order of removal, termination, or other disposition in the case.[420] When removal is ordered, the IJ must specify the country, or countries in the alternate, to which the applicant's removal may be directed.[421] If the IJ decides that the applicant is removable and orders the respondent removed, the IJ must advise the applicant of the decision and the consequences of the failure to depart the United States.[422] If the applicant does not waive

---

[411] 8 CFR §1003.3.

[412] *Id.*

[413] *Matter of Soleimani*, 20 I&N Dec. 99, 106 (BIA 1989) (finding that legacy INS could not rely on Israel's Law of Return to establish firm resettlement because it had submitted nothing of record regarding this law).

[414] *Abdille v. Ashcroft*, 242 F.3d 477, 490–91 (3d Cir. 2001).

[415] *Id.* (citing 8 CFR §1208.13(c)(2)(ii); *see also Matter of Annang*, 14 I&N Dec. 502 (BIA 1973).

[416] 8 CFR §1240.12(a).

[417] *Id.*

[418] *Id.*

[419] *Matter of S–H–*, 23 I&N Dec. 462 (BIA 2002).

[420] 8 CFR §§1240.12(a), (c).

[421] 8 CFR §1240.12(c).

[422] 8 CFR §1240.13(d).

appeal, the IJ must give the applicant the Notice of Appeal form (EOIR-26) and advise the applicant of the right to appeal to the BIA.[423]

3.4. ASYLUM PROCEDURES FOR STOWAWAYS

Stowaways arriving at a port of entry are not eligible to apply for admission or to be admitted.[424] If the stowaway indicates an intention to apply for asylum or a fear of persecution, a fear of torture, or a fear of return to the country of proposed removal, he or she must be referred for a "credible fear" interview under INA §235(b)(1)(B).[425] Credible fear interviews are conducted by asylum officers.[426] Stowaways are not considered applicants for admission and are not eligible for regular hearings under §240 of the INA.[427] If found to have a credible fear, however, stowaways are eligible for a hearing before an IJ conducted in accordance with the same rules as proceedings conducted under 8 CFR Part 1240, but the scope of review is limited to determining whether the individual is eligible for asylum, withholding of removal, or Convention Against Torture relief.[428]

3.4.1. Credible Fear

If the stowaway is found to have a credible fear of persecution, the asylum officer will issue to him or her Form I-863, Notice to Referral to Immigration Judge.[429] Before the IJ, the stowaway may only apply for asylum, withholding of removal, or relief under the Convention Against Torture.[430] The parties are prohibited from raising any other issue, including issues of admissibility, removability, eligibility for waivers, and eligibility for forms of relief other than asylum or withholding.[431]

3.4.2. No Credible Fear

If the stowaway is found not to have a credible fear, the asylum officer will provide the stowaway with written notice of the decision and will inquire whether the stowaway wishes to have the decision reviewed by an IJ.[432] The negative decision is issued on Form I-869, Record of Negative Credible Fear Finding and Request for Review by Immigration Judge.[433] If the stowaway does not request a review by an IJ, the asylum officer refers the

---

[423] *Id.*

[424] INA §235(a)(2); 8 USC §1225(a)(2).

[425] *Id.*; *see also* 8 CFR §1235.1(d)(4).

[426] INA §235(b)(1)(B); 8 USC §1225(b)(1)(B). For more information regarding the credible fear interview process, see ch. 5.

[427] INA §235(a)(2); 8 USC §1225(a)(2).

[428] *See* 8 CFR §§208.2(c)(1)(ii), 1208.2(c)(1)(ii); *see also* 8 CFR §§208.2(c)(3)(i), 1208.2(c)(3)(i), and 1235.1(d)(4).

[429] *See* 8 CFR §§208.2(c)(1)(ii), 1208.2(c)(1)(ii).

[430] 8 CFR §§208.2(c)(1), (2), 1208.2(c)(1), (2). See ch. 4 for more information regarding relief under the Convention Against Torture.

[431] 8 CFR §§208.2(c)(3)(i), 1208.2(c)(3)(i).

[432] 8 CFR §§208.30(g), 1208.30(g).

[433] 8 CFR §§208.30(g), 1208.30(g).

stowaway to the district director for completion of removal proceedings, in accordance with INA §235(a)(2).[434] It may be possible at this point, however, to arrange for a credible fear "reinterview."[435]

3.4.3. IJ Review of Negative Credible Fear Determination

If the stowaway requests a review of the negative credible fear determination by an IJ, the asylum officer must arrange for the stowaway's detention and serve him or her with a Form I-863, Notice of Referral to Immigration Judge.[436] If the IJ concurs with the asylum officer's determination, the case will be returned to DHS for removal of the stowaway.[437] The IJ's decision is final and may not be appealed.[438] The asylum office, however, may reconsider a negative credible fear finding after providing notice to the IJ.[439] Applicants who would like their claim reconsidered should arrange for a credible fear "reinterview."[440] If the IJ finds that the stowaway has a credible fear, the stowaway will be permitted to file an asylum application before the IJ in accordance with 8 CFR §1208.4(b)(3)(iii).[441] The IJ will make a decision on the asylum application and that decision may be appealed by ICE or the stowaway to the BIA.[442] If the asylum application is ultimately denied, ICE will remove the stowaway in accordance with INA §235(a)(2).[443] If the asylum application is ultimately approved, ICE must terminate removal proceedings in accordance with INA §235(a)(2).[444]

3.5. ASYLUM PROCEDURES FOR CHILDREN

Regrettably, children are all too often the victims of persecution and torture throughout the world. They are subjected to abusive child labor practices, are recruited by regular or irregular armies, are sold into prostitution or indentured servitude, and are subjected to various other human rights abuses. In the United States, a small but increasing number of children are seeking asylum.[445] Worldwide, refugee children comprise approximately half

---

[434] 8 CFR §§208.30(g), 1208.30(g).

[435] See ch. 5.2.9.

[436] 8 CFR §§208.30(g)(1)(i), 1208.30(g)(1)(i).

[437] 8 CFR §1208.30(g)(2)(iv)(A).

[438] Id.

[439] Id.

[440] See ch. 5.2.9.

[441] 8 CFR §1208.30(g)(2)(iv)(C).

[442] Id.

[443] Id.

[444] Id.

[445] See, e.g., J. Bhabha, "Crossing Borders Alone: The Treatment of Unaccompanied Children in the United States," 23 Immigration Law Today 23 (Mar./Apr. 2004); see also J. Bhabha and W. Young, "Through a Child's Eyes: Protecting the Most Vulnerable Asylum Seekers," 75 Interpreter Releases 757 (June 1, 1998); R. Bien, "Nothing to Declare but Their Childhood: Reforming U.S. Asylum Law to Protect the Rights of Children," 12 J.L. & Pol'y 797 (2004).

of the total refugee population.[446] As a result, children's asylum claims have received increasing attention by advocates, the Asylum Division, DHS, and the immigration courts.

In the most famous children's asylum case, legacy INS refused to consider the asylum application of six-year-old Elian Gonzalez from Cuba because it considered his application to be legally void. In upholding this determination, the Eleventh Circuit deferred to the following INS discretionary policy choices: (1) six-year-old children lack the capacity to sign and to submit personally an application for asylum; (2) six-year-old children must be represented by an adult in immigration matters; (3) absent special circumstances, the proper adult is the child's parent, even when the parent is not in the country; and (4) the fact that the parent lives in a totalitarian state in and of itself does not constitute a special circumstance requiring the selection of a nonparent representative.[447] The court was troubled, however, by the degree of obedience legacy INS paid to the wishes of the parent and by the fact that the child was from a Communist-totalitarian state that violated human rights and fundamental freedoms, but concluded that the policy choices were not unreasonable.[448]

Several years ago, the Office of International Affairs issued a memorandum to all asylum officers setting forth guidelines for adjudicating children's asylum claims.[449] The guidelines set forth various procedural safeguards, such as child-sensitive interviewing techniques and the presence of a trusted adult during the interview, to ensure that children's claims are properly and fairly adjudicated.[450] The guidelines also acknowledge that the harm a child fears or suffered may be relatively less than an adult and still qualify as persecution.[451] The guidelines also outline how children's claims should be analyzed under U.S. law.[452] In drafting these guidelines, the Office of International Affairs considered UNHCR's *Guidelines on Policies and Procedures in Dealing with Unaccompanied Children Seeking Asylum* (1997); *Refugee Children: Guidelines on Protection and Care* (1994); and *Policy on Refugee Children* (1993). It also looked to the Canadian Immigration and Refugee Board's *Child Refugee Claimants: Procedural and Evidentiary Issues*, which addresses such issues as the criteria for appointing a representative and the type of proceedings and manner of questioning in such cases.

While the IJs are not bound by the guidelines, the Office of the Chief Immigration Judge has recently issued an operating policies and procedures memorandum (OPPM) on the

---

[446] *See* UNHCR, EC/SCP/46, *Note on Refugee Children,* available at *www.unhcr.org/excom/EXCOM/ 3ae68ccc18.html.*

[447] *See Gonzalez v. Reno*, 212 F.3d 1338 (11th Cir. 2000).

[448] *Id.* at 1352–53.

[449] *See* INS Memorandum, J. Weiss, "Guidelines for Children's Asylum Claims" (Dec. 10, 1998), *published on* AILA InfoNet (*posted* Jan. 25, 1999), *reproduced in* 76 *Interpreter Releases* 1 and Appendix I (Jan. 4, 1999), and available at *www.nlada.org/Training/Train_Civil/Equal_Justice/2007_Materials/ 109_2007_Kerwin_handout7.*

[450] *Id.* at 5–15.

[451] *Id.* at 19.

[452] *Id.* at 16–27.

topic.[453] This OPPM incorporates by reference some of the child-questioning techniques referred to in the guidelines. In addition, the OPPM gives guidance to judges on a broad array of issues impacting children in immigration court proceedings, including basic legal principles, an appropriate courtroom setting, appropriate court procedures, the use of interpreters, and credibility assessments. With regard to a child's testimony, the OPPM cautions that it is generally unrealistic to expect a child to testify with the precision expected of an adult.[454] Similarly, UNHCR's *Handbook on Procedures and Criteria for Determining Refugee Status* (1992) notes that children's testimony should be given a liberal benefit of the doubt. The guidelines were relied on by the Sixth Circuit in finding that a minor girl who feared female genital mutilation if she returned to Ethiopia was eligible for asylum.[455]

The IJs also have received training on the adjudication of children's claims. In June 2000, the chief immigration judge authorized a pilot children's immigration court in Phoenix, where children were given access to pro bono counsel and child welfare specialists. This pilot children's court was so successful that it was expanded to eight additional locations.[456] Most recent statistics, however, are quite disappointing. Only 10 percent of children who appear in immigration court are represented.[457]

While some IJs attempt to ensure that unaccompanied children are represented by counsel, few if any other regulatory or statutory safeguards are available, even if the child is an asylum-seeker.[458]

---

[453] *See* EOIR Memorandum, D. Neal, "Operating Policies and Procedures Memorandum No. 07-01, Guidelines for Immigration Court Cases Involving Unaccompanied Alien Children" (May 22, 2007), *published on* AILA InfoNet at Doc. No. 07052360 (*posted* May 23, 2007).

[454] *Id.* at 7.

[455] *Abay v. Ashcroft*, 368 F.3d 634, 640 (6th Cir. 2004).

[456] *See* EOIR Fact Sheet, supra note 118, at 2; *see also* J. Bhabha, "David and Goliath? Detained Alien Children and the Right to Counsel," 7 *Bender's Immigr. Bull.* 582, 585 (May 15, 2002).

[457] *See* J. Bhabha, "Crossing Borders Alone," *supra* note 445, at 25. In 2006, 16,100 children applied for asylum in 26 European countries. Most of these children asylum-seekers were male. Only 27% of the 8,760 children asylum-seekers for whom information was available were female. UNHCR, "Number of Unaccompanied Children Seeking Asylum Steady Despite Wars and Forced Conscription" (Nov. 13, 2001), available at *www.unhcr.org/news/NEWS/3bf0dd74a.html*. In 2006, there were 7,746 unaccompanied children in DHS custody, more than three times the number of unaccompanied children detained in 1997. Congressional Research Service, Report for Congress, *Unaccompanied Alien Children: Policies and Issues* (Mar. 1, 2007) at 25–29; INS Fact Sheet, "INS' Office of Juvenile Affairs" (Aug. 1, 2002), *published on* AILA InfoNet (*posted* Aug. 12. 2002), and available at *www.immigration.com/newsletter1/insfactjuvenile.pdf* (asserting that there were 2,375 unaccompanied children in U.S. custody in 1997). For 2006, the top four countries of nationality of children in detention were El Salvador (31%), Honduras (28%), Guatemala (26%), and Mexico (7%). Congressional Research Service, Report for Congress, *supra*, at 28.

[458] *See, e.g., Chitay-Pirir v. INS*, 169 F.3d 1079, 1080 (7th Cir. 1999) (finding no error for refusal to appoint a guardian ad litem during immigration court proceedings for a minor aged 16 when he was represented by counsel and in the custody of the legacy INS); *Matter of Ponce-Hernandez*, 21 I&N Dec. 784 (BIA 1999) (in the case of a minor who failed to appear for his deportation hearing, the BIA found that legacy INS met its burden of proof in establishing deportability on the basis of a Record of Deportable Alien (Form I-213), which documented the minor's identity and alienage). *But see Lin v.*
continued

UNHCR, in its *Guidelines on Policies and Procedures in Dealing with Unaccompanied Children Seeking Asylum*,[459] recommends that an unaccompanied child be represented by an adult who would protect his or her interests and that the child have access to a qualified legal representative.[460] UNHCR further recommends that adjudicators give particular regard to the child's stage of development, his or her possibly limited knowledge of conditions in his or her home country, and the child's special vulnerability.[461]

Juvenile immigration cases must be heard in a timely manner. At least one court has found that the right to a speedy juvenile proceeding is recognized under the fundamental fairness guarantees of due process.[462]

The following are asylum regulations and policies that address children's claims:

3.5.1. Exception to One-Year Filing Deadline

For purposes of determining whether an individual is barred from asylum for failure to file within one year after his or her entry into the United States, the applicant may show "extraordinary circumstances" such as a "legal disability."[463] One example given in the regulations is a child's status as an "unaccompanied minor."[464] An "accompanied" minor may also meet the "extraordinary circumstances" exception, since the examples given are not an exhaustive list.[465] Also, since ageing-out of derivative status may materially affect eligibility for asylum,[466] it qualifies under the changed circumstances exception to the one-year filing deadline for asylum applications.[467]

3.5.2. Exception to Expedited Removal

As a general rule, an unaccompanied minor is not subject to expedited removal proceedings unless the minor: (1) has engaged in criminal activity, in the presence of a DHS officer, that would qualify as an aggravated felony if committed by an adult; (2) has been

---

Ashcroft, 377 F.3d 1014, 1026 (9th Cir. 2004), *overruled on other grounds by Thomas v. Gonzales*, 409 F.3d 1177, 1187 (9th Cir. 2005) (finding that minors are "entitled to trained legal assistance so their rights may be fully protected" in granting motion to reopen due to ineffective assistance of counsel); *Machado v. Ashcroft*, No. Cs-02-0066-FVS, Preliminary Injunction Order (E.D. Wash., Mar. 5, 2002) (legacy INS ordered to hire a lawyer for a child in its custody at government expense or release him from detention). For further discussion on the right to counsel for children in deportation proceedings, see J. Bhabha, "David and Goliath?," *supra* note 456.

[459] UNHCR, *Guidelines on Policies and Procedures in Dealing with Unaccompanied Children Seeking Asylum*, (Feb. 1997), available at *www.unhcr.org/publ/PUBL/3d4f91cf4.pdf*.

[460] *Id.* at ¶8.3.

[461] *Id.* at ¶8.6.

[462] *In re Thomas J.*, 811 A.2d 310 (Md. 2002).

[463] 8 CFR §§208.4(a)(5)(ii), 1208.4(a)(5)(ii).

[464] 8 CFR §§208.4(a)(5)(ii), 1208.4(a)(5)(ii).

[465] 8 CFR §§208.4(a)(5), 1208.4(a)(5); *see also El Himri v. Ashcroft*, 378 F.3d 932, 936 (9th Cir. 2004) (noting that the claim of a minor living with his parents was not time-barred).

[466] *See* this chapter, at 3.5.3.

[467] *See* 8 CFR §208.4(a)(4)(i)(C); *see also* INS Memorandum, *supra* note 449, at 28 n.48.

convicted or adjudicated delinquent of an aggravated felony within the United States or another country, and the inspecting officer has confirmation of that order; or (3) has previously been formally removed, excluded, or deported from the United States.[468]

If an unaccompanied minor is placed in expedited removal proceedings, the removal order must be reviewed and approved by the district director (DD) or deputy DD before the minor is removed from the United States.[469] Unaccompanied minors are, however, currently subject to reinstatement of removal proceedings.[470]

3.5.3. Aged-Out Children

Children who were listed as derivatives on their parent's asylum application sometimes reach the age of 21, *i.e.*, "age out," before the asylum interview. Under the Child Status Protection Act (CSPA), such children are still classified as children after they turn 21.[471] Similarly, children who are beneficiaries of derivative asylum sometimes turn 21 before their adjustment of status or before their I-730 Refugee/Asylee Relative Petition is adjudicated. Unfortunately, CSPA does not address these latter situations, but a USCIS memo does.[472]

Children Who Age Out Before the Asylum Interview

Children who are under 21 years of age at the time their parent files for asylum no longer age out of derivative status upon turning 21 years of age.[473]

Children Who Age Out Before Adjustment of Status

In the past, when the child was granted asylum as a derivative, but turned 21 years of age before an application for adjustment of status was filed, a *nunc pro tunc* (retroactive approval) procedure was permitted.[474] An aged-out derivative had to file an I-589 asylum application of his or her own.[475] Provided that the aged-out derivative remained unmarried, the asylum application was approved, *nunc pro tunc*, to the date of receipt of the original de-

---

[468] INS, *Inspector's Field Manual,* ch. 17.15(f)(4) (Mar. 1998), available at *www.asylumlaw.org*, as added by INS Memorandum, P. Virtue, "Unaccompanied Minors Subject to Expedited Removal" (Aug. 21, 1997), *published on* AILA InfoNet at Doc. No. 97082191 (*posted* Aug. 21, 1997).

[469] *Id.*

[470] *See* this chapter, at 3.6.

[471] *See* INA §208(b)(3); *see also* Child Status Protection Act, Pub. L. No. 107-208, 116 Stat. 927 (2002).

[472] *See* USCIS Interoffice Memorandum, W. Yates, "The Child Status Protection Act—Children of Asylees and Refugees" (Aug. 17, 2004), *published on* AILA InfoNet at Doc. No. 04091561 (*posted* Sept. 15, 2004); *see also* "The Child Status Protection Act: Breaking Down the Complicated 'Aging Out' Formula," 23 *Immigration Law Today* 32 (May/June 2004); AILF, Updated Practice Advisory on the Child Status Protection Act (Mar. 8, 2004), available at *www.ailf.org/lac/lac_pa_010504.pdf*.

[473] INA §208(b)(3). For additional guidance on this issue, see USCIS Memorandum, *supra* note 472; INS Memorandum, J. Langlois, "H.R. 1209—Child Status Protection Act" (Aug. 7, 2002), *published on* AILA InfoNet at Doc. No. 02090531 (*posted* Sep. 5, 2002).

[474] *See* INS Memorandum, *supra* note 449, at 28.

[475] *Id.*

rivative asylee status.[476] The aged-out derivative did not have to individually meet the refugee definition, but he or she was interviewed by an asylum officer to verify and to ensure that no mandatory bars or other disqualifications applied.[477] A fingerprint check had to be completed if the fingerprint check was more than 15 months old.[478] In light of CSPA, USCIS has issued a memo that provides that if the I-589 was filed by the principal when his or her child was under age 21, the child remains eligible for adjustment of status, unless the child turned 21 prior to August 2, 2002, and an adjustment application was not pending at the time the child turned 21.[479]

Children Who Age Out Before I-730 Is Filed

For asylum applications filed on or after August 2, 2002, a child who was under 21 at the time his or her parent filed for asylum continues to be eligible to have an I-730 filed on his or her behalf despite turning 21 before the I-730 is filed or approved.[480]

3.5.4. Detention of Children

Prior to 2001, families apprehended for entering the United States illegally were not regularly detained, because of the limited amount of family bed space.[481] However, after September 11, 2001, immigration policy changed and today, families and children are no longer routinely released.[482] In 2006, DHS had 7,746 unaccompanied children in DHS custody.[483]

Children seeking asylum defensively may be in DHS custody through part or all of their asylum proceedings. Regulations governing their release may be found at 8 CFR §1236.3. These regulations arose out of the settlement of the *Flores v. Reno* lawsuit regarding detention of children.[484] In addition, another case, *Flores v. Meese*, sets out a nationwide policy for the "detention, release, and treatment of minors in the custody of . . ." DHS.[485] Human rights groups have criticized DHS for its placement of children in detention facilities and also for its use of x-ray and dental examinations to determine age.[486]

---

[476] *Id.*

[477] *Id.*

[478] *Id.*

[479] *See* USCIS Memorandum, *supra* note 472.

[480] *See id.* For more information on filing I-730s, see this chapter, at 3.15.

[481] *Bunikyte v. Chertoff*, 2007 U.S. Dist. LEXIS 26166, *5 (D. Tex. 2007).

[482] *Id.*

[483] *See supra* note 457.

[484] *Flores v. Reno*, 507 U.S. 292 (1993); *see also* 75 *Interpreter Releases* 1020 (July 27, 1998).

[485] *See Flores v. Meese*, No. 85-cv-4544 (C.D. Cal. Sept. 1996); *see also Flores* Settlement P 9, Mot. Prel. Inj. Ex. A.

[486] *See, e.g.*, Physicians for Human Rights, *From Persecution to Prison: The Health Consequences of Detention for Asylum Seekers* (June 2003) at 129, available at http://physiciansforhuman rights.org/library/documents/reports/report-perstoprison-2003.pdf; *see also* Amnesty International USA, "'Why Am I Here?' Children in Immigration Detention," available at www.amnestyusa.org/refugee/usa_children_summary.html (stating that approximately one third of children

continued

Children are often detained in jail-like facilities in detention centers. The American Civil Liberties Union brought 17 lawsuits against Michael Chertoff, the Secretary of DHS, and six officials from ICE, on behalf of children detained at the T. Don Hutto detention facility in Taylor, TX.[487] These lawsuits contended that the Hutto facility violated the regulations arising out of *Flores v. Meese*, which ended in a 1997 court settlement that established minimum standards and conditions for the housing and release of all minors in federal immigration custody.[488] On August 27, 2007, a settlement was reached in the Hutto detention center litigation.[489] It is hoped that this settlement will improve the conditions for immigration children and their families.

Children must be advised of their rights.[490] In *Perez Funez v. INS District Director*, plaintiffs argued that minors are frequently coerced into choosing voluntary departure in lieu of pursuing relief that may be available to them.[491] As a result, USCIS is now required to provide written advice to children of their rights.[492]

3.6. REINSTATEMENT OF REMOVAL

Under INA §241(a)(5), the Secretary of Homeland Security, *i.e.*, DHS, may reinstate a previous order of removal against an individual who has illegally re-entered the United States after having been removed or having departed voluntarily under an order of removal, deportation, or exclusion.[493] Prior to applying affirmatively for asylum, always determine whether the applicant may be subject to INA §241(a)(5), *i.e.*, whether he or she (1) has been previously issued an order of removal, exclusion, or deportation, (2) was removed or departed voluntarily, or (3) illegally re-entered the United States.[494]

Courts have held that reinstatement of removal proceedings provides sufficient due process to ensure that an individual is not wrongfully deported or removed.[495]

---

are detained in "harsh conditions in secure, jail-like facilities . . ."); and this chapter, at 3.8.1. For information on procedural considerations for unaccompanied minors in immigration court proceedings, see this chapter, at 3.3.5.

[487] For information on the Hutto facility, see Women's Commission for Refugee Women & Children and Lutheran Immigration and Refugee Service, *Locking Up Family Values: The Detention of Immigrant Families* (Feb. 2007), available at *www.womenscommission.org/pdf/famdeten.pdf*.

[488] *Flores v. Reno*, Stipulated Settlement Agreement, No. CV 85-4544-RJK (C.D. Cal. 1997).

[489] *www.aclu.org/immigrants/detention/hutto.html*.

[490] *Perez-Funez v. District Director, INS*, 619 F. Supp. 656 (1985).

[491] *Id.*

[492] *Id.*

[493] INA §241(a)(5); 8 USC §1231(a)(5); 8 CFR §§241.8, 1241.8.

[494] For an excellent overview on current law regarding reinstatement and strategies for challenging the process, see AILF Practice Advisory, Reinstatement of Removal (updated July 11, 2006), available at *www.ailf.org/lac/reinstatment.pdf*.

[495] *Alvarenga-Villalobos v. Ashcroft*, 271 F.3d 1169 (9th Cir. 2001); *see also Velasquez-Gabriel v. Crocetti*, 263 F.3d 102 (4th Cir. 2001) (holding that reinstatement does not operate in an impermissibly retroactive manner).

CHAPTER 3 • ASYLUM AND WITHHOLDING OF REMOVAL PROCEDURES

The reinstatement of removal proceedings provision was added effective April 1, 1997, by IIRAIRA.[496] The provision applies to individuals who illegally re-entered the United States before that date, according to a recent Supreme Court case.[497]

> ➤ *Note*: Re-entering the United States without authorization after deportation or removal is punishable by a fine or by imprisonment of not more than two years.[498] An individual convicted of an aggravated felony who subsequently illegally re-enters may be sentenced to up to 20 years in prison.[499]

If the person is subject to this provision, the prior order is reinstated from its original date and may not be reopened or reviewed by an immigration judge.[500] Moreover, an individual subject to reinstatement of a removal order is not eligible for and may not apply for any relief under the INA and must be removed from the United States under the prior order of removal.[501]

> ➤ *Tip*—Does Reinstatement of Removal Apply in Your Case?—It may not. For example, reinstatement may not apply to individuals who enter the United States with facially valid visas or other entry documents.[502] It is important to review current case law on the topic. For an excellent overview, see the AILF Practice Advisory cited *supra* in footnote 492.

An exception to the general rule of no relief is for an individual who expresses a fear of returning to the country designated in the previous order of removal, deportation, or exclusion.[503] Such an individual will be referred to an asylum officer to determine whether the individual has a "reasonable fear" of persecution or torture pursuant to 8 CFR §1208.31.[504] The Asylum Division has exclusive jurisdiction to make reasonable fear determinations; EOIR, *i.e.*, an IJ, has exclusive jurisdiction to review reasonable fear determinations.[505] These procedures regarding reasonable fear determinations went into effect on March 22, 1999. Any applicants subject to reinstatement prior to March 22,

---

[496] IIRAIRA, Pub. L. No. 104-208, div. C, §305, 110 Stat. 3009, 3009-599.

[497] *Fernandez-Vargas v. Gonzales*, 126 S. Ct. 2422, 2434 (2006) (finding that INA §241(a)(5) was not impermissibly retroactive). *But see Valdez-Sanchez v. Gonzales*, 485 F.3d 1084, 1089–91 (10th Cir. 2007) (finding that DHS may not retroactively apply INA §241(a)(5) to an individual who illegally re-enters, marries a U.S. citizen and was granted adjustment of status all prior to IIRAIRA's effective date); *Faiz-Mohammed v. Ashcroft*, 395 F.3d 799, 810 (7th Cir. 2005) (finding that INA §241(a)(5) did not apply where the individual applied for adjustment prior to the enactment of IIRAIRA).

[498] INA §276(a); 8 USC §1326(a).

[499] INA §276(b); 8 USC §1326(b).

[500] INA §241(a)(5); 8 USC §1231(a)(5); 8 CFR §§241.8, 1241.8; *see also Morales-Izquierdo v. Gonzales*, 477 F.3d 691 (9th Cir. 2007) (finding that 8 CFR §241.8 comports with due process).

[501] INA §241(a)(5); 8 USC §1231(a)(5).

[502] *See Mora v. Smith*, No. C97-1758WD, slip op. (W.D. Wash., Dec. 17, 1997) (holding that reinstatement provision does not apply to individuals who entered with an I-688A employment authorization card).

[503] 8 CFR §§241.8(e), 1241.8(e).

[504] 8 CFR §§241.8(e), 1241.8(e).

[505] 8 CFR §§208.31(a), 1208.31(a).

1999, who were not served with a final decision should have been given an opportunity to seek relief under the new process.[506] Other exceptions to the reinstatement process are applicants for adjustment under the Haitian Refugee Immigrant Fairness Act (HRIFA) and the Nicaraguan Adjustment and Central American Relief Act (NACARA).[507]

3.6.1. Preliminary Procedures

If, during the course of the reinstatement process, an individual expresses a fear of returning to his or her country of removal, he or she must be referred to an asylum officer for a reasonable fear determination.[508] In the absence of exceptional circumstances, the reasonable fear determination will be conducted within 10 days of the referral.[509] The referring officer should give the applicant Form M-488, Information on Reasonable Fear Interview, and a list of legal services if the applicant is not represented.[510]

3.6.2. Definition of Reasonable Fear

The applicant will be determined to have a "reasonable fear of persecution or torture" if the applicant "establishes a reasonable possibility that he or she would be persecuted on account of his or her race, religion, nationality, membership in a particular social group, or political opinion, or a reasonable possibility that he or she would be tortured in the country of removal."[511] Torture is defined by regulation at 8 CFR §§208.18(a)(1), 1208.18(a)(1).[512] The reasonable fear standard is higher than the credible fear standard used in expedited removal proceedings.[513] According to the Asylum Division, it is the same standard used to establish a well-founded fear of persecution in the asylum context.[514]

3.6.3. No Bars Considered

When making a reasonable fear determination, the asylum officer is prohibited from considering whether the applicant is subject to any bars to withholding of removal.[515]

---

[506] *See* INS Memorandum, J. Langlois, "Implementation of Amendments to Asylum and Withholding of Removal Regulations, Effective March 22, 1999" (Mar. 18, 1999) at 6.

[507] 8 CFR §§241.8(d), 1241.8(d). For more information on these forms of relief, see ch. 6.6 and 6.7.

[508] 8 CFR §§208.31(a), 1208.31(a).

[509] 8 CFR §§208.31(b), 1208.31(b).

[510] *See* INS Memorandum, *supra* note 506, at 8.

[511] 8 CFR §§208.31(c), 1208.31(c).

[512] *See also* ch. 4.2.1.

[513] EOIR Memorandum, Office of Chief Immigration Judge, "Operating Policies and Procedures Memorandum No. 99-5: Implementation of Article 3 of the UN Convention Against Torture" (May 14, 1999), *published on* AILA InfoNet (*posted* June 4, 1999), and available at *www.usdoj.gov/eoir/efoia/ ocij/oppm99/99_5.pdf*; *see also* ch. 5.

[514] *See* INS Memorandum, *supra* note 506, at 12.

[515] 8 CFR §§208.31(c), 1208.31(c). See ch. 2.7.2 for a list of these mandatory bars.

Asylum officers are instructed, however, to elicit information related to possible bars and to flag cases with possible bars.[516]

3.6.4. Interview

The asylum officer must conduct the interview in a nonadversarial manner, separate and apart from the general public.[517] In most cases, the applicant will be detained. At the beginning of the interview, the asylum officer should determine that the applicant has an understanding of the reasonable fear determination process.[518] The asylum officer has the authority to administer oaths, verify the identity of the applicant, verify the identity of any interpreter, present and receive evidence, and question the applicant or any witnesses.[519] There is no need to submit a Form I-589 for the purposes of the reasonable fear screening process.[520]

Orientation

An asylum officer should first conduct an orientation with the applicant, which may be conducted by telephone.[521] The asylum officer should check whether the applicant has any medical problems and whether the applicant will have any special needs during the interview, such as an interpreter who speaks an unusual language.[522] During the interview, the asylum officer should ensure that the applicant has received and understood the M-488, has a list of pro bono representatives if unrepresented, and if represented, the officer should obtain or confirm information on how to contact the representative.[523]

Scheduling of Interview

In the absence of exceptional circumstances, the reasonable fear determination will be conducted within 10 days of the referral.[524] A case is not considered referred until the Asylum Office has received notice that a person requires a reasonable fear screening and has also received the A-file.[525] In determining whether the interview or adjudication should be delayed, the Asylum Office is instructed to err on the side of ensuring that the applicant is able to present his or her full claim, so long as there is no evidence of intentional delay tactics or abuse of process.[526] The interview should normally be scheduled approximately 48 hours after the orientation, unless the applicant states that he or she is

---

[516] *See* INS Memorandum, *supra* note 506, at 12.

[517] 8 CFR §§208.31(c), 1208.31(c).

[518] 8 CFR §§208.31(c), 1208.31(c).

[519] 8 CFR §§208.31(d), 1208.31(d).

[520] *See* INS Memorandum, *supra* note 506, at 7.

[521] *Id.* at 8.

[522] *Id.*

[523] *Id.*

[524] 8 CFR §§208.31(b), 1208.31(b).

[525] *See* INS Memorandum, *supra* note 506, at 7.

[526] *Id.* at 8.

ready to proceed sooner.[527] Generally, if the applicant is represented, the asylum officer should schedule the interview for a date and time that the representative may be present, unless the representative requests an interview date that will prevent the asylum officer from making a reasonable fear determination within the requisite 10-day period *and* it appears the representative's request is based on a delay tactic or convenience, rather than to address legitimate conflicts with commitments that cannot be rescheduled.[528]

Representation

The applicant may be represented by counsel or an accredited representative at the interview, at no expense to the government.[529] The representative should submit a Notice of Appearance, Form G-28, signed by the attorney or representative and the applicant. The representative may present a statement at the end of the interview.[530] The asylum officer, in his or her discretion, may limit the number of persons who may be present at the interview and the length of the representative's statement.[531] Representatives may participate in the interview by telephone if travel to a remote location is difficult on short notice, as long as their participation is at no expense to the government.[532]

Evidence

The applicant may present evidence, if available, relevant to the possibility of persecution or torture at the interview.[533] The asylum officer is instructed to elicit from the applicant any experiences of persecution, torture, or other harm that the applicant has experienced in the past, the basis of the applicant's fear that he or she would be persecuted or tortured in the future, whom the applicant fears, the applicant's knowledge of harm to individuals similarly situated, and any experiences of the applicant (in any country, including the United States) that may place the applicant at risk of persecution or torture.[534] The applicant must also be given the opportunity to explain any material discrepancies in his or her testimony, including inconsistencies, inability to provide detail, and perceived implausibility.[535]

Interpretation

If the applicant is unable to proceed effectively in English, and if the asylum officer is unable to proceed competently in the language chosen by the applicant, the asylum officer must arrange for an interpreter in conducting the interview.[536] The interpreter may not

---

[527] *Id.*

[528] *Id.* at 8–9.

[529] 8 CFR §§208.31(c), 1208.31(c).

[530] 8 CFR §§208.31(c), 1208.31(c).

[531] 8 CFR §§208.31(c), 1208.31(c).

[532] *See* INS Memorandum, *supra* note 506, at 9.

[533] 8 CFR §§208.31(c), 1208.31(c).

[534] *See* INS Memorandum, *supra* note 506, at 9.

[535] *Id.*

[536] 8 CFR §§208.31(c), 1208.31(c).

be a representative or employee of the applicant's country, or if stateless, the applicant's country of last habitual residence.[537] Before or during the interview, the applicant's request for a male or female interpreter should be accommodated when possible.[538] If the applicant, the applicant's representative, or the asylum officer believes that the interpreter is either not competent or not neutral, the officer may terminate the interview and request a different interpreter.[539] The applicant may provide his or her own interpreter.[540] If the applicant uses his or her own interpreter, the asylum officer is required to use a commercial interpreter to monitor the applicant's interpreter.[541]

Record

The asylum officer must create a summary of the material facts as stated by the applicant.[542] The asylum officer is required to place this information on Form I-899, Reasonable Fear Worksheet.[543] At the conclusion of the interview, the asylum officer must review the summary with the applicant and allow the applicant to correct any errors in the summary.[544]

3.6.5. Decision

The asylum officer must create a written record of his or her determination, including a summary of the material facts as stated by the applicant, any additional facts relied on by the asylum officer, and the asylum officer's determination of whether, in light of such facts, the applicant has established a reasonable fear of persecution or torture.[545] All reasonable fear cases must be reviewed by Asylum Headquarters before the determination is served on the applicant.[546]

Reasonable Fear—Withholding-Only Proceeding Before an IJ

If the asylum officer determines that the applicant has a reasonable fear of persecution or torture, he or she must inform the applicant and issue a Form I-863, Notice of Referral to an Immigration Judge, for a full consideration of the request for withholding only.[547] Such cases will be adjudicated in accordance with the provisions of 8 CFR §1208.16.[548] The chief immigration judge, however, has instructed IJs that in scheduling and adjudicating

---

[537] 8 CFR §§208.31(c), 1208.31(c).

[538] *See* INS Memorandum, *supra* note 506, at 12.

[539] *Id.*

[540] *Id.* at 10–11.

[541] *Id.*

[542] 8 CFR §§208.31(c), 1208.31(c).

[543] *See* INS Memorandum, *supra* note 506, at 9.

[544] 8 CFR §§208.31(c), 1208.31(c).

[545] 8 CFR §§208.31(c), 1208.31(c).

[546] *See* INS Memorandum, *supra* note 506, at 13; *see also* the USCIS webpage on reasonable fear screenings, available at *www.uscis.gov* (Click on the "Services and Benefits" tab, then the "Humanitarian Benefits" link, then the "Asylum" link, and finally the "Reasonable Fear Screenings" link.).

[547] 8 CFR §§208.31(e), 1208.31(e).

[548] 8 CFR §§208.31(e), 1208.31(e).

withholding-only cases, IJs should balance the dictates of due process concerns and regulatory compliance concerns.[549] A hearing notice, entitled Notice of Withholding-Only Hearing, must be sent to the applicant in care of his or her custodial authority and to his or her attorney, if any, via an appropriate overnight courier.[550]

An immigration judge is permitted, under 8 CFR §1208.16, to consider withholding of removal under INA §241(b)(3), withholding under the Convention Against Torture, and deferral of removal under the Convention Against Torture.[551] At the initial appearance before the IJ, the applicant will be given an adequate time to prepare and file a Form I-589 withholding of removal application.[552] Once the I-589 is received by the IJ, a copy will be forwarded to the Department of State, and the IJ must schedule a merits hearing.[553] The withholding-only proceeding may be conducted by video conference or telephonically.[554] If an interpreter is needed, the immigration court must provide one.[555] The applicant or the DHS may appeal the IJ's decision to the BIA.[556]

No Reasonable Fear—Removal or IJ Review

If the asylum officer determines that the applicant has not established a reasonable fear of persecution or torture, the asylum officer must inform the applicant in writing of the decision and must inquire whether the applicant wishes to have an IJ review the negative decision.[557] The asylum officer must use Form I-898, Record of Negative Reasonable Fear Interview Finding and Request for Review by Immigration Judge.[558] The applicant must indicate on Form I-898 whether he or she desires an IJ review.[559] An applicant who does not request an IJ review is subject to immediate removal from the United States.[560]

Withdrawals

An applicant referred for a reasonable fear interview may seek to withdraw his or her request.[561] An asylum officer must go over the withdrawal form with the applicant, either

---

[549] EOIR Memorandum, *supra* note 513, at 661.

[550] *Id.*

[551] For more detailed information regarding applying for relief under the Convention Against Torture, see ch. 4.

[552] EOIR Memorandum, *supra* note 513, at 661.

[553] *Id.*

[554] *Id.*

[555] *Id.*

[556] 8 CFR §§208.31(e), 1208.31(e).

[557] 8 CFR §§208.31(f), 1208.31(f).

[558] 8 CFR §§208.31(f), 1208.31(f).

[559] 8 CFR §§208.31(f), 1208.31(f).

[560] *See* INS Memorandum, *supra* note 506, at 5. *But see* ch. 5.2.9. Reinterviews may be available for reasonable-fear applicants as well.

[561] *See* INS Memorandum, *supra* note 506, at 15–16.

in person or telephonically, and with the assistance of an interpreter, if necessary.[562] Asylum Headquarters must concur with the withdrawal before the applicant is permitted to withdraw.[563]

3.6.6. Review of Negative Reasonable Fear Determination by IJ

If, upon receiving a negative reasonable fear determination, the applicant indicates a desire for an IJ review, the asylum officer must serve the applicant with Form I-863, Notice of Referral to the Immigration Judge.[564] The record of the determination, including copies of the I-863, the asylum officer's notes, the summary of material facts, and other materials on which the determination was based must be provided to the IJ with the negative determination.[565] It is likely that applicants who request a reasonable fear review will be detained at a DHS facility or in a federal, state, or local jail or prison. If the distance from the immigration court renders it impractical for the Asylum Office to file Form I-863 in person, the court administrator will allow the filing of Form I-863 by fax.[566] The hearing notice must be sent via an appropriate overnight courier to the applicant, in care of his or her custodial authority, and to the applicant's attorney, if any.[567]

The regulations do not describe how a reasonable fear review will be conducted. Because the proceedings resemble credible fear reviews, the chief immigration judge has instructed IJs that they should be modeled after credible fear review proceedings.[568] IJs are required to tape-record the reasonable fear review proceedings.[569] The proceedings may be conducted by video conference or telephonically.[570] If an interpreter is necessary, the immigration court must provide one.[571] Since the regulations do not specify whether an applicant has the right to be represented by counsel during the reasonable fear review, the chief immigration judge has instructed IJs that it is within their discretion whether to permit an applicant to be represented by counsel during the reasonable fear review.[572]

The IJ must make a de novo determination of whether the applicant has established a reasonable fear of persecution or torture.[573]

---

[562] *Id.*

[563] *Id.*

[564] 8 CFR §§208.31(g), 1208.31(g).

[565] 8 CFR §§208.31(g), 1208.31(g).

[566] EOIR Memorandum, *supra* note 513, at 659.

[567] *Id.*

[568] *Id.*

[569] *Id.* at 660.

[570] *Id.*

[571] *Id.*

[572] *Id.*

[573] *Id.*

Reasonable Fear

If, upon review of the asylum officer's negative reasonable fear determination, the IJ finds that the applicant has a reasonable fear of persecution or torture, the applicant is placed in withholding-only proceedings and the applicant may then submit Form I-589, Application for Asylum and Withholding of Removal.[574] The IJ may only consider the applicant's eligibility for withholding of removal under 8 CFR §1208.16, and must determine whether the applicant's removal must be withheld or deferred.[575] DHS or the applicant may appeal the IJ's decision whether removal must be withheld or deferred to the BIA.[576] The BIA may only review the IJ's decision regarding the applicant's eligibility for withholding or deferral of removal under 8 CFR §1208.16.[577]

No Reasonable Fear

If, upon review of the asylum officer's negative reasonable fear determination, the IJ concurs that the applicant does not have a reasonable fear of persecution or torture, the case will be returned to DHS for removal of the applicant.[578] There is no appeal from the IJ's decision.[579]

3.7. EXPEDITED REMOVAL FOR AGGRAVATED FELONS

The attorney general may initiate expedited proceedings to remove individuals convicted of an aggravated felony who are not permanent residents of the United States.[580] Under the Homeland Security Act of 2002, this authority extends to the DHS Secretary and other DHS officials.[581] At least three courts have held this expedited process applies to parolees.[582] Individuals in this expedited process are not eligible for any discretionary relief from removal.[583] They may be eligible, however, to apply for withholding of removal under INA §241(b)(3), withholding of removal under the Convention Against Torture, or deferral of removal under the Convention Against Torture.[584]

---

[574] *See* 8 CFR §§208.31(g)(2), 1208.31(g)(2); EOIR Memorandum, *supra* note 513, at 660.

[575] 8 CFR §§208.31(g)(2)(i), 1208.31(g)(2)(i).

[576] 8 CFR §§208.31(g)(2)(i), 1208.31(g)(2)(ii).

[577] 8 CFR §§208.31(g)(2)(i), 1208.31(g)(2)(ii); see also this chapter at 3.6.5 for more information on withholding-only proceedings.

[578] 8 CFR §§208.31(g)(1), 1208.31(g)(1).

[579] 8 CFR §§208.31(g)(1), 1208.31(g)(1). *But see* ch. 5.2.9. Reinterviews may be available for reasonable-fear applicants as well.

[580] INA §238(b); 8 USC §1228(b).

[581] *See* Homeland Security Act of 2002, Pub. L. No. 107-296, §§456, 1512, 1517, 116 Stat. 2135, 2200, 2310, 2311.

[582] *Bamba v. Riley*, 366 F.3d 195 (3d Cir. 2004); *Bazan-Reyes v. INS*, 256 F.3d 600 (7th Cir. 2001); *see also United States v. Hernandez-Vermudez*, 356 F.3d 1011 (9th Cir. 2004) (finding that 8 USC §1228(b) applies to immigrants who are not admitted to the United States).

[583] INA §238(b)(5); 8 USC §1228(b)(5).

[584] 8 CFR §§238.1(f)(3), 1238.1(f)(3). For more detailed information on the Convention Against Torture, see ch. 4.

CHAPTER 3 • ASYLUM AND WITHHOLDING OF REMOVAL PROCEDURES

To be subject to these expedited proceedings, the individual must: (1) be a noncitizen; (2) have not been lawfully admitted for permanent residence or have conditional permanent residence; (3) have been convicted of an aggravated felony and such conviction has become final; and (4) be deportable under INA §237(a)(2)(A)(iii) (*i.e.*, convicted of an aggravated felony).[585]

3.7.1. Administrative Removal Proceedings

Initiation

DHS must allege the above-mentioned elements in a Notice of Intent to Issue a Final Administrative Deportation Order (I-851) and serve it on the individual.[586] The I-851 must also advise the individual of: (1) the privilege of being represented by counsel; (2) the right to request withholding of removal to a particular country if he or she fears persecution or torture in that country; (3) the right to inspect evidence supporting the I-851; and (4) the right to rebut the charges in the I-851 within 10 calendar days (or 13 calendar days, if the service of the I-851 was by mail).[587] DHS must also provide the individual with a list of free legal services.[588]

Response to Notice of Intent (I-851)

In their responses, individuals may: (1) designate their choice for country of removal; (2) submit a written response rebutting the allegations supporting the charge in the I-851; (3) request the opportunity to review the DHS's evidence; (4) submit a statement indicating an intention to request withholding of removal under 8 CFR §1208.16; and/or (5) request in writing an extension of time for filing a response, stating the specific reasons why such an extension is necessary.[589] If an individual does not submit a timely response or concedes deportability, DHS will issue a final administrative order of removal.[590] If the individual requests withholding of removal, DHS will issue a final administrative order of removal and then immediately refer the individual to an asylum officer for a "reasonable fear" interview.[591]

Initiation of §240 Removal Proceedings

If the DHS trial attorney finds that the record raises an issue of material fact, he or she may issue a Notice to Appear to initiate removal proceedings under INA §240.[592] The

---

[585] *See* 8 CFR §§238.1(b), 1238.1(b).

[586] 8 CFR §§238.1(b)(2)(i), 1238.1(b)(2)(i).

[587] 8 CFR §§238.1(b)(2), 1238.1(b)(2).

[588] 8 CFR §§238.1(b)(2)(iv), 1238.1(b)(2)(iv).

[589] 8 CFR §§238.1(c)(1), 1238.1(c)(1).

[590] 8 CFR §§238.1(d)(1), 1238.1(d)(1).

[591] 8 CFR §§238.1(f)(3), 1238.1(f)(3); see this chapter at 3.7.2 for more information regarding the reasonable fear process.

[592] 8 CFR §§238.1(d)(2)(ii), 1238.1(d)(2)(ii).

officer may also initiate §240 proceedings if the officer finds the individual is "not amenable" to expedited proceedings under INA §238.[593]

Termination of §240 Removal Proceedings

If an individual is in §240 proceedings and meets the criteria for expedited proceedings for aggravated felons, the immigration judge, upon a motion by the DHS trial attorney, may terminate §240 proceedings to commence proceedings under INA §238.[594]

Judicial Review

Under the REAL ID Act, a petition for review filed with an appropriate court of appeals is the only means for judicial review of an order of removal.[595] This provision of the Act took effect immediately and applies to all removal order appeals, regardless of when the removal order was issued.[596] An individual may seek judicial review under INA §242 of a final administrative removal order issued pursuant to INA §238.[597] The REAL ID Act clarifies that federal appellate review in accordance with procedures under INA §242 is the only method available for review of any removal order issued under any provision of the INA.[598]

3.7.2. Reasonable Fear Determination by an Asylum Officer

The Asylum Division has exclusive jurisdiction to make reasonable fear determinations, and the EOIR, *i.e.*, an immigration judge, has exclusive jurisdiction to review reasonable fear determinations.[599] These procedures regarding reasonable fear determinations went into effect on March 22, 1999.[600]

Preliminary Procedures

If, during the course of the administrative removal process, an individual expresses a fear of returning to his or her country of removal, he or she must be referred to an asylum officer for a reasonable fear determination.[601] In the absence of exceptional circumstances, the reasonable fear determination will be conducted within 10 days of the referral.[602] The referring officer should give the applicant Form M-488, Information on Reasonable Fear Interview, and a list of legal services if the applicant is not represented.[603]

---

[593] 8 CFR §§238.1(d)(2)(iii), 1238.1(d)(2)(iii).

[594] 8 CFR §§238.1(e), 1238.1(e).

[595] INA §242(a)(5); 8 USC §1252(a)(5).

[596] REAL ID Act of 2005, Pub. L. No. 109-13, div. B, §106(b), 119 Stat. 231, 311.

[597] *See* INA §§238(b)(3), 242(a)(1); 8 USC §§1228(b)(3), 1252(a)(1).

[598] REAL ID Act of 2005, Pub. L. No. 109-13, div. B, §106(d), 119 Stat. 231, 311.

[599] 8 CFR §§208.31(a), 1208.31(a).

[600] 64 Fed. Reg. 8477 (Feb. 19, 1999).

[601] 8 CFR §§208.31(b), 1208.31(b).

[602] 8 CFR §§208.31(b), 1208.31(b).

[603] *See* INS Memorandum, *supra* note 506, at 8.

CHAPTER 3 • ASYLUM AND WITHHOLDING OF REMOVAL PROCEDURES   207

Definition of Reasonable Fear

The applicant will be determined to have a "reasonable fear of persecution or torture" if the applicant "establishes a reasonable possibility that he or she would be persecuted on account of his or her race, religion, nationality, membership in a particular social group or political opinion, or a reasonable possibility that he or she would be tortured in the country of removal."[604] Torture is defined by regulation at 8 CFR §1208.18(a).[605] This standard is higher than the credible fear standard used in expedited removal proceedings.[606] According to the Asylum Office, it is the same standard used to establish a well-founded fear of persecution in the asylum context.[607]

No Bars Considered

When making a reasonable fear determination, the asylum officer is prohibited from considering whether the applicant is subject to any bars to withholding of removal.[608] Asylum officers are instructed, however, to elicit information related to possible bars and to flag cases with possible bars.[609]

Interview

The asylum officer must conduct the interview in a nonadversarial manner, separate and apart from the general public.[610] In most cases, the applicant will be detained. At the beginning of the interview, the asylum officer should determine that the applicant has an understanding of the reasonable fear determination process.[611] The asylum officer has the authority to administer oaths, verify the identity of the applicant, verify the identity of any interpreter, present and receive evidence, and question the applicant or any witnesses.[612] There is no need to submit Form I-589 for the purposes of the reasonable fear screening process.[613]

Orientation

An asylum officer should first conduct an orientation with the applicant, which may be conducted by telephone.[614] The asylum officer should check whether the applicant has any medical problems and whether the applicant will have any special needs during the interview, such as an interpreter who speaks an unusual language.[615] During the inter-

---

[604] 8 CFR §§208.31(c), 1208.31(c).

[605] *See also* ch. 4.2.1.

[606] EOIR Memorandum, *supra* note 513, at 659; *see also* ch. 5.

[607] *See* INS Memorandum, *supra* note 506, at 12.

[608] 8 CFR §§208.31(c), 1208.31(c); see ch. 2.7.2 for a list of these mandatory bars.

[609] *See* INS Memorandum, *supra* note 506, at 12.

[610] 8 CFR §§208.31(c), 1208.31(c).

[611] 8 CFR §§208.31(c), 1208.31(c).

[612] 8 CFR §§208.31(d), 1208.31(d).

[613] *See* INS Memorandum, *supra* note 506, at 7.

[614] *See id.* at 8.

[615] *Id.*

view, the asylum officer should ensure that the applicant has received and understood the M-488 and has a list of pro bono representatives if unrepresented. If the applicant is represented, the officer should obtain or confirm information on how to contact the representative.[616]

Scheduling of Interview

In the absence of exceptional circumstances, the reasonable fear determination will be conducted within 10 days of the referral.[617] A case is not considered referred until the Asylum Office has received notice that a person requires a reasonable fear screening and has also received the A-file.[618] In determining whether the interview or adjudication should be delayed, the Asylum Office is instructed to err on the side of ensuring that the applicant is able to present his or her full claim, so long as there is no evidence of intentional delay tactics or abuse of process.[619] The interview should normally be scheduled approximately 48 hours after the orientation, unless the applicant indicates that he or she is ready to proceed sooner.[620] Generally, if the applicant is represented, the asylum officer should schedule the interview at a date and time the representative may be present, unless the representative requests an interview date that will prevent the asylum officer from making a reasonable fear determination within the requisite 10-day period *and* it appears the representative's request is based on a delay tactic or convenience, rather than to address legitimate conflicts with commitments that cannot be rescheduled.[621]

Representation

The applicant may be represented by counsel or an accredited representative at the interview, at no expense to the government.[622] The representative should submit a Notice of Appearance, Form G-28, signed by the representative and the applicant. The representative may present a statement at the end of the interview.[623] The asylum officer, in his or her discretion, may limit the number of persons who may be present at the interview and the length of the representative's statement.[624] Representatives may participate in the interview by telephone if travel to a remote location is difficult on short notice, as long as their participation is at no expense to the government.[625]

---

[616] *Id.*

[617] 8 CFR §§208.31(b), 1208.31(b).

[618] *See* INS Memorandum, *supra* note 506, at 7.

[619] *Id.* at 8.

[620] *Id.*

[621] *Id.* at 8–9.

[622] 8 CFR §§208.31(c), 1208.31(c).

[623] 8 CFR §§208.31(c), 1208.31(c).

[624] 8 CFR §§208.31(c), 1208.31(c).

[625] *See* INS Memorandum, *supra* note 506, at 9.

Evidence

The applicant may present at the interview evidence, if available, relevant to the possibility of persecution or torture.[626] The asylum officer is instructed to elicit from the applicant any experiences of persecution, torture, or other harm that the applicant has experienced in the past; the basis of the applicant's fear that he or she would be persecuted or tortured in the future; who the applicant fears; the applicant's knowledge of harm to individuals similarly situated; and any experiences of the applicant (in any country, including the United States) that may place the applicant at risk of persecution or torture.[627] The applicant must also be given the opportunity to explain any material discrepancies in his or her testimony—including inconsistencies, inability to provide detail, and perceived implausibility.[628]

Interpretation

If the applicant is unable to proceed effectively in English, and if the asylum officer is unable to proceed competently in the language chosen by the applicant, the asylum officer must arrange for an interpreter in conducting the interview.[629] The interpreter may not be a representative or employee of the applicant's country, or if stateless, the applicant's country of last habitual residence.[630] Before or during the interview, the applicant's request for a male or female interpreter should be accommodated when possible.[631] If the applicant, the applicant's representative, or the asylum officer believes that the interpreter is either not competent or not neutral, the officer may terminate the interview and request a different interpreter.[632] The applicant may provide his or her own interpreter.[633] If the applicant uses his or her own interpreter, the asylum officer is required to use a commercial interpreter to monitor the applicant's interpreter.[634]

Record

The asylum officer must create a summary of the material facts as stated by the applicant.[635] The asylum officer is required to place this information on Form I-899, Reasonable Fear Worksheet.[636] At the conclusion of the interview, the asylum officer must review the summary with the applicant and allow the applicant to correct any errors in the summary.[637]

---

[626] 8 CFR §§208.31(c), 1208.31(c).

[627] *See* INS Memorandum, *supra* note 506, at 9.

[628] *Id.*

[629] 8 CFR §§208.31(c), 1208.31(c).

[630] 8 CFR §§208.31(c), 1208.31(c).

[631] *See* INS Memorandum, *supra* note 506, at 12.

[632] *Id.*

[633] *Id.* at 10–11.

[634] *Id.*

[635] 8 CFR §§208.31(c), 1208.31(c).

[636] *See* INS Memorandum, *supra* note 506, at 9.

[637] 8 CFR §§208.31(c), 1208.31(c).

Decision

The asylum officer must create a written record of his or her determination, including a summary of the material facts as stated by the applicant, any additional facts relied on by the asylum officer, and the asylum officer's determination of whether, in light of such facts, the applicant has established a reasonable fear of persecution or torture.[638] All reasonable fear cases must be reviewed by Asylum Headquarters before the determination is served on the applicant.[639]

Reasonable Fear—Withholding-Only Proceeding Before an IJ

If the asylum officer determines that the applicant has a reasonable fear of persecution or torture, he or she must inform the applicant and issue a Form I-863, Notice of Referral to an Immigration Judge, for a full consideration of the request for withholding only.[640] Such cases will be adjudicated in accordance with the provisions of 8 CFR §1208.16 within 10 days of the issuance of the I-863.[641] The chief immigration judge, however, has instructed IJs that in scheduling and adjudicating withholding-only cases, IJs should balance the dictates of due process concerns and regulatory compliance concerns.[642] A hearing notice, entitled Notice of Withholding-Only Hearing, must be sent to the applicant in care of his or her custodial authority and to his or her attorney, if any, via an appropriate overnight courier.[643]

An immigration judge is permitted, under 8 CFR §§208.16, 1208.16, to consider withholding of removal under INA §241(b)(3), withholding under the Convention Against Torture, and deferral of removal under the Convention Against Torture.[644] At the initial appearance before the IJ, the applicant will be given an adequate time to prepare and file a Form I-589.[645] Once the I-589 is received by the IJ, a copy will be forwarded to the Department of State and the IJ must schedule a merits hearing.[646] The withholding-only proceeding may be conducted by video conference or telephonically.[647] If an inter-

---

[638] 8 CFR §§208.31(c), 1208.31(c).

[639] *See* INS Memorandum, *supra* note 506, at 13; *see also* the USCIS webpage on reasonable fear screenings, available at *www.uscis.gov* (Click on the "Services and Benefits" tab, then the "Humanitarian Benefits" link, then the "Asylum" link, and finally the "Reasonable Fear Screenings" link.).

[640] 8 CFR §§208.31(e), 1208.31(e).

[641] 8 CFR §§208.31(e), 1208.31(e).

[642] EOIR Memorandum, *supra* note 513, at 661.

[643] *Id.*

[644] For more detailed information regarding applying for relief under the Convention Against Torture, see ch. 4.

[645] EOIR Memorandum, *supra* note 513, at 661.

[646] *Id.*

[647] *Id.*

preter is needed, the immigration court must provide one.[648] The applicant or DHS may appeal the IJ's decision to the BIA.[649]

No Reasonable Fear—Removal or IJ Review

If the asylum officer determines that the applicant has not established a reasonable fear of persecution or torture, he or she must inform the applicant in writing of the decision and must inquire whether the applicant wishes to have an IJ review the negative decision.[650] The asylum officer must use Form I-898, Record of Negative Reasonable Fear Interview Finding and Request for Review by Immigration Judge.[651] The applicant must indicate on Form I-898 whether he or she desires an IJ review.[652] An applicant who does not request an IJ review is subject to immediate removal from the United States.[653]

Withdrawals

An applicant referred for a reasonable fear interview may seek to withdraw his or her request.[654] An asylum officer must go over the withdrawal form with the applicant, either in person or telephonically, and with the assistance of an interpreter, if necessary.[655] Asylum Headquarters must concur with the withdrawal before the applicant is permitted to withdraw.[656]

3.7.3. Review of Negative Reasonable Fear Determination by IJ

If, upon receiving a negative reasonable fear determination, the applicant indicates a desire for an IJ review, the asylum officer must serve the applicant with Form I-863, Notice of Referral to the Immigration Judge.[657] The record of the determination, including copies of the I-863, the asylum officer's notes, the summary of material facts, and other facts upon which the determination was based will be provided to the IJ with the negative determination.[658] It is likely that applicants who request a reasonable fear review will be detained at a DHS facility or in a federal, state, or local jail or prison. If the distance from the immigration court renders it impractical for the Asylum Office to file Form I-863 in person, the court administrator will allow the filing of Form I-863 by fax.[659] The hearing

---

[648] *Id.*

[649] 8 CFR §§208.31(e), 1208.31(e).

[650] 8 CFR §§208.31(f), 1208.31(f).

[651] 8 CFR §§208.31(f), 1208.31(f).

[652] 8 CFR §§208.31(f), 1208.31(f).

[653] *See* INS Memorandum, *supra* note 506, at 5. *But see* ch. 5.2.9. Reinterviews may be available for reasonable fear applicants as well.

[654] *See* INS Memorandum, *supra* note 506, at 15–16.

[655] *Id.*

[656] *Id.*

[657] 8 CFR §§208.31(g), 1208.31(g).

[658] 8 CFR §§208.31(g), 1208.31(g).

[659] EOIR Memorandum, *supra* note 513, at 659.

notice must be sent via an appropriate overnight courier to the applicant, in care of his or her custodial authority, and to the applicant's attorney, if any.[660]

The regulations do not describe how a reasonable fear review will be conducted. Because the proceedings resemble credible fear reviews, the chief immigration judge has instructed IJs that they should be modeled after credible fear review proceedings.[661] IJs are required to tape-record the reasonable fear review proceedings.[662] The proceedings may be conducted by video conference or telephonically.[663] If an interpreter is necessary, the immigration court must provide one.[664] Since the regulations do not specify whether an applicant has the right to be represented by counsel during the reasonable fear review, the chief immigration judge has instructed IJs that it is within their discretion whether to permit an applicant to be represented by counsel during the reasonable fear review.[665]

The IJ must make a de novo determination of whether the applicant has established a reasonable fear of persecution or torture.[666]

Reasonable Fear

If, upon review of the asylum officer's negative reasonable fear determination, the IJ finds that the applicant has a reasonable fear of persecution or torture, the applicant is placed in withholding-only proceedings and the applicant may then submit Form I-589, Application for Asylum and Withholding of Removal.[667] The IJ may only consider the applicant's eligibility for withholding of removal under 8 CFR §1208.16, and must determine whether the applicant's removal must be withheld or deferred.[668] DHS or the applicant may appeal to the BIA the IJ's decision whether removal must be withheld or deferred.[669] The BIA may only review the IJ's decision regarding the applicant's eligibility for withholding or deferral of removal under 8 CFR §1208.16.[670]

No Reasonable Fear

If, upon review of the asylum officer's negative reasonable fear determination, the IJ concurs that the applicant does not have a reasonable fear of persecution or torture, the

---

[660] *Id.*

[661] *Id.*

[662] *Id.* at 660.

[663] *Id.*

[664] *Id.*

[665] *Id.*

[666] *Id.*

[667] *See* 8 CFR §§208.31(g)(2), 1208.31(g)(2); EOIR Memorandum, *supra* note 513, at 8.

[668] 8 CFR §§208.31(g)(2)(i), 1208.31(g)(2)(i).

[669] 8 CFR §§208.31(g)(2)(ii), 1208.31(g)(2)(ii).

[670] 8 CFR §§208.31(g)(2)(ii), 1208.31(g)(2)(ii); *see also* this chapter at 3.7.2 for more information on withholding-only proceedings.

case will be returned to DHS for removal of the applicant.[671] There is no appeal from the IJ's decision.[672]

3.8. RELEASE FROM DETENTION

Due to the increase in detention space in the United States and the increasing use of detention by DHS, it is likely that an applicant for asylum, withholding of removal, or Convention Against Torture relief may be detained during part or all of the adjudication process. Detention of asylum-seekers has been criticized by human rights groups in the United States.[673] In 2004, DHS used detention as a tool to ensure removal after IJs issued decisions. Under pilot projects in three U.S. cities, DHS took into custody anyone issued a final order of removal by an immigration judge regardless of whether the individual reserved appeal. In addition, some individuals granted relief by the IJ were taken into custody if DHS reserved appeal in the case. Individuals taken into custody, could, if eligible, seek a bond from DHS and an IJ bond redetermination hearing. Upon completion of the pilot projects, DHS determined that this detention policy would not be implemented nationwide.[674]

DHS detains individuals at its own service processing centers and contract facilities,[675] as well as at Bureau of Prisons facilities and numerous local jails located throughout the United States. DHS has been criticized for conditions and practices in its facilities, as well as at local jails and prisons where DHS detainees are held.[676] In the past, DHS has also been criticized for using detention as a means of deterring asylum-seekers and for making detention decisions based on the nationality of the applicant.[677]

3.8.1. Who Is Eligible for Release

Under current law, regulations, and DHS policies, the following applicants for asylum, withholding of removal, or relief under the Convention Against Torture are eligible for release from detention:

---

[671] 8 CFR §§208.31(g)(1), 1208.31(g)(1).

[672] *Id. But see* ch. 5.2.9. Reinterviews may be available for reasonable fear applicants as well.

[673] *See, e.g.*, B. Frelick, "US Detention of Asylum Seekers and Human Rights," *Immigration Daily* (Apr. 20, 2005), available at *www.ilw.com*.

[674] For more information, see AILF Practice Advisory, ICE's Detention After Removal Hearing Program—Practical Suggestions and Legal Analysis for Potential Challenges (Apr. 9, 2004), available at *www.ailf.org/lac/lac_pa_041204.pdf*.

[675] See appx. 6E for list of facilities.

[676] *See, e.g.*, "ACLU Challenges Prison-Like Conditions at Hutto Detention Center," *supra* note 487; *see also Locking Up Family Values, supra* note 487; Human Rights First, *In Liberty's Shadow: U.S. Detention of Asylum Seekers in the Era of Homeland Security* (Jan. 2004), available at *www.humanrightsfirst.org/asylum/libertys_shadow/Libertys_Shadow.pdf*; Human Rights Watch, *Presumption of Guilt: Human Rights Abuses of Post-September 11 Detainees* (Aug. 2002), available at *www.hrw.org/reports/2002/us911*; Human Rights Watch, *Locked Away: Immigration Detainees in Jails in the United States* (Sept. 1998), available at *www.hrw.org/reports98/us-immig*.

[677] *See* UNHCR Advisory Opinion (Apr. 15, 2002), *reproduced in* 79 *Interpreter Releases* 620 (Apr. 29, 2002).

Individuals Found to Have a Credible Fear

Individuals in the expedited removal process who have been determined to have a "credible fear of persecution" are eligible for release from detention. The request for release must be made to the district director (DD) with jurisdiction over the place of detention.[678]

Noncriminals Who Have Made a Lawful or Illegal Entry or Who Fall Within the Definition of "Arriving Alien"

Individuals not subject to certain criminal grounds for detention who lawfully or illegally entered the United States and who have not yet been ordered removed, deported, or excluded may seek release from detention before an IJ.[679] Individuals who fall within the definition of "arriving alien," *i.e.*, who seek admission or transit at a U.S. port of entry, if placed in removal (*not* expedited removal) proceedings, may seek release from detention from the DD.[680]

Individuals Who Completed Their Criminal Sentences Prior to October 9, 1998, or with Final Orders of Removal Who Cannot Be Returned to Their Home Countries

An individual with a final order of removal, deportation, or exclusion is not eligible for release from detention unless the country designated for removal will not accept the individual. The landmark Supreme Court case *Zadvydas v. Davis*[681] prohibits the indefinite detention of noncitizens with final orders of removal where there is no likelihood of removal in the reasonable foreseeable future. In response to the Supreme Court's decision, legacy INS published interim regulations on November 14, 2001, setting forth the procedures for reviewing cases of individuals in detention with final orders of removal.[682] The case law and procedures for individuals in detention with final orders of removal are beyond the scope of this *Primer*.[683]

---

[678] *See* INS Memorandum, M. Pearson, "Expedited Removal: Additional Policy Guidance" (Dec. 30, 1997), *published on* AILA InfoNet at Doc. No. 97123091 (*posted* Dec. 30, 1997), and *reprinted in* 75 *Interpreter Releases* 270 (Feb. 23, 1998).

[679] *See* 8 CFR §1003.19(h)(2)(i).

[680] 8 CFR §1003.19(h)(2)(ii).

[681] *Zadvydas v. Davis*, 533 U.S. 678 (2001).

[682] *See* 66 Fed. Reg. 56967 (Nov. 14, 2001), codified at 8 CFR §241.13.

[683] For more information, see K. Glynn and S. Bronstein, *Systemic Problems Persist in U.S. Immigration and Customs Enforcement Custody Reviews for Indefinite Detainees* (Sept. 13, 2005), available at *www.cliniclegal.org/DSP/Indefinite2005FINALforRELEASE.pdf*; L. Joyce, "INS Detention Practices Post-*Zadvydas v. Davis*," 79 *Interpreter Releases* 809 (May 24, 2002). The General Accounting Office has recently criticized ICE's postorder custody reviews and recommended improvements. GAO, *Immigration Enforcement: Better Data and Controls Are Needed to Assure Consistency with the Supreme Court Decision on Long-Term Alien Detention* (May 2004), available at *www.gao.gov/new.items/d04434.pdf*.

Children

In 2006, there were 7,746 unaccompanied children in DHS custody, more than three times the number of unaccompanied children detained in 1997.[684] For 2006, the top four countries of nationality of children in detention were El Salvador (31%), Honduras (28%), Guatemala (26%), and Mexico (7%).[685]

Children, *i.e.*, individuals under the age of 18, are eligible for release from DHS custody pursuant to 8 CFR §1236.3.[686] These regulations on the release of children codify provisions of the *Flores v. Reno* settlement regarding detention of children.[687] DHS and legacy INS have been criticized for violating the terms of this settlement and for the conditions under which children are held.[688] Upon release from custody, DHS should serve both the adult to whom the child is released as well as the child with the Notice of Hearing and charging document.[689]

Moreover, children are often unrepresented in their immigration proceedings. At least one court has held that counsel must be appointed at government expense for a detained child.[690]

3.8.2. Who Is *Not* Eligible for Release

The following individuals under current law and regulations are not eligible for release from detention:

Individuals in Expedited Removal

An individual in the expedited removal process is not eligible for release from detention unless he or she is found to have a credible fear of persecution,[691] or he or she dem-

---

[684] Congressional Research Service, Report for Congress, *Unaccompanied Alien Children: Policies and Issues* (Mar. 1, 2007) at 25–29; INS Fact Sheet, "INS' Office of Juvenile Affairs" (Aug. 1, 2002), *published on* AILA InfoNet (*posted* Aug. 12. 2002), and available at *www.immigration.com/newsletter1/insfactjuvenile.pdf* (asserting that there were 2,375 unaccompanied children in U.S. custody in 1997).

[685] *Unaccompanied Alien Children*, *supra* note 684, at 28.

[686] *See* 8 CFR §§212.5(b)(3), 1212.5(b)(3).

[687] *Flores v. Reno*, 507 U.S. 292 (1993); *see also* 75 *Interpreter Releases* 1020 (July 27, 1998).

[688] *See, e.g.*, "ACLU Challenges Prison-Like Conditions at Hutto Detention Center," *supra* note 486; *see also Locking Up Family Values*, *supra* note 487; *From Persecution to Prison*, *supra* note 486, at 123 (criticizing DHS for detaining children and for its use of x-ray and dental examinations to determine age); Women's Commission for Refugee Women and Children, *Prison Guard or Parent?: INS Treatment of Unaccompanied Refugee Children* (May 2002), available at *www.womenscommission.org/pdf/ins_det.pdf*; Human Rights Watch, *Detained and Deprived of Rights: Children in the Custody of the U.S. Immigration and Naturalization Service* (Dec. 1998), available at *www.hrw.org/reports98/ins2*.

[689] *Flores-Chavez v. Ashcroft*, 362 F.3d 1150 (9th Cir. 2004).

[690] *See Machado v. Ashcroft*, No. Cs-02-0066-FVS, Preliminary Injunction Order (E.D. Wash., Mar. 5, 2002) (legacy INS ordered to hire a lawyer for a child in its custody at government expense or release him from detention). For further discussion on the right to counsel for children in deportation proceedings, see "David and Goliath?," *supra* note 456.

[691] *See* this chapter, at 3.8.1.

onstrates that "parole is required to meet a medical emergency or is necessary for a legitimate law enforcement purpose."[692]

Individuals Subject to Criminal Grounds of Deportation or Inadmissibility

Individuals subject to removal based on one or more of the grounds listed below may not seek release from detention, except if they completed the jail or prison sentence for the conviction prior to October 9, 1998 (and they do not have a final order of removal), or the designated country for removal will not accept them. The criminal grounds include: aggravated felony, crimes involving moral turpitude (unless one of two exceptions applies), two or more crimes involving moral turpitude, multiple criminal convictions if the aggregate sentence was five years or more, controlled-substance offenses, controlled-substance trafficking, certain firearms offenses, prostitution and commercialized vice offenses, and engaging in terrorist activities.[693] Such individuals are technically eligible for release under very restrictive criteria set forth in INA §236(c)(2), which allows the AG to release such individuals if necessary to provide protection to a witness or person cooperating in the investigation of major criminal activity and the individual would not be a danger to the safety of persons or property. Under the Homeland Security Act of 2002, this authority to release extends to the DHS secretary and DHS officials.[694] The Supreme Court addressed the issue of whether lawful permanent residents could be detained without bond while their removal hearings are pending under INA §236(c)(1) and found that they could be.[695]

Terrorists

Individuals subject to removal on terrorist grounds are not eligible for release from detention.[696] "Suspected terrorists" may also be detained under a controversial certification process contained in the USA PATRIOT Act.[697]

---

[692] 8 CFR §§235.3(b)(2)(iii), 1235.3(b)(2)(iii) (nonstowaways), 208.5(b)(2), 1208.5(b)(2) (stowaways).

[693] 8 CFR §1003.19(h)(2)(i). For a complete list, see INA §236(c)(1); 8 USC §1226(c)(1).

[694] *See* Homeland Security Act of 2002, Pub. L. No. 107-296, §§456, 1512, 1517, 116 Stat. 2135, 2200, 2310, 2311.

[695] *Demore v. Kim*, 538 U.S. 510 (2003). For practice tips on distinguishing the *Kim* decision, see AILF Practice Advisory, Mandatory Detention after *Demore v. Kim* (Aug. 29, 2003), available at *www.ailf.org/lac/lac_pa_083003.pdf*.

[696] INA §236(c)(1)(D); 8 USC §1226(c)(1)(D); 8 CFR §1003.19(h)(2)(i). *But see* INA §236(c)(2); 8 USC §1226(c)(2) (allowing the AG to release such individuals if necessary to provide protection to a witness or person cooperating in the investigation of major criminal activity and the individual would not be a danger to the safety of persons or property). This authority to release extends to the DHS Secretary and DHS officials. *See* Homeland Security Act of 2002, Pub. L. No. 107-296, §§456, 1512, 1517, 116 Stat. 2135, 2200, 2310, 2311.

[697] *See* INA §236A; 8 USC §1226a. For further discussion, see ch. 2.7.2; *see also* Office of the Inspector General, *The September 11 Detainees: A Review of the Treatment of Aliens Held on Immigration Charges in Connection with the Investigation of the September 11 Attacks* (June 2, 2003), available at *www.usdoj.gov/oig/special/0306/index.htm;* ACLU, *America's Disappeared: Seeking International Justice for Immigrants Detained After September 11* (Jan. 2004), available at *www.aclu.org/SafeandFree/SafeandFree.cfm?ID=14800&c=207*.

Individuals with Final Orders of Removal

An individual with a final order of removal, deportation, or exclusion is not eligible for release from detention unless the country designated for removal will not accept the individual. The landmark Supreme Court case *Zadvydas v. Davis*[698] prohibits the indefinite detention of noncitizens with final orders of removal where there is no likelihood of removal in the reasonable foreseeable future. In response to the Supreme Court's decision, legacy INS published interim regulations on November 14, 2001, setting forth the procedures for reviewing cases of individuals in detention with final orders of removal.[699] There has been criticism by courts on how DHS is implementing these regulations.[700] The case law and procedures for individuals in detention with final orders of removal is beyond the scope of this *Primer*.[701]

> *Tip*—For further information and a review of relevant case law, see M. Linsky and L. Palumbo, "A Practitioner's Guide to Representing Aliens Seeking Release on Bond in Removal Proceedings."[702]

3.8.3. Bond Hearings vs. Parole Requests

Recent changes to the law have altered the procedures for seeking release from detention. In cases in which a person is eligible for release from detention, the initial procedure for seeking release may be either a bond redetermination hearing before an IJ or a request for parole to the DD. The law is in a state of flux and may change depending on the outcome of federal court challenges to these procedures. Below is an overview of current release practices.

3.8.4. Bond Hearings

Individuals apprehended by DHS in the interior of the United States who are in removal proceedings and who are not subject to the criminal bars under INA §236(c)(1), who have physically entered the country (legally or illegally), and who do not have an administratively final order of removal, deportation, or exclusion, are generally eligible for a bond hearing before an IJ.[703] The BIA has also held that an individual initially screened for expedited removal, who was subsequently placed in removal proceedings under INA §240, is eligible for a custody redetermination hearing before an IJ.[704]

---

[698] *Zadvydas v. Davis*, 533 U.S. 678 (2001).

[699] *See* 66 Fed. Reg. 56967 (Nov. 14, 2001), codified at 8 CFR §241.13.

[700] *See, e.g., Gui v. Ridge*, 2004 WL 1920719 (M.D. Pa. 2004) (noting that 20 months awaiting removal and lack of evidence from ICE that removal to China was reasonably foreseeable entitled petitioner to release).

[701] For more information, see L. Joyce, "INS Detention Practices Post-*Zadvydas v. Davis*," 79 *Interpreter Releases* 809 (May 24, 2002).

[702] M. Linsky and L. Palumbo, "A Practitioner's Guide to Representing Aliens Seeking Release on Bond in Removal Proceedings," 1 *Immigration & Nationality Law Handbook* 219–29 (AILA 2004–05 Ed.).

[703] 8 CFR §1003.19(h)(2)(i). For a more in-depth overview of bond hearing law and procedures, see M. Linsky and L. Palumbo, *supra* note 702, at 219.

[704] *Matter of X–K–*, 23 I&N Dec. 731 (BIA 2005).

Procedure

The initial custody determination is made by DHS under 8 CFR §1236.1. An IJ may review that determination in a bond redetermination proceeding.[705] Bond redetermination hearings are generally informal and are usually not recorded. For information on local practices, contact experienced local immigration practitioners and the immigration court. See appendix 6B for a list of immigration court addresses and telephone numbers. It may also be helpful to observe several bond hearings prior to participating in one.

Application for an Initial Bond Redetermination

The request may be made orally, in writing, or, at the discretion of the IJ, by telephone.[706]

Venue

The request should be made to one of the following offices, in this designated order: (1) the immigration court having jurisdiction over the applicant's place of detention, (2) the immigration court having administrative control over the case, or (3) the Office of the Chief Immigration Judge in Falls Church, Virginia.[707]

Separate Proceeding

The bond redetermination hearing is separate and apart from, and may not form any part of, the removal proceedings.[708]

Basis for Decision

The IJ's determination regarding custody status or bond may be based on any information available to the IJ or that is presented to the IJ by DHS or the individual.[709]

Decision

The IJ will inform the parties orally or in writing of the decision and the reasons for the decision.[710]

Appeal

An appeal may be taken by DHS or the individual to the Board of Immigration Appeals on Form EOIR-26 within 30 calendar days of the IJ's decision.[711] The appeal is likely to take six months or longer and will not stay the removal proceedings.

DHS may seek an emergency stay of the IJ's bond decision. In some cases, DHS is entitled to an automatic stay of an IJ's bond redetermination, if the DD has denied the

---

[705] 8 CFR §1003.19(a).

[706] 8 CFR §1003.19(b).

[707] 8 CFR §1003.19(c).

[708] 8 CFR §1003.19(d).

[709] *Id.*

[710] 8 CFR §1003.19(f).

[711] 8 CFR §§1003.38, 1003.19(f). *See also* this chapter, at 3.10.

individual's request for release or has set a bond at $10,000 or more and the individual seeking release is subject to INA §236(c)(1), *i.e.*, criminal grounds for detention.[712]

Request for a Subsequent Bond Redetermination

After the initial bond redetermination by an IJ, a request for a subsequent redetermination may be made to the IJ.[713] The request must be made in writing and will be considered if there is a showing that the individual's circumstances have "changed materially" since the prior redetermination.[714] Even if the bond redetermination is on appeal to the BIA, the IJ retains jurisdiction to determine a subsequent bond based on materially changed circumstances.[715]

Burden of Proof

An individual who is not subject to a criminal ground of detention is generally eligible for a bond unless there is a finding that the individual is a threat to national security, likely to abscond, or a poor bail risk.[716] Factors that an IJ will consider in assessing an individual's eligibility for a bond include:

- Family ties in the United States
- Ties to the community
- Length of residence in the community
- Property in the United States
- Work history
- Failures to appear for criminal or immigration court hearings
- Criminal record and efforts toward rehabilitation
- Previous immigration violations
- Limited financial resources
- Any defenses to immigration charge
- Eligibility for relief in removal proceedings
- Likely duration of removal proceedings

---

[712] 8 CFR §1003.19(i). *But see Zavala v. Ridge*, 310 F. Supp. 2d 1071 (N.D. Calif. 2004) (finding that the automatic stay provision found at 8 CFR §1003.19(i)(2) violates due process). Note that some cases have also found 8 CFR §1003.19(i) to be unconstitutional. *See e.g., Ashley v. Ridge*, 288 F. Supp. 2d 662 (D.N.J. 2003); *Bezmen v. Ashcroft*, 245 F. Supp. 2d 446 (D. Conn. 2003); *Uritsky v. Ridge*, 286 F. Supp. 2d 842 (E.D. Mich. 2003).

[713] 8 CFR §1003.19(e).

[714] *Id.*

[715] *Matter of Valles*, 21 I&N Dec. 769 (BIA 1997).

[716] *See Matter of Patel*, 15 I&N Dec. 666 (BIA 1976), superseded by statute as stated in *Matter of Valdez-Valdez*, 21 I&N Dec. 703 (BIA 1997). *But see Matter of D–J–*, 23 I&N Dec. 572 (BIA 2003) (finding that AG has broad discretion in bond proceedings and may consider national security interests implicated when noncitizens arrive by sea and where such arrivals may encourage future mass migrations).

- Receipt of government benefits
- Complete address (not P.O. box) where applicant will reside upon release while case is pending

Documentary proof of any or all of these factors noted above should be submitted to the IJ at the bond redetermination hearing. Any documents in a language other than English should be translated into English and have a certificate of translation attached.[717]

3.8.5. Requests for Release (or Parole) to ICE District Directors

Individuals who are considered under current law *not* to be eligible for a bond hearing before an IJ include: (1) individuals seeking admission to the United States at a port of entry, *i.e.*, "arriving aliens," as defined in 8 CFR §1001.1(q); (2) individuals subject to INA §236(c); and (3) individuals subject to deportation based on security-related grounds.[718]

> *Note*: DHS's parole procedures change periodically as a result of changes in DHS policy or because of lawsuits filed on behalf of detainees.

Eligibility and Burden of Proof

Expedited Removal

An individual who is apprehended at a port of entry with false or no documents and is subject to expedited removal is not eligible for parole unless he or she demonstrates that "parole is required to meet a medical emergency or is necessary for a legitimate law enforcement purpose."[719]

Credible Fear Finding

An individual subject to expedited removal who is referred to a hearing before an IJ to apply for asylum, *i.e.*, who is found to have a "credible fear of persecution," may be released upon demonstrating his or her true identity, that he or she has a sponsor (a person with legal status willing to provide food and shelter), and that he or she will report for all immigration appointments and hearings. If the individual is subject to certain criminal or security-related bars, he or she is not likely to be paroled.[720]

---

[717] For a thorough analysis of these factors, see National Lawyers Guild, National Immigration Project, *Bond Practice Manual* (1994); *see also* Florence Immigrant and Refugee Rights Project, *All About Bonds* (Mar. 2002) (which contains a helpful bond worksheet), available at *www.firrp.org/documents/KyrMaterials/English/Bondsenglish.pdf*.

[718] 8 CFR §1003.19(h)(2)(i); *see Matter of Oseiwusu*, 22 I&N Dec. 19 (BIA 1998) (holding that an IJ has no authority over the custody of "arriving aliens," including an individual granted advance parole). These individuals may, however, request release from the district director, subject to the limitations discussed in this chapter at 3.8.2. and 3.8.4.

[719] 8 CFR §§235.3(b)(2)(iii), 1235.3(b)(2)(iii).

[720] *See* INS Memorandum, M. Pearson, "Expedited Removal: Additional Policy Guidance" (Dec. 30, 1997), *published on* AILA InfoNet at Doc. No. 97123091 (*posted* Dec. 30, 1997), and *reprinted in* 75 *Interpreter Releases* 270 (Feb. 23, 1998).

Others Arriving at a Port of Entry

An individual who is arriving at a port of entry who is not subject to expedited removal may be paroled upon demonstrating that there are "urgent humanitarian reasons" or there would be a "significant public benefit" if he or she is released or paroled.[721] An individual may meet this burden by showing that he or she has a serious medical condition, is pregnant, or a juvenile (if an appropriate relative or nonrelative may take custody).[722]

Arriving Individuals Subject to Criminal Grounds for Detention

An individual arriving at a port of entry or who has had his or her parole status revoked and who is subject to the criminal grounds for detention under INA §236(c)(1) may only be released on parole upon a showing that it is necessary to provide protection to a witness or person cooperating in the investigation of major criminal activity and the individual would not be a danger to the safety of persons or property.[723]

Procedure

The parole request should be made in writing to the DD having jurisdiction over the individual's place of detention. The request may be in the form of a letter and should include the individual's alien registration (or "A") number, reference to the applicable legal standard for release, the reasons why the individual meets the requirements for release, and the full address where the individual will reside if parole is granted. Also include any documents that support the application for a parole request, which may include: a letter from the sponsor, relative, or friend with whom the individual will reside upon release and proof of family ties in the United States, ties to the community, the individual's serious medical condition (if applicable), property in the United States, work history, evidence of rehabilitation (if the person has any criminal convictions), and likelihood of relief in removal proceedings. All non-English language documents should be translated into English and submitted with a certificate of translation.[724]

3.9. EMPLOYMENT AUTHORIZATION

An asylum applicant may be provided with employment authorization, but is not entitled to such authorization.[725] Moreover, employment authorization may not be granted prior to 180 days after the date of filing the application for asylum.[726] As a general rule, if an application for asylum is denied within the first 180 days, the applicant is ineligible for

---

[721] INA §212(d)(5)(A); 8 USC §1182(d)(5)(A).

[722] 8 CFR §§212.5(b)(1)–(3).

[723] *See* INA §236(c)(2); 8 USC §1226(c)(2).

[724] For a more thorough explanation of the parole process, see Florence Immigrant and Refugee Rights Project, *How to Apply to the Department of Homeland Security for Release from Immigration Custody* (Mar. 2002), available at *www.firrp.org/documents/KyrMaterials/English/ReleasefromINSCustody english.pdf*.

[725] INA §208(d)(2); 8 USC §1158(d)(2).

[726] INA §208(d)(2); 8 USC §1158(d)(2).

employment authorization throughout the immigration court and review process unless he or she is granted asylum by the IJ, the BIA, or a federal court.

> *Tip*—The procedures listed below are for individuals who applied for asylum on or after January 4, 1995.[727]

3.9.1. Eligibility

An asylum applicant who has not been convicted of an aggravated felony is eligible to apply for employment authorization in accordance with 8 CFR §§1274a.12(c)(8) and 1274a.13(a)(2).[728] However, an applicant whose asylum application has been denied by an asylum officer or by an IJ within 150 days after applying for asylum is ineligible for employment authorization.[729] Similarly, an applicant who fails to appear for an asylum interview or a hearing before an IJ is ineligible for employment authorization, unless the applicant demonstrates that the failure to appear was due to exceptional circumstances.[730]

3.9.2. Time for Filing

The application for employment authorization (Form I-765) should be submitted to USCIS "no earlier" than 150 days after the date the completed asylum application is filed.[731] One exception is for an applicant who has been recommended for approval, who may apply for employment authorization upon receipt of the notice of the recommended approval in less than 150 days.[732] If the asylum application has been returned as incomplete, the 150-day period will begin upon USCIS's receipt of a completed application.[733] Any delay requested or caused by the applicant will not be counted as part of the time period within which the applicant may not apply for employment authorization.[734]

> *Tip*—**Problems with Calculating the 180 Days**—"Clock" problems continue to plague asylum applicants and their representatives. EOIR recommends that if the immigration court has erroneously stopped the "clock" in a case, the matter should first be brought to the attention of the IJ and the court administrator.[735] If the IJ or court administrator fails to timely respond, the assistant

---

[727] *See* 8 CFR §§208.7(a)(3), 1208.7(a)(3).

[728] 8 CFR §§208.7(a)(1), 1208.7(a)(1).

[729] 8 CFR §§208.7(a)(1), 1208.7(a)(1).

[730] 8 CFR §§208.7(a)(4), 1208.7(a)(4).

[731] 8 CFR §§208.7(a)(1), 1208.7(a)(1); *see* appx. 9C.

[732] 8 CFR §§208.7(a)(1), 1208.7(a)(1); *see* 8 CFR §§274a.12(c)(8), 1274a.12(c)(8).

[733] 8 CFR §§208.7(a)(1), 1208.7(a)(1).

[734] 8 CFR §§208.7(a)(2), 1208.7(a)(2).

[735] For a list of immigration courts and their telephone numbers, see appx. 6B. For a more in-depth look at this issue, *see* AILF Practice Advisory, Employment Authorization and Asylum: Strategies to Avoid Stopping the Asylum Clock (Feb. 28, 2006), available at *www.ailf.org/lac/lac_pa_022806.pdf*.

chief immigration judge with responsibility for the court in question should be contacted.[736]

3.9.3. What to File

The applicant should file an Application for Employment Authorization (Form I-765) and proof that the application for asylum has been filed with USCIS or an IJ, or that it is pending before the BIA or federal court.[737]

3.9.4. Where to File

The application should be filed with the USCIS service center that has jurisdiction over the residence of the applicant.[738]

3.9.5. Fee

A filing fee is not required for an initial application. A fee is required for a renewal unless the applicant is eligible for a fee waiver under 8 CFR §§103.7(c), 1103.7(c).[739] The fee may be waived if the applicant is able to substantiate that he or she is unable to pay the application fee. Applicants must file an affidavit or unsworn declaration asking for the waiver, stating their belief that they are deserving of employment authorization, and the reasons for their inability to pay the fee.[740]

3.9.6. Adjudication Period

USCIS has 30 days from the date an application for employment authorization is filed to grant or deny the application.[741] No employment authorization may be issued, however, prior to the expiration of the 180-day period following the filing of an application for asylum that was filed on or after April 1, 1997.[742] Any delay requested or caused by the applicant will not be counted as part of the time period within which USCIS must respond to an application for employment authorization.[743]

> ➤ *Tip*—**No More Interim Employment Authorization Documents (EADs)**—In the past, when an applicant had waited longer than 30 days for an initial EAD or 90 days for a renewal, the local office of USCIS would

---

[736] For a list of assistant chief immigration judges and their territories, see appx. 6B.

[737] *See* appx. 9C, Instructions for Form I-765. No fee is required for initial applications.

[738] *See id.*

[739] *See id.*

[740] 8 CFR §§103.7(c), 1103.7(c).

[741] 8 CFR §§208.7(a)(1), 1208.7(a)(1).

[742] 8 CFR §§208.7(a)(1), 1208.7(a)(1).

[743] 8 CFR §§208.7(a)(2), 1208.7(a)(2).

issue an interim EAD. The local offices have been instructed that they no longer have the authority to issue interim EADs.[744]

3.9.7. Renewals

Employment authorization is renewable during the period of time necessary for the asylum officer or immigration judge to decide the asylum application and, if necessary, for the completion of any administrative or judicial review.[745] The applicant must file an I-765, the required fee (unless waived under 8 CFR §1103.7(c)) and proof that the applicant is continuing to pursue his or her application.[746] Depending on the stage of the applicant's immigration proceedings, he or she must submit either a copy of (1) the asylum denial, referral notice, or charging document for IJ proceedings, (2) a BIA receipt of timely appeal for applications pending at the BIA, or (3) the petition for review or habeas corpus date stamped by the appropriate court for claims pending in federal court.[747] In order for the employment authorization to be renewed before its expiration date, the I-765 must be filed 100 days before the expiration of the previously issued employment authorization.[748] Applications for renewals will be accepted up to 120 days before the expiration of the employment authorization documents.

3.9.8. Asylees and Withholding Grantees

Individuals who have received a final (*i.e.*, not subject to appeal) grant of asylum by the Asylum Division, IJ, or BIA are eligible for employment authorization as "asylees."[749] In the past, asylees have had to file an I-765, Application for Employment Authorization. Changes to the law under the Enhanced Border Security and Visa Entry Reform Act of 2002[750] required legacy INS, now DHS, to provide immediate employment authorization to asylees and substitutes the I-589, Application for Asylum (which already includes the applicant's photographs and fingerprints) for the I-765.[751]

A new policy, effective October 1, 2006, allows for the issuance of a two-year employment authorization document on form I-766 to individuals and their dependents granted asylum by USCIS's Asylum Division through the affirmative asylum process. Information

---

[744] *See* USCIS Public Notice, "USCIS Reminds Customers of Filing Change for Employments Authorization Documents" (revised Aug. 9, 2006), available at *www.uscis.gov/files/pressrelease/EADFilingCh072806PN.pdf.*

[745] 8 CFR §§208.7(b), 1208.7(b).

[746] 8 CFR §§208.7(c), 1208.7(c).

[747] 8 CFR §§208.7(c), 1208.7(c).

[748] Although 8 CFR §§208.7(d), 1208.7(d) state that the application must be filed 90 days before the expiration of the EAD, a USCIS Public Notice states that the application must be filed 100 days before, effective August 1, 2006. *See* USCIS Public Notice, *supra* note 744, at 2.

[749] 8 CFR §§274a.12(a)(5), 1274a.12(a)(5).

[750] Enhanced Border Security and Visa Entry Reform Act of 2002, Pub. L. No. 107-173, 116 Stat. 543.

[751] For more details, see 67 Fed. Reg. 64911 (Oct. 22, 2002).

on obtaining these EADs will be provided to individuals with notice of their asylum grant.[752]

Legacy INS also issued a memorandum to all regional directors clarifying that asylees are authorized to work whether or not they possess an employment authorization document (EAD).[753]

Individuals who receive a final (*i.e.*, not subject to appeal) grant of withholding of removal are also eligible for employment authorization.[754]

3.9.9. Social Security Cards

Asylum Applicants

Asylum applicants are eligible for Social Security cards upon receipt of their employment authorization document. Their cards, however, will bear the notation, "Valid for Work Only with DHS Authorization."

There is often a significant delay from the date employment authorization is granted until the immigration authorities notify the Social Security Administration that the applicant is authorized to work. There is a further delay of up to six weeks before an application for a social security number is processed. The lack of a Social Security number during this interim period should not result in a denial of employment or delay in beginning employment. Under Internal Revenue Service regulations,[755] an employer that has an employee who has not been issued a Social Security number can accept the following documentation for employment and payroll:

- Receipt for the application for a Social Security number along with the employee's name and address as shown on the receipt and the expiration date of the receipt; or
- Copy of the application for a Social Security card (Form SS-5) until the card is issued.[756]

> *Note*—What are the implications of using or having used a false Social Security number? For a thorough discussion of this issue, see C. Wheeler, "Immigration Consequences of Using a False Social Security Number," 8 *Bender's Immigr. Bull.* 952 (June 1, 2003).

---

[752] *See* USCIS Public Notice, "New Process for Issuing Employment Authorization Documents to Asylees" (Sept. 14, 2006), *published on* AILA InfoNet at Doc. No. 06091560 (*posted* Sept. 15, 2006), and available at *www.uscis.gov/files/pressrelease/AsyleeEAD.pdf*.

[753] *See* INS Memorandum, W. Yates, "The Meaning of 8 CFR 274a.12(a) as it Relates to Refugee and Asylee Authorization for Employment" (Mar. 10, 2003), *published on* AILA InfoNet at Doc. No. 03040140 (*posted* Apr. 1, 2003), and available at *www.uscis.gov/files/pressrelease/AsyleeEAD.pdf*; *see also* D. Cleveland, "An Asylee Does Not Need an Employment Authorization Document," *Navigating the Fundamentals of Immigration Law* 91 (AILA 2007–08 Ed.).

[754] 8 CFR §§274a.12(a)(10), 1274a.12(a)(10).

[755] 26 CFR §31.6011(b)-2(c)(2).

[756] These procedures are explained more fully in IRS Publication Circular E and Circular E Supplement, available at *www.irs.gov/publications/p15/index.html*.

Asylees

Asylees are eligible for "unrestricted" Social Security cards, *i.e.*, cards that do *not* bear the notation, "Valid for Work Only with DHS Authorization." Asylees also do not need employment authorization to apply for a Social Security card. They may apply immediately upon being granted asylum by the Asylum Office or the immigration court (provided DHS has not appealed the decision), or the BIA. To obtain the Social Security card, asylees may show any of the following documents:

- I-94 (with an "asylum granted" stamp);
- USCIS employment authorization document (showing the cite 8 CFR §274a.12(a)(5)); or
- original order of the immigration judge granting asylum (either with a waiver of appeal by DHS, or, if 30 days have passed, confirmation that DHS has not appealed by calling (800) 898-7180).[757]

There is often a significant delay from the date employment authorization is granted until the immigration authorities notify the Social Security Administration that the applicant is authorized to work. There is a further delay of up to six weeks before an application for a Social Security number is processed. The lack of a Social Security number during this interim period should not result in a denial of employment or delay in beginning employment. Under IRS regulations,[758] an employer that has an employee who has not been issued a Social Security number can accept the following documentation for employment and payroll:

- Receipt for the application for a Social Security number along with the employee's name and address as shown on the receipt and the expiration date of the receipt; or
- Copy of the application for a Social Security card (Form SS-5) until the card is issued.[759]

3.9.10. Federal Individual Tax ID Numbers

Asylum Applicants and Asylees

Both asylees and asylum applicants may need to apply to the Internal Revenue Service for an Individual Taxpayer Identification Number (ITIN).[760] Any individual who has a federal tax reporting or filing requirement and does not qualify for a Social Security number needs an ITIN.[761] An individual who lacks a Social Security number but wants to

---

[757] *See* SSA Memorandum, "Processing SSN Card Requests from Asylees—Information" (Apr. 4, 2001), available at *www.acf.dhhs.gov/programs/orr/policy/ssnasylee.htm*.

[758] 26 CFR §31.6011(b)-2(c)(2).

[759] These procedures are explained more fully in IRS Publication Circular E and Circular E Supplement, available at *www.irs.gov/publications/p15/index.html*.

[760] *See* the IRS webpage on ITINs, *www.irs.gov/individuals/article/0,,id=96287,00.html*.

[761] *Id.*

open a bank account also needs an ITIN, since banks are required to report any interest earned on their accounts.[762]

In order to obtain an ITIN, an individual must fill out a revised IRS Form W-7 and attach a federal income tax return (unless the individual qualified for an exception).[763] The individual must also provide proof of identity.[764] The IRS website lists the 13 types of documents that are acceptable for proving identity.[765]

ITINs are not a valid form of identification outside the tax system.[766]

3.9.11. Termination

Asylum Officer Denial

If the asylum application is denied by an asylum officer, the employment authorization terminates at the expiration of the employment authorization document (EAD) or 60 days after the denial of asylum, whichever is later.[767] Note that this does not apply to individuals whose cases are *referred* to immigration court.

IJ, BIA, or Federal Court Denial

If the asylum application is denied by an immigration judge, the BIA, or a federal court, the employment authorization terminates upon the expiration of the employment authorization document, *unless* the applicant has filed an appropriate request for administrative or judicial review.[768]

3.10. APPEALS TO BIA

> ➢ *Tip*—**Sweeping Changes to BIA Review**—In August 2002, Attorney General Ashcroft issued regulations that drastically changed the BIA appeals process. The regulations eliminated the BIA's de novo review of an IJ's factual findings and credibility determinations, increased the issuance of summary decisions, required simultaneous briefing by the parties if the noncitizen is in custody, and eliminated eight positions of the 23-member board.[769] The

---

[762] *See, e.g.*, NAFSA, Opening a Student Bank Account, *www.nafsa.org/knowledge_community_network.sec/international_student_3/international_student_4/practice_resources_18/driver_s_license_taxes/bank*.

[763] *www.irs.gov/individuals/article/0,,id=96287,00.html*. Form W-7 is available at *www.irs.gov/pub/irs-pdf/fw7.pdf*. The applicant's Form W-7, tax return, and proof of identity should be mailed to: Internal Revenue Service, Austin Service Center, ITIN Operation, P.O. Box 149342, Austin, TX, 78714-9342.

[764] *www.irs.gov/individuals/article/0,,id=96287,00.html*.

[765] *Id.*

[766] *Id.*

[767] 8 CFR §§208.7(b)(1), 1208.7(b)(1).

[768] 8 CFR §§208.7(b)(2), 1208.7(b)(2).

[769] *See* 67 Fed. Reg. 54878 (Aug. 26, 2002).

regulations should be read and re-read carefully before filing any appeal with the BIA.[770]

An individual whose asylum or withholding of removal claim is denied by an IJ may appeal the IJ's decision to the BIA.[771] DHS may also appeal an IJ decision to the BIA. Alternatively, the IJ may certify a decision to the BIA for its review.[772] The BIA has appellate jurisdiction over IJ decisions in exclusion, deportation, and removal proceedings.[773] The BIA may also review decisions of IJs regarding asylum applications filed by individuals who are not entitled to removal proceedings under INA §240.[774] Such individuals include crewmembers, stowaways, persons who have applied for admission or were admitted to the United States under the Visa Waiver Program, persons who have been ordered removed from the United States under INA §235(c) on security and related grounds, and individuals who are applicants for admission or who have been admitted under INA §101(a)(15)(S) as an informant.[775]

3.10.1. Notice of Right to File an Appeal

Applicants who are entitled to appeal to the BIA must be given notice of their right to appeal by the IJ.[776] Upon finding that an applicant is removable and ordering the applicant removed, the IJ must furnish the applicant with a Notice of Appeal (Form EOIR-26) and advise him or her of the right to appeal to the BIA within 30 days.[777] If an applicant waives his or her right to appeal, the immigration judge's order becomes final.[778] Prior to accepting the applicant's waiver of appeal, however, the IJ must also advise the applicant that he or she has the right to seek relief from removal.[779] Otherwise the applicant cannot make a considered and intelligent decision about whether to appeal.[780]

> ➢ *Note*—The BIA may not review an order of removal entered in absentia. An individual who received an in absentia removal order must file a motion to re-

---

[770] *See also* AILF Practice Advisory, Practicing Before the BIA under the New "Procedural Reforms" Rule (Jan. 10, 2003), available at *www.ailf.org/lac/lac_pa_topics.shtml#section2*; "BIA Procedural Reform Regulation: A Topical Summary," 79 *Interpreter Releases* 1457 (Sept. 30, 2002).

[771] 8 CFR §1003.1(b).

[772] 8 CFR §1003.7.

[773] 8 CFR §1003.1(b).

[774] 8 CFR §§1003.1(b)(9), 208.2(b), 1208.2(b).

[775] 8 CFR §§208.2(b), 1208.2(b). For a comprehensive overview of practice before the BIA, see the *Board of Immigration Appeals Practice Manual*, available at *www.usdoj.gov/eoir/vll/qapracmanual/apptmtn4.htm*, Questions and Answers Regarding Proceedings Before the Board, at *www.usdoj.gov/eoir/vll/qapracmanual/pracmanual/Q%2BAs/q%2Ba.pdf*, and Questions and Answers Regarding Oral Argument Before the Board, at *www.usdoj.gov/eoir/vll/qapracmanual/qaoral.pdf*.

[776] 8 CFR §1003.3(a)(1).

[777] 8 CFR §§1240.13(d), 1240.15.

[778] *See Matter of L–V–K–*, 22 I&N Dec. 976 (BIA 1999).

[779] *U.S. v. Arrieta*, 224 F.3d 1076, 1079 (9th Cir. 2000).

[780] *Id.*

open with the IJ.[781] If the individual did not receive oral warnings of the consequences of failing to appear, the individual may file a motion to reopen under the regulatory requirements found at 8 CFR §§1003.2(c) and 1003.23(b)(3).[782]

3.10.2. When to File

The Notice of Appeal must be *received* by the BIA within 30 calendar days after the IJ's oral decision was made or the IJ's written decision was mailed.[783] If the final date for filing falls on a Saturday, Sunday, or legal holiday, the appeal time shall be extended to the next business day.[784] The date of filing is the date the notice is *received* by the BIA.[785] An error by an overnight delivery service will *not* excuse a late filing.[786]

3.10.3. Where to File

The Notice of Appeal and all attachments must be sent to the Board of Immigration Appeals, Executive Office for Immigration Review, Office of the Chief Clerk, 5201 Leesburg Pike, Suite 1300, Falls Church, VA 22041; or, P.O. Box 8530, Falls Church, VA 22041. The telephone number for the BIA's Office of the Chief Clerk is (703) 605-1007. Public window hours are 8:00 am to 4:30 pm.

3.10.4. What to File

The applicant should file:

- A completed Notice of Appeal (Form EOIR-26) in English that lists specific details regarding why the applicant disagrees with the IJ's decision, including the specific findings of fact or conclusions of law that are being challenged on appeal, and citation to supporting authority.[787] If the applicant requests review by a three-member panel, the applicant may state in the Notice of Appeal the factual or legal basis for such a request under the standards set forth in 8 CFR §1003.1(e)(6).[788]

- A check or money order for the fee, currently $110, payable to the Department of Justice, or, if the applicant is unable to pay the filing fee, an Appeal Fee Waiver Request (Form EOIR-26A).[789]

- A Notice of Entry of Appearance as Attorney or Representative Before the Board (Form EOIR-27) if the applicant is represented on appeal.[790]

---

[781] *See Matter of Guzman-Arguera*, 22 I&N Dec. 722 (BIA 1999) and this chapter, at 3.3.5.

[782] *See Matter of M–S–*, 22 I&N Dec. 349 (BIA 1998) and this chapter, at 3.11.

[783] 8 CFR §§1003.3(a)(1), 1003.38(b).

[784] 8 CFR §1003.38(b).

[785] 8 CFR §1003.38(c).

[786] *Matter of Liadov*, 23 I&N Dec. 990 (BIA 2006). *But see Sun v. USDOJ*, 421 F.3d 105 (2d Cir. 2005); *Oh v. Gonzales*, 406 F.3d 611 (9th Cir. 2005).

[787] 8 CFR §1003.3(b).

[788] For tips on avoiding summary dismissal of your appeal, see this chapter, at 3.10.6.

[789] 8 CFR §1003.3(a)(1).

- Certificate of Service, certifying a copy was sent or delivered to ICE District Counsel.
- A change of address form (Form EOIR-33/BIA) if the applicant has changed his or her address.

> *Tip*—**Summary Dismissal**—The BIA may summarily dismiss an appeal that fails to give sufficient detail in the Notice of Appeal, that lacks an arguable basis in law or fact, or that was filed for an improper purpose, such as to cause unnecessary delay.[791]

3.10.5. Fee

The current filing fee for an appeal to the BIA is $110 and must be filed with the Notice of Appeal. Applicants who cannot pay the $110 filing fee should file a Fee Waiver Request (Form EOIR-26A) with their Notice of Appeal.[792] If no fee is filed or if the Fee Waiver Request does not establish the inability to pay the required fee, the appeal will not be deemed properly filed and the IJ decision will become final.[793]

3.10.6. Streamlined Process

Final regulations that permit a streamlined review process by the BIA were issued on October 18, 1999, and are found at 8 CFR §§1003.1 and 1003.2. Additional amendments to this process were issued on August 26, 2002.[794] The process was adopted to address the marked increase in the number of appeals filed with the BIA, which as of April 2002 had grown to a backlog of approximately 56,000 cases. The streamlined process allows for a single permanent board member to review the record on appeal and affirm the decision below without issuing an opinion in the case. Such an "affirmance without opinion" (AWO) is only issued if the result below was correct, any errors in the decision below were harmless or immaterial, and either the issues in the case are controlled by precedent or the factual or legal issues raised are so insubstantial that a three-member panel review is not warranted.[795] Since these streamlined procedures were issued in 2002, the backlog has been reduced to 28,000 as of January 2006.[796] Fewer than 20 percent of BIA decisions were AWOs in FY 2005.[797]

---

[790] *Id.*

[791] *See* 8 CFR §1003.1(d)(2). For tips on avoiding summary dismissal, see this chapter, at 3.10.6; *see also Vargas-Garcia v. INS*, 287 F.3d 882 (9th Cir. 2002) (holding BIA's summary dismissal resulted in denial of due process).

[792] 8 CFR §§1003.3(a)(1), 1003.8(c).

[793] 8 CFR §§1003.8(c), 1003.38(d).

[794] *See* 67 Fed. Reg. 54878 (Aug. 26, 2002).

[795] *See* 8 CFR §1003.1(a)(7).

[796] *See* EOIR Fact Sheet, "BIA Restructuring and Streamlining Procedures" (revised Mar. 9, 2006), *published on* AILA InfoNet at Doc. No. 06031013 (*posted* Mar. 10, 2006), and available at www.usdoj.gov/eoir/press/06/BIAStreamliningFactSheet030906.htm.

[797] *Id.*

> *Tip*—Is a Board Member's refusal to refer a case to a three-judge panel reviewable by a federal court? The circuits are split on this issue.[798]

To date, all circuits (except the D.C. Circuit, which does not appear to have addressed the issue) have upheld the AWO process and found it to be constitutional.[799]

In order to avoid this and other forms of summary dismissal, the Notice of Appeal should be as specific as possible. It would be useful to include one or more of the following statements and a description of the relevant facts from the case:

This appeal is not appropriate for affirmance without opinion under 8 CFR §1003.1(a)(7) because:

- This appeal raises substantial legal issues *[Identify legal issues or challenges to current precedent]*
- This appeal raises novel factual issues *[Describe issues]*
- The underlying facts are in dispute *[List facts in dispute]*
- The decision of the IJ was incorrect as a matter of law *[Describe error and cite case law, statute, or regulations]*
- The respondent meets the eligibility criteria for relief from removal (deportation) *[List form of relief and how respondent has met criteria]*
- Errors by the IJ (or DHS trial attorney) were significant and material *[Describe errors]*
- The proceedings deprived the respondent of his or her rights under the INA, the Due Process Clause of the Fifth Amendment, etc. *[List reasons why as specifically as possible]*

---

[798] The First, Third, and Ninth Circuits have held that a single member's refusal to refer the case to a three-judge panel is reviewable by a federal court in at least some situations. *See Haoud v. Ashcroft*, 350 F.3d 201, 206–08; *Purveegiin v. Gonzales*, 448 F.3d 684, 692 (3d Cir. 2006); *Chong Shin Chen v. Ashcroft*, 378 F.3d 1081, 1086–88 (finding the decision reviewable where the underlying issue was not controlled by existing Board or court precedent, and the factual and legal questions raised on appeal were not insubstantial). In contrast, the Second, Eighth, and Tenth Circuits have found these decisions to be discretionary and not subject to judicial review. *See Kambolli v. Gonzales*, 449 F.3d 454, 463 (2d Cir. 2006); *Bropleh v. Gonzales*, 428 F.3d 772, 779 (8th Cir. 2005); *Tsegay v. Ashcroft*, 386 F.3d 1347, 1353–58 (10th Cir. 2004). In the Sixth Circuit, the question remains unanswered. *Hassan v. Gonzales*, 403 F.3d 429, 437 (6th Cir. 2005).

[799] *Albathani v. INS*, 318 F.3d 365, 377 (1st Cir. 2003); *Zhang v. U.S. DOJ*, 362 F.3d 155, 157-59 (2d Cir. 2004); *Dia v. Ashcroft*, 353 F.3d 228, 244 (3d Cir. 2003); *Khattak v. Ashcroft*, 332 F.3d 250, 253 (4th Cir. 2003); *Soadjede v. Ashcroft*, 324 F.3d 830, 832–33 (5th Cir. 2003); *Denko v. INS*, 351 F.3d 717, 730 (6th Cir. 2003); *Duarte v. Ashcroft*, 83 Fed. Appx. 119, 122 (7th Cir. 2003) (not selected for publication in the Federal Reporter); *Ngure v. Ashcroft*, 367 F.3d 975, 981 (8th Cir. 2004), *reh'd denied*, 2004 U.S. App. LEXIS 18608 (8th Cir. 2004); *Falcon Carriche v. Ashcroft*, 350 F.3d 845, 852 (9th Cir. 2003); *Yuk v. Ashcroft*, 355 F.3d 1222, 1232 (10th Cir. 2004); *Mendoza v. U.S. Att'y Gen.*, 327 F.3d 1283, 1289 (11th Cir. 2003).

For guidance on challenging AWO decisions, see AILF Practice Advisory, Update on BIA Affirmance Without Opinion Litigation (Dec. 2003), available at *www.ailf.org/lac/lac_pa_120903.pdf*.

- Summary affirmance would deprive the respondent of his or her rights under the INA, the Due Process Clause of the Fifth Amendment, etc. *[List reasons why as specifically as possible]*[800]

3.10.7. Service on DHS

The applicant must serve DHS with a copy of the Notice of Appeal and all attachments.[801]

3.10.8. Automatic Stay of Removal

The decision of the IJ may *not* be executed: (1) during the time allowed for the filing of an appeal, unless a waiver of the right to appeal is filed; (2) while an appeal is pending before the BIA; or (3) while a case is before the BIA by way of certification.[802] Exceptions to this rule are: (1) an appeal from an IJ decision denying the applicant's motion to reopen or reconsider or to stay deportation, unless the BIA expressly grants a stay or the appeal is from a motion to reopen in an in absentia case under 8 CFR §§1003.6(b) and 1003.23(b)(1)(v); and (2) an appeal of a bond redetermination under 8 CFR §§1003.19(i) and 1236.1.

3.10.9. Briefs

If the applicant indicates that he or she will be filing a separate written statement or brief on the Notice of Appeal form, the BIA will send the parties a briefing schedule along with, in most cases, a transcript of the IJ proceedings.[803] If the applicant is *not* in custody, the appellant will be provided 21 days in which to file a brief or written statement, unless a shorter period is given by the BIA.[804] The appellee is given the same period of time.[805] If the applicant is in custody, both appellant and appellee are given 21 days to file simultaneous briefs, unless a shorter period of time is specified by the BIA. The BIA upon written motion may extend this period of time for up to 90 days for good cause shown.[806] Briefs in support of or opposition to the appeal must be filed directly with the BIA.[807] In its discretion, the BIA may consider a brief filed out

---

[800] The above examples were set forth in N. Wettstein, "How to Prevent Summary Dismissal of Your Appeal Before the BIA," 21 *Immigration Law Today* 284 (May 2002). If you are challenging the BIA's summary treatment of your appeal, you may wish to visit the website of the American Immigration Law Foundation *www.ailf.org*, for additional guidance. *See* M. Kenney, "How to Challenge a BIA 'Affirmance without Opinion,'" 21 *Immigration Law Today* 629 (Oct. 2002); *Vargas-Garcia v. INS*, 287 F.3d 882 (9th Cir. 2002) (one of a series of Ninth Circuit decisions that criticizes the BIA for failure to give adequate notice of the specificity required on the Notice of Appeal form (EOIR-26) to individuals who seek review).

[801] 8 CFR §1003.3(a)(1); *see* appx. 6D for a list of DHS district counsel addresses and telephone numbers.

[802] 8 CFR §1003.6.

[803] 8 CFR §1003.3(c)(1).

[804] *Id.*

[805] *Id.*

[806] *Id.*

[807] *Id.*

of time or may summarily dismiss the case for failure to file a brief.[808] All briefs must contain a certificate of service and the opposing party must be served with a copy of the brief.[809]

3.10.10. Oral Argument

If oral argument before the BIA is desired, a request should be included in the Notice of Appeal.[810] Oral argument is heard at the BIA's discretion and is not often granted.

3.10.11. Ineligibility/Waived Appeal

A Notice of Appeal may *not* be filed by an applicant who has waived appeal under 8 CFR §1003.39.

3.10.12. Departure from United States

The departure of a person who is the subject of deportation proceedings *prior* to appealing a decision in his or her case will constitute a waiver of his or her right to appeal.[811] The departure of a person who is the subject of deportation or removal proceedings, except for "arriving aliens" under 8 CFR §1001.1(q), while his or her appeal is *pending* will constitute a withdrawal of the appeal and the initial decision in the case will be final, as if no appeal had been taken.[812] One court has held that failure to give notice of the severe consequences of departing from the United States while an appeal is pending is a violation of due process.[813]

3.10.13. Interlocutory Appeal

The BIA may also consider interlocutory appeals. Although the BIA does not ordinarily entertain interlocutory appeals, it will rule on the merits of such appeals where it is necessary to address important jurisdictional questions regarding the administration of the immigration laws or to correct recurring problems in the handling of cases before IJs.[814]

---

[808] *Id.*; *see Kokar v. Gonzales*, 478 F.3d 803 (7th Cir. 2007) (finding summary dismissal was proper because no brief was filed); *Esponda v. U.S. Att'y Gen.*, 453 F.3d 1319 (11th Cir. 2006) (finding BIA abused its discretion in summarily dismissing appeal for failure to file a brief where Notice of Appeal set forth basis for appeal); *Singh v. Ashcroft*, 362 F.3d 1164 (9th Cir. 2003) (finding due process violation where BIA would not permit the late filing of a brief despite applicant demonstrating that briefing schedule was sent to the wrong address); *Garcia-Cortez v. Ashcroft*, 366 F.3d 749 (9th Cir. 2004) (finding that it was not appropriate for BIA to summarily dismiss case for failure to file a brief where the notice to appeal adequately set forth detailed reasons in support of the appeal). *But see Rioja v. Ashcroft*, 317 F.3d 514 (5th Cir. 2003) (upholding summary dismissal of the appeal where applicant indicated he would file a separate statement or brief and did not file one).

[809] 8 CFR §1003.3(c)(1).

[810] 8 CFR §1003.1(e)(7).

[811] 8 CFR §1003.3(e).

[812] 8 CFR §1003.4.

[813] *Martinez-de Bojorquez v. Ashcroft*, 365 F.3d 800 (9th Cir. 2004).

[814] *See, e.g., Matter of Morales*, 21 I&N Dec. 130 (BIA 1995–96) (finding that the immigration court did not have jurisdiction to proceed with the case of an *ABC* class member).

3.11. Motions to Reopen and Reconsider

If an individual has received an administratively final deportation, exclusion, or removal order, he or she may file a motion to reopen or reconsider with the IJ or BIA. Regulations regarding motions to reopen and reconsider impose strict time limitations, restrict the number of motions that may be filed, and allow for only a few narrow exceptions to the new limitations.

A motion to reopen, according to the BIA, seeks a second review of a case based on new or previously unavailable evidence.[815] If the motion involves facts regarding ineffective assistance of counsel that were previously unavailable to the applicant at the earlier stage, the motion is properly deemed a motion to reopen.[816] The BIA has noted that motions to reopen are "disfavored" and that it has broad discretion to deny such motions.[817] In contrast, a motion to reconsider "questions the [adjudicator's] decision for alleged errors in appraising the facts and law" and seeks a re-examination of the decision "in light of additional legal arguments, a change in law, or perhaps an argument or aspect of the case which was overlooked."[818]

> ➢ *Note*—An individual who was ordered removed in absentia should follow the procedures for filing a motion to reopen, discussed *infra*. One exception to this general rule is for individuals who did not receive written or oral notice of the consequences of the failure to appear.[819]

3.11.1. Who May Make a Motion

A motion to reopen or reconsider may be made by the BIA on its own motion, an IJ on his or her own motion, upon motion of DHS, or upon motion of the individual who has been ordered removed, deported, or excluded.[820] Only in exceptional circumstances will the BIA reopen proceedings *sua sponte*.[821] The time and numerical limitations listed below, however, do not apply to motions made by DHS if the basis of the motion is fraud or a crime that would terminate asylum.[822]

---

[815] *Matter of J–J–*, 21 I&N Dec. 976 at *4 n.1 (BIA 1997).

[816] *Siong v. INS*, 376 F.3d 1030, 1036 (9th Cir. 2004).

[817] *Matter of Gutierrez-Lopez*, 21 I&N Dec. 479 at *10 (BIA 1996).

[818] *Matter of J–J–*, 21 I&N Dec. 976 at *4, n.1 (citations omitted).

[819] *See Matter of G–Y–R–*, 23 I&N Dec. 181 (BIA 2001) (upholding an IJ's refusal to issue an in absentia order against an individual who was never advised of the consequences of her failure to provide legacy INS with a mailing address and who never received actual service of the NTA); *see also Matter of M–S–*, 22 I&N Dec. 349 (BIA 1998).

[820] 8 CFR §§1003.2(a), 1003.23(b)(1).

[821] *Matter of L–V–K–*, 22 I&N Dec. 976 (BIA 1999).

[822] 8 CFR §1003.23(b)(1).

CHAPTER 3 • ASYLUM AND WITHHOLDING OF REMOVAL PROCEDURES   235

3.11.2. Where to File

A motion to reopen or reconsider a decision of an IJ should be filed with the immigration court having administrative control over the record of proceeding.[823] If jurisdiction has vested with the BIA, the motion should be filed directly with the BIA. For decision information, including the court address, date of IJ decision, and BIA appeal information, call the EOIR Information Line at (800) 898-7180.

3.11.3. Jurisdiction

The BIA has jurisdiction over cases in which it has rendered a decision.[824] An IJ has jurisdiction in cases in which he or she has made a decision, unless jurisdiction has vested with the BIA.[825] Where the BIA dismisses an appeal solely for lack of jurisdiction, without adjudication on the merits, the IJ retains jurisdiction over any subsequent motion to reopen or reconsider.[826] The BIA, however, retains jurisdiction over a motion to reconsider its dismissal of an untimely appeal to the extent that the motion challenges the finding of untimeliness or requests consideration of the reasons for untimeliness.[827]

3.11.4. Standard of Review; Burden of Proof

The decision to grant or deny a motion to reopen or reconsider is within the discretion of the BIA or IJ and the motion may be denied even if the moving party has made out a prima facie case for relief.[828] A motion to reopen will not be granted unless it appears to the BIA or the IJ that the evidence sought to be offered is material and was not available and could not have been discovered or presented at a former hearing.[829] A motion to reopen will also not be granted for the purpose of allowing an applicant the opportunity to apply for discretionary relief if the applicant's right to apply for such relief was fully explained to him or her and an opportunity to apply was afforded to the applicant at a previous hearing, unless the relief is sought on the basis of circumstances that arose after the hearing.[830]

Additionally, if the applicant is filing a motion to reopen in order to apply for asylum, withholding of removal, or CAT relief, the motion must be accompanied by a completed

---

[823] 8 CFR §1003.23(b)(1)(ii).

[824] 8 CFR §1003.2(a).

[825] 8 CFR §1003.23(b)(1).

[826] *Matter of Lopez*, 22 I&N Dec. 16 (BIA 1998), *modifying Matter of Mladineo*, 14 I&N Dec. 591 (BIA 1974).

[827] *Id.*

[828] 8 CFR §§1003.2(a), 1003.23(b)(1)(iv); *see also Matter of Gutierrez-Lopez*, 21 I&N Dec. 479 at *10–11 (BIA 1996) (noting that the BIA may deny a motion to reopen even if the individual has made out a prima facie case if the relief would not be granted in the exercise of discretion).

[829] 8 CFR §§1003.2(c)(1), 1003.23(b)(3).

[830] 8 CFR §§1003.2(c)(1), 1003.23(b)(3); *see also Hailemichael v. Gonzales*, 454 F.3d 878, 883–84 (8th Cir. 2006) (finding that the IJ abused her discretion in granting DHS's motion to reopen because she failed to explain whether the documents submitted were material and unavailable at the time of the hearing).

application and all supporting documents.[831] The motion must also reasonably explain the failure to request asylum prior to the completion of proceedings.[832] An applicant demonstrates prima facie eligibility for relief where the evidence reveals a reasonable likelihood that the statutory requirements have been satisfied.[833] The showing need not be conclusive.[834] Courts have overturned denials of motions to reopen upon finding that the BIA abused its discretion.[835]

3.11.5. Limit on Number

A party may file only one motion to reconsider and one motion to reopen, unless one of the exceptions listed below applies.[836]

3.11.6. Time Limit for Filing

Motion to Reconsider—30 Days

A motion to reconsider must be filed with the IJ within 30 days of the date of entry of a final administrative order of removal, deportation, or exclusion.[837] A motion to reconsider must be filed with the BIA within 30 days after the mailing of the BIA decision.[838]

Motion to Reopen—90 Days

A motion to reopen must be filed with the IJ or the BIA within 90 days of the date of entry of a final administrative order of removal, deportation, or exclusion.[839] A motion to reopen a decision of the BIA following judicial review is untimely if it is filed more than 90 days after the date of the decision of the BIA, even if it is filed within 90 days of the order of the reviewing court.[840]

---

[831] 8 CFR §1003.23(b)(3).

[832] 8 CFR §§208.4(b)(3)(ii), 1208.4(b)(3)(ii); *see also Matter of R–R–*, 20 I&N Dec. 547 (BIA 1992) (finding that an asylum applicant must make a prima facie showing of his eligibility for asylum, as well as reasonably explain the failure to request asylum prior to the completion of deportation or exclusion proceedings).

[833] *Matter of S–V–*, 22 I&N Dec. 1306, 1308 (BIA 2000).

[834] *Id.*

[835] *See, e.g., Yang v. Gonzales*, 478 F.3d 133, 143 (2d Cir. 2007) (finding BIA erred in failing to consider the disbarment of the applicant's attorney in considering his motion to reopen); *Mejia v. Ashcroft*, 298 F.3d 873, 880 (9th Cir. 2002) (finding BIA abused its discretion by failing, contrary to settled law, to hold that an applicant was prima facie eligible for relief and for failing to address newly submitted evidence). For additional discussion of the BIA's standards for review, see ch. 2.8.1.

[836] 8 CFR §§1003.2(b)(2), 1003.2(c)(2), and 1003.23(b)(1).

[837] 8 CFR §1003.23(b)(1).

[838] 8 CFR §1003.2(b)(2).

[839] 8 CFR §§1003.2(c)(2), 1003.23(b)(1).

[840] *Matter of Susma*, 22 I&N Dec. 947 (BIA 1999).

3.11.7. Exceptions to the Numerical and Time Limitations

The limitations on the number and time periods for filing a motion to reconsider or reopen do not apply to the following:

Motion to Reopen an Order Entered In Absentia

If an individual was ordered deported or excluded in absentia, the time and numerical limitations do not apply to his or her motion to reopen.[841] If, however, the individual was ordered removed in absentia, the time limitations noted above do *not* apply, but the numerical limitations do.[842]

Changed Circumstances

The BIA or IJ may reopen a case to allow an applicant to apply or reapply for asylum, withholding of removal, or relief under the Convention Against Torture based on changed circumstances arising in the country of nationality or in the country to which deportation has been ordered if the evidence presented is material and was not available and could not have been discovered or presented at the previous hearing.[843] Motions to reopen cannot be based on changed personal circumstances, but must show a change in country conditions.[844] Applicants seeking to reopen asylum proceedings based on changed circumstances related to coercive population control methods must be careful to show specific evidence that they personally will suffer persecution as a result of the policies.[845]

If the applicant was previously denied asylum based upon a finding that the application was frivolous, the applicant is ineligible to file a motion to reopen or reconsider, or for a stay of removal.[846] In *Matter of G–C–L–*,[847] the BIA announced a withdrawal from

---

[841] 8 CFR §§1003.2(c)(3)(i), 1003.23(b)(4)(iii).

[842] 8 CFR §§1003.2(c)(3), 1003.23(b)(4)(ii).

[843] 8 CFR §§1003.2(c)(3)(ii), 1003.23(b)(4)(i); *see Malty v. Ashcroft*, 381 F.3d 942, 945–47 (9th Cir. 2004) (finding BIA abused its discretion in denying motion to reopen based on changed circumstances); *see also Mengistu v. Ashcroft*, 355 F.3d 1044, 1047 (7th Cir. 2004) (finding that the BIA's reliance on documents suggesting that Ethiopia had begun to withdraw its troops from Eritrea and that the United Nations had dispatched a peacekeeping mission was a "non sequitur" and did not address whether the applicant would face harm upon return); *Matter of A–N– & R–M–N–*, 22 I&N Dec. 953 (BIA 1999) (finding that asylum applicants from Afghanistan who were ordered deported in absentia need not demonstrate the cause of their failure to appear where their motion to reopen was based on changed country conditions).

[844] *Haddad v. Gonzales*, 437 F.3d 515, 517–18 (6th Cir. 2006); *Li Yong Zheng v. United States DOJ*, 416 F.3d 129, 130–31 (2d Cir. 2005).

[845] For example, in *Matter of S–Y–G–*, 24 I&N Dec. 247 (BIA 2007), the court rejected an applicant's motion to reopen asylum proceedings where the applicant claimed that the birth of her second child in the United States would lead to persecution in her home province in China. Although the applicant presented evidence that the province enforces general population control policies, the court held that such evidence was insufficient because it did not specifically show any likelihood that the applicant or similarly situated nationals would be persecuted.

[846] 8 CFR §1003.23(b)(4)(i).

[847] *Matter of G–C–L–*, 23 I&N Dec. 359 (BIA 2002).

its policy of automatically granting untimely motions to reopen for applicants fearing coercive population control methods. The BIA reasoned that it had been five years since the law had changed allowing for asylum on this basis and that the interest in finality of immigration proceedings took precedence.[848] Individuals wishing to reopen their cases based on coercive population control methods will have to show changed circumstances or another exception if their motion is not filed within 90 days.

Consent by All Parties

The time and numerical limitations do not apply to a motion to reopen or reconsider if all parties agree to the motion and the motion is jointly filed.[849] The procedure for requesting DHS's consent is to contact the district counsel's office that has jurisdiction over the case during the individual's immigration proceedings.[850] The request should be supported by affidavits or other evidence, including a complete copy of the application for relief.[851] The request should also include the proposed joint motion in a format that includes a signature block for the DHS attorney.[852]

DHS's consent will only be given in exceptional and compelling circumstances, according to a general counsel's office memorandum.[853] Factors DHS will consider are: (1) whether the new evidence is material; (2) whether the individual is statutorily eligible for relief; (3) whether the individual merits a favorable exercise of discretion; (4) the hardship to the individual and his or her U.S. citizen or legal permanent resident family members; (5) the individual's criminal history, if any; (6) the number and severity of the individual's immigration violations; (7) whether the individual has cooperated with, or his or her continued presence in the United States is desired for, a criminal or civil investigation or prosecution; and (8) whether the individual's removal is consistent with DHS objectives.[854]

DHS Motions Regarding Fraud or Crimes

If a motion to reopen or reconsider is filed by DHS in exclusion or deportation proceedings and the basis of the motion is fraud in the original proceeding or a crime that would support termination of asylum, the time and numerical limitations do not apply.[855]

---

[848] *Id.* at 362.

[849] 8 CFR §§1003.2(c)(3)(iii), 1003.23(b)(4)(iv).

[850] *See* "Office of the INS General Counsel, Revised Motions to Reopen Policy" (Dec. 23, 1997), *reprinted in* 75 *Interpreter Releases* 275 (Feb. 23, 1998). For a list of DHS district counsel offices, see appx. 6D.

[851] "Revised Motions to Reopen Policy," *supra* note 850.

[852] *Id.*

[853] *Id.*

[854] *Id.*

[855] 8 CFR §§1003.2(c)(3)(iv).

Equitable Tolling

At least two courts have held that numerical limitations on motions to reopen may be waived (or tolled) in cases in which an applicant has been defrauded by individuals purporting to provide legal representation.[856]

3.11.8. Contents of Motions

All motions must be filed in English or accompanied by a certified English translation.[857] If the moving party is represented by counsel, a Notice of Appearance must be filed on the appropriate form—Form EOIR-27 for the BIA or EOIR-28 for the IJ.[858] The motions also must include proof of service on the opposing party.[859] If the opposing party is DHS, the motion should be served on the district counsel for the district in which the case was completed before the IJ.[860] Motions filed with the BIA must be accompanied by a check or money order for $110, or a fee waiver request.[861] Motions filed with the IJ must be accompanied by a fee receipt.[862] The moving party may file a brief if it is included with the motion.[863] If oral argument is desired, a request should be made in the motion.[864]

To ensure the most efficient process of the motion, the BIA recommends that the motion be accompanied by a cover page containing the following information:

- Title (for example, "Respondent's Motion to Reopen");
- Full name of each respondent or applicant as it appears on the charging document;
- Alien registration (or "A") number for each respondent or applicant;
- Type of hearing or adjudication underlying the motion (for example, exclusion, deportation, removal, bond, or visa petition);
- Respondent's or applicant's custody status, *i.e.*, detained or not detained; and

---

[856] *See Rodriguez-Lariz v. INS*, 282 F.3d 1218, 1224 (9th Cir. 2002) (attorneys and nonattorney who failed to file a suspension application on time provided ineffective assistance of counsel and court remanded for BIA to grant second motion to reopen); *Iavorski v. INS*, 232 F.3d 124, 134–35 (2d Cir. 2000) (holding that ineffective assistance of counsel claim may be sufficient to justify equitable tolling, but applicant failed to exercise due diligence during period he sought to toll); *see also Fajardo v. INS*, 300 F.3d 1018, 1022 (9th Cir. 2002); *Varela v. INS*, 204 F.3d 1237, 1240 (9th Cir. 2000).

[857] 8 CFR §§1003.2(g)(1), 1003.23(b)(1).

[858] 8 CFR §§1003.2(g)(1), 1003.23(b)(1)(ii).

[859] 8 CFR §§1003.2(g)(1), 1003.23(b)(1)(ii).

[860] 8 CFR §§1003.2(g)(1), 1003.23(b)(1)(ii); *see* appx. 6D for a list of district counsel addresses and telephone numbers.

[861] 8 CFR §1003.2(g)(2).

[862] 8 CFR §1003.23(b)(1)(ii).

[863] 8 CFR §1003.2(g)(3).

[864] 8 CFR §1003.2(h).

- The adjudicator whose decision underlies the motion.[865]

The BIA also recommends that the body of the motion be filed on white, letter-sized paper, be typewritten or word-processed, and should clearly state the reasons for the motion. According to the BIA, any applications for relief filed with the motion should be included below the body of the motion. Any fees for these applications, however, should not be paid at the motion stage, but should be paid if and when the case is remanded to the IJ. Any new evidence, such as sworn affidavits, declarations under penalty of perjury, and documentary evidence should be submitted with the motion. Any material not in English must be accompanied by a certified English translation. A supporting brief may be filed and should be filed together with the motion, not separately. DHS has 13 days from the date of the filing of the motion to file a response. The BIA also recommends including a copy of the order or decision that is being challenged. Lastly, the BIA strongly encourages that the documents submitted have two holes punched 2.75 inches apart and centered at the top. Documents may be stapled at the top, but should not be bound on the side.[866]

Contents of Motion to Reconsider

A motion to reconsider must state the reasons for the motion by specifying the errors of fact or law in the prior IJ or BIA decision, and must be supported by pertinent legal authority.[867] A party may not seek reconsideration of a decision denying a previous motion to reconsider.[868] A motion to reconsider must state whether the validity of the exclusion, deportation, or removal order has been or is the subject of any judicial proceedings and, if so, the nature and date of the proceedings, the court in which the proceedings took place or is pending, and the result or status of the proceeding.[869] If the exclusion, deportation, or removal order is in effect, the motion to reconsider must include a statement by or on behalf of the individual subject to the order regarding whether he or she is the subject of any pending criminal proceedings and, if so, the current status of those proceedings.[870] Similarly, if the motion seeks discretionary relief, the motion must also include a statement by or on behalf of the moving party declaring whether he or she is the subject of any pending criminal prosecution and, if so, the nature and current status of the prosecution.[871]

Contents of Motion to Reopen

A motion to reopen must state the new facts that will be proved at the hearing to be held if the motion is granted and must be supported by affidavits or other evidentiary ma-

---

[865] *See BIA Practice Manual*, ch. 5 at 79–80, available at *www.usdoj.gov/eoir/vll/qapracmanual/pracmanual/chap5.pdf*.

[866] *See BIA Practice Manual*, ch. 3, available at *www.usdoj.gov/eoir/vll/qapracmanual/pracmanual/chap3.pdf*.

[867] 8 CFR §§1003.2(b)(1), 1003.23(b)(2).

[868] 8 CFR §§1003.2(b)(1), 1003.23(b)(2).

[869] 8 CFR §§1003.2(e), 1003.23(b)(1)(i).

[870] 8 CFR §§1003.2(e), 1003.23(b)(1)(i).

[871] 8 CFR §§1003.2(e), 1003.23(b)(1)(i).

terial.[872] A motion to reopen proceedings for the purpose of submitting an application for relief must be accompanied by the application and all supporting documentation.[873] A motion to reopen will not be granted unless it appears to the BIA or the IJ that the evidence sought to be offered is material and was not available and could not have been discovered or presented at a former hearing.[874] As with the motion to reconsider, a motion to reopen must state whether the validity of the exclusion, deportation, or removal order has been or is the subject of any judicial proceedings and, if so, the nature and date of the proceedings, the court in which the proceedings took place or is pending, and the result or status of the proceeding.[875] If the exclusion, deportation, or removal order is in effect, the motion to reopen must include a statement by or on behalf of the individual subject to the order regarding whether he or she is the subject of any pending criminal proceedings and, if so, the current status of those proceedings.[876] And, if the motion seeks discretionary relief, the motion must also include a statement by or on behalf of the moving party declaring whether he or she is the subject of any pending criminal prosecution and, if so, the nature and current status of the prosecution.[877]

3.11.9. Stay of Removal

The filing of a motion to reopen or reconsider does *not* stay the execution of any decision made in the case, except in the case of a motion to reopen an order entered in absentia.[878] A stay should be requested when the motion to reopen or reconsider is filed. Execution of the order will proceed unless a stay of execution is granted by the BIA, IJ, or DHS.[879]

3.11.10. Reply to Motion

For motions filed with the BIA, the opposing party has 13 days from the date of service of the motion to file a brief in opposition to the motion directly with the BIA.[880] The BIA may extend the time within which a brief is to be submitted.[881] A motion is deemed unopposed unless a timely response is made.[882] However, the BIA may in its discretion consider a brief filed out of time.[883] For motions filed with the IJ, the IJ may set and ex-

---

[872] 8 CFR §§1003.2(c)(1), 1003.23(b)(3).

[873] 8 CFR §§1003.2(c)(1), 1003.23(b)(3). *But see Matter of Yewondwosen*, 21 I&N Dec. 1025 (BIA 1997) (holding that the BIA or IJ may grant a motion to reopen where the individual fails to submit the application for relief in cases in which legacy INS/DHS joins in the motion).

[874] 8 CFR §§1003.2(c)(1), 1003.23(b)(3).

[875] 8 CFR §§1003.2(e), 1003.23(b)(1)(i).

[876] 8 CFR §§1003.2(e), 1003.23(b)(1)(i).

[877] 8 CFR §§1003.2(e), 1003.23(b)(1)(i).

[878] 8 CFR §§1003.2(f), 1003.23(b)(1)(v).

[879] 8 CFR §§1003.2(f), 1003.23(b)(1)(v).

[880] 8 CFR §1003.2(g)(3).

[881] *Id.*

[882] *Id.*

[883] *Id.*

tend time limits for motions to reopen or reconsider.[884] The IJ will deem the motion unopposed unless a timely response is made.[885]

3.11.11. Rulings on Motion

The BIA's rulings upon motions to reopen or reconsider must be made by written order.[886]

3.11.12. Departure from the United States

A moving party's departure from the United States while a motion to reopen or reconsider is pending constitutes a withdrawal of the motion.[887] Moreover, a motion to reopen or reconsider may not be filed on behalf of an individual who has departed the United States subject to a deportation, exclusion, or removal order.[888] At least one court has held, however, an IJ retains jurisdiction to reopen an in absentia case to address whether the applicant received notice of the hearing, even after the applicant had been removed.[889]

3.12. JUDICIAL REVIEW

The INA allows judicial review of orders of removal. Therefore, decisions denying asylum and withholding of removal may be reviewed by federal courts.[890] The most common avenue of review for individuals denied asylum or withholding of removal in proceedings under INA §240 is by filing a petition for review with a federal appeals court.[891] Arguably, because the REAL ID Act does not address habeas corpus review of detention, review may also be sought under a federal district court's general habeas corpus jurisdiction for individuals in DHS custody or subject to a final order of removal.[892] This section does not, however, address current law and procedures for filing a habeas petition.[893]

> *Tip*—**The REAL ID of 2005**—The REAL ID Act expanded the federal court of appeals jurisdiction so that many individuals previously barred from bringing petitions for review may now file such petitions. It did so by expanding

---

[884] 8 CFR §1003.23(b)(1)(iv).

[885] *Id.*

[886] 8 CFR §1003.2(i).

[887] 8 CFR §§1003.2(d), 1003.23(b)(1).

[888] 8 CFR §1003.23(b)(1).

[889] *Contreras-Rodriguez v. U.S. Att'y Gen.*, 462 F.3d 1314 (11th Cir. 2006).

[890] *See generally* INA §242; 8 USC §1252. For information on judicial review of Convention Against Torture decisions, see ch. 4.3.4.

[891] INA §242; 8 USC §1252.

[892] *See generally* 28 USC §§2241, 1651; U.S. Const. art. I, §9, cl. 2; *see also* L. Guttentag, "The 1996 Immigration Act: Federal Court Jurisdiction—Statutory Restrictions and Constitutional Rights," 74 *Interpreter Releases* 245 (Feb. 10, 1997).

[893] For further information regarding habeas petitions, see AILF Practice Advisory, Introduction to Habeas Corpus (Apr. 2006), available at *www.ailf.org/lac/lac_pa_0406.pdf.*

the jurisdiction of the courts of appeal to review all constitutional issues and questions of law related to a final order of removal. However, the REAL ID Act also eliminated habeas review over all final orders of removal. Any pending habeas corpus petition is automatically converted to a petition for review before the appropriate court of appeals.[894] For an excellent overview of these changes, see AILF Practice Advisory, How to File a Petition for Review (Oct. 25, 2006)[895] and AILF Practice Advisory, Judicial Review Provisions of the REAL ID Act (June 7, 2005).[896]

3.12.1. *Chevron* Deference

In general, where Congress delegates authority to an administrative agency to promulgate rules to implement a statute, that agency's interpretation of the statute is entitled to deferential review.[897] Under the rule of *Chevron* deference, substantial deference is given to an agency's interpretation of the statute it is charged with administering unless that interpretation is "arbitrary, capricious, or manifestly contrary to the statute."[898] Generally, a court will defer to the BIA's interpretation of the INA, because the BIA is charged with administration of that statute.[899]

However, there are exceptions to the application of *Chevron* deference to BIA determinations. For example, when a single member of the BIA decides a case through a non-precedential decision, such decisions are accorded no *Chevron* deference.[900] In addition, when the BIA is not charged with administration of a law, its interpretation of that law is reviewed *de novo*.[901] An important illustration of this rule is that when a BIA decision interprets federal or state criminal laws, courts review the decision *de novo*.[902]

3.12.2. No Review

Except as allowed for under the REAL ID Act,[903] a federal court is barred from reviewing the final removal orders in the following cases:

---

[894] REAL ID Act of 2005, Pub. L. No. 109-13, div. B, §106, 119 Stat. 231, 310–11.

[895] *www.ailf.org/lac/lac_pa_041706.pdf.*

[896] *www.ailf.org/lac/realid6705.pdf.*

[897] *United States v. Mead Corp.*, 533 U.S. 218, 226-27 (2001).

[898] *Chevron U.S.A. Inc. v. NRDC*, 467 U.S. 837, 844, 104 S. Ct. 2778 (1978).

[899] *Blake v. Gonzalez*, 481 F.3d 152, 156 (2d Cir. 2007).

[900] *Rotimi v. Gonzales*, 473 F.3d 55, 57 (2d Cir. 2007) (per curiam); *Garcia-Quintero v. Gonzales*, 455 F.3d 1006, 1012–14 (9th Cir. 2006).

[901] *Vargas-Sarmiento v. United States Dep't of Justice*, 448 F.3d 159, 165 (2d Cir. 2006).

[902] *Michel v. INS*, 206 F.3d 253, 252 (2d Cir. 2000); *Amibola v. Ashcroft*, 378 F.3d 173, 176 (2d Cir. 2004).

[903] INA §242(a)(2)(D); 8 USC §1252(a)(2)(D).

Negative Credible Fear Determination

A determination by an IJ that an individual failed to establish a credible fear of persecution in expedited removal proceedings is not reviewable in federal court (or by the BIA).[904]

Noncitizens Convicted of Certain Crimes

A federal court may not review a final order of removal of persons who have been convicted of: an aggravated felony, a crime involving moral turpitude (unless such crime falls within a narrow exception), two crimes involving moral turpitude, two crimes for which the aggregate sentences to confinement are five years or more, controlled substances offenses, controlled substance trafficking offenses, prostitution and prostitution-related offenses, commercialized vice offenses, certain firearms offenses, and miscellaneous treason, sedition, and sabotage offenses, or if the individual is a drug abuser or a drug addict.[905] If, however, the individual was placed in proceedings prior to April 1, 1997, the case may be a so-called "transitional" case in which judicial review is still available. A federal court, however, may review whether a crime or offense constitutes an aggravated felony or other bar to review.[906]

Reinstatement

An order of removal that is reinstated after an individual illegally re-enters the country is "not subject to being reopened or reviewed."[907]

3.12.3. Restrictions on Judicial Review

The following determinations made during the adjudication of an asylum or withholding claim are not reviewable:

Safe Third Country

A determination that the individual may not apply for asylum because he or she may be removed to a safe third country is not reviewable in federal court.[908]

One-Year Deadline

A determination that the individual is ineligible for asylum because there were no extraordinary circumstances causing the individual to file for asylum beyond the one-year deadline is not reviewable by a federal appeals court.[909] However, at least one court found that this determination is reviewable in habeas corpus proceedings in a federal district

---

[904] INA §§235(b)(1)(B)(iii)(III), (C); 8 USC §§1225(b)(1)(B)(iii)(III), (C).

[905] INA §242(a)(2)(C); 8 USC §1252(a)(2)(C).

[906] See ch. 2.7.2.

[907] INA §241(a)(5); 8 USC §1251(a)(5). See this chapter, at 3.6.

[908] INA §208(a)(3); 8 USC §1158(a)(3).

[909] INA §208(a)(3); 8 USC §1158(a)(3).

court.[910] Moreover, the REAL ID Act has since provided for direct judicial review by courts of appeal of constitutional claims or questions of law that were previously barred by other INA provisions that restricted jurisdiction to review of orders of removal.[911] Under the REAL ID Act, federal appeals courts have held that they have jurisdiction to review the BIA's denial of asylum based on failure to meet the one-year deadline if the one-year deadline issue constitutes a constitutional claim or a question of law.[912]

Previous Denial

A determination that an individual is ineligible for asylum because he or she was previously denied asylum and has failed to establish changed circumstances is not reviewable in federal court.[913]

Terrorist Bar

A court may not review a determination that an individual is barred from asylum because he or she is inadmissible for: (1) having engaged in terrorist activity; (2) being likely to engage in such activity; (3) having incited such activity; (4) being a representative of a terrorist organization (as designated by the secretary of state); (5) being a representative of a group that endorses terrorist activity; or (6) using his or her position of prominence to endorse or espouse terrorist activity.[914]

Expedited Removal

Individuals who are apprehended upon arrival with no documents or purportedly false documents have limited judicial review available through habeas corpus proceedings.[915] Such review is limited to issues of whether the individual is an alien, whether the individual was ordered removed in expedited proceedings, and whether the individual is a lawful permanent resident or was previously granted asylum or admitted as a refugee.[916]

---

[910] *See Kanivets v. Riley*, 320 F. Supp. 2d 297, 300–01 (E.D. Pa. 2004) (holding that the IJ erred in finding that the asylum application was time barred).

[911] INA §242(a)(2)(D); 8 USC §1252(a)(2)(D).

[912] *See Lin v. Gonzales*, 190 Fed. Appx. 301 (4th Cir. 2006); *Krisman v. Gonzales*, 199 Fed. Appx. 299 (4th Cir. 2006). *See also Spina v. Dep't of Homeland Sec.*, 70 F.3d 116, 123 (2d Cir. 2006); *Iasu v. Chertoff*, 426 F. Supp. 2d 1124 (D. Cal. 2006); *Walters v. Ashcroft*, 198 Fed. Appx. 78 (2d Cir. 2006); *Restrepo v. Winfrey*, 162 Fed. Appx. 311 (5th Cir. 2006); *Tilley v. Chertoff*, 144 Fed. Appx. 536 (6th Cir. 2005). *See also Moreno-Bravo v. Gonzales*, 463 F.3d 253 (2d Cir. 2006) (holding that any habeas petitions pending before an appellate court on the effective date of the REAL ID Act are properly converted to petitions for review and retained by that appellate court).

[913] INA §208(a)(3); 8 USC §1158(a)(3).

[914] INA §208(b)(2)(D); 8 USC §1158(b)(2)(D).

[915] INA §242(e)(2); 8 USC §1252(e)(2).

[916] INA §242(e)(2); 8 USC §1252(e)(2); *see also* ch. 5.

Discretionary Determinations by the IJ and BIA

Under the INA, no court is permitted to review discretionary determinations by the attorney general, other than the granting of asylum.[917] In a case involving an asylum applicant who sought habeas corpus review of a discretionary denial of asylum because his or her criminal convictions barred the filing of a petition for review, the reviewing court determined that it lacked jurisdiction to review the claim.[918] Courts have found jurisdiction to review a continuance denial.[919]

> ➢ *Tip*—**EAJA Fees**—Are you eligible to receive attorney's fees and costs? If you are successful before the federal court, you may be eligible to recover costs and fees under the Equal Access to Justice Act, 28 USC §2412(d) and 5 USC §504 et seq.[920]

3.12.4. Procedures

The following is an overview of the procedures for filing a petition for review with a federal appeals court.[921]

Time Limit

The petition for review must be filed not later than 30 days after the date of the final order of removal.[922] At least two courts have held that they are expressly prohibited from extending the time limit, even for good cause, because the rule for review of agency proceedings is strictly jurisdictional.[923]

Venue

The petition for review should be filed with the court of appeals for the judicial circuit in which the IJ completed proceedings.[924]

---

[917] INA §242(a)(2)(B)(ii); 8 USC §1252(a)(2)(B)(ii).

[918] *See Bakhtriger v. Elwood*, 360 F.3d 414 (3d Cir. 2004).

[919] *Zafar v. U.S. Att'y Gen.*, 461 F.3d 1357, 1360 (11th Cir. 2006).

[920] *See, e.g., Hua Fang v. Gonzales*, No. 03-71352, Filed order (Appellate Commissioner) (9th Cir. Oct. 30, 2006). For more information, see AILF Practice Advisory, Requesting Attorney's Fees Under the Equal Access to Justice Act (Apr. 7, 2006), available at *www.ailf.org/lac/EAJA_Fees_04_07_06.pdf*;

[921] For more comprehensive instructions, see AILF Practice Advisory, How to File a Petition for Review (Apr. 2006), available at *www.ailf.org/lac/lac_pa_041706.pdf*.

[922] INA §242(b)(1); 8 USC §252(b)(1).

[923] *Martinez-Serrano v. INS*, 94 F.3d 1256, 1258 (9th Cir. 1996); *Malvoisin v. INS*, 268 F.3d 74, 76 (2d Cir. 2001).

[924] INA §242(b)(2); 8 USC §1252(b)(2). For a list of websites for the U.S. courts of appeals, see appx. 6G.

What to File

- A petition for review.[925] Before filing the petition, it is important to review local court rules.
- A copy of the BIA decision.
- The filing fee or application for fee waiver. The fee for a petition for review is usually $100, but it is important to check local court rules.[926]
- A certificate of service stating that a copy of the petition was served on (mailed or delivered to) the attorney general, the Office of Immigration Litigation (OIL), and the ICE field office director or the most senior officer in the Detention and Removal Unit.[927]
- A motion to stay removal.[928]
- If applicant has been granted voluntary departure, a motion to stay the voluntary departure period.[929]

> ➢ **Beware**—A petitioner may not be entitled to review under the "Fugitive Disentitlement Doctrine," which applies to individuals who have been issued final orders of removal and fail to depart from the United States.[930]

Briefing Schedule

The petitioner's brief must be filed not later than 40 days after the administrative record is made available.[931] The reply brief must be filed not later than 14 days after the brief of the attorney general.[932] The court may extend these deadlines, but only if good cause is shown.[933] If the petitioner fails to file a brief within the time provided, the court must dismiss the appeal unless manifest injustice would result.[934]

---

[925] *See* appx. 5B.

[926] *See* appx. 6G for a list of websites for courts of appeals.

[927] For a list of addresses for the AG, OIL, and Field Office Directors, see appx. 6C.

[928] *See infra* this section.

[929] *See Nwakanma v. Ashcroft*, 352 F.3d 325 (6th Cir. 2004); *El Himri v. Ashcroft*, 344 F.3d 1261 (9th Cir. 2003); *see also* AILF Practice Advisory, Protecting the Voluntary Departure Period During Court of Appeals Review (updated Oct. 25, 2005), available at *www.ailf.org/lac/lac_pa_102505.pdf*.

[930] *See, e.g., Gao v. Gonzales*, 481 F.3d 173, 176 (2d Cir. 2007); *Garcia-Flores v. Gonzales*, 477 F.3d 439, 441 (6th Cir. 2007); *Sapoundjiev v. Ashcroft*, 376 F.3d 727, 728–29 (7th Cir. 2004); *Antonio-Martinez v. INS*, 317 F.3d 1089, 1093 (9th Cir. 2003); *Arana v. INS*, 673 F.2d 75, 77 (3d Cir. 1982). *But see Gutierrez-Almazan v. Gonzales*, 453 F.3d 956, 957 (7th Cir. 2006) (finding that the fugitive disentitlement doctrine did not apply where an alien voluntarily surrendered to authorities).

[931] INA §242(b)(3)(C); 8 USC §1252(b)(3)(C).

[932] INA §242(b)(3)(C); 8 USC §1252(b)(3)(C).

[933] INA §242(b)(3)(C); 8 USC §1252(b)(3)(C).

[934] INA §242(b)(3)(C); 8 USC §1252(b)(3)(C).

Scope of Review

The court must limit its review to the administrative record on which the order of removal is based.[935] Courts have found jurisdiction to review Visa Waiver Program asylum claims even though the BIA order does not expressly order removal.[936] The court is prohibited from hearing any cause or claim regarding the AG's decision or action to commence proceedings, adjudicate cases, or execute removal orders.[937] The administrative findings of fact are conclusive unless any reasonable adjudicator would be "compelled to conclude to the contrary."[938] The court may not rely on arguments in an agency's brief that are different from the grounds stated or discernible in the agency's decision itself.[939] The AG's discretionary judgment on whether to grant asylum is "conclusive unless manifestly contrary to law and an abuse of discretion."[940] Decisions regarding withholding of removal, however, are not discretionary and, therefore, would not be subject to this limitation on review of the AG's exercise of discretion.[941] These provisions are now also applicable to decisions, actions, and judgments by the secretary of the Department of Homeland Security under the Homeland Security Act of 2002.[942]

Stay of Removal

Filing the petition for review does not automatically stay the removal of an individual, unless the court orders a stay.[943] A stay should, therefore, be sought when filing the petition for review. Courts of appeal disagree regarding what standard should be met in a motion for a stay of removal filed in conjunction with a petition for review. Some courts apply the clear and convincing standard under INA §242(f)(2) (8 USC §1252(f)(2)).[944] Most, however, have held that the clear and convincing standard under INA §242(f)(2) does not apply to temporary stays for petitions for review.[945] It may be possible to return

---

[935] INA §242(b)(4)(A), 8 USC §1252(b)(4)(A).

[936] *Shehu v. U.S. Att'y Gen.*, 482 F.3d 652, 656 (3d Cir. 2007); *Kanacevic v. INS*, 448 F.3d 129, 134–35 (2d Cir. 2006); *Nreka v. U.S. Att'y Gen.*, 408 F.3d 1361, 1367 (11th Cir. 2005).

[937] INA §242(g); 8 USC §1252(g); *see also Reno v. American-Arab Anti-Discrimination Committee*, 525 U.S. 471 (1999).

[938] INA §242(b)(4)(B); 8 USC §1252(b)(4)(B).

[939] *See Mengistu v. Ashcroft*, 355 F.3d 1044, 1047–48 (7th Cir. 2004) (citing *Bowman Transportation, Inc. v. Arkansas-Best Freight System, Inc.*, 419 U.S. 281, 285–86 (1974)).

[940] INA §242(b)(4)(D); 8 USC §1252(b)(4)(D).

[941] *See, e.g., INS v. Cardoza-Fonseca*, 480 U.S. 421, 429 (1987).

[942] *See* Homeland Security Act of 2002, Pub. L. No. 107-296, §§456, 1512, 1517, 116 Stat. 2135, 2200, 2310, 2311.

[943] INA §242(b)(3)(B); 8 USC §1252(b)(3)(B).

[944] *See Weng v. U.S. Atty. Gen.*, 287 F.3d 1335 (11th Cir. 2002); *see also Ngarurih v. Ashcroft*, 371 F.3d 182, 195 n.13 (4th Cir. 2004) (citing with approval the clear and convincing standard in considering a petition for stay of removal).

[945] *See Hor v. Gonzales*, 400 F.3d 482, 485 (7th Cir. 2005); *Tesfamichael v. Gonzales*, 411 F.3d 169, 176 (5th Cir. 2005); *Faruqi v. DHS*, 360 F.3d 985, 988–89 (9th Cir. 2004); *Douglas v. Ashcroft*, 374 F.3d 230, 233–34 (3d Cir. 2004); *Bejjani v. INS*, 271 F.3d 670, 687–89 (6th Cir. 2001), *overruled on other grounds by Fernandez-Vargas v. Gonzales*, 126 S. Ct. 2422, 2427 (2006); *Arevalo v. Ashcroft*,
continued

to the United States if removal occurs and the applicant prevails on a petition for review.[946]

Motions to Reopen or Reconsider

Any review of a motion to reopen or reconsider must be consolidated with the review of the final order of removal.[947]

3.13. ADJUSTMENT OF STATUS FOR ASYLEES AND REFUGEES

An individual granted asylum or an individual admitted as a refugee may adjust to lawful permanent resident status one year after the grant of asylum or the admission as a refugee.[948]

3.13.1. Asylees

To qualify for adjustment of status, asylees must:

- apply for adjustment (using Form I-485);
- have been physically present in the United States for at least one year after being granted asylum;
- continue to meet the definition of refugee under INA §101(a)(42);
- not be "firmly resettled" in any foreign country; and
- be admissible as an immigrant under INA §212(a), except that the grounds of inadmissibility relating to lack of a proper travel document, labor certification, or likelihood of becoming a public charge do not apply. Moreover, the AG may waive *any* other ground of inadmissibility for humanitarian purposes, to ensure family unity, or when it is in the public interest, except for drug trafficking and security-related grounds.[949]

The application, with the appropriate fee, should be filed with the USCIS office designated in the instructions to the Application for Adjustment of Status (Form I-485).[950] Upon acceptance of the application, the applicant must submit to a medical examination to determine the mental and physical condition of the applicant.[951] An applicant may be

---

344 F.3d 1, 6–9 (1st Cir. 2003); *Mohammed v. Reno*, 309 F.3d 95, 98–100 (2d Cir. 2002); *see also Singh v. Ashcroft*, 375 F.3d 1007 (10th Cir. 2004) (motion must contain argument on likelihood of success on appeal, threat of irreparable harm, absence of harm to opposing party, and any risk of harm to public interest); *Rife v. Ashcroft*, 374 F.3d 606, 615 n.3 (8th Cir. 2004) (opting not to address the issue); AILF Practice Advisory, Applying for a Stay of Removal during Federal Court Proceedings (Oct. 24, 2005), available at *www.ailf.org/lac/stay_pa.pd/*.

[946] For more information, see AILF Practice Advisory, Return to the United States after Prevailing on a Petition for Review (Jan. 17, 2007), available at *www.ailf.org/lac/lac_pa_11607.pdf*.

[947] INA §242(b)(6); 8 USC §1252(b)(6).

[948] *See generally* INA §209; 8 USC §1159; 8 CFR §§209.1, 209.2, 1209.1, and 1209.2.

[949] INA §209(b), (c); 8 USC §1159(b), (c); 8 CFR §§209.2(a), 1209.2(a).

[950] 8 CFR §§209.2(c), 1209.2(c).

[951] 8 CFR §§209.2(d), 1209.2(d).

interviewed by a USCIS officer, or the interview may be waived.[952] After the interview or waiver, the applicant will be notified of the decision.[953] If the applicant is denied, he or she will be notified of the reasons for the denial and may renew the application before an IJ.[954] If the application is approved, USCIS will record the asylee's admission as a lawful permanent resident, as of the date one year before the date of approval.[955]

> *Tip*—**Waivers Under INA §209(c)**—Almost all grounds of excludability are waivable for asylees and refugees who seek to adjust their status. The only two exceptions are drug trafficking and security-related grounds. Sometimes Form I-602 is required. For guidance in this area, consult the USCIS memorandum on waivers under INA §209(c).[956] For more information on 209(c) waivers, see chapter 6.

Prior to the passage of the REAL ID Act in 2005, only 10,000 asylees could adjust each year.[957] If a number was not available, the asylee was supposed to be placed on a waiting list on a priority basis by the date the application was filed. The backlog of asylees awaiting adjustment grew significantly over the years. Before the REAL ID Act, it was estimated that a wait could be as long as 12 years. Fortunately, the REAL ID Act eliminated the wait by repealing the cap on adjustments for asylees.

3.13.2. Refugees

A person admitted as a refugee under INA §207 qualifies for adjustment of status if:

- his or her admission has not been terminated by the AG or DHS;
- he or she has been physically present in the United States for at least one year; and
- he or she is admissible as an immigrant under INA §212(a), except that the grounds of inadmissibility relating to lack of a proper travel document, labor certification, or likelihood of becoming a public charge do not apply. Moreover, the AG or DHS may waive *any* other ground of inadmissibility for humanitarian purposes, to ensure family unity, or when it is in the public interest, except for drug trafficking and security-related grounds.[958]

Refugees are required to appear before a DHS officer one year after their entry to determine their admissibility.[959] Unless there were medical grounds for exclusion at the

---

[952] 8 CFR §§209.2(e), 1209.2(e).

[953] 8 CFR §§209.2(f), 1209.2(f).

[954] 8 CFR §§209.2(f), 1209.2(f).

[955] 8 CFR §§209.2(f), 1209.2(f).

[956] USCIS Interoffice Memorandum, M. Aytes, "Waivers Under Section 209(c) of the Immigration and Nationality Act (AFM Update 05-33)" (Oct. 31, 2005), *published on* AILA InfoNet at Doc. No. 05110962 (*posted* Nov. 9, 2005), and available at *www.uscis.gov/files/pressrelease/209cAdjWvr 103105.pdf*.

[957] INA §209(b); 8 USC §1159(b) (2004).

[958] INA §§209(a), (c); 8 USC §§1159(a), (c); 8 CFR §§209.1, 1209.1.

[959] 8 CFR §§209.1(a)(1), 1209.1(a)(1).

time of the refugee's entry, no medical examination is required.[960] If the refugee is found to be admissible, he or she will be inspected and admitted for lawful permanent residence as of the date of his or her arrival in the United States.[961]

If the refugee is determined to be inadmissible, DHS may detain him or her and initiate removal proceedings.[962] If this happens, the refugee should request an NTA (which will reveal the grounds on which the government is seeking removal) and renew the request for adjustment in proceedings before an IJ.[963] While the hearing is pending, it is unclear whether the detainee will be able to seek a bond redetermination hearing before an IJ. The government has taken the position that unadjusted refugees revert after a year to "arriving alien" status and, thus, IJs have no jurisdiction over such individuals for bond hearing purposes.[964] However, this position contradicts the reasoning of the AG in *Matter of Jean*.[965] In that decision, the AG relied on INA §235(b)(2)(A); 8 USC §1225(b)(2)(A) in asserting the government's right to detain refugees who have stayed in the United States for more than a year but have been denied LPR status. The reliance on that provision, which governs the removal of aliens other than "arriving aliens," indicates that the AG did not consider refugees denied LPR status to revert to "arriving alien" status.

Do refugees lose their refugee status after they adjust to LPR status? At least one court has suggested that they may not.[966] Such individuals are, however, subject to removal.[967]

3.14. REFUGEE TRAVEL DOCUMENT

An asylee or refugee who wishes to travel temporarily outside of the United States and return to the United States must obtain a refugee travel document or a valid advance

---

[960] 8 CFR §§209.1(c), 1209.1(c).

[961] 8 CFR §§209.1(e), 1209.1(e).

[962] *See* INA §209(a); 8 USC §1159(a) (stating that refugees who have been in the United States for one year and have not yet acquired permanent residence status "*shall* . . . return or be returned to the custody of the Department of Homeland Security for inspection and examination") (emphasis added); *Matter of Jean*, 23 I&N Dec. 373, 381 (AG 2002) (reading INA §209(a) with INA §235(b)(2)(A); 8 USC §1225(b)(2)(A) in mind, and concluding that if a refugee who surrenders to DHS for inspection "'is not clearly and beyond a doubt entitled to be admitted,' he or she must be detained for a removal proceeding").

[963] *See* INA §235(b)(2)(A); 8 USC §1225(b)(2)(A) (ordering a proceeding under INA §240; 8 USC §1229a); 8 CFR §§209.1(e), 1209.1(e) (declaring that a refugee whose application for permanent residence has been denied must be notified in writing of the reasons for the denial and of the refugee's right to renew the request for permanent residence in removal proceedings under INA §240; 8 USC §1229a).

[964] 8 CFR §1003.19(h)(2)(i)(B) (declaring that IJs have no jurisdiction over bond hearings for arriving aliens in removal hearings).

[965] *Matter of Jean*, 23 I&N Dec. 373 (AG 2002).

[966] *See Smriko v. Ashcroft*, 387 F.3d 279, 281 (3d Cir. 2004) (in remanding AWO case to BIA, court suggests that applicant's argument that despite his adjustment of status to LPR, he still retains his refugee status, is supported by the INA and legislative history).

[967] *See Romanishyn v. Gonzales*, 455 F.3d 175, 186 (3d Cir. 2006) (holding that refugee who adjusted status is subject to removal even though his refugee status was never terminated).

parole document *prior* to his or her departure.[968] An application for a refugee travel document may be made by filing Form I-131 with DHS.[969]

> ➢ ***Warning*—Asylees and Legal Permanent Residents (LPR)**—Travel to the country of claimed persecution may result in the loss of asylee or LPR status. USCIS has recently issued a fact sheet that warns of the consequences that may result if an asylee or LPR returns to the country of claimed persecution.[970] Asylum may be terminated based on a fundamental change in circumstances, fraud, lack of a genuine fear of persecution, or because the asylee or LPR voluntarily availed himself or herself of the home country's protection.[971]

3.14.1. Who May File

The applicant for a refugee travel document must hold valid refugee status under INA §207, valid asylee status under INA §208, or must be a permanent resident as a direct result of his or her refugee or asylee status.[972] Asylum applicants who have not been granted asylum may be eligible for advance parole. If they return to the country of claimed persecution, however, even with advance parole, the application will be presumed to be abandoned and they may be denied re-entry, unless they are able to establish compelling reasons for return.[973]

3.14.2. Where to File

According to the Instructions to Form I-131, the form and required supporting evidence should be sent to: USCIS, Nebraska Service Center, P.O. Box 87131, Lincoln, NE 68501-7131. Note that USCIS forms are periodically revised. To obtain the most recent form, call USCIS or visit the USCIS website at *www.uscis.gov*.

3.14.3. Fee

There is a fee for filing Form I-131.[974] Note that filing fees periodically change, so it is important to check the regulations and form instructions.

3.14.4. What to File

The applicant should send the following:

- completed Form I-131 (which is also the application form for advance parole);

---

[968] 8 CFR §223.1(b).

[969] 8 CFR §223.2(a); *see also* appx. 9D, Form I-131.

[970] USCIS Fact Sheet, "Traveling Outside the United States as an Asylum Applicant, an Asylee, or a Lawful Permanent Resident Who Obtained Such Status Based on Asylum" (revised Jan. 4. 2007), *published on* AILA InfoNet at Doc. No. 06122875 (*first posted* Dec. 28, 2006), and available at *www.uscis.gov/files/pressrelease/AsylumTravel122706FS.pdf*.

[971] *Id.*

[972] 8 CFR §223.2(b)(2).

[973] 8 CFR §§208.8(b), 1208.8(b).

[974] 8 CFR §§103.7(b)(1), 1103.7(b)(1).

- a document issued by DHS showing the applicant's refugee or asylee status;
- a check or money order for the appropriate fee;
- two identical passport-style photographs;
- in some jurisdictions (New York, in particular), a refugee or asylee who has filed an application for adjustment of status may be required to request and receive advance parole prior to departing from the United States.[975]

In limited circumstances, a refugee or asylee *may* be granted a refugee travel document *after* his or her departure from the United States, if the refugee or asylee demonstrates that he or she: (1) did not intend to abandon his or her residence; (2) did not engage in activities inconsistent with his or her refugee or asylee status; and (3) has been outside of the United States for less than one year.[976] Such circumstances are narrow and, therefore, as a general rule a refugee or asylee should always obtain a travel document *prior* to departure. For individuals outside the United States for more than one year, humanitarian parole under INA §212(d)(5) may be available.[977]

As noted above, an asylee who travels to his or her home country may risk having his or her asylum status terminated for a number of reasons.[978] An asylum applicant who travels outside the United States while his or her application is pending without obtaining advance parole will be presumed to have abandoned his or her application.[979] If he or she returns to the country of claimed persecution, even with advance parole, his or her application will be presumed to be abandoned, unless he or she is able to establish compelling reasons for return.[980]

3.15. REFUGEE/ASYLEE RELATIVE PETITION (I-730)

The spouse and unmarried[981] children under 21 years of age of a refugee or an asylee may be admitted to the United States, upon approval of a Refugee/Asylee Relative Petition (Form I-730).[982]

---

[975] See appx. 9D, Form I-131, for additional instructions.

[976] 8 CFR §223.2(b)(2)(ii); *see also* INS Memorandum, B. Cooper, "Readmission of Asylees and Refugees Without Travel Documents" (Nov. 23, 1999), *published on* AILA InfoNet at Doc. No. 01050405 (*posted* May 4, 2001).

[977] INS Memorandum, *supra* note 976. For more information on Humanitarian Parole, see ch. 6.

[978] INA §208(c)(2)(D); 8 USC §1158(c)(2)(D); *see* this chapter, at 3.16.

[979] 8 CFR §§208.8(a), 1208.8(a).

[980] 8 CFR §§208.8(b), 1208.8(b).

[981] In an amicus brief filed with the Second Circuit, AILF argued that a child who was unmarried at the time of the asylum grant, notwithstanding a prior marriage that ended in divorce, was covered by the Child Status Protection Act and eligible for derivative asylee status. The Second Circuit remanded the case to the BIA and the BIA, agreeing with AILF's interpretation, remanded the case to the IJ. See AILF Legal Action Center, Litigation Clearinghouse Newsletter (Nov. 17, 2006) at 1, available at *www.ailf.org/lac/litclearinghouse/litclr_newsletter_111706.pdf.*

[982] *See generally* 8 CFR §§207.7, 208.21, and 1208.21; *see* also appx. 9B, Form I-730.

> *Tip*—Other relatives may be eligible for resettlement to the United States through the U.S. Refugee Resettlement Program. For more information, see J. Guilfoyle, "The Refugee Resettlement Program: How It Might Help the Relatives of Your Asylee Clients," 23 *Immigration Law Today* 48 (Sept./Oct. 2004).

3.15.1. Relationship

The spousal or parent-child relationship must have existed prior to the refugee's admission to the United States or the asylee's grant of asylum and must continue to exist at the time of the filing of the I-730 application.[983] Under the Child Status Protection Act of 2002 (CSPA), children who are under 21 when their parent files for asylum but turn 21 before asylum is granted are still considered "children" and eligible for derivative status.[984] A child who was *in utero* on the date of the asylum grant or refugee admission also is eligible for derivative status.[985] A person granted asylum may also apply on behalf of a step-child, if he or she married the child's parent before the child's 18th birthday. It may be possible for an asylum applicant who receives a recommended approval to marry prior to receipt of a final approval and, thereby, make his or her spouse eligible for an I-730 petition. Legacy INS has approved an I-730 petition in at least one such case.

3.15.2. Who May File

The I-730 may only be filed by the principal refugee or asylee.[986] Family members who derived their refugee or asylee status from the principal refugee or asylee are not eligible to file an I-730 on behalf of their spouses and children.[987]

3.15.3. Where to File

According to the Instructions to Form I-730, the form and required supporting evidence should be sent to: USCIS, Nebraska Service Center, P.O. Box 87730, Lincoln, NE 68501-7730. USCIS forms are periodically revised. To obtain the most recent form, contact USCIS or visit USCIS's website at *www.uscis.gov*.

3.15.4. When to File

The Form I-730 must be filed for each qualifying family member within two years of the refugee's admission to the United States or the asylee's grant of asylum.[988] The filing period may only be extended for humanitarian reasons.[989]

---

[983] 8 CFR §§207.7(c), 208.21(b), and 1208.21(b).

[984] INA §208(b)(3); 8 USC §1158(b)(3).

[985] 8 CFR §§207.7(c), 208.21(b), and 1208.21(b).

[986] 8 CFR §207.7(d); *see* 8 CFR §§208.21(c), (d), 1208.21(c), (d).

[987] 8 CFR §207.7(d).

[988] 8 CFR §§207.7(d), 208.21(c), (d), and 1208.21(c), (d).

[989] 8 CFR §§207.7(d), 208.21(c), (d), and 1208.21(c), (d).

3.15.5. Fee

There is no filing fee for Form I-730.[990]

3.15.6. What to File

A separate Form I-730 must be filed for each family member, and the supporting evidence should include:

- evidence that the applicant is a refugee or asylee;
- evidence of the claimed spousal or parent-child relationship, such as a marriage certificate and birth certificates; and
- a photograph of the family member for whom the applicant is filing.[991]

In the absence of a birth certificate, baptismal certificate, school or church records, it may be possible to establish parentage through DNA testing.[992]

3.15.7. Burden of Proof

The burden of proof is on the applicant to establish by a preponderance of the evidence that the family member is an eligible spouse or unmarried child under 21 years of age.[993] Ineligible family members include individuals previously granted asylum or refugee status, individuals convicted of a particularly serious crime or an aggravated felony, and individuals considered to be a danger to the security of the United States.[994]

3.15.8. No Appeal

There is no appeal from the denial of an I-730 by DHS.[995] The denial, however, is without prejudice to the consideration of a new petition or motion to reopen the refugee or asylee relative petition proceeding.[996]

3.16. TERMINATION OF ASYLUM AND WITHHOLDING

Asylum does not convey a right to remain permanently in the United States and may be terminated by the AG.[997] Withholding of removal or deportation may also be terminated.[998] The procedures and grounds for termination listed below are for applications

---

[990] 8 CFR §207.7(d).

[991] 8 CFR §§207.7(e), 208.21(c), (d), and 1208.21(c), (d); also see appx. 9B, Form I-730 for additional instructions regarding adopted children, step-children, and spouses with previous marriages, as well as acceptable secondary evidence of relationships.

[992] *See* "INS Issues Guidance on Blood and DNA Testing for Establishing Parentage," 77 *Interpreter Releases* 1096 (July 2000).

[993] 8 CFR §§207.7(e), 208.21(f), and 1208.21(f).

[994] See 8 CFR §§207.7(b), 208.21(a), and 1208.21(a) for additional categories.

[995] 8 CFR §§207.7(g), 208.21(e), and 1208.21(e).

[996] 8 CFR §§207.7(g), 208.21(e), and 1208.21(e).

[997] INA §208(c)(2); 8 USC §1158(c)(2); 8 CFR §§208.24(a), 1208.24(a).

[998] 8 CFR §§208.24(b), 1208.24(b).

that were granted after April 1, 1997. It is important to note that noncitizens who have been granted asylum or withholding of removal may *not* be deported or removed from the United States unless their asylum status or withholding order has been terminated.[999]

> ➢ *Beware*—Asylum may be terminated even after a person becomes a legal permanent resident.[1000]

3.16.1. Grounds for Terminating Asylum

A grant of asylum may be terminated by either the asylum officer who granted asylum or by an IJ or the BIA pursuant to a motion to reopen or in INA §240 proceedings if it is determined that the individual:

- was not eligible for asylum at the time it was granted and there is a showing of fraud in the application;
- no longer meets the definition of refugee, owing to a fundamental change in circumstances;
- engaged in the persecution of others;
- having been convicted by final judgment of a particularly serious crime, constitutes a danger to the community of the United States;
- has committed a serious nonpolitical crime outside of the United States;
- is a danger to the security of the United States;
- has engaged in terrorist activity;
- may be removed to a safe third country, pursuant to a bilateral or multilateral agreement;
- has voluntarily availed him- or herself of the protection of his or her home country or, if stateless, the country of last habitual residence; or
- has acquired a new nationality and enjoys the protection of the country of his or her new nationality.[1001]

3.16.2. Grounds for Terminating Withholding

A grant of withholding may be terminated by either the asylum officer who granted withholding or by an IJ or the BIA pursuant to a motion to reopen if it is determined that the individual:

- was not eligible for withholding at the time it was granted and there is a showing of fraud in the application;
- is no longer entitled to withholding due to a fundamental change in circumstances in the country to which removal was withheld;
- engaged in the persecution of others;

---

[999] 8 CFR §§208.22, 1208.22.
[1000] USCIS Fact Sheet, *supra* note 970.
[1001] *See* 8 CFR §§208.24(a)–(f), 1208.24(a)–(f); INA §208(c)(2); 8 USC §1158(c)(2).

- having been convicted by final judgment of a particularly serious crime, constitutes a danger to the community of the United States;
- has committed a serious nonpolitical crime outside of the United States; or
- is a danger to the security of the United States.[1002]

3.16.3. Procedures

Asylum Office

In cases in which the individual was granted asylum by the asylum officer, the individual must be given an interview with an asylum officer in which he or she will have the opportunity to present evidence. The individual must be given a notice of intent to terminate, with the reasons for termination, at least 30 days before the interview. If the asylum officer determines that the individual is no longer eligible for asylum or withholding of removal, the individual must be given written notice that his or her asylum or withholding of removal status, and any employment authorization status, have been terminated.[1003]

BIA or IJ

The BIA or IJ may reopen a case for the purpose of terminating a grant of asylum or withholding of removal or deportation made under the jurisdiction of an IJ. In such cases, DHS has the burden of establishing by a preponderance of the evidence one or more of the grounds for termination listed above.[1004] With regard to the fraud ground, the government must show that the applicant knew the statement or document was fraudulent at the time the applicant submitted it to the IJ.[1005] An IJ may terminate a grant of asylum or withholding of removal or deportation made by DHS at any time after the individual has been served with the notice to terminate. Terminations by IJs may also occur in conjunction with an exclusion, deportation, or removal proceeding.[1006]

3.16.4. Termination of Derivative Status

The termination of asylum status for a person who was the principal applicant will result in the termination of the asylum status of the spouse and minor child whose status was based on the asylum application of the principal. Such a termination, however, does not preclude the spouse or child from separately asserting an asylum or withholding of removal claim.[1007]

[1002] *See* 8 CFR §§208.24(b)–(e), 1208.24(b)–(e).

[1003] 8 CFR §§208.24(c), 1208.24(c).

[1004] 8 CFR §§208.24(f), 1208.24(f); *see also Ntangsi v. Gonzales*, 475 F.3d 1007, 1012-13 (8th Cir. 2007) (reversing termination of asylum status where neither the IJ nor the BIA placed the burden of proving fraud on the government)

[1005] *Ntangsi, supra* note 1004, at 1012.

[1006] 8 CFR §§208.24(f), 1208.24(f).

[1007] 8 CFR §§208.24(d), 1208.24(d).

3.17. Termination of Refugee Status

The AG or DHS may terminate the refugee status of any individual (and of any spouse or minor child who has derivative refugee status) if the AG or DHS determines that the individual was not in fact a refugee within the meaning of INA §101(a)(42); 8 USC §1101(a)(42) at the time of his or her admission to the United States.[1008] A refugee is, however, subject to removal even if his or her refugee status has not been terminated.[1009]

3.17.1. Procedure

The district director (DD) in the district where the individual is located must notify the individual in writing of DHS's intent to terminate the individual's refugee status. The individual has 30 days from the date the notice is served upon him or her, or delivered to his or her last known address, to present written or oral evidence to show why his or her refugee status should not be terminated.[1010] Upon termination of refugee status, the individual will be placed in expedited removal proceedings pursuant to INA §§235, 240, and 241.[1011]

3.17.2. No Appeal

There is no appeal from the termination of refugee status by the DD.[1012]

> ➢ *Tip*—**Effect of Adjustment of Status on Refugee Status**—UNHCR takes the position that a person admitted to the United States as a refugee continues to maintain refugee status even after the person adjusts status and becomes an LPR. The implication of this opinion is that because the person continues to be a refugee, the person should not be subject to removal on criminal grounds, but only on the cessation grounds in the Refugee Convention and Protocol.[1013]

[1008] INA §207(c)(4); 8 USC §1157(c)(4).

[1009] *See, e.g., Matter of Smriko*, 23 I&N Dec. 836, 840 (BIA 2005) (removal proceedings may be commenced against a refugee without prior termination of refugee status); *Romanishyn v. Gonzales*, 455 F.3d 175, 186 (3d Cir. 2006) (holding that refugee who adjusted status is subject to removal even though his refugee status was never terminated); *Kaganovich v. Gonzales*, 470 F.3d 894, 898 (9th Cir. 2006) (observing that "an alien who arrives in the United States as a refugee may be removed even if refugee status has never been terminated").

[1010] 8 CFR §207.9.

[1011] *Id.*

[1012] *Id.*

[1013] *See* "Becoming LPR Does Not Terminate Refugee Status, UNHCR Says," 80 *Interpreter Releases* 413 and Appendix III (Mar. 17, 2003). *See also Smriko v. Ashcroft*, 387 F.3d 279, 281 (3d Cir. 2004) (in remanding case to BIA, court suggests applicant's argument that despite his adjustment to LPR status he still retains his refugee status is supported by INA and legislative history).

CHAPTER 4
CONVENTION AGAINST TORTURE

A vivid, agonizing pain shot through my entire body as if a bolt of lightning had gone through me. Of all the beatings I have endured, I never felt anything to equal the instant of sheer pain produced by the impact of the rubber truncheon. It made every muscle in my body wince in sharp agony. It was something like the sensation produced when a dentist's drill strikes a nerve, but infinitely multiplied and spread over the entire nervous system. . . . "That fainting act won't get you anywhere," [Inspector Pick] was saying. "Those swipes behind the ear have been worked out by our greatest medical authorities. They are painful, I know, but you cannot faint or lose consciousness from them. . . . Get to work on him," he shouted. "Leave just enough of him to be questioned."*

4.1. The Implementing Legislation 260
4.2. Convention Against Torture—Key Provisions, U.S. Understandings, and Regulations 263
4.3. Procedures for Applying for Relief Under the Convention Against Torture 279

Another form of relief from removal is the protection of *nonrefoulement, i.e.*, nonreturn, under the United Nations Convention Against Torture and Other Cruel, Inhuman, or Degrading Treatment or Punishment (the Convention Against Torture, the Convention, or CAT).[1] The Convention Against Torture is a multilateral treaty that is intended not just to prevent torture, but to establish measures to eliminate torture and to compensate victims of torture. The United States signed the Convention on April 18, 1988, under President Ronald Reagan. Although the Senate adopted its resolution of advice and consent on October 27, 1990, the Convention did not take effect in the United States until November 20, 1994, one month after President Bill Clinton deposited the ratification with the U.N. Secretary General.[2]

The Convention Against Torture has become a safety net for individuals who do not qualify for asylum or withholding of removal. In many respects, the relief it provides is similar to withholding of removal. It prohibits the removal of an individual to a country where he or she would be tortured, but does not confer the possibility of adjustment of

---

* J. Karski, *Story of a Secret State* (1944). The passage is by Dr. Jan Karski, the late Professor Emeritus of Georgetown University, who was a courier for the Polish Underground during World War II, recounting one of his interrogations by the Gestapo.

[1] Convention Against Torture and Other Cruel, Inhuman or Degrading Treatment or Punishment, Dec. 10, 1984, 1465 U.N.T.S. 85 (entered into force June 26, 1987).

[2] *See* U.N. Doc. 571 Leg/SER. E/13, IV.9 (1995).

status to permanent residency. Nor does it confer derivative status on a spouse or minor children. It is, nevertheless, a valuable form of relief for individuals who may be barred from more traditional remedies such as asylum or withholding because of a criminal conviction or other bar. It is also valuable to individuals who are unable to establish that the persecution they fear is on account of their race, religion, nationality, membership in a particular social group, or political opinion.[3]

This chapter provides an overview of the protection available under the Convention Against Torture, the implementing legislation enacted in October 1998, the regulations that took effect in March 1999, and the policy memoranda issued by legacy Immigration and Naturalization Service (INS) General Counsel's Office, the Asylum Division, and the Executive Office for Immigration Review (EOIR).[4]

4.1. THE IMPLEMENTING LEGISLATION

On October 21, 1998, Article 3 of the Convention Against Torture was incorporated into U.S. domestic law when Congress passed and the President signed the Foreign Affairs Reform and Restructuring Act (FARRA).[5] Section 2242(a) of FARRA provides:

---

[3] *See* appx. 7C (chart comparing asylum, traditional withholding of removal, and Convention Against Torture relief); *see also Kalmalthas v. INS*, 251 F.3d 1279, 1283 (9th Cir. 2001) (noting that Convention Against Torture relief is both broader and narrower than a claim for asylum or withholding).

[4] For Expert Advice and Assistance on Convention Against Torture Claims, contact World Organization for Human Rights USA, 1725 K Street, N.W., Suite 610, Washington, DC 20006; phone (202) 296-5702; fax (202) 296-5704; e-mail: *woatusa@woatusa.org*; website: *www.humanrightsusa.org*.

[5] Foreign Affairs Reform and Restructuring Act of 1998 (FARRA), Pub. L. No. 105-277, div. G, 112 Stat. 2681, 2681-761 to 2681-854.

Section 2242 of FARRA provides:

"United States Policy With Respect to the Involuntary Return of Persons in Danger of Subjection to Torture"

> (a) Policy—It shall be the policy of the United States not to expel, extradite, or otherwise effect the involuntary return of any person to a country in which there are substantial grounds for believing the person would be in danger of being subjected to torture, regardless of whether the person is physically present in the United States.
>
> (b) Regulations—Not later than 120 days after the date of enactment of this Act, the heads of the appropriate agencies shall prescribe regulations to implement the obligations of the United States under Article 3 of the United Nations Convention Against Torture and Other Forms of Cruel, Inhuman or Degrading Treatment Punishment, subject to any reservations, understandings, declarations, and provisos contained in the United States Senate resolution of ratification of the Convention.
>
> (c) Exclusion of Certain Aliens—To the maximum extent consistent with the obligations of the United States under the Convention, subject to any reservations, understandings, declarations and provisos contained in the United States Senate resolution of ratification of the Convention, the regulations described in subsection (b) shall exclude from the protection of such regulations aliens described in section 241(b)(3)(B) of the Immigration and Nationality Act (8 USC 1231(b)(3)(B)).
>
> (d) Review and Construction—Notwithstanding any other provision of law, and except as provided in the regulations described in subsection (b), no court shall have jurisdiction to review the regulations adopted to implement this section, and nothing in this section shall be construed as providing any court jurisdiction to consider or review claims raised under the Convention or this section, or

continued

It shall be the policy of the United States not to expel, extradite, or otherwise effect the involuntary return of any person to a country in which there are substantial grounds for believing the person would be in danger of being subjected to torture, regardless of whether the person is physically present in the United States.

4.1.1. Regulations

FARRA required legacy INS, EOIR, and other government agencies to issue regulations implementing article 3 of the Convention Against Torture "[n]ot later than 120 days after the date of enactment" of FARRA[6] The regulations, however, would be subject to "any reservations, understandings, declarations, and provisos contained in the United States Senate resolution of the ratification of the Convention."[7] The regulations, issued on February 19, 1999, and later amended on December 6, 2000, set forth the procedures for applying for relief under the Convention.[8] In most cases, immigration judges have jurisdiction in the first instance to decide Convention Against Torture claims.

4.1.2. Possible Bars to Relief

FARRA mandated that "[t]o the maximum extent consistent with the obligations of the United States under the Convention" the regulations should exclude individuals barred from relief under the withholding of removal section of the Immigration and Nationality Act (INA).[9] Unlike the Refugee Convention and Protocol,[10] the Convention Against Torture does not contain any exceptions to relief, nor are any exceptions contained in U.S. Senate reservations, understandings, declarations, or provisos. Despite the lack of any exceptions, the regulations give a more precarious form of relief to individuals who are barred from withholding of removal.[11]

---

any other determination made with respect to the application of the policy set forth in subsection (a), except as part of the review of a final order of removal pursuant to section 242 of the Immigration and Nationality Act (8 USC §1252).

(e) Authority to Detain—Nothing in this section shall be construed as limiting the authority of the Attorney General to detain any person under any provision of law, including, but not limited to, any provision of the Immigration and Nationality Act.

(f) Definitions—

    (1) Convention Defined—In this section, the term "Convention" means the United Nations Convention Against Torture and Other Forms of Cruel, Inhuman or Degrading Treatment or Punishment, done at New York on December 10, 1984.

    (2) Same Terms as in Convention—Except as otherwise provided, the terms used in this section have the meanings given those terms in the Convention, subject to any reservations, understandings, declarations, and provisos contained in the United States Senate resolution of ratification of the Convention.

[6] *See* FARRA, *supra* note 5, at §2242(b), 112 Stat. 2681-822.

[7] *Id.*

[8] *See* this chapter, at 4.3.

[9] *See* FARRA, *supra* note 5, at §2242(c), 112 Stat. 2681-822.

[10] Convention Relating to the Status of Refugees, July 28, 1951, 189 U.N.T.S. 150 (entered into force Apr. 22, 1954); Protocol Relating to the Status of Refugees, 606 U.N.T.S. 267 (entered into force Oct. 4, 1967).

[11] *See* this chapter, at 4.3.2.

4.1.3. Judicial Review

FARRA permits judicial review of a Convention Against Torture claim, but only as part of a review of a final order of removal pursuant to §242 of the INA.[12] Arguably, this section of the legislation also permits a federal court to review the regulations implementing article 3.[13]

4.1.4. Detention

FARRA, moreover, in no way limits the attorney general's authority to detain individuals under the INA or any other provision of law. Individuals who have committed aggravated felonies or who are determined to be a threat to the security of the United States, therefore, may be subject to lengthy or indefinite detention despite being granted relief under the Convention.[14]

4.1.5. Definitions

Finally, and perhaps most importantly, FARRA provides that the terms used in the implementing legislation have the same meanings as the terms used in the Convention Against Torture, subject to any reservations, understandings, declarations, and provisos contained in the U.S. Senate resolution of ratification.[15] Thus, international law is increasingly becoming an important source for interpreting the new legislation and regulations.

4.1.6. Number of Cases Granted

Only four percent of CAT cases were granted by immigration courts in fiscal year 2006.[16] Nevertheless, it was a meaningful form of relief for the 578 individuals who might otherwise have been returned to their home countries.[17]

4.1.7. Prior Procedures for Relief Under the Convention

Prior to the passage of FARRA, both legacy INS and EOIR had taken the position that article 3 of the Convention Against Torture was not self-executing—meaning only that, absent implementing legislation, the treaty does not provide a rule that courts must enforce.[18] The Board of Immigration Appeals (BIA), in *Matter of H–M–V–*,[19] held that it

---

[12] *See* FARRA, *supra* note 5, at §2242(d), 112 Stat. 2681-822.

[13] *See* this chapter, at 4.3.4.

[14] *See* FARRA, *supra* note 5, at §2242(e), 112 Stat. 2681-822.

[15] *See* FARRA, *supra* note 5, at §2242(f), 112 Stat. 2681-822 to 2681-823.

[16] *See* U.S. Department of Justice, Executive Office for Immigration Review, Office of Planning, Analysis, & Technology, *FY 2006 Statistical Yearbook* (Feb. 2007), at M-1, available at www.usdoj.gov/eoir/statspub/fy06syb.pdf.

[17] *Id. See also Immigration Relief Under CAT for Serious Criminals and Human Rights Violators: Hearing Before the House Subcomm. on the Judiciary*, 108th Cong., 1st Sess. 45, Serial No. 34, at 11 (2003) (statement of C. Stewart Verdery, Asst. Secretary for Policy and Planning, Border and Transportation Security Directorate, U.S. Department of Homeland Security, estimating that 1,700 individuals had been granted CAT protection in the first four years after the implementing legislation was passed).

[18] *See, e.g., Foster v. Neilson*, 27 U.S. (2 Pet.) 253, 314 (1829), *overruled on other grounds by U.S. v. Percheman*, 32 U.S. 51 (1833).

[19] *Matter of H–M–V–*, 22 I&N Dec. 256 (BIA 1998).

lacked jurisdiction to adjudicate Convention Against Torture claims because there had been no legislation to implement article 3, no regulations had been promulgated with respect to article 3, and the U.S. Senate had declared that article 3 was not self-executing.[20]

Legacy INS, although taking the position that the Convention Against Torture was not self-executing, had remarked that the executive, as one of the political branches, may "act to protect rights a person may have under a treaty that is not self-executing."[21] As a result, legacy INS had established an informal process for presenting a claim under the Convention. That informal process ended on March 22, 1999, when the new regulations took effect.

4.2. CONVENTION AGAINST TORTURE—KEY PROVISIONS, U.S. UNDERSTANDINGS, AND REGULATIONS

For persons who fear being subjected to torture upon return to their home countries, the two most important provisions of the Convention Against Torture are article 1, which defines torture, and article 3, which sets forth the prohibition on returning an individual to torture. The Convention also provides for the establishment of a Committee Against Torture (Committee) that is made up of 10 experts and has the authority to hear claims between states that are parties to the Convention and claims by victims of a violation by a state party, but only if the state party recognizes the competence of the Committee to hear such claims.[22] To date, the United States has not recognized the competence of the Committee. Nevertheless, the case law of the Committee is a useful tool for interpreting, inter alia, a state's obligation under article 3 and the definition of torture.

> *Tip*—**U.S. Report to the United Nations Committee Against Torture**—As a state party to the Convention, the United States is required to report to the Committee on its compliance with the Convention. On May 6, 2005, the Department of State sent its second report to the Committee Against Torture, in which it reviewed U.S. efforts to comply with the Convention. The full text of the report is on the State Department website at *www.state.gov/g/drl/rls/45738.htm*. The 1999 report is also available, at *www.state.gov/www/global/human_rights/torture_index.html*.

Other significant provisions of the Convention include: article 2(1), the requirement that countries that are parties to the Convention take effective legislative, judicial, or other measures to prevent acts of torture in their territories; articles 2(2) and 2(3), the principles that torture cannot be justified by any exceptional circumstances, such as war or public emergency, nor may torture be justified if committed by an individual acting

---

[20] For an in-depth analysis of why article 3 should be considered to be self-executing, see K. Rosati, "United Nations Convention Against Torture: A Self-Executing Treaty that Prevents the Removal of Persons Ineligible for Asylum and Withholding of Removal," 26 *Denv. J. Int'l L. & Pol'y* 533–90 (1998).

[21] INS, *Basic Law Manual, U.S. Law and INS Refugee/Asylum Adjudications* (1994) at 11.

[22] *See* Convention Against Torture, *supra* note 1, arts. 17 to 24.

under an order from a superior officer or a public authority; article 4, the obligation to criminalize torture under domestic law; article 10, the duty to educate and inform law enforcement personnel, public officials, and others regarding the prohibition against torture; and articles 13 and 14, the obligation to provide methods of redress for victims of torture, including the right to compensation.

4.2.1. The Definition of Torture

The Convention Against Torture defines "torture" broadly as:

> any act by which severe pain or suffering, whether physical or mental, is intentionally inflicted on a person for such purposes as obtaining from him or a third person information or a confession, punishing him for an act he or a third person has committed or is suspected of having committed, or for any reason based on discrimination of any kind, when such pain or suffering is inflicted by or at the instigation of or with the consent or acquiescence of a public official or other person acting in an official capacity. It does not include pain or suffering arising only from, inherent in or incidental to lawful sanctions.[23]

Although the implementing legislation does not define torture, it specifically incorporates the Convention definition, subject to any U.S. Senate understanding or reservations.[24] The Convention definition is also found in the regulations issued by legacy INS and EOIR on February 19, 1999, at 8 CFR §§208.18(a)(1), 1208.18(a)(1).

The six basic elements of torture, detailed below, are:

- an intentional act;
- infliction of severe pain or suffering;
- under the custody or control of the offender;
- for a broad array of wrongful purposes;
- by or sanctioned by a public official;
- not arising out of lawful sanctions.

Intentional Act

The severe pain or suffering must be intentionally inflicted to meet the definition of torture. According to the regulations, "[i]n order to constitute torture, an act must be *specifically intended* to inflict severe physical or mental pain or suffering. An act that results in unanticipated or unintended severity of pain and suffering is not torture."[25] According to the BIA in *Matter of J–E–*, "specific intent" is defined as "intent to accomplish the precise criminal act that one is later charged with."[26] In contrast, "general intent" commonly "takes the form of recklessness . . . or negligence."[27] Moreover, the

---

[23] Convention Against Torture, *supra* note 1, art. 1.

[24] *See* FARRA, *supra* note 5, at §2242(f), 112 Stat. 2681-822 to 2681-823.

[25] 8 CFR §§208.18(a)(5), 1208.18(a)(5) (emphasis added).

[26] *Matter of J–E–*, 23 I&N Dec. 291, 301 (BIA 2002).

[27] *Id.* (finding that there is no evidence that Haitian authorities are intentionally and deliberately creating and maintaining harsh prison conditions in order to inflict torture, which appear to be a result of the

continued

CHAPTER 4 • CONVENTION AGAINST TORTURE

act itself need not be an affirmative act, but could be an omission, especially if the perpetrator has an affirmative duty to act. However, if there is no specific intent by authorities to inflict severe physical or mental pain or suffering, the claim will be denied.[28]

At least two courts have disagreed with the BIA's decision in *Matter of J–E–*. In *Zubeda v. Ashcroft*,[29] the Third Circuit noted that:

> Although the regulations require that the severe pain or suffering be 'intentionally inflicted,' we do not interpret this as a 'specific intent' requirement. Rather, we conclude that the Convention simply excludes severe pain and suffering that is the unintended consequence of an intentional act. The regulation does state: 'in order to constitute torture, an act must be specifically intended to inflict severe physical or mental pain or suffering.' [footnote omitted] However, the regulation immediately explains: [a]n act that results in unanticipated or unintended severity of pain and suffering is not torture.' The intent requirement therefore distinguishes between suffering that is the accidental result of an intended act, and suffering that is purposefully inflicted or the foreseeable consequence of deliberate conduct. However, this is not the same as requiring a specific intent to inflict suffering. . . . [R]equiring an alien to establish the specific intent of his/her persecutor could impose insurmountable obstacles to affording the very protections the community of nations sought to guarantee under the Convention Against Torture.

Likewise in *Lavira v. U.S. Attorney Gen.*,[30] the Third Circuit found that sending an HIV-positive prisoner to a disease-infested facility in Haiti can demonstrate a specific intent to torture on the part of the authorities. In that case, in addition to documentation of his HIV-positive status, the applicant submitted a detailed expert report on conditions in Haitian prisons. In at least two unpublished decisions, HIV-positive applicants have successfully argued that prison conditions in their home countries of Haiti and Cuba would amount to torture.[31]

In *Carry v. Holmes*,[32] the district court held that:

> In assessing intent, the appropriate question is not whether Haiti subjects detainees to indefinite detention with the specific intent to torture them, but whether Haitian

---

country's severe economic difficulties). *Accord Francois v. Gonzales*, 448 F.3d 645, 652 (3d Cir. 2006) (applicant failed to establish that prison conditions in Haiti constitute "torture"; citing with approval *Auguste v. Ridge*, 395 F.3d 123, 137 (3d Cir. 2005), which affirmed a district court's holding "that there must be some sort of underlying intentional direction of pain and suffering against a particular [applicant], more so than simply complaining of a general state of affairs"); *see also Al-Saher v. INS*, 268 F.3d 1143, 1147 (9th Cir. 2001) (noting beatings and burns inflicted by Iraqi officials were "specifically intended to inflict severe pain").

[28] *See Matter of J–E–*, 23 I&N Dec. at 300.

[29] *Zubeda v. Ashcroft*, 333 F.3d 463, 473–74 (3d Cir. 2003).

[30] *Lavira v. U.S. Attorney Gen.*, 478 F.3d 158, 170 (3d Cir. 2007).

[31] K. Musalo & M. Boyle, "Lesbian, Gay, Bisexual Transgender, and HIV Asylum Law," *Immigration & Nationality Law Handbook* 371, 386 (AILA 2007-08 Ed.).

[32] *Carry v. Holmes*, 1:02-cv-00369 (W.D.N.Y. July 22, 2003) at 23, available at *www.lexisnexis.com/practiceareas/immigration/pdfs/web426.pdf*.

officials intentionally, *i.e.*, deliberately or purposefully (as opposed to accidentally or negligently), inflict severe pain and suffering upon the detainees for the purpose of, inter alia, punishing them or intimidating them. See 8 C.F.R. §208.18(a)(1).

Infliction of Severe Pain or Suffering

The pain or suffering must be severe and may be either physical or mental. It does not include "lesser forms of cruel, inhuman or degrading treatment or punishment that do not amount to torture."[33] Sustained and severe beatings for a one-month period and being burned with cigarettes over an eight– to ten-day period is severe enough pain to meet the definition of torture.[34] Likewise, beatings, being forced to watch a rape, and threats that one's own wife will be raped amount to torture.[35] One court has held that forced sterilization would constitute torture under the CAT, and therefore an individual likely to be forcibly sterilized if removed qualifies for withholding under the CAT,[36] but simple deprivations of property are not included in the concept of torture.[37]

Physical Torture

Physical torture includes: beatings, burns, electrical shocks, exposure to excessive light or noise, sexual aggression, suspension, suffocation, and prolonged denial of sleep, food, hygiene, or medical assistance.[38] Rape is also increasingly recognized as a form of torture.[39]

---

[33] 8 CFR §§208.18(a)(2), 1208.18(a)(2).

[34] *Al-Saher v. INS*, 268 F.3d 1143, 1147 (9th Cir. 2001) (overturning BIA holding that Iraqi prisoner had not been tortured). *But see Ireland v. United Kingdom*, 2 Eur. Ct. H.R. 25 (1978) (finding that suspected terrorists who were subjected to wall standing, hooding, and constant loud hissing noise, and who were deprived of sleep, food, and drink by the British Army were subjected to inhuman and degrading treatment, but *not* torture; cited with approval in *Matter of J–E–*, 23 I&N Dec. 291, 298 (BIA 2002)).

[35] *Namo v. Gonzales*, 401 F.3d 453, 455 (6th Cir. 2005) (case remanded due to changed circumstances in Iraq).

[36] *Bi Zhu Lin v. Ashcroft*, 183 F. Supp. 2d 551, 553 (D. Conn. 2002) (noting that the immigration judge (IJ) found that forced sterilization was torture under the CAT). *But see Xiao v. Bd. of Immigration Appeals*, 165 Fed. Appx. 911, 914 (2d Cir. 2006) ("[I]t remains an open question whether forcible sterilizations may be recognized as torture.").

[37] *Jo v. Gonzales*, 458 F.3d 104, 109 (2d Cir. 2006) (finding that the regulations make clear that in order to come within the definition of torture, the mental anguish must have its origin in the treatment, actual or threatened, of a person).

[38] *See Torture and Other Cruel, Inhuman or Degrading Treatment or Punishment: Report of the Special Rapporteur*, U.N. ESCOR, Comm'n Hum. Rts., 41st Sess., ¶119, U.N. Doc. E/CN.4/1986/15 (1986); *see also Al-Saher v. INS*, 268 F.3d 1143, 1147 (9th Cir. 2001) (in reversing BIA, court held that beatings and burns suffered by an Iraqi prisoner amounted to torture as defined by Convention and regulations).

[39] *See Report of the Special Rapporteur on Violence Against Women, Its Causes and Consequences*, Comm'n Hum. Rts., 54th Sess., Provisional Agenda Item 9(a), ¶67, U.N. Doc. E/CN.4/1998/54 (1998); *see also Kioski v. Sweden*, Comm. No. 41/1996, *reported in Report of the Committee Against Torture*, U.N. GAOR, 51st Sess., Supp. No. 44, ¶9.6, U.N. Doc. A/51/44, at 86 (1996) (in which the Committee found substantial grounds for believing that a woman who had been the victim of past torture, including rape, would be subjected to torture if returned to Zaire). *But see Matter of J–E–*, 23 I&N Dec. 291 (BIA

continued

Mental Torture

Mental torture, according to the Senate in its resolution of advice and consent, includes:

prolonged mental harm caused by or resulting from: (1) the intentional infliction or threatened infliction of severe physical pain or suffering; (2) the administration or application, or threatened administration or application, of mind altering substances or other procedures calculated to disrupt profoundly the senses or the personality; (3) the threat of imminent death; or (4) the threat that another person will imminently be subjected to death, severe physical pain or suffering, or the administration or application of mind altering substances or other procedures calculated to disrupt profoundly the sense or personality.[40]

In dismissing an argument by a U.S. government attorney that assassination is not torture, the Seventh Circuit noted that "[e]ven if death itself is painless . . . the anticipation of it can be a source of acute mental anguish; if the threat of imminent albeit painless death were deliberately employed to cause such anguish, it would be a form of torture."[41] Torture of a U.S. citizen child, in the form of female genital mutilation (FGM), may also be the basis of a CAT claim for the noncitizen mother.[42]

Under the Custody or Control of the Offender

According to the regulations, "to constitute torture an act must be directed against a person in the *offender's* custody or physical control."[43] In most cases, an individual would be in the physical custody of his or her torturer. Arguably, individuals who are victims of widespread acts of barbarity, such as germ warfare or bombing campaigns, could contend that they were under the "control" of their torturers.[44]

For a Broad Array of Wrongful Purposes

There is no "on account of" requirement for Convention Against Torture relief as there is for asylum or traditional withholding of removal.[45] The Convention does require, however, that the torture be inflicted "for such purposes" as obtaining information or a confession, punishment, intimidation, coercion, or discrimination. It is important to note

---

2002) (indefinite detention, inhuman prison conditions, and police mistreatment of inmates in Haitian jails does not amount to torture).

[40] 136 Cong. Rec. S17491–92 (daily ed. Oct. 27, 1990). The regulations track verbatim the Senate understandings. *See* 8 CFR §§208.18(a)(4), 1208.18(a)(4).

[41] *Comollari v. Ashcroft*, 378 F.3d 694, 697 (7th Cir. 2004).

[42] *Nwaokolo v. Ashcroft*, 314 F.3d 303 (7th Cir. 2002) (finding BIA abused its discretion in denying motion to reopen).

[43] 8 CFR §§208.18(a)(6), 1208.18(a)(6) (emphasis added). *See Azanor v. Ashcroft*, 364 F.3d 1013, 1019 (9th Cir. 2004) (to qualify for CAT relief, an applicant need not show that she would likely face torture while under the custody or control of a public official, rather she may qualify for CAT by showing that she is under the custody and control of "private parties"); *Pascual-Garcia v. Ashcroft*, 73 Fed. Appx. 232, 234 (9th Cir. 2003) (holding that CAT relief does not require that torture occur while the victim is in the custody or control of the public official).

[44] *See also Comollari*, *supra* note 41, at 697 (questioning in dicta whether the victim of a sniper or car bomber would be under the custody or control of the offender).

[45] *See, e.g., Matter of S–V–*, 22 I&N Dec. 1306, 1311 (BIA 2000).

that the list is not exclusive, but indicates the type of motivation that typically underlies torture.[46] Torture based on a person's religion, ethnicity, duration of stay in the United States, and drug-related convictions are sufficient reasons for granting Convention Against Torture relief.[47] At least one commentator has suggested that the terms "intimidation" and "coercion" are such broad concepts that almost any reason for intentional torture would fall within these definitions.[48]

By or Sanctioned by a Public Official

To constitute "torture," the harm must be "inflicted by or at the instigation of or with the consent or acquiescence of a public official or any person acting in an official capacity."[49] One commentator has stated that this requirement "is perhaps the most significant limitation on Convention Against Torture relief, particularly when private groups such as organized private militias or 'death squads' are engaged in torture as a political weapon."[50]

Public Official or Person Acting in Official Capacity

As noted by the Senate, "[t]he Convention deals only with torture committed in the context of governmental authority, excluding torture that occurs as a wholly private act or, in terms more familiar in U.S. law, it applies to torture inflicted 'under color of law.'"[51] According to a decision by the Committee Against Torture, members of warring factions in Somalia, a country without a central government, "can fall within the phrase 'public officials or other persons acting in an official capacity,'" because, "de facto, [they] exercise certain prerogatives that are comparable to those normally exercised by legitimate governments."[52]

---

[46] *See* S. Exec. Rep. No. 101-30, at 14, 101st Cong., 2d Sess. 6 (1990) (report of the Senate Foreign Relations Committee recommending ratification of the Convention).

[47] *Matter of G–A–*, 23 I&N Dec. 366, 372 (BIA 2002) (an applicant's "criminal convictions in the United States, *however serious*, are not a bar to deferral of removal" under the Convention Against Torture) (emphasis added).

[48] *See* K. Rosati, "Finally! U.S. Law Implements Article 3 of the U.N. Convention Against Torture: An Analysis of the Legislation and Interim Regulations," 2 *Immigration & Nationality Law Handbook* 517, 526 (AILA 1999–2000 Ed.). *See also Camara v. Ashcroft*, 378 F.3d 361, 371 (4th Cir. 2004) (noting "the applicant need not prove the *reason* for torture") (emphasis in original). *But see Matter of J–E–*, 23 I&N Dec. 291, 300 (BIA 2002) (finding no evidence that Haitian government's practice of detaining all criminal deportees is for a "proscribed purpose").

[49] Convention Against Torture, *supra* note 1, art. 1. *See* 8 CFR §§208.18(a)(1), 1208.18(a)(1).

[50] *See* K. Rosati, *supra* note 48, at 522.

[51] *See* S. Exec. Rep. No. 101-30, *supra* note 46, at 14. *See also Khouzam v. Ashcroft*, 361 F.3d 161, 170–71 (2d Cir. 2004) (Egyptian police officers who torture suspects to extract confessions do so with consent or willful blindness of higher level government officials; overruling *Matters of Y–L–, A–G–, R–S–R–*, 23 I&N Dec. 270, 285 (AG 2002)).

[52] *Elmi v. Australia*, Comm. No. 120/1998, Committee Against Torture, 22d Sess. CAT/C/22/D/120/1998 (25 May 1999), ¶6.5, at 10. *But see Perinpanathan v. INS*, 310 F.3d 594, 599 (8th Cir. 2002) (torture by the LTTE, an illegal terrorist organization in Sri Lanka, cannot be considered torture by government officials).

Acquiescence

According to the Senate's understanding, to establish the acquiescence of a public official, the official must, "prior to the activity constituting torture, have awareness of such activity and thereafter breach his legal responsibility to intervene to prevent such activity."[53] "Awareness" includes "both actual knowledge and willful blindness."[54] Relying, in part, on the dictionary definition of "acquiescence," which is "silent or passive assent," the BIA held in *Matter of S–V–* that an applicant must do more than show that the government officials are aware of the activity but powerless to stop it.[55] The applicant must show that the government officials are "willfully accepting" of the guerrillas' torturous activities.[56] Unlike asylum, according to the BIA, Convention Against Torture relief does not extend to persons fleeing groups the government is "unable to control."[57]

The BIA's interpretation of the term "acquiescence" in *Matter of S–V–* has been rejected by a growing number of federal appeals courts. Governmental acquiescence has been defined to include governments who are *unable* and unwilling to protect their citizens and does not require actual knowledge of the tortuous conduct, only willful blindness.[58]

---

[53] 136 Cong. Rec. S17491–92 (daily ed. Oct. 27, 1990). *See also* 8 CFR §§208.18(a)(7), 1208.18(a)(7).

[54] *See* S. Exec. Rep. No. 101-30, *supra* note 46, at 9; *see also Cruz-Funez v. Gonzales*, 406 F.3d 1187, 1192 (10th Cir. 2005) (finding that "willful blindness" suffices to prove acquiescence); *Ontunez-Tursios v. Ashcroft*, 303 F.3d 341, 354 (5th Cir. 2002).

[55] *Matter of S–V–*, 22 I&N Dec. 1306, 1312 (BIA 2000) (denying motion to reopen to apply for Convention Against Torture relief by Colombian national who feared torture by guerrillas); *see also Mouawad v. Gonzales*, 479 F.3d 589, 596 (8th Cir. 2007) (holding that a government does not acquiesce to torture merely because it is aware of the torture but powerless to stop it, but finding IJ did not determine whether Hizballah commits acts of torture with consent of Lebanese government); *Chen v. Gonzales*, 470 F.3d 1131, 1142 (5th Cir. 2006) (finding the evidence did not compel the conclusion that Chinese officials will acquiesce to torture by snakeheads or money lenders).

[56] *Matter of S–V–*, *supra* note 55. *But see Cruz-Funez v. Gonzales*, 406 F.3d 1187, 1192 (10th Cir. 2005) (finding that willful acceptance is not required for a government to acquiesce); *Zheng v. Ashcroft*, 332 F.3d 1186, 1193 (9th Cir. 2003).

[57] *Matter of S–V–*, *supra* note 55 (citing *G.R.B. v. Sweden*, Comm. No. 83/1997, CAT/C/20/D/83/1997 (1997), a decision by the Committee Against Torture regarding fear of persecution by the Shining Path in Peru). *See also Menjivar v. Gonzales*, 416 F.3d 918, 923 (8th Cir. 2005) (upholding IJ's finding that the government did not acquiesce where police did not ignore threats and responding to the shooting by a gang within two hours); *Zeng v. Ashcroft*, 332 F.3d 1186, 1194–95 (9th Cir. 2003) (noting that correct inquiry is whether public officials would turn a blind eye to immigrant's torture by others); *Moshud v. Blackmun*, 68 Fed. Appx. 328 (3d Cir. 2003) (denying motion to reopen because FGM is illegal in Ghana and public officials have condemned the practice); *Ontunez-Turcios v. Ashcroft*, 303 F.3d 341, 354–55 (5th Cir. 2002) (holding that "willful blindness" is acquiescence under the CAT); *Matters of Y–L–, A–G–, R–S–R–*, 23 I&N Dec. 270, 280 (AG 2002) ("[V]iolence committed by individuals over whom the government has no reasonable control does not implicate the [Convention]."), *overruled in part on other grounds by Khouzam v. Ashcroft*, 361 F.3d 161, 170–71 (2d Cir. 2004) and *Zheng v. Ashcroft*, 332 F.3d 1186, 1196 (9th Cir. 2003).

[58] *See, e.g., Silva-Rengifo v. Att'y Gen. of US*, 473 F.3d 58, 65 (3d Cir. 2007) ("We cannot accept the Board's conclusion that the acquiescence that must be established under CAT requires actual knowledge of tortuous activity as required in *Matter of S–V–*"; an applicant need only show that the government was "willfully blind"); *Amir v. Gonzales*, 467 F.3d 921, 926 (6th Cir. 2006) (finding that *Matter continued*

In interpreting this term, a federal appeals court has held that actions by the Danish police, which included arresting the assailants, incarcerating them, and offering to admonish them when the victim asked that they not be punished further, did not constitute acquiescence.[59] In dicta, the court noted that under different circumstances, "such as where the authorities ignore or consent to severe domestic violence, the Convention [Against Torture] appears to compel protection for the victim."[60] If the immigration judge (IJ) or BIA fails to consider the question of whether a government acquiesces to torture, the case must be remanded.[61]

With regard to the requirement that the official have the "legal responsibility to intervene," it may be useful to look to the Convention itself, which includes numerous provisions directed at countries that are parties to the Convention to take effective legislative, judicial, or other measures to prevent acts of torture in their territories; to criminalize torture under domestic law; to educate and inform law enforcement personnel, public officials, and others regarding the prohibition against torture; and to review interrogation and custody procedures to prevent torture.[62] As one commentator has noted, "a violation of any of these international obligations, or a violation of any obligation found in domestic law, would arguably provide such a duty to intervene."[63] Rosati argues that if a government is unable or unwilling to control private groups that engage in torture, it has breached its legal responsibility to protect individuals within its jurisdiction and may, therefore, be acquiescing to the torture carried out by these groups.[64]

---

of S–V– directly conflicts with Congress's clear intent to include "willful blindness" in the definition of "acquiescence"); *Ornelas-Chavez v. Gonzales*, 458 F.3d 1052, 1060 (9th Cir. 2006) ("It is enough that public officials could have inferred the alleged torture was taking place, remained willfully blind to it, or simply stood by because of their inability or unwillingness to oppose it"; citing with approval *Zheng v. Ashcroft*, 332 F.3d 1186, 1194 (9th Cir. 2003)); *Ochoa v. Gonzales*, 406 F.3d 1166, 1172 (9th Cir. 2005) (finding that for relief under the CAT, an applicant "need only prove the government is aware of a third party's tortuous activity and does nothing to prevent it"); *Lopez-Soto v. Ashcroft*, 383 F.3d 228, 240 (4th Cir. 2004) (finding that "awareness includes both actual knowledge and willful blindness"); *Khouzam v. Ashcroft*, 361 F.3d 161, 171 (2d Cir. 2004) (finding that CAT relief does not require consent or approval to torturous conduct, only that government officials know of or remain willfully blind to an act and thereafter breach their legal responsibility to prevent it); *Ontunez-Tursios v. Ashcroft*, 303 F.3d 341 (5th Cir. 2002).

[59] *Ali v. Reno*, 237 F.3d 591, 598 (6th Cir. 2001).

[60] *Id.* (citing with approval, inter alia, B. Alexander, Note, "Convention Against Torture: A Viable Legal Alternative Remedy for Domestic Violence Victims," 15 *Am. U. Int'l L. Rev.* 895 (2000)).

[61] *Mouawad v. Gonzales*, 479 F.3d 589, 597 (finding IJ erred by failing to determine whether Hizballah commits acts of torture with consent of Lebanese government).

[62] *See* Convention Against Torture, *supra* note 1, arts. 2(1), 4, 10, and 11.

[63] K. Rosati, *supra* note 48, at 521–22.

[64] *Id.* at 522. *But see Matter of S–V–*, 22 I&N Dec. 1306, 1312 (BIA 2000) (holding that "acquiescence" does not include instances in which the government is unable to control the group that is feared, though the BIA's underlying definition of "acquiescence" is no longer good law in many jurisdictions, as shown *supra*, though it may continue to have weight in others).

Not Arising Out of Lawful Sanctions

The definition of torture does not include "pain or suffering arising only from, inherent in or incidental to lawful sanctions."[65] According to the Senate:

> the United States understands that "sanctions" include judicially imposed sanctions and other enforcement actions authorized by United States law or by judicial interpretation of such law. Nonetheless, the United States understands that a State Party could not through its domestic sanctions defeat the object and purposes of the Convention to prohibit torture.
>
> The United States understands that international law does not prohibit the death penalty, and does not consider this Convention to restrict or prohibit the United States from applying the death penalty consistent with the Fifth, Eighth, and/or Fourteenth Amendments to the Constitution of the United States, including any constitutional period of confinement prior to the imposition of the death penalty.[66]

The regulation regarding this issue provides: "Lawful sanctions include judicially imposed sanctions and other enforcement actions authorized by law, including the death penalty, but do not include sanctions that defeat the object and purpose of the [Convention] to prohibit torture."[67] Notably, the regulation omits the requirement, found in the Senate understanding, that the lawful sanction be "authorized by *United States* law."

The few cases construing this term have held that lawful sanctions do not include: imprisonment in a prison that is notorious for cruel and prolonged acts of torture against political opponents,[68] sustained beatings for one month and being burned with cigarettes over an eight- to ten-day period for misrepresenting religion and place of birth when applying for a job.[69]

Moreover, in order to determine if a sanction is lawful, the IJ or BIA must first determine if the sanction is permitted under the law of the country and whether the sanction is for a lawful purpose.[70] Lawful sanctions may include arrest and imprisonment for narcotics crimes in other countries.[71]

---

[65] Convention Against Torture, *supra* note 1, art. 1(1).

[66] 136 Cong. Rec. at S17491-92 and S36198-92 (daily ed. Oct. 27, 1990).

[67] 8 CFR §§208.18(a)(3), 1208.18(a)(3).

[68] *Hosseini v. Gonzales*, 471 F.3d 953, 960 (9th Cir. 2006) (finding that the Department of State country reports make clear that Iran's treatment of political opponents, including the MEK, goes far beyond what could reasonably be regarded as "lawful sanctions").

[69] *Al-Saher v. INS*, 268 F.3d 1143, 1147 (9th Cir. 2001); *see also Khouzam v. Ashcroft*, 361 F.3d 161, 169 (2d Cir. 2004) (in overturning the BIA, the court noted that "it would totally eviscerate the CAT to hold that once someone is accused of a crime it is a legal impossibility for any abuse inflicted on that person to constitute torture").

[70] *See, e.g., Habtemicael v. Ashcroft*, 370 F.3d 774, 781 (8th Cir. 2004) (in remanding the CAT claim for further fact finding, the court noted that the IJ made no findings as to whether the rebel group [the EPLF] had the status of a recognized government when the applicant was forced into its service or whether it had the authority to impress an Ethiopian citizen into military service against the Ethiopian government); *Carry v. Holmes, supra* note 32, at 20–22 (in denying government's motion to dismiss, the court noted that "there is nothing in the record to support the BIA's determination that indefinite detention of criminal deportees is permitted under Haitian law or that detention is being implemented

continued

As one commentator has noted, if the lawful sanctions exception is construed too broadly, it could be used to exclude brutal and torturous forms of punishment, such as stoning for adultery convictions.[72] Rosati asserts that to avoid the circular reasoning that the imposition of *any* lawful sanction would not defeat the object and purpose of the Convention because it is lawful and, therefore, outside of the definition of torture, it is necessary to determine whether the sanction would be authorized by U.S. law.[73] Because 8 CFR §§208.18(a)(3), 1208.18(a)(3) omit this requirement, which is found in the Senate understanding, it could also be argued that the regulations are *ultra vires*. With regard to the death penalty, Rosati notes:

> [I]f the method in which execution is conducted in another country is particularly barbarous or causes extreme pain and suffering, or if the imposition of death is not proportional to the crime committed, or if the death penalty is imposed without basic due process provided, advocates can argue that the imposition of the penalty in those circumstances constitutes torture.[74]

4.2.2. *Nonrefoulement* (Nonreturn) Provision

The *nonrefoulement* (nonreturn) provision in the Convention Against Torture prohibits, in absolute terms, the return of an individual to a country where he or she is in danger of being tortured. That provision states:

> No State Party shall expel, return (refouler) or extradite a person to another State where there are substantial grounds for believing that he or she would be in danger of being subjected to torture.[75]

This section will examine the following criteria for invoking the *nonrefoulement* provision:

- "More likely than not" standard
- Prospective only
- No internal relocation option
- Evidence to support claim
- Torture only
- No bars to protection

---

for a lawful purpose"). *But see Cadet v. Bulger*, 377 F.3d 1173, 1193 (11th Cir. 2004) (finding that the district court did not err in concluding that indefinite detention of criminal deportees in Haiti is lawful government sanction and not CAT-prohibited torture).

[71] *McDaniel v. INS*, 142 F. Supp. 2d 219, 224 (D. Conn. 2001) (finding the prosecution under Decree 33 in Nigeria does not amount to torture).

[72] *See* K. Rosati, *supra* note 48, at 524.

[73] *Id.*

[74] K. Rosati, *supra* note 48, at 525.

[75] Convention Against Torture, *supra* note 1, art. 3(1).

"More Likely Than Not" Standard

Both the Convention and implementing legislation require that there be "substantial grounds for believing [the person] would be in danger of being subjected to torture."[76] In interpreting this provision, the Senate, in its resolution of advice and consent, determined that "substantial grounds" means an individual must demonstrate it is "more likely than not that he [or she] would be tortured."[77] The regulations, similarly, place the burden on the individual to meet the "more likely than not" standard.[78] This is the same standard applied in withholding of removal claims.[79] In an unusual case in which an individual feared more than one entity in his home country, the Third Circuit held that the individual "is entitled to CAT protection if he is able to demonstrate that the cumulative probability of torture by the two entities exceeds 50%."[80] The attorney general has held that the "more likely than not" standard cannot be met by merely stringing together a series of suppositions where the evidence does not show that each step in the hypothetical chain of events is more likely than not to happen.[81] The Committee Against Torture has stated that the risk of torture "must be assessed on grounds that go beyond mere theory or suspicion," but "the risk does not have to meet the test of being highly probable."[82]

Prospective Only

Unlike asylum and traditional withholding of removal relief, which provide protection for individuals who have suffered past persecution, the Convention Against Torture protects individuals from future torture only.[83] Nevertheless, past torture is probative of whether an individual may be subjected to torture in the future. The regulations, therefore, specifically provide that "all evidence relevant to the possibility of future

---

[76] *See* id.; FARRA, *supra* note 5, at §2242(a), 112 Stat. 2681-822.

[77] 136 Cong. Rec. at S. 17492 (daily ed., Oct. 27, 1990).

[78] *See* 8 CFR §§208.16(c)(2), 1208.16(c)(2). *See also Berishaj v. Ashcroft*, 378 F.3d 314, 332 (3d Cir. 2004) (in rejecting a CAT claim, court noted there was "scant evidence" that it would be more likely than not that the applicant would be tortured upon return to Montenegro); *Cadet v. Bulger*, 377 F.3d 1173, 1180 (11th Cir. 2004); *Elien v. Ashcroft*, 364 F.3d 392, 398 (1st Cir. 2004); *Perinpanathan v. INS*, 310 F.3d 594, 599 (8th Cir. 2002) (burden of proof is on the applicant to establish it is more likely than not he or she would be tortured in proposed country of removal).

[79] *See Matter of M–B–A–*, 23 I&N Dec. 474 (BIA 2002) (evidence presented regarding the enforcement of Decree 33 in Nigeria was insufficient to establish that it was more likely than not the applicant would be tortured upon return); *Matter of J–E–*, 23 I&N Dec. 291, 303 (BIA 2002) (evidence of isolated acts of torture in Haitian prisons is insufficient to meet burden of proof).

[80] *Kamara v. Att'y General of the United States*, 420 F.3d 202, 213–14 (3d Cir. 2005).

[81] *Matter of J–F–F–*, 23 I&N Dec. 912, 917-18 (AG 2006) (overturning BIA's grant of deferral of removal under the CAT to a mentally ill man from the Dominican Republic convicted of rape).

[82] *A.A. v. Switzerland*, Comm. No. 268/2005, ¶8.3, CAT/C/38/D/268/2005 (May 11, 2007).

[83] *See, e.g., Niang v. Gonzales*, 422 F.3d 1187, 1202 (10th Cir. 2005) (finding that although past torture is a relevant consideration, it is only one factor in the assessment); *El Himri v. Ashcroft*, 378 F.3d 932, 938 (9th Cir. 2004) (in rejecting a CAT claim, the court noted that most of the violence against Palestinians in Kuwait ended when the constitutional government returned to Kuwait).

torture shall be considered, including, but not limited to . . . [e]vidence of past torture inflicted upon the applicant."[84]

No Internal Relocation Option

Despite the requirement that the torture feared must be by or at least sanctioned by a public official, an individual who fears torture must also address the issue of whether he or she could not relocate to another part of his or her home country where he or she is not likely to be tortured.[85] The Committee Against Torture has considered the following factors in determining whether an individual has an internal relocation option: the individual had to leave his or her native area, a new location inside his or her country did not prove secure, and indications that the individual was being sought by police in his or her home country.[86]

Evidence to Support Claim

As with asylum and traditional withholding of removal claims, an individual's testimony alone, if credible, may be sufficient to sustain the burden of proof without corroboration.[87] Likewise, the burden of proof is on the individual.[88] As noted above, the individual's burden of proof is "to establish that it is more likely than not he or she would be tortured if removed to the proposed country of removal."[89]

Credibility

An individual's credibility is an increasingly contested part of asylum and withholding of removal claims and, not surprisingly, is also an issue in Convention Against Torture claims. A past negative credibility determination in an asylum claim, however, will not necessarily carry over into a Convention Against Torture claim.[90] Nevertheless, some

---

[84] 8 CFR §§208.16(c)(3)(i), 1208.16(c)(3)(i). *See also Kioski v. Sweden*, Comm. No. 41/1996, *reported in Report of the Committee Against Torture*, U.N. GAOR, 51st Sess., Supp. No. 44, ¶9.3, U.N. Doc. A/51/44, at 86 (1996) (in which the Committee considered evidence of past detention and torture in finding that a woman from Zaire would be in danger of being subjected to torture upon return).

[85] *See* 8 CFR §§208.16(c)(3)(ii), 208.16(c)(2), 1208.16(c)(3)(ii), and 1208.16(c)(2); *see also Ramirez-Peyro v. Gonzales*, 477 F.3d 637, 641 (8th Cir. 2007) (finding the BIA could not engage in fact finding where the IJ made no specific findings about the geographic reach of the Juarez Drug Cartel in Mexico).

[86] *Alan v. Switzerland*, Comm. No. 21/1995, Supp. No. 44, ¶11.4, U.N. Doc. A/51/44, at 74–75 (1996) (finding, based on the evidence, that it was not likely that a "safe" area existed for the individual in Turkey).

[87] 8 CFR §§208.16(c)(2), 1208.16(c)(2). *See also Matter of J–E–*, 23 I&N Dec. 291, 302 (BIA 2002).

[88] 8 CFR §§208.16(c)(2), 1208.16(c)(2).

[89] 8 CFR §§208.16(c)(2), 1208.16(c)(2).

[90] *See Ramsameachire v. Ashcroft*, 357 F.3d 169, 184 (2d Cir. 2004); *Zubeda v. Ashcroft*, 333 F.3d 463, 476 (3d Cir. 2003) (noting that the "taint of the earlier adverse credibility determination" should not be allowed to "bleed through" to the CAT claim); *Camara v. Ashcroft*, 378 F.3d 361, 371–72 (4th Cir. 2004) (holding that the adverse credibility determination would not necessarily defeat the applicant's CAT claim where the applicant provided independent evidence that she would be tortured upon return); *Sivakaran v. Ashcroft*, 368 F.3d 1028, 1028 (8th Cir. 2004) (noting that the IJ's adverse credibility determination and adverse decisions on asylum and withholding are not determinative of the CAT claim); *Kalmalthas v. INS*, 251 F3d 1279, 1281 (9th Cir. 2001) (in vacating the BIA's denial of a motion to reopen, the court found that "country conditions alone can play a decisive role in granting relief under

continued

courts have found that the negative credibility determination in asylum could be used to deny a CAT claim.[91]

> *Tip*—The REAL ID Act changed how credibility determinations are made in nonasylum cases, including CAT claims. INA §240(c)(4)(C) allows the IJ to consider the totality of the circumstances in assessing an applicant's credibility, including demeanor, candor, plausibility, inconsistencies, and falsehoods (without regard to whether they go to the heart of the claim).

The Committee Against Torture has addressed credibility in numerous decisions. The Committee has found, for example, that "complete accuracy is seldom to be expected by victims of torture" and that inconsistencies in the presentation of the facts that are not material do not raise doubts about the general veracity of the claim.[92] With regard to claims of rape or sexual abuse, the Committee has found that it is reasonable for a victim to delay mentioning these grounds.[93] The Committee has stated: "It is well known that the loss of privacy and prospect of humiliation based on revelation alone of the acts concerned may cause both men and women to withhold the fact that they have been subjected to rape and/or other forms of sexual abuse until it appears absolutely necessary."[94] The Committee has also held that "it is not necessary that all the facts invoked by [the individual] should be proved; it is sufficient that the Committee should consider them to be sufficiently substantiated and reliable."[95]

All Evidence Relevant to the Possibility of Torture

In determining whether substantial grounds exist, *i.e.*, whether torture is more likely than not, the Convention Against Torture permits adjudicators to take into account "all relevant considerations including, where applicable, the existence in the State concerned of a consistent pattern of gross, flagrant or mass violations of human rights."[96]

---

the Convention," and the BIA failed to consider documentation of widespread torture against Tamil males in Sri Lanka); *Mansour v. INS*, 230 F.3d 902, 908 (7th Cir. 2000) (in vacating the BIA's denial of a motion to reopen by an Assyrian Christian from Iraq, the court noted, "[W]e are not comfortable with allowing a negative credibility determination in the asylum context to wash over the torture claim."). *But see Perinpanathan v. INS*, 310 F.3d 594, 599 (8th Cir. 2002) (finding that the applicant's lack of credibility in conjunction with his failure to document the reasons why he believed he would be tortured eliminated his eligibility for CAT relief).

[91] *Switzerland*, Comm. No. 268/2005, ¶8.3, CAT/C/38/D/268/2005 (May 11, 2007). *See, e.g.*, *Niang v. Gonzales*, 422 F.3d 1187, 1202 (10th Cir. 2005) (holding that "[h]ere, our review of Ms. Niang's CAT claim is controlled by the permissible finding that she is untruthful").

[92] *See, e.g.*, *Kioski v. Sweden*, Comm. No. 41/1996, *reported in Report of the Committee Against Torture*, U.N. GAOR, 51st Sess., Supp. No. 44, ¶9.3, U.N. Doc. A/51/44, at 86 (1996); *Tala v. Sweden*, Comm. No. 43/1996, Supp. No. 44, ¶10.3, U.N. Doc. A/51/44 at 62 (1996); *Alan v. Switzerland*, Comm. No. 21/1995, Supp. No. 44, ¶11.3, U.N. Doc. A/51/44, at 74 (1996).

[93] *V.L. v. Switzerland*, Comm. No. 262/2005, ¶8.8, CAT/C/37/D/262/2005 (Jan. 22, 2007).

[94] *Id.*

[95] *Aemei v. Switzerland*, Comm. No. 34/1995, Supp. No. 44, ¶9.6, U.N. Doc. A/52/44, at 78 (1997).

[96] Convention Against Torture, *supra* note 1, art. 3(2).

The regulations contain a similar, though somewhat expanded provision that requires the adjudicator, in assessing whether it is more likely than not that an individual will be tortured, to consider "all evidence relevant to the possibility of future torture," including but not limited to:

- evidence of past torture inflicted upon the individual;
- evidence that the individual could relocate to a part of the country of removal where he or she is not likely to be tortured;
- evidence of gross, flagrant, or mass violations of human rights within the country of removal; and
- other relevant evidence regarding conditions in the country of removal.[97]

As one court has noted, "country conditions alone can play a decisive role in granting relief under the Convention."[98] If the IJ or BIA fails to consider all evidence relevant to the possibility of future torture, the appropriate course of action is for a reviewing court to remand the case.[99] On occasion, courts have found that the record compelled the conclusion that the applicant would more likely than not face torture if returned to his or her country.[100] Notably, the absence of a pattern of gross, flagrant, or mass violations of human rights does not preclude an individual from Convention Against Torture protection.[101] However, general evidence of a country's human rights violations does not support a grant of relief under CAT if neither the general evidence nor particularized evidence concerning the applicant's own case demonstrate that the applicant is personally more likely than not to suffer torture upon return.[102]

The Committee Against Torture assesses evidence of past torture and evidence of gross, flagrant, or mass human rights violations. In reaching its decisions, it has considered, inter alia:

- the position of the United Nations High Commissioner for Refugees (UNHCR);[103]
- the U.S. Department of State Country Reports on Human Rights Practices;[104]

---

[97] *See* 8 CFR §§208.16(c)(3)(i)–(iv), 1208.16(c)(3)(i)–(iv); *see also Mapouya v. Gonzales*, 487 F.3d 396, 415 (finding the IJ erred by not addressing these four factors in assessing a CAT claim from Republic of Congo).

[98] *Kalmalthas v. INS*, 251 F.3d 1279, 1281 (9th Cir. 2001) (holding that BIA erred in denying motion to reopen based on previous asylum denial and negative credibility determination).

[99] *Mostafa v. Ashcroft*, 395 F.3d 622, 625-26 (6th Cir. 2005) (finding that the BIA failed to give adequate consideration to conditions in Iran and country condition reports submitted by the applicant).

[100] *See, e.g., Ali v. Achem*, 468 F.3d 462, 472–73 (7th Cir. 2006) (finding that a CAT applicant from Somalia would more likely than not face torture upon return, but remanding to the BIA to determine whether the torture would be at the instigation of or with the consent or acquiescence of a public official).

[101] *Matter of J–E–*, 23 I&N Dec. 291, 303 (BIA 2002).

[102] *Mu Xiang Lin v. DOJ*, 432 F.3d 156, 160 (2d Cir. 2005).

[103] *See Kioski v. Sweden*, Comm. No. 41/1996, *reported in Report of the Committee Against Torture*, U.N. GAOR, 51st Sess., Supp. No. 44, ¶9.5, U.N. Doc. A/51/44, at 86 (1996); *C.T. and K.M. v. Sweden*, Comm. No. 279/2005, ¶¶5.3 and 7.7, CAT/C/37/D/279/2005 (Dec. 7, 2006).

- reports by the United Nations Commission on Human Rights;[105]
- reports by Human Rights Watch;[106]
- ratification of the Convention Against Torture by the proposed country of return;[107]
- acts committed outside the country of origin;[108]
- medical evidence indicating the individual suffers from post-traumatic stress disorder (PTSD) and physical after-effects of past torture;[109] and
- publicity surrounding a particular case that increases the likelihood of torture upon return.[110]

Similarly, in the growing number of cases in the United States, courts have relied upon the following:

- the U.S. Department of State Country Reports on Human Rights Practices;[111]
- human rights reports by nongovernmental organizations (NGOs), such as Iranian Christians International;[112]
- State Department travel warnings;[113]
- State Department letter regarding whether failed asylum-seekers are subjected to torture;[114]
- reports from Bureau for International Narcotics and Law Enforcement of the Department of State regarding police corruption and abuses;[115]

---

[104] *See Tapia Paez v. Sweden*, Comm. No. 39/1996, Supp. No. 44, ¶7.2, U.N. Doc. A/52/44, at 89 (1997); *Dar v. Norway*, Comm. No. 249/2004, ¶2.5, CAT/C/38/D/249/2004 (May 16, 2007).

[105] *See Aemei v. Switzerland*, Comm. No. 34/1995, Supp. No. 44, ¶9.9, U.N. Doc. A/52/44, at 79 (1997).

[106] *See Tapia Paez v. Sweden*, Comm. No. 39/1996, Supp. No. 44, ¶3.2, U.N. Doc. A/52/44, at 87 (1997).

[107] *See Alan v. Switzerland*, Comm. No. 21/1995, Supp. No. 44, ¶11.5, U.N. Doc. A/51/44 at 75 (1996) (finding that despite Turkey's ratification of the Convention Against Torture, the practice of torture is still systematic in Turkey).

[108] *See Aemei v. Switzerland*, Comm. No. 34/1995, Supp. No. 44, ¶9.5, U.N. Doc. A/52/44, at 78 (1997) (individual was active in an illegal and dissident political organization in Switzerland that was monitored by the Iranian secret police); *El Rgeig v. Switzerland*, Comm. No. 280/2005, ¶¶5.3, 7.4, CAT/C/37/D/280/2005 (Nov. 30, 2006) (individual engaged in public demonstrations against Libya while in Switzerland).

[109] *See El Rgeig v. Switzerland*, Comm. No. 280/2005, ¶7.4, CAT/C/37/D/280/2005 (Nov. 30, 2006).

[110] *See Elmi v. Australia*, Comm. No. 120/1998, CAT/C/22/D/120/1998 (May 25, 1998), ¶6.8, at 10.

[111] *Hosseini v. Gonzales*, 471 F.3d 953, 960 (9th Cir. 2006) (relying on Department of State reports for Iran); *Zewdie v. Ashcroft*, 381 F.3d 804, 806 (8th Cir. 2004); *Perinpanathan v. INS*, 310 F.2d 594, 599 (8th Cir. 2002); *Al-Saher v. INS*, 268 F.3d 1143, 1147 (9th Cir. 2001); *Mansour v. INS*, 230 F.3d 902, 907–08 (7th Cir. 2000); *Matter of G–A–*, 23 I&N Dec. 366, 369 (BIA 2002).

[112] *Matter of G–A–*, *supra* note 111, at 369.

[113] *Id.* Travel warnings may be found at *www.travel.state.gov*.

[114] *Perinpanathan v. INS*, 310 F.3d 594, 599 (8th Cir. 2002) (the State Department letter concluded that several countries and UNHCR have monitored the return of thousands of Sri Lankans who had sought asylum, and that there was no evidence that the returnees have been tortured).

- the presence of international oversight or intervention by the International Committee for the Red Cross or UNHCR;[116]
- United Nations Committee Against Torture decisions, considered to be advisory only;[117]
- experts on judicial and penal system and the use of torture by police in the applicant's home country;[118]
- the lack of harm or threats to applicant on voluntary visits to home country;[119] and
- opinions of other governments adjudicating torture claims.[120]

Torture Only

The *nonrefoulement*, or nonreturn, provision of the Convention Against Torture protects individuals who would be subjected to "torture."[121] It does not apply in situations where individuals fear lesser forms of harm such as cruel, inhuman, or degrading treatment or punishment. Individuals fearing lesser forms of harm may qualify for asylum or withholding of removal if the harm they fear falls within the definition of persecution.[122] U.S. law and regulations similarly limit Convention Against Torture protection to individuals who would be tortured upon return.[123]

No Bars to Protection

Unlike asylum and withholding of removal, there are no bars to relief under the Convention Against Torture. If an individual demonstrates that there are "substantial grounds for believing [he or she] would be in danger of being subjected to torture," in a particular country, the individual cannot be returned there.[124]

---

[115] *Matters of Y–L–, A–G–, R–S–R–*, 23 I&N Dec. 270, 282 (AG 2002), *overruled in part on other grounds by Khouzam v. Ashcroft*, 361 F.3d 161, 170–71 (2d Cir. 2004) and *Zheng v. Ashcroft*, 332 F.3d 1186, 1196 (9th Cir. 2003). The latest report may be found at *www.state.gov/g/inl/rls/nrcrpt/2001/c6085.htm*.

[116] *Matter of G–A–*, *supra* note 111, at 371; *Matter of J–E–*, 23 I&N Dec. 291, 301 (BIA 2002).

[117] *Matter of S–V–*, 22 I&N Dec. 1306, 1313 n.1 (BIA 2000).

[118] *Khouzam v. Ashcroft*, 361 F.3d 161, 169 (2d Cir. 2004).

[119] *Matters of Y–L–, A–G–, R–S–R–*, 23 I&N Dec. 270 (AG 2002), *overruled in part on other grounds by Khouzam v. Ashcroft*, 361 F.3d 161, 170–71 (2d Cir. 2004) and *Zheng v. Ashcroft*, 332 F.3d 1186, 1196 (9th Cir. 2003).

[120] *Matter of J–E–*, *supra* note 116, at 297 (noting while these opinions are not binding, they are instructive).

[121] *See* Convention Against Torture, *supra* note 1, art. 3.

[122] *See* ch. 2.4.5.

[123] *See* FARRA, *supra* note 5, at §2242(a), 112 Stat. 2681-822; 8 CFR §§208.16(c)(2), 208.17(a), 1208.16(c)(2), and 1208.17(a).

[124] Convention Against Torture, *supra* note 1, art. 3(1). *See, e.g., Tebourski v. France*, Comm. No. 300/2006 ¶8.2, CAT/C/38/D/300/2006, (May 11, 2006) (individual convicted of terrorism charge in France should not have been deported to Tunisia, despite France's claim that he was a danger to domestic public order); *Tapia Paez v. Sweden*, Comm. No. 39/1996, Supp. No. 44, ¶14.5, U.N. Doc. A/52/44, at 94 (1997) (despite the denial of asylum to this former member of the Shining Path in Peru, the Committee found that "[t]he nature of the activities in which the person concerned engaged cannot be a material

continued

The implementing legislation, which was enacted on October 21, 1998, contains a provision requiring that the regulations implementing article 3 of the Convention exclude individuals who fall within the bars described in §241(b)(3)(B) of the INA, but only "to the maximum extent consistent with the obligations of the United States under the Convention."[125] Since there are no bars under the Convention or under any U.S. reservations, understandings, declarations, or provisos, advocates believed that this section would have no substantive effect. Nevertheless, legacy INS, in drafting the regulations, devised a process whereby individuals who would be subjected to torture are, in fact, barred from withholding of removal under the Convention Against Torture if they are barred under §241(b)(3) of the INA.[126] Such individuals are entitled to only the more precarious form of relief known as deferral of removal.[127]

4.3. Procedures for Applying for Relief Under the Convention Against Torture

4.3.1. Who Is Eligible to Apply

Individuals Physically Present

Under the Convention Against Torture regulations issued in February 1999, individuals physically present in the United States who are subject to various types of removal procedures are permitted to apply for relief under the Convention if they fear they will be subjected to torture upon return.[128] Unlike asylum, an individual cannot apply affirmatively for relief under the Convention Against Torture.[129] Only IJs, the BIA, or federal courts can grant relief under the Convention Against Torture.

Individuals subject to expedited removal, reinstatement of removal, or administrative removal for aggravated felonies are also permitted to apply for relief under the Convention Against Torture. Their claims are initially screened by an asylum officer.[130]

Individuals Not Physically Present

According to the implementing legislation, it is "the policy of the United States not to expel, extradite, or otherwise effect the involuntary return of any person to a country in

---

consideration when making a determination under Article 3"); *Khouzam v. Ashcroft*, 361 F.3d 161, 164 (2d Cir. 2004) (noting evidence of a past crime is not a bar to deferral of removal); *Vukmirovic v. Ashcroft*, 362 F.3d 1247, 1253 (9th Cir. 2004) (noting that even if the applicant was found to be a persecutor, he would be eligible for deferral of removal under CAT); *Matter of G–A–*, 23 I&N Dec. 366, 368 (BIA 2002) (an applicant's "criminal convictions in the United States, *however serious*, are not a bar to deferral of removal" under the Convention Against Torture) (emphasis added).

[125] *See* FARRA, *supra* note 5, at §2242(c), 112 Stat. 2681-822.

[126] *See* 8 CFR §§208.16(d)(2), 1208.16(d)(2).

[127] *See* 8 CFR §§208.17, 1208.17, and this chapter, at 4.3.2.

[128] See this chapter at 4.2.1 and 4.2.2 for an overview of the definition of torture and criteria for establishing relief under the Convention.

[129] *See* INS Memorandum, J. Langlois, "Implementation of Amendments to Asylum and Withholding of Removal Regulations, Effective March 22, 1999" (Mar. 18, 1999), at 6.

[130] *See* this chapter, at 4.3.7.

which there are substantial grounds for believing the person would be in danger of being subjected to torture, *regardless of whether the person is physically present in the United States.*"[131] The regulations issued by legacy INS and EOIR after the passage of FARRA only address procedures for individuals physically present in the United States. According to legacy INS, FARRA required the implementation of only article 3 of the Convention, which the agency reasoned, like article 33 of the Refugee Convention, does not extend to individuals outside of the United States. As justification for this position, legacy INS cited *Sale v. Haitian Centers Council, Inc.*[132] Legacy INS stated, however, that individuals interdicted in international waters will be screened for Convention Against Torture claims and will not be returned if they would be subjected to torture upon return. In addition, it appears that at least some individuals released from the Guantanamo prison facility who fear they will be tortured in their home countries have been sent to third countries by the United States.[133]

Diplomatic Assurances

The most controversial provision of the regulations implementing article 3 of the Convention is the provision allowing the attorney general, deputy attorney general, or the "INS Commissioner" (as the regulation was written prior to the creation of the Department of Homeland Security (DHS)) to determine, in consultation with the secretary of state, whether assurances from the proposed country of removal are sufficiently reliable to allow an individual's removal to that country.[134]

The first reported case in which diplomatic assurances were given was that of Hani Abdel Rahim Sayegh, a national of Saudi Arabia who was suspected of involvement in the bombing of Khobar Towers, a U.S. military complex in Saudi Arabia.[135] The Saudi government provided assurances that Sayegh would not be tortured if returned to Saudi Arabia, though he did face trial there and execution by beheading if convicted.[136] As a result of these assurances, Sayegh was returned to Saudi Arabia.

Once assurances are provided, an individual's claim for protection under the Convention Against Torture must not be considered further by an IJ, the BIA, or an asylum officer.[137] The

---

[131] FARRA, *supra* note 5, at §2242(a), 112 Stat. 2681-822 (emphasis added).

[132] *Sale v. Haitian Centers Council, Inc.*, 509 U.S. 155 (1993).

[133] T. Golden, "Chinese Leave Guantanamo for Albanian Limbo," *N.Y. Times*, June 10, 2007, at sec. 1, p. 1 (five Muslim men from the Uighur ethnic minority in Western China were found to pose no threat to the United States and released from Guantanamo prison in Cuba. They have been sent to Albania and are currently living in a refugee center there).

[134] *See* 8 CFR §§208.18(c), 1208.18(c). References to the legacy INS "Commissioner" after March 1, 2003, unless otherwise specified in the regulations, mean the director of USCIS, the commissioner of U.S. Customs and Border Protection (CBP), and the assistant secretary for U.S. Immigration and Customs Enforcement (ICE). 8 CFR §1.1(d).

[135] "Khobar Probe Figure Facing Deportation," *Washington Post*, Oct. 5, 1999, at p. A-10.

[136] *Id.*

[137] 8 CFR §§208.18(c)(3), 1208.18(c)(3).

IJ (and presumably the BIA) may, however, adjudicate any other pending applications, including asylum and withholding of removal under §241(b)(3) of the INA.[138]

At least one court has held that a CAT applicant must be provided the opportunity to challenge the reliability of diplomatic assurances.[139] In *Khouzam v. Hogan*, the U.S. District Court for the Middle District of Pennsylvania held that because the government had not provided the applicant with an opportunity to challenge the diplomatic assurances and had not provided any evidence to support its decision, the court would not reject the due process claims as barred by the political question doctrine.[140]

In a 2004 report on CAT, the Congressional Research Service (CRS) noted that although the use of diplomatic assurances did not appear to conflict with U.S. obligations under CAT, the United States is required under customary international law to exercise appropriate discretion in its use of diplomatic assurance.[141] The CRS report further states: "It could be argued, for example, that if a country demonstrated a consistent pattern of acting in a manner contrary to its diplomatic assurances to the United States, the United States would need to look beyond the face of these assurances before permitting transfer to that country."[142]

4.3.2. Types of Relief Available

As noted in this chapter at 4.2.2, although there are no bars to relief under the Convention Against Torture, legacy INS and EOIR have devised two separate forms of relief under the Convention. The first, called withholding of removal under the Convention Against Torture, is similar in many ways to withholding under INA §241(b)(3) ("traditional withholding"), including the bars to relief. The second, called deferral of removal under the Convention Against Torture, has no bars, but is a more precarious remedy that can be easily terminated.

Withholding Under the Convention Against Torture

To be eligible for withholding of removal under the Convention Against Torture, an individual must establish that it is more likely than not he or she would be subjected to torture if removed to his or her home country or other proposed country of removal.[143] Mandatory bars to this type of withholding—identical to the bars to traditional withholding under INA §241(b)(3)—are:

- conviction by final judgment of a particularly serious crime;

---

[138] EOIR Memorandum, M. Creppy, "Operating Policies and Procedures Memorandum No. 99-5: Implementation of Article 3 of the UN Convention Against Torture" (May 14, 1999), *published on* AILA InfoNet (*posted* June 4, 1999), and available at *www.usdoj.gov/eoir/efoia/ocij/oppm99/99_5.pdf*.

[139] See *Khouzam v. Hogan*, 497 F.Supp.2d 615 (M.D. Pa. 2007).

[140] *Id.* at 626 ("Because the Government has not provided Khouzam with an opportunity to challenge the reliability of the diplomatic assurances and has not presented any evidence to support its decision, the Court will not reject the due process claims as barred by the political question doctrine.").

[141] See CRS Report for Congress, *The U.N. Convention Against Torture: Overview of U.S. Implementation Policy Concerning the Removal of Aliens* (Mar. 11, 2004), at 12, available at *www.au.af.mil/au/awc/awcgate/crs/rl32276.pdf*.

[142] *Id.*

[143] See generally 8 CFR §§208.16(c), 1208.16(c); and this chapter, at 4.2.

- commission of a serious nonpolitical crime outside of the United States;
- participation in the persecution of others on account of race, religion, nationality, membership in a particular social group, or political opinion;
- danger to the security of the United States;
- engagement in terrorist activity, incitement of terrorist activity, or representation of a foreign terrorist organization;
- assistance in Nazi persecution; and
- engagement in genocide.[144]

Deferral Under the Convention Against Torture

To be eligible for deferral of removal under the Convention Against Torture, an individual must establish that it is more likely than not that he or she would be subjected to torture if removed to his or her home country or other proposed country of removal.[145] Unlike traditional withholding or withholding under the Convention Against Torture, there are no bars to relief.[146]

A grant of deferral, however, can be terminated more easily than withholding.[147] Moreover, a person who is granted deferral may be held in detention and is not entitled to employment authorization, though he or she may be released by U.S. Immigration and Customs Enforcement (ICE) or issued employment authorization by U.S. Citizenship and Immigration Services (USCIS).[148]

One commentator has suggested that the bars imposed for withholding of removal under the Convention Against Torture, the termination process for deferral of removal, the barriers to initiating a Convention Against Torture claim such as time and numerical limitations on motions to reopen, and the bar to relief if diplomatic assurances are received are all, arguably, invalid because they are beyond the scope of the implementing legislation.[149]

4.3.3. Applying for Convention Against Torture Relief

An individual may initiate a claim for Convention Against Torture relief by either requesting such relief before an IJ or by presenting evidence, including his or her testimony or information contained on the Form I-589, Application for Asylum and Withholding of Removal, that indicates that he or she may be tortured in the country of removal.[150] Question 4 in Part B of the I-589 specifically asks: "Are you afraid of being subjected to torture in your home country or any other country to which you may be returned?"

---

[144] For a more detailed discussion of these bars, see ch. 2.7.

[145] *See generally* 8 CFR §§208.17, 1208.17, and this chapter, at 4.2.

[146] *See, e.g., Matter of G–A–*, 23 I&N Dec. 366, 368 (BIA 2002) (an applicant's "criminal convictions in the United States, *however serious*, are not a bar to deferral of removal" under the Convention Against Torture) (emphasis added).

[147] *See* 8 CFR §§208.17(d), 1208.17(d); and this chapter, at 4.3.5.

[148] *See* 8 CFR §§208.17(c), 1208.17(c), and 241.3 to 241.5; *see also* this chapter, at 4.3.4, and ch. 3.9.

[149] K. Rosati, *supra* note 20.

[150] 8 CFR §§208.13(c)(1), 1208.13(c)(1). *See* EOIR Memorandum, *supra* note 138, at 8–9. *See also* Form I-589, reproduced in appx. 9A.

Where to File

The application should be filed in the same manner as any I-589.[151]

No Filing Fee

As with an application for asylum or traditional withholding, there is no filing fee.

4.3.4. The Immigration Court Hearing

The immigration court hearing, as a whole, is not significantly changed by the Convention Against Torture. The Convention, however, does add a form of protection from removal and results in additional considerations for IJs.[152]

Time Period

Unlike asylum claims, withholding of removal and deferral of removal claims under the Convention Against Torture are not subject to the 180-day "clock" (or period during which asylum claims must be decided).[153] A Convention Against Torture claim, however, will be adjudicated with all other claims for relief in removal proceedings.[154] Since there is no separate hearing for a Convention Against Torture claim, an individual who is applying for asylum as well as Convention Against Torture relief may be subject to the 180-day expedited docket.[155] At least one court has held that an immigration judge abused his discretion in failing to give a CAT applicant adequate time to complete his application due to the deficiencies with his legal representation.[156]

Steps in the Decision-Making Process

First, the IJ must determine whether it is more likely than not that the individual would be tortured if removed to the proposed country of removal.[157] Next, the IJ must determine whether the individual is subject to mandatory denial under one of the bars contained in INA §241(b)(3).[158]

If the individual has met his or her burden of proof and is not subject to a mandatory bar, the IJ must grant withholding of removal under the Convention Against Torture.[159] Such a grant has the same consequences as a grant under INA §241(b)(3), *i.e.*, the individual may not be removed to a country in which he or she would be subject to torture.

---

[151] *See* ch. 3.9.4.

[152] *See generally* EOIR Memorandum, *supra* note 138. Also see ch. 3.3 for a more in-depth discussion of the immigration court hearing process.

[153] *See* EOIR Memorandum, *supra* note 138, at 9.

[154] *Id.*

[155] For more information on the 180-day time period, *see* ch. 3.3.5.

[156] *Louis-Martin v. Ridge*, 322 F. Supp. 2d 556, 561–62 (M.D. Pa. 2004).

[157] 8 CFR §§208.16(c)(4), 1208.16(c)(4). For a further discussion of the more-likely-than-not standard, see this chapter, at 4.2.2.

[158] *See* 8 CFR §§208.16(c)(4), 1208.16(c)(4), 208.16(d)(2), and 1208.16(d)(2). A list of these mandatory bars may be found in this chapter at 4.3.2. A more in-depth analysis is contained in ch. 2.7.

[159] *See* 8 CFR §§208.16(c)(4), 1208.16(c)(4).

If the individual has met his or her burden of proof, but is subject to a mandatory bar, the IJ must deny withholding of removal under the Convention Against Torture and grant the individual deferral of removal.[160]

Right to Appeal

Administrative Review

The individual applicant or the ICE trial attorney may, under most circumstances, appeal the IJ's decision regarding relief under the Convention Against Torture to the BIA.[161] Exceptions to this general rule of the right to appeal are IJ reviews of negative credible fear determinations under the expedited removal process and IJ reviews of negative reasonable fear determinations under reinstatement of removal and administrative removal proceedings.[162]

Judicial Review

The individual may also seek judicial review of a denial of Convention Against Torture relief in federal court.[163] Such review is limited to review of final orders of removal under INA §242.[164] The regulations similarly acknowledge this right of judicial review.[165] The regulations note, however, that any appeal or petition regarding a claim under the Convention Against Torture "shall not be deemed to include or authorize the consideration of any administrative order or decision, or portion thereof, the appeal or review of which is restricted or prohibited by the [INA]."[166] In 2005, the REAL ID Act "consolidated judicial review of matters pertaining to removal orders in the courts of appeal and expanded appellate jurisdiction to include review of 'constitutional claims or questions of law.'"[167] Before passage of the REAL ID Act, courts did not have jurisdiction under the

---

[160] *See* 8 CFR §§208.16(c)(4), 1208.16(c)(4), 208.17(a), and 1208.17(a).

[161] *See* EOIR Memorandum, *supra* note 138, at 12. For additional information on filing an appeal with the BIA, see ch. 3.10.

[162] *See* this chapter, at 4.3.7.

[163] *See* FARRA, *supra* note 5, at §2242(d), 112 Stat. 2681-822.

[164] *Id. But see Kalmalthas v. INS*, 251 F.3d 1279, 1281 (9th Cir. 2001) (finding that denial of a motion to reopen constitutes a final order of removal for purposes of judicial review); *Khourassany v. INS*, 208 F.3d 1096, 1100 (9th Cir. 2000) (in denying motion to remand to file Convention Against Torture claim, court held that applicant should file motion to reopen with BIA).

[165] 8 CFR §§208.18(e)(1), 1208.18(e)(1).

[166] 8 CFR §§208.18(e)(1), 1208.18(e)(1). *See Fahim v. U.S. Attorney General*, 278 F.3d 1216, 1218 (11th Cir. 2002) (limiting review of CAT denial to whether any reasonable adjudicator would be compelled to conclude to the contrary); *Ali v. Reno*, 237 F.3d 591, 596 (6th Cir. 2001) (limiting its review of a CAT denial to whether the decision was manifestly contrary to law under INA §§242(b)(4)(B) and (C)). *See also Diakite v. INS*, 179 F.3d 553 (7th Cir. 1999) (holding that petitioner convicted of "serious" crimes must seek remedy under the Convention Against Torture in the administrative forum).

[167] *Hanan v. Gonzales*, 449 F.3d 834, 836 (8th Cir. 2006) (quoting 8 USC §1252(a)(2)(D), INA §242(a)(2)(D), and *Singh v. Gonzales*, 432 F.3d 533, 537 (3d Cir. 2006)). INA §242(a)(2)(D) reads: "Nothing in subparagraph (B) or (C), or in any other provision of this Act (other than this section) which limits or eliminates judicial review, shall be construed as precluding review of constitutional claims or questions of law raised upon a petition for review filed with an appropriate court of appeals in accordance with this section."

INA to review final orders of removal against noncitizens removable by reason of their commission of certain crimes.[168] Under the REAL ID Act, circuit courts are limited in their review to pure questions of law or the application of law to undisputed facts, but not factual issues standing alone.[169]

Although the REAL ID Act expanded appellate jurisdiction for aliens challenging a final removal order, it also eliminated habeas corpus review over final removal orders.[170] The INA now states that a petition for review filed with the appropriate court of appeals is the "sole and exclusive means for judicial review of "any cause or claim" under the CAT.[171] However, at least one court has found it has habeas corpus jurisdiction over a decision to terminate deferral of removal under the CAT. In *Khouzam v. Hogan*, the U.S. District Court for the Middle District of Pennsylvania interpreted the REAL ID Act as not precluding review of a deferral termination, as this CAT-related claim did not arise in the context of the ordinary removal process.[172]

Continued Detention After Grant of Deferral of Removal

An order granting deferral of removal does not alter ICE's authority to detain an individual who is otherwise subject to detention.[173] Decisions regarding release of individuals granted deferral are made pursuant to 8 CFR Part 1241.[174] As one commentator has mentioned, "prolonged detention . . . threatens to undermine the implementation of the Convention. . . . Given the conditions of detention in many [ICE] detention facilities and in the county jails across the country with which [ICE] contracts, a person eligible for deferral—a person who risks torture upon return—may logically decide to take his or her chances at home than to rot in indefinite detention in the US."[175] Rosati argues that individuals granted deferral should also be eligible for release under supervision pursuant to INA §241(a)(3) and 8 CFR §§241.3 to 241.5 after their 90-day removal period has expired.[176]

---

[168] *Calcano-Martinez v. INS*, 533 U.S. 348, 351–52 (2001) (citing INA §242(a)(2)(C); 8 USC §1252(a)(2)(C)). *See also Ramirez-Peyro v. Gonzales*, 477 F.3d 637, 641 (8th Cir. 2007); *Kamara v. Attorney General of the United States*, 420 F.3d 202, 210 (3d Cir. 2005).

[169] *Kamara, supra* note 168, at 211.

[170] INA §242(a)(4); 8 USC §1252(a)(4) ("Notwithstanding any other provision of law (statutory or non-statutory), including section 2241 of title 28, or any other habeas corpus provision, and sections 1361 and 1651 of such title, a petition for review filed with an appropriate court of appeals in accordance with this section shall be the sole and exclusive means for judicial review of any cause or claim under the [CAT], except as provided in subsection (e)."). Subsection (e) provides for very limited habeas review in expedited removal cases. *See also Kamara, supra* note 168, at 209–10. *But see Khouzam v. Hogan, supra* note 139, at *15–20.

[171] INA §242(a)(4); 8 USC §1252(a)(4). *But see Khouzam v. Hogan, supra* note 139, at *15–20.

[172] *See Khouzam v. Hogan, supra* note 139, at 623 (because a strict reading of INA §242(a)(4) and FARRA §2242(d) would eliminate any judicial review outside the context of an ordinary removal proceeding, the district court "interpret[ed] the REAL ID Act as not precluding habeas review of the . . . decision to terminate Khouzam's deferral of removal.").

[173] *See* FARRA, *supra* note 5, at §2242(e), 112 Stat. 2681-822; 8 CFR §§208.17(c), 1208.17(c).

[174] 8 CFR §§208.17(c), 1208.17(c).

[175] *See* K. Rosati, *supra* note 48, at 531–32.

[176] *Id.*

4.3.5. Termination of Convention Against Torture Protection

Withholding of Removal Under the Convention Against Torture

To terminate a grant of withholding of removal under the Convention Against Torture or under INA §241(b)(3), ICE must file a motion to reopen, which is subject to numerical and time limitations.[177] Only a few narrow exceptions are available to these numerical and time limitations, such as changed circumstances, fraud in the original proceeding, or a crime. Moreover, with regard to changed circumstances, ICE must show that the evidence supporting its motion is material and was not previously available.[178]

Deferral of Removal Under the Convention Against Torture

The grant of deferral of removal is a more precarious status that may be easily terminated.[179] For this reason, an individual granted deferral should routinely collect up-to-date information on the country to which his or her removal has been deferred to ensure a quick response to any motions filed by ICE.[180]

Motion for Hearing on Termination

To terminate a grant of deferral of removal, ICE must first file a motion to schedule a hearing to consider termination with the immigration court that issued the order granting deferral of removal.[181] If the motion is filed with another court, it must be rejected for lack of proper venue.[182] The motion must be granted if it is accompanied by evidence that is relevant to the possibility that the individual would be tortured in the country to which removal has been deferred and if the evidence was not presented at the previous hearing.[183] The ICE motion is not subject to the ordinary motion to reopen requirements.[184] The regulation does not address whether the IJ's decision on the motion to schedule a hearing is appealable.[185]

Notice of Hearing

The immigration court must provide notice to the individual of the time, place, and date of the hearing.[186] The notice must also inform the individual that he or she may sup-

---

[177] *See* 8 CFR §§208.24(f), 1208.24(f).

[178] See ch. 3.11 and 3.16.2 for further discussion regarding motions to reopen and termination of withholding.

[179] *See, e.g., Khouzam v. Hogan, supra* note 139. Here, the decision to terminate Khouzam's deferral was apparently made on January 24, 2007, and he would have been eligible for removal on June 1, 2007. *Id.* at 619. However, Khouzam was not informed of this decision until May 29, 2007, when he reported for a regular check-in with ICE. The district court stayed his removal, and at the time of press, Khouzam's fate was undetermined.

[180] *See* K. Rosati, *supra* note 48, at 531.

[181] 8 CFR §§208.17(d)(1), 1208.17(d)(1). *See also* EOIR Memorandum, *supra* note 138, at 11.

[182] EOIR Memorandum, *supra* note 138, at 11.

[183] *Id.* at 10.

[184] *Id.*

[185] *Id.* at 11.

[186] 8 CFR §§208.17(d)(2), 1208.17(d)(2).

plement the information in his or her initial application for relief under the Convention Against Torture.[187]

Submission of Supplemental Information

If the individual chooses to submit supplemental information, he or she must submit it within 10 calendar days of service of the notice, or 13 calendar days if service of the notice is by mail.[188]

Scheduling of Hearing

The hearing should not be scheduled earlier than 10 days for removal proceedings (14 days for deportation proceedings) after service of the notice.[189]

Department of State Comments

At the expiration of the 10– or 13-day period for supplementing the initial application, the immigration court will forward a copy of the original application, and any supplemental information that the individual or ICE has provided, to the Department of State (DOS), together with the time, place, and date of the termination hearing.[190] At its option, DOS may provide comments on the case in accordance with 8 CFR §§208.11, 1208.11.[191] DOS has the option of providing detailed country condition information, an assessment of the accuracy of the applicant's assertions regarding conditions in the applicant's home country, and any other information it believes to be relevant.[192]

De Novo Hearing

If ICE's motion is granted, the IJ must conduct a hearing and make a de novo determination as to whether the individual previously granted deferral is more likely than not to be subjected to torture.[193] The determination must be based on the record of the proceeding, the initial application, and any new evidence submitted by ICE or the individual.[194]

Burden of Proof

The burden of proof is on the individual previously granted deferral to establish that it is more likely than not that he or she would be tortured in the country to which removal has been deferred.[195]

Decision

If the IJ determines that it is more likely than not that the individual would be subjected to torture in the country to which removal has been deferred, the order of deferral

---

[187] 8 CFR §§208.17(d)(2), 1208.17(d)(2).
[188] 8 CFR §§208.17(d)(2), 1208.17(d)(2).
[189] EOIR Memorandum, *supra* note 138, at 11.
[190] 8 CFR §§208.17(d)(2), 1208.17(d)(2).
[191] 8 CFR §§208.17(d)(2), 1208.17(d)(2).
[192] 8 CFR §§208.11(a), (b), 1208.11(a), (b).
[193] 8 CFR §§208.17(d)(3), 1208.17(d)(3).
[194] 8 CFR §§208.17(d)(3), 1208.17(d)(3).
[195] 8 CFR §§208.17(d)(3), 1208.17(d)(3).

must remain in place.[196] If the individual has not met his or her burden of proof, the deferral of removal must be terminated.[197]

Appeal

Appeal of the IJ's decision lies with the BIA.[198]

Termination at the Request of the Individual

At any time while the grant of deferral of removal is in effect, the individual may make a written request to the immigration court to terminate the deferral order.[199] The immigration court must have administrative control of the case pursuant to 8 CFR §1003.11.[200] If the IJ is satisfied, based on the written record, that the individual's request is knowing and voluntary, the order of deferral will be terminated.[201] If the IJ determines that the individual's request is not knowing and voluntary, the individual's request may not serve as a basis for terminating the order of deferral.[202] If necessary, the IJ may calendar a hearing for the sole purpose of determining whether the individual's request is knowing and voluntary.[203]

Diplomatic Assurances

At any time while deferral of removal is in effect, the attorney general (AG) may determine whether deferral should be terminated based on diplomatic assurances forwarded by the secretary of state pursuant to 8 CFR §§208.18(c), 1208.18(c).[204] The secretary of state may forward assurances that the secretary of state has received from a specific country that the individual would not be tortured if he or she were removed to that country.[205] The AG, the deputy AG, or the "INS Commissioner" (as the regulation was written prior to the creation of DHS) must determine, in consultation with the secretary of state, whether the assurances are sufficiently reliable to allow the individual's removal to that country consistent with article 3 of the Convention Against Torture.[206] It is noteworthy that the regulations do not empower the AG to terminate a grant of withholding under the Convention Against Torture after receiving diplomatic assurances.[207]

---

[196] 8 CFR §§208.17(d)(4), 1208.17(d)(4).

[197] 8 CFR §§208.17(d)(4), 1208.17(d)(4).

[198] 8 CFR §§208.17(d)(4), 1208.17(d)(4).

[199] 8 CFR §§208.17(e)(1), 1208.17(e)(1).

[200] 8 CFR §§208.17(e)(1), 1208.17(e)(1).

[201] 8 CFR §§208.17(e)(2), 1208.17(e)(2).

[202] 8 CFR §§208.17(e)(2), 1208.17(e)(2).

[203] 8 CFR §§208.17(e)(2), 1208.17(e)(2).

[204] 8 CFR §§208.17(f), 1208.17(f).

[205] 8 CFR §§208.18(c), 1208.18(c).

[206] 8 CFR §§208.18(c), 1208.18(c). References to the legacy INS "Commissioner" after March 1, 2003, unless otherwise specified in the regulations, mean the director of USCIS, the commissioner of CBP, and the assistant secretary for ICE. 8 CFR §1.1(d).

[207] *See* K. Rosati, *supra* note 48, at 533.

4.3.6. Motions to Reopen

In cases in which an individual fears torture upon return to his or her home country, but did not request Convention Against Torture relief before an IJ, the individual may be eligible to file a motion to reopen. If a motion to reopen is granted for consideration of a Convention Against Torture claim, the IJ may also be able to consider other forms of relief available to the applicant, such as asylum.[208]

Individuals with Final Orders of Deportation, Exclusion, or Removal Before March 22, 1999

An individual whose order of removal became final before March 22, 1999 (the effective date of the implementing regulations) was permitted to file a motion to reopen within 90 days of the effective date of the regulations (or by June 21, 1999).[209]

Individuals with Final Orders of Deportation, Exclusion, or Removal After March 22, 1999

An individual whose order of removal became final after March 22, 1999, should have had the opportunity to raise a Convention Against Torture claim. The regulations, therefore, do not specifically address this category of cases. Nevertheless, an individual with a final order of removal issued after March 22, 1999, may be able to raise a claim under the Convention Against Torture by filing a motion to reopen under the procedures and requirements set forth in 8 CFR §§1003.2 and 1003.3.[210] At least one court has held that individuals in removal proceedings on or after March 22, 1999, may file a motion to reopen without having to establish a prima facie claim for CAT relief.[211]

Individuals with Requests for Convention Against Torture Relief Pending with Legacy INS on or Before March 22, 1999

No Final Decision

Any individual who filed a request with legacy INS for protection under article 3 of the Convention Against Torture on or before March 22, 1999, and whose request had not been finally decided by legacy INS, has been or should have been provided with written notice that after March 22, 1999, considerations for protection under the Convention Against Torture can only be obtained in accordance with the regulations, which became

---

[208] *See Johnson v. Ashcroft*, 286 F.3d 696, 700–05 (3d Cir. 2002) (finding BIA acted arbitrarily when it departed from established precedent that allows IJs to consider matters deemed appropriate in the IJ's discretion). For an overview of issues that have arisen with regard to motions to reopen, see M. Sklar, "New Convention Against Torture Procedures and Standards," 99-7 *Immigr. Briefings* (July 1999).

[209] 8 CFR §§208.18(b)(2), 1208.18(b)(2). *See Huang v. Ashcroft*, No. 03-16730, 2004 U.S. App. LEXIS 27903, at *2 (9th Cir. 2004) (holding that the time limit in 8 CFR §208.18(b)(2) [now also §1208.18(b)(2)] applies to all claims for protection under the CAT, without regard to the form of relief that might be granted).

[210] For further discussion, see ch. 3.11.

[211] *Qi Hang Guo v. USDOJ*, 422 F.3d 61, 64 (2d Cir. 2005) (holding that the controlling regulation, 8 CFR §208.18(b)(1) [now also at §1208.18(b)(1)] allows for an applicant to file a motion to reopen without having to establish a prima facie claim for CAT relief).

effective on March 22, 1999.[212] The notice also informed the individuals that they must file a motion to reopen with the immigration court or the BIA in order to seek relief under the Convention Against Torture.[213] In addition, the notice was accompanied by a stay of removal effective for 30 days after the service of the notice on the individual.[214] A motion to reopen for an individual falling within this category is not subject to the normal requirements for reopening.[215] Moreover, the regulations specifically provide that "[s]uch a motion *shall* be granted if it is accompanied by a copy of the notice ... or by other convincing evidence that the alien had a request pending with [legacy INS] for protection under Article 3."[216]

Denial by Legacy INS

If the individual's request was denied by legacy INS on or before March 22, 1999, the individual will be considered to have been "finally denied" withholding of removal and deferral of removal under the Convention Against Torture.[217] Arguably, such an individual could file a motion to reopen if he or she met the normal requirements for such a motion under 8 CFR §§1003.2 and 1003.3.

Grant by Legacy INS

If the individual's request was granted by legacy INS on or before March 22, 1999, the individual will be considered to have been granted withholding of removal under 8 CFR §§208.16(c), 1208.16(c), unless the individual is subject to a mandatory bar, in which case he or she will be considered to have been granted deferral of removal under 8 CFR §§208.17(a), 1208.17(a).[218]

4.3.7. Expedited Administrative Procedures

Individuals subject to special procedures for stowaways, expedited removal, reinstatement of removal, expedited removal for aggravated felonies, and "alien terrorist" and "terrorist" removal proceedings may also make a Convention Against Torture claim, which will be heard, in most cases, by an asylum officer.

Special Procedures for Stowaways Under INA §235(a)

A noncitizen stowaway who "indicates an intention to apply for asylum, or expresses a fear of persecution, a fear of *torture*, or a fear of return to the country of proposed removal" must be referred to an asylum officer "for a determination of credible fear of persecution or *torture*" pursuant to §235(b)(1)(B) of the INA.[219] If the stowaway is found to have a credible fear of torture, he or she should be placed in proceedings before an IJ for a determination only on eligibility for asylum, withholding of removal under INA

---

[212] 8 CFR §§208.18(b)(3)(ii), 1208.18(b)(3)(ii).

[213] 8 CFR §§208.18(b)(3)(ii)(A), 1208.18(b)(3)(ii)(A).

[214] 8 CFR §§208.18(b)(3)(ii)(A), 1208.18(b)(3)(ii)(A).

[215] 8 CFR §§208.18(b)(3)(ii)(A), 1208.18(b)(3)(ii)(A).

[216] 8 CFR §§208.18(b)(3)(ii)(A), 1208.18(b)(3)(ii)(A). (emphasis added).

[217] 8 CFR §§208.18(b)(4), 1208.18(b)(4).

[218] 8 CFR §§208.18(b)(4), 1208.18(b)(4).

[219] 8 CFR §1235.1(d)(4) (emphasis added). *See also* 8 CFR §§208.30, 1208.30.

§241(b)(3), or Convention Against Torture relief.[220] If the stowaway is found not to have a credible fear, the asylum officer will provide the stowaway with written notice of the decision and will inquire whether the stowaway wishes to have the decision reviewed by an IJ. If review is sought, the IJ will make a de novo determination on whether the stowaway has a credible fear.[221]

Expedited Removal Under INA §235(b)

A noncitizen arriving at a port of entry with false or no documents, who is subject to expedited removal under INA §235(b), and who "indicates an intention to apply for asylum, or expresses a fear of persecution, a fear of *torture*, or a fear of return to his or her country" must be referred to an asylum officer "for a determination of credible fear of persecution or *torture*."[222] If the individual is found to have a credible fear of torture, he or she should be placed in removal proceedings before an IJ under INA §240, "even if the [individual] does not have a credible fear of persecution."[223] If the individual is found not to have a credible fear, the asylum officer will provide written notice of the decision and will inquire whether the individual wishes to have the decision reviewed by an IJ. If the individual seeks IJ review, the IJ will make a de novo credible fear determination.[224]

Reinstatement of Removal Under INA §241(b)

An individual who, in the course of the reinstatement of removal process, expresses a fear of returning to the country of removal must be referred to an asylum officer for a "reasonable fear" interview.[225] The determination must be conducted within 10 days of the referral, in the absence of exceptional circumstances.[226] At the interview the asylum officer must determine whether the individual has a "reasonable fear" of persecution or torture, which is a higher screening standard than the credible fear standard.[227] A "reasonable fear" of torture is defined as "a reasonable possibility that he or she would be tortured in the country of removal."[228] If the asylum officer determines that the individual has a reasonable fear of persecution or torture, the case will be referred to an IJ for a hearing on withholding of removal (under either INA §241(b)(3) or the Convention Against Torture) or deferral of removal. If the asylum officer determines that the individual does not have a reasonable fear of persecution or torture, the individual will be given the opportunity to request an IJ review of the

---

[220] *See* INS Memorandum, *supra* note 129, at 4.

[221] EOIR Memorandum, *supra* note 138, at 6. See ch. 3.4 for additional information on procedures for stowaways, and ch. 5 for more information on expedited removal and the credible fear interview process.

[222] 8 CFR §§235.3(b)(4), 1235.3(b)(4) (emphasis added). *See also* 8 CFR §§208.30, 1208.30.

[223] *See* INS Memorandum, *supra* note 129, at 4.

[224] EOIR Memorandum, *supra* note 138, at 6. *See* ch. 5 for additional information on expedited removal and the credible fear process.

[225] 8 CFR §§208.31(b), 1208.31(b).

[226] 8 CFR §§208.31(b), 1208.31(b).

[227] *See* INS Memorandum, *supra* note 129, at 5.

[228] 8 CFR §§208.31(c), 1208.31(c).

negative reasonable fear determination.[229] The IJ review will be similar to a credible fear review, with the IJ making a de novo determination regarding whether the individual has a reasonable fear.[230] The reasonable fear standard, according to the Office of the Chief Immigration Judge, is higher than the credible fear standard and "is the standard used to adjudicate asylum applications."[231]

Expedited Removal for Persons Convicted of an Aggravated Felony Under INA §238(b)

An individual who, in the course of the expedited removal process for persons convicted of an aggravated felony, expresses a fear of returning to the country of removal must be referred to an asylum officer for a "reasonable fear" interview.[232] The determination must be conducted within 10 days of the referral, in the absence of exceptional circumstances.[233] At the interview the asylum officer must determine whether the individual has a "reasonable fear" of persecution or torture, which is a higher screening standard than the credible fear standard.[234] A "reasonable fear" of torture is defined as "a reasonable possibility that he or she would be tortured in the country of removal."[235] If the asylum officer determines that the individual has a reasonable fear of persecution or torture, the case will be referred to an IJ for a hearing on withholding of removal (under either INA §241(b)(3) or the Convention Against Torture) or deferral of removal. If the asylum officer determines that the individual does not have a reasonable fear of persecution or torture, the individual will be given the opportunity to request an IJ review of the negative reasonable fear determination.[236] The IJ review will be similar to a credible fear review, with the IJ making a de novo determination regarding whether the individual has a reasonable fear.[237] The reasonable fear standard, according to the Office of the Chief Immigration Judge, is higher than the credible fear standard and "is the standard used to adjudicate asylum applications."[238]

Alien Terrorist Administrative Removal Procedures Under INA §235(c)

An individual who is removable under INA §235(c) as an "alien terrorist" may request relief under the Convention Against Torture.[239] His or her request, however, may only be assessed by ICE.[240] The provisions of 8 CFR §§208, 1208 relating to consideration or

---

[229] *See* INS Memorandum, *supra* note 129, at 5.

[230] EOIR Memorandum, *supra* note 138, at 8.

[231] *Id.* For a further discussion of the reinstatement of removal process, see ch. 3.6.

[232] 8 CFR §§208.31(b), 1208.31(b).

[233] 8 CFR §§208.31(b), 1208.31(b).

[234] *See* INS Memorandum, *supra* note 129, at 5.

[235] 8 CFR §§208.31(c), 1208.31(c).

[236] *See* INS Memorandum, *supra* note 129, at 5.

[237] EOIR Memorandum, *supra* note 138, at 8.

[238] *Id.* For a further discussion of the expedited removal process for persons convicted of an aggravated felony, see ch. 3.7.

[239] 8 CFR §§208.18(d), 1208.18(d).

[240] 8 CFR §§208.18(d), 1208.18(d).

review by an IJ, the BIA, or an asylum officer do not apply in such cases.[241] Nevertheless, if ICE refers the case to an IJ pursuant to 8 CFR §§235.8(b)(2)(ii), (d), 1235.8(b)(2)(ii), (d), the IJ would have authority to consider the individual's claim under the Convention Against Torture.[242] According to legacy INS, only a few cases each year were handled under INA §235(c), and they typically involved highly sensitive issues and adjudication based on classified information under tight controls.[243]

Terrorist Removal Proceedings Under INA §501 et seq.

An individual subject to a removal order under INA §501 *et seq.*, the special terrorist removal proceedings, may not be removed if his or her removal would violate article 3 of the Convention Against Torture. A Convention Against Torture claim in these circumstances must be determined by the attorney general (or the secretary of Homeland Security), in consultation with the secretary of state.[244]

4.3.8. Employment Authorization

Employment Authorization When Removal Withheld Under the Convention Against Torture

Individuals granted withholding of removal under the Convention Against Torture are eligible for employment authorization.[245] Employment authorization is granted by filing Form I-765 with the appropriate USCIS service center and is not discretionary, *i.e.*, it will be granted automatically to individuals who demonstrate they have been granted withholding of removal under the Convention Against Torture. There is no filing fee for initial employment authorization or a renewal of employment authorization.[246]

Employment Authorization When Removal Deferred Under the Convention Against Torture

The interim regulations do not specifically provide for employment authorization for individuals granted deferral of removal under the Convention Against Torture. INA §241(a)(7), however, provides that an individual may be eligible for employment authorization if the AG makes a specific finding that "the removal of the alien is otherwise impracticable or contrary to the public interest." One commentator has argued that this provision of the INA should apply to individuals granted deferral of removal because the individual's removal is "impracticable" and it would be "contrary to the public interest" to remove an individual who would be subjected to torture.[247] Such individuals are likely

---

[241] 8 CFR §§208.18(d), 1208.18(d).

[242] *See* 64 Fed. Reg. 8478, 8484 (Feb. 19, 1999) (supplementary information).

[243] *Id.* at 8479.

[244] 28 CFR §200.1.

[245] 8 CFR §§274a.12(a)(10), 1274a.12(a)(10).

[246] *See* Form I-765, Application for Employment Authorization, reproduced in appx. 9C.

[247] *See* K. Rosati, *supra* note 48, at 532–33.

to be eligible for employment authorization at the discretion of the district director pursuant to 8 CFR §§274a.12(c)(18), 1274a.12(c)(18).[248]

---

[248] *See* Form I-765, Application for Employment Authorization, reproduced in appx. 9C.

CHAPTER 5
EXPEDITED REMOVAL

[I]n 15 percent of observed cases when arriving aliens expressed a fear of return to the inspector, the alien was not referred [for a credible fear interview].[*]

5.1. Statutory Provisions—INA §235(b)	295
5.2. How Expedited Removal Works in Practice	304
5.3. Oversight of the Expedited Removal Process	318

This chapter reviews current law, regulations, and policies applying to the expedited removal process that took effect April 1, 1997. The expedited removal provisions—the most controversial asylum changes included in the Illegal Immigration Reform and Immigrant Responsibility Act of 1996 (IIRAIRA)[1]—were the result of a perception by Congress that the asylum system was being abused by individuals arriving at ports of entry with false or no documents.[2] Many commentators have noted, however, that the abuses present in the early 1990s diminished significantly as a result of asylum reforms in 1995, and thus expedited removal was not necessary.[3] Nevertheless, as a result of changes under IIRAIRA, the expedited removal process is currently applied at every land, air, and sea port of entry in the United States. As asylum-seekers pass through this problem-plagued and often confusing process, it is important for attorneys and representatives to provide advice and assistance to ensure that individuals fleeing persecution are not mistakenly returned to their persecutors.[4]

5.1. STATUTORY PROVISIONS—INA §235(b)

5.1.1. What Is Expedited Removal

The expedited removal provisions of the Immigration and Nationality Act (INA) allow the Department of Homeland Security (DHS) to order the immediate removal of an individual arriving at a port of entry or, in some cases, of an individual already physically present in the

---

[*] U.S. Commission on International Religious Freedom, Report on Asylum Seekers in Expedited Removal, Vol. I: Findings and Recommendation, at 6 (Feb. 2005).

[1] Illegal Immigration Reform and Immigrant Responsibility Act of 1996 (IIRAIRA), Pub. L. No. 104-208, div. C, 110 Stat. 3009, 3009-546 to 3009-724.

[2] *See, e.g.*, B. Cooper, "Procedures for Expedited Removal and Asylum Screening Under [IIRAIRA]," 29 *Conn. L. Rev.* 1501, 1501–02 (1997).

[3] *See, e.g.*, U.S. Committee for Immigration Reform, *U.S. Refugee Policy: Taking Leadership, A Report to Congress* (June 1997), at 28–29; M. Pistone, *New Asylum Laws: Undermining an American Ideal* (Cato Institute 1998), at 7–8.

[4] Under regulations issued in 1999, individuals arriving at ports of entry who are subject to expedited removal may also apply for relief under the Convention Against Torture. *See infra* note 43.

United States, without further hearing or review.[5] If, however, the individual expresses a fear of persecution or a desire to apply for asylum, DHS will detain the individual and must refer the individual for a "credible fear" interview with an asylum officer (AO).[6] If the individual is found to have a credible fear of persecution, he or she is placed in regular §240 removal proceedings for full consideration of his or her asylum claim. An individual who expresses a fear of torture upon return will be interviewed to determine whether he or she has a credible fear of torture.[7]

5.1.2. Who Is Subject to Expedited Removal

Noncitizens Arriving at a Port of Entry with False or No Documents

Noncitizens are subject to expedited removal if the immigration officer at the port of entry determines that they are inadmissible under INA §§212(a)(6)(C) or (7) to the United States because they possess either false documents or no documents.[8] A false document may include a facially valid document that an individual obtained fraudulently or through willful misrepresentation of a material fact.[9] Expedited removal also applies to individuals seeking transit through the United States at a port of entry.[10]

Note on Canada: Noncitizens attempting to enter the United States at a land border port of entry with Canada must first establish that they are not ineligible for asylum and removable to Canada under the Safe Third Country Agreement,[11] through a threshold screening interview, in order to receive a credible fear interview.[12]

Noncitizens Interdicted in International or U.S. Waters and Brought to the United States

Noncitizens who are interdicted in international or U.S. waters and who are brought to the United States are also subject to expedited removal.[13]

Noncitizens Who Have Not Been "Admitted" or "Paroled" into the United States and Who Have Not Resided in the United States for Two Years or More

Expedited removal can be applied to individuals who entered the United States illegally—i.e., who have not been admitted or paroled—and who have not resided in the United States

---

[5] INA §235(b)(1)(A); 8 USC §1225(b)(1)(A).

[6] INA §235(b)(1)(A); 8 USC §1225(b)(1)(A).

[7] *See* 8 CFR §§208.30, 1208.30. *See also* ch. 4.

[8] INA §235(b)(1)(A)(i); 8 USC §1225(b)(1)(A)(i); 8 CFR §§235.3(b)(1)(ii), 1235.3(b)(1)(ii).

[9] INA §212(a)(6)(C); 8 USC §1182(a)(6)(C).

[10] 8 CFR §§235.3(b)(1)(i), 1235.3(b)(1)(i). See 8 CFR §§1.1(q), 1001.1(q) for the definition of an "arriving alien." *See also* Asylum Officer Basic Training Course (AOBTC), Lesson Plan on Credible Fear (April 14, 2006), at 7, *published on* AILA InfoNet at Doc. No. 06121861 (*posted* Dec. 18, 2006), and available at www.rmscdenver.org/documents/CredibleFear.pdf.

[11] Agreement Between the Government of the United States and the Government of Canada For Cooperation in the Examination of Refugee Status Claims from Nationals of Third Countries (Dec. 5, 2002), available at www.uscis.gov/files/article/appendix-c.pdf.

[12] 8 CFR §208.30(e)(6); *see also* the discussion of safe third countries in ch. 2.7.3.

[13] AOBTC, Lesson: Credible Fear, *supra* note 10, at 7.

for two or more years.¹⁴ Although initially the U.S. government did not apply expedited removal procedures to such individuals, it has begun to do so in recent years.

In November 2002, the legacy Immigration and Naturalization Service (INS) announced that it would immediately begin to place all aliens who arrived in the United States illegally by sea in expedited removal proceedings.¹⁵ The change was in response to what legacy INS perceived as a surge in illegal migration by sea, which it characterized as a threat to national security.¹⁶

In August 2004, DHS announced plans to expand the use of expedited removal to noncitizens who were in the United States less than 14 days and who were apprehended within 100 miles of the Mexican or Canadian border with the United States.¹⁷ The announcement, however, limited implementation to the following U.S. Customs and Border Protection (CBP) Border Patrol sectors: Laredo, McAllen, Del Rio, Marfa, El Paso, Tucson, Yuma, El Centro, San Diego, Blaine, Spokane, Havre, Grand Forks, Detroit, Buffalo, Swanton, and Houlton.¹⁸ In 2006, DHS announced that it was expanding this program to the entire U.S. border, including all coastal areas adjacent to the United States' maritime borders.¹⁹ If the noncitizen has been physically present in the United States for more than 14 days, he or she bears the burden of demonstrating this to the "satisfaction of the immigration officer" (usually a border patrol agent).²⁰ Lastly, to cover what it considered to be a "loophole" in the expedited removal process, DHS announced that it was expanding expedited removal to cover "illegal alien families."²¹ To accommodate these families subject to expedited removal, DHS announced the May 15, 2006, opening of a 500-bed detention facility in Texas that was specially equipped to meet family needs.²² There were soon allegations of mistreatment and prison-like conditions in this facility.²³

---

¹⁴ INA §235(b)(1)(A)(iii); 8 USC §1225(b)(1)(A)(iii).

¹⁵ *See* 67 Fed. Reg. 68924 (Nov. 13, 2002).

¹⁶ *Id.* at 68924. For an analysis and overview of how such provisions place asylum-seekers and refugees at risk, see L. Rosenberg, "The Courts and Interception: The United States' Interdiction Experience and Its Impact on Refugees and Asylum Seekers," 17 *Geo. Immigr. L.J.* 199, 215–18 (2003).

¹⁷ *See* 69 Fed. Reg. 48877 (Aug. 11, 2004).

¹⁸ *Id.* at 48880.

¹⁹ DHS Press Release, "Department of Homeland Security Streamlines Removal Process Along Entire U.S. Border" (Jan. 30, 2006), available at *www.dhs.gov/xnews/releases/press_release_0845.shtm*.

²⁰ *See* 69 Fed. Reg. 48877, 48880 (Aug. 11, 2004). For additional information, see AILF Practice Advisory, DHS Announces Unprecedented Expansion of Expedited Removal to the Interior (Aug. 13, 2004), available at *www.ailf.org/lac/lac_pa_081704.pdf*.

²¹ DHS/ICE News Release, "DHS Closes Loophole by Expanding Expedited Removal to Cover Illegal Alien Families" (May 15, 2006), available at *www.immigration.com/newsletter1/iceilegalfaml.pdf*.

²² *Id.*

²³ The ACLU brought 17 lawsuits against Michael Chertoff, the Secretary of DHS, and six officials from ICE, on behalf of children detained at the T. Don Hutto (Hutto) detention facility in Taylor, TX. See *www.aclu.org/immigrants/detention/28865prs20070306.html*; *see also* Women's Commission for Refugee Women & Children and Lutheran Immigration and Refugee Service, *Locking Up Family Values: The Detention of Immigrant Families* (Feb. 2007), available at *www.womenscommission.org/pdf/famdeten.pdf*. These lawsuits contended that the Hutto facility violated the regulations arising out of *Flores v. Meese,* which ended in a 1997 court settlement that established minimum standards and conditions for the housing and release of all minors in federal immigration custody. *Flores v. Reno*, Stipu-

Note that by regulation, the Attorney General (AG) is not required to publish a notice in the *Federal Register* prior to applying expedited removal in the interior if the delay caused by publication would adversely affect the interests of the United States or the effective enforcement of the immigration laws.[24]

Individuals Paroled into the United States After April 1, 1997

The definition of "arriving alien" includes an individual "paroled pursuant to §212(d)(5) of the Act."[25] Such individuals paroled after April 1, 1997, are subject to expedited removal upon the termination of parole.[26] Those parolees include individuals paroled pursuant to the Visa Waiver Pilot Program Contingency Plan, but not individuals with advance parole.[27]

5.1.3. Who Is *Not* Subject to Expedited Removal

Cuban Citizens or Nationals Arriving at a Port of Entry or Apprehended Within 100 Miles of the Border

Expedited removal does not apply to a native or citizen of a country in the Western Hemisphere with whose government the United States does not have full diplomatic relations and who arrives by aircraft at a port of entry.[28] This provision currently applies only to Cuban citizens and nationals. Expedited removal is also not applicable to any native or citizen of Cuba arriving by sea,[29] at a land port of entry, or apprehended within 100 air miles of a U.S. border.[30]

Pre–April 1, 1997, Parolees

An individual paroled into the United States under INA §212(d)(5) prior to April 1, 1997, is not subject to expedited removal.[31]

Unaccompanied Minors

DHS has implemented a policy of exempting unaccompanied minors, *i.e.*, persons under 18 years of age, from the expedited removal process. Under limited circumstances, however, DHS will place an unaccompanied minor in expedited removal. The circumstances are: (1) if the minor commits an aggravated felony in the immigration officer's presence; (2) if the minor has been convicted of or adjudicated delinquent of an aggra-

---

lated Settlement Agreement, No. CV 85-4544-RJK (C.D. Cal. 1997). On August 27, 2007, a settlement was reached in the Hutto detention center litigation. See *www.aclu.org/immigrants/detention/hutto.html*.

[24] *See* 8 CFR §§235.3(b)(1)(ii), 1235.3(b)(1)(ii).

[25] 8 CFR §§1.1(q), 1001.1(q). *See* INS Memorandum, "Policy Concerning Pre–April 1, 1997 Parolees" (June 30, 1997), *reproduced in* 74 *Interpreter Releases* 1247 (Aug. 18, 1997).

[26] AOBTC, Lesson: Credible Fear, *supra* note 10, at 7.

[27] *Id.*

[28] INA §235(b)(1)(F), 8 USC §1225(b)(1)(F).

[29] 67 Fed. Reg. 68925 (Nov. 13, 2002).

[30] 69 Fed. Reg. 48877 (Aug. 11, 2004); *see* U.S. Customs and Border Protection Memorandum, J. Ahern, "Treatment of Cuban Asylum Seekers at Land Border Ports of Entry" (June 10, 2005).

[31] *See* INS Memorandum, *supra* note 25.

vated felony in the United States or other country; or (3) if the minor has previously been formally removed, excluded, or deported from the United States.[32]

Stowaways

Stowaways are not technically subject to expedited removal procedures. Under INA §235(a)(2), stowaways are not eligible to apply for admission or to be admitted to the United States. If, however, they express a fear of return, they will be given a credible fear interview by an asylum officer. They are not, however, eligible for a hearing under INA §240.[33]

Crewmembers

Crewmembers who, whether on or off their vessel or other conveyance, indicate a fear of persecution in their home countries must be given an asylum application form to submit to the local DHS district director within 10 days.[34] The district director must, upon receiving the application, refer the individual to an immigration judge (IJ) for an asylum hearing.[35]

Individuals Seeking Entry Under VWPP

Individuals who are refused admission at a port of entry under the Visa Waiver Pilot Program (VWPP) (which expired on April 30, 1999) or the Visa Waiver Permanent Program (also VWPP) (effective October 20, 2000), and who request asylum in the United States, must be referred to an IJ for proceedings in immigration court.[36] Under the VWPP, nationals of certain designated countries are permitted to enter the United States without first obtaining a nonimmigrant visa.[37] Individuals entering with a passport from a VWPP country, even though they are not nationals of that country, are entitled to a hearing before an IJ and are not subject to expedited removal.[38]

Noncitizens Paroled into the United States with Advance Parole

Persons paroled into the United States pursuant to a grant of advance parole that was obtained prior to departure from the United States are not subject to expedited removal.[39]

Individuals with Additional Charges of Inadmissibility

Persons denied admission to the United States on charges other than having false or no documents under INA §§212(a)(6)(C) or 212(a)(7) are not subject to expedited removal.[40]

---

[32] *See* INS, *Inspector's Field Manual* (IFM), ch. 17.15(f), *reproduced in* 74 Interpreter Releases 1367 (Sept. 8, 1997).

[33] For asylum procedures for stowaways, see ch. 3.4.

[34] 8 CFR §§208.5(b), 1208.5(b).

[35] 8 CFR §§208.5(b), 1208.5(b).

[36] 8 CFR §217.4(a)(1).

[37] INA §217; 8 USC §1187.

[38] *See Matter of Kanagasundram*, 22 I&N Dec. 963 (BIA 1999).

[39] *See* AOBTC, Lesson: Credible Fear, *supra* note 10, at 8–9.

[40] *See* 8 CFR §§235.3(b)(3), 1235.3(b)(3).

LPRs, Asylees, Refugees, and Others with Additional Protections

An individual who claims under oath to be a lawful permanent resident (LPR), to have been previously admitted as a refugee, to have been previously granted asylum, or to be a U.S. citizen is entitled to administrative review of a removal order.[41]

5.1.4. Credible Fear Standard

In order to qualify for a hearing before an IJ, an individual who has expressed a fear of persecution or a desire to apply for asylum must establish—in an interview conducted by an AO—that he or she has a "credible fear of persecution." Credible fear of persecution under the INA means that there is:

> a *significant possibility*, taking into account the credibility of the statements made by the [individual] in support of [his or her] claim and other such facts as are known to the officer, that the [individual] could establish eligibility for asylum under [INA §] 208.[42]

An individual who indicates a fear of torture upon return to his or her home country will also be referred for a credible fear interview to determine whether he or she has a credible fear of torture.[43]

USCIS's Office of Refugee, Asylum and International Operations, which recently revised its Asylum Officer Basic Training Course lesson plan on credible fear, instructs that "the 'significant possibility' standard of proof can best be understood as requiring that the applicant 'demonstrate a *substantial and realistic possibility* of succeeding,' but not requiring the applicant to show that he or she is more likely than not going to succeed when before the immigration judge."[44] The lesson plan provides that "significant possibility" is intended to be "a low screening standard for admission into the usual full asylum process."[45] Additional revisions were made throughout the lesson plan to provide "greater balance" in guidance on credible fear determinations based on criticisms that the lesson plan sent a signal that there was a greater burden on asylum officers to support a negative credible fear determination than was on applicant's to establish a positive credible fear of torture.[46]

The lesson plan continues to instruct AOs that they should:

- Accord the benefit of the doubt to the applicant;
- Consider whether the case presents novel or unique issues;

---

[41] INA §235(b)(1)(C); 8 USC §1225(b)(1)(C); 8 CFR §§235.3(b)(5)(i), 1235.3(b)(5)(i). *But see Diaz v. Reno*, 40 F. Supp. 2d 984 (N.D. Ill. 1999) (holding that a U.S. citizen erroneously removed to Mexico under the expedited removal process was barred, under the doctrine of sovereign immunity, from suing the AG and the INS district director in their official capacity).

[42] INA §235(b)(1)(B)(v); 8 USC §1225(b)(1)(B)(v) (emphasis added).

[43] *See* 8 CFR §§208.30, 1208.30. For discussion of relief under the Convention Against Torture, see ch. 4.

[44] USCIS Memorandum, J. Langlois, "Increase of Quality Assurance Review for Positive Credible Fear Determinations and Release of Updated Asylum Officer Basic Training Course Lesson Plan, Credible Fear of Persecution and Torture Determinations" (Apr. 14, 2006), at 3 (emphasis in original); *see* AOBTC, Lesson: Credible Fear, *supra* note 10, at 13.

[45] *See* AOBTC, Lesson: Credible Fear, *supra* note 10, at 12, citing a statement by Sen. Orrin Hatch.

[46] USCIS Memorandum, *supra* note 44, at 3.

- Use legal interpretations most favorable to the applicant if there is disagreement among federal appeals courts or if the claim raises an unresolved issue of law.[47]

5.1.5. Withdrawal of Application for Admission

A person applying for admission may, in the AG's discretion and at any time, be permitted to withdraw his or her application for admission and depart immediately from the United States.[48] Under the Homeland Security Act of 2002, this discretion extends to the DHS secretary and other DHS officials.[49] Individuals given such permission, because they have not been issued a removal order, are not subject to the five-year bar to readmission. DHS reported that 128,328 individuals were permitted to withdraw their applications for admission in fiscal year (FY) 2003.[50] A person may dissolve his or her asylum claim at a later time in the credible fear process as well. An AO will interview the individual and complete a form entitled Request for Dissolution of the Credible Fear Process.[51] Making such a request, however, does not mean the individual will be allowed to withdraw and forego the issuance of an expedited removal order.[52] In 2005, the U.S. Commission on International Religious Freedom expressed concern that in a few observed instances immigration officials improperly encouraged asylum-seekers to withdraw their applications for admission and concluded that "Customs and Border Protection (CBP) quality assurance mechanisms are inadequate to ensure that all officers comply with the policy that all withdrawals be 'strictly voluntary.'"[53]

5.1.6. Judicial Review

The INA severely limits judicial review of expedited removal orders and the expedited removal process.[54]

Habeas Corpus Proceedings

An individual is entitled to habeas corpus proceedings, but the federal court may review only whether the individual (1) is an alien; (2) was ordered removed under INA §235(b)(1); or (3) is an LPR.[55] In determining whether an individual has been ordered removed, the court's inquiry is limited to whether such an order was issued and whether

---

[47] AOBTC, Lesson: Credible Fear, *supra* note 10, at 14.

[48] INA §235(a)(4), 8 USC §1225(a)(4).

[49] *See* Homeland Security Act of 2002, Pub. L. No. 107-296, §§456, 1512, 1517, 116 Stat. 2135, 2200, 2310, 2311.

[50] United States Commission on International Religious Freedom, Report on Asylum Seekers in Expedited Removal, Vol. I: Findings and Recommendations (Feb. 2005), at 32, available at *www.uscirf.gov/countries/global/asylum_refugees/2005/february/Volume%20I.pdf*.

[51] *See* INS Memorandum, J. Langlois, "Dissolution of Credible Fear Claims" (July 26, 2000).

[52] For further guidance on withdrawal of applications for admission, see this chapter, at 5.2.4.

[53] Report on Asylum Seekers in Expedited Removal, Vol. I, *supra* note 50, at 51.

[54] INA §§242(a)(2)(iii), (e); 8 USC §§1252(a)(2), (e).

[55] INA §242(e)(2); 8 USC §1252(e)(2).

it relates to the individual.[56] The court may not review whether the individual is actually inadmissible or entitled to any relief from removal.[57]

Limitations on Declaratory, Injunctive, and Equitable Relief

Except for the limited authority to challenge the validity of the expedited removal system, noted below, no court (except the Supreme Court) may enter declaratory, injunctive, or other equitable relief in any action pertaining to an expedited removal order.[58]

Prohibition on Certification of a Class Under Rule 23

No court may certify a class under Rule 23 of the Federal Rules of Civil Procedure in any action for which judicial review of the expedited removal process is authorized.[59]

Challenges to Validity of the System

An action may be brought in the U.S. District Court for the District of Columbia to determine only (1) whether the statute is constitutional and/or (2) whether a regulation, written policy directive, written policy guideline, or written procedure is consistent with the statute and is not otherwise a violation of law.[60] The action must be filed no later than 60 days after the date the challenged section, regulation, directive, guideline, or procedure is first implemented.[61] An order issued by the district court may be filed not later than 30 days after the order is issued.[62] The district court, court of appeals, and Supreme Court are required to expedite to the greatest extent possible the disposition of these challenges.[63] In March and May 1997, three actions were brought challenging expedited removal on behalf of asylum-seekers and other applicants for admission to the United States. The challenges were unsuccessful and the consolidated lawsuits were subsequently dismissed.[64]

Relief

If the court determines that the individual was not ordered removed or that he or she is an LPR, was admitted as a refugee under INA §207, or was granted asylum under INA §208, the court may not order a remedy or relief other than to require a hearing under INA §240.[65]

5.1.7. Consequences of Removal

An individual issued an order of removal under the expedited removal process or at the end of INA §240 proceedings is inadmissible to the United States for a period of five years,

---

[56] INA §242(e)(5); 8 USC §1252(e)(5).

[57] INA §242(e)(5); 8 USC §1252(e)(5).

[58] INA §§242(e)(1)(A), (f); 8 USC §§1252(e)(1)(A), (f).

[59] INA §242(e)(1)(B); 8 USC §1252(e)(1)(B).

[60] INA §242(e)(3)(A); 8 USC §1252(e)(3)(A).

[61] INA §242(e)(3)(B); 8 USC §1252(e)(3)(B).

[62] INA §242(e)(3)(C); 8 USC §1252(e)(3)(C).

[63] INA §242(e)(3)(D); 8 USC §1252(e)(3)(D).

[64] *See American Immigr. Lawyers Ass'n v. Reno*, 199 F.3d 1352 (D.C. Cir. Jan. 11, 2000), *aff'g* 18 F. Supp. 2d 38 (D.D.C. 1998). *See also* G. Neuman, "Federal Court Issues in Immigration Law," 78 *Tex. L. Rev.* 1661, 1668–79 (June 2000) (section on judicial review of expedited removal).

[65] INA §242(e)(4); 8 USC §1252(e)(4).

CHAPTER 5 • EXPEDITED REMOVAL

unless the AG consents to his or her admission.[66] Under the Homeland Security Act of 2002, this authority extends to the DHS secretary and other DHS officials.[67] If the individual is ordered removed a second time or has been convicted of an aggravated felony, he or she is inadmissible for a period of 20 years, unless the AG consents to his or her admission.[68]

5.1.8. Expedited Removal and Credible Fear Statistics

As a result of security measures taken after the September 11, 2001, terrorist attacks, the number of expedited removals from the United States has decreased dramatically. During FY 2001, 12,320 individuals were referred for a credible fear interview.[69] In FY 2003, the number of individuals referred dropped to 5,376.[70] The percentage of individuals referred for a credible fear interview found to have a credible fear was 93 percent from 2000 to 2003.[71] The percentage of asylum-seekers subject to expedited removal granted relief (either asylum or Convention Against Torture protection) was 28 percent from 2000 to 2004.[72] Notably, only 2 percent of unrepresented asylum-seekers were granted relief, while 25 percent of represented asylum-seekers were.[73]

While the number of people placed in expedited removal decreased in 2002, the number of asylum-seekers increased dramatically. For example, in FY 1998, 160,000 individuals were subject to expedited removal.[74] Of these individuals, 80,000 (or 50 percent) were permitted to withdraw their application for entry.[75] Of the remaining 80,000 individuals who were placed in the expedited removal process, 3,000 individuals expressed a fear of return or a desire to apply for asylum and were referred for a credible fear interview before an INS asylum officer.[76] About 18 percent of the expedited removal cases at airports were referred for a credible fear interview, in contrast to 0.4 percent (or four-tenths of 1 percent) of the cases at land ports of entry. Approximately 86 percent of the individuals referred to an asylum officer were found to have a "credible fear" of persecution and were referred for a hearing before an immigration judge.[77] In FY 1998, credible fear approval rates varied significantly depending on the asylum office conducting the interview. The Government Accountability Office (GAO) reported, for example, that the San Francisco asylum office's approval rate was 93 percent, while during the same seven-month period, the Houston and Miami asylum offices had a 59 percent approval rate.[78]

---

[66] INA §§212(a)(9)(A)(i), (iii); 8 USC §§1182(a)(9)(i), (iii).

[67] *See* Homeland Security Act of 2002, Pub. L. No. 107-296, §§456, 1512, 1517, 116 Stat. 2135, 2200, 2310, 2311.

[68] INA §§212(a)(9)(A)(i), (iii); 8 USC §§1182(a)(9)(i), (iii).

[69] Report on Asylum Seekers in Expedited Removal, Vol. I, *supra* note 50, at 32.

[70] *Id.*

[71] *Id.* at 33.

[72] *Id.*

[73] *Id.* at 34.

[74] INS Office of Public Affairs, *FY 1998 Update on Expedited Removals* (June 21, 1999).

[75] *Id.*

[76] *Id.*

[77] *Id.*

[78] *See* GAO, *Illegal Aliens: Changes in the Process of Denying Aliens Entry into the United States* 49 (Mar. 1998).

5.2. How Expedited Removal Works in Practice

5.2.1. Primary Inspection

When an individual arrives at a port of entry, he or she is inspected by an immigration officer at a primary inspection station. The primary inspector has only a few seconds to examine documents, run basic look-out queries, and ask pertinent questions.[79] Recent changes under the US-VISIT program also require individuals to be fingerprinted and photographed. If the immigration officer believes that the individual's documents are in order and that he or she is admissible to the United States, the individual is admitted. If, however, the primary inspector believes that there is a question about the individual's admissibility to the United States or that his or her documents are not in order, the inspector will refer the individual to secondary inspection.[80] Approximately 475 million people passed through primary inspection in the United States in 1996.[81] During the primary inspection stage, an individual does not have the right to representation unless he or she has become the focus of a criminal investigation and has been taken into custody.[82]

5.2.2. Secondary Inspection

Background

Millions of noncitizens are referred to secondary inspection each year.[83] Almost 10 million were referred in 1996.[84] Approximately 90 percent are admitted to the United States after they have been interviewed by a secondary inspector.[85] In order to determine whether the individual is subject to the expedited removal process, the secondary inspector questions the individual regarding his or her documents.[86]

No Right to Representation

As in primary inspection, a noncitizen in secondary inspection does not have the right to representation unless he or she has become the focus of a criminal investigation and has been taken into custody.[87] In at least one nonexpedited removal case, by stipulation, the applicant's attorney and CBP agreed to the presence of counsel at a deferred inspection interview.[88]

---

[79] 62 Fed. Reg. 10318 (Mar. 6, 1997) (supplementary information).
[80] *Id.*
[81] *Id.*
[82] 8 CFR §§292.5(b), 1292.5(b).
[83] 62 Fed. Reg. 10318 (Mar. 6, 1997) (supplementary information).
[84] *Id.*
[85] *Id.*
[86] *Id.*
[87] 8 CFR §§292.5(b), 1292.5(b).
[88] *See Torres v. Ridge*, No. C04-525JCC, Stipulation to Dismiss Plaintiff's Motion for a TRO (W.D. Wash. Apr. 13, 2004).

Record of Sworn Statement—Form I-867AB

During the secondary inspection interview, the inspector will seek to determine whether the noncitizen is in possession of a false document, invalid document, or no document.[89] If the inspector determines that the individual is subject to expedited removal, the inspector is required to take a sworn statement from the noncitizen on Form I-867AB, Record of Sworn Statement.[90] The inspector must read (or have read) to the noncitizen all information contained on the I-867A, create a record of the facts of the case and the statement made by the noncitizen during the questioning on the I-867A, and record the noncitizen's answers to questions on the I-867B. During the questioning in secondary inspection, the noncitizen must be given notice of the charges against him or her on Form I-860, Notice and Order of Expedited Removal, and must be given the opportunity to respond to those charges.[91] Following the questioning and recording of the noncitizen's statement, the inspector is required by regulation to read (or have read) to the noncitizen his or her statement.[92] The noncitizen must sign and initial each page of the statement and each correction.[93] Interpretative assistance must be used if necessary to communicate with the noncitizen.[94]

After consultation with nongovernmental organizations (NGOs) and the Office of United Nations High Commissioner for Refugees (UNHCR), legacy INS included the following information on the I-867A, directed specifically to potential asylum-seekers:

> You do not appear to be admissible or to have the legal papers authorizing your admission to the United States. This may result in your being denied admission and immediately returned to your home country without a hearing. If a decision is made to refuse your admission into the United States, you may be immediately removed from this country, and if so, you may be barred from reentry for a period of 5 years or longer.
>
> This may be your only opportunity to present information to me and the Immigration and Naturalization Service to make a decision. It is very important that you tell me the truth. If you lie or give misinformation, you may be subject to criminal or civil penalties, or barred from receiving immigration benefits or relief now or in the future.
>
> Except as I will explain to you, you are not entitled to a hearing or review.
>
> *U.S. law provides protection to certain persons who face persecution, harm or torture upon return to their home country. If you fear or have a concern about being removed from the United States or about being sent home, you should tell me so during this interview because you may not have another chance. You will have the opportunity to speak privately and confidentially to another officer about your fear*

---

[89] 62 Fed. Reg. 10318 (Mar. 6, 1997) (supplementary information).

[90] *See* 8 CFR §§235.3(b)(2)(i), 1235.3(b)(2)(i).

[91] 8 CFR §§235.3(b)(2)(i), 1235.3(b)(2)(i).

[92] 8 CFR §§235.3(b)(2)(i), 1235.3(b)(2)(i).

[93] 8 CFR §§235.3(b)(2)(i), 1235.3(b)(2)(i).

[94] 8 CFR §§235.3(b)(2)(i), 1235.3(b)(2)(i).

or concern. That officer will determine if you should remain in the United States and not be removed because of that fear.[95]

The I-867B requires the inspector to ask a series of questions regarding the noncitizen's fear of return to his or her home country. As noted above, interpretative assistance must be used if necessary to communicate with the noncitizen.[96] NGOs have expressed concern that, at some ports of entry, individuals are not afforded sufficient privacy to ensure confidentiality during the secondary inspection process. The questions that follow appear on the I-867B and were developed by legacy INS in consultation with NGOs and UNHCR:

- Why did you leave your home country or country of last residence?
- Do you have any fear or concern about being returned to your home country or being removed from the United States?
- Would you be harmed if you are returned to your home country or country of last residence?
- Do you have any questions or is there anything else you would like to add?[97]

Immigration inspectors are also instructed to inquire about the noncitizen's identity, alienage, and inadmissibility.[98] If a fear or concern is expressed during questioning, immigration inspectors have been instructed to ask follow-up questions to ascertain the general nature of the fear or concern.[99] If the noncitizen indicates an intention to apply for asylum or a fear of persecution, he or she should be referred to an AO.[100] Inspectors have been instructed to consider both verbal and nonverbal cues given by the noncitizen.[101] Additionally, inspectors have been advised that individuals expressing a fear based on personal disputes, domestic violence, sexual and child abuse, child custody problems, coercive marriage or family planning, female genital mutilation, AIDS, land or money disputes, whistle-blowing, and witnessing crimes should be referred to an AO.[102] Moreover, inspectors have been advised to "*not* go into detail on the nature of the [noncitizen's] fear of persecution or torture" and to "leave that" for the AO.[103]

> ➢ *Note*: A copy of the I-867AB is (or should be) given to each asylum-seeker referred for a credible fear interview. It is important to obtain and review this form with the asylum-seeker prior to the interview, IJ review, or IJ hearing. Statements or responses contained on the I-867AB have been used increas-

---

[95] Form I-867A (emphasis added). As noted above, this information must be read to every noncitizen subject to expedited removal.

[96] 8 CFR §§235.3(b)(2)(i), 1235.3(b)(2)(i).

[97] Form I-867B.

[98] 8 CFR §§235.3(b)(2)(i), 1235.3(b)(2)(i); IFM, *supra* note 32, at ch. 17.15(b)(2).

[99] INS Memorandum, C. Sale, IIRAIRA Wire #25 (Mar. 31, 1997) at ¶7, *published on* AILA InfoNet at Doc. No. 97033192 (*posted* Mar. 31, 1997).

[100] 8 CFR §§235.3(b)(2)(i), 1235.3(b)(2)(i); IFM, *supra* note 32, at ch. 17.15(b)(2).

[101] *See* IFM, *supra* note 32, at ch. 17.15(d).

[102] *Id.*

[103] *Id.* at ch. 17.15(b)(2) (emphasis added).

ingly for impeachment purposes at asylum hearings.[104] Under the REAL ID Act of 2005, a trier of fact may base a credibility determination on any prior statements made by an applicant.[105] If the asylum-seeker does not have a copy of the I-867AB, one may be obtained from the asylum office or DHS district counsel's office.[106]

The U.S. Court of Appeals for the Second Circuit has developed a four-part test to determine the reliability of an airport or other port-of-entry statement given by an asylum-seeker. The court noted that an adjudicator may take into account: (1) whether the record of the interview merely summarizes or paraphrases the applicant's statements rather than providing a verbatim account or transcript; (2) whether the questions posed to the applicant seem designed to elicit details of an asylum claim; (3) whether the applicant appears to have been reluctant to reveal information to immigration officials because of prior interrogation sessions or other coercive experiences in his or her home country; and (4) whether the applicant's answers to the questions posed suggest that the applicant did not understand English or the translations provided by the interpreter.[107]

Final Order

If the noncitizen does not express a fear of return or a desire to apply for asylum, has not established that he or she has a valid entry document, and has not been permitted to withdraw his or her application for entry, the immigration officer will issue a final order of removal after it has been reviewed and approved by a supervisory immigration officer.[108] The individual is not entitled to a hearing before an IJ or to an appeal to the Board of Immigration Appeals (BIA).[109] Upon issuance of a final order, the noncitizen must be detained

---

[104] *See, e.g., Simo v. Gonzales*, 445 F.3d 7, 12–13 (1st Cir. 2006) (upholding BIA's adverse credibility finding based on inconsistencies between applicant's airport interview and hearing testimony); *Guan v. Gonzales*, 432 F.3d 391, 395–96 (2d Cir. 2005) (finding that the IJ and BIA adverse credibility findings were based on substantial evidence insofar as they relied on inconsistencies between the applicant's airport interview and testimony before the IJ); *Zheng v. Gonzales*, 160 Fed. Appx. 501, 504 (7th Cir. 2005) (upholding IJ's adverse credibility determination, which relied on statements applicant made at the airport and during the credible fear interview, and which contradicted his testimony in immigration court); *Balogun v. Ashcroft*, 374 F.3d 492 (7th Cir. 2004) (upheld IJ's negative credibility determination based on discrepancies between airport statement and testimony); *Ramsameachire v. Ashcroft*, 357 F.3d 169 (2d Cir. 2004) (finding BIA did not err in basing adverse credibility determination on inconsistencies between airport statement and testimony at removal hearing); *but see Mohamed v. Gonzales*, 312 Fed. Appx. 126, 128 (9th Cir. 2005) (finding IJ could not base an adverse credibility determination on false statements an applicant made during an airport interview regarding which countries he passed through to get to the United States because this inconsistency did not go to the heart of the asylum claim).

[105] INA §208(b)(1)(B); 8 USC §1158(b)(1)(B).

[106] See appxs. 6A and 6C for a list of addresses and telephone numbers for these offices.

[107] *Ramsameachire v. Ashcroft*, 357 F.3d 169, 179–80 (2d Cir. 2004); *see also Guan v. Gonzales*, 432 F.3d at 396 (finding that airport interview could be used to support adverse credibility finding where (1) remarks were transcribed verbatim, (2) questions posed gave ample opportunity to describe persecution, (3) there was no indication of reluctance to reveal information, and (4) there was no evidence of translation problems).

[108] 8 CFR §§235.3(b)(7), 1235.3(b)(7).

[109] 8 CFR §§235.3(b)(2)(ii), 1235.3(b)(2)(ii).

unless the AG determines that parole is necessary to meet a medical emergency or a legitimate law enforcement objective.[110]

5.2.3. Expression of Fear and Form M-444

If a noncitizen expresses a fear of persecution, a fear of torture, a fear of return to his or her home country, or a desire to apply for asylum, the immigration inspector will refer him or her for a credible fear interview with an AO.[111] The immigration officer must provide the noncitizen with Form M-444, Information About Credible Fear Interview, in English or one of the 13 other languages into which the form has been translated.[112] The immigration officer must also explain Form M-444 to the noncitizen in a language he or she understands.[113] The form contains two signature lines, one for the interpreter (if one is used) and the other for the noncitizen to acknowledge receipt.[114]

The form contains information regarding the credible fear interview process, including notice that the asylum-seeker will have the opportunity to be interviewed by a specially trained AO, that he or she may consult with family members, friends, or other representative, and that he or she may contact UNHCR. The form will also contain a brief description of the credible fear legal standard, the right to an interpreter, the right to review by an IJ if the AO determines that he or she does not have a credible fear, and the consequences of failing to establish a credible fear of persecution.[115] The asylum-seeker should also be provided with a list of pro bono or nonprofit organizations that provide assistance free of charge in the area where he or she is detained.

5.2.4. Exceptions to Expedited Removal

As noted above in this chapter at 5.1.3, there are a number of individuals who are not subject to expedited removal. These exceptions are listed below with relevant cites to regulations and policies issued by legacy INS or DHS.

Applicants Permitted to Withdraw Their Applications for Admission

The AG may, in his or her discretion, permit any applicant for admission to withdraw his or her application for admission in lieu of expedited removal under INA §235(b)(1).[116] The applicant's decision to withdraw his or her application for admission must be made voluntarily.[117] An applicant, however, does not have the "right" to withdraw his or her application for admission.[118] Permission to withdraw an application for admission should *not* normally be granted unless the applicant intends and is able to depart the United States im-

---

[110] 8 CFR §§235.3(b)(2)(iii), 1235.3(b)(2)(iii).

[111] 8 CFR §235.3(b)(4).

[112] 8 CFR §235.3(b)(4)(i). *See also* "Expedited Removal in a Nutshell," 16 *AILA Monthly Mailing* 1021 (Dec. 1997).

[113] IFM, *supra* note 32, at ch. 17.15(d)(4).

[114] *Id.*

[115] 8 CFR §§235.3(b)(2)(i), 1235.3(b)(2)(i).

[116] 8 CFR §§235.4, 1235.4.

[117] 8 CFR §§235.4, 1235.4.

[118] 8 CFR §§235.4, 1235.4.

mediately.[119] Moreover, an applicant permitted to withdraw his or her application for admission will normally remain in carrier or DHS custody pending departure, unless the district director determines that parole of the applicant is warranted under 8 CFR §212.5(b).[120]

Factors

Chapter 17.2 of the *Inspector's Field Manual* (IFM) provides that an applicant should be permitted to withdraw his or her application for admission if it is determined to be in "the best interest of justice that a removal order not be issued."[121] Factors that may be considered by an inspector in determining whether an applicant should be permitted to withdraw his or her application for admission include: (1) the seriousness of the immigration violation; (2) previous findings of inadmissibility against the applicant; (3) intention on the part of the applicant to violate the law; (4) ability to easily overcome the ground of inadmissibility; (5) age or poor health of the applicant; and (6) other humanitarian or public interest considerations.[122] The IFM also acknowledges that detention space, workload, and resources may also affect whether applicants are permitted to withdraw their applications for admission.[123]

Unaccompanied Minors

Inspectors are also instructed to, whenever appropriate, permit unaccompanied minors to withdraw their application for admission rather than placing them in formal removal proceedings.[124] Before allowing the withdrawal, the inspector must be satisfied that the minor is capable of understanding the withdrawal process or that a responsible adult is aware of the actions taken and the minor's impending return.[125] When making such a decision, the inspector should make every effort to determine whether the minor has a fear of persecution.[126] According to legacy INS instructions, "if there is any doubt, *especially in the case of countries with known human rights abuses or where turmoil exists*," the minor should be placed in INA §240 removal proceedings.[127]

LPRs, Refugees, Asylees, and U.S. Citizens

If an applicant for admission who is subject to expedited removal claims to have been lawfully admitted for permanent residence (an LPR), admitted as a refugee or granted asylum, or claims to be a U.S. citizen, the immigration officer must attempt to verify the applicant's status.[128] If the status cannot be readily verified and the applicant claims under penalty of perjury that he or she is an LPR, an asylee, a refugee, or a U.S. citizen, his or her case will

---

[119] 8 CFR §§235.4, 1235.4.

[120] 8 CFR §§235.4, 1235.4.

[121] IFM, *supra* note 32, at ch. 17.2.

[122] *Id.*

[123] *Id.*

[124] *See* INS Memorandum, P. Virtue, "Unaccompanied Minors Subject to Expedited Removal" (Aug. 21, 1997), *published on* AILA InfoNet at Doc. No. 97082191 (*posted* Aug. 21, 1997).

[125] *Id.*

[126] *Id.*

[127] *Id.* (emphasis added).

[128] 8 CFR §§235.3(b)(5)(i), 1235.3(b)(5)(i).

be referred to an IJ for review.[129] There is no appeal from the IJ's decision.[130] Unlike asylum-seekers, such individuals are entitled to representation by counsel (at no expense to the government) at the IJ review.[131] Such individuals are also entitled to habeas corpus proceedings, but the court may only review whether the individual (1) is an alien; (2) was ordered removed under INA §235(b)(1); or (3) is an LPR.[132] The court may not review whether the individual is actually inadmissible or entitled to any relief from removal.[133]

If the immigration officer verifies the LPR, refugee, or asylee status of the applicant, but he or she appears to be inadmissible for other reasons, the officer may initiate regular removal proceedings against the alien under INA §240.[134]

Unaccompanied Minors

According to legacy INS and DHS, unaccompanied minors will normally be placed in regular INA §240 removal proceedings rather than in expedited removal proceedings.[135] In addition to charging them as not being in possession of valid entry documents, inspectors are instructed to charge minors as noncitizens likely to become a public charge under INA §212(a)(4), which renders the minor subject to regular §240 proceedings.[136] As a general rule, according to the legacy INS memorandum, a minor should not be charged as having fraudulent documents unless the minor "clearly understood" he or she was committing fraud or the minor is knowingly involved in criminal activity.[137]

Legacy INS noted, however, that under the following circumstances an unaccompanied minor may be placed in expedited removal proceedings: (1) the minor has, in the presence of an immigration officer, engaged in criminal activity that would qualify as an aggravated felony if committed by an adult; (2) the minor has been convicted or adjudicated delinquent of an aggravated felony within the United States or another country, and the inspecting officer has confirmation of that order; or (3) the minor has previously been formally removed, excluded, or deported from the United States.[138]

---

[129] 8 CFR §§235.3(b)(5)(iv), 1235.3(b)(5)(iv).

[130] 8 CFR §§235.3(b)(5)(iv), 1235.3(b)(5)(iv).

[131] *See* EOIR Memorandum, M. Creppy, "Interim Operating Policy and Procedure Memorandum 97-3: Procedures for Credible Fear and Claimed Status Reviews" (Mar. 25, 1997, as amended on Apr. 25, 1997), available at *www.usdoj.gov/eoir/efoia/ocij/oppm97/97-3.pdf*.

[132] INA §242(e)(2); 8 USC §1252(e)(2).

[133] INA §242(e)(5); 8 USC §1252(e)(5).

[134] 8 CFR §§235.3(b)(5)(ii), (iii), 1235.3(b)(5)(ii), (iii).

[135] *See* IFM, *supra* note 32, at ch. 17.15(f)(3); INS Memorandum, *supra* note 124.

[136] *See* 8 CFR §§235.3(b)(3), 1235.3(b)(3) (if INS charges an individual with additional grounds of inadmissibility other than seeking entry with false or no documents grounds, the individual is not subject to expedited removal).

[137] *See* IFM, *supra* note 32, at ch. 17.15(f)(3); INS Memorandum, *supra* note 124.

[138] IFM, *supra* note 32, at ch. 17.15(f)(4).

Pre–April 1, 1997, Parolees

Individuals paroled into the United States prior to April 1, 1997, are exempt from being subject to expedited removal.[139] This policy is reflected in the new definition of "arriving alien" in 8 CFR §§1.1(q), 1001.1(q).

Stowaways

Stowaways are not subject to expedited removal procedures. Under INA §235(a)(2), stowaways are not eligible to apply for admission or to be admitted to the United States. If, however, they express a fear of return, they will be given a credible fear interview by an AO. They are not, however, eligible for a hearing under INA §240.[140]

Crewmembers

Crewmembers who indicate a fear of persecution in their home countries whether on or off their vessel or other conveyance must be given an asylum application form and submit it to the local district director within 10 days.[141] The district director must, upon receiving the application, refer the individual to an IJ for an asylum hearing.[142]

Individuals Seeking Entry Under VWPP

Individuals who are refused admission at a port of entry under the Visa Waiver Pilot Program (VWPP) or the Visa Waiver Permanent Program (VWPP) and who request asylum in the United States must be referred to an IJ for proceedings in immigration court.[143] The proceedings are limited to a determination of eligibility for asylum or withholding or deferral of removal.[144] Under the VWPP, nationals of certain designated countries are permitted to enter the United States without first obtaining a visa.[145] Individuals entering with a passport from a VWPP country, even though they are not nationals of that country, are entitled to a hearing before an IJ and are not subject to expedited removal.[146]

5.2.5. Detention

A noncitizen who is subject to expedited removal or who has been issued a removal order in expedited removal proceedings "shall be detained" pending determination and removal, except that parole is permitted only when the AG determines, in the exercise of his or her discretion, that parole is required to meet a medical emergency or is necessary for a legitimate law enforcement objective.[147] The AG's discretion is delegated to DHS district directors.[148]

---

[139] See INS Memorandum, *supra* note 25; *see also* AOBTC, Lesson: Credible Fear, *supra* note 10, at 8.

[140] For asylum procedures for stowaways, see ch. 3.4.

[141] 8 CFR §§208.5(b), 1208.5(b).

[142] 8 CFR §§208.5(b), 1208.5(b).

[143] 8 CFR §217.4(a)(1).

[144] 8 CFR §§208.2(c)(3)(i), 1208.2(c)(3)(i).

[145] INA §217; 8 USC §1187.

[146] *See Matter of Kanagasundram*, 22 I&N Dec. 963 (BIA 1999).

[147] 8 CFR §§235.3(b)(2)(iii), 1235.3(b)(2)(iii).

[148] For information on procedures for requesting release on parole, see ch. 3.8.

In theory, a more generous standard for release is applied to individuals subject to expedited removal who have been found by an AO or IJ to have a "credible fear" of persecution. Such individuals may be paroled if they are able to establish: (1) their identity, (2) community ties, and (3) that they are not subject to any bars to asylum involving violence or misconduct.[149] Nevertheless, in some districts, asylum-seekers found to have a credible fear are denied any opportunity for release.[150]

5.2.6. Credible Fear Interviews

Rest Period

An individual who has expressed a fear of persecution or a desire to apply for asylum is allowed at least 48 hours to rest and prepare for the "credible fear" interview while he or she is detained at a DHS detention facility or local jail.[151] The individual may, however, request that the interview be conducted sooner, and the immigration inspector should convey that request to the asylum office.[152]

Location

The "credible fear" interview is conducted at DHS detention facilities, local jails or, in some areas, at DHS district offices.[153] The regulations provide that the interview must be "separate and apart from the general public."[154]

Interviewers

The credible fear interview is conducted by an asylum officer (AO).[155] The INA defines an AO as

> an immigration officer who (i) has had professional training in country conditions, asylum law, and interview techniques comparable to that provided to full time [asylum] adjudicators . . . , and (ii) is supervised by an officer who . . . has had substantial experience adjudicating asylum applications.[156]

---

[149] *See* INS Memorandum, M. Pearson, "Expedited Removal, Additional Policy Guidance" (Dec. 30, 1997), *published on* AILA InfoNet at Doc. No. 97123091 (*posted* Dec. 30, 1997).

[150] *See, e.g.*, United States Commission on International Religious Freedom, *Expedited Removal Study Report Card: 2 Years Later* (Feb. 8, 2007), at 5, available at *www.uscirf.gov/reports/scorecard_FINAL.pdf* (noting the wide variation in release rates across the country for FY 2003, from 0.5 percent in New Orleans to 98 percent in Harlingen, and that the average detention period for an asylum-seeker found to have a credible fear is 60 days); Lawyers Committee for Human Rights, *Refugees Behind Bars: The Imprisonment of Asylum Seekers in the Wake of the 1996 Immigration Act* (Aug. 1999), available at *www.humanrightsfirst.org/pubs/descriptions/behindbars.htm*; Lawyers Committee for Human Rights, *Slamming the Golden Door: A Year of Expedited Removal* (Mar. 1998), available at *www.humanrightsfirst.org/pubs/descriptions/golden.htm*; "Credible Fear Screening for Individuals in Expedited Removal," 16 *AILA Monthly Mailing* 1027 (Dec. 1997).

[151] *See* IFM, *supra* note 32, at ch. 17.15(b)(13). For the addresses and telephone numbers of DHS detention facilities, see appx. 6E.

[152] IFM, *supra* note 32, at ch. 17.15(b)(13).

[153] *See* 62 Fed. Reg. 10319 (Mar. 6, 1997) (supplementary information).

[154] 8 CFR §208.30(d).

[155] *Id.*

[156] INA §235(b)(1)(E); 8 USC §1225(b)(1)(E).

CHAPTER 5 • EXPEDITED REMOVAL 313

According to the Asylum Division, all AOs undergo a basic three-week training course.[157] In addition, all AOs conducting credible fear interviews receive specialized training in credible fear and expedited removal procedures.[158] The Asylum Division also conducts periodic quality assurance reviews of AO decisions to ensure that any problems that arise are corrected.[159]

Interview Procedures

The AO must conduct the credible fear interview in a nonadversarial manner.[160] At the time of the interview, the AO will verify whether the asylum-seeker received Form M-444, Information About Credible Fear Interview,[161] and whether he or she understands the credible fear determination process.[162] The AO will conduct the interview using Form I-870, Record of Determination/Credible Fear Work Sheet. The I-870 requires the AO to read the following information to the asylum-seeker:

> The purpose of this interview is to determine whether you may be eligible for asylum or protection from removal to a country where you fear persecution or torture. I am going to ask you questions about why you fear returning to your country or any other country you may be removed to. It is very important that you tell the truth during the interview and that you respond to all of my questions. This may be your only opportunity to give such information. Please feel comfortable telling me why you fear harm. U.S. law has strict rules to prevent the disclosure of what you tell me today about reasons why you fear harm. The information you tell me about the reasons for your fear will not be disclosed to your government, except in exceptional circumstances. The statements you make today may be used in deciding your claim and in any future immigration proceedings. It is important that we understand each other. If at any time I make a statement you do not understand, please stop me and tell me you do not understand so that I can explain it to you. If at any time you tell me something that I do not understand, I will ask you to explain.[163]

The I-870 is a five-page worksheet that the AO is required to complete during each credible fear interview. The AO is also required to create a summary of the material facts as stated by the asylum-seeker.[164] In cases in which credible fear is found, AOs are no longer required to prepare typed question-and-answer interview notes or write detailed assessments.[165] In addition to their statements, an asylum-seeker is permitted to present evidence during the interview, if available.[166] At the conclusion of the interview, the AO

---

[157] See "INS Reports on First Three Months of Expedited Removal," 74 *Interpreter Releases* 1101 (July 21, 1997).

[158] *Id.*

[159] *Id.*

[160] 8 CFR §208.30(d).

[161] *See* this chapter, at 5.2.3.

[162] 8 CFR §208.30(d).

[163] Form I-870 at 1.28.

[164] 8 CFR §208.30(d)(6).

[165] *See* INS Memorandum, J. Langlois, "Streamlining the Credible Fear Process" (Dec. 8, 2000), *published on* AILA InfoNet at Doc. No. 01013001 (*posted* Jan. 30, 2001).

[166] 8 CFR §208.30(d)(4).

must review the summary of material facts with the asylum-seeker and provide him or her with the opportunity to correct any errors.[167] Asylum officers are required to create a written record of their determination, including the summary, any additional facts upon which they relied, and their determination of whether, in light of such facts, the asylum-seeker has established a credible fear of persecution.[168]

A copy of the completed I-870 is available to asylum-seekers and their representatives or consultants. It is important to obtain a copy of the I-870, as well as the AO's written summary from the interview prior to an IJ review or IJ hearing. Statements made by asylum-seekers at the credible fear interview may be and have been used for impeachment purposes.[169]

> ➤ *Tip*—**Prior Statements under the REAL ID Act**—The REAL ID Act of 2005 allows immigration judges to base a credibility determination on prior statements made by the applicant, whether oral or written, and whether or not they were under oath.[170] It is, therefore, very important to obtain a copy of the I-870.

Role of Attorney, Representative, or Consultant

The asylum-seeker may consult with a person or persons of his or her choosing prior to the credible fear interview.[171] Such consultation must be at no expense to the government and may not unreasonably delay the process.[172] Any person or persons with whom the asylum-seeker chooses to consult may be present at the interview and may be permitted, in the discretion of the AO, to present a statement at the end of the interview.[173] The AO, in his or her discretion, may place reasonable limits on the number of people present at the interview and on the length of statement or statements made.[174] In practice, AOs appear to conduct these interviews in much the same way they conduct affirmative interviews, and allow for consultants to ask follow-up questions, provide documentation, and make closing statements. The Asylum Division encourages the use of consultants in the credible fear process and has noted that they generally facilitate the process and ensure that the asylum applicant's claim is fully elicited.[175]

---

[167] 8 CFR §208.30(d)(6).

[168] 8 CFR §208.30(e).

[169] *See, e.g., Simo v. Gonzales*, 445 F.3d 7, 12–13 (1st Cir. 2006) (upholding BIA's adverse credibility finding based on inconsistencies between applicant's airport interview and hearing testimony); *Zheng v. Gonzales*, 160 Fed Appx. 501, 504 (7th Cir. 2005) (upholding IJ's adverse credibility determination that relied on statements applicant made at the airport and during the credible fear interview that contradicted his testimony in immigration court)

[170] INA §208(b)(1)(B); 8 USC §1158(b)(1)(B).

[171] INA §235(b)(1)(B)(iv), 8 USC 1225(b)(1)(B)(iv); 8 CFR §208.30(d)(4).

[172] INA §235(b)(1)(B)(iv), 8 USC 1225(b)(1)(B)(iv); 8 CFR §208.30(d)(4).

[173] 8 CFR §208.30(d)(4).

[174] *Id.*

[175] *See* INS Memorandum, J. Langlois, "Role of Consultants in the Credible Fear Interview" (Nov. 14, 1997).

Interpretation

If the asylum-seeker is unable to proceed effectively with the interview in English, and if the AO is unable to proceed competently in a language chosen by the asylum-seeker, the AO must arrange for the assistance of an interpreter in conducting the interview.[176] The interpreter may *not* be a representative or employee of the asylum-seeker's country of nationality or, if the asylum-seeker is stateless, his or her country of last habitual residence.[177] In at least one reported case, a federal court reversed a negative credibility determination based, in part, on statements given at a credible fear interview where the AO used an Italian interpreter because an Amharic interpreter was not available.[178] The court found that it was error for the immigration judge to make a negative credibility determination without first assessing the applicant's Italian language skills.[179]

AOs have also been instructed to accommodate an asylum-seeker's special request for a male or female interpreter and for interpreters who do (or do not) speak certain dialects or have certain accents.[180] Asylum-seekers may also request that the interpreter be physically present at the interview if they would have difficulty presenting their claim through a telephonic interpreter.[181]

The Asylum Division encourages consultants to monitor the quality of the interpretation asylum-seekers receive and permits co-consultants fluent in English and the asylum-seeker's language to attend the credible fear interview.[182] The consultant or co-consultant may interrupt the interview to point out problems with the interpretation.[183] If the interpreter is not competent or not neutral, the AO should ask whether the asylum-seeker or his or her consultant would like to change interpreters.[184] Asylum-seekers may provide their own interpreter, provided that the interpretation is monitored by an interpreter from a commercial telephonic service.[185]

Dependents

An accompanying spouse or minor child may be included in the credible fear determination of the principal asylum-seeker, if the spouse or child so chooses.[186]

Confidentiality

The same confidentiality requirements that apply in asylum adjudications also apply to credible fear and reasonable fear interviews.[187]

---

[176] 8 CFR §208.30(d)(5).

[177] *Id.*

[178] *Ememe v. Ashcroft*, 358 F.3d 446 (7th Cir. 2004).

[179] *Id.* at 453.

[180] *See* INS Memorandum, J. Langlois, "Interpreters in the Credible Fear Process" (Feb. 10, 1998).

[181] *Id.*

[182] *Id.*

[183] *Id.*

[184] *Id.*

[185] *Id.*

[186] *See* 8 CFR §§208.30(b), 1208.30(b).

[187] *See* 8 CFR §§208.6, 1208.6. For discussion of the right to confidentiality, see ch. 3.3.5.

5.2.7. Asylum Officer's Credible Fear Decision

The AO's decision does not become final until reviewed by a supervisory AO.[188] Asylum officers have been instructed that an applicant who establishes a credible fear of torture, even if he or she does not have a credible fear of persecution (for asylum and withholding purposes), should be referred for a hearing before an IJ.[189]

If the AO determines that the asylum-seeker has a credible fear, the AO will inform the asylum-seeker and issue to him or her Form I-862, Notice to Appear, for full consideration of the asylum claim in proceedings under INA §240.[190] If the asylum-seeker is found *not* to have a credible fear of persecution, the AO will inform the asylum-seeker and issue to him or her Form I-869, Record of Negative Credible Fear Finding, on which the asylum-seeker must indicate whether he or she desires review by an IJ.[191] In the case of a negative credible fear determination, the AO must also issue Form I-860, Notice and Order of Expedited Removal, unless the asylum-seeker is a stowaway.[192]

5.2.8. Review by an IJ

The INA allows for a prompt review of a negative credible fear determination by an IJ.[193] The review must include the opportunity for the asylum-seeker to be heard and questioned by the IJ, either in person or by telephonic or video connection.[194] The review must be conducted as expeditiously as possible, "to the maximum extent practicable within 24 hours, but in no case later than 7 days after" the negative credible fear determination.[195]

Standard of Review

The IJ's review is a de novo review of the AO's negative credible fear determination.[196] The IJ must determine

> whether there is a significant possibility, taking into account the credibility of the statements made by the [asylum-seeker] in support of the [asylum-seeker's] claim and such other facts as are known to the [IJ], that the [asylum-seeker] could establish eligibility for asylum [under INA §208], withholding [under INA §241(b)(3),] or withholding under the Convention Against Torture.[197]

---

[188] 8 CFR §208.30(e)(4).

[189] *See* INS Memorandum, J. Langlois, "Implementation of Amendments to Asylum and Withholding of Removal Regulations, Effective March 22, 1999" (Mar. 18, 1999), at 4. For discussion of relief available to those who fear torture, see ch. 4.

[190] 8 CFR §208.30(f). See ch. 3.3 for information regarding §240 proceedings.

[191] 8 CFR §208.30(g)(1).

[192] *Id.* For discussion of the asylum procedures for stowaways, see ch. 3.4.

[193] INA §235(b)(1)(B)(iii)(III); 8 USC §1225(b)(1)(B)(iii)(III).

[194] INA §235(b)(1)(B)(iii)(III); 8 USC §1225(b)(1)(B)(iii)(III).

[195] INA §235(b)(1)(B)(iii)(III); 8 USC §1225(b)(1)(B)(iii)(III). *See* 8 CFR §1003.42(e) and EOIR Memorandum, M. Creppy, Operating Policies and Procedures Memorandum No. 99-5: Implementation of Article 3 of the UN Convention Against Torture (May 14, 1999), *published on* AILA InfoNet and also available at *www.usdoj.gov/eoir/efoia/ocij/oppm99/99_5.pdf*.

[196] 8 CFR §1003.42(d).

[197] *Id.* For discussion of withholding of removal under the Convention Against Torture, see ch. 4.

Procedures

If an asylum-seeker requests review of the AO's negative credible fear determination, the AO will serve the asylum-seeker with Form I-863, Notice of Referral to Immigration Judge.[198] The AO must provide the IJ with the record of the determination, including copies of the I-863, the AO's notes, the summary of material facts, and other materials on which the negative credible fear determination was based.[199] The record of proceeding created by the immigration court, however, "shall *not* be merged with any later proceeding" under §240.[200] Once the review is completed, the record of proceeding is "retired."[201]

Negative credible fear determinations, unlike other IJ hearings, may be reviewed by telephone conference call "*without* the [asylum-seeker's] consent."[202] If the asylum-seeker is detained at the same location as the immigration court (such as a DHS or contract facility), the IJ review will be conducted in person.[203] The IJ is required to audiotape the review and make the tape a part of the record of proceedings.[204]

The IJ may receive into evidence any oral or written statement that is material and relevant to any issue in the review.[205] According to the chief immigration judge, "credible fear review proceedings should *not* be as in-depth as a full asylum hearing."[206]

Role of Attorney, Representative, or Consultant

Asylum-seekers may *consult* with persons of their choosing *prior* to any review of the credible fear determination.[207] In a memorandum, the Office of the Chief Immigration Judge (OCIJ) has construed the statutory and regulatory provisions establishing that rule to mean that "[t]here is no right to *representation* prior to or *during* the review."[208] It is within the discretion of the IJ, according to the OCIJ, whether to permit persons with whom the asylum-seeker has consulted even to be "present" at the review.[209] The memorandum further notes that nothing in the statute, regulations, or the memorandum entitles an attorney to make an opening statement, call and question witnesses, cross-examine, object to written evidence, or make a closing argument.[210] For these reasons there is no need for the attorney or representative to file a Notice of Entry of Appearance (Form

---

[198] 8 CFR §208.30(g)(1)(i).

[199] 8 CFR §§208.30(g)(2)(ii), 1208.30(g)(2)(ii).

[200] 8 CFR §1003.42(b).

[201] *See* EOIR Memorandum, M. Creppy, "Interim Operating Policy and Procedure Memorandum 97-3: Procedures for Credible Fear and Claimed Status Reviews" (Mar. 25, 1997), at IV, available at *www.usdoj.gov/eoir/efoia/ocij/oppm97/97-3.pdf*.

[202] 8 CFR §1003.25(c) (emphasis added).

[203] *See* EOIR Memorandum, *supra* note 201, at VI.

[204] *Id.*

[205] 8 CFR §1003.42(c).

[206] *See* EOIR Memorandum, *supra* note 201, at VI (emphasis added).

[207] *See* INA §235(b)(1)(B)(iv); 8 USC §1225(b)(1)(B)(iv); *see also* 8 CFR §1003.42(c).

[208] *See* EOIR Memorandum, *supra* note 201, at VI (emphasis in original).

[209] *Id.* at n.10.

[210] *Id.*

EOIR-28).[211] As a result of this OCIJ memorandum, some IJs have not allowed attorneys and representatives to participate actively during the negative credible fear review.[212]

Interpreters

The immigration court is required to provide an interpreter if one is necessary.[213] If there is sufficient advance notice, the IJ should order a contract interpreter.[214] Given the expedited nature of the review, the Office of the Chief Immigration Judge anticipates that AT&T Language Line telephonic interpreters will be used extensively.[215]

Decision

If the IJ concurs with the AO's negative credible fear determination, the case will be returned to DHS for removal of the asylum-seeker.[216] If the IJ finds that the asylum-seeker possesses a credible fear of persecution, the IJ will vacate the order of the AO issued on Form I-860 and DHS will place the asylum-seeker in removal proceedings under INA §240, where the asylum-seeker may receive full consideration of his or her asylum claim.[217] The IJ has no authority to review an asylum-seeker's custody status, *i.e.*, make a bond or parole determination, in the course of reviewing a negative credible fear determination.[218]

No Appeal

There is no appeal from an IJ's decision on review of an adverse credibility determination.[219]

5.2.9. Credible Fear Reinterviews Prior to Departure

The Office of Refugee, Asylum, and International Operations may, at its discretion, offer a second credible fear interview to any asylum-seeker, even if he or she has failed to establish a credible fear of persecution before an AO or an IJ.[220] Reinterviews will occur if the asylum-seeker or his or her consultant makes a reasonable claim to the Office of Refugee, Asylum, and International Operations that compelling new information concerning the case exists and should be considered.[221]

5.3. OVERSIGHT OF THE EXPEDITED REMOVAL PROCESS

During the implementation of expedited removal, several governmental and nongovernmental groups have observed the expedited removal process in a variety of capacities, includ-

---

[211] *Id.*

[212] *See* "INS Reports on First Three Months of Implementation of Expedited Removal," 74 *Interpreter Releases* 1101, 1103 (July 21, 1997).

[213] 8 CFR §1003.42(c).

[214] *See* EOIR Memorandum, *supra* note 201, at VI.

[215] *Id.*

[216] 8 CFR §§208.30(f)(1), 1003.42(f).

[217] 8 CFR §1208.30(g)(2)(iv)(B). If the asylum-seeker is a stowaway, see ch. 3.4.

[218] 8 CFR §1003.42(g).

[219] 8 CFR §1003.42(f); *but see* this chapter, at 5.2.9.

[220] *See* INS Memorandum, *supra* note 149.

[221] *Id.* See appx. 6A for Office of Refugee, Asylum, and International Operations contact information.

ing as supervisors, as academics, or as consultants representing asylum-seekers during or after the process. It is, indisputably, a process that has drastically reduced the rights of noncitizens at ports of entry and dramatically increased the authority of immigration inspectors, AOs, and IJs. For these reasons, the expedited removal process is likely to be discussed and debated as long as the process is in existence. Some of the agencies and groups contributing to the ongoing discussion, along with their activities and reports, are cited below.

5.3.1. Quality Assurance

In an effort to ensure that all districts implement expedited removal correctly, USCIS's Office of Refugee, Asylum and International Operations announced in 2006 that it would increase the number and category of credible fear cases that are subject to mandatory quality review.[222] Beginning May 1, 2006, all positive credible fear determinations for individuals with odd-numbered A-numbers from the Arlington, Chicago, and Miami Asylum Offices became subject to mandatory quality assurance review. In addition, the following credible fear cases also require a quality assurance review by Asylum Headquarters before a decision is issued:

- Cases involving a negative credible fear of persecution and torture;
- Cases involving a negative credible fear of persecution, but a positive credible fear of torture;
- Positive credible fear determinations with an odd-numbered A-number for all inland cases;
- High-profile cases (*e.g.*, high-ranking foreign government officials or their family members, or any person whose case has been, or is likely to be, publicized);
- Claims based on domestic violence (*e.g.*, spousal abuse, child abuse, or violence between family members not in a spousal relationship);
- Positive credible fear determinations that involve a possible mandatory bar, except the bar of firm resettlement;
- Claims involving novel legal issues, or any case that a supervisory asylum prescreening officer believes should be reviewed by Asylum Headquarters;
- Claims involving individuals who appear to be incapable of testifying on their own behalf;
- Claims involving known or suspected human rights abusers or terrorists.[223]

The Office of Refugee, Asylum and International Operations also announced in 2006 the release of a new lesson plan on credible fear for its Asylum Officer Basic Training Course.[224] The lesson plan contains "significant changes" and, as a result, USCIS required all asylum office personnel to review and receive training on this revised lesson

---

[222] USCIS Memorandum, J. Langlois, "Increase of Quality Assurance Review for Positive Credible Fear Determinations and Release of Updated Asylum Officer Basic Training Course Lesson Plan, Credible Fear of Persecution and Torture Determinations" (Apr. 14, 2006), at 1.

[223] *Id.*

[224] *Id.*; *see* AOBTC, Lesson: Credible Fear, *supra* note 10.

plan.[225] The major changes in the lesson plan are revisions to the credible fear standard[226] and more "balanced" guidance on credible fear determinations after USCIS received criticism that there was a greater burden on asylum officers to support a negative credible fear determination.[227]

Asylum Headquarters has made available policy memoranda, the *Inspector's Field Manual*, and internal forms to NGOs and others, and has sought input from these groups when formulating policy and drafting forms.

5.3.2. Government Accountability Office Reports

Section 302(b) of IIRAIRA required the Government Accountability Office (GAO—formerly the General Accounting Office) to report on the implementation of the expedited removal process. GAO issued a report in March 1998 based on its review of legacy INS data and its observations from visits to five locations.[228] GAO reported that 79 percent of the individuals referred for a credible fear interview were found to have a credible fear by AOs.[229] The report, however, did not comment on the disparity in approval rates among asylum offices, ranging from a 93 percent approval rate in San Francisco to 59 percent in Houston and Miami.[230] GAO concluded that the immigration inspectors and supervisors documented that they followed certain legacy INS procedures 80 to 100 percent of the time.[231] Notably, GAO did not examine the quality or the correctness of the determinations made by inspectors, AOs, and IJs.

The International Religious Freedom Act of 1998 (IRFA) required a more in-depth study of the expedited removal process, particularly as it affected asylum-seekers.[232] The study, conducted by the GAO with the opportunity for participation by experts, had to be completed by September 1, 2000.[233] Specifically, the GAO was required to examine whether immigration officers were engaging in any of the following conduct when dealing with individuals who may be eligible to be granted asylum:

- Improperly encouraging such [individuals] to withdraw their applications for admission;

- Incorrectly failing to refer such [individuals] for an interview by an asylum officer for a determination of whether they have a credible fear of persecution . . . ;

- Incorrectly removing such [individuals] to a country where they may be persecuted;

---

[225] USCIS Memorandum, *supra* note 222, at 3.

[226] *See* this chapter, at 5.1.4.

[227] USCIS Memorandum, *supra* note 222, at 3.

[228] GAO, Report to Congressional Committees, *Illegal Aliens: Changes in the Process of Denying Aliens Entry into the United States* (Mar. 1998), at 4–5, available at *www.gao.gov/archive/1998/gg98081.pdf*.

[229] *Id.* at 7.

[230] *Id.* at 49.

[231] *Id.* at 4–5.

[232] *See* International Religious Freedom Act of 1998 (IRFA), Pub. L. No. 105-292, §605(a)(2), 112 Stat. 2787, 2814 (1998).

[233] *See* IRFA §§605(a), (b), 112 Stat. at 2814–15.

- Detaining such [individuals] improperly or in inappropriate conditions.[234]

In September 2000, GAO published its finding in a report entitled *Illegal Aliens: Opportunities Exist to Improve the Expedited Removal Process*. In this report, which was sharply criticized by the refugee advocacy community, GAO summarized its mostly paper review of legacy INS files and found:

- INS generally followed its own procedures for documenting expedited removal cases;
- INS generally followed its own procedures for documenting the credible fear process;
- Many asylum-seekers did not appear for their hearing after release.

As pointed out by the Expedited Removal Study in its critique of the GAO report, the questions posed by Congress in IRFA remain largely unanswered and the methodology employed by GAO was seriously flawed.[235] For example, the Expedited Removal Study's critique points out that in 2 percent of the randomly sampled 1,999 expedited removal files reviewed by GAO, legacy INS failed to refer individuals for a credible fear interview even though they had expressed a fear.[236] The Study points out that this could mean that as many as 900 individuals may not have been referred despite expressing a fear.[237]

5.3.3. U.S. Commission on International Religious Freedom Report

The U.S. Commission on International Religious Freedom was created by IRFA to monitor religious freedom in other countries and to advise Congress, the secretary of state, and the president on how best to promote religious freedom.[238] IRFA also contained provisions authorizing the Commission to designate experts in refugee and asylum law to conduct a study and submit a report—either with GAO or separately—on the expedited removal process.[239]

In 2003, the Commission designated attorney Mark Hetfield, Professor Kate Jastram, attorneys Robert Devine and Charles Kuck, Fritz Scheueren, and Dr. Craig Haney as experts to conduct the study. The Commission monitored seven ports of entry, interviewed almost 200 individuals in the expedited removal process, observed over 400 secondary inspection interviews, reviewed over 400 credible fear files, and visited 16 detention centers. The study was completed in 2004. The authorizing legislation for both the GAO study and the study by the Commission's designated experts included the grant of unrestricted access to all stages of the expedited removal process.[240]

---

[234] IRFA §605(a)(2), 112 Stat. at 2814.

[235] *See* The Expedited Removal Study, *Evaluation of the General Accounting Office's Second Report on Expedited Removal* (Oct. 2000), available at *http://w3.uchastings.edu/ers/reports/reports.htm*.

[236] *Id.* at 7.

[237] *Id.*

[238] For more information about the Commission and access to its country reports, see the Commission's website at *www.uscirf.gov*.

[239] *See* IRFA §§605(a)(1), (b)(1) 112 Stat. at 2814. For discussion of the GAO report, see this chapter, at 5.3.2.

[240] *See* IRFA §605(c)(1), 112 Stat. at 2815.

The Commission report was submitted to Congress in February 2005. The report is now publicly available online.[241]

The Commission looked at the same four questions that GAO reported on and made a series of findings and recommendation outlined in its report. Most notably, the Commission found:

1. At one port of entry, immigration officials were observed improperly encouraging asylum-seekers to withdraw their applications for admission.

2. In 15 percent of observed cases, inspectors failed to refer individuals who expressed a fear of return for a credible fear interview.

3. There was a very significant variation in asylum approval rates of individual immigration judges, and in 40 percent of the IJ denials, the IJ cited that the applicant's testimony was inconsistent with the claim presented to the inspector or the AO at the credible fear interview. Only 2 percent of unrepresented applicants were granted asylum, while 25 percent of represented applicants were granted.

4. In FY2003, only 0.5 percent of asylum-seekers in New Orleans were released prior to a decision in their case, while in Harlingen 98 percent were released.[242]

The Commission also presented DHS and EOIR with a series of recommendations to improve the expedited removal process and ensure that bona fide refugees are not returned to persecution. Two years after presenting these recommendations, the Commission issued a "report card" assessing how well the federal government agencies had implemented the recommendations.[243] Below is a summary of the grades[244] it gave:

CBP	F
ICE	D
USCIS (Asylum Office)	B
DHS (Agency-wide coordination)	D
DOJ/EOIR	C+
DHS and DOJ together	Grades from C to F

Update: The Commission's report was recently cited by the U.S. District Court for the Central District of California in its decision not to dissolve the *Orantes* injunction,

---

[241] www.uscirf.gov/countries/global/asylum_refugees/2005/february/index.html.

[242] *See* Report on Asylum Seekers in Expedited Removal, Vol. I, *supra* note 50, at 50–62.

[243] *See Expedited Removal Study Report Card: 2 Years Later*, *supra* note 150.

[244] A=Adopted and implemented; B=Largely adopted with progress in implementation; C=Largely adopted with little progress, or only partially adopted and implemented; D=Minimally addressed, but with little or no demonstration of ongoing commitment to address the objective of the recommendation; F=Rejected, or little evidence of meaningful action to address the objective of the recommendation. *Id.* at 13.

which prohibits DHS from coercing or otherwise improperly encouraging Salvadorans detained by immigration authorities to waive their rights. The court concluded that the "[d]ocumented levels of non-compliance with relevant standards indicate that the injunction is necessary to ensure that Salvadorans are able to exercise their right to apply for asylum freely and intelligently."[245]

5.3.4. Nongovernmental Organizations

Several nongovernmental organizations (NGOs), most notably the Expedited Removal Study, spent several years negotiating with legacy INS to obtain access to the expedited removal process, including secondary inspection. In January 2001, legacy INS finally granted NGOs access to the secondary-inspection phase of expedited removal, often referred to as the "black box."[246] These guidelines require that NGOs make requests to visit a port of entry in writing and at least two weeks before the requested visit. Access includes observing primary and secondary inspection and observing an individual secondary inspection interview if the person being interviewed consents.[247]

A report by the Expedited Removal Study, based primarily on anecdotal information from 736 cases, raised questions regarding the following: the accuracy of determinations made during the expedited removal process; the adequacy of expedited proceedings when complex legal or factual determinations, such as nexus and countrywide persecution, are required; whether the quality of interpretation may impact credible fear determinations; the importance of IJ review; the breadth of secondary inspection; parole; conditions of detention; notification of and access permitted to consular officers regarding asylum-seekers in detention; and the interrelation of expedited removal laws and refugee laws of other countries.[248]

A later report by the Expedited Removal Study raised concerns about access to the asylum process of individuals interdicted at sea, and legacy INS detention of Canada-bound asylum-seekers.[249] This report also analyzed data obtained from legacy INS and EOIR that showed:

- 91 percent of all persons subject to expedited removal were Mexican nationals;
- the San Ysidro (San Diego) port of entry had the highest number of people ordered removed under expedited removal (44 percent of all expedited removals in the country);

---

[245] *Orantes-Hernandez v. Gonzales*, 504 F. Supp. 2d 825 (C.D. Cal. 2007). For more on the *Orantes* case, *see* National Immigration Law Center, The *Orantes* Injunction and Expedited Removal (July 2006), available at www.nilc.org/immlawpolicy/removpsds/orantes&expremoval_2006-07.pdf.

[246] *See* INS Memorandum, M. Pearson, "Secondary Inspection Access Guidelines for Visits by Non-Governmental Organizations" (Jan. 22, 2001), *published on* AILA InfoNet at Doc. No. 01051505 (*posted* May 15, 2001).

[247] *Id.* at 2.

[248] *See* The Expedited Removal Study, *Report on the Second Year of Implementation of Expedited Removal* (May 1999), at 5, available at http://w3.uchastings.edu/ers/reports/1999/toc&exec_sum.pdf.

[249] *See* The Expedited Removal Study, *Report on First Three Years of Implementation of Expedited Removal* (May 2000), *reprinted in* 15 *Notre Dame J.L. Ethics & Pub. Pol'y* 1 (Special Issue 2001).

- 88 percent of individuals given a credible fear interview were found to have a credible fear.[250]

The last report issued by the Expedited Removal Study was a critique of GAO's Report on Expedited Removal.[251]

In addition, the Lawyers Committee for Human Rights (LCHR), now known as Human Rights First, issued a report that raised concerns regarding mistreatment of individuals at airports, inadequate translation, lack of access to counsel, and the detention of asylum-seekers found to have a credible fear of persecution.[252] LCHR also issued a more recent report on the continued detention of asylum-seekers who are held despite a finding that they possess a credible fear of persecution.[253] Another NGO, the Catholic Legal Immigration Network, which has staff attorneys at many detention facilities, has reported that individuals in the expedited removal process have been subjected to extended interrogations in secondary inspection, denied a meaningful opportunity to make telephone calls from detention centers, and have not been provided with copies of the required forms.[254]

5.3.5. United Nations High Commissioner for Refugees

Over the past decade, since the implementation of expedited removal, the Washington, D.C. Office of the United Nations High Commissioner for Refugees (UNHCR) has conducted a number of ad hoc visits to ports of entry to observe the expedited removal process, and has provided written comments directly to the legacy INS and DHS on its observations. UNHCR's access to expedited removal was formalized in a written agreement in February 2000, and is found in chapter 17.15(g) of the *Inspector's Field Manual*. Similar to the guidelines on NGO access referred to in the U.S. Commission on International Religious Freedom Report,[255] UNHCR must make its requests in writing and may observe both primary and secondary inspection.[256] UNHCR had commented on several occasions that it lacks resources, in personnel and finances, to monitor the process in a comprehensive manner and had stated that such monitoring might best be carried out by national organizations. In 2002, however, UNHCR initiated a more systematic approach for observing expedited removal procedures. From January through June of 2002, UNHCR—with funding from Harvard University's Carr Center for Human Rights at the Kennedy School of Government—conducted more in-depth field visits at Miami International Airport, John F. Kennedy Airport, Los Angeles International Airport, Newark Airport, and the San Ysidro land port of entry. UNHCR's report on its observations was given to DHS, but it was not shared with the public. However, findings from UNHCR's field visits were leaked to the *New York Times* and reported in an article on August 13,

---

[250] *Id.* at 5–6.

[251] *See supra* note 235. For more information on the Expedited Removal Study, see www.uchastings.edu/ers.

[252] *See Slamming the Golden Door: A Year of Expedited Removal, supra* note 150.

[253] *See Refugees Behind Bars: The Imprisonment of Asylum Seekers in the Wake of the 1996 Immigration Act, supra* note 150.

[254] *See* "Credible Fear Screening for Individuals in Expedited Removal," *supra* note 150.

[255] *See supra* note 241.

[256] *See* IFM, *supra* note 32, at ch. 17.15(g).

2004. According to the *New York Times*, UNHCR expressed concern in its report about airport inspectors who improperly notified consulates about asylum-seekers' identities, who intimidated and discouraged some individuals from seeking asylum, and who, in 14 cases known to UNHCR, improperly concluded that the individuals were not eligible for asylum.[257] UNHCR also issued an Information Bulletin in November 2003, in which it highlighted a number of continuing concerns about the expedited removal process, including inappropriate methods of questioning asylum-seekers, the poor quality of interpretation, the use of restraints at one port of entry, and the use of airport statements to impeach credibility.[258]

More recently, on February 8, 2007, UNHCR issued a press release welcoming the recommendations made by the U.S. Commission on International Religious Freedom in its 2005 report.[259] UNHCR stated that the changes recommended by the Commission would "ensure that refugees are not removed by the United States without an opportunity to apply for asylum and meaningfully present their case."[260] UNHCR also expressed concern about detention of asylum-seekers subject to expedited removal because of the remote detention facilities in which they are held and their lack of access to legal assistance.[261] The press release further notes that in the past six years, UNHCR has visited 48 detention centers in the United States and has observed that "many asylum seekers lack the basic tools to present their cases such as access to legal materials, telephones and interpreters."[262]

---

[257] R. Swarns, "U.N. Report Cites Harassment of Immigrants Who Sought Asylum at American Airports," *N.Y. Times*, Aug. 13, 2004, at A11.

[258] The Information Bulletin is available from the Washington Office of UNHCR, and may be requested by calling (202) 296-5191 or by sending an e-mail to *usawa@unhcr.org*.

[259] UNHCR Press Release, "United Nations Refugee Agency Welcomes Commission on International Religious Freedom's Expert Recommendations on Expedited Removal" (Feb. 8, 2007).

[260] *Id.*

[261] *Id.*

[262] *Id.*

Chapter 6
Other Forms of Relief

Imagination is more important than knowledge.[*]

6.1. "T" and "U" Visas for Victims of Trafficking in Persons	328
6.2. INA §209(c) Waiver for Refugees and Asylees	332
6.3. Temporary Protected Status	333
6.4. Humanitarian Parole	334
6.5. *ABC* Settlement	337
6.6. Nicaraguan Adjustment and Central American Relief Act	339
6.7. Haitian Refugee Immigration Fairness Act	341
6.8. Cuban Adjustment Act	343
6.9. Cancellation of Removal	344
6.10. Voluntary Departure	348
6.11. Registry	351
6.12. Waiver of Inadmissibility Under INA §212(h)	352
6.13. Family-Sponsored, Employment-Based, and Other Means of Regularizing Immigration Status in the United States	353
6.14. Citizenship	355
6.15. Private Bills	357

In addition to asylum and withholding of removal, other forms of relief may be available to persons facing removal from the United States. Persons fleeing persecution or torture should explore all forms of relief, many of which are easier to obtain than asylum and withholding of removal for qualified persons. New forms become available every year. In 2004, President Bush proposed a guestworker program that could provide lawful status to many of the estimated 10 million undocumented noncitizens in the United States. In the same year, two court settlements were reached in lawsuits pending from the last legalization or amnesty program enacted in 1986.[1] Listed below are the most common forms of relief, which are a good starting point. There are others less common, and those waiting to be discovered or developed. Don't be afraid to use your imagination.

---

[*] Albert Einstein, a refugee.
[1] For more information, see *www.legalizationusa.org*. Immigration law is constantly changing.

6.1. "T" AND "U" VISAS FOR VICTIMS OF TRAFFICKING IN PERSONS

In October 2000, Congress passed the Victims of Trafficking and Violence Protection Act (VTVPA) in response to the approximately 700,000 persons trafficked worldwide each year who are primarily women and children.[2] Estimates are between 14,500 and 50,000 of these individuals are trafficked into the United States annually.[3] In order to protect these victims from future harm, the VTVPA provides for two types of nonimmigrant (or temporary) visas, the "T" and the "U" visas. An individual who obtains a T or U visa may, after three years, obtain permanent residency. The VTVPA is particularly relevant to asylum-seekers because often, in desperation, they fall prey to human traffickers and other criminals when fleeing their dire situations at home—or, once on U.S. soil, become crime victims. All asylum applicants should be screened for possible relief under the VTVPA. If the applicant is currently in removal proceedings in immigration court, it may be possible to have the case administratively closed, continued, or even terminated to allow the applicant to apply to U.S. Immigration and Citizenship Services (USCIS) for a T or a U visa.[4]

6.1.1. T Visas

To receive T-1 classification under the VTVPA and regulations, an individual must:

- be a victim of a "severe form of trafficking of persons";
- be physically present in the United States or at a U.S. port of entry on account of such trafficking;
- have complied with "any reasonable request for assistance in the investigation or prosecution of acts of trafficking" or be under 15 years of age; and
- show he or she would suffer "extreme hardship involving unusual or severe harm upon removal."[5]

> ➢ *Tip*—For an excellent overview of T visas, see N. Walter, "Human Trafficking in the United States: Immigrant Victims Falling Through the Cracks," *Immigration & Nationality Law Handbook* 539 (AILA 2007–08 Ed.). For a more de-

---

[2] Victims of Trafficking and Violence Protection Act of 2000 (VTVPA), Pub. L. No. 106-386, §102(b)(1), 114 Stat. 1464, 1466. The VTVPA was amended and reauthorized by the Trafficking Victims Protection Reauthorization Act of 2003, Pub. L. No. 108-193, 117 Stat. 2875, and the Trafficking Victims Protection Reauthorization Act of 2005, Pub. L. No. 109-164, 119 Stat. 3558 (2006).

[3] VTVPA §102(b)(1), 114 Stat. 1466; *see also* U.S. Department of State, *Trafficking in Persons Report* (June 2004), available at *www.state.gov/g/tip/rls/tiprpt/2004*.

[4] *See* INS Interoffice Memorandum, J. Cronin, "Victims of Trafficking and Violence Protection Act of 2000 (VTVPA) Policy Memorandum #2—"T" and "U" Nonimmigrant Visas" (Aug. 30, 2001), *reprinted in* 78 *Interpreter Releases* 1758, appx. II (Nov. 12, 2001). For many other materials and documents useful when filing for a T or U visa, see the National Lawyers Guild's National Immigration Project website, at *www.nationalimmigrationproject.org/domestic-violence/domvioindex.htm#Content%20Sections*.

[5] *See* INA §101(a)(15)(T); 8 USC §1101(a)(15)(T); 8 CFR §214.11. *See also* USCIS Interoffice Memorandum, W. Yates, "Trafficking Victims Protection Reauthorization Act of 2003" (Apr. 15, 2004), *published on* AILA InfoNet at Doc. No. 04060110 (*posted* June 1, 2004).

tailed step-by-step guide, see U.S. Conference of Catholic Bishops, et al., *A Guide for Legal Advocates Providing Services to Victims of Human Trafficking* (2004), available at *www.cliniclegal.org/Publications/Freepublications/Human Trafficking.pdf*, and K. Kaufka, "T Nonimmigrant Visas and Protection and Relief for Victims of Human Trafficking: A Practitioner's Guide," 06-09 *Immigration Briefings* 1 (Sept. 2006).

Severe forms of trafficking include sex trafficking, involuntary servitude, debt bondage, peonage, and slavery.[6] Evidence that an individual is a victim of trafficking usually is provided by a law enforcement agency (LEA) endorsement, but such an endorsement is not an absolute requirement. A personal statement—one detailing the trafficking and good-faith attempts to secure the endorsement—may suffice.[7] An exception exists for victims under 15 years of age.[8]

In defining "extreme hardship," the regulations provide that such hardship cannot be based on mere economic detriment or the lack of social or economic opportunities.[9] Factors that may be considered include age, serious mental or physical illness, the impact of the lack of access to U.S. courts, and the likelihood of revictimization or harm from the trafficker in the home country.[10] The regulations for processing and adjudicating T visas were issued in 2002.[11]

In addition, the T visa holder may confer derivative T status to a spouse, child, parent, and unmarried siblings under 18 years of age.[12] T visa holders also are eligible for employment authorization[13] and medical and social service benefits.[14] The annual cap on T visas is 5,000 per year.[15] A T visa is granted for three years; at the expiration of the three-year period, the T visa holder is eligible to apply for permanent residency within 90 days.[16] Note that even though all of the grounds of inadmissibility apply, there is a national interest waiver available that waives all but grounds related to national security, public charge, international child abduction, and renunciation of U.S. citizenship to avoid taxation.[17]

---

[6] VTVPA §103(8), 114 Stat. 1470; 22 USC §7102(8).

[7] 8 CFR §214.11(h).

[8] *Id.*

[9] 8 CFR §214.11(i)(1).

[10] *Id.*

[11] *See* 67 Fed. Reg. 4784 (Jan. 31, 2002).

[12] INA §101(a)(15)(T); 8 USC §1101(a)(15)(T); *see also* 8 CFR §214.11(o)(1).

[13] INA §101(i)(2); 8 USC §1101(i)(2).

[14] VTVPA §§107(b)(1)(A), (B), 114 Stat. 1475.

[15] INA §214(o)(2); 8 USC §1184(o)(2); 8 CFR §214.11(m).

[16] 8 CFR §§214.11(p)(1), (2).

[17] *See* INA §212(d)(13)(B)(ii); 8 USC §1182(d)(13)(B)(ii); 8 CFR §§1212.16(b)(1), (c). For a more in-depth discussion of the T visa, see "INS Publishes Interim Rule Implementing 'T' Visa Requirements, Procedures for Trafficking Victims," 79 *Interpreter Releases* 173 (Feb. 4, 2002). A copy of Form I-914, Application for T Nonimmigrant Status, is available at *www.uscis.gov/files/form/i-914.pdf.*

> *Tip*—A trafficking victim may also meet the definition of refugee and qualify for asylum. See United Nations High Commissioner for Refugees (UNHCR), *Guidelines on International Protection: The Application of Article 1A(2) of the 1951 Convention and/or 1967 Protocol Relating to the Status of Refugees to Victims of Trafficking and Persons at Risk of Being Trafficked* (Apr. 2006).[18]

6.1.2. U Visas

A U visa is a form of relief available to individuals who have been victims of serious crimes in the United States (or crimes that violate the laws of the United States if outside of the United States) such as rape, torture, trafficking, incest, domestic violence, sexual assault, involuntary servitude, kidnapping, abduction, false imprisonment, extortion, perjury, and other offenses.[19] To qualify, individuals must demonstrate that they:

- suffered substantial physical or mental abuse as a result of having been a victim of criminal activity;
- possess information concerning the criminal activity; and
- have been helpful, are helpful, or are likely to be helpful to law enforcement or prosecutors.

Like the T visa, an applicant's primary evidence that he or she has been or is likely to be helpful to law enforcement or prosecutors is an LEA endorsement.[20]

As with the T visa, derivative status is available to the children, spouse, and, in some cases, the parent of a U visa holder.[21] The visa is granted for up to four years, after which the individual may apply for permanent residency. A waiver exists for all grounds of inadmissibility except for those related to Nazi persecution and genocide.[22] The annual cap on U visas is 10,000 per year.[23] U visas are adjudicated at the Vermont Service Center

---

[18] Available at *www.unhcr.org/publ/PUBL/443b626b2.pdf*.

[19] For the complete list, see INA §101(a)(15)(U)(iii); 8 USC §1101(a)(15)(U)(iii). *See also* USCIS Interoffice Memorandum, M. Aytes, "Applications for U Nonimmigrant Status; Revisions to Adjudicator's Field Manual (AFM) Chapter 39 (AFM Update AD06-11)" (Jan. 6, 2006), *published on* AILA InfoNet at Doc. No. 06011763 (*posted* Jan. 17, 2006).

[20] A sample LEA certification form is available on the asista.org website, at *http://asistaonline.org/legalresources/U_Visa/U_cert_form_with_instructions_2006.doc*, and the website of the National Immigration Project of the National Lawyers Guild, at *http://nationalimmigrationproject.org/DVPage/Instructions_for_Completing_U_Certification.doc*. Also see *www.nationalimmigrationproject.org/domestic-violence/domvioindex.htm#U%20Visa%20Documents* for U visa documents collected by the National Immigration Project.

[21] INA §101(a)(15)(U)(ii); 8 USC §1101(a)(15)(U)(ii).

[22] INA §212(d)(13); 8 USC §1182(d)(13).

[23] INA §214(o)(2); 8 USC §1184(o)(2).

CHAPTER 6 • OTHER FORMS OF RELIEF

(VSC), which, until recently, had jurisdiction to assess whether a U visa applicant is eligible for deferred action, even if the applicant is in removal proceedings.[24]

After many years of waiting,[25] the much anticipated U visa regulations were published on September 17, 2007, and went into effect on October 17, 2007.[26] A correction to these regulations was published on September 27, 2007, which provided that there is no filing fee for a U visa application.[27] In the past, when there were no regulations, "interim" U relief was available to U visa applicants.

> ➢ *Tip*—Those who received interim U relief are encouraged to apply for U nonimmigrant status within 180 days of the issuance of the regulations.[28]

To apply for U nonimmigrant status, an applicant must file:

- Form I-918, Supplement B, "U Nonimmigrant Status Certification";
- Any additional evidence regarding the qualifying crime, the physical or mental abuse suffered, the victim's helpfulness to the certifying agency, and the location of the crime;
- A statement by the victim regarding the facts of the victimization; and
- Form I-192, if the applicant is inadmissible.

U visa holders and their derivative family members are also be eligible for an automatic grant of employment authorization upon the grant of U nonimmigrant status.[29]

> ➢ *Tip*—**Helpful Website**—The U regulations were issued shortly before this 5th edition of the *Primer* was published. The dust has not yet settled regarding the U visa procedures. To stay up to date on the latest information on applying

---

[24] *See* USCIS Interoffice Memorandum, W. Yates, "Assessment of Deferred Action in Requests for Interim Relief from U Nonimmigrant Status Aliens in Removal Proceedings" (May 6, 2004), available at *www.uscis.gov/files/pressrelease/UPrcd050604.pdf*.

[25] Prior to the publication of the regulations, in response to the Department of Homeland Security's failure to issue them for almost seven years, organizations assisting U visa applicants had filed a lawsuit seeking the issuance of regulations. *See* Complaint, *Catholic Charities CYO v. Chertoff*, C07-01307-PJH (N.D. Cal. Mar. 6, 2007). A copy of the complaint is available at *http://vocesunidas.org/downloads/3-6-07UVisaComplaint-Updated.pdf*.

[26] 72 Fed. Reg. 53013 (Sept. 17, 2007).

[27] 72 Fed. Reg. 54813 (Sept. 27, 2007).

[28] The summary to the U visa regulations states: "Aliens who have been granted interim relief from USCIS are encouraged to file for U nonimmigrant status within 180 days of the effective date of this interim rule. USCIS will no longer issue interim relief upon the effective date of this rule; however, if the alien has properly filed a petition for U nonimmigrant status, but USCIS has not yet adjudicated that petition, interim relief will be extended until USCIS completes its adjudication of the petition. 72 Fed. Reg. 53013, 53014 (Sept. 17, 2007).

[29] 8 CFR §§214.14(c)(7), (f)(7).

for U nonimmigrant status, visit the website of Asista.org at *www.asista online.org*.

> *Tip*—**Prosecutorial Discretion**—At times it might be possible to convince immigration officials to exercise prosecutorial discretion and not file a Notice to Appear (NTA), or to rescind the issuance of an NTA, or to even join in a motion to reopen or remand. For guidelines from U.S. Immigration and Customs Enforcement's (ICE) Office of Principal Legal Advisor, see ICE Memorandum, W. Howard, "Prosecutorial Discretion" (Oct. 24, 2005), *published on* AILA InfoNet at Doc. No. 06050511 (*posted* May. 5, 2006). The memo instructs: "Where a 'U' or 'T' visa application has been submitted, it may be appropriate not to file an NTA until a decision is made on such an application." The recently issued regulations on U visas instruct that ICE counsel may agree, as a matter of discretion, to file a joint motion to terminate proceedings, while a petition for a U visa is being adjudicated by USCIS.[30]

6.2. INA §209(c) Waiver for Refugees and Asylees

A person admitted as a refugee or granted asylum is eligible for adjustment of status to lawful permanent residence one year after admission or after the grant of asylum.[31] The Immigration and Nationality Act (INA) permits the waiver of most grounds of inadmissibility, and provides that others do not apply.[32] All other grounds of inadmissibility that would otherwise bar the refugee or asylee from obtaining permanent resident status are waivable for "humanitarian purposes, to assure family unity, or when it is otherwise in the public interest."[33]

In a decision reversing the Board of Immigration Appeals' (BIA) grant of a waiver under INA §209(c), the attorney general (AG) ruled that individuals who commit violent or dangerous crimes will not be granted this discretionary waiver except in extraordinary circumstances resulting in exceptional or extremely unusual hardship.[34] More recently, in dicta, the BIA noted that "even nonviolent aggravated felonies will generally constitute significant negative factors militating strongly against a favorable exercise of discretion."[35]

A refugee or asylee who has not yet adjusted status and becomes deportable or inadmissible may be eligible for adjustment of status in removal proceedings,[36] provided the

---

[30] 8 CFR §214.14(c)(1)(i).

[31] INA §209, 8 USC §1159.

[32] INA §209(c), 8 USC §1159(c).

[33] INA §209(c); 8 USC §1159(c).

[34] *Matter of Jean*, 23 I&N Dec. 373 (AG 2002) (finding refugee convicted of manslaughter for killing a 19-month-old toddler in her care was not eligible for a waiver under §209(c)).

[35] *Matter of K–A–*, 23 I&N Dec. 661, 666 (BIA 2004) (nevertheless the BIA upheld the grant of adjustment of status to an asylee convicted of possession of forged instrument who was the mother of two U.S. citizen children, one of whom was disabled).

[36] *Id.* at 663–64 (BIA 2004); 8 CFR §§209.2(c), 1209.2(c).

CHAPTER 6 • OTHER FORMS OF RELIEF 333

inadmissibility is not on grounds that would disqualify him or her for adjustment. If in removal proceedings, refugees or asylees should inform the IJ that they wish to apply for adjustment of status. To seek such relief, they should submit an Application for Adjustment of Status (Form I-485) and an Application by Refugee for Waiver of Grounds of Excludability (Form I-602).[37]

> ➢ *Tip*—For a helpful how-to guide on INA §209(c) waivers, which includes sample waiver forms, see J. Ferguson, *AILA's Focus on Waivers Under the Immigration and Nationality Act* (AILA 2007).

6.3. TEMPORARY PROTECTED STATUS

In 1990, the United States enacted a temporary protected status (TPS) provision of the INA, which permits the AG to grant temporary safe haven in the United States to foreign nationals.[38] The AG may designate TPS for nationals of any country that is experiencing (1) an ongoing armed conflict posing serious threat to personal safety; (2) an environmental disaster resulting in a substantial, but temporary, disruption of living conditions; or (3) extraordinary and temporary conditions that prevent nationals from returning in safety.[39]

TPS is only granted to individuals already in the United States, usually to individuals present in the United States on the date the designation is made by the AG. It is generally not available to individuals who arrive after the date of initial designation. Exceptions to this general rule include the redesignations of Burundi, Liberia, Kosovo, Sierra Leone, and Sudan, which allowed individuals arriving after the initial designation date to apply for TPS.

An individual may be granted TPS if he or she:

- is a national of a country designated by the AG;
- has been continuously physically present in the United States since the effective date of the most recent designation;
- has been continuously residing in the United States since a date set by the AG;
- is admissible as an immigrant, except as provided for under 8 CFR §§244.3, 1244.3;
- has not been convicted of a felony or two or more misdemeanors in the United States and does not fall within one of the mandatory bars to withholding of removal; and
- timely registers for TPS or, if in valid status during the registration period, registers within 60 days from the expiration of such status.[40]

---

[37] *See* 8 CFR §1240.11(a).
[38] INA §244; 8 USC §1254a.
[39] INA §244(b)(1); 8 USC §1254a(b)(1).
[40] *See* 8 CFR §§244.2, 1244.2.

To apply for TPS, qualified individuals should complete an Application for Temporary Protected Status (Form I-821), together with an Application for Employment Authorization (Form I-765), and file them with the appropriate USCIS office according to the application instructions. Individuals granted TPS are permitted to remain in the United States and to obtain employment authorization during the period designated by the AG and any extensions of that period. Check the USCIS website at *www.uscis.gov* for the current fees for filing an I-821, employment authorization (if such authorization is requested), and fingerprinting. A waiver of such fees is available by filing a fee waiver request.[41] There is no fee when filing for an I-821 as part of a re-registration application. If an individual is in removal proceedings, DHS should agree to administratively close proceedings if the individual is *prima facie* eligible for TPS.[42] Note that if the individual wishes to eventually file for asylum, he or she must do so within a reasonable period after the expiration of TPS.[43]

To date, the AG's TPS designations have included nationals of the following countries or provinces: Angola, Bosnia-Herzegovina, Burundi, El Salvador, Guinea-Bissau, Honduras, Kosovo, Kuwait, Lebanon, Liberia, Montserrat, Nicaragua, Rwanda, Sierra Leone, Somalia, and Sudan.[44]

> ➤ *Tip*—Recipients of TPS may affirmatively apply for asylum while maintaining their TPS status.[45] TPS recipients may also apply for asylum after their TPS status terminates. If, however, a TPS recipient has been in the United States for more than one year, he or she should file for asylum within a "reasonable period" after his or her TPS status expires or he or she may be barred by the one-year filing deadline.[46]

6.4. HUMANITARIAN PAROLE

When an otherwise inadmissible individual needs temporary admission to the United States for urgent humanitarian reasons or for significant public benefit, the secretary of the Department of Homeland Security may provide that individual with temporary "hu-

---

[41] *See* 8 CFR §§244.20, 1244.20.

[42] *See* INS Memorandum, D. Carpenter, "Administrative Closure When Alien is Prima Facie Eligible for TPS or DED" (Feb. 7, 2002), *published on* AILA InfoNet at Doc. No. 02040338 (*posted* Apr. 3, 2002).

[43] *See* 8 CFR §§208.4(a)(5)(iv), 1208.4(a)(5)(iv) (providing that an "extraordinary circumstance" may include maintaining TPS status "until a reasonable period before the filing of the asylum application").

[44] To find the most recent designations and filing deadlines, visit the USCIS website at *www.uscis.gov* (Home > Services & Benefits > Humanitarian Benefits > Temporary Protected Status) or consult AILA InfoNet or *Interpreter Releases* for TPS information and notices. *See also* USCIS TPS Chart, appx. 7F. A useful "how-to" guide on TPS is available from the Immigrant Legal Resource Center in San Francisco ((415) 255-9499; *www.ilrc.org*).

[45] *See* ch. 3.2.

[46] *See* 8 CFR §§208.4(a)(5)(iv), 1208.4(a)(5)(iv) (providing that an "extraordinary circumstance" may include maintaining TPS status "until a reasonable period before the filing of the asylum application").

manitarian" parole.[47] Decisions to grant humanitarian parole are completely discretionary and are made by the secretary on a case-by-case basis.[48] The grant of parole lasts only as long as the emergency situation and may not exceed one year.[49]

Humanitarian parole is most frequently granted for critical medical treatment, attendance at funerals, and comparable emergency situations. Humanitarian parole may also be granted to refugees or asylees who travel outside of the United States and whose refugee travel documents expire. Another example of a successful petition for humanitarian parole is the case of a 21-year-old Nigerian university student who sustained an above-the-knee amputation as the result of a traffic accident in April 2006.[50] The Department of Homeland Security granted humanitarian parole to this student to enter the United States for three months to receive a prosthetic leg and to undergo rehabilitation.[51] His application contained letters and expert witness affidavits that demonstrated the discrimination and difficulty in obtaining employment that he would face if he were denied humanitarian parole and forced to live the rest of his life as an amputee.[52]

6.4.1. Who May File

Humanitarian parole may only be requested for persons located outside the United States, and may be filed by the prospective parolee, a sponsoring relative, an attorney, or any other interested individual or organization.[53]

6.4.2. What to File

Applicants for humanitarian parole must submit a Form I-131, Application for Travel Document, and a Form I-134, Affidavit of Support.[54] In addition, the applicant should include supporting evidence, including:

- evidence that the applicant has sufficient resources or financial support so that he or she will not become a public charge while in the United States, including a statement

---

[47] INA §212(d)(5)(A); 8 USC §1182(d)(5)(A).

[48] INA §212(d)(5)(A); 8 USC §1182(d)(5)(A); *see also* N. Bernstein, "A Contest of Suffering, With the U.S. as a Prize," *N.Y. Times,* Oct. 14, 2005, at B1 (reporting that only 20 percent of the 6,718 applications for humanitarian parole were approved by DHS between 2000 and 2005).

[49] *www.uscis.gov* (Services & Benefits tab, Visit the U.S. link, Humanitarian Parole link).

[50] *See www.bibdaily.com/pdfs/Henry%20Sunday.pdf.*

[51] Letter from Kenneth Leutbecker, Director, Parole and Humanitarian Assistance Branch, Office of International Affairs, U.S. Department of Homeland Security, to Christopher Nugent, Holland & Knight LLP, attorney for Henry Vusari Sunday (Apr. 24, 2007) (on file with Chris Nugent, Holland & Knight).

[52] The application also presented evidence that several organizations and individuals had already agreed to provide for this student's travel to the United States, his living expenses while in the United States, and all the fees related to the medical procedure. *See* Christopher Nugent, Memorandum in Support of Humanitarian Parole Application of Henry Vusari Sunday (Feb. 27, 2007) (on file with Chris Nugent, Holland & Knight).

[53] *www.uscis.gov* (Services & Benefits tab, Visit the U.S. link, Humanitarian Parole link).

[54] *Id.* These forms are available at *www.uscis.gov/files/form/I-131.pdf* and *www.uscis.gov/files/form/I-134.pdf*, respectively.

of how and by whom medical care, housing, transportation, and other subsistence needs will be met for the applicant;

- evidence of the claimed circumstances that led the applicant to seek humanitarian parole and the length of time for which parole is requested (not to exceed one year);
- a statement of why a U.S. visa cannot be obtained in lieu of humanitarian parole, including evidence of previous attempts to obtain visas;
- evidence of the relationship between the applicant and the sponsor; and
- information about the sponsor, including his or her name, date, place of birth, address, citizenship or immigration status, occupation, and financial resources.[55]

If an attorney is filing the application for humanitarian parole on behalf of the parolee, a G-28 Notice of Appearance must be included with the application materials.[56]

6.4.3. Fee

There is a filing fee for Form I-131. The fee is $305, and must be paid in the form of a cashier's check.[57] *Note*: Because filing fees change frequently, please consult the USCIS website for the latest fee information.

6.4.4. Where to File

Requests for humanitarian parole should be submitted to U.S. Citizenship and Immigration Services, ATTN: Chief, International Operations Division (Humanitarian Parole), 20 Massachusetts Avenue, NW, Suite 3300, Washington, DC 20529. However, applicants from Canada should submit their forms to the Director of the office that has jurisdiction over the area where the applicant plans to enter the United States.[58] In order to expedite the delivery and receipting of the application, USCIS strongly recommends the use of express mailing options with a return receipt service.[59]

6.4.5. When to File

Applications for humanitarian parole generally take 60-90 business days to process.[60]

6.4.6. No Appeal

Decisions regarding humanitarian parole are left solely to the discretion of the secretary of DHS, and there is no statutory provision for appeal.[61] However, if the applicant's circumstances change, a new application may be submitted as a new case for consideration. This requires another submission of the required forms and filing fee.[62]

---

[55] *www.uscis.gov* (Services & Benefits tab, Visit the U.S. link, Humanitarian Parole link).

[56] *Id.*

[57] *Id.*

[58] *Id.*

[59] *Id.*

[60] *Id.*

[61] INA §212(d)(5)(A); 8 USC §1182(d)(5)(A); *www.uscis.gov* (Services & Benefits tab, Visit the U.S. link, Humanitarian Parole link).

[62] *Id.*

6.5. *ABC* SETTLEMENT

Salvadoran and Guatemalan nationals who registered for relief under the *American Baptist Churches v. Thornburgh*[63] (*ABC*) settlement agreement are provided with certain benefits and procedural protections during the processing of their asylum applications. The settlement agreement is the result of a suit filed in U.S. District Court for the Northern District of California in 1985 against legacy INS, the Executive Office for Immigration Review (EOIR), and the U.S. Department of State (DOS). The plaintiffs, a certified class of Guatemalan and Salvadoran nationals, alleged that INS, EOIR, and DOS had discriminated against Salvadoran and Guatemalan asylum applicants. In 1990, the parties to the lawsuit reached a settlement, known as the *ABC* Settlement Agreement, which was approved by the court in 1991.

Under the terms of the settlement agreement, class members are entitled to a stay of deportation; administrative closure of pending immigration proceedings; an initial or de novo interview and adjudication by specially trained asylum officers; an adjudication pursuant to the asylum regulations published July 1, 1990; and employment authorization. Additionally, *ABC* class members may not be detained by DHS or removed from the United States while their claims are pending except under the limited circumstances noted below. *ABC* class members, however, may waive these rights.[64]

> *Note*: ABC class members were granted additional benefits under the Nicaraguan Adjustment and Central American Relief Act (NACARA), which was signed into law on November 19, 1997.[65]

6.5.1. Eligibility for *ABC* Class Member Benefits

Individuals who meet the following requirements are eligible for *ABC* class member benefits.

Salvadoran Nationals Who:

- were physically present in the United States on or before September 19, 1990 (there is no continuous physical presence requirement);
- submitted an *ABC* registration form or a TPS registration form (regardless of whether TPS was granted) to legacy INS between January 1 and October 30, 1991; and
- submitted an application for asylum on or before January 31, 1996 (or, because of a two-week grace period granted by legacy INS, before February 16, 1996) *or* submitted an application after the cut-off date but within 90 days of receiving Notice 5, a specific notice form under the *ABC* Settlement Agreement.

To verify if an individual is a member of the *ABC* class, send a fax to (703) 807-2438.

---

[63] *American Baptist Churches v. Thornburgh*, 760 F. Supp. 796 (N.D. Cal. 1991).

[64] *See, e.g., Matter of Gutierrez-Lopez*, 21 I&N Dec. 479 (BIA 1996) (holding that class member may waive *ABC* benefits to reopen case to apply for adjustment of status).

[65] *See* this chapter, at 6.6.

Guatemalan Nationals Who:

- were physically present in the United States on or before October 1, 1990 (there is no requirement of continuous physical presence);
- submitted an *ABC* registration form to legacy INS on or before December 31, 1991; and
- submitted an application for asylum on or before January 3, 1995.

To verify if an individual is a member of the *ABC* class, send a fax to (703) 807-2438.

> ➢ *Tip*—**Change of Address Procedures Announced**—USCIS announced that beginning on Oct. 4, 2005, all *ABC* class members must use form AR-11 to notify USCIS of any change of address. USCIS also announced that it was closing the *ABC* Project post office box used by 240,000 class members to submit changes of address.[66] The notice also instructs *ABC* class members to inform the asylum office with jurisdiction over their asylum application of any changes of address.[67]

6.5.2. Exclusions from Class Member Benefits

ABC class members who would otherwise be eligible for benefits are excluded if they:

- have been convicted of an aggravated felony; *or*
- were apprehended at the time of entry into the United States after December 19, 1990.

A determination of whether an individual was apprehended at the time of entry may only be made by an asylum officer, and not by an IJ or the BIA.[68]

6.5.3. Detention

An *ABC* class member may only be detained if he or she:

- has been convicted of a crime involving moral turpitude for which the sentence actually imposed exceeded a term of imprisonment in excess of six months;
- poses a national security risk; or
- poses a threat to public safety.

---

[66] *See* 70 Fed. Reg. 45410 (Aug. 5, 2005); *see also* USCIS Press Release, "Follow-Up Message: USCIS Announces New Address Change Procedures for *ABC* Class Members" (Nov. 30, 2005), *published on* AILA InfoNet at Doc. No. 05120165 (*posted* Dec. 1, 2005).

[67] 70 Fed. Reg. 45410 (Aug. 5, 2005).

[68] *See Matter of Morales*, 21 I&N Dec. 130 (BIA 1995) (finding that the IJ and BIA lack jurisdiction to determine whether an *ABC* class member was apprehended at the time of entry for purposes of determining eligibility under the *ABC* Settlement Agreement).

6.6. NICARAGUAN ADJUSTMENT AND CENTRAL AMERICAN RELIEF ACT

On November 19, 1997, the Nicaraguan Adjustment and Central American Relief Act (NACARA)[69] was signed into law. NACARA provides relief from the harsh provisions of the Illegal Immigration Reform and Immigrant Responsibility Act (IIRAIRA)[70] for Central Americans from Nicaragua, El Salvador, and Guatemala, as well as for individuals from several other countries. Cuban and Nicaraguan nationals receive the most generous treatment under NACARA in the form of lawful permanent residency status for those who qualify.

Salvadoran and Guatemalan nationals, as well as nationals from the former Soviet Union, the former Yugoslavia, and other Eastern European countries, receive the benefit of having their claims for suspension of deportation adjudicated under former INA §244(a).[71] Section 244(a) had more generous provisions for calculating continuous physical presence and for establishing hardship. In addition, individuals who are eligible to apply for relief under NACARA are not subject to the annual cap of 4,000.[72] Such individuals are, however, barred from seeking judicial review of the determination by the AG of whether they meet the requirements set forth below.[73]

The AG has authorized asylum officers (AOs) to make initial eligibility determinations regarding NACARA suspension claims for NACARA-eligible asylum-seekers and *ABC* class members with asylum applications pending before the Asylum Division. NACARA/*ABC* interviews are currently being conducted by AOs. The following proposed NACARA referrals to immigration court are reviewed by Asylum Headquarters' quality assurance team: those (1) based on discretionary factors, (2) based on good moral character, (3) based on the persecutor-of-others bar, (4) based on material support, or (5) based on an unusual legal issue.[74] Proposed grants are also reviewed by Asylum Headquarters if there are strong negative factors.[75] Persons covered by NACARA who are in removal proceedings may apply to an IJ for adjustment of status or suspension of deportation.

> *Note*: Final regulations implementing the adjustment of status provisions for Nicaraguan and Cuban nationals were issued in March 2000.[76] Interim regulations implementing the suspension of deportation and special rule cancellation of removal provisions for nationals of Guatemala, El Salvador, and former Soviet Bloc countries were issued in May 1999.[77]

The following is a summary of NACARA's provisions by country of origin.

---

[69] Nicaraguan Adjustment and Central American Relief Act (NACARA), Pub. L. No. 105-100, 111 Stat. 2160, 2193–201 (1997).

[70] Illegal Immigration Reform and Immigrant Responsibility Act of 1996, Pub. L. No. 104-208, div. C, 110 Stat. 3009, 3009-546 to 3009-724.

[71] NACARA §203(a)(1), 111 Stat. 2196–98. *See* this chapter, at 6.9.2.

[72] *See* this chapter, at 6.9.2.

[73] NACARA §§202(f), 203(a)(1), 111 Stat. 2196–98.

[74] USCIS Asylum Division, Quality Assurance Referral Sheet (revised Feb. 9, 2007).

[75] *Id.*

[76] *See* 65 Fed. Reg. 15846 (Mar. 24, 2000).

[77] *See* 64 Fed. Reg. 27856–81 (May 21, 1999).

6.6.1. Cuba

Cuban nationals who entered the United States prior to December 1, 1995, were eligible for lawful permanent residence provided they applied for adjustment of status before April 1, 2000.[78] Spouses, minor children, or unmarried adult sons and daughters of Cuban nationals who adjusted status under this provision were also eligible for adjustment of status, regardless of their entry date, if they applied before April 1, 2000.[79]

6.6.2. Nicaragua

Nicaraguan nationals who entered the United States prior to December 1, 1995, were eligible for lawful permanent residence provided they applied for adjustment of status before April 1, 2000.[80] Spouses, minor children, or unmarried adult sons and daughters of Nicaraguan nationals who adjusted under this provision were also eligible for adjustment of status, regardless of their entry date, if they applied before April 1, 2000.[81]

6.6.3. El Salvador

Salvadoran nationals are eligible to seek suspension of deportation under the provisions of law that existed prior to the passage of IIRAIRA if they:

- entered the United States on or before September 19, 1990, and registered for benefits under the *ABC* Settlement Agreement[82] or applied for TPS on or before October 31, 1991 (which automatically registered Salvadorans as *ABC* class members); *or*

- applied for asylum on or before April 1, 1990.[83]

The spouses, minor children, or unmarried adult sons and daughters of Salvadorans eligible for such relief may also have their cases adjudicated under pre-IIRAIRA rules.[84] In the cases of adult sons or daughters, they must demonstrate that they entered the United States on or before October 1, 1990.[85] Any grants of suspension are not subject to the annual cap of 4,000.[86] The regulations, which took effect on June 21, 1999, afford the principal applicants a rebuttable presumption that they would meet the extreme hardship requirement for suspension of deportation.[87]

---

[78] 8 CFR §§245.13(a), 1245.13(a); NACARA §§202(a)(1), (b)(1), 111 Stat. 2193–94.

[79] 8 CFR §§245.13(b), 1245.13(b); NACARA §§202(d), 111 Stat. 2195.

[80] 8 CFR §§245.13(a), 1245.13(a); NACARA §§202(a)(1), (b)(1), 111 Stat. 2193–94.

[81] 8 CFR §§245.13(b), 1245.13(b); NACARA §§202(d), 111 Stat. 2195.

[82] *See* this chapter, at 6.3.

[83] NACARA §203(a)(1), 111 Stat. 2196–98.

[84] *Id.*

[85] *Id.*

[86] *Id. See also* 8 CFR §§240.60 *et seq.*, 1240.60 *et seq.*

[87] 8 CFR §§240.64(d)(1), 1240.64(d)(1). For detailed instructions on analyzing and preparing a NACARA claim, *see* M. Silverman and L. Joaquin, "NACARA for Guatemalans, Salvadorans, and Former Soviet Bloc Nationals," 1 *Immigration & Nationality Law Handbook* 251 (AILA 2004–05 Ed.).

6.6.4. Guatemala

Guatemalan nationals are eligible to seek suspension of deportation under the provisions of law that existed prior to the passage of IIRAIRA if they:

- entered the United States on or before October 1, 1990, and registered for benefits under the *ABC* Settlement Agreement[88] on or before December 31, 1991; *or*
- applied for asylum on or before April 1, 1990.[89]

The spouses, minor children, or unmarried adult sons and daughters of Guatemalans eligible for such relief may also have their cases adjudicated under pre-IIRAIRA rules.[90] In the cases of adult sons or daughters, they must demonstrate that they entered the United States on or before October 1, 1990.[91] Any grants of suspension are not subject to the annual cap of 4,000.[92] The regulations, which took effect on June 21, 1999, afford the principal applicants a rebuttable presumption that they would meet the extreme hardship requirement for suspension of deportation.[93]

6.6.5. Former Soviet Union and Warsaw Pact Countries

Individuals are eligible to have their suspension of deportation claims considered under pre-IIRAIRA rules if they:

- entered the United States on or before December 31, 1990;
- filed an application for asylum on or before December 31, 1991; *and*
- at the time of filing, were nationals of the Soviet Union, Russia, any republic of the former Soviet Union, Latvia, Estonia, Lithuania, Poland, Czechoslovakia, Romania, Hungary, Bulgaria, Albania, East Germany, Yugoslavia, or any state of the former Yugoslavia.[94]

Unlike nationals from El Salvador and Guatemala, nationals of former Soviet Bloc countries have not been afforded the rebuttable presumption of extreme hardship in the determination of whether they qualify for suspension of deportation.

6.7. HAITIAN REFUGEE IMMIGRATION FAIRNESS ACT

The Haitian Refugee Immigration Fairness Act[95] (HRIFA) was signed into law on October 21, 1998. HRIFA permitted certain categories of Haitian nationals to apply for ad-

---

[88] *See* this chapter, at 6.3.

[89] NACARA §203(a)(1), 111 Stat. 2196–98.

[90] *Id.*

[91] *Id.*

[92] *Id. See also* 8 CFR §§240.60 *et seq.*, 1240.60 *et seq.*

[93] 8 CFR §§240.64(d)(1), 1240.64(d)(1).

[94] NACARA §203(a)(1), 111 Stat. 2196–98.

[95] Haitian Refugee Immigration Fairness Act (HRIFA), Pub. L. No. 105-277, div. A, §101(h), tit. IX (secs. 901–04), 112 Stat. 2681, 2681-538 to 2681-542.

justment of status to permanent residency. The final regulations, effective on their date of issuance, were released in March 2000.[96]

Principal beneficiaries must have filed their applications on or before March 31, 2000.[97] There is no application deadline for dependents. To be eligible for benefits as a principal beneficiary, a Haitian national:

- must have been physically present in the United States on December 31, 1995;[98]
- must have remained continuously physically present in the United States since December 31, 1995;[99]
- must not be inadmissible to the United States under any grounds of inadmissibility for which HRIFA does not specify an exception.[100]
- must belong to one of five classes set forth in §902(b)(1) of HRIFA.

The classes include any Haitian national who:

- filed for asylum before December 31, 1995;
- was paroled into the United States before December 31, 1995, after having been identified as having a credible fear of persecution, or paroled for emergency reasons or reasons deemed strictly in the public interest;
- was a child, i.e., unmarried and under 21 years of age, at the time of his or her arrival and on December 31, 1995; and either
    - arrived without parents and has remained in the United States without parents;
    - became orphaned after arriving in the United States; or
    - was abandoned by his or her parents or guardians prior to April 1, 1998, and has remained abandoned.[101]

The following grounds of inadmissibility under the INA do not apply to HRIFA applicants:

- §212(a)(4)—a noncitizen likely to become a public charge;
- §212(a)(5)—a noncitizen without a labor certification or proper qualifications for certain occupations;
- §212(a)(6)(a)—a noncitizen present without admission or parole;
- §212(a)(7)(a)—a noncitizen not in possession of a valid visa; and
- §212(a)(9)(B)—a noncitizen unlawfully present in the United States.[102]

---

[96] *See* 65 Fed. Reg. 15835 (Mar. 24, 2000); 8 CFR §§245.15, 1245.15.
[97] *See* 8 CFR §§245.15(c)(2)(i), 1245.15(c)(2)(i); HRIFA §902(a)(1)(A), 112 Stat. 2681-538.
[98] 8 CFR §§245.15(c)(1), 1245.15(c)(1).
[99] 8 CFR §§245.15(c)(4), 1245.15(c)(4).
[100] 8 CFR §§245.15(c)(3), 1245.15(c)(3).
[101] 8 CFR §§245.15(b)(1), 1245.15(b)(1); HRIFA §902(b)(1), 112 Stat. 2681-538 to 2681-539.
[102] 8 CFR §§245.15(e)(1), 1245.15(e)(1); HRIFA §902(a)(1)(B), 112 Stat. 2681-538.

To be eligible for benefits as a dependent beneficiary, an individual must be:

- a national of Haiti;
- the spouse, child, or unmarried son or daughter of a principal HRIFA beneficiary at the time the principal was granted adjustment of status;
- physically present in the United States; and
- not inadmissible to the United States under any grounds not excepted by HRIFA.[103]

6.8. CUBAN ADJUSTMENT ACT

The Cuban Adjustment Act (CAA) of 1966[104] provides an avenue for Cuban citizens or natives to become lawful permanent residents of the United States. Congress provided the attorney general with the discretion to provide legal permanent residency status to Cuban citizens or natives who have been admitted or paroled into the United States and have been present in the United States for at least one year following admission or parole.[105] The CAA also makes the applicant's spouse and children eligible to receive legal permanent residency.[106] The adjustment of status is purely discretionary, and an applicant may be granted adjustment of status even if he or she does not meet the ordinary requirements for adjustment under section 245 of the INA.[107]

Applicants seeking adjustment of status under the CAA may file with USCIS.[108] In addition, an IJ has jurisdiction in removal proceedings to adjudicate CAA applications from arriving applicants.[109] The applicant bears the burden of proving by a preponderance of the evidence that he or she is a Cuban citizen.[110] The applicant has no documents, he or she must be given the opportunity to explain why documents that would establish citizenship might be unavailable.[111] USCIS has found a Cuban passport to be the most persuasive evidence of Cuban citizenship, but other official Cuban documents, such as a Cuban Civil Registry document, a Cuban consular certificate of citizenship, or other official documents signed by a Cuban official with authority over such citizenship documents, may be persuasive in proving Cuban citizenship.[112]

---

[103] 8 CFR §§245.15(d), 1245.15(d); HRIFA §902(d), 112 Stat. 2681-539 to 2681-540.

[104] Pub. L. No. 89-732, 80 Stat. 1161 (1966) (8 USC §1255 note).

[105] 8 CFR §§245.2(a)(2)(ii), 1245.2(a)(2)(ii).

[106] *www.uscis.gov* (search for "Cuban Natives or Citizens Seeking Lawful Permanent Resident Status").

[107] *Id.*

[108] *See id.* (providing documentation requirements, applicable USCIS forms, and information on where and when to file).

[109] *See Matter of Artigas*, 23 I&N Dec. 99, 106 (BIA 2001) ("We find that an Immigration Judge has jurisdiction to consider an application for adjustment of status under the Cuban Adjustment Act made by a respondent charged in removal proceedings as an arriving alien without a valid visa.").

[110] *Matter of Buschini*, A98 064 379 (AAO 2006). USCIS designated *Matter of Buschini* as an adopted decision on June 30, 2006. *See www.uscis.gov/files/article/Buschini063006.pdf.*

[111] *Matter of Buschini, supra* note 110.

[112] *Id.*

However, a consular certificate stating that a person was born outside of Cuba to a Cuban citizen parent, but lacking a statement of citizenship, is not ordinarily accepted by USCIS as sufficient to prove Cuban citizenship.[113]

6.9. Cancellation of Removal

IIRAIRA dramatically altered two well-known forms of relief for individuals who had resided in the United States for long periods of time: relief under the repealed §212(c) and suspension of deportation under former §244(a). Both forms of relief, now more restrictive and renamed cancellation of removal, are set forth in INA §240A(a) (similar to former §212(c)) and §240A(b) (similar to suspension).[114]

Neither of these former sections, however, should be forgotten just yet. Section 212(c) may still apply in proceedings initiated prior to April 1, 1997. And by enacting NACARA, Congress has revived the old suspension of deportation section. NACARA permits potentially hundreds of thousands of Central Americans and Eastern Europeans who meet the requirements outlined above in this chapter at 6.5 to apply for relief under the more generous provisions of former §244(a). For these reasons, both the old and revamped forms of relief will be outlined briefly in this section.

6.9.1. Relief for Permanent Residents

Former §212(c)

Under the §212(c), as amended by the Antiterrorism and Effective Death Penalty Act of 1996,[115] individuals admitted for permanent residency who demonstrated seven years of lawful domicile in the United States could apply for a waiver of deportation, unless they had been convicted of almost any criminal offense.[116] Under this section, individuals in deportation proceedings could only seek a waiver for a ground of deportability that had a comparable exclusion ground.[117] A person who had entered without inspection, for example, could not seek a waiver of that ground under §212(c). In determining whether to grant a waiver, the IJ weighed the equities in the case, including rehabilitation and any showing of hardship to the individual or to his or her family.[118]

> ➢ *Tip*—Individuals placed in proceedings prior to April 24, 1996, or April 1, 1997, may have their claims adjudicated under earlier versions of §212(c), ac-

---

[113] *Id.*

[114] INA §§240A(a), (b); 8 USC §§1229b(a), (b).

[115] Pub. L. No. 104-132, 110 Stat. 1214.

[116] *See, e.g., Matter of Ponce de Leon*, 21 I&N Dec. 154 (BIA 1997) (finding a noncitizen convicted of an aggravated felony ineligible for §212(c) relief).

[117] *Matter of Jimenez-Santillano*, 21 I&N Dec. 567, 574 (BIA 1996) ("The essential analysis is to determine whether the deportation ground under which the alien has been adjudged deportable has a statutory counterpart among the exclusion grounds waivable by section 212(c).").

[118] *But see Matter of D–*, 20 I&N Dec. 915 (BIA 1994) (holding that allegations and evidence of a well-founded fear or clear probability of persecution have no place in a §212(c) adjudication).

cording to the Supreme Court's decision in *INS v. St. Cyr*.[119] Final regulations to implement *St. Cyr* were published on September 28, 2004.[120] Critics had complained that the proposed regulations were an evasion of the letter and spirit of the Supreme Court's ruling.[121]

New INA §240A(a)

Under the new cancellation of removal provision, §240A(a), the AG is permitted to cancel the removal of a person who is inadmissible or deportable if the individual:

- has been a lawful permanent resident (LPR) for not less than five years;
- has resided continuously in the United States for seven years after having been admitted in any status; and
- has not been convicted of an aggravated felony.[122]

The individual must also demonstrate that he or she merits such relief as a matter of discretion.[123] Favorable considerations include: family ties in the United States, residence of a long duration in the United States, evidence of hardship on the individual or his or her family, service in the U.S. Armed Forces, employment history, property or business ties in the United States, evidence of value and service to the community, proof of genuine rehabilitation, and other evidence of good character.[124] Adverse factors include: the nature and circumstances underlying the grounds for removal, significant violations of U.S. immigration laws, the existence of a criminal record, and other evidence of bad character.[125]

The period of continuous residence could include time accumulated in the United States in a nonimmigrant status.[126] The period of continuous residence stops accumulat-

---

[119] *See INS v. St. Cyr*, 533 U.S. 289 (2001).

[120] 69 Fed. Reg. 57826 (Sept. 28, 2004).

[121] *See* American Immigration Law Foundation (AILF) Practice Advisory, *St. Cyr* Regulations and Strategies for Applicants Who Are Barred from Section 212(c) Relief Under the Regulation (Oct. 19, 2004), available at www.ailf.org/lac/lac_pa_101904.pdf. *See also Atkinson v. Att'y Gen. of the U.S.*, 479 F.3d 222, 229–30 (3d Cir. 2007) (extending *St. Cyr* relief to all individuals convicted of pre-IIRAIRA aggravated felonies); *Hem v. Maurer*, 458 F.3d 1185, 1189 (10th Cir. 2006) (concluding that only objective reliance is necessary to sustain a retroactivity claim under 212(c), and that "litigants who proceed to trial but abandon their right to appeal when §212(c) relief is available have objectively relied on pre-IIRIRA law"); *Ponnapula v. Ashcroft*, 373 F.3d 480, 494–96 (3d Cir. 2004) (extending *St. Cyr* relief not only to individuals who entered plea agreements, but also to individuals offered plea agreements who went to trial on their criminal charges); *Alvarez-Hernandez v. Gonzales*, 401 F.3d 327, 334 (5th Cir. 2005) (finding that the date of a plea of guilty and not the date that the judgment of conviction is entered is determinative of whether the retroactive application of IIRAIRA's bar to 212(c) is applied).

[122] INA §240A(a); 8 USC §1229b(a).

[123] *See Matter of C–V–T–*, 22 I&N Dec. 7 (BIA 1998).

[124] *Id.* at 12.

[125] *Id.*

[126] *See Matter of Blancas-Lara*, 23 I&N Dec. 458 (BIA 2002) (time accumulated after applicant entered with border crossing card counts toward seven years of residence). *But see Matter of Koloamatangi*,

continued

ing upon the service of an Order to Show Cause (OSC) or a Notice to Appear (NTA), or when the individual commits an act that renders him or her inadmissible or deportable under certain criminal or security-related grounds, whichever occurs earlier.[127] Note that the law limits to 4,000 the annual number of individuals who may receive cancellation of removal and adjustment of status.[128]

> ➢ *Tip*—For more information on cancellation of removal under §240A(a), *see* R. Godinez and M. Kramer, "Advanced Issues in Criminal Alien Waivers," *Immigration & Nationality Law Handbook* 461, 464–67 (AILA 2007–08 Ed.).

6.9.2. Relief for Nonpermanent Residents

Old §244

Under pre-IIRAIRA §244(a), individuals who had resided in the United States for at least seven years, who could demonstrate good moral character, and who could show that their deportation would result in "extreme hardship" to themselves and/or their U.S. citizen or LPR spouse, parent, or child, could receive suspension of deportation and have their status adjusted for lawful permanent residency.[129] Individuals eligible to apply for suspension of deportation under NACARA, outlined above in this chapter at 6.5, will still have the benefit of these more generous provisions. It should be noted, however, that a claim of persecution may not be presented as a means of demonstrating "extreme hardship" for purposes of suspension of deportation.[130] For purposes of determining good moral character, the BIA has held that oral statements falsely made under oath to an AO constitute false testimony and disqualify an individual from suspension of deportation and voluntary departure.[131]

New §240A(b)

Under new §240A(b), for cancellation of removal and adjustment of status, an individual must demonstrate that that he or she:

---

23 I&N Dec. 548 (BIA 2003) (an individual who acquired LPR status through fraud or misrepresentation has never been "lawfully" admitted for permanent residence).

[127] *See* INA §240A(d); 8 USC §1229b(d); *Matter of N–J–B–*, 22 I&N Dec. 1057 (BIA 1997, AG 1997 and 1999). *See also Matter of Perez*, 22 I&N Dec. 689 (BIA 1999) (finding that an offense described in §240A(d) is deemed to end continuous residence or physical presence even if the offense was committed prior to the enactment of IIRAIRA). *But see Matter of Deanda-Romo*, 23 I&N Dec. 597 (BIA 2003) (where first of two crimes involving moral turpitude (CIMT) qualified as petty offense and did not render respondent inadmissible, he established requisite seven years).

[128] INA §240A(e); 8 USC §1229b(e).

[129] INA §244(a) (repealed); 8 USC §1254(a) (repealed).

[130] *See Gebremichael v. INS*, 10 F.3d 28 (1st Cir. 1993); *Farzad v. INS*, 802 F.2d 123 (5th Cir. 1986); *Kashefi-Zihagh v. INS*, 791 F.2d 708 (9th Cir. 1986); *Sanchez v. INS*, 707 F.2d 1523 (D.C. Cir. 1983).

[131] *Matter of R–S–J–*, 22 I&N Dec. 863 (BIA 1999).

- has been physically present in the United States for a continuous period of 10 years or more (or three years in the case of a battered spouse or child with a U.S. citizen or LPR spouse or parent[132]);

- has been a person of good moral character during that period;[133]

- has not been convicted of certain crimes (including certain crimes of moral turpitude, controlled-substance offenses, and aggravated felonies); and

- establishes that removal from the United States would result in "exceptional and extremely unusual hardship" to the individual's U.S. citizen or LPR spouse, parent, or child (or, in the case of a battered spouse or child, "extreme hardship" to the individual, or the individual's child or parent).[134]

Although the title of this section appears to limit relief to nonpermanent residents, the text of INA §240A(b) does not bar LPRs from relief. According to one commentator, denial of this relief to LPRs might violate the Equal Protection Clause of the U.S. Constitution.[135]

In determining whether an applicant meets the "exceptional and extremely unusual hardship" standard, the BIA has held that a single mother of six minor children (four of whom were U.S. citizens), with no immediate family in her home country, who was the sole support of her family, and who had limited financial resources, established eligibility for cancellation of removal.[136] In contrast, the BIA also has found that poor economic conditions, lack of family to assist with adjustment upon return, and diminished educational opportunities in the home country do not meet the "exceptional and extremely unusual hardship" standard.[137] The BIA has rejected an "unconscionable" standard as too high a burden of proof to demonstrate exceptional and extremely unusual hardship.[138]

Under this new cancellation of removal provision, the period of continuous residence terminates upon the service of an OSC or an NTA, or when the individual commits an act that renders him or her inadmissible or deportable under certain criminal or security-related grounds, whichever occurs earlier.[139] In calculating the 10-year period, at least one court has held that date of an individual's arrival in the United States should be counted, and concluded that a person who arrived on May 14, 1987, and who was served with an NTA on

---

[132] For more information on cancellation of removal under the Violence Against Women Act, *see* J. Dinnerstein, "Options for Immigrant Victims of Domestic Violence," *Immigration & Nationality Law Handbook* 482, 504–06 (AILA 2007–08 Ed.).

[133] *See Matter of Garcia-Hernandez*, 23 I&N Dec. 590 (BIA 2003) (petty offense CIMT does not bar the offender from establishing good moral character).

[134] INA §§240A(b)(1), (2); 8 USC §§1229b(b)(1), (2).

[135] *See* N. Wettstein, "Removal Proceedings, Cancellation of Removal, and Voluntary Departure," *Understanding the 1996 Immigration Act* 3–6 (Federal Publications 1997).

[136] *Matter of Recinas*, 23 I&N Dec. 467 (BIA 2002).

[137] *See Matter of Andazola*, 23 I&N Dec. 319 (BIA 2002).

[138] *See Matter of Monreal*, 23 I&N Dec. 56 (BIA 2001).

[139] *See* INA §240A(d); 8 USC §1229b(d); NACARA §203, 111 Stat. 2196; *see also Matter of Cisneros-Gonzalez*, 23 I&N Dec. 668 (BIA 2004) (service of a charging document in a prior proceeding does not end period of continuous presence with respect to application for cancellation in current proceeding); *Matter of Nolasco*, 22 I&N Dec. 632 (BIA 1999).

May 13, 1997, established he was physically present for 10 years.[140] The period of continuous residence terminates, however, when the individual is compelled to leave the United States under the threat of the institution of removal proceedings.[141]

Moreover, the new law limits to 4,000 the annual number of individuals who may receive cancellation of removal (or suspension of deportation) and adjustment of status.[142] As noted above in this chapter at 6.5, individuals eligible to have their suspension of deportation claims adjudicated under NACARA are not subject to the new rule for calculating continuous physical presence, nor are they subject to the cap of 4,000.

6.10. VOLUNTARY DEPARTURE

Individuals who fail to qualify for any of the forms of relief discussed above in this chapter may be eligible for voluntary departure.[143] Voluntary departure allows an otherwise removable noncitizen to depart from the United States at his or her own expense, within a specified time period, and without being issued an order of removal. In some cases, voluntary departure is preferable to an order of removal. Some commentators, however, caution that it is not always preferable to ask for voluntary departure.[144]

At the removal hearing, immigration judges (IJs) have a duty to provide individuals with information about the availability and requirements of voluntary departure and to provide individuals with an opportunity to apply prior to taking the pleadings in their cases.[145] Under IIRAIRA, a person issued a removal order may be barred from re-entering the United States for up to 20 years and may be subject to severe criminal and civil penalties if he or she re-enters without authorization.[146]

Voluntary departure does not require that an individual return to his or her home country if he or she is able to secure entry to a third country. IIRAIRA, however, also significantly altered this familiar form of relief, making it more difficult to obtain. If deportation or removal proceedings were commenced before April 1, 1997, arguably the old

---

[140] *See Lagandaon v. Ashcroft*, 383 F.3d 983 (9th Cir. 2004) (relying on the common-law definition of a year).

[141] *See Matter of Romalez-Alcaide*, 23 I&N Dec. 423 (BIA 2002). *But see Morales-Morales v. Ashcroft*, 384 F.3d 418, 428 (7th Cir. 2004) ("[W]hen an alien is simply returned to the border without voluntarily departing under threat of deportation . . . , there is no break in continuous physical presence.").

[142] INA §240A(e); 8 USC §1229b(e).

[143] *See* INA §240B; 8 USC §1229c.

[144] B. Bates, "Voluntary Departure: Do You Really *Want* It? If You Have It, Can You *Keep* It?" 1 *Immigration & Nationality Law Handbook* 123 (AILA 2004–05 Ed.) (noting that under some circumstances it is better to not obtain voluntary departure). *But see* "Voluntary Departure or Removal: Is There Any Difference?" 78 *Interpreter Releases* 1889 (Dec. 17, 2001) (concluding that for many individuals facing expulsion from the United States, there is no significant difference between a grant of voluntary departure and an order of removal).

[145] *Matter of Cordova*, 22 I & N Dec. 966 (BIA 1999) (BIA remanded case to IJ because IJ failed to advise individual of his eligibility for voluntary departure).

[146] *See* INA §§212(a)(9)(A)(i)–(iii), 276(b); 8 USC §§1182(a)(9)(A)(i)–(iii), 1326(b).

voluntary departure rules apply.¹⁴⁷ If removal proceedings were commenced after April 1, 1997, the procedures outlined below are applicable.¹⁴⁸

Under IIRAIRA, voluntary departure is available at two different stages of removal proceedings: *before* the conclusion of proceedings and *at* the conclusion of such proceedings.¹⁴⁹ These two types of voluntary departure have different requirements and benefits. Any decision regarding which one to choose should be carefully considered. Under IIRAIRA, the consequences for failing to depart voluntarily are much more severe.

Regulations prohibit administrative appeals regarding the amount of time granted for voluntary departure.¹⁵⁰ The statute itself prohibits judicial review of any regulation regarding eligibility for voluntary departure.¹⁵¹

6.10.1. Before the Conclusion of Removal Proceedings

An individual is eligible for voluntary departure prior to the institution of removal proceedings or before removal proceedings conclude if he or she:

- is not deportable for having been convicted of an aggravated felony or having engaged in terrorist activities;
- makes a request for voluntary departure prior to or at the master calendar hearing at which the case is initially calendared for a merits hearing;
- makes no additional requests for relief (or withdraws such requests prior to any grant of voluntary departure);
- concedes removability;
- waives appeal of all issues; and
- did not fail to depart in a timely manner after a previous grant of voluntary departure under INA §240B.¹⁵²

There is no statutory or regulatory requirement that the individual demonstrate that he or she has good moral character.¹⁵³ The waiver of appeal must be made on the record by the individual or his or her representative.¹⁵⁴

Voluntary departure *before* the conclusion of proceedings is not available to "arriving" noncitizens who are placed in removal proceedings at the time of their arrival in the United States, *i.e.*, individuals who, in the past, would have been in exclusion proceed-

---

[147] *See* IIRAIRA §309(c), 110 Stat. 3009-625 to 3009-626.

[148] *See also* "Voluntary Departure Under IIRAIRA: Standards and INS Implementation," 75 *Interpreter Releases* 79 (Jan. 16, 1998).

[149] *See Matter of Arguelles-Campos*, 22 I & N Dec. 811 (BIA 1999).

[150] 8 CFR §1240.26(g).

[151] INA §240B(e); 8 USC §1229c(e).

[152] 8 CFR §§1240.26(a), (b).

[153] *See Matter of Arguelles-Campos*, 22 I&N Dec. 811 (BIA 1999) (holding that individuals who apply prior to the conclusion of proceedings need not demonstrate good moral character or the financial means to depart the United States).

[154] *Matter of Ocampo-Ugalde*, 22 I&N Dec. 1301 (BIA 2000).

ings.[155] Such individuals may seek permission to withdraw their application for admission pursuant to INA §235(a)(4).

Generally, the Department of Homeland Security (DHS) or the IJ may grant voluntary departure for a period of up to 120 days.[156] The IJ, however, may only grant voluntary departure for a period of 30 days after the master calendar hearing at which the case is set for a merits hearing unless DHS counsel stipulates to a longer grant of voluntary departure.[157] Any extensions may only be granted by the DHS district director (DD), and the total period of time, including any extensions by the DD, may not exceed 120 days.[158]

One former exception to the 120-day limit on voluntary departure allowed individuals who were admitted to the United States as visitors and sought to remain in the United States for medical treatment to extend their period of voluntary departure.[159] This exception was permitted under the Three-Year Pilot Program Waiver that expired on September 30, 2003.[160]

Individuals may be required to post a voluntary departure bond that is surrendered when they depart the United States.[161] They must also present to DHS their passport or other travel document unless no document is required or DHS has possession of the document.[162]

6.10.2. At the Conclusion of Removal Proceedings

An immigration judge may grant voluntary departure at the conclusion of the removal proceedings if the individual demonstrates that he or she:

- has been present in the United States for a period of at least one year preceding the date the NTA was issued;
- is a person of good moral character for the preceding five years;
- has not been convicted of an aggravated felony and has not engaged in terrorist activities;
- has the means to depart the United States (i.e., travel documents) and the intention to do so;[163] and
- did not fail to depart in a timely manner after a previous grant of voluntary departure under INA §240B.[164]

---

[155] INA §240B(a)(4); 8 USC §1229c(a)(4).
[156] 8 CFR §§240.25(c), 1240.26(e).
[157] 8 CFR §1240.26(b)(1)(ii).
[158] 8 CFR §1240.26(f).
[159] INA §240B(a)(2); 8 USC §1229c(a)(2).
[160] *Id.*
[161] 8 CFR §§240.25(b), 1240.26(b)(3).
[162] 8 CFR §§240.25(b), 1240.26(b)(3).
[163] 8 CFR §1240.26(c).
[164] *See* 8 CFR §1240.26(a).

Such individuals are required to post a voluntary departure bond of not less than $500.[165] The IJ may only grant voluntary departure for a period of up to 60 days.[166] Any extensions may only be granted by the DD, and the total period of time, including extensions by the DD, may not exceed 60 days.[167] There is no judicial review from a denial of a request for voluntary departure at the conclusion of proceedings.[168] For purposes of determining good moral character, the BIA has held that oral statements falsely made under oath to an AO constitute false testimony and disqualify an individual from suspension of deportation and voluntary departure.[169]

6.10.3. Consequences for Failure to Depart

An individual who receives a grant of voluntary departure and fails to depart within the specified time period:

- is subject to a civil penalty of not less than $1,000 and not more than $5,000; and
- is ineligible, for a period of 10 years, for cancellation of removal, voluntary departure, adjustment of status, change of nonimmigrant status, or registry.[170]

6.10.4. Revocation

DHS may revoke the grant of voluntary departure without advance notice if it ascertains that the application should not have been granted. The revocation, however, must be communicated in writing and must cite the statutory basis for revocation. There is no appeal from the revocation of a grant of voluntary departure.[171]

6.11. REGISTRY

An individual may be eligible for adjustment of status in removal proceedings under a provision of law known as registry if the individual is not barred from applying for adjustment and establishes that he or she:

- entered the United States prior to January 1, 1972;
- has had his or her residence in the United States continuously since such entry;
- is a person of good moral character;

---

[165] 8 CFR §1240.26(c)(3).

[166] 8 CFR §1240.26(e).

[167] 8 CFR §1240.26(f).

[168] INA §240B(f); 8 USC §1229c(f).

[169] *Matter of R–S–J–*, 22 I&N Dec. 863 (BIA 1999).

[170] INA §240B(d); 8 USC §1229c(d). To avoid these harsh consequences, see AILF Practice Advisory, "Failure to Depart After a Grant of Voluntary Departure: The Consequences and Arguments to Avoid Them" (updated Feb. 21, 2006), available at *www.ailf.org/lac/lac_pa_022106.pdf*; AILF Practice Advisory, "Staying the Voluntary Departure Period when Filing a Motion to Reopen" (updated Dec. 16, 2005), available at *www.ailf.org/lac/lac_pa_121605.pdf*; and AILF Practice Advisory, "Protecting the Voluntary Departure Period During Court of Appeals Review" (amended Oct. 25, 2005), available at *www.ailf.org/lac/lac_pa_102505.pdf*.

[171] 8 CFR §240.25(f).

- is not ineligible for citizenship and is not deportable for having engaged in terrorist activity; and

- is not inadmissible for persecuting others under the Nazi regime, engaging in genocide, or on grounds that relate "to criminals, procurers and other immoral persons, subversives, violators of the narcotic laws or smugglers."[172]

Individuals have applied for registry in deportation proceedings.[173] At least one court has held that registry is available in exclusion proceedings.[174]

6.12. Waiver of Inadmissibility Under INA §212(h)

An individual in removal proceedings may also be eligible for a waiver of certain grounds of inadmissibility. Under INA §212(h), the AG may waive the following §212(a) grounds: commission of a crime involving moral turpitude; conviction of two or more offenses for which the aggregate sentence imposed is five years or more; prostitution and commercialized vice grounds; crimes where immunity was asserted to bar prosecution; or a single offense of simple possession of 30 grams or less of marijuana.[175] Federal courts do not have jurisdiction to review a decision of the AG to grant or deny a waiver under this subsection.[176]

An applicant for a waiver under §212(h) must establish that:

- his or her admission is not contrary to the national welfare, safety, or security of the United States, and that he or she has been rehabilitated, or

- in the case of an individual inadmissible on prostitution or procurement of prostitution grounds, that the activities occurred more than 15 years ago.[177]

In the case of an individual who is the spouse, parent, son, or daughter of a U.S. citizen or LPR, the individual may be eligible for a waiver under §212(h) if he or she establishes to the satisfaction of the AG that the denial of the waiver would result in extreme hardship to his or her U.S. citizen or LPR spouse, parent, son, or daughter.[178]

Waivers under §212(h) are *not* available to individuals who:

- have been convicted of (or who have admitted committing acts that constitute) murder or criminal acts involving torture, or an attempt or conspiracy to commit murder or a criminal act involving torture; and

---

[172] *See* INA §249; 8 USC §1259.

[173] *See, e.g., Matter of Sanchez-Linn*, 20 I&N Dec. 362 (BIA 1991) (rejecting a registry claim in deportation proceedings for failure to establish good moral character for a reasonable period of time since the commission of two serious crimes).

[174] *See Hernandez v. Chandler*, CA3-88-0224-R (N.D. Tex. June 23, 1989), *digested in* 66 *Interpreter Releases* 885 (Aug. 7, 1989).

[175] INA §212(h); 8 USC §1182(h). *See also* 8 CFR §§212.7, 1212.7.

[176] INA §212(h); 8 USC §1182(h). *See also* INA §242(a)(2)(B); 8 USC 1252(a)(2)(B).

[177] INA §212(h)(1)(A); 8 USC §1182(h)(1)(A).

[178] INA §212(h)(1)(B); 8 USC §1182(h)(1)(B).

- have previously been admitted to the United States as LPRs if either since the date of such admission they have been convicted of an aggravated felony or they have not lawfully resided continuously in the United States for a period of not less than seven years immediately preceding the date of initiation of proceedings to remove them from the United States.[179]

These restrictions added by IIRAIRA were effective on the date of enactment, September 30, 1996.[180] It is notable that non-LPRs convicted of aggravated felonies *are* permitted to seek a waiver under §212(h).[181] The following cases in federal appeals courts have held that §212(h) is constitutional and does not violate the Equal Protection Clause: *Camacho-Salinas v. United States AG*,[182] *De Fuentes v. Gonzales*,[183] *Latu v. Ashcroft*,[184] *Lukowski v. INS*,[185] *Taniguchi v. Schultz*,[186] *De Leon-Reynoso v. Ashcroft*,[187] *Jankowski-Burczyk v. INS*,[188] and *Lara-Ruiz v. INS*.[189]

> ➢ *Tip*—For more information on §212(h) waivers, see R. Godinez and M. Kramer, "Advanced Issues in Criminal Alien Waivers," *Immigration & Nationality Law Handbook* 461, 467–70 (AILA 2007–08 Ed.). *See also* J. Ferguson, *AILA's Focus on Waivers Under the Immigration and Nationality Act* (AILA 2007).

6.13. Family-Sponsored, Employment-Based, and Other Means of Regularizing Immigration Status in the United States

More conventional forms of immigration remedies also should not be overlooked. While such remedies may not be available in removal proceedings, they are routes to legal permanent resident (LPR) status in the United States. These remedies include obtaining LPR status through a spouse, parent, sibling, son, or daughter. For certain professional and skilled workers, it also may be possible to obtain temporary or permanent status through an employer. In addition, LPR status may be obtained under the diversity visa program. Individuals in temporary or nonimmigrant status also are permitted to remain in the United States while in valid status. The procedures for obtaining immigrant

---

[179] INA §212(h)(2); 8 USC §1182(h)(2). *See also Matter of Pineda-Castellanos*, 21 I&N Dec. 1017 (BIA 1997).

[180] *See Matter of Pineda-Castellanos, supra* note 179; *Matter of Yeung*, 21 I&N Dec. 610 (BIA 1997).

[181] *See Matter of Michel*, 21 I&N Dec. 1101 (BIA 1998).

[182] *Camacho-Salinas v. United States AG*, 460 F.3d 1343, 1348 (11th Cir. 2006).

[183] *De Fuentes v. Gonzales*, 462 F.3d 498, 506–08 (5th Cir. 2006).

[184] *Latu v. Ashcroft*, 375 F.3d 1012, 1020 (10th Cir. 2004).

[185] *Lukowski v. INS*, 279 F.3d 644, 647 (8th Cir. 2002).

[186] *Taniguchi v. Schultz*, 303 F.3d 950, 957–58 (9th Cir. 2002).

[187] *De Leon-Reynoso v. Ashcroft*, 293 F.3d 633, 640 (3d Cir. 2002).

[188] *Jankowski-Burczyk v. INS*, 291 F.3d 172, 178 (2d Cir. 2002).

[189] *Lara-Ruiz v. INS*, 241 F.3d 934, 947 (7th Cir. 2001); *see also Matter of Ayala-Arevalo*, 22 I & N Dec. 398 (BIA 1998) (finding that a §212(h) waiver is not available to an individual who claimed that his previous admission for permanent residency was not lawful because he concealed criminal activities).

or nonimmigrant status are beyond the scope of this *Primer*. The categories, however, are outlined below.[190]

> *Note*: **Asylum and Unlawful Presence**—Eligibility for certain immigration benefits may depend on the amount of time an individual has had an "unlawful presence" in the United States. Whether the period during which an individual's asylum application was pending will count as period of "unlawful presence" depends on a number of factors.[191]

6.13.1. Family-Sponsored Immigration

U.S. citizens may sponsor the following relatives for LPR status: spouses, unmarried children, parents, married children, and siblings. LPRs may sponsor spouses and unmarried children. There are an unlimited number of visas available to immediate relatives, *i.e.*, the spouses, minor unmarried children, and parents of U.S. citizens. In contrast, the remaining categories of relatives are subject to a preference system that for most categories, due to backlogs, requires relatives to wait until a visa becomes available. The USA PATRIOT Act[192] allows for certain relatives to self-petition if their relative petitions were terminated or rendered null because of the terrorist attacks of September 11, 2001, and in some cases, even if the relative petition had never been filed.[193]

6.13.2. Employment-Based Immigration

Noncitizens with special skills and talents needed in the United States may also be able to obtain LPR status. Employment-based categories include individuals of "extraordinary ability," "outstanding professors and researchers," noncitizens of "exceptional ability," professionals with advanced degrees, "skilled" workers, religious workers, and investors. Employment-based visas are also subject to a preference system that, for most categories, requires a noncitizen to wait for an available visa. The USA PATRIOT Act allows for certain noncitizens to self-petition if their labor certification applications were terminated or rendered null because of the terrorist attacks of September 11, 2001.[194]

---

[190] For more detailed information, see articles in the annual editions of *Immigration & Nationality Law Handbook*, available from AILA Publications at *www.ailapubs.org* or (800) 982-2839.

[191] *See* "INS Discusses the Exception to Unlawful Presence for Bona Fide Asylum Applicants," 76 *Interpreter Releases* 1289 (Aug. 30, 1999); *see also* Bureau of Citizenship and Immigration Services Memorandum, J. Podolny, "Interpretation of 'Period of Authorized Stay' by the Attorney General in Determining 'Unlawful Presence' Under INA Section 212(a)(9)(B)(ii)" (Mar. 27, 2003), *published on* AILA InfoNet as part of Doc. No. 03042140 (*posted* Apr. 21, 2003); K. Koenig, "Nuances of Unlawful Presence," *Immigration & Nationality Law Handbook* 847, 852–53 (AILA 2005–06 Ed.).

[192] Uniting and Strengthening America by Providing Appropriate Tools Required to Intercept and Obstruct Terrorism Act of 2001, Pub. L. No. 107-56, 115 Stat. 272.

[193] For additional information, see "INS Issues Guidance on Immigration Benefits for Terrorism Victims under USA PATRIOT Act," 79 *Interpreter Releases* 482 (Apr. 1, 2002).

[194] *Id.*

6.13.3. Diversity Visas

Individuals from countries that send few immigrants to the United States are eligible to register under the diversity visa program, also known as the visa lottery. Each year the Department of State designates the countries subject to the lottery and 50,000 visas are made available to nationals of those countries. Applicants for a diversity visa must have at least a high school education or its equivalent or, within the past five years, have two years of work experience in an occupation requiring at least two years of training or experience. The registration period for the 2009 Diversity Immigrant Visa Program was from October 3, 2007 to December 2, 2007.[195]

6.13.4. Nonimmigrant Visas

Nonimmigrant or temporary visas are available to the following categories of noncitizens: tourists, business visitors, noncitizens in transit, students, exchange visitors, temporary workers, treaty traders and investors, foreign government officials, intracompany transferees, foreign press representatives, and fiancé(e)s of U.S. citizens.[196]

6.13.5. Special Immigrant Juvenile Visas

A noncitizen juvenile may be eligible for legal permanent residency if he or she is present in the United States and meets the following requirements:

- has been declared dependent in a juvenile court and has been deemed eligible by that court for long-term foster care due to abuse, neglect, or abandonment;
- it has been determined in administrative or judicial proceedings that it is not in the juvenile's best interest to be returned to the juvenile's or his or her parents' previous country of nationality or country of last habitual residence;
- the AG expressly consents to the dependency order serving as a precondition to the grant of special immigrant juvenile visa status.[197]

The provision requiring the AG's consent was added in 1997.[198] At least one court has held that this provision may not be applied retroactively.[199] Another court ordered legacy INS to consent to the dependency hearing in state court.[200]

6.14. CITIZENSHIP

In some cases, an individual placed in removal proceedings may actually be a U.S. citizen or eligible to naturalize. Although such cases are unusual, the possibility should always be considered. By virtue of the Fourteenth Amendment to the U.S. Constitution,

---

[195] This and additional information on the diversity visa program may be obtained at www.dvlottery.state.gov.

[196] See generally INA §101(a)(15).

[197] INA §101(a)(27)(J); 8 USC §1101(a)(27)(J); see also 8 CFR §204.11.

[198] Pub. L. No. 105-119, §113, 111 Stat. 2439, 2460 (1997).

[199] See Gao v. Jenifer, 185 F.3d 548 (6th Cir. 1999).

[200] See Ramirez v. Sonchik, No. CIV 02-920 (D. Ariz. July 8, 2002); see also USCIS Memorandum, "Memorandum #3—Field Guidance on Special Immigrant Juvenile Visas" (May 27, 2004), available at www.uscis.gov/files/pressrelease/SIJ_Memo_052704.pdf.

any person born in the United States is a citizen of the United States. Two other ways of obtaining U.S. citizenship are addressed below. Also, the Child Citizenship Act of 2000[201] permitted many foreign-born children, including adopted children, to acquire citizenship automatically without formally naturalizing.[202]

6.14.1. Derivative Citizenship

An individual whose parent, grandparent, or, in some cases, great-grandparent was born in the United States may actually hold derivative U.S. citizenship, even though the individual has never resided in the United States and even if he or she currently holds lawful permanent residency. Derivative citizenship may be obtained by filing Form N-600 with USCIS. The rules regarding the acquisition of derivative U.S. citizenship are complex and vary depending on the year of the parent's, grandparent's, or great-grandparent's birth and period of residency in the United States.[203]

6.14.2. Naturalization

As odd as it may sound, an individual in removal proceedings may actually be able to naturalize and become a U.S. citizen. Not all grounds of removability are bars to U.S. citizenship. IJs are authorized to terminate removal proceedings when an individual has established prima facie eligibility for naturalization and the matter involves exceptionally appealing or humanitarian factors.[204] In such cases, however, it may be necessary for a federal court first to determine that the individual is eligible to naturalize before an IJ will terminate removal proceedings.[205]

On July 3, 2002, President George W. Bush issued Executive Order 13269, which allows for the expedited naturalization of noncitizens serving honorably in (or honorably discharged from) the Armed Forces of the United States on or after September 11, 2001, whether or not they have been lawfully admitted to the United States as permanent residents.[206]

---

[201] Child Citizenship Act of 2000, Pub. L. No. 106-395, 114 Stat. 1631.

[202] *See* INA §§320, 322; 8 USC §§1431, 1433; *see also* USCIS Fact Sheet, "The Child Citizenship Act of 2000" (Oct. 25, 2004), *published on* AILA InfoNet at Doc. No. 04110867 (*posted* Nov. 8, 2004).

[203] *See, e.g., Alcarez-Garcia v. Ashcroft*, 293 F.3d 1155 (9th Cir. 2002). For a useful chart on derivative citizenship, see *Kurzban's Immigration Law Sourcebook* (10th Ed. 2006), appx. B. *See also* D. Levy, "The Family in Immigration and Nationality Law: Part II," 92-10 *Immigration Briefings* (Oct. 1992).

[204] *See* 8 CFR §1239.2(f).

[205] *See, e.g., Gatcliffe v. Reno*, 23 F. Supp. 2d 581 (D.V.I. 1998) (finding that an individual had established good moral character and was eligible for naturalization despite having been convicted of an aggravated felony).

[206] *See* INS Memorandum, W Yates, "Implementation of Executive Order 13269" (July 17, 2002), *published on* AILA InfoNet at Doc. No. 02080946 (*posted* Aug. 9, 2002); *see also* J. Lockhart, "Naturalization through Active Duty Service in Armed Forces During Certain Periods of Military Hostilities Under INA Section 329," 04-10 *Immigration Briefings* 1 (Oct. 2004).

➤ *Tip*—In 2007, USCIS published a 65-page, comprehensive *Guide to Naturalization*.[207] For more information, see H. Hom, "Naturalization and Citizenship Requirements," *Navigating the Fundamentals of Immigration Law* 337 (AILA 2007–08 Ed.).

6.15. PRIVATE BILLS

When all else fails, an individual or family facing extreme or unusual hardship on removal may seek assistance from a member of Congress in the form of a private bill. A private bill could bestow permanent residency or even citizenship on a worthy candidate. The House Judiciary Committee's Subcommittee on Immigration and Claims has published a helpful guide on procedures and criteria for submitting private bills.[208] The guide notes that the Subcommittee reviews "only those cases that are of such an extraordinary nature that an exception to the law is needed."[209] Private bills commonly are submitted on behalf of: adopted children, doctors and nurses, persons involved with drugs or criminal activity, and persons seeking medical treatment.[210]

---

[207] Available at *www.uscis.gov/files/article/M-476.pdf*.

[208] *See* "Private Bill Procedures Guide Available from House Subcommittee," 79 *Interpreter Releases* 407 and Appendix IV (Mar. 18, 2002). *See also, AILA's Focus on Private Bills & Pardons in Immigration* (AILA 2007) by Anna Gallagher, *www.ailapubs.org*.

[209] *See* Committee on the Judiciary-Subcommittee on Immigration and Claims, *Rules on Procedure and Statement of Policy for Private Immigration Bills* (2002) at 3, *reproduced in* 79 *Interpreter Releases* 407 at Appendix IV.

[210] *Id.* at 4–5. For a more in-depth discussion of private bills, see A. Gallagher, "Remedies of Last Resort: Private Bills and Pardons," 06-02 *Immigration Briefings* (Feb. 2006) and *AILA's Focus on Private Bills & Pardons in Immigration* (AILA 2007). *See also* Congressional Research Service Report RL33024, M. Lee, *Private Immigration Legislation* (Feb. 28, 2007).

APPENDICES

Appendix 1—Interviewing and Intake
- 1A Interviewing Techniques 361
- 1B Sample Intake Form 365
- 1C Checklist for Bars to Asylum and Withholding of Deportation 369

Appendix 2—The Asylum Application
- 2A Checklist for Asylum Application (Form I-589) 371
- 2B Practice Pointers for Completing the Asylum Application 375
- 2C Sample Declaration 385

Appendix 3—Applying Affirmatively
- 3A Sample Letter to USCIS Service Center 391
- 3B Checklist for Preparing for the Asylum Interview 393
- 3C Sample Closing Statement 395

Appendix 4—Supporting Documentation
- 4A Checklist for Supporting Documentation 401
- 4B Sample Index of Supporting Documentation for Asylum Applicant from Iran 403
- 4C Sample Expert Affidavits (Country Conditions; Medical) 405
- 4D UNHCR Advisory Opinion on Cessation and Cancellation of Refugee Status 415

Appendix 5—Preparing for the Hearing
- 5A Practice Pointers on Direct and Cross-Examination of the Asylum Applicant 423
- 5B Sample Motion, Sample Petition for Review, and Sample Brief 429

Appendix 6—Contacts
- 6A Asylum Offices 473
- 6B Executive Office for Immigration Review 475
- 6C Address for Service of a Petition for Review 483
- 6D ICE Offices of Chief Counsel 487
- 6E Detention Facilities 495
- 6F Selected Resources for Country Condition Information 497
- 6G Useful Websites 499
- 6H Torture Treatment Programs 503

Appendix 7—Charts

7A	Affirmative and Defensive Asylum Process Chart	509
7B	Flowchart of Expedited Removal/Credible Fear Process	513
7C	A Comparison of the Forms of Protection Available Under U.S. Law	515
7D	Temporary Protected Status	517
7E	Benefits or Assistance Available to Asylees	519

Appendix 8—Resources

8A	Recommended Texts and Tools	523
8B	Resource Availability	525

Appendix 9—Forms

9A	Form I-589 and Instructions	527
9B	Form I-730 and Instructions	551
9C	Form I-765 and Instructions	557
9D	Form I-131 and Instructions	571

APPENDIX 1A
INTERVIEWING TECHNIQUES

A crucial and time-consuming part of representing or assisting an individual who is applying for asylum is gathering information about the claim from the applicant. It is often necessary to meet with the applicant on several occasions before beginning the task of completing the asylum application form. The interviewing process may be hampered because the applicant is often traumatized by his or her past experiences. Also, the applicant may initially lack the trust or confidence needed to share information about his or her past or the reasons for the harm he or she suffered. There may also be cultural or language barriers to overcome. Here are a few tips for getting over some of the hurdles you may encounter.

EXPLAIN YOUR ROLE AS AN ATTORNEY

Applicants for asylum come from a wide variety of backgrounds. Many may never have had contact with an attorney in their home countries. It is important to explain to the applicant that you represent him or her and that you do not work for the U.S. authorities. You should also note that you have a duty of confidentiality and may not reveal information to anyone without the applicant's permission.

DESCRIBE THE ASYLUM PROCESS

As Kafka's *The Trial* so aptly demonstrates, not knowing what to expect during a trial or hearing process can be frustrating, if not terrifying. Walk the applicant through the maze of the asylum process at the first interview and summarize the process at later interviews. It may be comforting for an applicant who is applying in removal proceedings to know that if he or she is not granted asylum by the immigration judge, there is an opportunity to appeal the decision to the Board of Immigration Appeals and, possibly, to a federal appeals court. In contrast, an applicant who seeks asylum in expedited removal proceedings should be informed of the need to fully present his or her claim at the "credible fear" interview, due to the swift and limited review of negative determinations.

EXPLAIN ASYLUM IN NONLEGAL TERMS

An applicant who understands the concept of asylum will be able to provide more relevant information to you during your interview sessions. Some applicants mistakenly believe that they must demonstrate that they will be persecuted for political reasons and are unaware of the other grounds for seeking asylum. It is also important to explain that the term persecution is broadly defined under U.S. law. Moreover, informing the applicant of the requirement that the persecution must be "on account of" one of the five enumerated grounds will prepare the applicant for your questions focusing on the reasons why the persecutor harmed or intends to harm him or her.

Schedule Several Meetings with the Applicant

An applicant who has met with you on several occasions will develop confidence in you and will most likely divulge more information about his or her asylum claim at each meeting. Some applicants may have been coached by smugglers or individuals from their home countries on the "story" they should tell U.S. authorities. Other applicants may conceal information that they believe may be harmful to their claims. It is important to impart to the asylum applicant the need to know the truth and all of the details regarding the applicant's fear of returning. At times, information that the applicant believes to be detrimental to his or her claim is actually helpful and may ultimately be the reason why he or she is granted asylum. Be prepared for your client's story to change as you discuss his or her claim over a period of time. It may, for example, take time for an applicant to reveal to you that he or she was sexually assaulted or took part in activities considered to be subversive in his or her home country.

Obtain a Competent Interpreter

If you and the applicant do not speak the same language, it is essential to obtain a competent interpreter for your interviews with the applicant. Before an interview, the interpreter should be instructed to provide exact translations of your questions and comments and of the applicant's responses. Be aware that applicants may not be able to relate certain aspects of their claims in the presence of a person of the opposite sex, or, in some cases, of the same sex. Ask the applicant if he or she would feel more comfortable with a male or female interpreter.

Learn About the Applicant's Country

In addition to human rights reports and current country condition reports, read as much as you can about the history of the applicant's country, its cultures, customs, religions, and traditions. There may even be movies or documentaries about the applicant's home country available at your local library or video store. The applicant's story will become clearer to you as you gain an understanding of his or her background.

Let the Applicant Play an Active Role in Developing the Claim

No one likes to feel helpless or powerless, including the applicant. Give the applicant assignments that will assist both you and the applicant in preparing his or her claim. Ask the applicant to write out his or her reasons for seeking asylum in a narrative form for your next interview. (If the applicant is unable to read and write, ask whether a family member or friend could assist or have the applicant tape record a narrative.) Ask the applicant to gather documents and letters in support of the claim, including identity documents, proof of membership in organizations or religious communities, or proof of military service. If he or she has access to a library or the Internet, the applicant may even be able to compile country condition reports for you. The applicant may also be able to identify family and friends who can corroborate parts of his or her claim. As an attorney, most likely a pro bono one, you need all of the help you can get, so don't overlook the applicant.

For additional interviewing techniques, you may wish to review:

- UNHCR Training Module RLD 4, Interviewing Applicants for Refugee Status (1995), available at *www.unhcr.org/publ/PUBL/3ae6bd670.pdf;* or
- S. Yale-Loehr, "Initial Interviews," *Navigating the Fundamentals of Immigration Law: Guidance and Tips for Successful Practice* (AILA 2007–08 Ed.).

APPENDIX 1B

SAMPLE INTAKE FORM

(This intake form may be used at an initial interview to obtain a general overview of the applicant's claim and to determine whether any bars to asylum may apply and whether any other forms of relief may be available to the applicant.)

Personal/Family Information

Applicant's Name _____

Address _____

Telephone No. _____ Fax No. _____

Any other names used _____

A# _____ Date of Birth _____ Sex _____ Marital Status _____

Place of Birth (POB) _____ Country of Citizenship _____
(if the country where applicant was born no longer exists, the applicant may be stateless)

POB of Mother _____, Father _____, Grandparents _____
(if a parent or grandparent was born in the U.S., the applicant may be a derivative U.S. citizen)

Is Spouse, Parent, Sibling, or Child a U.S. Citizen or Legal Permanent Resident? _____
(If yes, applicant may be able to immigrant to the United States through a family member)

Languages Spoken by Applicant _____

Other Countries of Residence _____

Type of Residency Permit, if any _____
(Applicant is not eligible for asylum if he or she was "firmly resettled" in a third country)

Religion _____ Ethnic Group _____

Profession/Work _____ Education _____
(An applicant who has a specialized skill or profession may qualify for an employment-based visa)

Present Employer, if any _____

Previous Employers _____
_____

Trafficking or Crime Victim _____
(Was the applicant a victim of a severe form of trafficking in persons or a victim of a serious crime? He or she may be eligible for a "T" or "U" visa, which eventually could lead to permanent residency. See ch. 6.)

Immigration Information

Date of Last Entry_____ Place of Last Entry _____

Manner of Last Entry (*e.g.*, with visa, without inspection, with false document, by claiming to be U.S. citizen) _____

Type of travel document (or passport) used, if any _____

Type of visa, if any _____ Date of expiration _____

Passport: Country _____ Date issued _____ Expiration Date _____
(In most cases, but not all, an applicant is a citizen of the country that issued his or her passport)

Present immigration status _____

Previous entries to the U.S., if any (including date/length of stay/manner of entry) _____
_____

Have any U.S. immigration petitions been filed on behalf of the applicant? _____

If so, what type and when? _____

Has the applicant previously applied for asylum in U.S.? _____ When? _____
(If yes, it is important to obtain any previously filed applications and note that the applicant may be ineligible for asylum unless he or she demonstrates changed country conditions)

Has the applicant previously obtained asylum, permanent residency or other immigration status in the U.S.? _____ If so, what type? _____ When? _____

Has the applicant ever appeared before an Immigration Judge? _____ When? _____
(If yes, it's important to question the applicant to determine if he or she has been previously deported from the United States, received voluntary departure, or whether the case was administratively closed)

APPENDIX 1B • SAMPLE INTAKE FORM

If in removal proceedings, how did applicant come to the attention of the DHS? _____
_____

Did the applicant make any statements to DHS? _____ When? _____ Where? _____
(If so, it's important to obtain all records from the DHS)

> *Make copies of any immigration documents and travel documents the applicant may have for his or her file. Also, file a Freedom of Information Act (FOIA) request form (Form G-639) as soon as possible to obtain a copy of the applicant's DHS file.*

Asylum Information

Reasons for fleeing home country _____
_____
_____

Actual physical or emotional harm (or torture) suffered by the applicant _____
_____

(If the applicant has suffered physical or emotional harm or has been subjected to torture, a physician or mental health professional may examine the applicant and submit a professional assessment of the applicant's physical and/or mental condition)

Reasons for fear of future harm (including any past harm to individuals similarly situated to the applicant, such as family members or friends) _____
_____
_____
_____

Who or what entities does the applicant fear? Is it the government or a government figure, the police, the military, a rival clan or ethnic group, members of a political party, death squads, or a rebel group? _____
_____

If it is a nongovernmental entity, could the applicant seek protection from the government?
_____
If not, why not? _____

Why is the person or groups the applicant fears seeking to harm him or her? _____
_____

What would happen to the applicant if he or she was returned to his or her home country?
_____

Would it be reasonable for the applicant to relocate to another part of the country? Why not?

APPENDIX 1C
CHECKLIST FOR BARS TO ASYLUM AND WITHHOLDING OF DEPORTATION

Bars to Asylum Only

☐ **Previous Denial.** If an asylum application was previously denied by an immigration judge or the Board of Immigration Appeals, the applicant is ineligible unless he or she demonstrates changed country conditions.

☐ **One-Year Deadline.** The applicant must file for asylum within one year after the date of his or her arrival in the United States, unless he or she demonstrates changed country conditions or extraordinary circumstances to excuse the delay.

☐ **Firm Resettlement.** Applicants are ineligible if they received an offer of permanent residency, citizenship, or other permanent status in a third country prior to coming to the United States, unless they demonstrate that their rights were restricted in that country or that they passed through that country in their flight from persecution, only remained as long as was necessary to arrange onward travel, and did not establish significant ties to the country.

☐ **Safe Third Country.** If the applicant can be sent to a safe third country pursuant to a bilateral or multilateral agreement, he or she is ineligible to apply for asylum. To date, one such agreement exists, between the United States and Canada.

☐ **Aggravated Felony.** An applicant convicted of an aggravated felony is barred from asylum.

Bars to Withholding of Removal and Asylum

☐ **Particularly Serious Crime.** An applicant convicted of an aggravated felony is deemed to have been convicted of a particularly serious crime for purposes of asylum. If he or she received an aggregate sentence of five years or more for an aggravated felony or felonies, the crime is deemed to be particularly serious for purposes of withholding of removal. Other crimes that are not aggravated felonies will be considered on a case-by-case basis to determine whether they are particularly serious.

☐ **Serious Nonpolitical Crime.** An applicant is ineligible for asylum and withholding if he or she committed a serious nonpolitical crime outside of the United States.

- ☐ **Persecutor of Others.** An applicant is ineligible for asylum or withholding if he or she engaged in the persecution of others on account of race, religion, nationality, membership in a particular social group, or political opinion.

- ☐ **Danger to the Security of the United States.** An applicant is ineligible for asylum or withholding if he or she is found to be a danger to the security of the United States. An applicant who is found to have engaged in terrorist activity is deemed to be a danger to the security of the United States for purposes of withholding.

- ☐ **Terrorism.** An applicant is ineligible for asylum and withholding of deportation if he or she is found to have engaged in terrorist activity, which includes providing even minimal support to a terrorist organization and even if the support was provided under duress. A waiver for individuals who provided material support "under duress" is available. An applicant is barred from asylum for inciting terrorist activity or for being a representative of a terrorist organization. Mere membership, however, is not a bar to asylum or withholding.

Bars to Withholding Only

- ☐ **Participation in Nazi Persecution.** An applicant is ineligible for withholding if he or she, under the direction of the Nazi government of Germany persecuted others on account of race, religion, national origin, or political opinion between March 23, 1933, and May 8, 1945.

- ☐ **Participation in Genocide.** An applicant is ineligible for withholding of removal if he or she engaged in genocide.

   Note that even if a bar mentioned above applies to the applicant, he or she may still be eligible for relief from deportation under the UN Convention Against Torture if he or she is likely to be subjected to torture by the government (or because of the government's acquiescence) if he or she is returned to his or her home country.

Appendix 2A

Checklist for Asylum Application (Form I-589)

Checklist for Form I-589

Now, more than ever, it is important for applicants to file complete and detailed applications for asylum. An incomplete or incorrectly filed application could delay the receipt of employment authorization and cause additional problems at the asylum interview or hearing before the immigration judge. An incomplete application may also cause the application to be filed beyond the one-year deadline, requiring additional proof that an earlier filing had been attempted.

> *Note*: Read the I-589 filing instructions completely and carefully. This checklist is not a substitute for the instructions.

☐ **Complete every question.** An unanswered question may result in the application being returned as incomplete. If the question addresses information provided in the applicant's declaration, provide a summary response and the notation "see attached declaration for additional information."

☐ **Attach a declaration from the applicant.** An effective way of presenting the asylum claim is in a narrative form in chronological order. A declaration allows the applicant to present his or her claim in this manner. Always include a summary of the claim at the beginning of the declaration. *See* appx. 2C, Sample Declaration.

☐ **List the applicant's spouse and *all* children.** This information should be given whether or not the spouse and children are present in the United States and should include all children regardless of their age or marital status.

☐ **Make sure the applicant signs the form.** The applicant should only sign a completed form and only after he or she has thoroughly reviewed the contents of the application and the declaration. By signing the form, the applicant certifies under penalty of perjury that the information and evidence submitted are true and correct. If it is determined that the applicant knowingly submitted a frivolous application, he or she may be permanently barred from obtaining any immigration benefits under the INA.

☐ **The preparer must also sign the form.** The only exception is if the preparer is an immediate family member (spouse, parent, or child) of the applicant. If anyone assisted the preparer, he or she must also sign the form. The preparer's failure to sign will result in the application being returned as incomplete.

☐ **Send by certified mail to the correct service center.** If the applicant is filing affirmatively (*i.e.,* he or she is not in removal proceedings) the application must be filed with a USCIS service center. Always file the application by certified mail, return receipt requested. *See* Section XII, "Where to File" in the instructions to the application. *(If, however, the applicant is applying for the first time in removal proceedings, the applicant must file the I-589 with the immigration court at a master calendar hearing.)*

CHECKLIST FOR FILING THE I-589

> *Note*: Read the I-589 filing instructions completely and carefully. This checklist is not a substitute for the instructions.

☐ The original and two copies of the completed, signed form, including any supplementary sheets, affidavits, and statements.

☐ Three copies of supporting documentation, including passports, travel documents, and identity documents, marriage certificate (if spouse is included in the application), birth certificates (for children under 21 included in the application), and documentation of country conditions. The applicant should take all original documents to the asylum interview. If the documents are numerous, it may be useful to make an index of the supporting documents and to tab each document for easy reference.

☐ Three copies of any medical reports, evaluations, or assessments submitted in support of the applicant's claim.

☐ An additional copy of the completed application for each family member present in the United States who is included in the application.

☐ One passport-style photograph for the applicant and each family member included in the application (taken no more than 30 days before submitting the application).

☐ Form G-28 (Notice of Entry of Appearance as Attorney or Representative) signed by the applicant and the attorney or accredited representative.

☐ **Translations.** Any documents in languages other than English must be accompanied by an English translation and a certificate of translation certifying that the translation is true and correct. The following is a sample certificate of translation:

I, _____, certify that I am fluent in both English and _____, and that this is a true and correct translation from _____ to English of the attached.

_____   _____
Date   Signature

See also Section X, "Organizing Your Application," in the instructions to the application.

Reminder: *Always keep a complete set of any documents submitted to the asylum office or immigration court!*

APPENDIX 2B
PRACTICE POINTERS FOR COMPLETING THE ASYLUM APPLICATION*

PRACTICE POINTERS FOR COMPLETING THE NEW I-589 (APPLICATION FOR ASYLUM AND WITHHOLDING OF REMOVAL) (Rev. 12/14/06)

The REAL ID Act, the USA PATRIOT Act, the Illegal Immigration and Immigrant Responsibility Act of 1996 (IIRAIRA), and the final asylum regulations changed various aspects of U.S. asylum law. More changes are expected. For this reason, it is important to consult the statute and regulations prior to completing any application for asylum and withholding of removal. Also, carefully read the instructions to the I-589 to ensure that you complete the form correctly and file it at the appropriate USCIS or immigration court location. The instructions also are filled with useful information, such as the telephone number to call for a list of voluntary agencies or pro bono attorneys and directions on where to file a change of address if the applicant moves.

These section-by-section practice pointers are provided to assist you in completing the I-589 effectively and to highlight several of the recent changes to asylum law. *Remember, every question must be answered.* If the question is not applicable to the applicant, write "not applicable," "N/A," or "none" in the space provided. If the applicant does not know the answer to a question, write "unknown" or "not known" in the space provided.

Part A. I—Information About You

- **Question 1—Alien Registration Number**

Alien Registration Number or A# refers to an eight-digit number beginning with the letter A that is assigned to individuals by DHS. If the applicant is *not* in removal proceedings, it is possible that he or she does not have an A#. If removal proceedings have been initiated, the A# may be found on the Notice to Appear (NTA). It is also possible that the applicant has more than one A# because the applicant may have filed for other forms of relief such as temporary protected status (TPS). All A#s should be listed.

- **Question 2—Social Security Number**

If the applicant does not have a valid Social Security number issued in his or her name, write "none" in the space provided.

---

* For a copy of Form I-589 (Rev. 12/14/06), see appx. 9A. Always check *www.uscis.gov* to ensure that you have the most current version of the I-589.

- **Questions 3–5—Name**

An applicant's last or first name may be hyphenated or contain two or more names. To ensure that you are identifying the applicant's first, middle, and last names correctly, refer to the applicant's identity documents, such as a national identity card or passport. List the applicant's last name in all capital letters.

- **Question 6—Aliases**

The applicant should list all names he or she has previously used, including the names used on any false identity documents, nicknames, and the applicant's maiden name, if any.

- **Question 7—Residence in the United States**

The applicant should list the place where he or she resides. This address determines the asylum office that has jurisdiction to adjudicate the applicant's claim. It is, therefore, imperative that the applicant notifies DHS, and if in removal proceedings, the immigration court, of any changes of address.

- **Question 8—Mailing Address in the United States**

If the applicant's mailing address is different from his or her residence, this section should be completed. This is also the address to which all interview and hearing notices will be sent.

- **Question 9—Sex**

If the applicant is a transgender applicant, you may wish to supplement the answer to this question on an attached sheet.

- **Question 10—Marital Status**

For an applicant who has a common-law marriage or relationship with a person that the applicant refers to as his or her spouse, you may wish to supplement the answer to this question on an attached sheet.

- **Question 11—Date of Birth**

An applicant may not know his or her exact date of birth. Write in the approximate year, if possible, in the space provided, *e.g.*, "approx. 19___."

- **Question 12—City and Country of Birth**

The applicant may have been born in a country that no longer exists. If the applicant is stateless, this point should be highlighted.

- **Question 13—Present Nationality**

This may be a difficult question for some applicants. Due to the recent dissolution and creation of numerous countries in recent history, there are many individuals who may lack a nationality. Prior to answering this question, it may be necessary to consult the nationality laws of the country of the applicant's birth or last habitual residence.

Although a passport may be *prima facie* evidence that the applicant is a citizen or national of the issuing country, it is not conclusive and the applicant may actually be stateless or a national of another country.

- **Question 14—Nationality at Birth**

There may be individuals who were conferred no nationality at birth and were, and perhaps continue to be, stateless. On the other hand, an individual may have been born in a country that no longer exists and may be stateless for this reason.

- **Question 15—Race, Ethnic, or Tribal Group**

List all of the applicant's racial, ethnic, and tribal groups, even if his or her claim in not based on membership in these groups.

- **Question 16—Religion**

Be as specific as possible. An Evangelical Christian, for example, may be at a greater risk of harm than Christians in general in a particular country.

- **Question 17—Check Each Box That Applies**

The applicant must identify whether he or she is in removal proceedings and whether he or she has ever previously been in removal proceedings. *Beware*!! If the applicant was previously in removal proceedings, it is important to determine the outcome of those proceedings for two reasons: (1) individuals previously denied asylum by an immigration judge or the Board of Immigration Appeals are not eligible to apply for asylum unless they demonstrate changed circumstances, and (2) individuals previously ordered deported, excluded, or removed from the United States may be subject to reinstatement of removal proceedings in which they are ineligible to apply for asylum. *See* ch. 3. To determine whether the applicant had an asylum application denied or was previously ordered removed, you may contact the Executive Office for Immigration Review information line ((800) 898-7180) or file a FOIA request with the Department of Homeland Security.

- **Question 18—Entry Questions**

If the applicant entered the country illegally and at a place other than a port of entry, write "EWI," *i.e.*, entry without inspection, or "EWA," *i.e.*, entry without admission, when responding to the status line in Question 18c. An I-94 is a white card given to noncitizens upon entry to the United States at a port of entry. Applicants who list previous entries to the United States should explain elsewhere in the application and/or in their declaration the reasons for not applying previously for asylum and why, if applicable, they returned to the country of claimed persecution.

> ➢ **Caution!** The applicant who is applying affirmatively should understand that this information, along with the information the applicant provides regarding his or her nationality, will in most cases be sufficient to establish his or her deportability or inadmissibility in removal proceedings, unless the applicant currently maintains a valid immigration status.

- **Question 19–21—Passport Information**

If the applicant obtained a passport and/or exit visa to leave his or her country, the applicant may wish to provide details regarding how he or she was able to obtain such documents if he or she fears the government that issued those documents. This information may be provided elsewhere in the application and/or in the applicant's declaration.

- **Questions 22–24—Languages**

Answers to these questions will assist the court in arranging for an interpreter for the hearing.

Part A. II—Information About Your Spouse and Children

These questions are self-explanatory. Please note that the application requires all children to be listed, regardless of age or marital status. As noted above, the information provided here, as elsewhere in the application, could be used to establish that an individual is removable (deportable) from the United States.

All persons "included" in the application will be granted asylum if the applicant is granted. A spouse, to be "included" in the application, must be present in the United States. Note that a spouse must still be "listed" on the application, even if the spouse is not in the United States. A child, to be "included" in the application, must be present in the United States, under 21 years of age, and unmarried. All children, however, must be "listed" on the application. The other reasons why a spouse or child may not be "included" in the application may be because he or she has U.S. citizenship or other legal immigration status or he or she is ineligible for asylum.

To list additional children, use copies of Supplement A (included in the I-589).

Part A. III—Information About Your Background

- **Question 1—Prior Residences Before Coming to United States**

If the applicant resided outside of his or her home prior to leaving, out of necessity or fear, that address must be listed, as well as his or her last address in the home country. USCIS notes in the filing instructions to Form I-589 that "no information indicating that you have applied for asylum will be provided to any government or country from which you claim a fear of persecution."

- **Question 2—Residences for Last Five Years**

This question is self-explanatory. Note that it is not unusual for an applicant to be reluctant to release the addresses of friends, relatives, or colleagues who assisted the applicant in fleeing the country or who sheltered the applicant upon arrival here.

- **Question 3—Education**

List all schools your client has attended, including primary school and trade or vocational schools.

- **Question 4—Employment**

Has the applicant been working without employment authorization in the United States? Now that asylum reform practically ensures, in most cases, that applicants do not have employment authorization until there has been a final adjudication of the claim, it is not uncommon for applicants to be working without a work permit. Should the employment be listed? Many applicants are reluctant to do so. It may be useful to ask other practitioners in your area about if and how the DHS trial attorneys and immigration judges view such employment to alleviate (in many cases) any fears the applicant has. Applicants must answer all questions truthfully.

- **Question 5—Parents and Siblings**

This question is self-explanatory. Note, however, that the asylum officer and the DHS trial attorney will question your client regarding why his parents and siblings, if still residing in the home country, are able to live there and the applicant is not.

Part B—Information About Your Application

The I-589 contains very limited space for providing information regarding the applicant's claim. It is recommended that the applicant prepare a separate declaration or affidavit regarding his or her claim and attach it to the I-589. If a more detailed declaration is attached, the applicant may then provide brief answers to the questions in this part and, after each answer, specifically refer to his or her declaration or affidavit. If the applicant wishes to provide a more detailed response to particular questions, he or she may use copies of Supplement B, included with the I-589. Read each of the questions carefully. The information requested in each is important for establishing eligibility for asylum. Such information should be included in the declaration.

- **Question 1—Why Are You Applying for Asylum, Withholding of Removal, or Convention Against Torture relief?**

Provide detailed information regarding the applicant's claim for asylum, withholding of removal, and/or CAT relief. Begin by providing a summary of the claim. The summary should include the basis for the fear, whether the applicant or the applicant's family or friends have experienced past persecution, and the reasons why the applicant fears persecution or torture if he or she is returned. If a declaration has been prepared, refer to the declaration for more details regarding the applicant's claim. The question also requests that the basis for the claim be specified, *i.e.*, race, religion, nationality, membership in a particular social group, political opinion, Convention Against Torture. All applicable grounds should be identified. It is common for more than one ground to be the basis of a claim.

(a) Question 1A—Mistreatment in Past

This is an important question requesting information regarding any past persecution suffered by the applicant or his or her family members. If past harm was suffered, the applicant should provide specific details regarding any and all occurrences. Note that the harm may have been inflicted by groups the government is unable or unwilling to control, which may include guerrilla groups, paramilitary groups or death squads, vigilante groups, or rival clans.

The applicant should include as part of the supporting documentation any documents that may relate to these incidents, including newspaper accounts, medical or psychological reports regarding the physical or mental harm inflicted, and statements from witnesses.

(b) Question 1B—Do You Fear Harm or Mistreatment If You Return?

The applicant should provide details regarding the harm he or she would face upon return. These details may be obtained from documents that show how individuals similarly situated to the applicant have been harmed in the applicant's home country. The applicant should also note any previous harm he or she, his or her family, or his or her colleagues have suffered in the past, or the threats they have received. If there has been a change in government, a cease-fire, or a peace agreement since the applicant left his or her home country, the applicant should provide details regarding why, in light of these events, he or she continues to fear returning. Again, it is preferable to provide a summary here and then refer to the applicant's detailed declaration attached to the application.

- **Question 2—Accusations, Charges, Arrests . . .**

The applicant should list any incident in which the applicant or his or her family member was accused, charged, arrested, detained, interrogated, convicted, sentenced, or imprisoned in any country other than the United States. In addition, the applicant should provide detailed information regarding each incident, preferably in his or her declaration. *Careful*! Is the applicant fleeing persecution or prosecution? An applicant who committed a serious nonpolitical crime outside of the United States is barred from asylum and withholding of removal, but is eligible for Convention Against Torture relief.

- **Question 3—Membership in Organizations or Groups**

These questions ask for information regarding the membership of the applicant or his or her family members in organizations or groups in the applicant's home country. Such groups may include ethnic groups, labor unions, religious groups or organizations, political parties, student groups, human rights groups, the press or media, military or paramilitary groups, civil patrols, or guerrilla organizations. If the applicant answers "yes" to this question, he or she must provide the names of the organizations, the dates of membership or affiliation, the purpose of the organization, the applicant's or his or her family member's duties as a member, and whether the applicant or his or her family member is still active.

There is no requirement that an asylum applicant be a member of a political party or other highly organized group to be granted asylum. He or she may simply be a member of a clan or ethnic minority that his or her family has belonged to for generations that is being targeted by the government or other group.

- **Question 4—Torture**

This question asks whether the applicant fears that he or she will be tortured upon return to his or her home country, and, if so, to explain why. The United States, as a signatory to the UN Convention Against Torture (CAT), may not return an individual to a country where he or she is likely to be tortured. Unlike asylum or withholding of removal, there are no bars to such protection and, furthermore, there is no requirement that the torture feared be on account of race, religion, nationality, membership in a particular social group, or political opinion. CAT defines "torture" broadly as "any act by which severe pain or suffering, whether physical or mental, is intentionally inflicted on a person." It does not, however, include pain or suffering arising only from, inherent in, or incidental to lawful sanctions. One limitation under CAT is that the torture must be at the hands of a public official, or with the consent or acquiescence of such official. See ch. 4 for more details.

Part C—Additional Information About Your Claim to Asylum

The six questions in this part seek information to determine whether the applicant may be barred from asylum or withholding of removal under one of the following grounds:

- **Question 1—Prior Applications for Asylum or Refugee Status in United States**

Did the applicant or any family members previously apply for asylum in the United States? If so, the applicant may be barred from reapplying without first establishing changed circumstances. Previous grants to other family members may help to bolster the applicant's claim and should be listed.

- **Question 2—Travel Through, Permanent Residence in, or Citizenship in Another Country (Safe Haven and Firm Resettlement)**

The applicant must list all of the countries the applicant, his or her spouse, and his or her children traveled through or resided in after leaving his or her home country prior to arriving in the United States. In addition, the applicant must give details for each country regarding the length of stay, status, reason for leaving, ability to return, and whether he or she applied for asylum or refugee status while in that country. This question is designed to elicit information regarding whether the applicant was "firmly resettled" in another country prior to entering the United States. An applicant who is determined to be firmly resettled is ineligible for asylum, but not withholding of removal. *See* ch. 2.

- **Question 3—Harm to Others (Persecutor Bar)**

If the applicant, his or her spouse, or the applicant's child caused harm or suffering to another person on account of race, religion, nationality, membership in a particular social group, or political opinion, the person who engaged in persecution is ineligible for asylum and withholding of removal.

- **Question 4—Return to Country of Claimed Persecution**

Applicants who returned to their home country must provide details regarding their return, the length of stay, purpose of trip, and the circumstances of the visit. If such a visit occurs after the filing of the application for asylum, the applicant is presumed to have abandoned his or her application unless he or she can demonstrate compelling reasons for returning. Applicants are also required to obtain advance parole prior to leaving the United States while an application for asylum is pending, or their application will be deemed abandoned.

- **Question 5—One-Year Deadline**

The applicant is asked to state whether his or her application is being submitted more than one year after his or her last arrival in the United States. If it is more than one year, the applicant is asked to explain why and is referred to the Filing Instructions for guidance. Persons are not eligible for asylum if they apply more than one year after their arrival in the United States unless they are able to demonstrate exceptional circumstances or changed circumstances. These terms are defined in the regulations at 8 CFR §§208.4, 1208.4. Whether one of these exceptions applies will be determined by the asylum officer, immigration judge, or the BIA.

- **Question 6—Crimes in United States**

This question asks not only about arrests, charges, and convictions in the United States, but also whether the applicant has "committed" any crimes. Is the applicant protected by the Fifth Amendment right not to incriminate him- or herself? *See* ch. 3 under the heading Rights. Note that if the applicant has been "convicted" of an aggravated felony in the United States, he or she is ineligible for asylum. If he she received a sentence of five years or more, regardless of any suspension of sentence, the applicant is also ineligible for withholding of removal. But see chapter 4 for information regarding relief under the Convention Against Torture.

Part D—Signature

The applicant must sign the application, certifying under penalty of perjury that the information is true and correct. This section also contains a warning that the information provided may be used in removal proceedings, even if the application is later withdrawn and that an applicant who knowingly files a frivolous application will be permanently ineligible for any benefits under the Immigration and Nationality Act. The applicant must also print his or her name and, if applicable, in his or her native alphabet.

Part E—Signature of Person Preparing Form

This part must be completed only if a person other than the applicant's spouse, parent, or child completed the application form. If a person other than the spouse, parent, or child of the applicant completed the form, he or she must declare that the form was completed at the request of the applicant, that the responses were provided by the applicant or based on information of which the preparer has knowledge, and that the completed application was read to the applicant in his or her native language before the applicant signed it, in the presence of the preparer. The preparer must also acknowledge that he or she is aware that the knowing placement of false information on this form is subject to civil penalties. The preparer must provide his or her name, address, and daytime telephone number.

Part F—To Be Completed at Interview

This part is completed when appearing before the asylum officer.

Part G—To Be Completed at Removal Hearing

This part is completed when appearing before an immigration judge.

APPENDIX 2C
SAMPLE DECLARATION

Declaration of _____ (A# _____)

I, _____, hereby declare under penalty of perjury that the following statements are true and correct to the best of my knowledge.

1. *[Summary of claim]* I am _____ years old, married, and a native and citizen of _____. I am fearful of returning to my home country. I believe that I or my family may be harmed, tortured, or killed because I have deserted from my home country's military, I have been accused of giving information to a government at war with my home government regarding a military base in my home country, and because I and my family members are _____, a persecuted ethnic and religious minority in my home country. Below I have provided a chronological account of the persecution I and my family have suffered in our home country.

2. I was born on _____ in _____. I am _____, a minority ethnic and religious group in my home country. I grew up in _____ and was raised following the traditions of my ethnic/religious group. In addition to our different language and manner of dressing, we have a different physical appearance than other nationals in our home country.

3. As a member of an ethnic and religious minority in my home country, I have been harassed and discriminated against throughout my life. I recall that in high school I and other students of the same ethnic and religious minority group were fearful of walking to and from school alone. The other students often beat and bullied us. They threw rocks at us and called us _____. They have been taught to hate members of our ethnic and religious group.

4. In high school, when I was approximately 15 years old, I participated with other students from my ethnic and religious minority group in about two or three nonviolent demonstrations in front of the county government office in _____, during which we called for rights for our ethnic and religious minority group. On demonstration occurred on _____, our ethnic minority's Independence Day celebration.

5. My high school was located in _____, a neighboring town of the ethnic and religious majority. Members of my family often traveled to this town to shop, study, or work. Almost every member of my family received the same type of harassment. My grandfather, who because of his traditional dress was easily identified as a member of our ethnic and religious minority group, experienced the most harassment. He often had rocks

thrown at him by the ethnic and religious majority group. I remember one incident that occurred in approximately the summer of _____ when I was walking with my sister, who was not dressed as the women of the ethnic and religious majority. Four men of the ethnic and religious majority group began to verbally and physically assault her. They used very strong foul language in addressing her and touched her in an unacceptable manner. I pushed my sister into a store and told her to call the police. I fought with the men for about 20 minutes. They punched me in the back and knocked me down. When the policeman arrived, I told him what had happened. He looked at me and asked me if I was _____, a member of the religious minority. The policeman, a member of the ethnic and religious majority group then said, "So what?" and left without taking a report.

6. In approximately _____, the government seized land owned by my family to build a military base. In order to force us to give up the land, the government on three occasions burned our crops on this land. In approximately _____, I decided to protest what I believed to be the unjust taking of our land. I contacted other families in the area who had their land taken also. I proposed that we go to the capital city, _____, with a letter asking the government to return our land. I was arrested by my government's secret police after I had finished speaking with one family whose land had been seized. The official name for the secret police is _____. They are undercover policemen who do not wear uniforms. I was told by these policemen that I was being arrested because I was "pushing people against the government." I was held for approximately six to eight hours. It was hard for the police to justify arresting me because I was from a religious family which did not, at the time, actively or openly oppose the government.

7. I attended the College of _____, in _____, the capital city, from _____ to _____. I remember one incident in which I invited other students of my religion to a party given at an off-campus location. The religious group organizing the party gave me 20 tickets to distribute at the college. I was told by the head of the student union that this party was against regulations and that only the student union had the right to plan student parties. The head of the student union told me that my religious minority group does not have a right to plan a party for only members of our group. The student union was a union established by the ruling political party in my home country. I was forced to sign a paper stating that I would not organize an event like this again. I had also refused to become a member of this ruling party.

8. Members of my ethnic and religious minority group were also discriminated against in the distribution of grants for students who qualified based on their academic standing. Even though I ranked at the top of my class, I did not receive a grant, nor did other members of my ethnic and religious minority group. I was also denied a scholarship to study for my Ph.D.

9. Another form of discrimination that I experienced was the denial of a permit to build a house. In _____, I purchased a lot on which I planned to build a house. After I purchased it, I attempted to build on it, but I was told by the state government that I was not permitted to build. I was told that the decision came from the capital city. Other members of my ethnic and religious minority group were denied similar requests to build homes. To the

present day, I am unable to build on this land. By not allowing us to build new houses, I believe that government is attempting to disperse my ethnic and religious minority group. The government also refuses to allow us to remodel or refurbish older houses. At the same time, the government is transferring members of the ethnic and religious majority group into our villages. I believe this is an attempt by the government to divide and weaken our group. I purchased the lot for _____, but it is not worth anything to me if I cannot build on it.

10. After my graduation, I began teaching in a high school in _____. I taught high school mathematics from _____ to _____. During the _____ school year, the Education Department asked all teachers to join the ruling political party. This is still the ruling party in my home country. I refused to become a member of the ruling party because the policies of this party favor only the ethnic and religious majority group in my home country. My supervisor threatened to transfer me out of the school I was teaching in as punishment for my refusal. Through the assistance of my father and through "gifts" to my supervisor, I was able to retain my position. My refusal, however, was a black mark on my record.

11. Since I was 18 years old, I have registered for military service in my home country every year. In _____, I failed to return to my home country to complete my military obligation. Initially, my military service was postponed until I finished my high school and university studies. Later, my military service was again postponed because there was a shortage of mathematics teachers in my home country after my college graduation. I was permitted to defer my military service during the time I was a teacher of mathematics.

12. From _____ to _____, I served in the military. I was in the reserves and fought in a war between my home country and a neighboring country. I witnessed many human rights abuses by both sides during this war. I suspected that the military was using _____ weapons against the neighboring country which resulted in the deaths of many of our own soldiers. I had to identify the body of my cousin who was burned by the use of these weapons.

13. As a soldier in the reserves, I again experienced discrimination because I am a member of an ethnic and religious minority. I was sometimes refused leave. I had to give my monthly paycheck to my supervisor in order to get the leave I had earned so that I could return home to see my family. Some soldiers who were members of the ethnic religious majority refused to eat with us. If we were seated at their table and shared food from a common tray, they would refuse to continue to take from the tray. They believed that members of our religious group were unholy. Because we were unable to eat with members of the ethnic and religious majority, we were often given smaller rations, about one-quarter of the standard ration.

14. In _____, I received an approval for a leave of absence from the Education Department, which I had applied for on four occasions in the past. I was accepted as a student by _____ University in the United States. My military service was once again postponed. *See* excerpt of my military record (attached at Tab _____).

15. I completed my Master's Degree at _____ University and continued my studies at _____ University for my Ph.D. I then transferred my studies to _____ University in _____. In _____, I began working at _____ University as a faculty associate with an H-1 visa.

16. I was required to return to my home country on _____ after I completed my studies. At that time, my country was engaged in a war with several neighboring countries. I was not in agreement with the government's objectives in that war. I did not want to fight in a war I did not believe in.

17. My failure to return is considered to be desertion from the military. I believe that if I am returned to my home country, I will be called before a military court. Deserters are dealt with very harshly by the military. Many deserters have been tortured and killed, especially if they have other family members who were deserters, as in my case.

18. My family members living in my home town also refused to fight. On _____, my home town was bombed by my own government because the people refused to abide by the government's policies and rebelled. Many houses and businesses were looted by government soldiers. Many of the residents, including my relatives, fled the country to _____. The eight members of my family who refused to fight in the war and fled from my home country are my brother, _____; my brother, _____; my nephew, _____; my nephew, _____, my first cousin, _____; my second cousin, _____; my brother-in-law, _____; and my first cousin, _____. All have been accepted as refugees in the United States, Canada, or Sweden. See Tabs _____, _____, _____, _____, _____, _____, _____, and _____.

19. One of my relatives, my cousin _____, became very ill while living in a refugee camp in _____. He needed medical assistance, but could not obtain it in the camp. He heard that the government had issued an amnesty for deserters and decided to return, hoping to receive medical assistance. He has not been heard from by our family since he turned himself into the military. We believe that he was executed for his desertion. Hanging is the standard punishment for desertion in my home country.

20. Several members of my family who sought refuge in a neighboring country were interviewed by individuals from the U.S. Catholic Conference. This organization later issued a report regarding their plight. *See* Tab _____. To assist them, I wrote to senators and representatives in the U.S. Congress on their behalf. *See* Letters at Tabs _____ and _____.

21. One of my brothers, _____, remained in our home country. On _____, he was arrested, interrogated, and tortured by members of the secret police in _____, and was transferred to the capital city. In their interrogation of my brother, the secret police accused me and my brother of supplying military information to the country fighting against my home country. They noted that our land that had been taken to build a military base was one of the first sites bombed during the war. They

played a tape recording of a call from me in the United States to my brother in which I discussed sending money to my sister-in-law to help her brother flee the country. He was later accepted as a refugee in Canada. The secret police called me a traitor when they played this tape for my brother. He suffered great physical and psychological abuse at the hands of the secret police and was forced to sign a statement that he would inform the police immediately when I and my family return to our home country. *See* Letter from my brother, _____, dated _____, Tab _____.

22. My wife, who is also included in my asylum application, has many family members who fled from our home country. Several of them have been granted refugee status in Sweden. The husband of one of her cousins, a prominent doctor, was hanged in _____ for opposing the government.

23. *[Closing Summary]* I fear returning to my home country for many reasons. I fear that I or my family members will be harmed, tortured, or killed because I am suspected of supplying military information to a government at war with my home country. I fear that I may be harmed, tortured, or killed because I deserted from the military when I did not return to complete my military service as required. Also, my family as a group has been sought out and accused of antigovernment activities. In addition, because I am a member of an ethnic and religious minority, I face even graver consequences. The government of my home country is notorious for the persecution of members of our group because of our cultural differences. The documents attached to my application demonstrate the government of my home country deals harshly with deserters, suspected traitors, government opponents, and members of my ethnic and religious minority group. *See* Supporting Documents at Tabs _____, _____, _____, _____, _____, _____, and _____.

_____
Date

_____
Signature of _____

APPENDIX 3A
SAMPLE LETTER TO USCIS SERVICE CENTER*

[Letterhead or Return Address]

[Date]

Via Certified Mail—Return Receipt Requested

USCIS [Texas, Nebraska, California, or Vermont] Service Center
[address]
[address]

Re: Asylum Application of _____; A# _____ [if available]

Dear Sir or Madam:

    Enclosed please find a completed Form I-589, Request for Asylum in the United States, submitted by Mr./Ms. _____ and the following attachments:

1. One (1) passport-style photograph of applicant,
2. Declaration [or Affidavit] of Mr./Ms. _____,
3. Form G-28, Notice of Appearance,
4. One (1) copy of Mr./Ms. _____'s passport (cover to cover),
5. One (1) copy of Mr./Ms. _____'s driver's license,
6. One (1) copy of Mr./Ms. _____'s marriage certificate *[if spouse is included in application and, if in a language other than English, include an English translation with a Certificate of Translation]*,
7. One (1) copy of birth certificate of _____ *[if child under 21 is included in application]*,

---

* If the applicant is in removal proceedings, the application must be filed with the immigration court. *Note: Carefully review the I-589's filing instructions. This sample letter is not a substitute for the filing instructions.*

8. One copy (1) of Affidavit of Dr. _____, attesting to the diagnosis that Mr./Ms. _____ suffers from Post Traumatic Stress Disorder with attached resume of Dr. _____ experience and education,

9. Documentation of country conditions, indexed and tabbed A–L, and

10. Two (2) additional copies of items 3 through 9 (above),

11. *[If spouse included]* For Mr./Ms. _____'s spouse, a copy of the completed I-589 (including the declaration of Mr./Ms. _____), with his/her photograph stapled at Part B,

12. Form G-28 for Mr./Ms. _____'s spouse,

13. *[If child included]* For Mr./Ms. _____'s child (under 21 years of age), a copy of the completed I-589 (including the declaration of Mr./Ms. _____), with his/her photograph stapled at Part B,

14. Form G-28 for Mr./Ms. _____'s child.

Please notify me of any and all interview dates scheduled for Mr./Ms. _____. Thank you for your attention to this matter.

Sincerely,

_____
Attorney for the Applicant

Certified mail receipt number _____

Appendix 3B
Checklist for Preparing for the Asylum Interview

☐ **Interpreter**. If the applicant is not fluent in English, he or she must bring an interpreter to the interview. A competent interpreter is essential for a successful interview. Always practice with the interpreter prior to the interview to ensure that the interpreter understands the applicant and is able to translate correctly the vocabulary used by you, the asylum officer, and the applicant. It is also important that the applicant feel comfortable with the interpreter and be able to discuss sensitive matters in the interpreter's presence.

☐ **Additional Documents**. If you obtain additional documents in support of the applicant's claim, take the original and three copies to the interview. If the documents are numerous, make an index to assist the asylum officer.

☐ **Prepare the Applicant**. Always give the applicant a copy of his or her asylum application and declaration. Ask him or her to read and re-read the application prior to the interview to refresh his or her memory regarding dates and events. If the applicant is illiterate, have the interpreter tape-record the contents of the application and declaration so that the applicant can listen several times to it prior to the interview. Instruct the applicant to tell the truth, to listen carefully to the asylum officer's questions, and to answer the questions asked, if he or she is able. Tell the applicant that it is acceptable to respond that he or she does not know an answer to a question, and that the applicant should not guess when answering a question. If the applicant's spouse or children are included on the application, also prepare them in the manner noted above if they will be testifying.

☐ **Note Any Corrections**. If any mistakes have been made on the application, submit a letter (and two copies) to the asylum officer noting the corrections on the day of the interview, prior to the start of the interview.

☐ **Mock Interviews**. If the applicant knows what to expect at the interview, he or she will be less nervous and better able to express him- or herself. Pretend you are the asylum officer and conduct an interview from beginning to end. Point out to the applicant instances in which he or she is not clearly expressing him- or herself.

☐ **Make a List of Key Points**. You will not be permitted to question the applicant at length during the interview, but most asylum officers will allow some follow-up questions by the attorney or representative. Make a list of key points that the applicant should make at the interview. As the applicant mentions these points during the interview, cross them off your list. If the applicant has not addressed a few of these points by the end of the interview, ask him or her questions to elicit responses regarding these points.

☐ **Take Detailed Notes at the Interview**. Asylum interviews are not videotaped or recorded. If you later want to change an asylum officer's findings, it is helpful to have detailed or verbatim notes from the interview.

☐ **Ask the Asylum Officer**. After asking the applicant any follow-up questions you may have, ask the asylum officer whether he or she sees any outstanding issues or problem areas, and offer to address them with additional evidence, if possible.

☐ **Prepare an Oral *and* Written Closing Statement**. Most asylum officers will allow attorneys to make a closing statement. You should take advantage of this opportunity and orally summarize why the applicant is eligible for and deserving of asylum at the conclusion of the interview. In addition, it is extremely helpful to submit, at the conclusion of your oral closing statement, a written closing statement that cites regulations, cases, and other authority regarding why the applicant should be granted asylum. *See* aapx. 3C, Sample Closing Statement.

APPENDIX 3C

SAMPLE CLOSING STATEMENT

[Letterhead]

[Date]

Via Hand Delivery

Asylum Officer
_____ Asylum Office
Department of Homeland Security
USCIS
[address]
[address]

CLOSING STATEMENT ON BEHALF OF _____; A# _____

Mr. _____, the principal asylum applicant in this case, and his wife through her derivative status, are eligible for and deserving of asylum under § 208 of the Immigration and Nationality Act (INA). Mr. _____'s asylum claim is based on both the past persecution he and his family have suffered and his and his family's well-founded fear of persecution if they are required to return to _____. Mr. _____ and his family suffered persecution at the hands of the _____ military and police because of their political opinion (imputed and actual), religion, race, and membership in a particular social group. Moreover, they have a well-founded fear of persecution in the future if they are returned to _____, based on the above-mentioned grounds.

As demonstrated by Mr. _____'s application, declaration, supporting documentation, and interview today, Mr. _____ fears persecution because: (1) he has been accused by the _____ military of supplying sensitive, strategic information to a government at war with _____; (2) he deserted from the _____ military by not returning to complete his military service; (3) he and his family have been accused of engaging in antigovernment activities; and (4) he is a member of an ethnic and religious minority group that has been persecuted by the _____ government.

Below, I have addressed the following legal issues in Mr. _____'s asylum claim: (1) that his persecutors have imputed a political opinion to him; (2) that he has a well-founded fear of persecution based on his refusal to serve in the _____ military; (3) that he faces persecution upon return because of his religion; and (4) that he faces persecution because of his race or membership in a particular social group because he is a member of an ethnic minority.

I. Political Opinion

Mr. _____ has been accused by the _____ military of supplying military information to a government at war with the government of his home country. (Mr. _____'s Declaration at para. ___, hereinafter "D. at ___.") His brother, _____, was arrested, interrogated, and brutally tortured by the _____ military based on the military's belief that Mr. _____ and his family members are politically opposed to the _____ government. (D. at ___.) The military also accused Mr. _____ and his family members of supporting _____, a group seeking to overthrow the government. (D. at ___.) Furthermore, Mr. _____'s desertion from the military, along with the desertion of numerous family members, has resulted in the government's belief that he and his family members are politically opposed to the _____ government. (D. at ___.)

In the past, Mr. _____ has demonstrated his actual opposition to the government by refusing to join the _____ Party, the ruling party of _____ (D. at ___.), by protesting the government's taking of his family's land, for which he was arrested (D. at ___.), and his desertion from the military (D. at ___.). Mr. _____'s asylum claim is, therefore, based on his actual and imputed political opinion.

Political opinions that give rise to asylum claims are defined as "opinions not tolerated by the authorities, which are critical of their policies or methods," and "such opinions [that] have come to the notice of the authorities or are attributed by them to the applicant." *United Nations Handbook on Procedures and Criteria for Determining Refugee Status*[1] (Geneva 1992) (hereinafter *UN Handbook*) at ¶80. An imputed political opinion, whether correctly or incorrectly attributed, is a basis for asylum within the meaning of INA § 208. *Ravindran v. INS*, 976 F.2d 754, 760 (1st Cir. 1992). The doctrine of imputed political opinion arose in recognition of the fact that "[i]f the persecutor thinks the person guilty of a political opinion, then that person is at risk," at as much risk, in fact, as a person who actually holds a political belief contrary to that of the persecutor. *Lazo-Majano v. INS*, 813 F.2d 1432, 1435 (9th Cir. 1987). This doctrine has been an integral part of the analyses in many asylum cases. *See, e.g., Aguilera-Cota v. INS*, 914 F.2d 1375, 1379 (9th Cir. 1990); *Beltran-Zavala v. INS*, 912 F.2d 1027, 1030 (9th Cir. 1990).

Under the imputed political opinion doctrine, the proper focus is not on the actual political beliefs of the victim, but rather on the "motivation of the persecutor." *Hernandez-Ortiz v. INS*, 777 F.2d 509, 516 (9th Cir. 1985). The BIA has concurred in the above-noted analysis for determining when persecution is on account of "political opinion." *See Matter of Maldonado-Cruz*, 19 I&N Dec. 509 (BIA 1988). In looking at the victim from the persecutor's perspective, one considers what particular conscious acts of the victim or other circumstances would cause the persecutor to attribute a political opinion to the victim. *Desir v. Ilchert*, 840 F.2d 723, 728 (9th Cir. 1988).

---

[1] It should be noted that the Supreme Court has held that the *UN Handbook* provides "significant guidance" in determining whether an asylum applicant meets the definition of "refugee." *INS v. Cardoza-Fonseca*, 480 U.S. 421, 438–39 & n.22 (1987).

Mr. _____ has demonstrated through his testimony, his asylum application, and the letter from his brother, _____ (found at Tab ___ of the Supporting Documentation), that the _____ military will harm, torture, or kill him because of his political opinions, imputed and real, if he is returned to _____. The accusations and threats made by the _____ military against Mr. _____ constitute direct evidence of his persecutors' motives. (D. at ___.) Moreover, the documentary evidence establishes that other individuals similarly accused of spying or opposing the government have been tortured and killed by the _____ government. (*See* Tabs ___, ___, ___, ___, ___, ___, ___, and ___ of the Supporting Documentation.)

II. Refusal to Serve in the Military

Mr. _____'s fear of persecution is also based on his refusal to serve in and desertion from the _____ military. Mr. _____ opposes serving in the military based on his moral beliefs and opposition to the objectives of the military. In his past military service, he became aware of the human rights abuses committed by the _____ military in the _____ war (D. at ___.) and does not want to participate in such abuses.

Mr. _____ qualifies for asylum based on his refusal to serve for two separate reasons. First, his refusal to serve is based on his moral convictions. Secondly, he qualifies based on the disproportionate treatment he is likely to suffer for his desertion based on his religion, nationality, membership in a particular social group, and political opinion.

The BIA recognized in *Matter of A.G.*, 19 I&N Dec. 502, 506 (BIA 1987), that a person may qualify for asylum based on his refusal to serve in the military "where the [person] would necessarily be required to engage in inhuman conduct as a result of the military service required by the government." Paragraph 170 of the *UN Handbook* further provides that "the necessity to perform military service may be the sole ground for a claim to refugee status . . . when a person can show that the performance of military service would have required participation in military action contrary to his genuine political, religious or moral convictions, or to valid reasons of conscience."

The documentary evidence submitted as Supporting Documentation at Tabs ___, ___, ___, ___, ___, ___, and ___ overwhelmingly demonstrates that the _____ military engaged in systematic human rights abuses throughout the _____ war. Many innocent civilians were targeted and killed by _____. Mr. _____'s desertion from the military by refusing to return to complete his military service was based on both his refusal to participate in the political objectives of the _____ government and his moral convictions. (D. at ___, ___, and ___.)

The *UN Handbook* at ¶169 also recognizes that a deserter may be considered a refugee if he "would suffer disproportionately severe punishment for the military offense based on his race, religion, nationality, membership of a particular social group or political opinion." The Supporting Documentation at Tabs ___, ___, ___, ___, and ___, demonstrates that members of Mr. _____'s religious and ethnic group suffer disproportionate punishment at the hands of the _____ military and police. Mr. _____ is likely to be tortured and executed for his act of desertion. (D. at ___.)

III. Religion

Mr. _____ and his family have suffered and are likely to suffer persecution in the future in _____ on account of their religious beliefs. Mr. _____ recounted in his declaration the widespread physical and verbal abuse, discrimination, and harassment that he and his family members suffered in _____ throughout their lives. (D. at ___, ___, ___, and ___.) These abuses continued through his higher education and military service. (D. at ___, ___, ___, and ___.)

The *UN Handbook* at ¶72 notes that "[p]ersecution for reasons of religion may assume various forms," including "serious measures of discrimination imposed on persons because they practise their religion or belong to a particular religious community."

In addition to Mr. _____'s declaration, the Supporting Documentation at Tabs ___ and ___ provides substantial evidence of the mistreatment and persecution of Mr. _____'s religious group in _____. The report, _____, lists numerous recent examples of the persecution of members of this religious group in _____. These individuals have been persecuted for refusing to join the ruling party, for having ties to the United States, because they are perceived to be opponents of the _____ government, and because they have deserted from the military. Mr. _____ falls into each of these categories and, therefore, has a well-founded fear of persecution because he is similarly situated to others who have been persecuted because of their religion. *See* 8 CFR §§208.13(b)(2), 1208.13(b)(2).

IV. Race; Membership in a Particular Social Group

Mr. _____ and his family also fear persecution because they are _____, an ethnic minority group in _____. This ethnic minority group could be characterized as either a race or particular social group according to the criteria set forth in the *UN Handbook* and the case law in the United States. The _____ people are a separate ethnic and linguistic group in _____, according to the Supporting Documentation at Tab ___. Mr. _____'s declaration chronicles his own efforts on behalf of his ethnic group (D at ___) and that his ethnic heritage was an additional cause of mistreatment, harassment, and discrimination (D. at ___, ___, and ___.).

The *UN Handbook* at ¶68 states that "[r]ace ... has to be understood in its widest sense to include all kinds of ethnic groups. ... Discrimination for reasons of race has found worldwide condemnations one of the most striking violations of human rights." The BIA has similarly defined "particular social group" as a group of individuals who "share a common, immutable characteristic ... which members of the group either cannot change, or should not be required to change, because it is fundamental to their individual identities or consciences." *Matter of Acosta*, 19 I&N Dec. 211, 233 (BIA 1985).

The _____ population in _____ has been continually and systematically oppressed by the government. The reports from _____ on the persecution of this ethnic group have been numerous and graphic. _____'s brutal treatment of this ethnic group has been labelled "genocide" by international human rights groups. *See* Supporting Documentation at Tabs ___, ___, ___, and ___.

Whether Mr. _____'s ethnicity is characterized as a particular social group or race, the harm he is likely to suffer because of it is the same. Mr. _____ and his family fear that they will be subjected to "genocide" if they are returned because of their ethnicity.

Mr. _____ also belongs to the particular social group of a family that has been singled out and targeted as being subversives and opponents of the government. His brother was arrested, interrogated, and brutally tortured because of his family is believed to be disloyalty to government. (D. at ___ and Supporting Documentation at Tabs ___ and ___.) As a member of a targeted "family," and Mr. _____ himself a target, he has a well-founded fear of persecution. Several of Mr. _____'s family members were interviewed and granted refugee status by the United States. *See* Supporting Documentation at Tabs ___, ___, ___, and ___. Mr. _____ also fears persecution because his family, as a group, has been sought out and targeted for persecution.

V. Conclusion

Based on the foregoing reasons, it is respectfully requested that Mr. _____ and his wife, _____, be granted asylum in the United States.

If you require any additional information regarding Mr. _____'s asylum claim, please do not hesitate to contact me at *[phone number]*.

Respectfully submitted,

_____
Attorney for the Applicants

Appendix 4A
Checklist for Supporting Documentation

After passage of the REAL ID Act of 2005, supporting documentation is more important than ever in establishing eligibility for asylum and withholding of removal. *See* chapter 2.6.3.

Supporting documentation may be obtained from obvious and a few not-so-obvious sources. You may find yourself testing the limits of your creativity. Below is a checklist to help with your research. But don't be surprised if your best leads come from the applicant.

Try to obtain:

- ☐ **Documents that specifically mention the applicant.** These may include identity documents, reports of the persecution suffered by the applicant, records that establish the applicant's ethnicity, religion, or nationality, and proof of the applicant's party or group memberships or affiliations. These may be documents that the applicant brought with him or her to the United States or, more likely, are documents obtained after the applicant arrived in the United States. Be creative! An affidavit from the applicant's rabbi in the United States may be submitted as proof of the applicant's religion. A picture of the applicant in his uniform may be submitted to demonstrate his service in the military. Statements from friends, neighbors, and relatives who witnessed an event or who may be able to substantiate the applicant's claim may also be submitted.

- ☐ **Medical reports and evaluations from health care professionals.** The harm the applicant suffered may be corroborated by the health care professionals who have examined or are treating the applicant. Submit reports, affidavits, X-rays, and photographs. See appendix 6H for a list of treatment centers and appendix 4C for a sample affidavit from a physician.

- ☐ **Expert Opinions.** Other sources of valuable information are experts from a variety of disciplines. Consider obtaining affidavits from academics who have studied the conditions in the applicant's country or a legal expert who can attest to the criminal penalties likely to be imposed on the applicant if returned. Another source is the Office of the United Nations High Commissioner for Refugees, which may verify the applicant's refugee status in a third country or offer an advisory opinion on a particular point of law. *See* appendix 4D.

- ☐ **Demonstrative evidence.** Consider the possibility of introducing, for example, a map of the applicant's escape route or a model or reproduction of the instrument or device used to harm or torture the applicant.

- ☐ **Country condition documentation.** This information is available from many sources, including Human Rights Watch, Amnesty International, the Department of State's *Country Reports on Human Rights Practices*, USCIS's Resource Informa-

☐ **Foreign Law.** If the applicant fears that he or she will be punished upon return to his or her home country for illegal exit, his or her sexual orientation, or other reasons that may be the basis of a claim, the law of the applicant's home country should be submitted. If nationality is at issue in the applicant's case, the nationality laws of the country of birth or last habitual residence should be submitted. The laws of many countries are available from the Library of Congress. *See* appendix 6G.

☐ **Proof of Attempts to Obtain Documents.** If the applicant has tried but failed to obtain documentation, those failed attempts could be submitted as evidence that the documentation is not available. The evidence may be in the form of a letter, a fax, or even phone bills (as proof of overseas calls). If attempts are made in-person, a nonparty witness might be able to submit an affidavit attesting to the encounter.

☐ **Proof of Why It Would Be Dangerous to Attempt to Obtain Documents.** Often asylum applicants are from countries where communication by telephone, fax, mail, and even e-mail is closely monitored. In such circumstances it would be unreasonable to expect an asylum applicant to obtain documents from his or her home country. It is necessary, however, to show why it is dangerous to even attempt to obtain these documents. Such proof may be available from country conditions experts or reports.

Note: Documentation should be paginated, indexed, tabbed, and highlighted for easy reference.

APPENDIX 4B
SAMPLE INDEX OF SUPPORTING DOCUMENTATION FOR ASYLUM APPLICANT FROM IRAN

Note: It is important to review and include documentation from the time of the persecution as well as current country conditions.

SAMPLE EVIDENTIARY INDEX
[An actual index, most likely, would include many more documents and would be annotated to include information contained in the document or report that is of particular significance to the applicant's claim.]

Table of Contents

	Tab
Declaration of **[Asylum Applicant]**	1
[Asylum Applicant's] National Identity Card and translation	2
[Asylum Applicant's] Marriage Certificate and translation	3
[Family Member's] Death Certificate and translation	4
[Asylum Applicant's] Proof of Employment as College Professor in Iran	5
Proof of Refugee Status of **[Asylum Applicant's Brother]** in Canada	6
[Asylum Applicant's] Membership Card for **[Human Rights Organization]**	7
Affidavit from President of Human Rights Organization re: **[Asylum Applicant's]** Membership and Participation in Human Rights Activities	8
Affidavit of Mental Health Professional re: Trauma Suffered by **[Asylum Applicant]**	9
Affidavit of Physician noting **[Asylum Applicant's]** Physical Scars are Consistent with Torture	10
Letters from **[Relatives]** and English Translations	11
DOS Country Reports on Human Rights Practice for 2006 (Feb. 2007), highlighting persecution of persons similarly situated to **[Asylum Applicant]**	12

DOS Country Reports on Human Rights Practice for 2005 (Feb. 2006),
highlighting persecution of persons similarly situated to **[Asylum Applicant]** 13

Amnesty International, *Iran: Civil Society Activists and
Human Rights Defenders Under Attack* (2004) 14

Amnesty International, *Iran: Five Years of Injustice and Impunity* (2004) 15

Human Rights Watch, *World Report 2007* 16

Translation of an Act Published on Pages 720–21 of the
Criminal Codes of the Islamic Republic of Iran 17

Travel Document Requirements for Citizens of the Islamic Republic of Iran 18

October 25, 2006, Article from *Persian Daily News* and English Translation 19

Map of Iran 20

Commendation of **[Asylum Applicant]** from **[State]** Correctional Employee 21

ICE Detainee Work Performance Report for **[Asylum Applicant]** 22

Letter from Mr. _____ of Local AA Chapter 23

United Nations Convention against Torture and Other Cruel,
Inhuman or Degrading Treatment or Punishment 24

Senate Resolution of Advice and Consent to Ratification of Torture Convention,
136 Cong. Rec. S17486 (Oct. 27, 1990) 25

United Nations High Commissioner for Refugees, *Handbook on Procedures
and Criteria for Determining Refugee Status* (1979) (relevant excerpts) 26

United Nations High Commissioner for Refugees, Factum of the Intervener,
filed in the Supreme Court of Canada 27

United Nations High Commissioner for Refugees, Advisory Opinion
for **[Asylum Applicant]** 28

APPENDIX 4C
SAMPLE EXPERT AFFIDAVITS

SAMPLE EXPERT AFFIDAVIT—COUNTRY CONDITIONS

Affidavit

State of Illinois }
County of Cook }

I, Heather McClure, being duly sworn, state as follows:

1. I, Heather McClure, am Resource Director of the Midwest Human Rights Partnership for Sexual Orientation (MHRPSO) in Chicago, Illinois. MHRPSO is a human rights project of the Heartland Alliance for Human Needs & Human Rights (formerly Travelers & Immigrants Aid), also in Chicago, Illinois. MHRPSO investigates and documents human rights violations against gay men, lesbians, and people with HIV/AIDS in Guatemala, and other focus countries. On January 23, 1997, I testified in the court of _____ to the authenticity of the documents I gathered in Guatemala City during a fact-finding trip from September 13–22, 1996. These documents were submitted to the court in January 1997, by _____, lawyer for the _____.

2. It has been brought to my attention that on the day of the aforementioned hearing, the court raised questions as to what constitutes or determines gay male identity. To help the court make its determination, I refer it to Attorney General Order No. 1895-94, dated June 19, 1994 (as reprinted in the "Task Force Update: Newsletter of the Lesbian and Gay Immigration Rights Task Force, Inc.," Fall 1996, Attachment A), and Stephen O. Murray's *Latin American Male Homosexualities* (University of New Mexico Press, 1995), a collection of anthropological essays that examine different homosexual practices throughout Latin America in relation to issues of family, society, culture, politics, economics, and ethnicity. Additional clarification is offered by (1) a mission statement describing the services of OASIS, a prominent HIV/AIDS prevention center in Guatemala City directed by Dr. Ruben Mayorga (Attachment B), and (2) a presentation of cases of patients with HIV/AIDS compiled by physicians affiliated with the Guatemalan Association for the Prevention and Control of AIDS (admitted into evidence by Judge _____ on January 23, 1997).

3. In Attorney General Order No. 1895-94, dated June 19, 1994, David A. Martin states legacy INS's position that "homosexuals do constitute a particular social group." Martin continues, "[a]ccordingly, our briefs should not pursue arguments that homosexuality fails to define a particular social group because it is not an immutable characteristic. Nor should the INS argue that homosexuals are too diverse and non-cohesive a group to qualify as a particular social group." As the documentation below illustrates, homosexuals in Guatemala do not share many of the cultural ways of life that, in large part, distinguish

U.S. homosexuals. Guatemalan homosexuals, nevertheless, still should be regarded as a particular social group with their own particular characteristics that have adapted in response to a history, and an economic and political system that are very different from those of the United States.

4. Both Dr. Murray's research and Dr. Mayorga's work in Guatemala City demonstrate that in Guatemala a homosexual man cannot be determined by the extent to which his sexual orientation is known to family, friends, and doctor; by his lack of membership in a gay organization; or by his involvement in heterosexual relationships (including marriage).

> a. Dr. Stephen Murray's research in Guatemala City reveals that "one major difference between North American and Latin American men engaged in recurrent homosexual relations is that Latin Americans live with their family of origin until they marry. . . . In my 1980 sample of homosexually active men in Guatemala City, the only men who did not live with their parents lived with wives of their own."
>
> b. Murray identifies reasons for the influence Latin American families exert over their children: "[B]esides greater centrality in socialization, the Latin American family retains economic functions. . . . In societies experienced by most as capricious and heartless, the family provides more than merely psychological shelter. If an individual is struck down by illness or injury and has no family to provide support, s/he will be reduced to begging in the streets. Examples of this horrific danger are readily visible." Continues Murray, "[B]ecause revelation of homosexuality is a basis for expulsion from the home, and because of the economic as well as psychological security provided by the family, homosexually active Latin Americans cultivate family relations to a greater extent than do those who can take them for granted."
>
> c. Further, Dr. Murray links the strong influence of the family to the lack of gay and lesbian organizations in Guatemala City (to date, none exists). Murray writes that the centrality of family is a long-enduring obstacle to gay self-identification and gay community-building because "[men's] residence with families scattered throughout cities precludes the development of gay neighborhoods." Without gay neighborhoods, such as those "gay ghettos" established in the United States after World War II, there exists in Guatemala tremendous obstacles to the formation of gay consciousness, culture, and community as these have developed in Anglo North America.
>
> d. As I testified on January 23, 1997, there are currently no gay or lesbian organizations in Guatemala. Though lesbians and gay men are involved in many prominent human rights and HIV/AIDS prevention and treatment organizations, they are not open about their sexual orientation, nor do they use their common sexual preferences as a basis for establishing gay and/or lesbian organizations. When I interviewed Guatemalans (gays, lesbians, and individuals of unidentified sexual orientation) as to why gays and lesbians were not more visible, I was told repeatedly that they are afraid they will be victims of violence, in addition to losing their jobs and the support of their families and friends.

e. The likelihood of violence against gays and lesbians is increased by a common misconception in Guatemalan society that lesbians and gay men are also "AIDS carriers." Conversely, people with HIV/AIDS are assumed to be gay or lesbian. AIDS-phobia and homophobia reinforce one another. Thus, there is a two-fold danger of being perceived, or exposed, as HIV-positive and/or homosexual—status in one group strongly implies membership within the other.

f. The presentation of cases of patients with HIV/AIDS compiled by physicians affiliated with the Guatemalan Association for the Prevention and Control of AIDS (admitted into evidence by Judge _____ on January 23, 1997) attests to additional risks that persons with HIV/AIDS take when they seek out medical care for HIV/AIDS in Guatemala. Case #7 (page 4) records that "there was no confidentiality of [the patient's] diagnosis within this hospital. Almost all of the doctors and nurses were made aware [of her HIV-positive status] and they asked her questions about her sexual conduct." On September 25, the patient was approached by "a journalist and a camera person" who wanted an interview. The patient "believes that it was one of the nurses of the hospital that contacted the press and television with her name and other confidential facts."

This case, like others documented by the Guatemalan Association for the Prevention and Control of AIDS, testifies to the lack of confidentiality afforded patients with HIV/AIDS (*see* Case #2). Given the tremendous social stigma associated with homosexuality (*see* documents admitted into evidence by Judge _____) and HIV/AIDS in Guatemala (*see* all patient cases), and the violence directed against gay men, lesbians, and persons with HIV/AIDS (*see* Cases #1 and #8, and other documents admitted into evidence by Judge _____), a gay man who seeks medical treatment for HIV/AIDS runs the risk of having his sexuality exposed to other doctors and nurses not responsible for his care, other patients, and society at large through the media. The consequences of such exposure could be the increased likelihood that he will be a target of violence, and will suffer other types of social rejection (including loss of job, family, and colleagues). If a gay man has no other alternative but to seek medical treatment for AIDS-related symptoms, it is highly probable that he will not divulge his sexuality for fear of possible exposure or retribution.

g. Additionally, Dr. Mayorga testifies in his affidavit dated September 19, 1996 (admitted into evidence on January 23, 1997), that "two gay men who have participated in OASIS' workshops were beaten upon leaving a gay bar (Metropolis) by a group of unknown men. They robbed them of a few personal items . . . and (the two men) suffered from bruises and cuts on their backs, necks and faces." Though it is not known whether the men's association with OASIS played a part in their perpetrators' motivations to attack them, it is evident that the general societal respect in the United States accorded gays and lesbians is not replicated in Guatemala. Instead, a gay Guatemalan man clearly endangers himself through his association with places deemed gay or lesbian (*e.g.*, bars), and may put himself at risk for affiliating himself with HIV/AIDS organizations perceived as sympathetic to gays and lesbians.

h. Thus, U.S. expectations that gay identity be defined through an individual's openness with his family about his sexual orientation, and membership in gay organizations, grows from the particular cultural and economic histories of Anglo-America. Similar criteria, when applied to Guatemalan gay men, obscures the very different family pressures, economic scarcity, and lack of a social safety net—as well as a dearth of institutions openly supportive of gay men, and risks of associating with those organizations—that help to define gay male identity in Guatemala.

i. Murray describes how gay men respond to severe homophobia and AIDS-phobia when he writes that gay men's association with like others is limited. He observes, "[F]or fear of having their reputation 'burned' (*quemada*) and their security thereby endangered, many persons involved in homosexual behavior avoid being seen with or being acknowledged by males who might be judged effeminate and also avoid places where homosexuals are known to congregate. The same pattern existed among homosexual Anglo Americans in the mid-1960s, although then and there it was fear of losing jobs more than Latin Americans' fear of the family learning of stigmatizing association." Dr. Mayorga's letter attests the very real fear of violence adds to men's concern that their families or employers will learn of their sexual orientation as a result of their involvement in organizations that might be perceived as places "where homosexuals are known to congregate."

j. Additional survival mechanisms gay men may adopt to avoid repercussions include living "double lives." As Dr. Murray explains, "Latinos [and others] can compartmentalize homosexuality—in space or time. According to Goode (1960), compartmentalization of roles is a common response to role strain; by no means is it unique to managing masculine self-presentation while engaged in homosexual behavior in Latin America. In Latin America, as in Anglo North America, there is 'a traditional difference between that which people know and that which they agree to admit that they know, that which they see and that which they speak of.'" (Henry James, quoted in Murray). One survival mechanism for gay men is marriage, or involvement in highly visible heterosexual relationships.

k. Both men's and women's social and professional standing in Guatemala is highly determined by their marital status. Consequently, the great majority of Guatemalans marry in their early- to mid-20s. A Guatemalan man who is unmarried by the age of approximately 30 is often suspected of being gay and may be victimized in the ways described above.

l. Though there are no exact statistics as to how many gay men marry, the AIDS epidemic in the last 10 years in Guatemala illustrates that a greater proportion of married men are involved in gay relationships than previously believed. Dr. Mayorga admits that "very little is know[n] about the spread of HIV among this population of men who have sexual relations with other men in developing countries and, in general, there are no prevention programs nor special attention designed with this population in mind. And [i]t is estimated that sexual activity among men is more frequent than previously thought. As an example, in the HIV/AIDS clinic of the St.

John of God General Hospital in Guatemala, of the 397 men with HIV/AIDS, 187 have had sexual relations with other men" (from OASIS Introduction). This same phenomenon, of married men having extramarital sex with other men (including gay sex workers), is prevalent enough that OASIS cites it as causally related to the increased transmission of HIV from husbands to their wives and to their children in utero.

5. In conclusion, the above demonstrates that a Guatemalan gay man's involvement in a marriage or other form of heterosexual relationship is not necessarily an indicator of his sexual practices or even his sexual identity. Instead, a gay man may choose to be married for the same reason he may decide never to reveal to his family or doctor the true nature of his sexual orientation: to avoid social and familial censure and, consequently, the risk of more serious repercussions, including physical violence, for being recognized as a gay man. Similarly, the failure of a gay man to involve himself in an organization that is sympathetic to gays and lesbians does not belie his sexuality; instead, it attests to the potential danger of association with such organizations. Indeed, the gap between sexual identity and sexual practice in Guatemala is a testament to the intensity and prevalence of homophobia and AIDS-phobia in that country, which can erupt into violence against individuals who are, or are perceived to be, gay and/or HIV-positive.

6. Finally, though _____ is in the United States, it is very difficult to "shake off" deeply ingrained mechanisms that, in Guatemala, are necessary for a gay man's physical, emotional, and economic survival. It is even more likely that these mechanisms will continue to determine a gay man's life in the United States if he remains in contact with his family, and is dependent for emotional support on a Guatemalan immigrant community shaped by the same cultural values that oppressed the gay male when he lived in Guatemala.

7. The process of "coming out" for lesbians and gay men is a gradual one and can take many years, even decades. Many American lesbians and gay men never reveal their sexual orientation to their families, doctors, colleagues, or employers; do not belong to gay and lesbian organizations; and have been married or are currently choosing to end marriages due to their sexual orientation.

8. _____ has had to struggle against additional obstacles, including the very real threat of state-sanctioned physical violence against those who are gay or lesbian (see MINUGUA, Report No. 22, Team No. 5, admitted into evidence) in a society whose judicial and security institutions have been identified as highly responsible for extensive human rights violations (documented by the U.S. Department of State and Amnesty International) against "undesirables" and "subversives," including homosexuals. In addition, widespread and severely debilitating social stigmas against gays, lesbians, and people with HIV/AIDS in Guatemala are realities most Americans never have to face. These challenges may have made _____'s ability to live as an openly gay man that much more difficult to achieve. Though these forces cannot erase his sexual orientation, they can define to a large extent the choices he feels he has, as a gay Guatemalan man, for expressing himself both in Guatemala and in the United States.

I declare under penalty of perjury that the foregoing is true and correct. Executed on this 3rd day of February 1997, in the City of Chicago, County of Cook, State of Illinois.

Subscribed and sworn to before me this ____ day of _____, ____

_____   _____
Notary Public   Heather McClure

SAMPLE EXPERT AFFIDAVIT—MEDICAL

OFFICE OF THE IMMIGRATION JUDGE
EXECUTIVE OFFICE FOR IMMIGRATION REVIEW

In the Matter of the Application
for Asylum and Withholding of
Removal of _____
a/k/a, _____

A # _____

**AFFIDAVIT OF
DOUGLAS SHENSON, MD, MPH**

STATE OF NEW YORK }
                   } ss.:
COUNTY OF THE BRONX }

DOUGLAS SHENSON, MD, MPH, being duly sworn, deposes and says:

1. I am an American physician licensed in the State of New York, currently working as an Assistant Professor in the Department of Epidemiology and Social Medicine, at Montefiore Medical Center/Albert Einstein College of Medicine. I am fully trained and board-eligible in the specialty of Internal Medicine.

2. I am a graduate of Tulane University School of Medicine and Tulane University School of Public Health and Tropical Medicine. In addition to holding medical and public health degrees, I have earned a bachelor's and a master's degree in Human Sciences from Oxford University in England. My clinical training was at the Residency Program in Social Internal Medicine at Montefiore Medical Center/Albert Einstein College of Medicine, where my last year I held the position of Chief Resident.

3. Since completing my clinical training, I have practiced in the Bronx. Because I speak French fluently, my colleagues have over the years referred to me a large number of West African and Haitian patients. I have been designated as an expert witness in the New York Eastern District court case of HIV-infected Haitian refugees seeking legal representation during their incarceration at Guantanamo U.S. Naval Base in Cuba.

4. I have a long-standing interest in medical human rights, and have published on the subject. I am on the Board of Directors of *Doctors of the World*, an American-based humanitarian and human rights group affiliated with the French organization, *Médecins du Monde*. I have received specialized postgraduate training in the use of medical skills for the documentation and treatment of human rights victims. Several human rights organizations have referred to me for evaluation individuals who have been subjected to torture or physical maltreatment in their homeland. These organizations include Physicians for

Human Rights, Church World Services, The Lawyers Committee for Human Rights, and PEN.

5. _____, Esq. requested that I conduct a physical examination of Mr. _____ in order to evaluate Mr. _____'s physical condition in light of his allegations that he was physically abused by government officials prior to this flight from _____ to this country.

6. I have had the opportunity to review the medical records that were provided to Mr. _____ through the Department of Homeland Security, by the Wackenhut Facility ("Wackenhut").

7. On January 19, 1993, I was able to visit Mr. _____ at Wackenhut, where he is currently being detained, and conducted a thorough clinical examination. During the course of that examination, Mr. _____ described the events surrounding his incarceration in _____. On February 81, 1992, four soldiers forcibly entered Mr. _____'s apartment and beat him severely. He was repeatedly hit in the face, on the head, and about the ears. He was kicked in the stomach when he fell to the ground. At one point, after getting up from the floor, he was pushed into a metal chair on which he gashed his right forearm. During the beating, one of the soldiers attacked him with a whip while another pinned his arms behind his back with a metal-buckled belt or cord. These beatings continued for approximately 15 minutes.

8. Mr. _____ was then bodily carried (with his arms still pinned back) and tossed into the back of a waiting van. He landed on his head and shoulders, apparently dislocating his right shoulder. He was then taken to _____ prison where he was held for 165 days. During his incarceration he received inadequate medical attention for his multiple injuries. His right shoulder was placed in a primitive cast, but was otherwise left unattended. He described to me the great fear he experienced during that period, not knowing when he would be released or what his fate might be.

9. Mr. _____ also described a variety of changes in his health which began following his beatings in the _____. He stated he now has great difficulty concentrating and is often forgetful. He suffers from frequent headaches, is unable to sleep at night and finds himself sleeping through much of the day. He is very sad and sometimes cries without any proximate cause. He is continuously anxious and has little appetite. He also states his hearing is impaired since his beatings.

10. On physical examination, Mr. _____ exhibits numerous scars. I asked him to point out how he sustained each one, and my findings are as follows: He has a 6 cm circular scar on the superior aspect of his right shoulder which follows the form of a crude buckle; he has a trailing 4 cm scar on the anterior aspect of his left shoulder consistent with a whipping; he has a 4 cm poorly joined scar on the medial surface of his left arm consistent with the "tearing" wound of a tightly bound rope; he has a well-joined 4 cm scar on his right forearm consistent with a cut from a sharp object such as a metal chair; he has a 3 cm trailing scar on the anterior aspect of his left thigh, which is also consistent with a

whipping wound; he has a 3 cm poorly healed scar on his right anterior shin, which he states resulted from an earlier sports accident.

11. Mr. _____ also has an asymmetrical hearing loss, with apparent sensorineural damage to his right ear (positive Weber Test). His tympanic membranes have been damaged, with probable perforation.

12. Based on my examination and experience in diagnosing other victims of physical maltreatment and torture, my assessment is that his multiple sights and symptoms are entirely consistent with the story he recounts. The fact that Mr. _____ attributes a rather dramatic scar to an unrelated sports accident persuades me further that he is telling the truth.

13. I would be willing to further explain my assessment, and answer any other questions relevant to this matter if requested to do so, whether in writing or orally.

Sworn to before me this
20th day of January 1993.

_____   _____

Notary Public   DOUGLAS SHENSON, MD, MPH

APPENDIX 4D

UNHCR ADVISORY OPINION ON CESSATION AND CANCELLATION OF REFUGEE STATUS

UNHCR
United Nations High Commissio
Haut Commissariat des Nations U

UNHCR

1775 K Street, NW
Suite 300
Washington, DC 20006

Tel.: 2022965191
Fax: 2022965660
Email: painter@unhcr.ch

28 February 2003

BY FACSIMILE & OVERNIGHT MAIL

Robert Pauw, Esq.
Gibbs, Houston & Pauw
1000 Second Avenue, Suite 1600
Seattle, WA 98104

Re: <u>Cessation and Cancellation of Refugee Status</u>

I am writing in response to your request for advice from the Office of the United Nations High Commissioner for Refugees ("UNHCR") on the issue of whether refugee status "ceases" or "terminates" once a refugee becomes a lawful permanent resident ("LPR") in his/her country of asylum. As explained in more detail below, LPR status does not "end" a person's refugee status. While LPR status is a positive and important step in the process of finding a durable solution for refugees, one's refugee status does not cease until one of the cessation clauses of the 1951 Convention relating to the Status of Refugees[1] ("the 1951 Convention") is implicated. Obtaining LPR status is not a basis for cessation of refugee status under the 1951 Convention. Similarly, refugee status is not "cancelled" unless there is some evidence of fraud or misrepresentation at the time that refugee status was recognized. Acquisition of LPR status would not be grounds for cancellation of refugee status.

The Office of the United Nations High Commissioner for Refugees

UNHCR has been charged by the United Nations General Assembly with responsibility for providing international protection to refugees and other persons within its mandate and for seeking permanent solutions to the problem of refugees by assisting governments and private organizations.[2] As set forth in its Statute, UNHCR fulfills its international protection mandate by, *inter alia*, "[p]romoting the conclusion and ratification of international conventions for the protection of refugees, supervising their application and proposing amendments thereto."[3] UNHCR's supervisory responsibility is mirrored in Article II of the 1967 Protocol relating to the Status of Refugees[4], to which the United States acceded in 1968. The Protocol incorporates the substantive provisions of the 1951 Convention.

The views of UNHCR are informed by over 50 years of experience supervising international refugee instruments. UNHCR is represented in 115 countries. UNHCR provides guidance in connection with the establishment and implementation of national procedures for refugee status determinations and also conducts such determinations under its mandate.

---

[1] 19 U.S.T. 6259 (1951).
[2] *See* Statute of UNHCR, UN Doc. A/RES/428(V), Annex, at paras. 1, 6 (1950).
[3] *Id.*, at para. 8(a).
[4] 19 U.S.T. 6223 (1967), art. 2.

UNHCR's interpretation of the provisions of the 1951 Convention and Protocol are, therefore, integral to the global regime for the protection of refugees.

Analysis

Under international refugee law, individuals can only lose their refugee status if they fall under one of the cessation clauses of the 1951 Convention or if their status is cancelled because of evidence of fraud or misrepresentation at the time that refugee status was initially recognized. Both of these grounds are considered below.

I. Cessation of Refugee Status

A. Cessation Clauses of the 1951 Convention relating to the Status of Refugees

1. General

Refugee status, as conceived in international law, is in most cases, a transitory phenomenon which lasts only as long as the reasons for fearing persecution in the country of origin persist. Once these reasons disappear, refugee status may be legitimately terminated.

The 1951 Convention contains six cessation clauses, which, when applied, will result in the termination of an individual's refugee status. These clauses apply only to persons who are refugees at the time of the clause's application. As noted in UNHCR's recently issued *Guidelines on Cessation of Refugee Status under Article 1C(5) and (6) of the 1951 Convention*,

> [w]hen interpreting the cessation clauses, it is important to bear in mind the broad durable solutions context of refugee protection informing the object and purpose of these clauses. Numerous Executive Committee Conclusions affirm that the 1951 Convention and principles of refugee protection look to durable solutions for refugees. Accordingly, cessation practices should be developed in a manner consistent with the goal of durable solutions.[5]

Given that application of such clauses results in the loss of refugee status, they are to be applied restrictively.[6] The cessation clauses are not penal in nature, and are not to be utilized

---

[5] UNHCR, *Guidelines on International Protection: Cessation of Refugee Status under Article 1C(5) and (6) of the 1951 Convention relating to the Status of Refugees (the "Ceased Circumstances" Clauses)*, UN Doc. HCR/GIP/02/03 (10 February 2003), at para. 6, citing Executive Committee Conclusions No. 29 (XXXIV) (1983), No. 50 (XXXIX) (1988), No. 58 (XL) (1989), No. 79 (XLVII) (1996), No. 81 (XLVIII) (1997), No. 85 (XLIX) (1998), No. 87 (L) (1999), No. 89 (L) (2000), and No. 90 (LII) (2001). The UNHCR Executive Committee is an intergovernmental group currently consisting of 60 Member States of the United Nations (including the United States) and the Holy See that advises the UNHCR in the exercise of its protection mandate.

[6] UNHCR, *Handbook on Procedures and Criteria for Determining Refugee Status Under the 1951 Convention and the 1967 Protocol relating to the Status of Refugees (" the Handbook")* (1979), at para. 116 (cessation clauses "are negative in character and ... should ... be interpreted restrictively"). The *Handbook* was prepared by UNHCR in 1979 at the request of Member States of the Executive Committee of the High Commissioner's Programme, including the US, to provide guidance to governments in applying the terms of the Convention and Protocol. The US Supreme Court in *INS v. Cardoza-Fonseca*, 480 U.S. 421, 439, n.22; 107 S.Ct. 1207, 1217 (1987), determined that, although the *Handbook* is not legally binding on US officials, it nevertheless provides "significant guidance" in construing the 1967 Protocol and in giving content to the obligations established therein. This position was reiterated by the Supreme Court in *INS v. Aguirre-*

for purposes of "punishing" a refugee otherwise found to meet the refugee definition under Article 1(A)(2).

The cessation clauses are found at Article 1(C) of the 1951 Convention. The first four cessation clauses "reflect a change in the situation of the refugee that has been brought about by himself,"[7] whereas the last two clauses address the situation where international protection is no longer justified due to changes in the country where persecution was feared. The cessation clauses are as follows:

(1) He has voluntarily re-availed himself of the protection of the country of his nationality; or
(2) Having lost his nationality, he has voluntarily re-acquired it; or
(3) He has acquired a new nationality, and enjoys the protection of the country of his new nationality; or
(4) He has voluntarily re-established himself in the country which he left or outside which he remained owing to a fear of persecution; orHe can no longer, because the circumstances in connexion with which he has been recognized as a refugee have ceased to exist, continue to refuse to avail himself of the protection of the country of his nationality ....
(5) Being a person who has no nationality he is, because the circumstances in connexion with which he has been recognized as a refugee have ceased to exist, able to return to the country of his former habitual residence ...

2. Cessation under Article 1C(3)

In considering whether acquisition of LPR status results in cessation of refugee status, particular reference should be made to Article 1C(3) of the 1951 Convention. Article 1C(3) makes clear that cessation based on effective protection in the country of refuge occurs only once a person has obtained a new nationality.[8] Once a refugee naturalizes, s/he should, in principle, be in a position to benefit from the protection afforded by that country to its citizens. International protection would therefore no longer be necessary and a durable solution will have been achieved.[9]

Naturalization alone, however, is not enough to trigger cessation under the 1951 Convention. Article 1C(3) requires that the person also "enjoys the protection of his new country of nationality." "This means that the refugee must secure and be able to exercise all the rights and benefits entailed by possession of the nationality of the country."[10] This carries particular importance, for example, in cases where the new nationality has been acquired through marriage. In such cases, the available protection "will depend on whether a genuine

---

Aguirre, 526 US 415, 427 (1999), where it stated that, while not binding on the Attorney General, the BIA or the US courts, the *Handbook* is a useful interpretative aid.

[7] *Handbook*, at para. 114.

[8] The analogous provision to Article 1C(3) under US law is found at INA Section 208(c)(2)(E) ("Asylum...may be terminated if the Attorney General determines that - ...(E) the alien has acquired a new nationality and enjoys the protection of the country of his or her new nationality.").

[9] *See* Atle Grahl-Madsen, *The Status of Refugees in International Law*, Vol. I (1972), at 396 ("If a refugee is naturalized in his country of refuge, he will immediately get all rights and benefits which the possession of that country entails, and it is only natural that he ceases to be a refugee.")

[10] UNHCR, *Note on the Cessation Clauses*, Executive Committee of the High Commissioner's Programme, Standing Committee, 8th meeting, UN Doc. EC/47/SC/CRP.30 (1997), at para. 15.

link has been established with the spouse's country."[11] As noted in UNHCR's *Guidelines on the Application of Cessation Clauses*, "two conditions therefore must be fulfilled in order to consider that a person who has acquired a new nationality enjoys the protection of new nationality: (1) the new nationality must be effective, in the sense that it must correspond to a genuine link between the individual and the State; and, (2) the refugee must be able and willing to avail himself or herself of the protection of the government of his or her new nationality. Only with effective national protection has a durable solution to the refugee's situation been achieved."[12]

3. Acquisition of Lawful Permanent Resident Status

It is clear from the text of the 1951 Convention, and its underlying rationale, that LPR status is not a sufficient basis for the cessation of refugee status. As noted in the *Handbook)*, the circumstances under which refugee status cease are "exhaustively enumerated…and no other reasons may be adduced by way of analogy to justify the withdrawal of refugee status."[13] This strict approach is important since refugees should not be subjected to constant review of their refugee status. Acquisition of LPR status is not one of the enumerated grounds and should not be applied by way of analogy to Article 1C(3). On the basis of the 1951 Convention's text alone, acquisition of LPR status is insufficient for purposes of cessation.

It is notable that, in the drafting of the 1951 Convention, a proposal to cease refugee status based on lengthy residence (ten years) in the country of asylum due to either refusal to avail oneself of the possibility of naturalization or ineligibility for naturalization due to "misbehaviour," was withdrawn after other delegates expressed serious reservations about it. Delegates noted that some refugees may be unable to naturalize or may be unwilling to abandon hopes of returning to their country of origin and retaining their citizenship there.[14]

LPR status also does not confer the degree of effective national protection that is necessary to ensure that international protection is no longer necessary. While the benefits of lawful permanent residence in the US are many, LPR status is not equivalent to US citizenship in important respects. Most notably, LPR status does not ensure protection from deportation, expulsion or extradition. For purposes of cessation of refugee status under Article 1C, this distinction is critical.[15]

B. Co-Existence of Refugee Status with Other Forms of Immigration Status

1. General

As noted earlier, and as made clear from the cessation clauses of the 1951 Convention, the ultimate goal for refugees is to find a durable solution to their situation. For purposes of cessation, the durable solution of effective national protection in the country of refuge occurs at the point of naturalization. It is understood, however, that a process of assimilation and

---

[11] UNHCR, *Guidelines on the Application of Cessation Clauses*, Inter-Office Memorandum No. 17/99, Field Office Memorandum No. 17-99 (1999), at para. 17.
[12] *Id.*, at para. 17.
[13] *Handbook*, at para. 116. *See also*, Grahl-Madsen, Vol. I, at 369 ("It is generally agreed that the enumeration of cessation clauses in Article 1C of the Refugee Convention…is exhaustive. In other words, once a person has become a refugee as defined in Article 1 of the Convention…he continues to be a refugee until he falls under any of those cessation clauses.").
[14] *See* UN Doc. A/Conf.2/SR23 (1951), at 21-25.
[15] Under appropriate circumstances, expulsion based on Articles 32 and 33(2) may be possible.

integration will occur before a refugee is naturalized. This process envisions a strengthening of the links between the refugee and the country of refuge, most notably through the acquisition of more permanent forms of legal status, such as lawful permanent residence.

As the connection between refugee and country of refuge strengthens, however, the individual's underlying status as a refugee remains constant, given that the particular needs of the refugee, be they protection-related (*e.g.*, from deportation) or otherwise (*e.g.*, family reunification)[16] will continue. The maintenance of refugee status better ensures that refugees will not refrain from integrating more fully in their host society for fear of losing the benefits that accompany refugee status. It also ensures that should the additional legal status granted them ever be rescinded, their refugee status will continue to provide protection. In this manner, refugee status and other forms of legal status in the country of refuge are co-extensive, not mutually exclusive. The additional legal status is, in effect, layered over the underlying refugee status that the individual continues to enjoy.

2.   *Articles 2-34 of the 1951 Convention*

The structure of the 1951 Convention reflects this "layering" of rights. Articles 2-34 detail the various rights and obligations of refugees under the 1951 Convention. These include, *inter alia*, the right to non-discrimination, religion, personal status, association, access to courts, and so forth. These rights, however, are not equally available to all refugees. Rather, many depend on the status, and the degree of integration, of the individual in the country of refuge.[17] For example, about half of the substantive provisions of the 1951 Convention refer to "refugees" without any distinction or qualification.[18] Other provisions, however, categorize the refugees to whom they apply, including refugees "in the territory" of the Contracting State[19], who have entered or are present "without authorization"[20], who are "lawfully" in the territory of a Contracting State[21], who are "lawfully staying" in the territory of a Contracting State[22], who are "lawfully resident" in the Contracting State,[23] who are "habitually resident",[24] and who can claim a "right of establishment."[25]

Those provisions of the 1951 Convention which detail the rights of refugees "lawfully" in the country of refuge, "lawfully staying" in the country of refuge, "lawfully residing" in the

---

[16] *See Handbook*, Chptr. VI, Principle of Family Unity.

[17] For a general discussion of this continuum of rights based on degree of connection between refugee and country of refuge, *see* James Hathaway and Anne Cusik, "Refugee Rights Are Not Negotiable," 14 *Geo. Immigr. L.J.*, 481, 491-98 (2000). *See also* Guy Goodwin-Gill, *The Refugee in International Law* (1996), at 307-309.

[18] *See, e.g.*, Articles 2 (general obligations), 3 (non-discrimination), 5 (rights granted apart from this Convention), 7 (exemption from reciprocity), 9 (provisional measures), 10 (continuity of residence), 13 (movable and immovable property), 16 (access to courts), 20 (rationing), 22 (public education), 29 (fiscal charges), 30 (transfer of assets), 33 (prohibition of expulsion or return), and 34 (naturalization).

[19] *See, e.g.*, Article 4 (religion), 27 (identity papers), and 28(1) (travel documents).

[20] Article 31 (refugees unlawfully in the country of refuge).

[21] *See, e.g.*, Articles 18 (self-employment), 26 (freedom of movement), and 32 (expulsion).

[22] *See, e.g.*, Articles 15 (right of association), 17 (wage-earning employment), 19 (liberal professions), 21 (housing), 23 (public relief), 24 (labor legislation and social security), and 28(1) (travel documents).

[23] *See, e.g.*, Paragraphs 6(1) and (3) and 11 of the Schedules to the 1951 Convention.

[24] *See, e.g.*, Articles 14 (artistic rights and industrial property), 16(2) (access to courts) and 16(3) (access to courts).

[25] As noted by Grahl-Madsen, "[t]he term 'right of establishment' is not used in any of the provisions of the Refugee Convention..., but the concept is found in the *travaux preparatoires* for the Refugee Convention, and it has got some expression in paragraph 6(1) and 11 of the two Schedules...."). Grahl-Madsen, Vol. II, at 334.

country of refuge, and so forth, envision that the refugee may have a legal status in the country of refuge in addition to, and distinct from, his/her refugee status. For some of these provisions, mere admission as an asylum-seeker or admission on a temporary visitor's visa may be sufficient to invoke the corresponding rights of the 1951 Convention.[26] Those refugees who enjoy some form of permanent or indefinite residence in the Contracting State, however, would be eligible for most, if not all, of the rights under the 1951 Convention, including those which require the greatest degree of connection between refugee and country of refuge, such as "habitual residence" or "right of establishment."[27] This would equally apply to refugees who obtain lawful permanent residence in the United States.

Consistent with the language and purpose of the substantive provisions of the 1951 Convention, therefore, refugees who acquire lawful permanent residence do not lose their refugee status, but rather benefit from an expanded range of rights under the 1951 Convention. In this regard, refugee status and LPR status co-exist. They are not mutually exclusive.

II. Cancellation of Refugee Status

The other manner by which individuals can lose their refugee status, albeit *ab anitio* or *ex tunc*, is through cancellation of refugee status.[28] Loss of refugee status through application of the cessation clauses must be clearly distinguished from loss of status as a result of annulment or cancellation. While the 1951 Convention does not specifically address cancellation, the *Handbook* provides the following:

> Article 1C does not deal with the cancellation of refugee status. Circumstances may, however, come to light that indicate that a person should never have been recognized as a refugee in the first place: *e.g.*, if it subsequently appears that refugee status was obtained by a misrepresentation of material facts, or that the person concerned possesses another nationality, or that one of the exclusion clauses would have applied to him had all of the relevant facts been known. In such cases, the decision by which he was determined to be a refugee will normally be cancelled.[29]

General principles of law, including that of *res judicata*, provide guidance on the cancellation of refugee status under the circumstances described in the *Handbook*. The principle of *res judicata* dictates that once a matter is judicially determined, it should not be subsequently reopened by the same parties.[30] However, on occasion, a decision may lose its final character due to new facts that indicate that the decision should never have been taken in the first place.

---

[26] *See, e.g.*, Grahl-Madsen, Vol. II, at 357 (refugees are 'lawfully' in territory if they possess proper travel documents, have observed frontier control formalities, and have not overstayed period and conditions of authorized stay, and are 'lawfully staying' in territory if they have been lawfully present for three months or are in possession of a residence permit authorizing stay for more than three months); Hathaway and Cusick, at 495 ("Where the laws of a state authorize the direct arrival of refugees who submit to a status determination or comparable procedure, it cannot sensibly be argued that refugees who avail themselves of this legal option are not lawfully present.")

[27] "[The 'right of establishment'] denotes a right to remain indefinitely in a territory (subject only to the provisions of Article 1C, 32 and 33 of the Refugee Convention). Such a right might be granted explicitly - by issuing an establishment permit or a residence permit valid for an indefinite period, etc. - or implicitly." Grahl-Madsen, Vol. II, at 358.

[28] The analogous "cancellation" provision under US law is found at 8 Code of Federal Regulations (CFR) Sections 207.9 ("Termination of Refugee Status") and 208.24(a)(1) ("Termination of asylum or withholding of removal or deportation").

[29] *Handbook*, at para. 117.

[30] UNHCR, *Note on Loss of Refugee Status through Cancellation* (1989), at para. 3.

UNHCR's *Note on Loss of Refugee Status through Cancellation*, states that the "circumstances that may call for an exception to the principle of *res judicata* include: (1) newly discovered evidence; (2) fraud, including concealment of material facts that there was a duty to disclose; and, (3) other misconduct in the proceedings."[31]

The principle of *res judicata* should be adhered to closely, and any exceptions should be applied restrictively. This is especially important given that the cancellation of refugee status could deprive individuals of acquired rights and interfere with legitimate expectations.[32] "The newly discovered evidence, fraud or other misconduct must, for example, be sufficiently material to have affected the outcome" and "must normally be intentional and manifest."[33] It should also be demonstrated "that the evidence could not readily have been discovered earlier, *i.e.*, at the time the decision was taken."[34] Any fraud or misconduct should be judicially determined.

Based on the above criteria, acquisition of LPR status would not be a basis for cancellation of refugee status. Acquisition of LPR status does not constitute newly discovered evidence, fraud, or other misconduct in the refugee status determination proceedings indicating that the person never should have been recognzied as a refugee in the first instance.

Conclusion

Based on the above analysis, it is UNHCR's opinion that an individual's refugee status does not cease if s/he becomes a lawful permanent resident. Similarly, acquisition of lawful permanent residence is not a basis for cancellation of refugee status.

We hope this information is useful. Please do not hesitate to contact our Office in writing should you wish to discuss this matter further.

Sincerely,

R. Andrew Painter
Senior Protection Officer

---

[31] *Id.*, at para. 4.
[32] *Id.*, at para. 9.
[33] *Id.*, at paras. 5-6.
[34] *Id.*, at para. 5.

Appendix 5A

Practice Pointers on Direct and Cross-Examination of the Asylum Applicant

As you prepare for your asylum hearing, it is helpful to outline your direct examination and anticipated cross-examination. Review the questions over and over with the asylum applicant during your interviews and, later, in a mock hearing. The following are useful tips to employ when preparing your direct examination and in anticipating the DHS attorney's cross-examination.

Starting

Begin your direct examination with simple questions that are easy for the applicant to answer and that will give the applicant time to become accustomed to testifying in court.

Concluding

End both your direct and re-direct with the strongest aspects of the applicant's claim.

Weak Points

Often it is helpful to address the weak points of the applicant's claim in your direct examination. If weak points are revealed only during cross-examination, the immigration judge may believe the applicant is evasive or dishonest.

Voluntary Departure

Ask voluntary departure questions at the beginning of the hearing, never at the end. Remember, it's better to end with the strongest points regarding the applicant's claim.

Cross-Examination

In asking the applicant anticipated cross-examination questions, always include questions that contain mistakes regarding the applicant's previous testimony. Advise the applicant of the importance of correcting such errors. Also, during the mock hearing, it is useful for the applicant to practice correcting these errors.

Emotional and Physical Harm

Ask questions not only about the events surrounding the applicant's claim, but also about the emotional and physical state of the applicant before, during, and after such events. It is important for the immigration judge to understand the trauma an individual may experience from witnessing such an event or its aftermath.

Objections

Advise the applicant that the DHS attorney may ask questions that are improper or irrelevant. Instruct the applicant that if an objection is made, the applicant should not answer the question until the matter is resolved by the immigration judge. If the applicant does not speak English, explain prior to the hearing that there may be untranslated discussions regarding questions, documents, or witnesses, and that these discussions are a normal part of the hearing.

Organization

In most cases, the best way to organize questions is chronologically. There may be cases, however, where a different order is preferable, especially if applicant fears more than one persecutor. For example, if the applicant fears both the government and a non-governmental actor, it may be best to organize questions chronologically, but separately, regarding each persecutor that the applicant fears.

Follow-Up Questions

An applicant may forget to mention a fact or detail of his or her claim while testifying. Make sure to ask nonleading follow-up questions during the direct and re-direct examination to elicit this information from the applicant. Practice this beforehand! It's hard not to be leading when your client has left out a small, but vital piece of information.

Comprehension

Applicants sometimes have difficulty understanding the immigration judge or DHS trial attorney because of their manner of speaking or the vocabulary they use. Advise the applicant that he or she should never answer a question that he or she does not understand. If an interpreter is being used, instruct the applicant to inform the immigration judge if he or she has difficulty understanding the interpreter.

DIRECT EXAMINATION OF THE APPLICANT

The Beginning—Simple Questions

Simple questions at the start of your direct examination will put the applicant at ease and allow him or her to become accustomed to answering questions in court. If an interpreter is used, these questions will allow the applicant to become accustomed to the accent and speech patterns of the interpreter, as well.

- Please state your full name.
- Where were you born?
- Are you a citizen of _____?
- How old are you?
- When were you born?
- Are you married?
- Where does your spouse live?
- How many children do you have?
- How old are they?
- Where do your children live?

Thorny Issues

Address the thornier issues in the case near the beginning of the direct examination, if possible. As noted above, it is better to save the stronger portions of the claim for later. Thorny issues that may arise in asylum claims include:

- Manner of entry into the United States (*e.g.*, use of false documents or illegal entry);
- Eligibility for voluntary departure (*see* chapter 6);
- Criminal convictions (in addition to questions regarding crimes and sentences, ask the applicant about his or her efforts toward rehabilitation and feelings of remorse for past actions);
- Reasons for remaining in the country of claimed persecution; and
- Lack of corroborating evidence. Note: if the applicant lacks proof of his or her identity, membership in a political party, or other aspect of his or her claim, the applicant must explain why he or she has been unable to obtain such evidence or why it would be unreasonable to attempt to obtain it.

The Middle—The Heart of the Claim

To begin this part of the direct examination, ask the applicant, "Why did you come to the United States?" or "Why did you leave your home country?" The applicant should begin with a brief summary of his or her claim, such as: *I came to the United States because I feared that I would be killed by the government because I am a member of _____, a religious minority, and I was an outspoken opponent of the government.* Then the applicant should be asked questions that elicit a chronological account of the harm he or she suffered and/or why he or she has a well-founded fear of persecution.

- Details matter! Ask probing questions so that the applicant provides as much detail as possible. Make sure, however, that you also ask these questions prior to the hearing so that you are not surprised in court by the applicant's responses.
- Be creative! Applicants who have difficulty remembering dates could establish approximate dates by providing details regarding the season, political events, religious celebrations, or even the ages of their children.
- Listen! Make sure that you, the interpreter, the DHS attorney, or the immigration judge do not inadvertently cut off the applicant's testimony. Always ask whether the applicant has any further comments if an interruption takes place.

The End—The Lasting Impression

End your direct examination with a summary of the strongest points of the applicant's claim. Sometimes this may be done by asking questions such as:

- Why did you leave your home country?
- Who or what did you leave behind?
- Have you been affected physically and emotionally by what has happened to you in your home country?
- In what way?

Applicants who have experienced or witnessed traumatic events may continue to experience emotional, as well as physical effects. If so, such applicants should also be referred for treatment. *See* appendix 6H for a list of treatment centers. It is also important to ask the applicant at or near the end of the direct examination:

- What do you think will happen to you if you are returned to your home country?
- Why?

Humanize your client. Let the immigration judge know what a responsible, respectable, honorable person she is. Does she help out in her neighborhood, church, school, or community? Is she a good mother? What activities does she do with her children? Is she attending classes? What are her future plans if she remains here? The DHS attorney might object that such questions are not relevant, but they are. They are relevant to whether the applicant merits asylum as a matter of discretion and most judges not only allow them, but are very interested in and swayed by the responses.

CROSS-EXAMINATION OF THE APPLICANT

In an effort to determine whether the applicant is eligible for or deserving of asylum or withholding of removal, the DHS attorney may ask the applicant questions regarding:

Family Members Who Have Remained in the Applicant's Home Country

If the applicant has family members who live in his or her home country, the applicant should indicate how the applicant's situation is different than that of his or her family members (if this is so) or provide information regarding why his or her family members have remained and the problems or difficulties, if any, they are experiencing.

Failure to Report Crimes or Abuses to the Police or Other Governmental Authority

If the applicant suffered harm in his or her home country, but failed to report it to the police, he or she will need to explain why. Was the applicant afraid of the authorities or would such a report have been futile or dangerous? These are areas that need to be explored when questioning the applicant prior to the hearing and addressed during direct examination.

Economic Reasons for Coming to the United States

The applicant may have chosen the United States as a country of refuge for a variety of reasons. The applicant may have friends or family members in the United States, or a desire to further his or her education, or he or she may have chosen the United States because of the freedoms enjoyed by its residents. It is also well known that may immigrants come to the United States to work. The applicant may have chosen the United States for any one or all of these reasons. If the applicant also came here believing that he or she would be able to find a job, in addition to fleeing the harm he or she experienced, the applicant should be truthful and acknowledge this. In answering, however, the applicant should reiterate the primary motive for leaving his or her home country.

Lack of Political Activity

Even though the applicant may not have been politically active in his or her home country, the applicant may still be eligible for asylum based on a political opinion imputed to him or her, or because of his or her race, religion, nationality, or membership in a particular social group. When the applicant is questioned about a lack of political activity, he or she should reiterate the basis for the asylum claim.

Failure to Mention an Event or Detail on the Asylum Application

When completing the asylum application, it is often useful to provide as many details as possible regarding the applicant's claim. Nevertheless, at the hearing, the applicant may (and almost always does) mention a fact or detail not included in the application. In response to a question by the DHS attorney regarding why the applicant failed to mention it on his or her asylum application, the applicant should offer an explanation. Was the applicant previously uncomfortable in speaking about a particular aspect of his or her claim? Did the applicant tell you and you decided to leave it out of the application? Or did the applicant, in preparing for the hearing, begin to remember more aspects and details regarding a particular event?

Inconsistencies in the Applicant's Testimony or Between the Testimony and the Application

We all make mistakes, but such mistakes could be fatal (literally) if they involve a material fact in the applicant's claim. Does the applicant have difficulty remembering? If so, the applicant should emphasize when answering questions that he or she has difficulty remembering and that the answers given are based on his or her recollection or are approximations. If the applicant makes a mistake when testifying or on his or her application, the applicant should state this in his or her answer. Individuals who have experienced or witnessed traumatic events may have difficulty remembering. If applicant is experiencing memory problems, you may wish to refer him or her for treatment. *See* appendix 6H. Applicants should also be advised that if the DHS attorney misstates their previous testimony or their statement on the application, they should correct such mistakes in their response.

Country Conditions

The applicant should be made aware of the country condition information submitted in his or her case. He or she also usually has firsthand knowledge of conditions in his or her country. Sometimes, however, the DHS attorney will ask a question that the applicant is unable to answer. The applicant should be instructed not to guess, and, if he or she is asked to guess, an objection should be made.

Misstatements Made upon Entry

The applicant may have made misstatements to an airport inspector or border patrol agent when he or she was apprehended. He or she may have made misrepresentations regarding his or her country of origin or reasons for coming to the United States. The applicant needs to explain why he or she made such statements. Occasionally, an applicant will claim that he or she did not make the misrepresentations that DHS claims were made. In such cases, it is important to request the opportunity to question the officer who reported that the applicant made such statements.

Failure to Apply for Asylum in Other Countries

Applicants may be questioned regarding whether they applied for asylum in any countries that they passed through en route to the United States. If the applicant did not apply in such countries, he or she will be asked why. Many applicants are unaware of asylum procedures in other countries or have fled their home countries with the intention of being reunited with friends and family members in the United States. The applicant should state his or her reasons for failing to apply in the countries he or she resided in or traveled through on the way to the United States.

Failure to Immediately Depart from the Country of Claimed Persecution

The applicant may have remained in his or her home country for several months or longer after he or she was harmed or threatened. It is important for the applicant to state when he or she decided to leave, the steps taken in arranging to leave, and the difficulties encountered in planning to leave.

Failure to Present Corroborating Evidence

The REAL ID Act imposes an even greater burden on the applicant to produce corroborating evidence in support of his or her claim. Often, it is unreasonable to expect the applicant to contact his or her home government, which has engaged in persecution, to corroborate the claim. Many times, individuals flee with little or nothing to prove their claim. The applicant should state any attempts made to locate corroborating evidence and, if no steps were taken, why it would be unreasonable to expect corroboration.

Manner of Entry

The applicant's manner of entry is almost always an issue in an asylum case. Did he or she enter legally on a valid passport? If so, DHS will argue either that the government is not really after the applicant because it would not have issued him or her a passport to leave the country or that the applicant committed fraud by telling a consular official overseas that he or she was coming to study or to visit as a tourist. Is the applicant better off in the eyes of DHS if he or she entered with a false passport and visa? Not really. DHS will argue that this is a person who lied to DHS inspectors at the airport to get into the United States and is probably lying now. What if the applicant resorted to using the services of a smuggler? DHS will ask detailed questions about the amount the applicant paid the smuggler and whether the smuggler informed him or her about what to say when seeking asylum. If the applicant is a victim of human traffickers, however, he or she may be eligible for a new form of relief under the Victims of Trafficking and Violence Protection Act. *See* chapter 6.1.

APPENDIX 5B

SAMPLE MOTION, SAMPLE PETITION FOR REVIEW, AND SAMPLE BRIEF

During the course of an asylum hearing in removal proceedings, it may become necessary to file one or more motions. You may wish to change venue if the applicant is released from detention or changes his or her address. Or you might want to reopen a case in which the applicant has been deported in absentia or in which his or her application for asylum has been previously denied. If the applicant is not removable from the United States and was erroneously placed in removal proceedings, you would, of course, file a motion to terminate proceedings. If the DHS trial attorney agrees with your position on a particular request, it is helpful to file a joint motion with the court. See appendix 6D for a list of telephone numbers and addresses of DHS chief counsel offices.

Most, if not all, immigration courts require that motions be submitted in writing. It is important to have a copy of the local immigration court rules before filing any motions. Copies may be obtained by contacting the immigration court or visiting the EOIR website at *www.usdoj.gov/eoir/efoia/ocij/locopproc.htm*. See appendix 6B for the telephone numbers and addresses of immigration courts throughout the United States.

If the motion or brief involves an issue that is novel or has been contested in other cases, you may be able to obtain sample motions or briefs on the issue from immigrant advocacy groups, or in some cases, directly from the attorneys who have prepared them. Some websites that maintain brief banks include: National Immigration Project of the National Lawyers Guild (*www.nationalimmigrationproject.org*), Center for Gender and Refugee Studies (*http://cgrs.uchastings.edu*), and The World Organization for Human Rights USA (*http://humanrightsusa.org*).

The sample motion in this appendix is a Motion to Change Venue. Rules and local practice regarding changes of venue vary from court to court and sometimes from judge to judge. If you are filing a motion to change venue and are unsure of the requirements, call the immigration court, as well as a local immigration attorney or local nonprofit agency, for more information. You should also read the most recent memorandum on changes of venue issued by the EOIR Office of the Chief Immigration Judge, "Operating Policy and Procedure Memorandum 01-02—Changes of Venue" (Oct. 9, 2001), available at *www.usdoj.gov/eoir/efoia/ocij/oppm01/OPPM01-02.pdf*.

Following the sample motion is a sample petition for review. The sample brief provided is the brief filed in *Matter of R–A–*, a gender-based, domestic violence asylum case. Sometimes immigration judges will request briefs from both parties on a narrow issue of law, such as whether an individual has been convicted of a particularly serious crime. A general brief regarding an applicant's eligibility for asylum and withholding may be submitted to the immigration judge prior to the hearing and is particularly useful in cases involving a novel legal argument.

Reminder: all motions and briefs must be filed with a certificate of service and must meet deadlines set by local operating procedures.

UNITED STATES DEPARTMENT OF JUSTICE
EXECUTIVE OFFICE FOR IMMIGRATION REVIEW
OFFICE OF THE IMMIGRATION JUDGE
HARLINGEN, TEXAS

In the Matter of:)
)   File No. A_____
_____   )
)   In Removal Proceedings
)
)
)

RESPONDENT'S MOTION REQUESTING CHANGE OF VENUE

    Respondent, _____, by and through her undersigned counsel, hereby requests this court to grant a change of venue of her removal hearing from Harlingen, Texas, to Houston, Texas, pursuant to 8 CFR §§1003.20 and 1240.1. Respondent requests a change of venue so that she may adequately prepare and present testimony in support of her request for asylum and withholding of removal. In support of this Motion, Respondent would show the following:

    1. Respondent currently resides at _____ St., Houston, TX _____, which is in the jurisdiction of the Houston Immigration Court.

    2. Respondent is represented by _____, an attorney who maintains her office at _____, Houston, TX, also within the jurisdiction of the Houston Immigration Court.

    3. Respondent has admitted the allegations of the Notice to Appear, conceded that she is removable, and has filed an application for asylum with this court.

    4. Because the issue of whether Respondent is removable has been resolved, there is no prejudice to the Department of Homeland Security if venue is changed to the Houston Immigration Court.

    5. In addition, Respondent's witnesses reside in the jurisdiction of the Houston Immigration Court. Moreover, Respondent is currently unemployed and is, therefore, unable to incur the cost of traveling to the Harlingen Immigration Court.

    6. Pursuant to *Baires v. INS*, 856 F.2d 89 (9th Cir. 1988) and *Chlomos v. U.S. Dept. of Justice*, 516 F.2d 310 (3d Cir. 1975), it would be an abuse of discretion to deny a change of venue in a case in which there would be little or no inconvenience to the government.

Based on the foregoing reasons, Respondent respectfully requests that venue in this case be changed to from Harlingen, Texas, to Houston, Texas.

Dated this _____ day of _____, 20___.

Respectfully submitted,

_____
Attorney for Respondent

[address]
[phone]

CERTIFICATE OF SERVICE

I certify that a true and correct copy of the foregoing Motion was served this _____ day of _____, 20___ on the DHS trial attorney at _____, Harlingen, TX by first-class U.S. mail, postage prepaid.

_____

UNITED STATES COURT OF APPEALS
FOR THE _____ CIRCUIT

_____)	
[name of Petitioner])	
)	
Petitioner,)	File No._____
)	
v.)	
)	A# _____
_____,)	
Attorney General,)	
)	
Respondent)	
_____)	

PETITION FOR REVIEW

The above named petitioner hereby petitions for the review of a final order of [deportation] [removal] entered by the Board of Immigration Appeals on _____ [date of BIA decision].

A copy of the BIA's decision is attached. To date, no court has upheld the validity of the order.

_____
[signature of attorney or petitioner]

Dated: _____

[(1) COMPLETE ALL BLANK SPACES EXCEPT "FILE NO.". THE COURT CLERK'S OFFICE WILL ASSIGN A NUMBER.
(2) ATTACH CERTIFICATE OF SERVICE AND THE BIA DECISIONS. CHECK LOCAL RULES FOR OTHER NECESSARY ATTACHMENTS.
(3) THIS DOCUMENT SHOULD BE SERVED ON THE ATTORNEY GENERAL, AND ON THE OFFICER OR EMPLOYEE OF DHS IN CHARGE OF THE DISTRICT IN WHICH THE FINAL ORDER OF REMOVAL WAS ENTERED. PETITIONER MAY ALSO WANT TO SERVE A COPY OF THE PETITION FOR REVIEW ON THE OFFICE OF IMMIGRATION LITIGATION, THE LOCAL DHS DISTRICT COUNSEL'S OFFICE, IF ANY, AND POSSIBLY THE LOCAL ICE REMOVAL OFFICERS.]

SAMPLE BRIEF

**UNITED STATES DEPARTMENT OF JUSTICE
ATTORNEY GENERAL JOHN ASHCROFT**

**BRIEF ON BEHALF OF RODI ALVARADO PEÑA
TO THE ATTORNEY GENERAL OF THE UNITED STATES**

Karen Musalo
Resident Scholar
University of California
Hastings College of Law
200 McAllister Street
San Francisco, CA 94102
(415) 565-4720

Attorney for Petitioner
Rodi Alvarado Peña

Table of Contents

	Page
Table of Authorities	i
I. Introduction and Procedural Background	1
II. Facts of the Case	4
III. Argument	9

1) Ms. Alvarado Has a Well-Founded Fear of Persecution on Account of her
   Social Group Membership and Political Opinion 9

    A. The Harm Ms. Alvarado Suffered Constitutes Persecution 9

    B. Ms. Alvarado was Persecuted on Account of her Membership in a
   Particular Social Group 11
   1. Ms. Alvarado s Social Group is Cognizable under the Law 12
   2. Ms. Alvarado was Persecuted on Account of her Social Group
      Membership 16

    C. Ms. Alvarado was Persecuted on Account of Her Political Opinion 20
   1. Ms. Alvarado s Resistance Constitutes a Political Opinion 22
   2. Ms. Alvarado was Persecuted on Account of her Political Opinion ... 24

    D. Ms. Alvarado has Suffered Atrocious Past Persecution and has
   Established a Well-founded fear of Future Persecution 25
   1. Ms. Alvarado has Established a Well-Founded Fear of Persecution ... 26
   2. Ms. Alvarado Qualifies for a Grant of Asylum Even in the Absence
      of a Well-founded Fear 29

IV. Conclusion 30

1) Ms. Alvarado Should be Granted Asylum 30

    A) Ms. Alvarado Should Be Granted Asylum on the Existing Record 30

    B) There are no Adverse Factors which Negatively Impact the Exercise
   of Discretion 32

Table of Authorities

Cases: Page

Matter of Acosta, 19 I. & N. Dec. 211 (BIA 1985) 12

Agbuya v. INS, 241 F.3d 1224 (9th Cir. 2001) 9

Ananeh-Firempong v. INS, 766 F.2d 621 (1st Cir. 1985) 12

Matter of B-, Int. Dec. 3251 (BIA 1995) 30

Baballah v. Ashcroft, 335 F.3d 981 (9th Cir. 2003) 17, 20

Bolanos-Hernandez v. INS, 767 F.2d 1277 (9th Cir. 1984) 17, 27

INS v. Cardoza-Fonseca, 480 U.S. 421 (1987) 27

Chang v. INS, 119 F.3d 1055 (3rd Cir. 1997) 23

Matter of Chen, 20 I. & N. Dec. 16 (BIA 1989) 29, 30

INS v. Elias-Zacarias, 502 U.S. 478 (1992) 16, 17

Fatin v. INS, 12 F.3d 1233 (3rd Cir. 1993) 12, 13, 15, 23

Gafoor v. INS, 231 F.3d 645 (9th Cir. 2000) 20

He v. Ashcroft, 328 F.3d 593 (9th Cir. 2003) 9

Hernandez-Montiel v. INS, 225 F.3d 1084 (9th Cir. 2000) 12

Hernandez-Ortiz v. INS, 777 F.2d 509 (9th Cir. 1995) 32

Matter of Kasinga, 21 I. & N. Dec. 357 (BIA 1996) .... *passim*

Kovac v. INS, 407 F.2d 102 (9th Cir. 1969) 9

Lal v. INS, 255 F.3d 998, *as amended*, 268 F.3d 1148 (9th Cir. 2001) 20, 29, 30

Lazo-Majano v. INS, 813 F.2d 1432 (9th Cir. 1987) 23, 29

Lopez-Galarza v. INS, 99 F.3d 954 (9th Cir. 1996) 29, 30

Lukwago v. Ashcroft, 329 F.3d 157 (3rd Cir. 2003) 15

Lwin v. INS, 144 F.3d 505 (7th Cir. 1998) 12, 15

Matter of Mogharrabi, 19 I. & N. Dec. 439 (BIA 1987) 12, 26, 27

Navas v. INS, 217 F.3d 646 (9th Cir. 2000) 9

Osorio v. INS, 18 F.3d 1017 (2nd Cir. 1994) 23

Rios v. Ashcroft, 287 F.3d 895 (9th Cir. 2002) 9, 17

Safaie v. INS, 25 F.3d 636 (8th Cir. 1994) 13

Sanchez-Trujillo v. INS, 801 F.2d 1571 (9th Cir. 1986) 12

Shoafera v. INS, 228 F.3d 1070 (9th Cir. 2000) 9

Singh v. INS, 94 F.3d 1353 (9th Cir. 1996) 9

Matter of S-P-, 21 I. & N. Dec. 486 (BIA 1996) 16, 17

INS v. Stevic, 467 U.S. 407 (1984) 27

Statutes & Regulations:

Immigration & Nationality Act § 101(a)(42)(A), 8 U.S.C. § 1101(a)(42)(A) (2003) 9

8 C.F.R. § 208.13 25

8 C.F.R. § 1208.13 .... 26, 29

Secondary Authority:

A) Legal Materials

Department of Justice, Immigration and Naturalization Service, *Asylum and Witholding Definitions*, 65 Fed. Reg. 76588 (Dec. 7, 2000) .... *passim*

Attorney General s Order No. 2379-2001 (January 19, 2001) 2

Phyllis Coven, Department of Justice, Immigration and Naturalization Service, Office of
International Affairs, *Considerations for Asylum Officers Adjudicating Asylum
Claims From Women* (1995) 10, 11, 13

Department of Justice, Immigration and Naturalization Service, *U.S. Law and INS
Refugee/Asylum Adjudications:* THE BASIC LAW MANUAL (1994) 10

INS v. Vallabhaneni, A76-724-694 (Transcript of June 21, 2001, BIA hearing en banc) 3

B) Scholarly Articles & Human Rights Materials

Copelon, Rhonda, *Recognizing the Egregious in the Everyday: Domestic Violence as
Torture*, 25 COLUM. HUM. RTS. L. REV. 291 (1994) 18

Kimberle Williams Crenshaw, *Mapping the Margins: Intersectionality, Identity Politics,
and Violence Against Women of Color, in* THE PUBLIC NATURE OF PRIVATE
VIOLENCE: THE DISCOVERY OF DOMESTIC ABUSE (1994) 20

R. Emerson Dobash and Russell Dobash, VIOLENCE AGAINST WIVES (1979) 21

Karl Hempel, M.D., *Domestic Violence*, THE HEALTH GAZETTE (1998) 20

Lawyers Committee for Human Rights, *Critique: Review of the U.S. Department of State's
Country Reports on Human Rights Practices for 1994* (July 1995) 7

V. Michael McKenzie, *Domestic Violence in America* (1995) 25

Thomas, Dorothy Q. and Michele E. Beasley, *Domestic Violence as a Human Rights
Issue*, 58 ALBANY L. REV. 1119 (1995) 18

Jennifer Tisdale, "Abuse of Women in Today's Guatemala," Guatemala Human Rights
Commission/USA, *Guatemala Bulletin* (Fourth Quarter 1992) 6

International Authority:

A) Cases & Statutes

*Islam (A.P.) v. Secretary of State for the Home Dept., and Regina v. Immigration
Appeal Tribunal and Another Ex Parte Shah (A.P.)*, [1999] 2 W.L.R. 1015
(House of Lords) (United Kingdom) 12, 19

Minister for Immigration and Multicultural Affairs v. Khawar [2002] HCA 14

(Australian High Court) 19

Refugee Appeal No. 71427/99, (Refugee Status Appeals Authority 2000)
(New Zealand) 12, 19

Canada (Attorney General) v. Ward, [1993] 2 S.C.R. 689 12

Refugee Act 1996 (Ireland) 11

Refugees Act 1998, Act No. 130 ¶1(xxi) (South Africa) 11

B) Governmental Asylum Guidelines

Department of Immigration and Multicultural Affairs, *Refugee and Humanitarian Visa Applicants: Guidelines on Gender Issues for Decision Makers* (July 1996) (Australia) 11

Immigration and Refugee Board of Canada, *Guideline 4: Women Refugee Claimants Fearing Gender-Related Persecution: Update* (Nov. 25, 1996) 11

Immigration Appeal Authority, *Asylum Gender Guidelines* (November 2000) (United Kingdom) 11

C) United Nations Materials

UNHCR, Guidelines on International Protection: Gender-Related Persecution within the context of Article 1A(2) of the 1951 Convention and/or its 1967 Protocol relating to the Status of Refugees (HCR/GIP/02/01, 7 May 2002) 11

UNHCR, Guidelines on International Protection: Membership in a Particular Social Group within the context of Article 1A(2) of the 1951 Convention and/or its 1967 Protocol relating to the Status of Refugees (HCR/GIP/02/02, 7 May 2002) 11, 19

UN Commission on Human Rights, 52nd Sess., Item 9 (a) of the Provisional Agenda, *1996 Report of the Special Rapporteur on Violence Against Women, its Causes and Consequences*, Resolution 1995/85, E/CN.4/1996/53 (1996) 10, 21

UN Declaration on the Elimination of Violence against Women, G.A. Res. 48/104, U.N. GAOR Supp. (No. 49), at 217, U.N. Doc. A/48/49 (1993) 23

I. Introduction and Procedural Background

Ms. Rodi Alvarado Peña [Ms. Alvarado or Respondent] was subjected to more than ten years of unspeakably brutal violence at the hands of her husband, Francisco Osorio. (Record (Rec.) at 4-6.)[1] The violence which Osorio inflicted upon her caused severe physical injury and extreme mental anguish. (Rec. at 693-705.) Ms. Alvarado could neither escape Osorio within Guatemala, nor secure any protection whatsoever from the official authorities. (Rec. at 241-43; 700-02.) None of these facts are in dispute.

On the basis of this record, on September 20, 1996, an Immigration Judge (IJ) granted Ms. Alvarado asylum in the United States. (Rec. at 197.) The IJ ruled that the harm she suffered constituted persecution, that the government of Guatemala was unwilling to protect her, and that the persecution was on account of two of the required statutory grounds social group membership and political opinion. (Rec. at 190-97.) The social group was defined by nationality, gender, and marital status (Guatemalan women, who have been involved intimately with Guatemalan male companions, who believe that women are to live under male domination) (Rec. at 193), and the political opinion was that of opposition to male domination. (Rec. at 196.)

The former Immigration and Naturalization Service (INS) appealed the decision. On June 11, 1999, in a sharply divided 10-5 vote, the BIA reversed the IJ s grant of asylum to Ms. Alvarado. (Rec. at 27.) The Board accepted that the husband s violent abuses rose to the level of persecution, and that Ms. Alvarado had been unable to obtain state protection. (Rec. at 11.) However, the BIA majority rejected the IJ s ruling that the persecution was on account of social

---

[1] Note that all citations to the record are to the Certified Administrative Record produced for the appeal from the June 1999 BIA decision to the Ninth Circuit Court of Appeals, which appeal was later stayed.

group membership and political opinion. (Rec. at 11-27.)

Counsel for Ms. Alvarado filed a timely Petition for Review with the Ninth Circuit Court of Appeals on July 9, 1999, and simultaneously sought certification of the decision by then Attorney General Janet Reno. The Ninth Circuit Court of Appeals stayed proceedings pending a decision by Attorney General Reno on the request for certification. In December 2000 and January 2001, the Department of Justice (DOJ) and Attorney General Reno took two separate but related actions related to Ms. Alvarado s case. On December 7, 2000, the DOJ issued a Proposed Rule[2] which directly addresses the issues raised in Ms. Alvarado s case, and on January 19, 2001, the Attorney General accepted certification, vacated the BIA s decision, and directed the Board to decide the case pursuant to this rule, when issued in final form.[3] The Commentary to the Proposed Rule explicitly states that it removes certain barriers that the *In re R-A-* decision seems to pose to claims that domestic violence, against which a government is either unwilling or unable to provide protection, rises to the level of persecution of a person on account of membership in a particular social group.[4] The Proposed Rule, which is now under the jurisdiction of the

---

[2] Department of Justice, Immigration and Naturalization Service, *Asylum and Withholding Definitions*, 65 Fed. Reg. 76588 (Dec. 7, 2000) [hereinafter Proposed Regulation or Proposed Rule].

[3] The order reads as follows:
Pursuant to 8 C.F.R. § 3.1(h)(1)(iii), the Acting Commissioner of the Immigration and Naturalization Service has referred to the Attorney General for review the June 11, 1999, decision of the Board of Immigration Appeals (Board) that overturned the Immigration Judge s decision dated September 20, 1996. The June 11, 1999 decision of the Board is hereby vacated and the matter is remanded to the Board for reconsideration. I direct the Board to stay reconsideration of the decision until after the proposed rule published at 65 Fed. Red. 76588 (Dec. 7, 2000) is published in final form. The Board should then reconsider the decision in light of the final rule.
Attorney General s Order No. 2379-2001 (January 19, 2001).

[4] Supplementary Information to Proposed Regulation, *supra* note 2, at 76589 [hereinafter Commentary].

Department of Homeland Security (DHS), has not yet been published in final form; however, the government is on record as stating that the regulation represents its best interpretation of the refugee definition.[5]

On February 21, 2003, Attorney General John Ashcroft directed the Board of Immigration Appeals to certify to him the decision in *Matter of R-A-*. On March 24, 2003, Ms. Alvarado's counsel requested permission to brief the issues, and asked for clarification as to whether the Proposed Rule continued to represent the agency's best interpretation of the refugee definition. The request for clarification noted that meaningful briefing requires that counsel be put on notice of any departure from this position.[6] The request to brief was denied by the Attorney General on September 5, 2003, and on November 4, 2003, 62 members of the House of Representatives made an appeal to the Attorney General that he allow briefing; their request was representative of sustained Congressional interest in the case and the issues it raises regarding the protection of women victims of gender violence.[7] On December 8, 2003, Attorney General Ashcroft issued an

---

[5] Among the forums in which this position has been stated for the record include before the BIA during the June 21, 2001, en banc argument of the case, *INS v. Vallabhaneni*, A76-724-694 (Transcript of June 21, 2001, BIA hearing en banc, at 45-46).

[6] The letter stated:
[C]larification is necessary regarding the status of the Proposed Rule. The DOJ has publicly taken the position that the Proposed Rule represents its interpretation of the refugee definition. Counsel requests clarification as to whether this continues to be the DOJ's position, and whether it is the position of the Department of Homeland Security (DHS). Meaningful briefing requires that counsel be put on notice of any departure from this position.
Letter from Karen Musalo to Attorney General John Ashcroft, dated March 24, 2003.

[7] In addition to the letters regarding the denial of briefing from members of Congress, *see* (1) Letter of May 2, 2003, to Attorney General John Ashcroft and Department of Homeland Security Secretary Thomas J. Ridge from 15 members of the Senate (in support of gender-based asylum and expressing concern about Rodi Alvarado's case); (2) Letter of February 27, 2003, to Attorney General Ashcroft from 49 members of the House of Representatives (in support of gender-based asylum and expressing concern about Rodi Alvarado's case); (3) Letter of September 29, 2000, to Attorney General Janet Reno from eight

order for both parties to submit briefs; this brief is submitted pursuant to that order. There have been no official statements by DOJ or DHS that the Proposed Rule no longer represents the government's position; thus it will be assumed that it continues to represent the government's best interpretation of the refugee definition.

II. Facts of the Case

The facts of Ms. Alvarado's claim for asylum are undisputed; both the immigration judge and the BIA found Ms. Alvarado to be credible in all respects. Ms. Alvarado was sixteen years of age when she married her husband Francisco Osorio, a former soldier in the Guatemalan military. From the inception of their marriage Osorio subjected her to violent physical and sexual abuse. He would "hit or kick Ms. Alvarado whenever he felt like it, wherever [they] happened to be: in the house, on the street, on the bus." (Rec. at 694.) He would mistreat her when he was drunk and when he was sober. (Rec. at 328.) Her husband dislocated her jaw when her menstrual period was 15 days late (Rec. at 694); kicked her violently in the spine when she failed to heed his demand that she abort her three to four month old fetus (Rec. at 694); kicked her in her genital

---

members of the Senate (urging immediate action to reverse the Board's denial in *Matter of R-A-*); (4) Letter of September 18, 2000, to Attorney General Janet Reno from 54 members of the House of Representatives (in support of gender-based asylum and requesting a meeting to discuss the issue); (5) Letter of February 14, 2000, to Attorney General Reno from seven members of the Senate (asking the Attorney General to reverse the BIA's decision in an honor killing case, referring to *Matter of R- A-* and expressing concern that "the BIA lacks sufficient understanding of current standards in both United States asylum law and policy and international human rights law."); (6) Letter of December 2, 1999, to Attorney General Reno from five members of the Senate, asking the Attorney General to clarify the gender guidelines for asylum and reinstate the grant in *Matter of R-A-*); (7) Letter of September 16, 1999, to Attorney General Reno from 53 members of the House of Representatives (expressing concern about the denial of asylum to Rodi Alvarado and asking the Attorney General to reinstate the grant in *Matter of R-A-*); (8) Letter of July 22, 1999, to Attorney General Janet Reno from the Congressional Hispanic Caucus (supporting Ms. Alvarado's asylum claim and requesting certification of *Matter of R-A-*).

area so violently that she suffered internal hemorrhaging (Rec. at 695); and brutally raped her time and time again, both vaginally and anally, beating her before and during the unwanted sex. (Rec. at 694-95.) Osorio, who had guns and knives at his ready disposal, pistol-whipped Ms. Alvarado, broke windows and mirrors with her head, punched, and slapped her, threatened her with his machete, and dragged her down the street by her hair. (Rec. at 697-700.)

Ms. Alvarado's efforts to escape her husband within Guatemala were futile. She sought refuge at her brother's and parents' homes, but her husband was always able to track her down. (Rec. at 238.) On one occasion, in the hope of evading her husband, Ms. Alvarado took her older child out of school, and rented a room outside of the city. Although she told no one where she had gone, Osorio found her, and proceeded to beat and kick her into unconsciousness in front of their two children. (Rec. at 696-97.)

After more than ten years of this violent abuse, Ms. Alvarado decided that the only way to save her life was to flee Guatemala. (Rec. 702-03.) This was a very wrenching decision for her, because in leaving, she had to abandon the people she care[d] about most — her family and her two year old son, and seven year old daughter. (Rec. at 705.) Although the pain of separation was, and continues to be, tremendous, Ms. Alvarado believes it is for the best, because if her husband had succeeded in his efforts to kill her, her children would have no mother at all. (Rec. at 706.)

Osorio repeatedly expressed his opinion that he had the right to treat Ms. Alvarado as he did, because of her gender and their relationship; the abuse was accompanied by statements such as "You're my woman, you do what I say" (Rec. at 696), "You're my woman, and I can do whatever I want" (Rec. at 695), "You don't order me" (Rec. at 694), and "I can do it if I want to. (Rec. at 697.)

As this record makes abundantly clear, Osorio was correct in his assertions that because Ms. Alvarado was his woman he could do to her whatever he wanted with complete impunity. Neither the police nor the courts of Guatemala intervened once over the entire course of this decade-long brutal marital relationship. The police did not come when called by a desperate Ms. Alvarado on the telephone, and they never took any steps to arrest Osorio or require him to appear in response to written complaints which Ms. Alvarado filed. (Rec. at 700-02.) Osorio enjoyed the same impunity within the court system; when Ms. Alvarado went before a judge, he told her that he would not interfere in domestic matters or disputes. (Rec. at 243.) The police had communicated essentially the same thing, telling Ms. Alvarado that they would not provide her any assistance because she should take care of it at home. (Rec. at 700.)

Extensive record evidence on country conditions in Guatemala demonstrates that the absolute failure of protection to Ms. Alvarado by law enforcement and judicial personnel is not an aberration. To the contrary, such failure of protection is the norm, and reflects deeply entrenched attitudes regarding the subordinate status of women in Guatemalan society. Women suffer *de jure* as well as the *de facto* discrimination. The Guatemalan Civil Code accords legal primacy to the husband in the marital relationship;[8] such provisions have led international bodies to express

---

[8] Rec. at 739:
Guatemalan women are even discriminated against legally. The Guatemalan civil code [sic] recognizes the male as a married couple s legal representative...A husband can legally forbid his wife to engage in activities outside the home. The husband also has the primary authority in disposing of joint property.

Jennifer Tisdale, Abuse of Women in Today s Guatemala, Guatemala Human Rights Commission/USA, *Guatemala Bulletin*, Fourth Quarter 1992.

concern over the discrimination institutionalized in law in Guatemala.[9] Beyond the Guatemalan Civil Code, many other norms in Guatemalan law are discriminatory and contradict the principle of equality guaranteed in the Constitution. (Rec. at 737.) These *de jure* denials of equality are compounded by discrimination in the administration of justice and application of the law. (Rec. at 737.)

Gross gender inequality in Guatemala is not a recent phenomena; women historically have been oppressed, (Rec. at 739) and cultural norms persist that conceive of women as subordinate to men[.] (Rec. at 737.) All of this has led to a situation wherein the conditions women live in are among the worst in Latin America. (Rec. at 739.) The education of women is considered unimportant because [a woman s] place is [in] the home. (Rec. at 742.) More than 80% of the illiterate persons in Guatemala are female (Rec. at 742), and the country has the highest rate of females without formal education in all of Latin America. (Rec. at 742.)

The *de jure* and *de facto* subordinate status of women is inextricably related to the broad acceptance of violence against them; this violence is tolerated...and legitimized by laws and customs (Rec. at 736) and what is culturally taught and learned about what a woman is and the role she must play are significant factors sustaining...violence toward women[.] (Rec. at 744.)

---

[9] Rec. at 398:
Members of the UN Committee on the Elimination of Discrimination against Women reported in April that Guatemala s report and presentation to the Committee increased their concern at the discrimination institutionalized in law. They also expressed alarm that Guatemala s Constitutional Court had ruled that none of the country s Civil Code required change, despite Guatemala s ratification of the Convention on the Elimination of Discrimination against Women, which was automatically incorporated into domestic law and requires that states not discriminate on the basis of gender.

Lawyers Committee for Human Rights, *Critique: Review of the U.S. Department of State s Country Reports on Human Rights Practices for 1994* (July 1995).

Domestic violence has reached epidemic proportions in Guatemala; a 1990 survey of 1,000 women reported that 48% had been battered by their partners, who used [f]ists, feet, knives, razor blades, sledge hammers and pieces of wood to attack them. (Rec. at 423.) Out of every ten women murdered, four are killed by their husbands. (Rec. at 740.) Other statistics are equally grim: an officer of a Fire Fighters Corps responsible for women and children...determined that in a six hour shift, 90 per cent of women treated for physical injuries had been attacked by their partners (Rec. at 423), and a doctor reported that 75 per cent of women admitted to his hospital with injuries were victims of spousal abuse. (Rec. at 423.)

Although they are the victims of these brutal assaults, women are most often portrayed as the provocator[s] of the abuse (Rec. at 425), reinforcing the societal attitudes of discrimination and ignorance regarding the human rights of women[.] (Rec. at 425.) As was Ms. Alvarado s experience, women who turn to the police or the courts confront the attitude that domestic violence is not a real problem, or even a human rights violation. (Rec. at 429.) Both the police and the courts generally encourage women seeking their help to keep the problem to themselves. (Rec. at 429.) As of 1994, a year before Ms. Alvarado fled Guatemala, there were no shelters for battered women in the country. (Rec. at 431.)

III. Argument

1) Ms. Alvarado Has a Well-Founded Fear of Persecution on Account of her Social Group Membership and Political Opinion

In order to qualify for refugee status, an individual is required to show that she has suffered past persecution or has a well-founded fear of future persecution on account of race, religion, nationality, political opinion or membership in a particular social group. Immigration & Nationality Act (INA) § 101(a)(42)(A), 8 U.S.C. § 1101(a)(42)(A) (2003). The persecution must be by the government, or individuals that the government is unable or unwilling to control. *He v. Ashcroft*, 328 F.3d 593, 603 (9th Cir. 2003); *Navas v. INS*, 217 F.3d 646, 655-56 (9th Cir. 2000) . As the uncontroverted evidence in this case establishes, Ms. Alvarado meets the refugee definition because she has been persecuted, and reasonably fears future persecution, on account of her memberhip in a gender-defined particular social group, and on account of her political opinion of resistance to the brutal abuse meted out by her husband; this abuse occurred in a situation where the government of Guatemala failed to provide even the least measure of protection.

A. The Harm Ms. Alvarado Suffered Constitutes Persecution

Courts have long held that threats to life or freedom, or other egregious physical and psychological harms, inflicted by the government or by persons the government is unable or unwilling to control, constitute persecution. *See, e.g., He v. Ashcroft, supra; Rios v. Ashcroft*, 287 F.3d 895, 900 (9th Cir. 2002); *Agbuya v. INS*, 241 F.3d 1224 (9th Cir. 2001), *Shoafera v. INS*, 228 F.3d 1070 (9th Cir. 2000), *Singh v. INS*, 94 F.3d 1353 (9th Cir. 1996), *Kovac v. INS*, 407 F.2d 102, 105-07 (9th Cir. 1969).

Because domestic abuse involves severe and repeated physical and psychological harm that poses an immediate threat to a woman s life and freedom, the Department of Justice has expressly recognized domestic violence as a type of mistreatment that constitutes persecution under U.S. asylum laws.[10] Indeed, because of its severe nature and intentional infliction by its perpetrator, the harm resulting from domestic violence has been found so abhorrent as to fit the definition of torture.[11]

Throughout the litigation of this case, neither the government (previously the INS) nor the BIA has contested that the harm Ms. Alvarado suffered was more than sufficient (Rec. at 11) to constitute persecution. Likewise, neither the government nor the BIA contested that Ms. Alvarado was unable to avail herself of any assistance from the government. And they could not have reasonably done so: the utter failure of the Guatemalan government to respond is established through Ms. Alvarado's account of her repeated but futile attempts to obtain assistance from the police and courts, coupled with the documentary evidence that government officials do not view domestic violence as a real problem, or even a human rights violation. (Rec. at 429.) Given the severity of the physical and psychological abuse she suffered, and the extreme degree, intensity, duration and frequency of that harm, there can be no question that Ms. Alvarado was persecuted within the meaning of the statute.

---

[10] *See* Phyllis Coven, Department of Justice, Immigration and Naturalization Service, Office of International Affairs, *Considerations for Asylum Officers Adjudicating Asylum Claims From Women* 4 (1995); Rec. at 649-52 [DOJ Gender Guidelines]; Department of Justice, Immigration and Naturalization Service, *U.S. Law and INS Refugee/Asylum Adjudications:* THE BASIC LAW MANUAL (1994).

[11] *See* U.N. Commission On Human Rights, 52nd Sess., Item 9 (a) of the Provisional Agenda, *1996 Report of the Special Rapporteur on Violence Against Women, its Causes and Consequences*, Resolution 1995/85, E/CN.4/1996/53 (1996), at 14, ¶ 50 (indicating that domestic violence should be understood and treated as a form of torture).

B. Ms. Alvarado was Persecuted on Account of her Membership in a Particular Social Group

The IJ who granted Ms. Alvarado protection ruled that the brutal domestic violence she suffered was causally linked to her membership in a social group defined by the characteristics of gender, marital status, and nationality. The judge's recognition of a gender-defined social group, and her finding of a nexus between the harm and the described group, is based on well-established precedent, and is fully supported by the record in this case. Furthermore, the recognition that claims of gender-persecution come within the protection of the refugee definition, is consistent with international trends,[12] and has been affirmed by the most recent guidance from the Office of the United Nations High Commissioner for Refugees.[13]

---

[12] Among the countries accepting gender claims are Australia, Austria, Canada, Germany, New Zealand, Spain, the United Kingdom, and the United States. *See infra* notes 16, 33; International Gender Asylum Decisions and Law, available at <http://www.uchastings.edu/cgrs/law/intl.html>. Countries with legislation specific to asylum claims based on gender-based persecution includes Ireland, Denmark and South Africa. *See, e.g.,* Refugee Act 1996 ¶ 1 (Ireland) (defining social group to include "a group of persons whose defining characteristic is their belonging to the female or the male sex...."); Refugees Act 1998, Act No. 130 ¶ 1(xxi) (South Africa) (defining social group to include "a group of persons of particular gender...."); *see also* International Gender Asylum Decisions and Law, *supra*. Gender guidelines for asylum claims have been issued by a wide range of countries, led by the United States and Canada. *See, e.g.,* DOJ Gender Guidelines, *supra* note 10; Immigration and Refugee Board of Canada, *Guideline 4: Women Refugee Claimants Fearing Gender-Related Persecution: Update* (Nov. 25, 1996); Immigration Appeal Authority, *Asylum Gender Guidelines* (November 2000) (United Kingdom), available at <http://www.iaa.gov.uk/32.htm>; Australian Department of Immigration and Multicultural Affairs, *Refugee and Humanitarian Visa Applicants: Guidelines on Gender Issues for Decision Makers* (July 1996), available at <http://www.uchastings.edu/cgrs/law/guidelines/aust.pdf>. Other countries with gender guidelines include the Netherlands, Norway, and Sweden. *See* Governmental Gender Guidelines for Asylum Adjudicators, available at <http://www.uchastings.edu/cgrs/law/guidelines.html>.

[13] UNHCR, Guidelines on International Protection: Gender-Related Persecution within the context of Article 1A(2) of the 1951 Convention and/or its 1967 Protocol relating to the Status of Refugees (HCR/GIP/02/01, 7 May 2002) (hereinafter "UNHCR Gender Guidelines"); UNHCR, Guidelines on International Protection: Membership in a Particular Social Group within the context of Article 1A(2) of the 1951 Convention and/or its 1967 Protocol relating to the Status of Refugees , ¶ 19 (HCR/GIP/02/02, 7 May 2002) (hereinafter "UNHCR Social Group Guidelines").

1. Ms. Alvarado's Social Group is Cognizable under the Law

In its seminal *Acosta*[14] decision, the BIA ruled that for the particular social group ground to be interpreted consistently with the other statutory grounds, the defining characteristics of the group must be either immutable or fundamental. The immutable/fundamental criteria test is widely accepted by federal courts across the United States,[15] and has been frequently cited with approval by foreign tribunals.[16] It has recently been adopted by the Ninth Circuit,[17] as an alternative to its long-standing voluntary associational relationship [18] test, and it has been incorporated into the Proposed Rule.[19]

The social group recognized by the IJ in Ms. Alvarado's case is defined by gender, marital status, and nationality, each of which meet the *Acosta* criteria. First, the BIA in *Acosta* explicitly identified sex as the type of immutable or fundamental characteristic by which a social group

---

[14] *Matter of Acosta,* 19 I. & N. Dec. 211 (BIA 1985), *overruled on other grounds by Matter of Mogharrabi,* 19 I. & N. Dec. 439 (BIA 1987).

[15] *See, e.g., Lwin v. INS,* 144 F.3d 505, 511-112 (7th Cir. 1998) (applying *Acosta* to find that Burmese students share common immutable characteristics); *Fatin v. INS,* 12 F.3d 1233 (3rd Cir. 1993) (gender could define a social group pursuant to *Acosta*); *Ananeh-Firempong v. INS,* 766 F.2d 621 (1st Cir. 1985) (individuals of a specific ethnic group associated with the former government constitute a particular social group).

[16] *See, e.g., Islam (A.P.) v. Secretary of State for the Home Dept., and Regina v. Immigration Appeal Tribunal and Another Ex Parte Shah (A.P.),* [1999] 2 W.L.R. 1015 (House of Lords) (United Kingdom) (relying on and quoting *Acosta*'s influential, important and seminal reasoning) (Opinions of Lord Steyn, Lord Hoffman and Lord Hope); Refugee Appeal No. 71427/99, ¶97 (Refugee Status Appeals Authority 2000) (New Zealand) (relying on the good working rule from *Acosta*); *Canada (Attorney General) v. Ward,* [1993] 2 S.C.R. 689, 736-37 (discussing and quoting from *Acosta* at length).

[17] *Hernandez-Montiel v. INS,* 225 F.3d 1084, 1092-93 (9th Cir. 2000).

[18] *Sanchez-Trujillo v. INS,* 801 F.2d 1571 (9th Cir. 1986).

[19] Proposed Regulations, *supra* note 2, at 76598.

could be defined. In 1996 the BIA applied that principle in its landmark *Kasinga* ruling, where it held that a social group defined by gender in combination with other chacteristics is cognizable. *Matter of Kasinga,* 21 I. & N. Dec. 357 (BIA 1996). The social group in *Kasinga* was defined by gender, ethnicity, bodily integrity, and opposition to female genital mutilation ([y]oung women of the Tchamba-Kunsuntu Tribe who have not had FGM, as practiced by the tribe, and who oppose the practice. *Id.* at 365.

The federal courts have also recognized that gender could appropriately define a particular social group under U.S. asylum laws. *See Fatin v. INS*, 12 F.3d 1233, 1240-41 (3rd Cir. 1993); *Safaie v. INS*, 25 F.3d 636, 640 (8th Cir. 1994) (We agree with the Third Circuit that a group of women, who refuse to conform... may well satisfy the definition.). Notably, prior to the Board s decision in *Kasinga,* the DOJ itself observed that the *Acosta* social group formulation supported the cognizability of a social group based on gender, either alone or as part of a combination.[20] The Commentary to the Proposed Rule affirms the viability of gender-defined social groups, stating that to be immutable, the common trait must be unchangeable, or truly fundamental to an applicant s identity. Gender is clearly such an immutable trait. [21]

Second, although marital status is not inherently immutable, there are circumstances such as prevail in Ms. Alvarado s case where marital status constitutes an immutable trait.[22] Ms. Alvarado s brutal and domineering husband simply would not permit her to leave the

---

[20] DOJ Gender Guidelines, *supra* note 10, at 13-15; Rec. at 649-52.

[21] Commentary, *supra* note 4, at 76593.

[22] The Commentary to the Proposed Rule recognizes this principle, stating that there may be circumstances in which an applicant s marital status could be considered immutable. *Id.*

relationship, and there was no one in Guatemala who would intervene on her behalf. Osorio transformed what should have been a consensual relationship into one that was immutable, and he could do this because the authorities of Guatemala abdicated their responsibility to protect Ms. Alvarado. Osorio hunted her down every time she attempted to leave him, and told her on numerous occasions that she could neither escape him in life[23] or in death.[24] His threats continued even after she fled Guatemala; Ms. Alvarado's sister recounted in a letter that Osorio had said "if she comes back, I will not let her live." (Rec. at 686.)

Osorio could both make and carry through on his threats with impunity because of the institutionalized discrimination against women in Guatemala, and the absolute failure of governmental protection. (Rec. at 429-30, 736-37, 739, 742, 744.) It is in this respect that nationality becomes a defining characteristic of the social group: it acts as a limiting and contextualizing factor to the characteristics of gender and marital status, an explicit recognition that social group cognizability is not determined in the abstract, but in the context of particular countries, societies and cultures.

---

[23] On one occasion Ms. Alvarado told Osorio she wanted to get far away from him so he could not find her. He replied:

[Y]ou will suffer much worse than what I have done to you so far...If you ever try to leave, I will come find you. And when I find you, I could kill you, but I'm not going to do that. I will break your legs. I will cripple you so that you will be in a wheelchair for the rest of your life. I will mark your face so it will be scarred forever, it will be twisted and deformed.

(Rec. at 704.)

On another occasion Osorio pulled out a machete in the middle of the night, and taunted her, saying:

Just you wait, you can't hide, even if you are buried underground, you can't hide from me...you can't get away...I will cut off your legs so you can't get away any more.

(Rec. at 698.)

[24] Once when Ms. Alvarado was so desperate about her circumstances that she attempted to take her own life, through an overdose, Osorio said, "If you want to die, go ahead. But from here, you are not going to leave." (Rec. at 699-700.)

The inclusion of nationality as a characteristic of Ms. Alvarado's social group is analogous to the inclusion of tribal affiliation (*e.g.*, "women of the Tchamba-Kunsuntu Tribe") as a social group characteristic in the *Kasinga* decision. In each case the characteristic limits the social group from the potentially larger group; in *Kasinga*, the characteristic of tribal affiliation limited the social group from a larger group defined solely by gender, intact genitalia and opposition to female genital mutilation. In Ms. Alvarado's case, the characteristic of nationality limits the group from one defined exclusively by gender and marital status without reference to geographical limits. Characteristics that reference country or region can be found as a matter of routine in refugee cases involving the particular social group ground. *See, e.g., Lukwago v. Ashcroft*, 329 F.3d 157, 171 (3rd Cir. 2003) ("social group of children *from Northern Uganda* who are abducted and enslaved ... ") (emphasis added); *Lwin*, 144 F.3d at 512 ("social group of parents of *Burmese* student dissidents") (emphasis added); *Fatin*, 12 F.3d at 1241 ("social group of *Iranian* women who refuse to conform") (emphasis added).

The Proposed Rule explicitly adopts an approach which incorporates the evaluation of societal conditions, norms and attitudes into the determination of social group cognizability. Included in its list of "factors that may be considered... in deciding whether a particular social group exists" [25] are whether the "group is recognized to be a societal faction or is otherwise a recognized segment of the population *in the country in question*" or whether "*the society in which the group exists* distinguishes members of the group for different treatment or status than is accorded to other members of the society." [26]

---

[25] Proposed Regulations, *supra* note 2, at 76594.

[26] *Id.* at 76598 (emphasis added).

These factors from the Proposed Rule lend further support to the cognizability of Ms. Alvarado s social group. The record in this case establishes that in Guatemala, women as a recognized segment of the population are singled out for different (*i.e.*, discriminatory) treatment. Women who are married are subject to discrimination on the basis of both their gender and their marital status. The bias is enshrined in the laws, where women have lesser rights than men. (Rec. at 739.) It is evidenced in the discrimination in the administration of justice and application of the law (Rec. at 737) which allow the police and the courts to respond dismissively to their serious complaints of maimings and death threats by their husbands. And it is evident in the pervasive and persistent attitudes that women [are] subordinate to men. (Rec. at 737.) The Commentary to the Proposed Rule specifically notes the relevance of evidence that the institutions of the society at hand offer fewer protections or benefits to members of the group than to other members of society. [27] This is certainly the case for women in Guatemala.

2. Ms. Alvarado was Persecuted on Account of her Social Group Membership

The statutory language on account of requires that there be a causal relationship, or nexus, between the persecution and one of the enumerated grounds. Nexus is established when the persecutor is motivated by a cognizable ground in inflicting the harm, or the harm is directed at the applicant because of the protected characteristic. *INS v. Elias-Zacarias*, 502 U.S. 478, 482-83 (1992); *Kasinga*, 21 I. & N. Dec. 357; *Matter of S-P-*, 21 I. & N. Dec. 486 (BIA 1996).

> [A]n applicant does not bear the unreasonable burden of establishing the exact motivation of a persecutor where different reasons for actions are possible. *Matter of Fuentes*, 19 I&N Dec. 658, 662 (BIA 1988). Rather, an asylum applicant bear[s] the burden of

---

[27] *Id.* at 76594.

establishing facts on which a reasonable person would fear that the danger arises on account of his race, religion, nationality, membership in a particular social group, or political opinion.

Id. at 489-90. Further, it is well-established that nexus may be established by either direct or circumstantial evidence. *Elias-Zacarias*, 502 U.S. at 482-83; *Baballah v. Ashcroft*, 335 F.3d 981, 990 (9th Cir. 2003); *Rios v. Ashcroft*, 287 F.3d at 900. Significantly, in *Kasinga,* the Board ruled that societal and cultural factors are also to be taken into account in determining nexus. 21 I. & N. Dec. at 366-67. The Proposed Rule also adopts this approach.[28]

At issue in this case is whether Osorio tormented and abused Ms. Alvarado because she was his *wife*, a status which incorporates gender and marital status. Osorio's comments and actions throughout the course of the relationship leave no doubt on this point. Time and time again in the midst of the vicious abuse, and in response to Ms. Alvarado's protestations Osorio affirmed his right to do as he did because she was his wife: "You're my woman, you do what I say" (Rec. at 696); "You're my woman, and I can do whatever I want" (Rec. at 695); "You don't order me" (Rec. at 694), and "I can do it if I want to." (Rec. at 697.) It was clear to Ms. Alvarado that her husband's animus was not personal to her as an *individual*, but directed towards her as his *wife*; when directly questioned on this point, she testified that her husband would batter any woman to whom he was married. (Rec. at 325.)

Persecutors are often not as vocal about their motives as was Osorio. *See, e.g., Bolanos-Hernandez v. INS*, 767 F.2d 1277, 1285 (9th Cir. 1984) ("Persecutors are hardly likely to provide their victims with affidavits attesting to their acts of persecution."). However, even if he had remained silent, the record would have been more than sufficient to establish the nexus

---

[28] *Id.* at 76593.

between his brutal persecution of Ms. Alvarado and her status as his wife. The extensive body of literature on domestic violence directly address its purposes and motivations, and make quite clear the gender and marital status link. The following is but a small sample of excerpts from scholarly literature on the issue which was *admitted into the record* in this case:

> Wife-beating is, therefore, not an individual, isolated or aberrant act,.... but a social license, a duty or sign of masculinity, deeply ingrained in culture, widely practiced, denied and completely or largely immune from sanction. *It is inflicted on women in the position of wives* for their actual or suspected failure to properly carry out their role, for their failure to produce, serve or be properly subservient[.] [29]

> [V]iolence against *wives* is a function of the belief...that men are superior and that *the women they live with* are their possessions or chattels that they can treat as they wish and as they consider appropriate. [30]

> Domestic violence has been revealed [to be] gender specific....[O]f all spousal violence crimes, ninety-one percent were victimizations of *women by their husbands or ex-husbands.* [31]

> Domestic violence is not gender-neutral...severe, repeated domestic violence is overwhelmingly initiated by *men and inflicted upon women.* [32]

Osorio s own words and actions, coupled with an understanding of domestic violence provides direct evidence that the persecution was motivated by gender and marital status.

However, there is still more evidence on this point. The BIA held in *Kasinga* that the nexus

---

[29] Copelon, Rhonda, *Recognizing the Egregious in the Everyday: Domestic Violence as Torture*, 25 COLUM. HUM. RTS. L. REV. 291, 335 (1994); (Exhibit 2-J) (emphasis added).

[30] *Id* at 304; (Exhibit 2-J) (emphasis added).

[31] Thomas, Dorothy Q. and Michele E. Beasley, *Domestic Violence as a Human Rights Issue*, 58 ALBANY L. REV. 1119, 1128 (1995); (Exhibit 2-M) (emphasis added).

[32] Copelon, *supra* note 29 at 303 (Exhibit 2-J)(emphasis added).

determination includes an analysis of societal and cultural norms;[33] this approach is reiterated in the Commentary to the Proposed Rule:

> [E]vidence about patterns of violence in the society against individuals similarly situated to the applicant may also be relevant to the on account of determination. For example, in the domestic violence context, an adjudicator would consider any evidence that the abuser uses violence to enforce power and control over the applicant because of the social status that a woman may acquire when she enters into a domestic relationship. This would include any direct evidence about the abuser s own actions, as well as any circumstantial evidence that such patterns of violence are *(1) supported by the legal system or social norms in the country in question, and (2) reflect a prevalent belief within society, or within relevant segments of society....*[34] [Emphasis added.]

The evidence is clear on these points. The legal system in Guatemala supports the patterns of violence by abdicating its responsibility to intervene to protect victims of domestic battering. The prevalent beliefs within society, which support and perpetuate the violence, include the beliefs that women are subordinate to men (Rec. at 737), that domestic violence as a social problem is unimportant (Rec. at 429), and that the woman is to blame when familial violence takes place.

---

[33] The approach to determining nexus which considers the abuser s actions within the societal / country context has been widely accepted; it is commonly referred to as a bifurcated nexus analysis. *See, e.g., Minister for Immigration and Multicultural Affairs v. Khawar* [2002] HCA 14 (Australian High Court), available at <http://scaleplus.law.gov.au/html/highcourt/0/2002/0/2002041114.htm>; *Islam, supra* note 16; Refugee Appeal No. 71427/99, *supra* note 16, ¶106 (New Zealand); UNHCR Social Group Guidelines, *supra* note 13. The British House of Lords illustrated its rationale by reference to the persecution of Jews prior to the Second World War:
> Suppose oneself in Germany in 1935.... [S]uppose that the Nazi government in those early days did not actively organise violence against Jews, but pursued a policy of not giving any protection to Jews subjected to violence by neighbours. A Jewish shopkeeper is attacked by a gang organised by an Aryan competitor who smash his shop, beat him up and threaten to do it again if he remains in business. The competitor and his gang are motivated by business rivalry and a desire to settle old personal scores, but *they would not have done what they did unless they knew that the authorities would allow them to act with impunity.* And the ground upon which they enjoyed impunity was that the victim was a Jew.... An essential element in the persecution, the failure of the authorities to provide protection, is based upon race.

Islam, supra, ¶133 (Lord Hoffman) (emphasis added).

[34] Commentary, *supra* note 4, at 76593.

(Rec. at 425.) The social norms and beliefs include such a broad acceptance of domestic violence that a man can batter his wife in public or drag her by the hair down the street, as Osorio did to Ms. Alvarado and no one will lift a finger to stop the violence.

C. Ms. Alvarado was Persecuted on Account of Her Political Opinion

The IJ who granted Ms. Alvarado s claim for asylum made the finding that she had resisted her husband s brutal acts of domination. (Rec. at 196.) The IJ ruled that her resistance was the expression of a political opinion against male domination, and constituted a challenge to [Osorio s] opinion that women are to be subordinate to men. (Rec. at 196.) Osorio s violent behavior towards his wife was meant to punish her for the actual opinion she held, or the opinion he attributed to her that men have no right to treat women in the manner in which he treated her.

Asylum claims often involve overlapping grounds of persecution. *See, e.g.*, *Baballah v. Ashcroft*, 335 F.3d 981 (ethnicity and religion); *Gafoor v. INS*, 231 F.3d 645 (9th Cir. 2000) (race and imputed political opinion); *Lal v. INS*, 255 F.3d 998, *as amended*, 268 F.3d 1148 (9th Cir. 2001) (religion and political opinion). The IJ s ruling that Osorio was motivated *both* by Ms. Alvarado s status as his wife and her political opinion of resistance is supported by the record as well as by scholarly literature regarding the phenomenon of domestic violence. Most experts recognize that domestic violence is a tool aimed at gaining power in order to control the intimate partner, [35] that it is part of a broad-scale system of domination of women,[36] and that it must be

---

[35] Karl Hempel, M.D., *Domestic Violence*, THE HEALTH GAZETTE (1998), available at <http://www.tfn.net/HealthGazette/domestic.html>.

[36] Kimberle Williams Crenshaw, *Mapping the Margins: Intersectionality, Identity Politics, and Violence Against Women of Color*, *in* THE PUBLIC NATURE OF PRIVATE VIOLENCE: THE DISCOVERY OF

understood in its social and cultural context as the extension of the domination and control of husbands over their wives. [37]

That men use spousal abuse as a means by which to perpetuate male domination and patriarchal social systems has likewise been recognized by many international organizations. For example, in a special report on the causes and consequences of violence against women, the United Nations Special Rapporteur on Violence Against Women concluded that [i]n intimate violence, male supremacy, ideology and conditions &confer upon men the sense of entitlement, if not the duty, to chastise their wives. [38]

This understanding of domestic violence explains why Osorio would escalate his abuse upon the least sign of resistance on Ms. Alvarado s part. Furthermore, because domestic violence is quintesssentially about issues of power and subordination in intimate relationships, domestic violence is necessarily motivated by status (*i.e.* social group) as well as by resistance (*i.e.* insubordination). Osorio s rage at Ms. Alvarado s resistance is consonant with an understanding of domestic violence as purposeful behavior intended to exert power, to eradicate resistance and to perpetuate subordination.

1. Ms. Alvarado s Resistance Constitutes a Political Opinion

Ms. Alvarado did not agree with the prevailing social and cultural norms of male domination and abuse. Her disagreement was expressed within the context of her relationship

---

DOMESTIC ABUSE 93, 93 (1994).

[37] R. Emerson Dobash and Russell Dobash, VIOLENCE AGAINST WIVES 15 (1979).

[38] *1996 Report of the Special Rapporteur*, *supra* note 11, at 7, ¶ 3.

with Osorio. Although she was terrorized by him, she demonstrated her resistance through both her words and her actions. On a number of occasions, when he was in the throes of tormenting her, she spoke up and directly challenged him, protesting his right to force sex on her (Rec. at 695); to rape her anally (Rec. at 696); and to use her head as a battering ram against furniture. (Rec. at 697.) On other occasions she expressed her resistance by her actions: she reported his abuse to the police (Rec. at 700); she attempted to use the judicial system (Rec. at 701); contrary to his demands that she not leave him, she fled to her parents and brother s home, and then to a rented room in an effort to resist his control. (Rec. at 696.) She went to seek medical treatment, even though she knew he would be enraged. (Rec. at 696.) And finally, when none of that was successful in vindicating her right to be free of abuse, she flouted his assertion of absolute authority over her by leaving his sphere of control, and fleeing to the United States. (Rec. at 702.)

Testimony by a psychotherapist who treated her in the United States affirms the depth of Ms. Alvarado s belief in her right not to be abused by her spouse. The psychotherapist, Dr. Linda Bersing, is an expert on women s issues and Latin America who has counseled women for more than two decades. She testified that Ms. Alvarado was quite different from other women with whom she had met over the years. (Rec. at 305) The difference, she testified, was that Ms. Alvarado had a will...to fight ; she believed she had the right to do something and she was really determined , and unlike other women who might end up believing that they deserve the abuse, she did not accept her situation. (Rec. at 306.)

Courts have long held that the term political opinion extends to a range of beliefs and philosophies, and is not limited to notions regarding political parties and ideologies. *See, e.g.,*

Chang v. INS, 119 F.3d 1055, 1063 (3rd Cir. 1997) (an asylum seeker need not call herself a dissident or articulate resistance in terms of a particular ideology); *Osorio v. INS*, 18 F.3d 1017, 1030 (2nd Cir. 1994) (holding that refugee law does not require that [the asylum seeker] be a politician and ruling that to require an individual to state which political party he belongs to, which political philosophy he espouses or which political leaders he supports...betrays an impoverished view of what political opinions are....); *Lazo-Majano v. INS*, 813 F.2d 1432, 1435 (9th Cir. 1987), *overruled on other grounds by Fisher v. INS*, 79 F.3d 955 (9th Cir. 1996) (*en banc*) (views of a poor domestic and washerwoman who does not participate in politics nonetheless political).

Feminism has been expressly recognized as a political opinion. *See, e.g., Fatin*, 12 F.3d at 1242 (In this case, if the petitioner s political opinion is defined simply as feminism, she would presumably satisfy the first element [establishing a political opinion], *for we have little doubt that feminism qualifies as a political opinion* within the meaning of the relevant statutes. (Emphasis added)). A woman s deeply held opinion that her husband does not have the right to violate her physical and psychological integrity is one of the most fundamental expressions of feminism, because freedom from domestic violence is a necessary condition for the attainment of all other societal equalities.[39] Ms. Alvarado believes in the right to this equality, and her words and actions

---

[39] The United Nations Declaration on the Elimination of Violence Against Women recognizes that violence against women is the essential and ultimate social mechanism by which women are forced into a subordinate position as compared to men. Declaration on the Elimination of Violence against Women, G.A. Res. 48/104, U.N. GAOR Supp. (No. 49), at 217, U.N. Doc. A/48/49 (1993).

throughout her relationship were an expression of this belief, and were not simply the articulation of the common human desire not to be harmed or abused.[40]

2. Ms. Alvarado was Persecuted on Account of her Political Opinion

As discussed above, the extensive literature establishes that the fundamental purpose of domestic violence is to punish, humiliate, and exercise power over the victim on account of her gender (Rec. at 39) and to extinguish any actual or perceived dissent. Osorio was motivated to batter Ms. Alvarado because of her status as his wife, and he was motivated to batter her because she resisted and challenged his right to exert absolute power and control over her.

There was not a single time when Ms. Alvarado resisted Osorio that he did not respond by even more brutal treatment. Osorio vowed to kill her for leaving him. (Rec. at 704.) When she tried to escape by renting a room, he beat her unconscious. (Rec. at 696.) When she refused his command to go to the hospital to abort their child, he battered her and attempted to induce a miscarriage. (Rec. at 694.) He pulled a machete on her when she refused to go for a walk in the middle of the night. (Rec. at 698.)

The least hint of resistance, or questioning of his authority resulted in escalated abuse: Osorio became enraged when she asked him not to drink so much (Rec. at 694); he threatened to kill her when she tried to resist forced sex: Just do it, or I'll finish you off. (Rec. at 695.) When Ms. Alvarado simply remarked that Osorio had arrived home late, he hit and punched her, saying that he didn't have to answer to her. (Rec. at 699.) Perhaps most telling of all are Osorio's

---

[40] The BIA made this characterization of Ms. Alvarado's opinions in its decision reversing the IJ. (Rec. at 13.)

threats to his wife as to what he would do should she ever leave him which would be the ultimate throwing off of his authority. He told her:

> [Y]ou will suffer much worse than what I have done to you so far...If you ever try to leave, I will come find you. And when I find you, I could kill you, but I m not going to do that. I will break your legs. I wil cripple you so that you will be in a wheelchair for the rest of your life. I will mark your face so it will be scarred forever, it will be twisted and deformed. (Rec. at 704.)

The fact that Osorio was motivated to punish Ms. Alvarado for her resistance is evident in the sequence of events the repeated cycles of resistance, followed by violence and threats of violence. The conclusion that the battering was, in part, politically-motivated, is reinforced by the scholarly literature on domestic violence, which as detailed above recognizes it as purposeful conduct, intended to extinguish resistance, and to dominate and control.[41]

D. Ms. Alvarado has Suffered Atrocious Past Persecution and has Established a Well-founded fear of Future Persecution

A well-founded fear of persecution may be presumed if an asylum applicant establishes past persecution. The regulations in force when Ms. Alvarado s case was adjudicated provided that the presumption could be rebutted only upon a showing by a preponderance of the evidence that country conditions had changed to such an extent that the fear of persecution was no longer well-founded. 8 C.F.R. § 208.13(b)(1)(i). Current regulations provide for rebuttal upon proof by a preponderance 1) of a fundamental change in circumstances such that the applicant no longer has a well-founded fear of persecution ; or 2) that the applicant could avoid persecution by

---

[41] *See* V. Michael McKenzie, DOMESTIC VIOLENCE IN AMERICA 8 (1995) ([s]pousal battery is a choice men exercise intentionally and purposefully to resolve conflict and achieve their goals of dominance, and coercive control of women).

internal relocation within the country of origin if, under all the circumstances, it would be reasonable to expect her to do so. 8 C.F.R. §§ 1208.13(b)(1)(i)(A) & (B).

Even in cases where the presumption of a well-founded fear has been rebutted, asylum may be granted in the exercise of discretion when the applicant has demonstrated compelling reasons for being unwilling or unable to return to the country arising out of the severity of the past persecution or there is the reasonable possibility that the applicant may suffer other serious harm upon removal to the home country. 8 C.F.R. §§ 1208.13(b)(1)(iii)(A) & (B).

It is undisputed that Ms. Alvarado has suffered past persecution, and there is no evidence in the record of changed country conditions, changed circumstances, or reasonable internal relocation, which could rebut the presumption in her favor of a well-founded fear. Even in the absence of the regulatory presumption, the record evidence establishes that a reasonable person in Ms. Alvarado s circumstances would fear persecution. *Matter of Mogharrabi*, 19 I. & N. Dec. 439 (BIA 1987). Moreover, given the duration and extreme severity of the abuse, and its ongoing physical and psychological effects, Ms. Alvarado qualifies for a grant of protection even in the absence of a well-founded fear of persecution.

1. Ms. Alvarado has Established a Well-Founded Fear of Persecution

The IJ ruled that Ms. Alvarado was entitled to the regulatory presumption of a well-founded fear on the basis of her past persecution, and that there was no evidence that conditions in Guatemala had changed to such an extent ... to obviate the Respondent s need for protection. (Rec. at 192.) There is no evidence to support a rebuttal even under the revised regulation s broader grounds; there have been no changed circumstances, and the record is clear on the futility of Ms. Alvarado's attempts to escape her husband through internal relocation. (Rec. at 235, 238-240.)

Ms. Alvarado can establish a well-founded fear of persecution even in the absence of the regulatory presumption. An applicant's fear is well-founded if it is subjectively genuine and objectively reasonable, or if a "reasonable person" in the circumstances would fear persecution. *INS v. Cardoza-Fonseca*, 480 U.S. 421, 430-43 (1987); *Mogharrabi*, 19 I. & N. Dec. at 445. The particular facts of this case, considered in the context of scholarly research on domestic violence, can only lead one to the conclusion that any reasonable person in Ms. Alvarado's circumstances would fear persecution.

Osorio asserted on numerous occasions that Ms. Alvarado could never escape him. (Rec. at 699-700.) He tracked her down on every occasion that she did attempt to leave, and among the many threats that he made was that he would make her suffer worse than ever before should she attempt to leave him. (Rec. at 704.) His threats against her did not cease with her departure from Guatemala; Ms. Alvarado's sister recounted that Osorio has "her under a death threat" (Rec. at 679), and that "if she comes back he will not let her live." [42] (Rec. at 686.) The gravity of these threats is underscored by the literature on domestic violence, *see supra* at section B.2, and by observations made by the Violence Against Women Office (VAWO) of the Department of Justice, which were incorporated into the Commentary to the Proposed Regulation:

---

[42] Ms. Alvarado has more than met the "well-founded fear" burden for asylum; on these facts, she has also met the higher standard of "clear probability" required for restriction on removal. *INS v. Stevic*, 467 U.S. 407 (1984). A clear probability of persecution may be shown where a specific threat is made by a person with the will and ability to carry it out. *Bolanos-Hernandez*, 767 F.2d at 1285. As amply demonstrated by the record, Osorio has both the will and ability to carry out his threat that he will not let her live.

> [I]n relationships involving domestic violence, past behavior is a strong predictor of future behavior by the abuser. *See, e.g.*, United States Department of Justice, Understanding Domestic Violence: A Handbook for Victims and Professionals. ... [D]omestically and internationally, domestic violence centers on power and control over the victim. Consequently, when victims attempt to flee the abusive relationship, or otherwise assert their independence, abusers often pursue them and escalate the violence to regain or reassert control. *See, e.g.*, United States Department of Justice, Stalking and Domestic Violence under the Violence Against Women Act (1998). *The risk to lethality to the victim is typically greatest when she attempts to escape the abuse, and in contrast to other persecution cases where the persecutor s desire to harm the victim may wane if the victim leaves, the victim s attempt to leave typically increases the abuser s motivation to locate and harm her.*[43]

The VAWO also commented that because of the abuser s intimate relationship with the victim, he is likely to possess important information about where the victim could go or to whom she would turn for assistance. [44]

Therefore, it is clear that Osorio s threats should be taken seriously, and that Ms. Alvarado may be assumed to be at higher risk now than she was at any point in her relationship with Osorio (*i.e.*, escape puts victim at the greatest risk to lethality). The VAWO s observations are also particularly relevant to the issue of internal relocation, as they recognize the ability intimate partners have to locate the victim. Osorio has demonstrated his ability through his past successes in tracking down Ms. Alvarado. The fact that they have children together is also a significant consideration; should Ms. Alvarado be forced to return to Guatemala, there is no doubt that she would want to see her children, who have been residing with Osorio s parents. (Rec. at 705.) This would certainly make it virtually a foregone conclusion that Osorio would be able to locate Ms. Alvarado.

---

[43] Commentary, *supra* note 4, at 76595 (emphasis added; some citations omitted).

[44] *Id.* at 76596.

2. Ms. Alvarado Qualifies for a Grant of Asylum Even in the Absence of a Well-founded Fear

An applicant may obtain asylum even if she has no well-founded fear in the future, provided that she has compelling reasons arising out of the severity of the past persecution for being unwilling to return. 8 C.F.R. § 1208.13(b)(1)(iii). *See also Lal*, 255 F.3d at 1002; *Lopez-Galarza v. INS*, 99 F.3d 954, 960-63 (9th Cir. 1996); *Matter of Chen*, 20 I & N. Dec. 16 (BIA 1989). Assuming *arguendo* that Ms. Alvarado could not establish a well-founded fear of persecution, she would still qualify for asylum because the harm which she suffered was exceptionally severe and atrocious.

Persecution is stamped on every page of this record. Although this observation was made by Ninth Circuit jurist John T. Noonan upon reading the record in the *Lazo-Majano* case, *see* 813 F.2d at 1434, it could just as well have been said about the record in the instant case. It is impossible to read the record in Ms. Alvarado s case without reaching the conclusion that her home had become a virtual torture chamber, where her husband was at liberty to rape, sodomize, whip, kick, and beat her. Bones were dislocated, internal hemorrhaging occurred, flesh was cut and bruised, and sexually transmitted diseases were passed on.

The physical harm was extreme and long-lasting; in her affidavit, Ms. Alvarado testified that she suffers from severe, recurring headaches from being hit and kicked in the head, dragged by the hair, or her head used as a battering ram. (Rec. at 705.) She still suffers from severe abdominal pains and irregular menstrual periods from the rapes and blows to her abdomen and genital area, and has recurring pains in her arm and chest from being pulled across the bed when her husband would force sex upon her. (Rec. at 696, 705.)

But it is not only the physical harms which have ongoing consequences for Ms. Alvarado; she continues to suffer from the psychological and emotional repercussions of this exceptionally brutal abuse. She regularly has nightmares that she is back in Guatemala, and the thought of this makes her so desperate and fearful that she cannot get back to sleep. (Rec. at 704-05.)

There can be no doubt that Ms. Alvarado s abuse rises to the severity of harm necessary for a grant of asylum even in the absence of a well-founded fear of persecution. The physical and psychological harm she endured are equivalent to that present in cases where asylum was granted on the basis of severe past persecution. *See, e.g., Lopez-Galarza*, 99 F.3d 954 (female applicant imprisoned for 15 days, repeatedly raped and subjected to other physical abuse); *Matter of B-*, Int. Dec. 3251 (BIA 1995) (Afghan interrogated, physically abused, detained for 15 months, and forced to serve in the Army because of assistance to the mujahideen); *Chen*, 20 I. & N. Dec. 16 (Chinese applicant and his family suffered brutal physical and psychological mistreatment over more than a decade during the Cultural Revolution). In addition, although it is not a requirement, Ms. Alvarado not only endured atrocious forms of persecution in the past, but she continues to suffers from ongoing physical and emotional consequences arising from the ten years of battering and torment. *See Lal*, 255 F.3d at 1006 (although existence of lasting physical or emotional disability may sometimes be a factor in determining the severity of an applicant's past persecution, it has not been a requirement.).

IV. Conclusion

1) **Ms. Alvarado Should be Granted Asylum**

    A. **Ms. Alvarado Should Be Granted Asylum on the Existing Record**

Ms. Alvarado has suffered tremendously for the last twenty years of her life. From 1984, the date of her marriage, until 1995, when she fled Guatemala, she was the victim of her husband's unrestrained brutality. And from 1995 to 2004, she has suffered what is now almost a decade of separation from her children. When she left Guatemala, her son was a toddler; he is now nearly twelve years old; her daughter, who was a young girl, is in her late teens. Because they live with Osorio's parents, she has had only the most minimal contact with them over the years.

As detailed in Part I, *supra*, Ms. Alvarado's claim for asylum has been pending for almost *ten years* since 1995, when she first appeared before an immigration judge. Each delay has increased her anguish over her separation from her children, as well as her feeling of insecurity regarding her ultimate fate.

The record in Ms. Alvarado's case is extremely well-developed. Her declaration is detailed, her testimony was extensive, and the documentary evidence regarding relevant conditions in Guatemala is comprehensive. Extensive briefing, including that of *amicus curiae*, has occurred at each step of adjudication, and has included in-depth discussion of the scholarly literature on domestic violence. Furthermore, current briefing has addressed Ms. Alvarado's eligibility for protection not only under existing caselaw, but pursuant to the Proposed Regulations as well. Factors relevant under the Proposed Regulations are well-developed in the existing record, and a remand is not required to further develop the record for these purposes.

Ms. Alvarado's case is ripe for decision. Justice and fairness require an adjudication on the existing record, and on the basis of the arguments that have been submitted throughout the past decade in this case. To further delay a decision in this case is to deny Ms. Alvarado the opportunity to regain the peace of mind that comes with a resolution of her claim for protection, and more importantly the opportunity for family reunification at long last.

B.   There are no Adverse Factors which Negatively Impact the Exercise of Discretion

Asylum is a discretionary remedy, and may be denied in the exercise of discretion by the Attorney General, or his delegates. However, where an individual has established a well-founded fear of persecution, asylum should only be denied in the exercise of discretion on the basis of genuine compelling factors factors important enough to warrant returning a *bona fide* refugee to a country where he may face a threat of imminent danger to his life or liberty. *Hernandez-Ortiz v. INS*, 777 F.2d 509, 519 (9th Cir. 1995). Not only are there no compelling factors which would justify a denial in this case there are simply no adverse factors *whatsoever*. Ms. Alvarado has established statutory eligibility, and in the total absence of negative factors, should be granted relief in the exercise of discretion.

Respectfully Submitted,

———————————————
Karen Musalo, Resident Scholar
Stephen Knight, Research Fellow (on brief)
University of California
Hastings College of Law
200 McAllister Street
San Francisco, CA 94102
(415) 565-4720

DATED: February 18, 2004

DECLARATION OF SERVICE BY MAIL
Matter of Rodi Alvarado Peña

I, Stephen Knight, declare that I am at least 18 years of age, that I am not a party to the within cause, that my business address is Center for Gender & Refugee Studies, UC Hastings College of the Law, 200 McAllister Street, San Francisco, CA, 94102. On February 18, 2004, I served

BRIEF ON BEHALF OF RODI ALVARADO PEÑA TO THE ATTORNEY GENERAL OF THE UNITED STATES

on the person listed below by placing a true copy thereof in a prepaid sealed envelope with first-class postage thereon fully prepaid, in the United States mail at San Francisco, California, addressed as follows:

> George R. Martin
> Acting Chief Appellate Counsel
> U.S. I.C.E.
> U.S. D.H.S.
> 5113 Leesburg Pike, Suite 200
> Falls Church, VA 22041

I declare under penalty of perjury under the laws of the State of California that the foregoing is true and correct. Executed on February 18, 2004, at San Francisco, California.

_____
Stephen Knight

APPENDIX 6A
ASYLUM OFFICES

Office of Refugee, Asylum, and International Operations
20 Massachusetts Avenue, NW, Suite 3300, Washington, DC 20591
(202) 272-1601, (202) 272-1676 (fax)
Lori Scialabba, *Director*

U.S. Citizenship and Immigration Services Asylum Division
20 Massachusetts Avenue, NW, Washington, DC 20591
(202) 272-1663, (202) 272-1681 (fax)
Joseph Langlois, *Chief*
Joanna Ruppel, *Deputy*

Arlington, VA (ZAR)
Ann Palmer, Director
1525 Wilson Boulevard, Suite 300
Arlington, VA 22209
(703) 525-8141 x1308
(703) 812-8455 (fax)

Jurisdiction: DC, western PA, MD, VA, WV, NC, GA (except Atlanta expedited removal and stowaways cases, which are handled by NY), AL, and SC

Chicago, IL (ZCH)
Kenneth Madsen, Director
401 LaSalle Street, 8th Floor
Chicago, IL 60605
(312) 353-9607; 9608; 9609; 9610
(312) 886-0204 (fax)

Jurisdiction: IL, IN, MI, WI, MN, ND, SD, KS, MO, OH, IO, NE, MT, ID, and KY

Houston, TX (ZHN)
Marie Hummert, Director
16630 Imperial Valley Drive, Suite 200
Houston, TX 77060

Mailing Address:
P.O. Box 670626
Houston, TX 77267-0626
(281) 774-4830
(281) 774-5823 (fax)

Jurisdiction: LA, AR, MS, TN, TX, OK, NM, CO, UT, and WY

Los Angeles, CA (ZLA)
George Mihalko, Director
1585 S. Manchester St.
Anaheim, CA 92802

Mailing Address:
P.O. Box 65015
Anaheim, CA 91815-5015
(714) 808-8205
(714) 635-9136 (fax)

Jurisdiction: AZ, southern CA (within the jurisdiction of the Los Angeles and San Diego district offices), southern NV (within the jurisdiction of the Las Vegas Suboffice), HI, and Guam

Miami, FL (ZMI)
Erich Cauller, Director
99 S.E. 5th Street, 1st Floor
Miami, FL 33131
(305) 530-6076 x310
(305) 530-6070 (fax)

Jurisdiction: FL, Puerto Rico, and the U.S. Virgin Islands

Newark, NJ (ZNK)
Susan Raufer, Director
1200 Wall Street, West
Lyndhurst, NJ 07071
(201) 531-0555 x256
(201) 531-1877 (fax)

Jurisdiction: NY (within the boroughs of Manhattan and the Bronx, the Buffalo District Office), PA (excluding the jurisdiction of the Pittsburgh Suboffice), CT, DE, ME, MA, NH, NJ, PA, RI, and VT

Rosedale, NY (ZNY)
Patricia Jackson, Director
One Cross Island Plaza
Rosedale, NY 11422
(718) 723-5954 x1002
(718) 723-1121 (fax)

Jurisdiction: NY (excluding the jurisdiction of the Buffalo District Office and the boroughs of Manhattan and the Bronx)

San Francisco, CA (ZSF)
Emilia Bardini, Director
75 Hawthorne St., 3rd Fl., South Wing
San Francisco, CA 94105
(415) 293-1285
(415) 293-1269 (fax)

Mailing Address:
P.O. Box 77530
San Francisco, CA 94107

Jurisdiction: northern CA (within the jurisdiction of the San Francisco District Office), northern NV (within the jurisdiction of the Reno Suboffice), OR, WA, and AK

APPENDIX 6B
EXECUTIVE OFFICE FOR IMMIGRATION REVIEW

BOARD OF IMMIGRATION APPEALS
OFFICE OF THE CHIEF CLERK
5201 Leesburg Pike, Suite 1300, Falls Church, VA 22041;
or P.O. Box 8530, Falls Church, VA 22041
(703) 605-1007

OFFICE OF THE CHIEF IMMIGRATION JUDGE
5107 Leesburg Pike, Suite 2500, Falls Church, VA 22041, (703) 305-1247

David L. Neal
Chief Immigration Judge

Brooke B. Grandle
Counsel to the Chief Immigration Judge

Scott M. Rosen
Special Counsel to the Chief Immigration Judge

Edward F. Kelly
Special Counsel to the Chief Immigration Judge

ASSISTANT CHIEF IMMIGRATION JUDGES

Rico Bartolomei
Area of responsibility: East Mesa, El Centro, Eloy, Florence, Imperial, Phoenix, San Diego, Tucson
Back-up: Gary W. Smith

Sarah Burr
Area of responsibility: Fishkill, New York, Ulster, Varick
Back-up: Anne J. Greer

David W. Crosland
Area of responsibility: Krome, Miami
Back-up: Phillip T. Williams

Larry R. Dean
Area of responsibility: Dallas, El Paso, El Paso SPC, Harlingen, Houston, Houston SPC, Port Isabel, San Antonio
Back-up: Gary W. Smith

Thomas Fong
Area of responsibility: Lancaster, Los Angeles, San Pedro
Back-up: Anne J. Greer

Anne J. Greer
Area of responsibility: Baltimore, Batavia, Buffalo, Denver, Salt Lake City
Back-up: Phillip T. Williams

Stephen Griswold
Area of responsibility: Portland, San Francisco, Seattle, Tacoma
Back-up: Michael C. McGoings

Michael C. McGoings
Area of responsibility: Bloomington, Chicago, Honolulu, HQIC, Memphis, New Orleans, Oakdale
Back-up: Gary W. Smith

Gary W. Smith
Area of responsibility: Arlington, Atlanta, Boston, Cleveland, Hartford, Philadelphia, York
Back-up: Michael C. McGoings

Phillip T. Williams
Area of responsibility: Detroit, Elizabeth, Las Vegas, Newark, Orlando, San Juan
Back-up: Anne J. Greer

MaryBeth Keller (Acting)
Area of responsibility: Conduct and Professionalism

IMMIGRATION COURTS AND JUDGES

ARIZONA

Eloy
1705 E. Hanna Rd.
Suite 366
Eloy, AZ 85231
(520) 466-3671

Immigration Judges
John W. Davis
Sean H. Keenan
Thomas M. O'Leary

Florence
3260 N. Pinal Pkwy. Ave.
Florence, AZ 85232
(520) 868-3341

Immigration Judges
Bruce A. Taylor
Scott M. Jefferies

Phoenix
200 East Mitchell Dr.
Suite 200
Phoenix, AZ 85012
(602) 640-2747

Immigration Judges
LaMonte S. Freerks
Wendell Hollis
John W. Richardson

Tucson
160 N. Stone Ave.
Suite 300
Tucson, AZ 85701-1502
(520) 670-5212

CALIFORNIA

East Mesa
East Mesa CCA
446 Alta Road
San Diego, CA 92158
(619) 661-3327

Immigration Judge
Zsa Zsa De Paolo

El Centro
1115 N. Imperial Ave.
El Centro, CA 92243
(760) 353-2328

Immigration Judge
Jack H. Weil

Imperial
2409 La Brucherie Rd.
Imperial, CA 92251
(760) 355-0070

Immigration Judges
Dennis R. James
Jack W. Staton

Lancaster
Mira Loma Facility
45100 N. 60th St., West

APPENDIX 6B • EXECUTIVE OFFICE FOR IMMIGRATION REVIEW

Lancaster, CA 93536
(661) 942-8633

Immigration Judges
William J. Nickerson, Jr.
Robert O. Vicars

Los Angeles
606 S. Olive St., 15th Fl.
Los Angeles, CA 90014
(213) 894-2811

Immigration Judges
David C. Anderson
Ira E. Bank
Lori Bass
Christine A. Bither
Isabel A. Bronzina
Alison Daw
Dorothy Dunkel-Bradley
Thomas Y.K. Fong
Gilbert T. Gembacz
Anthony T. Giattina
Anna Ho
Jan D. Latimore
William J. Martin, Jr.
Lorraine J. Munoz
Renee L. Renner
Stephen L. Sholomson
Christine E. Stancill
A. Ashley Tabaddor
Frank Travieso
Mimi Tsankov
Gita Vahid-Tehrani
John F. Walsh
Richard D. Walton

San Diego
401 West "A" Street
Suite 800
San Diego, CA 92101
(619) 557-6052

Immigration Judges
Anthony Atenaide
Kenneth A. Bagley
Robert J. Barrett
Richard J. Bartolomei, Jr.
Ignacio P. Fernandez
Henry Ipema, Jr.
John C. Williams

San Francisco
120 Montgomery Street
Suite 800
San Francisco, CA 94104
(415) 705-4415

Immigration Judges
Lawrence N. DiCostanzo
Loreto Geisse
Stephen Griswold
Miriam R. Hayward
Carol A. King
Dana Leigh Marks
Anthony S. Murry
Tue Phan-Quang
Beverley M. Phillips
George W. Proctor
Laura L. Ramirez
Brian H. Simpson
Bette Kane Stockton
Marilyn J. Teeter
Polly A. Webber
Michael J. Yamaguchi
Robert Yeargin

San Pedro
San Pedro Service
Processing Center
2001 Seaside Ave.
Rm. 136
San Pedro, CA 90731
(310) 241-2424

Immigration Judges
Rose C. Peters
D.D. Sitgraves

COLORADO

Denver
Byron G. Rogers
Fed. Building
1961 Stout St.
Rm. 1403
Denver, CO 80294
(303) 844-5815

Immigration Judges
David J. Cordova
Donn L. Livingston
James P. Vandello

CONNECTICUT

Hartford
AA Ribicoff Fed. Bldg.
& Courthouse
450 Main St., Rm. 509
Hartford, CT 06103-3015
(860) 240-3881

Immigration Judge
Michael W. Straus

FLORIDA

Bradenton
515 11th Street West
Bldg. A , Rm. 300
Bradenton, FL 34205
(941) 749-1044

Miami
One Riverview Square
333 S. Miami Ave.
Suite 700
Miami, FL 33130
(305) 530-6455

Immigration Judges
Scott G. Alexander
Kevin G. Bradley
Teofilo Chapa
David W. Crosland
J. Daniel Dowell
Mahlon F. Hanson
Rodger C. Harris
Carey Holliday

Michael C. Horn
Denise A. Marks Lane
Stephen E. Mander
Nancy R. McCormack
Mark H. Metcalf
Pedro A. Miranda
Adam Opaciuch
John Opaciuch
Charles J. Sanders
Bruce W. Solow
Elisa M. Sukkar
Lilliana Torreh-Bayouth
Earle Wilson

Miami
Krome North Processing Center
18201 SW 12th St.
Bldg. #1, Suite C
Miami, FL 33194
(305) 530-7196

Mailing Address:
P.O. Box 940998
Miami, FL 33194

Immigration Judges
Rex J. Ford
Kenneth S. Hurewitz
Denise N. Slavin

Orlando
80 North Hughey Ave
Suite 203
Orlando, FL 32801
(407) 648-6565

Immigration Judges
Victoria L. Ghartey
Rafael B. Ortiz-Segura

GEORGIA

Atlanta
Martin Luther King Jr. Federal Bldg.
77 Forsyth St., Rm. 112
Atlanta, GA 30303
(404) 331-0907

Immigration Judges
William A. Cassidy
Wayne K. Houser, Jr.
J. Dan Pelletier
Grace A. Sease

HAWAII

Honolulu
PJKK Federal Building
300 Ala Moanu Blvd.
Rm. 8-112
Honolulu, HI 96850
(808) 541-1870

Immigration Judge
Dayna Beamer

ILLINOIS

Chicago
55 East Monroe St.
Suite 1900
Chicago, IL 60603-5701
(312) 353-7313

Immigration Judges
Glen Bower
O. John Brahos
Carlos Cuevas
James R. Fujimoto
Jennie L. Giambastiani
George Katsivalas
Robert D. Vinikoor
Craig M. Zerbe

Chicago (detained)
536 Clark Street
Room B1330/1320
Chicago, IL 60605
(312) 353-1387

Immigration Judge
George Katsivalas

LOUISIANA

New Orleans
One Canal Place
365 Canal Street
Suite 2450
New Orleans, LA 70130
(504) 589-3992

Immigration Judge
William Stogner

Oakdale
1900 E. Whatley Road
Oakdale, LA 71463
(318) 335-0365

Immigration Judges
John A. Duck, Jr.
James Nugent
Agnelis L. Reese

MARYLAND

Baltimore
George Fallon Federal Building
31 Hopkins Plaza
Rm. 440
Baltimore, MD 21201
(410) 962-3092

Immigration Judges
Bruce M. Barrett
Lisa Dornell
Jill H. Dufresne
John F. Gossart, Jr.
Elizabeth A. Kessler

MASSACHUSETTS

Boston
JFK Federal Building
15 New Sudbury St.
Rm. 320
Boston, MA 02203
(617) 565-3080

Immigration Judges
Francis L. Cramer
Matthew J. D'Angelo
Robin Feder
Paul M. Gagnon
Eliza C. Klein
Leonard I. Shapiro

MICHIGAN

Detroit
P.V. McNamara Federal Building
477 Michigan Avenue, Suite 440
Detroit, MI 48226
(313) 226-2603

Immigration Judges
Elizabeth A. Hacker
Marsha K. Nettles
Robert D. Newberry

MINNESOTA

Bloomington
7850 Metro Parkway
Suite 320
Bloomington, MN 55425
(612) 725-3765

Immigration Judges
Joseph R. Dierkes
Kristin W. Olmanson

NEVADA

Las Vegas
3365 Pepper Lane
Suite 200
Las Vegas, NV 89120
(702) 458-0227

Immigration Judges
Harry L. Gastley
Ronald L. Mullins
Irene Weiss

NEW JERSEY

Elizabeth
625 Evans Street
Rm. 148A
Elizabeth, NJ 07201
(973) 693-4113

Immigration Judges
Dorothy Harbeck
Mirlande Tadal

Newark
970 Broad Street
Rm. 1135
Newark, NJ 07102
(973) 645-3524

Immigration Judges
Henry S. Dogin
Annie S. Garcy
Frederic G. Leeds
Eugene Pugliese
Margaret R. Reichenberg
Alberto J. Riefkohl

NEW YORK

Batavia
4250 Federal Drive
Rm. F108
Batavia, NY 14020
(585) 345-4300

Immigration Judge
John B. Reid

Buffalo
130 Delaware Ave.
Suite 410
Buffalo, NY 14202
(716) 551-3442

Immigration Judges
Philip J. Montante, Jr.
Michaelangelo Rocco

Fishkill
Downstate Correctional Facility
121 Red Schoolhouse Rd.
Fishkill, NY 12524
(845) 831-3657

New York City
26 Federal Plaza
12th Floor, Rm. 1237
New York, NY 10278
(917) 454-1040

Immigration Judges
Steven R. Abrams
Terry A. Bain
Javier Balasquide
Noël A. Brennan
Joanna M. Bukszpan
Sarah M. Burr
Jeffrey S. Chase
George T. Chew
Paul A. DeFonzo
Annette S. Elstein
Noel Anne Ferris
Vivienne E. Gordon-Uruakpa
Theresa Holmes-Simmons
Sandy K. Hom
Brigitte Laforest
Elizabeth A. Lamb
Margaret McManus
Philip L. Morace
Thomas Mulligan
Barbara A. Nelson
Patricia A. Rohan
Douglas B. Schoppert
Helen Sichel
William P. Van Wyke
Gabriel C. Videla
Robert D. Weisel

Ulster
Ulster Correctional Facility
Berme Road
P.O. Box 800
Napanoch, NY 12458
(845) 647-5506

Immigration Judge
Roger Sagerman

Varick Street
201 Varick Street
Rm. 1140
New York, NY 10014
(212) 620-6279

Immigration Judges
Alan L. Page
Alan A. Vomacka

OHIO

Cleveland
801 W. Superior Ave
Suite 13-100
Cleveland, OH 44113
(216) 802-1100

Immigration Judge
D. William Evans, Jr.

OREGON

Portland
1220 SW Third Ave.
Suite 218
Portland, OR 97204
(503) 326-6341

Immigration Judge
Michael H. Bennett

PENNSYLVANIA

Philadelphia
1600 Callowhill Street
Suite 400
Philadelphia, PA 19130
(215) 656-7000

Immigration Judges
Charles M. Honeyman
Rosalind K. Malloy
Miriam K. Mills

York
3400 Concord Road
Suite #2
York, PA 17402
(717) 755-7555

Mailing Address:
P.O. Box 20370
York, PA 17402

Immigration Judges
Andrew R. Arthur
Walter A. Durling

PUERTO RICO

Guaynabo (San Juan)
San Patricio Office Ctr.
#7 Tabonuco St.
Rm. 401
Guaynabo, PR
00968-4605
(787) 749-4386

Immigration Judge
Irma Lopez-Defillo

TENNESSEE

Memphis
Clifford B. Davis
Federal Building
167 N. Main Rm. 460
Memphis, TN 38103
(901) 544-3818

Immigration Judges
Lawrence O. Burman
Charles E. Pazar

TEXAS

Dallas
1100 Commerce Street,
Suite 404
Dallas, TX 75242
(214) 767-1814

Immigration Judges
D. Anthony Rogers
Deitrich H. Sims

El Paso
700 E. San Antonio St.
Suite 675
El Paso, TX 79901
(915) 534-6020

Immigration Judges
Robert Hough
Richard R. Ozmun

Thomas Roepke

El Paso
Service Processing Center
8915 Montana Avenue
El Paso, TX 79925
(915) 225-0750

Immigration Judge
William L Abbott

Harlingen
2009 W. Jefferson Ave
Suite 300
Harlingen, TX 78550
(956) 427-8580

Immigration Judges
Howard Achtsam
David Ayala
Margaret D. Burkhart
William C. Peterson
Eleazar Tovar

Houston
2320 LaBranch Street,
Rm. 2235
Houston, TX 77004
(713) 718-3870

Immigration Judges
Jimmie L. Benton
Chris A. Brisack
Philip S. Law
Howard Rose
Mimi S. Yam
Clarease Rankin Yates
William K. Zimmer

Houston
Houston Service
Processing Center
5520 Greens Road
Houston, TX 77032
(281) 987-2112

Los Fresnos
Port Isabel Processing
Center

27991 Buena Vista Blvd.
Building 37
Los Fresnos, TX 78566
(956) 547-1789

Mailing Address:
201 East Jackson Street
Harlingen, TX 78550-0000

San Antonio
800 Dolorosa Street
Suite 300
San Antonio, TX 78207
(210) 472-6637

Immigration Judges
Gary D. Burkholder
John D. Carté
Susan E. Castro
Larry R. Dean
Glenn P. McPhaul
Bertha A. Zuniga

UTAH

Salt Lake City
5500 W. Amelia Earhart Dr.
Suite 160
Salt Lake City, UT 84116
(801) 524-3000

Immigration Judge
William Nixon

VIRGINIA

Arlington
901 N. Stuart St.
Suite 1300
Arlington, VA 22203
(703) 235-2307

Immigration Judges
John M. Bryant
M. Christopher Grant
Wayne R. Iskra
Garry D. Malphrus
Brian M. O'Leary
Paul W. Schmidt
Thomas G. Snow

Headquarters
5107 Leesburg Pike
Suite 1850
Falls Church, VA 22041
(703) 305-0273

Immigration Judges
Charles Adkins-Blanch
Roxanne C. Hladylowycz
Robert P. Owens
Jeffrey L. Romig

WASHINGTON

Seattle
1000 Second Ave.
Suite 2500
Seattle, WA 98104
(206) 553-5953

Immigration Judges
Kenneth Josephson
Edward R. Kandler
Victoria E. Young

Tacoma
1623 East J Street
Tacoma, WA 98421
(206) 553-5953

APPENDIX 6C

ADDRESSES FOR SERVICE OF A PETITION FOR REVIEW

ATTORNEY GENERAL
Attorney General
U.S. Department of Justice
950 Pennsylvania Avenue, NW
Washington, DC 20530-0001

OFFICE OF IMMIGRATION LITIGATION
Thomas W. Hussey, Director
Office of Immigration Litigation
U.S. Department of Justice/Civil Division
1331 Pennsylvania Avenue, NW
Washington, DC 20004

OFFICE OF DETENTION AND REMOVAL—FIELD OFFICES

Service must also be made on the Field Office Director or, where none exists, the most senior officer in the Detention & Removal Unit. Counsel will need to contact the local ICE office to obtain the name and position title of the appropriate local officer and to verify the mailing address for service on this individual (as some offices are now using P.O. Box addresses).

Headquarters

Director, Office of Detention and Removal
801 I St, NW
Suite 900
Washington, DC 20536
Phone: (202) 305-2734

Field Offices

Atlanta
Field Office Director
77 Forsyth St., SW, Suite 117
Atlanta, GA 30303
Phone: (404) 331-2765
Area of Responsibility: Georgia, North Carolina, South Carolina

Baltimore
Field Office Director
31 Hopkins Plaza, Suite 630
Baltimore, MD 21201
Phone: (410) 962-2037
Area of Responsibility: Maryland

Boston
Field Office Director
John F. Kennedy, Federal Bldg.
Govt. Center, 17th Flr.
Room 1775
Boston, MA 02203
Phone: (617) 565-3304
Area of Responsibility: Connecticut, Maine, Massachusetts, New Hampshire, Vermont, Rhode Island

Buffalo
Field Office Director
130 Delaware Avenue
Buffalo, NY 14202
Phone: (716) 551-4741 x2500
Area of Responsibility: Upstate New York

Chicago
Field Office Director
10 W. Congress, Suite 400

Chicago, IL 60605
Phone: (312) 347-2400
Area of Responsibility: Illinois, Indiana, Kansas, Kentucky, Missouri, Wisconsin

Dallas
Field Office Director
8101 N. Stemmons Frwy
Dallas, TX 75247
Phone: (214) 905-5860
Area of Responsibility: North Texas, Oklahoma

Denver
Field Office Director
4730 Paris Street
Denver, CO 80239
Phone: (303) 371-1067
Area of Responsibility: Colorado, Wyoming

Detroit
Field Office Director
333 Mt. Elliott St.
Detroit, MI 48207
Phone: (313) 568-6049 x4079
Area of Responsibility: Michigan, Ohio

El Paso
Field Office Director
1545 Hawkins Blvd
El Paso, TX 79925
Phone: (915) 225-0888
Area of Responsibility: Southwest Texas, New Mexico

Houston
Field Office Directo
126 Northpoint Drive
Houston, TX 77060
Phone: (281) 774-4968
Area of Responsibility: Southeast Texas

Los Angeles
Field Office Director
300 North Los Angeles Street,
Room 7631A
Los Angeles, CA 90012
Phone: (213) 830-7911
Area of Responsibility: Central California

Miami
Field Office Director
7880 Biscayne Blvd.
Miami, FL 33138
Phone: (305) 762-3622
Area of Responsibility: Florida, Puerto Rico, U.S. Virgin Islands

Newark
Field Office Director
Hemisphere Building, Suite 512
Routes 1 and 9 South
Newark, NJ 07114
Phone: (973) 645-3666
Area of Responsibility: New Jersey

New Orleans
Field Office Director
DHS/ICE
1250 Poydras, Suite 325
New Orleans, LA 70113
Phone: (504) 599-7947
Area of Responsibility: Alabama, Arkansas, Louisiana, Mississippi, Tennessee

New York
Field Office Director
26 Federal Plaza, Rm. 1104
New York, NY 10278
Phone: (212) 264-3972
Area of Responsibility: The five boroughs (counties of NYC) and the following counties in New York: Westchester, Putnam, Dutchess, Ulster, Rockland, Nassau, and Suffolk

Philadelphia
Field Office Director
1600 Callowhill Street, 5th Floor
Philadelphia, PA 19130
Phone: (215) 656-7164

APPENDIX 6C • ADDRESSES FOR SERVICE OF A PETITION FOR REVIEW

Area of Responsibility: Delaware, Pennsylvania, West Virginia

Phoenix
Field Office Director
2035 N. Central Avenue
Phoenix, AZ 85004
Phone: (602) 379-3426
Area of Responsibility: Arizona

Salt Lake City
Field Office Director
5272 S. College Drive
Suite 100
Salt Lake City, UT 84123
Phone: (801) 313-4260
Area of Responsibility: Utah, Idaho, Montana, Nevada

San Antonio
Field Office Director
8940 Fourwinds Drive
San Antonio, TX 78239
Phone: (210) 967-7055
Area of Responsibility: Central South Texas

San Diego
Field Office Director
880 Front Street, #2232
San Diego, CA 92101
Phone: (619) 557-6117
Area of Responsibility: Southern California

San Francisco
Field Office Director
630 Sansome Street, Rm 590
San Francisco, CA 94111
Phone: (415) 844-5512
Area of Responsibility: Northern California, Hawaii, Guam

Seattle
Field Office Director
12500 Tukwila International Blvd.
4th Floor
Seattle, WA 98168
Phone: (206) 835-0650
Area of Responsibility: Alaska, Oregon, Washington

St. Paul
Field Office Director
2901 Metro Dr., Suite 100
Bloomington, MN 55425
Phone: (9525) 853-2550
Area of Responsibility: Iowa, Minnesota, Nebraska, North Dakota, South Dakota

Washington, DC
Field Office Director
2675 Prosperity Avenue
Fairfax, VA 22031
Phone: (703) 285-6200
Area of Responsibility: District of Columbia, Virginia

APPENDIX 6D
ICE OFFICES OF CHIEF COUNSEL

Arlington, Virginia (WAS)

Office of the Chief Counsel
Immigration and Customs Enforcement
U.S. Department of Homeland Security
901 N. Stuart Street, Suite 708
Arlington, VA 22203

Mailing Address: Same as above

Telephone: (703) 235-2700

Atlanta, Georgia (ATL)

Office of the Chief Counsel
Immigration and Customs Enforcement
U.S. Department of Homeland Security
77 Forsyth Street SW, Room 385
Atlanta, GA 30303

Mailing Address: Same as above

Telephone: (404) 331-6831

Baltimore, Maryland (BAL)

Office of the Chief Counsel
Immigration and Customs Enforcement
U.S. Department of Homeland Security
Fallon Federal Building
31 Hopkins Plaza, Room 730
Baltimore, MD 21201

Mailing Address: Same as above

Telephone: (410) 962-0773

Boston, Massachusetts (BOS)

Office of the Chief Counsel
Immigration and Customs Enforcement
U.S. Department of Homeland Security
John F. Kennedy Federal Bld'g, Rm. 425
Government Center
Boston, MA 02203

Mailing Address:
Office of the Chief Counsel
Immigration and Customs Enforcement
U.S. Department of Homeland Security
P.O. Box 8728
JFK Station
Boston, MA 02114

Telephone: (617) 565-3140

Hartford Suboffice (HAR)

Office of Chief Counsel
Immigration and Customs Enforcement
U.S. Department of Homeland Security
Ribicoff Federal Building, Room 483
450 Main Street
Hartford, CT 06103-3060

Telephone: (860) 240-3615

Buffalo, New York (BUF)

Office of the Chief Counsel
Immigration and Customs Enforcement
U.S. Department of Homeland Security
130 Delaware Avenue, Room 203
Buffalo, NY 14202

Mailing Address: Same as above

Telephone: (716) 551-4741 x3200/3285

Buffalo Federal Detention Facility

Office of the Chief Counsel
Immigration and Customs Enforcement
U.S. Department of Homeland Security
4250 Federal Drive
Batavia, NY 14020

Telephone: (585) 344-5135

Chicago, Illinois (CHI)

Office of the Chief Counsel
Immigration and Customs Enforcement
U.S. Department of Homeland Security
55 East Monroe Street, Suite 1700
Chicago, IL 60603

Mailing Address: Same as above

Telephone: (312) 984-2400

Dallas, Texas (DAL)

Office of the Chief Counsel
Immigration and Customs Enforcement
U.S. Department of Homeland Security
8101 N. Stemmons Freeway
Dallas, TX 75247

Mailing Address:
Office of the Chief Counsel
Immigration and Customs Enforcement
U.S. Department of Homeland Security
P.O. Box 561363
Dallas, TX 75356-1363

Telephone: (214) 905-5780

Denver, Colorado (DEN)

Office of the Chief Counsel
Immigration and Customs Enforcement
U.S. Department of Homeland Security
5445 DTC Parkway, Suite 530
Englewood, CO 80111

Mailing Address:
Office of the Chief Counsel
Immigration and Customs Enforcement
U.S. Department of Homeland Security
4730 Paris Street, Albrook Center
Denver, CO 80239

Telephone: (303) 721-3109

Salt Lake City Suboffice

Office of the Chief Counsel
Immigration and Customs Enforcement
U.S. Department of Homeland Security
5272 S. College Drive, Suite 100
Salt Lake City, UT 84123

Mailing Address: Same as above

Telephone: (801) 313-4302

Detroit, Michigan (DET)

Office of the Chief Counsel
Immigration and Customs Enforcement
U.S. Department of Homeland Security
Federal Building
333 Mt. Elliott Street, 2nd Floor
Detroit, MI 48207

Mailing Address: Same as above

Telephone: (313) 568-6033

Cleveland Suboffice (CLE)

Office of the Chief Counsel
Immigration and Customs Enforcement
U.S. Department of Homeland Security
Anthony J. Celebrezze Federal Bldg.
1240 E. 9th Street, Room 585
Cleveland, OH 44199

Telephone: (216) 535-0520
Fax: (216) 522-4733

Cincinnati Suboffice (CLE)

Office of the Chief Counsel
Immigration and Customs Enforcement
U.S. Department of Homeland Security
550 Main Street, Room 4001
Cincinnati, OH 45202

Telephone: (513) 684-3033

El Paso, Texas (ELP)

Office of the Chief Counsel
Immigration and Customs Enforcement
U.S. Department of Homeland Security
1545 Hawkins Boulevard, Room 275
El Paso, TX 79925

Mailing Address:
Office of the Chief Counsel
Immigration and Customs Enforcement
U.S. Department of Homeland Security
c/o 1 Stop Postal
P.O. Box 122
1535 Hawkins Boulevard, Suite B
El Paso, TX 79925
Telephone: (915) 225-1803

Honolulu, Hawaii (HHW)

Office of the Chief Counsel
Immigration and Customs Enforcement
U.S. Department of Homeland Security
595 Ala Moana Boulevard
Honolulu, HIi 96813-4999

Mailing Address: Same as above

Telephone: (808) 532-2149

Houston, Texas (HOU)

Office of the Chief Counsel
Immigration and Customs Enforcement
U.S. Department of Homeland Security
126 Northpoint Drive, Room 2020
Houston, TX 77060

Mailing Address:
Office of the Chief Counsel
Immigration and Customs Enforcement
U.S. Department of Homeland Security
P.O. Box 670049
Houston, TX 77267-0049

Telephone: (281) 774-4746

Huntsville Suboffice

Office of the Chief Counsel
Immigration and Customs Enforcement
U.S. Department of Homeland Security
Huntsville Office
7405C1 Highway 75 South
Huntsville, TX 77340

Mailing Address:
Office of the Chief Counsel
Immigration and Customs Enforcement
U.S. Department of Homeland Security
Huntsville Office
P.O. Box 237
Huntsville, TX 77342-0237

Telephone: (936) 730-3746/3748

Los Angeles, California (LOS)

Office of the Chief Counsel
Immigration and Customs Enforcement
U.S. Department of Homeland Security
606 South Olive Street, 8th Floor
Los Angeles, CA 90014

Mailing Address: Same as above

Telephone: (213) 894-2805

Las Vegas Suboffice

Immigration and Customs Enforcement
U.S. Department of Homeland Security
Trial Attorney Unit
3373 Pepper Lane
Las Vegas, NV 89120

Mailing Address: Same as above

Telephone: (702) 433-7288

Miami, Florida (MIA)

Office of the Chief Counsel
Immigration and Customs Enforcement
U.S. Department of Homeland Security
333 S. Miami Avenue, Suite 200
Miami, FL 33130

Telephone: (305) 400-6160

Newark, New Jersey (NEW)

Office of the Chief Counsel
Immigration and Customs Enforcement
U.S. Department of Homeland Security
970 Broad Street, Room 1104B
Newark, NJ 07102

Telephone: (973) 645-2318/2601/3091/6294

New Orleans, Louisiana (NOL)

Office of the Chief Counsel
Immigration and Customs Enforcement
U.S. Department of Homeland Security
1250 Poydras Street, Room 325
New Orleans, LA 70113

Telephone: (504) 599-7938

Please note that the chief counsel is stationed at Oakdale.

Oakdale Federal Alien Detention Facility (OAK)

Office of the Chief Counsel
Immigration and Customs Enforcement
U.S. Department of Homeland Security
1010 E. Whatley Road
Oakdale, LA 71463

Mailing Address:
Litigation Unit
Immigration and Customs Enforcement
U.S. Department of Homeland Security
P.O. Box 1128
Oakdale, LA 71463-1128

Telephone: (318) 335-0713

Memphis Suboffice

Immigration and Customs Enforcement
U.S. Department of Homeland Security
Clifford Davis Federal Building
167 North Main Street, Room 1036
Memphis, TN 38103-1876

Telephone: (901) 521-3301

New York, New York (NYC)

Office of the Chief Counsel
Immigration and Customs Enforcement
U.S. Department of Homeland Security
26 Federal Plaza, Room 1130
New York, NY 10278

Mailing Address:
Office of the Chief Counsel
Immigration and Customs Enforcement
U.S. Department of Homeland Security
P.O. Box 3507
New York, NY 10008-3507

Telephone: (212) 264-5916

APPENDIX 6D • ICE OFFICES OF COUNSEL

Varick Street Service Processing Center

Immigration and Customs Enforcement
U.S. Department of Homeland Security
Service Processing Center
Litigation Unit
201 Varick Street, Room 1130
New York, NY 10014

Telephone: (212) 337-2638/2639

Orlando, Florida (ORL)

Office of the Chief Counsel
Immigration and Customs Enforcement
U.S. Department of Homeland Security
80 N. Hughey Avenue, Suite #200
Orlando, FL 32801

Mailing Address: Same as above

Telephone: (407) 236-9932

Philadelphia, Pennsylvania (PHI)

Office of the Chief Counsel
Immigration and Customs Enforcement
U.S. Department of Homeland Security
1600 Callowhill Street, 4th Floor
Philadelphia, PA 19130

Mailing Address: Same as above

Telephone: (215) 656-7146

Phoenix, Arizona (PHO)

Office of the Chief Counsel
Immigration and Customs Enforcement
U.S. Department of Homeland Security
2035 N. Central Avenue, Room 266
Phoenix, AZ 85004

Mailing Address:
Office of the Chief Counsel
Immigration and Customs Enforcement
U.S. Department of Homeland Security
P.O. Box 25158
Phoenix, AZ 85002

Telephone: (602) 379-3164/3586/4007

Service Processing Center (FLO)

Immigration and Customs Enforcement
U.S. Department of Homeland Security
Service Processing Center
Trial Attorney Unit
3250 N. Pinal Parkway Avenue
Florence, AZ 85232

Telephone: (520) 868-3081/3127/3310

Eloy Detention Facility (EAZ)

Immigration and Customs Enforcement
U.S. Department of Homeland Security
Trial Attorney Unit
Eloy Detention Facility
1705 East Hanna Road
Eloy, AZ 85231

Telephone: (520) 464-3032

Tucson Suboffice

Immigration and Customs Enforcement
U.S. Department of Homeland Security
Trial Attorney Unit
6431 S. Country Club Road
Tucson, AZ 85706-5907

Mailing Address: Same as above

Telephone: (520) 670-4789

St. Paul, Minnesota (SPM)

Office of the Chief Counsel
Immigration and Customs Enforcement
U.S. Department of Homeland Security
2901 Metro Drive, Suite 100
Bloomington, MN 55425

Mailing Address:
Office of the Chief Counsel
Immigration and Customs Enforcement
U.S. Department of Homeland Security
P.O. Box 11898
St. Paul, MN 55111-0898

Telephone: (612) 313-9070

Omaha Suboffice (OMA)

Office of the Chief Counsel
Immigration and Customs Enforcement
U.S. Department of Homeland Security
1717 Avenue H
Omaha, NE 68110

Mailing Address: Same as above

Telephone: (402) 536-4800

San Antonio, Texas (SNA)

Office of the Chief Counsel
Immigration and Customs Enforcement
U.S. Department of Homeland Security
8940 Fourwinds Drive, Room 5045
San Antonio, TX 78239

Mailing Address:
Office of the Chief Counsel
Immigration and Customs Enforcement
U.S. Department of Homeland Security
P.O. Box 1939
San Antonio, TX 78297-1939

Telephone: (210) 967-7050

Harlingen Suboffice (HLG)

Office of the Chief Counsel
Immigration and Customs Enforcement
U.S. Department of Homeland Security
1717 Zoy Street
Harlingen, TX 78552

Mailing Address:
Office of the Chief Counsel
Immigration and Customs Enforcement
U.S. Department of Homeland Security
P.O. Box 1711
Harlingen, TX 78551

Telephone: (956) 389-7051

San Diego, California (SND)

Office of the Chief Counsel
Immigration and Customs Enforcement
U.S. Department of Homeland Security
880 Front Street, Room 2246
San Diego, CA 92101-8834

Mailing Address: Same as above

Telephone: (619) 557-5578

San Francisco, California (SFR)

Office of the Chief Counsel
Immigration and Customs Enforcement
U.S. Department of Homeland Security
120 Montgomery Street, Suite 200
San Francisco, CA 94111

Mailing Address:
Office of the Chief Counsel
Immigration and Customs Enforcement
U.S. Department of Homeland Security
P.O. Box 26449
San Francisco, CA 94126-6449

Telephone: (415) 705-4604/4486/4686

San Juan, Puerto Rico (SAJ)

Office of the Chief Counsel
Immigration and Customs Enforcement
U.S. Department of Homeland Security
San Patricio Office Plaza Center
7 Tabonuco Street, Suite 100
Guaynabo, PR 00968

Mailing Address:
Office of the Chief Counsel
Immigration and Customs Enforcement
U.S. Department of Homeland Security
GPO Box 365068
San Juan, PR 00936-5068

Telephone: (787) 706-2352/2353/2354

Seattle, Washington (SEA)

Office of the Chief Counsel
Immigration and Customs Enforcement
U.S. Department of Homeland Security
1000 Second Avenue, Suite 2900
Seattle, WA 98104

Mailing Address: Same as above

Telephone: (206) 553-2366

Northwest Detention Center

Immigration and Customs Enforcement
U.S. Department of Homeland Security
Detention and Removal Operations
Attn: Litigation Section
Northwest Detention Center
1623 East J Street, Suite 2
Tacoma, WA 98421

Telephone: (253) 779-6015

Portland Suboffice (POO)

Office of the Chief Counsel
Immigration and Customs Enforcement
U.S. Department of Homeland Security
Federal Office Building
511 NW Broadway, Room 318
Portland, OR 97209

Mailing Address:
Office of the Chief Counsel
Immigration and Customs Enforcement
U.S. Department of Homeland Security
P.O. Box 3361
Portland, OR 97208-3361

Telephone: (503) 326-2059

APPENDIX 6E
DETENTION FACILITIES

For additional information or updates, see *www.ice.gov/pi/dro/facilities.htm*.

Federally Owned Facilities*

Buffalo
Batavia FDF
4250 Federal Drive
Batavia, NY 14020
(585) 343-0814
Officer-in-Charge
Charles Mule

El Paso
El Paso SPC
8915 Montana Avenue
El Paso, TX 79925
(915) 225-1941
Officer-in-Charge
Alfredo Campos

Harlingen
Port Isabel SPC
27991 Buena Vista Rd
Los Fresnos, TX 78566
(956) 547-1700
Officer-in-Charge
Officer Beemer

Los Angeles
San Pedro SPC
2001 S. Seaside Ave.
Terminal Island
San Pedro, CA 90731
(310) 241-2300
Officer-in-Charge
Rudolph Garcia

Miami
Krome North SPC
18201 SW 12th Street
Miami, FL 33194
(305) 207-2001
Officer-in-Charge
Wesley Lee

New York
Varick Street SPC
201 Varick Street
New York, NY 10014
(212) 620-3449
Detainee message service
(212) 242-9893

Oakdale, LA
FDC Oakdale
2105 E. Whately Rd
Oakdale, LA 71463
(318) 335-4466
[mailing address]
P.O. Box 5010
Oakdale, LA 71463

Phoenix
Florence SPC
3250 N. Pinal Parkway
Florence, AZ 85232
(520) 868-5862
Officer-in-Charge
David A. Kollus

San Diego
El Centro SPC
1115 North Imperial Ave.
El Centro, CA 92243-1739
(760) 336-46000
Officer-in-Charge
Robert Rillamas

San Juan
Aguadilla SPC
505 Gun Road
Aguadilla, PR 00604
(787) 890-3600 / 3611
[mailing address]
P.O. Box 250480
Aguadilla, PR 00604
Officer-in-Charge
Jerry Collaza

Seattle
[Correctional Services Corp.]
Northwest Detention Center
1623 East J Street, Suite 2
Tacoma, WA 98421-1615
(253) 779-6000
[detainee mailing address]
Detainee Detention Number
1623 East J St, Suite 5
Tacoma, WA 98421

---

* All these facilities, except for Seattle and Oakdale, are ICE-owned and -operated service processing centers (SPCs) or federal detention facilities (FDFs). The Seattle facility is federally owned, but contractor-operated. Oakdale is owned and operated by Bureau of Prisons (part of DOJ).

Contractor-Owned and -Operated Detention Facilities

Denver
[Global Expertise Outsourcing (GEO)]
Aurora Contract Detention Facility
11901 E. 30th Avenue
Aurora, CO 80010
(303) 361-0701 (detainee information)
(303) 361-6612 (contacting detainees)

GEO Warden:
J. Alexander

ICE Supervisory Deportation Officer:
Robert Lindly, (303) 361-0723

Houston
[Corrections Corp. of America]
Houston Processing Center
15850 Export Plaza Dr.
Houston, TX 77032
(281) 449-1481

Officer-in-Charge
Douglas Henkel,
Assistant Field Office Director

Warden
Robert Lacy, Jr.

Newark
[Corrections Corp. of America]
Service Processing Center
625 Evans Street
Elizabeth, NJ 07201
(973) 622-7157

Warden
Charlotte Collins

Phoenix
[Corrections Corp. of America]
Eloy Detention Center
1705 East Hanna Road
Eloy, AZ 85231
(520) 466-4141

ICE Officer-in-Charge
John K. Crowther (Acting)

Warden
Bruno Stolc

San Antonio
[Corrections Corp. of America]
Laredo Contract Detention Facility
4702 E. Saunders
Laredo, TX 78041
(210) 727-4118

[ICE Office]
4602 E. Saunders
Laredo, TX 78041

Officer-in-Charge
Conrad Agagan, (956) 729-9620

Warden
Jose L. Hinojosa, (956) 727-4118

San Diego
[Corrections Corp. of America]
P.O. Box 438150
San Diego, CA 92143-9020
(619) 661-9119

Warden
Joe Easterling

Juvenile Shelter Care Facilities

Juveniles apprehended by the DHS are held in juvenile detention centers or in shelter care facilities located throughout the United States.

APPENDIX 6F
SELECTED RESOURCES FOR COUNTRY CONDITION INFORMATION

Amnesty International National Refugee Office 600 Pennsylvania Ave., S.E. Washington, DC 20003 (202) 544-0200 (202) 675-8569 fax E-mail: *refugee@aiusa.org* *www.amnesty.org*	Disseminates reports on persons imprisoned as prisoners of conscience or without trial and persons subject to unfair trial for political reasons, as well as reports on torture, disappearance, and execution. To obtain information to support asylum cases, send copy of I-589 with biographical statement of the applicant and cover letter from the attorney with the specific information desired. Four weeks' notice required. Publishes annual survey, *Amnesty International Report*.
Freedom House 120 Wall St., 26th Flr. New York, NY 10005 (212) 514-8040 (212) 514-8055 *or* 1301 Connecticut Ave. NW, Floor 6 Washington DC 20036 (202) 296-5101 (202) 293 2840 fax *www.freedomhouse.org*	Encourages development and existence of free institutions around the world. Operates research/documentation center and clearinghouse. Publishes *Nations in Transit* country reports, *Freedom in the World*, a survey of political rights and civil liberties, and various special reports.
Human Rights Watch 350 Fifth Ave., 34th Floor New York, NY 10017-6104 (212) 290-4700 (212) 736-1300 fax *or* 1630 Connecticut Ave., NW Suite 500 Washington, DC 20009 (202) 612-4321 (202) 612-4333 fax *www.hrw.org*	Monitors human rights violations of all types around the world. Made up of the following projects: Africa, the Americas, Asia, Europe, Middle East, Arms, Free Expression, Prison, and Women's Rights. Each regional project publishes a newsletter and reports on human rights violations in specific countries. Publishes newsletter and annual survey, *Human Rights Watch World Report*.

Human Rights First (formerly Lawyers Committee for Human Rights) 333 Seventh Ave., 13th Flr. New York, NY 10001 (212) 845-5200 (212) 845-5299 fax *or* 100 Maryland Ave., NE Suite 500 Washington, DC 20002 (202) 547-5692 (202) 543-5999 fax *www.humanrightsfirst.org*	Publishes human rights reports on various countries, with emphasis on abuses against the legal community and the judicial process. Also publishes annual critiques of the Department of State annual report on human rights conditions throughout the world. Refugee project promotes pro bono legal representation to asylum applicants. Provides training in international human rights and refugee law.
U.S. Government Printing Office Superintendent of Documents P.O. Box 371954 Pittsburgh, PA 15250-7954 (202) 512-1800 (202) 512-2250 fax *www.access.gpo.gov*	Publishes U.S. government documents and reports. Also supplies subscriptions to government publications. Publishes *Country Reports on Human Rights Practices*, the Department of State's annual report to Congress on individual, political, civil, and worker rights and human rights violations in countries throughout the world. Includes discussions on political and extrajudicial killings, disappearance, torture, arrest and detention, fair trial, civil liberties, and discrimination based on religion, race, sex, language, social status, and disability.
U.S. Committee for Refugees and Immigrants 1717 Massachusetts Ave., NW Suite 200 Washington, DC 20036 (202) 347-3507 (202) 347-3418 fax E-mail: *irsa@irsa-uscr.org* *www.refugees.org*	Public information arm of the Immigration & Refugee Services of America. Produces series of issue papers on individual countries and other country reports based on onsite visits. Publishes monthly newsletter *Refugee Reports*, and annual assessment of worldwide refugee situations in *World Refugee Survey*.
United Nations High Commissioner for Refugees 1775 K St., NW Suite 300 Washington, DC 20006 (202) 296-5191 (202) 296-5660 fax E-mail: *usawa@unhcr.org* *www.unhcr.org*	Promotes U.S. compliance with international standards of refugee protection. Assists asylum seekers and their representatives in effectively presenting their asylum claims to U.S. officials. Provides information on country conditions and human rights situations worldwide. Also assists in verifying refugee status in other countries. Maintains RefWorld online database, containing a vast collection of reports relating to situations in countries of origin, policy documents and positions, and documents relating to international and national legal frameworks.

APPENDIX 6G
USEFUL WEBSITES

U.S. Government Websites

(a) U.S. Citizenship and Immigration Services (USCIS)—*www.uscis.gov*

    This site contains a great deal of useful information, including:
- Immigration and Nationality Act
- Title 8 of the Code of Federal Regulations
- *Federal Register* excerpts
- Forms (including G-28, I-589, I-131, I-730, I-765)
- Affirmative Asylum Procedures Manual
- Policy memoranda

(b) Resource Information Center—*www.uscis.gov* ("Education and Resources" tab; then "Asylum Resources" hyperlink)

(c) Executive Office for Immigration Review—*www.usdoj.gov/eoir*

    This site contains:
- *Immigration Judges' Benchbook*—*www.usdoj.gov/eoir/statspub/benchbook.pdf*
- EOIR asylum statistics—*www.usdoj.gov/eoir/statspub.htm*
- BIA precedent decisions, *www.usdoj.gov/eoir/vll/libindex.html*, including a headnote table, *www.usdoj.gov/eoir/vll/intdec/chart/42403hdnttable.htm*
- BIA Practice Manual–*www.usdoj.gov/eoir/bia/qapracmanual/BIA_Practice_Man_FullVer.pdf*
- Questions and answers
- Information on immigration courts, including local rules, addresses, and phone numbers

(d) U.S. Department of State—*www.state.gov* (includes the human rights reports, *www.state.gov/g/drl/hr*, and *Annual Report on Religious Freedom*, *www.state.gov/g/drl/rls/irf*)

(e) Office of Personnel Management—*www.opm.gov* (includes a publication on citizenship laws of the world, *www.opm.gov/extra/investigate/IS-01.pdf*)

(f) Office of Refugee Resettlement (includes information on public benefits available asylees and refugees)—*www.acf.dhhs.gov/programs/orr*

(g) Government Printing Office daily updates of CFR—*http://ecfr.gpoaccess.gov*

(h) Library of Congress, for U.S. laws and laws of other countries—*www.loc.gov/law/guide*

Canadian Government Website

Immigration and Refugee Board of Canada—*www.irb-cisr.gc.ca/index.htm*

Nongovernmental Organizations (NGO) Websites

The following sites are excellent sources of information on country conditions and immigrants rights:

(a) Amnesty International—*www.amnesty.org*

(b) asylumlaw.org—*www.asylumlaw.org*

(c) Center for Gender and Refugee Studies—*http://cgrs.uchastings.edu*

(d) Freedom House—*www.freedomhouse.org*

(e) HRI (Human Rights Internet)—*www.hri.ca*

(f) Human Rights Watch—*www.hrw.org*

(g) HuriSearch—*www.hurisearch.org*

(h) International Crisis Group—*www.crisisgroup.org/home/index.cfm*

(i) International Rehabilitation Council for Torture Victims—*www.irct.org*

(j) National Immigration Law Center—*www.nilc.org*

(k) National Immigration Project of the National Lawyers Guild—*www.nationalimmigrationproject.org*

(l) Refugee Law Center—*www.refugeelawcenter.org*

(m) U.S. Committee for Refugees and Immigrants—*www.refugees.org*

(n) University of Minnesota Human Rights Library—*www1.umn.edu/humanrts*

(o) Women's Human Rights net—*www.whrnet.org*

United Nations Websites

(a) United Nations High Commissioner for Refugees—*www.unhcr.org*

   This website contains:
   - country-specific information about refugees
   - 1951 UN Convention Relating to the Status of Refugees
   - 1967 Protocol Relating to the Status of Refugees
   - UNHCR's *Handbook on Procedures and Criteria for Determining Refugee Status*
   - International Protection Guidelines

(b) United Nations Human Rights Council—*www.ohchr.org/english/bodies/hrcouncil*

   This website contains:
   - Committee Against Torture decisions—*www.ohchr.org/english/bodies/cat/index.htm*

- United Nations human rights treaties
- United Nations documents, reports, and publications

Legal Websites

(a) AILA InfoNet—*www.aila.org*; a member service of the American Immigration Lawyers Association, InfoNet provides news of recent legislation, regulatory activity, agency meetings, and more.

(b) ASIL Guide to Electronic Resources for International Law—*www.asil.org/resource/home.htm*; includes a guide to researching international law on the Internet.

(c) University of Minnesota Human Rights Library asylum and refugee resources — *www1.umn.edu/humanrts/center/asylum/refugee_index.html*; includes refugee treatises and instruments, UNHCR country of origin information, selected U.S. cases, and other publications.

(d) University of Michigan refugee caselaw site—*www.refugeecaselaw.org*; this site collects, indexes, and publishes selected recent court decisions from federal and supreme court decisions from the United States, Great Britain, Canada, Australia, New Zealand, Austria, Germany, and Switzerland.

(e) American Immigration Law Foundation—*www.ailf.org*; AILF's Legal Action Center provides mentoring and practice materials to attorneys across the country on all issues relating to immigration, including asylum. Its practice advisories, available online, address cutting-edge issues in immigration law, including asylum and appeal issues.

(f) Georgetown Law Library, Center for Applied Legal Research, Asylum Case Research Guide—
www.ll.georgetown.edu/intl/guides/CALSAsylumLawResearchGuide.cfm; this page describes some basic sources for research on behalf of individuals seeking asylum in the United States.

(g) Cornell University Law School, Legal Information Institute—*www.law.cornell.edu*; includes federal and state court decisions, U.S. Code, U.S. Constitution, Code of Federal Regulations, basic legal information, international law, United Nations materials, laws of foreign countries.

(h) Refugee Law Reader—*www.refugeelawreader.org*; includes cases, documents, articles, and others materials regarding refugee law, with a particular focus on the European asylum system.

(i) Researching Refugee Law, by Marci Hoffman (UC Berkeley)—
www.law.berkeley.edu/library/staff/mhoffman/refugees.html#us

(j) National Legal Aid and Defenders Association, Defending Immigrants Partnership webpage—*www.nlada.org/Defender/Defender_Immigrants*; includes charts analyzing the immigration consequences of state convictions, recent cases and news stories.

(k) LexisNexis—Immigration Law Cases of Interest—*www.lexisnexis.com/practiceareas/immigration/immigration_cases.asp*; includes cases from around the country, many unpublished and not available elsewhere.

(l) TRAC Immigration reports—*http://trac.syr.edu/immigration/reports*; includes data from immigration courts relating to asylum

Websites for U.S. Courts of Appeal

First Circuit—*www.ca1.uscourts.gov*
Second Circuit—*www.ca2.uscourts.gov*
Third Circuit—*www.ca3.uscourts.gov*
Fourth Circuit—*www.ca4.uscourts.gov*
Fifth Circuit—*www.ca5.uscourts.gov*
Sixth Circuit—*www.ca6.uscourts.gov*
Seventh Circuit—*www.ca7.uscourts.gov*
Eighth Circuit—*www.ca8.uscourts.gov*
Ninth Circuit—*www.ca9.uscourts.gov*
Tenth Circuit—*www.ca10.uscourts.gov*
Eleventh Circuit—*www.ca11.uscourts.gov*
D.C. Circuit—*www.cadc.uscourts.gov*
Federal Circuit—*www.cafc.uscourts.gov*

Other Sources

AILA's Guide to Technology and Legal Research for the Immigration Lawyer (AILA 3d Ed. 2003)
AILA*Link*

APPENDIX 6H
TORTURE TREATMENT PROGRAMS

* Contact persons ♦ Member of National Consortium of Torture Treatment Programs

ACCESS Psychosocial Rehabilitation Center for Survivors of Torture ♦
*Husam Abdulkhaleq
habdulkhaleq@accesscommunity.org
Ph: (313) 216-2202
Fax: (313) 584-3622
6450 Maple Street
Dearborn, MI 48126
www.accesscommunity.org

Advocates for Survivors of Trauma and Torture ♦
*Karen Hanscom, Maria Brown
klh@astt.org
mbrown@astt.org
Ph: (410) 464-9006
Fax: (410) 464-9010
431 E. Belvedere Avenue
Baltimore, MD 21212
www.astt.org

Asian Association of Utah (provisional member)
*Shu Cheng, Buu Diep
shuc@aau-slc.org
buud@aau-slc.org
Ph: (801) 467-6060
Fax: (801) 486-8007
1588 South Major St.
Salt Lake City, UT 84115
www.aau-slc.org

Bellevue/NYU Program for Survivors of Torture ♦
*Allen Keller, Carol Prendergast
ask45@aol.com
prendc02@med.nyu.edu
Ph: (212) 994-7169; (212) 994-7158
Fax: (212) 994-7177
462 First Ave., CD710
New York, NY 10016
www.survivorsoftorture.org

Boat People SOS, Inc.
*Thao Nguyen, Tuyet Duong
thao.nguyen@bpsos.org
tuyet.duong@bpsos.org
Ph: (281) 530-6888
11205 Bellaire Blvd., Suite B22
Houston, TX 77072
www.bpsos.org

Boston Center for Refugee Health and Human Rights ♦
*Lin Piwowarczyk, Michael Grodin
piwo@bu.edu
grodin@bu.edu
Ph: (617) 414-5082; (617) 414-4794
Fax: (617) 414-4796
Boston Medical Center Dowling 7
1 Boston Medical Center Place
Boston, MA 02118-2393
www.bcrhhr.org

Center for Survivors of Torture ♦
*Manuel Balbona, Sharmin DeMoss
manuel@cstdallas.org
sharmin@cstdallas.org
Ph: (214) 827-2314
Fax: (214) 887-4101
4123 Junius Street
P.O. Box 720668
Dallas, TX 75206
Central Texas Outreach Office
Phone: (512) 358-4612
Fax: (512) 358-4612
5124 Burnet Road
Austin, TX 78756
www.cstdallas.org

Center for Survivors of Torture (AACI) ♦
*Armina Husic
armina.husic@aaci.org
Ph: (408) 975-2379
Fax: (408) 975-2745
2400 Moorpark Ave., Ste. 300
San Jose, CA 95128
www.aaci.org/center-for-survivors-of-torture.htm

**Center for Survivors of
Torture and War Trauma** ♦
*Sherry Hogan-Smith, Jean Abbott
sherryh@stlcenterforsurvivors.org
jeanabbott4400@yahoo.com
Ph: (314) 533-4114; (314) 371-6500 x1148
Fax: (314) 533-4114
1077 S. Newstead
St. Louis, MO 63110
www.stlcenterforsurvivors.org

**Center for the Prevention and
Resolution of Violence** ♦
*Beverly Blashill, Robert Robin
bevblas@yahoo.com
rrobin@gci.net
Ph: (520) 628-7525
Fax: (520) 628-4309
738 N. 5th Avenue, Suite 104
Tucson, AZ 85705
www.hopifoundation.org

Center for Victims of Torture ♦
*Douglas Johnson, Pete Dross
djohnson@cvt.org
pdross@cvt.org
Minneapolis Healing Center
Ph: (612) 436-4800
Fax: (612) 436-2606
717 East River Road
Minneapolis, MN 55455
St. Paul Healing Center
Ph: (612) 436-4800
Fax: (612) 436-2604
649 Dayton Avenue
St. Paul, MN 55104
www.cvt.org

**Cross Cultural Counseling Center,
International Institute of New Jersey** ♦
*Sara Kahn, Kay Itzigsohn
skahn@iinj.org,
kitzigsohn@iinj.org
Ph: (201) 653-3888 x112 or x108
Fax: (201) 963-0252
One Journal Square Plaza, 4th Floor
Jersey City, NJ 07306
West New York Office
444 60th Street, 2nd Floor
West New York, NJ 07093
Phone: (201) 758-0022
Fax: (201) 758-1675
www.iinj.org

**DeKalb County Board of Health -
Center for Torture and Trauma Survivors** (provisional member)
*Kitty Kelley
kakelley@gdph.state.ga.us
Ph: (404) 297-7156; (404) 294-3800
Fax: (404) 508-7844
445 Winn Way, Suite 150
Decatur, GA 30030
www.dekalbhealth.net

**Doctors of the World-USA, Inc.
Human Rights Clinic** ♦
*Vandana Tripathi, Hari Acharya
Vandana.Tripathi@dowusa.org
hari.acharya@dowusa.org
Ph: (212) 226-9890
80 Maiden Lane, Suite 607
New York, NY 10038
www.doctorsoftheworld.org/projects/hr.cfm

F.I.R.S.T. Project, Inc. ♦
*Maria Prendes-Lintel, Jason Varga
mlintel@firstproject.org
jvarga@firstproject.org
Ph: (402) 488-6760
Fax: (402) 489-2296
1919 S. 40th Street, Suite 111
Lincoln, NE 68506
www.firstproject.org

**Florida Center for Survivors of
Torture—A Program of Gulf Coast
Jewish Family Services, Inc.** ♦
*Michael Bernstein, Stacie Blake
Mbernstein@gcjfs.org
SBlake@gcjfs.org
Pinellas Office:
14041 Icot Blvd.
Clearwater, FL 33760
Phone: (727) 450-7273
Fax: (727) 450-7285
Hillsborough Office:
13542 N. Florida Ave.
Tampa, FL 33613
Phone: (813) 987-6700
Fax: (813) 987-6588
Pasco Office:
6014 U.S. Hwy 19, Suite 201
New Port Richey, FL 33613
Phone: (727) 816-1550
Fax: (727) 816-1553
www.gcjfs.org/fl-center-survivors.htm

Appendix 6H • Torture Treatment Programs

Harvard Program in Refugee Trauma ♦
*Richard Mollica, Jim Lavelle
rmollica@partners.org
jlavelle@partners.org
Ph: (617) 876-7879
Fax: (617) 876-2360
Department of Psychiatry
Massachusetts General Hospital
22 Putnam Ave.
Cambridge, MA 02139
www.hprt-cambridge.org

**Institute for the Study of
Psychosocial Trauma** ♦
*Carlos Gonsalves
cjgons@mac.com
Ph: (650) 424-1314
Fax: (650) 424-0304
380 Edlee Avenue
Palo Alto, CA 94306

**International Survivors Center
c/o International Institute of Boston** ♦
*Lauren Shebairo, Kathleen Flinton
kflinton@iiboston.org
lshebairo@iiboston.org
Ph: (617) 695-9990
Fax: (617) 695-9191
One Milk Street
Boston, MA 02109
www.iiboston.org

**International Trauma Studies
Program-Refuge** ♦
*Jack Saul
info@itspnyc.org
Ph: (212) 691-4499
Fax: (212) 807-1809
155 Avenue of the Americas, 4th Floor
New York, NY 10013
http://itspnyc.org

Khmer Health Advocates ♦
*Heang Tan, Theanvy Kuoch
htan@khmerhealthadvocates.org
tkuoch@khmerhealthadvocates.org
Ph: (860) 561-3345
Fax: (860) 561-3538
29 Shadow Lane
W. Hartford, CT 06110
www.KhmerHealthAdvocates.org
www.CambodianHealth.org

Liberty Center for Survivors of Torture ♦
*Denise Michultka, Godelive Muttu
denisem@lcfsinpa.org
godelivem@lcfsinpa.org
Ph: (215) 747-7500 x252
Fax: (215) 747-7707
231 N. 63rd Street
Philadelphia, PA 19139-1111
www.lcfsinpa.org/survivors_torture

Lowell Community Health Center, Inc.
(provisional member)
*Sheila Och, Dorcas Grigg-Saito
sheilaOC@lchealth.org
dorcasgr@lchealth.org
Ph: (978) 746-7870
Fax: (978) 275-9890
585-597 Merrimack St.
Lowell, MA 01854
www.lchealth.org

**Lutheran Immigration and Refugee
Service, Detained Torture Survivors
Legal Support Network** ♦ (associate member)
*Annie Sovcik
asovcik@lirs.org
Ph: (410) 230-2744
Fax: (410) 230-2893
700 Light Street
Baltimore, MD 21230
www.lirs.org/What/programs/torturesurvivor.htm

Minnesota Advocates for Human Rights
*Michele Garnett McKenzie, Jennifer Prestholdt
mckenzie@mnadvocates.org
jprestholdt@mnadvocates.org
Ph: (612) 341-3302
Fax: (612) 341-2971
650 3rd Ave. S., #550
Minneapolis, MN 55402-1940
www.mnadvocates.org

**Program for Survivors of Torture
and Severe Trauma (PSTT) at CMHS** ♦
*Sonali Gupta, Dorothy Kiburi
sgupta@cmhs.org
dkiburi@cmhs.org
Ph: (703) 533-3302 x167; x130
Fax: (703) 237-2083
701 W. Broad Street, Suite 305

Falls Church, VA 22046
www.cmhsweb.org

Program for Torture Victims ♦
*Michael Nutkiewicz, Ana Deutsch, Jose Quiroga
nutkiewicz@ptvla.org
adeutsch@ptvla.org
jquirogamd@aol.com
Ph: (213) 747-4944
Fax: (213) 747-4662
3655 S Grand Ave., #290
Los Angeles, CA 90007
www.ptvla.org

Rocky Mountain Survivors Center ♦
*Ernie Duff, Izabela Lundberg
eduff@rmscdenver.org
ilundberg@rmscdenver.org
Ph: (303) 321-3221 x206
Fax: (303) 321-3314
1547 Gaylord St.
Denver, CO 80206
www.rmscdenver.org

Safe Horizon/Solace
Ph: (718) 899-1233
2 Lafayette Street, 3rd Floor
New York, NY 10007
www.safehorizon.org

St. Anselm's Cross-Cultural Community Center
Peter Nguyen
peternguyen@anselmcenter.org
Ph: (714) 537-0608 x334
Fax: (714) 537-7606
13091 Galway Street
Garden Grove, CA 92844
www.anselmcenter.org

Survivors International ♦
*Uwe Jacobs
info@survivorsintl.org
Ph: (415) 546-2080
Fax: (415) 546-2084
703 Market Square, #301
San Francisco, CA 94103
www.survivorsintl.org

Survivors of Torture, International ♦
Kathi Anderson*
kanderson@notorture.org
survivors@notorture.org
Ph: (619) 278-2407
Fax: (619) 294-9429
P.O. Box 151240
San Diego, CA 92175
www.notorture.org

The Center for Justice and Accountability ♦
(associate member)
*Pamela Merchant
pmerchant@cja.org
center4justice@cja.org
Ph: (415) 544-0444
Fax: (415) 544-0456
870 Market St., Suite 684
San Francisco, CA 94102
www.cja.org

The Marjorie Kovler Center for the Treatment of Survivors of Torture, of the Heartland Alliance for Human Needs and Human Rights ♦
*Mary Fabri, Mary Lynn Everson
mrfabri@ heartlandalliance.org
meverson@heartlandalliance.org
Ph: (773) 381-4070
Fax: (773) 381-4073
1331 W. Albion
Chicago, IL 60626
www.heartlandalliance.org

Torture Abolition and Survivors Support Coalition International ♦ (associate member)
*Orlando Tizon, Sister Dianna Ortiz
otizon@tassc.org
diortiz@tassc.org
Ph: (202) 529-2991
Fax: (202) 529-8334
4121 Harewood Road, NE Suite B
Washington, DC 20017
www.tassc.org

Torture Treatment Center of Oregon ♦
*J. David Kinzie, Crystal Riley
kinziej@ohsu.edu
rileyc@ohsu.edu
Ph: (503) 494-6148; (503) 494-6140
Fax: (503) 494-6143
Intercultural Psychiatric Program
Department of Psychiatry (UHN88)
Oregon Health and Science University
3181 S.W. Sam Jackson Park Road
Portland, OR 97201-3098

Utah Health and Human Rights Project ♦
*Susan Ritter, Mollie Murphy Dale
susan@uhhp.org
mollie@uhhp.org
Ph: (801) 363-4596
Fax: (801) 363-6068
309 East 100 South, Suite 11
Salt Lake City, UT 84110

War Trauma Recovery Project
*Chris Huber, Priscilla Schulz
wtr@stlouis.missouri.org
Ph: (314) 771-7061
P.O. Box 63100
St. Louis, MO 63163

APPENDIX 7A
AFFIRMATIVE AND DEFENSIVE ASYLUM PROCESS CHART

AFFIRMATIVE	DEFENSIVE
(*See* chapter 3 and appendices 2 and 3 for a more in-depth examination of each step in the affirmative process.)	(*See* chapter 3 and Appendices 2 and 5 for a more in-depth examination of each step in the defensive process.)
Interview Potential Applicant During the initial interviews with the applicant, it is important to determine: (1) that the applicant has a basis for submitting a claim; (2) that the applicant is eligible to apply affirmatively; (3) that the applicant is not barred from seeking asylum; and (4) that the applicant is not subject to reinstatement of removal because he or she was previously removed or ordered deported and subsequently re-entered the United States illegally.	**Interview Potential Applicant** During the initial interviews with the applicant, it is important to determine whether he or she: (1) has a basis for submitting a claim; (2) is eligible for any *other* relief in removal proceedings (*see* chapter 6); (3) was referred by an asylum officer after an affirmative or credible fear interview; and (4) is subject to a bar to asylum or withholding of removal.
Prepare the Application In addition to answering all of the questions on Form I-589, Application for Asylum and Withholding of Removal, it is useful to prepare a declaration of the applicant that gives a detailed, chronological account of the basis for the applicant's fear of returning to his or her home country. *See* appendix 2B for practice pointers.	**Release from Detention** If the applicant is detained, release from detention may be sought at a bond hearing before an IJ or from the ICE district director with jurisdiction over the applicant's place of custody. *See* chapter 3.8.
File the Application Carefully read and follow the instructions on the I-589 and file the application with the correct number of copies and the required documentation at the appropriate USCIS service center. USCIS will send an acknowledgment of receipt of the application or will return the application if it is not complete or has been incorrectly filed.	**Prepare the Application** In addition to answering all of the questions on Form I-589, Application for Asylum and Withholding of Removal, it is useful to prepare a declaration of the applicant that gives a detailed, chronological account of the basis for the applicant's fear of returning to his or her home country. *Note*: The information provided on the asylum application may be used to satisfy DHS's burden of proof in removal proceedings. If the applicant previously filed for asylum affirmatively or defensively or has had a credible fear interview under the expedited removal process, it is imperative that copies of the previous applications, statements, and/or interview notes be obtained prior to preparing the applicant's I-589.

AFFIRMATIVE	DEFENSIVE
(*See* chapter 3 and appendices 2 and 3 for a more in-depth examination of each step in the affirmative process.)	(*See* chapter 3 and Appendices 2 and 5 for a more in-depth examination of each step in the defensive process.)
Notice of Interview An interview will normally be scheduled within 45 days after the application is filed. A notice will be sent to the applicant approximately two weeks before the interview informing the applicant of the date, time, and location of the interview. *Note*: Always inform USCIS and the asylum office of any change of address to ensure that the interview notice and decision information is received.	**Master Calendar Hearings** At the applicant's master calendar, the following matters will be addressed: **Pleadings** The IJ will read the allegations and charges in the Notice to Appear and will ask the applicant or his or her attorney to respond to them. **Filing of the Application** Carefully read and follow the instructions on the I-589 and file the application with the correct number of copies and the required documentation at the immigration court. The application must be filed at a master calendar hearing. **Motions** The IJ will consider a variety of motions at this stage, including motions for a continuance, for change of venue, and for withdrawal or substitution of counsel.
Asylum Interview The applicant will be interviewed by an asylum officer who has reviewed the application submitted by the applicant. If the applicant does not speak English fluently, he or she must bring an interpreter to the interview. The applicant may be represented by counsel at the interview and may bring witnesses and submit additional documentation. *See* appendix 3B for a checklist.	**Hearing on Deportability or Inadmissibility** If the charge or charges on the Notice to Appear are contested, the IJ may schedule a separate hearing on whether the applicant is subject to removal from the United States. If the IJ finds that the applicant is not subject to removal, applying for relief from removal is no longer necessary.
Employment Authorization	
The Application for Employment Authorization, Form I-765, may be submitted "no earlier" than 150 days after the date the completed asylum application is filed. An individual is ineligible for employment authorization if he or she has been convicted of an aggravated felony or if his or her application for asylum was denied by an asylum officer or IJ within 150 days after submitting his or her application. See chapter 3.9 for more information regarding employment authorization for asylum applicants.	

APPENDIX 7A • AFFIRMATIVE AND DEFENSIVE ASYLUM PROCESS CHART

AFFIRMATIVE	DEFENSIVE
(*See* chapter 3 and appendices 2 and 3 for a more in-depth examination of each step in the affirmative process.)	(*See* chapter 3 and Appendices 2 and 5 for a more in-depth examination of each step in the defensive process.)
Decision The asylum officer may grant, deny, or refer an asylum claim. At the end of the asylum officer interview, the applicant will be informed where and when he or she must appear to acknowledge receipt of the asylum officer's written decision. If the interview is conducted on a circuit ride by the asylum officer, the decision may be mailed to the applicant. **Grant** An applicant is eligible to apply for permanent residency one year after he or she has granted asylum. Prior to granting asylum, the asylum office must check the identity of the applicant against all appropriate records and databases maintained by the secretaries of DHS and State and the attorney general, including the Automated Visa Lookout System. **Denial** An applicant will only be issued a denial if he or she is in lawful status. Prior to issuing a denial, the asylum officer must provide the applicant with a Notice of Intent to Deny and allow the applicant to submit a rebuttal.	**Merits Hearing on Requested Relief (Individual Calendar Hearing)** If the applicant has been determined to be subject to removal, his or her application for asylum and withholding and any other form of relief sought will be considered by the IJ at an individual calendar hearing. A hearing on the merits is usually completed within 180 days after the application is filed with the IJ.
Referral If the asylum claim is not granted and the applicant appears to be deportable or inadmissible, he or she will be issued a Notice to Appear for removal proceedings. *See* DEFENSIVE side of the Asylum Process Chart.	**Appeal to BIA** The IJ's decision to grant or deny asylum or withholding of removal may be appealed by the applicant *or* DHS to the Board of Immigration Appeals within 30 days after the date of the IJ's decision.
No Appeal/Motions to Reopen or Reconsider There is no appeal from an asylum officer's decision. An applicant who is referred for removal proceedings may renew his or her request for asylum before an IJ. Under some circumstances it may be possible to file a motion to reopen or reconsider with Asylum HQ or the asylum office that issued the decision. *See* chapter 3.2.5.	**Judicial Review** A negative decision by the BIA may be appealed to a federal court *unless* the contested issue involves one or more of the following determinations, which are not reviewable: (1) the availability of a safe third country; (2) the one-year filing deadline; (3) the previous denial bar; or (4) the terrorist bar. *See* chapter 3.12.

AFFIRMATIVE	DEFENSIVE
(*See* chapter 3 and appendices 2 and 3 for a more in-depth examination of each step in the affirmative process.)	(*See* chapter 3 and Appendices 2 and 5 for a more in-depth examination of each step in the defensive process.)
No Appeal/Motions to Reopen or Reconsider	**Judicial Review**
There is no appeal from an asylum officer's decision. An applicant who is referred for removal proceedings may renew his or her request for asylum before an IJ. Under some circumstances it may be possible to file a motion to reopen or reconsider with Asylum HQ or the asylum office that issued the decision. *See* chapter 3.2.5.	A negative decision by the BIA may be appealed to a federal court *unless* the contested issue involves one or more of the following determinations, which are not reviewable: (1) the availability of a safe third country; (2) the one-year filing deadline; (3) the previous denial bar; or (4) the terrorist bar. *See* chapter 3.12.

APPENDIX 7B
FLOWCHART OF EXPEDITED REMOVAL/CREDIBLE FEAR PROCESS

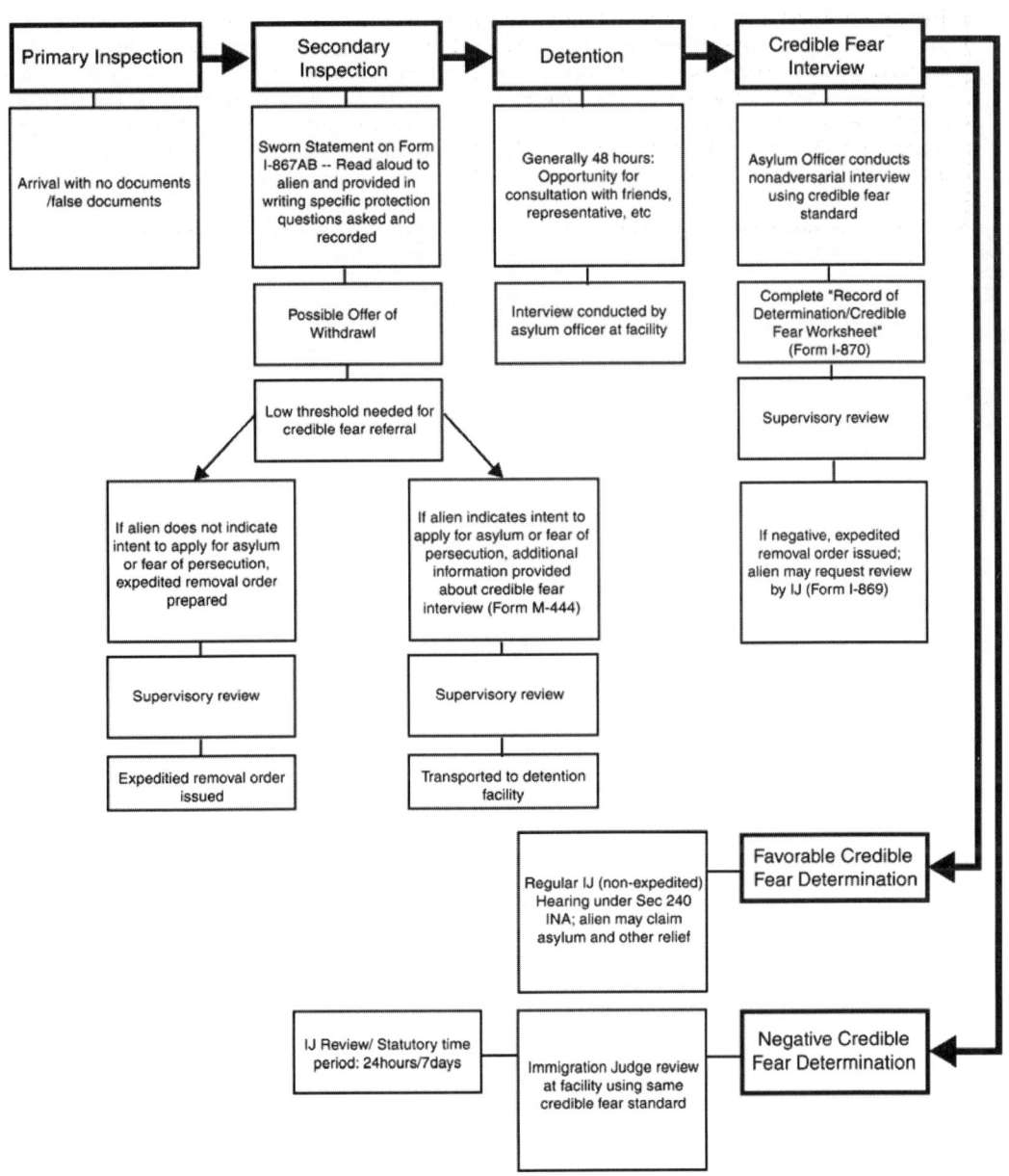

APPENDIX 7C

A COMPARISON OF THE FORMS OF PROTECTION AVAILABLE UNDER U.S. LAW

Protection under article 3 of the Convention Against Torture (CAT) is not the same as asylum or as withholding of removal. The following chart, adapted from legacy INS materials (and *not* necessarily the view of the author), compares these forms of protection:

Asylum	Withholding of Removal	CAT Relief
Not a treaty obligation	A treaty obligation (art. 33)	A treaty obligation
Discretionary	Mandatory	Mandatory
One-year filing deadline	No filing deadline	No filing deadline
Standard requires a *well-founded fear of persecution* on account of race, religion, nationality, membership in a particular social group, or political opinion in the country in question. Harm feared must be on account of a protected ground.	Standard requires that it is *more likely than not that the person would be persecuted* on account of race, religion, nationality, membership in a particular social group, or political opinion in the country in question. Harm feared must be on account of a protected ground.	Standard requires that the person is *more likely than not to be tortured* in the country in question. Harm feared need not be on account of a protected ground.
Persons ineligible for protection include certain criminals, terrorists, persecutors.	Persons ineligible for protection include certain criminals, terrorists, persecutors.	No bars to protection for deferral of removal applicants.
Basis for adjustment to legal permanent resident status.	Not basis for adjustment to legal permanent resident status.	Not basis for adjustment to legal permanent resident status.
Immediate family members may be granted same status derivatively.	Family members may not be granted derivative status.	Family members may not be granted derivative status.
Grant confers permission to remain in United States.	Grant prohibits only removal to country of risk; does not prohibit removal to nonrisk country.	Grant prohibits only removal to country of risk; does not prohibit removal to nonrisk country.

APPENDIX 7D
TEMPORARY PROTECTED STATUS

The Temporary Protected Status (TPS) statute and DHS regulations (INA §244 and 8 CFR Part 244) provide eligible aliens from designated countries a temporary stay of removal and employment authorization for the designated TPS period and for any extensions. For eligibility information, please see 8 CFR Part 244. TPS does not lead to permanent resident status. When a TPS designation ends, beneficiaries revert to the immigration status they had prior to TPS (unless that benefit has expired or been terminated) or to any other status they may have been granted while in TPS. Chart current through October 2007.

Country	Designation Date	Current Expiration Date	Federal Register Cite (most recent)
Burundi	11/04/1997	5/02/2009	72 FR 61172 (10/29/2007)
El Salvador	03/09/2001	03/09/2009	72 FR 46649 (08/21/2007)
Honduras	01/05/1999	01/05/2009	72 FR 29529 (05/29/2007)
Nicaragua	01/05/1999	01/05/2009	69 FR 64088 (05/29/2007)
Somalia	09/16/1991	03/17/2008	71 FR 42653 (07/27/2006)
Sudan	11/04/1997	11/02/2008	72 FR 10541 (03/08/07)

Note: The designation of Liberia for TPS was terminated effective 12:01 a.m. October 1, 2007. 71 Fed. Reg. 55000 (Sept. 20, 2006). DHS granted an 18-month extension of employment authorization, through March 31, 2009, to those Liberians with TPS status as of September 30, 2007, who are provided deferred enforced departure in accordance with President Bush's Memorandum to Secretary of Homeland Security, Michael Chertoff, dated September 12, 2007. 72 Fed. Reg. 53596 (Sept. 19, 2007).

Note: TPS for Burundi has been terminated, effective May 2, 2009. 72 Fed. Reg. 61172 (Oct. 29, 2007).

APPENDIX 7E
BENEFITS OR ASSISTANCE AVAILABLE TO ASYLEES

The benefits and forms of assistance listed in this chart are applicable to individuals who have already been granted asylum.

Type of Benefit or Assistance	Description	Eligibility Period for Asylees (from date of asylum grant)
Employment authorization document (EAD)	Document issued by USCIS free of charge to asylees that provides evidence that the holder is authorized to work in the United States (Form I-765). Once an asylee's EAD expires, the asylee may offer other documents as proof of employment eligibility, but may still want to renew the EAD as proof of identity if a green card has not yet been received. The filing fee for renewing an EAD is $340, but fee waivers are available for individuals who are unable to pay the fee.	2 years (may be renewed for a fee)
Social Security card	Provides documentation necessary for employment, Social Security benefits, and other government services, and is also often required by other businesses like banks and credit companies. Because some services and benefits provided to asylees require asylees to enroll within 31 days of the date they are granted asylum, it is important that asylees apply for Social Security numbers quickly. Asylees receive unrestricted Social Security cards. *www.ssa.gov/pubs/10002.html*	No time limit
State driver's license or ID card	Requirements for obtaining a driver's license or identification card vary by state. Common requirements include proof of identity, proof of legal presence, proof of in-state residency, and proof of a Social Security number (if one has been issued). In some jurisdictions, asylees or applicants for asylum may present an application for asylum along with documentation from USCIS or U.S. immigration court indicating either receipt or approval of the application as proof of identity and legal presence. Unexpired EADs or Form I-94 Records of Arrival and Departure stamped Asylee may also be accepted as valid documentation in some jurisdictions. The websites of local motor vehicle departments list the acceptable forms of identification and proof of residency.	Varies by state

Type of Benefit or Assistance	Description	Eligibility Period for Asylees (from date of asylum grant)
Match grant	Selectively provides job counseling and placement, case management, cash, and living assistance. Serves as an alternative to RCA (below) and is administered through nonprofit groups participating in the federal match grant program, with the objective of helping asylees quickly become self-sufficient. Must be enrolled within 31 days of asylum grant date.* www.acf.hhs.gov/programs/orr/programs/match_grant_prg.htm	180 days
Temporary Assistance to Needy Families (TANF)	A monthly cash payment to low-income asylees with children under the age of 18, regardless of the children's immigration status. www.acf.dhhs.gov/programs/ofa	5 years (but may be extended at state option)
Supplemental Security Income (SSI)	Provides monthly cash payments to low-income asylees who are 65 or older, blind, or disabled and unable to work. Must be certified by the Social Security Administration. www.ssa.gov/pubs/11000.html	7 years (with exceptions)
Medicaid	Reimburses payments to health care providers for medical expenses of certain low-income individuals, primarily pregnant women, families with children, the elderly, and the disabled. Guidelines regarding eligibility and services vary by state. www.cms.hhs.gov/home/medicaid.asp	7 years (but may be extended at state option)
Refugee Cash and Medical Assistance (RCA & RMA)	Provide federally funded, state administered benefits to asylees who meet the financial requirements of TANF and Medicaid, but are not eligible for these programs because they fail to meet other nonfinancial requirements. Like TANF, the amount of assistance received under RCA varies based on local rules and family size. Most jurisdictions require that an adult receiving RCA participate in employment training. Asylees may also be eligible for emergency cash relief for limited periods. Children ineligible for TANF may usually renew their RCA benefits indefinitely. Some jurisdictions require that the asylee apply within 30 days of receiving asylum. www.acf.hhs.gov/programs/orr/programs/cma.htm	8 months

APPENDIX 7E • BENEFITS OR ASSISTANCE AVAILABLE TO ASYLEES

Type of Benefit or Assistance	Description	Eligibility Period for Asylees (from date of asylum grant)
Food stamps	Provides coupons or debit cards that may be redeemed at grocery stores. Amount provided varies based on family size and income and usually requires that an able-bodied adult recipient register for an employment assistance program or be employed. May be provided indefinitely to children of asylees, although renewal of benefits may be required. *www.fns.usda.gov/fsp*	7 years (but may be extended at state option)
Torture treatment centers	Provides rehabilitative services to asylees who have been the victims of torture. Federal grants from the Office of Refugee Resettlement (ORR) provide funding for treatment of physical and psychological effects of torture, social and legal services, and research and training for health care providers. Refer to Appendix 6H for a listing of torture treatment programs and contact information. *www.acf.hhs.gov/programs/orr/programs/services_survivors_torture.htm*	No time limit
Medical screening	In states where available, an assessment conducted by the state department of public health, which may include early diagnosis and treatment of illnesses, screening for TB, parasites, and hepatitis, as well as school vaccinations for asylee children.	Varies by state, but is strongly recommended where available and should be arranged within 90 days of asylum grant
Refugee social services	Provide services to refugees, including English language training, employability services, case management, social adjustment services, and interpretation services, with the objective of facilitating early economic self-sufficiency and social adjustment. *www.acf.hhs.gov/programs/orr/programs/ref_social_prg.htm*	5 years (except for some refugee social services, which are provided pursuant to discretionary grants without time limits)

* An asylee may be enrolled within 31 days of *notification* of grant of asylum if an exception letter to the program guidelines is obtained from the ORR Matching Grant Team.

APPENDIX 8A
RECOMMENDED TEXTS AND TOOLS

The following books and publications are additional sources of information regarding asylum and refugee law that may be useful as you prepare your case:

Texts

- USCIS, Office of International Division, Asylum Division, *Affirmative Asylum Procedures Manual* (available at *www.uscis.gov/files/nativedocuments/Affrm AsyManFNL.pdf*)

- *Immigration & Nationality Law Handbook* (AILA) (annual editions)

- D. Anker, *Law of Asylum in the United States*

- G. Goodwin-Gill & J. McAdam, *The Refugee in International Law*

- A. Grahl-Madsen, *The Status of Refugees in International Law*

- J. Hathaway, *The Law of Refugee Status*

- National Immigrant Justice Center, *Basic Procedural Manual for Asylum Representation: Affirmatively and in Removal Proceedings*

- Immigration Equality & Midwest Immigrant and Human Rights Center, *Winning Asylum, Withholding and CAT Cases Based on Sexual Orientation, Transgender Identity and/or HIV Positive Status* ("LGBT/HIV Asylum Manual") (available at *www.immigrationequality.org/manual_template.php*)

- R. Jobe, M. Silverman, & L. Katzman, *Winning Asylum Cases* (Immigrant Legal Resource Center)

- Immigration and Naturalization Service, *Basic Law Manual—U.S. Law and INS Refugee/Asylum Adjudications*

- D. Kesselbrenner & L. Rosenberg, *Immigration Law and Crimes* (West loose-leaf service)

- V. Kot, *The Impact of Cultural Factors on Credibility in the Asylum Context* (Immigrant Legal Resource Center)

- I. Kurzban, *Kurzban's Immigration Law Sourcebook* (AILA) (biennial editions)

- D. Martin, *Asylum Case Law Sourcebook* (West) (biennial editions)

- Midwest Immigrant and Human Rights Center, *Immigration and You: A Manual for Children* (available at *www.asylumlaw.org/docs/children/MIHRC_childrens_man ual_2004.pdf*)

- P. Schrag, *A Well-Founded Fear: The Congressional Battle to Save Political Asylum in America*
- UNHCR, *Handbook on Procedures and Criteria for Determining Refugee Status* (available at *www.unhcr.org/publ/PUBL/3d58e13b4.pdf*)
- UNHCR, *Collection of International Instruments and Legal Texts Concerning Refugees and Others of Concern to UNHCR* (four-volume set available at *www.unhcr.org/publ/PUBL/455c460b2.html*)

Periodicals

- *Immigration Law Today* (AILA) (bimonthly)
- *Bender's Immigration Bulletin*, Matthew Bender (bimonthly)
- *Immigration Briefings*, available on Westlaw (monthly)
- National Immigration Project of the National Lawyers Guild (quarterly news bulletins; membership required)
- *Immigrants' Rights Update*, National Immigration Law Center (available at *www.nilc.org/pubs/iru/index.htm*)

Online databases

- AILA*Link*, *www.ailalink.org* (AILA)
- RefWorld, *www.refworld.org* (UNHCR)

Appendix 8B
Resource Availability

The UNHCR Handbook
- UNHCR, 1775 K Street, N.W., Suite 300, Washington, DC 20006 Fax: (202) 296-5660; e-mail: *usawa@unhcr.org*
- Also available on UNHCR's website at *www.unhcr.org/publ/PUBL/3d58e13b4.pdf*

Sources for Researching Customary International Law
- Georgetown University International Law Library: *www.ll.georgetown.edu/staff/int/index.cfm*
- Restatement (Third) of Foreign Relations Law
- UNHCR's website: *www.unhcr.org*
- UNHCR's RefWorld website: *www.refworld.org*

Foreign Case Law and Statutes
- Law libraries with a foreign law collection
- *www.refugeecaselaw.org*: a website of the University of Michigan Law School, containing refugee and asylum cases from the highest courts of Australia, Austria, Canada, Germany, New Zealand, Switzerland, the United Kingdom, and the United States
- The Office of Personnel Management's *Citizenship Laws of the World* (March 2001), available at *www.opm.gov/extra/investigate/IS-01.pdf*
- Library of Congress Law Library, 101 Independence Avenue, S.E., Washington, DC 20540, (202) 707-5079; website: *www.loc.gov/law/public/law.html* (contains the Global Legal Information Network (GLIN), with laws from numerous countries)
- UNHCR's Washington Office (address above); *usawa@unhcr.ch* provides assistance in determining refugee status or "firm resettlement" of asylum applicants in third countries

Immigration and Nationality Act
- Law libraries, under Title 8 of the U.S. Code
- USCIS website: *www.uscis.gov*
- AILA Publications (*www.ailapubs.org;* (800) 982-2839): AILA*Link* (*www.ailalink.org*) and *Immigration & Nationality Act* (annual editions)
- Title 8 of the U.S. Code is available at *www.gpoaccess.gov/uscode/index.html*. Print copies are available for purchase from the Superintendent of Documents, U.S. Government Printing Office, P.O. Box 371954, Pittsburgh, PA 15250-7954. Tel: (202) 512-1800; fax: (202) 512-2104; online at *http://bookstore.gpo.gov*

Title 8 of the Code of Federal Regulations
- Law libraries
- USCIS website: *www.uscis.gov*
- Title 8 of the Code of Federal Regulations is available for purchase from the Superin-

tendent of Documents, U.S. Government Printing Office (address, phone, fax, and website above)
- AILA Publications (*www.ailapubs.org;* (800) 982-2839): AILA*Link* (*www.ailalink.org*) and *Immigration Regulations* (CFR) (annual editions)

BIA Decisions
- Law libraries with an immigration law collection
- EOIR Virtual Law Library: *www.usdoj.gov/eoir/vll/libindex.html*
- AILA Publications (*www.ailapubs.org;* (800) 982-2839): AILA*Link* (*www.ailalink.org*)
- AILA InfoNet (*www.aila.org*) and *Immigration Law Today* (AILA)
- Current decisions: Superintendent of Documents, U.S. Government Printing Office (address above)

Legacy INS, DHS, and EOIR Policy Directives, Memoranda, and Statements
- Law libraries with an immigration law collection
- AILA Publications (*www.ailapubs.org;* (800) 982-2839): AILA*Link* (*www.ailalink.org*)
- AILA InfoNet (*www.aila.org*)
- USCIS website: *www.uscis.gov*
- ICE website: *www.ice.gov*
- EOIR website: *www.usdoj.gov/eoir*

Field Manuals
- asylumlaw.org website: *www.asylumlaw.org*
- C. Gordon, S. Mailman, & S. Yale-Loehr, *Immigration Law and Procedure*, vol. 10 (Matthew Bender)
- AILA Publications (*www.ailapubs.org;* (800) 982-2839): AILA*Link* (*www.ailalink.org*)
- Lexis and Westlaw

Detention Operations Manual
- ICE website: *www.ice.gov/partners/dro/opsmanual/index.htm*

Affirmative Asylum Procedures Manual
- USCIS website: *www.uscis.gov/files/nativedocuments/AffrmAsyManFNL.pdf*

Basic Law Manual
- Law libraries with an immigration law collection

Asylum Officer Basic Training Course lesson plans
- Rocky Mountain Survivors Center website: *www.rmscdenver.org/legal_aobtc.html*

APPENDIX 9A

FORM I-589 AND INSTRUCTIONS

Department of Homeland Security
U.S. Citizenship and Immigration Services
U.S. Department of Justice
Executive Office for Immigration Review

OMB No. 1615-0067; Expires 12/31/07

I-589, Application for Asylum and for Withholding of Removal

Instructions

What Is the Purpose of This Form?

This form is used to apply for asylum in the United States and for withholding of removal (formerly called "withholding of deportation"). This application may also be used to apply for protection under the Convention Against Torture. You may file this application if you are physically present in the United States and you are not a U.S. citizen.

NOTE: You **must** submit an application for asylum within one year of arriving in the United States, unless there are changed circumstances that materially affect your eligibility for asylum or extraordinary circumstances directly related to your failure to file within one year. (See **Page 5** of the Instructions, Part 1: Filing Instructions, Section V, "Completing the Form," Part C, for further explanation.)

You may include in your application your spouse and unmarried children who are under 21 years of age and physically present in the United States. You **must** submit certain documents for your spouse and each child included, as required by these instructions. Children 21 years of age or older and married children must file separate Form I-589 applications. If you are granted asylum and your spouse and/or any unmarried children under the age of 21 are outside the United States, you may file Form I-730, Refugee and Asylee Relative Petition, for them to gain similar benefits.

Instruction Sections: Filing Information and How Your Application Will Be Processed.

The instructions are divided into two sections.

The first section has filing information. This section discusses basic eligibility criteria and guides you through filling out and filing the application.

The second section explains how your application will be processed. This section also describes potential interim benefits available while your application is pending.

Please read these instructions carefully. The instructions will help you complete your application and understand how it will be processed. If you have questions about your eligibility, how to complete the form or the asylum process, you may wish to consult an attorney or other qualified person to assist you. (See **Page 4** of the Instructions, Part I, Filing Instructions, Section IV, "Right to Counsel.")

Additional Information on Websites.

Additional information concerning asylum and withholding of removal is available on the following websites: Department of Homeland Security (DHS), U.S. Citizenship and Immigration Services (USCIS): **http://www.uscis.gov** and U.S. Department of Justice (DOJ), Executive Office for Immigration Review (EOIR): **http://www.usdoj.gov/eoir**.

WARNING: Applicants in the United States illegally are subject to removal if their asylum or withholding claims are not granted by an asylum officer or an immigration judge. Any information provided in completing this application may be used as a basis for the institution of, or as evidence in, removal proceedings, even if the application is later withdrawn.

Applicants determined to have knowingly made a frivolous application for asylum will be permanently ineligible for any benefits under the Immigration and Nationality Act (INA). You may not avoid a frivolous finding simply because someone advised you to provide false information in your asylum application.

If filing with USCIS, unexcused failure to appear for an appointment or to provide biometrics (such as fingerprints) and other biographical information within the time allowed may delay eligibility for employment authorization and result in an asylum officer dismissing your asylum application or referring it to an immigration judge. Applicants and eligible dependents in removal proceedings who fail without good cause to provide DHS with their biometrics or their biographical information as required within the time allowed may have their applications found abandoned by the immigration judge. See sections 208(d)(5)(A) and 208(d)(6) of the INA and 8 Code of Federal Regulations (CFR) sections 208.10, 1208.10, 208.20, 1003.47(d) and 1208.20.

Table of Contents

Instructions for Form I-589	1
Part 1. Filing Instructions	2
I. Who May Apply and Filing Deadlines	2
II. Basis of Eligibility	2
A. Asylum	2
B. Withholding of Removal	2
C. Deferral of Removal Under the Convention Against Torture	3
D. Legal Sources Relating to Eligibility	3
III. Confidentiality	4
IV. Right to Counsel	4
V. Completing the Form	4
Part A. I. Information About You	4
Part A. II. Spouse and Children	5
Part A. III. Information About Your Background	5
Part B. Information About Your Application	5
Part C. Additional Information About Your Application	5
Part D. Your Signature	6
Part E. Signature of Person Preparing Form, If Other Than You	6
Part F. To Be Completed at Asylum Interview, If Applicable	6
Part G. To Be Completed at Removal Hearing, If Applicable	6
VI. Required Documents and Required Number of Copies That You Must Submit With Your Application	6
VII. Additional Evidence That You Should Submit	7
VIII. Fee	7
IX. Biometrics, Including Fingerprints and Photographs	7
X. Organizing Your Application	7
XI. Incomplete Asylum Applications	8
XII. Where to File	8
Part 2. Information Regarding Post-Filing Requirements	9
I. Notification Requirements When Your Address Changes	9
II. Asylum Interview Process	9
III. Status While Your Application Is Pending	10
IV. Travel Outside the United States	10
V. Employment Authorization While Your Application Is Pending	10
VI. Privacy Act Notice	10
VII. Paperwork Reduction Act Notice	10
Supplements to Form I-589	11

Part 1. Filing Instructions.

I. Who May Apply and Filing Deadlines.

You may apply for asylum irrespective of your immigration status and even if you are in the United States unlawfully.

You MUST file this application within one year after you arrived in the United States, unless you can show that there are changed circumstances that affect your eligibility for asylum or extraordinary circumstances that prevented you from filing within one year. (See Page 5 of the Instructions, Part I: Filing Instructions, Section V, "Completing the Form," Part C, for further explanation of this requirement.)

If you have previously been denied asylum by an immigration judge or the Board of Immigration Appeals, you must show that there are changed circumstances that affect your eligibility for asylum.

The determination of whether you are permitted to apply for asylum will be made once you have had an asylum interview with an asylum officer or a hearing before an immigration judge. Even if you are not eligible to apply for asylum for the reasons stated above, you may still be eligible to apply for withholding of removal under section 241(b)(3) of the INA or under the Convention Against Torture before the Immigration Court.

II. Basis of Eligibility.

A. Asylum.

In order to qualify for asylum, you must establish that you are a refugee who is unable or unwilling to return to his or her country of nationality, or last habitual residence in the case of a person having no nationality, because of persecution or a well-founded fear of persecution on account of race, religion, nationality, membership in a particular social group or political opinion. This means that you must establish that race, religion, nationality, membership in a particular social group or political opinion was or will be at least one central reason for your persecution or why you fear persecution. (See section 208 of the INA; 8 CFR sections 208 and 1208, et seq.)

If you are granted asylum, you and any eligible spouse or child included in your application will be permitted to remain and work in the United States and may eventually adjust to lawful permanent resident status. **If you are not granted asylum, the Department of Homeland Security (DHS) may use the information you provide in this application to establish that you are removable from the United States.**

B. Withholding of Removal.

Your asylum application is also considered to be an application for withholding of removal under section 241(b)(3) of the INA, as amended. It may also be considered an application for withholding of removal under the Convention Against Torture if you checked the box at the top of **Page 1** of the application form, or if the evidence you present indicates that you may be tortured in the country of removal. (See 8 CFR sections 208.13(c)(1) and 1208.13(c)(1).) If asylum is not granted, you may still be eligible for withholding of removal.

Regardless of the basis for the withholding application, you will not be eligible for withholding if you:

(1) Assisted in Nazi persecution or engaged in genocide;

(2) Have persecuted another person;

(3) Have been convicted by a final judgment of a particularly serious crime and therefore represent a danger to the community of the United States;

(4) Are considered for serious reasons to have committed a serious non-political crime outside the United States; or

(5) Represent a danger to the security of the United States. (See section 241(b)(3) of the INA; 8 CFR sections 208.16 and 1208.16.)

i. Withholding of Removal Under Section 241 (b)(3) of the INA.

In order to qualify for withholding of removal under section 241(b)(3) of the INA, you must establish that it is more likely than not that your life or freedom would be threatened on account of race, religion, nationality, membership in a particular social group or political opinion in the proposed country of removal.

If you obtain an order withholding your removal, you cannot be removed to the country where your life or freedom would be threatened. This means that you may be removed to a third country where your life or freedom would not be threatened. Withholding of removal does not adhere derivatively to any spouse or child included in the application. They would have to apply for such protection on their own.

If you are granted withholding of removal, this would not give you the right to bring your relatives to the United States. It also would not give you the right to become a lawful permanent resident of the United States.

ii. Withholding of Removal Under the Convention Against Torture.

The Convention Against Torture refers to the United Nations Convention Against Torture and other Cruel, Inhuman or Degrading Treatment or Punishment.

To be granted withholding of removal to a country under the Convention Against Torture, you must show that it is more likely than not that you would be tortured in that country.

"Torture" is defined in Article 1 of the Convention Against Torture and at 8 CFR sections 208.18(a) and 1208.18(a). For an act to be considered torture, it must be an extreme form of cruel and inhuman treatment, it must cause severe physical or mental pain and suffering and it must be specifically intended to cause severe pain and suffering.

Torture is an act inflicted for such purposes as obtaining from the victim or a third person information or a confession, punishing the victim for an act he or she or a third person has committed or is suspected of having committed, or intimidating or coercing the victim or a third person or for any reason based on discrimination of any kind.

Torture must be inflicted by or at the instigation of, or with the consent or acquiescence of, a public official or other person acting in an official capacity. The victim must be in the custody or physical control of the torturer. Torture does not include pain or suffering that arises only from, is inherent in or is incidental to lawful sanctions, although such actions may not defeat the objective and purpose of the Convention Against Torture.

Form I-589, Application for Asylum and for Withholding of Removal, will be considered an application for withholding of removal under the Convention Against Torture if you tell the immigration judge that you would like to be considered for withholding of removal under the Convention Against Torture, or if it is determined that evidence indicates that you may be tortured in the country of removal.

To apply for withholding of removal under the Convention Against Torture, you must check the box at the top of **Page 1** of the application and fully complete Form I-589.

You should include a detailed explanation of why you fear torture in response to Part B, Question 4, of the application. In your response you should write about any mistreatment you experienced or any threats made against you by a government or somebody connected to a government.

Only immigration judges and the Board of Immigration Appeals may grant withholding of removal or deferral of removal under the Convention Against Torture. If you have applied for asylum, the immigration judge will first determine whether you are eligible for asylum under section 208 of the INA and for withholding of removal under section 241(b)(3) of the INA. If you are not eligible for either asylum under section 208 of the INA or withholding of removal under section 241(b)(3) of the INA, the immigration judge will determine whether the Convention Against Torture prohibits your removal to a country where you fear torture.

As implemented in U.S. law, Article 3 of the Convention Against Torture prohibits the United States from removing you to a country in which it is more likely than not that you would be subject to torture. The Convention Against Torture does not prohibit the United States from returning you to any other country where you would not be tortured. This means that you may be removed to a third country where you would not be tortured. Withholding of removal under the Convention Against Torture does not allow you to adjust to lawful permanent resident status or to petition to bring family members to come to, or remain in, the United States.

C. Deferral of Removal Under the Convention Against Torture.

If it is more likely than not that you will be tortured in a country but you are ineligible for withholding of removal, your removal will be deferred under 8 CFR sections 208.17(a) and 1208.17(a). Deferral of removal does not confer any lawful or permanent immigration status in the United States and does not necessarily result in release from detention. Deferral of removal is effective only until it is terminated. Deferral of removal is subject to review and termination if it is determined that it is no longer more likely than not that you would be tortured in the country to which your removal is deferred or if you request that your deferral be terminated.

D. Legal Sources Relating to Eligibility.

The documents listed below are some of the legal sources relating to asylum, withholding of removal under section 241(b)(3) of the INA, and withholding of removal or deferral of removal under the Convention Against Torture. These sources are provided for reference only. You do not need to refer to them in order to complete your application.

- Section 101(a)(42) of the INA, 8 U.S.C. 1101(a)(42) (defining "refugee");

- Section 208 of the INA, 8 U.S.C. 1158 (regarding eligibility for asylum);
- Section 241(b)(3) of the INA, 8 U.S.C. 1231(b)(3) (regarding eligibility for withholding of removal);
- Title 8 of the CFR sections 208 and 1208, et seq.;
- Article 3 of the Convention Against Torture and Other Cruel, Inhuman or Degrading Treatment or Punishment as ratified by section 2242(b) of the Foreign Affairs Reform and Restructuring Act of 1998 and 8 CFR section 208, as amended by the Regulations Concerning the Convention Against Torture: Interim Rule, 64 FR 8478-8492 (February 19, 1999) (effective March 22, 1999); 64 FR 13881 (March 23, 1999);
- The 1967 United Nations Protocol relating to the Status of Refugees;
- The 1951 Convention relating to the Status of Refugees; and
- The Office of the United Nations High Commissioner for Refugees, Handbook on Procedures and Criteria for Determining Refugee Status (Geneva, 1992).

III. Confidentiality.

The information collected will be used to make a determination on your application. It may also be provided to other government agencies (federal, state, local and/or foreign) for purposes of investigation or legal action on criminal and/or civil matters and for issues arising from the adjudication of benefits. However, no information indicating that you have applied for asylum will be provided to any government or country from which you claim a fear of persecution. Regulations at 8 CFR sections 208.6 and 1208.6 protect the confidentiality of asylum claims.

IV. Right to Counsel.

Immigration law concerning asylum and withholding of removal or deferral of removal is complex. You have a right to provide your own legal representation at an asylum interview and during immigration proceedings before the Immigration Court, at no cost to the United States Government.

If you need or would like help to complete this form and to prepare your written statements, assistance from pro bono (free) attorneys and/or voluntary agencies may be available. Voluntary agencies may help you for no fee or a reduced fee, and attorneys on the list referred to below may take your case for no fee. If you have not already received from USCIS or the Immigration Court a list of attorneys and accredited representatives, you may obtain a list by calling **1-800-870-3676** or visiting the U. S. Department of Justice (DOJ), Executive Office for Immigration Review (EOIR) website at: **http://www.usdoj.gov/eoir/probono/states.htm**.

Representatives of the United Nations High Commissioner for Refugees (UNHCR) may be able to assist you in identifying persons to help you complete the application. The UNHCR website provides useful country conditions information and also has links to other reliable sources. You may also, if you wish, forward a copy of your application and other supporting documents to the UNHCR.

(For instructions on where to file the original, please see **Page 8** of the Instructions, Part 1: Filing Instructions, Section XII, "Where to File.") The current address of the UNHCR is:

United Nations High Commissioner for Refugees
1775 K Street, NW, Suite 300
Washington, DC 20006
Telephone: (202) 296-5191
Website: **http://www.unhcr.ch**

Calls from Detention Centers and Jails: Between the hours of 2 and 5 p.m. (Eastern Standard Time), Monday, Wednesday and Friday, asylum-seekers in detention centers and jails may call UNHCR collect at **(202) 296-5191** or may call UNHCR's toll-free number at: **(888) 272-1913**.

V. Completing the Form.

Type or print all of your answers in black ink on the Form I-589. Your answers must be completed in English. Forms completed in a language other than English will be returned to you. Provide the specific information requested about you and your family. **Answer all the questions asked.**

If any question does not apply to you or you do not know the information requested, answer "none," "not applicable" or "unknown."

Provide detailed information and answer the questions as completely as possible. Applications filed with missing information may be returned to you as incomplete. If you need more space, attach the Supplement A or B Forms (included in the application package) and/or an additional sheet(s) indicating the question number(s) you are answering.

You are strongly urged to attach additional written statements and documents that support your claim. Your written statements should include events, dates and details of your experiences that relate to your claim for asylum.

NOTE: Please put your Alien Registration Number (A#) (if any), name (exactly as it appears in Part A. I. of the form), signature, and date on each supplemental sheet and on the cover page of any supporting documents.

You will be permitted to amend or supplement your application at the time of your asylum interview before an asylum officer and at your hearing in Immigration Court by providing additional information and explanations about your asylum claim.

Part A. I. Information About You.

This part asks for basic information about you. "Alien Registration Number" (A#) refers to your DHS file number. If you do not already have an A#, DHS will assign one to you.

You must provide your residential street address (the address where you physically live) in the United States in Part A. I., Question 7, of the asylum application. You may also provide a mailing address, if different from the address where you reside, in Question 8. If someone else is collecting your mail for you at your mailing address, you may enter that person's name in the "In Care Of" field in your response to Question 8. If your mailing address is a post office box, include that address in Question 8 **and** include a residential address where you physically live in Question 7.

In Question 12, use the current name of the country. Do not use historical, ethnic, provincial or other local names.

APPENDIX 9A • I-589

If you entered the country with inspection, the Form I-94 number (#) referred to in Question 18b is the number on Form I-94, Arrival-Departure Record, given to you when you entered the United States. In Question 18c, enter the date and status as it appears on the Form I-94. If you did not receive a Form I-94, write "None." If you entered without being inspected by an immigration officer, write "No Inspection" in Question 18c in the current status or status section.

Part A. II. Spouse and Children.

You should list your spouse and all of your children in this application, regardless of their age, marital status, whether they are in the United States or whether or not they are included in this application or filing a separate asylum application.

You may ask to have included in your asylum application your spouse and/or any children who are under the age of 21 years and unmarried, if they are in the United States. Children who are married and/or children who are 21 years of age or older must file separately for asylum by submitting their own Form I-589 asylum applications.

If you apply for asylum while in proceedings before the Immigration Court, the immigration judge may not have authority to grant asylum to any spouse or child included in your application who is not also in proceedings.

When including family members in your asylum application, you **must** submit one additional copy of your completed asylum application and primary documentary evidence establishing your family relationship for each family member, as described below:

- If you are including your spouse in your application, submit three copies of your marriage certificate and three copies of proof of termination of any prior marriages.
- If you are including any unmarried children under 21 years of age in your application, submit three copies of each child's birth certificate.

If you do not have and are unable to obtain these documents, you must submit secondary evidence. Secondary evidence includes, but is not limited to, medical records, religious records and school records. You may also submit an affidavit from at least one person for each event you are trying to prove. Affidavits may be provided by relatives or others. Persons providing affidavits need not be United States citizens or lawful permanent residents.

Affidavits must:

- Fully describe the circumstances or event(s) in question and fully explain how the person acquired knowledge of the event(s);
- Be sworn to or affirmed by persons who were alive at the time of the event(s) and have personal knowledge of the event(s) (date and place of birth, marriage, etc.) that you are trying to prove; and
- Show the full name, address and date and place of birth of each person giving the affidavit and indicate any relationship between you and the person giving the affidavit.

If you submit secondary evidence or affidavits, you must explain why primary evidence (e.g., birth or marriage certificate) is unavailable. You may explain the reasons primary evidence is unavailable using the Supplement B Form or additional sheets of paper. Attach this explanation to your secondary evidence or affidavits.

If you have more than four children, complete the Supplement A Form for each additional child or attach additional pages and documentation providing the same information asked in Part A. II. of the Form I-589.

Part A. III. Information About Your Background.

Please answer Questions 1 through 5, providing details as requested for each question. Your responses to the questions concerning the places you have lived, your education, and your employment history should be in reverse chronological order starting with your current residence, education, employment and working back in time.

Part B. Information About Your Application.

This part asks specific questions relevant to eligibility for asylum, for withholding of removal under section 241(b)(3) of the Act or for withholding of removal under the Convention Against Torture. At Question 1, please check the box(es) next to the reason(s) that you are completing this application. For all other questions, please check "Yes" or "No" in the box provided.

If you answer "Yes" to any question, explain in detail using the Supplement B Form or additional sheets of paper as needed.

You should clearly describe any of your experiences, or those of family members or others who have had similar experiences that may show that you are a refugee.

If you have experienced harm that is difficult for you to write down and express, you should be aware that these experiences may be very important to the decision-making process regarding your request to remain in the United States. At your interview with an asylum officer or hearing with an immigration judge, you will need to be prepared to discuss the harm you have suffered. If you are having trouble remembering or talking about past events, we suggest that you talk to a lawyer, an accredited representative or a health professional who may be able to help you explain your experiences and current situation.

Part C. Additional Information About Your Application.

Check "Yes" or "No" in the box provided for each question. If you answer "Yes" to any question, explain in detail using the Supplement B Form or additional sheets of paper as needed.

If you answer "Yes" to Question 5, you must explain why you did not apply for asylum within the first year after you arrived in the United States. The government will accept as an explanation certain changes in the conditions in your country, certain changes in your own circumstances and certain other events that may have prevented you from applying earlier.

For example, some of the events the government might consider as valid explanations include, but are not limited to, the following:

- You have learned that human rights conditions in your country have worsened since you left;
- Because of your health, you were not able to submit this application within a year after you arrived;
- You previously submitted an application, but it was returned to you because it was not complete, and you submitted a complete application within a reasonable amount of time.

Federal regulations specify some of the other types of events that may also qualify as valid explanations for why you filed late. These regulations are found at 8 CFR sections 208.4 and 1208.4. The list in the regulations is not all-inclusive, and the government recognizes that there are many other circumstances that might be acceptable reasons for filing more than one year after arrival.

If you are unable to explain why you did not apply for asylum within the first year after you arrived in the United States or your explanation is not accepted by the government, you may not be eligible to apply for asylum, but you could still be eligible for withholding of removal.

Part D. Your Signature.

You must sign your application in Part D and respond to the questions concerning any assistance you received to complete your application, providing the information requested. Sign after you have completed and reviewed the application.

If it is determined that you have knowingly made a frivolous application for asylum, you can be permanently ineligible for any benefits under the INA. (See section 208(d)(6) of the INA.)

According to regulations at 8 CFR sections 208.20 and 1208.20, an application is frivolous if any of its material elements is deliberately fabricated. (See Instructions, Part 1: Filing Instructions, Section IV, "Right to Counsel," in the event that you have any questions.) Please note that you may not avoid a frivolous finding simply because someone advised or told you to provide false information on your asylum application.

Part E. Signature of Person Preparing Form, If Other Than You.

Any person, other than an immediate family member (your spouse, parent(s) or children), who helped prepare your application must sign the application in Part E and provide the information requested.

Penalty for Perjury.

All statements in response to questions contained in this application are declared to be true and correct under penalty of perjury. You and anyone, other than an immediate family member, who assists you in preparing the application must sign the application under penalty of perjury. Your signature is evidence that you are aware of the contents of this application. Any person assisting you in preparing this form, other than an immediate family member, must include his or her name, address and telephone number and sign the application where indicated in Part E.

Failure of the preparer to sign will result in the application being returned to you as an incomplete application.

If USCIS or EOIR later learns that you received assistance from someone other than an immediate family member and the person who assisted you **willfully** failed to sign the application, this may result in an adverse ruling against you.

Title 18, United States Code (U.S.C.), Section 1546(a), provides in part:

> Whoever knowingly makes under oath, or as permitted under penalty of perjury under Section 1746 of Title 28, knowingly subscribes as true, any false statement with respect to a material fact in any application, affidavit, or other document required by the immigration laws or regulations prescribed thereunder, or knowingly presents any such application, affidavit, or other document containing any such false statement shall be fined in accordance with this title or imprisoned not more than ten years, or both.
>
> If aggravating factors exist, the maximum term of imprisonment could reach 25 years.

If you knowingly provide false information on this application, you or the preparer of this application may be subject to criminal penalties under Title 18 of the U.S.C. and to civil penalties under section 274C of the INA, 8 U.S.C. 1324c.

Part F. To Be Completed at Asylum Interview, If Applicable.

Do not sign your application in Part F before filing this form. You will be asked to sign your application in this space at the conclusion of the interview regarding your claim.

NOTE: You must, however, sign Part D of the application.

Part G. To Be Completed at Removal Hearing, If Applicable.

Do not sign your application in Part G before filing this form. You will be asked to sign your application in this space at the hearing before the immigration judge.

NOTE: You must, however, sign Part D of the application

You are again reminded that, if is determined that you have knowingly made a frivolous application for asylum, you can be permanently ineligible for any benefits under the INA. (See section 208(d)(6) of the INA.)

According to regulations at 8 CFR sections 208.20 and 1208.20, an application is frivolous if any of its material elements is deliberately fabricated. Again, please note that you may not avoid a frivolous finding simply because someone advised or told you to provide false information on your asylum application.

VI. Required Documents and Required Number of Copies That You Must Submit With Your Application.

You must submit the following documents to apply for asylum and withholding of removal:

- **The completed, signed original and two copies of your completed application, Form I-589**, and the original and two copies of any supplementary sheets and supplementary statements. If you choose to submit additional supporting material, see **Page 7** of the Instructions, Part 1: Filing Instructions, Section VII, "Additional Evidence That You Should Submit." You **must** include three copies of each document. You should make and keep an additional copy of the completed application for your own records.

- **An additional copy of your completed application, Form I-589**, with supplementary statements, for each family member listed in Part A. II, whom you want to have included in your application.

- **Three copies of primary or secondary evidence** of relationship, such as birth or school records of your children, marriage certificate or proof of termination of marriage, for each family member listed in Part A. II. whom you want to have included in your application.

NOTE: If you submit an affidavit, you must submit the original and two copies. (For affidavit requirements, see **Pages 4 and 5** of the Instructions, Part 1: Filing Instructions, Section V, "Completing the Form," Part A. II.)

APPENDIX 9A • I-589   533

- **One passport-style photograph** of yourself and of each family member listed in Part A. II. who is included in your application. The photos must have been taken no more than 30 days before you file your application. Using a pencil, print the person's complete name and A Number (if any) on the back of his or her photo.

- **Three copies of all passports or other travel documents** (cover to cover) in your possession and three copies of any U.S. Immigration documents, such as a Form I-94, Arrival-Departure Record, for you and each family member included in your application, if you have such documents.

- **If you have other identification documents** (for example, birth certificate, military or national identification card, driver's license, etc.), it is recommended that you submit three copies with your application and bring the original(s) with you to the interview.

Documents filed with this application should be photocopies. If you choose to send an original document, USCIS or the Immigration Court may keep that original document for its records.

Translation of documents not in English is required. Any document in a language other than English must be accompanied by an adequate English translation that the translator has certified as complete and correct and by the translator's certification that he or she is competent to translate into English the language used in the document.

VII. Additional Evidence That You Should Submit.

You should submit reasonably available corroborative evidence showing (1) the general conditions in the country from which you are seeking asylum and (2) the specific facts on which you are relying to support your claim.

If evidence supporting your claim is not reasonably available or you are not providing such corroboration at this time, you must explain why, using the Supplement B Form or additional sheets of paper.

Supporting evidence may include, but is not limited to, newspaper articles, affidavits of witnesses or experts, medical and/or psychological records, doctors' statements, periodicals, journals, books, photographs, official documents or personal statements or live testimony from witnesses or experts.

If you have difficulty discussing harm you have suffered in the past, you may wish to submit a health professional's report explaining this difficulty.

VIII. Fee.

There is no fee for filing this application.

IX. Biometrics, Including Fingerprints and Photographs.

Applicants for asylum are subject to a biometrics check of all appropriate records and other information databases maintained by the Attorney General and Secretary of State.

You and your eligible spouse or children over the age of 14 years listed on your asylum application must provide biometrics. You and your spouse and children will be given instructions on how to complete this requirement. You will be notified in writing of the time and location of the Application Support Center where you must go to be fingerprinted and photographed.

If filing with USCIS, unexcused failure to appear for a scheduled appointment or to provide your required biometrics, including fingerprints and photograph, or to provide other biographical information within the time allowed, may delay eligibility for employment authorization and/or result in an asylum officer dismissing your asylum application or referring it to an immigration judge. For applicants before an immigration judge, such failure without good cause may constitute an abandonment of your asylum application and result in the denial of employment authorization. (See 8 CFR section 1003.47(d).)

At the time you file your Form I-589, Application for Asylum and for Withholding of Removal, you **must** submit photographs as specified on **Page 6** of the Instructions, Part 1: Filing Instructions, Section VI, "Required Documents and Required Number of Copies That You Must Submit With Your Application."

X. Organizing Your Application.

Put your application together in the following order, forming one complete package (if possible, secure with binder clips and rubber bands so that material may be easily separated):

- Your original Form I-589, with all questions completed, and the application signed by you in Part D and signed by any preparer in Part E; and

- One passport-style photograph of you stapled to the form at Part D.

Behind your original Form I-589, attach in the following order:

- One Form G-28, Notice of Entry of Appearance as Attorney or Representative, signed by you and the attorney or representative, if you are represented by an attorney or representative;

- The originals of all supplementary sheets and supplementary statements submitted with your application;

- One copy of any additional supporting documentation;

- One copy of the evidence of your relationship to your spouse and unmarried children under 21 years of age to be included in your applicaiton, if any; and

- Two copies of the items listed above in your original package, except your photograph.

If you are including family members in your application, attach one additional package for each family member. Arrange each family member's package as follows:

- One copy of your completed, signed Form I-589 and supplementary sheets submitted with the original application. In Part A. II., staple in the upper right corner one passport-style photo of the family member to be included; and

- One copy of Form G-28, if any.

For example, if you include your spouse and two children, you should submit your original package, plus two duplicates for you, plus one package for your spouse and one package for each child, for a total of six packages. Be sure each has the appropriate documentation.

NOTE: Any additional pages submitted should include your printed name (exactly as it appears in Part A. I. of the form), A Number (if any), signature and date.

XI. Incomplete Asylum Applications.

An asylum application that is incomplete will be returned to you by mail within 30 days of receipt of the application by USCIS. An application that has not been returned to you within 30 days of having been received by USCIS will be considered complete, and you will receive written acknowledgement of receipt from USCIS.

The filing of a complete application starts the 150-day period you must wait before you may apply for employment authorization. If your application is not complete and is returned to you, the 150-day period will not begin until you resubmit a complete application. (See **Page 10** of the Instructions, Part 2: Information Regarding Post-Filing Requirements, Section V, "Employment Authorization," for further information regarding eligibility for employment authorization.)

An application will be considered incomplete in each of the following cases:

- The application does not include a response to each of the questions contained in the Form I-589;
- The application is unsigned;
- The application is submitted without the required photograph;
- The application is sent without the appropriate number of copies for any supporting materials submitted; or
- You indicated in Part D that someone prepared the application other than yourself or an immediate family member and the preparer failed to complete Part E of the asylum application.

XII. Where to File.

Although USCIS will confirm in writing its receipt of your application, you may wish to send the completed forms by registered mail (return receipt requested) for your own records.

If you are in proceedings in Immigration Court:

If you are currently in proceedings in Immigration Court (that is, if you have been served with Form I-221, Order to Show Cause and Notice of Hearing; Form I-122, Notice to Applicant for Admission Detained for Hearing Before an Immigration Judge; Form I-862, Notice to Appear; or Form I-863, Notice of Referral to Immigration Judge), you are required to file your Form I-589 with the Immigration Court having jurisdiction over your case.

At the Master Calendar hearing, counsel for DHS will provide you with a form entitled *Instructions For Submitting Certain Applications In Immigration Court and For Providing Biometric and Biographical Information to U.S. Citizenship and Immigration Services* (Pre-Filing Instructions) that you must follow. The Pre-Filing Instructions may also be obtained at **http://www.uscis.gov**. The following paragraphs describe the Pre-Filing Instructions that you will have to follow.

In addition to filing your Form I-589, Application for Asylum and for Withholding of Removal, with the immigration judge and serving a copy on the appropriate Immigration and Customs Enforcement (ICE) Office of Chief Counsel, you must also complete the following requirements before the immigration judge can grant relief or protection in your case.

Send the following three items to the address below:

(1) A clear copy of the first three pages of your completed Form I-589 that you will be filing or have filed with the Immigration Court, which must include **your full name, current residential address, current mailing address and A Number. Do not** submit any documents other than the first three pages of the completed Form I-589;

(2) A copy of Form EOIR-28, Notice of Entry of Appearance as Attorney or Representative Before the Immigration Court, if you are represented; and

(3) A copy of the Pre-Filing Instructions provided by counsel for DHS that you received at your first Master Calendar hearing in immigration removal proceedings.

USCIS Nebraska Service Center
Defensive Asylum Application With Immigration Court
P.O. Box 87589
Lincoln, NE 68501-7589

Please note that there is no filing fee required for Form I-589 applications.

After the three items are received at the USCIS Nebraska Service Center, **you will receive**:

- A USCIS receipt notice indicating that USCIS received your Form I-589 application and
- An Application Support Center (ASC) notice for you and any eligible spouse and children included in your Form I-589 application who are also in removal proceedings. Each ASC notice will indicate the individual's unique receipt number and will provide instructions for each person to appear for an appointment at a nearby ASC for collection of biometrics (such as your photograph, fingerprints and signature). If you do not receive the ASC notice in three weeks, call **1-800-375-5283.**

NOTE: If you also mail applications for other forms of relief that you are applying for while in removal proceedings, as specified by the Pre-Filing Instructions (see side B) provided by counsel for DHS at your Master Calendar hearing, you will receive two notices with different receipt numbers. You must wait for and take both scheduling notices to your ASC appointment.

You (and your eligible spouse and children) must then:

- **Attend** the biometrics appointment at the ASC and obtain a **biometrics confirmation** document before leaving the ASC and
- **Retain** your ASC biometrics confirmation as proof that your biometrics were taken and bring it to your future Immigration Court hearings.

NOTE: If the instructions above should change for submitting copies of the first three pages of your asylum application to the USCIS Nebraska Service Center for purposes of receiving the receipt notice and ASC scheduling appointment, you will be provided the changed instructions, either at the Master Calendar hearing or at another point in the Immigration Court proceedings. Please follow the instructions you are provided, or else you may not receive the ASC biometrics scheduling notice in a timely manner.

APPENDIX 9A • I-589   535

If you are not in proceedings in Immigration Court:

Mail your completed Form I-589 and any other additional information to the USCIS Service Center as indicated below.

If you live in Alabama, Arkansas, Colorado, Commonwealth of Puerto Rico, District of Columbia, Florida, Georgia, Louisiana, Maryland, Mississippi, New Mexico, North Carolina, Oklahoma, western Pennsylvania in the jurisdiction of the Pittsburgh Suboffice*, South Carolina, Tennessee, Texas, U.S. Virgin Islands, Utah, Virginia, West Virginia or Wyoming, mail your application to:

USCIS Texas Service Center
Attn: Asylum
P.O. Box 851892
Mesquite, TX 75185-1892

If you live in Alaska, northern California*, Idaho, Illinois, Indiana, Iowa, Kansas, Kentucky, Michigan, Minnesota, Missouri, Montana, Nebraska, northern Nevada in the jurisdiction of the Reno Suboffice*, North Dakota, Ohio, Oregon, South Dakota, Washington or Wisconsin, mail your application to:

USCIS Nebraska Service Center
P.O. Box 87589
Lincoln, NE 68501-7589

If you live in Arizona, southern California*, Hawaii, southern Nevada in the jurisdiction of the Las Vegas Suboffice* or the Territory of Guam, mail your application to:

USCIS California Service Center
P.O. Box 10589
Laguna Niguel, CA 92607

If you live in Connecticut, Delaware, Maine, Massachusetts, New Hampshire, New Jersey, New York, eastern Pennsylvania excluding the jurisdiction of the Pittsburgh Suboffice*, Rhode Island or Vermont, mail your application to:

USCIS Vermont Service Center
Attn: Asylum
75 Lower Welden Street
St. Albans, VT 05479

*NOTE: For applicants in the states of California, Nevada and Pennsylvania who may be unsure of which Service Center to use for mailing applications, call the USCIS National Customer Service Center or your local asylum office for more specific information. The National Customer Service Center and the asylum offices serving those states are listed below with their public information numbers.

National Customer Service Center:

| Toll Free Number | 800-375-5283 |
| TDD Hearing Impaired | 800-767-1833 |

For California or Nevada:

| Los Angeles Asylum Office | 714-808-8199 |
| San Francisco Asylum Office | 415-293-1234 |

For Pennsylvania:

| Newark Asylum Office | 201-531-0555 |
| Arlington Asylum Office | 703-235-4100 |

Information concerning asylum offices and where to file asylum applications is also available on the USCIS website at: http://www.uscis.gov.

Pursuant to 8 CFR section 208.4(b)(5), the following categories of individuals are not entitled to an asylum interview at a USCIS Asylum Office:

(1) Certain alien crewmembers;

(2) Certain stowaways;

(3) Visa Waiver Program applicants for admission;

(4) Visa Waiver Program overstays and status violators;

(5) Certain aliens ordered removed under section 235(c) of the INA on security related grounds; and

(6) Certain non-immigrants admitted pursuant to section 101(a)(15)(S) of the INA (e.g., witnesses and informants).

Individuals subject to these special categories who file asylum applications with USCIS Service Centers will be served with a Form I-863, Notice of Referral to Immigration Judge, when they appear at the USCIS Asylum Office and will be referred to Immigration Court for an asylum-only hearing.

Part 2. Information Regarding Post-Filing Requirements.

I. Notification Requirements When Your Address Changes.

If you change your address, you must inform USCIS in writing within ten days of moving.

While your asylum application is pending before the asylum office, you must notify the asylum office on Form AR-11, Alien's Change of Address Card, or by a signed and dated letter notifying USCIS within ten days after you change your address.

The address that you provide on the application, or the last change of address notification that you submitted, will be used by USCIS for mailing. Any notices mailed to that address will constitute adequate service, except that personal service may be required for the following: Form I-122, Notice to Alien Detained for Hearing by an Immigration Judge; Form I-221, Order to Show Cause; Form I-862, Notice to Appear; Form I-863, Notice of Referral to Immigration Judge; and Form I-860, Notice and Order of Expedited Removal.

If you are already in proceedings in Immigration Court, you must notify the Immigration Court on EOIR Form 33, Alien's Change of Address Card, of any changes of address within five days of the change in address. You must send the notification to the Immigration Court having jurisdiction over your case. You must also notify USCIS on Form AR-11, Alien's Change of Address Card, or by a signed and dated letter within ten days after you change your address.

II. Asylum Interview Process.

If you are not in proceedings in Immigration Court, you will be notified by the USCIS asylum office of the date, time and place (address) of a scheduled interview.

USCIS suggests that you bring a copy of your Form I-589 asylum application with you when you have your asylum interview. An asylum officer will interview you under oath and make a determination concerning your claim. In most cases, you will not be notified of the decision in your case until a date after your interview.

You have the right to legal representation at your interview, at no cost to the U.S. Government. (See **Page 4** of the Instructions, Part I: Filing Instructions, Section IV, "Right to Counsel.") You also may bring witnesses with you to the interview to testify on your behalf.

If you are unable to proceed with the asylum interview in fluent English, you must provide, at no expense to USCIS, a competent interpreter fluent in both English and a language that you speak fluently.

Your interpreter must be at least 18 years of age. The following persons cannot serve as your interpreter: your attorney or representative of record, a witness testifying on your behalf at the interview or a representative or employee of your country. Quality interpretation may be crucial to your claim. Such assistance must be obtained at your expense prior to the interview.

Failure without good cause to bring a competent interpreter to your interview may be considered an unexcused failure to appear for the interview. Any unexcused failure to appear for an interview may prevent you from receiving employment authorization, and your asylum application may be dismissed or referred directly to the Immigration Court.

If you are hearing-impaired and require the services of a sign language interpreter in your language, one will be provided for you. Please contact the asylum office with jurisdiction over your case as soon as you receive a notice for your asylum interview to notify the office that you will need a sign language interpreter in your language, so that accommodations can be made in advance.

If available, you must bring some form of identification to your interview, including any passport(s), other travel or identification documents or Form I-94, Arrival-Departure Record. You may bring to the interview any additional available items documenting your claim that you have not already submitted with your application. All documents must be submitted in triplicate.

If members of your family are included in your application for asylum, they must also appear for the interview and bring any identity or travel documents they have in their possession.

III. Status While Your Application Is Pending.

While your case is pending, you will be permitted to remain in the United States. After your asylum interview, if you have not been granted asylum and appear to be removable under section 237 of the INA, 8 U.S.C. 1227, or inadmissible under section 212 of the INA, 8 U.S.C. 1182, your application will be referred to the Immigration Court by the asylum office.

IV. Travel Outside the United States.

If you leave the United States without first obtaining advance parole from USCIS using Form I-131, Application for a Travel Document, it will be presumed that you have abandoned your application. If you obtain advance parole and return to the country of claimed persecution, it will be presumed that you abandoned your application, unless you can show that there were compelling reasons for your return.

NOTE: The application process for advance parole varies depending on your personal circumstances. Using InfoPass, check with your local USCIS District Office for application instructions. Additional information on obtaining advance parole is available from the USCIS website at **http://www.uscis.gov**.

V. Employment Authorization While Your Application Is Pending.

You will be granted permission to work if your asylum application is granted.

Simply filing an application for asylum does not entitle you to employment authorization. You may request permission to work if your asylum application is pending and 150 days have lapsed since your application was accepted by USCIS or the Immigration Court. (See 8 CFR sections 208.7(a)(1) and 1208.7(a)(1).) Any delay in the processing of your asylum application that you request or cause shall not be counted as part of the 150-day period.

If your asylum application has not been denied within 180 days from the date of filing a complete asylum application, you may be granted permission to work by filing Form I-765, Application for Employment Authorization, with USCIS. Follow the instructions on that application and submit it with a copy of evidence as specified in the instructions that you have a pending asylum application.

Each family member whom you have asked to be included in your application and who also wants permission to work must submit a separate Form I-765.

You may obtain copies of Form I-765 by calling the USCIS forms line at 1-800-870-3676 or from the USCIS website at: **http://www.uscis.gov**.

VI. Privacy Act Notice and General Information.

The authority to collect this information is contained in Title 8 of the United States Code. Furnishing the information on this form is voluntary; however, failure to provide all of the requested information may result in the delay of a final decision or denial of your request.

- Do You Need Forms or Information?

To order USCIS forms, call our toll-free forms line at **1-800-870-3676**. You can also order USCIS forms and obtain information on immigration laws, regulations and procedures by telephoning our National Customer Service Center toll-free at **1-800-375-5283** or visiting the USCIS website at **www.uscis.gov**.

VII. Paperwork Reduction Act Notice.

Under the Paperwork Reduction Act, an agency may not conduct or sponsor an information collection and a person is not required to respond to a collection of information unless it displays a currently valid OMB control number.

We try to create forms and instructions that are accurate, can be easily understood and that impose the least possible burden on you to provide us with information. Often this is difficult because some immigration laws are very complex.

APPENDIX 9A • I-589

The estimated average time to complete and file this application is as follows: (1) 2 hours to learn about the form, (2) 5 hours to complete the form and (3) 5 hours to assemble and file the application, for the total estimated average burden hours of 12 hours per application. The estimated time to complete the form will vary depending on the complexity of your individual circumstances.

If you have comments regarding the accuracy of this estimate or suggestions for making this form simpler, write to U.S. Citizenship and Immigration Services, Regulatory Management Division, 111 Massachusetts Avenue, N.W., 3rd Floor, Suite 3008, Washington, DC 20529, OMB No. 1615-0067. **Do not mail your completed application to this Washington, D.C., address.**

Supplements to Form I-589.

Form I-589, Supplement A - For use to complete Part A. II.

Form I-589, Supplement B - For use to complete Parts B and C and to provide additional information for any other part of the application.

Department of Homeland Security
U.S. Citizenship and Immigration Services

U.S. Department of Justice
Executive Office for Immigration Review

OMB No. 1615-0067, Expires 12/31/07

I-589, Application for Asylum and for Withholding of Removal

START HERE - Please type or print in black ink. See the Instructions for information about eligibility and how to complete and file this application. There is **NO filing fee for this application.**

NOTE: Please check this box if you also want to apply for withholding of removal under the Convention Against Torture. ☐

Part A. I. Information about you.

1. Alien Registration Number(s) (A#s) *(If any)*	2. U.S. Social Security Number *(If any)*

3. Complete Last Name	4. First Name	5. Middle Name

6. What other names have you used? *(Include maiden name and aliases.)*

7. Residence in the U.S. *(Where you physically reside.)*   Telephone Number ( )

Street Number and Name   Apt. Number

City	State	Zip Code

8. Mailing Address in the U.S.
(If different than the address in No. 7)
In Care Of *(If applicable):*   Telephone Number ( )

Street Number and Name   Apt. Number

City	State	Zip Code

9. Gender: ☐ Male ☐ Female   10. Marital Status: ☐ Single ☐ Married ☐ Divorced ☐ Widowed

11. Date of Birth *(mm/dd/yyyy)*   12. City and Country of Birth

13. Present Nationality *(Citizenship)*	14. Nationality at Birth	15. Race, Ethnic or Tribal Group	16. Religion

17. Check the box, a through c, that applies: **a.** ☐ I have never been in Immigration Court proceedings.
b. ☐ I am now in Immigration Court proceedings.   **c.** ☐ I am **not** now in Immigration Court proceedings, but I have been in the past.

18. Complete 18 a through c.
a. When did you last leave your country? *(mmm/dd/yyyy)* _____ b. What is your current I-94 Number, if any? _____
c. Please list each entry into the U.S. beginning with your most recent entry.
List date *(mm/dd/yyyy)*, place, and your status for each entry. *(Attach additional sheets as needed.)*

Date _____ Place _____ Status _____ Date Status Expires: _____
Date _____ Place _____ Status _____
Date _____ Place _____ Status _____

19. What country issued your last passport or travel document?	20. Passport #	21. Expiration Date *(mm/dd/yyyy)*
	Travel Document #	

22. What is your native language? *(Include dialect, if applicable.)*   23. Are you fluent in English? ☐ Yes ☐ No   24. What other languages do you speak fluently?

For EOIR use only.	Action: Interview Date: _____ Asylum Officer ID#: _____	For USCIS use only. Decision: Approval Date: _____ Denial Date: _____ Referral Date: _____

Form I-589 (Rev. 12/14/06) Y

APPENDIX 9A • I-589

Part A. II. Information about your spouse and children.

Your spouse. ☐ I am not married. *(Skip to **Your children**, below.)*

1. Alien Registration Number (A#) *(If any)*	2. Passport/ID Card No. *(If any)*	3. Date of Birth *(mm/dd/yyyy)*	4. U.S. Social Security No. *(If any)*
5. Complete Last Name	6. First Name	7. Middle Name	8. Maiden Name
9. Date of Marriage *(mm/dd/yyyy)*	10. Place of Marriage	11. City and Country of Birth	
12. Nationality *(Citizenship)*	13. Race, Ethnic or Tribal Group	14. Gender ☐ Male ☐ Female	

15. Is this person in the U.S. ?
☐ Yes *(Complete Blocks 16 to 24.)* ☐ No *(Specify location.)* _____

16. Place of last entry in the U.S.	17. Date of last entry in the U.S. *(mm/dd/yyyy)*	18. I-94 No. *(If any)*	19. Status when last admitted *(Visa type, if any)*
20. What is your spouse's current status?	21. What is the expiration date of his/her authorized stay, if any? *(mm/dd/yyyy)*	22. Is your spouse in Immigration Court proceedings? ☐ Yes ☐ No	23. If previously in the U.S., date of previous arrival *(mm/dd/yyyy)*

24. If in the U.S., is your spouse to be included in this application? *(Check the appropriate box.)*

☐ Yes *(Attach one photograph of your spouse in the upper right corner of Page 9 on the extra copy of the application submitted for this person.)*

☐ No

Your children. Please list **all** of your children, regardless of age, location or marital status.

☐ I do not have any children. *(Skip to Part A. III., **Information about your background.**)*

☐ I have children.   Total number of children: _____ .

(NOTE: Use Supplement A Form I-589 or attach additional sheets of paper and documentation if you have more than four children.)

1. Alien Registration Number (A#) *(If any)*	2. Passport/ID Card No. *(If any)*	3. Marital Status *(Married, Single, Divorced, Widowed)*	4. U.S. Social Security No. *(If any)*
5. Complete Last Name	6. First Name	7. Middle Name	8. Date of Birth *(mm/dd/yyyy)*
9. City and Country of Birth	10. Nationality *(Citizenship)*	11. Race, Ethnic or Tribal Group	12. Gender ☐ Male ☐ Female

13. Is this child in the U.S. ?
☐ Yes *(Complete Blocks 14 to 21.)* ☐ No *(Specify location.)* _____

14. Place of last entry in the U.S.	15. Date of last entry in the U.S. *(mm/dd/yyyy)*	16. I-94 No. *(If any)*	17. Status when last admitted *(Visa type, if any)*
18. What is your child's current status?	19. What is the expiration date of his/her authorized stay, if any? *(mm/dd/yyyy)*	20. Is your child in Immigration Court proceedings? ☐ Yes ☐ No	

21. If in the U.S., is this child to be included in this application? *(Check the appropriate box.)*

☐ Yes *(Attach one photograph of your child in the upper right corner of Page 9 on the extra copy of the application submitted for this person.)*

☐ No

Form I-589 (Rev. 12/14/06) Y Page 2

Part A. II. Information about your spouse and children. (Continued.)

1. Alien Registration Number (A#) *(If any)*	2. Passport/ID Card No. *(If any)*	3. Marital Status *(Married, Single, Divorced, Widowed)*	4. U.S. Social Security No. *(If any)*
5. Complete Last Name	6. First Name	7. Middle Name	8. Date of Birth *(mm/dd/yyyy)*
9. City and Country of Birth	10. Nationality *(Citizenship)*	11. Race, Ethnic or Tribal Group	12. Gender ☐ Male ☐ Female

13. Is this child in the U.S. ?
☐ Yes *(Complete Blocks 14 to 21.)* ☐ No *(Specify location.)*

14. Place of last entry in the U.S.	15. Date of last entry in the U.S. *(mm/dd/yyyy)*	16. I-94 No. *(If any)*	17. Status when last admitted *(Visa type, if any)*
18. What is your child's current status?	19. What is the expiration date of his/her authorized stay, if any? *(mm/dd/yyyy)*	20. Is your child in Immigration Court proceedings? ☐ Yes ☐ No	

21. If in the U.S., is this child to be included in this application? *(Check the appropriate box.)*
☐ Yes *(Attach one photograph of your child in the upper right corner of Page 9 on the extra copy of the application submitted for this person.)*
☐ No

1. Alien Registration Number (A#) *(If any)*	2. Passport/ID Card No. *(If any)*	3. Marital Status *(Married, Single, Divorced, Widowed)*	4. U.S. Social Security No. *(If any)*
5. Complete Last Name	6. First Name	7. Middle Name	8. Date of Birth *(mm/dd/yyyy)*
9. City and Country of Birth	10. Nationality *(Citizenship)*	11. Race, Ethnic or Tribal Group	12. Gender ☐ Male ☐ Female

13. Is this child in the U.S.?
☐ Yes *(Complete Blocks 14 to 21.)* ☐ No *(Specify location.)*

14. Place of last entry in the U.S.	15. Date of last entry in the U.S. *(mm/dd/yyyy)*	16. I-94 No. *(If any)*	17. Status when last admitted *(Visa type, if any)*
18. What is your child's current status?	19. What is the expiration date of his/her authorized stay, if any? *(mm/dd/yyyy)*	20. Is your child in Immigration Court proceedings? ☐ Yes ☐ No	

21. If in the U.S., is this child to be included in this application? *(Check the appropriate box.)*
☐ Yes *(Attach one photograph of your child in the upper right corner of Page 9 on the extra copy of the application submitted for this person.)*
☐ No

1. Alien Registration Number (A#) *(If any)*	2. Passport/ID Card No. *(If any)*	3. Marital Status *(Married, Single, Divorced, Widowed)*	4. U.S. Social Security No. *(If any)*
5. Complete Last Name	6. First Name	7. Middle Name	8. Date of Birth *(mm/dd/yyyy)*
9. City and Country of Birth	10. Nationality *(Citizenship)*	11. Race, Ethnic or Tribal Group	12. Gender ☐ Male ☐ Female

13. Is this child in the U.S. ?
☐ Yes *(Complete Blocks 14 to 21.)* ☐ No *(Specify location.)*

14. Place of last entry in the U.S.	15. Date of last entry in the U.S. *(mm/dd/yyyy)*	16. I-94 No. *(If any)*	17. Status when last admitted *(Visa type, if any)*
18. What is your child's current status?	19. What is the expiration date of his/her authorized stay, if any? *(mm/dd/yyyy)*	20. Is your child in Immigration Court proceedings? ☐ Yes ☐ No	

21. If in the U.S., is this child to be included in this application? *(Check the appropriate box.)*
☐ Yes *(Attach one photograph of your child in the upper right corner of Page 9 on the extra copy of the application submitted for this person.)*
☐ No

APPENDIX 9A • I-589

Part A. III. Information about your background.

1. Please list your last address where you lived before coming to the U.S. If this is not the country where you fear persecution, also list the last address in the country where you fear persecution. *(List Address, City/Town, Department, Province, or State and Country.)*
(NOTE: *Use Supplement B, Form I-589 or additional sheets of paper, if necessary.)*

Number and Street *(Provide if available)*	City/Town	Department, Province or State	Country	Dates From *(Mo/Yr)*	To *(Mo/Yr)*

2. Provide the following information about your residences during the past five years. List your present address first.
(NOTE: Use Supplement B, Form I-589 or additional sheets of paper, if necessary.)

Number and Street	City/Town	Department, Province or State	Country	Dates From *(Mo/Yr)*	To *(Mo/Yr)*

3. Provide the following information about your education, beginning with the most recent.
(NOTE: Use Supplement B, Form I-589 or additional sheets of paper, if necessary.)

Name of School	Type of School	Location *(Address)*	Attended From *(Mo/Yr)*	To *(Mo/Yr)*

4. Provide the following information about your employment during the past five years. List your present employment first.
(NOTE: Use Supplement B, Form I-589 or additional sheets of paper, if necessary.)

Name and Address of Employer	Your Occupation	Dates From *(Mo/Yr)*	To *(Mo/Yr)*

5. Provide the following information about your parents and siblings (brothers and sisters). Check the box if the person is deceased.
(NOTE: Use Supplement B, Form I-589 or additional sheets of paper, if necessary.)

Full Name	City/Town and Country of Birth	Current Location
Mother		☐ Deceased
Father		☐ Deceased
Sibling		☐ Deceased
Sibling		☐ Deceased
Sibling		☐ Deceased
Sibling		☐ Deceased

Form I-589 (Rev. 12/14/06) Y Page 4

Part B. Information about your application.

(NOTE: Use Supplement B, Form I-589 or attach additional sheets of paper as needed to complete your responses to the questions contained in Part B.)

When answering the following questions about your asylum or other protection claim (withholding of removal under 241(b)(3) of the INA or withholding of removal under the Convention Against Torture) you should provide a detailed and specific account of the basis of your claim to asylum or other protection. To the best of your ability, provide specific dates, places and descriptions about each event or action described. You should attach documents evidencing the general conditions in the country from which you are seeking asylum or other protection and the specific facts on which you are relying to support your claim. If this documentation is unavailable or you are not providing this documentation with your application, please explain why in your responses to the following questions.

Refer to Instructions, Part 1: Filing Instructions, Section II, "Basis of Eligibility," Parts A - D, Section V, "Completing the Form," Part B, and Section VII, "Additional Evidence That You Should Submit," for more information on completing this section of the form.

1. Why are you applying for asylum or withholding of removal under section 241(b)(3) of the INA, or for withholding of removal under the Convention Against Torture? Check the appropriate box(es) below and then provide detailed answers to questions A and B below:

    I am seeking asylum or withholding of removal based on:

    ☐ Race   ☐ Political opinion
    ☐ Religion   ☐ Membership in a particular social group
    ☐ Nationality   ☐ Torture Convention

    A. Have you, your family, or close friends or colleagues ever experienced harm or mistreatment or threats in the past by anyone?

      ☐ No   ☐ Yes

      If "Yes," explain in detail:

      (1) What happened;
      (2) When the harm or mistreatment or threats occurred;
      (3) Who caused the harm or mistreatment or threats; and
      (4) Why you believe the harm or mistreatment or threats occurred.

    B. Do you fear harm or mistreatment if you return to your home country?

      ☐ No   ☐ Yes

      If "Yes," explain in detail:

      (1) What harm or mistreatment you fear;
      (2) Who you believe would harm or mistreat you; and
      (3) Why you believe you would or could be harmed or mistreated.

Part B. Information about your application. (Continued.)

2. Have you or your family members ever been accused, charged, arrested, detained, interrogated, convicted and sentenced, or imprisoned in any country other than the United States?

☐ No ☐ Yes

If "Yes," explain the circumstances and reasons for the action.

3.A. Have you or your family members ever belonged to or been associated with any organizations or groups in your home country, such as, but not limited to, a political party, student group, labor union, religious organization, military or paramilitary group, civil patrol, guerrilla organization, ethnic group, human rights group, or the press or media?

☐ No ☐ Yes

If "Yes," describe for each person the level of participation, any leadership or other positions held, and the length of time you or your family members were involved in each organization or activity.

B. Do you or your family members continue to participate in any way in these organizations or groups?

☐ No ☐ Yes

If "Yes," describe for each person your or your family members' current level of participation, any leadership or other positions currently held, and the length of time you or your family members have been involved in each organization or group.

4. Are you afraid of being subjected to torture in your home country or any other country to which you may be returned?

☐ No ☐ Yes

If "Yes," explain why you are afraid and describe the nature of torture you fear, by whom, and why it would be inflicted.

Part C. Additional information about your application.

(**NOTE:** *Use Supplement B, Form I-589 or attach additonal sheets of paper as needed to complete your responses to the questions contained in Part C.*)

1. Have you, your spouse, your child(ren), your parents or your siblings ever applied to the U. S. Government for refugee status, asylum or withholding of removal?

   ☐ No   ☐ Yes

   If "Yes," explain the decision and what happened to any status you, your spouse, your child(ren), your parents or your siblings received as a result of that decision. Please indicate whether or not you were included in a parent or spouse's application. If so, please include your parent or spouse's A-number in your response. If you have been denied asylum by an Immigration Judge or the Board of Immigration Appeals, please describe any change(s) in conditions in your country or your own personal circumstances since the date of the denial that may affect your eligibility for asylum.

2. **A.** After leaving the country from which you are claiming asylum, did you or your spouse or child(ren) who are now in the United States travel through or reside in any other country before entering the United States?   ☐ No   ☐ Yes

   B. Have you, your spouse, your child(ren) or other family members, such as your parents or siblings, ever applied for or received any lawful status in any country other than the one from which you are now claiming asylum?

   ☐ No   ☐ Yes

   If "Yes" to either or both questions (2A and/or 2B), provide for each person the following: the name of each country and the length of stay, the person's status while there, the reasons for leaving, whether or not the person is entitled to return for lawful residence purposes, and whether the person applied for refugee status or for asylum while there, and if not, why he or she did not do so.

3. Have you, your spouse or your child(ren) ever ordered, incited, assisted or otherwise participated in causing harm or suffering to any person because of his or her race, religion, nationality, membership in a particular social group or belief in a particular political opinion?

   ☐ No   ☐ Yes

   If "Yes," describe in detail each such incident and your own, your spouse's or your child(ren)'s involvement.

Form I-589 (Rev. 12/14/06) Y Page 7

APPENDIX 9A • I-589

Part C. Additional information about your application. (Continued.)

4. After you left the country where you were harmed or fear harm, did you return to that country?

   ☐ No   ☐ Yes

   If "Yes," describe in detail the circumstances of your visit(s) (for example, the date(s) of the trip(s), the purpose(s) of the trip(s) and the length of time you remained in that country for the visit(s).)

5. Are you filing this application more than one year after your last arrival in the United States?

   ☐ No   ☐ Yes

   If "Yes," explain why you did not file within the first year after you arrived. You should be prepared to explain at your interview or hearing why you did not file your asylum application within the first year after you arrived. For guidance in answering this question, see Instructions, Part 1: Filing Instructions, Section V. "Completing the Form," Part C.

6. Have you or any member of your family included in the application ever committed any crime and/or been arrested, charged, convicted and sentenced for any crimes in the United States?

   ☐ No   ☐ Yes

   If "Yes," for each instance, specify in your response: what occurred and the circumstances, dates, length of sentence received, location, the duration of the detention or imprisonment, the reason(s) for the detention or conviction, any formal charges that were lodged against you or your relatives included in your application and the reason(s) for release. Attach documents referring to these incidents, if they are available, or an explanation of why documents are not available.

Part D. Your Signature.

I certify, under penalty of perjury under the laws of the United States of America, that this application and the evidence submitted with it are all true and correct. Title 18, United States Code, Section 1546(a), provides in part: Whoever knowingly makes under oath, or as permitted under penalty of perjury under Section 1746 of Title 28, United States Code, knowingly subscribes as true, any false statement with respect to a material fact in any application, affidavit, or other document required by the immigration laws or regulations prescribed thereunder, or knowingly presents any such application, affidavit, or other document containing any such false statement or which fails to contain any reasonable basis in law or fact - shall be fined in accordance with this title or imprisoned for up to 25 years. I authorize the release of any information from my immigration record that U.S. Citizenship and Immigration Services (USCIS) needs to determine eligibility for the benefit I am seeking.

Staple your photograph here or the photograph of the family member to be included on the extra copy of the application submitted for that person.

WARNING: Applicants who are in the United States illegally are subject to removal if their asylum or withholding claims are not granted by an asylum officer or an immigration judge. Any information provided in completing this application may be used as a basis for the institution of, or as evidence in, removal proceedings even if the application is later withdrawn. Applicants determined to have knowingly made a frivolous application for asylum will be permanently ineligible for any benefits under the Immigration and Nationality Act. You may not avoid a frivolous finding simply because someone advised you to provide false information in your asylum application. If filing with USCIS, unexcused failure to appear for an appointment to provide biometrics (such as fingerprints) and your biographical information within the time allowed may result in an asylum officer dismissing your asylum application or referring it to an immigration judge. Failure without good cause to provide DHS with biometrics or other biographical information while in removal proceedings may result in your application being found abandoned by the immigration judge. See sections 208(d)(5)(A) and 208(d)(6) of the INA and 8 CFR sections 208.10, 1208.10, 208.20, 1003.47(d) and 1208.20.

Print your complete name.	Write your name in your native alphabet.

Did your spouse, parent or child(ren) assist you in completing this application? ☐ No ☐ Yes *(If "Yes," list the name and relationship.)*

_____ _____ _____ _____
  (Name)   *(Relationship)*   *(Name)*   *(Relationship)*

Did someone other than your spouse, parent or child(ren) prepare this application? ☐ No ☐ Yes *(If "Yes," complete Part E.)*

Asylum applicants may be represented by counsel. Have you been provided with a list of persons who may be available to assist you, at little or no cost, with your asylum claim? ☐ No ☐ Yes

Signature of Applicant *(The person in Part A.I.)*

[_____]
Sign your name so it all appears within the brackets

Date *(mm/dd/yyyy)* _____

Part E. Declaration of person preparing form, if other than applicant, spouse, parent or child.

I declare that I have prepared this application at the request of the person named in Part D, that the responses provided are based on all information of which I have knowledge, or which was provided to me by the applicant, and that the completed application was read to the applicant in his or her native language or a language he or she understands for verification before he or she signed the application in my presence. I am aware that the knowing placement of false information on the Form I-589 may also subject me to civil penalties under 8 U.S.C. 1324c and/or criminal penalties under 18 U.S.C. 1546(a).

Signature of Preparer	Print Complete Name of Preparer		
Daytime Telephone Number ( )	Address of Preparer: Street Number and Name		
Apt. No.	City	State	Zip Code

Form I-589 (Rev. 12/14/06) Y Page 9

APPENDIX 9A • I-589

Part F. To be completed at asylum interview, if applicable.

NOTE: *You will be asked to complete this Part when you appear for examination before an asylum officer of the Department of Homeland Security, U.S. Citizenship and Immigration Services (USCIS).*

I swear (affirm) that I know the contents of this application that I am signing, including the attached documents and supplements, that they are ☐ all true or ☐ not all true to the best of my knowledge and that correction(s) numbered ____ to ____ were made by me or at my request. Furthermore, I am aware that if I am determined to have knowingly made a frivolous application for asylum I will be permanently ineligible for any benefits under the Immigration and Nationality Act and that I may not avoid a frivolous finding simply because someone advised me to provide false information in my asylum application.

Signed and sworn to before me by the above named applicant on:

_____   _____
Signature of Applicant   Date *(mm/dd/yyyy)*

_____   _____
Write Your Name in Your Native Alphabet   Signature of asylum officer

Part G. To be completed at removal hearing, if applicable.

NOTE: *You will be asked to complete this Part when you appear before an immigration judge of the U.S. Department of Justice, Executive Office for Immigration Review (EOIR), for a hearing.*

I swear (affirm) that I know the contents of this application that I am signing, including the attached documents and supplements, that they are ☒ all true or ☐ not all true to the best of my knowledge and that correction(s) numbered ____ to ____ were made by me or at my request. Furthermore, I am aware that if I am determined to have knowingly made a frivolous application for asylum I will be permanently ineligible for any benefits under the Immigration and Nationality Act and that I may not avoid a frivolous finding simply because someone advised me to provide false information in my asylum application.

Signed and sworn to before me by the above named applicant on:

_____   _____
Signature of Applicant   Date *(mm/dd/yyyy)*

_____   _____
Write Your Name in Your Native Alphabet   Signature of immigration judge

Form I-589 (Rev. 12/14/06) Y Page 10

Supplement A, Form I-589

A # (If available)	Date
Applicant's Name	Applicant's Signature

List all of your children, regardless of age or marital status.
(NOTE: Use this form and attach additional pages and documentaton as needed, if you have more than four children.)

1. Alien Registration Number (A#) (If any)	2. Passport/ID Card Number (If any)	3. Marital Status (Married, Single, Divorced, Widowed)	4. U.S. Social Security Number (If any)
5. Complete Last Name	6. First Name	7. Middle Name	8. Date of Birth (mm/dd/yyyy)
9. City and Country of Birth	10. Nationality (Citizenship)	11. Race, Ethnic or Tribal Group	12. Gender ☐ Male ☐ Female

13. Is this child in the U.S.? ☐ Yes (Complete blocks 14 to 21.) ☐ No (Specify location.)

14. Place of last entry in the U.S.	15. Date of last entry in the U.S. (mm/dd/yyyy)	16. I-94 Number (If any)	17. Status when last admitted (Visa type, if any)
18. What is your child's current status?	19. What is the expiration date of his/her authorized stay, if any? (mm/dd/yyyy)	20. Is your child in Immigration Court proceedings? ☐ Yes ☐ No	

21. If in the U.S., is this child to be included in this application? (Check the appropriate box.)
   ☐ Yes (Attach one photograph of your child in the upper right corner of Page 9 on the extra copy of the application submitted for this person.)
   ☐ No

1. Alien Registration Number (A#) (If any)	2. Passport/ID Card Number (If any)	3. Marital Status (Married, Single, Divorced, Widowed)	4. U.S. Social Security Number (If any)
5. Complete Last Name	6. First Name	7. Middle Name	8. Date of Birth (mm/dd/yyyy)
9. City and Country of Birth	10. Nationality (Citizenship)	11. Race, Ethnic or Tribal Group	12. Gender ☐ Male ☐ Female

13. Is this child in the U.S.? ☐ Yes (Complete blocks 14 to 21.) ☐ No (Specify location.)

14. Place of last entry in the U.S.	15. Date of last entry in the U.S. (mm/dd/yyyy)	16. I-94 Number (If any)	17. Status when last admitted (Visa type, if any)
18. What is your child's current status?	19. What is the expiration date of his/her authorized stay, if any? (mm/dd/yyyy)	20. Is your child in Immigration Court proceedings? ☐ Yes ☐ No	

21. If in the U.S., is this child to be included in this application? (Check the appropriate box.)
   ☐ Yes (Attach one photograph of your child in the upper right corner of Page 9 on the extra copy of the application submitted for this person.)
   ☐ No

Form I-589 Supplement A (Rev. 12/14/06) Y

APPENDIX 9A • I-589

Supplement B, Form I-589

Additional information about your claim to asylum.

A# *(If available)*

Date

Applicant's Name

Applicant's Signature

NOTE: *Use this as a continuation page for any additional information requested. Please copy and complete as needed.*

Part

Question

Form I-589 Supplement B (Rev. 12/14/06) Y

APPENDIX 9B

FORM I-730 AND INSTRUCTIONS

Department of Homeland Security
U.S. Citizenship and Immigration Service

OMB No.1615-0037; Expires 08/31/07

I-730, Refugee/Asylee Relative Petition

Instructions

NOTE: Read these instructions carefully. If you do not follow the instructions, U.S. Citizenship and Immigration Services (USCIS) may have to return your petition, which may delay final action. If more space is needed to complete an answer, continue on a separate sheet(s) of paper. USCIS is comprised of offices of the former Immigration and Naturalization Service (INS).

1. Who May File This Petition?

If you have been admitted to the United States as a refugee or if you have been granted status in the United States as an asylee, **and as the principal applicant within the previous two years,** you may file this petition. Approval of the I-730 petition for a relative abroad does not guarantee visa issuance. A separate Form I-730 must be filed for each family member.

You are not eligible to file this petition if:

- You were granted status in the United States as a derivative beneficiary or as an accompanying or following-to-join family member; or
- You were admitted to the United States as a refugee more than two years ago (see *NOTE below), or
- You were granted status in the United States as an asylee more than two years ago (see *NOTE below).

*NOTE: The two-year limitation may be waived by USCIS for humanitarian reasons. Please attach a detailed explanation why the petitioner could not file within two years of being granted status. USCIS will make a decision based upon the explanation.

2. Who Is Eligible to Receive Accompanying or Following-to-Join Benefits?

Your spouse and/or your unmarried child(ren) under (21) years of age, whether inside or outside of the United States, are eligible for accompanying or following-to-join benefits **provided** that the family member(s) qualify under the conditions described below.

If you are a refugee:

- The relationship between you and your relative must have existed on the date you were admitted to the United States as a refugee and must continue to exist.

  -- If the person you are filing for is a child who was conceived but not yet born on the date you were admitted to the United States, the relationship will be considered to exist as of the date you were admitted to the United States.

  -- The mother of such child is not an eligible relative unless the mother was married to you, the principal refugee, when you were admitted to the United States.

If you are an asylee:

- The relationship between you and your relative must have existed on the date you were granted asylum in the United States and must continue to exist.

  -- If the person you are filing for is a child who was conceived but not yet born on the date you were granted asylum in the United States, the relationship will be considered to exist as of the date you were granted asylum in the United States.

  -- The mother of such child is not an eligible relative unless the mother was married to you, the principal asylee, when you were granted asylum in the United States.

- In all cases, if the family member you are filing for is your child, the child must be under 21 years of age when the petition is filed and continue to be unmarried at the time of approval.

- A spouse or child must be otherwise admissible as an immigrant (for refugee relatives) or not subject to the mandatory bars of 8 CFR 208.21 (for asylee relatives).

A petition may not be approved for the following persons:

- A spouse or child who has previously been granted refugee or asylee status.

- An adopted child, if the adoption took place after the child became 16 years old, or if the child has not been in legal custody and living with the adoptive parent(s) for at least two years.

- A stepchild, if the marriage that created this relationship took place after the child became 18 years old.

- A husband or wife, if each was not physically present at the marriage ceremony and the marriage was not consummated.

- A husband or wife, if it is determined that such alien has attempted or conspired to enter into a marriage for the purpose of evading immigration laws.

- A parent, sister, brother, grandparent, grandchild, nephew, niece, uncle, aunt, cousin or in-law.

3. What Are the General Filing Instructions?

Type or print legibly in black ink.

If you need extra space to complete any item, attach a separate continuation sheet. Indicate the item number, date and sign each sheet.

Answer all questions fully and accurately. Portions left unanswered may result in a Request for Evidence. If the previous marriages portion does not apply to you, please state "none." For all others that do not apply to you, please state "N/A."

Copies. In all cases, you should submit one readable photocopy of each required document to USCIS. If a copy of a document is submitted, USCIS may at any time require that the original document be submitted for review.

Translation. Documents in a foreign language must be accompanied by a complete English translation. The translator must certify that the translation is accurate and that he or she is competent to translate. Original documents submitted when not required will remain a part of the record.

4. What Documents Do You Need to Prove Eligibility and a Family Relationship?

Certain documents are required to be submitted with this petition to show that you are eligible to file this petition and to show that a relationship exists between you and your relative. (If the documents described below are not available, see **Sections 4** and **5** of these instructions):

* In all cases, submit **evidence of your status** as a refugee or asylee in the United States.
* In all cases, submit a recently taken clear **photograph** of the family member you are filing for.
* If you are petitioning for your **husband or wife,** submit your marriage certificate. If you and/or your spouse were previously married to other people, submit evidence of the legal termination of the previous marriage(s). Evidence of any legal name change must also be submitted, if applicable.
* If you are petitioning for your **child** and you are the **natural mother,** whether the child was born in or out of wedlock, submit the child's birth certificate showing both the child's name and your name. Evidence of any legal name change must also be submitted if the names on the birth certificate do not match the names on the petition.
* If you are petitioning for your **child** and you are the **natural father,** submit the child's birth certificate showing both the child's name and your name. If you were married to the child's mother, submit your marriage certificate. If you and/or the child's mother were previously married to other people, submit evidence of the legal termination of the previous marriage(s). If you were not married to the child's mother, submit evidence that the child was legitimated by civil authorities, submit evidence that a bona fide parent/child relationship exists or existed between you and the child. Evidence of a bona fide parent/child relationship should prove that you have emotional and financial ties to the child, and that you have shown genuine general welfare. Such evidence may include (but is not limited to) the following:

-- Money order receipts;
-- Canceled checks showing financial support of the child;
-- Income tax returns in which you claim the child as a dependent and member of your household;
-- Medical or insurance records that include the child as a dependent;
-- School records for the child;
-- Correspondence between you and the child;
-- Notarized affidavits of reliable persons who are knowledgeable about the relationship. Evidence of any legal name change must also be submitted, if applicable.

* If you are petitioning for your **stepchild,** whether the child was born in or out of wedlock, submit the child's birth certificate and the marriage certificate between you and the child's natural parent. If you and/or the child's natural parent were ever previously married to other people, submit evidence of the legal termination of the previous marriage(s). Evidence of any legal name changes must also be submitted, if applicable.
* If you are petitioning for your **adopted child,** submit a certified copy of the adoption decree and evidence that you resided together with the child for at least two years. If you were granted legal custody of the child prior to the adoption, submit a certified copy of the court order granting custody. Evidence of any legal name changes must also be submitted, if applicable.

5. What If a Document Is Not Available?

If the documents described above are not available from the civil authorities, you may submit the following, as secondary evidence, along with a statement from the appropriate civil authority certifying that the required document(s) is(are) not available.

* *Religious institution record:* A certificate under the seal of the religious institution where the baptism, dedication or comparable rite occurred within two months after birth, showing the date and place of the child's birth, the date of the religious ceremony, and the names of the child's parents.
* *School record:* A letter from the authorities of the school (s) attended, showing the date of admission to the school, the child's date and place of birth and the names of both parents, if shown on the school records.
* *Census record:* State or federal census record showing name, place of birth, and date of birth or the age of the person(s) listed.

APPENDIX 9B • I-730

6. What If Secondary Evidence is Not Available?

If the secondary evidence described above is not available, you can submit affidavits. If you submit affidavits, they must overcome the absence of primary and secondary evidence.

Affidavits:

Submit written statements sworn to or affirmed by two persons who were living at the time and who have personal knowledge of the event you are trying to prove: for example, the date and place of birth, marriage or death. The persons making the affidavits do not have to be United States citizens.

Each affidavit should contain the following information regarding the person making the affidavit: his or her full name, address, date and place of birth and his or her relationship to you (if any); full information concerning the event; and complete details concerning how the person acquired the knowledge of the event.

7. Where Do You File This Form?

Nebraska Service Center Filings

File Form I-730 with the Nebraska Service Center if you, the petitioner, currently live in the following states:

Alaska, Arizona, California, Colorado, Guam, Hawaii, Idaho, Illinois, Indiana, Iowa, Kansas, Michigan, Minnesota, Missouri, Montana, Nebraska, Nevada, North Dakota, Ohio, Oregon, South Dakota, Utah, Washington, Wisconsin or Wyoming.

The mailing address you should use is:

USCIS - Nebraska Service Center
P.O. Box 87730
Lincoln, NE 68501-7730

Texas Service Center Filings

File Form I-730 with the Texas Service Center if you, the petitioner, currently live in the following states:

Alabama, Arkansas, Connecticut, Florida, Georgia, Kentucky, Louisiana, Maine, Maryland, Massachusetts, Mississippi, New Hampshire, New Jersey, New Mexico, New York, North Carolina, South Carolina, Oklahoma, Pennsylvania, Puerto Rico, Rhode Island, Tennesse, Texas, Vermont, Virginia, U.S. Virgin Islands, West Virginia or Washington, DC.

The mailing address you should use is:

USCIS - Texas Service Center
P.O. Box 852824
Mesquite, TX 75185

8. What Are the Penalties for Committing Marriage Fraud?

- Title 8, United States Code, Section 1325, states that any person who knowingly enters into a marriage contract for the purpose of evading any provision of the immigration laws shall be imprisoned for not more than five years, or fined not more than $250,000, or both.

- Title 18, United States Code, Section 1001, states that whoever willfully and knowingly falsifies a material fact, makes a false statement or makes use of a false document will be fined up to $10,000 or imprisoned up to five years, or both.

9. What Is Our Authority for Collecting This Information?

USCIS requests the information on the form to carry out the immigration laws contained in Title 8, United States Code, Sections 1157(c)(2) and 1158(b)(3). USCIS needs this information to determine whether a person is eligible for immigration benefits. The information you provide may also be disclosed to other federal, state, local and foreign law enforcement and regulatory agencies during the course of the investigation required by USCIS. You do not have to give this information. However, if you refuse to give some or all of it, your petition may be denied.

10. USCIS Forms and Information.

To order USCIS forms, call our toll-free number at **1-800-870-3676.** You can also get USCIS forms and information on immigration laws, regulations and procedures by telephoning our National Customer Service Center at **1-800-375-5283** or visiting our internet website at www.uscis.gov.

11. Use InfoPass for Appointments

As an alternative to waiting in line for assistance at your local USCIS office, you can now schedule an appointment through our internet-based system, **InfoPass**. To access the system, visit our website at www.uscis.gov. Use the **InfoPass** appointment scheduler and follow the screen prompts to set up your appointment. **InfoPass** generates an electronic appointment notice that appears on the screen. Print the notice and take it with you to your appointment. The notice gives the time and date of your appointment, along with the address of the USCIS office.

12. Paperwork Reduction Act.

An agency may not conduct or sponsor an information collection and a person is not required to respond to a collection of information unless it displays a currently valid OMB control number. The public reporting burden for this collection of information is estimated to average 35 minutes per response, including the time for reviewing instructions, searching existing data sources, gathering and maintaining the data needed and completing and reviewing the collection of information. Send comments regarding this burden estimate or any other aspect of this collection of information, including suggestions for reducing this burden, to: **U.S. Citizenship and Immigration Services, Regulatory Management Division, 111 Massachusetts Avenue, N.W., Suite 3008, Washington, DC 20529. OMB No. 1615-0037. Do not mail your petition to this address.**

Check List.

- Did you answer each question on the Form I-730 petition according to the instructions on the form?
- Did you sign and date the petition?
- Did you submit proof of your status as a refugee or asylee in the United States?
- Did you submit documented proof of relationship, including those needing copies and/or translations?
- Did you submit the beneficiary photo?
- Did you provide the beneficiary's address where he or she is residing now?
- Did you provide the beneficiary's name and address as written in the language of his or her country of residence?

APPENDIX 9B • I-730

OMB No. 1615-0037, Expires 08/31/07

Department of Homeland Security
U.S. Citizenship and Immigration Services

I-730, Refugee/Asylee Relative Petition

DO NOT WRITE IN THIS BLOCK - FOR USCIS OFFICE ONLY

Section of Law
- [ ] 207 (c)(2) Spouse
- [ ] 207 (c)(2) Child
- [ ] 208 (b)(3) Spouse
- [ ] 208 (b)(3) Child

Action Stamp

Receipt

Reviewed For Material Support

Date:

Remarks

START HERE - Please type or print legibly in black ink.

Petitioner Status:
- [ ] Refugee
- [ ] Asylee
- [ ] Lawful Permanent Resident based on previous Refugee status
- [ ] Lawful Permanent Resident based on previous Asylee status

I am filing this petition for my:
- [ ] Spouse
- [ ] Unmarried child under 21 years of age who is:
- [ ] Biological Child
- [ ] Stepchild
- [ ] Adopted Child

Number of relatives I am filing for: _____ (_____ of _____)

Part 1. Information about you.

Family Name (Last Name), Given Name (First Name), Middle Name

Address - C/O

Street Number and Name | Apt. #

City | State or Province

Country | Zip/Postal Code | Gender: a. [ ] Male b. [ ] Female

Date of Birth (mm/dd/yyyy) | Country of Birth

Country of Citizenship/Nationality | Telephone Number Country and City/Area Code

Alien Registration Number(A#) | U.S. Social Security # (If applicable,)

Other Name(s) Used (Including maiden name)

State If Married, Date (mm/dd/yyyy) and Place of Present Marriage:

State If Previously Married, Name(s) of Prior Spouse(s):

Date(s) Previous Marriage(s) Ended: (mm/dd/yyyy)

If Granted Refugee Status, Date (mm/dd/yyyy) and Place Admitted to the United States:

Date (mm/dd/yyyy) and Place Refugee or Asylee status was granted:

Part 2. Information about your alien relative.

Family Name (Last Name), Given Name (First Name), Middle Name

Address - C/O

Street Number and Name | Apt. #

City | State or Province

Country | Zip/Postal Code | Gender: a. [ ] Male b. [ ] Female

Date of Birth (mm/dd/yyyy) | Country of Birth

Country of Citizenship/Nationality | Telephone Number Country and City/Area Code

Alien Registration Number (If any,) | U. S. Social Security # (If any,)

Other Name(s) Used (Including maiden name)

State If Married, Date (mm/dd/yyyy) and Place of Present Marriage:

State If Previously Married, Name(s) of Prior Spouse(s):

Date(s) Previous Marriage(s) Ended: (mm/dd/yyyy)

To Be Completed by
Attorney or Representative, if any.
[ ] Fill in box if G-28 is attached to represent the petitioner.

Volag #

Atty State License #

Form I-730 (Rev. 09/18/06) N

Part 2. Information about your alien relative. (Continued.)

Name and address of your alien relative in the language written in the country where he or she now resides.

Family Name _____ Given Name _____ Middle Name _____

Address - C/O _____

Street Number and Name/Apt. # _____

City/State or Province _____

Country/Zip/Postal Code _____

Part 3. Processing Information.

1. Check One:
   a. ☐ The person named in **Part 2** is now in the United States.
   b. ☐ The person named in **Part 2** is now outside the United States. (Please indicate the location of the American Consulate or Embassy where your relative will apply for a visa.)

   American Consulate/Embassy at: _____
   City and Country

2. Is the person named in **Part 2** in deportation or removal proceedings in the United States?
   a. ☐ No
   b. ☐ Yes *(Please explain below or on a separate sheet(s) of paper.)*

Part 4. Signature.

*Read the information on penalties in the instructions before completing this section and sign below. If someone helped you to prepare this petition, he or she must complete **Part 6**.*

I certify or, if outside the United States, I swear or affirm, under penalty of perjury under the laws of the United States of America, that this petition and the evidence submitted with it, is all true and correct. I authorize the release of any information from my record which U.S. Citizenship and Immigration Services needs to determine eligibility for the benefit I am seeking.

Signature _____ Print Name _____ Date _____ Daytime Telephone Number _____

NOTE: *If you do not completely fill out this form or fail to submit the required documents listed in the instructions, your relative may not be found eligible for the requested benefit and this petition may be denied.*

Part 5. Signature of person preparing form, if other than petitioner above. (Sign below.)

I declare that I prepared this petition at the request of the above person and it is based on all of the information of which I have knowledge.

Signature _____ Print Full Name _____ Date _____ Daytime Telephone Number _____

Firm Name and Address _____ E-Mail Address (If any.) _____

APPENDIX 9C

FORM I-765 AND INSTRUCTIONS

OMB No. 1615-0040; Expires 08/31/08

Department of Homeland Security
U.S. Citizenship and Immigration Services

Instructions for I-765, Application for Employment Authorization

Instructions

Please read these instructions carefully to properly complete this form. If you need more space to complete an answer, use a separate sheet(s) of paper. Write your name and Alien Registration Number (A #), if any, at the top of each sheet of paper and indicate the part and number of the item to which the answer refers.

The filing addresses provided on this form reflect the most current information as of the date this form was last printed. If you are filing Form I-765 more than 30 days after the latest edition date shown in the lower right-hand corner, please visit our website at www.uscis.gov **before you file**, and check the Forms and Fees page to confirm the correct filing address and version currently in use. Check the edition date located in the lower right-hand corner of the form. If the edition date on your Form I-765 matches the edition date listed for Form I-765 on the online Forms and Fees page, your version is current and will be accepted by USCIS. If the edition date on the online version is later, download a copy and use the online version. If you do not have internet access, call the National Customer Service Center at 1-800-375-5283 to verify the current filing address and edition date. **Improperly filed forms will be rejected, and the fee returned, with instructions to resubmit the entire filing using the current form instructions.**

Index

	Page No.
What Is the Purpose of This Form	1
Who May File This Form I-765	1
Required Documentation	6
What Is the Filing Fee	7
Where to File	8
Processing Information	12
Other Information	10

What Is the Purpose of This Form?

Certain aliens who are temporarily in the United States may file a Form I-765, Application for Employment Authorization, to request an Employment Authorization Document (EAD). Other aliens who are authorized to work in the United States without restrictions should also use this form to apply to USCIS for a document evidencing such authorization. Please review **Eligibility Categories** to determine whether you should use this form.

If you are a Lawful Permanent Resident, a Conditional Resident, or a nonimmigrant authorized to be employed with a specific employer under 8 CFR 274a.12(b), please do **not** use this form.

Definitions.

Employment Authorization Document (EAD): Form I-688, Form I-688A, Form I-688B, Form I-766, or any successor document issued by USCIS as evidence that the holder is authorized to work in the United States.

Renewal EAD: An EAD issued to an eligible applicant at or after the expiration of a previous EAD issued under the same category.

Replacement EAD: An EAD issued to an eligible applicant when the previously issued EAD has been lost, stolen, mutilated, or contains erroneous information, such as a misspelled name.

Interim EAD: An EAD issued to an eligible applicant when USCIS has failed to adjudicate an application within 90 days of receipt of a properly filed EAD application or within 30 days of a properly filed initial EAD application based on an asylum application filed on or after January 4, 1995. The interim EAD will be granted for a period not to exceed 240 days and is subject to the conditions noted on the document.

Who May File This Form I-765?

USCIS adjudicates a request for employment authorization by determining whether an applicant has submitted the required information and documentation, and whether the applicant is eligible. In order to determine your eligibility, you must identify the category in which you are eligible and fill in that category in **Question 16** on the Form I-765. Enter only **one** of the following category numbers on the application form. For example, if you are a refugee applying for an EAD, you should write "(a)(3)" at **Question 16**.

For easier reference, the categories are subdivided as follows:

	Page No.
Asylee/Refugee and their Spouses and children	1
Nationality Categories	2
Foreign Students	2

Form I-765 Instructions (Rev. 07/30/07) Y

Eligible Dependents of Employees of Diplomatic Missions, International Organizations or NATO 3
Employment-Based Nonimmigrants 3
Family-Based Nonimmigrants 4
Adjustment of Status Categories 4
Other Categories 5

1. **Asylee/Refugee Categories.**

    A. **Refugee--(a)(3).** File your EAD application with either a copy of your Form I-590, Registration for Classification as Refugee, approval letter or a copy of a Form I-730, Refugee/Asylee Relative Petition, approval notice.

    B. **Paroled as a Refugee--(a)(4).** File your EAD application with a copy of your Form I-94, Arrival and Departure Record.

    C. **Asylee (Granted Asylum)--(a)(5).** File your EAD application with a copy of the USCIS letter, or judge's decision, granting you asylum. It is not necessary to apply for an EAD as an asylee until 90 days before the expiration of your current EAD.

    D. **Asylum Applicant (With a Pending Asylum Application) Who Filed for Asylum on or After January 4, 1995–(c)(8).** (For specific instructions for applicants with pending asylum claims, see Page 5).

2. **Nationality Categories.**

    A. **Citizen of Micronesia, the Marshall Islands or Palau—(a)(8).** File your EAD application if you were admitted to the United States as a citizen of the Federated States of Micronesia (CFA/FSM), the Marshall Islands (CFA/MIS), or Palau, pursuant to agreements between the United States and the former trust territories.

    B. **Deferred Enforced Departure (DED) / Extended Voluntary Departure—(a)(11).** File your EAD application with evidence of your identity and nationality.

    C. **Temporary Protected Status (TPS)—(a)(12).** File your EAD application with Form I-821, Application for Temporary Protected Status. If you are filing for an initial EAD based on your TPS status, include evidence of identity and nationality as required by the Form I-821 instructions.

    D. **Temporary Treatment Benefits** --(c)(19). For an EAD based on 8 CFR 244.5. Include evidence of nationality and identity as required by the Form I-821 instructions.

      1. Extension of TPS status: include a copy (front and back) of your last available TPS document: EAD, Form I-94 or approval notice.

      2. Registration for TPS only without employment authorization: file the Form I-765, Form I-821, and a letter indicating that this form is for registration purposes only. No fee is required for the Form I-765 filed as part of TPS registration. (Form I-821 has separate fee requirements.)

    E. **NACARA Section 203 Applicants Who Are Eligible to Apply for NACARA Relief With USCIS--(c)(10).** See the instructions to Form I-881, Application for Suspension of Deportation or Special Rule Cancellation of Removal, to determine if you are eligible to apply for NACARA 203 relief with USCIS.

    If you are eligible, follow the instructions below and submit your Form I-765 at the same time you file your Form I-881 application with USCIS:

      1. If you are filing a Form I-881 with USCIS, file your EAD application at the same time and at the same filing location. Your response to Question 16 on the Form I-765 should be "(c)(10)."

      2. If you have already filed your I-881 application at the service center specified on the Form I-881, and now wish to apply for employment authorization, your response to **Question 16** on Form I-765 should be **"(c)(10)."** You should file your EAD application at the Service Center designated in "Where to File" of these instructions.

      3. If you are a NACARA Section 203 applicant who previously filed a Form I-881 with USCIS, and the application is still pending, you may renew your EAD. Your response to **Question 16** on Form I-765 should be **"(c)(10)."** Submit the required fee and the EAD application to the service center designated in "Where to File" of these instructions.

    F. **Dependent of TECRO E-1 Nonimmigrant—(c).** File your EAD application with the required certification from the American Institute in Taiwan if you are the spouse, or unmarried dependent son or daughter of an E-1 employee of the Taipei Economic and Cultural Representative Office.

3. **Foreign Students.**

   A. **F-1 Student Seeking Optional Practical Training in an Occupation Directly Related to Studies—(c)(3)(i).** File your EAD application with a Certificate of Eligibility of Nonimmigrant (F-1) Student Status (Form I-20 A-B/I-20 ID) endorsed by a Designated School Official within the past 30 days.

   B. **F-1 Student Offered Off-Campus Employment Under the Sponsorship of a Qualifying International Organization-- (c)(3)(ii).** File your EAD application with the international organization's letter of certification that the proposed employment is within the scope of its sponsorship, and a Certificate of Eligibility of Nonimmigrant (F-1) Student Status -- For Academic and Language Students (Form I-20 A-B/ -20 ID) endorsed by the Designated School Official within the past 30 days.

   C. **F-1 Student Seeking Off-Campus Employment Due to Severe Economic Hardship--(c)(3)(iii).** File your EAD application with Form I-20 A-B/I-20 ID, Certificate of Eligibility of Nonimmigrant (F-1) Student Status -- For Academic and Language Students, and any evidence you wish to submit, such as affidavits, that detail the unforeseen economic circumstances that cause your request, and evidence you have tried to find off-campus employment with an employer who has filed a labor and wage attestation.

   D. **J-2 Spouse or Minor Child of an Exchange Visitor--(c)(5).** File your EAD application with a copy of your J-1's (principal alien's) Certificate of Eligibility for Exchange Visitor (J-1) Status (Form IAP-66). You must submit a written statement, with any supporting evidence showing, that your employment is not necessary to support the J-1 but is for other purposes.

   E. **M-1 Student Seeking Practical Training After Completing Studies—(c)(6).** File your EAD application with a completed Form I-539, Application to Change/Extend Nonimmigrant Status. Form I-20 M-N, Certificate of Eligibility for Nonimmigrant (M-1) Student Status -- For Vocational Students endorsed by the Designated School Official within the past 30 days.

4. **Eligible Dependents of Employees of Diplomatic Missions, International Organizations, or NATO.**

   A. **Dependent of A-1 or A-2 Foreign Government Officials--(c)(1).** Submit your EAD application with Form I-566, Inter-Agency Record of Individual Requesting Change/Adjustment to, or from, A or G Status; or Requesting A, G, or NATO Dependent Employment Authorization, through your diplomatic mission to the Department of State (DOS). The DOS will forward all favorably endorsed applications directly to the Nebraska Service Center for adjudication.

   B. **Dependent of G-1, G-3 or G-4 Nonimmigrant–(c)(4).** Submit your EAD application with a Form I-566, Inter-Agency Record of Individual Requesting Change/Adjustment to or from A or G Status; or Requesting A, G, or NATO Dependent Employment Authorization, through your international organization to the Department of State (DOS). [In New York City, the United Nations (UN) and UN missions should submit such applications to the United States Mission to the UN (USUN).] The DOS or USUN will forward all favorably endorsed applications directly to the Nebraska Service Center for adjudication.

   C. **Dependent of NATO-1 Through NATO-6--(c)(7).** Submit your EAD application with Form I-566, Inter-Agency Record of Individual Requesting Change/ Adjustment to, or from, A or G Status; or Requesting A, G or NATO Dependent Employment Authorization, to NATO SACLANT, 7857 Blandy Road, C-027, Suite 100, Norfolk, VA 23551-2490. NATO/SACLANT will forward all favorably endorsed applications directly to the Nebraska Service Center for adjudication.

5. **Employment-Based Nonimmigrant Categories.**

   A. **B-1 Nonimmigrant Who is the Personal or Domestic Servant of a Nonimmigrant Employer--(c)(17)(i).** File the EAD application with:

   1. Evidence from your employer that he or she is a B, E, F, H, I, J, L, M, O, P, R, or TN nonimmigrant and you were employed for at least one year by the employer before the employer entered the United States or your employer regularly employs personal and domestic servants and has done so for a period of years before coming to the United States; and

2. Evidence that you have either worked for this employer as a personal or domestic servant for at least one year or, evidence that you have at least one year's experience as a personal or domestic servant; and

3. Evidence establishing that you have a residence abroad which you have no intention of abandoning.

B. **B-1 Nonimmigrant Domestic Servant of a U.S. Citizen-- (c)(17)ii).** File your EAD application with:

1. Evidence from your employer that he or she is a U.S. citizen; and

2. Evidence that your employer has a permanent home abroad or is stationed outside the United States and is temporarily visiting the United States or the citizen's current assignment in the United States will not be longer than four 4 years; and

3. Evidence that he or she has employed you as a domestic servant abroad for at least six months prior to your admission to the United States.

C. **B-1 Nonimmigrant Employed by a Foreign Airline–(c)(17)(iii).** File your EAD application with a letter from the airline fully describing your duties and indicating that your position would entitle you to E nonimmigrant status except for the fact that you are not a national of the same country as the airline or because there is no treaty of commerce and navigation in effect between the United States and that country.

D. **Spouse of an E-1/E-2 Treaty Trader or Investor--(a)(17).** File your EAD application with evidence of your lawful status and evidence you are a **spouse** of a principal E-1/E-2, such as your Form I-94. (Other relatives or dependents of E-1/E-2 aliens who are in E status are not eligible for employment authorization and may not file under this category.)

E. **Spouse of an L-1 Intracompany Transferee– (a)(18).** File your EAD application with evidence of your lawful status and evidence you are a **spouse** of a principal L-1, such as your I-94. (Other relatives or dependents of L-1 aliens who are in L status are not eligible for employment authorization and may not file under this category.)

6. **Family-Based Nonimmigrant Categories.**

A. **K-1 Nonimmigrant Fiance(e) of U.S. Citizen or K-2 Dependent--(a)(6).** File your EAD application if you are filing within 90 days from the date of entry. This EAD cannot be renewed. Any EAD application other than for a replacement must be based on your pending application for adjustment under (c)(9).

B. **K-3 Nonimmigrant Spouse of U.S. Citizen or K-4 Dependent--(a)(9).** File your EAD application along with evidence of your admission such as copies of your Form I-94, passport, and K visa.

C. **Family Unity Program–(a)(13).** If you are filing for initial or extension Family Unity benefits complete and submit Form I-817, Application for Voluntary Departure Under the Family Unity Program. An Employment Authorization Document (EAD) will be issued if your I-817 is approved, no I-765 application is necessary.

If your non-expired Family Unity EAD is lost or stolen file an I-765 application with proper fee(s), along with a copy of your approval notice for Family Unity benefits, to request a replacement.

D. **LIFE Family Unity--(a)(14).** If you are applying for initial employment authorization pursuant to the Family Unity provisions of section 1504 of the LIFE Act Amendments, or an extension of such authorization, you should not be using this form. Please obtain and complete a Form I-817, Application for Family Unity Benefits. If you are applying for a replacement EAD that was issued pursuant to the LIFE Act Amendments Family Unity provisions, file your EAD application with the required evidence listed in the "Required Document" section of these instructions.

E. **V-1, V-2 or V-3 Nonimmigrant--(a)(15).** If you have been inspected and admitted to the United States with a valid V visa, file this application along with evidence of your admission, such as copies of your Form I-94, passport, and K visa. If you have been granted V status while in the United States, file this application along with evidence of your V status, such as an approval notice. If you are in the United States but you have not yet filed an application for V status, you may file this application at the same time as you file your application for V status. USCIS will adjudicate this application after adjudicating your application for V status.

APPENDIX 9C • I-765

7. **EAD Applicants Who Have Filed for Adjustment of Status.**

   A. **Adjustment Applicant—(c)(9).** File your EAD application with a copy of the receipt notice or other evidence that your Form I-485, Application for Permanent Residence or Adjust Status, is pending. You may file Form I-765 together with your Form I-485.

   B. **Adjustment Applicant Based on Continuous Residence Since January 1, 1972—(c)(16).** File your EAD application with your Form I-485, Application for Permanent Residence; a copy of your receipt notice; or other evidence that the Form I-485 is pending.

   C. **Renewal EAD for National Interest Waiver Physicians:** If you are filing for a renewal EAD based on your pending adjustment status and an approved National Interest Waiver Physician petition, you must also include evidence of your meaningful progress toward completing the national interest waiver obligation. Such evidence includes documentation of employment in any period during the previous 12 months (e.g. copies of W-2 forms). If you did not work as a national interest waiver physician during any period of the previous 12 months, you must explain and provide a statement of future intent to work in the national interest waiver employment.

8. **Other Categories.**

   A. **N-8 or N-9 Nonimmigrant—(a)(7).** File your EAD application with the required evidence listed in the "Required Document" section of these instructions.

   B. **Granted Withholding of Deportation or Removal (a)(10).** File your EAD application with a copy of the Immigration Judge's order. It is not necessary to apply for a new EAD until 90 days before the expiration of your current EAD.

   C. **Applicant for Suspension of Deportation—(c)(10).** File your EAD application with evidence that your Form I-881, Application for Suspension of Deportation, or EOIR-40, is pending.

   D. **Paroled in the Public Interest—(c)(11).** File your EAD application if you were paroled into the United States for emergent reasons or reasons strictly in the public interest.

   E. **Deferred Action—(c)(14).** File your EAD application with a copy of the order, notice or document placing you in deferred action and evidence establishing economic necessity for an EAD.

   F. **Final Order of Deportation—(c)(18).** File your EAD application with a copy of the order of supervision and a request for employment authorization which may be based on, but not limited to the following:

      1. Existence of a dependent spouse and/or children in the United States who rely on you for support; and

      2. Existence of economic necessity to be employed;

      3. Anticipated length of time before you can be removed from the United States.

   G. **LIFE Legalization Applicant—(c)(24).** We encourage you to file your EAD application together with your Form I-485, Application to Register Permanent Residence or Adjust Status, to facilitate processing. However, you may file Form I-765 at a later date with evidence that you were a CSS, LULAC, or Zambrano class member applicant before October 1, 2000 and with a copy of the receipt notice or other evidence that your Form I-485 is pending.

   H. **T-1 Nonimmigrant—(a)(16).** If you are applying for initial employment authorization as a T-1 nonimmigrant, file this form only if you did not request an employment authorization document when you applied for T nonimmigrant status. If you have been granted T status and this is a request for a renewal or replacement of an employment authorization document, file this application along with evidence of your T status, such as an approval notice.

   I. **T-2, T-3, or T-4 Nonimmigrant—(c)(25).** File this form with a copy of your T-1's (principal alien's) approval notice and proof of your relationship to the T-1 principal.

Required Documentation.

All applications must be filed with the documents required below, in addition to the particular evidence required for the category listed in "Who May File This Form I-765" with fee, if required.

If you are required to show economic necessity for your category, submit a list of your assets, income and expenses.

Please assemble the documents in the following order:

1. Your application with the filing fee. See **"What Is the Filing Fee"** for details.

2. If you are mailing your application to USCIS, you must also submit:

   A. A copy of Form I-94 Departure Record (front and back), if available. If you are filing an I-765 under the (c) (9) category, an I-94 record need not submitted.

   B. A copy of your last EAD (front and back). If no prior EAD has been issued, you must submit a copy of a federal government issued identity document, such as a passport showing your picture, name, and date of birth; a birth certificate with photo ID; a visa issued by a foreign consulate; or a National ID document with photo and/or fingerprint. The identity document photocopy must clearly show the facial features of the applicant and the biographical information.

   C. You **must** submit two identical color photographs of yourself taken within 30 days of the filing of this application. The photos must have a white to off-white background, be printed on thin paper with a glossy finish, and be unmounted and unretouched.

   The passport-style photos must be 2" x 2." The photos must be in color with full face, frontal view on a white to off-white background. Head height should measure 1" to 1 3/8" from top of hair to bottom of chin, and eye height is between 1 1/8" to 1 3/8" from bottom of photo. Your head must be bare unless you are wearing a headdress as required by a religious order of which you are a member. Using pencil or felt pen, lightly print your name and Alien Receipt Number on the back of the photo.

Special Filing Instructions for Those With Pending Asylum Applications ((c)(8)).

Asylum Applicant (with a pending asylum application) who Filed for Asylum on or after January 4, 1995. *You must wait at least 150 days following the filing of your asylum claim before you are eligible to apply for an EAD. If you file your EAD application early, it will be denied. File your EAD application with:*

1. A copy of the USCIS acknowledgement mailer which was mailed to you; or

2. Other evidence that your Form I-589 was filed with USCIS; or

3. Evidence that your Form I-589 was filed with an Immigration Judge at the Executive Office for Immigration Review (EOIR); or

4. Evidence that your asylum application remains under administrative or judicial review.

Asylum Applicant (with a pending asylum application) who filed for Asylum and for Withholding of Deportation prior to January 4, 1995 and is *NOT* in Exclusion or Deportation Proceedings.

You may file your EAD application at any time; however, it will only be granted if USCIS finds that your asylum application is not frivolous. File your EAD application with:

1. A complete copy of your previously filed Form I-589; AND

2. A copy of your USCIS receipt notice; or

3. A copy of the USCIS acknowledgement mailer; or

4. Evidence that your Form I-589 was filed with EOIR; or

5. Evidence that your asylum application remains under administrative or judicial review; or

6. A copy of the USCIS acknowledgement mailer; or

Asylum applicant (with a pending asylum application) who filed an Initial Request for Asylum prior to January 4, 1995, and *IS IN* Exclusion or Deportation Proceedings. If you filed your Request for Asylum and Withholding of Deportation (Form I-589) prior to January 4, 1995 and you ARE IN exclusion or deportation proceedings, file your EAD application with:

1. A date-stamped copy of your previously filed Form I-589; or

APPENDIX 9C • I-765 563

2. A copy of Form I-221, Order to Show Cause and Notice of Hearing, or Form I-122, Notice to Applicant for Admission Detained for Hearing Before Immigration Judge; or

3. A copy of EOIR-26, Notice of Appeal, date stamped by the Office of the Immigration Judge; or

4. A date-stamped copy of a petition for judicial review or for *habeas corpus* issued to the asylum applicant; or

5. Other evidence that you filed an asylum application with EOIR.

Asylum application under the ABC Settlement Agreement—(c)(8). If you are a Salvadoran or Guatemalan national eligible for benefits under the ABC settlement agreement, American Baptist Churches v. Thornburgh, 760 F. Supp. 976 (N.D. Cal. 1991), please follow the instructions contained in this section when filing your Form I-765.

You must have asylum application (Form I-589) on file either with USCIS or with an immigration judge in order to receive work authorization. Therefore, please submit evidence that you have previously filed an asylum application when you submit your EAD application. You are not required to submit this evidence when you apply, but it will help USCIS process your request efficiently.

If you are renewing or replacing your EAD, you must pay the filing fee.

Mark your application as follows:

1. Write "ABC" in the top right corner of your EAD application. You must identify yourself as an ABC class member if you are applying for an EAD under the ABC settlement agreement.

2. Write "(c)(8)" in **Section 16** of the application.

You are entitled to an EAD without regard to the merits of your asylum claim. Your application for an EAD will be decided within 60 days if: (1) you pay the filing fee, (2) you have a complete, pending asylum application on file, and (3) write "ABC" in the top right corner of your EAD application. If you do not pay the filing fee for an initial EAD request, your request may be denied if USCIS finds that your asylum application is frivolous. However, if you cannot pay the filing fee for an EAD, you may qualify for a fee waiver under 8 CFR 103.7(c).

What is the Filing Fee?

The filing fee for Form I-765 is $340.00.

Exceptions:

Initial EAD: If this is your initial application and you are applying under one of the following categories, a filing fee is **not** required:

1. (a)(3) Refugee;
2. (a)(4) Paroled as Refugee;
3. (a)(5) Asylee;
4. (a)(7) N-8 or N-9 nonimmigrant;
5. (a)(8) Citizen of Micronesia, Marshall Islands or Palau;
6. (a)(10) Granted Withholding of Deportation;
7. (a)(11) Deferred Enforced Departure;
8. (a)(16) Victim of Severe Form of Trafficking (T-1);
9. (c)(1), (c)(4), or (c)(7) Dependent of certain foreign government, international organization, or NATO personnel; or
10. (c)(8) Applicant for asylum [an applicant filing under the special ABC procedures must pay the fee].

Renewal EAD: If this is a renewal application and you are applying under one of the following categories, a filing fee is **not** required:

1. (a)(8) Citizen of Micronesia, Marshall Islands, or Palau;
2. (a)(10) Granted Withholding of Deportation;
3. (a)(11) Deferred Enforced Departure; or
4. (c)(l), (c)(4), or (c)(7) Dependent of certain foreign government, international organization, or NATO personnel.

Replacement EAD: If this is your replacement application and you are applying under one of the following categories, *a* filing fee is **not** required:

1. (c)(l), (c)(4), or (c)(7) Dependent of certain foreign government, international organization, or NATO personnel.

Form I-765 Instructions (Rev. 07/30/07) Y Page 7

Incorrect Card: No fee is required if you are filing only because the card issued to you was incorrect due to a USCIS administrative error. However, if the error was not caused by USCIS, both application and biometrics fees are required.

You may be eligible for a fee waiver under 8 CFR 103.7(c).

USCIS will use the Poverty Guidelines published annually by the Department of Health and Human Services as the basic criteria in determining the applicant's eligibility when economic necessity is identified as a factor.

The Poverty Guidelines will be used as a guide, but not as a conclusive standard, in adjudicating fee waiver requests for employment authorization applications requiring a fee.

Use the following guidelines when you prepare your check or money order for the Form I-765 fee:

1. The check or money order must be drawn on a bank or other financial institution located in the United States and must be payable in U.S. currency; and

2. Make the check or money order payable to **U.S. Department of Homeland Security**, unless:

   A. If you live in Guam and are filing your petition there, make it payable to **Treasurer, Guam**.

   B. If you live in the U.S. Virgin Islands and are filing your petition there, make it payable to **Commissioner of Finance of the Virgin Islands**.

NOTE: If you filed a Form I-485, Application to Register Permanent Residence or Adjust Status, as of July 30, 2007, no fee is required to also file a request for employment authorization on Form I-765. You may file the I-765 concurrently with your I-485, or you may submit the I-765 at a later date. If you file Form I-765 separately, you must also submit a copy of your Form I-797C, Notice of Action, receipt as evidence of the filing of an I-485 as of July 30, 2007.

NOTE: Please spell out U.S. Department of Homeland Security; do not use the initials "USDHS" or "DHS."

Notice to Those Making Payment by Check. If you send us a check, it will be converted into an electronic funds transfer (EFT). This means we will copy your check and use the account information on it to electronically debit your account for the amount of the check. The debit from your account will usually take 24 hours, and will be shown on your regular account statement.

You will not receive your original check back. We will destroy your original check, but we will keep a copy of it. If the EFT cannot be processed for technical reasons, you authorize us to process the copy in place of your original check. If the EFT cannot be completed because of insufficient funds, we may try to make the transfer up to two times.

How to Check If the Fees Are Correct.

The form fee on this form is current as of the edition date appearing in the lower right corner of this page. However, because USCIS fees change periodically, you can verify if the fees are correct by following one of the steps below:

1. Visit our website at **www.uscis.gov**, select "Immigration Forms" check the appropriate fee;

2. Review the Fee Schedule included in your form package, if you called us to request the form; or

3. Telephone our National Customer Service Center at **1-800-375-5283** and ask for the fee information.

Where to File?

E-Filing Form I-765: Certain Form I-765 filings may be electronically filed (E-Filed) with USCIS. Please view our website at www.uscis.gov for a list of who is eligible to e-file this form and instructions.

If your response to **Question 16** is **(a)(3)**, admitted as a refugee, **(a)(4)**, paroled as a refugee, **(a)(5)**, asylum granted, **(a)(7)**, N-8 or N-9 nonimmigrant, or **(a)(8)**, admitted as citizen of the Federated States of Micronesia or of the Marshall Islands mail your application to:

> USCIS
> Nebraska Service Center
> P.O. Box 87765
> Lincoln, NE 68501-7765

For private courier (non-USPS) deliveries:

> USCIS
> Nebraska Service Center
> 850 S. Street
> Lincoln, NE 68508-1225

If your response to **Question 16** is:

1. **(a)(10)**, an alien granted withholding of deportation or removal;

2. **(c)(11)**, an alien paroled into the United States temporarily for emergency reasons, or reasons deemed strictly in the public interest;

APPENDIX 9C • I-765

3. **(c)(14)**, an alien who has been granted deferred action, (exception: if the grant of deferred action was based on an approved Form I-360 petition filed for a battered or abused spouse or child file your Form I-765 with the Vermont Service Center at the address below);

4. **(c)(16)**, an alien who has filed an application for creation of record of lawful admission for permanent residence; or

5. **(c)(18)**, an alien against whom a final order of deportation or removal exists and who is released on an order of supervision, mail your application to the following address:

   USCIS
   P.O. Box 805887
   Chicago, IL 60680-4120

If your response to **Question 16** is **(c)(14)**, an alien who has been granted deferred action based on an approved Form I-360 petition filed for a battered or abused spouse or child, **(a)(16)**, victim of trafficking, or **(c)(25)**, immediate family member of a T-1 victim of severe form of trafficking in persons, send your application to (this address may be used for both US Postal Service and private courier deliveries):

   USCIS
   Vermont Service Center
   Attn: I-765
   75 Lower Welden St.
   St. Albans, VT 05479-0001

If your response to **Question 16** is **(a)(14)**, an alien granted family unity benefits under Section 1504 of the LIFE Act, or **(c)(24)**, an alien who has filed for adjustment pursuant to section 1104 of the LIFE Act, mail your application to:

   USCIS
   P.O. Box 7219
   Chicago, IL 60680-7219

If your response to **Question 16** is **(a)(15)**, any alien in V nonimmigrant status, mail your application to:

   USCIS
   P.O. Box 7216
   Chicago, IL 60680-7216

If your response to **Question 16** is **(a)(12)**, alien granted Temporary Protected Status, or **(c)(19)**, alien who has a pending application for TPS, mail your application according to the instructions in the Federal Register notice for your particular country's TPS designation.

If you need to replace a valid lost, stolen or mutilated Temporary Protected Status EAD, send your application to (this address may be used for both US Postal Service and private courier deliveries):

   USCIS
   Vermont Service Center
   Attn: TPS
   75 Lower Welden St.
   St. Albans, VT 05479-0001

If your response to **Question 16** is **(c)(1)**, alien spouse or unmarried dependent child, son or daughter of a foreign government official, or **(c)(4)**, eligible dependent of a G-1, G-3 or G-4 non-immigrant, or **(c)(7)**, dependent of a NATO 1 through NATO 7, submit your application through your principal's sponsoring organization. Your application will be reviewed and forwarded by DOS, USUN, or NATO/SACLANT to the Nebraska Service Center following certification of your eligibility for an EAD.

If your response to **Question 16** is **(c)(8)** under the special ABC filing instructions, and you are filing your Form I-589 Application for Asylum and this application together, mail your applications to the office where you will file your asylum application. Otherwise, for all other (c)(8) filings, see additional instructions below.

If your response to **Question 16** is **(c)(9)** and you filed your I-485 application with the USCIS Chicago Lockbox Facility, file your Form I-765 with the following address (if you filed your Form I-485 with a USCIS service center, see instructions below):

USCIS Lockbox Addresses:

   For United States Postal Service (USPS) deliveries:

   USCIS
   P.O. Box 805887
   Chicago, IL 60680-4120

   For private courier (non-USPS) deliveries:

   USCIS
   Attn: FBASI
   427 S. LaSalle, 3rd Floor
   Chicago, IL 60605-1029

Otherwise, if you filed your I-485 adjustment application with a USCIS service center, you must file Form I-765 at the Nebraska Service Center or the Texas Service Center, depending on where you live (see the following addresses).

Nebraska Service Center Filings

File Form I-765 alone or concurrently with Form I-485 with the Nebraska Service Center if you live in:

Alaska, Arizona, California, Colorado, Guam, Hawaii, Idaho, Illinois, Indiana, Iowa, Kansas, Michigan, Minnesota, Missouri, Montana, Nebraska, Nevada, North Dakota, Ohio, Oregon, South Dakota, Utah, Washington, Wisconsin or Wyoming.

If you are filing Form I-765 alone, mail your Form I-765 package to:

USCIS
Nebraska Service Center
P.O. Box 87765
Lincoln, NE 68501-7765

If you are filing Form I-765 concurrently with Form I-485, mail to:

USCIS
Nebraska Service Center
P.O. Box 87485
Lincoln, NE 68501-7485

For private courier (non-USPS) deliveries:

USCIS
Nebraska Service Center
850 S. Street
Lincoln, NE 68508-1225

Texas Service Center Filings

File Form I-765 with the Texas Service Center if you live in:

Alabama, Arkansas, Connecticut, Florida, Georgia, Kentucky, Louisiana, Maine, Maryland, Massachusetts, Mississippi, New Hampshire, New Jersey, New Mexico, New York, North Carolina, South Carolina, Oklahoma, Pennsylvania, Puerto Rico, Rhode Island, Tennessee, Texas, Vermont, Virginia, U.S. Virgin Islands, West Virginia or Washington, DC.

If you are filing Form I-765 concurrently with Form I-485, mail your Form I-765 to the address you will use to file Form I-485.

If you are filing Form I-765 alone, mail your Form I-765 package to:

USCIS
Texas Service Center
P.O. Box 851041
Mesquite, TX 75185-1041

For private courier (non-USPS) deliveries:

USCIS
Texas Service Center
4141 North St. Augustine Road
Dallas, TX 75227

If your response to **Question 16** is:

1. **(a)(6)**, alien admitted as a nonimmigrant fiancé(e) pursuant to section 101(a)(15) (K)(i);
2. **(a)(11)**, alien granted extended voluntary departure by the Secretary as a member of a nationality group pursuant to a request by the Secretary of State;
3. **(a)(13)**, alien granted voluntary departure under the Family Unity Program;
4. **(a)(17)**, spouse of a treaty trader, investor;
5. **(a)(18)**, spouse of an intracompany transferee;
6. **(c)(2)**, alien spouse or unmarried dependent son or daughter of an employee of the Coordination Council for North American Affairs;
7. **(c)(3)(i)**, F-1 student seeking optional practical training;
8. **(c)(3)(ii)**, F-1 student offered employment under the sponsorship of an international organization;
9. **(c)(3)(iii)**, F-1 student seeking employment because of severe economic hardship;
10. **(c)(5)**, spouse or minor child of an exchange visitor (J-2);
11. **(c)(6)**, M-1 student seeking employment for practical training;
12. **(c)(8)**, an alien who has filed an application for asylum or withholding of deportation or removal;
13. **(c)(17)(i)**, a visitor for business (B-1) who is the personal or domestic servant who is accompanying or following to join an employer;
14. **(c)(17)(ii)**, a domestic servant of a U.S. citizen accompanying or following to join his or her U.S. citizen employer who has a permanent home or is stationed in a foreign country; or
15. **(c)(17)(iii)**, an employee of a foreign airline engaged in international transportation of passengers freight:

mail your application to the appropriate Service Center depending on where you live (see chart on the following page).

APPENDIX 9C • I-765

If you live in:		Mail your application to:
Connecticut D.C. Maryland New Hampshire New York Puerto Rico Vermont West Virginia	Delaware Maine Massachusetts New Jersey Pennsylvania Rhode Island Virginia U.S.V.I.	For both US Postal Service and private courier deliveries: USCIS Vermont Service Center ATTN: I-765 75 Lower Welden Street St. Albans, VT 05479-0001
Arizona Guam Nevada	California Hawaii	US Postal Service deliveries: USCIS California Service Center P.O. Box 10765 Laguna Niguel, CA 92607-1076 For private courier (non-USPS) deliveries: USCIS California Service Center 24000 Avila Road 2nd Floor, Room 2312 Laguna Niguel, CA 92677
Alabama Florida Kentucky Mississippi North Carolina South Carolina Texas	Arkansas Georgia Louisiana New Mexico Oklahoma Tennessee	US Postal Service deliveries: USCIS Service Center Texas Service Center P.O. Box 851041 Mesquite, TX 75185-1041 For private courier (non-USPS) deliveries: USCIS Texas Service Center 4141 N St. Augustine Rd Dallas, TX 75227
Alaska Idaho Indiana Kansas Minnesota Montana North Dakota Oregon Utah Wisconsin	Colorado Illinois Iowa Michigan Missouri Nebraska Ohio South Dakota Washington Wyoming	US Postal Service deliveries: USCIS Service Center Nebraska Service Center P.O. Box 87765 Lincoln, NE 68501-7765 For private courier (non-USPS) deliveries: USCIS Nebraska Service Center 850 S. Street Lincoln, NE 68508-1225

If your response to **Question 16** is:

1. **(a)(9)**, admitted as a K-3 spouse or K-4 dependant; or

2. **(c)(10)**, and you are a NACARA 203 applicant eligible to apply for relief with USCIS, or if your I-881 application is still pending with USCIS and you wish to renew your EAD:

mail your EAD application with the required fee to the appropriate USCIS service center below:

If you live in Alabama, Arkansas, Colorado, Connecticut, Delaware, the District of Columbia, Florida, Georgia, Louisiana, Maine, Maryland, Massachusetts, Mississippi, New Hampshire, New Jersey, New Mexico, New York, North Carolina, Oklahoma, Pennsylvania, Puerto Rico, Rhode Island, South Carolina, Tennessee, Texas, Utah, the U.S. Virgin Islands, Vermont, Virginia, West Virginia or Wyoming, send your application to (this address may be used for both US Postal Service and private courier deliveries):

USCIS
Vermont Service Center
Attn: I-765
75 Lower Welden St.
St. Albans, VT 05479-0001

If you live in Alaska, Arizona, California, the Commonwealth of Guam, Hawaii, Idaho, Illinois, Indiana, Iowa, Kansas, Kentucky, Michigan, Minnesota, Missouri, Montana, Nebraska, Nevada, North Dakota, Oregon, Ohio, South Dakota, Washington or Wisconsin, mail your application to:

USCIS
California Service Center
P.O. Box 10765
Laguna Niguel, CA 92607-1076

For private courier (non-USPS) deliveries:

USCIS
California Service Center
24000 Avila Road
2nd Floor, Room 2312
Laguna Niguel, CA 92677

NOTE: You should submit the fee for the EAD application on a separate check or money order. Do not combine your check or money order with the fee for the Form I-881.

If your response to **Question 16** is **(c)(10)** and you are not eligible to apply for NACARA 203 relief with USCIS, but you are eligible for other deportation or removal relief, mail your application to the following address:

USCIS
P.O. Box 805887
Chicago, IL 60680-4120

Questions Regarding Form I-765

For additional information about Form I-765, including how to file your application or filing locations not mentioned, call the USCIS National Customer Service Center at **1-800-375-5283** or visit our website at **www.uscis.gov**.

Processing Information.

Any Form I-765 that is not signed or accompanied by the correct fee, will be rejected with a notice that the Form I-765 is deficient. You may correct the deficiency and resubmit the Form I-765. An application or petition is not considered properly filed until accepted by USCIS.

Initial processing. Once a Form I-765 has been accepted, it will be checked for completeness, including submission of the required initial evidence. If you do not completely fill out the form, or file it without required initial evidence, you will not establish a basis for eligibility and we may deny your Form I-765.

Requests for more information or interview. We may request more information or evidence, or we may request that you appear at a USCIS office for an interview. We may also request that you submit the originals of any copy. We will return these originals when they are no longer required.

Interim EAD. If you have not received a decision within 90 days of receipt by USCIS of a properly filed EAD application or within 30 days of a properly filed initial EAD application based on an asylum application filed on or after January 4, 1995, you may obtain interim work authorization by appearing in person at your local USCIS district office. You must bring proof of identity and any notices that you have received from USCIS in connection with your application for employment authorization.

Approval. If approved, your EAD will either be mailed to you or you may be required to appear at your local USCIS office to pick it up.

Denial. If your application cannot be granted, you will receive a written notice explaining the basis of your denial.

Penalties.

If you knowingly and willfully falsify or conceal a material fact or submit a false document with this Form I-765, we will deny the Form I-765 and may deny any other immigration benefit.

In addition, you will face severe penalties provided by law and may be subject to criminal prosecution.

USCIS Forms and Information.

To order USCIS forms, call our toll-free number at **1-800-870-3676**. You can also get USCIS forms and information on immigration laws, regulations and procedures by telephoning our National Customer Service Center at **1-800-375-5283** or visiting our internet website at **www.uscis.gov**.

As an alternative to waiting in line for assistance at your local USCIS office, you can now schedule an appointment through our internet-based system, **InfoPass**. To access the system, visit our website. Use the **InfoPass** appointment scheduler and follow the screen prompts to set up your appointment. **InfoPass** generates an electronic appointment notice that appears on the screen.

Paperwork Reduction Act.

Authority for Collecting This Information. The authority to require you to file Form I-765, Application for Employment Authorization, when applying for employment authorization is found at sections 103(a) and 274A(h)(3) of the Immigration and Nationality Act. Information you provide on your Form I-765 is used to determine whether you are eligible for employment authorization and for the preparation of your Employment Authorization Document if you are found eligible. Failure to provide all information as requested may result in the denial or rejection of this application. The information you provide may also be disclosed to other federal, state, local and foreign law enforcement and regulatory agencies during the course of the USCIS investigations.

An agency may not conduct or sponsor an information collection and a person is not required to respond to a collection of information unless it displays a currently valid OMB control number. The public reporting burden for this collection of information is estimated at 3 hours and 25 minutes per response, including the time for reviewing instructions, completing and submitting the form. Send comments regarding this burden estimate or any other aspect of this collection of information, including suggestions for reducing this burden, to: U.S. Citizenship and Immigration Services, Regulatory Management Division, 111 Massachusetts Avenue, N.W., 3rd Floor, Suite 3008, Washington, DC 20529. OMB No. 1615-0040. **Do not mail your application to this address.**

APPENDIX 9C • I-765

OMB No. 1615-0040; Expires 08/31/08

Department of Homeland Security
U.S. Citizenship and Immigration Services

I-765, Application for Employment Authorization

Do not write in this block.

Remarks	Action Block	Fee Stamp
A#		

Applicant is filing under §274a.12 _____

☐ Application Approved. Employment Authorized / Extended *(Circle One)* until _____ (Date).
_____ (Date).

Subject to the following conditions: _____

☐ Application Denied.
  ☐ Failed to establish eligibility under 8 CFR 274a.12 (a) or (c).
  ☐ Failed to establish economic necessity as required in 8 CFR 274a.12(c)(14), (18) and 8 CFR 214.2(f)

I am applying for:
  ☐ Permission to accept employment.
  ☐ Replacement *(of lost employment authorization document)*
  ☐ Renewal of my permission to accept employment *(attach previous employment authorization document).*

1. Name (Family Name in CAPS) (First) (Middle)

11. Have you ever before applied for employment authorization from USCIS?
  ☐ Yes (If yes, complete below) ☐ No
  Which USCIS Office? Date(s)

2. Other Names Used (Include Maiden Name)

  Results (Granted or Denied - attach all documentation)

3. Address in the United States (Number and Street) (Apt. Number)

  (Town or City) (State/Country) (ZIP Code)

12. Date of Last Entry into the U.S. (mm/dd/yyyy)

4. Country of Citizenship/Nationality

13. Place of Last Entry into the U.S.

5. Place of Birth (Town or City) (State/Province) (Country)

14. Manner of Last Entry (Visitor, Student, etc.)

6. Date of Birth (mm/dd/yyyy)   7. Gender
  ☐ Male ☐ Female

15. Current Immigration Status (Visitor, Student, etc.)

8. Marital Status ☐ Married ☐ Single
  ☐ Widowed ☐ Divorced

16. Go to **Part 2** of the Instructions, Eligibility Categories. In the space below, place the letter and number of the category you selected from the instructions (For example, (a)(8), (c)(17)(iii), etc.).

9. Social Security Number (Include all numbers you have ever used) (if any)

  Eligibility under 8 CFR 274a.12

10. Alien Registration Number (A-Number) or I-94 Number (if any)

  ( ) ( ) ( )

Certification.

Your Certification: I certify, under penalty of perjury under the laws of the United States of America, that the foregoing is true and correct. Furthermore, I authorize the release of any information that the U.S. Citizenship and Immigration Services needs to determine eligibility for the benefit I am seeking. I have read the Instructions in **Part 2** and have identified the appropriate eligibility category in **Block 16**.

Signature	Telephone Number	Date

Signature of person preparing form, if other than above: I declare that this document was prepared by me at the request of the applicant and is based on all information of which I have any knowledge.

Print Name	Address	Signature	Date

Remarks	Initial Receipt	Resubmitted	Relocated		Completed		
			Rec'd	Sent	Approved	Denied	Returned

Form I-765 (Rev. 07/30/07) Y

APPENDIX 9D
FORM I-131 AND INSTRUCTIONS

Department of Homeland Security
U. S. Citizenship and Immigration Services

OMB No. 1615-0013; Expires 11/30/07

I-131, Application for Travel Document

DO NOT WRITE IN THIS BLOCK		FOR USCIS USE ONLY (except G-28 block below)
Document Issued ☐ Reentry Permit ☐ Refugee Travel Document ☐ Single Advance Parole ☐ Multiple Advance Parole Valid to: _____	**Action Block**	**Receipt**
If Reentry Permit or Refugee Travel Document, mail to: ☐ Address in Part 1 ☐ American embassy/consulate at: _____ ☐ Overseas DHS office at: _____		☐ Document Hand Delivered On _____ By _____ *To be completed by Attorney/Representative, if any.* Attorney State License # _____ ☐ Check box if G-28 is attached.

Part 1. Information about you. *(Please type or print in black ink.)*

1. A #
2. Date of Birth *(mm/dd/yyyy)*
3. Class of Admission
4. Gender Male ☐ Female ☐
5. Name *(Family name in capital letters)* *(First)* *(Middle)*
6. Address *(Number and Street)* Apt. #
   City State or Province Zip/Postal Code Country
7. Country of Birth
8. Country of Citizenship
9. Social Security # *(if any.)*

Part 2. Application type *(check one).*

a. ☐ I am a permanent resident or conditional resident of the United States and I am applying for a reentry permit.

b. ☐ I now hold U.S. refugee or asylee status and I am applying for a refugee travel document.

c. ☐ I am a permanent resident as a direct result of refugee or asylee status and I am applying for a refugee travel document.

d. ☐ I am applying for an advance parole document to allow me to return to the United States after temporary foreign travel.

e. ☐ I am outside the United States and I am applying for an advance parole document.

f. ☐ I am applying for an advance parole document for a person who is outside the United States. *If you checked box "f", provide the following information about that person:*

1. Name *(Family name in capital letters)* *(First)* *(Middle)*
2. Date of Birth *(mm/dd/yyyy)*
3. Country of Birth
4. Country of Citizenship
5. Address *(Number and Street)* Apt. # Daytime Telephone # *(area/country code)*
   City State or Province Zip/Postal Code Country

Form I-131 (Rev. 07/30/07)Y

Part 3. Processing information.

1. Date of Intended Departure *(mm/dd/yyyy)*

2. Expected Length of Trip

3. Are you, or any person included in this application, now in exclusion, deportation, removal or recission proceedings? ☐ No ☐ Yes *(Name of DHS office)*:

If you are applying for an Advance Parole Document, skip to Part 7.

4. Have you ever before been issued a reentry permit or refugee travel? *for the last document issued to you)*: ☐ No ☐ Yes *(Give the following information*

Date Issued *(mm/dd/yyyy)*: Disposition *(attached, lost, etc.)*:

5. Where do you want this travel document sent? *(Check one)*

a. ☐ To the U.S. address shown in **Part 1** on the first page of this form.

b. ☐ To an American embassy or consulate at: City: Country:

c. ☐ To a DHS office overseas at: City: Country:

d. If you checked "b" or "c", where should the notice to pick up the travel document be sent?

☐ To the address shown in **Part 2** on the first page of this form.
☐ To the address shown below:

Address *(Number and Street)* Apt. # Daytime Telephone # *(area/country code)*

City State or Province Zip/Postal Code Country

Part 4. Information about your proposed travel.

Purpose of trip. *If you need more room, continue on a seperate sheet(s) of paper.*	List the countries you intend to visit.

Part 5. Complete only if applying for a reentry permit.

Since becoming a permanent resident of the United States (or during the past five years, whichever is less) how much total time have you spent outside the United States?

☐ less than six months ☐ two to three years
☐ six months to one year ☐ three to four years
☐ one to two years ☐ more than four years

Since you became a permanent resident of the United States, have you ever filed a federal income tax return as a nonresident, or failed to file a federal income tax return because you considered yourself to be a nonresident? *(If "Yes," give details on a separate sheet(s) of paper.)* ☐ Yes ☐ No

Part 6. Complete only if applying for a refugee travel document.

1. Country from which you are a refugee or asylee:

If you answer "Yes" to any of the following questions, you must explain on a separate sheet(s) of paper.

2. Do you plan to travel to the above named country? ☐ Yes ☐ No

3. Since you were accorded refugee/asylee status, have you ever:
a. returned to the above named country? ☐ Yes ☐ No
b. applied for and/or obtained a national passport, passport renewal or entry permit of that country? ☐ Yes ☐ No
c. applied for and/or received any benefit from such country (for example, health insurance benefits). ☐ Yes ☐ No

4. Since you were accorded refugee/asylee status, have you, by any legal procedure or voluntary act:
a. reacquired the nationality of the above named country? ☐ Yes ☐ No
b. acquired a new nationality? ☐ Yes ☐ No
c. been granted refugee or asylee status in any other country? ☐ Yes ☐ No

Form I-131 (Rev. 07/30/07)Y Page 2

APPENDIX 9D • I-131

Part 7. Complete only if applying for advance parole.

On a separate sheet(s) of paper, please explain how you qualify for an advance parole document and what circumstances warrant issuance of advance parole. Include copies of any documents you wish considered. *(See instructions.)*

1. For how many trips do you intend to use this document? ☐ One trip ☐ More than one trip

2. If the person intended to receive an advance parole document is outside the United States, provide the location (city and country) of the American embassy or consulate or the DHS overseas office that you want us to notify.

City

Country

3. If the travel document will be delivered to an overseas office, where should the notice to pick up the document be sent:

   ☐ To the address shown in **Part 2** on the first page of this form.

   ☐ To the address shown below:

   Address *(Number and Street)*   Apt. #   Daytime Telephone # *(area/country code)*

   City   State or Province   Zip/Postal Code   Country

Part 8. Signature. *Read the information on penalties in the instructions before completing this section. If you are filing for a reentry permit or refugee travel document, you must be in the United States to file this application.*

I certify, under penalty of perjury under the laws of the United States of America, that this application and the evidence submitted with it are all true and correct. I authorize the release of any information from my records that the U.S. Citizenship and Immigration Services needs to determine eligibility for the benefit I am seeking.

Signature   Date *(mm/dd/yyyy)*   **Daytime Telephone Number** *(with area code)*

Please Note: If you do not completely fill out this form or fail to submit required documents listed in the instructions, you may not be found eligible for the requested document and this application may be denied.

Part 9. Signature of person preparing form, if other than the applicant. *(Sign below.)*

I declare that I prepared this application at the request of the applicant and it is based on all information of which I have knowledge.

Signature   Print or Type Your Name

Firm Name and Address   Daytime Telephone Number *(with area code)*

Fax Number *(if any.)*   Date *(mm/dd/yyyy)*

3. Advance Parole Document.

> **Travel Warning**
>
> Before you apply for an advance parole document, read this travel warning carefully.
>
> A. If you have been unlawfully present in the United States for more than 180 days but less than one year and you leave before removal proceedings are started against you, you may be inadmissible for three years from the date of departure.
>
> B. If you have been unlawfully present in the United States for one year or more, you may be inadmissible for ten years from the date of departure regardless of whether you left before, during or after removal proceedings.
>
> C. Unlawful presence is defined as being in the United States without having been inspected and admitted or paroled (illegal entry), or after the period of authorized stay has expired.
>
> D. However, certain immigration benefits and time spent in the United States while certain applications are pending may place you in a period of authorized stay. These include, but are not limited to, a properly filed adjustment of status application, Temporary Protected Status (TPS), deferred enforced departure (DED), asylum and withholding of removal.
>
> E. Although advance parole may allow you to return to the United States, your departure may trigger the three-or ten-year bar, if you accrued more than 180 days of unlawful presence **BEFORE** the date you were considered to be in a period of authorized stay.
>
> F. Therefore, if you apply for adjustment of status after you return to the United States, resume an adjustment application that was pending before you left, or return to a status that requires you to establish that you are not inadmissible, you will need to apply for and receive a waiver of inadmissibility before your adjustment application may be approved or your status continued.
>
> G. Generally, only those persons who can establish extreme hardship to their U.S. citizen or lawful permanent resident spouse or parent may apply for the waiver for humanitarian reasons, to assure family unity or when it is otherwise in the public interest. (See sections 209(c), 212(a)(9) and 244(c) of the Immigration and Nationality Act for more information on unlawful presence and the available waivers.)

A. *If you are outside the United States and need to visit the United States temporarily for emergent humanitarian reasons:*

1. You may apply for an advance parole document. However, your application must be based on the fact that you cannot obtain the necessary visa and any required waiver of inadmissibility. Parole under these conditions is granted on a case-by-case basis for temporary entry, according to such conditions as prescribed.

2. A person in the United States may file this application on your behalf. In so doing, he or she should complete **Part 1** of the form with information about him or herself.

B. *If you are in the United States and seek advance parole:*

1. You may apply if you have an adjustment of status application pending and you seek to travel abroad for emergent personal or bona fide business reasons; or

2. You may apply if you are classified as a refugee or asylee and you seek to travel abroad for emergent personal or bona fide business reasons, or you are traveling to Canada to apply for a U.S. immigrant visa. (See **Part 2, Refugee Travel Document on Page of 2 of these instructions,** for additional information on refugee/asylee travel); or

3. You may apply if you have been granted Temporary Protected Status or another immigration status that allows you to return to that status after a brief, casual and innocent absence (as defined in 8 CFR 244.1) from the United States.

C. *An advance parole document may not be issued to you if:*

1. You held J-1 nonimmigrant status and are subject to the two-year foreign residence requirement as a result of that status; or

2. You are in exclusion, deportation, removal or recission proceedings.

D. *If you travel before the advance parole document is issued, your application will be deemed abandoned if:*

1. You depart from the United States; or

2. The person seeking advance parole attempts to enter the United States before a decision is made on the application.

APPENDIX 9D • I-131   575

General Instructions.

Step 1. Fill Out the Form I-131

1. Type or print legibly in black ink.

2. If extra space is needed to complete any item, attach a continuation sheet, indicate the item number, and date and sign each sheet.

3. Answer all questions fully and accurately. State that an item is not applicable with "N/A." If the answer is none, write "none."

Step 2. General requirements

1. **Initial Evidence.**

   We may request additional information or evidence, or we may request that you appear at a USCIS office for an interview. You must file your application with all the required evidence. If you do not submit the required evidence, it will delay the issuance of the document you are requesting.

   All applications must include a **copy of an official photo identity document showing your photo, name and date of birth.** (Example: a valid government issued driver's license; passport identity page; Form I-551, Permanent Resident Card or any other official identity document.) The copy must **clearly** show the photo and identity information. **A Form I-94, Arrival/Departure Document, is not acceptable as a photo identity document.**

   If you are applying for a:

   A. *Reentry Permit.*

   You **must** attach:

   1. A copy of the front and back of your Form I-551, Permanent Resident Card; or

   2. If you have not yet received your Form I-551, a copy of the biographic page(s) of your passport and a copy of the visa page showing your initial admission as a permanent resident, or other evidence that you are a permanent resident; or

   3. A copy of the Form I-797, Notice of Action, approval notice of an application for replacement of your Permanent Resident Card or temporary evidence of permanent resident status.

   B. *Refugee Travel Document.*

   You **must** attach a copy of the document issued to you by the USCIS or former INS showing your refugee or asylee status and the expiration date of such status.

   C. *Advance Parole Document.*

   1. *If you are in the United States,* you must attach:

      a. A copy of any document issued to you by the USCIS or former INS showing your present status in the United States; and

      b. An explanation or other evidence showing the circumstances that warrant issuance of an advance parole document; or

      c. If you are an applicant for adjustment of status, a copy of the USCIS or former INS receipt as evidence that you filed the adjustment application;

      d. If you are traveling to Canada to apply for an immigrant visa, a copy of the U.S. consular appointment letter.

   2. *If you are applying for a person who is outside the United States,* you **must** attach:

      a. A statement of how and by whom medical care, transportation, housing, and other expenses and subsistence needs will be met; and

      b. An Affidavit of Support (Form I-134), with evidence of the sponsor's occupation and ability to provide necessary support; and

      c. A statement explaining why a U.S. visa cannot be obtained, including when and where attempts were made to obtain a visa; and

      d. A statement explaining why a waiver of inadmissibility cannot be obtained to allow issuance of a visa, including when and where attempts were made to obtain a waiver, and a copy of any USCIS or former INS decision on your waiver request; and

      e. A copy of any decision on an immigrant petition filed for the person, and evidence regarding any pending immigrant petition; and

      f. A complete description of the emergent reasons explaining why advance parole should be authorized and including copies of any evidence you wish considered, and indicating the length of time for which the parole is requested.

2. **Photographs.**

   A. *If you are filing for a reentry permit or a refugee travel document, or if you are in the United States and filing for an advance parole document:*

   You **must** submit two identical color photographs of yourself taken within 30 days of the filing of this application.

The photos must have a white to off-white background, be printed on thin paper with a glossy finish, and be unmounted and unretouched. **NOTE: Digital photos are not acceptable.**

Passport-style photos must be 2" x 2." The photos must be in color with full face, frontal view on a white to off-white background. Head height should measure 1" to 1 3/8" from top of hair to bottom of chin, and eye height is between 1 1/8" to 1 3/8" from bottom of photo. Your head must be bare unless you are wearing a headdress as required by a religious order of which you are a member. Using pencil or felt pen, lightly print your name and Alien Receipt Number on the back of the photo.

B. *If the person seeking advance parole is outside the United States:*

1. If you are applying for an advance parole document and you are outside the United States, do not submit the photographs with your application. Prior to issuing the parole document, the U.S. embassy or consulate or DHS office abroad will provide you with information regarding the photograph requirements.

2. If you are filing this application for an advance parole document for another person, submit the required photographs of the person to be paroled.

Invalidation of Travel Document.

Any travel document obtained by making a material false representation or concealment in this application will be invalid.

A travel document will also be invalid if you are ordered removed or deported from the United States.

In addition, a refugee travel document will be invalid if the United Nations Convention of July 28, 1951, shall cease to apply or shall not apply to you as provided in Article 1C, D, E or F of the Convention.

Copies. Unless specifically required that an original document be filed with an application or petition, an ordinary legible photocopy may be submitted. Original documents submitted when not required will remain a part of the record, even if the submission was not required.

Translations. Any document containing foreign language submitted to the Service shall be accompanied by a full English language translation which the translator has certified as complete and accurate, and by the translator's certification that he or she is competent to translate from the foreign language into English.

Where To File?

E-Filing Form I-131

Certain Form I-131 filings may be electronically filed (E-filed) with USCIS. Please view our website at **www.uscis.gov** for a list of who is eligible to e-file this form and instructions.

1. **Travel Documents.**

   If you are applying for a refugee travel document based on your refugee or asylum status or you are a permanent resident as a direct result of your refugee or asylee status in the U.S., file your Form I-131 with the Nebraska Service Center at the below address:

   USCIS Nebraska Service Center
   P.O. Box 87131
   Lincoln, NE 68501-7131

2. **Reentry Permits.**

   If you are a Lawful Permanent Resident or a Conditional Permanent Resident and are applying for a reentry permit, file your Form I-131 with the Nebraska Service Center at the below address:

   USCIS Nebraska Service Center
   P.O. Box 87131
   Lincoln, NE 68501-7131

3. **Advance Parole.**

   A. **For adjustment of status applications (Form I-485) filed with the USCIS Chicago Lockbox Facility:**

   Submit Form I-131 either concurrently with Form I-485 or alone to the same address you used to file your I-485 application (a complete list of the adjustment of status applications filed with the USCIS Chicago Lockbox Facility is found on Form I-485):

   USCIS Lockbox Addresses:

   For United States Postal Service (USPS) deliveries:

   USCIS
   P.O. Box 805887
   Chicago, IL 60680-4120

   For private courier (non-USPS) deliveries:

   USCIS
   Attn: FBASI
   427 S. LaSalle - 3rd Floor
   Chicago, IL 60605-1029

APPENDIX 9D • I-131

B. For battered spouses and children applying for adjustment of status:

If you are filing as a battered or abused spouse or child and you are filing your I-131 concurrently with Form I-485 send both forms to the address you will use to file Form I-485. If you are requesting advanced parole based on a pending I-485, file your Form I-131 using the same address you used to file Form I-485.

C. For special immigrant international employees:

If you are a special immigrant international organization employee or eligible relative and you are applying for advance parole concurrently with Form I-485, use the filing address listed on Form I-485 for both forms. If you are filing a Form I-131 based on a pending Form I-485, file Form I-131 with the Nebraska Service Center using the following address:

USCIS Nebraska Service Center
P.O. Box 87131
Lincoln, NE 68501-7131

D. For aliens granted refugee or asylee status who have filed or will file an adjustment of status application:

If you have been granted refugee or asylee status and you are applying for advance parole concurrently with Form I-485 use the filing address listed on Form I-485 for both forms. If you are filing a Form I-131 based on a pending Form I-485, file Form I-131 with the Service Center where your Form I-485 is pending (see addresses to the Nebraska and Texas Service Centers below).

E. For Immigrant Investors:

If you are an immigrant investor and you are applying for advance parole concurrently with Form I-485, use the filing address lised on Form I-485 for both forms. If you are filing a Form I-131 based on a pending Form I-485, file Form I-131 with the Texas Service Center using the following address:

USCIS Texas Service Center
P.O. Box 851182
Mesquite, TX 75185-1182

E. For applicants covered under the Haitian Refugee Immigrant Fairness Act (HRIFA):

If you are either the dependent spouse or child of a HRIFA principal or a HRIFA principal who has a Form I-485 pending you may file your Form I-131 using the following address:

USCIS Nebraska Service Center
P.O. Box 87245
Lincoln, NE 68501-7245

F. For other adjustment of status applications (Form I-485) filed at a USCIS Service Center including the following:

1. Based on an underlying Form I-140 petition;
2. Based on an underlying Form I-360 petition not previously mentioned; **or**
3. Others not previously mentioned.

If you are applying for advance parole concurrently with Form I-485, use the filing address listed on Form I-485 for both forms. If you are filing a Form I-131 based on a pending Form I-485, file Form I-131 with the Nebraska Service Center or Texas Service Center, depending on where you live.

1. **Nebraska Service Center Filings:**

   File your Form I-131 with the Nebraska Service Center if you live in the following states: Alaska, Arizona, California, Colorado, Guam, Hawaii, Idaho, Nevada, Illinois, Indiana, Iowa, Kansas, Michigan, Minnesota, Missouri, Montana, Nebraska, North Dakota, Ohio, Oregon, South Dakota, Utah, Washington, Wisconsin or Wyoming.

   USCIS Nebraska Service Center
   P.O. Box 87131
   Lincoln, NE 68501-7131

2. **Texas Service Center Filings:**

   File your Form I-131 with the Texas Service Center if you live in the following states: Alabama, Arkansas, Connecticut, Delaware, Florida, Georgia, Kentucky, Louisiana, Maine, Maryland, Massachusetts, Mississippi, New Hampshire, New Jersey, New Mexico, New York, North Carolina, Pennsylvania, Puerto Rico, Rhode Island, South Carolina, Oklahoma, Tennessee, Texas, Vermont, Virginia, U.S. Virgin Islands, West Virginia and the District of Columbia.

   USCIS Texas Service Center
   P.O. Box 851182
   Mesquite, TX 75185-1182

G. For individuals with Temporary Protected Status (TPS)

If you have been granted Temporary Protected Status and you are applying for advance parole, mail Form I-131 to the Vermont Service Center, regardless of where you live in the U.S.

USCIS Vermont Service Center
Attn: I-131
75 Lower Welden Street
St. Albans, VT 05479-0001

H. For beneficiaries outside the U.S. making the request on humanitarian grounds, of a Private Bill, and in removal proceedings:

If you are:

1. The beneficiary of a Private Bill,
2. In removal proceedings or
3. Outside the U.S. and are applying for advance parole on humanitarian grounds or the request is being filed on your behalf.

Then mail Form I-131 to the following address:

U.S. Citizenship and Immigration Services
Attn: Chief, International Operations Division
(Humanitarian Parole)
20 Massachusetts Avenue, NW, Room 3300
Washington, DC 20529

I. Questions Regarding Form I-131.

For additional information about Form I-131, including how to file your application or filing locations not mentioned, call the USCIS National Customer Service Center at **1-800-375-5283** or visit our website at **www.uscis.gov**.

What Is the Filing Fee?

The filing fee for a Form I-131 is **$305.00**.

Use the following guidelines when you prepare your check or money order for the Form I-131 fee:

1. The check or money order must be drawn on a bank or other financial institution located in the United States and must be payable in U.S. currency; and

2. Make the check or money order payable to **U.S. Department of Homeland Security**, unless:

   A. If you live in Guam and are filing your petition there, make it payable to **Treasurer, Guam**.

   B. If you live in the U.S. Virgin Islands and are filing your petition there, make it payable to **Commissioner of Finance of the Virgin Islands**.

NOTE: If you filed a Form I-485, Application to Register Permanent Residence or Adjust Status, as of July 30, 2007, no fee is required to also file a request for advance parole on Form I-131. You may file the I-131 concurrently with your I-485, or you may submit the I-131 at a later date. If you file Form I-131 separately, you must also submit a copy of your Form I-797C, Notice of Action, receipt as evidence of the filing of an I-485 as of July 30, 2007.

NOTE: Please spell out U.S. Department of Homeland Security; do not use the initials "USDHS" or "DHS."

Notice to Those Making Payment by Check. If you send us a check, it will be converted into an electronic funds transfer (EFT). This means we will copy your check and use the account information on it to electronically debit your account for the amount of the check. The debit from your account will usually take 24 hours, and will be shown on your regular account statement.

You will not receive your original check back. We will destroy your original check, but we will keep a copy of it. If the EFT cannot be processed for technical reasons, you authorize us to process the copy in place of your original check.

You will not receive your original check back. We will destroy your original check, but we will keep a copy of it. If the EFT cannot be processed for technical reasons, you authorize us to process the copy in place of your original check. If the EFT cannot be completed because of insufficient funds, we may try to make the transfer up to two times.

How to Check If the Fees Are Correct.

The form fee on this form is current as of the edition date appearing in the lower right corner of this page. However, because USCIS fees change periodically, you can verify if the fees are correct by following one of the steps below:

1. Visit our website at **www.uscis.gov**, select "Immigration Forms" and check the appropriate fee;
2. Review the Fee Schedule included in your form package, if you called us to request the form; or
3. Telephone our National Customer Service Center at **1-800-375-5283** and ask for the fee information.

Address Changes.

If you change your address and you have an application or petition pending with USCIS, you may change your address on-line at **www.uscis.gov**, click on "Change your address with USCIS" and follow the prompts or by completing and mailing Form AR-11, Alien's Change of Address Card, to:

U.S. Citizenship and Immigration Services
Change of Address
P.O. Box 7134
London, KY 40742-7134

APPENDIX 9D • I-131

For commercial overnight or fast freight services only, mail to:

U.S. Citizenship and Immigration Services
Change of Address
1084-I South Laurel Road
London, KY 40744

Processing Information.

Any Form I-131 that is not signed or accompanied by the correct fee, will be rejected with a notice that the Form I-131 is deficient. You may correct the deficiency and resubmit the Form I-131. An application or petition is not considered properly filed until accepted by USCIS.

Initial processing. Once a Form I-131 has been accepted, it will be checked for completness, including submission of the required initial evidence. If you do not completely fill out the form, or file it without required initial evidence, you will not establish a basis for eligibility and we may deny your Form I-131.

Requests for more information or interview. We may request more information or evidence, or we may request that you appear at a USCIS office for an interview. We may also request that you submit the originals of any copy. We will return these originals when they are no longer required.

Decision. The decision on a Form I-131 involves a determination of whether you have established eligiblity for the requested benefit. You will be notified of the decision in writing.

What If You Claim Nonresident Alien Status on Your Federal Income Tax Return?

If you are an alien who has established residence in the United States after having been admitted as an immigrant or adjusted status to that of an immigrant, and are considering the filing of a nonresident alien tax return or the non-filing of a tax return on the ground that you are a nonresident alien, you should carefully review the consequences of such actions under the Immigration and Nationality Act.

If you file a nonresident alien tax return or fail to file a tax return, you may be regarded as having abandoned residence in the United States and as having lost your permanent resident status under the Act. As a consequence, you may be ineligible for a visa or other document for which permanent resident aliens are eligible.

You may also be inadmissible to the United States if you seek admission as a returning resident, and you may become ineligible for adjustment of status as a permanent resident or naturalization on the basis of your original entry.

USCIS Forms and Information.

To order USCIS forms, call our toll-free number at **1-800-870-3676**. You can also get USCIS forms and information on immigration laws, regulations and procedures by telephoning our National Customer Service Center at **1-800-375-5283** or visiting our internet website at **www.uscis.gov**.

As an altenative to waiting in line for assistance at your local USCIS office, you can now schedule an appointment through our internet-based system, **InfoPass**. To access the system, visit our website. Use the **InfoPass** appointment scheduler and follow the screen prompts to set up your appointment. **InfoPass** generates an electronic appointment notice that appears on the screen.

Penalties.

If you knowingly and willfully falsify or conceal a material fact or submit a false document with this Form I-131, we will deny the Form I-131 and may deny any other immigration benefit.

In addition, you will face severe penalties provided by law and may be subject to criminal prosecution.

Privacy Act Notice.

We ask for the information on this form, and associated evidence, to determine if you have established eligibility for the immigration benefit for which you are filing. Our legal right to ask for this information can be found in the Immigration and Nationality Act, as amended. We may provide this information to other government agencies. Failure to provide this information, and any requested evidence, may delay a final decision or result in denial of your Form I-131.

Paperwork Reduction Act.

An agency may not conduct or sponsor an information collection and a person is not required to respond to a collection of information unless it displays a currently valid OMB control number. The public reporting burden for this collection of information is estimated at 55 minutes per response, including the time for reviewing instructions, completing and submitting the form. Send comments regarding this burden estimate or any other aspect of this collection of information, including suggestions for reducing this burden, to: U.S. Citizenship and Immigration Services, Regulatory Management Division, 111 Massachusetts Avenue, N.W., 3rd Floor, Suite 3008, Washington, DC 20529. OMB No. 1615-0013. **Do not mail your application to this address.**

Department of Homeland Security
U. S. Citizenship and Immigration Services

OMB No. 1615-0013, Expires 11/30/07

I-131, Application for Travel Document

DO NOT WRITE IN THIS BLOCK		FOR USCIS USE ONLY (except G-28 block below)
Document Issued ☐ Reentry Permit ☐ Refugee Travel Document ☐ Single Advance Parole ☐ Multiple Advance Parole Valid to: _____	**Action Block**	**Receipt**
If Reentry Permit or Refugee Travel Document, mail to: ☐ Address in Part 1 ☐ American embassy/consulate at: _____ ☐ Overseas DHS office at: _____		☐ Document Hand Delivered On _____ By _____ *To be completed by Attorney/Representative, if any.* Attorney State License # _____ ☐ Check box if G-28 is attached.

Part 1.   Information about you. *(Please type or print in black ink.)*

1. A #

2. Date of Birth *(mm/dd/yyyy)*

3. Class of Admission

4. Gender   Male ☐   Female ☐

5. Name *(Family name in capital letters)*   *(First)*   *(Middle)*

6. Address *(Number and Street)*   Apt. #

City   State or Province   Zip/Postal Code   Country

7. Country of Birth

8. Country of Citizenship

9. Social Security # *(if any.)*

Part 2.   Application type *(check one).*

a. ☐   I am a permanent resident or conditional resident of the United States and I am applying for a reentry permit.

b. ☐   I now hold U.S. refugee or asylee status and I am applying for a refugee travel document.

c. ☐   I am a permanent resident as a direct result of refugee or asylee status and I am applying for a refugee travel document.

d. ☐   I am applying for an advance parole document to allow me to return to the United States after temporary foreign travel.

e. ☐   I am outside the United States and I am applying for an advance parole document.

f. ☐   I am applying for an advance parole document for a person who is outside the United States. *If you checked box "f", provide the following information about that person:*

1. Name *(Family name in capital letters)*   *(First)*   *(Middle)*

2. Date of Birth *(mm/dd/yyyy)*

3. Country of Birth

4. Country of Citizenship

5. Address *(Number and Street)*   Apt. #   Daytime Telephone # *(area/country code)*

City   State or Province   Zip/Postal Code   Country

Form I-131 (Rev. 07/30/07)Y

APPENDIX 9D • I-131

Part 3. Processing information.

1. Date of Intended Departure *(mm/dd/yyyy)*

2. Expected Length of Trip

3. Are you, or any person included in this application, now in exclusion, deportation, removal or recission proceedings? ☐ No ☐ Yes *(Name of DHS office):*

If you are applying for an Advance Parole Document, skip to Part 7.

4. Have you ever before been issued a reentry permit or refugee travel? ☐ No ☐ Yes *(Give the following information for the last document issued to you):*

Date Issued *(mm/dd/yyyy):*   Disposition *(attached, lost, etc.):*

5. Where do you want this travel document sent? *(Check one)*
   a. ☐ To the U.S. address shown in **Part 1** on the first page of this form.
   b. ☐ To an American embassy or consulate at: City: Country:
   c. ☐ To a DHS office overseas at: City: Country:
   d. If you checked "b" or "c", where should the notice to pick up the travel document be sent?
      ☐ To the address shown in **Part 2** on the first page of this form.
      ☐ To the address shown below:

Address *(Number and Street)*   Apt. #   Daytime Telephone # *(area/country code)*

City   State or Province   Zip/Postal Code   Country

Part 4. Information about your proposed travel.

Purpose of trip. *If you need more room, continue on a seperate sheet(s) of paper.*   List the countries you intend to visit.

Part 5. Complete only if applying for a reentry permit.

Since becoming a permanent resident of the United States (or during the past five years, whichever is less) how much total time have you spent outside the United States?
☐ less than six months   ☐ two to three years
☐ six months to one year   ☐ three to four years
☐ one to two years   ☐ more than four years

Since you became a permanent resident of the United States, have you ever filed a federal income tax return as a nonresident, or failed to file a federal income tax return because you considered yourself to be a nonresident? *(If "Yes," give details on a separate sheet(s) of paper.)*   ☐ Yes ☐ No

Part 6. Complete only if applying for a refugee travel document.

1. Country from which you are a refugee or asylee:

If you answer "Yes" to any of the following questions, you must explain on a separate sheet(s) of paper.

2. Do you plan to travel to the above named country?   ☐ Yes ☐ No

3. Since you were accorded refugee/asylee status, have you ever:
   a. returned to the above named country?   ☐ Yes ☐ No
   b. applied for and/or obtained a national passport, passport renewal or entry permit of that country?   ☐ Yes ☐ No
   c. applied for and/or received any benefit from such country (for example, health insurance benefits).   ☐ Yes ☐ No

4. Since you were accorded refugee/asylee status, have you, by any legal procedure or voluntary act:
   a. reacquired the nationality of the above named country?   ☐ Yes ☐ No
   b. acquired a new nationality?   ☐ Yes ☐ No
   c. been granted refugee or asylee status in any other country?   ☐ Yes ☐ No

Form I-131 (Rev. 07/30/07)Y Page 2

Part 7. Complete only if applying for advance parole.

On a separate sheet(s) of paper, please explain how you qualify for an advance parole document and what circumstances warrant issuance of advance parole. Include copies of any documents you wish considered. *(See instructions.)*

1. For how many trips do you intend to use this document? ☐ One trip ☐ More than one trip

2. If the person intended to receive an advance parole document is outside the United States, provide the location (city and country) of the American embassy or consulate or the DHS overseas office that you want us to notify.

City

Country

3. If the travel document will be delivered to an overseas office, where should the notice to pick up the document be sent:

☐ To the address shown in **Part 2** on the first page of this form.

☐ To the address shown below:

Address *(Number and Street)* Apt. # Daytime Telephone # *(area/country code)*

City State or Province Zip/Postal Code Country

Part 8. Signature.
Read the information on penalties in the instructions before completing this section. If you are filing for a reentry permit or refugee travel document, you must be in the United States to file this application.

I certify, under penalty of perjury under the laws of the United States of America, that this application and the evidence submitted with it are all true and correct. I authorize the release of any information from my records that the U.S. Citizenship and Immigration Services needs to determine eligibility for the benefit I am seeking.

Signature Date *(mm/dd/yyyy)* Daytime Telephone Number *(with area code)*

Please Note: *If you do not completely fill out this form or fail to submit required documents listed in the instructions, you may not be found eligible for the requested document and this application may be denied.*

Part 9. Signature of person preparing form, if other than the applicant. *(Sign below.)*

I declare that I prepared this application at the request of the applicant and it is based on all information of which I have knowledge.

Signature Print or Type Your Name

Firm Name and Address Daytime Telephone Number *(with area code)*

Fax Number *(if any.)* Date *(mm/dd/yyyy)*

Form I-131 (Rev. 07/30/07)Y Page 3

TABLE OF FEDERAL COURT DECISIONS, STATE COURT DECISIONS, AND DECISIONS OF FOREIGN TRIBUNALS

Federal Court Decisions

Abankwah v. INS, 185 F.3d 18 (2d Cir. 1999) 34, 60, 80, 87
Abay v. Ashcroft, 368 F.3d 634 (6th Cir. 2004) 34, 36, 60, 64, 89, 91, 191
Abdalla v. INS, 43 F.3d 1397 (10th Cir. 1994) 127, 128
Abdel-Masieh v. INS, 73 F.3d 579 (5th Cir. 1996) 38, 44, 75
Abdille v. Ashcroft, 242 F.3d 477 (3d Cir. 2001) 101, 127, 187
Abebe v. Gonzales, 432 F.3d 1037 (9th Cir. 2005) 60
Abedini v. INS, 971 F.2d 188 (9th Cir. 1992) 75, 76, 92
Abu-Hasirah v. Dep't of Homeland Sec., 478 F.3d 474 (2d Cir. 2007) 179
Accardi v. Shaughnessy, 347 U.S. 260 (1954) 166
Acewicz v. INS, 984 F.2d 1056 (9th Cir. 1993) 95
Adebisi v. INS, 952 F.2d 910 (5th Cir. 1992) 51
Agada v. Ashcroft, 368 F.3d 867 (8th Cir. 2004) 92
Agbuya v. INS, 219 F.3d 962 (9th Cir. 2000), *amended,* 241 F.3d 1224 (9th Cir. 2001) . 41, 54, 73
Aguilera-Cota v. INS, 914 F.2d 1375 (9th Cir. 1990) 51, 54, 83
Aguirre-Aguirre; INS v., 526 U.S. 415 (1999) 5, 109, 110, 136
Aguirre-Tello; United States v., 353 F.3d 1199 (10th Cir. 2003) 167
Ahmad v. INS, 163 F.3d 457 (7th Cir. 1999) 45, 46
Ahmadshah v. Ashcroft, 396 F.3d 917 (8th Cir. 2005) 46, 98
Ahmed v. Gonzales, 467 F.3d 669 (7th Cir. 2006) 30, 33
Ahmetovic v. INS, 62 F.3d 48 (2d Cir. 1995) 105
Ahumada-Aguilar; United States v., 295 F.3d 943 (9th Cir. 2002) 149, 169
Ai Feng Yuan v. U.S. Dep't of Justice, 416 F.3d 192 (2d Cir. 2005) 56
Air France v. Saks, 470 U.S. 392 (1985) 20
Akhtar v. U.S. Attorney Gen., 138 Fed. Appx. 481 (3d Cir. 2005) 68
Alaka v. U.S. Attorney Gen., 456 F.3d 88 (3d Cir. 2006) 108
Alarcon-Chavez v. Gonzales, 403 F.3d 343 (5th Cir. 2005) 179
Albathani v. INS, 318 F.3d 365 (1st Cir. 2003) 228
Alcarez-Garcia v. Ashcroft, 293 F.3d 1155 (9th Cir. 2002) 354
Alexandrov v. Gonzales, 442 F.3d 395 (6th Cir. 2006) 144
Al-Harbi v. INS, 242 F.3d 882 (9th Cir. 2001) 54
Ali v. Achem, 468 F.3d 462 (7th Cir. 2006) 274
Ali v. Ashcroft, 346 F.3d 873 (9th Cir. 2003) 2
Ali v. Ashcroft, 394 F.3d 780 (9th Cir. 2005) 128
Ali v. Reno, 237 F.3d 591 (6th Cir. 2001) 127, 268, 282
Ali v. Reno, 829 F. Supp. 1415 (S.D.N.Y. 1993) 113
Al Khouri v. Ashcroft, 362 F.3d 461 (8th Cir. 2004) 82, 159, 166, 169, 170
Almuhtaseb v. Gonzales, 453 F.3d 743 (5th Cir. 2006) 70, 133
Al Najjar v. Ashcroft, 257 F.3d 1262 (11th Cir. 2001) 29
Al-Saher v. INS, 268 F.3d 1143 (9th Cir. 2001) 263, 264, 269, 275
Alsamhouri v. Gonzales, 484 F.3d 117 (1st Cir. 2007) 159

Alvarenga-Villalobos v. Ashcroft, 271 F.3d 1169 (9th Cir. 2001) 195
Alvarez-Flores v. INS, 909 F.2d 1 (1st Cir 1990) 51
Alvarez-Hernandez v. Gonzales, 401 F.3d 327 (5th Cir. 2005) 343
American-Arab Anti-Discrimination Comm.; Reno v., 525 U.S. 471 (1999) 245
American Baptist Churches (ABC) v. Thornburgh, 760 F. Supp. 796 (N.D. Calif. 1991) 335
American Immigration Lawyers Ass'n v. Reno, 199 F.3d 1352 (D.C. Cir. Jan. 11, 2000),
  aff'g 18 F. Supp. 2d 38 (D.D.C. 1998) 300
Amibola v. Ashcroft, 378 F.3d 173 (2d Cir. 2004) 240
Amir v. Gonzales, 467 F.3d 921 (6th Cir. 2006) 267
Ananeh-Firempong v. INS, 766 F.2d 621 (1st Cir. 1985) 51
Andia v. Ashcroft, 359 F.3d 1181 (9th Cir. 2004) 181
Andriasian v. INS, 180 F.3d 1033 (9th Cir. 1999) 42, 103, 166
Ang v. Gonzales, 430 F.3d 50 (1st Cir. 2005) 49
Angoucheva v. INS, 106 F.3d 781 (7th Cir. 1997) 59
Antonio-Martinez v. INS, 317 F.3d 1089 (9th Cir. 2003) 244
Arana v. INS, 673 F.3d 75 (3d Cir. 1982) 244
Arboleda v. U.S. Attorney Gen., 434 F.3d 1220 (11th Cir. 2006) 73, 74, 100
Arevalo v. Ashcroft, 344 F.3d 1 (1st Cir. 2003) 245
Arriaga-Barrientos v. INS, 937 F.2d 411 (9th Cir. 1991) 51, 54, 91, 92
Arrieta; United States v., 224 F.3d 1076 (9th Cir. 2000) 226
Arteaga v. INS, 836 F.2d 1227 (9th Cir. 1988) 54, 71
Aruta v. INS, 80 F.3d 1389 (9th Cir. 1996) 54
Arvizu; United States v., 122 S. Ct. 744 (2002) 165
Ashley v. Ridge, 288 F. Supp. 2d 662 (D.N.J. 2003) 217
Auguste v. Ridge, 395 F.3d 123 (3d Cir. 2005) 263
Augustin v. Sava, 735 F.2d 32 (2d Cir. 1984) 171
Avetova-Elisseva v. INS, 213 F.3d 1192 (9th Cir. 2000) 72, 93
Avila v. Rivkind, 724 F. Supp. 945 (S.D. Fla. 1989) 113
Awolesi v. Ashcroft, 341 F.3d 227 (3d Cir. 2003) 135
Azanor v. Ashcroft, 364 F.3d 1013 (9th Cir. 2004) 265
Azarshahy v. Ilchert, 1994 WL 446040 (N.D. Cal., August 10, 1994) 78
Azhgirevich v. Gonzales, 185 Fed. Appx. 72 (2d Cir. 2006) 40
Aziz v. Gonzales, 478 F.3d 854 (8th Cir. 2007) 143–144
Azzouka v. Meese, 820 F.2d 585 (2d Cir. 1987) 113
Baballah v. Ashcroft, 367 F.3d 1067 (9th Cir. 2004) 34, 35, 40, 42, 44, 46, 64, 91
Bace v. Ashcroft, 352 F.3d 1133 (7th Cir. 2003) 33, 38, 40, 95, 135
Bah v. Gonzales, 462 F.3d 637 (6th Cir. 2006) 61
Baires v. INS, 856 F.2d 89 (9th Cir. 1988) 161
Bakhtriger v. Elwood, 360 F.3d 414 (3d Cir. 2004) 243
Balasubramanrim v. INS, 143 F.3d 157 (3d Cir. 1998) 83
Balleteros-Ruiz; United States v., 319 F.3d 1101 (9th Cir. 2003) 173
Balliu v. Gonzales, 467 F.3d 609 (7th Cir. 2006) 38
Balogun v. Ashcroft, 374 F.3d 492 (7th Cir. 2004) 305
Bamba v. Riley, 366 F.3d 195 (3d Cir. 2004) 203
Bandari v. INS, 227 F.3d 1160 (9th Cir. 2000) 41, 44, 76, 83
Banks v. Gonzalez, 453 F.3d 449 (7th Cir. 2006) 31, 84, 183
Baptiste v. U.S. Attorney Gen., 229 Fed.Appx. 66 (3d Cir. 2007) 68
Barapind v. Enomoto, 400 F.3d 744 (9th Cir. 1986) 109
Barreto-Claro v. U.S. Attorney Gen., 275 F.3d 1334 (11th Cir. 2001) 144, 159
Barry v. Gonzales, 445 F.3d 741 (4th Cir. 2006) 34

© *2007 American Immigration Lawyers Association*

Bastanipour v. INS, 980 F.2d 1129 (7th Cir. 1992) 44, 51
Bazan-Reyes v. INS, 256 F.3d 600 (7th Cir. 2001) 203
Begzatowski v. INS, 278 F.3d 665 (7th Cir. 2002) 36, 71
Beharry v. Reno, 183 F. Supp. 2d 584 (E.D.N.Y 2002), *rev'd,* 329 F.3d 51 (2d Cir. 2003) 7
Behzadpour v. U.S., 946 F.2d 1351 (8th Cir. 1991) 75, 76
Bejjani v. INS, 271 F.3d 670 (6th Cir. 2001) 245
Belishta v. Ashcroft, 378 F.3d 1078 (9th Cir. 2004) 100
Bellido v. Ashcroft, 367 F.3d 840 (8th Cir. 2004) 36, 76, 83, 87, 92
Berdo v. INS, 432 F.2d 824 (6th Cir. 1970) 35
Berishaj v.Ashcroft, 378 F.3d 314 (3d Cir. 2004) 271
Bernal-Garcia v. INS, 852 F.2d 144 (5th Cir. 1988) 51
Berri v. Gonzales, 468 F.3d 390 (6th Cir. 2006) 159
Beskovic v. Gonzales, 467 F.3d 223 (2d Cir. 2006) 37
Bezmen v. Ashcroft, 245 F. Supp. 2d 446 (D. Conn. 2003) 217
Bhatt v. Reno, 172 F.3d 978 (7th Cir. 1999) 31, 33, 80, 92
Bilokumsky v. Tod, 263 U.S. 149 (1923) 168
Bi Zhu Lin v. Ashcroft, 183 F. Supp. 2d 551 (D. Conn. 2002) 264
Blake v. Gonzales, 473 F.3d 55 (2d Cir. 2007) 240
Blanco-Lopez v. INS, 858 F.2d 531 (9th Cir. 1988) 54
Boakai v. Gonzales, 447 F.3d 1 (1st Cir. 2006) 133
Bockou Essohou v. Gonzales, 471 F.3d 518 (4th Cir. 2006) 74
Boer-Sedano v. Gonzales, 418 F.3d 1082 (9th Cir. 2005) 67, 74, 100
Bolanos-Hernandez v. INS, 767 F.2d 1277 (9th Cir. 1984) 40, 92
Bolshakov v. INS, 133 F.3d 1279 (9th Cir. 1998) 136
Borja v. INS, 175 F.3d 732 (9th Cir. 1999) 36
Bowman Transp., Inc. v. Arkansas-Best Freight Sys., Inc., 419 U.S. 281 (1974) 245
Boyanivskyy v. Gonzales, 450 F.3d 286 (7th Cir. 2006) 182
Boykov v. INS, 109 F.3d 413 (7th Cir. 1997) 90
Bradvica v. INS, 128 F.3d 1009 (7th Cir. 1997) 37, 136
Briones v. INS, 175 F.3d 727 (9th Cir. 1999) 41, 54
Bropleh v. Gonzales, 428 F.3d 772 (8th Cir. 2005) 228
Brown v. Gardner, 513 U.S. 115 (1994) 15
Brue v. Gonzales, 464 F.3d 112 (10th Cir. 2006) 133
Bucur v. INS, 109 F.3d 399 (7th Cir. 1997) 35, 43
Bunikyte v. Chertoff, 2007 U.S. Dist. LEXIS 26166 (D. Tex. 2007) 194
Buschini, Matter of, A98 064 379 (AAO 2006) 341, 342
Bustos-Torres v. INS, 898 F.2d 1053 (5th Cir. 1990) 182
Cabrera-Perez v. Gonzales, 456 F.3d 109 (3d Cir. 2006) 179
Cadet v. Bulger, 377 F.3d 1173 (11th Cir. 2004) 270, 271
Calcano-Martinez v. INS, 533 U.S. 348 (2001) 132, 283
Camacho-Salinas v. United States AG, 460 F.3d 1343 (11th Cir. 2006) 351
Camara v. Ashcroft, 378 F.3d 361 (4th Cir. 2004) 85, 266, 272
Campos-Sanchez v. INS, 164 F.3d 448 (9th Cir. 1998) 131
Canas-Segovia v. INS, 970 F.2d 599 (9th Cir. 1992) 44, 53
Cano-Merida v. INS, 311 F.3d 960 (9th Cir. 2002) 166, 167
Cao v. U.S. Att'y. Gen., 407 F.3d 146 (3d Cir. 2005) 57
Capric v. Ashcroft, 355 F.3d 1075 (7th Cir. 2004) 26, 37, 93, 138
Cardenas v. INS, 294 F.3d 1062 (9th Cir. 2002) 74
Cardoza-Fonseca; INS v., 480 U.S. 421 (1987) 4, 5, 10, 25, 26, 27, 30, 79, 245
Carry v. Holmes, 1:02-cv-00369 (W.D.N.Y. July 22, 2003) 263, 269

Castellano-Chacon v. INS, 341 F.3d 533 (6th Cir. 2003) 49, 70
Castillo v. INS, 951 F.2d 1117 (9th Cir. 1991) 71
Castillo-Arias v. U.S. Attorney Gen., 446 F.3d 1190 (11th Cir. 2006), *cert. denied*,
    127 S. Ct. 977 (Jan. 8, 2007) 48, 49, 51
Castillo-Villagra v. INS, 972 F.2d 1017 (9th Cir. 1992) 95
Castro-Cortez v. INS, 239 F.3d 1037 (9th Cir. 2001) 146, 156, 157
Castro-O'Ryan v. INS, 847 F.2d 1307 (9th Cir. 1988) 169
Castro-Perez v. Gonzales, 409 F.3d 1069 (9th Cir. 2005) 72
Catholic Charities CYO v. Chertoff, C07-01307-PJH (N.D. Cal. Mar. 6, 2007) 329
Ceballos-Castillo v. INS, 904 F.2d 519 (9th Cir. 1990) 83
Chacon-Botero v. U.S. Attorney Gen., 427 F.3d 954 (11th Cir. 2005) 134
Chakir v. Gonzales, 466 F.3d 563 (7th Cir. 2006) 45
Cham v. Gonzales, 445 F.3d 683 (2d Cir. 2006) 167
Chand v. INS, 222 F.3d 1066 (9th Cir. 2000) 33
Chandi v. Gonzales, 2007 U.S. App. LEXIS 8593 (9th Cir. 2007) 160
Chang v. INS, 119 F.3d 1055 (3d Cir. 1997) 34, 52, 75, 76, 77, 137
Chavarria v. Gonzales, 446 F.3d 508 (3d Cir. 2006) 35, 90
Chavarria v. U.S. Dep't of Justice, 722 F.2d 666 (11th Cir. 1984) 95
Cheema v. Ashcroft, 372 F.3d 1147 (9th Cir. 2004), *amended by* 383 F.3d 848
    (9th Cir. 2004) 113, 115, 185
Chen v. Ashcroft, 381 F.3d 221 (3d Cir. 2004) 56
Chen v. Ashcroft, 94 Fed. Appx. 930, 2004 WL 835786 (3d Cir. 2004) 112
Chen v. Gonzales, 417 F.3d 303 (2d Cir. 2005) 57, 65
Chen v. Gonzales, 434 F.3d 212 (3d Cir. 2005) 77
Chen v. Gonzales, 457 F.3d 670 (7th Cir. 2006) 56
Chen v. Gonzales, 470 F.3d 1131 (5th Cir. 2006) 267
Chen v. INS, 195 F.3d 198 (4th Cir. 1999) 58, 135
Chen v. INS, 266 F.3d 1094 (9th Cir. 2001) 57
Chen v. INS, 359 F.3d 121 (2d Cir. 2004) 32, 35, 44, 45, 85
Chen v. United States, 434 F.3d 144 (2d Cir. 2006) 49
Chen v. U.S. Attorney Gen., 463 F.3d 1228 (11th Cir. 2006) 81
Cheo v. INS, 162 F.3d 1227 (9th Cir. 1998) 128
Chevron, USA, Inc. v. Natural Resources Defense Council, 467 U.S. 837,
    104 S. Ct. 2778 (1984) 136, 137, 240
Chitay-Pirir v. INS, 169 F.3d 1079 (7th Cir. 1999) 178, 191
Choeum v. INS, 129 F.3d 29 (1st Cir. 1997) 27, 105, 109
Chong Shin Chen v. Ashcroft, 378 F.3d 1081 (9th Cir. 2004) 228
Chouchkov v. INS, 220 F.3d 1077 (9th Cir. 2000) 91
Cifuentes-Villatoro v. Ashcroft, 71 Fed. Appx. 750 (9th Cir. 2003) 71
Ciorba v. Ashcroft, 323 F.3d 539 (7th Cir. 2003) 37, 172
Circu v. Gonzales, 450 F.3d 990 (9th Cir. 2006) 166
Colmenar v. INS, 210 F.3d 967 (9th Cir. 2000) 172
Comollari v. Ashcroft, 378 F.3d 694 (7th Cir. 2004) 265
Contreras-Rodriguez v. U.S. Attorney Gen., 462 F.3d 1314 (11th Cir. 2006) 239
Cordero-Trejo v. INS, 40 F.3d 482 (1st Cir. 1994) 44, 85, 92, 93
Coronado-Durazo v. INS, 123 F.3d 1323 (9th Cir. 1997) 173
Crespo-Gomez v. Richard, 780 F.2d 932 (11th Cir. 1986) 105
Cruz-Diaz v. INS, 86 F.3d 330 (4th Cir. 1996) 64
Cruz-Espinoza v. INS, 45 F.3d 308 (9th Cir. 1995) 172
Cruz-Funez v. Gonzales, 406 F.3d 1187 (10th Cir. 2005) 267

© 2007 *American Immigration Lawyers Association*

Cuban-American Bar Ass'n, Inc. v. Christopher, 43 F.3d 1412 (11th Cir. 1995) 141
Cunanan v. INS, 856 F.2d 1373 (9th Cir. 1988) 184
Daiga v. INS, 183 F.3d 797 (8th Cir. 1999) 82
Dalton v. Ashcroft, 257 F.3d 200 (2d Cir. 2001) 107
Damaize-Job v. INS, 787 F.2d 1332 (9th Cir. 1986) 83, 94
Damko v. INS, 430 F.3d 626 (2d Cir. 2005) 35
Daneshvar v. Ashcroft, 355 F.3d 615 (6th Cir. 2004) 79
Daubert v. Merrell Dow Pharms., 509 U.S. 579 (1993) 183
Davila-Bardales v. INS, 27 F.3d 1 (1st Cir. 1994) 16
Dawoud v. Gonzales, 424 F.3d 608 (7th Cir. 2005) 85
Debab v. INS, 163 F.3d 21 (1st Cir. 1998) 40
De Fuentes v. Gonzales, 462 F.3d 498 (5th Cir. 2006) 351
De La Llana-Castellon v. INS, 16 F.3d 1093 (10th Cir. 1994) 95
De Leon-Barrios v. INS, 116 F.2d 391 (9th Cir. 1997) 83, 132
De Leon-Reynoso v. Ashcroft, 293 F.3d 633 (3d Cir. 2002) 351
Delgado v. U.S. Att'y Gen., 487 F.3d 855 (11th Cir. 2007) 141
Demarest v. Manspeaker, 498 U.S. 184 (1991) 15
De Morales v. INS, 116 F.3d 145 (5th Cir. 1997) 180
Demore v. Kim, 538 U.S. 510 (2003) 213
Denko v. INS, 351 F.3d 717 (6th Cir. 2003) 228
Desta v. Ashcroft, 329 F.3d 1179 (10th Cir. 2003) 127, 161
Detroit Free Press v. Ashcroft, 303 F.3d 681 (6th Cir. 2002) 163
DeValle v. INS, 901 F.2d 787 (9th Cir. 1990) 51
Dhine v. Slattery, 3 F.3d 613 (2d Cir. 1993) 103
Dhoumo v. BIA, 416 F.3d 172 (2d Cir. 2005) 28
Dia v. Ashcroft, 353 F.3d 228 (3d Cir. 2003) 228
Diakite v. INS, 179 F.3d 553 (7th Cir. 1999) 282
Diallo v. Ashcroft, 381 F.3d 687 (7th Cir. 2004) 37, 127
Diallo v. Gonzales, 447 F.3d 1247 (10th Cir. 2006) 133
Diallo v. INS, 232 F.3d 279 (2d Cir. 2000) 26, 31, 85
Diaz v. Reno, 40 F. Supp. 2d 984 (N.D. Ill. 1999) 298
Disu v. Ashcroft, 338 F.3d 13 (1st Cir. 2003) 83
Djedovic v. Gonzales, 441 F.3d 547 (7th Cir. 2006) 71
Dobrota v. INS, 195 F.3d 970 (7th Cir. 1999) 95
Doe v. *See name of opposing party*
Doherty, In re, 599 F. Supp. 270 (S.D.N.Y. 1984) 115
Doherty; INS v., 502 U.S. 314 (1992) 136
Douglas v. Ashcroft, 374 F.3d 230 (3d Cir. 2004) 245
Doumbia v. Gonzales, 472 F.3d 957 (7th Cir. 2007) 181
Duarte v. Ashcroft, 83 Fed. Appx. 119 (7th Cir. 2003) 228
Duarte de Guinac v. INS, 179 F.3d 1156 (9th Cir. 1999) 36, 42, 71, 87
Dunat v. Henry, 297 F.2d 744 (3d Cir. 1961) 35
Dusky v United States, 362 U.S. 402 (1960) 176
Dwomoh v. Sava, 696 F. Supp. 970 (S.D.N.Y. 1988) 77, 110
Echeverria-Hernandez v. INS, 923 F.2d 688, *vacated,* 946 F.2d 1481 (9th Cir. 1991) 7
Efe v. Ashcroft, 293 F.3d 899 (5th Cir. 2002) 144, 159
El Himri v. Ashcroft, 344 F.3d 1261 (9th Cir. 2003) 244
El Himri v. Ashcroft, 378 F.3d 932 (9th Cir. 2004) 123, 192, 271
Elias-Zacarias; INS v., 502 U.S. 478 (1992) 39, 40, 52, 72, 135, 138
Elien v. Ashcroft, 364 F.3d 392 (1st Cir. 2004) 49, 51, 271

Elnager v. INS, 930 F.2d 784 (9th Cir. 1991) 45
El Rescate Legal Servs., Inc. v. EOIR, 959 F.2d 742 (9th Cir. 1992) 171
Elzour v. Ashcroft, 378 F.3d 1143 (10th Cir. 2004) 127
Ememe v. Ashcroft, 358 F.3d 446 (7th Cir. 2004) 83, 313
Escobar v. Gonzales, 417 F.3d 363 (3d Cir. 2005) 51, 65
Espinoza v. INS, 45 F.3d 308 (9th Cir. 1995) 181
Esponda v. U.S. Attorney Gen., 453 F.3d 1319 (11th Cir. 2006) 230
Essohou v. Gonzales, 471 F.3d 518 (4th Cir. 2006) 100
Estrada-Escobar v. Ashcroft, 376 F.3d 1042 (10th Cir. 2004) 54
Estrada-Posadas v. INS, 924 F.2d 916 (9th Cir. 1991) 54
Eta-Ndu v. Gonzales, 411 F.3d 977 (8th Cir. 2005) 86
Etchu-Njang v. Gonzales, 403 F.3d 577 (8th Cir. 2005) 136
Etugh v. INS, 921 F.2d 36 (3d Cir. 1991) 74
Ezeagwuna v. Ashcroft, 301 F.3d 116 (3d Cir. 2002), *rev'd,* 325 F.3d 396 (3d Cir. 2003) 182
Fahim v. U.S. Attorney Gen., 278 F.3d 1216 (11th Cir. 2002) 282
Faiz-Mohammed v. Ashcroft, 395 F.3d 799 (7th Cir. 2005) 195
Fajardo v. INS, 300 F.3d 1018 (9th Cir. 2002) 236
Falcon Carriche v. Ashcroft, 350 F.3d 845 (9th Cir. 2003) 228
Fano v. O'Neill, 806 F.2d 1262 (5th Cir. 1987) 15
Farah v. Ashcroft, 348 F.3d 1153 (9th Cir. 2003) 144, 159
Farbakhsh v. INS, 20 F.3d 877 (8th Cir. 1994) 128
Faruqi v. DHS, 360 F.3d 985 (9th Cir. 2004) 245
Farzad v. INS, 802 F.2d 123 (5th Cir. 1986) 344
Fatin v. INS, 12 F.3d 1233 (3d Cir. 1993) 33, 38, 49, 62
Fedunyak v. Gonzales, 477 F.3d 1126 (9th Cir. 2007) 52
Felzcerek v. INS, 75 F.3d 112 (2d Cir. 1996) 182
Fergiste v. INS, 138 F.3d 14 (1st Cir. 1998) 98
Fernandez-Roque v. Smith, 599 F. Supp. 1103 (N.D. Ga. 1984) 16
Fernandez-Vargas v. Gonzales, 126 S. Ct. 2422 (2006) 195, 245
Feroz v. INS, 22 F.3d 225 (9th Cir. 1994) 105
Fesseha v. Ashcroft, 333 F.3d 13 (1st Cir. 2003) 37
Filartiga v. Pena-Irala, 630 F.2d 876 (2d Cir. 1980) 7
Firmansjah v. Gonzales, 424 F.3d 598 (7th Cir. 2005) 127
Fisher v. INS, 79 F.3d 955 (9th Cir. 1996) 62
Flores v. Meese, No. 85-cv-4544 (C.D. Cal. Sept. 1996) 194
Flores v. Reno, Stipulated Settlement Agreement, No. CV 85-4544-RJK (C.D. Cal. 1997) 194
Flores; Reno v., 507 U.S. 292 (1993) 166, 194, 213
Flores-Chavez v. Ashcroft, 362 F.3d 1150 (9th Cir. 2004) 177, 178, 181, 213
Flores-Portillo v. Ashcroft, 103 Fed. Appx. 852 (5th Cir. 2004) 65
Floroiu v. Gonzales, 481 F.3d 970 (7th Cir. 2007) 46, 132, 167
Foroglou v. INS, 170 F.3d 68 (1st Cir. 1999) 71, 72
Foster v. Neilson, 27 U.S. (2 Pet.) 253 (1829) 9, 260
Francois v. Gonzales, 448 F.3d 645 (3d Cir. 2006) 263
Francois v. INS, 283 F.3d 926 (8th Cir. 2002) 31, 39, 92, 95, 101
Gafoor v. INS, 231 F.3d 645 (9th Cir. 2000) 42
Gailius v. INS, 147 F.3d 34 (1st Cir. 1998) 40, 85, 95, 136, 137, 163
Galina v. INS, 213 F.3d 955 (7th Cir. 2000) 85, 95
Galvez-Vergara v. Gonzales, 484 F.3d 798 (5th Cir. 2007) 179
Gao v. Board of Immigration Appeals, 482 F.3d 122 (2d Cir. 2007) 83
Gao v. Gonzales, 440 F.3d 62 (2d Cir. 2006) 50, 63, 99

© 2007 American Immigration Lawyers Association

TABLE OF FEDERAL DECISIONS, STATE DECISIONS, AND FOREIGN TRIBUNALS

Gao v. Gonzales, 481 F.3d 173 (2d Cir. 2007) 244
Gao v. Jenifer, 185 F.3d 548 (6th Cir. 1999) 353
Garcia-Cortez v. Ashcroft, 366 F.3d 749 (9th Cir. 2004) 230
Garcia-Flores v. Gonzales, 477 F.3d 439 (6th Cir. 2007) 244
Garcia-Guzman v. Reno, 65 F. Supp. 2d 1077 (N.D. Cal. 1999) 161, 170
Garcia-Martinez v. Ashcroft, 371 F.3d 1066 (9th Cir. 2004) 59, 138
Garcia-Quintero v. Gonzales, 455 F.3d 1006 (9th Cir. 2006) 240
Garrovillas v. INS, 156 F.3d 1010 (9th Cir. 1998) 36, 37, 84, 90
Gatcliffe v. Reno, 23 F. Supp. 2d 581 (D.V.I. 1998) 354
Ge v. Ashcroft, 367 F.3d 1121 (9th Cir. 2004) 55
Gebrekidan v. Clark, 2006 U.S. Dist. LEXIS 83687 (W.D. Wash. 2006) 160
Gebremichael v. INS, 10 F.3d 28 (1st Cir. 1993) 91, 344
Georgis v. Ashcroft, 328 F.3d 962 (7th Cir. 2003) 80, 83, 185
Ghaly v. INS, 58 F.3d 1425 (9th Cir. 1995) 132, 136
Ghounem v. INS, 378 F.3d 740 (8th Cir. 2004) 180
Giday v. Gonzales, 434 F.3d 543 (7th Cir. 2006) 35, 71
Gilaj v. Gonzales, 408 F.3d 275 (6th Cir. 2005) 136
Girma v. INS, 283 F.3d 664 (5th Cir. 2002) 41, 132, 135, 136
Gjeci v. Gonzales, 451 F.3d 416 (7th Cir. 2006) 159, 166
Gjerazi v. Gonzales, 435 F.3d 800 (7th Cir. 2006) 86
Gomes v. Gonzales, 429 F.3d 1264 (9th Cir. 2005) 45, 93, 99
Gomez v. INS, 947 F.2d 660 (2d Cir. 1991) 51, 63, 65
Gomez-De Leon v. INS, 2002 U.S. Dist. LEXIS 13606 (D. Conn. 2002) 69
Gonahasa v. INS, 181 F.3d 538 (4th Cir. 1999) 31, 85
Gonzales; Doe v., 484 F.3d 445 (7th Cir. 2007) 109, 111
Gonzales-Neyra v. INS, 122 F.3d 1293 (9th Cir. 1997), *amended,* 133 F.3d 726
  (9th Cir. 1998) 27, 40, 90, 135
Gonzalez v. Reno, 212 F.3d 1338 (11th Cir. 2000) 190
Gonzalez-DeLeon; United States v., 32 F. Supp. 2d 925 (W.D. Tex. 1998) 169
Gonzalez-Rivera v. INS, 22 F.3d 1441 (9th Cir. 1994) 165
Grava v. INS, 205 F.3d 1177 (9th Cir. 2000) 52
Gu v. Gonzales, 454 F.3d 1014 (9th Cir. 2005) 45
Guan v. Gonzales, 432 F.3d 391 (2d Cir. 2005) 305
Guan v. INS, 453 F.3d 129 (2d Cir. 2006) 137
Guevara-Flores v. INS, 786 F.2d 1242 (5th Cir. 1986) 25
Gui v. Ridge, 2004 WL 1920719 (M.D. Pa. 2004) 215
Gui Cun Liu v. Ashcroft, 372 F.3d 529 (3d Cir. 2004) 185
Gumbol v. INS, 815 F.2d 406 (6th Cir. 1987) 45, 46
Guo v. Ashcroft, 361 F.3d 1194 (9th Cir. 2004) 40, 44, 137
Gutierrez-Almazan v. Gonzales, 453 F.3d 956 (7th Cir. 2006) 244
Gutierrez-Chavez v. INS, 298 F.3d 824 (9th Cir. 2002) 132
Gutierrez-Roque v. INS, 954 F.2d 769 (D.C. Cir. 1992) 95
Habtemicael v. Ashcroft, 370 F.3d 774 (8th Cir. 2004) 269
Haddad v. Gonzales, 437 F.3d 515 (6th Cir. 2006) 235
Hagi v. Ashcroft, 359 F.3d 1044 (8th Cir. 2004) 99
Hailmichael v. Gonzales, 454 F.3d 878 (8th Cir. 2006) 233
Hajiani-Niroumand v. INS, 26 F.3d 832 (8th Cir. 1994) 83
Hamama v. INS, 78 F.3d 233 (6th Cir. 1996) 105
Hanaj v. Gonzales, 446 F.3d 694 (7th Cir. 2006) 79, 82, 86
Hanan v. Gonzales, 449 F.3d 834 (8th Cir. 2006) 282

© *2007 American Immigration Lawyers Association*

Haoud v. Ashcroft, 350 F.3d 201 (1st Cir. 2003) 228
Hartooni v. INS, 21 F.3d 336 (9th Cir. 1994) 82, 137
Hassan v. Gonzales, 403 F.3d 429 (6th Cir. 2005) 228
Hayek v. Gonzales, 445 F.3d 501 (1st Cir. 2006) 133
He v. Ashcroft, 328 F.3d 593 (9th Cir. 2003) 171
Hem v. Maurer, 458 F.3d 1185 (10th Cir. 2006) 343
Hernandez v. Chandler, CA3-88-0224-R (N.D. Tex. June 23, 1989) 350
Hernandez v. Reno, 258 F.3d 806 (8th Cir. 2001) 111, 112
Hernandez-Barrera v. Ashcroft, 373 F.3d 9 (1st Cir. 2004) 38, 96, 98
Hernandez-Gil v. Gonzales, 476 F.3d 803 (9th Cir. 2007) 170
Hernandez-Montiel v. INS, 225 F.3d 1084 (9th Cir. 2000) 50, 66, 169
Hernandez-Ortiz v. Gonzales, 496 F.3d 1042 (9th Cir. 2007) 64
Hernandez-Vermudez; United States v., 356 F.3d 1011 (9th Cir. 2004) 203
Hernandez-Vivas v. INS, 23 F.3d 1557 (9th Cir. 1994) 136
Hong v. U.S. Attorney Gen., 165 Fed. Appx. 995 (3d Cir. 2006) 65
Hor v. Gonzales, 421 F.3d 497 (7th Cir. 2005) 86, 134, 245
Hose v. INS, 180 F.3d 992 (9th Cir. 1999) 132
Hosseini v. Gonzales, 471 F.3d 953 (9th Cir. 2006) 269, 275
Hoxha v. Ashcroft, 319 F.3d 1179 (9th Cir. 2003) 135
Hua Fang v. Gonzales, No. 03-71352, Filed order (Appellate Comm'r)
    (9th Cir. Oct. 30, 2006) 243
Huaman Cornelio v. BIA, 979 F.2d 995 (4th Cir. 1992) 54, 94
Huang v. Ashcroft, No. 03-16730, 2004 U.S. App. LEXIS 27903 (9th Cir. 2004) ... 287
Huang v. Gonzales, 453 F.3d 142 (2d Cir. 2006) 167
Huang v. INS, 421 F.3d 125 (2d Cir. 2005) 58, 103, 104, 136
Humanitarian Law Project v. U.S. Dep't of Justice, 352 F.3d 382 (9th Cir. 2003) ... 115
Iasu v. Chertoff, 426 F. Supp. 2d 1124 (D. Cal. 2006) 122, 134, 242
Iavorski v. INS, 232 F.3d 124 (2d Cir. 2000) 236
In re. *See name of party*
INS v. *See name of opposing party*
Islami v. Gonzales, 412 F.3d 391 (2d Cir. 2005) 71
Ivanishvili v. Gonzales, 433 F.3d 332 (2d Cir. 2006) 33, 44
Ivezaj v. INS, 84 F.3d 215 (6th Cir. 1996) 95
Jacinto v. INS, 208 F.3d 725 (9th Cir. 2000) 170
Jadaan v. Gonzales, 211 Fed. Appx. 422 (6th Cir. 2006) 176
Jahed v. INS, 356 F.3d 991 (9th Cir. 2004) 36, 41, 136
Jama v. Immigration & Customs Enforcement, 543 U.S. 335 (2005) 161
Jankowski-Burczyk v. INS, 291 F.3d 172 (2d Cir. 2002) 351
Janusiak v. INS, 947 F.2d 46 (3d Cir. 1991) 75
Jarbough v. U.S. Attorney Gen., 483 F.3d 184 (3d Cir. 2007) 133
Jiang v. Gonzales, 474 F.3d 25 (1st Cir. 2007) 186
Jian Hui Shao v. BIA, 465 F.3d 497 (2d Cir. 2006) 58
Jibril v. Gonzales, 423 F.3d 1129 (9th Cir. 2005) 81
Jo v. Gonzales, 458 F.3d 104 (2d Cir. 2006) 264
Jobson v. Ashcroft, 326 F.3d 367 (2d Cir. 2003) 107
Johnson v. Ashcroft, 286 F.3d 696 (3d Cir. 2002) 287
Jorge-Tzoc v. Gonzales, 435 F.3d 146 (2d Cir. 2006) 64
Juiang Hui v. U.S. Attorney Gen., 174 Fed. Appx. 627 (2d Cir. 2006) 160
Kabamba v. Gonzales, 162 Fed. Appx. 337 (5th Cir. 2006) 86
Kaczmarczyk v. INS, 933 F.2d 588 (7th Cir. 1991) 95, 177

Kaganovich v. Gonzales, 470 F.3d 894 (9th Cir. 2006) 254
Kaiser v. Ashcroft, 390 F.3d 653 (9th Cir. 2004) 100
Kalaj v. Gonzales, 201 Fed. Appx. 345 (6th Cir. 2006) 170
Kalmalthas v. INS, 251 F.3d 1279 (9th Cir. 2001) 258, 272, 274, 282
Kalubi v. Ashcroft, 364 F.3d 1134 (9th Cir. 2004) 81, 102, 103, 104, 117, 135
Kamara v. U.S. Attorney Gen., 420 F.3d 202 (3d Cir. 2005) 271, 283
Kamboli v. Gonzales, 449 F.3d 454 (2d Cir. 2006) 228
Kanacevic v. INS, 448 F.3d 129 (2d Cir. 2006) 244
Kanivets v. Riley, 320 F. Supp. 2d 297 (E.D. Pa. 2004) 45, 122, 125, 242
Kapcia v. INS, 944 F.2d 702 (10th Cir. 1991) 76
Karouni v. Gonzales, 399 F.3d 1163 (9th Cir. 2005) 66, 68
Kashefi-Zihagh v. INS, 791 F.2d 708 (9th Cir. 1986) 344
Kastigar v. United States, 406 U.S. 441 (1972) 168
Kaur v. Gonzales, 418 F.3d 1061 (9th Cir. 2005) 83
Kebede v. Ashcroft, 366 F.3d 808 (9th Cir. 2004) 60, 82
Kerciku v. INS, 314 F.3d 913 (7th Cir. 2003) 80, 132, 136, 166, 182
Key v. Heckler, 754 F.2d 1545 (9th Cir. 1985) 170
Khalaf v. INS, 909 F.2d 589 (1st Cir. 1990) 45
Khan v. INS, 237 F.3d 1143 (9th Cir. 2001) 185
Khano v. INS, 999 F.2d 1203 (7th Cir. 1993) 83
Khattak v. Ashcroft, 332 F.3d 250 (4th Cir. 2003) 228
Khourassany v. INS, 208 F.3d 1096 (9th Cir. 2000) 282
Khouzam v. Ashcroft, 361 F.3d 161 (2d Cir. 2004) 168, 266, 267, 268, 269, 276, 277
Khouzam v. Hogan, 497 F.Supp.2d 615 (M.D. Pa. 2007) 279, 283, 284
Kiareldeen v. Ashcroft, 273 F.3d 542 (3d Cir. 2001) 171, 172, 184
Kiareldeen v. Reno, 71 F. Supp. 2d 402 (D.N.J. 1999), *rev'd sub nom.*
   Kiareldeen v. Ashcroft, 273 F.3d 542 (3d Cir. 2001) 119, 168, 172, 184
Kibinda v. U.S. Attorney Gen., 477 F.3d 113 (3d Cir. 2007) 37
Kifleyesus v. Gonzales, 462 F.3d 937 (8th Cir. 2006) 144
Kimumwe v. Gonzales, 431 F.3d 319 (8th Cir. 2005) 66
Kllokoqi v. Gonzales, 439 F.3d 336 (7th Cir. 2005) 84
Knauff v. Shaughnessy, 338 U.S. 537 (1950) 166
Knezevic v. Ashcroft, 367 F.3d 1206 (9th Cir. 2004) 31, 35, 38, 42, 46, 92, 99
Kofa v. INS, 60 F.3d 1084 (4th Cir. 1995) 105
Kojevnikova v. Reno, 173 F.3d 844 (2d Cir. 1999) 36, 44, 96
Kokar v. Gonzales, 478 F.3d 803 (7th Cir. 2007) 230
Konstantinova v. INS, 195 F.3d 528 (9th Cir. 1999) 173
Korablina v. INS, 158 F.3d 1038 (9th Cir. 1998) 30, 33, 44, 98
Kossov v. INS, 132 F.3d 405 (7th Cir. 1998) 160
Kotasz v. INS, 31 F.3d 847 (9th Cir. 1994) 93
Koudriachova v. Gonzales, 490 F.3d 255 (2d Cir. 2007) 49
Kourski v. Ashcroft, 355 F.3d 1038 (7th Cir. 2004) 79, 82, 86
Kovac v. INS, 407 F.2d 102 (9th Cir. 1969) 35
Koval v. Gonzales, 418 F.3d 798 (7th Cir. 2005) 182, 183, 184
Kozulin v. INS, 218 F.3d 1112 (9th Cir. 2000) 77
Krastev v. INS, 292 F.3d 1268 (10th Cir. 2002) 100
Kratchmarov v. Heston, 172 F.3d 551 (8th Cir. 1999) 31, 94
Krisman v. Gonzales, 199 Fed. Appx. 299 (4th Cir. 2006) 122, 242
Krotova v. Gonzales, 416 F.3d 1080 (9th Cir. 2005) 33, 73
Krouchevski v. Ashcroft, 344 F.3d 670 (7th Cir. 2003) 83, 137

Lagandaon v. Ashcroft, 383 F.3d 983 (9th Cir. 2004) 346
La Guerre v. Reno, 164 F.3d 1035 (7th Cir. 1998) 166
Laipenieks v. INS, 750 F.2d 1427 (9th Cir. 1985) 112
Lal v. INS, 255 F.3d 998, *amended on reh'g,* 268 F.3d 1148 (9th Cir. 2001) 39, 101
Landon v. Plasencia, 459 U.S. 21 (1982) 166
Lara-Ruiz v. INS, 241 F.3d 934 (7th Cir. 2001) 351
Lata v. INS, 204 F.3d 1241 (9th Cir. 2000) 132
Latu v. Ashcroft, 375 F.3d 1012 (10th Cir. 2004) 351
Lavira v. U.S. Attorney Gen., 478 F.3d 158 (3d Cir. 2007) 68, 106, 263
Lee v. Ashcroft, 368 F.3d 218 (3d Cir. 2004) 107, 134
Leocal v. Ashcroft, 543 U.S. 1, 125 S.Ct. 377 (2004) 107
Leva-Montalvo v. INS, 173 F.3d 749 (9th Cir. 1999) 53
Lewis v. U.S. Dep't of Justice, 34 Fed. Appx. 774 (Fed. Cir. 2002) 173
Lhanzom v. Gonzales, 430 F.3d 847 (7th Cir. 2005) 44
Li v. Ashcroft, 356 F.3d 1153 (9th Cir. 2004) 56, 57
Li v. Gonzales, 405 F.3d 171 (4th Cir. 2005) 35, 56
Li v. INS, 92 F.3d 985 (9th Cir. 1996) 51, 91
Li v. U.S. Attorney Gen., 400 F.3d 157 (3d Cir. 2005) 90
Lim v. INS, 224 F.3d 929 (9th Cir. 2000) 26, 78, 79, 89, 90, 92
Lin v. Ashcroft, 377 F.3d 1014 (9th Cir. 2004) 57, 166, 191
Lin v. Gonzales, 190 Fed. Appx. 301 (4th Cir. 2006) 122, 242
Lin v. Gonzales, 2007 U.S. App. LEXIS 3041 (2d Cir. 2007) 68
Lin v. U.S. Dep't of Justice, 494 F.3d 296 (2d Cir. 2007) 55, 56
Liti v. Gonzales, 411 F.3d 631 (6th Cir. 2005) 100
Li Yong Zheng v. U.S. Dep't of Justice, 416 F.3d 129 (2d Cir. 2005) 235
Lopez v. Ashcroft, 366 F.3d 799 (9th Cir. 2004) 138
Lopez v. Gonzales, 127 S. Ct. 625 (2006) 107
Lopez-Gomez v. Ashcroft, 263 F.3d 442 (5th Cir. 2001) 74, 99, 107
Lopez-Mendoza; INS v., 468 U.S. 1032 (1984) 165, 168
Lopez-Soto v. Ashcroft, 383 F.3d 228 (4th Cir. 2004) 49, 268
Lopez-Zeron v. U.S. Dep't of Justice, 8 F.3d 636 (8th Cir. 1993) 54
Louis-Martin v. Ridge, 322 F. Supp. 2d 556 (M.D. Pa. 2004) 281
Lu v. Ashcroft, 2004 U.S. App. LEXIS 3003 (No. 02-74281, 9th Cir. 2004) 53
Lukowski v. INS, 279 F.3d 633 (8th Cir. 2002) 351
Lukwago v. Ashcroft, 329 F.3d 157 (3d Cir. 2003) 48, 49, 65, 71, 78, 135, 136
Lusingo v. Gonzales, 420 F.3d 193 (3d Cir. 2005) 64
Lwin v. INS, 144 F.3d 505 (7th Cir. 1998) 48, 49, 50
Ma v. Ashcroft, 361 F.3d 553 (9th Cir. 2004) 55, 56
M.A. v. INS, 899 F.2d 304 (4th Cir. 1990) 30, 71, 76
Mabasa v. Gonzales, 455 F.3d 740 (7th Cir. 2006) 125, 133
Machado v. Ashcroft, No. Cs-02-0066-FVS, Preliminary Injunction Order
 (E.D. Wash., Mar. 5, 2002) 169, 191, 213
Maharaj v. Gonzales, 450 F.3d 961 (9th Cir. 2006) (en banc) 126
Maini v. INS, 212 F.3d 1167 (9th Cir. 2000) 44, 73
Makadji v. Gonzales, 470 F.3d 450 (2d Cir. 2006) 128
Makonnen v. INS, 44 F.3d 1378 (8th Cir. 1995) 78
Maldonado v. U.S. Attorney Gen., 188 Fed. Appx. 101 (3d Cir. 2006) 66
Maldonado-Cruz v. INS, 883 F.2d 788 (9th Cir. 1990) 54
Malty v. Ashcroft, 381 F.3d 942 (9th Cir. 2004) 234
Malvoisin v. INS, 268 F.3d 74 (2d Cir. 2001) 243

Mandycz; United States v., 199 F. Supp. 2d 671 (D. Mich. 2002) 177
Manimbao v. Ashcroft, 329 F.3d 655 (9th Cir. 2003) 138
Mansour v. INS, 230 F.3d 902 (7th Cir. 2000) 273, 275
Mapouya v. Gonzales, 487 F.3d 396 (6th Cir. 2007) 167, 274
Margalli-Olvera v. INS, 43 F.3d 345 (8th Cir. 1994) 16
Margos v. Gonzales, 443 F.3d 593 (7th Cir. 2006) 96, 98
Marshi, Matter of, A26 980 386 (AG 2004) 125, 182
Martinez-de Bojorquez v. Ashcroft, 365 F.3d 800 (9th Cir. 2004) 231
Martinez-Ruiz v. Gonzales, 479 F.3d 762 (11th Cir. 2007) 35
Martinez-Serrano v. INS, 94 F.3d 1256 (9th Cir. 1996) 243
Martins v. INS, 972 F.2d 657 (5th Cir. 1992) 105
Mashiri v. Ashcroft, 383 F.3d 1112 (9th Cir. 2004) 74
Mathews v. Eldridge, 424 U.S. 319 (1976) 177
Matter of. *See name of real party*
Mazariegos v. U.S. Attorney Gen., 241 F.3d 1320 (11th Cir. 2001) 99
McAllister v. U.S. Attorney Gen., 444 F.3d 178 (3d Cir. 2006) 115
McDaniel v. INS, 142 F. Supp. 2d 219 (D. Conn. 2001) 270
McMullen v. INS, 788 F.2d 591 (9th Cir. 1986) 109, 110
McNary v. Haitian Refugee Center, Inc., 498 U.S. 479 (1991) 15
Mead Corp.; United States v., 533 U.S. 218 (2001) 240
Meidiansyah v. U.S. Attorney Gen., 468 F.3d 763 (11th Cir. 2006) 144
Mejia v. Ashcroft, 298 F.3d 873 (9th Cir. 2002) 233
Mendoza v. U.S. Attorney Gen., 327 F.3d 1283 (11th Cir. 2003) 229
Mengistu v. Ashcroft, 355 F.3d 1044 (7th Cir. 2004) 234, 245
Menjivar v. Gonzales, 416 F.3d 918 (8th Cir. 2005) 72, 267
Mezvrishvili v. U.S. Attorney Gen., 467 F.3d 1292 (11th Cir. 2006) 46
Mgoian v. INS, 184 F.3d 1029 (9th Cir. 1999) 50, 91, 136, 138
Michel v. INS, 206 F.3d 253 (2d Cir. 2000) 240
Mikhael v. INS, 115 F.3d 299 (5th Cir. 1997) 31
Miranda v. Arizona, 384 U.S. 436 (1966) 168
Miranda-Alvarado v. Gonzales, 449 F.3d 915 (9th Cir. 2006) 110, 111
Mirzoyan v. Gonzales, 457 F.3d 217 (2d Cir. 2006) 35
Mitreva v. Gonzales, 417 F.3d 761 (7th Cir. 2005) 40, 93
Mohamed v. Gonzales, 312 Fed. Appx. 126 (9th Cir. 2005) 305
Mohammed v. Gonzales, 400 F.3d 785 (9th Cir. 2005) 34, 39, 49, 61, 63
Mohammed v. Reno, 309 F.3d 95 (2d Cir. 2002) 245
Mohideen v. Gonzales, 416 F.3d 567 (7th Cir. 2005) 41
Molina v. INS, 170 F.3d 1247 (9th Cir. 1999) 54
Montecino v. INS, 915 F.2d 518 (9th Cir. 1990) 52
Montilla v. INS, 926 F.2d 162 (2d Cir. 1991) 165
Mora v. Smith, No. C97-1758WD (W.D. Wash., Dec. 17, 1997) 196
Morales v. Gonzales, 472 F.3d 689 (9th Cir. 2007) 134
Morales v. INS, 208 F.3d 323 (1st Cir. 2000) 136, 172
Morales-Izquierdo v. Gonzales, 477 F.3d 691 (9th Cir. 2007) 196
Morales-Morales v. Ashcroft, 384 F.3d 418 (7th Cir. 2004) 346
Moreno-Bravo v. Gonzales, 463 F.3d 253 (2d Cir. 2006) 242
Moshud v. Blackmun, 68 Fed. Appx. 328 (3d Cir. 2003) 267
Mosquera-Perez v. INS, 3 F.3d 553 (1st Cir. 1993) 105
Mostafa v. Ashcroft, 395 F.3d 622 (6th Cir. 2005) 274
Mouawad v. Gonzales, 479 F.3d 589 (8th Cir. 2007) 267, 268

Muhanna v. Gonzales, 399 F.3d 582 (3d Cir. 2005) 144
Mukamusoni v. Ashcroft, 390 F.3d 110 (1st Cir. 2004) 69, 123
Mulanga v. Ashcroft, 349 F.3d 123 (3d Cir. 2003) 53, 80, 82, 87
Murray v. The Charming Betsy, 6 U.S. (2 Cranch) 64 (1804) 2
Mussie v. INS, 172 F.3d 329 (4th Cir. 1999) 128
Mu Xiang Lin v. U.S. Dep't of Justice, 432 F.3d 156 (2d Cir. 2005) 274
Myslymi v. Gonzales, 216 Fed. Appx. 571 (7th Cir. 2007) 182
Nabulwala v. Gonzales, 479 F.3d 972 (8th Cir. 2007) 66
Nahrvani v. Gonzales, 399 F.3d 1148 (9th Cir. 2005) 128
Naizgi v. Gonzales, 455 F.3d 484 (4th Cir. 2006) 100
Nakibuka v. Gonzales, 421 F.3d 473 (7th Cir. 2005) 92
Nakimbugwe v. Gonzales, 475 F.3d 281 (5th Cir. 2007) 121, 133
Namo v. Gonzales, 401 F.3d 453 (6th Cir. 2005) 264
Nasir v. INS, 122 F.3d 484 (7th Cir. 1997) 136, 137
Navas v. INS, 217 F.3d 646 (9th Cir. 2000) 36, 40
Nazarova v. INS, 171 F.3d 478 (7th Cir. 1998) 180
Nee Hao Wong v. INS, 550 F.2d 521 (9th Cir. 1977) 176, 177
Nelson v. INS, 232 F.3d 258 (1st Cir. 2000) 37, 61, 176
Ngarurih v. Ashcroft, 371 F.3d 182 (4th Cir. 2004) 245
Ngure v. Ashcroft, 367 F.3d 975 (8th Cir. 2004) 33, 45, 75, 76, 93, 228
Niam v. Ashcroft, 354 F.3d 652 (7th Cir. 2004) 85, 132, 183
Niang v. Gonzales, 422 F.3d 1187 (10th Cir. 2005) 49, 50, 61, 63, 271, 273
Niang v. Gonzales, 492 F.3d 505 (4th Cir. 2007) 26
Nibagwire v. Gonzales, 450 F.3d 153 (4th Cir. 2006) 180
North Jersey Media Group, Inc. v. Ashcroft, 308 F.3d 198 (3d Cir. 2002) 163
Nreka v. U.S. Attorney Gen., 408 F.3d 1361 (11th Cir. 2005) 244
Ntangsi v. Gonzales, 475 F.3d 1007 (8th Cir. 2007) 254
Nugent v. Ashcroft, 367 F.3d 162 (3d Cir. 2004) 107
Nwakanma v. Ashcroft, 352 F.3d 325 (6th Cir. 2004) 244
Nwaokolo v. Ashcroft, 314 F.3d 303 (7th Cir. 2002) 265
Ochoa v. Gonzales, 406 F.3d 1166 (9th Cir. 2005) 268
Ofosu v. McElroy, 933 F. Supp. 237 (S.D.N.Y. 1995) 111
Oh v. Gonzales, 406 F.3d 611 (9th Cir. 2005) 226
Olarte v. INS, 1995 U.S. App. LEXIS 7796 (9th Cir. 1995) 48
Oliva-Muralles v. Ashcroft, 328 F.3d 25 (1st Cir. 2003) 40
Ontunez-Tursios v. Ashcroft, 303 F.3d 341 (5th Cir. 2002) 40, 49, 267, 268
Orantes-Hernandez v. Gonzales, 504 F. Supp. 2d 825 (C.D. Cal. 2007) 321
Orantes-Hernandez v. Thornburgh, 919 F.2d 549 (9th Cir. 1990) 169
Orhorhaghe v. INS, 38 F.3d 488 (9th Cir. 1994) 165
Ornelas-Chavez v. Gonzales, 458 F.3d 1052 (9th Cir. 2006) 268
Ornelas v. Ruiz, 161 U.S. 502 (1896) 110
Osorio v. INS, 18 F.3d 1017 (2d Cir. 1994) 41, 52
Osorio v. INS, 99 F.3d 928 (9th Cir. 1996) 83, 138
Ouda v. INS, 324 F.3d 445 (6th Cir. 2003) 29, 35
Ozdemir v. INS, 46 F.3d 6 (5th Cir. 1994) 76
Palavra v. INS, 287 F.3d 690 (8th Cir. 2002) 94, 135
Pan v. Gonzales, 449 F.3d 408 (2d Cir. 2006) 56
The Paquete Habana, 175 U.S. 677 (1900) 7, 8
Paramasamy v. Ashcroft, 295 F.3d 1047 (9th Cir. 2002) 81, 82
Paripovic v. Gonzales, 418 F.3d 240 (3d Cir. 2005) 29

Pascual-Garcia v. Ashcroft, 73 Fed. Appx. 232 (9th Cir. 2003) 265
Pasha v. Gonzales, 433 F.3d 530 (7th Cir. 2005) 183
Pasquini v. Morris, 700 F.2d 658 (11th Cir. 1983) 15
Pavlovich v. Gonzales, 476 F.3d 613 (8th Cir. 2007) 161
Pavlyk v. Gonzales, 469 F.3d 1082 (7th Cir. 2006) 52
Pedro-Mateo v. INS, 224 F.3d 1147 (9th Cir. 2000) 1, 72
People's Mojahedin Org. of Iran v. U.S. Dep't of State, 182 F.3d 17 (DC Cir. 1999) 116
Percheman; United States v., 32 U.S. 51 (1833) 9, 260
Perez-Funez v. District Director, INS, 619 F. Supp. 656 (1985) 195
Perez-Quiroz v. Gonzales, 2007 U.S. App. LEXIS 4515 (9th Cir. 2007) 165
Perinpanathan v. INS, 310 F.3d 594 (8th Cir. 2002) 266, 271, 273, 275
Perkovic v. INS, 33 F.3d 615 (6th Cir. 1994) 47, 76
Phommasoukha v. Gonzales, 408 F.3d 1011 (8th Cir. 2005) 35, 38
Pickering v. Gonzales, 454 F.3d 525 (6th Cir. 2006) 108
Pitcherskaia v. INS, 118 F.3d 641 (9th Cir 1997) 36, 37, 67
Podio v. INS, 153 F.3d 506 (7th Cir. 1999) 172
Ponce-Leiva v. Ashcroft, 331 F.3d 369 (3d Cir. 2003) 169
Ponnapula v. Ashcroft, 373 F.3d 480 (3d Cir. 2004) 343
Pop v. INS, 270 F.3d 527 (7th Cir. 2001) 45
Popova v. INS, 273 F.3d 1251 (9th Cir. 2001) 15, 40, 44
Prasad v. INS, 47 F.3d 336 (9th Cir. 1995) 76
Prichard-Ciriza v. INS, 978 F.2d 219 (5th Cir. 1992) 169
Pronsivakulchai v. Gonzales, 461 F.3d 903 (7th Cir. 2006) 171
Purveegiin v. Gonzales, 448 F.3d 684 (3d Cir. 2006) 228
Qi Hang Guo v. U.S. Dep't of Justice, 422 F.3d 61 (2d Cir. 2005) 287
Qu v. Gonzales, 399 F.3d 1195 (9th Cir. 2005) 56
Qui v. Ashcroft, 329 F.3d 140 (2d Cir. 2003) 56, 81, 136, 138
Quomsieh v. Gonzales, 479 F.3d 602 (8th Cir. 2007) 45
Raffington v. Cangemi, 399 F.3d 900 (8th Cir. 2005) 68
Raffington v. INS, 340 F.3d 720 (8th Cir. 2003) 51
Ramadam v. Gonzales, 479 F.3d 646 (9th Cir. 2007) (en banc) 125, 133
Ramirez v. Sonchik, No. CIV 02-920 (D. Ariz. July 8, 2002) 285, 353
Ramirez-Peyro v. Gonzales, 477 F.3d 637 (8th Cir. 2007) 272, 283
Ramos v. Ashcroft, 371 F.3d 948 (7th Cir. 2004) 164
Ramsameachire v. Ashcroft, 357 F.3d 169 (2d Cir. 2004) 272, 305
Ravindran v. INS, 976 F.2d 754 (1st Cir. 1992) 51, 94
Recinos de Leon v. Gonzales, 400 F.3d 1185 (9th Cir. 2005) 167
Refahiyat v. INS, 29 F.3d 553 (10th Cir. 1994) 46
Reno v. *See name of opposing party*
Restrepo v. Winfrey, 162 Fed. Appx. 311 (5th Cir. 2006) 122, 134, 242
Reyes-Guerrero v. INS, 192 F.3d 1241 (9th Cir. 1999) 79
Rife v. Ashcroft, 374 F.3d 606 (8th Cir. 2004) 127, 245
Rioja v. Ashcroft, 317 F.3d 514 (5th Cir. 2003) 230
Rios v. Ashcroft, 287 F.3d 895 (9th Cir. 2002) 36, 92, 95
Rios-Berrios v. INS, 776 F.2d 859 (9th Cir. 1985) 168
Rivas-Martinez v. INS, 997 F.2d 1143 (5th Cir. 1993) 72
Rivera-Castaneda v. INS, 6 Fed. Appx. 604 (9th Cir. 2001) 48
Rivera-Moreno v. INS, 213 F.3d 481 (9th Cir. 2000) 54
Rizal v. Gonzales, 442 F.3d 84 (2d Cir. 2006) 46
Rodriguez-Lariz v. INS, 282 F.3d 1218 (9th Cir. 2002) 236

Rodriguez-Matamoros v. INS, 86 F.3d 158 (9th Cir. 1996) 91
Romanishyn v. Gonzales, 455 F.3d 175 (3d Cir. 2006) 248, 254
Rotimi v. Gonzales, 473 F.3d 55 (2d Cir. 2007) 240
Rreshpja v. Gonzales, 420 F.3d 551 (6th Cir. 2005) 51
Rusu v. INS, 296 F.3d 316 (4th Cir. 2002) 164
Safaie v. INS, 25 F.3d 636 (8th Cir. 1994) 49, 51, 63
Sagarminaga v. INS, 113 F.3d 1247 (10th Cir. 1997) 54
Sagaydak v. Ashcroft, 405 F.3d 1035 (9th Cir. 2005) 133
Sahi v. Gonzales, 416 F.3d 587 (7th Cir. 2005) 32, 33
Saidane v. INS, 129 F.3d 1063 (9th Cir. 1997) 172, 182, 184
St. Cyr; INS v., 533 U.S. 289 (2001) 122, 132, 343
St. John v. Ashcroft, 43 Fed. Appx. 281 (10th Cir. 2002) 107
Salaam v. INS, 229 F.3d 1234 (9th Cir. 2000) 86
Salazar v. Ashcroft, 359 F.3d 45 (1st Cir. 2004) 27, 126, 127
Sale v. Haitian Centers Council, Inc., 509 U.S. 155 (1993) 141, 278
Saleh v. INS, 962 F.2d 234 (2d Cir. 1992) 45, 76
Salkeld v. Gonzales, 420 F.3d 804 (8th Cir. 2005) 66
Sall v. Gonzales, 437 F.3d 229 (2d Cir. 2006) 127
Salta v. INS, 314 F.3d 1076 (9th Cir. 2002) 180
Samedov v. Gonzales, 422 F.3d 704 (8th Cir. 2005) 31
Sanchez v. INS, 707 F.2d 1523 (D.C. Cir. 1983) 344
Sanchez-Trujillo v. INS, 801 F.2d 1571 (9th Cir. 1986) 48, 49, 65
Sangha v. INS, 103 F.3d 1482 (9th Cir. 1997) 53, 80, 90
Sapoundjiev v. Ashcroft, 376 F.3d 727 (7th Cir. 2004) 244
Secaida-Rosales v. INS, 331 F.3d 297 (2d Cir. 2003) 82, 88, 136, 137
Selami v. Gonzales, 423 F.3d 621 (6th Cir. 2005) 144
Selgeka v. INS, 184 F.3d 337 (4th Cir. 1999) 166
Senathirajah v. INS, 157 F.3d 210 (3d Cir. 1998) 76, 80, 83, 131
Setiadi v. Gonzales, 437 F.3d 710 (8th Cir. 2006) 99
Shah v. INS, 220 F3d 1062 (9th Cir. 2000) 85, 86
Shahinaj v. Gonzales, 481 F.3d 1027 (8th Cir. 2007) 66, 132, 167
Shan Liao v. U.S. Dep't of Justice, 293 F.3d 61 (2d Cir. 2002) 36, 57, 88, 135, 136
Sharif v. INS, 87 F.3d 932 (7th Cir. 1996) 35, 53, 63
Sharma v. INS, 89 F.3d 545 (9th Cir. 1996) 180
Shaughnessy v. Mezei, 345 U.S. 206 (1953) 166
Shehu v. Gonzales, 443 F.3d 435 (5th Cir. 2006) 98
Shehu v. U.S. Attorney Gen., 482 F.3d 652 (3d Cir. 2007) 244
Shoafera v. INS, 228 F.3d 1070 (9th Cir. 2000) 34, 42, 47
Shou Yung Guo v. Gonzales, 463 F.3d 109 (2d Cir. 2006) 58
Silva v. Gonzales, 455 F.3d 26 (1st Cir. 2006) 134
Silva-Rengifo v. U.S. Attorney Gen., 473 F.3d 58 (3d Cir. 2007) 267
Simo v. Gonzales, 445 F.3d 7 (1st Cir. 2006) 305, 312
Singh v. Ashcroft, 362 F.3d 1164 (9th Cir. 2003) 230
Singh v. Ashcroft, 367 F.3d 1139 (9th Cir. 2004) 171
Singh v. Ashcroft, 375 F.3d 1007 (10th Cir. 2004) 245
Singh v. Gonzales, 432 F.3d 533 (3d Cir. 2006) 282
Singh v. Ilchert, 63 F.3d 1501 (9th Cir. 1995) 75, 76, 88, 138
Singh v. Ilchert, 69 F.3d 375 (9th Cir. 1995) 76, 88
Singh v. INS, 94 F.3d 1353 (9th Cir. 1996) 43
Singh v. INS, 134 F.3d 962 (9th Cir. 1998) 33, 37

© *2007 American Immigration Lawyers Association*

Singh v. INS, 213 F.3d 1050 (9th Cir. 2000) 179
Singh v. INS, 292 F.3d 1017 (9th Cir. 2002) 83
Singh v. Moschorak, 53 F.3d 1031 (9th Cir. 1995) 75
Singh-Kaur v. INS, 183 F.3d 1147 (9th Cir. 1999) 83, 137
Siong v. INS, 376 F.3d 1030 (9th Cir. 2004) 231
Sivaainkaran v. INS, 972 F.2d 161 (7th Cir. 1992) 95
Sivakaran v. Ashcroft, 368 F.3d 1028 (8th Cir. 2004) 272
Smriko v. Ashcroft, 387 F.3d 279 (3d Cir. 2004) 248, 255
Soadjede v. Ashcroft, 324 F.3d 830 (5th Cir. 2003) 228
Sotelo-Aquije v. Slattery, 17 F.3d 33 (2d Cir. 1994) 72
Spina v. Department of Homeland Sec., 70 F.3d 116 (2d Cir. 2006) 122, 134, 242
Sterkaj v. Gonzales, 439 F.3d 273 (6th Cir. 2006) 144
Stevic; INS v., 467 U.S. 407 (1984) 26
Stoyanov v. INS, 172 F.3d 731 (9th Cir. 1999) 84, 131, 166
Subhan v. Ashcroft, 383 F.3d 591 (7th Cir. 2004) 166
Sultani v. Gonzales, 455 F.3d 878 (8th Cir. 2006) 128
Sun v. U.S. Dep't of Justice, 421 F.3d 105 (2d Cir. 2005) 226
Tagaga v. INS, 228 F.3d 1030 (9th Cir. 2000) 76
Tamara-Gomez v. Gonzales, 447 F.3d 343 (5th Cir. 2006) 40, 104
Tamas-Mercea v. Reno, 222 F.3d 417 (7th Cir. 2000) 37
Taniguchi v. Schultz, 303 F.3d 950 (9th Cir. 2002) 351
Tapiero de Orjuela v. Gonzales, 423 F.3d 666 (7th Cir. 2005) 49
Tarubac v. INS, 182 F.3d 1114 (9th Cir. 1999) 36, 41, 52, 98
Tawadrus v. Ashcroft, 364 F.3d 1099 (9th Cir. 2004) 169
Tchoukhrova v. Gonzales, 404 F.3d 1181, *reh'g en banc denied,* 430 F.3d 1222
    (9th Cir. 2005), *vacated,* 127 S. Ct. 57 (2006) 50, 64
Tesfamichael v. Gonzales, 469 F.3d 109 (5th Cir. 2006) 29, 30, 245
Tewabe v. Gonzales, 446 F.3d 533 (4th Cir. 2006) 82
Thavendran v. Gonzales, 211 Fed. Appx. 74 (2d Cir. 2007) 93
32 County Sovereignty Comm. v. U.S. Dep't of State, 292 F.3d 797 (D.C. Cir. 2002) 116
Thomas v. Gonzales, 409 F.3d 1177 (9th Cir. 2005) (en banc), *vacated,* 547 U.S. 183
    (2006) 49, 50, 54, 66, 166, 169, 191
Tian Ming Lin v. Gonzales, 473 F.3d 48 (2d Cir. 2007) 58
Tilley v. Chertoff, 144 Fed. Appx. 536 (6th Cir. 2005) 122, 134, 242
Torres v. Ridge, No. C04-525JCC (W.D. Wash. Apr. 13, 2004) 302
Toure v. U.S. Attorney Gen., 443 F.3d 310 (3d Cir. 2006) 87
Toussaint v. Gonzales, 455 F.3d 409 (3d Cir. 2006) 51
Tsegay v. Ashcroft, 386 F.3d 1347 (10th Cir. 2004) 228
Tu Kai Yang v. Gonzales, 427 F.3d 1117 (8th Cir. 2005) 99
Tun v. Gonzales, 485 F.3d 1014 (8th Cir. 2005) 167, 171, 182, 183
Turcios v. INS, 821 F.2d 1396 (9th Cir. 1987) 136
Umanzor-Alvarado v INS, 896 F.2d 14 (1st Cir. 1990) 54
Un v. Gonzales, 415 F.3d 205 (1st Cir. 2005) 35, 38
United States v. *See name of opposing party*
Uritsky v. Ridge, 286 F. Supp. 2d 842 (E.D. Mich. 2003) 217
Uwais v. Gonzales, 478 F.3d 513 (2d Cir. 2007) 41, 53
Uwase v. Ashcroft, 349 F.3d 1039 (7th Cir. 2003) 82, 137
Valansi v. Ashcroft, 278 F.3d 203 (3d Cir. 2002) 107
Valdez-Sanchez v. Gonzales, 485 F.3d 1084 (10th Cir. 2007) 195
Vang v. INS, 146 F.3d 1114 (9th Cir. 1998) 128

Varela v. INS, 204 F.3d 1237 (9th Cir. 2000) 236
Vargas-Garcia v. INS, 287 F.3d 882 (9th Cir. 2002) 227, 229
Vargas-Sarmiento v. United States Dep't of Justice, 448 F.3d 149 (2d Cir. 2006) 240
Vasha v. Gonzales, 410 F.3d 863 (6th Cir. 2005) 167
Vasile v. Gonzales, 417 F.3d 766 (7th Cir. 2005) 134
Velarde v. INS, 140 F.3d 1305 (9th Cir. 1998) 136
Velasco v. INS, 87 Fed. Appx. 35, 2004 WL 78208 (9th Cir. 2004) 174
Velasquez-Gabriel v. Crocetti, 263 F.3d 102 (4th Cir. 2001) 195
Velazquez v. Ashcroft, 103 Fed. Appx. 142 (9th Cir. 2004) 136
Ventura v. INS, 264 F.3d 1150 (9th Cir. 2001) 54, 90, 91
Ventura; INS v., 537 U.S. 12 (2002) 91
Vera-Valera v. INS, 147 F.3d 1036 (9th Cir. 1998) 53
Vladimirova v. Ashcroft, 377 F.3d 690 (7th Cir. 2004) 35, 99
Voci v. Gonzales, 409 F.3d 607 (3d Cir. 2005) 36
Vongsakdy v. INS, 171 F.3d 1203 (9th Cir. 1999) 39, 79, 101
Vujisic v. INS, 224 F.3d 578 (7th Cir. 2000) 71, 95
Vukmirovic v. Ashcroft, 362 F.3d 1247 (9th Cir. 2004) 112, 277
Vumi v. Gonzales, 502 F.3d 150 (2d Cir. 2007) 49
Walters v. Ashcroft, 198 Fed. Appx. 78 (2d Cir. 2006) 122, 134, 242
Wang v. Ashcroft, 341 F.3d 1015 (9th Cir. 2003) 26, 34, 57, 82
Wang v. Gonzales, 152 Fed. Appx. 761 (11th Cir. 2005) 56, 57, 66
Wangchuck v. DHS, 448 F.3d 524 (2d Cir. 2006) 28
Weinberger v. Rossi, 456 U.S. 25 (1982) 2
Weng v. U.S. Attorney Gen., 287 F.3d 1335 (11th Cir. 2002) 245
Wiransane v. Ashcroft, 366 F.3d 889 (10th Cir. 2004) 78, 86, 92, 138
Woodby v. INS, 385 U.S. 276 (1966) 162
Xiao v. Bd. of Immigration Appeals, 165 Fed. Appx. 911 (2d Cir. 2006) 264
Xiao Ji Chen v. U.S. Dep't of Justice, 434 F.3d 144 (2d Cir. 2006) 133–34
Xie v. INS, 434 F.3d 136 (2d Cir. 2006) 111
Xiong v. INS, 173 F.3d 601 (7th Cir. 1999) 107
Yadegar-Sargis v. INS, 297 F.3d 596 (7th Cir. 2002) 63
Yakovenko v. Gonzales, 477 F.3d 631 (8th Cir. 2007) 99, 133
Yan v. Gonzales, 438 F.3d 1249 (10th Cir. 2006) 46
Yang v. Gonzales, 427 F.3d 1117 (8th Cir. 2005) 57, 74, 183, 233
Yang v. McElroy, 277 F.3d 158 (2d Cir. 2002) 95
Yang v. U.S. Attorney Gen., 418 F.3d 1198 (11th Cir. 2005) 57
Yepes-Prado v. INS, 10 F.3d 1363 (9th Cir. 1993) 16, 131
Yong Hao Chen v. INS, 195 F.3d 198 (4th Cir. 1999) 93
Yuanliang Liu v. U.S. Dep't of Justice, 455 F.3d 106 (2d Cir. 2006) 160
Yuk v. Ashcroft, 355 F.3d 1222 (10th Cir. 2004) 229
Zadvydas v. Davis, 533 U.S. 678 (2001) 212, 215
Zafar v. U.S. Attorney Gen., 461 F.3d 1357 (11th Cir. 2006) 243
Zahedi v. INS, 222 F.3d 1157 (9th Cir. 2000) 76, 87
Zahren v. Gonzales, 487 F.3d 1039 (7th Cir. 2007) 161
Zarate-Martinez; United States v., 133 F.3d 1194 (9th Cir. 1998) 173
Zavala v. Ridge, 310 F. Supp. 2d 1071 (N.D. Calif. 2004) 217
Zavala-Bonilla v. INS, 730 F.2d 562 (9th Cir. 1984) 83
Zehatye v. Gonzales, 453 F.3d 1182 (9th Cir. 2006) 71
Zewdie v. Ashcroft, 381 F.3d 804 (8th Cir. 2004) 275
Zhang v. Gonzales, 434 F.3d 993 (7th Cir. 2006) 56

© *2007 American Immigration Lawyers Association*

Zhang v. Reno, 27 F. Supp. 2d 476 (S.D.N.Y. 1998) 55
Zhang v. U.S. Dep't of Justice, 362 F.3d 155 (2d Cir. 2004) 228
Zhao v. U.S. Dep't of Justice, 265 F.3d 83 (2d Cir. 2001) 57
Zheng v. Ashcroft, 332 F.3d 1186 (9th Cir. 2003) 267, 268, 276
Zheng v. Gonzales, 409 F.3d 804 (7th Cir. 2005) 56
Zheng v. Gonzales, 160 Fed. Appx. 501 (7th Cir. 2005) 305, 312
Zheng v. U.S. Attorney Gen., 451 F.3d 1287 (11th Cir. 2006) 37
Zhen Nan Lin v. U.S. Dep't of Justice, 459 F.3d 255 (2d Cir. 2006) 174
Zhu v. Ashcroft, 382 F.3d 521 (5th Cir. 2004) 172
Zubeda v. Ashcroft, 333 F.3d 463 (3d Cir. 2003) 263, 272

State Court Decisions

Thomas J., In re, 811 A.2d 310 (Md. 2002) 192
Zaim R., In re, 13 Misc.3d 180, 822 N.Y.S.2d 368 (N.Y. Fam. Ct. 2006) 178

Decisions of Foreign Tribunals

A.A. v. Switzerland, Comm. No. 268/2005, CAT/C/38/D/268/2005 (May 11, 2007) 271, 273
Aemei v. Switzerland, Comm. No. 34/1995, Supp. No. 44 (1997) 273, 275
Alan v. Switzerland, Comm. No. 21/1995, Supp. No. 44 (1996) 272, 273, 275
C.T. and K.M. v. Sweden, Comm. No. 279/2005, CAT/C/37/D/279/2005 (Dec. 7, 2006) 274
Dar v. Norway, Comm. No. 249/2004, CAT/C/38/D/249/2004 (May 16, 2007) 275
El Rgeig v. Switzerland, Comm. No. 280/2005, CAT/C/37/D/280/2005 (Nov. 30, 2006) 275
Elmi v. Australia, Comm. No. 120/1998, CAT/C/22/D/120/1998 (May 25, 1998) 266, 275
G.R.B. v. Sweden, Comm. No. 83/1997, CAT/C/20/D/83/1997 (1997) 267
Ireland v. United Kingdom, 2 Eur. Ct. H.R. 25 (1978) 264
Kioski v. Sweden, Comm. No. 41/1996 (1996) 264, 272, 273, 274
Tala v. Sweden, Comm. No. 43/1996, Supp. No. 44 (1996) 273
Tapia Paez v. Sweden, Comm. No. 39/1996, Supp. No. 44 (1997) 275, 276
Tebourski v. France, Comm. No. 300/2006, CAT/C/38/D/300/2006 (May 11, 2006) 276
V.L. v. Switzerland, Comm. No. 262/2005, CAT/C/37/D/262/2005 (Jan. 22, 2007) 273

TABLE OF ADMINISTRATIVE DECISIONS (BIA, IJ, AG)

___, Matter of, A43 163 062 (IJ Oct. 3, 2000) (Florence, AZ) 107
___, Matter of, A71 498 940 (IJ Oct. 31, 1995) (New York, NY) 50, 67
___, Matter of, A76 512 001 (IJ Oct. 18, 2000) 50, 61, 74
___, Matter of, A94 097 292 (BIA, June 21, 2000) 143
___, Matter of, [file no. redacted] (BIA Aug. 8, 2007) 124
___, Matter of, (IJ Dec. 20, 2000) (Baltimore, MD) 33, 50, 67
A–A–, Matter of, 22 I&N Dec. 140 (BIA 1998) 181
A– and Z–, Matter of, A72 190 893, A72 793 219 (IJ Dec. 20, 1994) 62
Abu, Matter of, A29-499-143 (IJ Dec. Feb. 19, 1997) 7
Acosta, Matter of, 19 I&N Dec. 211 (BIA 1985) 16, 33, 48, 49, 51, 70, 79
A–E–M–, Matter of, 21 I&N Dec. 1157 (BIA 1998) 7, 33, 37, 74, 91, 92
A–G–, Matter of, 19 I&N Dec. 502 (BIA 1987) 71
A–G–F–F–, Matter of, [number not provided] (IJ July 9, 2004) (New York, NY) 66, 67
A–H–, Matter of, 23 I&N Dec. 774 (AG 2005) 102, 111
A–K–, Matter of, 24 I&N Dec. 275 (BIA 2007) 60, 91
Ali, Matter of, 21 I&N Dec. 1058 (BIA 1997) 180
Alvarado-Alvino, Matter of, 22 I&N Dec. 718 (BIA 1999) 107
Amaya-Castro, Matter of, 21 I&N Dec. 583 (BIA 1996) 178
A–M–E– & J–G–U–, Matter of, 24 I&N Dec. 69 (BIA 2007) 49
A–M–L–, Matter of, [number not provided] (IJ Nov. 21, 2001) (Phoenix, AZ) 50
A–N–, Matter of, A73 603 840 (IJ Dec. 22, 2000) 62
A–N– & R–M–N–, Matter of, 22 I&N Dec. 953 (BIA 1999) 234
Andazola, Matter of, 23 I&N Dec. 319 (BIA 2002) 345
Annang, Matter of, 14 I&N Dec. 502 (BIA 1973) 101, 187
Anselmo, Matter of, 20 I&N Dec. 25 (BIA 1989) 16, 17
A–P–, Matter of, 21 I&N Dec. 468 (BIA 1999) 165
Arguelles-Campos, Matter of, 22 I&N Dec. 811 (BIA 1999) 347
Artigas, Matter of, 23 I&N Dec. 99 (BIA 2001) 341
A–S–, Matter of, 21 I&N Dec. 1106 (BIA 1998) 81, 131
A–T–, Matter of, 24 I&N Dec. 296 (BIA 2007) 39, 61
Ayala-Arevalo, Matter of, 22 I&N Dec. 398 (BIA 1998) 351
B–, Matter of, 20 I&N Dec. 427 (BIA 1991) 109
B–, Matter of, 21 I&N Dec. 66 (BIA 1995) 82, 104, 131
Ballester-Garcia, Matter of, 17 I&N Dec. 592 (1980) 110
B–A–S–, Matter of, 22 I&N Dec. 57 (1998) 179
B–B–, Matter of, 22 I&N Dec. 309 (BIA 1998) 88
B–F–O–, Matter of, A78 677 043 (BIA Nov. 6, 2001) 101
Blancas-Lara, Matter of, 23 I&N Dec. 458 (BIA 2002) 343
Boromand, Matter of, 17 I&N Dec. 450 (BIA 1980) 81, 131
Burbano, Matter of, 20 I&N Dec. 872 (BIA 1994) 131
Buschini, Matter of, A98 064 379 (AAO 2006) 341, 342
C–, Matter of, 20 I&N Dec. 529 (BIA 1992) 105, 108
C–A–, Matter of, 23 I&N Dec. 951 (BIA 1985) 48, 51
C–A–L–, Matter of, 21 I&N Dec. 754 (BIA 1997) 40, 72, 79
C–C–, Matter of, 23 I&N Dec. 899 (BIA 2006) 58
Chen, Matter of, 20 I&N Dec. 16 (BIA 1989) 38, 39, 69, 101, 104
Cisneros-Gonzalez, Matter of, 23 I&N Dec. 668 (BIA 2001) 345
Cordova, Matter of, 22 I&N Dec. 966 (BIA 1999) 346
C–V–T–, Matter of, 22 I&N Dec. 7 (BIA 1998) 343
C–Y–Z–, Matter of, 21 I&N Dec. 915 (BIA 1997) 55, 56

D–, Matter of, 20 I&N Dec. 827 (BIA 1994) 182
D–, Matter of, 20 I&N Dec. 915 (BIA 1994) 342
Dass, Matter of, 20 I&N Dec. 120 (BIA 1989) 31, 85
Deanda-Romo, Matter of, 23 I&N Dec. 597 (BIA 2003) 344
Deportation Proceedings of Doherty, 12 Op. O.L.C. 1 (1988) 17
Devison, Matter of, 22 I&N Dec. 1362 (BIA 2000) 64, 108
D–J–, Matter of, 23 I&N Dec. 572 (AG 2003) 16, 217
D–L– & A–M–, Matter of, 20 I&N Dec. 409 (BIA 1991) 128
D–V–, Matter of, 21 I&N Dec. 77 (BIA 1993) 25, 30, 37, 38, 41, 45, 61
Enamorado, Matter of, A77 530 541 (IJ Nov. 22, 1999) (Harlingen, TX) 70
E–P–, Matter of, 21 I&N Dec. 860 (BIA 1997) 81, 92
E–S– and A–M–, Matter of, [file no. redacted] (IJ Mar. 20, 2003) (Phoenix, AZ) 70
Exilus, Matter of, 18 I&N Dec. 276 (BIA 1982) 77
Faronda-Blandon, Matter of, A74 979 517 (IJ June 15, 2001) 50
Fatoumata Toure, Matter of, A24 876 244 (BIA 1990) 28
Fedorenko, Matter of, 19 I&N Dec. 57 (BIA 1984) 112
Fefe, Matter of, 20 I&N Dec. 116 (BIA 1989) 80
Frentescu, Matter of, 18 I&N Dec. 244 (1982) 107, 108, 109
Fuentes, Matter of, 19 I&N Dec. 658 (BIA 1988) 40, 41, 51, 87
G–A–, Matter of, 23 I&N Dec. 366 (BIA 2002) 45, 78, 266, 275, 276, 277, 280
Garcia-Flores, Matter of, 17 I&N Dec. 325 (BIA 1980) 15, 165
Garcia-Hernandez, Matter of, 23 I&N Dec. 590 (BIA 2003) 345
G–C–L–, Matter of, 23 I&N Dec. 359 (BIA 2002) 55, 235
Gharadaghi, Matter of, 19 I&N Dec. 311 (BIA 1985) 103
G–N–C–, Matter of, 22 I&N Dec. 281 (BIA 1998) 146, 156, 157
Gomez-Gomez, Matter of, 23 I&N Dec. 522 (BIA 2002) 179
Gonzalez, Matter of, 19 I&N Dec. 682 (BIA 1988) 110
Gonzalez-Lopez, Matter of, 20 I&N Dec. 644 (BIA 1993) 181
Grijalva, Matter of, 19 I&N Dec. 713 (BIA 1988) 184
Grijalva, Matter of, 21 I&N Dec. 472 (BIA 1996) 180
Guevara, Matter of, 20 I&N Dec. 238 (1991) 168
Gutierrez, Matter of, 16 I&N Dec. 226 (BIA 1977) 170
Gutierrez-Lopez, Matter of, 21 I&N Dec. 479 (BIA 1996) 231, 233, 335
Gutierrez-Martinez, Matter of, A17 945 476 (BIA Mar. 9, 2004) 107
Guzman-Arguera, Matter of, 22 I&N Dec. 722 (BIA 1999) 179, 226
G–Y–R–, Matter of, 23 I&N Dec. 181 (BIA 2001) 178, 181, 232
H–, Matter of, 21 I&N Dec. 337 (BIA 1996) 20, 38, 39, 50, 73, 74, 98, 101, 102, 104
H–M–, Matter of, 20 I&N Dec. 683 (BIA 1993) 76, 95
H–M–V–, Matter of, 22 I&N Dec. 256 (BIA 1998) 9, 260
Izatula, Matter of, 20 I&N Dec. 149 (BIA 1990) 76, 77
J–B–N– & S–M–, Matter of, 24 I&N Dec. 208 (BIA 2007) 42
J–E–, Matter of, 23 I&N Dec. 291 (BIA 2002) 262, 263, 264, 266, 271, 272, 274, 276
Jean, Matter of, 23 I&N Dec. 373 (AG 2002) 103, 108, 109, 174, 247, 248, 330
J–F–F–, Matter of, 23 I&N Dec. 912 (AG 2006) 68, 271
J–H–S–, Matter of, 24 I&N Dec. 196 (BIA 2007) 58
Jimenez-Santillano, Matter of, 21 I&N Dec. 567 (BIA 1996) 342
J–J–, Matter of, 21 I&N Dec. 976 (BIA 1997) 120, 126, 231
J–M–, Matter of, [number not provided] (BIA May 31, 2007) 68
Juarez, Matter of, 19 I&N Dec. 664 (BIA 1988) 109
J–W–S–, Matter of, 24 I&N Dec. 185 (BIA 2007) 58
K, Matter of, 20 I&N Dec. 418 (BIA 1991) 105
K–, Matter of, 20 I&N Dec. 418 (BIA 1991) 105
K–A–, Matter of, 23 I&N Dec. 661 (BIA 2004) 330
Kanagasundram, Matter of, 22 I&N Dec. 963 (BIA 1999) 156, 297, 309

Table of Administrative Decisions

Kasinga, Matter of, 21 I&N Dec. 357 (BIA 1996) 33, 34, 37, 50, 60, 63, 73, 82, 102
Koloamatangi, Matter of, 23 I&N Dec. 548 (BIA 2003) 343–44
K–R–Y– and K–C–S–, Matter of, 24 I&N Dec. 133 (BIA 2007) 28, 127
K–S–, Matter of, 20 I&N Dec. 715 (BIA 1993) 17
Kulle, Matter of, 19 I&N Dec. 318 (BIA 1985) 81, 131
Leon-Orosco and Rodriguez-Colas, Matter of, 19 I&N Dec. 136 (AG 1984) 16
Liadov, Matter of, 23 I&N Dec. 990 (BIA 2006) 226
Liao, Matter of, A44 197 294 (BIA Oct. 22, 1999) 171
Long Sheng, Matter of, A71 800 016 (IJ Baltimore, June 23, 1993) 186
Lopez, Matter of, 22 I&N Dec. 16 (BIA 1998) 232
L–S–, Matter of, 22 I&N Dec. 645 (BIA 1999) 106
L–S–J–, Matter of, 21 I&N Dec. 973 (BIA 1997) 16, 131
L–V–K–, Matter of, 22 I&N Dec. 976 (BIA 1999) 173, 226, 232
Maccaud, Matter of, 14 I&N Dec. 429 (BIA 1973) 94
Marshi, Matter of, A26 980 386 (AG 2004) 125, 182
Martinez-Recinos, Matter of, 23 I&N Dec. 175 (BIA 2001) 107
Matter of. *See name of real party*
M–B–A–, Matter of, 23 I&N Dec. 474 (BIA 2002) 271
McMullen, Matter of, 19 I&N Dec. 90 (1984) 110
M–D–, Matter of, 23 I&N Dec. 540 (BIA 2002) 180
Medina, Matter of, 19 I&N Dec. 734 (BIA 1988) 7, 8
Mejia-Andino, Matter of, 23 I&N Dec. 533 (BIA 2002) 178
Michel, Matter of, 21 I&N Dec. 1101 (BIA 1998) 160, 351
Mladineo, Matter of, 14 I&N Dec. 591 (BIA 1974) 232
Mogharrabi, Matter of, 19 I&N Dec. 439
    (BIA 1987) 16, 25, 26, 30, 31, 33, 48, 49, 51, 53, 70, 79, 80, 92
Morales, Matter of, 21 I&N Dec. 130 (BIA 1995) 173, 231, 336
M–S–, Matter of, 22 I&N Dec. 349 (BIA 1998) 179, 226, 232
M–V–, Matter of, [number withheld] (BIA 2002), ... 176
N–B–, Matter of, 22 I&N Dec. 590 (BIA 1999) 179
Ngum, Matter of, A27 709 543 (BIA Dec. 13, 1999) 78
N–J–B–, Matter of, 22 I&N Dec. 1057 (BIA 1997, AG 1997 and 1999) 344
N–M–A–, Matter of, 22 I&N Dec. 312 (BIA 1998) 97, 101
Nolasco, Matter of, 22 I&N Dec. 632 (BIA 1999) 345
Ocampo-Ugalde, Matter of, 22 I&N Dec. 1301 (BIA 2000) 347
O–D–, Matter of, 21 I&N Dec. 1079 (BIA 1998) 79, 82, 86
O–D–, Matter of, 21 I&N Dec. 1079 (BIA 1998) 79, 82
Oseiwusu, Matter of, 22 I&N Dec. 19 (BIA 1998) 218
O–Z– & I–Z–, Matter of, 22 I&N Dec. 23 (BIA 1998) 37, 47
Patel, Matter of, 15 I&N Dec. 666 (BIA 1976) 217
Pearson, Matter of, A72 472 870 (IJ Mar. 27, 1997) 115
Perez, Matter of, 22 I&N Dec. 689 (BIA 1999) 344
Pineda-Castellanos, Matter of, 21 I&N Dec. 1017 (BIA 1997) 351
P–L–P–, Matter of, 21 I&N Dec. 887 (BIA 1997) 145, 156
Ponce de Leon, Matter of, 21 I&N Dec. 154 (BIA 1997) 342
Ponce-Hernandez, Matter of, 21 I&N Dec. 784 (BIA 1999) 162, 178, 182, 191
Pula, Matter of, 19 I&N Dec. 467 (BIA 1987) 26, 80, 89, 102, 103
Q–T–M–T–, Matter of, 21 I&N Dec. 639 (BIA 1996) 12, 105, 106
Quist, Matter of, A79 468 512 (BIA July 9, 2004) 60
R–, Matter of, 20 I&N Dec. 621 (BIA 1992) 41, 54, 75
R–A–, Matter of, 22 I&N Dec. 906 (AG 2001) 62
R–A–, Matter of, 23 I&N Dec. 694 (AG 2005) 62
Ramos, Matter of, 23 I&N Dec. 336 (BIA 2002) 107
Recinas, Matter of, 23 I&N Dec. 467 (BIA 2002) 345

Reyes-Diaz, Matter of, [number not provided] (IJ Aug. 2, 2001) (Los Angeles, CA) 50
Rivera, Matter of, 19 I&N Dec. 688 (BIA 1988) 161
Rivera, Matter of, 21 I&N Dec. 599 (BIA 1996) 180
R–O–, Matter of, 20 I&N Dec. 455 (BIA 1992) 72
Rodriguez-Coto, Matter of, 19 I&N Dec. 208 (BIA 1985) 109
Rodriguez-Majano, Matter of, 19 I&N Dec. 811 (BIA 1988) 111, 112, 116
Rodriguez-Palma, Matter of, 17 I&N Dec. 465 (BIA 1980) 110
Romalez-Alcaide, Matter of, 23 I&N Dec. 423 (BIA 2002) 346
R–R–, Matter of, 20 I&N Dec. 547 (BIA 1992) 71, 94, 233
R–S–J–, Matter of, 22 I&N Dec. 863 (BIA 1999) 344, 349
S–A–, Matter of, 21 I&N Dec. 1050 (BIA 1997) 180
S–A–, Matter of, 22 I&N Dec. 1328 (BIA 2000) 37, 45, 62, 72, 73, 82, 131
Salama, Matter of, 11 I&N Dec. 536 (BIA 1966) 35
Salim, Matter of, 18 I&N Dec. 311 (BIA 1982) 71
Sanchez and Escobar, Matter of, 19 I&N Dec. 276 (BIA 1985) 48
Sanchez-Linn, Matter of, 20 I&N Dec. 362 (BIA 1991) 350
Santos, Matter of, A29 564 781 (IJ Dec. Aug. 24, 1990) 7
Santos-Lopez, Matter of, 23 I&N Dec. 419 (BIA 2002) 106, 107
Sanudo, Matter of, 23 I&N Dec. 968 (BIA 2006) 107
S–B–, Matter of, 24 I&N Dec. 42 (BIA 2006) 14, 81
S–H–, Matter of, 23 I&N Dec. 462 (BIA 2002) 131, 187
Sharmin, Matter of, A73 556 833 (IJ Sept. 27, 1996) 50, 59, 62, 63
Shirdel, Matter of, 19 I&N Dec. 33 (BIA 1984) 102
Singh, Matter of, 21 I&N Dec. 998 (BIA 1997) 180
Singh, Matter of, A78 494 845 (BIA Nov. 23, 2001) 171
S–L–L–, Matter of, 24 I&N Dec. 1 (BIA 2006) 56
Small, Matter of, 23 I&N Dec. 448 (BIA 2002) 107
S–M–J–, Matter of, 21 I&N Dec. 722 (BIA 1997) 20, 31, 80, 85, 86, 87, 88, 89, 184, 186
Smriko, Matter of, 23 I&N Dec. 836 (BIA 2005) 254
Soleimani, Matter of, 20 I&N Dec. 99 (BIA 1989) 101, 104, 128, 187
S–P–, Matter of, 21 I&N Dec. 486 (BIA 1996) 41, 53, 54, 76, 85, 88
S–S–, Matter of, 21 I&N Dec. 121 (BIA 1995) 79
Susma, Matter of, 22 I&N Dec. 947 (BIA 1999) 234
S–V–, Matter of, 22 I&N Dec. 1306 (BIA 2000) 233, 265, 267, 268, 276
Sweetser, Matter of, 22 I&N Dec. 709 (BIA 1999) 107
S–Y–G–, Matter of, 24 I&N Dec. 247 (BIA 2007) 58, 235
T–, Matter of, 20 I&N Dec. 571 (BIA 1992) 41, 76
Taylor, Matter of, 24 Immigr. Rptr. B1-184 (BIA 2002) 69
Toboso-Alfonso, Matter of, 20 I&N Dec. 819 (BIA 1990) 37, 50, 66, 109
Tomas, Matter of, 19 I&N Dec. 464 (BIA 1987) 171
T–Z–, Matter of, 24 I&N Dec. 163 (BIA 2007) 35
U–H–, Matter of, 23 I&N Dec. 355 (BIA 2002) 114
Valdez-Valdez, Matter of, 21 I&N Dec. 703 (BIA 1997) 217
Valles, Matter of, 21 I&N Dec. 769 (BIA 1997) 217
Vigil, Matter of, 19 I&N Dec. 572 (BIA 1988) 54, 65, 71, 72
Villalta, Matter of, 20 I&N Dec. 142 (BIA 1990) 51, 72, 91
Vivas, Matter of, 16 I&N Dec. 68 (BIA 1977) 184
V–T–S–, Matter of, 21 I&N Dec. 792 (BIA 1997) 33, 37, 50, 88
W–F–, Matter of, 21 I&N Dec. 503 (BIA 1996) 180
X–K–, Matter of, 23 I&N Dec. 731 (BIA 2005) 215
X–P–T–, Matter of, 21 I&N Dec. 634 (BIA 1996) 55
Yanez-Garcia, Matter of, 23 I&N Dec. 390 (BIA 2002) 106
Y–B–, Matter of, 21 I&N Dec. 1136 (BIA 1998) 31, 80, 86, 89
Y–C–, Matter of, 23 I&N Dec. 286 (BIA 2002) 123

© 2007 American Immigration Lawyers Association

Yeung, Matter of, 21 I&N Dec. 610 (BIA 1997) 351
Yewondwosen, Matter of, 21 I&N Dec. 1025 (BIA 1997) 238
Y–L–, Matter of, 24 I&N Dec. 151 (BIA 2007) 143, 144
Y–L–, Matter of, 23 I&N Dec. 270 (AG 2002) 106, 132, 266, 267, 276
Y–L–, A–G–, R–S–R–, Matters of, 23 I&N Dec. 270 (AG 2002) 106, 132, 266, 267, 276
Y–T–L–, Matter of, 23 I&N Dec. 601 (BIA 2003) 39, 55, 97, 98

TABLE OF COURT AND ADMINISTRATIVE DECISIONS SORTED BY COUNTRY

Afghanistan
Ahmadshah v. Ashcroft, 396 F.3d 917 (8th Cir. 2005) 46, 98
A–N– & R–M–N–, Matter of, 22 I&N Dec. 953 (BIA 1999) 234
B–, Matter of, 21 I&N Dec. 66 (BIA 1995) 82, 104
Feroz v. INS, 22 F.3d 225 (9th Cir. 1994) 105
Izatula, Matter of, 20 I&N Dec. 149 (BIA 1990) 76, 77
Mashiri v. Ashcroft, 383 F.3d 1112 (9th Cir. 2004) 74
N–M–A–, Matter of, 22 I&N Dec. 312 (BIA 1998) 97, 101
Salim, Matter of, 18 I&N Dec. 311 (BIA 1982) 71
Shirdel, Matter of, 19 I&N Dec. 33 (BIA 1984) 102
Sultani v. Gonzales, 455 F.3d 878 (8th Cir. 2006) 128

Albania
Bace v. Ashcroft, 352 F.3d 1133 (7th Cir. 2003) 33, 38, 40, 95, 135
Comollari v. Ashcroft, 378 F.3d 694 (7th Cir. 2004) 265
Kerciku v. INS, 314 F.3d 913 (7th Cir. 2003) 80, 132, 136, 166, 182
Pasha v. Gonzales, 433 F.3d 530 (7th Cir. 2005) 183
Shahinaj v. Gonzales, 481 F.3d 1027 (8th Cir. 2007) 66, 132, 167

Algeria
Debab v. INS, 163 F.3d 21 (1st Cir. 1998) 40

Argentina
Maldonado v. U.S. Attorney Gen., 188 Fed. Appx. 101 (3d Cir. 2006) 66

Armenia
Avetova-Elisseva v. INS, 213 F.3d 1192 (9th Cir. 2000) 72, 93
Mgoian v. INS, 184 F.3d 1029 (9th Cir. 1999) 50, 91, 136, 138

Australia
Sultani v. Gonzales, 455 F.3d 878 (8th Cir. 2006) 128

Azerbaijan
Andriasian v. INS, 180 F.3d 1033 (9th Cir. 1999) 42, 103, 166

Bangladesh
A–S–, Matter of, 21 I&N Dec. 1106 (BIA 1998) 81, 131
Gomes v. Gonzales, 429 F.3d 1264 (9th Cir. 2005) 45, 93, 99
Khan v. INS, 237 F.3d 1143 (9th Cir. 2000) 185
Sharmin, Matter of, A73 556 833 (IJ Sept. 30, 1996) 50, 59, 62, 63

Bolivia
Andia v. Ashcroft, 359 F.3d 1181 (9th Cir. 2004) 181
Bellido v. Ashcroft, 367 F.3d 840 (8th Cir. 2004) 36, 76, 83, 87, 92
Rioja v. Ashcroft, 317 F.3d 514 (5th Cir. 2003) 230

Bosnia-Herzegovina
Bradvica v. INS, 128 F.3d 1009 (7th Cir. 1997) 37, 136
Knezevic v. Ashcroft, 367 F.3d 1206 (9th Cir. 2004) 31, 35, 38, 42, 46, 92, 99
Palavra v. INS, 287 F.3d 690 (8th Cir. 2002) 94, 135
Smriko v. Ashcroft, 387 F.3d 279 (3d Cir. 2004) 248, 255
Vukmirovic v. Ashcroft, 362 F.3d 1247 (9th Cir. 2004) 112, 277

Bulgaria
Angoucheva v. INS, 106 F.3d 781 (7th Cir. 1997) 59
Kratchmarov v. Heston, 172 F.3d 551 (8th Cir. 1999) 31, 94
Krouchevski v. Ashcroft, 344 F.3d 670 (7th Cir. 2003) 83, 137
L–V–K–, Matter of, 22 I&N Dec. 976 (BIA 1999) 173, 226, 232
Popova v. INS, 273 F.3d 1251 (9th Cir. 2001) 37, 40, 44
Stoyanov v. INS, 172 F.3d 731 (9th Cir. 1999) 84, 131, 166
Vladimirova v. Ashcroft, 377 F.3d 690 (7th Cir. 2004) 35, 99

Burkina Faso
A–A–, Matter of, 22 I&N Dec. 140 (BIA 1998) 181

Burma
Lwin v. INS, 144 F.3d 505(7th Cir. 1998) 48, 49

Cambodia
Choeum v. INS, 129 F.3d 29 (1st Cir. 1997) 27, 105, 109
Yuk v. Ashcroft, 355 F.3d 1222 (10th Cir. 2004) 229

Cameroon
Daiga v. INS, 183 F.3d 797 (8th Cir. 1999) 82
Ezeagwuna v. Ashcroft, 301 F.3d 116 (3d Cir. 2002) 182

Canada
Dalton v. Ashcroft, 257 F.3d 200 (2d Cir. 2001) 107
Maccaud, Matter of, 14 I&N Dec. 429 (BIA 1973) 94

Chile
Castro-O'Ryan v. INS, 847 F.2d 1307 (9th Cir. 1987) 169

China
___, Matter of, A76 512 001 (IJ Oct. 18, 2000) 50, 61, 74
Ai Feng Yuan v. U.S. Dep't of Justice, 416 F.3d 192 (2d Cir. 2005) 55
Cao v. U.S. Attorney Gen., 407 F.3d 146 (3d Cir. 2005) 57
C–C–, Matter of, 23 I&N Dec. 899 (BIA 2006) 58
Chang v. INS, 119 F.3d 1055 (3d Cir. 1997) 34, 52, 75, 76, 77, 137
Chen, Matter of, 20 I&N Dec. 16 (BIA 1989) 38, 39, 69, 101, 104
Chen v. Ashcroft, 94 Fed. Appx. 930, 2004 WL 835786 (3d Cir. 2004) 112
Chen v. Gonzales, 417 F.3d 303 (2d Cir. 2005) 57, 65
Chen v. Gonzales, 434 F.3d 212 (3d Cir. 2005) 77
Chen v. Gonzales, 457 F.3d 670 (7th Cir. 2006) 56
Chen v. Gonzales, 470 F.3d 1131 (5th Cir. 2006) 267
Chen v. INS, 195 F.3d 198 (4th Cir. 1999) 58, 135
Chen v. INS, 266 F.3d 1094 (9th Cir. 2001) 57

Chen v. INS, 359 F.3d 121 (2d Cir. 2004) 32, 35, 45, 85
C–Y–Z–, Matter of, 21 I&N Dec. 915 (BIA 1997) 55, 56
Gao v. Gonzales, 440 F.3d 62 (2d Cir. 2006) 50, 63, 99
G–C–L–, Matter of, 23 I&N Dec. 359 (BIA 2002) 55, 235
Ge v. Ashcroft, 367 F.3d 1121 (9th Cir. 2004) 55
Gui Cun Liu v. Ashcroft, 372 F.3d 529 (3d Cir. 2004) 185
Guo v. Ashcroft, 361 F.3d 1194 (9th Cir. 2004) 40, 44, 137
He v. Ashcroft, 328 F.3d 593 (9th Cir. 2003) 171
Huang v. INS, 421 F.3d 125 (2d Cir. 2005) 58
J–H–S–, Matter of, 24 I&N Dec. 196 (BIA 2007) 58
Jian Hui Shao v. BIA, 465 F.3d 497 (2d Cir. 2006) 58
J–W–S–, Matter of, 24 I&N Dec. 185 (BIA 2007) 58
Li v. Ashcroft, 356 F.3d 1153 (9th Cir. 2004) 56, 57
Li v. Gonzales, 405 F.3d 171 (4th Cir. 2005) 35, 56
Li v. INS, 92 F.3d 985 (9th Cir. 1996) 51, 91
Lin v. Ashcroft, 377 F.3d 1014 (9th Cir. 2004) 57, 166, 191
Lin v. Gonzales, 2007 U.S. App. LEXIS 3041 (2d Cir. 2007) 68
Lin v. U.S. Dep't of Justice, 494 F.3d 296 (2d Cir. 2007) 55, 56
Lu v. Ashcroft, 2004 U.S. App. Lexis 3003 (No. 02-74281, 9th Cir. 2004) 53
Ma v. Ashcroft, 361 F.3d 553 (9th Cir. 2004) 55
Pan v. Gonzales, 449 F.3d 408 (2d Cir. 2006) 56
Qui v. Ashcroft, 329 F.3d 140 (2d Cir. 2003) 56, 81, 136, 138
Shan Liao v. U.S. Dep't of Justice, 293 F.3d 61 (2d Cir. 2002) 36, 57, 88, 135, 136
Shou Yung Guo v. Gonzales, 463 F.3d 109 (2d Cir. 2006) 58
S–L–L–, Matter of, 24 I&N Dec. 1 (BIA 2006) 56
S–Y–G–, Matter of, 24 I&N Dec. 247 (BIA 2007) 58, 235
Tian Ming Lin v. Gonzales, 473 F.3d 48 (2d Cir. 2007) 58
Tu Kai Yang v. Gonzales, 427 F.3d 1117 (8th Cir. 2005) 99
Wang v. Ashcroft, 341 F.3d 1015 (9th Cir. 2003) 26, 34, 57, 82
Wang v. Gonzales, 152 Fed. Appx. 761 (11th Cir. 2005) 56, 57, 66
Weng v. U.S. Attorney Gen., 287 F.3d 1335 (11th Cir. 2002) 245
X–P–T–, Matter of, 21 I&N Dec. 634 (BIA 1996) 53
Yang v. Gonzales, 427 F.3d 1117 (8th Cir. 2005) 57, 74, 183, 233
Yang v. McElroy, 277 F.3d 158 (2d Cir. 2002) 95
Yang v. U.S. Attorney Gen., 418 F.3d 1198 (11th Cir. 2005) 57
Y–C–, Matter of, 23 I&N Dec. 286 (BIA 2002) 123
Y–T–L–, Matter of, 23 I&N Dec. 601 (BIA 2003) 39, 55, 97, 98
Zhang v. Gonzales, 434 F.3d 993 (7th Cir. 2006) 56
Zhang v. Reno, 27 F. Supp. 2d 476 (S.D.N.Y. 1998) 55
Zhao v. U.S. Dep't of Justice, 265 F.3d 83 (2d Cir. 2001) 57
Zheng v. Ashcroft, 332 F.3d 1186 (9th Cir. 2003) 267, 268, 276
Zheng v. Gonzales, 409 F.3d 804 (7th Cir. 2005) 56
Zhen Nan Lin v. U.S. Dep't of Justice, 459 F.3d 255 (2d Cir. 2006) 174
Zhu v. Ashcroft, 382 F.3d 521 (5th Cir. 2004) 172

Colombia
Campos-Sanchez v. INS, 164 F.3d 448 (9th Cir. 1998) 131
Faronda-Blandon, Matter of, A74 979 517 (IJ June 15, 2001) 50
Gutierrez-Chavez v. INS, 298 F.3d 824 (9th Cir. 2002) 132
Mosquera-Perez v. INS, 3 F.3d 553 (1st Cir. 1993) 105
Reyes-Guerrero v. INS, 192 F.3d 1241 (9th Cir. 1999) 79

S–V–, Matter of, 22 I&N Dec. 1306 (BIA 2000) 233, 265, 267, 268, 276

Columbia
Arboleda v. U.S. Attorney Gen., 434 F.3d 1220 (11th Cir. 2006) 73, 74, 100
Tapiero de Orjuela v. Gonzales, 423 F.3d 666 (7th Cir. 2005) 49

Cuba
Artigas, Matter of, 23 I&N Dec. 99 (BIA 2001) 341
Avila v. Rivkind, 724 F. Supp. 945 (S.D. Fla. 1989) 113
B–, Matter of, 20 I&N Dec. 427 (BIA 1991) 109
Ballester-Garcia, Matter of, 17 I&N Dec. 592 (1980) 110
Barreto-Claro v. U.S. Attorney Gen., 275 F.3d 1334 (11th Cir. 2001) 144, 159
Buschini, Matter of, A98 064 379 (AAO 2006) 341, 342
Crespo-Gomez v. Richard, 780 F.2d 932 (11th Cir. 1986) 105
D–, Matter of, 20 I&N Dec. 915 (BIA 1994) 342
D–L– & A–M–, Matter of, 20 I&N Dec. 409 (BIA 1991) 128
Fernandez-Roque v. Smith, 599 F. Supp. 1103 (N.D. Ga. 1984) 16
Gonzalez v. Reno, 212 F.3d 1338 (11th Cir. 2000) 190
Leon-Orosco and Rodriguez-Colas, Matter of, 19 I&N Dec. 136 (AG 1984) 16
Rodriguez-Coto, Matter of, 19 I&N Dec. 208 (BIA 1985) 109
Rodriguez-Palma, Matter of, 17 I&N Dec. 465 (BIA 1980) 110
Rodriguez-Roman v. INS, 98 F.3d 416 (9th Cir. 1996) 77
Toboso-Alfonso, Matter of, 20 I&N Dec. 819 (BIA 1990) 37, 50, 66, 109

Democratic Republic of Congo
Essohou v. Gonzales, 471 F.3d 518 (4th Cir. 2006) 74, 100
Kabamba v. Gonzales, 162 Fed. Appx. 337 (5th Cir. 2006) 86
Kalubi v. Ashcroft, 364 F.3d 1134 (9th Cir. 2004) 81, 102, 103, 104, 117, 135
Mapouya v. Gonzales, 487 F.3d 396 (6th Cir. 2007) 167, 274
Mulanga v. Ashcroft, 349 F.3d 123 (3d Cir. 2003) 53, 80, 82, 87
Zubeda v. Ashcroft, 333 F.3d 463 (3d Cir. 2003) 263, 272

Dominican Republic
Devison, Matter of, 22 I&N Dec. 1362 (BIA 2000) 64, 108
J–F–F–, Matter of, 23 I&N Dec. 912 (AG 2006) 68, 271
R–S–R–, Matter of, 23 I&N Dec. 270 (AG 2002) 106, 132

Egypt
Ali v. Reno, 829 F. Supp. 1415 (S.D.N.Y. 1993) 113
Elnager v. INS, 930 F.2d 784 (9th Cir. 1991) 45
Fahim v. U.S. Attorney Gen., 278 F.3d 1216 (11th Cir. 2002) 282
Ghaly v. INS, 58 F.3d 1425 (9th Cir. 1995) 132, 136
Khouzam v. Ashcroft, 361 F.3d 161 (2d Cir. 2004) 266, 267, 268, 269, 276, 277
Malty v. Ashcroft, 381 F.3d 942 (9th Cir. 2004) 234
Ramadam v. Gonzales, 479 F.3d 646 (9th Cir. 2007) (en banc) 125, 133
Salama, Matter of, 11 I&N Dec. 536 (BIA 1966) 35
Tawadrus v. Ashcroft, 364 F.3d 1099 (9th Cir. 2004) 169

El Salvador
Acosta, Matter of, 19 I&N Dec. 211 (BIA 1985) 16, 33, 48, 49, 51, 79

A–G–, Matter of, 19 I&N Dec. 502 (BIA 1987), *aff'd sub nom.* M.A. v. INS,
899 F.2d 304 (4th Cir. 1990) 71
Aguilera-Cota v. INS, 914 F.2d 1375 (9th Cir. 1990) 51, 54, 83
Alvarez-Flores v. INS, 909 F.2d 1 (1st Cir 1990) 51
Arteaga v. INS, 836 F.2d 1227 (9th Cir. 1988) 54, 71
Baires v. INS, 856 F.2d 89 (9th Cir. 1988) 161
Bernal-Garcia v. INS, 852 F.2d 144 (5th Cir. 1988) 51
Blanco-Lopez v. INS, 858 F.2d 531 (9th Cir. 1988) 54
Bolanos-Hernandez v. INS, 767 F.2d 1277 (9th Cir. 1984) 40, 92
Canas-Segovia v. INS, 970 F.2d 599 (9th Cir. 1992) 44, 53
DeValle v. INS, 901 F.2d 787 (9th Cir. 1990) 51
Echeverria-Hernandez v. INS, 923 F.2d 688, *vacated,* 946 F.2d 1481 (9th Cir. 1991) 7
Fuentes, Matter of, 19 I&N Dec. 658 (BIA 1988) 40, 41, 51, 87
Gomez v. INS, 947 F.2d 660 (2d Cir. 1991) 51, 63, 65
Gonzales; Doe v., 484 F.3d 445 (7th Cir. 2007) 109, 111
Guevara-Flores v. INS, 786 F.2d 1242 (5th Cir. 1986) 25
Gutierrez-Lopez, Matter of, 21 I&N Dec. 479 (BIA 1996) 231, 233, 335
G–Y–R–, Matter of, 23 I&N Dec. 181 (BIA 2001) 178, 181, 232
Hernandez-Barrera v. Ashcroft, 373 F.3d 9 (1st Cir. 2004) 38, 96, 98
Hernandez-Vivas v. INS, 23 F.3d 1557 (9th Cir. 1994) 136
Leva-Montalvo v. INS, 173 F.3d 749 (9th Cir. 1999) 53
M.A. v. INS, 899 F.2d 304 (4th Cir. 1990) 71, 76
Maldonado-Cruz v. INS, 883 F.2d 788 (9th Cir. 1990) 54
Martinez-Recinos, Matter of, 23 I&N Dec. 175 (BIA 2001) 107
Medina, Matter of, 19 I&N Dec. 734 (BIA 1988) 7, 8
Menjivar v. Gonzales, 416 F.3d 918 (8th Cir. 2005) 72, 267
Molina v. INS, 170 F.3d 1247 (9th Cir. 1999) 54
Montecino v. INS, 915 F.2d 518 (9th Cir. 1990) 52
Morales, Matter of, 21 I&N Dec. 130 (BIA 1995) 173, 231, 336
Navas v. INS, 217 F.3d 646 (9th Cir. 2000) 36, 40
Orantes-Hernandez v. Gonzales, 504 F. Supp. 2d 825 (C.D. Cal. 2007) 321
Rios-Berrios v. INS, 776 F.2d 859 (9th Cir. 1985) 168
Rivas-Martinez v. INS, 997 F.2d 1143 (5th Cir. 1993) 72
Rivera-Moreno v. INS, 213 F.3d 481 (9th Cir. 2000) 54
R–O–, Matter of, 20 I&N Dec. 455 (BIA 1992) 72
Rodriguez-Majano, Matter of, 19 I&N Dec. 811 (BIA 1988) 111, 112, 116
Sanchez and Escobar, Matter of, 19 I&N Dec. 276 (BIA 1985), *aff'd sub nom.*
Sanchez-Trujillo v. INS, 801 F.2d 1571 (9th Cir. 1986) 48, 49, 65
Sanchez v. INS, 707 F.2d 1523 (D.C. Cir. 1983) 344
Santos-Lopez, Matter of, 23 I&N Dec. 419 (BIA 2002) 106, 107
Umanzor-Alvarado v INS, 896 F.2d 14 (1st Cir. 1990) 54
Velasco v. INS, 2004 WL 78208 (9th Cir. 2004) 174
Vigil, Matter of, 19 I&N Dec. 572 (BIA 1988) 54, 65, 71, 72
Villalta, Matter of, 20 I&N Dec. 142 (BIA 1990) 51, 72, 91
Zavala-Bonilla v. INS, 730 F.2d 562 (9th Cir. 1984) 83

Eritrea
Francois v. INS, 283 F.3d 926 (8th Cir. 2002) 31, 39, 92, 95, 101
Gebrekidan v. Clark, 2006 U.S. Dist. LEXIS 83687 (W.D. Wash. 2006) 160
Giday v. Gonzales, 434 F.3d 543 (7th Cir. 2006) 35, 71
Zehatye v. Gonzales, 453 F.3d 1182 (9th Cir. 2006) 71

Ethiopia
Abay v. Ashcroft, 368 F.3d 634 (6th Cir. 2004) 34, 60, 64, 89, 91, 191
Abebe v. Gonzales, 432 F.3d 1037 (9th Cir. 2005) 60
Desta v. Ashcroft, 329 F.3d 1179 (10th Cir. 2003) 127, 161
Dhine v. Slattery, 3 F.3d 613 (2d Cir. 1993) 103
Ememe v. Ashcroft, 358 F.3d 446 (7th Cir. 2004) 83, 313
Gebrekidan v. Clark, 2006 U.S. Dist. LEXIS 83687 (W.D. Wash. 2006) 160
Gebremichael v. INS, 10 F.3d 28 (1st Cir. 1993) 91, 344
Georgis v. Ashcroft, 328 F.3d 962 (7th Cir. 2003) 80, 83, 185
Giday v. Gonzales, 434 F.3d 543 (7th Cir. 2006) 35, 71
Girma v. INS, 283 F.3d 664 (5th Cir. 2002) 41, 132, 135, 136
Habtemicael v. Ashcroft, 370 F.3d 774 (8th Cir. 2004) 269
Kebede v. Ashcroft, 366 F.3d 808 (9th Cir. 2004) 60, 82
Mengistu v. Ashcroft, 355 F.3d 1044 (7th Cir. 2004) 234, 245
Mussie v. INS, 172 F.3d 329 (4th Cir. 1999) 128
Shoafera v. INS, 228 F.3d 1070 (9th Cir. 2000) 34, 42, 47
Zewdie v. Ashcroft, 381 F.3d 804 (8th Cir. 2004) 275

Fiji
Chand v. INS, 222 F.3d 1066 (9th Cir. 2000) 33
Gafoor v. INS, 231 F.3d 645 (9th Cir. 2000) 42
Lal v. INS, 255 F.3d 998, *amended on reh'g,* 268 F.3d 1148 (9th Cir. 2001) 39, 101
Lata v. INS, 204 F.3d 1241 (9th Cir. 2000) 132
Prasad v. INS, 47 F.3d 336 (9th Cir. 1995) 76
Sharma v. INS, 89 F.3d 545 (9th Cir. 1996) 180
Singh v. INS, 134 F.3d 962 (9th Cir. 1998) 33, 37
Tagaga v. INS, 228 F.3d 1030 (9th Cir. 2000) 76

Gambia
___, Matter of, *[file no. redacted]* (BIA Aug. 8, 2007) 124
Quist, Matter of, A79 468 512, (BIA July 9, 2004) 60

Germany
Kulle, Matter of, 19 I&N Dec. 318 (BIA 1985) 81, 131
Mashiri v. Ashcroft, 383 F.3d 1112 (9th Cir. 2004) 74
Nahrvani v. Gonzales, 399 F.3d 1148 (9th Cir. 2005) 128

Ghana
Abankwah v. INS, 185 F.3d 18 (2d Cir. 1999) 60, 80, 87
Ananeh-Firempong v. INS, 766 F.2d 621 (1st Cir. 1985) 51
Annang, Matter of, 14 I&N Dec. 502 (BIA 1973) 101, 187
Dwomoh v. Sava, 696 F. Supp. 970 (S.D.N.Y. 1988) 77, 110
Moshud v. Blackmun, 68 Fed. Appx. 328 (3d Cir. 2003) 267
M–S–, Matter of, 22 I&N Dec. 349 (BIA 1998) 179, 226, 232
Ofosu v. McElroy, 933 F. Supp. 237 (S.D.N.Y. 1995) 111

Gibraltar
Shaughnessy v. Mezei, 345 U.S. 206 (1953) 166

Greece
Foroglou v. INS, 170 F.3d 68 (1st Cir. 1999) 71, 72

Guatemala
Aguirre-Aguirre; INS v., 526 U.S. 415 (1999) 5, 109, 110, 136
A–M–L–, Matter of, *[number not provided]* (IJ Nov. 21, 2001) 50
Arriaga-Barrientos v. INS, 937 F.2d 411 (9th Cir. 1991) 51, 54, 91, 92
C–A–L–, Matter of, 21 I&N Dec. 754 (BIA 1997) 40, 72
Cano-Merida v. INS, 311 F.3d 960 (9th Cir. 2002) 166, 167
Ceballos-Castillo v. INS, 904 F.2d 519 (9th Cir. 1990) 83
Chitay-Pirir v. INS, 169 F.3d 1079 (7th Cir. 1999) 178, 191
Cordero-Trejo v. INS, 40 F.3d 482 (1st Cir. 1994) 44, 85, 92, 93
De Leon-Barrios v. INS, 116 F.3d 391 (9th Cir. 1997) 83, 132
Duarte de Guinac v. INS, 179 F.3d 1156 (9th Cir. 1999) 36, 42, 71, 87
Elias-Zacarias; INS v., 502 U.S. 478 (1992) 39, 40, 52, 72, 135, 138
E–S– and A–M–, Matter of, *[file no. redacted]* (IJ Mar. 20, 2003) (Phoenix, AZ) 70
Estrada-Posadas v. INS, 924 F.2d 916 (9th Cir. 1991) 54
Garcia-Martinez v. Ashcroft, 371 F.3d 1066 (9th Cir. 2004) 59, 138
G–Y–R–, Matter of, 23 I&N Dec. 181 (BIA 2001) 178, 181, 232
Hernandez v. Reno, 258 F.3d 806 (8th Cir. 2001) 111, 112
Jacinto v. INS, 208 F.3d 725 (9th Cir. 2000) 170
Juarez, Matter of, 19 I&N Dec. 664 (BIA 1988) 109
Lopez v. Ashcroft, 366 F.3d 799 (9th Cir. 2004) 138
Lopez-Gomez v. Ashcroft, 263 F.3d 442 (5th Cir. 2001) 74, 99
Mazariegos v. Office of the United States AG, 241 F.3d 1320 (11th Cir. 2001) 99
Mendoza v. U.S. Attorney Gen., 327 F.3d 1283 (11th Cir. 2003) 229
Morales v. INS, 208 F.3d 323 (1st Cir. 2000) 136, 172
Oliva-Muralles v. Ashcroft, 328 F.3d 25 (1st Cir. 2003) 40
Osorio v. INS, 18 F.3d 1017 (2d Cir. 1994) 41, 52
Pascual-Garcia v. Ashcroft, 73 Fed. Appx. 232 (9th Cir. 2003) 265
Pedro-Mateo v. INS, 224 F.3d 1147 (9th Cir. 2000) 51, 72
Ponce-Leiva v. Ashcroft, 331 F.3d 369 (3d Cir. 2003) 169
R–A–, Matter of, 22 I&N Dec. 906 (AG 2001) 62
R–A–, Matter of, 23 I&N Dec. 694 (AG 2005) 62
Rios v. Ashcroft, 287 F.3d 895 (9th Cir. 2002) 36, 92, 95
Sagarminaga v. INS, 113 F.3d 1247 (10th Cir. 1997) 54
Secaida-Rosales v. INS, 331 F.3d 297 (2d Cir. 2003) 82, 88, 136, 137
Tomas, Matter of, 19 I&N Dec. 464 (BIA 1987) 171
Varela v. INS, 204 F.3d 1237 (9th Cir. 2000) 236
Velasquez-Gabriel v. Crocetti, 263 F.3d 102 (4th Cir. 2001) 195
Ventura v. INS, 264 F.3d 1150 (9th Cir. 2001) 54, 90, 91

Guinea
Camara v. Ashcroft, 378 F.3d 361 (4th Cir. 2004) 85
Dia v. Ashcroft, 353 F.3d 228 (3d Cir. 2003) 228
Fatoumata Toure, Matter of, A24 876 244 (BIA 1990) 28
M–D–, Matter of, 23 I&N Dec. 540 (BIA 2002) 180
S–B–, Matter of, 24 I&N Dec. 42 (BIA 2006) 14, 81

Guinea-Bissau
Bah v. Gonzales, 462 F.3d 637 (6th Cir. 2006) 61

Haiti

Augustin v. Sava, 735 F.2d 32 (2d Cir. 1984) 171
Baptiste v. U.S. Attorney Gen., 229 Fed.Appx. 66 (3d Cir. 2007) 68
Cadet v. Bulger, 377 F.3d 1173 (11th Cir. 2004) 270, 271
Carry v. Holmes, 1:02-cv-00369 (W.D.N.Y. July 22, 2003) 263, 269
D–, Matter of, 20 I&N Dec. 827 (BIA 1994) 182
D–J–, Matter of, 23 I&N Dec. 572 (AG 2003) 16, 217
D–V–, Matter of, 21 I&N Dec. 77 (BIA 1993) 25, 30, 37, 38, 41, 45, 61
Elien v. Ashcroft, 364 F.3d 392 (1st Cir. 2004) 271
E–P–, Matter of, 21 I&N Dec. 860 (BIA 1997) 92
Exilus, Matter of, 18 I&N Dec. 276 (BIA 1982) 77
Fefe, Matter of, 20 I&N Dec. 116 (BIA 1989) 80
Fergiste v. INS, 138 F.3d 14 (1st Cir. 1998) 98
Francois v. Gonzales, 448 F.3d 645 (3d Cir. 2006) 263
J–E–, Matter of, 23 I&N Dec. 291 (BIA 2002) 262, 263, 264, 266, 271, 272, 274, 276
Jean, Matter of, 23 I&N Dec. 373 (AG 2002) 103, 108, 109, 174, 247, 248, 330
Lavira v. U.S. Attorney Gen., 478 F.3d 158 (3d Cir. 2007) 68, 106
Leocal v. Ashcroft, 543 U.S. 1, 125 S. Ct. 377 (2004) 107
Louis-Martin v. Ridge, 322 F. Supp. 2d 556 (M.D. Pa. 2004) 281
L–S–J–, Matter of, 21 I&N Dec. 973 (BIA 1997) 16, 131
Malvoisin v. INS, 268 F.3d 74 (2d Cir. 2001) 243
McNary v. Haitian Refugee Center, Inc., 498 U.S. 479 (1991) 15
St. Cyr; INS v., 533 U.S. 289 (2001) 122, 132, 343
Y–L–, Matter of, 23 I&N Dec. 270 (AG 2002) 106, 132, 266, 267, 276

Honduras

Castellono-Chacon v. INS, 341 F.3d 533 (6th Cir. 2003) 70
Castro-Perez v. Gonzales, 409 F.3d 1069 (9th Cir. 2005) 72
Enamorado, Matter of, A77 530 541 (IJ Nov. 22, 1999) (Harlingen, TX) 70
Escobar v. Gonzales, 417 F.3d 363 (3d Cir. 2005) 51, 65
Flores-Portillo v. Ashcroft, 103 Fed. Appx. 852 (5th Cir. 2004) 65
Kotasz v. INS, 31 F.3d 847 (9th Cir. 1994) 93
Lopez-Zeron v. U.S. Dep't of Justice, 8 F.3d 636 (8th Cir. 1993) 54
Ontunez-Tursios v. Ashcroft, 303 F.3d 341 (5th Cir. 2002) 40, 267

Hungary

Berdo v. INS, 432 F.2d 824 (6th Cir. 1970) 35

India

___, Matter of, (IJ Dec. 20, 2000) (Baltimore, MD) 33, 50, 67
Bhatt v. Reno, 172 F.3d 978 (7th Cir. 1999) 31, 33, 80, 92
Cheema v. Ashcroft, 383 F.3d 848 (9th Cir. 2004) 113, 115
Dass, Matter of, 20 I&N Dec. 120 (BIA 1989) 31, 85
Dhoumo v. BIA, 416 F.3d 172 (2d Cir. 2005) 28
K–S–, Matter of, 20 I&N Dec. 715 (BIA 1993) 17
Maini v. INS, 212 F.3d 1167 (9th Cir. 2000) 44, 73
P–L–P–, Matter of, 21 I&N Dec. 887 (BIA 1997) 145, 156
R–, Matter of, 20 I&N Dec. 621 (BIA 1992) 41, 54, 75
Sangha v. INS, 103 F.3d 1482 (9th Cir. 1997) 53, 80, 90
Shah v. INS, 220 F.3d 1062 (9th Cir. 2000) 85, 86

© 2007 American Immigration Lawyers Association

Singh v. Ashcroft, 367 F.3d 1139 (9th Cir. 2004) 171
Singh v. Ilchert, 69 F.3d 375 (9th Cir. 1995) 53, 75, 76, 88
Singh v. INS, 292 F.3d 1017 (9th Cir. 2002) 83
Singh v. Moschorak, 53 F.3d 1031 (9th Cir. 1995) 75
Singh-Kaur v. INS, 183 F.3d 1147 (9th Cir. 1999) 83, 137
Wangchuck v. DHS, 448 F.3d 524 (2d Cir. 2006) 28

Indonesia
A–G–F–F–, Matter of, *[number not provided]* (IJ July 9, 2004) 66, 67
Setiadi v. Gonzales, 437 F.3d 710 (8th Cir. 2006) 99
Wiransane v. Ashcroft, 366 F.3d 889 (10th Cir. 2004) 78, 86, 92, 138

Iran
Abedini v. INS, 971 F.2d 188 (9th Cir. 1992) 75, 76, 92
Azarshahy v. Ilchert, 1994 WL 446040 (N.D. Cal., Aug. 10, 1994) 78
Bandari v. INS, 227 F.3d 1160 (9th Cir. 2000) 41, 44, 76, 83
Bastanipour v. INS, 980 F.2d 1129 (7th Cir. 1992) 44, 51
Behzadpour v. U.S., 946 F.2d 1351 (8th Cir. 1991) 75, 76
Boromand, Matter of, 17 I&N Dec. 450 (BIA 1980) 81, 131
Daneshvar v. Ashcroft, 355 F.3d 615 (6th Cir. 2004) 79
Farbakhsh v. INS, 20 F.3d 877 (8th Cir. 1994) 128
Farzad v. INS, 802 F.2d 123 (5th Cir. 1986) 344
Fatin v. INS, 12 F.3d 1233 (3d Cir. 1993) 33, 38, 49, 62
Fisher v. INS, 79 F.3d 955 (9th Cir. 1996) 62
G–A–, Matter of, 23 I&N Dec. 366 (BIA 2002) 45, 266, 275, 276, 277, 280
Gharadaghi, Matter of, 19 I&N Dec. 311 (BIA 1985) 103
Hajiani-Niroumand v. INS, 26 F.3d 832 (8th Cir. 1994) 83
Hartooni v. INS, 21 F.3d 336 (9th Cir. 1994) 82, 137
H–M–V–, Matter of, 22 I&N Dec. 256 (BIA 1998) 9, 260
Hosseini v. Gonzales, 471 F.3d 953 (9th Cir. 2006) 269, 275
Jahed v. INS, 356 F.3d 991 (9th Cir. 2004) 36, 41, 136
Kashefi-Zihagh v. INS, 791 F.2d 708 (9th Cir. 1986) 344
Mogharrabi, Matter of, 19 I&N Dec. 439
   (BIA 1987) 16, 25, 26, 30, 31, 33, 49, 51, 53, 70, 79, 80, 92
Mostafa v. Ashcroft, 395 F.3d 622 (6th Cir. 2005) 274
Nahrvani v. Gonzales, 399 F.3d 1148 (9th Cir. 2005) 128
Refahiyat v. INS, 29 F.3d 553 (10th Cir. 1994) 46
Safaie v. INS, 25 F.3d 636 (8th Cir. 1994) 51, 63
Sharif v. INS, 87 F.3d 932 (7th Cir. 1996) 53, 63
Soleimani, Matter of, 20 I&N Dec. 99 (BIA 1989) 101, 104, 128, 187
U–H–, Matter of, 23 I&N Dec. 355 (BIA 2002) 114
Yadegar-Sargis v. INS, 297 F.3d 596 (7th Cir. 2002) 63
Zahedi v. INS, 222 F.3d 1157 (9th Cir. 2000) 76, 87

Iraq
Al-Harbi v. INS, 242 F.3d 882 (9th Cir. 2001) 54
Ali v. Reno, 237 F.3d 591 (6th Cir. 2001) 127, 268, 282
Al-Saher v. INS, 268 F.3d 1143 (9th Cir. 2001) 263, 264, 269, 275
Aziz v. Gonzales, 478 F.3d 854 (8th Cir. 2007) 143–144
Gumbol v. INS, 815 F.2d 406 (6th Cir. 1987) 46
Hamama v. INS, 78 F.3d 233 (6th Cir. 1996) 105

© 2007 American Immigration Lawyers Association

Mansour v. INS, 230 F.3d 902 (7th Cir. 2000) 273, 275
Margos v. Gonzales, 443 F.3d 593 (7th Cir. 2006) 96, 98
S–H–, Matter of, 23 I&N Dec. 462 (BIA 2002) 131, 187

Ireland
Doherty, In re, 599 F. Supp. 270 (S.D.N.Y. 1984) 115
McAllister v. U.S. Attorney Gen., 444 F.3d 178 (3d Cir. 2006) 115
McMullen, Matter of, 19 I&N Dec. 90 (1984), *aff'd sub nom.* McMullen v. INS (II),
788 F.2d 591 (9th Cir. 1986) 110
Pearson, Matter of, A72 472 870 (IJ Mar. 27, 1997) (New York, NY) 115

Israel
Baballah v. Ashcroft, 367 F.3d 1067 (9th Cir. 2004) 34, 35, 40, 42, 44, 46, 64, 91
Khourassany v. INS, 208 F.3d 1096 (9th Cir. 2000) 282
Kiareldeen v. Reno, 71 F. Supp. 2d 402 (D.N.J. 1999) 119, 168, 171, 172, 184
Valansi v. Ashcroft, 278 F.3d 203 (3d Cir. 2002) 107

Italy
Pasquini v. Morris, 700 F.2d 658 (11th Cir. 1983) 15

Ivory Coast
Bamba v. Riley, 366 F.3d 195 (3d Cir. 2004) 203
Camara v. Ashcroft, 2004 WL 2203983 (3d Cir. 2004) 272

Jamaica
Jobson v. Ashcroft, 326 F.3d 367 (2d Cir. 2003) 107
Nugent v. Ashcroft, 367 F.3d 162 (3d Cir. 2004) 107
Raffington v. Cangemi, 399 F.3d 900 (8th Cir. 2005) 68
Raffington v. INS, 340 F.3d 720 (8th Cir. 2003) 51

Jordan
A–N–, Matter of, A73 603 840 (IJ Dec. 22, 2000) 62
H–, Matter of, 21 I&N Dec. 337 (BIA 1996) 20, 38, 39, 50, 74, 98, 101, 102, 104
Khalaf v. INS, 909 F.2d 589 (1st Cir. 1990) 45
Letter Opinion by Robert Esbrook, A77 827 289 (Chicago Asylum Office, Feb. 25, 2002) 61

Kenya
Ngure v. Ashcroft, 367 F.3d 975 (8th Cir. 2004) 33, 45, 75, 76, 93, 228

Kosovo
Selgeka v. INS, 184 F.3d 337 (4th Cir. 1999) 166
Shehu v. Gonzales, 443 F.3d 435 (5th Cir. 2006) 98

Kuwait (Palestinian)
El Himri v. Ashcroft, 378 F.3d 932 (9th Cir. 2004) 123, 192, 271
Ouda v. INS, 324 F.3d 445 (6th Cir. 2003) 29, 35

Kyrgyzstan
Kanivets v. Riley, 320 F. Supp. 2d 297 (E.D. Pa. 2004) 122, 125, 242
Kanivets v. Riley, 2004 WL 1211956 (E.D. Pa. 2004) 45

© *2007 American Immigration Lawyers Association*

Laos
A–P–, Matter of, 21 I&N Dec. 468 (BIA 1999) 165
L–S–, Matter of, 22 I&N Dec. 645 (BIA 1999) 106
Siong v. INS, 376 F.3d 1030 (9th Cir. 2004) 231
Vang v. INS, 146 F.3d 1114 (9th Cir. 1998) 128
Vongsakdy v. INS, 171 F.3d 1203 (9th Cir. 1999) 39, 79, 101
Xiong v. INS, 173 F.3d 601 (7th Cir. 1999) 107

Latvia
Galina v. INS, 213 F.3d 955 (7th Cir. 2000) 85, 95
Kossov v. INS, 132 F.3d 405 (7th Cir. 1998) 160
Laipenieks v. INS, 750 F.2d 1427 (9th Cir. 1985) 112

Lebanon
Albathani v. INS, 318 F.3d 365 (1st Cir. 2003) 228
Al Khouri v. Ashcroft, 362 F.3d 461 (8th Cir. 2004) 82, 159, 166, 169, 170
Karouni v. Gonzales, 399 F.3d 1163 (9th Cir. 2005) 66, 68
Marshi, Matter of, A26 980 386 (AG Feb. 13, 2004) 125, 182
Mikhael v. INS, 115 F.3d 299 (5th Cir. 1997) 31
Mouawad v. Gonzales, 479 F.3d 589 (8th Cir. 2007) 267, 268

Liberia
Diakite v. INS, 179 F.3d 553 (7th Cir. 1999) 282
J–J–, Matter of, 21 I&N Dec. 976 (BIA 1997) 110, 126, 231
Johnson v. Ashcroft, 286 F.3d 696 (3d Cir. 2002) 287
K–, Matter of, 20 I&N Dec. 418 (BIA 1991) 105
Kofa v. INS, 60 F.3d 1084 (4th Cir. 1995) 105
S–M–J–, Matter of, 21 I&N Dec. 722 (BIA 1997) 20, 31, 80, 85, 86, 87, 88, 89, 184, 186

Lithuania
Gailius v. INS, 147 F.3d 34 (1st Cir. 1998) 40, 85, 95, 136, 137, 163

Macedonia
Begzatowski v. INS, 278 F.3d 665 (7th Cir. 2002) 36, 71

Mali
A–T–, Matter of, 24 I&N Dec. 296 (BIA 2007) 39, 61
Makadji v. Gonzales, 470 F.3d 450 (2d Cir. 2006) 128

Mauritania
Diallo v. Ashcroft, 381 F.3d 687 (7th Cir. 2004) 37, 127
Diallo v. INS, 232 F.3d 279 (2d Cir. 2000) 26, 31, 85
Makadji v. Gonzales, 470 F.3d 450 (2d Cir. 2006) 128
M–D–, Matter of, 21 I&N Dec. 1180 (BIA 1998) 180
O–D–, Matter of, 21 I&N Dec. 1079 (BIA 1998) 79, 82, 86
Y–B–, Matter of, 21 I&N Dec. 1136 (BIA 1998) 31, 86, 89

Mexico
Alvarado-Alvino, Matter of, 22 I&N Dec. 718 (BIA 1999) 107
Boer-Sedano v. Gonzales, 418 F.3d 1082 (9th Cir. 2005) 67, 74, 100
Fano v. O'Neill, 806 F.2d 1262 (5th Cir. 1987) 15

Garcia-Flores, Matter of, 17 I&N Dec. 325 (BIA 1980) 15, 165
Hernandez-Montiel v. INS, 225 F.3d 1084 (9th Cir. 2000) 50, 66, 169
Margalli-Olvera v. INS, 43 F.3d 345 (8th Cir. 1994) 16
Ponce de Leon, Matter of, 21 I&N Dec. 154 (BIA 1997) 342
Ramirez-Peyro v. Gonzales, 477 F.3d 637 (8th Cir. 2007) 272, 283
Rodriquez-Lariz v. INS, 282 F.3d 1218 (9th Cir. 2002) 236
Yanez-Garcia, Matter of, 23 I&N Dec. 390 (BIA 2002) 106

Moldova
Bakhtriger v. Elwood, 360 F.3d 414 (3d Cir. 2004) 243

Montenegro
Berishaj v. Ashcroft, 378 F.3d 314 (3d Cir. 2004) 271
Capric v. Ashcroft, 355 F.3d 1075 (7th Cir. 2004) 26, 37, 93, 138

Morocco
S–A–, Matter of, 22 I&N Dec. 1328 (BIA 2000) 37, 45, 62, 72, 73, 82, 131

Nicaragua
Awolesi v. Ashcroft, 341 F.3d 227 (3d Cir. 2003) 135
B–F–O–, Matter of, A78 677 043 (BIA Nov. 6, 2001) 101
Cardoza-Fonseca; INS v., 480 U.S. 421 (1987) 4, 5, 10, 25, 26, 27, 30, 79, 245
Castillo v. INS, 951 F.2d 1117 (9th Cir. 1991) 71
Chavarria v. U.S. Dep't of Justice, 722 F.2d 666 (11th Cir. 1984) 95
Damaize-Job v. INS, 787 F.2d 1332 (9th Cir. 1986) 83, 94
De La Llana-Castellon v. INS, 16 F.3d 1093 (10th Cir. 1994) 95
Gutierrez-Roque v. INS, 954 F.2d 769 (D.C. Cir. 1992) 95
H–M–, Matter of, 20 I&N Dec. 683 (BIA 1993) 76, 95
N–J–B–, Matter of, 22 I&N Dec. 1057 (BIA 1997, AG 1997 and 1999) 344
Osorio v. INS, 99 F.3d 928 (9th Cir. 1996) 83, 138
Rodriguez-Matamoros v. INS, 86 F.3d 158 (9th Cir. 1996) 91
R–R–, Matter of, 20 I&N Dec. 547 (BIA 1992) 71, 94, 233
Taylor, Matter of, 24 Immigr. Rptr. B1-184 (BIA 2002) 69

Nigeria
Adebisi v. INS, 952 F.2d 910 (5th Cir. 1992) 51
Agada v. Ashcroft, 368 F.3d 867 (8th Cir. 2004) 92
Azanor v. Ashcroft, 364 F.3d 1013 (9th Cir. 2004) 265
Balogun v. Ashcroft, 374 F.3d 492 (7th Cir. 2004) 305
Disu v. Ashcroft, 338 F.3d 13 (1st Cir. 2003) 83
Efe v. Ashcroft, 293 F.3d 899 (5th Cir. 2002) 144, 159
K–A–, Matter of, 23 I&N Dec. 661 (BIA 2004) 330
Martins v. INS, 972 F.2d 657 (5th Cir. 1992) 105
M–B–A–, Matter of, 23 I&N Dec. 474 (BIA 2002) 271
McDaniel v. INS, 142 F. Supp. 2d 219 (D. C.T. 2001) 270
Nwakanma v. Ashcroft, 352 F.3d 325 (6th Cir. 2004) 244
Nwaokolo v. Ashcroft, 314 F.3d 303 (7th Cir. 2002) 265
Salaam v. INS, 229 F.3d 1234 (9th Cir. 2000) 86

Pakistan
Ahmad v. INS, 163 F.3d 457 (7th Cir. 1999) 45, 46

Akhtar v. U.S. Attorney Gen., 138 Fed. Appx. 481 (3d Cir. 2005) 68
Kaiser v. Ashcroft, 390 F.3d 653 (9th Cir. 2004) 100
Khattak v. Ashcroft, 332 F.3d 250 (4th Cir. 2003) 228
Nasir v. INS, 122 F.3d 484 (7th Cir. 1997) 136, 137
Sahi v. Gonzalez, 416 F.3d 587 (7th Cir. 2005) 32
S–P–, Matter of, 21 I&N Dec. 486 (BIA 1996) 41, 53, 54, 76, 85, 88

Palestine
Azzouka v. Meese, 820 F.2d 585 (2d Cir. 1987) 113
Kiareldeen v. Reno, 71 F. Supp. 2d 402 (D.N.J. 1999) 119, 168, 171, 172, 184

Peru
A–E–M–, Matter of, 21 I&N Dec. 1157 (BIA 1998) 7, 37, 74, 91, 92
Cardenas v. INS, 294 F.3d 1062 (9th Cir. 2002) 74
Davila-Bardales v. INS, 27 F.3d 1 (1st Cir. 1994) 16
Estrada-Escobar v. Ashcroft, 376 F.3d 1042 (10th Cir. 2004) 54
Gonzales-Neyra v. INS, 122 F.3d 1293 (9th Cir. 1997), *amended,* 133 F.3d 726
(9th Cir. 1998) 27, 40, 90, 135
Huaman Cornelio v. BIA, 979 F.2d 995 (4th Cir. 1992) 54, 94
J-M-, Matter of, *[number not provided]* (BIA May 31, 2007) 68
Miranda-Alvarado v. Gonzales, 449 F.3d 915 (9th Cir. 2006) 110, 111
Salazar v. Ashcroft, 359 F.3d 45 (1st Cir. 2004) 27, 126, 127
Salkeld v. Gonzales, 420 F.3d 804 (8th Cir. 2005) 66
Sotelo-Aquije v. Slattery, 17 F.3d 33 (2d Cir. 1994) 72
Vera-Valera v. INS, 147 F.3d 1036 (9th Cir. 1998) 53

Philippines
Agbuya v. INS, 219 F.3d 962 (9th Cir. 2000), *amended by* 241 F.3d 1224
(9th Cir. 2001) 41, 54, 73
Borja v. INS, 175 F.3d 732 (9th Cir. 1999) 36
Briones v. INS, 175 F.3d 727 (9th Cir. 1999) 41, 54
Colmenar v. INS, 210 F.3d 967 (9th Cir. 2000) 172
Fajardo v. INS, 300 F.3d 1018 (9th Cir. 2002) 236
Garrovillas v. INS, 156 F.3d 1010 (9th Cir. 1998) 37, 84, 90
Grava v. INS, 205 F.3d 1177 (9th Cir. 2000) 52
Hose v. INS, 180 F.3d 992 (9th Cir. 1999) 132
Lim v. INS, 224 F.3d 929 (9th Cir. 2000) 26, 78, 79, 89, 90, 92
Manimbao v. Ashcroft, 329 F.3d 655 (9th Cir. 2003) 138
Mejia v. Ashcroft, 298 F.3d 873 (9th Cir. 2002) 233
S–P–, Matter of, 21 I&N Dec. 486 (BIA 1996) 41, 53, 54, 76, 85, 88
Tarubac v. INS, 182 F.3d 1114 (9th Cir. 1999) 36, 41, 52, 98
V–T–S–, Matter of, 21 I&N Dec. 792 (BIA 1997) 37, 50, 88

Poland
Acewicz v. INS, 984 F.2d 1056 (9th Cir. 1993) 95
Felzcerek v. INS, 75 F.3d 112 (2d Cir. 1996) 182
Janusiak v. INS, 947 F.2d 46 (3d Cir. 1991) 75
Kaczmarczyk v. INS, 933 F.2d 588 (7th Cir.) 95, 177
Kapcia v. INS, 944 F.2d 702 (10th Cir. 1991) 76
Kulle, Matter of, 19 I&N Dec. 318 (BIA 1985) 81, 131

Portugal
Ramos, Matter of, 23 I&N Dec. 336 (BIA 2002) 107

Romania
C–, Matter of, 20 I&N Dec. 529 (BIA 1992) 105, 108
Ciorba v. Ashcroft, 323 F.3d 539 (7th Cir. 2003) 37, 172
Dobrota v. INS, 195 F.3d 970 (7th Cir. 1999) 95
Floroiu v. Gonzales, 481 F.3d 970 (7th Cir. 2007) 46, 132, 167
Frentescu, Matter of, 18 I&N Dec. 244 (1982) 107, 108, 109
Pop v. INS, 270 F.3d 527 (7th Cir. 2001) 45
Rusu v. INS, 296 F.3d 316 (4th Cir. 2002) 164

Russia
Avetova-Elisseva v. INS, 213 F.3d 1192 (9th Cir. 2000) 72, 93
Bolshakov v. INS, 133 F.3d 1279 (9th Cir. 1998) 136
Iavorski v. INS, 232 F.3d 124 (2d Cir. 2000) 236
Kojevnikova v. Reno, 173 F.3d 844 (2d Cir. 1999) 36, 44, 96
Kourski v. Ashcroft, 355 F.3d 1038 (7th Cir. 2004) 82, 86
Kozulin v. INS, 218 F.3d 1112 (9th Cir. 2000) 77
Pitcherskaia v. INS, 118 F.3d 641 (9th Cir 1997) 37, 67
Tchoukhrova v. Gonzales, 404 F.3d 1181, *rehearing en banc denied*, 430 F.3d 1222 (9th Cir. 2005), *vacated*, 127 S. Ct. 57 (2006) 50, 64

Rwanda
Mukamusoni v. Ashcroft, 390 F.3d 110 (1st Cir. 2004) 69, 123
Uwase v. Ashcroft, 349 F.3d 1039 (7th Cir. 2003) 82, 137

Senegal
A-K-, Matter of, 24 I&N Dec. 275 (BIA 2007) 60, 91
Niang v. Gonzales, 422 F.3d 1187 (10th Cir. 2005) 49, 50, 61, 63, 271, 273
Niang v. Gonzales, 492 F.3d 505 (4th Cir. 2007) 26

Serbia
Paripovic v. Gonzales, 418 F.3d 240 (3d Cir. 2005) 29

Somalia
Abdille v. Ashcroft, 242 F.3d 477 (3d Cir. 2001) 101, 127, 187
Ali v. Achem, 468 F.3d 462 (7th Cir. 2006) 274
Ali v. Ashcroft, 346 F.3d 873 (9th Cir. 2003) 2
Farah v. Ashcroft, 348 F.3d 1153 (9th Cir. 2003) 144, 159
H–, Matter of, 21 I&N Dec. 337 (BIA 1996) 20, 38, 39, 50, 74, 98, 101, 102, 104
Hagi v. Ashcroft, 359 F.3d 1044 (8th Cir. 2004) 99
Mohammed v. Gonzales, 400 F.3d 785 (9th Cir. 2005) 34, 39, 49, 61, 63

South Africa
D–V–, Matter of, 21 I&N Dec. 77 (BIA 1993) 30, 37, 38, 41, 45, 61
Thomas v. Ashcroft, 359 F.3d 1169 (9th Cir. 2004) 50
Thomas v. Gonzales, 409 F.3d 1177 (9th Cir. 2005) (en banc), *vacated*, 547 U.S. 183 (2006) 49, 50, 54, 66, 166, 169, 191

South Korea
K–R–Y– and K–C–S–, Matter of, 24 I&N Dec. 133 (BIA 2007) 28, 127
Lee v. Ashcroft, 368 F.3d 218 (3d Cir. 2004) 107, 134

Sri Lanka
Balasubramanrim v. INS, 143 F.3d 157 (3d Cir. 1998) 83
Kalmalthas v. INS, 251 F.3d 1279 (9th Cir. 2001) 258, 272, 274, 282
Kanagasundram, Matter of, 22 I&N Dec. 963 (BIA 1999) 156, 297, 309
Paramasamy v. Ashcroft, 295 F.3d 1047 (9th Cir. 2002) 81, 82
People's Mojahedin Org. of Iran v. U.S. Dep't of State, 182 F.3d 17 (D.C. Cir. 1999) 116
Perinpanathan v. INS, 310 F.3d 594 (8th Cir. 2002) 266, 271, 273, 275
Ramsameachire v. Ashcroft, 357 F.3d 169 (2d Cir. 2004) 272, 305
Ravindran v. INS, 976 F.2d 754 (1st Cir. 1992) 51, 94
Senathirajah v. INS, 157 F.3d 210 (3d Cir. 1998) 76, 80, 83, 131
Sivaainkaran v. INS, 972 F.2d 161 (7th Cir. 1992) 95
Sivakaran v. Ashcroft, 368 F.3d 1028 (8th Cir. 2004) 272
S–P–, Matter of, 21 I&N Dec. 486 (BIA 1996) 41, 53, 54, 76, 85, 88
T–, Matter of, 20 I&N Dec. 571 (BIA 1992) 41, 76
Thavendran v. Gonzales, 211 Fed. Appx. 74 (2d Cir. 2007) 93

Sudan
Abdalla v. INS, 43 F.3d 1397 (10th Cir. 1994) 127
Abdel-Masieh v. INS, 73 F.3d 579 (5th Cir. 1996) 38, 44, 75
Niam v. Ashcroft, 354 F.3d 652 (7th Cir. 2004) 85, 132, 183

Suriname
Nelson v. INS, 232 F.3d 258 (1st Cir. 2000) 37, 61, 176
Tamas-Mercea v. Reno, 222 F.3d 417 (7th Cir. 2000) 37

Syria
Khano v. INS, 999 F.2d 1203 (7th Cir. 1993) 83

Tanzania
Lusingo v. Gonzales, 420 F.3d 193 (3d Cir. 2005) 64

Togo
___, Matter of, A71 498 940 (IJ Oct. 31, 1995) (New York, NY) 50, 67
Kasinga, Matter of, 21 I&N Dec. 357 (BIA 1996) 33, 37, 50, 60, 63, 73, 82, 101

Trinidad
Beharry v. Reno, 183 F. Supp. 2d 584 (E.D.N.Y. 2002), *rev'd,* 329 F.3d 51 (2d Cir. 2003) 7
Small, Matter of, 23 I&N Dec. 448 (BIA 2002) 107

Turkey
Ozdemir v. INS, 46 F.3d 6 (5th Cir. 1994) 76

Uganda
Gonahasa v. INS, 181 F.3d 538 (4th Cir. 1999) 31, 85
Lukwago v. Ashcroft, 329 F.3d 157 (3d Cir. 2003) 49, 65, 71, 78, 135, 136
Nabulwala v. Gonzales, 479 F.3d 972 (8th Cir. 2007) 66
Shan Liao v. U.S. Dep't of Justice, 293 F.3d 61 (2d Cir. 2002) 36, 57, 88, 135, 136

Ukraine
Denko v. INS, 351 F.3d 717 (6th Cir. 2003) 228
Fedorenko, Matter of, 19 I&N Dec. 57 (BIA 1984) 112
Korablina v. INS, 158 F.3d 1038 (9th Cir. 1998) 30, 33, 44, 98
Koval v. Gonzales, 418 F.3d 798 (7th Cir. 2005) 182, 183, 184
Nazarova v. INS, 171 F.3d 478 (7th Cir. 1998) 180
O–Z– & I–Z–, Matter of, 22 I&N Dec. 23 (BIA 1998) 47
Podio v. INS, 153 F.3d 506 (7th Cir. 1999) 172
Yakovenko v. Gonzales, 477 F.3d 631 (8th Cir. 2007) 99, 133

Uruguay
Acosta, Matter of, 19 I&N Dec. 211 (BIA 1985) 16, 33, 48, 49, 51, 79

Vietnam
C–V–T–, Matter of, 22 I&N Dec. 7 (BIA 1998) 343
Q–T–M–T–, Matter of, 21 I&N Dec. 639 (BIA 1996) 12, 105, 106

Yemen
Saleh v. INS, 962 F.2d 234 (2d Cir. 1992) 45, 76

Yugoslavia
Ahmetovic v. INS, 62 F.3d 48 (2d Cir. 1995) 105
Begzatowski v. INS, 278 F.3d 665 (7th Cir. 2002) 36, 71
Capric v. Ashcroft, 355 F.3d 1075 (7th Cir. 2004) 26, 37, 93, 138
Dunat v. Henry, 297 F.2d 744 (3d Cir. 1961) 35
Ivezaj v. INS, 84 F.3d 215 (6th Cir. 1996) 95
Kovac v. INS, 407 F.2d 102 (9th Cir. 1969) 35
Perkovic v. INS, 33 F.3d 615 (6th Cir. 1994) 47, 76
Pula, Matter of, 19 I&N Dec. 467 (BIA 1987) 26, 80, 89, 94, 102, 103
Vujisic v. INS, 224 F.3d 578 (7th Cir. 2000) 71, 95

Zimbabwe
Kimumwe v. Gonzales, 431 F.3d 319 (8th Cir. 2005) 66
Mabasa v. Gonzales, 455 F.3d 740 (7th Cir. 2006) 125, 133

SUBJECT-MATTER INDEX

A

ABC Settlement, 145, 146, 335–36
Abuse-of-discretion standard, 131, 136
Adjudicator's Field Manual, 15
Adjustment of status, 246–48, 255
    and ageing-out, 193
    waiver under INA §209(c), 330–31
Administrative notice of changed country conditions, 94–96
Advance parole status, 249, 297
Advisals in removal proceedings, 159, 195
AEDPA. *See* Antiterrorism and Effective Death Penalty Act of 1986
Affidavits vs. declarations, 186
Affirmative Asylum Procedures Manual, 15
Affirmative procedures, 145–55
    biometrics, 148
    for children, 154, 155
    decision to grant, deny, or refer, 151–53
    failure to appear, 150–51
    filing procedures, 146–47
    identity checks, 151
    interpreters, 148–49
    interviews, 147–48
    motion to reopen/reconsider. *See* Motion to reopen/reconsider
    no appeals, 153
    State Department comments, 150
Afghanistan, 74, 98, 130
Ageing-out, 192, 193–94, 250
Aggravated felonies, 105–8, 134, 142
    expedited removal proceedings, 203–11, 290
    no review of removal order, 241
    re-entering after deportation or removal, 196
    release from detention, ineligibility for, 214
AIDS-related discrimination. *See* HIV-positive/AIDS status
Albania, 46, 51, 66
Alien terrorist removal courts, 118–19, 291
Al-Qaida, 115
American Civil Liberties Union, 194
Amnesty International, 84
Angola, 332

Antiterrorism and Effective Death Penalty Act of 1986 (AEDPA)
    eligibility of members of terrorist organizations, 116–17
    judicial review of removal orders, 132

nonrefoulement provision, 12
    serious crimes, 106
    waiver of deportation, 342
Appeals, 225–31
    See also Judicial review
    automatic stay of removal, 229–30, 245
    bond hearings, 216–17
    briefs, 230, 244
    Convention Against Torture claims, 282–83
    deferral of removal, 286
    departure from U.S., effect of, 231
    expedited removal order, 305
    family member petition (Form I-730), 252
    fees, 227–28
    filing, 227, 243–44
    humanitarian parole, 334
    interlocutory appeals, 231
    negative credible fear decision, 316
    notice of right to, 187, 226
    oral argument, 230
    procedure, 243–46
    right to, 173
    scope of review, 244–45
    service on DHS, 229
    streamlined process, 228–29
    termination of refugee status, 255
    time period, 226, 243
    venue, 243
    waiver of, 230
    where to file, 227
Arakan Liberation Party (ALP), 118
Argentina, 66
Armed robbery, 109
Armenia, 103
Arranged marriages, 50, 61
Arriving aliens, 212, 296
Asylum Office Basic Training Course (AOBTC), 20, 29, 120, 121, 124
Attorney General
    detention of suspected terrorists, 17
    grant of asylum by, 25
    prosecutorial discretion, 330
    standard of review, 131
Attorneys. *See* Representation
AUC (United Self-Defense Forces of Colombia), 116
Authentication of documents, 185–86
Automated Visa Lookout System, 151
Automatic stay of removal, 229–30, 245
Azerbaijan, 103

B

Bangladesh, 99
Bars to asylum and withholding of removal, 104–19, 142
   criminal convictions, 105–10, 142
   danger to U.S. security, 112–13, 142
   discretionary denials, 102–4
   participation in persecution of others, 110–12, 142
   serious nonpolitical crimes, 109–10, 142
   terrorism-related bars, 113–19, 142
Bars to asylum only, 119–30
   aggravated felonies, 105–8, 142
   firm resettlement, 126–28, 142
   one-year filing deadline, 120–26, 142
   prior asylum denial, 119–20, 142
   safe third country, removal to, 129–30, 142
   statutory bars, 13
Bars to withholding of removal only, 130, 142
Basic Law Manual, 20
Basque Homeland and Freedom (ETA), 115
Battery, 109
Benefit of the doubt, 88–89
Biometrics, 148, 157–58
Board of Immigration Appeals (BIA), 225–31
   code of conduct, 167
   decisions, 16
   representation before, 143
   standard of review, 130–31
Bond hearings, 211, 215–18
Bosnia-Herzegovina, 332
Brazil, 66
Briefs on appeal, 230, 244
Burden of proof, 79–101
   of asylum applicant, 25, 79–80, 102
   benefit of the doubt, 88–89
   bond hearings, 217–18
   changed country conditions, 94–96
   corroboration, 84–88
   deferral of removal, 286
   discovery, 184
   family and friends, persecution of, 91–92
   family member petition (Form I-730), 252
   foreign law, 101
   fundamental change in circumstances, 97–98, 120
   humanitarian asylum, 100–101
   information provided by applicant may be used to satisfy government's, 144
   internal relocation alternative, reasonableness of, 98–99
   motion to reopen/reconsider, 232–33
   nonrefoulement, 272
   parole requests, 218
   possession of valid passport, 94
   presumption of future persecution based on past persecution, 96–101
   "similarly situated" standard, 92–93
   specific threat of harm, 89–90
   testimony and credibility, 80–84
Burglary, 109
Burma, 50
Burundi, 130, 332
Bush administration's admission of refugees, 141

C

Canada, 129–30, 141, 190, 294, 295
Cancellation of removal, 342–46
Capital Area Immigration Rights (CAIR) Coalition, 70
Center for Gender and Refugee Studies (University of California, Hastings College of Law), 60
Central American countries, 46, 69–70
   See also specific countries
Change of address for pending application, 150–51, 227
Change of nationality as ground for termination of asylum, 253
Change of venue, 161
Changed circumstances
   See also Fundamental change in circumstances
   and late filing, 124–26
   motion to reopen, 234–35
   review of, 138
   termination of asylum or withholding due to, 253
Changed country conditions, 94–96
Chevron deference, 240
Child Citizenship Act of 2000, 354
Child Status Protection Act of 2002 (CSPA), 250
Children
   See also Unaccompanied children
   advisals in removal proceedings, 195
   affirmative procedures for, 155
   ageing-out, 192, 193–94
   asylum procedures for, 189–95
   belonging to particular social group, 63–65
   credible fear interview of parent, 313
   derivative status, 250–51
   detention of, 194–95, 213
   exception to expedited removal, 192, 308

Subject-Matter Index

exception to one-year filing deadline, 122, 192
Headquarters review of cases, 154
interviews, 148, 190, 193
representation of, 191, 213
special immigrant juvenile visas, 353
speedy proceeding, 192
step-children, 251
in utero, 251
Chin National Front/Chin National Army (CNF/CAN), 118
Chin National League for Democracy (CNLD), 118
China, 51, 52, 61, 74, 77, 99, 141, 174, 186
  one-child policy, 55–58, 97
Citizenship, 353–55
Class certification, 300
Classified information used in asylum proceedings, 118–19, 184–85
Clear and convincing standard for one-year filing deadline, 120–21
Closed hearings, 163
Code of conduct for IJs and BIA, 167
Coercive population control, 55–58, 97, 235
Colombia, 49, 73, 99, 115
Committee Against Torture, 261, 266
  on credibility determination, 273
  on evidence of past torture and human rights violations, 274–76
  U.S. report to, 261
Communist Party Marxist (India), 73
Compulsory military service, 70–72
Confidentiality
  credible fear interview, 313
  notice of, 144–45
  right to, 173–76
Congo, Republic of, 61, 74, 99, 130
Congressional Research Service on diplomatic assurances and U.S. obligations under CAT, 279
Conscription, 70–72
Constitutional rights in removal proceedings, 165–76
Continuances, 159
Convention Against Torture (CAT), 8–9, 257–92
  See also Nonrefoulement
  administrative review, 282
  alien terrorist removal procedures, 291
  appeals, 282–83
  application procedures under, 277–92
    eligibility, 277–79
    Form I-589, 280–81
    presence of individual applicant, 277–78
  types of relief available, 279–80
  and criminal prosecution, 76
  deferral of removal under, 280, 284–87
  definition of torture, 262–70
  detention, 260, 283–84
  and diplomatic assurances, 278–79, 286–87
  and disabled persons, 68
  employment authorization, 291–92
  and expedited removal proceeding, 209, 289
  immigration court hearing, 281–84
  implementing legislation, 258–61
  INS and EOIR memoranda on, 19
  judicial review, 282–83
  key provisions, 261–77
  motion to reopen, 287–88
  number of cases in U.S., 260
  prior procedures for relief, 260–61
  regulations issued in U.S. under, 259
  and reinstatement of removal, 200, 289–90
  stowaways, 289
  termination of protection under, 284–87
  and terrorist removal proceedings, 291
  U.S. as signatory, 257
  and withholding of removal, 279–80
Convention on the Rights of the Child, 9
Convictions. *See* Criminal convictions
Corroboration, 84–88, 134, 137
Country conditions documentation, 84–88
Countrywide persecution, 73–75
Credibility of applicant, 80–84
  and *nonrefoulement,* 272–73
  review of negative credible-fear determination, 173, 241, 314–16
  standard of review, 131, 137–38
Credible fear determination. *See* Fear of persecution
Crewmembers, 146, 297, 309
Criminal convictions, 103, 142
  See also Aggravated felonies
  delinquency, adjudication of, 108
  judicial review of removal orders for, 134
  no review of removal order, 241
  nonaggravated felonies, 108–9
  parole for those subject to criminal grounds for detention, 218
  postconviction relief, 108
  serious crimes, 105, 106, 142, 253
  serious nonpolitical crimes, 109–10, 142, 253
  termination of asylum caused by, 253
Cuba, 66, 77, 113, 118, 128, 141, 189–90, 296, 337, 338
Cuban Adjustment Act of 1966 (CAA), 341–42
Customary international law, 7–8

© *2007 American Immigration Lawyers Association*

D

Danger to U.S. security. *See* National security-related cases
De novo review, 131, 132, 136, 225, 240, 285
Death penalty, 269
Decision and order of IJ, 187
Deferral of removal under CAT, 280, 284–87
Delinquency, adjudication of, 108
Denial of application, 151–52
    employment authorization termination due to, 225
    mandatory denials, 162
Denmark, 127
Departure from U.S.
    effect on appeal, 231
    effect on asylee status, 250
    effect on motion to reopen, 239
    travel documents for refugees, 248–50
    voluntary departure, 346–49
Deportability determination, 162
Derivative citizenship, 354
Derivative status, 250–52
    termination of, 254
Desertion from military service, 70–72
Designation of country of removal, 160–61
Detention
    of *ABC* class member, 336
    of children, 194–95
    of Convention Against Torture claimants, 260, 283–84
    FARRA provisions, 260
    pending expedited removal determination, 309–10
    release from, 211–19
    of suspected terrorists, 119
    upon expedited removal order, 305–6
Detention and Deportation Officer's Field Manual, 15
Detention Operations Manual, 15
Diplomatic assurances and Convention Against Torture (CAT), 278–79, 286–87
Diplomats, 154
Disabled persons, 64, 68–69
    See also Mental disabilities
Discovery, 184
Discretionary denials, 102–4, 154
    judicial review, 242–43
Diversity visas, 353
Documentation of country conditions, 84–88
Domestic violence, 62
Dominican Republic, 141
Draft-evasion, 70–72
Drug addiction, 134, 214, 241
Drug possession and other drug offenses, 109, 214, 241
Drug trafficking offenses, 51, 106, 134, 214, 241, 247
Due process rights, 166–68

E

Ecuador, 141
Eighth Amendment, 269
El Salvador, 51, 174, 213, 332, 335, 337, 338
Eligibility to apply, 140–45
    affirmative procedures, 145–46
    asylum, 140
    withholding of removal, 140–41
Emergency situations and humanitarian parole, 333
Employment authorization, 219–25
    adjudication period, 221
    application (Form I-765), 221, 222
    asylees and withholding grantees, 222–23
    Convention Against Torture claims, 291–92
    eligibility, 220
    federal individual tax ID numbers, 224
    fee, 221
    renewals, 221–22
    Social Security cards, 223–24
    termination, 225
    time for filing, 220
    where to file, 221
Employment-based immigration, 351, 352
Entry of appearance, 158
Equal Access to Justice Act (EAJA), 243
ETA (Basque Homeland and Freedom), 115
Ethiopia, 61, 89, 128, 191
Ethnicity. *See* Nationality
Evidence, 181–87
    aggravated felons in expedited removal proceedings, 207
    reinstatement of removal, 199
    right to present, examine, and object to, 171–72
Executive Office for Immigration Review (EOIR)
    forms. *See* Forms
    regulations, 8–9
Executive Order 13269 for noncitizens serving in U.S. Armed Forces, 354
Expedited removal proceedings, 13, 140, 293–323
    See also Habeas corpus jurisdiction
    aggravated felons, 203–11, 290
    administrative proceedings, 203–5

© 2007 American Immigration Lawyers Association

evidence, 207
initiation of removal proceedings, 204
interpreters, 207–8
judicial review, 204–5
notice of intent (Form I-851), 203–4
reasonable fear determination, 205–9
record, 208
representation, 207
response to notice of intent (Form I-851), 204
termination of removal proceedings, 204
withdrawal of request for reasonable fear interview, 209
challenges to validity of the system, 300
consequences of removal, 300–301
and Convention Against Torture, 209, 289
crewmembers, 297
described, 293–94, 302–16
detention pending determination and removal, 309–10
exceptions from, 296–98, 306–9
false or no documents at port of entry, 289, 294, 303–5
final order, 305–6
Form I-860 (Notice and Order of Expedited Removal), 303
Government Accountability Office reports, 318–19
illegal aliens with nonresidence in U.S. for two or more years, 294–96
individuals subject to, 294–96
interdicted noncitizens, 294
judicial review, 18, 242, 299–300
NGO access to secondary inspections, 321–22
oversight of, 316–23
primary inspection, 302
quality assurance, 317–18
relief, 300
secondary inspections, 302–6
NGO access to, 321–22
statutory provisions, 293–301
stowaways, 297
unaccompanied children, 192, 296–97
UNHCR review and recommendations, 303–4, 322–23
U.S. Commission on International Religious Freedom study, 319–21
Experts, 182–84
Extraordinary/exceptional circumstances
failure to appear, 179–80
late filing, 122–24

Extreme hardship, 326, 327

F

Factual findings, review of, 138
Failure to appear, 150–51, 178–81
Fair trial, lack of, 76
False information on application, 144
False or no documents at port of entry, 218, 242, 289, 294, 303–5
Falun Gong, 53
Family and friends, persecution of, 91–92
Family reunification, 104, 250–52, 352
Family-sponsored immigration, 351, 352
FARC (Revolutionary Forces of Colombia), 73, 116
FBI, requests to for rap sheets, 105
Fear of persecution
credible fear determination
administrative review, 314–16
expedited removal, 301, 314
Form M-444 (Information About Credible Rear Interview), 306
interviews, 188–89, 306, 310–13, 316
parole requests, 218
release from detention, 212
stowaways, 188–89
reasonable fear. *See* Reasonable fear
standard for, 25–26, 196
well-founded, 30–32
family and friends, persecution of, 91–92
"similarly situated" standard, 92–93
Federal courts
decisions, 17–18
standard of review, 131–38
Federal Rules of Evidence, 182
Fees
affirmative applications, 147
appeals, 227–28
CAT applications, 281
EAJA recovery of, 243
employment authorization, 221
humanitarian parole, 334
motion to reopen/reconsider, 236
refugee travel applications, 249
Relative Petition (Form I-730), 251
removal proceedings, 157–58
Temporary Protected Status applications, 332
U visa applications, 329
Felonies. *See* Aggravated felonies; Criminal convictions
Female genital mutilation (FGM), 50, 60–61, 63,

73
Field manuals, 15–16
Fifth Amendment, 168–69, 269
Filing deadline, 120–26
  See also One-year filing deadline
Filing procedures, 146–47
  fee, 147
  incomplete applications, 147
  where to file, 146–47
Fingerprint cards, 105
Fingerprints. *See* Biometrics
Firearms offenses, 134, 214, 241
Firm resettlement, 126–28, 142
  foreign laws, construction of, 21, 187
Forced abortion, sterilization, or other pregnancy control methods, 55–58
Foreign Affairs Reform and Restructuring Act of 1998 (FARRA)
  bars to relief, 259
  definitions, 260
  detention, 260
  judicial review, 260
  prohibiting return to country where individual will be subject to torture, 25, 258–59
  regulations under, 259
Foreign language documents, 187
Foreign laws, 20–21, 101
Foreign terrorist organizations, designation as, 115
Form AR-11 (change of address), 150–51
Form EOIR-26 (Notice of Appeal), 187, 226, 227
Form EOIR-26A (Appeal Fee Waiver Request), 227
Form EOIR-27 (Notice of Entry of Appearance as Attorney or Representative), 227
Form EOIR-28 (Notice of Appearance), 158, 315–16
Form EOIR-33/BIA (Change of Address), 227
Form G-28 (Notice of Appearance), 149, 158, 198, 207
Form G-639 (FOIA request), 184
Form I-131 (Application for Travel Document), 248, 333
Form I-134 (Affidavit of Support), 333
Form I-485 (Application for Adjustment of Status), 246, 331
Form I-589 (Application for Asylum and Withholding of Removal), 146–47, 173, 202, 280–81
Form I-730 (Refugee/Asylee Relative Petition), 250–52
Form I-765 (Application for Employment Authorization), 221, 222
Form I-821 (Applications for Temporary Protected Status), 332
Form I-851 (Notice of Intent to Issue a Final Administrative Deportation Order), 203
Form I-860 (Notice and Order of Expedited Removal), 303
Form I-862. *See* Notice To Appear (NTA)
Form I-863 (Notice of Referral), 201, 210, 315
Form I-867AB (Record of Sworn Statement), 303–5
Form I-898 (Record of Negative Reasonable Fear Interview Finding and Request for Review), 201, 209
Form I-899 (Reasonable Fear Worksheet), 200, 208
Form I-918 (U Nonimmigrant Status Certification), 329
Form M-444 (Information About Credible Rear Interview), 306
Form M-488 (Information on Reasonable Fear Interview), 197
Former Soviet Union countries, 29, 46, 339
  See also specific countries
Fourteenth Amendment, 269, 353
Fourth Amendment, 165
Fraud, 236, 252, 253
Freedom of Information Act (FOIA) request (Form G-639), 184
Frivolous applications, notice of consequences of filing, 143–44, 235
Fugitive Disentitlement Doctrine, 244
Fundamental change in circumstances, 97–98

G

Gambia, 123–24
Gang-related claims, 69–70
Gender-based claims, 25, 51, 59–63
  referral procedure, 153
Geneva Conventions, 10
Genocide, participation in, 130, 142
Gonzalez, Elian, 189–90
Government Accountability Office reports, 318–19
Grant of application, 151–52
Grounds of persecution
  imputed protected grounds, 42
  mixed motives, 41–42
  "on account of," 39–40
  race, religion, nationality, political views, or group membership, 26

See also individual treatment of each topic
Guatemala, 42, 50, 62, 99, 213, 335–36, 337, 339
Guinea-Bissau, 61, 332

H

Habeas corpus jurisdiction, 122, 133–34, 239, 242, 283, 299–300
Hague Convention Abolishing the Requirement of Legalisation for Foreign Public Documents (1961), 185
Haiti, 130, 141, 263
Haitian Refugee Immigration Fairness Act of 1998 (HRIFA), 339–41
Hamas, 115
Handbook on Procedures and Criteria for Determining Refugee Status (UNHCR), 5
Harvard Immigration and Refugee Clinic Program, 60
Hazardous neutrality, 54
Headquarters Court (HQIC), 164
Hearing-impaired applicants, 149
Hearings. *See* Removal proceedings
Hearsay, 184
Hezbollah, 125
Historical background of U.S. asylum law, 23–25
HIV-positive/AIDS status, 19, 50, 67–68
Homeland Security Act of 2002, 25, 26, 129, 143, 145, 174, 299
Homeland Security Department
 detention facilities used by, 211–12
 gender-based asylum claims, 25
 identification of terrorist organizations, 118
 waiver of inadmissibility by, 117, 129
Homosexuality, 66–67
Honduras, 51, 213, 332
Human Rights First, 118
Human Rights Watch, 84
Human trafficking, 51, 326–30
Humanitarian asylum, 100–101, 103, 330
Humanitarian parole, 332–34
Hutto detention center litigation, 194–95

I

Identity checks, 151
IIRAIRA. *See* Illegal Immigration Reform and Immigrant Responsibility Act of 1996
Illegal aliens and expedited removal process, 294–96

Illegal Immigration Reform and Immigrant Responsibility Act of 1996 (IIRAIRA), 12–13
 aggravated felonies, definition of, 105
 cancellation of removal provisions, 342
 effect on asylum status and filing time, 24
 expedited removal provisions, 293
 judicial review of removal orders, 132, 133, 134
 limitations on court review of asylum, 17–18
 refugee, defined, 12, 56
 reinstatement of removal, 195
 standards of review, 135
 voluntary departure, 347
Illness as reason for failing to file in one year, 122, 123
Immigration and Nationality Act of 1952 (INA), 24
 refugee, defined, 27–28
Immigration court procedures, 155–87
 code of conduct for IJs, 167
 Convention Against Torture cases, 281–84
 eligible applicants, 156–57
 fees, 157–58
 hearings, 158–87
 recusal of IJ, 167–68
 stowaways, 188–89
 where to file, 157
Imputed membership in particular social group, 49
Imputed nationality, 47
Imputed political opinion, 53–54
Imputed protected grounds, 42
Imputed race, 43
Imputed religion, 46
In absentia orders, 173, 179–81, 231, 234
Inadmissibility determination, 162
Incompetents. *See* Mental disabilities
Incomplete applications, 147
India, 73, 75
Individual Taxpayer Identification Number (ITIN), 224
Indonesia, 99
Ineffective assistance of counsel, 122–23
Ineligibility for asylum, 102–30, 142
 See also headings starting "Bars"
Informants, 146
Inspector's Field Manual, 15
Interdiction on U.S. waters, 141, 294
Interim employment authorization documents (EADs), 221
Interlocutory appeals, 231
Internal relocation alternative, 98–99

© *2007 American Immigration Lawyers Association*

International Convention on the Prevention and Punishment of Genocide, 130
International Covenant on Civil and Political Rights, 43
International Religious Freedom of Act of 1998 (IRFA), 43, 318
International sources of asylum law, 1–10
Interpreters, 148–49, 171
    aggravated felons in expedited removal proceedings, 207
    credible fear determination review, 316
    credible fear interviews, 313
    reinstatement of removal, 199
Interviews, 147–48
    aggravated felons in expedited removal proceedings, 206–7
    children, 148, 190, 193
    credible fear interviews, 188–89, 306, 310–13, 316
    nonadversarial nature of, 147–48
    reinstatement of removal, 197–200
    stowaways and credible fear, 188–89
    time period, 147
Iran, 51, 63, 114, 116, 128
Iraq, 46, 54, 98, 130, 141
Irish Republican Army (IRA), 115, 116
Israel, 101, 128

J

Jamaica, 51
Jordan, 61, 66, 94
Judicial process, lack of, 76
Judicial review, 239–46
    Chevron deference, 240
    Convention Against Torture claims, 260, 282–83
    and criminal conviction, 134
    of denial based on late filing, 122
    of expedited removal process, 18, 242, 299–300
    FARRA provisions, 260
    motion to reopen/reconsider consolidated with, 246
    of removal orders, 131–38
    restrictions on, 241–43
    revised standards of review, 135–36
Juveniles. *See* Children

K

Karen National Union/Karen National Liberation Army (KNU/KNLA), 118
Karenni National Progressive Party (KNPP), 118
Kayan New Land Party (KNLP), 118
Kidnapping, 109
Kosovo, 332
Kuwait, 332

L

Last habitual residence, defined, 29
Late arrival, 179
Late filing. *See* One-year filing deadline
Lawful permanent residents (LPRs), 140, 166, 242, 248–49, 252, 255, 298, 307–8, 345, 351
Lawyers Committee for Human Rights (LCHR), 322
Lebanon, 66, 125, 332
LGBT/HIV Asylum Manual, 67, 68
Liberation Tigers of Tamil Eelam (LTTE), 115, 116
Liberia, 61, 88, 130, 332
Location of hearings, 164–65

M

Mandatory detention of suspected terrorists, 119
Master calendar hearings, 158–61
Material Support Exemption Worksheet, 118
Material support to terrorist organization, 118, 153
Medical treatment and humanitarian parole, 333
Membership in particular social group, 26, 47–51
    and children, 64
    and "disfavored" group, 93
    and gang membership, 69–70
    and gender-based claims, 63
    imputed membership, 49
Memoranda, 18–20
Mental disabilities, 51, 68–69, 122, 176–77
Mental torture, 265
Merits hearings, 163–65
Mexico, 67, 74, 99, 213, 295, 321
Minors. *See* Children
Mixed motives, 41–42
Montserrat, 332
Moral turpitude, crimes involving, 134, 214, 241
Morocco, 62
Motion to dismiss, 156
Motion to reopen/reconsider, 153–54, 231–39
    burden of proof, 232–33
    changed circumstances alleged, 120
    consent by parties, 235–36

consolidation with judicial review, 246
contents of motion, 236–38
Convention Against Torture cases, 287–88
crime supporting termination as basis, 236
departure from U.S., effect of, 239
equitable tolling, 236
fee, 236
filing with affirmative application after prior denial, 146
fraud as basis, 236
in absentia order, 179, 181
jurisdiction, 232
limit on number, 233, 234–35
reply to, 238–39
rulings on, 239
standard of review, 232–33
and stay of removal, 238
time limit for filing, 234, 235–36
where to file, 232
who may make, 232
Motions during removal proceeding, 161

N

National Immigration Project of the National Lawyers Guild, 107
National Legal Aid & Defender Association's Defending Immigrants Partnership, 107–8
National security-related cases, 112–13, 142, 153, 247, 253
See also Terrorism; Treason and sedition
Nationality, 26, 28–29, 46–47
imputed nationality, 47
Naturalization, 354
Nazi persecution, participation in, 130, 142
Negative credible fear decision, review of, 173, 241, 314–16
Negative reasonable fear decision, review of, 201–3, 209–11
Neutrality in political opinion, 54
New People's Army (Philippines), 73
New York and advance parole status prior to travel, 249
Nicaragua, 332, 337, 338
Nicaraguan Adjustment and Central American Relief Act of 1997 (NACARA), 154, 337–39, 342
Nonaggravated felonies, 108–90
Nongovernmental actors, persecution by, 72–73, 74
Nongovernmental organizations (NGOs), access to secondary inspections, 321–22
Nonimmigrant visas, 353

Nonpermanent residents, relief for, 344–46
Nonrefoulement
Convention Against Torture provision, 270–77
evidence to support claim, 272–76
IIRAIRA provision, 12
"more likely than not" standard, 271
no bars to protection, 276–77
no internal relocation option, 272
prospective only, 271–72
Refugee Act provision, 11
Refugee Convention provision, 4–5
torture only, 276
Northern Ireland, 115
Notable applicants, 154
Notes and assessments of asylum officer, 172
Notice of Appeal (Form EOIR-26), 187, 226, 227, 229
Notice of Appearance (Form EOIR-28), 158
Notice of Appearance (Form G-28) for representative, 149, 158, 198, 207
Notice of Intent to Issue a Final Administrative Deportation Order (Form I-851), 203
Notice of Referral (Form I-863), 201, 210, 315
Notice requirements, 142–45
confidentiality, 144–45
deferral of removal, notice of hearing, 285
frivolous applications, 143–44
information may be used to initiate removal proceedings, 144
intent to terminate asylum, 253
representation, right to, 142–43
Notice To Appear (NTA), 145–46, 156, 330

O

Office of Chief Immigration Judge OPPM on children, 190
Office of Legal Counsel decisions, 17
Off-the-record remarks, 168
One-child policy, 55–58, 97
One-year filing deadline, 120–26, 142
changed circumstances related to late filing, 124–26
child applicants and exception, 192
extraordinary circumstances related to late filing, 122–24
judicial review, 133, 241–42
Operations Instructions (OIs), 15
Oral argument
appeals, 230
motion to reopen/reconsider, 236
Overseas investigations, 174
Overseas processing and admissions, 141–42

© 2007 American Immigration Lawyers Association

P

Pakistan, 99
Palestine Liberation Organization, 113, 114
Palestinians, 29, 94
Parole requests, 218–19
 burden of proof, 218
 humanitarian parole, 332–34
Parolees exempt from expedited removal, 296, 309
Participation in persecution of others, 110–12, 142, 153, 253
Passports, possession of, 94
Past persecution
 as basis for asylum, 38–39
 discretionary grant of asylum, 104
 and presumption of future persecution, 96–101
PATRIOT Act. *See* USA PATRIOT Act
Permanent residency, application for, 26
Persecution, 32–39
 countrywide, 73–75
 credible fear of. *See* Fear of persecution
 defined, 32–34
 examples of, 34–38
 of family and friends, 91–92
 fear of. *See* Fear of persecution
 grounds of. *See* Grounds of persecution
 participation in persecution of others, 110–12, 142, 153, 253
 past persecution. *See* Past persecution
 prosecution vs., 75–77
 reasonable fear of. *See* Reasonable fear
Peru, 66, 68, 111
Philippines, 73, 78
Physical disabilities, 68–69, 122
Physical torture, 264
Pilot children's immigration court, 191
Pleadings, 160
Policy directives, 18–20
Political opinion, 26, 52–58
 actual acts, words, and beliefs, 52–53
 coercive population control, 55–58
 imputed, 53–54
 neutrality, 54
 unexpressed, 53
Port of entry
 false or no documents at, 218, 242, 289, 294, 303–5
 parole upon arriving at, 218
Postconviction relief, 108
Presidency Advisory Council on AIDS, 19, 67
Presumption of future persecution based on past persecution, 96–101
Prior asylum denial, 119–20, 142, 154, 196, 242
Prior statements and credibility determination, 312
Priorities for refugees, 141
Private bills, 355
Pro bono representation, 142–43, 149
Prosecution vs. persecution, 75–77
Prosecutorial discretion, 330
Prostitution, 51, 134, 214, 241, 350
Protocol, 1–7
 refugee, defined, 4
 U.S. accession to, 24
Punishment
 for criminal conduct, 75–77
 for illegal departure, 77

Q

Quality Assurance Program, 153, 317–18

R

Race as grounds, 26, 42–43
 definition of race, 42
 imputed race, 43
Rap sheets, requests for, 105
Rape, 51, 59–63, 264, 328
REAL ID Act of 2005
 on credibility determination, 81, 83, 84, 87, 134, 137, 273, 305, 312
 effect on asylum provisions, 25
 on judicial review of asylum decisions, 14, 133, 240
 on judicial review of removal orders, 204–5, 242, 282–83
 mixed motives, 41–42
 on one-year filing deadline, 122
 standards of review, 135
 terrorism provisions, 113–14, 116, 117
 waiver of inadmissibility, 117
 on well-founded fear of persecution, 31
Reasonable fear
 defined, 197, 205
 determination
  aggravated felons, 205–9
  reinstatement of removal, 200–201
 interview, 196–97
  withdrawal of request, 201, 209
Reasonable Fear Worksheet (Form I-899), 200, 208
Record of Negative Reasonable Fear Interview Finding and Request for Review (Form I-898), 201, 209

© 2007 American Immigration Lawyers Association

Re-entering after deportation or removal, 195–96
Referral of application, 152–53
Refugee Act of 1980, 10–11
   asylum provision, 11
   definition of refugee, 11
   nonrefoulement provision, 11
Refugee Convention, 1–7
   on fundamental change in circumstances, 97
   on removal after adjustment of status, 255
   serious nonpolitical crimes, bar for, 109
Refugee Resettlement Program, 250
Refugee *sur place*, 77–78
Refugees
   expedited removal, exemption from, 298
   IIRAIRA definition of, 12, 56
   INA definition of, 27–28
   overseas processing and admissions, 141–42
   Protocol definition of, 4
   Refugee Act definition of, 11
   travel documents, 248–50
Registry, 349–50
Regulations, 14–15
Reinstatement of removal, 195–203
   and Convention Against Torture, 289–90
   decision, 200–201
   evidence, 199
   interpreters, 199
   interviews, 197–200
   no reasonable fear decision, 201, 202–3
   no review, 241
   preliminary procedures, 196–97
   reasonable fear, defined, 197
   reasonable fear determination, 200–201
   record, 200
   review of negative reasonable fear decision, 201–3
   withholding-only proceeding, 200–201
Relative petition (Form I-730), 250–52
Release from detention, 211–19
   bond hearings, 215–18
   eligible individuals, 212–13
      arriving aliens, 212
      children, 213
      credible fear determination, 212
      refusal of home country to accept individual designated for removal, 212
   noneligible individuals, 213–15
      criminal grounds of deportation or inadmissibility, 214
      expedited removal process, 214
      final orders of removal, 215
      terrorists, 214
   parole requests vs. bond hearings, 215
   requests to ICE district directors, 218–19
Religion as grounds, 43–46
   imputed religion, 46
Remaining in home country for extended period, 78–79
Removal proceedings, 158–87
   See also Expedited removal proceedings; Immigration court procedures
   advisals, 159
   affidavits vs. declarations, 186
   appeal, right to, 173
   authentication of documents, 185–86
   children, 189–95
   classified evidence, 184–85
   closed hearing, 163
   confidentiality, right to, 173–76
   constitutional and statutory rights, 165–76
   continuances, 159
   Convention Against Torture cases, 281–84, 291
   decision and order, 187
   deportability determination, 162
   designation of country of removal, 160–61
   discovery, 184
   due process rights, 166–68
   entry of appearance, 158
   evidence, 181–87
      right to present, examine, and object to, 171–72
   experts, 182–84
   failure to appear, consequences of, 178–81
   Fifth Amendment privilege, 168–69
   foreign language documents, 187
   foreign law, 187
   Fourth Amendment rights, 165
   Headquarters Court (HQIC), 164
   hearsay, 184
   inadmissibility determination, 162
   incompetents, 176–77
   information provided by applicant may be used to initiate, 144, 156
   interpreters, 171
   late arrival, 179
   location of hearings, 164–65
   mandatory denials, 162
   master calendar hearings, 158–61
   merits hearing, 163–65
   motions, 161
   notes and assessments of asylum officer, 172
   pleadings, 160
   removability phase, 162
   representation, right to, 159, 160, 169–70

self-incrimination privilege, 168–69
Sixth Amendment rights, 169–70
State Department concerns, 162–63
stowaways, 188–89
time period, 158
unaccompanied minors, 177–78
videoconferenced hearing, 163
voluntary departure at conclusion of, 348–49
voluntary departure before conclusion of, 347–48
witnesses, 182–84
    right to cross-examine, 172
Reopening case
    See also Motion to reopen/reconsider
    to terminate asylum or withholding, 254
Reply to motion to reopen, 238–39
Representation
    aggravated felon in expedited removal proceeding, 207
    of children, 191, 213
    credible fear determination review, 315
    credible fear interview, 312
    Notice of Appearance (Form G-28), 149, 158, 198
    primary inspection, 302
    reinstatement of removal, 198–99
    right to, 142–43, 159, 160
    secondary inspection, 302
Revocation of voluntary departure, 349
Revolutionary Forces of Colombia (FARC), 73, 116
Robbery, 110
Russia, 64, 66
Rwanda, 123, 130, 332

S

Safe third country, removal to, 129–30, 142, 161, 241, 253
Safe-country agreement with Canada, 129–30, 294
Saudi Arabia, 29, 66, 278
Self-incrimination privilege, 168–69
Serious crimes, conviction of, 105, 106, 142, 253
Serious nonpolitical crimes, 109–10, 142, 253
Service of appeal on DHS, 229
Sexual orientation, 66–67
Shining Path, 116
Sierra Leone, 61, 332
Sign-language interpreters, 149
"Similarly situated" standard, 92–93
Sixth Amendment, 169–70
Social Security cards, 223–24

Somalia, 49, 50, 61, 73, 128, 266, 332
Special immigrant juvenile visas, 353
Specific threat of harm, 89–90
Spouses
    credible fear interview of spouse, 313
    derivative status, 250–51
Standard of review, 130–38
    abuse-of-discretion standard, 131, 136
    before Attorney General, 131
    before BIA, 130–31
    of changed circumstances, 138
    credibility determinations, 131, 137–38
    credible fear determination, 314
    de novo standard, 131, 132, 136
    of factual findings, 138
    before federal courts, 131–38
    motion to reopen/reconsider, 232–33
    revised standards, 135–36
    statutory construction, 136–37
State Department
    affirmative applications, procedure for, 150
    concerns in deferral of removal, 285
    concerns in removal proceedings, 162–63
    designation of foreign terrorist organizations, 116
    priorities for refugees, 141
    reports, 84
State drug offenses, 106
Statelessness, 28–29
Statutes, 10–14
Stay of removal, 229–30, 238, 245
Stowaways, 146, 188–89, 289, 297, 309
Sudan, 61, 332
Suspected terrorists, mandatory detention of, 119

T

T visas, 326–28
Taliban, 98
Tamil Tigers, 115
Temporary Protected Status (TPS), 123, 331–32
Termination of asylum and withholding, 252–54
Terrorism, 113–19, 142
    alien terrorist removal courts, 118–19, 291
    and Convention Against Torture claims, 291
    engaging in terrorist activity, 113–15
    individuals in positions of prominence who endorse terrorist activity, 116
    mandatory detention of suspected terrorists, 119
    material support to terrorist organization, 118
    members of terrorist organizations, 116–17
    no judicial review of terrorist bar, 242
    representative of foreign terrorist

organization, 115–16
representative of political or social groups that endorse terrorist activity, 116
termination of asylum due to, 253
waiver of certain grounds of inadmissibility, 117–18
Testimony and credibility of applicant, 80–84
Theft, 110
Tibetan Mustangs, 118
Time period
  appeals, 226, 243
  Convention Against Torture claims, 281
  employment authorization, 220
  interviews, 147
  motion to reopen/reconsider, 234, 235
  removal proceedings, 158
  T visas, 327
Torture
  See also Convention Against Torture (CAT)
  acquiescence of public official, 262, 267
  credible fear of, 154
  under custody or control of offender, 265
  elements of, 262–70
  infliction of severe pain or suffering, 264–65
  intentional act, 262–64
  mental torture, 265
  nonrefoulement. See Nonrefoulement
  not arising out of lawful sanctions, 269–70
  physical torture, 264
  by public official, 266–68
  reasonable fear of, 154
  sanctioned by public official, 266–68
  for wrongful purposes, 265–66
Totality of circumstances, 102, 118
Travel documents, 248–50
Treason and sedition, 134, 241
Treaties, 9–10
Trokosi, 50, 63

U

U visas, 328–30
Uganda, 61, 64, 66
Ukraine, 99
UN Committee Against Torture. *See* Committee Against Torture
UN Convention. *See* Refugee Convention
UN High Commissioner for Refugees (UNHCR)
  on confidentiality of proceedings, 175–76
  on definition of persecution, 32
  Executive Committee Conclusions, 6
  on expedited removal process, 303–4, 322–23
  guidance, 5
  Guidelines on International Protection, 43–44, 328
  guidelines on refugee and unaccompanied children, 190
  guidelines on refugee women, 59
  on interdiction (interception), 141
  on mixed motives, 41
  on removal after adjustment of status, 255
  reports and other publications, 6
  on well-founded fear of persecution, 30
UN Protocol. *See* Protocol
Unable or unwilling to return, 30
Unaccompanied children, 63–64, 155, 177–78, 191
  See also Children
  expedited removal proceedings, 192, 296–97, 308
  release from detention, 213
  withdrawal of application for admission, 307
Unauthorized stays, 77
Unexpressed political opinion, 53
United Self-Defense Forces of Colombia (AUC), 116
Universal Declaration of Human Rights, 43
U.S. Coast Guard. *See* Interdiction on U.S. waters
U.S. Commission on International Religious Freedom (USCIRF), 43, 319–21, 323
U.S. Committee for Refugees, 115
USA PATRIOT Act, 13–14
  bars for terrorism, 116
  effect on asylum provisions, 25
  limitations on court review of asylum, 17–18
  self-petitions allowed under, 352
  suspected terrorists, detention of, 119
US-VISIT program, 302

V

V visas, 326
Venue
  appeals, 243
  bond hearings, 216
Victims of trafficking, 51, 326–30
Victims of Trafficking and Violence Protection Act of 2000 (VTVPA), 326
Videoconferenced hearings, 163
Visa Waiver Pilot Program (VWPP), 297, 309
Visa waiver status, 145, 146, 153, 156, 296
Voluntary associational relationship, 49
Voluntary departure, 346–49

W

Waiver of appeal, 230
Waiver of inadmissibility, 117–18
  under §212(h), 350–51
Waiver under §209(c), 330–31
Warsaw Pact countries, 339
Withdrawal of application for admission, 299, 306–7
Withdrawal of request for reasonable fear interview, 201, 209
Withholding of removal
  asylum officers' authority, 146
  bars to, 130
  compared to asylum, 26
  under Convention Against Torture, 279–80
  eligibility to apply for, 140–41
  and firm resettlement, 126
  ineligibility for, 102–30, 142
  reinstatement of removal determination, 200–201
  standard for relief, 26–27
  standard of review, 130–38
  termination of, 252, 253
Witnesses, 146, 168, 172, 182–84
Women
  arranged marriages, 50, 61
  asylum guidelines from INS, 18
  gender-based claims, 25, 51, 59–63, 153
World Trade Center bombing (1993), 112

Z

Zimbabwe, 66, 125, 130